THE GERMAN RIGHT, 1918–1930

The failure of the Weimar Republic and the rise of National Socialism remains one of the most challenging problems of twentieth-century European history. *The German Right, 1918–1930* sheds new light on this problem by examining the role that the non-Nazi Right played in the destabilization of Weimar democracy in the period before the emergence of the Nazi Party as a mass party of middle-class protest. Larry Eugene Jones identifies a critical divide within the German Right between those prepared to work within the framework of Germany's new republican government and those irrevocably committed to its overthrow. This split was greatly exacerbated by the course of German economic development in the 1920s, leaving the various organizations that comprised the German Right defenceless against the challenge of National Socialism. At no point was the disunity of the non-Nazi Right in the face of Nazism more apparent than in the September 1930 Reichstag elections.

LARRY EUGENE JONES is Professor Emeritus in the Department of History at Canisius College in Buffalo, New York, where he has taught since 1968. His previous publications include the award-winning *German Liberalism and the Dissolution of the Weimar Party System, 1918–1933* (1988) and *Hitler versus Hindenburg: The 1932 Presidential Elections and the End of the Weimar Republic* (2015).

THE GERMAN RIGHT, 1918–1930

Political Parties, Organized Interests, and Patriotic Associations in the Struggle against Weimar Democracy

LARRY EUGENE JONES

Canisius College, New York

CAMBRIDGE
UNIVERSITY PRESS

CAMBRIDGE
UNIVERSITY PRESS

University Printing House, Cambridge CB2 8BS, United Kingdom

One Liberty Plaza, 20th Floor, New York, NY 10006, USA

477 Williamstown Road, Port Melbourne, VIC 3207, Australia

314–321, 3rd Floor, Plot 3, Splendor Forum, Jasola District Centre, New Delhi – 110025, India

79 Anson Road, #06–04/06, Singapore 079906

Cambridge University Press is part of the University of Cambridge.

It furthers the University's mission by disseminating knowledge in the pursuit of education, learning, and research at the highest international levels of excellence.

www.cambridge.org
Information on this title: www.cambridge.org/9781108494076
DOI: 10.1017/9781108643450

First published 2020

Printed in the United Kingdom by TJ International Ltd. Padstow, Cornwall

A catalogue record for this publication is available from the British Library.

Library of Congress Cataloging-in-Publication Data
Names: Jones, Larry Eugene, author.
Title: The German right, 1918–1930 : political parties, organized interests, and patriotic associations in the struggle against Weimar Democracy / Larry Eugene Jones, Canisius College, New York.
Description: Cambridge, United Kingdom ; New York : Cambridge University Press, 2020. | Includes bibliographical references and index.
Identifiers: LCCN 2019038331 (print) | LCCN 2019038332 (ebook) | ISBN 9781108494076 (hardback) | ISBN 9781108713863 (paperback) | ISBN 9781108643450 (epub)
Subjects: LCSH: Germany–Politics and government–1918-1933. | Conservatism–Germany–History–20th century. | Political parties–Germany–History–20th century. | Deutschnationale Volkspartei–History. | Nationalism–Germany–History–20th century. | Pangermanism–GermanyHistory–20th century.
Classification: LCC DD240 .J588 2020 (print) | LCC DD240 (ebook) | DDC 943.085–dc23
LC record available at https://lccn.loc.gov/2019038331
LC ebook record available at https://lccn.loc.gov/2019038332

ISBN 978-1-108-49407-6 Hardback

Dedicated to the memory of my mother
Lila Maurine Berg Jones
(1909–1996)

CONTENTS

18   The September Earthquake   555

     Epilogue: The Price of Disunity   589

     Select Bibliography   598
     Index   610

FIGURES

ix

ACKNOWLEDGMENTS

This book has its origins in the 1960s, a time when the United States found itself in the midst of a crisis that severely tested the strength and resilience of its democratic institutions. As a young graduate student at the University of Wisconsin-Madison, I was quickly swept up in the wave of student protest that was engulfing American campuses throughout the country and became an embittered opponent of the Viet Nam War. This coincided with my introduction to Marxism, first under the tutelage of Richard DeGeorge at the University of Kansas and then under that of Harvey Goldberg and William Appleman Williams at Wisconsin. Even though I never thought of myself as a Marxist in anything more than a vague, undefined sense of the word, my encounter with Marxism was very much at the center of my approach to the study of history in general and continues to inform my inquiry into the failure of Weimar Germany and the rise of Nazism.

Recent developments in American political life notwithstanding, my subsequent studies on modern German history quickly convinced me that the political cultures of the two countries were so dissimilar that something analogous to the Nazi seizure of power in Germany was inconceivable here in America. At the very least, American democratic institutions were much more firmly rooted in American political culture than those of the Weimar Republic and had consistently proven themselves more resilient to the pressures of economic crisis than their Weimar counterpart. Moreover, the feudal relics that had played such an instrumental role in bringing about the collapse of Weimar democracy were totally absent from the American political experience, particularly after the defeat of the South in the American Civil War. Yet even as it became clear that the German model had lost much of its relevance for understanding the American political experience, the failure of Weimar democracy and the triumph of Nazism remained very much at the heart of my scholarly agenda for the half-century or so that I have been a professional historian.

Why Weimar failed was very much at the center of my study of German liberalism that appeared with the University of North Carolina Press in 1988. By then, however, I had come to realize that the failure of German liberalism was only part of the story and had already begun to collect material on right-wing political organizations in the Weimar Republic for a parallel study of the German

Right. Hopes that this might lead to a follow-up publication in fairly short order – a draft manuscript was already under way as early as 1990 – were, however, put on hold with the fall of the Berlin wall and the unrestricted access this suddenly afforded historians like myself to the troves of material in the Deutsches Zentralarchiv and other East German archives. The fact that I was now able to access not only the records of a plethora of right-wing parties, interest groups, and patriotic associations that had been previously unavailable to historians in the west but also the private papers of a select group of right-wing politicians meant that much of what I had already written would have to be redone. Similarly, my success in gaining access to materials on the politics of Germany's Catholic aristocracy through the auspices of the Vereinigte Westfälische Adelsarchive in Münster added a new dimension to my study on the German Right that would require a further revision of my timetable for publication.

It is difficult for the author of a book that has been as long in gestation as this to remember, let alone thank, all of those without whose help and counsel its publication would never have been possible. I was particularly fortunate to spend two years each studying with two of the most influential scholars of their time, first from 1963 to 1966 as a Fulbright scholar with Karl Dietrich Bracher at the University of Bonn and then from 1975 to 1977 as a Humboldt fellow with Hans Mommsen at the University of the Ruhr in Bochum. Bracher's *Die Auflösung der Weimarer Republik* was the first German-language book in my library, and Hans went on to become one of my closest professional friends. Both had a decisive impact on the way I came to read the political history of the Weimar Republic, and I remain profoundly grateful for their inspiration, support, and generosity. That I had the opportunity to study with Bracher and Mommsen at a formative stage in my career was a stroke of enormous good fortune that I probably never fully appreciated at the time but that with the benefit of historical hindsight becomes clearer and clearer every day of my professional career. I am also deeply indebted to Theodore Hamerow, my dissertation advisor at Wisconsin, for his counsel and encouragement during the early years of my career. Likewise, I remain deeply indebted to Georg Iggers for his friendship and constant curiosity about my work. Similarly, both Gerald Feldman and Henry A. Turner, Jr., were particularly supportive of my work in the early stages of my career, even to the point of sharing materials in their possession that helped me fill important gaps in the narrative I was trying to put together. I am particularly grateful to Professor Feldman for having invited me to take part from 1978 to 1983 in the international project on "Inflation und Wiederaufbau in Deutschland und Europa 1914–1924" that was funded by a grant from the Volkswagen-Stiftung. My involvement in this project was instrumental in helping me understand the impact of the runaway inflation of the early 1920s and the measures that were taken to stabilize the currency in 1923–24 on Germany's political development and the swing to the Right that took place in various stages after 1924.

Over the years my work has benefited from conversations and collaborative undertakings with a wide range of historians that have helped shape this book. In the fall of 1998 I had the privilege of participating in a conference in Toronto organized by James Retallack on Saxony that helped me grasp the importance of regional history and just how significant regional differences were in understanding the politics of the German Right. The following spring I attended the second of two symposia in Bad Homburg that Heinz Reif organized on the theme of "Elitenwandel in der gesellschaftlichen Moderni-sierung: Adel und Bürgertum im 19. und 20. Jahrhundert" that complemented and contextualized my own work on the politics of the Rhenish-Westphalian aristocracy. Then in the spring of 2004 I had the privilege of co-organizing a conference on Kuno Graf von Westarp, in my mind the most important of the conservative politicians in the Weimar Republic, at the ancestral estate of Westarp's grandson Hans Freiherr Hiller von Gaertringen. The conference provided important new perspectives on Westarp's political leadership that were subsequently incorporated into the book at hand. During a break from my study of the German Right to complete a book on the 1932 presidential elections that Cambridge University Press published in 2015, I edited a collection of essays on the German Right in the Weimar Republic that appeared with Berghahn Books in 2014. I remain deeply indebted to the scholars who contributed articles to this volume for the way in which this helped me flesh out my knowledge of right-wing politics in Weimar Germany. Then in May 2015 I had the good fortune to participate in a workshop at Harvard University organized by Daniel Ziblatt to solicit comments and criticism of the manuscript he was preparing for Oxford University Press on *Conservative Parties and the Birth of Democracy*. This was a particularly valuable experience for me in that it helped clarify arguments in my own work and situate it in a broader theoretical context.

Of my own contemporaries, none has played a more important role in highlighting the complexity and nuances of right-wing politics in Germany from 1890 to 1933 than Geoff Eley. Although there remain significant differ-ences in the way we each approach the history of the German Right – particularly in the latter stages of the Weimar Republic – I still find Geoff's criticism of my work thoughtful, carefully nuanced, and provocative. I am also indebted to Wolfram Pyta for his cooperation in co-editing the results of the Westarp conference in 2006 and for his continued interest in my work. Recently I have worked closely with Hermann Beck first in organizing sessions for the annual meetings of the German Studies Association but more recently in co-editing a collection of essays on the Nazi seizure of power for Berghahn Books. Hermann is a knowledgeable and discerning student of the German Right, and I greatly value his counsel. Of my more established colleagues, I am particularly grateful to Shelley Baranowski, Winfried Becker, Joseph Ben-dersky, Wolfgang Hardtwig, Peter Hayes, Konrad Jarausch, Stefan Malinowski,

William Patch, Karsten Ruppert, Charles Sidman, and Bernd Weisbrod for the exchange of ideas that we have had over the years, while a cohort of younger scholars including Alex Burkhardt, Andy Daum, Daniela Gasteiger, Björn Hofmeister, Barry A. Jackisch, Rainer Orth, Michael O'Sullivan, André Postert, Mark Ruff, Edward Snyder, Kevin Spicer, and Benjamin Ziemann and their willingness to share the results of their research with me have reassured me that the future of Weimar political history lies in good hands. This list is not exhaustive, and I apologize to anyone whose name I might have omitted.

I am also grateful to numerous colleagues in the profession who have helped me gain access to the materials upon which this book is based. No one has been more helpful in this regard than my long-time friend Hans-Dieter Kreikamp, who worked as an archivist at the German Federal Archives (or Bundesarchiv) in Koblenz and Berlin and who unfailingly responded to my requests for copies of materials I needed for my work. Without his help and support I would never have been able to complete this study. I am also grateful to Hans-Dieter and his wife Tania for their gracious hospitality on the occasion of my visits to Berlin. I also owe an enormous debt of gratitude to Friedrich Freiherr Hiller von Gaertringen, who granted me access to the papers of his grandfather Kuno Graf von Westarp at the very beginning of my career and remained a valuable source of information and counsel until his death in 1999. Karl Mayer, a professional archivist and local historian who worked closely with Friedrich and his brother Hans to ensure their accessibility to future generations of historians, performed an invaluable service by organizing approximately two-thirds of the collection. An indispensable source on the history of the German Right, the Westarp papers remain in family possession, where Verena Gräfin von Zeppelin-Aschhausen, their current custodian, is committed to making the collection available to research scholars like myself. And lastly, I would like to extend a special word of gratitude to Horst Conrad, Werner Friese, and the staff of the Westfälisches Archivamt in Münster, who by affording me access to the archives of the Westphalian aristocracy helped me achieve what would prove to be a major breakthrough in my research on the politics of the German Right.

The completion of this work would not have been possible without the generous help and support of a large number of archives, libraries, and research institutes. Here I would like to express my gratitude to the staff of the Bundesarchiv in Berlin-Lichterfelde and Koblenz, the Bundesarchiv-Militärabteilung in Freiburg im Breisgau, and the Politisches Archiv des Auswärtigen Amts in Berlin for providing access to materials in their possession. I am particularly grateful to the Bildarchiv of the Bundesarchiv for permission to use the images of right-wing politicians and right-wing campaign material that are to be found throughout the book. Important material on the history of the German Right was also to be found in state, regional, and municipal archives, in particular in the Bayerisches Hauptstaatsarchiv in Munich, the

Brandenburgisches Hauptlandesarchiv in Potdam, the Landesarchiv Berlin, the Landesarchiv Nordrheinland-Westfalen in Münster, the Landesarchiv Baden-Württemberg, the Hauptstaatsarchiv Stuttgart, the Niedersächsisches Staatsarchiv in Osnabrück, the Sächsisches Hauptstaatsarchiv in Dresden, and the Staatsarchiv Hamburg as well as in the municipal archives of Braunschweig, Dresden, Mönchen-Gladbach, Paderborn, Stuttgart, and Wuppertal. Corporate archives also proved to be a valuable source of information on the German Right. In this respect I am particularly grateful to the Historisches Archiv Friedrich Krupp GmbH in Essen for access to the papers of Gustav Krupp von Bohlen und Halbach, to the Rheinisch-Westfälisches Wirtschaftsarchiv zu Köln for access to the papers of the Gutehoffnungshütte's Paul Reusch, to the Siemens Historical Institute in Berlin (and its predecessor, the Werner von Siemens Institut für die Geschichte des Hauses Siemens in Munich) for access to the papers of Carl Friedrich von Siemens, to the ThyssenKrupp Konzernarchiv, Außenstelle Hoesch-Archiv, in Dortmund for access to the papers of Fritz Springorum, and to the Unternehmensarchiv Bayer A.G. in Leverkusen for access to the papers of Carl Duisberg. And lastly, I would like to thank private research institutes that made their holdings available for this project, namely the Archiv für Christlich-Demokratische Politik an der Konrad-Adenauer-Stiftung in Sankt-Augustin the Forschungsstelle für Zeitgeschichte in Hamburg, the Institut für Zeitgeschichte in Munich, and the Kommission für Zeitgeschichte in Bonn. I remain profoundly grateful to all of those who have helped me assemble the material upon which this book is based and for the service they provide all historians.

None of the research upon which this book is based would have been possible without the generous financial support I have received from a variety of sources over the course of my career. I am particularly grateful to my home institution Canisius College for the sabbaticals and numerous small research grants that I have received from the college since arriving in Buffalo in the fall of 1968. These made it possible for me to return to Germany for extended periods of research on an almost yearly basis. In addition to the fellowships I received from the Fulbright Program and the Alexander von Humboldt-Stiftung at the beginning of my career, I have held major grants from the American Council of Learned Societies, the National Endowment of the Humanities, the National Humanities Center, the German Marshall Fund, and the Woodrow Wilson International Center for Scholars as well as smallers grants-in-aid from the American Philosophical Society and the Deutscher Akademischer Austauschdienst. Were it not for the generosity of these organizations and their donors, this book could never have been completed.

No less important was the encouragement and patient support I have received from Cambridge University Press. I remain deeply indebted first and foremost to Lewis Bateman, who first contacted me when he was at Princeton University Press, solicited and oversaw the publication of my first book on the history of German liberalism during the Weimar Republic, and then demonstrated enormous patience as he waited for the completion of my manuscript on the German Right. When it became apparent that things were not moving as quickly as we had hoped, it was Lew who suggested that I take a break from this project to write a book on the 1932 presidential elections. That was without a question one of the best pieces of editorial advice I have ever received. Following Lew's retirement in 2016, this project was handed over first to Michael Watson and then to Liz Friend-Smith, who shepherded it through the approval process before placing it in the capable hands of Ian McIver, Ishwarya Mathavan, and particularly my copy-editor Barbara Wilson for guiding me through the production process. All of this was done with a professionalism and a respect for the author's instincts and predilections that made publication much less onerous than it has been for many of my colleagues in the profession.

I would be remiss if I did not also express my gratitude to those of my colleagues at Canisius who have been supportive of my work during my long tenure at the college. I think in particular of the old guard of Tom Banchich, Dave Costello, Walt Sharrow, Ed Neville, and Jim Valone who made Canisius a welcome and comforing place to teach, and of the younger cohort of Richard Bailey, René de la Pedraja, Dave Devereux, Bruce Dierenfield, Julie Gibert, and Steve Maddox. What we all share in common is a deep and abiding commitment to the humanities and to excellence in teaching and scholarship. The bridge between these two groups is Nancy Rosenbloom, my colleague, wife, and the mother of our two sons, Matthew and Daniel Rosenbloom-Jones. All three have endured my fascination with German history with a mixture of amusement, patience, and good humor, but it is Nancy who has had to put up with my moments of distraction, my annoying work habits and late nights at the computer, and everything else that has gone into the completion of this book. Never did Nancy doubt the value of what I was doing, either as a work of historical scholarship or as a part of who I am. And for that she has my deepest thanks and love.

The person to whom I owe the greatest debt of gratitutde is the person to whose memory this book is dedicated, my mother Lila Maurine Berg Jones. My brother Ron and I grew up poor in a small farm town in south central Kansas in what was at the time the heart of the dust bowl. My mother, who had abandoned her dreams of becoming a concert pianist with the onset of the Great Depression and became a school teacher by default, valued education above all else and was committed to making certain that Ron and I received the best education possible. No sacrifice was too great in order to make this part of her dream come true. In retrospect, I doubt if I ever really told my mother how greatly I appreciated all that she had done for the two of us and that it was only through her love and sacrifice that I was able to achieve my own dreams as a scholar and teacher. May this book be a fitting tribute to her memory and sacrifice.

Buffalo, New York

ABBREVIATIONS

Organizations

ADGB	Allgemeiner Deutscher Gewerkschaftsbund/General German Trade-Union Federation
ADI	Arbeitsausschuß deutschnationaler Industrieller/Coordinating Committee of German National Industrialists
ADV	Alldeutscher Verband/Pan-German League
AKD	Arbeitsgemeinschaft Katholischer Deutscher/Coalition of Catholic Germans
BBB	Bayerischer Bauernbund/Bavarian Peasants' League
BBMB	Bayerischer Bauern- und Mittelstandsbund/Bavarian Peasant and Middle Class League
BDI	Bund der Industriellen/League of Industrialists
BER	Bund zur Erneuerung des Reiches/ League for the Regeneration of the Reich
BdL	Agrarian League/Bund der Landwirte
BLB	Bayerischer Landbund/Bavarian Rural League
BrLB	Brandenburgischer Landbund/Brandenburg Rural League
BMP	Bayerische Mittelpartei/Bavarian Middle Party
BVP	Bayerische Volkspartei/Bavarian People's Party
CDI	Centralverband Deutscher Industrieller/Central Association of German Industrialists
CNBLP	Christlicher-nationale Bauern- und Landvolkpartei/Christian-National Peasants and Farmer's Party
CSRV	Christlich-soziale Reichsvereinigung/Christian-Social Reich Union
CSVD	Christlich-Sozialer Volksdienst/Christian-Social People's Service
CVD	Christlicher Volksdienst/Christian People's Service
CVP	Christliche Volkspartei/Christian People's Party
DAAP	Deutsche Arbeiter- und Angestelltenpartei/German Workers and Employees' Party
DAG	Deutsche Adelgenossenschaft/German Nobles' Society
DAP	Deutsche Arbeitspartei/German Worker's Party

DBP	Deutsche Bauernpartei/German Peasants' Party
DDGB	Deutsch-demokratischer Gewerkschaftsbund/German Democratic Trade Union Federation
DDP	Deutsche Demokratische Partei/German Democratic Party
DGB	Deutscher Gewerkschaftsbund/German Trade-Union Federation
DHK	Deutscher Herrenklub/German Gentlemen's Club
DHR	Deutscher Hochschulring/German University Ring
DHV	Deutschnationaler Handlungsghilfen-Verband/German National Union of Commercial Employees
DIHT	Deutscher Industrie- und Handelstag/German Chamber of Commerce and Industry
DIV	Deutsche Industriellen-Vereinigung/German Industrialists' Association
DKP	Deutsche Konservative Partei/German Conservative Party
DLB	Deutscher Landbund/German Rural League
DLV	Deutscher Landarbeiterverein/German Farm Workers' Union
DNAB	Deutschnationaler Arbeiterbund/German National Workers' League
DNJ	Deutschnationaler Jugendbund/German National Youth League
DNVP	Deutschnationale Volkspartei/German National People's Party
DRKB	Deutsche Reischskriegerbund Kyffhäuser/German Reich Warriors' Kyffhäuser League
DSTB	Deutschvölkischer Schutz- und Trutzbund/German-Racist Protection and Defense League
DStP	Deutsche Staatspartei/German State Party
DvAG	Deutschvölkische Arbeitsgemeinschaft/German-Racist Coalition
DVFP	Deutschvölkische Freiheitspartei/German-Racist Freedom Party
DVLP	Deutsche Vaterlandspartei/German Fatherland Party
DVP	Deutsche Volkspartei/German People's Party
EWB	Einwohnerwehren Bayerns/Bavarian Civil Defense Leagues
Gaä	Gemeinsamer Ausschuß/Joint Committee
GCG	Gesamtverband der christlichen Gewerkschaften Deutschlands/United Federation of Christian Trade Unions
GdA	Gewerkschaftsbund der Angestellten/Federation of Employee Unions
Gedag	Gesamtverband deutscher Angestelltengewerkschaften/United Federation of German Employee Unions
GKE	Genossenschaft katholischer Edelleute in Bayern/Association of Catholic Nobles in Bavaria
HAPAG	Hamburg-Amerikanische Packetfahrt-Actien-Gesellschaft/Hamburg-America Line
KPD	Kommunistiche Partei Deutschlands/German Communist Party
KVP	Konservative Volkspartei/Conservative People's Party
NDB	Nationalverband Deutscher Berufsverbände/National Federation of German Professional Unions

NLV   Nationalliberale Vereinigung der Deutschen Volkspartei/Nationalliberale
         Vereinigung der Deutschen Volkspartei
NSDAP   Nationalsozialistische Deutsche Arbeiterpareti/National Socialist
         German's Worker Party
NSDFP   Nationalsozialistische Deutsche Freiheitspartei/National Socialist German
         Freedom Party
NSFP   Nationalsozialistische Freiheitspartei/National Socialist Freedom Party
Orgesch Organisation Orgesch/Organization Orgesch
RDI   Reichsverband der Deutschen Industrie/National Federation of German
         Industry
RFKP   Reichs- und Freikonservative Partei/Imperial and Free Conservative Party
RLB   Reichs-Landbund/National Rural League
RLHV   Reichsverband landwirtschaftlicher Hausfrauenvereine/National
         Federation of Agricultural Housewives' Associations
RPL   Reichspropagandaleitung der NSDAP/Reich Propaganda Leadership of
         the NSDAP
RvA   Reichsbund vaterländischer Arbeitervereine/National Alliance of
         Patriotic Workers' Clubs
SLB   Sächischer Landbund/Saxon Rural League
SPD   Sozialdemokratische Partei Deutschlands/Social Democratic Party of
         Germany
TLB   Thüringer Landbund/Thüringian Rural League
VDA   Vereinigung der Deutschen Arbeitgeberverbände/Federation of German
         Employer Associations
VdBD   Vereinigung der christlichen Bauernvereine Deutschlands/Association of
         Christian Peasant Unions of Germany
VDESI   Verein Deutscher Eisen- und Stahlindustrieller/Association of German
         Iron and Steel Industrialists
VKE   Verein katholischer Edelleute Deutschlands/Association of Catholic
         Nobles of Germany
VKF   Vereinigung Konservativer Frauen/Association of Conservative Women
VKV   Volkskonservative Vereinigung/People's Conservative Association
VNR   Volksnationale Reichsvereinigung/People's National Reich Association
VRP   Reichspartei für Volksrecht und Aufwertung/Reich Party for People's
         Justice and Revaluation
VSB   Völkisch-Sozialer Block/Racist Social Bloc
VVVB   Vereinigte Vaterländische Verbände Bayerns/United Patriotic Leagues of
         Bavaria
VVVD   Vereinigte Vaterländische Verbände Deutschlands/United Patriotic
         Leagues of Germany
WBB   Westfälischer Bauernbund/Westphalian Peasants' Union
WBP   Württembergische Bürgerpartei/Württemberg Burgher Party

WBWB	Württembergischer Bauern-und Weingärterbund/Württemberg Peasants and Winegrowers' League
WP	Wirtschaftspartei or Reichspartei des Deutschen Mittelstandes/Business Party or Reich Party of the German Middle Class
ZAG	Zentralarbeitsgemeinschaft der industriellen und gewerblichen Arbeitgeber- und Arbeitnehmerverbände/Central Association of Industrial and Commercial Employer and Employee Associations
ZdL	Zentralverband der Landarbeiter/Central Association of Farm Laborers

Archives

ACDP Sankt-Augustin	Archiv für Christlich-Demokratische Politik, Sankt Augustin
BA Berlin	Bundesarchiv Berlin-Lichterfelde, Berlin
BA Bildarchiv	Bundesarchiv, Bildarchiv, On-Line
BA Koblez	Bundesarchiv Koblenz, Koblenz
BA-MA Freiburg	Bundesarchiv-Militärarchiv, Freiburg im Breisgau
Bayer AG	Unternehmensarchiv Bayer AG, Leverkusen
BHStA Munich	Bayerische Hauptstaatsarchiv, Munich
BLHA Potsdam	Brandenburgischer Landeshauptstaatsarchiv, Potsdam
DHV-Archiv Hamburg	Archiv des Deutschen Handels- und Industrieangestellten-Verband, Hamburg
FZH Hamburg	Forschungsstelle für Zeitgeschichte in Hamburg, Hamburg
GLA Karlsruhe	Landesarchiv Baden-Württemberg, Generallandesarchiv Karlsruhe, Karlruhe
GStA Berlin-Dahlem	Geheimes Staatsarchiv Preußischer Kulturbesitz, Berlin
HA Krupp	Historisches Archiv, Friedrich Krupp GmbH, Essen
IfZ Munich	Institut für Zeitgeschichte, Munich
KfZ Bonn	Kommission für Zeitgeschichte, Bonn
LA Berlin	Landesarchiv Berlin, Berlin
LaNRW Münster	Landesarchiv Nordrhein-Westfalen, Münster
NSStA Osnabrück	Niedersächsisches Landesarchiv/Staatsarchiv Osnabrück, Osnabrück
PA AA Berlin	Politisches Archiv des Auswärtigen Amts, Berlin
RWWA Cologne	Rheinisch-Westfälisches Wirtschaftsarchiv zu Köln, Cologne
SHI Berlin	Siemens Historical Institute, Berlin
SHStA Dresden	Sächsisches Hauptstaatsarchiv, Dresden
StA Braunschweig	Stadtarchiv Braunschweig, Braunschweig
StA Hamburg	Staatsarchiv Hamburg, Hamburg
StA Köln	Stadtarchiv Köln, Cologne
StA Mönchen-Gladbach	Stadtarchiv Mönchen-Gladbach, Mönchen-Gladbach

StA Paderborn	Stadtarchiv Paderborn, Paderborn
TKA Dortmund	ThyssenKrupp Konzenarchiv, Außenstelle Hoesch, Dortmund
VWA Münster	Vereinigte Westfälische Adelsarchive, Münster

~

Introduction

Setting the Context

Germany's defeat in World War I, the collapse of the Hohenzollern monarchy, and the founding of the Weimar Republic marked the beginning of a dramatic new phase in the history of the German Right. The question that faced the leaders of Germany's conservative establishment as they reacted to the traumatic events of 1918–19 was whether they would be able to adapt to the revolutionary changes that had taken place in the structure of German political life or whether they would retreat to the entrenched positions they had held in the last years of the Second Empire. The possibilities that faced Germany's conservative leadership were open, and it was by no means certain – and certainly not in 1918–19 – which of these two paths would be taken. Yet despite promising signs from within Germany's conservative establishment that something new might emerge from the ruins of the old order, the leaders of the German Right would consistently opt for policies over the course of the next decade that denied rather than affirmed the possibility of a democratic future. The reasons for this are indeed complex and resist reduction to a common denominator such as the weight of historical tradition, the force of German nationalism, the fear of Bolshevism, or the anti-liberal animus of Germany's conservative elites. All of these factors – and others as well – were involved, though in differing degrees at different points in time. As this would suggest, the responses to the question posed above even within the German Right were extremely varied, just as the players who were involved in crafting those responses were diverse and represented divergent, if not contradictory, interests. By no means, however, was the way in which all of this was eventually resolved somehow fixed or pre-determined. In other words, it was the specific actions of specific individuals or groups of individuals at specific points in time that shaped the course of events that ultimately determined the fate of Germany's experiment in democracy.[1]

---

[1] Larry Eugene Jones, "Why Hitler Came to Power: In Defense of a New History of Politics," in *Geschichtswissenschaft vor 2000. Perspektiven der Historiographiegeschichte, Geschichtstheorie, Sozial- und Kulturgeschichte. Festschrift für Georg G. Iggers zum 65. Geburtstag*, ed. Konrad H. Jarausch, Jörn Rüsen and Hans Schleier (Hagen, 1991), 256–76. In a similar vein, though from a different conceptual perspective, see Geoff Eley, *Nazism as*

The consequences of what happened on the German Right were indeed enormous. Recent scholarship has suggested that an essential precondition for the smooth transition from authoritarian to democratic government was the existence of a strong, resilient party on the Right that was committed to pursuing its objectives within the framework of the new democratic system. A case in point, as Daniel Ziblatt argues in his recent book on *Conservative Parties and the Birth of Democracy*, is the Conservative Party in Great Britain, a party that adapted itself to the exigencies of democratic politics and that by the end of the nineteenth century had evolved into a bulwark of British democracy. The absence of such a party, Ziblatt goes on to argue, severely undermined efforts to establish a viable democratic order and greatly enhanced the likelihood of a return to authoritarian rule in one form or another, often in a form that was more authoritarian and more brutal in its opposition to the forces of democratic change than the one it had replaced. The perfect counterpoint is the case of Germany before 1933, where forces on the Right never succeeded in achieving the degree of political cohesiveness that would have enabled them to assume the mantle of their British counterpart.[2]

The disunity of the German Right was very much a defining feature of the German party system and the way it evolved in the Weimar Republic. The purpose of this study is to examine why a party like the Conservative Party in Great Britain never succeeded in establishing itself as a durable political force in pre-Nazi Germany. Political parties constituted a particularly important feature of Weimar's political landscape. They were, after all, indispensable vehicles for the mediation of social, economic, and political power between the individual, his social class, and the state. At the same time, political parties objectified the basic values of the different "social-cultural milieu" that consti-tuted Germany's political culture. In this respect, political parties not only represented the material interests of specific sectors of German society but also helped articulate the subjective images of the world – or what Max Weber called *Weltbilder* – by which the different segments of the German population came to understand their role in Germany's political system. As Weber wrote in the introduction to his comparative study on the economic ethic of world religions: "Not ideas but material and ideal interests directly govern men's conduct. Yet very frequently the 'world images' that have been created by 'ideas' have, like switchmen, determined the tracks along which action has been pushed by the dynamic of interest."[3]

Fascism: Violence, Ideology, and the Ground of Consent in Germany, 1930–1945 (London and New York, 2013), 13–22.

[2] Daniel Ziblatt, *Conservative Parties and the Birth of Democracy* (Cambridge, 2017), 1–21.

[3] Max Weber, "The Social Psychology of the World Religions," in *From Max Weber: Essays in Sociology*, ed. Hans Gerth and C. Wright Mills (Oxford, 1948), 268.

In his classic formulation of this argument, the German sociologist M. Rainer Lepsius attributed the remarkable stability of the German party system from the founding of the Second Empire in 1871 to the outbreak of the Great Depression at the end of the 1920s to the fact that during this period Germany's political parties functioned as the political "action committees" of four relatively homogeneous, yet structurally complex, political subcultures, or what Lepsius chose to call "social-moral milieus."[4] The strength of Lepsius's approach is that it employs both social and cultural criteria to understand the relationship between Germany's political parties and the different subcultures they represented. This is particularly useful in the case of the German Center Party (Deutsche Zentrumspartei), which had served as the political representative of Germany's sociologically diverse Catholic population since its founding in 1871. Germany's Protestant population, on the other hand, was split into two distinct subcultures, one feudal, rural, and conservative and the other bourgeois, urban, and liberal. The German working class, with its plethora of political, economic, and cultural organizations, constituted the fourth and final subculture upon which the German party system rested.[5]

According to Lepsius, the net effect of this situation was to create a political culture in which the various German parties were concerned more with defending the material and cultural assets of the specific subcultures with which they were identified than with effecting their integration into a national political culture.[6] While this state of affairs may have inhibited the emergence of a homogeneous political culture similar to those that developed in France, Great Britain, or the United States, it nevertheless produced a remarkably high degree of politicization on the part of the Wilhelmine electorate. By the outbreak of World War I, Germany had developed an electoral system in which voters took their right to vote seriously and, in the case of an overwhelming majority of all German voters, exercised that right as a politically meaningful act by which they affirmed their loyalties to the respective subculture to which they belonged. Even if electoral outcomes had little effect upon the personnel or policies of those in control of the existing political system, the cleavages between Germany's different subcultures endowed the right to vote with a significance that was more than purely symbolic. This was no less true of conservatives from east of the Elbe River than it was of Catholics or

[4] M. Rainer Lepsius, "Parteiensystem und Sozialstruktur: zum Problem der Demokratisierung der deutschen Gesellschaft," in *Wirtschaft, Geschichte und Wirtschaftsgeschichte. Festschrift zum 65. Geburtstag von Friedrich Lütge*, ed. Wilhelm Abel, Knut Borchardt, Hermann Kellerbenz, and Wolfgang Zorn (Stuttgart, 1956), 382. See also Wolfram Pyta, *Dorfgemeinschaft und Parteipolitik 1918–1933. Die Verschränkung von Milieu und Parteien in den protestantischen Landgebieten Deutschlands in der Weimarer Republik* (Düsseldorf, 1996).

[5] Lepsius, "Parteiensystem und Sozialstruktur," 383–92.

[6] Ibid., 383.

workers. Even though German conservatives may have had profound reservations about the legitimacy of representative institutions, they nevertheless came to use the ballot not only to defend their vested class interests against the incursion of commercial and industrial capitalism but also to affirm the specific cultural and religious values that were inseparably intertwined with the Prussian way of life.[7]

Much of the following study focuses on the history of the German National People's Party (Deutschnationale Volkspartei or DNVP), a party that was firmly anchored in Germany's predominantly Protestant national-conservative milieu and that served as its primary political representative from the time of its founding in late 1918 through the end of the Weimar Republic. Though still mostly rural, this milieu was no longer as homogeneous as it had been at the beginning of the nineteenth century and had undergone considerable diversification in the preceding half-century. This study is not a conventional party history of the DNVP but seeks to examine the party's development from 1918 to 1930 against the background of what was happening to the larger milieu of which it was a part. In this respect, this project draws not just upon the theoretical insights of Lepsius but upon the more historically rooted applications of the milieu thesis in the works of Karl Rohe, Frank Bösch, and Helga Matthiesen, the last two of which deal specifically with the national-conservative milieu that is the primary focus of this project.[8] A specific goal of this undertaking is to situate the DNVP in the milieu with which it was identified even as that milieu was undergoing a series of dramatic changes in the wake of economic and political modernization. To do this, it will be necessary to place the development of the DNVP in the broader context of its relationships with the various interest groups that constituted the material base of Germany's national-conservative milieu with specific attention devoted to the tensions this produced at various levels of the party organization. This, in turn, will entail a careful study of the aspirations of organized economic interests and how they sought to promote those interests not just within the DNVP but within the German party system as a whole. It will also focus on how the Stahlhelm, the Pan-German League (Alldeutscher

[7] Stanley Suval, *Electoral Politics in Wilhelmine Germany* (Chapel Hill, NC, 1985), 55–63, 97–106. See also Gerhard A. Ritter, "The Social Bases of the German Political Parties, 1867–1920," in *Elections, Parties, and Political Traditions: Social Foundations of German Parties and Party Systems, 1867–1987*, ed. Karl Rohe (Oxford, 1990), 27–52.

[8] For a reassessment of the Lepsius thesis, see Karl Rohe, "German Elections and Party Systems in Historical and Regional Perspective: An Introduction," in *Elections, Parties, and Political Traditions*, ed. Rohe, 1–26, as well as the more specialized applications of the milieu thesis by Frank Bösch, *Das konservative Milieu. Vereinskultur und lokale Sammlungspolitik in ost- und westdeutschen Regionen (1900–1960)* (Göttingen, 2002), and Helge Matthiesen, *Greifswald in Vorpommern. Konservative Milieu im Kaiserreich, in Demokratie und Diktatur 1900–1930* (Düsseldorf, 2000), esp. 75–301.

Verband or ADV), and the various groups that comprised Germany's patriotic Right resisted efforts to use the DNVP as the vehicle for the representation of organized economic interests and how they struggled to reassert the primacy of the national moment in German political life over the purely economic. With the increasing fragmentation of Germany's bourgeois party system in the second half of the 1920s and early 1930s, the focus of the manuscript is broadened to include a detailed analysis of those parties that broke away from the DNVP in an attempt to establish themselves as independent forces on the German Right. The political fragmentation of Germany's bourgeois Right posed a particular challenge to the patriotic Right and its struggle to salvage the national movement from descent into the morass of interest politics, most notably in the 1929 crusade against the Young Plan.

The underlying question is, as Thomas Mergel defined it in a widely cited article in the *Historische Zeitschrift*, how and why did the DNVP not evolve into a German version of British Tory democracy, that is, as a state-supporting conservative party committed to pursuing its objectives within the framework of Germany's republican system of government.[9] Mergel's answer to this question, however, was too narrowly focused on the years from 1928 to 1930 to provide an altogether satisfying answer to the question he had posed. In fact, what happened between 1928 and 1930 was not, as Mergel would have us believe, so much a turning point, a path not taken, as the logical conse- quence of what had already happened, of other paths not taken, in the earlier history of the party. The purpose of this study will be to place the events of 1928 to 1930 in a broader historical perspective by identifying earlier points in the history of the DNVP – for example, in the struggle over the party program in April 1920, the racist crisis of 1922, the split over the Dawes Plan in 1924, the Locarno conflict of 1925, and the DNVP's difficulties as a member of the fourth Marx cabinet in 1927–28 – when the DNVP missed the opportunity to redefine itself in a way that might have contributed to the stabilization of the Weimar system. At the same time, Mergel runs the risk of overestimating the actual potential of the DNVP to develop into a moderate state-supporting conservative party along the lines of the Conservative Party in Great Britian. As Manfred Kittel reminds us in a sharp critique of Mergel's thesis, party leaders often found their hands tied by the strong anti-system sentiment that existed in broad sectors of the DNVP's popular base, a sentiment that could be easily mobilized by those on the party's right wing who adamantly opposed any sort of accommodation with the hated Weimar system.[10] One could argue

---

[9] Thomas Mergel, "Das Scheitern des deutschen Tory-Konservatismus. Die Umformung der DNVP zu einer rechtsradikalen Partei 1928–1932," *Historische Zeitschrift* 276 (2003): 323–68.

[10] Manfred Kittel, "'Steigbügelhalter' Hitlers oder 'stille Republikaner'? Die Deutschnatio- nalen in neuer politikgeschichtlicher und kulturalistischer Perspektive," in *Geschichte der*

that the prospects of a development such as that envisaged by Mergel would have become even more difficult with the economic collapse of the late 1920s.

A somewhat more skeptical assessment of the DNVP's political prospects is to be found in Maik Ohnezeit's monograph on the party's development from its founding in the last months of 1918 to Alfred Hugenberg's election to the DNVP party chairmanship in October 1928.[11] This work is based on extensive research in the surviving party records and the private papers of Count Kuno von Westarp, who served as chairman of the DNVP Reichstag delegation from 1924 to 1928 and as the party's national chairman from 1926 to 1928. It contains a wealth of information on the party's organizational structure and on the decision-making process within the party as a whole. Moreover, Ohnezeit is particularly sensitive to the fissures within the party's social base and the effect these had upon the DNVP's ability to articulate a coherent vision and to pursue a clear and consistent course of action. Yet for all its many virtues, Ohnezeit's study of the DNVP is deficient in several key respects. Most importantly, it does not situate the DNVP's political fortunes during the period under investigation in the general framework of German social and economic development over the same period of time. Similarly, Ohnezeit devotes insufficient attention to special-interest organizations like the National Federation of German Industry (Reichsverband der deutschen Industrie or RDI) and the National Rural League (Reichs-Landbund or RLB) and patriotic associations like the Stahlhelm and Pan-German League (Alldeutscher Verband or ADV) and the demands they placed upon the DNVP's national leadership. It is important, therefore, to view the DNVP's history in the Weimar Republic not just in its own terms but as part of the larger German Right to which it belonged. Third, Ohnezeit's study is essentially a study of the DNVP from the perspective of Berlin and does not adequately address the enormous regional diversity that existed throughout the party organization. A member of the DNVP in Bavaria, for example, had interests and concerns different from those of his counterpart in Württemberg, and both viewed party affairs through a lens that was substantially different from that of their party colleagues in East Prussia or Mecklenburg. Here too it is necessary to broaden the focus that Ohnezeit brings to bear upon the DNVP and its place in the politics of the Weimar Republic.

The development of the German Right in the Weimar Republic was profoundly affected by the general course of German social and economic development. One of the major objectives of this study will be to explore the impact

---

Politik. Alte und neue Wege, ed. Hans-Christof Kraus and Thomas Nicklas, Historische Zeitschrift, Beiheft 44 (Munich, 2007), 201–35.

[11] Maik Ohnezeit, Zwischen "schärfster Opposition" und dem "Willen zur Macht." Die Deutschnationale Volkspartei (DNVP) in der Weimarer Republik 1918–1928 (Düsseldorf, 2011).

of developments in the economy of the Weimar Republic on the DNVP and the interest groups that constituted its material base. The Weimar economy passed through three distinct phases, each with profound implications for the social and economic constituencies that formed the backbone of the DNVP's electorate.[12] Although the runaway inflation of the early 1920s helped keep employment levels high and thus helped hold the radicalization of the German working class in check, it wreaked havoc on the urban middle classes and those sectors of society whose wealth was primarily in the form of paper mark assets. The DNVP was able to capitalize upon the distress that broad sectors of the German middle class experienced as a result of the great inflation, a factor that no doubt helped account for its dramatic victories in the May and December 1924 Reichstag elections. But the stabilization of the German currency at the end of 1923 and the return to normalcy from 1925 to 1929 were accompanied by a sharp increase in unemployment, the collapse of agricultural prices on the world market, and a revolt on the part of small investors who felt victimized by the government's failure to embrace a full and equitable revaluation of the losses they had suffered during the great inflation. This coincided with the DNVP's entry into the government in 1925 and 1927 and the emergence of special-interest parties that articulated their appeals for support in the language of economic self-interest. The heavy losses the DNVP suffered in the May 1928 Reichstag elections bore dramatic testimony to the success with which special-interest parties were able to mobilize the support of specific sectors of the Nationalist electorate. This, in turn, set the stage for a bitter leadership conflict that ended with the defeat of those who had been responsible for the DNVP's two experiments at governmental participation and the triumph of those on the party's extreme right wing who were irreconcilably opposed to any form of collaboration with the hated Weimar system.

The third phase in the economic history of the Weimar Republic began with the outbreak of the world economic crisis in the fall of 1929 and was marked by the end of effective parliamentary rule and the turn to government by presidential decree. In many respects, this represented the fulfillment of what the more moderate elements on the German Right had been hoping for ever since the founding of the Weimar Republic and created opportunities for the pursuit of a conservative agenda that had not existed since the end of the Second Empire. Moderate conservatives both within and outside the DNVP would rally behind the banner of Reich President Paul von Hindenburg and the experiment in government by presidential decree in the hope that this might allow them to reposition themselves as the driving force in German political life. All of this presented the DNVP with a series of challenges that

---

[12] For an overview, see Harold James, "The Weimar Economy," in *Weimar Germany*, ed. Anthony McElligott (Oxford, 2009), 102–26.

would ultimately determine whether it would evolve into the state-supporting conservative party that would play its role in the stabilization of Weimar democracy or remain steadfast in its implacable opposition to the hated Weimar system. Would the DNVP succeed in withstanding the forces of social and political disintegration that the world economic crisis had unleashed throughout the German nation? Would the moderates regain control of the DNVP, or would they be left with no alternative but to try to establish themselves as a viable force outside the orbit of the DNVP? Or would the DNVP somehow manage to reestablish itself as the basis upon which the various elements of a badly fragmented German polity reconstituted themselves as an effective and viable political force? These were indeed critical questions, and the fate of the Weimar Republic would hang in the balance. No less critical was the way in which the DNVP and the forces of the German Right would react to the emergence of the NSDAP as a mass political movement toward the end of the 1920s. Would the DNVP be able to sustain itself as a viable political force in the face of challenge from a party that was more radical both in its recipe for a solution to various ills that bedeviled the German nation and in the methods by which it sought to translate that recipe into reality? Would a badly fragmented German nation discover in nationalism, anti-Marxism, antisemitism, or any combination thereof the ideological basis upon which it could reconstitute itself as the decisive force in German political life? And if so, would the NSDAP replace the DNVP as the party political basis upon which this would take place?[13]

The men who would face these challenges would, for the most part, have defined themselves as conservatives. But, as Oded Heilbronner argued in 2003 in a thought-provoking review of recent literature, the relationship between conservatism and the conservative German Right is problematic and defies any easy one-to-one correlation.[14] In fact, many of those who rose to leadership on the German Right both before and after World War I came not from conservative but from liberal backgrounds.[15] The study of what conservatism meant in its German context is further complicated by the lack of a scholarly consensus over what the term conservatism actually means.[16]

---

[13] In this respect, see Larry Eugene Jones, "Germany's Conservative Elites and the Problem of Political Mobilization in the Weimar Republic," in *Transformations of Populism in Europe and the Americas: History and Recent Tendencies*, ed. John Abromheit, Bridget Maria Chesterton, Gary Marotta, and York Norman (London, 2016), 32–48.

[14] Oded Heilbronner, "The German Right: Has It Changed?" *German History* 21 (2003): 541–61, here 542–46.

[15] Geoff Eley, *Reshaping the German Right: Radical Nationalism and Political Change after Bismarck* (New Haven and London, 1980), 101–15.

[16] Much of what follows identifies themes originally addressed in Larry Eugene Jones and James Retallack, "German Conservatism Reconsidered: Old Problems and New Directions," in *Between Reform and Reaction: Studies in the History of German Conservatism*

Problems of definition stem in large measure from the fact that, unlike liberalism or socialism, conservatism did not originate as an ideology with a fully articulated concept of human nature, the state, and society, but as a reaction to the sudden and dramatic changes that began to transform the face of Europe in the second half of the eighteenth century. In terms of its basic ideological contours, conservatism rejected the liberal doctrine of natural rights in favor of an organic theory of the state and society that affirmed the priority of the general welfare of the whole over the private rights of the individual. In its critique of liberal theories of the state and society, German conservatism drew much of their inspiration from the writings of Edmund Burke and his rejection of the universalist principles that in his mind had led to the outbreak of the French Revolution.[17] In Germany, however, this was reinforced by two further tendencies that gave German conservatism its characteristic form. The first of these was a literary movement known as romanticism and the revolt against reason that had begun in France with the writings of Jean Jacques Rousseau but found many of its most ardent supporters in Germany. The romantics stressed the primacy of feeling and sentiment over reason and replaced the liberal theory of society and its emphasis upon the pursuit of private self-interest with the concept of an organic society in which the welfare of the whole assumed priority over the interests of any of its constituent parts.[18] The second was the wave of nationalist indignation that swept much of Germany following Napoleon's humiliation of Prussia in 1806–07 and that found expression in Johann Gottlieb Fichte's famous *Addresses to the German Nation* from the winter of 1807–08.[19] The symbiosis of German conservatism with romanticism and nationalism provided those who were committed to the preservation of existing social, economic, and political hierarchies with a coherent and emotionally compelling defense of tradition against the corrosive forces of the modern world.[20]

It would take the better part of the next forty years and the revolutionary upheaval of 1848–49 for those who subscribed to these principles to coalesce into political organizations of their own. In this respect, Sigmund Neumann

---

from 1789 to 1945, ed. Larry Eugene Jones and James N. Retallack (Providence, RI, and Oxford, 1993), 1–30, esp. 3–8.

[17] On the German misreading of Burke, see Karl Mannheim, "Conservative Thought," in *From Karl Mannheim*, ed. and with an introduction by Kurt H. Wolff (New York, 1971), 132–222, esp. 140.

[18] Ibid., 142–52. On Rousseau's impact on German political thought, see David James, *Rousseau and German Idealism: Freedom, Dependence, and Necessity* (Cambridge, 2013), 91–142.

[19] Matthew Levinger, *Enlightened Nationalism: The Transformation of Prussian Political Culture, 1806–1848* (New York and Oxford, 2009), 97–99.

[20] Mannheim, "Conservative Thought," 152–60.

distinguished between two antithetical strands within nineteenth-century German conservatism that he identified as "romantic" and "liberal" conservatism and that came together in the period after 1848 to produce a higher synthesis he labelled "realistic conservatism." As representative figures of these three stages in the development of German conservatism, Neumann selected the romantic conservatives Justus Möser and Ludwig von der Marwitz, the liberal conservatives Joseph Maria von Radowitz and Moritz August von Bethmann-Hollweg, and the realistic conservative Otto von Bismarck.[21] In a similar vein, Klaus Epstein in his seminal study of the genesis of German conservative thought from 1770 to 1806 not only stressed the historical specificity of German conservatism as a defense of the *ancient régime* against the universalist principles of the Enlightenment and French Revolution, but also offered a comprehensive definition of conservatism that embraced three distinct ideal types: status quo conservatism, reform conservatism, and reactionaries.[22] The definition of conservative in the German context would become even more complicated with the emergence of "conservative revolutionaries" in the last decades of the nineteenth century. The conservative revolutionaries – epitomized by the likes of Paul de Lagarde, Julius Langbehn, and Arthur Moeller van den Bruck – rejected the ideologies of the nineteenth century, including conservatism itself, as moribund and sterile and evinced a deep-seated animosity to the various manifestations of cultural and political modernity. They espoused a particular hostility toward the materialism of the industrial age and called for the spiritual renewal of the German nation in apocalyptic tones that drew much of their inspiration from the writings of Friedrich Nietzsche. They were also quick to identify the Jew as one of the principal beneficiaries of the modern age and embraced a particularly virulent form of antisemitism that was gaining ever wider acceptance within Germany's conservative establishment.[23] Antisemitism was a well-established and highly recognizable component of right-wing ideology both before and after World War I.

For the most part, the conservative revolutionaries – or "young conservatives" as they preferred to call themselves in the Weimar Republic – remained on the fringes of German political life and exercised little in the way of direct influence on the politics of Germany's conservative elites before World War I. While the study of their ideas is a valuable exercise in and of itself, it is more

---

[21] Sigmund Neumann, *Die Stufen des preußischen Konservativismus. Ein Beitrag zum Staats- und Gesellschaftsbild Deutschlands im 19. Jahrhundert* (Berlin, 1930). See also Hans Jürgen Puhle, "Conservatism in Modern German History," *Journal of Contemporary History* 13 (1978): 689–720.

[22] Klaus Epstein, *The Genesis of German Conservatism* (Princeton, NJ, 1966), 7–11.

[23] See the classic study by Fritz Stern, *The Politics of Cultural Despair: A Study in the Rise of the Germanic Ideology* (Berkeley, CA, and Los Angeles, 1961).

important to place those ideas in a specific historical context and to understand just how those ideas reproduced themselves in the actions of individual men and women. Even then, it is difficult to establish with any degree of precision the exact relationship between thought and action, particularly in the absence of detailed biographical information that can reveal the motives behind the action. In other words, the extent to which ideas influence the political behavior of individual men and women is not always that easy to discern. In the case of Weimar conservatism, however, there was a complex and highly variegated network of clubs, associations, and affiliated publications that enabled Germany's young conservatives to propagate their ideas well beyond the reach of what had been previously possible. One of the distinctive features of Weimar culture was the emergence of revolutionary new modes of communicative discourse that greatly facilitated the exchange and dissemination of ideas.[24] Any study of the German Right in the Weimar Republic would therefore be remiss if it did not also examine the relationship between the network of clubs and organizations through which Germany's young conservative intelligentsia propagated its critique of Weimar political life and the political parties, economic interest organizations, and patriotic associations through which it tried to gain influence.[25] In this respect, however, it would be a serious mistake to assume that Germany's young conservative intelligentsia represented a singular voice with a singular vision of Germany's political future. In point of fact, there was little in the way of ideological cohesion within the ranks of young conservatives, with some embracing a German version of British Tory democracy and others identifying themselves as conservative revolutionaries with nothing but disdain for any compromise with the existing political order. Despite the appeal these ideas held for Weimar's conservative elites, the sheer range of viewpoints within the ranks of Germany's young conservative intelligentsia was indeed daunting and defied the emergence of an ideological consensus upon which the various elements of a badly fragmented German Right might presumably coalesce.[26]

The one area, however, in which the revolutionary conservatives of the late Wilhelmine era are to be cited for their prescience is with respect to the so-called "Jewish question." Antisemitism in one form or another had been a well-defined feature of German life ever since the late Middle Ages and

---

[24] In this respect, see Thomas Mergel, *Parlamentarische Kultur in der Weimarer Republik. Politische Kommunikation, symbolische Politik und Öffentlichkeit im Reichstag* (Düsseldorf, 2002).
[25] This has been persuasively argued in Geoff Eley, "The German Right from Weimar to Hitler: Fragmentation and Coalescence," *Central European History* 48 (2015): 100–13, esp. 107–12.
[26] On this point, see Klemens von Klemperer, *Germany's New Conservatism: Its History and Dilemma in the Twentieth Century*, 2nd printing with a foreword by Sigmund Neumann (Princeton, NJ, 1968), 71–190.

assumed a new virulence after the emancipation of German Jewry in the middle of the nineteenth century. The antisemitism of the German Right was a hodge-podge of different threads of antisemitic thought and practice. Some of it was rooted in inherited religious prejudice, both Lutheran and Catholic. Some of it was of a more recent provenance and had to do with the perception that since their emancipation in the previous century the Jews had come to exert an influence over German social, economic, and cultural life that was incommensurate with their meager numbers. Some of it stemmed from the way in which the Christian-Social tradition of Adolf Stoecker at the end of the nineteenth century had identified Jewishness with the worst excesses of an unbridled capitalism. Some of it was certainly related to the increasingly palpable fear of Bolshevism and social revolution that gripped Europe's propertied classes in the wake of World War I. And some of it was rooted in an aggressive and virulent form of racism and in a racial theory of history that saw the Jews as the heart and soul of a vast and multi-faceted conspiracy aimed at the subjugation, if not the destruction, of the German nation and the last remaining reservoirs of unpolluted Aryan racial stock.[27]

The precise place and function of antisemitism in the development of the German Right both before and after World War I remains a matter of considerable disagreement among historians and students of modern German history.[28] On the one hand, historians have been quick to take note of the fact that antisemitism appears to have become a fairly ubiquitous feature of German political culture by the middle of the nineteenth century and that its potency was greatly intensified by the financial crisis of the 1870s and the onset of the great depression that would last for the next twenty years.[29] On the other hand, efforts to found new political parties that relied first and foremost on antisemitism as a way of attracting mass political support met with repeated failure in the period before 1914.[30] The problem is compounded by the fact that the decade of the 1890s witnessed the emergence of a plethora

---

[27] The preceding has been excerpted from Larry Eugene Jones, "Conservative Antisemitism in the Weimar Republic: A Case Study of the German National People's Party," in *The German Right in the Weimar Republic: Studies in the History of German Conservatism, Nationalism, and Antisemitism*, ed. Larry Eugene Jones (New York and Oxford, 2014), 79–107, here 96.

[28] In this respect, see Oded Heilbronner, "From Antisemitic Peripheries to Antisemitic Centres: The Place of Antisemitism in Modern German History," *Journal of Contemporary History* 35 (2000): 559–76.

[29] For example, see Peter G. J. Pulzer, *The Rise of Political Antisemitism in Germany and Austria* (New York, London, and Sydney, 1964), esp. 75–126. See also Klaus von See, *Freiheit und Gemeinschaft. Völkisch-nationales Denken in Deutschland zwischen Französischer Revolution und Erstem Weltkrieg* (Heildeberg, 2001), esp. 112–74.

[30] Richard S. Levy, *The Downfall of the Anti-Semitic Political Parties in Imperial Germany* (New Haven, CT, and London, 1975), esp. 225–53.

of organizations on the moderate to the radical Right that unhesitatingly placed antisemitism and the search for a solution to the so-called Jewish question at the core of their existence. The most important of these was the Pan-German League, an organization that had been founded in the early 1890s in an effort to mobilize popular support for an imperialist agenda that would transform Germany from a European into a world power but that by the turn of the century had become one of the German Right's most outspoken and unrelenting voices in the struggle against the threat of Jewish world domination.[31] But the agitation of the Pan-German League was only one aspect of a far more radical transformation of German political life in the late nineteenth century that marked the eclipse of National Liberal hegemony and the emergence of a new and more stridently populist form of German nationalism.[32] To highlight the differences between these organizations and those that had come into existence at an earlier stage in Germany's political development, historians such as Geoff Eley and James Retallack have adopted the term "New Right" to distinguish populist and nationalist organizations like the ADV, the German Naval League (Deutscher Flottenverein), and the Society for the Eastern Marshes (Deutscher Ostmarkenverein) from older and more established forms of conservative political engagement.[33] To be sure, not all of the organizations that belonged to the "New Right" embraced the ADV's antisemitism or the sense of urgency it attached to the quest for a solution to Germany's "Jewish question." But antisemitism would become an increasingly prominent feature of right-wing political culture as organizations as diverse as the German Conservative Party (Deutschkonservative Partei or DKP), the Agrarian League (Bund der Landwirte or BdL), and the German National Union of Commercial Employees (Deutschnationaler Handlungsgehilfen-Verband or DHV) all

[31] On the founding and early history of the ADV, see Rainer Hering, *Konstruierte Nation. Der Alldeutsche Verband 1890 bis 1939* (Hamburg, 2003), 110–33, as well as Björn Hofmeister, "Between Monarch and Dictatorship: Radical Nationalism and Social Mobilization of the Pan-German League, 1914–1939" (Ph.D. diss., Georgetown University, 2012), 25–67.

[32] In this respect, see the two seminal essays by Geoff Eley, "Reshaping the Right: Radical Nationalism and the German Navy League, 1898–1908," *Historical Journal* 21 (1978): 327–54, and idem, "The Wilhelmine Right: How It Changed," in *Society and Politics in Wilhelmine Germany*, ed. Richard J. Evans (London and New York, 1978), 112–35, as well as Eley, *Reshaping the German Right*, 19–98. See also Peter Walkenhorst, *Nation – Volk – Rasse. Radikaler Nationalismus im Deutschen Kaiserreich 1890–1914* (Göttingen, 2007), 38–79.

[33] On this distinction, see Geoff Eley, "Conservatives and Radical Nationalists in Germany: the Production of Fascist Potentials, 1912–28," in *Fascists and Conservatives: The Radical Right and the Establishment in Twentieth-Century Europe*, ed. Martin Blinkhorn (London, 1990), 50–70, esp. 61–65, and James Retallack, *The German Right, 1860–1920. Political Limits of the Authoritarian Imagination* (Toronto, 2006), 76–107.

incorporated antisemitic language of one sort or another into their official programmatic statements.

Antisemitism would become a well-defined trademark of Germany's political culture well before the outbreak of World War I. The failure of antisemitic parties to establish themselves as a viable force in German political life might very well suggest that antisemitism had become such a ubiquitous feature of German political life that antisemitic parties were unnecessary or superfluous. This also might suggest that while antisemitism ran broadly throughout the different sectors of German bourgeois society, it did not run all that deeply and that it lacked the emotional intensity to transform itself into an effective and durable political movement. Just how all of this would be sorted out in both theory and practice would remain one of the most vexing challenges for the DNVP and its allies on the German Right in the Weimar Republic. Germany would experience a veritable explosion of antisemitism in the first years after the end of World War I, an explosion fueled by the trauma of defeat and inflation, the fear of Bolshevism, and a conspiratorial theory of history that portrayed the Jew as the archenemy of the German people and as the architect of all the misfortunes that had befallen Germany.[34] Much of this temporarily abated with the economic and political stabilization of the Weimar Republic in the second half of the 1920s. But with the onset of the world economic crisis at the end of the 1930s, antisemitism regained much its earlier virulence with devastating consequences for the fate of Weimar democracy.

The September 1930 Reichstag elections represented a dramatic turning point in the history of the Weimar Republic. The shift to government by presidential decree in the spring of 1930 and the increasing reliance upon the special emergency powers that the Weimar Constitution had invested in the office of the Reich presidency effectively destroyed the last vestiges of parliamentary government at the national level. The emergence of the NSDAP as a mass political party in the 1930 Reichstag elections fundamentally altered the calculus of right-wing politics in the Weimar Republic and amounted to a decisive break with established patterns of parliamentary discourse. Not only had the forces on the moderate Right, including those that had recently broken away from the DNVP in the second of two major secessions on the party's left wing, failed to come together into some sort of united front during the campaign, but the DNVP went down to a major defeat that saw it completely eclipsed on the radical Right by the NSDAP. With more than six million votes and 107 deputies in the Reichstag, the NSDAP was the second largest party in the newly elected parliament and stood on the threshold of a bid for power that would end with Adolf Hitler's appointment as chancellor less than two

---

[34] Werner Jochmann, "Die Ausbreitung des Antisemitismus," in *Deutsches Judentum in Krieg und Revolution 1916–1923. Ein Sammelband,* ed. Werner E. Mosse (Tübingen, 1971), 409–510.

years later. In the wake of these developments. the complex and multi-tiered interrelationships that had developed between organized economic interests and political parties in the first years of the Weimar Republic – in fact, these relationships had already begun to take shape before the outbreak of World War but were greatly accentuated by the transition to parliamentary democracy in 1918–19 – completely unraveled. Any chance that the DNVP or any other constellation of forces on the German Right might evolve into a state-supporting conservative party capable of facilitating the transition from authoritarian to democratic government was dealt a well-neigh fatal blow by the verdict of September 1930. By this point, the more traditional elements on the German Right were no longer capable of offering any sort of effective resistance to the rise of National Socialism and the appeal it held for diverse sectors of the German population. To the contrary, the divisions on the German Right only played into the hands of the Nazis and greatly facilitated their march to power. The disunity of the German Right thus constituted a precondition for the Nazi rise to power that was every bit as important as the schism on the socialist Left or the fragmentation of the German middle.

1

Revolution and Realignment

World War I was a catastrophe for virtually every sector of German society with the possible exception of workers in the war industries and the industrialists and managers who profited from their control of the warime economy. The rest of the economy – and in particular agriculture, the retail sector, and small and middle-sized manufacturing – was decimated by acute shortages of manpower, energy, raw materials, and capital.[1] As the war entered its third year in the fall of 1916, the sense of national euphoria and affirmation of national unity that had greeted its outbreak two years earlier gave way to a mixture of disillusionment, stoic resignation, and outright bitterness over the way in which Germany's political leadership had failed to deliver on its promise of a quick, decisive victory.[2] In the public eye, blame for the catastrophic series of events that had befallen Germany over the preceding decade rested squarely on the shoulders of those conservative elites in the government and military who were responsible for Germany's entry into the war and the conduct of the German military effort. This represented a dramatic intensification of the crisis of conservative hegemony that had been simmering severe ever since the *Daily Telegraph* affair in the fall of 1908 and that now found its most sensational expression in the passage of the Reichstag's Peace Resolution in June 1917. Not only did the passage of the Peace Resolution represent a direct challenge to the political prerogatives of Germany's conservative elites, but it brought together the three components of the political alliance – the Social Democrats, the Center, and the left-liberal Progressive People's Party (Fortschrittliche Volkspartei) – that would vie for power through the remainder of the war and into the postwar period.[3] Just how the leaders of Germany's

---

[1] On the social effects of World War I, see Jürgen Kocka, *Klassengesellschaft im Krieg. Deutsche Sozialgeschichte 1914–1918* (Göttingen, 1973), esp. 65–195; Gerald D. Feldman, *Army, Industry, and Labor in Germany, 1914–1918* (Princeton, NJ, 1966), 459–77; and Roger Chickering, *Imperial Germany and the Great War, 1914–1918* (Cambridge, 1998), 95–131.

[2] Chickering, *Imperial Germany*, 132–67.

[3] Klaus Epstein, "Der Interfraktionelle Ausschuß und das Problem der Parlamentarisierung 1917–1918," *Historische Zeitschrift* 191 (1960) 562–84.

conservative parties would respond to the military defeat of 1918 and to the revolution that would sweep away the institutions through which Germany's conservative elites had exercised their political hegemony for almost half a decade remained an open question as they turned their attention to the challenges of survival in a radically transformed new order.

The Many Faces of Wilhelmine Conservatism

Before the outbreak of World War I no less than four conservative parties had dotted Germany's political landscape.[4] Of these, the oldest and most important was the German Conservative Party. Ever since its founding in 1876, the DKP had functioned as the political instrument of East Elbian aristocrats fearful that Prussia's absorption into the new German Empire would infringe upon their own historic rights and privileges. The party, whose parliamentary strength had peaked in the late 1880s when it had elected no fewer than eighty deputies to the Reichstag, had fallen upon hard times since the turn of the century, polling only 9.2 percent of the popular vote and electing just forty-two deputies in the 1912 Reichstag elections.[5] Since 1911 leadership of the party had rested in the hands of a special three-man committee consisting of Ernst von Heydebrand und der Lasa, Oskar von Normann, and Karl Stackmann. The first of these three had also served as chairman of the party's delegation to the Prussian Landtag since 1906, while his counterpart in the Reichstag, Count Kuno von Westarp, had assumed his post as late as 1913. In terms of its basic ideological orientation, the DKP was unequivocally committed not only to the preservation of the Hohenzollern monarchy and the defense of aristocratic privilege, but also to the maintenance of Prussian hegemony over the rest of the Reich. Above all else, the leaders of the DKP were adamantly opposed to the democratization of the existing political system and categorically rejected any reform of the Prussian franchise that might undermine the powers of the crown and aristocracy. In the last years before the outbreak of World War I, however, the leaders of the DKP came to feel as if they and all they stood for was under siege from below.[6] Whether they

---

[4] Volker Stalmann, "Vom Honoratrioren- zum Berufspolitiker: Die konservativen Parteien," in *Regierung, Parlament und Öffentlichkeit im Zeitalter Bismarcks. Politikstil im Wandel*, ed. Lothar Gall and Dieter Langewiesche (Paderborn, 2003), 91–125.

[5] For further details, see James N. Retallack, *Notables of the Right: The Conservative Party and Political Mobilization in Germany, 1876–1918* (Boston, 1988), as well as the anthology of Retallack's articles published under the title *The German Right, 1860–1920: Political Limits of the Authoritarian Imagination* (Toronto, Buffalo, NY, and London, 2006).

[6] James Retallack, "Heydebrand and Westarp: Leaving behind the Second Reich," in James Retallack, *Germany's Second Reich: Portraits and Pathways* (Toronto, Buffalo, and London, 2015), 202–34.

and the interests they represented would survive the transition to the age of parliamentary democracy remained to be seen.

The DKP's counterpart outside of Prussia was the Imperial and Free Conservative Party (Reichs- und freikonservative Partei or RFKP), more popularly known inside Prussia proper as the Free Conservatives.[7] Like its Prussian counterpart, the RFKP had been founded in the mid-1870s as a consequence of the split that the unification of Germany had produced within conservative ranks between those who supported and those who opposed unification on the terms proffered by the Iron Chancellor Otto von Bismarck. Whereas the leaders of the DKP feared that Prussia's absorption into the newly founded German Empire would lead to the loss of historic rights and privileges for the Prussian aristocracy, the Free Conservatives were less heavily committed to the defense of Prussian privilege and more closely tied to Germany's emerging industrial elite than the DKP. With the appointment of Bernhard von Bülow as chancellor in 1900, the Free Conservatives resolved their differences with the DKP and joined it, the Center, and the National Liberals in the so-called Bülow Bloc that coalesced behind the chancellor after the 1903 Reichstag elections and that functioned as an unofficial parliamentary coalition before falling apart in the dispute over a reform of the federal tax system in 1908–09. Throughout all of this, the RFKP's strength at the polls continued to plummet from a peak of 13.6 percent of the popular vote in the late 1870s to 3.0 percent in 1912.[8]

The declining electoral fortunes of the DKP and RFKP extended as well to the two remaining conservative parties of any note, the Christian-Social Party (Christlich-soziale Partei) and the German-Racist Party (Deutschvölkische Partei). The Christian-Socials traced their origins to the 1870s, when Adolf Stoecker, the court pastor of Wilhelm I, had tried to counter the appeal of a newly reunified socialist movement by founding a party of his own, the Christian-Social Workers' Party (Christlich-soziale Arbeiterpartei).[9] The real target of Stoecker's strategy, however, was not so much the German worker as the independent middle class of small shopkeepers and artisans. In an attempt to capitalize upon the economic distress this sector of German society had experienced since the onset of the "great depression," Stoecker and his associates not only called for the introduction of legislation that would protect the independent middle class against the vicissitudes of a market economy but,

---

[7] Matthias Alexander, *Die Freikonservative Partei 1890–1918. Gemäßigter Konservatismus in der konstitutionellen Demokratie* (Düsseldorf, 2000), esp. 27–42.

[8] Ibid., 268–346. See also Georg von Below, *Die politische Lage im Reich und in Baden* (Heidelberg, 1910).

[9] On the Christian-Social movement, see Martin Spahn, "Die christlichsoziale Bewegung," *Hochland* 26 (1929): 164–82. See also Norbert Friedrich, *"Die christlich-soziale Fahne empor!" Reinhard Mumm und die christlich-soziale Bewegung* (Stuttgart, 1997), 60–114.

more importantly, tried to place the blame for its economic difficulties on the Jewish control of German financial institutions.[10] The Christian-Socials, however, experienced a great deal of difficulty establishing themselves as an independent political entity, and at the beginning of the 1880s they entered into a special arrangement with the German Conservative Party.[11] This alliance lasted until the mid-1890s, at which time Stoecker and his followers decided to sever their ties with the DKP and refound their party amidst a new and indeed more highly charged wave of agitation against the social and economic influence of German Jewry. Although Franz Behrens and the generation of Christian-Socials who gained control of the party after Stoecker's political retirement in 1907 moderated their antisemitism in favor of a heightened emphasis upon the social gospel of Lutheranism and what it had to offer the German worker,[12] the Christian-Social Party never elected more than a handful of deputies in any national election and remained at best a marginal factor in Wilhelmine political life.[13]

If in the last years before the outbreak of World War I the Christian-Socials were in the process of retreating from the more extreme antisemitism of Stoecker and his generation, this could not be said of the German-Racist Party. This party, which had been created through the merger of the German Social Party (Deutschsoziale Partei) and the German Reform Party (Deutsche Reformpartei) in March 1914, was dominated by a leadership cadre that subscribed to the most virulent brand of racial antisemitism the nineteenth century had to offer. Whereas the antisemitism of the Christian-Socials had been primarily religious and economic in nature, the leaders of the German-Racist Party regarded the Jew as a racial parasite that had to be expunged from all aspects of German life or else the German people would experience the slow death of racial decay.[14] This particular brand of antisemitism, however, was no more attractive to the average German than that of the Christian-Socials – a

---

[10] On Stoecker, see Werner Jochmann, "Stoecker als nationalkonservativer Politiker und antisemitischer Agitator," in Günter Brakelmann, Martin Greschat, and Werner Jochmann, *Protestantismus und Politik. Werk und Wirkung Adolf Stoeckers* (Hamburg, 1982), 123–98, as well as Klaus Motschmann, "Ein aussichtsloser Kampf um die innere Einheit Deutschlands – Adolf Stoecker (1834–1909)," in *Konservative Politiker in Deutschland. Eine Auswahl biographischer Porträts aus zwei Jahrzehnte*, ed. Hans-Christoph Kraus (Berlin, 1995), 206–33.

[11] Retallack, *Notables of the Right*, 36–53.

[12] For example, see the reports by Mumm and Behrens in *Bericht über den Christlich-sozialen Parteitag am 6., 7. und 8. September 1913 in Bielefeld* (Bielefeld, n.d. [1913]), 8–20.

[13] Levy, *Anti-Semitic Parties*, 245–47.

[14] Stefan Breuer, *Die Völkischen in Deutschland. Kaiserreich und Weimarer Republik* (Darmstadt, 2008), 68–83. See also Werner Bergmann, "Völkischer Antisemitismus im Kaiserreich," in *Handbuch zur Völkischen Bewegung 1871–1918*, ed. Uwe Puschner, Walter Schmitz, and Justus H. Ulbricht (Munich, 1996), 449–63.

fact to which the weakness of its two forerunners in the 1912 Reichstag elections clearly attested – with the result that the German-Racist Party too had been effectively relegated to the margins of German political life by the time war broke out in August 1914.[15] Appearances notwithstanding, the weakness of Germany's antisemitic parties in the last decade before the outbreak of World War I did not necessarily mean that German society had become any more tolerant of Jews or that antisemitism was no longer a relevant issue in Wilhelmine politics. To the contrary, this might very well suggest that antisemitism had become such a pervasive and widely accepted feature of right-wing politics in Wilhelmine Germany that single-issue parties such as the German-Racist Party were no longer necessary or viable.[16]

The last decade of the Second Empire was marked by a political stalemate that neither the champions nor the opponents of reform were able to turn to their advantage.[17] Under these circumstances, the forces on the German Right tried to shore up their position following their defeat in the March 1912 Reichstag elections by founding the Cartel of Productive Estates (Kartell des schaffenden Stände) as the rallying point around which the various social and economic groups that supported their political agenda could unite. Among the organizations that came together in August 1913 to form the Cartel of Productive Estates were the Agrarian League, the Central Association of German Industrialists (Centralverband Deutscher Industrieller or CDI), the Association of German Peasant Unions (Vereinigung der christlichen Bauernvereine Deutschlands or VdB), and the Imperial German Middle-Class League (Reichsdeutscher Mittelstandsverband).[18] But the cartel, whose program amounted to a virtual declaration of war against the Social Democrats and their allies in the struggle for a democratic reform of German political life, failed to win the support of prominent conservative parliamentarians like Heydebrand and Westarp and remained little more than an empty specter devoid of lasting influence upon Germany's political development.[19]

---

[15] Levy, *Anti-Semitic Parties*, 251–53. See also Uwe Lohalm, *Völkischer Radikalismus. Die Geschichte des Deutschvölkischen Schutz- und Trutz-Bundes 1919–1923* (Hamburg, 1970), 68–71.

[16] For example, see Peter Walkenhorst, *Nation – Volk – Rasse. Radikaler Nationalismus im Deutschen Kaiserreich 1890–1914* (Göttingen, 2006).

[17] For further details, Wolfgang J. Mommsen, "The Latent Crisis of the Wilhelmine Empire: The State and Society in Germany, 1890–1914," in Wolfgang J. Mommsen, *Imperial Germany, 1867–1918: Politics, Culture, and Society in an Authoritarian State*, trans. by Richard Deveson (London, 1995), 141–62.

[18] Dirk Stegmann, *Die Erben Bismarcks. Parteien und Verbände in der Spätphase des wilhelminischen Deutschlands. Sammlungspolitik 1897–1918* (Cologne, 1970), 360–68.

[19] Retallack, *Notables of the Right*, 214–15.

World War I and the Fatherland Party

The extent to which the anxiety that Germany's conservative elites felt over their inability to contain or suppress the challenge for democratic reform may have contributed to the recklessness that Germany's political leadership displayed during the July crisis of 1914 and remains a question of immense complexity and enduring controversy.[20] Still, there can be little doubt that the disarray of the German Right on the eve of World War I severely handicapped the efforts of Germany's conservative leadership to steer a clear and unequivocal course of action during the first years of the war. The dilemma in which Germany's conservative elites found themselves was complicated by the fact that the proclamation of the *Burgfrieden* and the enthusiasm with which the Social Democrats embraced the call to arms in August 1914 intensified the split between those like Chancellor Theobald von Bethmann Hollweg who sought to build a broad domestic consensus for the conduct of the war and those on the far Right who persisted in their demagogy against organized labor. The situation was complicated even further by the indecisive nature of the war itself and the conflict this engendered both outside and within the cabinet. As the war entered its third year, Bethmann Hollweg's enemies on the extreme Right intensified their campaign against his conduct of the war and demanded his removal from office so that military victory, replete with extensive territorial conquests on both the eastern and western fronts, might be possible.[21] Not only did agitation of this sort have a polarizing effect upon German political life as a whole, but it also succeeded in bringing the leadership of Germany's conservative parties more and more into the orbit of the radical Right.[22]

At no point were the polarization of German political life and the radicalization of the German Right more apparent than following the passage of the Peace Resolution in the summer of 1917. The adoption of the Peace Resolution was significant not only as a barometer of German war-weariness but also because it signalled a shift in the balance of power within the Reichstag from those parties that were opposed to the democratization of German political life to those that sought a thorough reform of the existing political system and the establishment of a viable parliamentary democracy.[23] Rocked by what the passage of the Peace Resolution meant for its hegemonial aspirations both at

---

[20] See the essay by Mommsen cited above, n. 18, as well as the classic statement of this argument by Wolfgang J. Mommsen, "Domestic Factors in German Foreign Policy before 1914," in Mommsen, *Imperial Germany*, 163–88.

[21] For further details, see Heinz Hagenlücke, *Deutsche Vaterlandspartei. Die nationale Rechte am Ende des Kaiserreiches* (Düsseldorf, 1997), 49–142.

[22] For example, see Retallack, *Notables of the Right*, 215–20, and Friedrich, "*Christlich-soziale Fahne*," 109–14.

[23] For further details, see Chickering, *Imperial Germany*, 160–67.

home and abroad, the German Right responded by launching the German
Fatherland Party (Deutsche Vaterlandspartei or DVLP). After a series of
preliminary meetings that were conducted with the utmost secrecy in late
August and early September 1917,[24] the Fatherland Party held its first public
rally in Berlin's Philharmonic Hall on 24 September with Wolfgang Kapp,
Admiral Alfred von Tirpitz, and Duke Johann Albrecht zu Mecklenburg as the
featured speakers. In one speech after another, the founders of the new party
hailed the DVLP as a radically new political construction consecrated in the
spirit of August 1914, that mystical moment in which all partisan differences
dissolved in a mood of popular euphoria as a united German nation went to
war.[25] Only by invoking the spirit of those sacred August days and by uniting
all those Germans who placed love of nation before partisan or sectarian
interest would it be possible, as the DVLP's first chairman Alfred Tirpitz
claimed, for Germany to crush the forces of defeatism at home and secure
an honorable peace commensurate with the sacrifices of the German people
and Germany's mission as a world power.[26]

The driving force behind the founding of the German Fatherland Party was
Wolfgang Kapp, a former official in the Prussian civil administration who had
spearheaded the campaign against Bethmann Hollweg in 1915–16.[27] Kapp,
who enjoyed close ties to the leaders of the Pan-German League, envisaged the
Fatherland Party as a platform for launching the candidacy of the one-time
naval minister Tirpitz for the chancellorship. But Tirpitz, who had endeared
himself to the extreme Right by resigning from the cabinet in March 1916 in
protest against the government's refusal to resume unrestricted submarine
warfare, shared none of the anti-Catholic, antisocialist animus, or even anti-
Jewish animus that lay at the heart of the Pan-German ideology and embraced
a concept of national inclusiveness that had little in common with that of
Kapp and his supporters on the far Right. Its internal divisions notwithstanding, the Fatherland Party recruited nearly a million members in the first year
of its existence and developed a broad base of support that clearly eclipsed that
of any of Germany's nonsocialist parties. The key to the DVLP's success lay
not merely in the massive support it received from its benefactors in German
industry but more importantly from Tirpitz's refusal to embroil the new party

[24] Hagenlücke, *Vaterlandspartei*, 143–64.

[25] Remarks of Gottfried Traub in Deutsche Vaterlands-Partei, *Deutsche Ziele. Reden bei der
    ersten öffentlichen Partei-Kundgebung* (Berlin, n.d. [1917]), 25–30. See also Jeffrey Ver-
    hey, *The Spirit of 1914: Militarism, Myth, and Mobilization in Germany* (Cambridge,
    2000), 178–85.

[26] Speech by Tirpitz in DVLP, ed., *Deutsche Ziele*, 5–15. See also Deutsche Vaterlandspartei,
    Landesverband Bayern, *Was will die Deutsche Vaterlandspartei?* (Diessen vor München,
    n.d. [1917–18]), esp. 7–10.

[27] See the broadside by Wolfgang Kapp, *Die nationalen Kreise und der Reichskanzler.
    Denkschrift* (Königsberg, 1916).

in the struggle over domestic political issues such as electoral reform for fear that this might alienate constituencies he deemed vital for the success of the party's struggle for an honorable peace replete with territorial acquisitions on both the western and eastern fronts. Not surprisingly, the DVLP met with a cool response from the leaders of the German Conservative Party and failed to attract significant support outside the ranks of Germany's educated and propertied bourgeoisie.[28]

While the government generally welcomed the support it received from the Fatherland Party and its efforts to mobilize public opinion for the war effort, the DVLP remained on the periphery of the decision-making process and never succeeded in exercising the influence over governmental policy for which Tirpitz and Kapp had been hoping. Though temporarily buoyed in the spring of 1918 by military success in the east and by improved prospects for victory in the west, Tirpitz and the leaders of the Fatherland Party lamented the lack of support they had received from Germany's political parties in their efforts to overcome the partisan divisions that in their mind continued to undermine Germany's will to win.[29] In the meantime, war-weariness continued to take its toll on the national will to fight with serious consequences for the DVLP. As contributions from heavy industry dried up and membership dues no longer sufficed to cover the expenses of the party's elaborate propaganda apparatus, the DVLP found itself in such a severe financial crisis by the summer of 1918 that even Tirpitz began to despair of its prospects.[30] Not even the founding of the German Workers and Employees' Party (Deutsche Arbeiter- und Angestelltenpartei or DAAP) in March 1918 as a front for attracting the support of working-class and white-collar elements that otherwise would have remained aloof from the Fatherland Party could reverse the DVLP's flagging fortunes.[31] With the collapse of the much-vaunted

[28] See Hagenlücke, *Vaterlandspartei*, 248–371, and Stegmann, *Erben Bismarcks*, 497–518. See also Dirk Stegmann, "Vom Neokonservatismus zum Proto-Faschismus: Konservative Partei, Vereine und Verbände 1893–1920," in *Deutscher Konservatismus im 19. und 20. Jahrhundert. Festschrift für Fritz Fischer*, ed. Dirk Stegmann, Bernd-Jürgen Wendt, and Peter-Christian Witt (Bonn, 1983), 218–23. For DVLP's regional profile, see Hans Peter Müller, "Die Deutsche Vaterlandspartei in Württemberg 1917/18 und ihre Erbe. Besorgte Patrioten oder rechte Ideologen?" *Zeitschrift für Württembergische Landesgeschichte* 59 (2000): 217–45, and Dirk Stegmann, "Die Deutsche Vaterlandspartei in Schleswig-Holstein 1917–1918. Konservative Sammlungsbewegungen in der Provinz," *Demokratische Geschichte* 20 (2009): 41–75. On Tirpitz and the Pan-Germans, see Raffael Scheck, *Alfred von Tirpitz and German Right-Wing Politics, 1914–1930* (Atlantic Highlands, NJ, 1998), 65–81.

[29] Tirpitz's speech at the second party congress of the DVLP, 19 Apr. 1918, in *Mitteilungen der Deutschen Vaterlands-Partei*, 29. Apr. 1918, no. 12.

[30] Scheck, *Tirpitz*, 73–74.

[31] On the DAAP, see Hagenlücke, *Vaterlandspartei*, 344–51, and Dirk Stegmann, "Zwischen Repression und Manipulation: Konservative Machteliten und Arbeiter- und Ange-

"Michael's Offensive" in the late summer of 1918 and the growing realization that Germany would have to settle at best for a negotiated peace without significant territorial gains, the DVLP's call for an honorable peace was all but drowned out in the rising tide of war-weariness and economic hardship.[32]

While the Fatherland Party was effectively paralyzed by the deteriorating military situation and the erosion of popular support for a continuation of the war, the parliamentary leaders of Germany's conservative parties moved quickly to salvage what they could of their own political position. With Germany's military collapse in the fall of 1918, most German conservatives conceded that far-reaching changes in Germany's political system were unavoidable. Under these circumstances, political fragmentation was a luxury German conservatives could no longer afford. Exploratory negotiations between representatives of the various conservative parties had taken place sporadically throughout the war, but with the rapidly deteriorating situation at the front and the growing specter of revolution at home they assumed even greater urgency. The leaders of the German Conservative Party had initiated a comprehensive revision of the 1893 Tivoli party program in the spring of 1918 and had entered into confidential negotiations with the other conservative parties about the establishment of closer ties between their respective organizations. The DKP's efforts to revise its party program were essentially complete by the end of October 1918, and on 7 November the DKP executive committee met in emergency session in Berlin to appoint a special commission under Westarp's chairmanship to bring the negotiations with the leaders of the other right-wing parties to a successful conclusion.[33] These developments, however, were quickly overtaken when just two days later Kaiser Wilhelm II announced his abdication and the Social Democrats' Philipp Scheidemann proclaimed the founding of a republic from the balcony of the Reichstag.

The Search for Conservative Unity

Though not entirely unexpected, the collapse of the Hohenzollern monarchy on 9 November 1918 sent shock waves throughout the German conservative establishment. By no means, however, was the upheaval confined to Prussia, as popular demonstrations in Munich, Stuttgart, Leipzig, and elsewhere heralded the collapse of the monarchal order throughout Germany. Stunned by these developments, Westarp left Berlin and did not follow up on his party's

stelltenbewegung 1910–1918. Ein Beitrag zur Vorgeschichte der DAP/NSDAP," *Archiv für Sozialgeschichte* 12 (1972): 351–432.

[32] For further details, see Hagenlücke, *Vaterlandspartei*, 372–85.

[33] Kuno von Westarp, *Die Regierung des Prinzen Max von Baden und die Konservative Partei 1918* (Berlin, n.d. [1928]), 112–14.

decision to initiate negotiations with the other right-wing parties about their consolidation into a single conservative party.[34] It was not until after the leaders of the various conservative parties came together more or less by coincidence at the funeral of Baron Karl Friedrich von Gamp-Massaunen, the parliamentary leader of the Free Conservatives who had died on 15 November, that negotiations to found a united conservative party were resumed.[35] Representatives from the four conservative parties met repeatedly over the course of the next week before issuing an appeal on 22 November that announced the founding of the German National People's Party.[36] The appeal took great pains to portray the DNVP as a totally new political party and, at the insistence of the Free Conservatives and Christian-Socials, assiduously avoided language that might identify it too closely with the prewar DKP.[37] Above all else, the appeal emphasized the sociological heterogeneity of the DNVP and insisted that the new party, as its name suggested, was a people's party that appealed across class, confessional, and regional lines to all sectors of the German population.[38]

Both the Christian-Socials and Free Conservatives were quick to endorse the founding of the DNVP and to recommend it to their followers as the proud heir to their own political traditions. The Christian-Socials had played a

[34] Kuno von Westarp, *Konservative Politik im Übergang vom Kaiserreich zur Weimarer Republik*, ed. Friedrich Freiherr Hiller von Gaertringen with assistance from Karl J. Mayer and Reinhold Weber (Düsseldorf, 2001), 13–15. See also Daniela Gasteiger, *Kuno von Westarp (1864–1945). Parlamentarismus, Monarchismus und Herrschaftsutopien im deutschen Konservatismus* (Berlin, 2018), 149–56.

[35] Westarp, *Konservative Politik*, ed., Hiller von Gaertringen, 17–18. See also Hans Erdmann von Lindeiner-Wildau, "Konservatismus," in *Volk und Reich der Deutschen. Vorlesungen gehalten in der Deutschen Vereinigung für Staatswissenschaftliche Fortbildung*, ed. Bernhard Harms, 3 vols. (Berlin, 1929), 2: 49.

[36] There is no official protocol of the negotiations that culminated in the founding of the DNVP. For Westarp's role, see "Mein Anteil an den Gründungsverhandlungen der Deutschnationalen Volkspartei," n.d., Nachlass Kuno Graf von Westarp, Archiv der Freiherrn Hiller von Gaertringen, Gärtringen (hereafter cited as NL Westarp, Gärtringen), II/1, as well as Westarp, *Konservative Politik*, ed. Hiller von Gaertringen, 20–22. See also the detailed report prepared by Brauer for Heydebrand, 24 Nov. 1918, records of the Deutschkonservative Partei, Bundesarchiv Berlin (hereafter cited as BA Berlin), Bestand R 8003, 2/2–10. For further information, see Lewis Hertzman, "The Founding of the German National People's Party, November 1918–January 1919," *Journal of Modern History* 30 (1958): 24–36; Jan Striesow, *Die Deutschnationale Volkspartei und die Völkisch-Radikalen 1918–1922* (Frankfurt a.M., 1981), 9–43, and Ohnezeit, *Zwischen "schärfster Opposition,"* 30–46.

[37] Westarp to Kreth, 10 Jan. 1919, BA Berlin, Nachlass Kuno Graf von Westarp, 37/6–8.

[38] "Gründungsaufruf der Deutschnationalen Volkspartei," 22 Nov. 1918, reprinted in the *Neue Preußische (Kreuz-Zeitung)*, 24 Nov. 1918, no. 595. See also Henning von Koß, *Die Parteien und ihre Programme im Lichte der Wirklichkeit. Ein politischer Wegweiser*, Deutschnationale Politik, no. 5 (Berlin, n.d. [1919]), 39.

particularly prominent role in the deliberations that had led to the founding of the DNVP, and Wilhelm Wallbaum, their present chairman, wasted no time in petitioning the members of his party's executive committee for authorization to conclude the merger with the DNVP after negotiations with Adam Stegerwald and the leaders of the Christian labor movement on the founding of an interconfessional Christian workers' party had broken down.[39] Though initially more reluctant than most of his colleagues to support the new party, Stoecker's son-in-law and Christian-Social parliamentarian Reinhard Mumm stepped into the breach and succeeded in rallying the Christian-Social organization throughout the country to the DNVP's political banner.[40] In a parallel action, the leaders of the Imperial and Free Conservative Party, who along with the Christian-Socials had been the driving force behind the founding of the DNVP, voted at a meeting of the RFKP central committee (Hauptausschuß) on 13 December to instruct all party members to join the DNVP and to place their party's resources at the disposal of the DNVP.[41] It was a somewhat different situation within the German Conservative Party. Heydebrand, Westarp, and their party colleagues were aggravated over the way in which the Christian-Socials and Free Conservatives had wrested leadership of the movement for conservative unity from their hands and were far less than enthusiastic about the emerging shape of the DNVP.[42] Although Westarp and his associates found themselves the target of a virtual putsch that had been organized and conducted by leaders of the DKP organization outside of Berlin, there was little their opponents could do but endorse the new party. At a meeting of the DKP executive committee on 3 December party leaders threw their full support behind the DNVP, though without authorizing the dissolution of their own party.[43] Westarp's strategy as the DKP's chief liaison to the DNVP was first to bring the DKP as intact as possible into the new party and second to mould the new party as much as possible in the spirit of the

---

[39] Wallbaum to the CSP central executive committee (Hauptvorstand), 27 Nov. 1918, BA Berlin, Nachlass Reinhard Mumm, 31/7–8. See also Mumm, *Christlich-soziale Gedanke*, 88–130, and Friedrich, *Christlich-soziale Fahne*, 177–88.

[40] Mumm to Dietrich, 18 Nov. 1918, BA Berlin, NL Mumm, 277/20–22. See also Friedrich, *Christlich-soziale Fahne*, 187, and Helmut Busch, "Reinhard Mumm als Reichstagsabgeordneter," *Jahrbuch des Vereins für Westfälische Kirchengeschichte* 65 (1972): 189–217, esp. 190, n. 4. See also the correspondence between Heuser and Mumm, 12–15 Nov. 1918, BA Berlin, NL Mumm, 277/13–15, and Veidt to Mumm, 16 Nov. 1918, ibid., 277/18–19.

[41] For the rationale behind this decision, see Georg von Below, *Recht und Notwendigkeit der Deutschnationalen Volkspartei*, Vortragsentwurf, no. 1 (Berlin, n.d. [1919]).

[42] For example, see Westarp to Klasing, 25 Mar. 1919, BA Berlin, NL Westarp, 37/42–43. On Westarp's strategy, see Gasteiger, *Westarp*, 159–78.

[43] Westarp, *Konservative Politik*, ed. Hiller von Gaertringen, 24–25. See also Westarp's undated memorandum on the meeting of the DKP executive committee, 3 Dec. 1919, as well as the memorandum from the DKP executive committee to the party's state and provincial organizations, n.d., both in NL Westarp, Gärtringen, II/1.

DKP.[44] In a similar vein, the leaders of the minuscule German-Racist Party realized that they too had no choice but to cast their lot with the DNVP, though clearly with the intention of using it into an instrument for the propagation of their racist and antisemitic propaganda.[45]

At the same time that the various right-wing parties were lining up in support of the DNVP, the new party also received surprisingly strong support from another source, namely, former liberals who had been active in the Fatherland Party. Here the central figure was Gottfried Traub, a Protestant pastor who had belonged to the left-liberal Progressive People's Party (Fortschrittliche Volkspartei) before the war but who had become increasingly involved in the activities of the DVLP during the war aims controversy of 1917–18. After the collapse of November 1918 Traub had hoped that those National Liberals who had not aligned themselves with the German Democratic Party (Deutsche Demokratische Partei or DDP) would find their way to the DNVP and was disappointed by the decision of Gustav Stresemann, the parliamentary leader of the all but defunct National Liberal Party (Nationalliberale Partei or NLP), to found a new party of his own, the German People's Party (Deutsche Volkspartei or DVP), instead of joining the DNVP.[46] In this regard Traub worked closely with Georg Wilhelm Schiele, a conservative who had played a prominent role in the Fatherland Party, in drafting plans for the creation of a Section for the Liberal Bourgeoisie (Abteilung für das liberale Bürgertum) within the DNVP as a way of uniting liberal and conservative behind its banner.[47] These efforts received strong support from press magnate Alfred Hugenberg, himself a product of that National Liberal milieu that had crystallized during the struggle for German unification and an outspoken and uncompromising nationalist who had joined the DNVP shortly after its founding.[48] On 10 December the national committee (Reichsausschuß) of the Fatherland Party met in Berlin to initiate its liquidation and agreed, at

---

[44] Westarp to Kreth, 10 Jan. 1919, BA Berlin, NL Westarp, 37/6–8.

[45] Fricke, "Deutschvölkische Partei," in *Lexikon zur Parteiengeschichte*, ed. Fricke et al., 1:561.

[46] Gottfried Traub, "Wie ich deutschnationale wurde," in *Deutscher Aufstieg. Bilder aus der Vergangenheit und Gegenwart der rechtsstehenden Parteien*, ed. Hans von Arnim and Georg von Below (Berlin, 1925), 423–40. On Traub's involvement in the DNVP, see Willi Heinrichs, *Gottfried Traub (1869–1956). Liberaler Theologe und extremer Nationalprotestant* (Waltrop, 2001), 280–86. On the founding of the DVP, see Larry Eugene Jones, *German Liberalism and the Dissolution of the Weimar Party System, 1918–1933* (Chapel Hill, NC, 1988), 15–29.

[47] See Schiele to Hugenberg, 5 Dec. 1918, and Traub, 6 Dec. 1918, Bundesarchiv Koblenz (hereafter cited as BA Koblenz), Nachlass Alfred Hugenberg, 46/59–60, 52–53, as well as the entries in Traub's diary for 22 Nov.–5 Dec. 1918, BA Koblenz, Nachlass Gottfried Traub, 8/6–8, and Traub's unpublished memoirs, ibid., 5/72–73.

[48] Heidrun Holzbach, *Das "System Hugenberg." Die Organisation bürgerlicher Sammlungspolitik vor dem Aufstieg der NSDAP* (Stuttgart, 1981), 70–73.

Traub's urging, to place what little remained of its resources at the disposal of the DNVP.[49] By providing the DNVP with immediate access to the DVLP's rank-and-file membership, which tended to be more bourgeois and nationalist than aristocratic or conservative in its basic political orientation, this only helped confirm the DNVP's image of itself as a new and socially comprehensive *Sammelpartei* unencumbered by the stigma of the prewar DKP.

Diversity in Unity

The founding of the German National People's Party met with an enthusiastic response not just from conservative strongholds east of the Elbe[50] but from conservative and nationalist circles throughout the country. In areas as diverse as Bavaria, Württemberg, Saxony, and Thuringia, news of the party's founding provided local conservatives with a sense of the direction in which they should be headed and galvanized them into action. In Bavaria, where the National Liberals were quick to cast their lot with the left-liberal German Democratic Party,[51] Franconian conservatives under the leadership of school teacher Hans Hilpert reacted to the collapse of their efforts to reach an accord with the state NLP by officially launching a party of their own, the Bavarian Middle Party (Bayerische Mittelpartei or BMP), in Nuremburg on 10 December 1918.[52] Hilpert and his supporters were also anxious to stem the tide of defections among Munich conservatives led by Baron Wilhelm von Pechmann to the

---

[49] Protocol of the meeting of the DVLP national committee, 10 Dec. 1918, BA Koblenz, Nachlass Wolfgang Kapp, 7.

[50] For example, see Wilhelm Kähler, *Die Gründung der Deutschnationalen Volkspartei. Vortrag, gehalten als Einführung in das Verständnis ihrer Ziele, vor der Greifswalder Studentenschaft* (Greifswald, n.d. [1919]), 13–15. For further details, see Bert Becker, "Revolution und rechte Sammlung. Die Deutschnationale Volkspartei in Pommern 1918/19," in *Geist und Gestalt im historischen Wandel. Facetten deutscher und europäischer Geschichte 1789-1989. Festschrift für Siegfried Bahne*, ed. Bert Becker and Horst Lademacher (Münster, New York, Munich, and Berlin, 2000), 211–30, as well as Matthiesen, *Greifswald in Vorpommern*, 82–97.

[51] Larry Eugene Jones, "Nationalism, Particularism, and the Collapse of the Bavarian Liberal Parties, 1918-1924," *Jahrbuch zur Liberalismus-Forschung* 14 (2002): 105–42, here 110–18.

[52] On the founding of the BMP, see Wengg to Weilnböck, 23 Nov. 1918, and Hilpert to Weilnböck, 21 Nov. and 5 Dec. 1918, BA Koblenz, Nachlass Luitpold von Weilnböck, 46b. For further details, see Hilpert, "Die Gründung der Bayerischen Mittelpartei und ihre Notwendigkeit," *Blätter der bayerischen Mittelpartei* 1, no. 14 (7 Dec. 1919): 79–82, and no. 15 (21 Dec. 1919): 88–91. See also Manfred Kittel, "Zwischen völkischem Fundamentalismus und gouvernementaler Taktik. DNVP-Vorsitzender Hans Hilpert und die bayerischen Deutschnationalen," *Zeitschrift für bayerische Landesgeschichte* 59 (1996): 849–901, esp. 856–61, and Elina Kiiskinen, *Die Deutschnationale Volkspartei in Bayern (Bayerische Mittelpartei) in der Regierungspolitik des Freistaats während der Weimarer Zeit* (Munich, 2005), 38–44.

Bavarian People's Party (Bayerische Volkspartei or BVP), a party that Georg
Heim, Sebastian Schlittenbauer, and the leaders of the Bavarian branch of the
Christian Peasant Unions had founded in Regensburg four weeks earlier as a
Bavarian alternative to the German Center Party.[53] In the meantime, the BMP
party leadership tried to shore up its political prospects by negotiating a
merger with the Bavarian branch of the Agrarian League, the bastion of
agrarian conservatism in prewar Franconia. Although these negotiations failed
to produce the desired result, the Bavarian BdL nevertheless encouraged its
members to vote for the BMP – and by extension for the DNVP as well – in
the upcoming state and national elections.[54]

A similar pattern emerged in Württemberg, where leaders of the bourgeois
Right reacted to the collapse of the imperial order by founding the Württemberg Burgher Party (Württembergische Bürgerpartei or WBP) at a demonstration in Stuttgart on 19 December 1918. Here the initial impulse came from
Walter Hirzel and Gustav Beißwänger, the latter a one-time disciple of left-
liberal Friedrich Naumann who hoped that it might be possible to unite the
Württemberg bourgeoisie in all of its social and political diversity into a single
political party. But when Johannes Hieber and the left wing of the Württemberg National Liberals merged with the prewar German People's Party to form
the state chapter of the newly founded German Democratic Party, Beißwänger
and his supporters became increasingly dependent upon the leaders of the
Württemberg branch of the German Conservative Party, who up to this time
had done their best to avoid the political limelight.[55] In the meantime, the
Burgher Party had begun to receive important declarations of support from
former National Liberals like Wilhelm Bazille and Gottlob Egelhaaf as well as
from many who had not affiliated themselves with any of Württemberg's
prewar parties.[56] All of this made it possible for the WBP's founders to portray

---

[53] For further details, see Weber to Weilnböck, 23 Nov. 1918, BA Koblenz, NL Weilnböck,
46b. On the founding of the BVP, see Claudia Friemberger, *Sebastian Schlittenbauer und
die Anfänge der Bayerischen Volkspartei* (St. Ottilien, 1998), 46–62, 98–102.

[54] Report on the meeting of the executive committee of the Bavarian BdL, 21 Dec. 1918, BA
Koblenz, NL Weilnböck, 46b.

[55] See Ernst Marquardt, "Kaempfer fuer Deutschlands Zukunft und Ehre. Umrisszeichnungen aus der Geschichte der deutschnationalen Volkspartei Württembergs," unpublished
manuscript from 1934 in the Württembergische Landesbibliothek Stuttgart, 10–14. See
also Hans Peter Müller, "Die Bürgerpartei/Deutschnationale Volkspartei (DNVP) in
Württemberg 1918-1933. Konservative Politik und die Zerstörung der Weimarer Republik," *Zeitschrift für Württembergische Landesgeschichte* 61 (2002): 375–433, esp. 376–69,
and Reinhold Weber, *Bürgerpartei und Bauernbund in Württemberg. Konservativen
Parteien im Kaiserreich und in der Weimarer Republik (1895 bis 1933)* (Düsseldorf,
2004), 121–32.

[56] On Bazille, see Hans Peter Müller, "Wilhelm Bazille. Deutschnationaler Politiker, württembergischer Staatspräsident 1874-1934," *Lebensbilder aus Baden-Württemberg* 21
(2005): 480–517, esp. 486–93.

the Burgher Party as an entirely new conservative *Sammelpartei* that sought to rescue the German nation from the morass in which it currently found itself.[57] But whatever concessions the founders of the Burgher Party might have made to attract National Liberal support were undercut by the fact that in campaign for the elections to the National Assembly the WBP renewed the DKP's long-standing alliance with Theodor Körner alt of the Württemberg Peasants and Winegrowers' League (Württembergischer Bauern- und Weingärtnerbund or WBWB).[58] As the Württemberg section of the Agrarian League, the WBWB had been a bastion of Württemberg conservatism before the war and espoused an unabashedly antisemitic and antirepublican line that undercut the more moderate profile the Burgher Party hoped to project.[59]

The founding of the Bavarian Middle Party and the Württemberg Burgher Party afforded the DNVP access to new and potentially significant voter constituencies in regions where the conservative parties had not performed all that well before the war. Moreover, both BMP and WBP would conclude electoral alliances with the state affiliates of the newly founded German People's Party, which had been so decimated by defections to the left-liberal German Democratic Party that they lacked the organization to conduct campaigns of their own.[60] In Saxony and Thuringia, on the other hand, the DNVP's state organizations were more firmly integrated into the national party from the very outset. The DKP had been a well-established feature of the Saxon political landscape long before the outbreak of World War I and relied upon an old and deeply rooted tradition of political antisemitism to mobilize opposition against liberal efforts to reform Saxony's political institutions.[61] On 5 December the leaders of the Saxon DKP endorsed the DNVP and encouraged its members to support it in the upcoming national and state elections.[62] At the same time,

[57] *Richtlinien für die Politik der Württ. Bürgerpartei* (Stuttgart, n.d.), esp. 1–2, 9–14, reprinted in *Jahrbuch der Württ. Bürgerpartei – Deutschnationalen Volkspartei Württembergs 1921*, ed. W. Haller-Ludwigsburg (N.p., n.d. [1921]), 18–31.

[58] Müller, "Bürgerpartei," 385–87.

[59] For further details, see Hans Peter Müller, "Landwirtschaftliche Interessenvertretung und völkisch-antisemitische Ideologie. Der Bund der Landwirte/Bauernbund in Württemberg 1895–1918," *Zeitschrift für Württembergische Landesgeschichte* 53 (1994): 263–300. For the flavor of the WBWB's antisemitism, see Theodor Körner alt, ed., *Das grune Buch der Bauernpolitik. Ein politisches Handbuch für Wähler in Stadt und Land* (Stuttgart, 1931), 22–23.

[60] Wolfgang Hartenstein, *Die Anfänge der Deutschen Volkspartei 1918–1920* (Düsseldorf, 1962), 65.

[61] On this point, see James Retallack, "Conservatives and Antisemites in Baden and Saxony," *German History* 17 (1999): 507–26. See also Retallack, *The German Right*, 273–324, as well as his magnum opus *Red Saxony: Election Battles and the Spectre of Democracy in Germany, 1860–1918* (Oxford, 2016), 199–231, 255–68.

[62] Unpublished memoirs of Albrecht Philipp, "Mein Weg: Rückschau eines Siebzigjährigen auf allerlei Geschenisse und Menschen, Dritte Teil: Abgeordnetenjahre in der

the Saxon branch of the Agrarian League, which was in the process of reconstituting itself as the Saxon Rural League (Sächsischer Landbund or SLB), decided not to follow the example of its Württemberg counterpart by forming an independent party of its own but threw its full support behind the DNVP at both the state and national levels.[63] In the neighboring state of Thuringia, on the other hand, none of the prewar conservative parties were in a position to assume the initiative, which passed into the hands of local farm leaders who, in breaking away from the Junker-dominated Agrarian League, formed an independent agricultural interest organization of their own, the Thuringian Rural League (Thüringer Landbund or TLB). Though allied with the DNVP at the national level, the founders of the TLB moved quickly to transform their organization from a simple lobby for the representation of agricultural economic interests into a regional political party with a diversified social base recruited from precisely those elements that had come to form the backbone of the DNVP's electoral constituency in other parts of the country.[64]

From the outset, the founders of the German National People's Party conceived of their new party as a sociologically and confessionally heterogeneous conservative *Sammelpartei* that sought to explode the ecological boundaries of prewar German conservatism.[65] In this respect, the DNVP resembled more the wartime German Fatherland Party than the prewar German Conservative Party. The East-Elbian aristocrats who had dominated the DKP before the war had been pushed to the background as a new cadre of conservative leaders recruited in large part from the ranks of the Free Conservatives, Christian-Socials, and German Fatherland Party came to the fore.[66] Nowhere was the shift in leadership more evident than in the election of Oskar Hergt as the DNVP's national chairman at the first meeting of the DNVP executive

---

Weimarer Republik (1919–1930)," Sächsisches Hauptstaatsarchiv Dresden (hereafter cited as SHStA Dresden), Nachlass Albrecht Philipp, 5/3–7.

[63] See Benjamin Lapp, *Revolution from the Right: Politics, Class, and the Rise of Nazism in Saxony, 1919–1933* (Atlantic Highlands, NJ, 1997), 21–52, esp. 26–27.

[64] For further details, see Guido Dressel, *Der Thüringer Landbund – Agrarischer Berufsverband als politische Partei in Thüringen 1919–1933* (Weimar, 1998), 12–30, and Jochen Grass, *Studien zur Politik der bürgerlichen Parteien Thüringens in der Weimarer Zeit 1920–1932. Ein Beitrag zur Landesgeschichte* (Hamburg, 1997), 120–36, 168–83.

[65] For example, see Peter-Christian Witt, "Eine Denkschrift Otto Hoetzschs vom 5. November 1918," *Vierteljahrshefte für Zeitgeschichte* 21 (1973): 337–53.

[66] Becker, "Revolution und rechte Sammlung," 215–20. This was also true in West Germany. See Gisbert Jörg Gemein, "Politischer Konservatismus am Rhein und in Westfalen in der Weimarer Zeit am Beispiel der Deutschnationalen Volkspartei," in *Rheinland-Westfalen im Industriezeitalter. Beiträge zur Landesgeschichte des 19. und 20. Jahrhunderts*, ed. Kurt Düwell and Wolfgang Köllmann, vol. 3: *Vom Ende der Weimarer Republik bis zum Land Nordrhein-Westfalen* (Wuppertal, 1984), 62–75.

committee on 9 December 1918.[67] A career civil servant who had served as Prussian Finance Minister in 1917–18, Hergt had not belonged to any of the prewar conservative parties and was thus not identified with any of the factions that had come together to found the DNVP. Hergt was thus ideally suited to promote the DNVP's image as a comprehensive conservative *Sammelpartei* open to all of those who, regardless of class, confession, or geographical region, were willing to work together in bringing about the rebirth of the German phoenix from the ashes of defeat and revolution. At the same time, however, Hergt was unschooled in the ways of party politics, and it was by no means clear that he was equal to the task of negotiating the conservative ship of state through the uncharted waters of mass democracy.[68] Whether he and his supporters would succeed in transforming the DNVP into a genuine people's party capable of accommodating itself to the demands of the new political order was far from certain.

Conflicting Messages

German conservatives entered the campaign for the January 1919 elections to the National Assembly with enormous liabilities. The widespread disillusionment that had accompanied the military and political collapse of November 1918 left German conservatives at a profound psychological disadvantage in the period leading up to the elections. Their prospects were particularly depressing in former conservative strongholds east of the Elbe, where socialist agitators had already started to organize farm laborers into the German Farm Workers' Union (Deutscher Landarbeiterverein or DLV), a union affiliated with socialist labor,[69] while in the cities and towns the conservatives were slow in mobilizing their supporters for the upcoming elections to the National Assembly and the various constitutional assemblies that were being convened

---

[67] Meeting of the DNVP executive committee, 19 Dec. 1918, BA Koblenz, NL Traub, 50/96–100. See also the report from Marx to an unidentified recipient, 24 Dec. 1918, Landesarchiv Nordrhein-Westfalen Münster, Archiv des Westfälisch-Lippischer Wirtschaftsverband (hereafter cited as LaNRW Münster), Nachlass Clemens Graf von Schorlemer-Lieser, Bestand C113, Bestand B, vol. 42.

[68] On Hergt, see Annelise Thimme, *Flucht in den Mythos. Die Deutschnationale Volkspartei und die Niederlage von 1918* (Göttingen, 1969), 34–45.

[69] For an overview, see Jens Flemming, "Landarbeiter zwischen Gewerkschaften und 'Werkgemeinschaft.' Zum Verhältnis von Agrarunternehmern und Landarbeiterbewegung in der Anfangsphase der Weimarer Republik," *Archiv für Sozialgeschichte* 14 (1974): 351–418. On the situation in Pomerania, see Shelley Baranowski, *The Sanctity of Rural Life: Nobility, Protestantism, and Nazism in Weimar Prussia* (New York and Oxford, 1995), 40–41, and Daniel Hildebrand, *Landbevölkerung und Wahlverhalten. Die DNVP im ländlichen Raum Pommerns und Ostpreußens 1918–1924* (Hamburg, 2004).

Figure 1.   Photograph of Oskar Hergt, DNVP party chairman from 1918 to 1924 and vice chancellor and Reich minister of justice in 1927–28. Reproduced with permission from the Bundesarchiv Berlin, Bild 183-2009-0316-500

in different German states.[70] The leaders of the new conservative party also found themselves competing for the votes of the German people under circumstances radically different from those that had existed before the war. The most important of these differences involved the introduction of universal suffrage and the elimination of the discriminatory franchises in Prussia and elsewhere that had allowed Germany's upper classes to retain political power in the face of an increasingly determined challenge from below.[71] These changes made it incumbent upon the leaders of the DNVP to broaden their

---

[70] Hans-Joachim Bieber, *Bürgertum in der Revolution. Bürgerräte und Bürgerstreiks in Deutschland 1918-1920* (Hamburg, 1992), 71–77. On the disorganization of urban conservatives in the aftermath of the November Revolution, see the entries for 7–14 Jan. 1919, in Georg Schönath, "Göttinger Tagebuch Oktober 1918 bis März 1919," *Göttinger Jahrbuch* 24 (1976): 171–203, as well as Günter Hollenburg, "Bürgertum und Revolution in Frankfurt a.M. 1918/19," *Blätter für deutsche Landesgeschichte* 115 (1979): 69–120, and Günter Hollenburg, "Die bürgerlichen Schichten zwischen Sammlung und sozialliberaler Koalition 1918/19," *Vierteljahrshefte für Zeitgeschichte* 27 (1979): 392–430.

[71] For an overview, see Gerhard A. Ritter, "Kontinuität und Umformung des deutschen Parteiensystems 1918-1920," in *Entstehung und Wandel der modernen Gesellschaft. Festschrift für Hans Rosenberg zum 65. Geburtstag*, ed. Gerhard A. Ritter (Berlin, 1970), 342–84.

party's base of support if they hoped to compete in any sort of meaningful way for control of the state. In this respect, however, party strategists found themselves at a severe disadvantage. For not only did the political momentum rest with those parties that identified themselves with Germany's fledgling republican order, but the consolidation of the different conservative party organizations that had come together to found the DNVP was far from complete by the time the campaign was under way. This, along with the short time in which the DNVP had to prepare for the election, severely handicapped party leaders when it came to articulating their message and mobilizing those sectors of the German population that were still reeling from the shock of the lost war and collapse of the old imperial order.

In the campaign for the elections to the National Assembly, DNVP party strategists went to great lengths to portray their party as an entirely new party unencumbered by the mistakes of the past and inspired by the dream of reconciling all of those of genuine national feeling in a new and enduring conservative synthesis.[72] As the thirty-seven-year-old Prussian civil servant Ulrich von Hassell wrote for the *Neue Preußische (Kreuz-)Zeitung* in early January 1919, it was the task of the DNVP to rescue all that was "eternal and valuable from the past" for the creation of the new. This, Hassell continued, could take place only on the "basis of a strong national state" that is firmly anchored in German ethnicity, or *Deutschtum*, and inspired by a genuine social and Christian spirit. "Then and only then," concluded Hassell, "would the party build the bridges between the old and new and win the generations of the past and future for its political mission, that is, only if it organizes itself for the new age as a truly new party."[73] Hassell's initiative received strong support from those who wished to put as much distance between themselves and the prewar DKP. Nowhere was this more apparent than in the "Ziele der Deutschnationalen Volkspartei," the only comprehensive programmatic statement the DNVP released in the short time that remained before the January elections. This statement stressed the party's commitment "to cooperate on the basis of any form of government in which law and order prevailed." Although the statement categorically rejected a one-sided socialist republic, it did not preclude cooperation on the basis of the republican form of government as long as all sectors of society could take part in the decision-making process. Still, the Nationalists remained committed to monarchism as the system of

[72] Ohnezeit, *Zwischen "schärfster Opposition,"* 159–64. See also Lewis Hertzman, *DNVP: Right-Wing Opposition in the Weimar Republic, 1918–1924* (Lincoln, NB, 1963); and Jan Striesow, *DNVP und die Völkisch-Radikalen,* 44–63.

[73] Hassell, "Grundsätzliches zur Deutschnationale Volkspartei," n.d. [Jan. 1919], BA-Berlin, NL Mumm, 276/7. See also Gregor Schöllgen, "Wurzeln konservativer Opposition. Ulrich von Hassell und der Übergang vom Kaiserreich zur Weimarer Republik," *Geschichte in Wissenschaft und Unterricht* 38 (1987): 478–89.

government that experience had shown to be the best guarantor of public order and security and that had contributed in no small measure to the greatness of Prussia and Germany.[74] At the same time, the "Ziele der Deutschnationalen Volkspartei" committed the DNVP to the struggle against dictatorship and terrorism, the preservation of free enterprise and private property, and the end of wartime economic controls with special attention devoted to the threat of socialization in agriculture, the economic plight of the German middle class, and the right of workers to organize for the improvement of their social and economic circumstances. In a similar vein, the party committed itself to help those who had been disabled or who had lost their husbands and fathers in the Great War.[75]

All of this was designed to present the DNVP in the most favorable light possible, that is, as a dynamic and socially comprehensive conservative party with a social conscience and a genuine concern for the material and moral welfare of all sectors of German society.[76] What the "Ziele," however, did not reveal was a darker side to the DNVP's propaganda that surfaced in other party publications. For at the same time that the DNVP tried to portray itself as a positive and progressive conservative party, it also preyed upon the fears of Bolshevism to which events first in Russia and then closer to home had given rise.[77] Party strategists also evoked the "Stab-in-the-Back Legend" to mobilize popular sentiment against the political legacy of the November Revolution. The DNVP blamed the revolution for everything from the undisciplined retreat of German troops from the front and the Allied seizure of locomotives and rolling stock to the food shortages and other deprivations at home.[78] Moreover, attacks

---

[74] *Ziele der Deutschnationalen Volkspartei*, Deutschnationale Flugschrift, no. 2 (Berlin, n.d. [1919]), 4. For a particularly eloquent statement of the DNVP's ideological profile, see Friedrich Brunstäd, "Die Weltanschauung der Deutschnationalen Volkspartei," in *Der nationale Wille. Werden und Wirken der Deutschnationalen Volkspartei 1918–1928*, ed. Max Weiß (Essen, 1928), 54–82.

[75] Ibid., 4–8.

[76] In a similar vein, see Karl Helfferich, *Rede des Herrn Staatsministers Dr. Helfferich gehalten am 7. Januar 1919 in der Öffentliche Versammlung der Deutschnationalen Volkspartei in Greifswald* (Greifswald, n.d. [1919], esp. 9–14.

[77] For example, see "Gegen den Bolschewismus. Die dringendsten Pflichten eines Deutschen," n.d. [1918–19], DNVP-Werbeblatt, no. 56, Bayerisches Hauptstaatsarchiv, Munich, Abteilung V, Flugblattsammlung-60 (hereafter cited as BHStA Munich), Abt. V, F-60.

[78] "Das Verdienst der Revolution," n.d. [1918–19], DNVP-Werbeblatt, no. 33, BHStA Munich, Abt. V, F-60. The DNVP targeted veterans of World War I for this propaganda. See "Soldaten!," n.d. [1918–19], DNVP-Werbeblatt, no. 20, ibid. On the "Stab-in-the-Back Legend," see Friedrich Hiller von Gaertringen, "'Dolchstoß'-Diskussion und 'Dolchstoßlegende' im Wandel von vier Jahrzehnten," in *Geschichte und Gegenwartsbewußtsein. Historische Betrachtungen und Untersuchungen. Festschrift für Hans Rothfels zum 70. Geburtstag*, ed. Waldemar Besson and Friedrich Hiller von Gaertringen (Göttingen, 1963), 122–60, and Boris Barth, *Dolchstoßlegenden und politische Desintegration. Das*

on the legacy of the November Revolution were frequently laced with strong doses of antisemitism. The last years of World War I had witnessed a veritable explosion of antisemitism at all levels of German society, and the racists in the DNVP were anxious to tap into this sentiment as quickly and effectively as possible.[79] One DNVP leaflet entitled "Wählt keine Judenlisten" could not have been more explicit about the relationship between the revolutionary upheavals at the end of 1918 and the influence of international Jewry: "The political collapse of our Fatherland," it claimed, "can be traced first and foremost to the destructive influence and single-minded [*zielbewußte*] activity of international Jewry... The revolutions are the star of Judas."[80]

Such attacks became more frequent as the campaign drew to a climax and stood in sharp contrast to the conciliatory language of the "Ziele der Deutschnationalen Volkspartei." Even relative moderates like Friedrich Edler von Braun who campaigned in Bavaria on the joint ticket shared by the DVP and DNVP felt compelled to address the Jewish question. While acknowledging the great service that individual Jews had rendered Germany in the areas of scholarship, literature and art and carefully dissociating himself from the agitation of radical antisemites, Braun continued:

> The Jewish question is one of the most deeply touching problems of the current scene, and one can not ignore it in formulating quidelines for policy. The Jews are a people without a home and destroy every national body in which they gain a decisive influence, for they are international and cosmopolitan in their disposition and historical development and must therefore necessarily disrupt the processes of national development. Proof of this can be seen in their close connection with Social Democracy, whose teachings come from Marx and Lassalle and is therefore born from the Jewish spirit. So also was the majority of the leaders of the revolution in Russia and Germany Jews. Here I do not need to remind you of their names but only point to the fact that far more than a half of the ministers in the revolutionary government consisted of Jews ... It is gainst this overgrowth of the Jewish influence [*Überwuchern des jüdischen Einflusses*] in politics, against its domination of capital and the press, that we must turn and protect ourselves if we are not to fail in our obligations to our own people. We must protect the German oak from the being choked by the these usurous weeds [*Wucherpflanze*] if one day we do not want to appear decayed and rotten to the core.[81]

Traume der deutschen Niederlage im Ersten Weltkrieg 1914–1933 (Düsseldorf, 2003), esp. 301–21.

[79] Jochmann, "Ausbreitung des Antisemitismus," 409–510, esp. 412–86.

[80] *Im Deutschen Reich* 25 (1919): 71, cited in Striesow, *DNVP und die Völkisch-Radikalen*, 61. See also Jones, "Conservative Antisemitism," 79–107.

[81] [Friedrich Edler von Braun], *Wahlrede des Kandidaten der Bayerischen Mittelpartei (Deutsch-Nationale Volkspartei in Bayern und der Deutschen Volkspartei (Nationalliberale Partei) Staatsrat von Braun* (Augsburg, n.d. [1918–19], 6.

Figure 2. Antisemitic handout for the 1919 elections to the Weimar National Assembly designed by Otto v. Kursell, January 1919. Reproduced with permission from the Bundesarchiv Berlin, Plakat 0002-033-052

What this revealed was an almost schizophrenic contradiction in the party's self-image that was temporarily obscured by the turmoil of 1918–19 but that would become increasingly apparent with the passage of time. At the heart of this contradiction lay the fact that the DNVP embraced two fundamental and ultimately irreconcilable tendencies, one a governmental conservatism associated with the likes of Hergt, Westarp, and Karl Helfferich that was prepared to pursue its objectives within the framework of the existing political order and the other a radical nationalism that was unconditionally opposed to Germany's new republican order and sought nothing less than its total destruction. The fact that the DNVP's national headquarters was still in the process of being established and was therefore unable to exercise much control over the activities of the party's regional and local organizations further compromised its ability to develop a unified and coherent electoral message. In tayloring their party's campaign propaganda to local conditions, the DNVP's local leaders focused on issues of immediate concern that frequently diverged from the thrust of the party's national campaign. The fear of revolution and rejection of the new republican order was frequently much stronger at the local and regional levels of the DNVP's national organization than among those who had assumed leadership of the party in Berlin, a fact that only further undermined the coherence of the DNVP's campaign for the 1919 elections to the National Assembly and undercut the conciliatory tenor the party's national leadership sought to project in programmatic statements such as the "Ziele der Deutschnationalen Volkspartei." This was particularly true in Bavaria and Württemberg, where the DNVP's regional affiliates were still nominally independent of the national party and relied much more heavily than the party's Berlin leadership upon antisemitism as a way of mobilizing their electorates.[82]

One area in which all party leaders were in essential agreement, however, was the need to mobilize the women's vote.[83] In the last decades of the Second Empire, women had become increasingly active in a wide range of conservative and right-wing political organizations, including the Association of Conservative Women (Vereinigung Konservativer Frauen or VKF) that had been founded in 1913 as a women's auxiliary of the DKP.[84] The founding of the VKF, however, was only one sign of the widespread mobilization of conservative women in the years before and during the war, a phenomenon that also included the formation of charitable and confessional organizations like the Protestant Women's Aid (Evangelische Frauenhilfe) and German Protestant Women's League (Deutsch-Evangelischer Frauenbund), housewives' organizations like the National Federation of Agricultural Housewives' Associations (Reichsverband landwirtschaftlicher Hausfrauenvereine or RLHV) and its urban counterpart the Federation of German Housewives' Associations (Verband Deutscher Hausfrauenvereine) as well as the emergence of patriotic associations like the Patriotric Women's Club (Vaterländischer Frauenverein or VFV), the Naval League of German Women (Flottenbund Deutscher Frauen), and the Women's Club of the German Colonial Society (Frauenbund der deutschen Kolonialgesellschaft).[85] For most of the women involved in

---

[82] On the decentralized character of the DNVP party organization, see Ohnezeit, *Zwischen "schärfster Opposition,"* 47–59. On the relative autonomy of the party affiliates in Bavaria and Württemberg, see Striesow, *DNVP und die Völkisch-Radikalen,* 213–32, and Müller, "Burgerpartei," 380–85.

[83] Roger Chickering, "'Casting Their Gaze More Broadly': Women's Patriotic Activism in Imperial Germany," *Past and Present* 118 (1988): 156–85. See also Christiane Streubel, "Frauen der politischen Rechten in Kaiserreich und Republik. Ein Überblick und Forschungsbericht," *Historical Social Research* 28 (2003): 103–66.

[84] For further details, see Kirsten Heinsohn, "Im Dienste der deutschen Volksgemeinschaft: Die 'Frauenfrage' und konservative Parteien vor und nach dem Ersten Weltkrieg," in *Nation, Politik und Geschlect. Frauenbewegungen und Nationalismus in der Moderne,* ed. Ute Planert (Frankfurt a.M. and New York, 2000), 131–46.

[85] Streubel, "Frauen der politischen Rechten," 110–24. See also Andrea Süchting-Hänger, *Das "Gewissen der Nation." Nationales Engagement und politisches Handeln konservativer Frauenorganisationen 1900 bis 1937* (Düsseldorf, 2002), esp. 19–90. On the RLHV, see Renate Bridenthal, "Organized Rural Women and the Conservative Mobilization of the

Figure 3. DNVP campaign placard designed by an unidentified graphic artist for the 1919 elections to the Weimar National Assembly, January 1919. Reproduced with permission from the Bundesarchiv Berlin, Plakat 002-004-016

these organizations, their service in the national cause was seen as an attempt to advance and legitimate their claims to a more responsible role in shaping the course of their country's political future. Their male counterparts, some of whom were organized in the German League against Women's Emancipation (Deutscher Bund gegen die Frauenemanzipation),[86] remained deeply suspicious of the increased activism of conservative women in the years before the outbreak of World War I and were strongly opposed to the more emancipatory impulses that had manifested themselves in the women's movement. But the war had intensified the degree of political activism on the part of German women everywhere and made it impossible for the leaders of Germany's conservative establish to ignore their demands for a stronger voice in German political life.[87]

For the most part, the founders of the DNVP were ambivalent about the enfranchisement of women. For although they recognized the role that women had played in a number of patriotic organizations both before and during the war, old-line conservatives like Westarp were opposed to the enfranchisement of women for fear that this would benefit the parties of the moderate and radical Left.[88] But with the enactment of a new electoral law based upon the principle of proportional representation and the extension of the franchise to all women over twenty-one years of age, the leaders of the DNVP could no longer afford to ignore the dramatic changes that this entailed for Germany's political landscape. Women had already played an important role in the new party's internal deliberations, and on 6 December 1918 the DNVP party leadership established the National Women's Committee of the German National People's Party (Reichsfrauenausschuß der Deutschnationalen Volkspartei) as the first step toward the mobilization of the women's vote for the upcoming elections to the National Assembly.[89] This committee, chaired by

German Countryside in the Weimar Republik," in *Between Reform, Reaction, and Resistance: Studies in the History of German Conservatism from 1789 to 1945*, ed. Larry Eugene Jones and James Retallack (Providence, RI, and Oxford, 1993), 375–405, esp. 375–82. On the VFV, see Andrea Süchting-Hänger, "'Gleichgroße mutige Helferinnen' in der weiblichen Gegenwelt: Der Vaterländischer Frauenverein und die Politisierung konservativer Frauen 1890–1914," in *Nation, Politik und Geschlecht*, ed. Ute Planert, 215–33.

[86] Ute Planert, *Antifeminismus im Kaiserreich. Diskurs, soziale Formation und politische Mentalität* (Göttingen, 1998), 118–51.

[87] Süchting-Hänger, *"Gewissen der Nation,"* esp. 90–122.

[88] Westarp, *Konservative Politik*, ed. Hiller von Gaertringen, 114–15. See also Matthew Stibbe, "Anti-Feminism, Nationalism and the German Right, 1914–1920: A Reappraisal," *German History* 20 (2002): 185–210.

[89] Annagrete Lehmann, "Ziel und Entwicklung der deutschnationalen Frauenarbeit," in *Der nationale Wille. Werden und Wirken der Deutschnationalen Volkspartei 1918–1928*, ed. Max Weiß (Essen, 1928), 319–36. See also Süchting-Hänger, *"Gewissen der Nation,"* 127–43, and Raffael Scheck, "German Conservatism and Female Political Activism in the Early Weimar Republic," *German History* 15 (1997): 34–55, as well as Christiane

the conservative feminist and social activist Margarete Behm, unleashed a flurry of activity in the time that still remained before election day, portraying women as the defender of the nation's moral virtue and articulating an essentially conservative view of women and their role in German society.[90] At the same time, the DNVP reassured women of its support in the struggle for their political rights. In its campaign appeal from 22 December the DNVP not only commended German women for "their admirable accomplishments during the war" but welcomed them as an "equal partner in the restoration of our nation" and promised its full support in the struggle for the "full right to participate in structuring public life."[91]

Financing the Campaign

The Nationalist campaign for the Weimar and Prussian constitutional assemblies required enormous sums of money. In the ten weeks between the founding of the party in late November and the convocation of the Weimar National Assembly in early February 1919 the DNVP's national headquarters in Berlin raised nearly 2.4 million marks. Of this amount, 800,000 marks covered printing costs and other expenses direcly related to the campaign, while another 500,000 marks were used to subsidize the party's local and regional chapters. As a result, the party was left with a balance of approximately one million marks for the post-election period.[92] These funds came from essentially three sources. In the first place, the DNVP was able to raise an estimated 300,000 marks from wealthy individuals who contributed three, four, and occasionally five digit sums.[93] This money was supplemented by sizable contributions from the Central Association of German Conservatives (Hauptverein der Deutschkonservativen), the executive body of the German Conservative Party and the trustee of the DKP's financial assets. The Central

Streubel, *Radikale Nationalistinnen. Agitation und Programmatik rechter Frauen in der Weimarer Republik* (Frankfurt and New York, 2006), 107–16, and Kirsten Heinsohn, *Konservative Parteien in Deutschland 1912 bis 1933. Demokratisierung und Partizipation in geschlechthistorischer Perspektive* (Düsseldorf, 2010), 62–82.

[90] For example, see *Die Frauen und die DNVP*, Deutschnationale Flugschrift, no. 4 (Berlin, n.d. [1918]). See also Julie Sneeringer, *Winning Women's Votes: Propaganda and Politics in Weimar Germany* (Chapel Hill, NC, and London, 2002), 42–51.

[91] "Wahlaufruf der Deutschnationalen Volkspartei," n.d. [22 Dec. 1918], Werbeblatt no. 10, BHStA Munich, Abt. V, F-60.

[92] Detailed information on the DNVP's finances for 1918–19 are to be found in a volume entitled "DNVP 1918/19," NL Westarp, Gärtringen, II/2. See also Ohnezeit, *Zwischen "schärfster Opposition,"* 74–83.

[93] Westarp to Roesicke, 27 Jan. 1919, BA Berlin, NL Westarp, 39/77. For further details, see Westarp, *Konservative Politik*, ed. Hiller von Gaertringen, 29–30. See also Kreth to the Central Association of German Conservatives, 1 Feb. 1919, appended to Kreth to Westarp, 1 Feb. 1919, BA Berlin, NL Westarp, 37/21.

Association raised 550,000 marks from its own provincial associations for the DNVP's use in the campaign, while another 200,000 marks came from large landowners who had formerly belonged to the DKP's delegation in the Herrenhaus, or upper house of the Prussian legislature.[94] But as important as these contributions may have been in helping to establish the DNVP as a viable political force in the elections to the Weimar and Prussian constitutional assemblies, by far the greatest share of the party's funds came from industrial sources.

Before 1914 Germany's right-wing parties had received the bulk of their industrial funding through the auspices of the Commission for the Collection, Administration, and Allocation of the Industrial Campaign Fund (Kommission zur Sammlung, Verwaltung und Verwendung des industriellen Wahlfonds), a body that had been established in 1909 under the aegis of the Central Association of German Industrialists (Centralverband der Deutschen Industrieller or CDI) and that had served from the last years of the Second Empire to the early years of the Weimar Republic as a major conduit of funds from heavy industry to the parties of the political Right.[95] But in October 1917 the Commission for the Industrial Campaign Fund suspended its collections[96] and was slow to react to the dramatic changes that took place in Germany's political system in November 1918.[97] It was not until the very end of November 1918 that the Commission for the Industrial Campaign Fund resumed its collections in preparation for the upcoming elections to the National Assembly and constitutional assemblies in the various German states.[98] In the meantime, Carl Friedrich von Siemens and a group of Berlin industrialists had stepped into the void that had been created by the inactivity of the Commission for the Industrial Campaign Fund by establishing the Curatorium for the Reconstruction of German Economic Life (Curatorium für den Wiederaufbau des deutschen Wirtschaftslebens). Although Siemens belonged to the newly founded German Democratic Party, the Curatorium

---

[94] Westarp to Heydebrand, 20 Jan. 1919, NL Westarp, Gärtringen, II/78, also in BA Berlin, R 8003, 2/20–28.

[95] On the Commission for the Industrial Campaign Fund, see "Die industriellen Wahlfonds," n.d., appended to a letter from Johannes Flathmann to the administration of the Gutehoffnungshütte (GHH) in Oberhausen, 7 Mar. 1912, as well as Flathmann's letter to the GHH administration, 15 Apr. 1913, in the corporate records of the Gutehoffnungshütte, Rheinisch-Westfälisches Wirtschaftsarchiv zu Köln, Cologne (hereafter cited as RWWA Cologne), Abt. 130, Allgemeine Verwaltung der GHH, 300106/117.

[96] Flathmann to Reusch, 8 Oct. 1917, RWWA Cologne, Abt. 130, Allgemeine Verwaltung der GHH, 300106/117.

[97] For example, see Flathmann to Friedburg, 18 Nov. 1918, records of the Deutsche Volkspartei, BA Koblenz, Bestand R 45 II, 1/59–63.

[98] Flathmann to Reusch, 28 Nov. 1918, RWWA Cologne, Abt. 130, Allgemeine Verwaltung der GHH, 300106/117.

was an ostensibly nonpartisan organization whose primary purpose was to prevent a socialist victory in the elections to the Weimar National Assembly and included industrialists who supported parties other than the DDP.[99]

The DNVP was represented in the Curatorium by Ernst von Borsig, a leading figure in the Berlin machine manufacturing industry who had taken part in the founding of the Commission for the Industrial Campaign Fund in 1909–10 and was now a member of the small circle of Berlin industrialists who belonged to the Curatorium.[100] Not only did Borsig's firm contribute 120,000 marks to the Curatorium for a special account opened in the name of the Association of Berlin Metal Industrialists (Verband Berliner Metall-Industrieller),[101] but he no doubt had a hand in funneling 500,000 of the more than 3,000,000 marks the Curatorium raised for use in the 1919 elections to the DNVP just days before the elections took place.[102] Borsig's firm also contributed another 100,000 marks to the "Efforts at Public Enlightenment" (Volksaufklärungs-Bestrebungen) that Jakob Wilhelm Reichert, business manager of the Association of German Iron and Steel Industrialists (Verein deutscher Eisen- und Stahlindustrieller or VDESI) and a DNVP candidate for the National Assembly, had launched in early December 1918.[103] Though never part of the DNVP's official campaign budget, these funds nevertheless worked to the party's benefit in the 1919 campaign for the Weimar National Assembly.

The fact that the DNVP was dependent upon a non-partisan agency like the Curatorium for the Reconstruction of German Economic Life for such a large part of its campaign budget did not sit well with all quarters of the party. Concerned that this might compromise the party's ability to wage an effective and uncompromising struggle against Germany's new republican system, press magnate and former director of the Krupp Steel Works Alfred Hugenberg stepped into the breach and began to raise money on his own.

---

[99] Siemens, "Kuratorium für dem Wiederaufbau des deutschen Wirtschaftslebens," n.d. [4 Feb. 1919], Siemens Historical Institute, Berlin (hereafter cited as SHI Berlin), Nachlass Carl Friedrich von Siemens, 4/Lf 646. For further details, see Larry Eugene Jones, "Carl Friedrich von Siemens and the Industrial Financing of Political Parties in the Weimar Republic," in Christian Jansen, Lutz Niethammer, and Bernd Weisbrod, eds., Von der Aufgabe der Freiheit. Politische Verantwortung und bürgerliche Gesellschaft im 19. und 20. Jahrhundert. Festschrift für Hans Mommsen zum 5. November 1995 (Berlin, 1995), 231–46, esp. 232–35.

[100] On the membership of the Curatorium, see Siemens to Ziegler, 11 June 1919, SHI Berlin, NL Siemens, 4 Lf/646. On Borsig, see Werner Müller and Jürgen Stockfisch, "Borsig und die Demokratie," Beiträge, Dokumente, Informationen des Archivs der Hauptstadt der Deutschen Demokratischen Republik 4, no. 1 (1967): 1–44.

[101] Memorandum, "Betr. Zahlung der Firma für Zweck der Volksaufklärung der Wahlpropaganda, usw.," 21 Feb. 1919, Borsig Zentralverwaltung GmbH, Landesarchiv Berlin, Rep. A-226 (hereafter cited as LA Berlin), 59/29–30.

[102] Curatorium to the DNVP, 14 Jan. 1919, SHI Berlin, NL Siemens, 4 Lf/646.

[103] Reichert to Borsig, 3 Dec. 1918, LA Berlin, Zentralverwaltung Borsig GmbH, 59/2.

Like Reichert, Hugenberg was a DNVP candidate for the National Assembly. He belonged, however, with Traub and Schiele to that contingent of former liberals who had joined the DNVP on the premise that it represented the best chance of bringing about the fundamental changes in German political life they thought essential if Germany was to free itself from the yoke of Social Democracy.[104] Before the war Hugenberg had played an active role in the founding and organisation of the Pan-German League and stood on the extreme right wing of the DNVP. Relying heavily upon funding from his associates in the German coal industry, Hugenberg collected over two million marks for the DNVP in the first months of the Weimar Republic. 750,000 marks of this amount went directly to the party's national headquarters in Berlin in the last weeks before the 1919 elections – with another 250,000 to follow shortly thereafter – while 500,000 marks went to the party's regional organizations in Westphalia and the Rhineland.[105] Further assistance would be forthcoming during the course of the year.

Relief and Disappointment

The DNVP was slow in mobilizing its resources for the campaign for the National Assembly and found itself at a distinct disadvantage vis-à-vis its opponents in staking out its claim to the loyalties of the German voter. The DNVP found itself forced on to the defensive by the military and political collapse of November 1918 and faced a formidable task in reformulating conservative ideals and objectives in a language that was palatable to an electorate that had been radicalized by four years of war and hardship. Nowhere was this more apparent than in former conservative strongholds east of the Elbe, where socialist agitators were hard at work organizing local farm laborers into unions that openly challenged the hegemony of local rural elites. While the leaders of the Agrarian League tried to counter developments in the countryside by throwing the full weight of their influence and prestige behind the DNVP,[106] the effect this had upon a radicalized rural electorate was minimal. In towns and cities as well, local conservatives were slower than their political rivals in responding to the radically different circumstances that had been created by the collapse of the imperial order and in organizing themselves for the upcoming elections. Still, for all of the challenges that it faced in the campaign for the elections to the National Assembly, the DNVP succeeded in casting itself as a dynamic, new conservative party untarnished by the follies of the past, in

---

[104] Hugenberg, "Die Deutschnationalen – eine Reformpartei," in Alfred Hugenberg, *Streiflichter aus Vergangenheit und Gegenwart* (Berlin, 1927), 122–30.

[105] Correspondence between Hergt and Roesicke, 5–20 Mar. 1919, BA Berlin, Nachlass Gustav Roesicke, 4a/36–39.

[106] Roesicke to Weilnböck, 5 Dec. 1918, BA Koblenz, NL Weilnböck, 46b.

establishing at least the beginnings of a new national organization in areas where conservatives had not been particularly strong before the war, and in mobilizing extensive financial resources for use in the campaign. Buoyed by the widespread social and political unrest that existed throughout the country, the prospects of Germany's conservative establishment were by no means as bleak on the eve of the election as they had been in November 1918.

By all accounts, the leaders of the DNVP were both gratified and surprised by their party's performance in the elections first to the National Assembly on 19 January 1919 and then to the Prussian constitutional assembly seven days later. If nothing else, the outcome of the elections fully vindicated the enormous effort the leaders of Germany's conservative establishment had expended on behalf of the DNVP. Even if the party emerged from the elections with only 10.3 percent of the popular vote, this was more than twice the 4.4 percentage share of the popular vote that the German People's Party, its principal rival on the German Right, received. This, in turn, entitled the DNVP to forty-four seats in the constitutional convention that was scheduled to convene in Weimar at the beginning of February. In the elections to the Prussian constitutional convention a week later the DNVP fared slightly better, taking 11.2 percent of the popular vote and winning forty-eight seats. Victory at the polls, on the other hand, belonged to the two socialist parties, which received over 45 percent of the popular vote between them. But the fact that they had failed to achieve an absolute majority meant that the more moderate of the two working-class parties, in this case the Majority Social Democratic Party, would have to share power with the Center and German Democratic Party, which received 19.7 and 18.5 percent of the popular vote respectively and held a combined total of 166 seats in the newly elected National Assembly.[107] To be sure, a socialist majority in the National Assembly had been averted, but power at Weimar would clearly rest in the hands of those parties that were committed to establishment of a German republic.

The leaders of the DNVP were no doubt relieved that the socialist parties had failed to gain an absolute majority in the Weimar National Assembly and that the establishment of a socialist dictatorship, if this was ever a real possibility, had been averted. In assessing the outcome of the elections, the leaders of the DNVP had reason to be both surprised and concerned. One of the most disturbing aspects of the election was the devastating losses the DNVP had sustained in former conservative strongholds east of the Elbe River. For example, in the two East Elbian districts of East Prussia and Pomerania the DNVP's share of the popular vote in comparison to that the two most prominent conservative parties – the DKP and RFKP – had received

[107] Jürgen Falter, Thomas Lindenberger, and Siegfried Schumann, *Wahlen und Abstimmungen in der Weimarer Republik. Materialien zum Wahlverhalten 1919–1933* (Munich, 1986), 67, 101.

in the 1912 Reichstag elections sank from 38.5 to 11.9 and 45.4 to 23.9 percent respectively.[108] What this reflected was not just the radicalization of the rural proletariat in eastern Germany but also the success with which the two socialist parties were able to mobilize the frustration and bitterness of farm laborers for the campaigns in the elections to the National Assembly.[109] At the same time, however, the DNVP was able to compensate for part of these losses by a stronger performance in large and middle-sized cities than the prewar conservative parties. For example, the DNVP was able to increase its share of the popular vote in cities with more than 100,000 inhabitants from 3.5 to 10.4 percent vis-à-vis what the DKP and RFKP had received in 1912, while in communities with less than 2,000 inhabitants the DNVP recorded modest gains over and above what its predecessors had received seven years earlier.[110]

Perhaps the most startling aspect of the 1919 election results was the fact that Germany's newly enfranchised women voters supported the DNVP to a significantly higher degree than their male counterparts. Contrary to the expectations of Westarp and other conservative opponents of women's suffrage, women voters did not automatically support the parties that had championed their enfranchisement but turned out in great number for the DNVP. In those precincts where election results were broken down by gender, between 55 and 60 percent of the Nationalist vote came from women. Only the Center, where women constituted approximately 60 percent of the party's electorate, received a higher share of its votes from women than the DNVP, whereas the DVP received slightly more and the DDP slightly less than half of its votes from women voters. The two socialist parties, on the other hand, fared much more poorly with anywhere from 35 to 45 percent of its popular vote from women. Had only men voted in the elections to the National Assembly, the two socialist parties would almost certainly have received an absolute majority between them. The enfranchisement of women, the unexpectedly high rate of voter participation by women voting for the first time, and the clear preference of women voters for those parties like the Center and DNVP that placed a high premium upon the defense of traditional religious and moral values all played a critical role in preventing a socialist majority in the National Assembly.[111]

---

[108] Ritter, "Kontinuität und Unformung," 367. On Pomerania, see Bert Becker, "Verwaltung und höhere Beamtenschaft in Pommern 1918/19," in *Pommern zwischen Zäsur und Kontinuität 1918, 1933, 1945, 1989,* ed. Bert Becker and Kyra T. Inachin (Schwerin, 1999), 39–68, esp. 52–61.

[109] Martin Schumacher, *Land und Politik. Eine Untersuchung über politische Parteien und agrarische Interessen 1914–1923* (Düsseldorf, 1978), 189–215, 236–47, 294–316.

[110] Ritter, "Kontinuität und Unformung," 370.

[111] The electoral data on women's voting in the elections to the Weimar National Assembly is extremely sparse and incomplete. The earliest and still most thorough analysis of women's voting behavior in the Weimar Republic is R. Hartwig, "Wie die Frauen im Deutschen Reich von ihrem Wahlrecht Gebrauch machen," *Allgemeines Statistisches Archiv* 17 (1928): 497–512.

The founding of the German National People's Party and the consolidation of Germany's prewar right-wing parties into a single political party represented an important milestone in the history of German conservatism. Yet while the founders of the DNVP could take credit for having mobilized women and urban voters who had not previously voted conservative, they were understandably disappointed that their party had not performed better at the polls, lamenting in particular its unexpectedly poor performance in former conservative strongholds east of the Elbe. While the reconquest of the German countryside would remain one of the DNVP's top priorities, party leaders would also turn their attention to the long-term – and, in many ways, more daunting – task of anchoring their party as firmly as possible in Germany's conservative milieu. This task would not be made any easier by the extremely high degree of interest articulation that had characterized Germany's social and economic development in the decades preceding the outbreak of World War I. Having survived its baptism at the polls in the January 1919 elections to the Weimar and Prussian constitutional assemblies, the DNVP possessed considerable potential for future growth if its leaders could only find the formula that would allow them to reconcile the divergent and often antagonistic interests that constituted the infrastructure of the German Right into a viable and cohesive political organization.

2

Infrastructure of the German Right

In addition to the various parties through which German conservatives had sought to articulate and promote their vested class interests, there existed a wide array of special-interest organizations that had emerged between the founding of the Second Empire and its collapse a half century later. In 1876 the leaders of German heavy industry had founded the Central Association of German Industrialists in an attempt to combat the economic liberalism of the early Second Empire and to pressure the government into adopting protective tariffs for iron and steel. It was not until the 1890s, however, that special-interest organizations began to proliferate with the founding of the Agrarian League, the League of Industrialists (Bund der Industriellen or BDI), and the German National Union of Commercial Employees. Efforts to reform the German tax system in 1907–08 provided further impetus to the emergence of special-interest organizations and led to the founding of the Hansa-Bund for Commerce, Trade and Industrie (Hansa-Bund für Gewerbe, Handel und Industrie) and the German Peasants' League (Deutscher Bauernbund) under the leadership of political liberals who sought to break the monopoly of power held by Germany's conservative establishment. Conservatives responded to the challenge that not only this but, more importantly, the rapid growth of Social Democracy posed to their political hegemony by trying to unite the more traditional elements of the urban and rural middle classes, first through the founding of the Imperial German Middle-Class League in 1911 and then with the creation of the Cartel of Productive Estates (Kartell der schaffenden Stände) in 1913.[1]

By the outbreak of World War I, an elaborate network of interrelationships, or *Querverbindungen*, had developed between political parties and the newly emergent economic interest organizations. At no point was this more apparent than in the campaign for the 1912 Reichstag elections, when industrial,

---

[1] For further details, see Dirk Stegmann, *Die Erben Bismarcks. Parteien und Verbände in der Spätphase des Wilhelminischen Deutschlands. Sammlungspolitik 1897–1918* (Cologne, 1970), as well as Hans-Jürgen Puhle, "Parlament, Parteien und Interessenverbände 1890–1914," in *Das kaiserliche Deutschland. Politik und Gesellschaft 1870–1918*, ed. Michael Stürmer (Düsseldorf, 1970), 340–77.

agricultural, and middle-class interest organizations entered into alliances with the various non-socialist parties in an attempt to influence the outcome of the election. The collapse of November 1918, however, temporarily immobilized Germany's conservative elites and severely shook the system of *Querverbindungen* they had built up over the course of the previous decade. The democratization of the political system would present Germany's conservative elites with a whole range of new problems that required fundamentally different strategies from those they had pursued before the war. For at the same time that the introduction of proportional representation greatly enhanced the significance of those special-interest organizations with a mass membership base, it also weakened those organizations like the Agrarian League and Central Association of German Industrialists that functioned as lobbies for specific sectors of Germany's economic elite.[2] The ability of Germany's conservative elites to survive the dramatic changes that had taken place in their political environment since the end of 1918 would depend in no small measure upon the success with which they were able to reach across class lines and enter into accommodations with potential allies in the working, white-collar, and middle classes.

Industry and Big Business

For the most part, Germany's industrial leaders proved far more flexible in adjusting to the far-reaching changes that had taken place in the structure of German political life than their counterparts in the agrarian sector.[3] In November 1918 Germany's industrial leadership moved quickly to consolidate its position in face of the revolutionary upheaval that had taken grip of the country by entering into a special agreement with the leaders of the socialist labor unions to form the Central Association of Industrial and Commercial Employer and Employee Associations (Zentralarbeitsgemeinschaft der industriellen und gewerblichen Arbeitgeber- und Arbeitnehmerverbände or ZAG).[4] This represented a radical departure from the alliances that Germany's industrial leadership had cultivated with the Junkers and the middle class before the

---

[2] See Gerhard Schulz, "Räte, Wirtschaftsstände und Verbandswesen am Anfang der Weimarer Republik," in *Gesellschaft, Parlament und Regierung. Zur Geschichte des Parlamentarismus in Deutschland*, ed. Gerhard A. Ritter (Düsseldorf, 1974), 355–66.

[3] For an overview, see Eduard Hamm, "Die wirtschaftspolitische Interessenvertretung," in *Volk und Reich der Deutschen. Vorlesungen gehalten in der Deutschen Vereinigung für Staatswissenschaftliche Fortbildung*, ed. Bernhard Harms, 3 vols. (Berlin, 1929), 2:426–59.

[4] Gerald D. Feldman, "German Business Between War and Revolution: The Origins of the Stinnes-Legien Agreement," in *Entstehung und Wandel der modernen Gesellschaft. Festschrift für Hans Rosenberg zum 65. Geburtstag*, ed. Gerhard A. Ritter (Berlin, 1970), 312–41.

war and involved tacit recognition of the role that organized labor was going to play in shaping Germany's political future. What industry hoped to gain from this arrangement, as the DNVP's Jakob Wilhelm Reichert explained to a group of businessmen from the Rhineland and Westphalia on 30 December 1918, was not merely a way of circumventing economic experimentation and increased regulation by the new democratic state but also a means of increasing its influence upon the legislative process by establishing a common front with organized labor.[5] A month later the German business community took a further step toward this end when the Central Association of German Industrialists merged with the League of Industrialists to found the National Federation of German Industry (Reichsverband der Deutschen Industrie or RDI). The official founding of the new organization took place at a special demonstration in Berlin on 12 April 1919, where Kurt Sorge, a Berlin industrialist with close ties to Ruhr heavy industry and a member of the German People's Party, was elected as its national president.[6]

Ironically, the reorganization of German economic life on the basis of an alliance between industry and labor represented a triumph for the more conservative elements of the German industrial community and helped secure the predominance of German big business over smaller and less highly concentrated industrial enterprises.[7] The conservative triumph was further reflected not only in the election of Sorge as president of the RDI,[8] but also in the preferential treatment that representatives of heavy industry received in the selection of personnel for the RDI executive committee and presidium and in the exclusion of the DVP's Gustav Stresemann, one of Germany's most prominent liberals, from a position in the RDI leadership.[9] Conservative business interests also controlled the Federation of German

---

[5] Jakob Wilhelm Reichert, *Entstehung, Bedeutung und Ziel der "Arbeitsgemeinschaft." Vortrag, gehalten vor der Vereinigung der Handelskammern des rheinisch-westfälischen Industriebezirks zu Essen-Ruhr am 30. Dezember 1918* (Berlin, 1919), 8–9, 11–12.

[6] *Bericht über die Gründungsversammlung des Reichsverbandes der deutschen Industrie Berlin, den 12. April 1919*, Veröffentlichungen des Reichsverbandes der deutschen Industrie, no. 1 (Berlin, 1919). For further details, see Stephanie Wolff-Röhe, *Der Reichsverband der Deutschen Industrie 1919–1924/25* (Frankfurt a.M., 2001), 47–73.

[7] Feldman, "German Business between War and Revolution," 340.

[8] For Sorge's political orientation, see his letter to Hugenberg, 19 May 1919, BA Koblenz, Nachlass Alfred Hugenberg, 27/165–70.

[9] See Stresemann to the League of Industrialists, 30 and 31 Mar. 1919, Politisches Archiv des Auswärtigen Amts, Berlin (hereafter cited as PA AA Berlin), NL Gustav Stresemann, 114/122926–27, 122937–42. See also Friedrich Zunkel, "Die Gewichtung der Industriegruppen bei der Etablierung des Reichsverbandes der Deutschen Industrie," in *Industrielles System und politische Entwicklung in der Weimarer Republik. Verhandlungen des Internationalen Symposiums in Bochum vom 12.–17. Juni 1973*, ed. Hans Mommsen, Dietmar Petzina, and Bernd Weisbrod (Düsseldorf, 1974), 637–47.

Employer Associations (Vereinigung der Deutschen Arbeitgeberverbände or VDA), which had been founded in 1913 to provide the entire industrial community with a single voice in matters of social and economic policy. After the November Revolution, the VDA became almost totally subordinate to the RDI and heartily endorsed the alliance that industry had concluded with organized labor under the auspices of the Zentralarbeitsgemeinschaft.[10] Even if the German Chamber of Commerce and Industry (Deutscher Industrie- und Handelstag or DIHT) remained under liberal influence,[11] conservative business interests still controlled two of the three *Spitzenverbände*, or peak associations, that represented the German business community on a national basis. The same interests also exercised a controlling voice over the policies of influential regional lobbies such as the Association for the Protection of the Common Economic Interests in the Rhineland and Westphalia (Verein zur Wahrung der gemeinsamen wirtschaftlichen Interessen in den Rheinland und Westfalen), an organization more commonly known as the Langnamverein.[12]

All of these organizations espoused a policy of complete neutrality with respect to the various parties that dotted Weimar's political landscape. *Überparteilichkeit*, or non-partisanship, quickly became a favorite slogan of conservative economic interests in the Weimar Republic and underscored their general estrangement from the existing party system and their lack of commitment to the parliamentary form of government that Germany had inherited from the November Revolution.[13] This, however, did not prevent them from extending financial assistance to the very parties that they treated with such disdain. Economic self-interest made it imperative for them to support the parties that were preparing to wage the struggle in parliament against Social Democratic demands for the socialization of German industry.[14] Although the RDI established an industrial fund of its own and began to solicit

---

[10] Ernst von Borsig, *Industrie und Sozialpolitik. Das sozialpolitische Programm der Vereinigung der Deutschen Arbeitgeberverbände*, Schriften der Vereinigung der Deutschen Arbeitgeberverbände, no. 4. (Berlin, n.d. [1924]), 7–12.

[11] On the DIHT, see Wolfgang Hardtwig, *Freiheitliches Bürgertum in Deutschland. Der Weimarer Demokrat Eduard Hamm zwischen Kaiserreich und Widerstand* (Stuttgart, 2018), 202–34.

[12] On the Langnamverein, see Bernd Weisbrod, *Schwerindustrie in der Weimarer Republik. Interessenpolitik zwischen Stabilisierung und Krise* (Wuppertal, 1978), 169–86.

[13] Fritz Blaich, "Staatsverständnis und politische Haltung der deutschen Unternehmer 1918–1930," in *Die Weimarer Republik 1918–1933. Politik – Wirtschaft – Gesellschaft*, ed. Karl Dietrich Bracher, Manfred Funke, and Hans-Adolf Jacobsen (Bonn, 1987), 158–78.

[14] For an overview of this process, see Theodor Eschenburg, *Probleme der modernen Parteifinanzierung*, Tübinger Universitätsreden, 13 (Tübingen: J. C. B. Mohr (Paul Siebeck), 1961), esp. 5–12.

donations for the struggle against Social Democracy at the beginning of
1922,[15] its organizational statutes barred it from making direct contributions
to political parties. To circumvent this restriction, Germany's industrial elite
bypassed the RDI to work through what political scientists have labeled
"multi-party conveyor organizations."[16] The oldest of these conduits was the
Commission for the Collection, Administration, and Allocation of the Industrial Campaign Fund. Founded in 1909 under the auspices of the Central
Association of German Industrialists,[17] the Commission for the Industrial
Campaign Fund was dominated by conservative industrialists who were determined to resist the forces of democratic change that had surfaced with such
threatening potential in the last years before the outbreak of the war.[18] The
driving force behind the Commission was its general secretary, Johannes
Flathmann, a former National Liberal who joined the DVP immediately after
its founding in the winter of 1918 and who adamantly opposed the creation of
a united liberal party through a merger with the DDP.[19] Temporarily immobilized by the turmoil that had accompanied the collapse of the Second
Empire, the Commission was not sufficiently organized to play a significant
role in the elections to the National Assembly. By the spring of 1919, however,
it had begun to recover from the lethargy that had gripped it at the height of
the November Revolution and was in the process of using funds that Ruhr
heavy industry had placed at its disposal to influence the two parties that stood
furthest to the Right, the DVP and DNVP.[20] Here the immediate goal was to
bring about closer political and organizational ties between the two right-wing
parties in hopes that together they might be able to thwart Social Democratic

[15] See Schweighoffer and Herle to Silverberg, 7 Jan. 1922, BA Koblenz, Nachlass Paul
Silverberg, 238/6, and Bücher to Silverberg, 16 Jan. 1922, ibid., 238/8, as well as the RDI's
appeal for the creation of an industrial fund, n.d., ibid., 238/2–4.
[16] Arnold J. Heidenheimer and Frank C. Langdon, *Business Associations and the Financing
of Political Parties: A Comparative Study of the Evolution of Practices in Germany,
Norway, and Japan* (The Hague, 1968), 9–13. The section on Germany is badly flawed
and factually inaccurate.
[17] Circular from the Commission for the Collection, Administration, and Allocation of the
Industrial Campaign Fund to the members of the Central Association of German
Industrialists, 14 Jan. 1910, SHI Berlin, NL Siemens, 4/Lf 646.
[18] In this respect, see "Der industrielle Wahlfonds," n.d., appended to Meyer and Flathmann
to the GHH, 7 Mar. 1912, as well as a second letter from Meyer and Flathmann to the
GHH, 15 Apr. 1913, both in RWWA Cologne, Abt. 130, Allgemeine Verwaltung der
GHH, 300106/117.
[19] Flathmann to Friedberg, 18 Nov. 1918, BA Koblenz, R 45 II, 301/59–63.
[20] See Flathmann to Stresemann, 21 Mar. 1919, PA AA Berlin, NL Stresemann, 206/
137704–07, as well as the circular from the Commission for the Industrial Campaign
Fund, Sept. 1919, RWWA Cologne, Abt. 130, Allgemeine Verwaltung der GHH, 300106/
117.

schemes for a reorganization of the German economy along lines inimical to the best interests of big business.[21]

The second of the three conduits upon which German industry relied to finance the parties of its choice was of more recent vintage. Founded in December 1918 on the initiative of Berlin industrialist Carl Friedrich von Siemens,[22] the Curatorium for the Reconstruction of German Economic Life was created for the immediate purpose of preventing the socialist parties from gaining an absolute majority in the elections to the Weimar National Assembly.[23] Behind this more immediate concern lay a long-range strategic objective, namely, that of filling the void that had been left by the immobilization of the Commission for the Collection, Administration, and Allocation of the Industrial Campaign Fund.[24] Siemens and his associates were particularly interested in the newly created German Democratic Party because, of all of Germany's nonsocialist parties, it offered the best prospect of developing into a bourgeois *Sammelpartei* capable of stemming the tide of social and political radicalism that was sweeping the country. Not only did Siemens himself join the DDP, but the Curatorium donated more than a million marks to DDP for use in the January 1919 elections to the National Assembly, while the DVP and DNVP each received 500,000 marks.[25] The Center also approached the Curatorium for assistance in its campaign for the National Assembly but was rebuffed.[26]

Originally Siemens and the founders of the Curatorium for the Reconstruction of German Economic Life hoped for an accommodation with the Commission for the Industrial Campaign Fund that would further rationalize the process by which industry financed those parties that were favorably disposed

---

[21] See Vögler to Hugenberg, 31 Oct. and 8 Dec. 1919, BA Koblenz, NL Hugenberg, 29/402–04, and 49/36–38, as well as Vögler to Stresemann, 9 Feb. 1920, PA AA Berlin, NL Stresemann, 220/140114–16.

[22] Text of Siemens's speech in the Berlin Chamber of Commerce (Berliner Handelskammer), 4 Feb. 1919, SHI Berlin, NL Siemens, 4/Lf 646. See also Larry Eugene Jones, "Carl Friedrich von Siemens and the Industrial Financing of Political Parties in the Weimar Republic," in *Von der Aufgabe der Freiheit. Politische Verantwortung und bürgerliche Gesellschaft im 19. und 20. Jahrhundert. Festschrift für Hans Mommsen zum 5. November 1995*, ed. Christian Jansen, Lutz Niethammer, and Bernd Weisbrod (Berlin, 1995), 231–46.

[23] Siemens to Ziegler, 11 June 1919, SHI Berlin, NL Siemens, 4/Lf 646.

[24] Speech by before the Berlin Chamber of Commerce, 4 Feb. 1919, SHI Berlin, NL Siemens, 4/Lf 646.

[25] See the breakdown of the Curatorium's disbursements for the elections to the National Assembly, n.d., SHI Berlin, NL Siemens, 4/Lf 646. See also Siemens to Deutsch, 2 Jan. 1919; Leidig (DVP) to Siemens, 5 Jan. 1919; and the Curatorium to the DNVP, 14 Jan. 1919, ibid.

[26] Pfeiffer to Siemens, 17 Jan. 1919, SHI Berlin, NL Siemens, 4/Lf 646.

to the interests of German big business.[27] Negotiations between the Curatorium and the Commission, however, broke down in the late spring of 1919,[28] with the result that the Curatorium confined its solicitations to Berlin while the Commission concentrated its efforts in the Rhineland and Westphalia. The obstacle here was the reluctance of the conservatives who were in control of the Commission for the Industrial Campaign Fund to share responsibility for the disbursement of funds with the more liberal elements around Siemens.[29] The way in which Ruhr heavy industry tried to monopolize control over the use of industrial campaign funds was hardly acceptable to the leaders of the German chemical industry, who in December 1922 established a special commission of their own under the nominal chairmanship of DVP Reichstag deputy Wilhelm Ferdinand Kalle.[30] The creation of the "Kalle Committee," as this commission was unofficially known, was motivated in large part by the determination of Carl Duisberg and the leaders of the chemical industry to counter the growing influence that Ruhr heavy industry the more conservative elements of the German industrial community seemed to be gaining over the various bourgeois parties.[31] The "Kalle Commmittee" differed from the Commission for the Industrial Campaign Fund and the Curatorium for the Reconstruction of German Economic Life in that it did not limit its support to campaign contributions but made annual donations to the DDP, DVP, and Center that, when translated into their post-inflationary equivalents, ranged from 100,000 to 200,000 marks apiece.[32]

In the period immediately following the end of World War I, the primary objective behind the industrial financing of political parties had been to prevent the socialists from gaining an absolute majority in the elections to the National Assembly.[33] Once the revolutionary threat had abated, however,

---

[27] Proposal for a merger of the two organizations that was approved at a meeting of the Curatorium, 9 May 1919, SHI Berlin, NL Siemens, 4/Lf 646.

[28] Minutes of a joint meeting of the Curatorium and the Commission for the Industrial Campaign Fund, 15 May 1919, SHI Berlin, NL Siemens, 4/Lf 646.

[29] Remarks by Flathmann at the meeting cited in the previous note, as well as Vögler to Hugenberg, 27 Oct. and 8 Dec. 1919, BA Koblenz, NL Hugenberg, 49/36–42.

[30] Duisberg to Wolff, 29 Jan. 1923, Unternehmensarchiv Bayer AG, Leverkusen (hereafter cited as Bayer AG Leverkusen), Autographen-Sammlung Duisberg. On the composition of the "Kalle Committee," see Paul Moldenhauer, "Politische Erinnerungen," BA Koblenz, Nachlass Paul Moldenhauer, 1/136. See also Peter Hayes, *Industry and Ideology: IG Farben in the Nazi Era* (Cambridge, 1987), 48–52.

[31] For Duisberg's antipathy towards Ruhr heavy industry, see his letter to Weinberg, 24 Sept. 1923, Bayer AG Leverkusen, Vorakten der IG Farben, 4B/20.

[32] On the disbursement patterns of the "Kalle Committee," see the depositions from Pfeiffer and Kalle, 8 Sept. 1947, Stadtarchiv Nürnberg, Bestand KV-Prozesse, Fall 6, Nr. X 3.

[33] For example, see Meyer and Flathmann to Reusch, 28 Nov. 1918, RWWA Cologne, Abt. 130, Allgemeine Verwaltung der GHH, 300106/117. See also Kalle to Duisberg, 1 Oct. 1924, Bayer AG Leverkusen, Vorakten der IG Farben, 4B/20.

industry adopted a more aggressive strategy by trying to use its financial leverage to secure the election of deputies who were favorably disposed to industrial interests and could influence the policies of their respective parties in industry's favor.[34] Although this strategy succeeded in bringing men like Siemens and the DVP's Hugo Stinnes into the Reichstag,[35] it did not necessarily mean that the parties to which they belonged had become pawns of the German industrial establishment. If anything, Germany's industrial leadership remained disgruntled over their lack of leverage over the policies of the different bourgeois parties. In the meantime, the German big business became increasingly divided between those industrialists like Siemens, Duisberg, and Kalle who sought to pursue their objectives within the framework of the existing political system and those like the DNVP's Alfred Hugenberg who remained irreconcilably opposed to the new political order and sought to subvert it in any way possible. Coupled with Flathmann's deteriorating health, this split immobilized the Commission for the Industrial Campaign Fund during the runaway inflation of the early 1920s and led to its eclipse as an effective broker of industrial influence. Hugenberg and his associates were quick to take advantage of this situation by establishing what amounted to a virtual monopoly over the collection and disbursement of funds for the right-wing DNVP.[36] Although the Curatorium for the Reconstruction of German Economic Life and the "Kalle Committee" continued to support the more moderate bourgeois parties after the stabilization of the mark in the winter of 1923–24, the demise of the Commission for the Collection, Administration, and Allocation of the Industrial Campaign Fund only strengthened Hugenberg's position as the self-appointed spokesman for the more conservative elements of the Ruhr industrial establishment.

Agriculture

Although the November Revolution had led to far-reaching changes in the organization and representation of German industrial interests, these changes did little to dislodge the more conservative elements of the German industrial community from the citadels of power and influence they had occupied before the war. If anything, the creation of the *Zentralarbeitsgemeinschaft* and the

---

[34] Siemens to Fischer, 7 Nov. 1919, SHI Berlin, NL Siemens, 4/Lf 646.

[35] See Siemens to the chairman of the DDP, Bezirksverband Berlin, 9 Dec. 1919, SHI Berlin, NL Siemens, 4/Lf 555, as well as Flathmann to Stinnes, 19 Apr. 1920, Archiv für Christlich-Demokratische Politik (hereafter cited as ACDP Sankt Augustin), Nachlass Hugo Stinnes, I-220/002/4.

[36] Hugenberg and Reichert, "An die industriellen Freunde der Deutschnationalen Volkspartei," Oct. 1924, Landesarchiv Berlin (hereafter cited as LA Berlin), Zentralverwaltung Borsig GmbH, 7/77.

founding of the National Federation of German Industry had only helped industrial conservatives consolidate their position first vis-à-vis organized labor and secondly with respect to the less highly concentrated elements of the German business community. The recovery of Germany's conservative elites from the revolutionary upheaval of 1918–19 could also be seen in the case of German agriculture. The position of Germany's rural conservatives had been severely weakened by the war and above all by the radicalizing effects of wartime economic controls upon small and middle-sized peasant producers. To be sure, agrarian conservatives in the Weimar Republic were never as influential or as powerful as they had been before the war. Nor did they possess the agility or financial resources of their counterparts in the German industrial community. Still, the wave of agrarian radicalism that swept the countryside in the aftermath of World War I caught them off-guard and forced them onto the defensive. Without the agility or financial resources of their counterparts in the German industrial community, it was unclear whether Germany's agricultural elites would be able to regain control of the countryside and reclaim their role as the dominant voice in the German agricultural community.[37]

Before the war the bastion of conservative influence in the countryside had been the Agrarian League, an organization established in 1893 by East Elbian landowners with close ties to the prewar German Conservative Party in an attempt to protect their vital interests as grain producers against the trade policies of the new chancellor Leo von Caprivi.[38] By no means, however, was the Agrarian League the only organization that claimed to represent the interests of German agriculture. In the first decade of the twentieth century, the predominance of the Agrarian League within the German agricultural community was directly challenged, first by the establishment of the Association of German Peasant Unions (Vereinigung der deutschen Bauernvereine or VdB) in 1900 and then with the founding of the German Peasants' League under liberal leadership in 1909. Both of these organizations were founded by farm leaders who deeply resented the way in which the Agrarian League's demands for high agricultural tariffs had sacrificed the interests of small and middle-sized peasants

---

[37] For an overview, see Jens Flemming, *Landwirtschaftliche Interessen und Demokratie. Ländliche Gesellschaft, Agrarverbände und Staat 1890–1925* (Bonn, 1978), 161–251.

[38] Hans-Jürgen Puhle, *Agrarische Interessenpolitik und preußischer Konservatismus im wilhelminischen Reich. Ein Beitrag zur Analyse des Nationalismus in Deutschland am Beispiel des Bundes der Landwirte und der Deutsch-Konservativen Partei* (Hanover, 1966), 23–36. See also Shelley Baranowski, "Continuity and Contingency: Agrarian Elites, Conservative Institutions, and East Elbia in Modern German History," *Social History* 12 (1987): 285–308.

to those of large landed agriculture.[39] The economic deprivation of World War I and in particular governmental controls over agricultural prices and production did much to radicalize small and middle-sized peasants throughout the country and severely strained their loyalties to the political system of which the East Elbian Junkers were such a conspicuous part. When the war finally ended in November 1918, no element of German society, with the exception of the industrial working class, was as profoundly alienated from the old imperial regime as the German peasantry.[40] And nowhere was this disaffection more apparent than in Bavaria, where the leaders of the 25,000-member Bavarian Peasants' League (Bayerischer Bauernbund or BBB) not only participated in the overthrow of the Wittelsbach dynasty but actively supported the provisional government that assumed office in early November 1918 under the leadership of Independent Socialist Kurt Eisner.[41]

The radicalization of Germany's rural population held immediate and far-reaching implications for the social and political hegemony of Germany's conservative rural elites. At the very least, the introduction of a democratic franchise throughout the Reich – and particularly the abolition of the three-class franchise in Prussia – meant that German conservatives were now far more dependent upon the support of the rural voter than they had been even before the outbreak of World War I. In an attempt to head off the collapse of the badly compromised and increasingly defunct Agrarian League, rural conservatives took it upon themselves to create a series of regional agrarian leagues, or *Landbünde*, in Brandenburg, Pomerania, and other parts of the country in what was generally portrayed as a spontaneous rebellion on the part of Germany's rural population.[42] In the spring of 1919 Germany's rural conservatives then tried to bring this development under their control by

---

[39] Ibid., 144–47. On the German Peasants' League, see Karl Böhme, *Der Bauernstand in Freiheit und Knechtschaft* (Berlin, 1924), 89–97. For further details, see George S. Vascik, "The German Peasant League and the Limits of Rural Liberalism in Wilhelmine Germany," *Central European History* 24 (1991): 147–75.

[40] Robert G. Moeller, "Dimensions of Social Conflict in the Great War: The View from the Countryside," *Central European History* 14 (1981): 142–68.

[41] On the BBB's involvement in the Bavarian revolution, see *Der Bayerische Bauernbund im Jahre 1919*, Flugschriften des Bayerischen Bauernbundes, no. 1 (Munich, n.d. [1920]), 1–5, as well as Georg Eisenberger, *Mein Leben für die Bauern. Erinnerungen eines Bauernführers*, with an introduction and edited by Johann Kirchinger (Munich, 2013), esp. 116–19. For further details, see Heinz Haushofer, "Der Bayerische Bauernbund (1893–1933)," in *Europäische Bauernparteien im 20. Jahrhundert*, ed. Heinz Gollwitzer (Stuttgart and New York, 1977), 562–86.

[42] Memorandum from Levetzow to the BdL's provincial, state, and district chairmen, 28 Feb. 1919, BA Koblenz, NL Weilnböck, 20b. For further details, see Heinrich Muth, "Die Entstehung der Bauern- und Landarbeiterräte im November 1918 und die Politik des Bundes der Landwirte," *Vierteljahreshefte für Zeitgeschichte* 21 (1973): 1–58.

creating the Coalition of German Agriculture (Arbeitsgemeinschaft der deutschen Landwirtschaft) as an umbrella organization that claimed to represent the collective interests of the entire agricultural estate.[43] Although the founders of the new organization were prepared to make concessions to small and middle-sized farmers in an effort to secure their cooperation, the fact that only the Junker-dominated Agrarian League agreed to join the coalition – both the Christian peasant unions and the German Peasants' League declined to do so – revealed the lack of any genuine consensus within the German agricultural community.[44] That being the case, the founders of the Coalition of German Agriculture decided to recast their organization as the German Rural League (Deutscher Landbund or DLB), in which the various provincial agrarian organizations that had surfaced since the end of the war would be invited to participate on the basis of regional autonomy.[45]

The German Rural League was much more decentralized in its underlying organizational structure than the prewar Agrarian League and afforded regional farm organizations such as the Brandenburg Rural League (Brandenburgischer Landbund or BrLB) much greater autonomy in the conduct of their own affairs than the BdL's regional chapters had enjoyed before the war.[46] The DLB's objectives were two-fold: firstly, to enhance the representation of agricultural economic interests at all levels of the governmental process and, secondly, to cultivate a greater occupational awareness throughout the German agricultural community. With respect to the first of these objectives, the DLB refused to identify itself with any of the existing political parties in favor of a policy of complete non-partisanship or *Überparteilichkeit* that enabled it to pursue its goals in concert with any party that might serve its purpose.[47] By the end of 1919 the DLB claimed nearly half a million registered members with over 150 individual chapters and regional affiliates in Brandenburg, Brunswick, Lower Saxony, Mecklenburg, Pomerania, Silesia, and Thuringia.[48] In the meantime, the leaders of the German Rural League had entered

---

[43] Protocol of the founding of the Coalition of German Agriculture, 14 Apr. 1919, BA Koblenz, NL Weilnböck, 20b. See also the coalition's statutes and guidelines, or *Richtlinien*, as well as its appeal "Landwirte, schließt Euch zusammen!," n.d., ibid.

[44] For the position of the Christian peasant unions, see August Crone-Münzebrock, ed., *Die Organisation des deutschen Bauernstandes* (Berlin, n.d. [1920]), 44–47. For a general overview, see Klaus Müller, "Agrarische Interesenverbände in der Weimarer Republik," *Rheinische Vierteljahresblätter* 38 (1974): 386–405.

[45] For the official version of these developments, see Deutscher Landbund, ed., *Der Landbundgedanke. Zur Organisation des deutschen Landvolkes* (Berlin, n.d. [1919]), 4–11. See also Flemming, *Landwirtschaftliche Interessen*, 169–97.

[46] Rainer Pomp, *Bauern und Grossgrundbesitzer auf ihrem Weg ins Dritte Reich. Der Brandenburgische Landbund 1918–1933* (Berlin, 2011), 35–59.

[47] DLB, *Landbundgedanke*, 11–13, 31–32.

[48] Ibid., 7.

into negotiations with the prewar Agrarian League as the first step towards the creation of a single organization capable of representing the corporate interests of the entire agricultural community. For Gustav Roesicke and the leaders of the BdL, the imperative behind the negotiations was the need to provide agricultural interests – and particularly those of large landed agriculture – with the most effective parliamentary representation possible.[49] Negotiations between the two organizations were anything but easy and often took place in the face of a peasant animus toward large landed agriculture so strong it threatened the negotiations with collapse.[50] In the final analysis, however, the logic of interest politics prevailed, and on 1 January 1921 the German Rural League and Agrarian League formally merged their organizations to found the National Rural League (Reichs-Landbund or RLB).[51]

The National Rural League differed from the prewar Agrarian League in three important respects. In the first place, the negotiators for the DLB had succeeded in persuading the leaders of the BdL to adopt a far more decentralized organizational structure for the RLB than they had originally been prepared to accept, with the result that the RLB's regional affiliates enjoyed much greater autonomy than had ever been the case within the BdL. Secondly, the RLB sought to achieve a greater degree of parity between large landed agriculture and small and middle-sized family farmers than had ever existed in the Junker-dominated Agrarian League. The desire to present at least the appearance of such parity was reflected in the fact that Karl Hepp, a farm activist from Hesse-Nassau and an outspoken advocate of small and middle-sized agricultural interests, was elected along with the BdL's Gustav Roesicke as one of the RLB's two presidents at its first national congress in March 1921.[52] And thirdly, the RLB adopted at the DLB's insistence a policy of complete neutrality with respect to the existing political parties.[53] This policy represented a dramatic departure from the close alliance that the BdL had established first with the German Conservative Party before the war and then

---

[49] Roesicke's remarks at a meeting of the DLB executive committee, 16 Dec. 1919, records of the Reichs-Landbund, BA Berlin, Bestand R 8034 I, 1/242–43.

[50] Report for Roesicke on the negotiations in Stettin, Nov. 15, 1920, BA Berlin, R 8034 I, 1/41–43.

[51] On the negotiations between the BdL and DLB, see the protocol of the critical meetings between the leadership of the two organizations on 10 August and 4 October 1920, BA Berlin, R 8034 I, 1/280–91, as well as Paul Boetticher, *Der Bund der Landwirte 1918–1920. Ein Schlußkapitel* (Berlin, 1925), 51–60. See also Flemming, *Landwirtschaftliche Interessen*, 229–51, and Stephanie Merkenich, *Grüne Front gegen Weimar. Reichs-Landbund und agrarische Lobbyismus 1918–1933* (Düsseldorf, 1998), 57–72.

[52] *Reichs-Landbund. Agrarpolitische Wochenschrift* 1, no. 5 (12 Mar. 1921): 69.

[53] See point eight in *Programm und Leitsätze des Reichs-Landbundes (Beschlossen von der Vertreterversammlung des Reichs-Landbundes am 10. November 1921)* (Berlin, n.d., [1921]), 8.

with the newly founded DNVP after the November Revolution. This too was reflected in the election of Hepp, who unlike most of the RLB's national leadership belonged not to the DNVP, but to the liberal German People's Party.[54] Still, the question as to whether or not all of this was merely a fig leaf designed to conceal the continued dominance of Germany's conservative rural elites in the articulation and representation of agricultural economic interests remained essentially unanswered. In Bavaria and Württemberg, for example, the RLB's state affiliates – in this case, the Bavarian Rural League (Bayerischer Landbund or BLB) and the Württemberg Peasants and Wine Growers' League (Württembergischer Bauern- und Weingärtner Bund or WBWB) – remained in the hands of virtually the same men who had directed the affairs of local Agrarian League chapters before the war.[55]

Over the course of the next several years, the National Rural League developed into one of the most influential economic interest organizations in all of Germany. In terms of its basic ideological orientation, the RLB was militantly anti-socialist and categorically rejected the accomplishments of the November Revolution as a betrayal of the German peasant. The real key to the RLB's success, however, lay not so much in its ideology as in its relentless campaign against the controlled economy in agriculture. During the war the government had imposed strict controls over agricultural prices and production in an effort to combat the threat of inflation. When these controls were retained after the end of hostilities in order to assure a steady and relatively inexpensive supply of food to the cities, they encountered strong and vociferous resistance from virtually every sector of the German agricultural community. This reaction was fueled in large part by the runaway inflation of the early 1920s. Even though the inflation made it possible for farmers to dispose of mortgages against their property on extremely favorable terms, they complained bitterly that the continuation of the controlled economy in agriculture sacrificed their vital interests to those of the urban consumer.[56] As the struggle

---

[54] For Hepp's political views, see his letter to Stresemann, 4 Sept. 1921, PA AA Berlin, NL Stresemann, 231/141458–60.

[55] On the situation in Bavaria, see Alois Hundhammer, *Die landwirtschaftliche Berufsvertretung in Bayern* (Munich, 1926), 57–68. For the WBWB's political orientation, see Theodor Körner alt, ed., *Wahlhandbuch zu den Land- und Reichstagswahlen 1924. Zum Gebrauch und zur Aufklärung für die württembergischen Wähler* (Stuttgart, 1924), 41–63. On the continuity of leadership in the WBWB, see Hans Peter Müller, "Wilhelm Vogt. Württembergischer Bauernbundpolitiker und bäuerlicher Standesvertreter im Kaiserreich und in der Weimarer Republik 1854–1938," *Lebensbilder aus Baden-Württemberg* 18 (1994): 395–417.

[56] For further details, see Robert G. Moeller, "Winners as Losers in the German Inflation: Peasant Protest over the Controlled Economy, 1920–1923," in *Die Deutsche Inflation. Eine Zwischenbilanz/The German Inflation Reconsidered*, ed. Gerald D. Feldman, Carl-Ludwig Holtfrerich, Gerhard A. Ritter, and Peter-Christian Witt (Berlin and New York, 1982), 255–82.

over the controlled economy drew to a climax in 1921–22, the National Rural League quickly assumed the leadership of efforts to dismantle governmental controls over agricultural prices and production.[57] At the same time, the leaders of the RLB routinely castigated those parties that continued to support the controlled economy in agriculture as traitors to the German peasantry in a transparent attempt to translate peasant frustration over the continuation of governmental economic controls into a general mandate for political change.[58]

By the time that governmental controls over agricultural prices and production were eventually abandoned in the middle of 1923, Germany's rural conservatives had succeeded in reestablishing themselves as the dominant force within the German agricultural community. Not only did the RLB embrace more than 1.7 million members – or 5.6 million if one includes family members, farm laborers, employees, and representatives of other professions – by the beginning of 1924,[59] but the RLB was in the firm control of political conservatives who were determined to use their influence to protect large landed agriculture against the twin dangers of economic competition from abroad and democratic change at home.[60] Conservative hegemony in the countryside was further enhanced by the physical suppression of the socialist labor movement among the farm workers in Brandenburg and Pomerania[61] and by the strategic alliance that evolved in much of Eastern Prussia between local landowning elites and the National Farm Workers' League (Reichsland-arbeiterbund), a "yellow" union that was a pariah from t,he perspective of both the socialist and Christian labor movements on account of its refusal to recognize the principle of collective bargaining as enshrined in the *Zentralar-beitsgemeinschaft*. This, however, did not prevent Franz Behrens and the Central Association of Farm Laborers (Zentralverband der Landarbeiter or ZdL), a Christian farm workers' union founded under conservative leadership in 1913,[62] from concluding a similar arrangement for its affiliates in Silesia and

---

[57] Karl Hepp, *Lage und Aufgaben der deutschen Landwirtschaft. Nach einem Vortrag gehalten in Darmstadt am 1. April 1921 auf dem Parteitag der Deutschen Volkspartei in Hessen*, Aufklärungsschriften der Deutschen Volkspartei in Hessen, no. 13 (Darmstadt, 1921), 9–11.

[58] Josef Kaufhold, *Die Sünden der Demokratischen Partei und des Deutschen Bauernbundes an der Landwirtschaft*, Deutschnationale Flugschrift, no. 134 (Berlin, 1922).

[59] [Reichs-Landbund], *Übersicht über die Entwicklung des Organisationswesens in der deutschen Landwirtschaft* (Berlin, 1924), 21.

[60] See Dieter Gessner, *Agrarverbände in der Weimarer Republik. Wirtschaftliche und soziale Voraussetzungen agrarkonservativer Politik vor 1933* (Düsseldorf, 1976), 28–65.

[61] Jens Flemming, "Die Bewaffnung des 'Landvolks'. Ländliche Schutzwehren und agrarischer Konservatismus in der Anfangsphase der Weimarer Republik," *Militärgeschichtliche Mitteilungen* 26 (1979): 7–36.

[62] On the founding and goals of the ZdL, see *Zehn Jahre christlich-nationale Landarbeiterbewegung 1913–1923. Eine Festschrift zur Erinnerung an das 10jährige Bestehen des Zentralverbandes der Landarbeiter*, ed. Hauptvorstand des Zentralverbandes (Berlin

Prussian Saxony.[63] The increasingly close relationship that evolved between the RLB and the farm workers' movement, whether of "yellow" or Christian provenance, helped keep the latter from falling under the influence of the Christian trade-union movement.[64]

Catholic rural conservatives were no less successful than their Protestant counterparts in reasserting their social and political hegemony in the face of the dramatic changes that had taken place with the collapse of the Second Empire and the establishment of the Weimar Republic.[65] To be sure, the Catholic nobility in the Rhineland, Westphalia, and Bavaria felt every bit as threatened by the triumph of democracy as the landowning classes of East Elbia. Moreover, the situation was complicated by the fact that the Catholic peasantry did not always share the animus of many Catholic nobles towards the Center. If anything, the initial response on the part of the Catholic peasantry in the Rhineland had been to rally to the support of the Center and to close ranks for the more effective representation of its interests within the party, if for no other reason than to prevent the Center from becoming too heavily dependent upon the Christian labor unions.[66] Still, control of the enormously influential Rhenish and Westphalian peasant associations remained in the hands of unabashed conservatives like Clemens von Loë-Bergerhausen and Engelbert Kerckerinck zur Borg, who not only criticized the Center for its willingness to share governmental responsibility with the Social

1923), 6–13. On the ZdL's relationship to the DNVP, see Franz Behrens, *Die ländlichen Arbeiter und die Politik. Ein politisches Handbuch für Land-, Forst- und andere ländliche Arbeiter, Angestellten und deren Frauen*, ed. by Reichsarbeiterausschuß der Deutschnationalen Volkspartei (Berlin, 1920).

[63] For a defense of this alliance, see Franz Behrens, "Landarbeiterbewegung und Wirtschaftsfriede," in *Die christlich-nationale Landarbeiterbewegung und die Hebung der landwirtschaftlichen Produktion als Voraussetzung des deutschen Wiederaufstiegs. Drei Vorträge*, Schriftenreihe des Zentralverbandes der Landarbeiter, no. 13 (Berlin, 1922), 27–40. For further details, see Jens Flemming, "Großagrarische Interessen und Landarbeiterbewegung. Überlegungen zur Arbeiterpolitik des Bundes der Landwirte und des Reichslandbundes in der Anfangsphase der Weimarer Republik," in *Industrielles System und politische Entwicklung in der Weimarer Republik*, ed. Mommsen, Petzina, and Weisbrod, 745–62.

[64] On the choices facing Christian farm labor, see Jens Flemming, "Zwischen Industrie und christlich-nationaler Arbeiterschaft. Alternativen landwirtschaftlicher Bündnispolitik in der Weimarer Republik," in *Industrielle Gesellschaft und politisches System. Beiträge zur politischen Sozialgeschichte. Festschrift für Fritz Fischer zum 70. Geburtstag*, ed. Dirk Stegmann, Bernd Jürgen Wendt, and Peter-Christian Witt, 259–76. Bonn, 1978.

[65] Larry Eugene Jones, "Catholic Conservatives in the Weimar Republic: The Politics of the Rhenish-Westphalian Aristocracy, 1919–1933," *German History* 18 (2000): 61–85.

[66] For example, see Bolling's remarks in Christliche Bauernschaft der Rheinlande, *Bericht über die erste vorbereitende Versammlung am 29. Januar 1919 in Köln* (Cologne, 1919), 8–10.

Democrats[67] but used peasant frustration over the continuation of wartime economic controls to consolidate their own position as leaders of the most important regional agricultural interest organizations. The Center's relations with the Rhenish and Westphalian peasant associations remained strained throughout the Weimar Republic despite the fact that the party continued to command the respect and loyalty of the local peasantry.[68] In the Catholic parts of Bavaria, on the other hand, leadership of the Bavarian Christian Peasants' Association (Bayerischer Christlicher Bauernverein) remained in the control of Catholic conservatives who were closely allied to the Bavarian People's Party and who harbored at best an ambivalent attitude towards the Weimar Republic.[69]

For the most part Germany's rural conservatives were able to contain the wave of social and political radicalism that gripped the German countryside in the wake of the November Revolution. Whatever concessions Germany's rural elites had been obliged to make in the reassertion of their social and political hegemony seemed inconsequential in light of the strong position they had managed to carve out for themselves in the National Rural League and other agricultural interest organizations. Not only had Germany's rural elites managed to survive the social and political upheaval of 1918–19 with much of their prewar power base intact, but they were well positioned for an assault upon Germany's fledgling republican order if and when the appropriate opportunity presented itself. As in the case of German industry, the forces of social and political conservatism in German agriculture demonstrated remarkable resiliency in rebounding from the collapse of the Second Empire and were far from dormant in the newly established Weimar Republic.

Christian-National Labor

A third arena in which the vitality of German conservatism made itself apparent was the Christian labor movement and its affiliated white-collar unions. To be sure, the conservatism of the Christian labor movement differed

---

[67] Engelbert von Kerckerinck zur Borg, *Unsere Stellung zur Zentrumspartei. Vortrag in der Generalversammlung des Vereins kath. Edelleute zu Münster am 4. Febr. 1919* (Münster, n.d. [1919]). See also Kerckerinck zur Borg to the archbishop of Cologne, 29 Dec. 1918, and Erzberger, 14 July 1919, Vereinigte Westfälische Adelsarchive Münster (hereafter cited as VWA Münster), Nachlass Engelbert Freiherr von Kerckerinck zur Borg, 139. See also Friedrich Keinemann, *Vom Krummstab zur Republik. Westfälischer Adel unter preußischer Herrschaft 1802–1945* (Bochum, 1997), 365–90, and Gerhard Kratzsch, *Engelbert Reichsfreiherr von Kerckerinck zur Borg. Westfälischer Adel zwischen Kaiserreich und Weimarer Republik* (Münster, 2004), 135–53.

[68] Robert G. Moeller, *German Peasants and Agrarian Politics, 1914–1924: The Rhineland and Westphalia* (Chapel Hill, NC, 1986), 74–91, 116–38.

[69] Hundhammer, *Berufsvertretung*, 34–56.

sharply from that of the National Rural League or the German industrial establishment, so much so, in fact, that many of its most prominent leaders would have questioned the designation conservative. Still, the leaders of the Christian labor movement subscribed to an organic theory of society and rejected the glorification of the individual that had become such a prominent feature of both the economic and cultural dimensions of modern life. More importantly, the leaders of the Christian labor movement were unabashedly nationalistic, so much so that they preferred to refer to their movement as not simply Christian, but as Christian-national.[70] This distinction was particularly important because those within the German working class who either implicitly or explicitly embraced the basic values of the conservative *Weltanschauung* represented a distinct minority. Before the war, the working-class and white-collar movements had been split into three ideological camps: Social Democratic, liberal, and Christian-national. Of these three, the Social Democratic was clearly the strongest, claiming more than a quarter million members as opposed to the approximately 342,000 and 106,000 workers who were affiliated with the Christian-national and liberal labor movements respectively.[71] Within the German white-collar movement, on the other hand, the situation was reversed with the Christian-national and liberal unions claiming an estimated 450,000 and 91,000 members respectively, while the socialist white-collar unions could account for only about 81,000 members.[72] Although the war produced a much higher degree of unionization within both the working-class and white-collar sectors of the German labor force, this tended to favor the socialist unions at the expense of their Christian and liberal rivals. By the end of 1919 the socialist unions had increased their membership to almost five-and-a-half million, whereas the Christian-national and liberal unions recorded membership increases to 858,000 and 190,000 respectively. Within the German white-collar movement, on the other hand, conservative unions now accounted for more than 430,000 members, while the liberal and socialist white-collar unions claimed the support of an estimated 68,000 and 146,000 members respectively. For the conservative unions this approximated prewar membership levels, for the liberal unions it reflected the loss of

---

[70] For the ideological orientation of the Christian trade unions, see *Die geistigen Grundlagen der christlich-nationalen Arbeiterbewegung* (Berlin-Wilmersdorf, 1923), as well as the subsequent revision of this statement by Elfriede Nebgen, *Geistige Grundlagen der christlichen Arbeiterbewegung*, ed. Gesamtverband der christlichen Gewerkschaften Deutschlands (Berlin-Wilmersdorf, 1928). For further details, see Michael Schneider, *Die Christlichen Gewerkschaften 1894–1933* (Bonn, 1982), 543–54.

[71] Emil Lederer, "Die Gewerkschaftsbewegung 1918/19 und die Entfaltung der wirtschaftlichen Ideologien in der Arbeiterklasse," *Archiv für Sozialwissenschaft und Sozialpolitik* 47 (1920/21): 221–26.

[72] Emil Lederer, "Die Bewegung der Privatangestellten seit dem Herbst 1918," *Archiv für Sozialwissenschaft und Sozialpolitik* 47 (1920–21): 585–619.

approximately 25 percent of their prewar membership, and for the socialist unions it represented an increase of more than 80 percent over the number of those who had been affiliated before 1914.[73]

The collapse of 1918 and the increasing radicalization of the German working class forced the leaders of the Christian labor movement and its affiliated white-collar unions into an essentially defensive posture. The leader of the Christian labor movement was Adam Stegerwald, a member of the Center Party who had served as chairman of the United Federation of Christian Trade Unions (Gesamtverband der christlichen Gewerkschaften Deutschlands or GCG) since 1903. Germany's military defeat and the collapse of the monarchy had come as a bitter shock to the profoundly conservative Stegerwald, who desperately sought to shore up his own movement in the face of what threatened to develop into a mass exodus of Christian workers to the socialist labor movement.[74] It was against the background of these developments that Stegerwald briefly explored the possibility of creating an interconfessional Christian workers' party with Franz Behrens and the leaders of the Christian-national labor movement. Stegerwald had grown increasingly critical of his own party during the latter stages of World War I and felt that the impending collapse of the old imperial order would usher in a far-reaching realignment of the existing party system.[75] Four days after the fall of the monarchy Heinrich Brauns from the People's Association for Catholic Germany (Volksverein für das katholische Deutschland) proposed the transformation of the German Center Party into a sociologically heterogeneous interconfessional people's party whose fundamental orientation would no longer be exclusively Catholic but Christian in the broadest sense of the word.[76] Not only did Brauns' proposal to expand the Center's political base by opening its doors to Evangelical Christians meet with a warm reception

[73] Jürgen Kocka, *Klassengesellschaft im Krieg. Deutsche Sozialgeschichte 1914–1918* (Göttingen, 1973), 51–57, 76–82.

[74] See Bernhard Forster, *Adam Stegerwald (1874–1945). Christlich-nationaler Gewerkschafter – Zentrumspolitiker – Mitbegründer der Unionsparteien* (Düsseldorf, 2003), 208–20.

[75] Stegerwald, "Das Alte stürzt!," *Deutsche Arbeit* 3, no. 11 (Nov. 1918): 481–97. See also Stegerwald to Brauweiler, 3 Sept. 1918, Stadtarchiv Mönchen-Gladbach (hereafter cited as StA Mönchen-Gladbach), Nachlass Heinz Brauweiler, Bestand 15, 173. For Stegerwald's reasons, see his letter to Becker, 22 Nov. 1918, appended to Stegerwald to Brauns, 22 Nov. 1918, records of the Volksverein für das katholische Deutschland, BA Berlin, Bestand R 8115 I, 180/20–25. For further details, see Forster, *Stegerwald*, 208–20; Larry Eugene Jones, "Adam Stegerwald und die Krise des deutschen Parteiensystems. Ein Beitrag zur Deutung des 'Essener Programms' vom November 1920," *Vierteljahrshefte für Zeitgeschichte* 27 (1979): 1–29; and William L. Patch, Jr., *Christian Trade Unions in the Weimar Republic, 1918–1933: The Failure of "Corporate Pluralism"* (New Haven, CN, 1985), 38–45.

[76] Brauns to Marx and Kastert, 13 Nov. 1918, BA Berlin, R 8115 I, 180/4–5, also in the Stadtarchiv Köln (hereafter cited as StA Köln), Nachlass Wilhelm Marx, 222/72–73.

from party leaders in the Rhineland and west Germany,[77] but it complemented a similar appeal that a group of Center politicians in Berlin had issued
for the renewal of the Center as a "Christian people's party" committed to the
preservation of Christian values and institutions in a time of revolutionary
upheaval.[78]

In a proclamation issued just days after the collapse of the monarchy, the
executive committee of the United Federation of Christian Trade Unions
expressed its full and unequivocal support for the establishment of a democratic people's state on the basis of a free and united German Reich.[79] At the
same time, the leaders of the Christian labor movement took note of the
creation of the *Zentralarbeitsgemeinschaft* and realized that this would require
them to work more closely with the socialist labor movement in order to keep
German big business from dictating the new organization's agenda and policies.[80] To Stegerwald, these developments signaled a fundamental renewal
and reorganization of German political life that only further dramatized the
need for a sweeping realignment of the German party system.[81] But Stegerwald's efforts to unite the non-socialist elements of the German working and
white-collar classes into a single political party were hurt from the outset by
the government's decision to hold the elections to the Weimar National
Assembly in the middle of January 1919 and not in February as originally
planned.[82] Without the time to complete arrangements for the founding of a
new party or to resolve some of the outstanding differences that existed in the
area of cultural policy,[83] the leaders of the Christian labor movement came
under enormous pressure to affiliate with either the Center or one of the new
political parties that had surfaced since the collapse of the Second Empire in
order to make sure that Christian labor was adequately represented at
Weimar. Under these circumstances, both Franz Behrens, a Protestant labor

---

[77] For example, see Becker to Stegerwald, 19 Nov. 1918, BA Berlin, R 8115 I, 180/12–17, also
in StA Köln, NL Marx, 222/78–83.

[78] *Das neue Zentrum und die politische Neuordnung*, ed. Generalsekretariat der Zentrumspartei (Berlin, n.d. [1918]).

[79] *Zentralblatt der christlichen Gewerkschaften Deutschlands* 18, no. 24 (18 Dec. 1918):
193–94.

[80] Bechly, Behrens, and Stegerwald to the members of the executive committee and advisory
council of the German Labor Congress, 28 Nov. 1918, BA Berlin, Nachlass Johannes
Giesberts, 94/14–15.

[81] Stegerwald to the executive committees of the Christian labor unions, 30 Nov. 1918, BA
Berlin, NL Giesberts, 94/16–21. For similar sentiments within the Evangelical workers'
movement, see Gutsche, "Wirtschaftsrevolution und Christlich-nationale Arbeiterbewegung," *Evangelisch-soziale Stimmen* 14, no. 11 (30 Nov. 1918): 42–43.

[82] Stegerwald to Spahn, 31 Jan. 1919, BA Koblenz, Nachlass Martin Spahn, 19.

[83] Gutsche's remarks of 18 Dec. 1918, quoted in Heinrich Imbusch, "10 Jahre Deutscher
Gewerkschaftsbund," in *Der Deutsche 1921–1931. Jubliäums-Nummer vom 1. April
1931*, 3.

leader who had served alongside Stegerwald in the leadership of the German Labor Congress (Deutscher Arbeiter-Kongreß) before the war, and the leaders of the Evangelical workers' movement rallied to the banner of the newly founded German National People's Party in early December 1918.[84] This sounded the death knell of Stegerwald's efforts to found an interconfessional Christian people's party, with the result that he and those of his supporters who belonged to the Center had no choice but to renew their ties to the party, though without necessarily abandoning hope that it might reform itself along the lines that he and his associates in the Christian labor movement had recommended.[85] By the same token, Fritz Baltrusch and Georg Streiter from the United Federation of Christian Trade Unions and Wilhelm Gutsche from the newly founded German Trainmen's Union (Gewerkschaft deutscher Eisenbahner), all of whom had actively supported the creation of an inter-confessional Christian workers' party, decided to cast their lot with Gustav Stresemann and the German People's Party.[86]

As efforts to create an interconfessional Christian workers' party ran out of steam in the first weeks of December 1918, Stegerwald and his associates began to focus their attention instead upon the consolidation of all of Germany's nonsocialist unions in a new trade-union federation. On 20 November 1918 Stegerwald and Gustav Hartmann, chairman of the liberal Federation of German Labor Associations (Verband der deutschen Gewerkvereine), announced the founding of the German Democratic Trade-Union Federation (Deutsch-demokratischer Gewerkschaftsbund or DDGB) as an umbrella organization in which the non-socialist elements of the German working class – liberal as well as conservative – could unite.[87] Similar developments were under way within the German white-collar movement, where Hans Bechly, chairman of the influential and unabashedly conservative German National Union of Commercial Employees met with representatives from more liberal white-collar unions throughout the first half 1919 in an attempt

---

[84] On the breakdown of these negotiations, see Gutsche to Stresemann, 14 Dec. 1918, PA AA Berlin, NL Stresemann, 183/134088–91.

[85] Stegerwald to Spahn, 31 Jan. 1919, BA Koblenz, NL Spahn, 19.

[86] Gutsche to Stresemann, 14 Dec. 1918, PA AA Berlin, NL Stresemann, 183/134088–91. See also Baltrusch to Stresemann, 12 Dec. 1918, ibid., 183/134018–19.

[87] On the founding of the DDGB, see Stegerwald to the executive committees of the Christian labor unions, 30 Nov. 1918, BA Berlin, NL Giesberts, 94/16–21, as well as Wilhelm Wiedfeld, *Der Deutsche Gewerkschaftsbund* (Leipzig, 1933), 12–23. See Steger-wald's speech at the DDGB's founding ceremonies, 20 Nov. 1918, in *Zwecke und Ziele des Deutsch-demokratischen Gewerkschaftsbundes,* Schriften des Deutsch-demokratischen Gewerkschaftsbundes, no. 1 (Berlin, 1919), 1–8, as well as the report in *Zentralblatt der christlichen Gewerkschaften Deutschlands* 28, no. 24 (18 Nov. 1918): 203–05. For further details, see Hartmut Roder, *Der christlich-nationale Deutsche Gewerkschaftsbund (DGB) im politisch-ökonomischen Kräftefeld der Weimarer Republik* (Frankfurt am Main, Bern, and New York, 1986), 235–38, as well as Forster, *Stegerwald,* 206–08.

to lay the foundation for a united white-collar union known as the Federation of Employee Unions (Gewerkschaftsbund der Angestellten or GdA).[88] But in the summer of 1919, just as preparations for the official founding of the new white-collar union were drawing to a close, the leaders of the DHV announced that they were withdrawing from further negotiations so as not to compromise the integrity of their struggle against the so-called Weimar system.[89] In a parallel development, Stegerwald's efforts to consolidate the non-socialist elements of the German working class suffered a similar fate when the German Democratic Trade Union Federation fell apart on 14 November 1919 as a result of supposedly irreconcilable ideological differences between the Christian and liberal labor unions.[90]

These developments revealed the extent to which prewar ideological divisions continued to frustrate the unity and effectiveness of the German labor movement in the immediate postwar period. In both cases, however, the impulse that led to the breakdown of negotiations came from the more conservative elements of the working-class and white-collar movements and was driven by the fear that their affiliation with more liberal unions under the aegis of the German Democratic Trade-Union Federation or the Federation of Employee Unions might identify them too closely with Germany's new republican system. Following the collapse of the DDGB and the DHV's withdrawal from negotiations to found the GdA, the leaders of the Christian-national labor movement concentrated their efforts on uniting all of those who shared their basic ideological orientation into a single trade-union federation. These efforts drew to a successful conclusion with the official founding of the German Trade-Union Federation (Deutscher Gewerkschaftsbund or DGB) on 22 November 1919.[91] The DGB rested upon three organizational pillars, each of which represented a particular branch or "estate" of the German labor force. In addition to the United Federation of Christian Trade Unions that served as the representative for more than a million industrial workers, there was the United Federation of German Employee Unions (Gesamtverband deutscher Angestellten-Gewerkschaften or Gedag) under the leadership of the DHV's Bechly and the United Federation of German Civil Servant Unions (Gesamtverband der deutschen Beamten-Gewerkschaften) under the leadership of Wilhelm Gutsche from the newly established German Trainmen's

---

[88] Heinz-Jürgen Priamus, *Angestellte und Demokratie. Die nationalliberale Angestelltenbewegung in der Weimarer Republik* (Stuttgart, 1979), 72–82.

[89] For further details, see Iris Hamel, *Völkischer Verband und nationale Gewerkschaft. Der Deutschnationale Handlungeshilfen-Verband 1893–1933* (Hamburg, 1967), 169–73.

[90] "Die christlichen Gewerkschaften im Jahre 1919," *Zentralblatt der christlichen Gewerkschaften Deutschlands* 20, no. 20 (27 Sept. 1920): 204.

[91] Wiedfeld, *Deutsche Gewerkschaftsbund*, 24–30. See also Schneider, *Christliche Gewerkschaften*, 486–96, and Roder, *Gewerkschaftsbund*, 254–63.

Union (Gewerkschaft deutscher Eisenbahner).[92] By the fall of 1920, the German Trade-Union Federation could claim the support of almost two million members.[93] Although it may have been eclipsed in terms of total membership by the socialist General German Trade-Union Federation (Allgemeiner Deutscher Gewerkschaftsbund or ADGB), the Christian trade-union movement was no longer the negligible factor in German working-class politics that it had been before the war.[94]

The real strength of the Christian labor movement throughout the Weimar Republic lay not so much in the size of its membership as in the extent of its political contacts. Unlike the National Rural League which, despite its disclaimers to the contrary, was essentially tied to one political party, the German Trade-Union Association was an organization whose leaders were to be found in all of Germany's bourgeois parties with the exception of the DDP. For although Stegerwald and many of his associates in the leadership of the United Federation of Christian Trade Unions belonged to the Center, they were flanked on the left by Hans Bechly, Otto Thiel, and Wilhelm Gutsche from the DVP and on the right by Franz Behrens, Reinhard Mumm, and Emil Hartwig from the DNVP. The network of alliances, or *Querverbindungen*, that the Christian labor movement forged with the various non-socialist parties in the first years of the Weimar Republic thus afforded Stegerwald and his associates a degree of political leverage that not even the much larger ADGB enjoyed. At the same time, however, the tension between those unions like Heinrich Imbusch's Union of Christian Mine Workers (Gewerkverein Christlicher Bergarbeiter) or Georg Wieber's Christian Metal Workers' Union of Germany (Christlicher Metallarbeiterverband Deutschlands) that were allied to the Center and therefore supported the new republican system and those like Franz Behrens' Central Association of Farm Workers that were allied to the DNVP and therefore rejected Weimar was frequently so great that it threatened to paralyze the entire movement. What many regarded as the ultimate source of the DGB's political strength was at the same time a threat to its unity and continued effectiveness.

On the extreme right wing of the Christian-national labor movement stood the German National Union of Commercial Employees. Established in 1893 by a handful of political antisemites under the leadership of Wilhelm Schack, the DHV had evolved over the course of the next quarter decade from a small racist organization that served as little more than a forum for the

---

[92] Brüning to Stegerwald, 24 Sept. 1921, ACDP Sankt-Augustin, Nachlass Adam Stegerwald, I-206/014. See also Brüning's memorandum of 24 Nov. 1921, appended to his letter to Stegerwald, 23 (sic) Nov. 1921, ibid., I-206/018.

[93] Schneider, *Christliche Gewerkschaften*, 492.

[94] For the DGB's accomplishments on behalf of German labor, see Deutscher Gewerkschaftsbund, ed., *Aus der Arbeit des D.G.B.* (Berlin-Wilmersdorf, n.d. [1926]).

dissemination of antisemitic propaganda into the largest of Germany's white-collar unions representing an estimated 200,000 thousand salesmen and clerical employees throughout the country by the end of 1919.[95] The DHV recruited the bulk of its membership from the ranks of those middle-class elements whose economic independence had been undermined by the advanced pace of industrialization and economic rationalization of the late nineteenth century.[96] In the meantime, the leadership of the DHV had been transferred to a new generation of political pragmatists who no longer regarded the struggle against the so-called Jewish threat as important as that for the social, economic, and spiritual welfare of the German salaried employee. The new generation of DHV leaders was epitomized by Hans Bechly, a member of the prewar National Liberal Party who was elected to the chairmanship of the DHV in 1909. Under Bechly's leadership the DHV began to cultivate closer ties with all of Germany's non-socialist parties while maintaining an official policy of neutrality with respect to the individual parties themselves. Bechly thus put an end to the DHV's close identification with the more reactionary elements on the German Right in favor of a policy that encouraged it to cultivate closer ties with all parties that were prepared to support its basic objectives.[97]

Following the collapse of 1918, the DHV moved quickly to reestablish its influence within the white-collar movement and to combat the forces of social and political revolution that had plunged the nation into chaos.[98] For the leaders of the DHV, the November Revolution was little more than an ill-fated attempt to replace a hierarchical social and political order that had outlived its usefulness with a new order that was every bit as repressive and exploitive as the one it sought to replace. In their crusade against the social and political legacy of the November Revolution, the leaders of the DHV not only sought to

---

[95] Hamel, *Völkischer Verband*, 52–122.

[96] Jürgen Kocka, "Vorindustrielle Faktoren in der deutschen Industrialisierung. Industrie-bürokratie und 'neuer Mittelstand'," in *Das kaiserliche Deutschland. Politik und Gesellschaft 1870–1918*, ed. Michael Stürmer (Düsseldorf, 1970), 265–86.

[97] Hans Bechly, *Die Deutschnationale Handlungsgehilfenbewegung und die politischen Parteien. Vortrag gehalten auf dem Zwölften deutschen Handlungsgehilfentage am 18. Juni 1911 in Breslau* (Hamburg, 1911).

[98] For further details, see Richard Döring and Bruno Plintz, eds., *Der Deutschnationale Handlungsgehilfen-Verband in der Reichshauptstadt von 1895–1925. Ein Beitrag zur Geschichte der Berliner Handlungsgehilfen-Bewegung* (Berlin, n.d. [1926]), 115–51, as well as the unpublished memoirs of Max Habermann, "Der Deutschnationale Handlungsgehilfen-Verband im Kampf um das Reich 1918–1933. Ein Zeugnis seines Wollens und Wirkens" (1934), archives of the Deutscher Handels- und Industrieangestellten-Verband, Hamburg (hereafter cited as DHV-Archiv Hamburg), 8–14.

mobilize white-collar support with an appeal that was as anti-capitalist as it was anti-Marxist[99] but also exploited the friction between the working-class and white-collar sectors of the socialist labor movement to gain admission to the *Zentralarbeitsgemeinschaft*.[100] At the same time, the DHV tried to secure a foothold within the various non-socialist parties that had emerged from the ruins of the Second Empire. Following the collapse of efforts to create an interconfessional Christian workers' party in early December 1918, Bechly took part in the official founding of the German People's Party and worked closely with party chairman Gustav Stresemann and DHV secretary Otto Thiel to secure a foothold for the DVP in Germany's growing white-collar population.[101] Other DHV officials, in the meantime, joined the DNVP, Center, and German Democratic Party in accordance with its professed policy of nonpartisanship.[102] In his keynote address at the DHV's Brunswick congress in May 1920, Bechly went to great pains to reaffirm the union's prewar policy of nonpartisanship and publicly urged its members to promote the DHV's social, economic, and cultural objectives by working within all of Germany's non-socialist parties. For although they harbored a deep and abiding animus towards the republican system of government, Bechly and the leaders of the DHV also realized that the only way in which they could influence the legislative process on the behalf of those they represented was to work through the existing political parties. The DHV's immediate objective, therefore, was to secure the election of key union officials to the national parliament, where they would be able to persuade the parties to which they belonged to support legislation beneficial to the interests and welfare of the white-collar employee.[103] At the same time, the DHV leadership worked closely with Stegerwald and his associates to prevent the growing animosity between the

[99] For example, see Hans Bechly, *Der nationale Gedanke nach der Revolution. Vortrag, gehalten am vierzehnten Deutschen Handlungsgehilfentag in Leipzig, vom 18. bis 20. Oktober 1919* (Hamburg, n.d. [1919]), 17–20, 22–36, and Hans Blechly, *Volk, Staat und Wirtschaft. Vortrag gehalten auf dem sechzehnten Deutschen Handlungsgehilfentag in Königsberg/Pr. am 29. Juni 1924* (Hamburg, 1924).
[100] Habermann, "Der DHV im Kampf um das Reich," DHV-Archiv Hamburg, 14.
[101] Gutsche to Stresemann, 14 Dec. 1918, PA AA Berlin, NL Stresemann, 183/134088–91. Bechly involvement in the founding of the DVP, see the minutes of the DVP's founding ceremonies, 15 Dec. 1918, BA Koblenz, R 45 II, 301/227–37.
[102] For example, see the essays by Lambach (DNVP), Thiel (DVP), Gehrig (Center), and Richter (DDP), in *Jahrbuch für Deutschnationale Handlungsgehilfen für 1921*, ed. Deutschnationaler Handlungsgehilfen-Verband (Hamburg, 1921), 50–83.
[103] Hans Bechly, *Staat, Gesellschaft und Politik. Vortrag, gehalten auf dem Verbandstage in Braunschweig am 15. und 16. Mai 1920* (Hamburg, n.d. [1920]), 6–12. See also the correspondence between the DHV's national leadership and Gehrig, 28 Jan–5 Feb. 1921, ACDP Sankt-Augustin, Nachlass Otto Gehrig, I-087/001/1.

Center and DNVP from further undermining the unity and effectiveness of the Christian labor movement.[104]

The Christian-national labor movement was something of a historical anachronism that was anything but a sociologically and ideologically homogeneous factor in German political life. Its supporters were spread out through at least three parties, two of which officially supported the Weimar Republic and a third that actively opposed it. With the exception of those workers' associations that belonged to the so-called yellow trade-union movement, however, the leaders and affiliated unions of the Christian-national labor movement were committed to pursuing their goals within the framework of Germany's new republican system despite whatever political or ideological reservations they may have had about it. The political pragmatism of the Christian-national labor movement would have a moderating effect upon the German Right as it mobilized its resources for its struggle against Weimar democracy.

The Middle Classes

If political and ideological divisions threatened the unity and effectiveness of the Christian labor movement, this was even more true of the last and most deeply divided sector of Germany's conservative milieu, the so-called middle class or *Mittelstand*. In fact, the very term *Mittelstand* was something of a fiction and suggested a much higher degree of sociological cohesiveness on the part of those intermediary strata that lay between the two extremes of capital and labor than actually existed.[105] Not only were the German middle strata deeply fragmented along social, political, and ideological lines, but the degree of interest articulation was more pronounced here than within any other sector of German society. For in addition to the salaried employees who preferred to identify themselves more with the social and cultural values of the *Mittelstand* than with those of the industrial proletariat, the so-called middle class also included the artisanry and small business sector, the liberal professions such as law, medicine, and journalism, and the professional civil service including state employees, teachers, and university professors. To compound the situation, each of these groups was represented by a wide range of interest organizations, some of which defined themselves by region and others by ideology. In the final analysis, it was precisely the plethora of special interest organizations within the German middle strata that militated so

---

[104] Correspondence between Bechly and Stegerwald, 28 Sept.–3 Oct. 1921, ACDP Sankt-Augustin, NL Stegerwald, I-206/014, as well as Habermann, "Der DHV im Kampf um das Reich," DHV-Archiv Hamburg, 15–17.

[105] For example, see David Blackbourn, "The *Mittelstand* in German Society and Politics, 1870–1914," *Social History*, no. 4 (1977): 409–33.

decisively against their social and political cohesiveness. Moreover, the economic burden of the lost war and the struggle over how this burden was to be distributed throughout German society as a whole only intensified the general level of interest antagonism within the German middle strata and made it even more difficult to blend these interests together into something resembling a cohesive social force.[106] The social and economic fragmentation of the German middle strata thus mirrored what was happening to German society as a whole and served as the special case of a more general process that was to become more and more pronounced as the decade of the 1920s wound to a close.

Properly speaking, only a part of the so-called German middle class could rightly be identified as belonging to Germany's conservative milieu. Many of those in the liberal professions, for example, had long identified themselves with the basic values and institutions of the German liberal tradition, although even here an erosion of liberal commitment had become increasingly apparent in the late nineteenth and early twentieth centuries.[107] The same could be said of the state civil service, although here the bureaucracy's professed *Überparteilichekeit* concealed an underlying commitment to conservative values and institutions at the same time that it prevented the civil service from becoming too closely identified with the program or ideology of a particular political party.[108] Still, the sustained assault against the prerogatives of the professional bureaucracy and the erosion of its economic substance in the first years of the Weimar Republic led Germany's civil servants to become more aggressive in the defense of their special interests with the founding of the German Civil Servants' Association (Deutscher Beamtenbund) in December 1918. Although the leaders and membership of the German Civil Servants' Association were recruited by and large from the ranks of Germany's liberal parties, these developments had a radicalizing effect upon the civil service and made its rank-and-file membership increasingly susceptible to the agitation of Germany's right-wing parties.[109]

---

[106] Hans Mommsen, "Die Auflösung des Bürgertums seit dem späten 19. Jahrhundert," in *Bürger und Bürgerlichkeit im 19. Jahrhundert*, ed. Jürgen Kocka (Göttingen, 1987), 288–315.

[107] See Konrad H. Jarausch, *The Unfree Professions: German Lawyers, Teachers, and Engineers, 1900–1950* (New York and Oxford, 1990), esp. 78–114, and Kenneth F. Ledford, *From General Estate to Special Interest: German Lawyers, 1878–1933* (Cambridge, 1996), 245–99.

[108] Peter-Christian Witt, "Konservatismus als Überparteilichkeit. Die Beamten der Reichskanzlei zwischen Kaiserreich und Weimarer Republik 1900–1933," in *Deutscher Konservatismus im 19. und 20. Jahrhundert. Festschrift für Fritz Fischer*, ed. Dirk Stegmann, Bernd Jürgen Wendt, and Peter-Christian Witt (Bonn, 1983), 234–41.

[109] Andreas Kunz, *Civil Servants and the Politics of Inflation in Germany, 1914–1924* (Berlin and New York, 1986), 132–58, 207–08, 377–82.

Of all the groups that comprised the German middle strata, none was more firmly entrenched in Germany's conservative milieu than the so-called economic *Mittelstand* of artisans and small, independent businessmen. Before the war this particular sector of the German middle strata had been represented by the ostensibly nonpartisan German Middle-Class Association (Deutsche Mittelstandsvereinigung) following its founding in 1904 and then from 1911 on by the more militantly conservative Reich German Middle-Class League. With the creation of the Cartel of Productive Estates in 1913, the DKP assumed the political leadership of an alliance that resisted a reform of Germany's political system and provided propagandist support for the German war effort in the first years of World War I.[110] But the collapse of the Second Empire and the wave of revolutionary turmoil that accompanied the end of the war sent a shockwave through the various sectors of Germany's conservative milieu and left it politically adrift. In the campaign for the elections to the Weimar National Assembly, for example, the Middle-Class Association for Political Enlightenment (Mittelstandsvereinigung für politische Aufklärung) in Greifswald was so obsessed with the fear of socialism and the threat of expropriation that they withheld their endorsement from any single party and urged their supporters to vote for any one of the three nonconfessional bourgeois parties – that is, for the DDP, DVP, or DNVP – in order to prevent Social Democracy from gaining the absolute majority it needed to use the National Assembly as an instrument of class domination.[111] The severe economic hardship that the artisanry and small business sector experienced after World War I would only intensify the resentment that these sectors of Germany's middle-class economy harbored toward the Weimar Republic and would accelerate their descent into the camp of the anti-republican German Right.[112]

All of this worked to the advantage of the DNVP, which moved quickly to anchor itself as firmly as possible in Germany's conservative milieu in the predominantly Protestant areas of Germany that ran from Hesse through Saxony and Thuringia into Pomerania, Mecklenburg, and the Prussian provinces to the east of the Elbe. With the exception of Saxony, this area lacked significant industrial development and was predominantly rural with a

[110] Stegmann, *Erben Bismarcks*, 249–56. See also Heinrich August Winkler, *Mittelstand, Demokratie und Nationalsozialismus. Die politische Entwicklung von Handwerk und Kleinhandel in der Weimarer Republik* (Cologne, 1972), 40–64.

[111] For example, see the brochures the Mittelstandsvereinigung für politische Aufklärung distributed in the campaign for the National Assembly, especially *Was steht für den Kleinbesitz auf dem Lande bei den Wahlen auf dem Spiel?*, Flugschrift 1; *Welcher Partei soll bei den Wahlen der Handwerker seine Stimme geben?*, Flugschrift 2; and *Die Zukunft der Angestellten und die Wahlen zur Nationalversammlung*, Flugschrift 3, all published in Greifswald at the end of 1918 and beginning of 1919.

[112] Winkler, *Mittelstand*, 65–83, 128–34.

scattering of small and middle-sized cities. Everyday life was organized around a rich and variegated associational structure that included everything from veterans' organizations and the Lutheran Church and its activities to artisan guilds, salesmen's associations, and shooting clubs. Even local taverns played an important role in fostering a high degree of sociability between individuals whose social and economic interests might not have had all that much in common. What united these elements, however, was the sense of having been left behind and the threat that this posed to their sense of place in Germany's political future.[113] The task of giving this a coherent political voice fell to a quartet of "mentors," or what Wolfgram Pyta calls *Meinungsführer* – the large peasant or *Großbauer*, the manor lord or *Gutsherr*, the country parson, and the village school teacher – who would exercise enormous influence over the voting behavior of the local population. After some initial hesitancy following the collapse of the Second Empire, these *Meinungsführer* began to line up in support of the DNVP, thus enabling the party to establish itself as an agrarian *Volkspartei* that represented Germany's rural conservative milieu in all of its sociological heterogeneity up until the onset of the agrarian crisis and widespread peasant protest at the end of the 1920s.[114]

The principal challenge facing the DNVP as it sought to unite the various forces on the German Right into a cohesive political force was to anchor itself as firmly as possible in the various sectors of Germany's conservative milieu. This would be no easy task in light of the fact that this milieu was anything but a homogeneous bloc. On the contrary, Germany's conservative milieu was riven by all sorts of structural contradictions that would only become deeper with the passage of time. The general course of German social and economic development since unification in 1871 had only intensified the degree of interest articulation and antagonism at all levels of German society and had made the task of forging the disparate social and economic groups that comprised Germany's conservative milieu into a cohesive political force all the more difficult. At the same time, the challenge of determining how the social and economic cost of Germany's lost war would be distributed throughout German society as a whole made it imperative for influential economic interest organizations like the National Federation of German Industry, the National Rural League, and the German Trade-Union Federation to set aside whatever ideological reservations they may have had about Germany's new

---

[113] For two excellent regional studies on the DNVP and the conservative milieu of the Weimar Republic, see Matthiesen, *Greifswald in Vorpommern*, 75–301, and Bösch, *Das konservative Milieu*, 35–133.

[114] Pyta, *Dorgemeinschaft und Parteipolitik 1918–1933. Die Verschränkung von Milieu und Parteien in den protestantischen Landgebieten Deutschlands in der Weimarer Republik* (Düsseldorf, 1996), 83–162.

republican system and to work within that system in order to protect and
advance the social and economic interests of those whom they sought to
represent. This, in turn, placed an increasingly heavy burden on relations
between those who were hoping to gain access to the corridors of power in
order to promote the vital interests of their respective constituencies and those
on the extreme Right who remained implacably opposed to collaboration with
the republican system of government on any terms whatsoever. The tensions
this produced within the German Right would remain more or less obscured
as long as the German National People's Party – at this time the primary
political representative of Germany's conservative milieu – refused to waver in
its unconditional opposition to the system of government that Germany had
inherited from the November Revolution. What might happen once it had
become clear that the Weimar Republic had indeed survived the trauma of its
birth was far from certain.

3

Forging a Conservative Synthesis

The leaders of the German National People's Party had every reason to be satisfied with the outcome of the 1919 elections in the Reich and Prussia. Operating under circumstances that could only be described as difficult, the DNVP had survived its first test at the polls with flying colors. Still, the problems facing party leaders following the elections were formidable. First and foremost was the disunity of the DNVP delegation to the Weimar National Assembly. The Nationalist delegation was anything but a cohesive unit, consisting of disparate elements ranging from governmental conservatives like Clemens von Delbrück and Count Arthur von Posadowsky-Wehner, large landowners like Gustav Roesicke and Martin Schiele, labor leaders like Franz Behrens and Wilhelm Wallbaum to Pan-German nationalists like Alfred Hugenberg and Käthe Schirmacher, political antisemites like Albrecht von Graefe-Goldebee and Wilhelm Bruhn, and refugees from the now defunct Fatherland Party like Gottfried Traub.[1] Little united these groups save their shared antipathy to the social and political legacy of the November Revolution and their simmering discontent over the lost war and Germany's weakness in the deliberations at the Paris Peace Conference. To mold these groups into a cohesive and effective parliamentary delegation was the DNVP's first order of business as it regrouped for the bitter political struggles that lay ahead in 1919.

In a larger sense, however, the disunity of the DNVP's delegation to the Weimar National Assembly only mirrored the situation within the party as a whole. Here the task of forging a viable and durable synthesis may have been even more daunting than that of unifying the delegation. For in addition to the ideological diversity that was so distinctive of the DNVP's delegation at Weimar, the party's national organization had to cope with regional differences of enormous scale and magnitude. The DNVP's national party organization had come together in the fall and early winter of 1918 as a loose, if not inchoate, coalition of different regional organizations, some of which were still

---

[1] For a portrait of the Nationalist delegation to the National Assembly, see Gottfried Traub, *Erinnerungen. Wie ich das "Zweite Reich" erlebte. Tagebuchnotizen aus der Hitlerzeit* (Stuttgart, 1998), 190–91. See also Christian F. Trippe, *Konservative Verfassungspolitik 1918–1923. Die DNVP als Opposition in Reich und Ländern* (Düsseldorf, 1995), 64–70.

dominated by prewar agrarian elites while others were entirely new construc-
tions that represented much different social and political constituencies. In the
months that lay ahead the DNVP's national leadership would have to find a
formula that would allow it to consolidate the diverse social, economic, and
regional constituencies that comprised the party's material base into a cohesive
and effective political organization. To do this, DNVP strategists needed to
anchor the new party as firmly as possible in Germany's conservative milieu
and, if possible, to extend conservative influence into those sectors of the
population that had remained outside the embrace of prewar German
conservatism.[2]

In Search of an Identity

The internal consolidation of the DNVP was inextricably related to the task of
developing a party program that would reconcile the values, interests, and
concerns of the diverse factions that constituted the DNVP's material base.
The party's earliest programmatic statements, such as the election appeal of
22 November 1918 or "Die Ziele der Deutschnationalen Volkspartei" from
mid-December, were characteristically vague and offered little insight into
how the party stood on specific social, economic, and cultural issues. Although
the DNVP party leadership would not appoint a committee to draft a party
program until September 1919, internal wrangling over the form and content
of the program began almost immediately after the elections. Here the initiative came from a group of self-styled young conservatives led by Ulrich von
Hassell. On 15 February 1919 Hassell and his associates convened the State-
Political Coordinating Committee of the German National People's Party
(Staatspolitische Arbeitsgemeinschaft der Deutschnationalen Volkspartei) as
a forum for bringing together the different constituencies that were represented within the DNVP for a free and candid exchange of ideas.[3] Hassell's
primary objective was to ensure that the new party was as comprehensive as
possible and that it appealed to a broad cross-section of the German electorate.[4] Over the course of the next twelve months Hassell and his supporters
organized a series of lectures on a wide range of topics of relevance to
Germany's postwar conservative agenda. Of particular concern was how the

---

[2] For example, see Peter-Christian Witt, "Eine Denkschrift Otto Hoetzschs vom 5. November 1918," *Vierteljahrshefte für Zeitgeschichte* 21 (1973): 337–53. See also the memorandum from Meyer, 27 Jan. 1919, appended to Winterfeld to Hergt, 6 Feb. 1919, records of
the Deutschnationale Volkspartei, BA Berlin, Bestand R 8005, 1/82–98.

[3] Hassell's remarks at the official founding of the State Political Coordinating Committee, 15
Feb. 1919, BA Berlin, NL Mumm, 293/137–38. See also Hassell to Mumm, 7 Feb. 1919,
ibid., 293/143.

[4] Hassell, "Die Lebensnotwendigkeiten der Deutschnationalen Volkspartei," *Eiserne Blätter*
1, no. 12 (21 Sept. 1919): 209–13.

party should go about attracting the support of workers, farm laborers, women, and Catholics, as well as the position the party would take on the so-called Jewish question.[5] The purpose of this, as Hassell explained on the eve of the DNVP's Berlin party congress in July 1919, was to make certain that the DNVP did not deteriorate into a one-sided agrarian party like the prewar DKP. Calling for the creation of a strong national, unitary, and organic state, Hassell exhorted his supporters to embrace three basic principles as the ideological foundation of the DNVP: a Christian concept of the world, a social concept of the nation, and an organic concept of the state. Then and only then, Hassell concluded, would the DNVP become "the great right-wing party of the future [*die große Rechtspartei der Zukunft*] that will lead our fatherland once more to better times."[6]

Hassell and his associates believed that only the creation of a entirely new conservative party free from the social, regional, and confessional prejudices of Germany's prewar conservative parties could lead the German people from the ruins of war and revolution to unity and a new sense of its national destiny.[7] Hassell's vision of the DNVP as a socially and confessionally heterogeneous conservative *Sammelpartei* stood in sharp contrast to the objectives of the hard-line Prussian conservatives around Ernst Heydebrand von der Lasa and Count Kuno von Westarp. Although Westarp had played a major role in persuading his colleagues in the Central Association of German Conservatives to throw their support behind the newly founded DNVP,[8] its leaders remained profoundly critical of the new party's composition and looked forward to the day when they could take control of the party and purge it of those they regarded as politically unreliable.[9] For his own part, Hergt had made his acceptance of the DNVP party chairmanship in December 1918 contingent upon the dissolution of the Central Association of German Conservatives,[10]

---

[5] These lectures were given at "evening workshops," or *Arbeitsabende*, that the State Political Coordinating Committee held throughout 1919 and early 1920. For the most part, the transcripts of these lectures can be found in BA Berlin, R 8005, vol. 327.

[6] Hassell, "Die Aufgaben einer großen politischen Partei in der Gegenwart," 11 July 1919, BA Berlin, R 8005, 327/78–79.

[7] Hassell, "Wir jungen Konservativen. Ein Aufruf," *Der Tag*, 24 Nov. 1918. For the broader context, see Peter Fritzsche, "Breakdown or Breakthrough? Conservatives and the November Revolution," in *Between Reform, Reaction, and Resistance: Studies in the History of German Conservatism from 1789 to 1945*, ed. Larry Eugene Jones and James Retallack (Providence, RI, and Oxford, 1993), 299–328.

[8] Westarp, *Konservative Politik*, ed. Hiller von Gaertringen, 29–30. On Westarp's career in Weimar politics, see Larry Eugene Jones, "Kuno Graf von Westarp und die Krise des deutschen Konservativismus in der Weimarer Republik," in *"Ich bin der letzte Preuße": Kuno Graf von Westarp und die deutsche Politik (1900–1945)*, ed. Larry Eugene Jones and Wolfram Pyta (Cologne, Weimar, and Vienna, 2006), 109–46.

[9] Westarp to Klasing, 25 Mar. 1919, BA Berlin, NL Westarp, 37/42–43.

[10] Hergt to [Dietrich], 19 Dec. 1918, NL Westarp, Gärtringen, II/1.

but ran into strong opposition from Westarp, who declared in a meeting with the DNVP party chairman in late January 1919 that for the moment the Central Association would not dissolve itself but would continue its activities outside the public eye.[11] Westarp succeeded in fending off Hergt's demand that the Central Association initiate dissolution proceedings immediately at a meeting of the DNVP executive committee on 31 January by reminding the DNVP party chairman that only a DKP party congress was authorized to undertake such a step and that the outcome of such a meeting could not be predicted given the widespread uneasiness with the DNVP that existed in conservative circles throughout the country.[12]

Westarp's thinly veiled threat of a conservative secession on the DNVP's right wing was sufficient to blunt the thrust of Hergt's offensive against the Central Association of German Conservatives until the DNVP revisited the issue at the first meeting of the DNVP central executive committee in April 1919. Refusing to go ahead with the dissolution of the old party, Heydebrand and the erstwhile leaders of the now defunct DKP maintained that it was essential to preserve the Central Association of German Conservatives as an independent organization with sufficient resources to wage its own campaign in support of conservative values and principles.[13] These sentiments received strong support from Westarp, who convened a special session of the Central Association's Berlin leadership on the eve of the first meeting of the DNVP central executive committee to publish a resolution that defended the continued existence of the old conservative party as a "state-political necessity" to preserve the historical legacy of the Prussian state and the values for which it had always stood.[14] This set the stage for a furious exchange before the DNVP central executive committee during which Westarp defended the Central Association and its refusal to close shop against the attacks of those like Hassell, Traub, and Siegfried von Kardorff who conceived of the DNVP as a totally new political creation unencumbered by the follies of the past.[15] The conflict over the DNVP's identity, however, was far from over.

---

[11] Westarp to Heydebrand, 13 Feb. 1919, ibid., II/79.

[12] Ibid.

[13] Heydebrand to Westarp, 16 Feb. 1919, NL Westarp, Gärtringen, II/79.

[14] "Erklärung der Konservativen Parteileitung," *Kreuz-Zeitung*, 13 Apr. 1919, quoted in Westarp, *Konservative Politik*, ed. Hiller von Gaertringen, 38–39. See also Westarp to Heydebrand, 7 Apr. 1919, NL Westarp, Gärtringen, II/79.

[15] *Erste Tagung des Hauptvorstandes der Deutschnationalen Volkspartei im Festsaal der Preußischen Landes-Versammlung in Berlin am 15. und 16. April 1919*, Deutschnationale Tagungsberichte, no. 1 (Berlin, 1919), 11–16. See also the report to Heydebrand, 17 Apr. 1919, BA Berlin, R 8003, 2/49–51, as well as Westarp, *Konservative Politik*, ed. Hiller von Gaertringen, 36–42.

Defining Itself at Weimar

As the initial skirmishes over the identity and program of the DNVP were taking shape, party leaders had begun to make progress on the other two problems that had faced them in early 1919, namely the lack of unity within the DNVP delegation to the Weimar National Assembly and the need to consolidate the various groups that constituted the party's material base into a comprehensive national organization. To be sure, the internal consolidation of the DNVP was greatly assisted by the fact that all elements of the party were unconditionally opposed to the governmental coalition that assumed power at Weimar in early February 1919.[16] Even then, the first meetings of the DNVP delegation at Weimar were raucous affairs that lacked an agenda and clear, decisive leadership. The delegation was in fact so disorganized that the deputies could not even agree upon which issues should be dealt with first.[17] Gradually, however, a modicum of order and a sense of priorities began to emerge as experienced governmental conservatives led by Posadowsky-Wehner and Delbrück began to assert control and as the delegation itself began to focus on those issues on which there was little, if any, disagreement.[18] On no issue was there greater unanimity than on that of monarchism. Virtually every member of the DNVP's Weimar delegation believed that monarchism represented the form of government that was best suited to the German character. When Posadowsky-Wehner rose up in defense of the "old system" on 14 February, his impassioned remarks met with enthusiastic support from every faction within the delegation.[19] Although many Nationalists may have been dismayed by the abdication and flight of Kaiser Wilhelm II, a commitment to the restoration of the monarchical form of government remained the one issue upon which virtually every member of the Nationalist delegations in Weimar and Berlin could agree.[20]

[16] See Adolf von Posadowsky-Wehner, Siegfried von Kardorff, and Oskar Hergt, *Die Abrechnung mit der Revolution. Reden in der Verfassunggebenden Deutschen National-versammlung in Weimar am 27. März 1919 und in der Verfassunggebenden Preußischen Landesversammlung in Berlin am 26. und 27. März 1919*, Deutschnationale Parlaments-reden, nos. 3–4 (Berlin, 1919).

[17] On the DNVP delegation at Weimar, see the excerpts from the diary of DNVP deputy Ulrich Kahrstedt, 3–7 Feb. 1919, BA Koblenz, NL Traub, 8/14–15.

[18] Fur further details, see Westarp, *Konservative Politik*, ed. Hiller von Gaertringen, 257–305.

[19] Traub, *Erinnerungen*, 192.

[20] For example, see Axel von Freytagh-Loringhoven, *Politik. Eine Einführung in Gegen-wartsfragen* (Munich, 1919), 89–136. See also Friedrich Freiherr Hiller von Gaertringen, "Zur Beurteilung des 'Monarchismus' in der Weimarer Republik," in *Tradition und Reform in der deutschen Politik. Gedenkschrift für Waldemar Besson*, ed. Gotthard Jaspers (Frankfurt a.M., 1976), 138–86.

An issue of no less significance as a unifying factor in the DNVP's early development was the status of the Lutheran church and the place of religious education in the German school system. In the campaign for the elections to the National Assembly, the DNVP had devoted an inordinate amount of attention to warning against the dangers that besieged the Lutheran Church and committed itself as unequivocally as possible to the defense of Christian culture and institutions against the rising tide of individualism, secularization, and religious indifference.[21] The fact that no less than eight of the forty-two Nationalist deputies elected to the Weimar National Assembly were Lutheran pastors underscored the importance the party attached to religious issues and the fate of the Church in postwar German society. At Weimar, however, the DNVP had little direct influence over the policies of the national cabinet since it did not belong to the governmental coalition that the Majority Socialists, Center, and DDP formed in early February 1919. But Mumm, Traub, and the leaders of the party's Evangelical faction nutured close ties with their counterparts in the two liberal parties and worked closely with them to prevent the disestablishment of the Lutheran Church and other measures that would seriously weaken its standing in German society.[22] At the same time, the leaders of the DNVP's Evangelical faction could count on the support of the Center Party to protect the principle of confessional education against the efforts of those who wanted to secularize the German school system from top to bottom. Mumm would later regard the role he had played in preserving the privileged status of the Lutheran Church in post-revolutionary Germany as the single most significant accomplishment of his political career.[23]

The significance of monarchism and the defense of the prerogatives of the Lutheran Church as issues around which the party faithful could rally, however, were quickly eclipsed by two issues that dominated the Nationalists' political agenda in the second half of 1919: the struggle against the Allied peace terms and the ratification of Germany's new constitution. Originally the DNVP's foreign policy specialists had hoped that American influence would temper France's desire for a peace of retribution and were prepared to accept a peace based upon the principles of Woodrow Wilson's "Fourteen Points."[24]

---

[21] *Ziele der Deutschnationalen Volkspartei*, Deutschnationale Flugschrift, no. 2 (Berlin, n.d. [1919]), 10. See also Wilhelm Kähler, "Deutschnationale Kulturpolitik" in *Der nationale Wille. Werden und Wirken der Deutschnationalen Volkspartei 1918–1928*, ed. Max Weiß (Essen, 1928), 178–203, esp. 196–200.

[22] Traub, *Erinnerungen*, 147–48. See also Ludwig Richter, *Kirche und Schule in den Beratungen der Weimarer Nationalversammlung* (Düsseldorf, 1996), esp. 304–20.

[23] Reinhard Mumm, *Der christlich-soziale Gedanke. Bericht über ein Lebensarbeit in schwerer Zeit* (Berlin, 1933), 97–102. See also Friedrich, *"Die christlich-soziale Fahne empor!"*, 196–204.

[24] See the report by Hoetzsch in *Erste Tagung des Hauptvorstandes der DNVP*, 8–9. as well as the resolution adopted by the DNVP Central Committee, 16 Apr. 1919, ibid., 11.

None of this, however, sat well with old-line conservatives like Westarp, who railed against the earliest reports emanating from the Allied camp as signs of an impending *Gewaltfriede* to which the DNVP would remain irreconcilably opposed.[25] By the same token, Westarp denounced the way in which the governing councils of Wilson's League of Nations were constituted as further proof of a concerted Allied strategy to block Germany's return to great power status and to enforce the provisions of a truly Draconian peace.[26] When the Allies presented the German delegation at Paris with their peace terms on 7 May 1919, any chance that the DNVP might ratify the treaty completely evaporated as the balance within the Nationalist delegation to the National Assembly shifted in favor of those like Westarp who were intractably opposed to acceptance of the Allied peace terms. The Nationalists moved quickly to position themselves at the head of the national protest to which the publication of the Allied peace terms had given rise.[27]

In denouncing the proposed peace treaty as a *Gewaltfriede* that was being imposed upon Germany at the point of a bayonet,[28] the leaders of the DNVP were anxious not to be outdone by the rival DVP, whose national party chairman Gustav Stresemann was every bit as uncompromising as the Nationalists in his denunciation of Versailles as a "death sentence" aimed at the annihilation and enslavement of the German people.[29] For their own part, the Nationalists rejoiced in the sense of national solidarity with which Germany's political leadership greeted the Allied peace proposal and that manifested itself most dramatically in the historic session of the National Assembly on 12 May, when all parties from the Majority Socialists to the DNVP came together to reject Allied peace terms as an insult to Germany's national honor.[30] By the same token, the leaders of the DNVP expressed great dismay when this solidarity began to evaporate as the national cabinet under Majority Socialist Philipp Scheidemann wrestled with Allied demands that Germany accept the terms of the proposed peace treaty without amendment or reservation. The Nationalists were particularly indignant over the possibility that the

---

[25] Kuno von Westarp, *Gewaltfriede und Deutschnationale Volkspartei. Rede vom 15. Januar 1919*, Konservative Flugschrift, no. 14 (Berlin, n.d. [1919]).
[26] Kuno von Westarp, *Deutschland im Völkerbund*, Deutschnationale Politik, no. 1 (Berlin, n.d. [1919].
[27] For example, see Otto Hoetzsch, "Die Außenpolitik der Deutschnationalen Volkspartei," in *Der nationale Wille*, ed. Weiß, 83–117, esp. 85–90.
[28] Hans Erdmann von Lindeiner-Wildau, *Wie der Gewaltfriede aussieht*, Deutschnationale Flugschrift, no. 17 (Berlin, n.d. [1919]). In a similar vein, see Karl Helfferich, *Die Friedensbedingungen. Ein Wort an das deutsche Volk* (Berlin, 1919).
[29] [Gustav Stresemann], *Dr. Stresemanns Rede gegen den Vernichtungsfrieden, gehalten am Sonnabend, den 24. Mai 1919, in Stade*, Sonderabdruck aus dem "Stader Tageblatt" (N.p. [Stade], n.d. [1919], 8ff.
[30] Traub, *Erinnerungen*, 195–97.

government might accede to Allied demands that it accept the treaty intact, including Articles 227-30 that required Germany to surrender officers and other high officials responsible for the conduct of the war to the Allies for trial as war criminals and Article 231 that assigned Germany sole responsibility for the outbreak of World War I.[31] The Nationalists regarded these as non-negotiable "points of honor," and when the national government failed to secure Allied concessions on these points, not even an offer from Reich President Friedrich Ebert to place the formation of a new government in the hands of the DNVP could soften the party's opposition to acceptance of Allied peace terms.[32]

As it became increasingly clear that rejection of Allied peace terms would most likely lead to the occupation and possible dismemberment of the German Reich, Delbrück and a handful of followers in the DNVP's Weimar delegation were willing to provide the national government with a measure of political cover as long as this did not entail acceptance of those articles of the proposed peace treaty that constituted an insult to Germany's national honor.[33] But the furor over Allied peace terms severely weakened the position of the DNVP moderates and enabled those like Westarp who were most strongly opposed to an accommodation with the government to gain control of the delegation and set the tone of its policy toward the Allies. On 22 June 1919 the DNVP delegation to the Weimar National Assembly voted along with DVP delegation and a majority of the Democratic delegation against acceptance of the Allied peace terms.[34] Supported by both the Majority and Independent Socialists, the Center, and a minority of the Democratic delegation, the national government headed now by Majority Socialist Gustav Bauer succeeded in finding a parliamentary majority for acceptance of the Allied peace terms, setting the stage for the formal signing of the treaty that would take place in the Hall of Mirrors at the Versailles Palace in the outskirts of Paris on 28 June 1919.

The significance of the struggle against Versailles as a catalyst for the internal consolidation of the DNVP cannot be overemphasized. The struggle against Versailles temporarily papered over the divisions that had bedeviled the DNVP ever since its founding at the end of 1918 and provided party leaders with an issue of such enormous emotional force that they were able to unite the various constituencies that made up the DNVP's popular base

---

[31] For the Nationalist position, see Karl Helfferich, *Der Friede von Versailles. Rede an die akademische Jugend gehalten am 26. Juni 1919 im Auditorium Maximum der Berliner Universität*, Deutschnationale Flugschrift, no. 20 (Berlin, n.d. [1919]).

[32] Traub, *Erinnerungen*, 202.

[33] Entry in Kahrstedt's diary, 21 June 1919, BA Koblenz, NL Traub, 8/18.

[34] Traub, *Erinnerungen*, 203-05.

behind their crusade for the restoration of Germany's national honor.[35] At the same time, those moderates who had been moving ever so slowly in the direction of an accommodation with the national government found themselves stymied by the depth of anti-government feeling that had been unleashed by the struggle against the Versailles Treaty. In his keynote address at the DNVP's first party congress in Berlin on 12–13 July 1919, party chairman Oskar Hergt took special pains to stress the all-inclusive character of the new party and called upon all of those who shared the DNVP's indignation over the terms of the "Versailles Dictate" to join it in the struggle for right and justice before God and the bar of history.[36] But the harshest words came from Westarp, a former member of the prewar German Conservative Party who had been relegated to the sidelines in the 1919 elections to the National Assembly. Westarp was determined to use the campaign against Versailles to consolidate and strengthen the conservative foothold in the DNVP at the expense of the party's more moderate leaders like Hergt, Otto Hoetzsch, and Clemens von Delbrück.[37] Labeling Versailles a disgrace and humiliation for Germans at home and abroad, Westarp called upon the DNVP to become the heart and soul of German resistance against the enslavement of the German nation. "Freedom from the slavery of the Versailles Peace Treaty," argued Westarp, "that is the task of all politics, that is the goal of every political struggle. . .It is our task to loosen the frightful chains that bind Germany hand and foot through unrelenting effort, to protect German *Volkstum* and German values whenever the opportunity presents itself, and then to be ready with watchful eyes and unshakable resolve, to be ready to shake off the bonds of slavery!"[38]

The DNVP's struggle against Versailles would set the stage for the next major struggle the party would face, the struggle over ratification of the Weimar Constitution. That the DNVP would not vote for the new constitution was a foregone conclusion. As a party committed to the monarchical form of government as the form of government best suited to the traditions and character of the German people,[39] the DNVP could not possibly have supported the republican constitution that the parties of the Weimar coalition had drafted without irreparably compromising its political and ideological

---

[35] For example, see Westarp to Heydebrand, 20 June 1919, NL Westarp, Gärtringen, II/80.

[36] Oskar Hergt, *Gegenwart und Zukunft der Deutschnationalen Volkspartei. Rede auf dem Parteitag der Deutschnationalen Volkspartei in Berlin am 12. und 13. Juli 1919*, Deutschnationale Flugschrift, no. 21 (Berlin, 1919).

[37] Westarp to Heydebrand, 28 May and 7 July 1919, NL Westarp, Gärtringen, II/80.

[38] Kuno von Westarp, *Deutschlands Zukunftsaufgaben in der auswärtigen Politik. Rede auf dem Parteitag der Deutschnationalen Volkspartei in Berlin am 12. und 13. Juli 1919*, Deutschnationale Flugschrift, no. 24 (Berlin, 1919), 7.

[39] Excerpts from Delbrück's speech in the National Assembly, 28 Feb. 1919, quoted in Westarp, *Konservative Politik*, ed. Hiller von Gaertringen, 264–65.

integrity. Still, this did not prevent individual Nationalists from taking part in the deliberations that accompanied the establishment of the new constitutional order at both the national and state levels. In fact, governmental conservatives like Delbrück and Adelbert Düringer in the Weimar National Assembly and Hergt and Hoetzsch in the Prussian Constitutional Assembly as well as their counterparts in Bavaria, Württemberg, and elsewhere worked diligently to establish a constitutional framework for the defense of conservative institutions, interests, and values in Germany's new republican order.[40] Here the Nationalists pursued three goals. First, they sought to strengthen the authority of the state – admittedly a paradox in view of their opposition to the republican form in which the state currently existed – by decoupling the exercise of executive authority from the vicissitudes of the constantly shifting party configurations in the Reichstag and state legislative bodies and by increasing the powers and prerogatives of the Reich President and state executives at the expense of popularly elected legislatures.[41] Second, they sought to prevent the dismemberment of Prussia for the purposes of creating a unitary German state. Accordingly, the Nationalists fought to preserve as much as possible of Prussia's territorial and institutional integrity within the framework of a new federal arrangement that guaranteed the individual German states a substantial measure of autonomy from the central government in Berlin.[42] Third, the Nationalists sought to sidetrack socialist efforts to include elements of the revolutionary *Rätesystem*, or system of revolutionary councils, in the new constitutional order and called for the reorganization of German economic life along corporatist lines and the creation of a separate legislative chamber for the representation of social, economic, and vocational interests.[43]

On none of these issues would the Nationalists have a significant impact upon the outcome of the deliberations that culminated in the presentation of the draft constitution to the Weimar National Assembly in mid-July 1919. While it was unlikely that even under the best of circumstances the DNVP would have supported the new constitutional order that was taking shape in Weimar and elsewhere, Nationalist opposition to the new constitution quickly hardened in the wake of Versailles, and on 31 July 1919 the DNVP joined the German People's Party and Independent Socialists in voting against its ratification.[44] The resounding "No" with which the DNVP greeted the adoption of the new constitution, however, was more than a simple vote. It was a symbolic act that defined the DNVP as a party of "resistance" against the deplorable

[40] For further details, see Trippe, *Konservative Verfassungspolitik*, 62–90.
[41] Axel von Freytagh-Loringhoven, "Verfassungsfragen," in *Der nationale Wille*, ed. Weiß, 143–53, esp. 146.
[42] Ibid., 145–46. See also Westarp, *Konservative Politik*, ed. Hiller von Gaertringen, 270–72.
[43] Westarp, *Konservative Politik*, ed. Hiller von Gaertringen, 294–97.
[44] Freytagh-Loringhoven, "Verfassungsfragen," 145.

conditions that had been created by the lost war and the political revolution that followed. It was a "No" directed as much against the spirit of the Weimar Constitution as it was against the specific provisions of the constitution with which the Nationalists took issue. The Nationalists disputed the legitimacy of the National Assembly to write a new constitution and rejected the principle of popular sovereignty upon which the new constitution rested. The DNVP's vote against the Weimar Constitution was, as one of the party's leading constitutional theorists put it, not just a vote rejecting the new constitutional order but a vote against the spirit of Weimar and all the constitution presumably stood for.[45]

The DNVP's votes against the Versailles Peace Treaty and the Weimar Constitution were defining moments in the party's early history and established the DNVP as a party of "negative integration," that is, as a party that sought to consolidate the diverse and potentially antagonistic constituencies that constituted its material base by stressing not what these constituencies held in common, but what they opposed in common. In the final analysis, it was the struggle against the twin evils of Versailles and Weimar that bound the DNVP together into a cohesive political force. Not only did this struggle obscure the divisions that existed within the DNVP's rank-and-file, but it gave the different constituencies within the party a sense of mission and purpose without which the DNVP might very well have broken apart into its constituent elements. It was what party activist Hans Erdmann von Lindeiner-Wildau called the "unity of the no [*Gemeinsamkeit der Nein*]" that defined the DNVP in the first years of existence and that presented party leaders with the key to its internal consolidation. It remained to be seen whether it would ever be possible to transform this "unity of the no" into a "unity of the yes" that would allow the DNVP to perform positive and constructive work on the basis of the new political order to which the architects of the Weimar Constitution had given birth.[46]

Building a Social Constituency

The DNVP's Berlin party congress in mid-July 1919 represented a milestone in the party's internal consolidation.[47] By then the DNVP was already well into the process of integrating the various social, economic, and vocational

---

[45] Axel von Freytagh-Loringhoven, "Der Geist der neuen Verfassung," in *Jahrbuch 1920 der Deutschnationalen Volkspartei* (Berlin, n.d. [1920]), 87–102.

[46] Hans von Lindeiner-Wildau, "Konservatismus," in *Volk und Reich der Deutschen*, ed. Bernhard Harms, 3 vols. (Berlin, 1929), 2:58–59. In a similar vein, see David P. Walker, "The German Nationalist People's Party: The Conservative Dilemma in the Weimar Republic," *Journal of Contemporary History* 14 (1979): 627–47.

[47] For the official record of the DNVP's Berlin party congress, see *Der erste Parteitag der Deutschnationalen Volkspartei am 12. und 13. Juli 1919 in Berlin. Stenographischer Bericht*, Sonderausgabe der *Post* (Berlin, 1919).

groups upon which it depended for the bulk of its electoral support into its own organizational structure through the creation of vocational committees, or *berufsständische Fachausschüsse*.[48] The leaders of the DNVP took a particular interest in their party's efforts to win the support of the German worker and white-collar employee. Before the war German conservatives, with the exception of the Christian-Socials, had paid little more than lip service to the social and economic interests of the German working class. But the abolition of the three-class franchise in Prussia and the introduction of a new electoral system based upon the principle of proportional representation had made it incumbent upon the leaders of the DNVP to expand their party's base of support into Germany's working and white-collar population. Here the initiative came from Emil Hartwig, a forty-five-year-old trade-union secretary from the Evangelical-Social Academy (Evangelisch-soziale Schule) in Bethel and the general secretary of the Christian-Social movement since 1906. In late November 1918 Hartwig and his associates issued an appeal on the DNVP's behalf to the leaders of the Christian-Social labor movement throughout the country, and in January 1919 they founded the Reich Workers' Committee of the DNVP (Reichsarbeiterausschuß der Deutschnationalen Volkspartei) to facilitate recruitment of the German worker and combat the rising tide of social and political radicalism within the industrial working class.[49]

Hartwig's efforts, which received their impetus from the social gospel of German Lutheranism and were aimed at improving the spiritual as well as the material welfare of the industrial worker,[50] were complemented by those of Franz Behrens in the countryside. Like Hartwig, the forty-six-year-old Behrens subscribed to Luther's school gospel but concentrated his efforts not on the industrial worker in predominantly urban areas but upon the farm laborer in East Prussia and elsewhere. In December 1912 Behrens had founded the Central Association of German Forest, Farm, and Vineyard Workers (Zentralverband der Forst-, Land- und Weinbergsarbeiter Deutschlands) – an organization subsequently renamed the Central Association of Farm

---

[48] Max Weiß, "Organisation," in *Der nationale Wille*, ed. Weiß, 362–90, here 386–89.

[49] See "An unsere Standesgenossen in Stadt u. Land," *Evangelisch-soziale Stimmen* 14, no. 12 (31 Dec. 1918): 42–43. See also *Die deutschnationale Arbeiter-Bewegung, ihr Werden und Wachsen*, ed. Bundesvorstand des Deutschnationalen Arbeiterbundes (Berlin, n.d. [1925]), 10. For further details, see Amrei Stupperich, *Volksgemeinschaft oder Arbeitersolidarität. Studien zur Arbeitnehmerpolitik in der Deutschnationalen Volkspartei (1918–1933)* (Göttingen and Zurich, 1982), esp. 17–52, and Maik Ohnezeit, *Zwischen "schärfster Opposition,"* 62–64.

[50] Speech by Hartwig in *Die erste deutschnationale Arbeitertagung in Hagen i. W.* (N.p., n.d. [1919]), 1–4. On the Evangelical workers' movement, see the reports by Werbeck, Grunz, and Rudolf in *Die EAV.-Bewegung, ihr Werden und Wollen. Der 24. Vertretertag des Gesamtverbandes evangelischer Arbeitervereine Deutschlands in Halle a.S. vom 27.–29. Juni 1925* (Berlin, n.d. [1925]), 12–31.

Laborers – that sought to contain the spread of Marxism in the German countryside by integrating the farm worker as firmly as possible into the Christian-national labor movement.[51] In July 1919 Behrens was given the opportunity to address the DNVP's national party congress in Berlin in what as a clear sign of just how important the worker's vote was to the party's future growth and development. Behrens reminded the party faithful not only that the full and complete integration of the German worker into the political fabric of the nation as a whole was one of the DNVP's most cherished objectives but also, in what could only have been a direct shot at the anti-union sentiments on the DNVP's right wing, that the worker was fully entitled to organize for the purpose of securing his material interests in the workplace and society at large.[52] Behrens's speech afforded the leaders of the DNVP's labor wing the official imprimatur they needed to intensify their efforts to integrate the German worker into the DNVP's organizational framework. These efforts drew to a preliminary climax in early November 1919 when the leaders of the DNVP's labor wing convened the first German National Workers' Conference (Deutschnationale Arbeitertagung) in Hagen. Here Hartwig and Behrens stressed not just their commitment to the material welfare of the German worker but, more importantly, the importance of not losing sight of the spiritual dimension of the current political struggle. For, as Behrens insisted, the collapse of 1918 was more than a military and political collapse; it was a spiritual collapse that manifested itself first in the profiteering and racketeering of the lost war and then in the triumph of revolutionary socialism and its crusade to de-Christianize German life. For Behrens and the leaders of the DNVP's labor wing, the challenge was not to succumb to the rising tide of materialism and self-interest that had led to the collapse of 1918 but to use the collapse as the point of departure for the moral and spiritual rebirth of the German nation, a rebirth that could take place only on the basis of the German National People's Party.[53]

Similar developments were under way within the German white-collar movement. Here the central figure was Friedrich Frahm, a forty-four-year-old official in the German National Union of Commercial Employees who in January 1919 had been elected to the Prussian Constitutional Assembly. In its appeal to the German salaried employee, the DNVP adopted the DHV's

---

[51] On the ZdL, see *Zehn Jahre christlich-nationale Landarbeiterbewegung 1913–1923. Eine Festschrift zur Erinnerung an das 10 jährige Bestehen des Zentralverbandes der Land-arbeiter*, ed. Vorstand des Zentralverbandes der Landarbeiter (Berlin, 1923), 6–13.

[52] Franz Behrens, *Arbeiterschaft und Deutschnationale Volkspartei. Rede auf dem Parteitag der Deutschnationalen Volkspartei in Berlin am 12. u. 13. Juli 1919*, Deutschnationale Flugschrift, no. 23 (Berlin, 1919).

[53] Speech by Behrens in *Die erste deutschnationale Arbeitertagung in Hagen i. W.* (N.p., n.d. [1919]), 5–10.

position that the white-collar workforce constituted an "estate," or *Stand*, that distinguished it in particular from the industrial working class below it.[54] While this distinction reflected the high degree of status consciousness that existed in the more conservative sectors of Germany's white-collar population, it did not stand in the way of close cooperation between the white-collar and working-class representatives within the DNVP.[55] Following the example of Hartwig and his associates, the leaders of the DNVP's white-collar wing founded the Reich Committee for Sales Clerks and Private Employees (Reichs-ausschuß für kaufmännische und Privatangestellten) under Frahm's chair-manship in early 1919.[56] But unlike the DNVP's workers' committee, the committee for salaried employees never developed a particularly prominent profile within the party organization, in part because the DNVP's white-collar contingent already had a powerful voice in the DHV and did not need the strong internal presence that was essential to the legitimacy of the DNVP's working-class wing. This, however, did not keep Walther Lambach, a thirty-four-year-old DHV offical who replaced Frahm as chairman of the DNVP's Reich Committee for Sales Clerks and Private Employees in the summer of 1920, from developing into an articulate and indefatigable advocate of white-collar interests within the DNVP. Speaking at the DNVP's second party congress in Hanover in October 1920, Lambach outlined an ambitious social program which, if effectively implemented, would lead to the creation of a genuine *Volksgemeinschaft* in which the worker and white-collar employee would take their place as equals in the fabric of the German nation.[57]

Through its ties to the Evangelical workers' movement, the Central Associ-ation of Farm Laborers, and the German National Union of Commercial Employees, the DNVP established a foothold in the German working and white-collar classes that was unprecedented in the history of German conservatism. Yet as promising as these ties were, by no means were they as important for the future of the DNVP as its relations with the German agricultural community. Agriculture constituted the heart and soul of the conservative milieu in which the DNVP was situated and which the DNVP sought to unite into a cohesive political force. But, as in the case of labor, the organizational infrastructure of German agriculture had undergone profound changes during World War I and the ensuing revolution. The war and revolution had had a radicalizing effect upon Germany's rural population and seriously eroded the influence of the land-owning aristocracy east of the

---

[54] Walther Lambach, "Angestelltenfragen," in *Der nationale Wille*, ed. Weiß, 225–33.
[55] Stupperich, *Volksgemeinschaft oder Arbeitersolidarität*, 13.
[56] Ibid., 22–24.
[57] Walther Lambach, *Unser Weg zur deutschen Volksgemeinschaft. Rede auf dem 2. Partei-tage der Deutschnationalen Volkspartei in Hannover am 25. Oktober 1920*, Deutschna-tionale Flugschrift, no. 79 (Berlin, 1920).

Elbe and elsewhere.[58] At the same time, the introduction of a democratic franchise throughout the Reich – and particularly the abolition of the three-class franchise in Prussia – meant that German conservatives were now far more dependent upon the support of the rural voter than they had ever been before the outbreak of the war. The success with which German conservatives were able to reconstitute their hegemony in the countryside would have profound implications for the future of the DNVP and its efforts to reinvigorate political conservatism as a factor in German political life.

In the immediate aftermath of the November Revolution, Gustav Roesicke and the leaders of the Agrarian League lined up behind the DNVP and actively supported it in the elections to the Weimar and Prussian constitutional assemblies.[59] The DNVP, in return, waged an aggressive campaign designed to disabuse German peasants and farm workers of the democratic sentiments that might have captured their support as a result of the war and the deteriotaring economic situation in the countryside.[60] Whatever its short-comings from the perspective of the East Elbian landowners might have been,[61] the DNVP remained the party of preference for the vast majority of Germany's Protestant rural voters. At Weimar as many as sixteen of the forty-five Nationalist deputies were either farmers or estate owners, while in the Prussian constitutional assembly seven of the party's fifty deputies had close ties to Prussian agriculture. Still, the percentage of deputies with an agricultural pedigree was significantly less than what it had been for the German Conservative Party before the war. Outside of Prussia the DNVP received far-reaching support from the BdL's one-time regional affiliates in Bavaria, Württemberg, Saxony, and Thuringia even though in some cases those affiliates maintained complete organizational independence from the DNVP's district organizations.[62] More than anything else, it was the DNVP's unrelenting struggle against the wartime controls that the government had imposed on agricultural prices and production to combat the threat of inflation that

[58] See Flemming, *Landwirtschaftliche Interessen*, 76–160, and Robert G. Moeller, *German Peasants*, 43–67.

[59] Roesicke to Wangenheim, Winckel, and Weilnböck, 10 Dec. 1918, BA Berlin, Nachlass Conrad von Wangenheim, 13/132–34, also in BA Koblenz, NL Weilnböck, 46b.

[60] See Oskar Thomas, *Demokratie, Landwirtschaft und Landarbeiterschaft*, Deutschnationale Flugschrift, no. 29 (Berlin, n.d. [1919].

[61] For example, see Levetzow to Wangenheim, 5 Feb. 1919, BA Berlin, NL Roesicke, 4a/294.

[62] For further details, see Martin Schumacher, *Land und Politik. Eine Untersuchung über politische Parteien und agrarische Interessen 1914–1923* (Düsseldorf, 1978), 477–80. On the situation in Württemberg, see Hans Peter Müller, "Landwirtschaftliche Interessenvertretung und völkisch-antisemitische Ideologie. Der Bund der Landwirte/Bauernbund in Württemberg 1895–1918," *Zeitschrift für Württembergische Landesgeschichte* 53 (1994): 263–300, and Reinhold Weber, *Bürgerpartei und Bauernbund in Württemberg. Konservative Parteien im Kaiserreich und in Weimar (1895 bis 1933)* (Düsseldorf, 2004), 121–31.

defined the DNVP's agrarian profile.[63] Of all the parties at Weimar, none was more uncompromising in its demands for an end to these controls than the DNVP. At the same time, the DNVP championed the cause of the farm laborer and called for a comprehensive program of rural resettlement aimed at repopulating the countryside and transforming the farm laborer into an independent peasant proprietor.[64] The DNVP's long-term goal was to restore the hegemonic relationships that had existed in the countryside before the war and that had been overturned by the spread of socialism into rural Germany in the revolutionary turmoil of the immediate postwar period.

The Quest for Synthesis

As successful as the DNVP was in establishing footholds within both the Christian labor movement and organized agriculture, by no means were its efforts in the immediate postwar period confined to these social strata. By the end of 1919 the DNVP had also established vocational committees for the state civil service, teachers, doctors and those in the medical profession, students, university professors, the economic middle class, and ex-servicemen and veterans of the recent war in addition to those that had already been constituted for workers, white-collar employees, and agriculture.[65] It was no idle claim when Nationalist party chairman Oskar Hergt asserted at the DNVP's Berlin party congress earlier in the year that "no party could claim to be as deeply rooted in all sectors of the population, in all parts of the nation" as the DNVP.[66] But the precise content of what Hergt meant when he portrayed the DNVP as a conservative *Sammelpartei* open to all Germans regardless of region, class, or confession remained vague and uncertain. Whenever Hergt tried to spell out what this was supposed to mean in terms of the party's social and economic policy, he became immediately embroiled in controversy. Speaking in the Prussian Constitutional Assembly on 25 September 1919, Hergt outlined a six-point program for the restoration of order throughout the country that he hoped would serve as the basis upon which all of the parties in the Reichstag, including his own DNVP, could unite. Most of the recommendations contained in Hergt's so-called *Ordnungsprogramm*, such as his call for an end to the controlled economy and for the suspension

---

[63] Moeller, "Winners as Losers in the German Inflation," 255–82.

[64] Joseph Kaufhold, *Die Deutschnationale Volkspartei und die Landwirtschaft*, Deutschnationale Politik, no. 8 (Berlin, 1920), esp. 4–16. See also Albert Arnstadt, "Landwirtschaft und Deutschnationale Volkspartei," *Jahrbuch 1920 der Deutschnationalen Volkspartei* (Berlin, n.d. [1920]), 24–27.

[65] "Geschäftsbericht der Hauptgeschäftsstelle der Deutschnationalen Volkspartei (Juli 1919 bis Oktober 1920)," n.d., BA Berlin, NL Mumm, 276/91–95.

[66] Hergt, *Gegenwart und Zukunft*, 3.

of all efforts at socialization, were fairly innocuous and enjoyed widespread, if not unanimous, support within the DNVP. But when Hergt also had the temerity to suggest that the DNVP should be prepared to enter the national government and that Germany's propertied classes should bear their fare share of the burden for the reconstruction of the Fatherland,[67] his remarks met with a stony silence from Westarp and the leaders of the party's right wing, a silence that underscored just how difficult the task of reconciling the interests of the various constituencies that made up the party's material base was going to be.[68]

Under these circumstances, the party leadership continued its work on drafting a comprehensive party program that could reconcile the diverse social and economic interests that constituted the DNVP's material base. At Berlin the DNVP party leadership had empanelled a special commission for the purpose of drafting a comprehensive party program.[69] The commission consisted of fifteen members recruited from the various factions that had come together to form the DNVP at the end of 1918, and its task was to draft a program that did not merely highlight the DNVP's reasons for rejecting the existing state of affairs but presented a set of positive objectives capable of attracting the support of the German people. As Hans Erdmann von Lindeiner-Wildau, the DNVP's managing secretary, declared at the first meeting of the program commission on 29 September 1919: "The people should not come to us because we have not taken part in the stupidity of others but because we can show the path to recovery."[70] The commission's work was divided into four subcommittees, one to draft the preamble and the other three for sections on "nation and state," "spiritual life," and "economic life."[71] The deliberations were tedious and difficult, in part because they afforded the old-line Prussian conservatives affiliated with the Central Association of German Conservatives an opportunity to secure for themselves a decisive influence over the party's self-image and future political development.[72] At the same

---

[67] Oskar Hergt, *Das Ordnungsprogramm der Deutschnationalen Volkspartei. Rede in der Preußischen Landes-Versammlung am Freitag, 26. September 1919*, Deutschnationale Flugschrift, no. 31 (Berlin, 1919).

[68] For Westarp's reaction to Hergt's speech, see his letters to Heydebrand from 1 Oct. 1919 and 7 Jan. 1920, NL Westarp, Gärtringen, II/80.

[69] Westarp, *Konservative Politik*, ed. Hiller von Gaertringen, 93. For further details, see Hertzman, *DNVP*, 79–92, and Ohnezeit, *Zwischen "schärfster Opposition,"* 88–99.

[70] Statement by Lindeiner-Wildau at the meeting of the DNVP program commission, 29 Sept. 1919, BA Berlin, NL Westarp, 114/6. See also the memorandum that Lindeiner-Wildau attached to his letter to Hergt, 27 May 1919, BA Berlin, R 8005, 3/233–37.

[71] Minutes of the first meeting of the DNVP program commission, 29 Sept. 1919, BA Berlin, NL Westarp, 114/5–9. See also the entry in Kahrstedt's diary, 29 Sept. 1919, NL Westarp, Gärtringen, II/4.

[72] See Heydebrand's remarks at a meeting of Nationalist politicians in the Breslau general secretariat of the DKP, 8 July 1919, appended to Kube to Heydebrand, 26 July 1919, NL

time, DNVP moderates were anxious to recapture the ground they had lost to the conservatives in the struggle against Versailles and to reclaim leadership of the party.[73] The two factions were on a collision course that would ultimately determine the character and nature of the DNVP.

Behind the Central Association of German Conservatives and its efforts to gain a stronger foothold in the German National People's Party stood the by no means inconsiderable resources of Prussia's land-owning aristocracy. In Prussia, as throughout the Reich as a whole, the land-owning aristocracy – along with the monarchy, the military, the ministerial bureaucracy, and the Lutheran state church – constituted one of the pillars of Germany's prewar conservative establishment. Although industrialization and economic modernization in the last decades of the Second Empire had done much to erode the place of the land-owning aristocracy in German economic life, the titled nobility still possessed a measure of social prestige and political influence that was no longer commensurate with its economic substance. The military and political collapse of 1918 and the apparent triumph of socialism in the immediate postwar period were accompanied not just by the loss of the privileged status the aristocracy had enjoyed under the Prussian constitution but also by the disruption of traditional hegemonic relationships in the countryside and the fear that the new government might expropriate large landed agriculture.[74] The leaders of the Central Association of German Conservatives regarded the DNVP with deep suspicion and had joined it only in the hope of transforming it into an instrument of their own political will.[75] As

Westarp, Gärtringen, II/79, as well as Schröter (Central Association of German Conservatives) to Westarp, 14 Aug. 1919, BA Berlin, NL Westarp, 37/118–22. See also Daniela Gasteiger, "From Friends to Foes: Count Kuno von Westarp and the Transformation of the German Right," in *The German Right in the Weimar Republic. Studies in the History of German Conservatism, Nationalism, and Antisemitism*, ed. Larry Eugene Jones (New York and Oxford, 2014), 48–78, esp. 59–71.

[73] For example, see Delbrück to Hergt, 22 Aug. 1919, BA Koblenz, Nachlass Siegfried von Kardorff, 10/50–59.

[74] See Wolfgang Zollitsch, "Die Erosion des traditionellen Konservatismus. Ländlicher Adel in Preußen zwischen Kaiserreich und Weimarer Republik," in *Parteien im Wandel. Vom Kaiserreich zur Weimarer Republik. Rekrutierung – Qualifizierung – Karrieren*, ed. Dieter Dowe, Jürgen Kocka, and Heinrich August Winkler (Munich, 1999), 161–82, as well as Stephan Malinowski, *Vom König zum Führer. Sozialer Niedergang und politische Radikalisierung im deutschen Adel zwischen Kaiserreich und NS-Staat* (Berlin, 2003), 198–259, and Eckart Conze, "'Only a Dictator Can Help Us Now': Aristocracy and the Radical Right in Germany," in *European Aristocracies and the Radical Right, 1918–1939*, ed. Karina Urbach (Oxford, 2007), 129–47.

[75] On hard-line Prussian conservatives and their relationship to the DNVP, see Jens Flemming, "Konservatismus als 'nationalrevolutionäre Bewegung.' Konservative Kritik an der Deutschnationalen Volkspartei 1918–1933," in *Deutscher Konservatismus im 19. und 20. Jahrhundert. Festschrift für Fritz Fischer*, ed. Dirk Stegmann, Bernd-Jürgen Wendt, and Peter-Christian Witt (Bonn, 1983), 295–331, and Rainer Pomp,

the association's chairman, Westarp used his appointment to the all-important subcommittee on "Nation and State" to tie the DNVP as tightly as possible to the ideological pretensions of the Prussian conservatives and to derail the efforts of the two other subcommittee members, Ulrich von Hassell from the DNVP's State Political Coordinating Committee and former Free Conservative Siegfried von Kardorff, to cast the DNVP as a broadly based, all-inclusive conservative party.[76]

The conflict over the shape and content of the DNVP party program drew to a climax in the period preceding the meeting of the DNVP program committee on 29 January 1920, at which time the final outlines of the program were to be approved. On 21 December 1919 Kardorff wrote to Westarp and identified foreign policy, monarchism, and federalism as areas of continuing disagreement. Kardorff criticized in particular the bellicose tone of the Westarp's stance toward the Allies, his efforts to identify the party as unabashedly as possible with a restoration of the Hohenzollern monarchy, and the conservatives' preference for the more decentralized federal structure of the old Bismarckian Reich over the unitary state.[77] Undeterred by these developments, the DNVP's State Political Coordinating Committee continued to work on the party program before submitting its draft to the party chairman in late January 1920. Intended only as a general statement of the principles upon which the party was based, this draft carefully avoided any reference to the Hohenzollerns in its endorsement of the monarchical form of government and gracefully skirted the issue of Prussia with little more than an innocuous bromide against its dismemberment. At the same time, the draft stressed the national concept, the Christian faith, and the unity of all Germans as the three principles upon which the rebirth of the German nation was to take place.[78] None of this set well with old-line Prussian conservatives like Oskar von der Osten, a former DKP parliamentarian who had been appointed to the DNVP program committee and who took issue with the draft's failure to commit the party to the restoration of the Hohenzollerns and the decentralized federal structure of the Bismarckian Reich at the same time that he criticized

"Brandenburgischer Landadel und die Weimarer Republik. Konflikte um Oppositionsstrategien und Elitenkonzepte," in *Adel und Staatsverwaltung in Brandenburg im 19. und 20. Jahrhundert. Ein historischer Vergleich*, ed. Kurt Adamy and Kristina Hübener (Berlin, 1996), 185–218, esp. 186–96.

[76] "Staat und Volk (Nicht Volk und Staat)," n.d. [Jan. 1920], BA Berlin, NL Westarp, 114/49–52. See also Westarp, *Konservative Politik*, ed. Hiller von Gaertringen, 94–95.

[77] Kardorff to Westarp, 21 Dec. 1919, BA Berlin, NL Westarp, 114/11–12. See also Kardorff "Richtlinien für eine Erweiterung des Programms der Deutschnationalen Volkspartei," n.d., BA Koblenz, NL Kardorff, 16/3–14.

[78] "Programm der Deutschnationalen Volkspartei," n.d., BA Berlin, NL Westarp, 114/108–17, appended to Trotha to Hergt, 28 Jan. 1920, ibid. 114/19–22.

Kardorff's unqualified endorsement of parliamentarism and a democratic franchise.[79]

Another issue that required further clarification was the Jewish question. Despite the affinity that many conservative Jews felt for the parties of the German Right,[80] the antisemites within the DNVP had become increasingly active in the latter stages of the campaign for the Weimar and Prussian constitutional assemblies and were pressing the party leadership to adopt a clear and unequivocal stand against the danger that Jews presumably posed to Germany's national life. This coincided with a dramatic upsurge in the general level of antisemitism throughout German society as organizations on the racist Right intensified their attacks against the so-called Jewish threat.[81] While it is no doubt true that even the most moderate of the DNVP party leaders like Clemens von Delbrück harbored a bias against Jews that was particularly strong toward those Eastern European Jews, or *Ostjuden*, who had entered Germany after the war,[82] few were willing to make antisemitism a fundamental tenet of the DNVP's official program or embrace the radical demands for the exclusion of Jews from German economic, political, and cultural life. While some like Kardorff called upon the DNVP to dissociate itself from antisemitism altogether,[83] most preferred to cloak their antisemitism in more general statements calling for the preservation of Germany's Christian culture or the protection of Germany's unique ethnic character or *Volkstum*. In neither case, however, was this sufficiently pointed to satisfy the leaders of the party's antisemitic faction, who continued to pressure the party leadership for a bolder and more defiant statement on the Jewish threat to Germany's national life. As a result, the party's national leaders eventually gave in and included a sentence in the draft party program that specifically identified "the increasingly dangerous dominance of Jewry in government and public life since the revolution" as a threat to the unique ethnic character of the German nation.[84] Even this did not go far enough to satisfy the more rabid antisemites within the party.[85]

The DNVP concluded its initial deliberations on the new party program in January 1920 and immediately began to revise and edit it in anticipation of its

---

[79] Osten to Kardorff, 9 Jan. 1920, BA Berlin, NL Westarp, 114/14–16.

[80] For example, see the recent publication by Philipp Nielsen, *Between Heimat and Hatred: Jews and the Right in Germany, 1871–1935* (Oxford, 2019), 135–43.

[81] Both of these organizations are discussed in greater detail in chapter 5.

[82] For example, see Delbrück to Hergt, 22 Aug. 1919, BA Koblenz, NL Kardorff, 10/50–59.

[83] Kardorff to Hergt, 21 Aug. 1919, BA Koblenz, NL Kardorff, 10/46–47.

[84] Westarp, *Konservative Politik*, ed. Hiller von Gaertringen, 108–09. For further details, see Striesow, *DNVP und die Völkisch-Radikalen*, 146–62, and Jochmann, "Ausbreitung des Antisemitismus," 486–500.

[85] Graefe-Goldbee, "Partei u. Judenfrage," 5 Feb. 1920, NL Westarp, Gärtringen, VN 29.

official adoption later that spring.[86] In the meantime, the party continued to develop and expand its organizational base in preparation for the upcoming national elections. On 13 March 1920 the DNVP concluded an agreement with the Bavarian Middle Party whereby the latter would become part of the DNVP national party organization with concessions regarding its autonomy in Bavarian state politics.[87] By the same token, the DNVP had begun to normalize its relations with the Württemberg Burgher Party, although here negotiations would drag on for some time and not reach a final conclusion until November 1920. In both cases, the Bavarian Middle Party and the Württemberg Burgher Party would continue to function as the DNVP's state affiliates under their original names and with greater independence from the DNVP's central headquarters in Berlin than the party's state, provincial, and district organizations in other parts of the country generally enjoyed.[88]

One area, however, in which the DNVP was not able to record much progress was in its relationship to the German People's Party. The DNVP party leadership had hoped for a merger with the DVP after the elections to the National Assembly but had been stalled by the DVP's reluctance to commit itself to anything more elaborate than the creation of a special committee to coordinate strategy between the parties' Weimar delegations.[89] The fact that the DVP and DNVP both opposed acceptance of the Versailles Peace Treaty and ratification of the Weimar Constitution did much to revive hopes that a merger of the two parties might still be in the works. Not only did Hergt explicitly address such a possibility in his keynote speech at the DNVP's Berlin party congress in July 1919,[90] but industrial interests in the two right-wing parties strongly supported the establishment of closer political ties between the two parties, if for no other reason than to strengthen the

---

[86] "Richtlinien der Deutschnationalen Volkspartei," n.d. [13. Jan, 1920], BA Berlin, NL Westarp, 114/83–85.

[87] Agreement signed by Hergt, Graef, and Hilpert, 13 Mar. 1920, BA Berlin, R 8005/27/46. See also "Anschluß der Bayerischen Mittelpartei an die Deutschnationale Volkspartei," *Blätter der bayerischen Mittelpartei* 2, no. 10 (9 Mar. 1920): 37–40, as well as Hans Hilpert, *Die Deutschnationalen in Bayern. Rede auf dem dritten Parteitage der Deutschnationalen Volkspartei in München am 2. Sept. 1921*, Deutschnationale Flugschrift, no. 116 (Berlin, 1921), 3–4. For further details, see Elina Kiiskinen, *DNVP in Bayern*, 70–76.

[88] Resolution adopted at the WBP delegate congress in Stuttgart, 4–7 Nov. 1920, in *Jahrbuch der Württ. Bürgerpartei – Deutschnationale Volkspartei Württembergs*, ed W. Haller-Ludwigsburg (Stuttgart, 1921), 96. See also Bazille, "Der Anschluß der Bürgerpartei an die Deutschnationale Volkspartei," *Blätter der Württembergischen Bürgerpartei. Halbmonatschrift der Württembergischen Bürgerpartei* 1, no. 2 (24 Oct. 1920): 12–13.

[89] Hergt's comments at a meeting of the DNVP's organizational representatives, 7–8 Feb. 1919, BA Berlin, R 8005, 1/195–201.

[90] Hergt, *Gegenwart und Zukunft*, 9. See also Hans Erdmann von Lindeiner-Wildau, *Wir und die Deutsche Volkspartei*, Deutschnationale Flugschrift, no. 77 (Berlin, 1921).

bourgeois presence and the influence of industry in parliament.[91] But Stresemann and the leaders of the DVP were extremely wary of any accommodation
with the Nationalists that might restrict their own party's freedom of movement and ability to act independently of the larger and more conservative
DNVP.[92] In a review of the DNVP's Berlin congress, the DVP's Julius Curtius
poured cold water on the proposal by stressing the profound ideological
differences that separated the two parties and by asking whether the unresolved divisions within the DNVP made it a suitable partner for a merger.[93] At
the same time, Stresemann and the leaders of the DVP went to great efforts to
dissociate themselves from the increasingly virulent antisemitism from within
the ranks of the DNVP. To be sure, neither Stresemann nor his supporters
were immune from the antisemitic prejudice that had surfaced with such a
vengeance in the immediate postwar period. But, by the same token, they
regarded Nationalist attacks against German Jews as excessive and dismissed
them as evidence of the DNVP's political immaturity.[94]

The Perils of Putschism

Despite its rebuff at the hands of the DVP, the DNVP was slowly, but surely,
positioning itself for the new national elections that were scheduled for some
yet undetermined time in the near future. All of this, however, was suddenly
thrown into confusion when on the morning of 13 March 1920 an insurgent
military force under the command of General Walther von Lüttwitz marched
on Berlin, forced the legitimate government to flee the city to safety in the
south, and installed a new government under Wolfgang Kapp, the onetime
chairman of the now defunct German Fatherland Party, with the ultimate aim
of establishing a national dictatorship that would prepare the way for a
restoration of the monarchy. For the most part, the putschists were members
of free corps units that had made their mark in the struggle against Bolshevism

---

[91] See Vögler to Hugenberg, 17 Oct. 1919, BA Koblenz, NL Hugenberg, 49/39–42; 31
Oct. 1919, ibid. 29/402–04; and 9 Dec. 1919, ibid. 49/36–38.

[92] For example, see Gustav Stresemann, *Die Deutsche Volkspartei und ihr politisches Programm. Rede auf dem Leipziger Parteitag der Deutschen Volkspartei am 18. Oktober 1919*,
Flugschriften der Deutschen Volkspartei, no. 11 (Berlin, 1919), 22–23.

[93] Julius Curtius, "Die deutschnationale Volkspartei, ihre Zusammensetzung, Grundsätze,
Taktik nach dem Berliner Parteitag vom 12. und 13. Juli 1919," *Deutsche Stimmen* 31,
no. 41 (19 Oct. 1919): 708–17. For the DVP's perspective, see Hartenstein, *Anfänge der
DVP*, 131–42, and Ludwig Richter, *Die Deutsche Volkspartei 1918–1933* (Düsseldorf,
2002), 76–87.

[94] For the DVP's position on the "Jewish question," see the resolution adopted by the DVP
managing committee, 28 Jan. 1920, PA AA Berlin, NL Stresemann, 220/140063. For
Stresemann's position, see Jonathan Wright, "Liberalism and Anti-Semitism in Germany:
The Case of Gustav Stresemann," in *Liberalism, Anti-Semitism, and Democracy: Essays in
Honour of Peter Pulzer*, ed. Henning Tewes and Jonathan Wright (Oxford, 2001), 102–26.

but were now threatened with dissolution as a result of Allied pressure on the Bauer government. Preparations for the putsch lay in the hands of the National Association (Nationale Vereinigung), a shadowy organization that had been founded by Erich Ludendorff in the fall of 1919 and that enjoyed particularly close ties to the DNVP party leadership.[95] The assault against Germany's fledgling republic enjoyed widespread support among the aristocratic and bourgeois elites east of the Elbe, where it excited hopes that the verdict of November 1918 might be reversed.[96] At the same time, the Kapp-Lüttwitz putsch constituted a major crisis for the DNVP, if not so much by virtue of the undertaking's ignominious collapse four days later as for the fact that prominent members of the party, including Westarp and Traub, were actively involved in its preparation, though not necessarily in its execution. Moreover, many party leaders had extensive foreknowledge of the putsch and secretly supported its objectives even though they might not have been directly involved in the putsch itself.[97] The problem now confronting party leaders was how could they best extricate themselves from the mess that had been created by the abortive putsch without doing serious damage to the progress they had recorded in building up their party's national organization or to their prospects in the upcoming national elections. Their task was complicated by the fact that the putsch had exposed serious fault lines within the DNVP and threatened to weaken, if not destroy, its fragile unity with a major secession on the party's left wing.

In the period leading up to the putsch, Hergt and the DNVP party leadership had intensified their attacks against the Bauer government and the parties of the Weimar Coalition in anticipation of new elections in the Reich and Prussia that would, they hoped, bring their party substantial gains at the polls.[98] At the same time, Hergt and other party moderates did their best to dissociate themselves from the schemes of right-wing reactionaries and discouraged Lüttwitz and his supporters from going ahead with their plans for a

---

[95] For further details, see Johannes Erger, *Der Kapp-Lüttwitz Putsch. Ein Beitrag zur deutschen Innenpolitik 1919/20* (Düsseldorf, 1967), as well as the documentation in *Der Kapp-Lüttwitz-Ludendorff-Putsch. Dokumente*, ed. Erwin Könnemann and Gerhard Schulze (Munich, 2002), 1–134.

[96] See Axel Schildt, "Der Putsch der 'Prätorianer, Junker und Alldeutschen.' Adel und Bürgertum in den Anfangswirren der Weimarer Republik," in *Adel und Bürgertum in Deutschland II. Entwicklungslinien und Wendepunkte im 20. Jahrhundert*, ed. Heinz Reif (Berlin, 2001), 103–25.

[97] For further details, see Westarp, *Konservative Politik*, ed. Hiller von Gaertringen, 200–41, and Traub, *Erinnerungen*, 224–69.

[98] For example, see Oskar Hergt, *Dieser Regierung kein Vertrauen*, Deutschnationale Flugschrift, no. 39 (Berlin, n.d. [1920]), esp. 3–8. See also Westarp to Heydebrand, 16 Feb. 1920, NL Westarp, Gärtringen, II/80.

military coup d'etat.[99] The DNVP headquarters in Berlin, however, reacted to the news of the putsch on the morning of 13 March with "frivolous jubilation and hopeful joyousness [*eitel Jubel und Hoffnungsfreudigkeit*]," all in the naïve belief that the new age for which the Nationalists had so fervently hoped had finally arrived.[100] But almost immediately party leaders began to distance themselves from the putsch as the utter hopelessness of the undertaking became more and more apparent. Now the best party leaders could hope for was to use their connections with the putschists to seek a return of constitutional government, though under circumstances in which their negotiating posture would have been greatly improved. Here Hergt and the leaders of the DNVP's delegation to the Weimar National Assembly sought an accomodation between Kapp and the legitimate government in temporary exile in Stuttgart that would pave the way for new national elections, the election of a new Reich president by popular vote, the formation of new cabinets in the Reich and Prussia consisting of specialists chosen for their expertise and not for their party affiliation, and a general amnesty for all of those on the Left and the Right from arrest and prosecution.[101] In their first public reaction to the putsch on the evening of 13 March the Nationalists thus tempered their rejection of the undertaking with sharp criticism of the Weimar government for having breached the new constitution by failing to call for new elections once the Weimar National Assembly had completed its work. In the same breadth, the DNVP pledged itself to work in close concert with all of those forces committed to the preservation of peace, order, freedom, and national honor.[102]

Initially Hergt had hoped that Stresemann and the DVP would support his party's efforts to pressure the exile government in Stuttgart into reaching an agreement with Kapp that would lead to the fulfillment of these and other conditions.[103] But with Kapp's resignation and the capitulation of the putschists on 17 March, the situation in which the DNVP party leadership found

---

[99] See excerpts from Hergt's speech before the Prussian constitutional assembly, 13 Jan. 1920, and Posadowsky-Wehner's warning against a putsch in the National Assembly, 9 Mar. 1920, quoted in *Die Deutschnationale Volkspartei und der Militärputsch vom 13. März 1920*, Deutschnationale Politik, no. 10 (Berlin, 1920), 5. On Lindeiner-Wildau's efforts to dissuade the putschists, see Westarp, *Konservative Politik*, ed. Hiller von Gaertringen, 203–04, as well as Lindeiner-Wildau's memorandum, n.d. [19–20 Mar. 1920], BA Berlin, R 8005, 5/48–56.

[100] Report to Heydebrand, 1 Apr. 1920, BA Berlin, R 8003, 2/105–10.

[101] Reports by Schiele before the DNVP delegation to the Weimar National Assembly, 16 Mar. 1920, BA Berlin, NL Mumm, 276/137–42, and by Graef in the meeting on 17 Mar. 1920, ibid., 147–53. See also Westarp to Heydebrand, 13 Mar. 1920, NL Westarp, Gärtringen, II/80.

[102] Statement by the DNVP party leadership, 13 Mar. 1920, BA Berlin, R 8005, 6/114.

[103] Hergt's remarks at a meeting of the DNVP delegation to the Weimar National Assembly, 16 Mar. 1920, BA Berlin, NL Mumm, 276/138–39, 142.

itself suddenly became immensely more complicated. The leaders of the DNVP moved quickly to shift attention from their contacts with the putschists before the march on Berlin to the chaotic conditions in Germany that had supposedly led to the insurrection in the first place. In a statement issued on 18 March the DNVP party leadership launched a blistering attack against the Weimar government for having failed to live up to the terms of the constitution it had set in place and for having created precisely those circumstances that had led to the military uprising. According to this account, the DNVP had only entered into negotiations with the Kapp regime to stabilize a situation that had been created by the incompetence of the central government and, in particular, by its failure to resist Allied demands for the dissolution of the volunteer military units that were necessary to contain the threat of the revolutionary Left.[104]

The DNVP's statements of 13 and 18 March were little more than disingenuous ploys to conceal the extent to which members of the party had been involved in the preparation of the putsch and to disguise the sympathy that news of the putsch had elicited within the party's rank-and-file. Not only did this do little to repair the DNVP's public image, but it only exposed and exacerbated the deepening divisions that existed within the party. For while old-line Prussian conservatives like Westarp and the leaders of the party's antisemitic faction generally supported the putsch,[105] the DNVP's governmental conservatives were openly critical of their party's connection to the putsch and feared that it would interrupt or delay what they saw as a decisive shift to the right on the part of the German middle classes in the lead-up to the elections.[106] Among the most outspoken critics of the DNVP's posture during the Kapp-Lüttwitz putsch was Kardorff, the nominal leader of the DNVP's Free Conservative faction and a Nationalist deputy in the Prussian constitutional assembly. As a member of the DNVP program committee, Kardorff was already disturbed by the way in which old-line Prussian conservatives like Westarp and Osten had side-stepped moderates like himself in drafting the new party program.[107] In February 1920 Kardorff had in fact been so

---

[104] Statement issued by the DNVP party leadership, 18 Mar. 1920, BA Berlin, R 8005, 5/ 69–70, quoted in *DNVP und Militärputsch*, 7–8. See also "Der 13. März und die Deutschnationale Volkspartei," n.d., BHStA Munich, Abt. V, Flugblattsammlung 60/ 1920, and *Wir klagen die Regierung an! Reden der deutschnationalen Abgeordneten Düringer, Behrens und Hergt zum Kappschen Militärputsch in der Deutschen National-versammlung und in der Preußischen Landesversammlung am 30. März 1920*, Deutsch-nationale Parlamentsreden, Heft 16 (Berlin, 1920).

[105] Gasteiger, *Westarp*, 178–85.

[106] Comments by Delbrück at a meeting of the DNVP delegation to the Weimar National Assembly, 17 Mar. 1920, BA Berlin, NL Mumm, 276/147–53.

[107] Kardorff to Westarp, 21 Dec. 1919, BA Berlin, NL Westarp, 114/ 11–12.

infuriated by the sharp criticism a speech he had delivered in Berlin had provoked from the party's right wing that he stepped down as vice-chairman of the Nationalist delegation to the Prussian constitutional assembly and resigned from the delegation's executive committee.[108] But none of this would be to much avail.

At the decisive meeting of the DNVP central executive committee on 9 April Westarp used his rhetorical talents to beat back the moderates and to insinuate key conservative planks into the DNVP party program.[109] At the same time, Westarp did his best to disabuse his supporters in the Central Association of German Conservatives of their plans for a break with the DNVP and to reassure them that collaboration with the DNVP represented the only possibility of accomplishing a conservative agenda.[110] For Kardorff, who was already fuming over the DNVP's flirtation with the putschists and the preferential treatment it showed antisemites in the selection of candidates for the upcoming elections, the meeting of the DNVP central executive committee on 9 April 1920 was the final straw. Joined by two other members of the DNVP's Free Conservative faction – Otto Arendt and Otto von Dewitz – Kardorff met with the DVP party chairman Gustav Stresemann on 15 April 1920 to finalize plans for their defection to the German People's Party.[111] Two days later, the three issued a sharply worded statement in which they denounced "the increasing prominence of extreme right-wing personalities in the DNVP and their influence upon the development of the party" and announced their decision to join the DVP. Affirming their unconditional commitment to the spirit and letter of the Weimar Constitution, Kardorff and his associates pledged themselves to work within the DVP for the consolidation of all social classes into a genuine *Volksgemeinschaft* and to cooperate with all of those, including the Majority Socialists, who shared their respect for the principles of constitutional government.[112] By no means, however, was Kardorff's defection an isolated incident. Only ten days earlier another former Free Conservative, university professor Johann Victor Bredt, had announced his resignation from the DNVP – though with much less fanfare than Kardorff – as a protest

---

[108] Kardorff to Hergt, 23 Feb. 1920, PA AA Berlin, NL Stresemann, 221/140215–17.
[109] Speech by Westarp before the DNVP central executive committee, 9 Apr. 1920, NL Westarp, Gärtringen, II/80. See also Westarp, *Konservative Politik*, ed. Hiller von Gaertringen, 100–12.
[110] Westarp to Heydebrand, 9 Apr. 1920, NL Westarp, Gärtringen, II/80.
[111] Stresemann's memorandum of a meeting with Arendt, Dewitz, Kardorff, and the DDP's Jordan, 15 Apr. 1920, PA AA Berlin, NL Stresemann, 213/138848.
[112] Statement by Arendt, Dewitz, and Kardorff, n.d., appended to Kardorff's letter to Stresemann, 17 Apr. 1920, BA Koblenz, NL Kardorff, 13/145–47. See also Hartenstein, *Anfänge der DVP*, 195–99.

against the unbridled enthusiasm that local party activists in his home city of Marburg an der Lahn had shown for the failed Kapp putsch.[113]

What this revealed was a broad pattern of discontent among DNVP moderates who had become distressed by their party's slow but steady drift to the right since the summer of 1919. It was thus with a certain sense of urgency that the DNVP party leadership resumed its work on the new party program before finally publishing it on 18 April 1920 under the title "Grundsätze der Deutschnationalen Volkspartei."[114] At the same time, party leaders tried to mollify the DNVP moderates by allowing the publication of the draft that had been prepared by the DNVP's State Political Coordinating Committee under the title *Nationales Manifest der Deutschnationalen Volkspartei*.[115] By highlighting the national, Christian, and social principles to which all sectors of the DNVP were dedicated, these two documents helped party leaders limit the scope of the Free Conservative defections and prevent a full-fledged secession on the party's left wing. As a compromise between the various factions that had come together in the DNVP, however, the new party program had its shortcomings and fell short of satisfying everyone in the party. The leaders of the DNVP's moderate wing were particularly disappointed with the concessions that had been made to the conservatives because they had made a merger with the DVP impossible and only isolated the DNVP from less conservative bourgeois forces in the middle and moderate Right.[116] By the same token, the leaders of the DNVP's Christian-Social wing were frustrated by the program's failure to recognize labor unions as a legitimate form of working-class organization and to grant the German worker parity as a fully entitled member of the *Volksgemeinschaft*.[117] Nor were old-line Prussian conservatives satisfied with the new program despite the critical role that Westarp had played in its formulation. For although Westarp urged his associates in the Central Association of German Conservatives to accept the program despite its admitted imperfections, he also lamented its failure to ground the DNVP sufficiently in

[113] Joh. Victor Bredt, *Erinnerungen und Dokumente 1914 bis 1933*, ed. Martin Schumacher (Düsseldorf, 1970), 158. See also Martin Grosch, *Johann Victor Bredt. Konservative Politik zwischen Kaiserreich und Nationalsozialismus. Eine politische Biographie* (Berlin, 2014), 177–82.

[114] *Grundsätze der Deutschnationalen Volkspartei* (Berlin, n.d. [1920]), also published in *Der nationale Wille*, ed. Weiß, 391–400.

[115] Staatspolitische Arbeitsgemeinschaft der Deutschnationalen Volkspartei, *Nationales Manifest der Deutschnationalen Volkspartei*, Apr. 1920, in BA Berlin, NL Mumm, 277/208a–d.

[116] Kanitz to Hergt, 15 Apr. 1920, BA Berlin, R 8005, 3/231–32.

[117] "Forderungen der deutschnationalen Arbeitervertreter an die Parteileitung," 24 Mar. 1920, BA Berlin, NL Mumm, 469/75.

the values of the Prussian tradition and objected to the concessions it had supposedly made to the principles of parliamentary government.[118]

To the Polls

Its imperfections notwithstanding, the "Grundsätze der Deutschnationalen Volkspartei" effectively defined the ideological tenor of the DNVP's campaign for the new national elections that were set for 6 June 1920. By portraying the DNVP as a national party dedicated to the rebirth of the German nation through its unification and emancipation from foreign domination, as a Christian party committed to revitalizing the spiritual and moral foundations of Germany's national life, and as a social party seeking the reconciliation of all strata of German society in a greater *Volksgemeinschaft*, the new program highlighted those ideals that all of those in the party held in common and could embrace without equivocation. At the same time, DNVP campaign strategists complemented their party's vigorous affirmation of its national, Christian, and social character with a series of specific appeals targeting the material concerns of the different social and vocational groups that constituted the party's popular base.[119] Speaking before the German National Civil Servants' Association (Deutschnationaler Beamtenbund) on 26 April 1920, Westarp reiterated the DNVP's commitment to the preservation of a professional civil service free from external political influence and called upon the government to implement cost-of-living adjustments so that civil servant salaries could keep pace with the rising costs of food and other consumer products.[120] On 5 May Westarp turned his attention to the plight of the independent middle class, the artisanry, and the small business sector in a speech in the Berlin suburb of Charlottenburg. Responding to the charge that the DNVP, as a party of large landed agriculture, was indifferent to the plight of the urban middle class, Westarp cited the long history of conservatism's involvement with the middle class and reminded government officials of their constitutional obligation to provide the middle class with the assistance it needed in order to sustain itself in the struggle between Jewish finance capital and the organized proletariat.[121]

---

[118] Westarp to Heydebrand, 15 Apr. 1920, NL Westarp, Gärtringen, II/80, excepts of which are quoted in Westarp, *Konservative Politik*, ed. Hiller von Gaertringen, 111.

[119] For further details, see Ohnezeit, *Zwischen "schärfster Opposition,"* 207–18.

[120] Kuno von Westarp, *Die Beamtenfrage. Rede in der Versammlung des Deutschnationalen Beamtenbundes am 26. April 1920 in den Kammersälen in Berlin*, Deutschnationale Flugschrift, no. 59 (Berlin, 1920).

[121] Kuno von Westarp, *Rede über Mittelstand, Handwerk und Kleinhandel. Gehalten in der Versammlung der Deutschnationalen Volkspartei in Charlottenburg am 5. Mai 1920*, Deutschnationale Flugschrift, no. 60 (Berlin, n.d. [1920]). See also Kuno von Westarp, *Getrennt marschieren, vereint—geschlagen werden!*, Deutschnationale Flugschrift, no. 58

While DNVP party strategists made a concerted effort to mobilize the support of an increasingly beleaguered German middle class, they continued to reach out to workers and white-collar employees. Here the Nationalists were able to draw upon the resources of the Evangelical workers' movement and the various Christian labor unions that had coalesced into the German Trade-Union Federation and whose leaders encouraged their followers to support the DNVP as one of several parties whose ideological objectives were compatible with their own.[122] By the same token, Hans Bechly from the German National Union of Commercial Employees used the organization's Brunswick congress in May 1920 to secure the passage of a resolution that urged its members to promote the DHV's social, economic, and cultural objectives by working within all of Germany's nonsocialist parties.[123] But as important as all of this might have been to those who conceived of the DNVP as a socially heterogeneous conservative *Sammelpartei*, no one received more attention from party strategists than the German farmer. Not only did the farmer constitute the social backbone of German conservatism, but the Nationalists were particularly concerned that regional agricultural interest organizations might field their own slate of candidates as part of a national agrarian ticket with devastating consequences for the DNVP's electoral prospects.[124]

No task in the campaign for the 1920 Reichstag elections was more important for the DNVP party leadership than the reestablishment of conservative hegemony throughout the German countryside. In this regard, the Nationalists received strong support from the leaders of the Agrarian League, who regarded the DNVP and DVP as the only parties worthy of agriculture's support.[125] Germany's conservative rural elites were anxious to contain the wave of social and political radicalism that had swept the countryside in the wake of the November Revolution. This was particularly true in conservative strongholds east of the Elbe, where the Social Democrats had experienced considerable success in organizing disgruntled farm laborers and peasants under the auspices of the German Farm Workers' Union.[126] Working closely

(Berlin, n.d. [1920]). In a similar vein, see Ernst Mentzel, *Die Mittelstandspolitik und die Parteien*, Deutschnationale Flugschrift, no. 30 (Berlin, 1919).

[122] "Richtlinien des Deutschen Gewerkschaftsbundes für die Reichstagswahlen," *Zentralblatt der christlichen Gewerkschaften Deutschlands* 20, no. 12 (7 Juni 1920): 109–10.

[123] Hans Bechly, *Staat, Gesellschaft und Politik. Vortrag, gehalten auf dem Verbandstage in Braunschweig am 15. und 16. Mai 1920* (Hamburg, n.d. [1920]), 6–12.

[124] Kanitz to Hergt, 26 Apr. 1920, BA Berlin, R 8005, 3/225–26.

[125] Roesicke before the executive committee of the German Rural League, 16 Dec. 1919, BA Berlin, R 8034 I, 2/242–46.

[126] For further details, see Flemming, *Landwirtschaftliche Interessen und Demokratie*, 76–160, as well as Mechthild Hempe, *Ländliche Gesellschaft in der Krise. Mecklenburg in der Weimarer Republik* (Colgone, Weimar, and Vienna, 2002), 71–103.

with the BdL's regional affiliates in Pomerania, Brandenburg, and elsewhere, East-Elbian estate owners went so far as to arm extra-legal paramilitary units in an attempt to break the back of the DLV by force and to restore the patriarchal relationships between lord and peasant that had existed before the war.[127] At the same time, the DNVP's Franz Behrens and his associates in the Central Association of Farm Laborers were hard at work organizing farm workers from throughout the east under the banner of the Christian-national labor movement in hopes of establishing a viable alternative to the socialist-led DLV.[128] Although these efforts invariably cut across those of the estate owners and their allies in the BdL, they nevertheless helped the DNVP position itself as the party of preference in the rural areas east of the Elbe.[129] This scenario repeated itself, though with distinctive regional nuances, in Bavaria, where the leaders of the Bavarian Rural League concluded an electoral alliance with the DNVP's state affiliate, the Bavarian Middle Party,[130] and in Württemberg, where Theodor Körner alt, Wilhelm Vogt, and their conferederates in the leadership of the Württemberg Peasants and Wine Growers' League ran their own slate of candidates only to affiliate themselves with the DNVP Reichstag delegation after the elections.[131]

In its bid for the support of the German farmer, the DNVP and its allies in the German agricultural community also relied upon what was more than just an innocuous dose of antisemitism. Antisemitism had been a hallmark of prewar rural political culture not just in the conservative strongholds east of the Elbe[132] but also in regions with historically liberal profiles like Württemberg and Schleswig-Holstein.[133] Frustrated by the DNVP's failure to include a

---

[127] Hempe, *Ländliche Gesellschaft*, 213–70.

[128] Behrens's report in Zentralverband der Landarbeiter, *Verhandlungs-Bericht über den 1. Verbandstag in Berlin am 16.–19. Mai 1920* (Berlin, 1920), 3–7.

[129] Daniel Hildebrand, *Landbevölkerung und Wahlverhalten. Die DNVP im ländlichen Raum Pommern und Ostpreußen 1918–1924* (Hamburg, 2004), 227–39.

[130] See "Mittelpartei und Landwirtschaft," in *Die Ziele der bayer. Mittelpartei (Deutschnationale Volkspartei in Bayern)*, ed. Geschäftsstelle der bayerischen Mittelpartei (Nuremburg, 1920), 22–27. See also Kittel, "Zwischen völkischem Fundamentalismus und gouvrementaler Taktik," 861–68.

[131] For the WWBB's political goals in 1920, see *Richtlinien der württemb. Bauernpolitik. Politische Bemerkungen zu den Richtlinien. Zweck, Ziel und Aufgaben des Bundes der Landwirte/Württemb. Bauern- u. Weingärtnerbund. Die landwirtschaftlichen Organisationen Württembergs*, ed. Württ. Bauern- und Weingärtnerbund, Schriften zur Wahlbewegung, no. 2 (Stuttgart, 1920), 3–15.

[132] Hans Reif, "Antisemitismus in den Agrarverbänden Ostelbiens während der Weimarer Republik," in *Ostelbische Agrargesellschaft im Kaiserreich und in der Weimarer Republik. Agrarkrise – junkerliche Interessenpolitik – Modernisierungsstrategien*, ed. Heinz Reif (Berlin, 1994), 378–411.

[133] On this point, see Hans Peter Müller, "Antisemitismus im Königreich Württemberg zwischen 1871 und 1914," *Jahrbuch des Vereins für Württembergisch Franken* 86 (2002): 547–83, and Peter Wulf, "Antisemitismus in bürgerlichen und bäuerlichen Parteien und

more aggressive plank on the so-called Jewish question in the new party program it promulgated in April 1920, the leaders of the DNVP's racist wing redoubled their efforts to move antisemitism to the center of the party's campaign for the 1920 Reichstag elections. DNVP racists celebrated what they saw as a major victory when they succeeded in blocking the nomination of Anna von Gierke, a member of the DNVP delegation to the Weimar National Assembly and a conservative feminist renown for her work in the field of social and child welfare, to a secure candidacy in the 1920 Reichstag elections on account of her mother's Jewish ancestry. Both Gierke and her father Otto, a highly respected professor of law at the University of Berlin, subsequently resigned from the party in what was clearly another setback for the leaders of the DNVP's moderate wing.[134] Although the leaders of the DNVP's racist wing rejoiced at the rejection of Gierke's candidacy, the incident severely compromised efforts by the DNVP party leadership to counter the impression of a sharp swing to the right that had been created by the secession of the Free Conservatives under Kardorff.[135] At the same time, DNVP racists and their supporters in the German-Racist Protection and Defense League (Deutsch-völkischer Schutz- und Trutzbund or DSTB) moved quickly to transform the DNVP into an instrument of their own political agenda at both the regional and national levels of the DNVP party organization. For their own part, Hergt and the DNVP leadership did little to oppose these efforts and more or less acquiesced in the racists' takeover of their party's campaign in the 1920 Reichstag elections.[136]

The Gierke affair also cut across the DNVP's efforts to win the support of German women. Having entrenched themselves in the party's national organization with the founding of the DNVP's National Women's Committee in December 1918, the party's women activists had spent most of the following year consolidating their position within the party and, through the person of Leonore Kühn, played an important role in drafting the new party program the DNVP promulgated in April 1920.[137] All of this was part of a fundamental reassessment by conservatives of the place of women in Germany's national

Verbände in Schleswig-Holstein (1918–1924)," Jahrbuch für Antisemitismusforschung 11 (2002): 52–75..

[134] See the letters from Otto and Anna von Gierke to the DNVP party leadership, 12 May 1920, in Otto von Gierke, Einige Wünsche an die Deutschnationale Volkspartei, Als Manuskript gedruckt (Berlin, n.d. [1920]), 22–29. For a Nationalist critique of the DNVP's position on antisemitism, see Friedrich von Oppeln-Bronikowski, Antisemitismus? Eine unparteiische Prüfung des Problems (Charlottenburg, 1920).

[135] For example, see Weiß to Westarp, 4 May 1920, NL Westarp, Gärtringen, II/5.

[136] Striesow, DNVP und die Völkisch-Radikalen, 233–42.

[137] For further details, see Süchting-Hänger, "Gewissen der Nation," 143–49, and Raffael Scheck, Mothers of the Nation: Right-Wing Women in Weimar Germany (Oxford and New York, 2004), 24–32.

life and stemmed in no small measure from recognition of the critical role that women voters had played salvaging the DNVP's electoral fortunes in the 1919 elections to the Weimar National Assembly.[138] In the 1920 campaign the DNVP's women activists were careful to distance themselves from Gierke and, with the notable exception of committee chairwoman Margarete Behm, lined upon behind the DNVP racists and their efforts to cast the DNVP as the vanguard of racial purity.[139] As in the 1919 elections to the National Assembly, the DNVP once again projected an essentially conservative image of women and their role in Germany's national life, highlighting the virtues of domesticity, religion, and patriotic sacrifice. Above all, DNVP campaign propaganda insisted, it was the task and responsibility of women to protect the cherished values of Germany's national culture – family, faith, nation, racial hygiene – against the forces of decay that had been unleashed by the November Revolution and that had become synonymous with the hated Weimar system.[140]

Underlying the DNVP's propaganda in the campaign for the 1920 Reichstag elections was a pervasive and powerful antisystem bias that stood in sharp contrast to the hopes of party moderates that the elections would pave the way to their party's entry into the national government. For the leaders of the DNVP the elections were a referendum on the November Revolution, the consequences of which were portrayed as a disaster for virtually every sector of German society, including the German worker.[141] Speaking at a party rally in Berlin-Schöneberg on 29 April, Westarp called for an "annihilating [*vernichtende*] settling of accounts" with the new system, a system that in the area of foreign policy had forced Germany to accept the "disgraceful peace of Versailles" while at home it had placed the nation at the mercy of undisciplined masses and had subjected the productive elements in the city and countryside to the dictatorship of organized labor and its allies on the radical Left. The coming election, Westarp continued, would decide whether it would be possible for the German people to forge "a new national feeling" rooted in

---

[138] See Matthew Stibbe, "Anti-Feminism, Nationalism and the German Right, 1914–1920: A Reappraisal," *German History* 20 (2002): 185–210, and Kirsten Heinsohn, "Das konservative Dilemma und die Frauen. Anmerkungen zum Scheitern eines republikanischen Konservatismus in Deutschland," in *"Ich bin der letzte Preuße": Der politische Lebensweg des konservativen Politikers Kuno Graf von Westarp (1864–1945)*, ed. Larry Eugene Jones and Wolfram Pyta (Cologne, Weimar, and Vienna, 2005), 77–107, as well as Kirsten Heinsohn, *Konservative Parteien in Deutschland*, 82–93.

[139] Sneeringer, *Winning Women's Votes*, 50.

[140] Ibid., 42–51.

[141] For example, see Joseph Kaufhold, *Die Folgen der Revolution*, Deutschnationale Flugschrift, no. 53 (Berlin, 1920), as well as the two DNVP campaign leaflets "Am 6. Juni Freiheit!," n.d. [May 1920], and "Um die Freiheit," n.d. [May 1920], both in the Nachlass Berthold Freiherr Hiller von Gaertringen, Archiv des Freiherren Hiller von Gaertringen, Gärtringen (hereafter cited as NL Hiller, Gärtringen).

the "living forces of Christianity," in monarchism, and in the tried and true traditions of Prussian-German history. Then and only then would the German people be able to free itself from the yoke of slavery at home and abroad and embark upon a new era in pursuit of Germany's national greatness.[142]

Westarp's appeal to the "living forces of Christianity" was not empty rhetoric but an essential component of the DNVP's campaign to mobilize the support of conservative Christians who felt a deep sense of concern over the place of religion in German public life after the upheavals of 1918–19. Before the war the German Lutheran Church had constituted one of the main pillars of support for the forces of political conservatism both inside and outside of Prussia. But the collapse of the Hohenzollen monarchy and the subsequent disestablishment of the church by the Weimar and Prussian constitutional assemblies deprived the Lutheran Church of the privileged position it had enjoyed before 1914 and caused widespread alarm among conservative Christians who perceived this as the first in a series of assaults upon their religious and cultural values.[143] In the campaign for the 1920 Reichstag elections the DNVP positioned itself, as it had in 1919, as the defender of the vital interests of the Lutheran Church and Germany's Protestant population.[144] At the same time, however, the leaders of the DNVP also made a concerted bid for the support of German Catholics who had become estranged from the Center Party as a result of its dramatic shift to the left in the last years of World War I.[145] In January 1920 Hergt issued what amounted to a programmatic statement by the DNVP party leadership when, in a letter to the district organization in Münster, he called for an end to the confessional tensions that had become so deeply embedded in the fabric of German political life and stressed that all of those, Catholic as well as Protestant, who embraced the struggle for Germany's national regeneration would be welcomed as full and equal members of the party.[146]

---

[142] Speech by Westarp before the DNVP local organization in Berlin-Schöneberg, 29 Apr. 1920, BA Berlin, NL Westarp, 125/11–17.

[143] Kurt Nowak, *Evangelische Kirche und Weimarer Republik. Zum politischen Weg des deutschen Protestantismus zwischen 1918 und 1932* (Göttingen, 1981), 17–52, esp. 25–31.

[144] In this respect, see Wilhelm Kähler, "Die Kulturpolitik der Deutschnationalen Volks-partei," in *Jahrbuch der Erziehungswissenschaft und Jugendkunde*, ed. Erich Stern, 3 (1927): 5–30.

[145] For example, see the flyer from the DNVP national headquarters "Katholische Glau-bensgenosssen!," 21 May 1920, Werbeblatt no. 129, as well as the campaign leaflet from the Württemberg Burgher Party, "Katholiken und Zentrumsleute gegen Erzberger," n.d. [1920], both in NL Hiller, Gärtringen.

[146] For the text of Hergt's letter, 2 Jan. 1920, see *Politisches Handwörterbuch (Führer-ABC)*, ed. Max Weiß (Berlin, 1928), 319. See also Landsberg-Steinfurt, "Darf ein Katholik deutschnational sein?," *Eiserne Blätter* 1, no. 41 (18 Apr. 1920): 717–20.

Despite the optimism with which the DNVP party leadership entered the campaign, the party's campaign effort was hampered by lingering financial difficulties that were only partly resolved by the time of the elections. In building up a strong and comprehensive national party organization, the leaders of the DNVP had decided not to burden the party's state and regional organizations with the responsibility of sharing the funds they had raised locally with the party headquarters in Berlin. As a result, party leaders in Berlin found themselves short of funds for use in the campaign and had to turn, as the DVP and other non-socialist parties had already begun to do, to potential backers in the German business community.[147] The DNVP's principal source of financial support in the 1920 campaign was the Commission for the Collection, Administration, and Allocation of the Industrial Campaign Fund, where its general secretary Johannes Flathmann worked closely with Alfred Hugenberg in collecting and distributing campaign funds to the DNVP and DVP.[148] To be sure, Germany's industrial leaders – including Carl Friedrich von Siemens, the driving force behind the Commision's principal rival in the solicitation of industrial campaign funds, the Curatorium for the Reconstruction of German Economic Life – would have preferred to support one rather than two right-wing parties and were disappointed when efforts to unite the DVP and DNVP broke down in late 1919.[149] As a result, Siemens' Curatorium ended up donating 775,000 marks to the campaign coffers of each of the two right-wing parties.[150] In the meantime, the fact that Flathmann was able to secure the nomination of Hugo Stinnes, Kurt Sorge, and Reinhold Quaatz to secure candidacies on the DVP ticket meant that it and not the DNVP would become the party of preference for the Commission for the Industrial Campaign Fund and its financial supporters in the Ruhr.[151]

A Mixed Verdict

If the 1920 Reichstag elections was to be a referendum on the social and political legacy of the November Revolution, then the leaders of the DNVP could not have been altogether pleased with the outcome. To be sure, Hergt

---

[147] Hergt and Dryander to Springorum, 7 May 1920, ThyssenKrupp Konzernarchiv, Außenstelle Hoesch-Archiv, Dortmund (hereafter cited as TKA Dortmund), Nachlass Fritz Springorum, F 4e 3.

[148] Heidrun Holzbach, Das "System Hugenberg." Die Organisation bürgerlicher Sammlungspolitik vor dem Aufstieg der NSDAP (Stuttgart, 1981), 78–82.

[149] On the course of these negotiations, see Stresemann to Baumgärtel, 10 Dec. 1919, PA AA Berlin, NL Stresemann, 208/138114–16.

[150] Hergt and Dryander to the Curatorium, 9 June 1920, SHI Berlin, NL Siemens, 4/Lf 646.

[151] For further details, see Flathmann to Stinnes, 19 Apr. 1920, and Osius to Stinnes, 20 Apr. 1920, ACDP Sankt-Augustin, NL Stinnes, 002/4, as well as Flathmann to Stresemann, 4 May 1920, PA AA Berlin, NL Stresemann, 212/138646–51.

and his associates could derive a measure of satisfaction from the fact that their party had improved upon its performance in the elections to the Weimar National Assembly by more than a million votes, increasing its share of the popular vote from 10.3 to 15.1 percent and its representation in the national parliament from twenty-nine to sixty-six seats. At the same time, however, the DNVP's gains in the 1920 Reichstag were eclipsed by those of its only rival on the German Right, the German People's Party, which increased its share of the popular vote from 4.4 to 13.9 percent and entered the new Reichstag with a delegation sixty-two strong.[152] The fact that the DVP had outperformed the DNVP by a substantial margin rankled Nationalist party leaders, who immediately found themselves embroiled in a heated public dispute over the role that antisemitism and the excesses of the party's antisemitic wing had played in the DNVP's disappointing performance vis-à-vis the DVP.[153] On the more positive side, party leaders were pleased with the fact that the DNVP had succeeded in recapturing a much of the terrain it had surrendered to the two socialist parties in 1919 in the predominantly rural areas east of the Elbe. In East Prussia, for example, the DNVP increased its share of the popular vote from 11.9 to 30.9 percent, in Pomerania and Mecklenburg from 23.9 to 35.5 and 13.1 to 20.6 percent respectively. The party also benefited from strong gains in Frankfurt an der Oder, Württemberg, Thuringia, Schleswig-Holstein, and Franconia, all districts in which the support of local farm organizations contributed susbstantially to the DNVP's success at the polls. Outside of Hamburg, where the DNVP increased its share of the popular vote from 3.5 to 12.4 percent, the party's gains in districts with a more predominantly urban profile lagged significantly behind that in districts with large rural populations. In Berlin, for example, the DNVP was able to increase its share of the popular vote from 9.3 to just 11.5 percent, while in Breslau the party improved upon its 15.3 percentage share of the popular vote in 1919 by a mere 3.1 percent.[154]

The election outcome revealed a sharp swing to the right in which all of the parties that belonged to the Weimar Coalition suffered substantial losses. Of the 466 deputies elected to the Reichstag, the three government parties could claim the support of only 225. The Majority Socialists saw their share of the popular vote reduced from 37.9 percent in the elections to the Weimar National Assembly to 21.6 percent in 1920, while the Independent Socialists actually improved upon their share of the popular vote from 7.6 percent in 1919 to 18.6 in 1920. In the meantime, the newly founded German

---

[152] Falter, Lindenberger, and Schumann, *Wahlen und Abstimmungen*, 41, 67–68.

[153] Graef, "Die Lehren des Wahlausfalls," *Unsere Partei* 2, no. 17 (June–July 1920): 1–6.

[154] Falter, Lindenberger, and Schumann, *Wahlen und Abstimmungen*, 67–68. See also Gerhard A. Ritter, "Kontinuität und Umformung des deutschen Parteiensystems 1918–1920," in *Entstehung und Wandel der modernen Gesellschaft. Festschrift für Hans Rosenberg zum 65. Geburtstag*, ed. Gerhard A. Ritter (Berlin, 1970), 342–76, here 367.

Communist Party (Kommunistische Partei Deutschlands or KPD) receieved
1.7 percent of the popular vote in its first national campaign.[155] The German
Democratic Party, whose campaign had been carefully crafted to resassure
middle-class voters that collaboration with the Majority Socialists had been
necessary to expedite Germany's political stabilization, lost more than half of
the votes it had received in the elections to the Weimar National Assembly and
saw its share of the popular vote fall from 18.5 percent in 1919 to a 8.3 percent
in 1920. Defections from the left-liberal DDP accounted in no small measure
for the impressive gains recorded by its liberal rival, the DVP, whose leaders
proved remarkably successful in exploiting the anxieties that the DDP's
performance as a member of the governmental coalition had aroused among
its middle-class supporters.[156] Nor was the Center, the third member of the
Weimar Coalition, immune from the sting of defeat. Reeling from the defection of its entire Bavarian organization to the Bavarian People's Party that had
been founded in the immediate wake of the November Revolution, the Center
lost a third of the vote it had received in the elections to the Weimar National
Assembly and saw its parliamentary delegation reduced from eighty eight – or
seventy, if one subtracts the eighteen deputies who defected to the BVP – to
sixty-eight mandates.[157] That these losses were far less severe than those of the
other coalition parties did little to diminish the enormity of the defeat that the
parties of the Weimar Coalition had suffered at the polls on 6 June 1920.

The outcome of the 1920 Reichstag elections resulted in fundamental and
permanent changes in Germany's political landscape. The parties of the
Weimar Coalition would never recover the majority they had held in the
National Assembly. Beset by defections to the Left and the Right, the parties
that identified themselves with Germany's new republican order remained on
the defensive for the remainder of the Weimar Republic. In the short term, this
meant that the parties of the Weimar Coalition had lost their mandate to
govern and that political stability could be achieved only by extending the
governmental coalition to the left to include the Independent Socialists or to
the right to include the DVP. Neither was a particularly attractive option. At
the same time, the bitter defeat that the German electorate had handed the
parties of the Weimar Coalition created a new set of opportunities for the
German Right. Would the DNVP capitalize upon the weakness of Germany's
republican parties by joining the government itself and reshape Germany's

---

[155] Heinrich August Winkler, *Von der Revolution zur Stabilisierung. Arbeiter und Arbeiterbewegung in der Weimarer Republik 1918 bis 1924* (Berlin and Bonn, 1984), 350–59.

[156] Jones, *German Liberalism*, 76–80. See also Hartenstein, *Anfänge der DVP*, 224–53.

[157] Rudolf Morsey, *Die Deutsche Zentrumspartei 1917–1923* (Düsseldorf, 1966), 320–24.

political future from within the existing system of government? Or would it remain steadfast in its opposition to the new republican order and stay the course that had served it so well in the first year and a half of its existence? How these questions were answered would have a profound impact not just upon the future of the DNVP but on that of the Weimar Republic itself.

4

Growth and Consolidation

The Reichstag elections of 6 June 1920 marked an important milestone in the development of the German Right after World War I. Capitalizing upon the sense of moral outrage to which the imposition of the Versailles Peace Treaty had given rise, the DNVP had weathered the Kapp putsch to establish itself as the party of national opposition to the Weimar Republic and all that it purportedly stood for. The early years of the Weimar Republic were to be good years for the DNVP and other right-wing organizations. For the humiliation of Versailles was to be followed by the London Ultimatum of May 1921 and the partition of Upper Silesia later that fall, and the price increases of the last years of the war and the early postwar period was to develop into a full-fledged inflation that severely undermined whatever confidence Germany's urban and rural middle classes might have had in the newly established republican system. This was a situation in which not just the DNVP, but all right-wing organizations, including those much more radical than the DNVP, flourished. The problem confronting the leaders of the DNVP was how best to consolidate their party's position on the German Right and to harness the forces of counterrevolution that had been unleashed by the fear of Bolshevism, the humiliation of Versailles, and the rapidly deteriorating economic situation.

Reaffirming the Hard Line

With sixty-two seats in the newly elected Reichstag – a number that would climb to sixty-six as a result of later elections in the contested areas of Schleswig-Holstein, East Prussia, and Upper Silesia – the DNVP easily retained its position as the largest opposition party in parliament. The parties of the Weimar Coalition no longer commanded the strength to form a new majority government and would have to bring either the Independent Socialists or the German People's Party into the governmental coalition in order to achieve a parliamentary majority. But Stresemann and the leaders of the German People's Party, whose parliamentary strength had increased by nearly three-fold, categorically rejected an accommodation with either socialist party, hoping instead to move the fulcrum of power to the right by excluding the socialists from the government. Ideally Stresemann would like to have shored up his own right flank by tying the DNVP to the new governmental coalition, but that was unlikely in light of strong opposition from both the Center and German Democratic Party to a coalition with the Nationalists.[1] At the same time, many of the moderates in the DNVP Reichstag delegation were intrigued by the possibility of entering the government despite strong resistance from Count Westarp and the leaders of the DNVP's right wing. The issue became moot when a minority government consisting of the Center, DDP, and DVP assumed office under the leadership of the Center's Konstantin Fehrenbach on 20 June 1920.[2]

In outlining his party's position before the Reichstag on 28 June, DNVP party chairman Oskar Hergt chastised the Majority Socialists for their refusal to share governmental responsibility with the DVP and reiterated his own party's willingness to form a coalition government with all of Germany's bourgeois parties.[3] Several days later Karl Helfferich, Germany's wartime minister of finance and a newly elected member of the DNVP Reichstag delegation, sharply attacked the government parties for their failure to accept the results of the recent elections by forming a new cabinet whose parliamentary mandate was still dependent upon the Majority Socialists. The disastrous situation in which the Reich found itself and the difficult negotiations that lay ahead for the German people both at home and abroad, Helfferich concluded, mandated a government with the broadest possible base of support in the Reichstag. And on this point, he concluded, the government parties could not have failed more miserably.[4] Yet in their willingness to broach the possibility of sharing governmental responsibility with other nonsocialist parties, Hergt and Helfferich found themselves at odds with the leaders of their own party's right wing. Hergt had been fully prepared to read a declaration expressing the DNVP's willingness to share governmental responsibility with any party, including the Majority Socialists, that was prepared to work together in the reconstruction of the German fatherland. But Westarp and his supporters on the DNVP's right wing were so strongly opposed to any such gesture by the DNVP leadership that they threatened to form a separate parliamentary

[1] See Wright, *Stresemann*, 163–67, and Richter, *Deutsche Volkspartei*, 217–22.
[2] Morsey, *Deutsche Zentrumspartei*, 329–34.
[3] Oskar Hergt and Karl Helfferich, *Der Block der Mitte. Reden des Reichstagsabgeordnete Hergt und Helfferich am 28. Juni und 2. Juli 1920 im Reichstage*, Deutschnationale Parlamentsreden, no. 17 (Berlin, 1920), 10–15.
[4] Ibid., 28–36. See also Albrecht Philipp, *Die deutschnationale Fraktion des Reichstags und die Reichsregierungen Fehrenbach u. Dr. Wirth (Juni 1920–August 1921, Hanbuch-Folge, no. 5 (Berlin, 1921), 3–6.

delegation until Hergt desisted and agreed to strike any such statement from his speech to the Reichstag.[5]

Uncertainty over the DNVP's political course persisted through the summer and early fall of 1920 until its annual party congress in Hanover in late October 1920.[6] In his keynote address on the morning of 25 October, Hergt moved quickly to dispel the uncertainty that existed in much of the party by declaring it a "sacred duty" for the DNVP "to wage opposition against the domination of the existing parliamentary system" and pledged the party to reject "a politics of compromise" in any form whatsoever. Hergt went on to draw a sharp distinction between the political course of his own party and that of its major rival on the Right, the German People's Party. Whereas the DVP presumably strived for a programmatic understanding with the Majority Socialists, the DNVP explicitly rejected a pact with Social Democracy in its present form and made its willingness to collaborate with Social Democracy at any point in the future contingent upon its radical ideological reorientation. The goal of the DNVP, Hergt concluded with an obvious eye to the upcoming Prussian state elections, was to transform the Prussian state into a bastion of law and order – in the terminology of the day an *Ordnungsstaat* – from which it could conquer the rest of the Reich. This would be possible, however, only if the DNVP remained true to its sacred mission and resisted the temptation to seek power in the existing system of government.[7]

Hergt's speech constituted a clear and unequivocal rebuff to those both within and outside the party who hoped that the DNVP might set aside its ideological objections to the existing system of government and play a more constructive role in the solution of the myriad problems facing Germany's political leadership. Hergt's vigorous reaffirmation of the DNVP's role as an opposition party ushered in a period of relative calm in the DNVP's internal development that lasted until the Prussian Landtag elections in February 1921. The intransigence of the DNVP party leadership was also reflected in two further speeches on the first day of the congress, the first an impassioned call for a revision of the Versailles Peace Treaty from Albrecht von Graefe-Goldebee of the DNVP's racist faction[8] and the second an appeal by Paul

---

[5] On the split in the DNVP Reichstag delegation, see Westarp to Heydebrand, 28 June 1920, NL Westarp, Gärtringen, II/80–81, and Traub, 3 July 1920, BA Koblenz, NL Traub, 50/87–89.

[6] For the official record of the Hanover party congress, see "Ergebnisse der 2. Parteitages in Hannover," *Unsere Partei* 2, nos. 23–24 (Nov. 1920): 1–20. See also the entries in the diary of Max von Gallwitz, 23–26 Oct. 1920, BA-MA Freiburg, Nachlass Max von Gallwitz, 36.

[7] Oskar Hergt, *Unser Ziel. Rede auf dem 2. Parteitag der Deutschnationalen Volkspartei in Hannover am 25. Oktober 1920*, Deutschnationale Flugschrift, no. 75 (Berlin, 1920).

[8] Albrecht von Graefe-Goldebee, *Die Revision von Versailles. Rede auf dem 2. Parteitage der Deutschnationalen Volkspartei in Hannover am 25. Oktober 1920*, Deutschnationale Flugschrift, no. 72 (Berlin, 1920).

Baecker of the *Deutsche Tageszeitung* for the creation of a new German Reich that included not only the areas that had been severed from Germany after World War I but also the German-speaking populations of Austria and the newly created state of Czechoslovakia.[9] If nothing else, the speeches by Graefe-Goldebee and Baecker underscored the psychological inability of the DNVP party leadership to accept the reality of the lost war and exposed just how unsuited it was to the task of sharing responsibility with Germany's other political parties in the conduct of German foreign policy.[10]

Aside from Hergt's speech, the other major highlight of the Hanover congress was an elaborate discourse by Walther Lambach on the DNVP's goals and aspirations in the area of social policy. Just elected to the Reichstag as a liaison to the German National Union of Commercial Employees, the thirty-five-year-old union official outlined an ambitious social program that aimed at the creation of a genuine *Volksgemeinschaft* in which the worker and white-collar employee would take their place alongside that of the farmer, the businessman, and representatives of other vocations.[11] In a similar vein, Paul Rüffer from the DNVP's fledgling working-class wing expressed satisfaction with the success of its efforts to secure a foothold within the DNVP's national organization and reaffirmed their loyalty to the party and its struggle for the welfare of the German worker.[12] Yet while both efforts drew much of their impetus from the social gospel of German Protestantism, party leaders were also hopeful of attracting the support of Catholic conservatives who had become estranged from the German Center Party.[13] In this respect, the Nationalists were intent upon expanding their party's political base into sectors of the population that had fallen outside the orbit of prewar German conservatism but now, because of the twin shock of defeat and revolution, were ripe for recruitment to the conservative cause. For the moment, however, party leaders chose not to endanger their party's fragile unity by assuming the burden of governmental responsibility but opted instead to rally the party faithful around what Hans Erdmann von Lindeiner-Wildau, the DNVP's

---

[9] Paul Baecker, *Die deutsche Frage. Rede auf dem zweiten Parteitage der Deutschnationalen Volkspartei in Hannover am 25. Oktober 1920*, Deutschnationale Flugschrift, no. 78 (Berlin, 1920).

[10] Thimme, *Flucht in den Mythos*, 61–95. See also Boris Barth, *Dolchstoßlegenden und politische Desintegration. Das Traume der deutschen Niederlage im Ersten Weltkrieg 1914–1933* (Düsseldorf, 2003), 302–21.

[11] Walther Lambach, *Unser Weg zur deutschen Volksgemeinschaft. Rede auf dem 2. Parteitag der Deutschnationalen Volkspartei in Hannover am 25. Oktober 1920*, Deutschnationale Flugschrift, no. 79 (Berlin, 1920).

[12] Paul Rüffer, "Die Stellung des deutschnationalen Arbeiters zur äußeren und inneren Politik," in *Deutschnationale Arbeitertagung in Hannover am Dienstag, den 26. Oktober 1920*, Deutschnationale Flugschrift, no. 88 (Berlin, n.d. [1920]), 3–27.

[13] Entry in Gallwitz's diary, 25 Oct. 1920, BA-MA Freiburg, NL Gallwitz, 36.

general secretary from the party's founding until the fall of 1921, epigrammatically termed the "unity of the no."[14]

Coming after a brief flirtation with the possibility of entering the government in the aftermath of the June 1920 elections, the DNVP's return to the path of uncompromising opposition to Germany's new republican order represented a decisive victory for the party's right wing. Here the principal impulse came from the leaders of the party organizations from east of the Elbe, most notably East Prussia and Pomerania. The DNVP's East Elbian organizations had been caught off guard by the collapse of the old imperial order and had struggled with great difficulty to establish themselves in the face of a radicalized rural population.[15] But by the summer of 1920 the pendulum had begun to swing back in their favor, and in the June elections they managed to reconquer much of the terrain they had surrendered in the elections to the Weimar National Assembly. Reinvigorated by the resurrection of their electoral base in the second half of 1919 and early 1920, the DNVP's East Prussian and Pomeranian organizations now began to assert themselves all the more vigorously in the DNVP's internal affairs. Nowhere was this more apparent than at a special congress of the DNVP's Pomeranian district organization in Greifswald on 5–6 November 1920. The keynote speaker was none other than Albrecht von Graefe-Goldebee, one of the DNVP's most outspoken antisemites and an unrelenting opponent of Germany's new republican system. Not only was Graefe quick to invoke the "stab-in-the-back legend" with all of its antisemtic overtones as an explanation for the disasters that befell Germany between 1914 and 1918, but he categorically rejected any compromise with the system that these disasters had left in their wake.[16] Whether or not intransigence of this sort could be reconciled with the aspirations of those who had rallied to the DNVP's banner in the hope that it might play a more positive role in the reconstruction of German social and economic life was far from certain.

Catholics on the Right

While the DNVP's Hanover congress helped restore a sense of calm within the party and set the stage for its campaign for the upcoming Prussian Landtag elections, it was soon eclipsed by an event that dramatized just how unstable Germany's political landscape was. Speaking at the first postwar congress of the Christian trade-union movement in Essen on 21 November 1920, Adam

---

[14] Hans Erdmann von Lindeiner-Wildau, "Konservatismus," in *Volk und Reich der Deutschen*, ed. Bernhard Harms, 3 vols. (Berlin, 1929), 2:35–61, here pp. 58–61.

[15] For further details, see Hildebrand, *Landbevölkerung und Wahlverhalten*, 159–78.

[16] Speech by Graefe-Goldebee in *Deutschnationaler Parteitag für Vorpommern. Am 6. und 7. November 1920 in Greifswald* (Greifswald, n.d. [1920]), 11–20.

Stegerwald caused a political sensation when, much to the dismay of his own party colleagues and to the astonishment of virtually everyone else, he called for the creation of an interconfessional people's party resting upon the four pillars of Christianity, democracy, nationalism, and social equality. Claiming that neither the Catholic nor the Protestant sector of the population was sufficiently strong to create such a party by itself, Stegerwald argued that only the creation of an entirely new party that embraced the best of both confessions and that appealed across class lines to all sectors of German society could bring about the material and spiritual rehabilitation of the German people.[17] A profoundly conservative Catholic who was deeply disturbed by the emergence of Matthias Erzberger as the driving force in the Center after the end of World War I,[18] Stegerwald feared that the growing emnity between the DNVP and Center might destroy the effectiveness of his own movement, particularly after the Christian labor unions reaffirmed its loyalty to the republican form of government in the wake of the ill-fated Kapp-Lüttwitz putsch.[19] In the build-up to the 1920 Reichstag elections Christian labor leaders tried to insulate their movement against further damage by reiterating the principle of non-partisanship upon which the German Trade-Union Federation had been founded. In May 1920 the DGB issued a set of guidelines in May 1920 that left its affiliated unions free to endorse the candidates of their choice without regard for party affiliation as long as those candidates embraced the ideals and principles of the Christian-national labor movement.[20]

Stegerwald's and his associates continued to decry the increasing fragmentation of the German party system and the effect it was having upon the unity and effectiveness of their own movement.[21] Stegerwald's concern was directly related to a series of developments that directly affected the effectiveness of his

---

[17] Adam Stegerwald, *Deutsche Lebensfragen. Vortrag gehalten auf dem 10. Kongreß der christlichen Gewerkschaften Deutschlands am 21. November 1920 in Essen* (Cologne, 1920), 39–42. On the political calculations that lay behind this appeal, see Stegerwald to Schofer, 3 Aug. 1921, and Brüning to Stegerwald, 4 Aug. 1921, both in ACDP Sankt Augustin, NL Stegerwald, I-206/018. See also Leo Schwering, "Stegerwalds und Brünings Vorstellungen über Parteireform und Parteiensystem," in *Staat, Wirtschaft und Politik in der Weimarer Republik. Festschrift für Heinrich Brüning*, ed. Ferdinand A. Hermens and Theodor Schieder (Berlin, 1967), 23–40, as well as Jones, "Stegerwald," 1–29, and Forster, *Stegerwald*, 279–90. For further information on the Essen congress, see Roder, *Gewerkschaftsbund*, 264–82.

[18] See Stegerwald's attack on Erzberger at the meeting of the Center Reichstag delegation, 19 Oct. 1920, BA Koblenz, Nachlass Rudolf ten Hompel, 20.

[19] Resolution of the GCG executive committee, 7–8 Apr. 1920, in *Zentralblatt der christlichen Gewerkschaften Deutschlands* 20, no. 9 (26 Apr. 1920): 77–78.

[20] "Richtlinien des Deutschen Gewerkschaftsbundes für die Reichstagswahlen," in *Zentralblatt der christlichen Gewerkschaften Deutschlands* 20, no. 12 (7 Juni 1920): 109–10.

[21] Adam Stegerwald, *Sittliche Kraft oder rohe Gewalt? Mahnruf der christlich-nationalen Arbeiterschaft an das deutsche Volk. Vortrag, gehalten auf der Kundgebung der christlichen*

own Center Party. The founding of the Bavarian People's Party and the end of its parliamentary alliance with the Center in January 1920, the emergence of the Christian People's Party (Christliche Volkspartei or CVP) in the Rhineland and the western parts of Germany, and the sympathy of Catholic conservatives who had formerly belonged to the Center for the right-wing DNVP gave rise to widespread concern about the Center's survival as a viable factor in German political life.[22] It was against the background of these developments that Stegerwald and his lieutenants, the most important of whom was DGB secretary Heinrich Brüning, decided to resume their efforts on behalf of a reform of the German party system. In September 1920 Christian labor leaders drafted an eight-page memorandum entitled "Arbeiterbewegung und Politik" that outlined the case for the creation of an interconfessional and socially heterogeneous people's party open to all of those who were prepared to cooperate in the reconstruction of the German fatherland on a Christian, national, democratic, and social basis.[23] The ideas contained in this memorandum quickly found their way into Stegerwald's speech at Essen and became the nucleus of what came to be known as his "Essen Program."

Stegerwald's appeal for the founding of an interconfessional and socially heterogenous Christian people's party was addressed in large part to conservative Catholics who opposed the Center's sharp swing to the left in the last years of World War I. Catholic support for the Center had already begun to unravel in the last years before the outbreak of the war.[24] This trend continued into the early years of the Weimar Republic as Catholic nobles, Catholic workers, Catholic peasants, and representatives of the Catholic middle class began to

---

Gewerkschaften in Fredenbaum zu Dortmund am 25. April 1920 (Cologne, 1920). See also Sedlmayr to Kaiser, 31 May 1920, BA Koblenz, Nachlass Jakob Kaiser, 250.

[22] For example, see Heinrich Triepel, *Krisis in der Zentrumspartei?* (Opladen, n.d. [1920]). For further details, see Morsey, *Zentrumspartei*, 273–310.

[23] "Arbeiterbewegung und Politik. Als Manuskript gedruckt für die Führer der christlich-nationalen Arbeiterbewegung," Sept. 1920, ACDP Sankt Augustin, NL Stegerwald, I-206/001/2.

[24] For example, see Engelbert von Kerckerinck zur Borg, *Unsere Stellung zur Zentrumspartei. Vortrag in der Generalversammlung des Vereins kath. Edelleute zu Münster am 4. Febr. 1919* (Münster, n.d. [1919]), Vereinigte Westfälische Adelsarchive, Münster (hereafter cited as WVA Münster), Nachlass Hermann von Lüninck, 807. See also Gerhard Kratzsch, *Engelbert Reichsfreiherr von Kerckerinck zur Borg. Westfälischer Adel zwischen Kaiserreich und Weimarer Republik* (Münster, 2004), 113–33. On Catholic conservative estrangement from the Center, see Horst Gründer, "Rechtskatholizismus im Kaiserreich und in der Weimarer Republik unter besonderer Berücksichtigung der Rheinlande und Westfalens," *Westfälische Zeitschrift* 134 (1984): 107–55, and Christoph Hübner, *Die Rechtskatholiken, die Zentrumspartei und die katholische Kirche in Deutschland bis zum Reichskonkordat von 1933. Ein Beitrag zur Geschichte des Scheiterns der Weimarer Republik* (Berlin, 2014), 155–234, as well as Friedrich Keinemann, *Vom Krummstab zur Republik. Westfälischer Adel unter preußischer Herrschaft 1802–1945* (Dortmund, 1997), 364–84.

turn away from the Center in search of a new political home.[25] DNVP
strategists were quick to take note of this and saw an opportunity to broaden
the base of their political movement by reaching out to Catholics and other
groups that had not previously been identified with the conservative cause.
Here the initiative came from a prominent Westphalian noble, Baron Alfred
von Landsberg-Steinfurt, who took it upon himself to issue an appeal on
behalf of the DNVP calling for all "national Germans" to set aside their
confessional differences and unite against the common threat that "the marriage of Anglo-Saxon lust for world power with the international masonic-
Jewish struggle for world domination through the power of money" posed to
all Christians irrespective of denomination.[26] In June 1919 Landsberg's older
brother Engelbert von Landsberg-Velen, also a highly respected Westphalian
noble, was invited to speak before the DNVP's State Political Coordinating
Committee on the topic of "Die Deutschnationale Volkspartei und der Katholizismus." Here the elder Landsberg called upon the DNVP to take the lead in
overcoming the historic schism between Catholic and Protestant and to unite
the two confessions against all those forces in the modern world that
threatened the unity and vitality of the German nation.[27] Five months later
Engelbert von Landsberg-Velen had an opportunity to act upon his own
advice when he and a handful of other DNVP Catholics met in Berlin to lay
the foundation for the creation of a national Catholic committee that would
assist the party leadership in winning the support and votes of Catholics in
areas with a significant Catholic population such as Silesia, Westphalia, the
Rhineland, Berlin, and possibly Bavaria.[28]

Landsberg and his associates clearly had an eye on the Reichstag elections
that were scheduled to take place in early 1920 and were optimistic of
achieving a decisive breakthrough into the ranks of the dissident elements

[25] Johannes Schauff, *Das Wahlverhalten der deutschen Katholiken im Kaiserreich und in der
Weimarer Republik. Untersuchungen aus dem Jahre 1928*, ed. Rudolf Morsey (Mainz,
1975), 70–107.

[26] Landsberg-Steinfurt, "Zusammenschluß aller nationalen Deutschen," n.d. [1919], VWA
Münster, Nachlass Engelbert Freiherr von Kerckerinck zur Borg, 139. For further details,
see Larry Eugene Jones, "Catholic Conservatives in the Weimar Republic: The Politics of
the Rhenisch-Westphalian Aristocracy, 1918–1933," *German History* 18 (2000): 60–85,
here 61–63.

[27] Landsberg-Velen, "Die Deutschnationale Volkspartei und der Katholizismus," *15. Arbeits-
abend der Staatspolitischen Arbeitsgemeinschaft der Deutschnationalen Volkspartei, 13.
Juni 1919*, 91–97, BA Berlin, R 8005, 327. See also the preliminary draft of Landsberg's
speech with his handwritten corrections under the title "Katholizismus u. nationale
Politik. Vortrag in der Staatspolitischen Arbeitsgemeinschaft der Deutschnationalen
Volkspartei in Berlin am 13. Juni 1919," VWA Münster, Nachlass Hermann Graf zu
Stolberg-Stolberg, Haus Westheim, 170.

[28] Notes on the meeting of the DNVP Catholic committee, 5 Nov. 1919, VWA Münster,
Nachlass Engelbert Freiherr von Landsberg-Velen, Haus Drensteinfurt, E1.

on the Center's right wing.[29] Their efforts received what amounted to the party's official imprimatur when, in an oft-cited letter to the leaders of the DNVP's district organization in Münster on 2 January 1920, DNVP party chairman Hergt reiterated his party's conviction that the "life forces of Christianity" constituted "an essential and indispensable foundation for the wholesome development of the German fatherland." In the same breath, Hergt stressed the DNVP's eagerness to welcome "all of those – Catholic and Protestant alike – who embraced a national politics … as equal and fully entitled members" of the party and insisted that it was the duty of all national-thinking Germans to do whatever they could to eliminate confessional tensions from German public life so as not to further complicate the already difficult task of Germany's national recovery on the basis of its Christian and national values.[30] In the short term, however, the DNVP's hopes of achieving a major breakthrough into the ranks of the Center's right wing never materialized, in large part because Catholic conservatives in the Rhineland and Westphalia chose not to affiliate themselves with the DNVP but rather to launch a new Catholic party of their own, the Christian People's Party. The architect of the new party was Baron Hermann von Lüninck, a Westphalian noble who argued that the Center had lost its historic character as a "Christian-conservative party" and that it was therefore necessary for Catholic conservatives like himself to found a new Catholic party for those who could no longer tolerate the direction in which the Center was headed. The party that Lüninck had in mind would be conservative and monarchist in terms of its basic political orientation and committed to the defense of those religious and cultural values that lay at the heart of the old Center's political mission.[31]

From December 1919 through the spring of 1920 Lüninck worked closely with Baron Clemens von Loë-Bergerhausen from the Rhenish Peasants' Union (Rheinischer Bauernverein) and Heinz Brauweiler of the *Düsseldorfer Tagesblatt* in establishing the foundations of the new party.[32] The CVP made its

---

[29] Landsberg-Steinfurt, "Darf ein Katholik deutschnational sein?" *Eiserne Blätter* 1, no. 41 (18 Apr. 1920): 717–20.

[30] "Die Deutschnationale Volkspartei und die Katholiken," 2 Jan. 1920, in *Politisches Handwörterbuch (Führer-ABC)*, ed. Max Weiß (Berlin, 1928), 319.

[31] In this respect, see Hermann von Lüninck, *Das Zentrum am Scheidewege* (Munich, 1920), and Hermann von Lüninck, "Die politische Vertretung des deutschen Katholizismus," ibid., no. 9 (1 May 1920): 555–72.

[32] Notes on a meeting of the CVP executive committee, 13 Apr. 1920, StA Mönchen-Gladbach, NL Brauweiler, 162. On the founding of the CVP, see Lüninck to Hermann zu Stolberg-Stolberg, 26. Feb. 1920, VWA Münster, NL Hermann zu Stolberg-Stolberg, 167, and Lüninck to Josef zu Stolberg-Stolberg, 12, 14, and 19 Apr. 1920, all in VWA Münster, Nachlass Josef Graf zu Stolberg-Stolberg, 330. For further details, see Reis, "Die deutschnationalen Katholiken," 262–92. On Brauweiler's role in launching the CVP, see the unpublished dissertation by Carina Simon, "Heinz Brauweiler. Eine politische Biographie

public debut in Cologne on 13 April 1920 with an appeal that denounced "the frightful revolution from the Left" and called for "Germany's rebirth out of the womb of Christianity." This broadside was directed almost exclusively against the Center, which was condemned for having abandoned the social and religious values that lay at the heart of its political mission and was therefore responsible for the deep spiritual and political crisis that had descended upon the German people.[33] In the June 1920 Reichstag elections the Christian People's Party fielded its own slate of candidates in the four districts along the lower and middle Rhine – Cologne-Aachen, Koblenz-Trier, and the two Düsseldorf districts – and received over 65,000 votes without either the resources or time to develop an effective party organization.[34] The CVP's success at the polls not only confirmed the deepening crisis in which the Center Party had found itself since the summer of 1917, but it lent renewed encouragement to those within the DNVP who were hopeful of breaking the Center's hold on the political loyalties of Germany's Catholic conservatives. At the same time, the CVP's performance in the 1920 Reichstag elections under-scored the need for the DNVP to preempt the challenge of the new party by intensifying its own efforts to win the support of Catholic conservatives who could no longer countenance the direction in which the Center was presumably headed.

On 10 August 1920 Landsberg-Velen and a handful of his closest associates met in Berlin with Lindeiner-Wildau and Graef-Anklam from the DNVP's national headquarters to finalize preparations for the creation of a special committee for Catholics within the DNVP's organizational structure. Landsberg-Velen, who had previously served as chairman of the Catholic Committee of the DNVP's State Political Coordinating Committee, was chosen to chair the new committee.[35] The purpose of this committee was to make certain that the legacy of the *Kulturkampf* had been extinguished at all

---

im Zeichen des antidemokratischen Denkens" (Ph. D. diss., Universität Kassel, 2016), 101–06.

[33] "Aufruf! An unsere christlichen Gesinnungsgenossen in Stadt und Land!," n.d. [13 Apr. 1920], VWA Münster, NL Josef Graf zu Stolberg-Stolberg, 327.

[34] *Die Christliche Volkspartei*, ed. Generalsekretariat der Christlichen Volkspartei, Rhei-nische Bücherei, no. 1 (Koblenz, n.d. [1921]), esp. 17–29.

[35] Report of the constituitive assembly of the "Reich Committee of Catholics in the German National People's Party," Berlin, 10 Aug. 1920, VWA Münster, NL Landsberg, E1, also in LaNRW Münster, NL Schorlemer-Lieser, C113/B 42. See also Lejeune-Jung to Stolberg, 23 Aug. 1920, VWA Münster, NL Josef zu Stolberg, 324. For further details, see Reiß, "Die deutschnationalen Katholiken," 349–412; Hübner, *Rechtskatholiken*, 235–64, and Larry Eugene Jones, "Catholics on the Right: The Reich Catholic Committee of the German National People's Party, 1920–33," *Historisches Jahrbuch* 126 (2006): 221–67, here 223–30.

levels of the party organization, to advise party leaders on matters of concern to German Catholics, and to assist the party in representing "the religious, cultural, ecclesiastical, and political interests of German Catholics" as vigorously as possible.[36] Its ultimate goal, as Paul Lejeune-Jung wrote to the Center's Martin Spahn in the summer of 1921, was the "de-confessionalization" of German political life and the creation of a Christian platform upon Catholics and Protestants could stand in unity.[37] The official founding of the DNVP's new Catholic committee took place on 25 October 1920 at the DNVP's second annual party congress in Hanover.[38] The ceremonies were modest with between twenty-five to thirty party members in attendance. The fact, however, that the participants included more Protestants than Catholics and that the founding ceremonies of the DNVP's Catholic committee took place in Hanover's Lutheran Guild House (Evangelisches Vereinhaus)[39] could only have sent a confusing message to the very Catholics the DNVP was targeting for recruitment. At the same time, Landsberg-Velen and his associates tried to overcome whatever reservations of the Catholic church hierarchy may have had about their undertaking by sending a letter to the Catholic bishops and the recently appointed Papal Nuncio Eugenio Pacelli in which they outlined the reasons that had led him and his fellow Catholics to join the DNVP and requested that the party to which they now belonged be accorded the same support and understanding historically reserved for the Center.[40] But this overture encountered a cool response from the German episcopacy and did little to soften the essentially negative attitude of Germany's Catholic hierarchy to the DNVP and its solicitation of Catholic votes.[41] The obstacles confronting the leaders of the DNVP's Reich Catholic Committee in their efforts to secure a breakthrough into the right wing of the Center were indeed formidable.

---

[36] "Aufgaben der Ausschüsse der Katholiken in der Deutschnationalen Volkspartei," n.d., VWA Münster, NL Landsberg, E1, also in *Über die politische und parteipolitische Stellung der katholischen Deutschen. Von einem solchen* (Berlin, n.d. [1921]), 47–48.

[37] Lejeune-Jung to Spahn, 21 July 1921, BA Koblenz, Nachlass Martin Spahn, 172.

[38] Landsberg, "Der Reichsausschuß der Katholiken in der Deutschnationalen Volkspartei," *Katholisches Korrespondenzblatt, Werbe-Nummer* (n.d.), 2–3. See also Viktor Lukassowitz, *Wir Katholiken in der Deutschnationalen Volkspartei* (Breslau, n.d. [2001]), 134–38.

[39] Report of unknown provenance on the founding of the DNVP's National Committee for Catholics, 25 Oct. 1920, BA Koblenz, Nachlass Josef Wirth, 62. See also the entry in Gallwitz's diary, 25 Oct. 1920, BA-MA Freiburg, NL Gallwitz, 36.

[40] Undated copies of the letter addressed to Pacelli and the *Denkschrift* accompanying it are to be found in VWA Münster, NL Landsberg, E4, and in Stadtarchiv Paderborn (hereafter cited as StA Paderborn), "Dokumentation Paul Lejeune-Jung," Bestand S 2/125.

[41] Minutes of the DNVP's Reich Catholic Committee, 3 Feb. 1921, VWA Münster, NL Landsberg, E1.

The Prussian Campaign

The first test for DNVP's Reich Catholic Committee would come in the campaign for the Prussian state elections on 20 February 1921. From the perspective of the DNVP, Prussia had been the driving force behind the process of German unification in the previous century and embodied all of those traditions that were associated with Germany's rise as a great power. It was to these traditions, the Nationalists asserted, that Germany would have to return if she was ever to regain the great-power status she had enjoyed before World War I. But Prussia had been controlled by the parties of the Weimar Coalition ever since the elections to the Prussian constitutional assembly in early 1919, a position from which they had encouraged the dismemberment of Prussia by granting far-reaching autonomy to its various provinces. The call for new elections thus afforded the leaders of the DNVP an opportunity not only to break the Weimar Coalition's hold on power in Prussia but also to put a stop to its efforts to destroy the very institutions that were essential for Germany's return to great-power status.[42] At the same time, the Nationalists sought to use the Prussian campaign as a public referendum on the policies of the Fehrenbach cabinet since assuming office in the summer of 1920. DNVP strategists thus pursued a two-fold goal in the 1921 Prussian campaign. For just as they hoped that the results of the February election would produce a fundamental change in the policies and composition of the Prussian government, they also they sought to inflict such heavy damage upon the three parties that supported the Fehrenbach cabinet – the Center, DDP, and DVP – that the national government's mandate to rule would be seriously compromised. This would then provide the Nationalists with the leverage they needed to force a change of government in the Reich as well. The conquest of Prussia represented the first step toward the reestablishment of conservative hegemony throughout the rest of Germany at the same time that it constituted an essential prerequisite for the success of this endeavor.[43]

Hergt opened the Nationalist campaign in the Prussian Landtag elections with a major programmatic speech in Berlin's Philharmonic Hall on 9 January 1921. His speech began with a brief but nonetheless dramatic sketch of the desperate diplomatic situation in which Germany found itself sign the ratification of the Versailles Treaty and attacked the Fehrenbach government and the parties that supported it for Germany's diplomatic weakness. In the course of his remarks Hergt took special pains to include Stresemann's German

---

[42] "Preußenprogramm der Deutschnationalen Volkspartei, n.d. [Jan. 1921], NL Westarp, Gärtringen, VN 32.

[43] Undated draft of its election appeal for the Prussian campaign, NL Westarp, Gärtringen, VN 30, as well as Kreth to Oldenburg-Januschau, 27 Oct. 1920., ibid., II/5. For further details, see Ohnezeit, *Zwischen "schärfster Opposition,"* 222–26.

People's Party in his condemnation of the Fehrenbach cabinet and cited in particular its failure to block acceptance of the recent reparations accord that Germany had signed at Spa as a sign of the DVP's unreliability in matters of foreign policy. By the same token, the DVP was also held responsible for the continuation of Erzberger's fiscal policies under Joseph Wirth, his successor at the ministry of finance, and for the government's refusal to schedule new Prussian elections as soon as possible. All of this, concluded Hergt, suggested that the DVP was unwilling to pursue any course of action that might jeopardize the possibility of a coalition with the Majority Socialists. This, to his way of thinking, constituted nothing less than a betrayal of the mandate the DVP had received in the June 1920 Reichstag elections.[44] By targeting the DVP in this fashion, Hergt and the leaders of the DNVP were trying to reverse the victory the DVP had scored at the polls in the most recent Reichstag elections and to reestablish their party as the dominant force on the German Right. Stresemann and the leaders of the DVP immediately countered this strategy by inviting all of those, including the DNVP and the Majority Socialists, who were prepared to set aside their domestic differences for the sake of greater national solidarity in the conduct of German foreign policy to join the DVP and other government parties in the creation of a "national unity front."[45] When the Nationalists rejected this proposal on 2 February 1921,[46] Stresemann immediately seized upon the DNVP's refusal to participate in a broadly based "war cabinet" embracing all of those who had rallied to the German war effort in August 1914 as a sign of its unreliability in matters of Germany's national interest and assailed the Nationalists for placing short-term electoral gains ahead of the need for national unity in the face of Allied pressure.[47]

While Hergt made the DVP the principal target of his attack in his speech in Berlin's Philharmonic Hall, by no means did the Nationalists exempt the Center from its invective against the national government and the parties that supported it.[48] With the creation of the DNVP's Reich Catholic Committee

[44] Oskar Hergt, *Auf zum Preußenkampf. Rede am Sonntag, den 9. Januar 1921, in der Philharmonie in Berlin*, Deutschnationale Flugschrift, no. 93 (Berlin, 1921), esp. 10–13.

[45] *Nationalliberale Correspondenz. Pressedienst der Deutschen Volkspartei*, 17 Jan. 1921, no. 13.

[46] On these negotiations, see *Die Bemühungen der Deutschen Volkspartei um die Bildung einer nationalen Einheitsfront*, ed. DVP, Reichsgeschäftsstelle (Berlin, n.d. [1921]), 1–9. For the DVP's position, see Stresemann to Hergt, 3 and 10 Feb. 1921, PA AA Berlin, NL Stresemann, 237/142456–58, 142503–04.

[47] [Stresemann], "Zur Frage der nationalen Einheitsfront," *Deutsche Stimmen* 33, no. 8 (20 Feb. 1921): 113–17.

[48] For example, see Walther Graef-Anklam, *Preußenpolitik. Rede in der Preuß. Landesversammlung am 14. Januar 1921*, Deutschnationale Flugschrift, no. 99 (Berlin, n.d. [1921]), 10–11.

the Nationalists began to target the Center's electoral base in the same way that it had attacked that of the DVP. The campaign found the Center very much on the defensive, in part because it was still recoiling from the heavy losses it had sustained in the June 1920 Reichstag elections[49] but also because Stegerwald's appeal at Essen for the creation of a "sociologically heterogeneous, interconfessional Christian people's party" had given rise to a new round of doubts about the Center's future existence. Speaking at a seminar for DNVP activists in December 1920, Paul Lejeune-Jung cited Stegerwald's Essen appeal as further evidence of the deepening crisis in which the Center found itself and as a sign of the political realignment that had been taking place among German Catholics since the last years of the war. A former Centrist who had defected to the DNVP earlier in the year and was now Landsberg-Velen's second-in-command in the leadership of the DNVP's Reich Catholic Committee, Lejeune-Jung claimed that under Erzberger the Center had rebaptized itself as a middle party and in so doing had jettisoned the religious and conservative principles upon which it had been founded. The only way the Center could revive its flagging electoral fortunes, Lejeune-Jung concluded, was to evoke the specter of a new *Kulturkampf*, whereas the DNVP sought to exclude confessional differences from German political life and hoped to unify the two confessions in the defense of Germany's Christian culture.[50] The Center responded by denouncing the DNVP's appeal for an interconfessional defense of Germany's Christian culture as little more than a ploy to dupe well-meaning Catholics into embracing an essentially Lutheran vision of what that culture should be and took particular umbrage at the anti-Catholic polemics on the part of prominent DNVP Protestants.[51] The leaders of the DNVP's Reich Catholic Committee responded to this charge by attacking the Center for injecting divisive confessional issues into the campaign at a time when the

---

[49] On the situation in the Center, see the minutes of the conference of representatives of the Center's provincial and state committees in Würzburg, 12 Sept. 1920, records of the German Center Party, ACDP Sankt Augustin, Bestand VI-051, 081.

[50] Paul Lejeune-Jung, *Das Zentrum. Vortrag im politischen Lehrgang der Deutschnationalen Volkspartei am 17. Dezember 1920*, Deutschnationale Flugschrift, no. 83 (Berlin, 1921), 2–4, 7–8. See also Lejeune-Jung's comments at the 82nd evening workshop of the DNVP's State Political Coordinating Committee on "Stegerwald und wir," 12 Oct. 1921, NL Westarp, Gärtringen, II/8. On Lejeune-Jung's political career, see Franz-Josef Weber, "Paul Lejeune-Jung (1882–1944)," in *Deutsche Patrioten in Widerstand und Verfolgung 1933–1945. Paul Lejeune-Jung – Theodor Roeningh – Josef Wirmer – Georg Frhr. von Boeselager. Ein Gedenkschrift der Stadt Paderborn*, ed. Friedrich Gerhard Hohmann (Paderborn, 1986), 7–19.

[51] For example, see Franz Steffen, *Deutschnationale Volkspartei – Christentum – Katholizismus. Eine grundsätzliche Auseinandersetzung* (Berlin, 1922), esp. 38–93. See also "Wahlkampfmethoden der Deutschnationalen Volkspartei," *Mitteilungen der Deutschen Zentrumspartei* 2, nos. 7–8 (28 Feb. 1921): 56–61.

need for national unity was greater than ever.[52] At the same time, the DNVP Catholics repeatedly challenged the Center's credentials as a "true" representative of Germany's Catholic population and asked whether it, by virtue of its close identification with Germany's new republican system, had effectively abdicated its commitment to defend its interests.[53]

With their attacks against the DVP and Center, DNVP campaign strategists clearly hoped to accelerate the swing to the right that had made itself felt in the June 1920 Reichstag elections. As in the past, the DNVP supplemented its broadsides against political rivals with direct appeals to the social and economic interests of the various vocational groups that constituted its material base. For example, the DNVP appealed to the farmer by pointing to its efforts to dismantle the controlled economy in agriculture and end government controls over agricultural prices and production,[54] to the salaried employee by championing a reform and expansion of the exiting program of white-collar insurance and addressing the housing shortage that weighed so heavily upon the welfare of Germany's white-collar population,[55] to the wage laborer by urging a reform of the existing system of unemployment insurance and the creation of workers' courts to adjudicate disputes with management,[56] to the civil servant by stressing its commitment to defend the historic rights of the professional civil service in the face of the leveling pressures of the modern democratic state,[57] to the public school teacher not only by reaffirming the Christian foundations of German public education, but also by supporting measures to alleviate the salary inequities teachers had experienced as a result of the postwar inflation,[58] and lastly to the independent middle class and small

---

[52] Declaration adopted by the DNVP's Reich Catholic Committee, 3 Feb. 1921, VWA Münster, NL Landsberg, E1, and published in the *Katholisches Korrespondenzblatt* 1, no. 2 (8 Apr. 1921): 1–2. See also Reichsausschuß der Katholiken in der Deutschnationalen Volkspartei, *Die Deutschnationale Volkspartei und der katholische Volksteil Deutschlands*, Deutschnationales Rüstzeug, Sonder-Lieferung 1 (Berlin, n.d. [1921]).

[53] *Der Kampf gegen die deutschnationalen Katholiken*, ed. Landes-Ausschuß der Katholiken in der deutschnationalen Volkspartei für die Provinz Westfalen (Münster, 1921).

[54] Josef Kaufhold, *Die Tätigkeit der Deutschnationalen Volkspartei für die Landwirtschaft im Reichstage*, Deutschnationale Flugschrift, no. 70 (Berlin, n.d. [1920]. See also Emil Ebersbach, *Die Tätigkeit der Deutschnationalen Volkspartei in der verfassungsgebenden Preußischen Landesversammlung* (Berlin, n.d. [1920]), 15–19.

[55] Gustav Lindenberg, *Politische Aufgaben der Angestellten*, Deutschnationale Flugschrift, no. 56 (Berlin, 1920), 16–18. See also Paul Krellmann, *Die Privatangestellten und die Deutschnationale Volkspartei*, Deutschnationale Flugschrift, no. 100 (Berlin, 1921), 5–11.

[56] *Arbeiterfragen in der Preußenversammlung*, Deutschnationale Flugschrift, no. 64 (Berlin, 1920), 2–4.

[57] "Ein Jahr Deutschnationale Beamtenschaft," n.d. [Feb. 1921], NL Westarp, Gärtringen, VN 32. See also Ebersbach, *Tätigkeit*, 22–29.

[58] Viktor Lukassowitz, *Die Tätigkeit der Deutschnationalen Volkspartei in der Preuß. Landesversammlung für die Volksschule und ihre Lehrer*, Deutschnationale Flugschrift, no. 74 (Berlin, n.d. [1920]), 2–4, 12–18. See also Ebersbach, *Tätigkeit*, 25–26, 29–31.

business sector by reminding it of its unequivocal commitment to the struggle against socialism in all of its mriad forms.[59] But one issue that did not figure as prominently in the DNVP's Prussian campaign as it had in the party's previous campaigns was antisemitism. After the 1920 Reichstag elections Hergt and the party's more moderate leaders had concluded that the agitation of the DNVP's antisemitic wing had damaged their party's performance at the polls.[60] But the decision to mute the antisemitic rhetoric that had played such a prominent role in the 1919 and 1920 campaigns came under a sharp attack from Graef-Anklam and party racists at the DNVP's national headquarters in a way that seriously exacerbated the rift within the party on the so-called Jewish question. As the former general and DNVP Reichstag deputy Max von Gallwitz noted in his diary after a particularly heated session of the DNVP Reichstag delegation, the issue was so divisive that the unity of the party itself was at stake.[61]

For all of the energy the leaders of the DNVP had invested in the crusade to free Prussia from the grips of the Weimar Coalition outcome of the Prussian elections on 20 February 1921 proved a bitter disappointment. DNVP party leaders could derive a measure of satisfaction from the fact that their party had improved upon its performance in the 1919 elections to the Prussian consti- tutional assembly by approximately 1.1 million votes and had increased its percentage share of the Prussian vote from 11.2 in 1919 to 18.0 in 1921, thus extending a string of victories that had begun with the 1920 Reichstag elec- tions.[62] But the Nationalists had anticipated even more significant gains than those their party actually achieved and were particularly annoyed by the fact that the rival DVP had outperformed the DNVP by increasing its popular vote by almost 1.4 million votes and its share of the Prussian vote from 5.7 to 14.0 percent.[63] And while the Center lost more nearly a quarter of its 1919 vote, it actually improved upon its performance in the 1920 Reichstag elections by more than a percentage point, an outcome that party officials attributed in part to the Center's success in recapturing much of the ground it had surrendered in 1920 to the Christian People's Party in Koblenz-Trier and to the DNVP in

---

[59] Gustav Budjuhn, *Mittelstandsfragen. Vortrag im Politischen Lehrgang der Deutschnatio- nalen Volkspartei am 15. Dezember 1920*, Deutschnationalen Flugschrift, no. 81 (Berlin, 1921), 3–6, 10–12, and Gustav Budjuhn, *Gewerbliche Mittelstandspolitik in der Preu- ßischen Landesversammlung*, Deutschnationale Flugschrift, no. 92 (Berlin, 1921).

[60] For example, see Kahrstedt, "Kritik," *Eiserne Blätter* 1, no. 50 (20 June 1920): 864–66, and Kahrstedt, "Nochmals zum Antisemitismus," ibid., 2, no. 4 (25 July 1920): 51–55.

[61] Entry in Gallwitz's diary, 31 Jan. 1921, BA-MA Freiburg, NL Gallwitz, 36.

[62] Falter, Lindenberger, and Schumann, *Wahlen und Abtimmungen*, 101.

[63] Letter from Ada Gräfin von Westarp to Gertraude Freifrau Hiller von Gaertringen, 23 Feb. 1921, NL Westarp, Gärtringen.

other parts of the Rhineland and Westphalia.[64] What this suggested was that the DNVP's Reich Catholic Committee had not been particularly successfully in winning the support of Catholic conservatives who had become disillusioned with the Center's shift to the left. Despite their gains at the polls, the DNVP and DVP had failed to break the hold the parties of the Weimar coalition held over Prussian political life and that they were still confronted by a parliamentary majority that was firmly committed to the republican system of government. Although the government parties had seen their mandate in the Prussian Landtag reduced from 304 to 211 seats, they still held a slim parliamentary majority that left their control of the state government weakened but essentially intact.[65] If the outcome of the Prussian Landtag elections was to have any political fallout, it would not be in Prussia but in the Reich.

Retreat into Demagogy

The results of the Prussian Landtag elections in February 1921 confirmed the swing to the right that had taken place in Germany's political landscape since the summer of 1919. The political mandate of the Fehrenbach cabinet was severely weakened by the election outcome, and pressure for the extension of the government to the right continued to mount in the wake of the DNVP's victory at the polls. Acting on his own initiative and without encouragement from the DVP's coalition partners,[66] Stresemann wrote to Hergt in late February and proposed that representatives from their two parties meet to discuss the circumstances under which the DNVP might enter the government. Hergt promptly responded that his party fully recognized the dangers inherent in Germany's diplomatic situation and was therefore willing to discuss entering into negotiations aimed at the formation of a "broad-based coalition born out of national need [*aus der nationalen Not geborenen Gesamtkoalition*]," though without explicitly committing himself or his party to a coalition with the Majority Socialists.[67] On 2 March Stresemann and two other members of his party – Alfred Zapf and Adolf Kempkes – met with Hergt, Helfferich, and Westarp from the DNVP. This time Hergt indicated that his party was not only willing to enter into formal negotiations about the creation

---

[64] Alois Kloecker, *Der erste Preußische Landtag. Ein Handbuch über die preußischen Landtagswahlen und den Landtag* (Berlin, 1921), 24–44.

[65] Dietrich Orlow, *Weimar Prussia, 1918–1925: The Unlikely Rock of Democracy* (Pittsburgh, PA, 1986), 77–81.

[66] Stresemann's notes on a meeting with the leaders of the other government parties, 22 Feb. 1921, PA AA Berlin, NL Stresemann, 237/142497–502.

[67] Hergt to Stresemann, 25 Feb. 1921, PA AA Berlin, NL Stresemann, 237/142520–21. No copy of Stresemann's letter to Hergt has survived.

of a "national unity front," but that it was also prepared to make far-reaching concessions to make the formation of such a front possible. In return, Hergt stipulated that the government in Prussia should be reorganized along the same lines as in the Reich and that certain Social Democratic demands, such as those for socialization of industry, be shelved for the duration of the proposed unity front. Skeptical that either the DDP or Center would go along with such an arrangement, Stresemann suggested that, should these efforts fail, the DVP would then seek to reorganize the government in Prussia along the lines of the bourgeois minority coalition that currently governed the Reich. In this case, Stresemann insisted, the support of the DNVP would be crucial and a test of just how serious the party was about sharing the burden of governmental responsibility.[68]

The following day Stresemann met with the DNVP party leaders again, this time with representatives from the two parties' delegations to the newly elected Prussian Landtag. Once again the two parties affirmed their willingness to join a broadly based coalition government stretching from the DNVP to the Majority Socialists, but only if the government in Prussia was reorganized along the same lines on which the national government was taking shape.[69] But this was a condition to which the Center would not accede, and in the second week of March Carl Trimborn, the Center's national party chairman, announced that his party would not take part in a reorganization of the Prussian cabinet and would insist instead upon the retention of the existing governmental coalition.[70] Trimborn's declaration, which spelled an end to Stresemann's efforts to bring the DNVP into the government, could only have brought a sigh of relief from those in the DNVP who were not yet prepared to share the burden of governmental responsibility. There remained, however, a remote possibility that Stresemann might still be asked to form a new government that could conceivably include representatives from the DNVP. But when the Allied Supreme Council in London issued an ultimatum on 5 May 1921 that threatened occupation of the Ruhr if Germany did not accept an Allied schedule for the payment of reparations with Germany's total obligation set at 132 billion gold marks, Stresemann informed the other government parties that he could not assume responsibility for the formation of a new

---

[68] Memorandum of a meeting of the DVP's Stresemann, Kempkes, and Zapf with the DNVP's Hergt, Helfferich, and Westarp, 2 Mar. 1921, BA Koblenz, R 45 II, 355/93–97.
[69] For the DNVP's position, see Westarp to Traub, 2 Apr. 1921, NL Westarp, Gärtringen, II/83.
[70] Stresemann's remarks at a meeting of the DVP managing committee, 8 Mar. 1921, BA Koblenz, R 45 II/355/143–73, reprinted in *Nationalliberalismus in der Weimarer Republik. Die Führungsgremien der Deutschen Volkspartei 1918–1933*, ed. Eberhard Kolb and Ludwig Richter, 2 vols. (Düsseldorf, 1999), 1:404–16. See also Stresemann's memorandum, 9 Mar. 1921, PA AA Berlin, NL Stresemann, 237/142566–69. For further details, see Wright, *Stresemann*, 167–79, and Richter, *Deutsche Volkspartei*, 223–39.

government if that also meant that he and his party would have to vote for the unconditional acceptance of the allied ultimatum.[71]

Stresemann's announcement cleared the way for the installation of Joseph Wirth, a member of the Center's left wing closely identified with the much reviled Erzberger, as the new chancellor on 9 May 1921.[72] With Wirth's appointment as chancellor, the DNVP retreated once again to the comfort of unconditional opposition.[73] No Nationalist was more effective in mobilizing the passions of its electorate in the immediate postwar period than Karl Helfferich. Born in 1872, Helfferich had a long and distinguished career as one of Germany's leading experts in the field of public finance before the outbreak of World War I. During the war he had risen to the post of state secretary in the Reich Ministry of Finance and had become as one of chancellor Theobald von Bethmann Hollweg's most trusted political advisors with his appointment as vice chancellor and Reich minister of the interior in 1916. But his close wartime ties to Bethmann had made him persona non grata in conservative circles during the latter stages of the war, and he failed in his efforts to secure a candidacy on the Nationalist ticket in the elections to the Weimar National Assembly.[74] Helfferich languished on the margins of German political life for several months before launching his political comeback with a impassioned speech against Germany's acceptance of the Versailles Peace Treaty at the University of Berlin on 26 June 1919. Helfferich would use this as an occasion to resume his crusade against the one person whom he held more responsible than any other for the humiliation of Versailles, Reich Finance Minister Matthias Erzberger. Not only had Erzberger been the driving force behind the passage of the Peace Resolution in July 1917, but it was Erzberger who had travelled to Compiegne in November 1918 to sign the armistice that ended the war. And now it was Erzberger who, in apparent indifference to the deep sense of national outrage to which the publication of the Allied peace terms had given rise, went to Versailles and signed a treaty that constituted the epitome of German disgrace. And for this, Helfferich concluded, Erzberger had earned for himself the title of "debaucher of the Reich [*Reichsverderber*]."[75]

---

[71] Wright, *Stresemann*, 179–81.

[72] For further details, see Ulrike Hörster-Philipps, *Joseph Wirth 1879–1956. Eine politische Biographie* (Paderborn, 1998), 98–115.

[73] For further details, see Philipp, *Die Deutschnationale Fraktion*, 136–52, as well as Wilhelm Bazille, "Die Annahme des Londoner Ultimatums im Reichstag," *Nationale Blätter*, ed. Württembergische Bürgerpartei 1, no. 19 (19 June 1921): 153–57.

[74] John G. Williamson, *Karl Helfferich, 1872–1924: Economist, Financier, Politician* (Princeton, NJ, 1971), 60–285.

[75] Karl Helfferich, *Der Friede von Versailles. Rede an die akademische Jugend gehalten am 26. Juni 1919 im Auditorium Maximum der Berliner Universität*, Deutschnationale Flugschrift, no. 20 (Berlin, n.d. [1919]).

Figure 4. Photograph of Karl Helfferich, DNVP Reichstag deputy from 1920 to 1924 and the party's most prominent critic of German reparations policy. Reproduced from the private collection of the author

Helfferich's attacks against Erzberger and his famous battle-cry "Fort mit Erzberger" quickly moved him to the center of Germany's political stage.[76] The crusade against Erzeberger drew to a preliminary climax in the spring of 1920 when the beleagured finance minister sued Helfferich for slander and lost his case in court.[77] The role that Helfferich played in bringing about Erzberger's political disgrace no doubt helped him win election to the Reichstag in June 1920, whereupon he was quickly accepted into the inner councils of the Nationalist party leadership and became one of Hergt's most trusted advisors.[78] Helfferich resumed his attacks against Erzberger following the former finance minister's attempts at political rehabilitation in early 1921 and emerged as one of the German Right's most unrelenting and effective critics of the "policy of fulfillment" that Wirth and his foreign minister Walther

[76] See Helfferich's wartime speeches against Erzberger in Karl Helfferich, *Fort mit Erzberger!* (Berlin, 1919).
[77] See Karl Helfferich, *Wer ist Erzberger? Rede im Prozeß Erzberger-Helfferich (Sitzung vom 20. Januar 1920)*, Deutschnationale Flugschrift, no. 44 (Berlin, n.d. [1920]).
[78] Westarp to Heydebrand, 30 Mar. 1921, NL Westarp, Gärtringen, II/85.

Rathenau initiated upon assuming office in May 1921. An expert in the area of public finance, Helfferich postulated a direct relationship between the onset of the inflation in the early 1920s and efforts by Erzberger, Wirth, and their Social Democratic allies to finance the payment of reparations through the expropriation of Germany's propertied classes. Helfferich was thus able to lay the increasing economic hardship that the German middle classes experienced in the first years of the Weimar Republic at the doorstep of those republican politicians who were committed to fulfilling the terms of the Versailles Peace Treaty and the London Ultimatum.[79] Helfferich's speeches from 1919 to 1923 were masterpieces of political demagogy that enabled the DNVP to translate nationalist frustration over the Versailles peace settlement and middle-class anxiety over the collapse of the mark into a mandate for repudiation of the Weimar Republic. The Nationalists were thus able to shift the focus of middle-class anxiety over the collapse of the German currency from the economic to the political arena. Only the repudiation of the London Ultimatum and all future reparations demands, the Nationalists argued, would make it possible for Germany to recover from the ravages of war and inflation. And this would require not just a change of goverments but, more importantly, a change of governmental systems.[80]

Tweaking the Nationalist Profile

Though temporarily shaken by Erzberger's assassination by right-wing extremists on 24 August 1921 and stunned by allegations that held the DNVP accountable for Erzberger's murder, neither Helfferich nor the leaders of the DNVP let this deter them from their emotionally charged crusade against the policy of fulfillment and the political system they held responsible for Germany's diplomatic impotence.[81] Erzberger's murder and the crusade against fulfillment formed the immediate context for the DNVP's third annual party congress in Munich in the first week of September 1921.[82] Party strategists were eager to secure an organizational foothold in Bavaria, a predominantly

---

[79] Karl Helfferich, *Schuldknechtschaft! 155 Milliarden jährliche Reichsausgabe. Reichstags-rede am 6. Juli 1921* (Berlin, 1921), 4–22.

[80] For samples of Helfferich's rhetoric, see Karl Helfferich, *Steuerkompromiß und nationale Opposition. Reichstagsreden vom 16. und 20, März 1922* (Berlin, 1922), and idem, *Deutschlands Not. Reichstagsrede, gehalten am 23. Juni 1922* (Berlin, 1922).

[81] Karl Helfferich, *Deutschland in den Ketten des Ultimatums*, Deutschnationale Flugschrift, no. 107 (Berlin, 1921).

[82] On the Munich congress, see Pflug's report at the 81st evening workshop of the DNVP's State Political Coordinating Committee on "Der Münchener Parteitag," 19 Sept. 1921, NL Westarp, Gärtringen, II/8, as well as the detailed report in "Der Parteitag der Deutsch-nationalen Volkspartei in München," supplement to the *Nationale Blätter*, ed. Württem-bergische Bürgerpartei 2, no. 1 (9 Oct. 1921): 9–12.

Catholic state in which conservatives had not fared particularly well before 1914 and where disgruntlement over the Center's political course had led to the founding of a separate Catholic party in the form of the Bavarian People's Party. By holding the 1921 party congress in the citadel of Bavarian Catholicism, the DNVP hoped to take advantage of the growing rift that had developed between Munich and Berlin over the disarmament of Bavaria's civilian defense units, or *Einwohnerwehren*, at the same time that they sought to help the Bavarian DNVP secure a breakthrough into the ranks of Bavaria's Catholic conservataives who were in the process of launching their own political party, the Bavarian Royal Party (Bayerische Königspartei) to the right of the BVP.[83] Given the deep-seated hostility that broad sectors of Bavaria's propertied classes felt toward the policies emanating from Berlin, the leaders of the DNVP sought to insinuate their party as skillfully as possible into the Bavarian equation and mobilize a source of electoral support that had previously stood well outside the orbit of political conservatism.[84]

In his keynote address on the evening of 1 September 1921, DNVP party chairman Oskar Hergt reaffirmed his party's unconditional opposition to the national government and its domestic and foreign policies. Refering to the recent Allied demarché calling for the partition of Upper Silesia despite the outcome of the League of Nations conducted there, Hergt declared: "In the area of domestic politics our position commits us to the sharpest opposition against the national government as the bearer of the ultimatum and the policies that led to it. And if we had not yet arrived at the resolve to wage the strongest possible opposition," Hergt continued, "then after the events of the last days it would be more necessary than ever." Then, towards the end of his speech, Hergt entoned what would become the *Leitmotiv* of the congress when he dedicated the DNVP to the "consolidation of all those national elements at home that have taken a stand against international insanity, that are committed to the struggle for national self-determination, and that are fighting alongside us in the battle for the freedom of Germany's national economy."[85]

On the second day of the congress Friedrich Brunstäd, a Lutheran theologian from the University of Erlangen, spoke on the topic of "Völkisch-nationale Erneuerung." Highly regarded in right-wing circles as an eloquent and

---

[83] Rudolf Endres, "Der Bayerische Heimat- und Königsbund," in *Land und Reich/Stamm und Nation. Probleme und Perspektiven bayerischer Geschichte. Festgabe für Max Spindler zum 90. Geburtstag*, ed. Andreas Kraus, 4 vols. (Munich, 1984): 3: 415–36, esp. 416–18.

[84] On the DNVP in Bavaria, see Kittel, "Zwischen völkischen Fundamentalismus und gouvernementaler Taktik," 868–77.

[85] Oskar Hergt, *Deutschnationale Politik im Reich und Preußen. Rede auf dem dritten Parteitage der Deutschnationalen Volkspartei in München am 1. September 1921*, Deutschnationale Flugschrift, no. 118 (Berlin, 1921), 17–19.

articulate spokesman for the Christian-social philosophy of the state, Brunstäd took it upon himself to sketch out the ideological and spiritual foundation upon which the consolidation of German Right should take place. Denouncing the atomization and fragmentation of modern mass society, Brunstäd stressed the organic character of state, society, and nation, all of which were rooted in and derived their vitality from the life of the *Volk*.[86] Brunstäd was followed by Hans Hilpert, chairman of the DNVP in Bavaria who portrayed his party as the only truly national force in Bavarian political life and recounted the role it had played in the reestablishment of law and order following the Munich soviet of 1919.[87] And on the following day Helfferich produced a detailed, if not depressing, analysis of Germany's financial situation in which he denounced the Wirth government for its financial irresponsibility and attacked in particular the high rate of direct taxation on income and property to which Wirth had resorted as assault upon the institution of private property.[88] But the greatest sensation of the Munich congress was reserved for Martin Spahn, a prominent Catholic intellectual who announced to the great jubilation of the DNVP's Reich Catholic Committee that he was leaving the Center to join the DNVP in its crusade for a united German Right. That the DNVP should be meeting in the heart of Bavaria, continued Spahn, was both proof that the DNVP embodied a new and more comprehensive species of German conservatism and an invitation to Catholics throughout the country to rethink their political sympathies and join forces with the Nationalists in the creation of a greater German Right. In the DNVP, Spahn concluded, "we Catholics see the embryo of an emerging great united Right" whose mission it will be to lay the groundwork for the resurrection of Bismarck's political masterpiece, the German Empire.[89]

Spahn was a major figure in the young conservative intelligentsia of the early Weimar Republic, and his defection to the DNVP sent shock waves

---

[86] Friedrich Brunstäd, *Volkisch-nationale Erneuerung. Rede auf dem dritten Parteitage der Deutschnationalen Volkspartei in München am 2. September 1921*, Deutschnationale Flugschrift, no. 119 (Berlin, 1921).

[87] Hans Hilpert, *Die Deutschnationalen in Bayern. Rede auf dem dritten Parteitage der Deutschnationalen Volkspartei in München am 2. September 1921*, Deutschnationale Flugschrift, no. 116 (Berlin, 1921).

[88] Karl Helfferich, *Die Lage der deutschen Finanzen. Rede auf dem dritten Parteitage der Deutschnationalen Volkspartei in München am 3. September 1921*, Deutschnationale Flugschrift, no. 121 (Berlin, 1921).

[89] Martin Spahn, *Der Weg zur deutschen Rechten. Rede auf dem dritten Parteitag der Deutschnationalen Volkspartei in München am 2. Sept. 1921*, Deutschnationale Flugschrift, no. 115 (Berlin, 1921). See also Martin Spahn, "Mein Wechsel der politischen Partei," *Das neue Reich. Wochenschrift für Kultur, Politik und Volkswirtschaft* 3, no. 8 (20 Nov. 1921): 136–39. For further information, see Gabriele Clemens, *Martin Spahn und der Rechtskatholizismus in der Weimarer Republik* (Mainz, 1983), 145–68.

through the ranks of the German Center Party. As young Catholic intellectuals responded to Spahn's appeal for the creation of a united German Right with notable enthusiasm,[90] the leaders of the DNVP's Reich Catholic Committee moved to capitalize upon the excitement generated by Spahn's announcement and redoubled their efforts to secure a breakthrough into the right wing of the Center.[91] Yet while these efforts received strong and unequivocal support from Hergt and the DNVP's national leadership,[92] they caused considerable alarm among the party's Evangelical leaders, who complained that the creation of the DNVP's Reich Catholic Committee had given Catholics too much influence within the party organization and began to agitate for permission to organize a similar committee for themselves. At the end of October the DNVP's official party correspondence published an appeal calling for the creation of a Evangelical Reich Committee (Evangelischer Reichsausschuß) and inviting interested party members to the official founding of the new committee in Berlin on the anniversary of Martin Luther's birthday, 10 November 1921.[93] In December 1921 Reinhard Mumm, university professor Wilhelm Kähler, and Carl Günther Schweitzer were elected as co-chairs of the new committee. Although the DNVP was committed to the principle of confessional parity, the DNVP's Evangelical Reich Committee was dominated by conservative Lutherans who regarded their primary mission to be the defense of the Lutheran Church in an age of rampant individualism and secularism.[94] As such, its members had little intrinsic interest in cooperating with Catholics on issues of common concern and actually saw the creation of the Evangelical Reich Committee as a way to preempt the formation of an interconfessional committee consistent with the DNVP's professed commitment to parity between Catholic and Lutheran.

The DNVP's two confessional committees stood outside the organizational structure that party leaders had created for the vocational and professional committees representing agriculture, workers, white-collar employees, civil servants, teachers, and the independent middle class. This was also true of the DNVP's committees for women and youth. Women had played an important role in the mobilization of the Nationalist vote in the 1919 and 1920 elections and had worked closely with women from other parties to

---

[90] For example, see Everding to Spahn, 6 Sept. 1921, BA Koblenz, NL Spahn, 177.

[91] Lejeune-Jung to Spahn, 1 Oct. 1921, BA Koblenz, NL Spahn, 172.

[92] Hergt to Landsberg, 17 Nov. 1921, VWA Münster, NL Landsberg, E5.

[93] *Korrespondenz der Deutschnationalen Volkspartei* 4, no. 255 (29 Oct. 1921).

[94] For example, see Wilhelm Kähler, *Politik und Kirche. Die Wahrnehmung der evangelischen Belange in der Deutschnationalen Volkspartei*, Deutschnationale Flugschrift, no. 170 (Berlin, 1924). See also Nobert Friedrich, "'National, Sozial, Christlich'. Der Evangelische Reichsausschuß der Deutschnationalen Volkspartei in der Weimarer Republik," *Kirchliche Zeitgeschichte* 6 (1993): 290–311.

organize opposition to the Versailles Peace Treaty.[95] Still, women in the DNVP complained about being underrepresented in the inner councils of the party leadership and felt that they were not being taken seriously by the party's male leaders.[96] The DNVP's women activists were also stung by the fact that Anna von Gierke, one of three women who had been elected to the Weimar National Assembly on the Nationalist ticket, had been denied an opportunity to run for reelection in 1920 because of her mother's Jewish ancestry.[97] In preparation for the 1921 Munich party congress the DNVP's Reich Women's Committee circulated a set of guidelines designed to shape the party's position on issues related to the status of women. Reflecting the ideas and influence of the committee's first chairwomen, Christian-Social labor leader Margarete Behm, this document was essentially a catalog of political demands that touched upon everything from the struggle against filth and trash in the theater and cinema to the creation of parity between men and women in access to education, compensation in the workplace, and the choice of a professional career outside the home.[98] From the perspective of the DNVP party leadership, however, such a document was ill-suited as an instrument for the recruitment of women and was subsequently replaced by a more grandoise statement of the party's goals for women that had been drafted by Magdalene von Tiling, a prominent Lutheran theologians with a decidedly more conservative cast of mind than Behm. This document, entitled "Grundsätze deutschnationaler Frauenarbeit," was more ideological in tone and sacrificed the emphasis that the earlier statement had placed on practical measures aimed at achieving parity between men and women for a more traditional definition of the role of women in home and society.[99] This shift of emphasis toward a

---

[95] See Raffael Scheck, "German Conservatism and Female Political Activism in the Early Weimar Republic," *German History* 15 (1997): 34-55, and Raffael Scheck, "Women Against Versailles: Maternalism and Nationalism of Female Bourgeois Politicians in the Early Weimar Republic," *German Studies Review* 22 (1999): 21-42. See also Sneeringer, *Winning Women's Votes*, 42-51.

[96] Comments by Diers and Lehmann in the 27th evening work session (*Arbeitsabend*) of the DNVP's State Political Coordinating Committee, 14 Nov. 1919, BA Berlin, R 8005, 327/52-55.

[97] Westarp, *Konservative Politik*, ed. Hiller von Gaertringen, 143.

[98] "Richtlinien der Deutschnationalen Volkspartei für Frauenfragen," DNVP-Werbeblatt, no. 106, n.d. [1921], NL Westarp, Gärtringen, VN 35, republished as "Deutschnationale Frauenpolitik. Richtlinien der Deutschnationalen Volkspartei für Frauenfragen," in *Jahrbuch 1921 der Deutschnationalen Volkspartei* (Berlin, n.d. [1921]), 30-32. For further details, see Raffael Scheck, "Women on the Weimar Right: The Role of Female Politicians in the Deutschnationale Volkspartei (DNVP)," *Journal of Contemporary History* 36 (2001): 547-60, esp. 551-54.

[99] Annagrete Lehmann, "Ziel und Entwicklung der deutschnationalen Frauenarbeit," in *Der nationale Wille*, ed. Weiß, 326-28. On the background of this statement, see Jordan to Westarp, 18 Aug. 1921, NL Westarp, Gärtringen, VN 35. See also Andrea

more conservative conception of the German woman and her place in German society was further reflected in the speech that Paula Mueller-Otfried delivered at the 1921 Munich party congress on the role that women were to play in the rebirth of the German nation.[100] The extent to which this would help or hinder the recruitment of German women remained to be seen.

The recruitment of German youth posed a different set of problems. In Weimar political parlance the term "youth" was generally reserved for those who had been born since the turn of the century and whose formative life experience had been the deprivation of the war and the immediate postwar period. In many respects, this was a superfluous generation whose access to economic opportunity and political power was blocked by a gerontocracy that had survived the collapse of 1918 with most of its prerogatives intact. In a broader sense, however, the term "younger generation" was frequently used to include those who had been born in the 1880s and 1890s and whose social and political values had been shaped first by their involvement in the prewar German youth movement and then by their experiences at the front in World War I. In either case, the members of these two cohort groups tended to be deeply alienated from the basic values and institutions of both prewar and postwar German political life. Overcoming this alienation and integrating the so-called younger generation into the fabric of German political life would remain one of the difficult challenges that faced the parties of the Weimar Republic.[101]

Of all of the major parties of the Weimar Republic, the DNVP was the last to create its own youth organization. Like the rival German People's Party, the DNVP chose to work through the German National Youth League (Deutschnationaler Jugendbund or DNJ), an ostensibly nonpartisan youth

---

Süchting-Hänger, *"Gewissen der Nation,"* 143–49, 193–212; and Kirsten Heinsohn, "'Volksgemeinschaft' als gedachte Ordnung. Zur Geschlechterpolitik in der Deutschnationalen Volkspartei," in *Geschlechtergeschichte des Politischen. Entwürfe von Geschlecht und Gemeinschaft im 19. und 20. Jahrhundert*, ed. Gabriele Boukrif, et al (Münster, 2002), 83–106.

[100] Paula Mueller-Otfried, *Die Mitarbeit der Frau bei der Erneuerung unseres Volkes. Rede auf dem dritten Parteitage der Deutschnationalen Volkspartei in München am 2. September 1921*, Deutschnationale Flugschrift, no. 117 (Berlin, 1921). In a similar vein, see Elisabeth Spohr, "Die soziale Aufgabe der deutschnationalen Frau," in *Deutschnationaler Parteitag für Vorpommern*, 20–25.

[101] On the role of generational cleavages in Weimar political culture, see Detlev J. K. Peukert, *Die Weimarer Republik. Krisenjahre der klassischen Moderne* (Frankfurt am Main, 1987), 25–31. On the challenges of organizing German youth for political purposes, see Krabbe, *Jugendorganisationen bürgerlicher Parteien*, 35–41, and Larry Eugene Jones, "Generational Conflict and the Problem of Political Mobilization in the Weimar Republic," in *Elections, Mass Politics, and Social Change in Modern Germany: New Perspectives*, ed. Larry Eugene Jones and James Retallack (Cambridge, 1992), 347–69.

organization in which all of those who were committed to the reconstruction of the Fatherland on the basis of Germany's Christian culture could unite.[102] Under the leadership of the DNVP's Wilhelm Foellmer,[103] the DNJ enrolled 90,000 members in the first year of its existence and seemed well on its way to establishing itself as a mass organization for the more nationalistic elements of Germany's bourgeois youth.[104] But at its Nuremberg congress in August 1921 the DNJ splintered into three separate factions: the Young German League (Jungdeutscher Bund), the Young National League (Jungnationaler Bund), and what still remained of the badly decimated DNJ. The fragmentation and subsequent demise of the DNJ left the leaders of the DNVP with no alternative but to found their own youth organization. Acting on an initiative that Frank Glatzel, a young conservative activist with close ties to the German National Union of Commercial Employees and co-founder of the Young German League in August 1919, had taken at the DNVP's 1920 party congress,[105] the party's youth leaders met in Hanover at the beginning of 1922 to found the National Federation of DNVP Youth Groups (Reichsverband der Jugendgruppen der Deutschnationalen Volkspartei), an organization that renamed itself the Bismarck Youth of the German National People's Party (Bismarckjugend der Deutschnationalen Volkspartei) later that fall.[106] Unlike youth organizations attached to the Center or DDP, the Bismarck Youth was completely subordinated to the DNVP party organization and had no autonomous existence of its own.[107] Even then, the Bismarck Youth proved relatively successful in the first year or so of its existence in recruiting new party members from the ranks of the younger generation. By the middle of 1923, however, these efforts began to

[102] Westarp, *Konservative Politik*, ed. Hiller von Gaertringen, 153–55.

[103] Foellmer's brief report at a meeting of the DNVP's organizational representatives, 7–8 Feb. 1919, BA Berlin, R 8005, 1/200.

[104] On the founding and program of the DNJ, see Wilhelm Foellmer, *Der deutschnationale Jugendbund. Vorschläge und Anregungen* (Berlin, 1919).

[105] Speech by Glatzel at the DNVP Hanover party congress, 25 Oct. 1920, BA Berlin, R 8005, 53/332–34, reprinted in *Parteijugend zwischen Wandervogel und politischer Reform. Eine Dokumentation zur Geschichte der Weimarer Republik*, ed. Wolfgang R. Krabbe (Münster, 2000), 49–50.

[106] "Geschäftsbericht der Hauptgeschäftsstelle der Deutschnationalen Volkspartei (September 1921 bis Oktober 1922)," NL Westarp, Gärtringen, 88. For further details, see "Der Bismarckjugend der Deutschnationalen Volkspartei," in *Die deutschen Jugendverbände. Ihre Ziele, ihre Organisation sowie ihre neuere Entwicklung und Tätigkeit*, ed. Hertha Siemering (Berlin, 1931), 255–58, as well as Wolfgang R. Krabbe, "Die Bismarckjugend der Deutschnationalen Volkspartei," *German Studies Review* 17 (1994): 9–32.

[107] Konrad Meyer, *Organisationsfragen. Vortrag, gehalten am 23. September 1925 auf der deutschnationalen Schulungswoche*, Deutschnationale Flugschrift, no. 226 (Berlin, 1925), 12–14.

stagnate, and it was not until the end of the decade that the Bismarck Youth was able to recover any sort of momentum.[108]

In a parallel move, the DNVP also took steps to improve and consolidate its ties to labor and industry. Ever since the founding of the DNVP in the last days of 1918 Emil Hartwig, Paul Rüffer, and the leaders of the party's Christian-Social faction had been busy at work building up the Reich Workers' Committee of the DNVP.[109] By the time of the DNVP's Hanover party congress in October 1920, the leaders of the party's working-class movement could claim 15,000 registered members in fifteen district organizations across the country in addition to an estimated 45,000 to 50,000 workers and white-collar employees who belonged to the party but not to their organization.[110] In fact, the leaders of the DNVP's labor wing had been so successful in building up their organization that they demanded and received a charter that was fundamentally different from that of other party organs. At Munich Hartwig and his associates received permission to reconstitute the Reich Workers' Committee as the German National Workers' League (Deutschnationaler Arbeiterbund or DNAB), a body that reported to the DNVP's national and district leadership but enjoyed a corporate existence of its own within the DNVP party organization. This unique, if not awkward situation afforded the DNAB a measure of independence within the party organization that none of the DNVP's other vocational committees enjoyed.[111]

Just as the leaders of the DNVP were trying to solidify their party's position among the nonsocialist elements of the German labor movement, they also sought to improve ties to the German industrial establishment. The DNVP had received substantial support from both the Curatorium for the Reconstruction of German Economic Life and the Commission for the Collection, Administration, and Allocation of the Industrial Campaign Fund in the 1920 Reichstag elections and the 1921 elections to the Prussian Landtag despite the fact that for many industrialists the DVP remained the party of preference by virtue of its unequivocal commitment to the free enterprise system.[112] Most of the

---

[108] Krabbe, "Bismarckjugend," 20–27.

[109] For further details, see *Die deutschnationale Arbeiter-Bewegung, ihr Werden und Wachsen*, ed. Bundesvorstand des Deutschnationalen Arbeiterbundes (Berlin, n.d. [1925]), 10–29. See also Emil Hartwig, "Deutschnationale Arbeiterbewegung," in *Der nationale Wille*, ed. Weiß, 215–24.

[110] "Geschäftsbericht der Hauptgeschäftsstelle der Deutschnationalen Volkspartei (Juli 1919 bis Oktober 1920)," n.d., BA Berlin, NL Mumm, 276/91–95.

[111] On the DNAB, see *Aufbau und Tätigkeit des Deutschnationalen Arbeiterbundes*, ed. Bundesvorstand des Deutschnationalen Arbeiterbundes (Berlin, 1925), 6–31.

[112] On industrial support of the DNVP's campaigns in 1920, see Dryander to the Curatorium for the Reconstruction of German Economic Life, 9 June 1920, SHI Berlin, NL Siemens, 4/Lf 646, and Flathmann to Hugenberg, 16 June 1920, BA Koblenz, NL Hugenberg, 15/37. For 1921 see the memorandum of Siemens's meeting with Vögler,

money the DNVP received from the Commission for the Industrial Campaign Fund was funneled through film and press magnate Alfred Hugenberg, a member of the DNVP Reichstag delegation with extensive contacts to German industry and the Germany business community.[113] The purpose of this support was not just to strengthen the non-socialist parties to the point where they could block further socialist experimentation with the economy but also to elect deputies who either came from industry or who were sympathetic to industrial concerns.[114] Industrialists close to the DNVP would have preferred a merged with the DVP and occasionally intervened when the rhetoric between the two parties threatened to become too inflamatory.[115] But as the two right-wing parties drifted further apart in 1920–21, the leaders of the DNVP's industrial wing became increasingly concerned about their lack of influence within the party and moved to organize themselves more effectively for the sake of a stronger voice on issues related to industrial matters. In 1919 the party had established the Reich Industrial Committee of the DNVP (Reichs-Industrieausschuß der Deutschnationalen Volkspartei) under the chairmanship of DNVP Reichstag deputy Jakob Wilhelm Reichert,[116] but this committee had had little effect upon the party's economic and fiscal policies. In an effort to correct this situation, Hugenberg and Reichert met with approximately fifty party members who were either industrialists or enjoyed close ties to industry at the DNVP's 1921 party congress in Munich to found the Coordinating Committee of German National Industrialists (Arbeitsausschuß deutschnationaler Industrieller or ADI).[117]

The purpose of this organization, as Reichert explained at the ADI's official founding on 2 September 1921, was to make certain that economic factors received adequate attention within the party by providing DNVP industrialists from all parts of the Reich with a forum from which they could offer their views on policy issues affecting their welfare. The committee would pursue this objective first by compiling a comprehensive list of all the entrepreneurs and high-level corporate employees who belonged to the party and second by making it possible for those party members who were active in industry to meet and exchange views with those Nationalist deputies in the Reichstag and

---

n.d. [Feb. 1921], SHI Berlin, NL Siemens, 4/Lf 646) and Dryander to Hugenberg, 23 Feb. 1921, BA Koblenz, NL Hugenberg, 11/193–94.

[113] Holzbach, Das "System Hugenberg," 70–89.

[114] Hugenberg to Dryander, 15 Jan. 1921, BA Koblenz, NL Hugenberg, 11/313–16, and Flathmann to Hugenberg, 7 and 10 Feb. 1921, ibid., 20/60–64.

[115] For example, see the correspondence between Stresemann and Vögler, 3–9 Feb. 1920, PA AA Berlin, NL Stresemann, 220/140087–90, 140114–16.

[116] "Geschäftsbericht der Hauptgeschäftsstelle der Deutschnationalen Volkspartei (Juli 1919 bis Oktober 1920)," n.d., BA Berlin, NL Mumm, 276/91–95.

[117] Report of the ADI's first meeting, 2 Sept. 1921, Staatsarchiv Hamburg (hereafter cited as StA Hamburg), corporate archives of Blohm und Voß GmbH, 1210/11.

the various state parliaments.[118] The committee, which reserved for itself the right to form subcommittees at the district level of the party's national organization, would solidify its ties to the party leadership by inviting a member of the DNVP's Reich Vocational Committee (Berufsständischer Reichsausschuß der Deutschnationalen Volkspartei) to serve on its executive committee. At the same time, the committee would appoint Abraham Frowein and Fritz Tänzler as liasons to the National Federation of German Industry and the Federation of German Employer Associations to mediate between the party and the most influential of Germany's industrial lobbies.[119] The committee was to be headed by Hugenberg himself, who along with Reichert and the ADI's business manager would represent the ADI and its concerns to the DNVP party leadership.[120] The one task that did not fall within the ADI's purview was the collection of campaign funds from the DNVP's industrial backers, although that would change with the demise of the Commission for the Industrial Campaign Fund in the wake of the great inflation of 1922–23.[121]

By the summer of 1922 the leaders of the DNVP had succeeded in creating a comprehensive party organization that securely anchored their party in virtually every corner of Germany's conservative milieu. The DNVP was far more successful that any of its prewar predecessors in attracting a broad and socially diversified base of support. To be sure, the DNVP had been able to take advantage of the fact that as an opposition party it was spared the unpopular choices that the parties of the Weimar coalition as well as the German People's Party had to make in allocating the social cost of Germany's lost war. The legitimacy of Germany's new republican order as well as that of those parties with which the republic had become identified had been severely compromised by the disgrace of the Versailles Peace Treaty and the uncontrollable inflation of the early 1920s. All of this helped create a situation into which the DNVP, as the party that was most resolutely opposed to the new republican order, could insinuate itself with consummate ease.

---

[118] Reichert's remarks at the meeting of the ADI, 2 Sept. 1921, StA Hamburg, Blohm und Voß GmbH, 1210/11.

[119] Report by Willamowitz-Moellendorf at the meeting of the ADI, 2 Sept. 1921, StA Hamburg, Blohm und Voß GmbH, 1210/11.

[120] Report of the first meeting of the ADI, 2 Sept. 1921, StA Hamburg, Blohm und Voß GmbH, 1210/11. See also the ADI statutes, adopted at a meeting of the ADI on 4 Nov. 1921, ibid., 1210/2.

[121] Hugenberg and Reichert, "An die industriellen Freunde der Deutschnationalen Volkspartei," Oct. 1924, StA Hamburg, Blohm und Voß GmbH, 1210/11.

5

The Radical Right

By the beginning of 1922 the German National People's Party was well on its way to developing a comprehensive party organization that was securely anchored in virtually every sector of Germany's conservative milieu. Yet for all of its success in the early years of the Weimar Republic, the DNVP still remained deeply divided on fundamental questions of tactics and strategy. For although the party drew much of its integrative potential from its unremitting hostility to Germany's republican system, there remained an unresolved conflict between those who were prepared to work within the existing political system to bring about a conservative regeneration of the German state and those who rejected collaboration with Germany's fledgling republican order in any form whatsoever. This last sentiment was particularly strong among the plethora of patriotic societies and paramilitary organizations that had surfaced in Germany since the last years of the Second Empire and that stood outside the orbit of party control. What these organizations hoped to create was a sense of national identity sufficiently powerful in terms of its emotional appeal to override the social and economic cleavages that had become so deeply embedded in the fabric of Germany's political life. Most of these organizations were militantly anti-Marxist, and many regarded the Jewish problem as the ultimate source of Germany's national weakness. The oldest of Germany's patriotic societies – the Pan-German League, the German Naval League, the Society for the Eastern Marches – all traced their origins to the crisis of National Liberal hegemony in the 1880s and to the dramatic transformation that took place in the structure of the German Right in the last decade of the nineteenth century.[1] Most of these organizations, however, would disappear from Germany's political landscape after the end of World War I, while those that survived the collapse of 1918–19 were eclipsed by paramilitary organizations that drew their impetus from the explosion of violence that had

---

[1] Geoff Eley, "Reshaping the Right: Radical Nationalism and the German Navy League, 1898–1908," *Historical Journal* 21 (1978): 327–54, as well as his more detailed study *Reshaping the German Right: Radical Nationalism and Political Change after Bismarck* (New Haven and London, 1980), 19–98.

accompanied the collapse of the Second Empire and the birth of the Weimar Republic.

What the patriotic Right brought to German political culture was a new and more stridently populist tone that was directed not just against Marxists and Jews but also against established political elites and the organizations through which they exercised their social and political hegemony.[2] Not only did this reflect the general decline in civility and the heightened propensity to violence that characterized German political culture after World War I,[3] but it posed a direct challenge to the authority of the DNVP party leadership, which valued the patriotic societies as allies in the struggle against the Weimar system but experienced considerable difficulty in harnessing them to the strategic goals of the party.[4] The organizations of the patriotic Right, on the other hand, generally looked upon the world of party politics with great disdain and consistently portrayed themselves as *überparteilich*, that is, as associations that stood above the incessant haggling of the individual political parties. The patriotic societies were also extremely critical of the role that organized economic interests had come to play in the German political process and regarded it as their special mission to free Germany's national life from the tyranny of economic self-interest. Only after the grip of special interests had been broken would Germany's national rebirth be possible.

The Pan-German League

Of all the organizations on the prewar patriotic Right that survived the collapse of 1918–19, none was more important than the Pan-German League. When the Pan-German League – or, more correctly, its immediate predecessor, the General German League (Allgemeiner Deutscher Verband) – was established as an offshoot of the German Colonial Society (Deutsche Kolonialgesellschaft) in 1891, its threefold purpose was to mobilize patriotic

---

[2] This has been persuasively argued in Peter Fritzsche, *Rehearsals for Fascism: Populism and Political Mobilization in Weimar Germany* (New York and Oxford, 1990), esp. 3–16, and Geoff Eley, "Conservatives – Radical Nationalists – Fascists: Calling the People into Politics, 1890–1930," in *Transformations of Populism in Europe and the Americas: History and Recent Tendencies*, ed. John Abromeit et al. (London, 2016), 15–31.

[3] Bernd Weisbrod, "Gewalt in der Politik. Zur politischen Kultur in Deutschland zwischen den beiden Weltkriegen," *Geschichte in Wissenschaft und Unterricht* 43 (1992): 391–404. On the violence that accompanied the birth of the Weimar Republic, see Mark Jones, *Founding Weimar: Violence and the German Revolution of 1918–1919* (Cambridge, 2017).

[4] For the DNVP's attitude towards the patriotic Right, see Otto Schmidt-Hannover, *Die vaterländische Bewegung und die Deutschnationale Volkspartei. Vortrag, gehalten in Berlin am 28. März 1924*, Deutschnationale Flugschrift, no. 167 (Berlin, 1924), and Max Weiß, "Wir und die vaterländische Bewegung," in *Der nationale Wille. Werden und Wirken der Deutschnationalen Volkspartei 1918–1928*, ed. Max Weiß (Essen, 1928), 351–61.

consciousness at home, support the aspirations of ethnic Germans abroad, and promote the extension of German power and the creation of a colonial empire throughout the world.[5] Plagued by internal disorganization, declining membership, and chronic financial difficulties, the General German League reconstituted itself as the Pan-German League in 1894 and under the chairmanship of Ernst Haase expanded its national membership from an estimated 7,700 at the end of 1895 to more than 10,000 by the middle of 1897 before reaching a peak of approximately 23,000 in 1901.[6] At the same time, the Pan-Germans became increasingly critical of the general weakness that characterized the conduct of national affairs under Bismarck's successors to the chancellorship. In 1903 Heinrich Claß, Haase's heir apparent as the ADV's national chairman, delivered a blistering attack against the government of Bernhard von Bülow that reflected the organization's increasing radicalization and its disaffection from the symbols and institutions of the Second Empire.[7]

With Claß's election to the ADV national chairmanship in February 1908, the triumph of the more radical elements within the Pan-German League was effectively secured. Galvanized not only by the diplomatic embarrassment that Germany had suffered in the First Moroccan Crisis but more recently by the Kaiser's indiscretions in connection with the *Daily Telegraph* affair, the ADV portrayed itself as the leader of the "national opposition" whose mission was to redeem the national cause from those, including the Kaiser, who had served it with little more than weakness, incompetence, and betrayal.[8] For his own part, the thirty-five-year-old Claß was a psychologically insecure individual who harbored a deep and abiding hatred for those whom he deemed as enemies of Germany's historic mission, most notably Marxists and Jews. His ascendancy to the ADV's national leadership was accompanied by an intensification of Pan-German tirades against the predominant position that Jews had allegedly secured for themselves in German cultural, economic, and political life since their formal emancipation with the founding of the Second Empire in 1871.

---

[5] Roger Chickering, *We Men Who Feel Most German: A Cultural Study of the Pan-German League, 1886–1914* (Boston, 1984), 49. In addition to the book by Chickering, see also Rainer Hering, *Konstruierte Nation. Der Alldeutsche Verband 1890 bis 1939* (Hamburg, 2003), esp. 110-62; Barry A Jackisch, *The Pan-German League and Radical Nationalist Politics in Interwar Germany, 1918–39* (Farnham, 2012); and Björn Hofmeister, "Between Monarchy and Dictatorship: Radical Nationalism and Social Mobilization of the Pan-German League, 1914–1939" (Ph.D. diss., Georgetown University, 2012).

[6] Chickering, *We Men Who Feel Most German*, 57, 213.

[7] Ibid., 214-17. See also Claß, "Wandlungen in der Weltstellung des Deutschen Reiches," in *Zwanzig Jahre alldeutscher Arbeit und Kämpfe*, ed. Hauptleitung des Alldeutschen Verbandes (Leipzig, 1910), 157-227. See also Heinrich Claß, *Wider den Strom. Vom Werden und Wachsen der nationalen Opposition im alten Reich* (Leipzig, 1932), 91-97.

[8] Claß's speech, "Zusammenbruch der reichsdeutschen Politik und seine Folgen," 21 Nov. 1908, in *Zwanzig Jahre*, ed. ADV, 389-98.

Claß and his associates subscribed to a particularly virulent brand of racial antisemitism that regarded Jews as biologically inferior to their Aryan counterparts and demanded nothing less than their total exclusion from all aspects of German life.[9]

In the last years before the outbreak of World War I, the Pan-Germans became increasingly outspoken in their criticism of the Kaiser and routinely denounced the policies of his chancellor, Theobald von Bethmann Hollweg, as both the source and symbol of Germany's national weakness. Nowhere was the depth of Pan-German alienation from the symbols and institutions of the Second Empire more apparent than in the book that Claß, writing under the pseudonym of Daniel Frymann, published in 1912 under the title *Wenn ich der Kaiser wär'*. Here Claß denounced the Social Democratic gains in the recent Reichstag elections as a symptom of a deeper political crisis that was to be traced back in all of its myriad manifestations to a campaign of domestic subversion by Jews and their political acolytes. Only through the creation of a *völkisch* dictatorshp in which Jews were deprived of their rights and Socialists expelled from the country would it be possible to overcome the alienation of the *Volk* from the state and thus create a new Germany in which all classes and confessions were reconciled to each other in support of a dynamic and expansionist foreign policy throughout the world.[10] As its title suggested, Claß's book was both an attempt to cloak the Pan-German agenda in the symbols of royal authority and a direct attack upon the Kaiser for having failed to undertake the sweeping reform of Germany's domestic political system that was necessary if the nation was ever to fulfill its historic mission as a world power. Nor did Claß's attacks abate with the outbreak of World War I. Claß's memoirs record the jubilation he and his colleagues felt at the outbreak of hostilities in the fall of 1914, and they were quick to place themselves in the vanguard of those who demanded territorial annexations in both the east and the west as a *conditio sine qua non* for an end to the war.[11]

---

[9] Report by Kuhlenbeck, "Die politischen Ergebnisse der Rassenforschung," at the ADV congress in Wurms, 15–17 June 1905, in *Zwanzig Jahre*, ed. ADV, 272–75. On Claß's rise to the ADV leadership, see Johannes Leicht, *Heinrich Claß 1868–1953. Die politische Biographie eines Alldeutschen* (Paderborn, 2012), 113–25. On the ADV's conversion to antisemitism, see Chickering, *We Men Who Feel Most German*, 230–45, and Hering, *Konstruierte Nation*, 187–219.

[10] Leicht, *Claß*, 151–64. See also Björn Hofmeister, "Weltanschauung, Mobilisierungsstrukturen und Krisenerfahrungen. Antisemitische Radikalisierung des Alldeutschen Verbandes als Prozess 1912–1920," *Jahrbuch für Antisemitismusforschung* 24 (2015): 120–153, esp. 134–44.

[11] Heinrich Claß, "Der Alldeutsche Verband," *Der Panther. Monatsschrift für Politik und Volkstum*, 3, no.10 (Oct. 1915): 1137–47. See also the memorandum Claß released on 28 Aug. 1914 in Heinrich Claß, *Zum deutschen Kriegsziel. Eine Flugschrift* (Munich, 1917).

Through the creation of ancillary organizations such as the Independent Committee for a German Peace (Unabängiger Ausschuß für einen deutschen Frieden),[12] the Pan-Germans were able to exercise enormous influence upon the formation of public opinion during the war. But as the war dragged on, their exasperation over Germany's failure to secure a quick military victory and the vehemence of their attacks against those who either questioned the wisdom of the war or could be held responsible for its conduct began to mount.[13] Following the passage of the Peace Resolution in the summer of 1917, the Pan-Germans threw their support behind the German Fatherland Party, a militantly nationalistic party that had been founded without Pan-German participation in September 1917. Whereas the ADV was an elitist organization whose prewar membership had never exceeded 23,000,[14] the Fatherland Party was a mass political party that claimed a greatly exaggerated total of 1.25 million members at the height of its influence in the summer of 1918.[15] As it became ever more clear in the fall of 1918 that Germany was about to lose the war, the Pan-Germans found themselves forced more and more to the margins of German political life. At a meeting of the ADV managing committee in late October 1918 Claß and other Pan-German leaders railed against the domestic reforms of Max von Baden and his government's peace overtures toward the Allies. At the same time, the committee laid the groundwork for an intensification of its crusade against the Jews in postwar Germany by making preparations for the creation of a new organization devoted to the dissemination of racist and antisemitic propaganda. At the close of the meeting, the ADV published a resolution calling for the formation of a "cabinet of national defense" that would reestablish the spirit of August 1914 and that was committed to pursuing the war to the only acceptable conclusion, total victory.[16]

Following the German collapse in November 1918, the Pan-Germans were so severely compromised by their rabid support for Germany's most extreme

---

[12] See Unabhängiger Ausschuß für einen Deutschen Frieden, *Durch deutschen Sieg zum Deutschen Frieden. Mahnruf ans Deutsche Volk. Fünf Reden zur Lage gehalten am 19. Januar 1917 in der Versammlung des "Unabhängiger Ausschuß für einen Deutschen Frieden im Sitzungssaale des Abgeordnetenhauses zu Berlin* (Berlin, 1917).

[13] For example, see Max Kloß, *Die Arbeit des Alldeutschen Verbandes im Kriege. Rede, gehalten auf der Tagung des Alldeutschen Verbandes zu Kassel, am 7. Oktober 1917* (Munich, 1917), esp. 10–15.

[14] Chickering, *We Men Who Feel Most German*, 213.

[15] Hagenlücke, *Vaterlandspartei*, 143–64. On the shifting political landscape in the late Second Empire, see Dirk Stegmann, "Vom Neokonservatismus zum Proto-Faschismus: Konservative Parteien, Vereine und Verbände 1893–1920," in *Deutscher Konservatismus im 19. und 20. Jahrhundert. Festschrift für Fritz Fischer*, ed. Dirk Stegmann, Bernd Jürgen Wendt, and Peter-Christian Witt (Bonn, 1983), 199–230, esp. 180–87.

[16] Resolution of the ADV managing committee, 19–20 Oct. 1918, records of the Alldeutscher Verband, Bestand R 8048 (hereafter cited as BA Berlin, R 8048), 121/67–68.

war aims that they found themselves relegated to the periphery of Germany's national political life.[17] This, however, did little to moderate its radicalism or its political militancy. Meeting in Bamberg on 16 February 1919, the ADV managing committee drafted what amounted to a virtual declaration of war against Germany's emerging democratic system and called upon its supporters throughout the country to help rescue the future of the German people from the forces of decay and revolution. The "Bamberg Declaration" became the basis of ADV policy throughout the Weimar Republic and demanded, among other things, the restoration of the German empire, the reacquisition of Germany's lost territories, the incorporation of Austria into a greater Germany and, most ominously, the struggle against "all forces that inhibited or damaged the racial development of the German people – including in particular the fetish for foreign things [*Fremdsucht*] and the Jewish predominance [that had made themselves manifest] in virtually every aspect of German political, economic and cultural life."[18] With the proclamation of the "Bamberg Declaration," the antisemitism that had never been far from the surface of the ADV's prewar campaign for an expansionist foreign policy now became a clear and unmistakable feature of its postwar political profile. For not only did Claß and the leaders of the ADV hold Jews directly responsible for Germany's military defeat and for the collapse of the old imperial order, but they insisted that the systematic elimination of the Jewish influence from all aspects of their country's national life constituted an essential precondition for Germany's national recovery.[19]

For all of its fury, the "Bamberg Declaration" did little more than confirm the Pan-German League's virtual isolation in the new and radically different circumstances that had been created by the collapse of the monarchy and the establishment of the Weimar Republic. Their predicament was compounded by the fact that the newly founded German National People's Party seemed a particularly awkward instrument for the conquest of political power and did little to reassure them about the future of their own political agenda. Under these circumstances, Claß and the leaders of the ADV began to explore the possibility of closer relations with other right-wing organizations, including the nascent National Socialist German Workers' Party that had been founded

[17] The essentially defensive character of the ADV's postwar posture is clearly reflected in Alldeutscher Verband, Hauptleitung, ed., *Der Alldeutsche Verband. Eine Aufklärungsschrift* (Berlin, n.d. [ca. 1918]). See also Jackisch, *Pan-German League*, 13–29.

[18] For the text of the "Bamberger Erklärung," see *Alldeutsche Blätter*, 29, no. 9 (1 Mar. 1919): 65–69.

[19] Speech by Claß, "Der Einfluß des Judentums, der deutsche Zusammenbruch und die Wiederaufrichtung," at the ADV's first postwar congress in Berlin, 1 Sept. 1919, in *Alldeutsche Blätter* 29, no. 36 (6 Sept. 1919): 304. See also Georg Fritz, "Die Überwindung der jüdischen Fremdherrschaft," in *Deutschvölkisches Jahrbuch 1920*, ed. Georg Fritz (Weimar, 1920), 63–74.

in Munich under the leadership of Adolf Hitler.[20] At the same time, they decided to shift the focus of their activities from the political to the cultural arena and to concentrate their efforts on the dissemination of racist and antisemitic ideas throughout the public at large. In October 1919 the leaders of the ADV founded the German-Racist Protection and Defense League both as a forum for the propagation of their ideas and as a crystallization point around which all of those who shared those ideas could unite.[21] According to its official charter, the DSTB's purpose was to enlighten the public about the nature and extent of the Jewish peril and to combat that peril with all the economic and political means at its disposal. In fulfilling this mandate, the DSTB saturated the German public with a steady stream of racist and anti-semitic literature that, by the account of its general secretary Alfred Roth, produced more than twenty million pieces of propaganda in 1920 alone.[22] At the same time, the DSTB sought to establish a foothold for itself within the right-wing DNVP in hopes of transforming it into an instrument of the racist cause.[23]

The early years of the Weimar Republic were heady days for political antisemites like Claß and Roth. Germany's defeat in World War I and the emergence of the "Stab-in-the-Back Legend," the omnipresent threat of Bolshevism and social revolution, the runaway inflation of the early 1920s and, last but certainly not least, the large-scale influx of east European Jews combined to excite the antisemitic prejudices of the German people and to transform what in the Second Empire had been a general, yet essentially benign, undercurrent of antisemitic bias into open hostility.[24] To be sure, this

---

[20] For further details, see Joachim Petzold, "Claß und Hitler. Über die Förderung der frühen Nazibewegung durch den Alldeutschen Verband und dessen Einfluß auf die nazistische Ideologie," *Jahrbuch für Geschichte* 21 (1980): 247–88, See also Leicht, *Claß*, 285–97, and Barry A. Jackisch, "Continuity and Change on the German Right: The Pan-German League and Nazism, 1918–1939," in *The German Right in the Weimar Republic: Studies in the History of German Conservatism, Nationalism, and Antisemitism*, ed. Larry Eugene Jones (New York and Oxford, 2014), 166–93, esp. 166–73.

[21] Uwe Lohalm, *Völkischer Radikalismus. Die Geschichte des Deutschvölkischen Schutz- und Trutz-Bundes 1919–1923* (Hamburg, 1970), 19–24. See also Breuer, *Völkischen in Deutschland*, 150–60.

[22] Alfred Roth, *Aus der Kampfzeit des Deutschvölkischen Schutz- und Trutzbundes. Eine Erinnerungsschrift* (Hamburg, 1939), 19–23. See also Uwe Lohalm and Martin Ulmer, "Alfred Roth und der Deutschvölkische Schutz- und Trutz-Bund. 'Schrittmacher für das Dritte Reich'," in *Wegbereiter des Nationalsozialismus. Personen, Organisationen und Netzwerke der extremen Rechten zwischen 1918 und 1933*, ed. Daniel Schmidt, Michael Sturm, and Livi Massimiliao (Essen, 2015), 21–36.

[23] For further details, see Striesow, *DNVP und die Völkisch-Radikalen*, 102–62, 233–447.

[24] See Jochmann, "Die Ausbreitung des Antisemitismus," 409–510, as well as Heinrich August Winkler, "Die deutsche Gesellschaft der Weimarer Republik und der Antisemitismus – Juden als Blitzableiter," in *Vorurteil und Völkermord. Entwicklungslinien des*

was an environment in which the political message of the Pan-German League and the German-Racist Protection and Defense League found a ready audience, and there is no doubt that their relentless propaganda against the Jew and the influence he allegedly exercised over the various aspects of Germany's national life did indeed strike a resonant chord in diverse sectors of German society. Yet for all of the resonance that antisemitic propaganda began to experience in the immediate postwar period, neither the Pan-German League nor the German-Racist Protection and Defense League were able to break out of the political isolation in which they found themselves during the first years of the Weimar Republic.

Racism and the DNVP

Of the various parties that had emerged from the November revolution, only the DNVP held any real appeal for the Pan-German League and its allies in the German-Racist Protection and Defense League.[25] Racial antisemites like Ferdinand Werner, Wilhelm Bruhn, and Albrecht von Graefe-Goldebee had been involved in the DNVP since its founding in November 1918 and had used the Nationalist campaign for the 1919 elections to the Weimar and Prussian constitutional assemblies as a forum for the dissemination of their propaganda. Encouraged by their role in the 1919 elections, DNVP racists with close ties to the DSTB made a concerted effort to have an antisemitic plank inserted into the DNVP's official party program at the DNVP's Berlin party congress in the summer of 1919, but were rebuffed by party moderates who feared that this might offend significant elements of Germany's bourgeois and middle-class electorates.[26] After the DNVP's disappointing performance in the 1920 Reichstag elections in which its gains at the polls failed to keep pace with those of the rival DVP, the leader's of the DNVP's racist faction were quick to attribute this to the party's failure to highlight the Jewish question as prominently as it should have.[27] Party moderates, on the other hand, maintained that the excesses of the antisemites had offended potential voters and were thus responsible for the DNVP's poor showing relative to that of the DVP in the 1920 elections.[28]

Antisemitismus, ed. Wolfgang Benz and Werner Bergmann (Freiburg, Basel, and Vienna, 1997), 341–62.

[25] Axel von Freytagh-Loringhoven, "Der Alldeutsche Verband und die Parteien," *Alldeutsche Blätter* 30, no. 28 (16 Oct. 1920): 226–27.

[26] Streisow, *DNVP und die Völkisch-Radikalen*, 130–62. See also Breuer, *Völkischen in Deutschland*, 183–93, and Jones, "Conservative Antisemitism," 79–107.

[27] See Freytagh-Loringhoven to Westarp, 20 July 1920, NL Westarp, Gärtringen, VN 25.

[28] See Kahrstedt, "Kritik," *Eiserne Blätter* 1, no. 50 (20 June 1920): 864–66, and Kahrstedt, "Nochmals zum Antisemitismus," ibid., 2, no. 4 (25 July 1920): 51–55.

Following the 1920 elections in which no fewer than six racists were elected to the Reichstag on the Nationalist ticket, the party's racist faction intensified its efforts to force a change in the DNVP's organizational statutes aimed at barring Jews from party membership.[29] At the same time, the party's racists were particularly active in efforts to organize support from university students on the basis of a radical nationalist and antisemitic program.[30] For its own part, the DNVP's national leadership was becoming increasingly wary of the negative effects that the agitation of Wulle and his associates was having upon the party's electoral prospects and was looking for a way to rein the antisemites in before further damage was done. In his speech on the DNVP's cultural program at the 1920 Hanover party congress Karl Bernhard Ritter, a Protestant pastor and a deputy in the Prussian Landtag, signaled the party's disapproval of radical antisemitism by devoting not so much as a single word to Germany's supposed Jewish problem.[31] Party leaders also made a concerted, though not wholly successful, effort to mute the antisemitic demagogy of the party's racist wing in the 1921 elections to the Prussian Landtag for fear that, if unrestrained, its antics might drive potential voters away from the party.[32] Even Reinhard Mumm, one of the DNVP's most prominent Protestant leaders and a candid Christian anti-Semite in his own right, rejected racial antisemitsm and particularly the way its more radical exponents used antisemitism to justify "malicious attacks on the Old Testament."[33] The crowning indignity, however, came at the DNVP's Munich party congress in September 1921 when Friedrich Brunstäd, a professor at the University of Erlangen and one of the party's preeminent ideologues, defined the Jewish problem in a fashion that infuriated the party's antisemites. For while Brunstäd admitted that "the Jewish question was in truth a German question," he also contended that "the struggle against Jewry is but a small part of the overall struggle for the soul of our people. In essence it is a question of the soul. The Jewish problem will be solved when every German man and every German woman solves it for themselves ... This struggle will not be decided by individual legal measures but by the return

---

[29] Streisow, *DNVP und die Völkisch-Radikalen*, 242–69.
[30] For example, see the recent contribution by Benjamin Ziemann, "Martin Niemöller als völkisch-nationaler Studentenpolitiker in Münster 1919 bis 1923," *Vierteljahrshefte für Zeitgeschichte* 67 (2019): 209–34, esp. 212–18.
[31] Karl Bernhard Ritter, *Volkstum und deutsche Zukunft. Ein deutschnationales Kulturprogramm*, Deutschnationale Flugschrift, no. 71 (Berlin, n.d. [1920]).
[32] Entry in Gallwitz's diary, 31 Jan. 1921, BA-MA Freiburg, NL Gallwitz, 36.
[33] Mumm, "Die Judenfrage vom christlichen Standpunkt," 5 Apr. 1921, BA Berlin, NL Mumm, 356/22.

of the German people to health and by overcoming the danger of degenerating into an amorphous mass [*Massenwerdung*]."[34]

This was a formula for the solution of Germany's so-called Jewish problem and a prescription for Germany's racial regeneration with which the more militant racists within the DNVP could not possibly agree.[35] For the racists Brunstäd's speech was but the last in a long series of indignities they had suffered at the hands of the party leadership, and it only strengthened their determination to do what they could to reverse the direction in which they saw their party headed.[36] Led by the triumvirate of Albrecht von Graefe-Goldebee, Wilhelm Henning, and Reinhold Wulle, the DNVP's racist wing held international Jewry responsible for the increasingly desperate situation in which Germany found itself and demanded that the DNVP pursue a more aggressively antisemitic campaign against those German Jews whom they saw as instruments of international Jewry.[37] Henning was particularly critical of DNVP moderates for their eagerness to work within the framework of the existing political system and their willingness to sacrifice their party's basic principles for the sake of short-term political gains. Such an attitude, Henning argued in a position paper he wrote at the end of June, led to softness and inconsequence and crippled the strong will that was necessary to achieve power.[38]

Henning's worst fears could only have been confirmed when on 25 November 1921 the DNVP party representation (Parteivertretung) rejected three motions that would have had effectively barred Jews from membership in the party and then proceeded to adopt by a relatively narrow 103 to 81 margin a resolution introduced by Helfferich that blocked a change in the party statutes on the so-called Jewish question. According to the terms of this resolution, the party's district organizations were barred from amending their statutes to exclude Jews from party membership, although precisely how this

---

[34] Friedrich Brunstäd, *Völkisch-nationale Erneuerung. Rede auf dem 3. Parteitag der Deutschnationalen Volkspartei im München am 2. September 1921*, Deutschnationale Flugschrift, no. 119 (Berlin, 1921), 16–17.

[35] For example, see Brauer to Heydebrand, 4 Nov. 1921, NL Westarp, Gärtringen, II/82, 40–41, as well as the discussion on "Die völkische Frage" at the 85th evening workshop of the DNVP's State Political Coordinating Committee, 23 Nov. 1921, NL Westarp, Gärtringen, II/8. In a similar vein, see Wangenheim (Deutschvölkischer Arbeitsring) to Hergt, 22 Aug. 1921, BA Berlin, R 8005, 3/131, and Schultz to the DNVP national headquarters, 26 Aug. 1921, ibid., 3/116–17.

[36] "Darstellung des Abgeordneten Henning über die Ereignisse, die zu seinem Ausschluß aus der Fraktion geführt haben," n.d. [Sept.–Oct. 1922], NL Westarp, Gärtringen, VN 88. See also Striesow, *DNVP und die Völkisch-Radikalen*, 341–420; Lewis Hertzman, *DNVP*, 124–64, and most recently Ohnezeit, *Zwischen "schärfster Opposition,"* 134–58.

[37] Graefe-Goldebee to Westarp, 8 Jan. 1922, NL Westarp, Gärtringen, VN 25.

[38] Henning, "Gedanken zur grundsätzlichen Haltung unserer Partei," 30 June 1921, BA Berlin, NL Mumm, 277/269–70.

would pertain to the two or three district organizations that had already adopted a so-called Jewish paragraph remained unclear.[39] The leaders of the DNVP's racist wing were infuriated over this turn of events and decided that the time to organize themselves and their followers at both the national and district levels of the DNVP organization had arrived.[40] But their efforts faced strong opposition from Hergt, Helfferich, and Hugenberg, while Westarp, who privately agreed with Graefe on the nature of the Jewish threat, remained cool to the idea of a separate racist organization within the party.[41]

In their crusade to free the German nation from the grip of international Jewry, the DNVP racists focused much of their venom on the person of Walther Rathenau, a prominent Jewish industrialist and intellectual who had been appointed first minister of reconstruction and then foreign minister in the Wirth cabinet.[42] But when Rathenau moved to center stage with the conclusion of the Rapallo Treaty with Soviet Russia in the last days of the Genoa conference in April 1922, the DNVP party leadership antagonized the party's racist wing by refraining from a full-scale attack against Rapallo.[43] By the same token, the Nationalists decided not to press for a no-confidence vote against the Wirth government prior to the chancellor's trip to Paris at the end of May in search of an international loan that would have helped stabilize the mark and allow for the German economy to recover from the ravages of the inflation.[44] The crisis came to a head when in the June issue of the *Konservative Monatsschrift* Henning broke with the party leadership and launched a particularly scurrilous attack on Rathenau and his alleged betrayal of Germany at Rapallo.[45] When Rathenau was assassinated by right-wing extremists on his way to the German foreign office the morning of 24 June, the tables were suddenly reversed as the DNVP found itself reviled as a "party of murderers" whom the government and its backers held directly responsible for having created the climate in which such an atrocity could take place. No words took a greater toll upon party morale than those of the chancellor Joseph Wirth, when on the day after Rathenau's murder he attacked the DNVP party chairman Hergt for not having taken a clear and unequivocal stand against those who had done so much to poison Germany's national life. Then, turning to the Right, Wirth concluded with words that struck deep into the heart of the

[39] Brauer to Heydebrand, 1 Dec. 1921, NL Westarp, Gärtringen, II/82.
[40] Ibid.
[41] Brauer to Heydebrand, 16 Jan. 1922, ibid.
[42] For example, see Alfred Roth, *Rathenau – "Der Kandidat des Auslandes"* (Hamburg, 1922).
[43] Brauer to Heydebrand, 24 Apr. 1922, NL Westarp, Gärtringen, II/82.
[44] Memorandum by Westarp, 2 June 1922, appended to Brauer to Heydebrand, 2 June 1922, NL Westarp, ibid.
[45] Henning, "Das wahre Gesicht des Rapallo-Vertrags," *Konservative Monatsschrift* 79, no. 6 (June 1922): 521–26.

DNVP: "There stands the enemy that pours its poison into the wounds of the nation. There stands the enemy. And let there be no doubt on this, this enemy stands on the Right!"[46]

Wirth's words and the unmitigated passion with which they were spoken constituted a direct challenge to Hergt and the leaders of the DNVP. After his speech in the Reichstag Wirth went to Hergt and declared that he could only believe in the DNVP's innocence in the matter of Rathenau's murder if it drew a clear and unequivocal line between it and the group of radical racists around Henning. At a meeting of the DNVP party representation on 4 July, a group of party moderates led by Adelbert Düringer, Otto Hoetzsch, and Count Gerhard von Kanitz pressed for Henning's expulsion from the party and demanded – apparently with Hergt's tacit support – that the party draw a clear line between itself and the racists who had helped set the stage for Rathenau's murder.[47] Helfferich, an early target of Wirth's polemics because of his attacks upon first Erzberger and then Rathenau, was an adamant opponent of antisemitism in any form whatsoever and sided with Hergt and those who believed that a purge of the party's racist wing was essential to restore the its respectability and credibility as a future coalition partner.[48] The question of the DNVP's position on racism and antisemitism thus became inextricably intertwined with that of its future role in the national government. Efforts to force the racists from the party also received support from the DNVP's industrial backers, who were as disturbed over the racists' increasingly intemperate diatribes against the capitalist economic order as they were over their anti-semitic excesses.[49] With the quadrumvirate of Hergt, Helfferich, Hoetzch, and Hugenberg leading the charge, the DNVP Reichstag delegation formally expelled Henning from the delegation, though not from the party, by more than a two-thirds majority at meetings of both the delegation and the party executive committee on 19 July.[50] Not even this, however, was sufficient to placate Düringer, who announced his resignation from the DNVP on the following day in protest against its failure to take a clear and unequivocal stand against racial antisemitism.[51] For Henning, on the other hand, his

[46] Joseph Wirth, *Reden während der Kanzlerschaft* (Berlin, 1925), 397–406.
[47] Brauer to Heydebrand, 8 July 1922, NL Westarp, Gärtringen, II/83. See also "Darstellung des Abgeordneten Henning über die Ereignisse, die zu seinem Ausschluß aus der Frak-tion geführt haben," n.d. [Sept.–Oct. 1922], NL Westarp, Gärtringen, 88.
[48] Williamson, *Helfferich*, 368–71.
[49] Frowein to Hergt, 8 July 1922, BA Berlin, R 8005, 3/30–32.
[50] Brauer to Heydebrand, 20 July 1922, NL Westarp, Gärtringen, II/83. See also Henning, "Darstellung des Abgeordneten Henning...," (see n. 46). For a defense of the party's action, see "Zur Abwehr," 29 July 1922, BA Berlin, NL Mumm, 277/281–87.
[51] On Düringer, see Weiß to Traub, 7 July 1922, BA Koblenz, NL Traub, 50/93–94, as well as Thomas Wirth, *Adelbert Düringer: Jurist zwischen Kaiserreich und Republik* (Mann-heim, 1989), 177–80.

expulsion from the Reichstag delegation was only the most recent example of the campaign of defamation and slander the party had waged against his personal honor.[52]

Stung by Henning's expulsion, Graefe-Goldebee and Wulle announced their resignation from the DNVP Reichstag delegation as a sign of solidarity with their beleaguered colleague, but they remained in the party in order to continue their crusade for racist ideas within the DNVP.[53] In justifying their step, Graefe-Goldebee and the leaders of the DNVP's racist wing claimed that only a complete overhaul of the party leadership and Henning's reinstatement to full membership in the DNVP Reichstag delegation would allow the party to fulfill its mission as an instrument of Germany's racial and national regeneration.[54] In their efforts to remake the DNVP in the racist image, the leaders of the DNVP's racist wing enjoyed strong support at the local and regional levels of the Nationalist party organization not just in former conservative bastions east of the Elbe but also in Bavaria.[55] Westarp, who was fully aware of the sympathy the racists enjoyed at the base of the DNVP party organization, was determined to prevent a secession and mediated between the racists and the party leadership in hopes that a break could still be avoided.[56] Westarp readily conceded the threat that Jewish domination posed to German economic, cultural, and political life but cautioned against attributing all of Germany's ills to Jewish machinations or making the struggle against Jewry the sole object of the DNVP's political mission. As Westarp insisted in a statement released to the German press on 22 August 1922, the struggle against the threat of Jewish dominance must be subordinated to the overall strategic goals of the party.[57]

---

[52] Henning, "'Des Nächsten Ehre.' An die Deutschnationale Volkspartei," 1 Aug. 1922, NL Westarp, Gärtringen, VN 88.

[53] Brauer to Heydebrand, 20 July 1922, NL Westarp, Gärtringen, II/83. See also Wulle, "Die Vorgänge in der deutschnationalen Volkspartei," n.d. [July 1922], NL Westarp, Gärtringen, VN 87.

[54] Protocol of a meeting of approximately forty DNVP racists convened by Wulle, 31 July 1922, NL Westarp, Gärtringen, VN 25. See also Brauer to Heydebrand, 18 July 1922, ibid., II/83.

[55] See the letters from the DNVP headquarters in Pomerania to Westarp, 20 July 1922, NL Westarp, Gärtringen, VN 87, and from Koennecke of the DNVP headquarters in Potsdam II, 25 July 1922, ibid·, VN 88. On the situation in Bavaria, see Xylander to Hergt, 6 July 1922, BA Berlin, R 8005, 3/38–40, as well as Dungern to Westarp, 11 Sept. 1922, ibid., VN 89.

[56] See Westarp's letters to Heydebrand, 2 Aug. 1922, NL Westarp, Gärtringen, II/82; Marcinowski, 22 Sept. 1922, ibid., VN 86; and Dungern, 28 Sept. 1922, ibid., VN 89.

[57] Statement by Westarp, 22 Aug. 1922, quoted in Walther Graef (Anklam), "Der Werdegang der Deutschnationalen Volkspartei 1918–1928," in Der nationale Wille, ed. Weiß, 42. See also Westarp, Konservative Politik, ed. Hiller von Gaertringen, 139–49, as well as Gasteiger, Westarp. 189–95, and Stephan Malinowski, "Kuno Graf von Westarp – ein

Secession

The threat of a general secession on the part of the DNVP's racist wing placed Westarp and those who had formerly belonged to the prewar German Conservative Party in an increasingly difficult situation.[58] For although Westarp and indeed many of his associates from the former DKP sympathized with Graefe and his bias against Jews, Westarp felt a strong sense of loyalty to the DNVP and was committed to maintaining party unity in face of the racist challenge. On 14 August Westarp met with Wulle and other members of the party's racist faction and succeeded in tempering their desire for a confrontation with the DNVP party leadership.[59] At a meeting of the DNVP executive committee on 14–15 September 1922 Westarp was successful in defending Graefe-Goldebee and Wulle from efforts by party moderates to have them, along with Henning, expelled from the party, but he was unable to persuade Hergt and the DNVP party leadership to make a conciliatory gesture toward the racists that might have preserved the unity of the party.[60] Westarp's efforts to mediate between the racists and the DNVP party leadership suffered another blow when on the second day of the meeting the leaders of the DNVP's racist wing announced the establishment of the German-Racist Coalition (Deutschvölkische Arbeitsgemeinschaft or DvAG) as a special organization within the DNVP that would presumably keep those who shared their concern about the urgency of the so-called Jewish threat from leaving the party.[61] In his efforts to prevent the racists from leaving the party, Westarp received strong support from a surprising source, the Pan-German League. On 19 September Baron Leopold von Vietinghoff-Scheel and Baron Axel von Freytagh-Loringhoven from the Pan-German leadership met with a contingent of DNVP racists in an attempt to dissuade them from leaving the party. Vietinghoff-Scheel cautioned the racists in particular against plans to found a new party of their own.[62]

---

missing link im preußischen Adel. Anmerkungen zur Einordnung eines untypischen Grafen," in *"Ich bin der letzte Preuße": Der politische Lebensweg des konservativen Politikers Kuno Graf von Westarp (1864–1945)*, ed. Larry Eugene Jones and Wolfram Pyta (Cologne, Weimar, and Vienna, 2006), 9–32.

[58] For example, see Brauer to Heydebrand, 20 July 1922, NL Westarp, Gärtringen, II/83.

[59] Report on the meeting of 14 Aug. 1922, BA Berlin, NL Mumm, 277/276–78.

[60] Brauer to Heydebrand, 19 Sept. 1922, NL Westarp, Gärtringen, II/83. See also the report on the meeting of the DNVP party representation, 15 Sept. 1922, SHStA Dresden, NL Philipp, 13.

[61] Brauer to Heydebrand, 19 Sept. 1922, NL Westarp, Gärtringen, II/83. See also Kube to Westarp, 20 Sept. 1922, NL Westarp, Gärtringen, VN 87, as well as the comments by Graefe-Goldebee, Henning, and Butzbach at a meeting of the DNVP executive committee, 28–29 Sept. 1922, in a report by Weiß, 2 Oct. 1922, ibid., VN 87. For further details, see Graefe-Goldebee to Westarp, 17 Sept. 1922, ibid., VN 88.

[62] Brauer to Heydebrand, 20 Sept. 1922, NL Westarp, Gärtringen, II/83.

On 28 September 1922 the DNVP racists officially launched the German-Racist Coalition at a small meeting in Berlin-Charlottenburg. Graefe-Goldebee was elected chairman of the seven-member executive committee responsible for organizing all of those within the DNVP who shared their commitment to Germany's racial and national regeneration. In addition to Graefe-Goldebee, the committee also included Henning and Wulle, the latter as its executive secretary. Although the DvAG would function as an independent organization within the DNVP and organize its followers into separate cells at the local and provincial levels of the DNVP's national organization, the founders of the DvAG took special pains to stress that it was not their intention "to throw down the gauntlet" to the DNVP. "Our struggle," the communiqué continued, "has never been directed against the party but always against a system within the party."[63] This disclaimer did little to reassure the DNVP party representation, which was meeting in Berlin that very weekend to discuss, among other items, the problem the racists had created with the founding of their own organization. Declaring "the existence of the German-Racist Coalition with an organization of its own within the DNVP as incompatible with the vital interests, unity, and solidarity of the party,"[64] the party leadership handed Graefe-Goldebee and his associates a stinging rebuff that left their continued presence in the DNVP in doubt.[65]

Given the gravity of the situation, the DNVP party leadership decided to refer the question of the DvAG's future status to the DNVP party congress that was scheduled to meet in Görlitz in late October 1922. The action that the DNVP party representation had taken at its meeting in Berlin constituted a clear victory for Hergt and the moderates who were in control of the party executive committee and prompted a disgruntled Westarp to remark that one day the conservatives too would have to leave the party because after the racists had left it would be impossible to halt the DNVP's drift to the left.[66] Westarp's efforts to mediate between the racists and the DNVP party leadership were repeatedly thwarted by the latter's intransigence and its determination to subject the party's racist faction to party discipline.[67] By the third week of October the rupture had become irreparable. Hergt and particularly Helfferich were relentless in their crusade to drive the racists from the party and to block the reinstatement of Graefe-Goldebee and Wulle to the DNVP

[63] "Die Gründung der Deutschvölkischen Arbeitsgemeinschaft," n.d. [Oct. 1922], NL Westarp, Gärtringen, VN 88. See also Graefe-Goldebee to Westarp, 17 Sept. 1922., ibid., as well as the agenda for the meeting on 28 Sept. 1922, appended to Kube to Westarp, 20 Sept. 1922, ibid., VN 87.

[64] Memoranda from Weiß to the party's state and regional organizations, 2 and 4 Oct. 1922, NL Westarp, Gärtringen, VN 87. See also Brauer to Heydebrand, 3 Oct. 1922, ibid., II/83.

[65] Graefe-Goldebee to Westarp, 23 Sept. 1922, NL Westarp, Gärtringen, VN 25.

[66] Brauer to Heydebrand, 3 Oct. 1922, NL Westarp, Gärtringen, II/83.

[67] Brauer to Heydebrand, 13 Oct. 1922, ibid.

Reichstag delegation in the period that led up to the Görlitz congress. As it was, only thirteen members of the delegation joined Westarp in his efforts to negotiate a compromise that would have made it possible for the racists to remain in the party, while thirty-six deputies supported the DNVP party leadership in attaching conditions to the reinstatement of the racists that Graefe-Goldebee and his associates would find impossible to accept.[68]

The DNVP's Görlitz party congress 25–28 October 1922 was dominated from beginning to end by the racist question. In comparison to the party's most recent congress at Munich, the Görlitz congress was a much more subdued affair. Whereas at Munich the DNVP had celebrated its success in building a comprehensive organization that firmly anchored the party in Germany's conservative milieu, at Görlitz party leaders were anxious to paper over the divisions that the racist conflict had opened up within party and to prevent the conflict over the party's handling of the racist issue from triggering a full-fledged secession on the DNVP's right wing. In his keynote address on the first day of the congress, Nationalist party chairman Hergt went out of his way to pacify the more radical elements on the party's right wing by reaffirming as categorically as possible the DNVP's unconditional opposition to the republican form of government and its steadfast refusal to join the other non-socialist parties in a coalition government committed to fulfilling the terms of the Versailles Peace Treaty.[69] Then, in one of the featured speeches on the last day of the congress, Max Wallraf from the DNVP Prussian Landtag delegation went to great pains to portray the DNVP as a *völkisch* party opposed to all alien influences upon Germany's national life.[70] But none of this did much to placate the leaders of the DNVP's German-Racist Coalition, whose demands for a "reformation" of the DNVP at all levels of its national organization evoked nothing but a deaf response at the upper echelons of the Nationalist party leadership. Mediation between the two groups became pointless, and on 28 October 1922 the faction around Graefe-Goldebee, Wulle, and Henning used a change in the party statutes that prohibited the existence of separate organizations like the German-Racist Coalition within the DNVP party apparatus as the pretext for severing their ties to the party.[71] Two months later, the secessionists formally reconstituted themselves as the German-Racist Freedom

---

[68] Brauer to Heydebrand, 18 Oct. 1922, ibid.

[69] Oskar Hergt, *Von deutscher Not. Rede auf dem Vierten Deutschnationalen Reichsparteitage in Görlitz am 27. Oktober 1922*, Deutschnationale Flugschrift, no. 140 (Berlin, 1922).

[70] Max Wallraf, *Die deutschen Parteien am Schweidewege! Rede auf dem Vierten Deutschnationalen Reichsparteitage in Görlitz am 28. Oktober 1922*, Deutschnationale Flugschrift, no. 139 (Görlitz, 1922), 11–12.

[71] "Vertrauliche Information: Görlitzer Parteitag. Gründung der Deutschvölkischen Arbeitsgemeinschaft außerhalb der Partei," n.d. [ca. Okt.–Nov. 1922], NL Westarp, Gärtringen, VN 88.

Party (Deutschvölkische Freiheitspartei or DVFP), thus putting the final touches on their break with the Nationalist party organization.[72]

The founding of the German-Racist Freedom Party reverberated throughout the DNVP organization and threatened the party with a mass secession of its racist wing.[73] In an attempt to shore up their flank, the DNVP party leadership authorized the creation of a special organization within the party for those racists who had remained with the DNVP.[74] But what proved decisive in the DNVP's efforts to contain the racist secession was the strong support it received from Claß and the Pan-German League. For although the Pan-Germans espoused a racial antisemitism that was virtually indistinguishable from that of Graefe-Goldebee and Wulle, they remained adamantly opposed to the founding of the new racist party and threw their full support behind the DNVP in the critical days following the Görlitz congress. Longstanding animosities between Claß and Graefe-Goldebee no doubt played a decisive role in shaping the ADV's response to these developments as the Pan-Germans held the founders of the new party responsible for the splintering of the antisemitic movement and never wavered in their belief that their agenda could be advanced only in collaboration with the DNVP.[75] The key figure in this regard was Baron Axel von Freytagh-Loringhoven, a Nationalist deputy in the Prussian Landtag from Breslau who enjoyed close ties to the Pan-German leadership. Not only did Freytagh-Loringhoven go head-to-head with Graefe-Goldebee in keeping the DNVP's rank-and-file from bolting the party,[76] but he took the lead in organizing the DNVP's racist wing into a special committee within the DNVP party apparatus.[77] The official founding of the DNVP's National Racist Committee (Völkischer Reichsausschuß der Deutschnationalen Volkspartei) under the chairmanship of Walther Graef-Anklam, a member of the Nationalist delegation to the Prussian Landtag, in early 1923 represented Freytagh-Loringhoven's crowning achievement in that it not only stemmed the defection of DNVP racists to the DVFP but provided the Pan-Germans with an organizational foothold in the DNVP. The stated purpose of this committee was first to create greater awareness of the threat of Jewish dominance in the German press, second to fight with all legal means the efforts of international Jewry to destroy the German economy, and third to unite all

---

[72] Reimer Wulff, "Die deutschvölkische Freiheitspartei 1922–1928" (Ph.D. diss. Universität Marburg, 1968), 6–14. See also Breuer, *Völkischen in Deutschland*, 194–208.

[73] For example, see Weiß (DNVP Reichsgeschäftsstelle) to Westarp, 23 Jan. 1923, NL Westarp, Gärtringen, VN 37. See also Merkel (DNVP Potsdam I) to Westarp, 8 Feb. 1923, ibid.

[74] *Korrespondenz der DNVP*, 1 Nov. 1922, no. 215.

[75] Jackisch, *Pan-German League*, 46–49, 54–62.

[76] Hamel (DNVP Mecklenburg-Schwerin) to Westarp, 8 Jan. 1923, NL Westarp, Gärtringen, VN 37. See also Graefe-Goldebee to Claß, 8 Jan. 1923, BA Berlin, R 8048, 226/38–39.

[77] For example, see Freytagh-Loringhoven to Claß, 6 Aug. 1923, BA Berlin, R 8048, 209/177.

German-racist elements on the basis of the DNVP for concerted action against the onslaught of international and Jewish dominated forces.[78]

By no means did the outcome of the racist conflict within the DNVP mean that the party had purged itself of antisemitism or that it was now prepared to seek a more responsible role in determining Germany's political future. In point of fact, antisemitism itself was never at issue for the vast majority of those who were involved in the conflict. Antisemitism was a well defined feature of Germany's conservative milieu long before the conflict ever erupted, and only a handful of those who belonged to the DNVP's inner councils denied the existence of a "Jewish question" in Germany's national life. What was really at stake in the racist conflict of 1921–22 was not the existence of a "Jewish threat" but the means with which the struggle against this threat was to be waged and just where this particular struggle ranked in relationship to the other issues that faced the party. Whereas the racists around Graefe-Goldebee, Henning, and Wulle believed that no issue was more important than the struggle for Germany's racial regeneration, the DNVP party leadership argued that the struggle against the influence that German and international Jewry presumably exercised over German cultural, economic, and political life had to be subordinated to other issues of more immediate import, issues such as the fight against Versailles and the policy of fulfillment and the struggle for the rehabilitation of German agriculture. The struggle against the Jewish dominance of Germany's national life could wait until after these more immediate issues had been addressed.[79]

The Paramilitary Right

Party leaders faced a similar, though less vexing problem with the various paramilitary organizations that had sprung up across the country in the wake of World War I. The war – and particularly its duration – had had a brutalizing effect on those who had served at the front and made it difficult for many to reintegrate themselves into civilian life after the end of the war. The situation was further exacerbated by the continuation of fighting long after the official conclusion of hostilities in the fall of 1918 and by the threat that the spread of Bolshevism throughout central and eastern Europe posed to the

---

[78] Minutes of the meeting of the DNVP National Racist Committee, 22 Apr. 1923, BA Berlin, R 8005, 361/230–31, also in BA R 8048, 223/5–6. See also Graef-Anklam, "Die völkischen Zielen der Deutschnationalen Volkspartei," n.d. [Apr. 1923], ibid., 223/219. See also Jackisch, Pan-German League, 96–100, and Hofmeister, "Between Monarchy and Dictatorship," 271–82.

[79] "Zu den Angriffen der Deutschvölkischen Freiheitspartei," n.d. [ca. Jan. 1923], SHStA Dresden, NL Philipp, 13.

propertied classes throughout the area.[80] While the vast majority of those Germans who had served at the front were able to find their way back into the German workforce and returned to what passed for normal civilian life, others found the transition difficult and tried to preserve what they could of their experience at the front by joining special combat units that were fully committed to the use of violence in defense of the existing social and economic order. The founding of the Weimar Republic was marked by a dramatic escalation of political violence as militant organizations on the Left and the Right fought for control of the streets. The first years after the end of war witnessed the emergence of any number of paramilitary combat leagues, some of which were militantly opposed to Germany's new republican system and others that were motivated more by the fear of Bolshevism than anything else. In almost all cases, these organizations drew their impetus from the collapse of established political authority, disorder on the home front to which veterans of the Great War were returning, the apparent triumph of political radicalism, and with it the ubiquitous, if not imagined, threat of Bolshevism. The old order had indeed collapsed, and German veterans of the Great War, drawing their inspiration from the sense of solidarity to which fighting at the front had forged, saw themselves as harbingers of a new era from which the social, economic, and political cleavages of the world into which they had been born would be banished.[81]

The initial and by far most widespread phenomena of this sort in Germany were the so-called Free Corps, or *Freikorps*, that had been formed by soldiers returning from the eastern front where exposure to large numbers of Eastern European Jews and ideological indoctrination on the dangers of Bolshevism had left them vulnerable to the antisemitic histrionics of the Pan-German League and German-Racist Protection and Defense League.[82] Despite their militancy and high political profile, the Free Corps encompassed only a small fraction of those who had served at the front with an estimated membership of

---

[80] For further details, see Robert Gerwarth, "The Central European Counter-Revolution: Paramilitary Violence in Germany, Austria, and Hungary after the Great War," *Past and Present* 200 (2008): 175–209, as well as the introduction by Robert Gerwarth and John Horne, "Paramilitarism in Europe after the Great War: An Introduction," in *War in Peace: Paramilitary Violence in Europe after the Great War*, ed. Robert Gerwarth and John Horne (Oxford, 2012): 1–18.

[81] On the contours of paramilitary violence in postwar Germany, see Dirk Schumann, *Political Violence in the Weimar Republic, 1918–1933: Fight for the Streets and Fear of Civil War*, trans. by Thomas Dunlap (New York and Oxford, 2009), 3–34.

[82] Bernhard Sauer, "Freikorps und Antisemitismus in der Frühzeit der Weimarer Republik," *Zeitschrift für Geschichtswissenschaft* 56 (2008): 5–29. See also Joachim Schroeder, "Der Erste Weltkrieg und der 'jüdische Bolschewismus'," in *Nationalsozialismus und Erster Weltkrieg*, ed. Krumeich (Essen, 2010), 77–96 and Brian E. Crim, "'Our Most Serious Enemy': The Specter of Judeo-Bolshevism in the German Military Community, 1914–1923," *Central European History* 44 (2011): 624–41.

400,000 as opposed to the thirteen million Germans who had been mobilized between 1914 and 1918.[83] The Free Corps were notorious for their lack of discipline and committed atrocities that led to their forced dissolution in 1920. While many of those affected by this action subsequently made their way into the ranks of the fledgling National Socialist German Workers' Party, the persistence of the "red scare" prompted the creation of volunteer civilian defense leagues known as *Einwohnerwehren* for the ostensible purpose of defending the existing social order against the threat of the radical Left. In Prussia the *Einwohnerwehren* played a critical role in stabilizing bourgeois social and economic power during a period of revolutionary turmoil and received strong support from both civilian and military authorities even after the Versailles Treaty expressly prohibited the existence of any organization outside of the 100,000-man Reichswehr that bore arms or otherwise concerned itself with military matters.[84] Nowhere were the *Einwohnerwehren* more important than in Bavaria, where they played a decisive role in the reestablishment of law and order following the suppression of the Munich soviet in the spring of 1919 and enjoyed the support and protection of influential government officials, not the least of whom was Gustav von Kahr, the Bavarian minister president from March 1920 to September 1921. Not only did Kahr rely upon the civilian defense leagues to contain the plebeian unrest that threatened to spread to Bavaria following the collapse of the Kapp putsch, but his patronage helped shield the Bavarian defense leagues against Allied efforts to force their dissolution.[85]

Following the suppression of the *Einwohnerwehren* in Prussia and elsewhere, Kahr provided the political cover that made it possible for forestry official Georg Escherich to organize the various defense units that had sprung up in Bavaria, Austria, and other parts of the country into an organization that bore his name, Organization Escherich (Organisation Escherich or Orgesch).

---

[83] For a contemporary overview of this phenomenon, see Frank Glatzel, "Wehrverbände und Politik," in *Politische Praxis 1926*, ed. Walther Lambach (Hamburg, n.d. [1926]), 313–28. For more scholarly treatments, see Kristian Mennen, "'Milksops' and 'Bemedalled Old Men': War Veterans and the War Youth Generation in the Weimar Republic," *Fascism* 6 (2017): 13–41, here 19. On the reintegration of World War I veterans into postwar German society, see Richard Bessel, "Militarismus im innenpolitischen Leben der Weimarer Republik. Von den Freikorps zur SA," in *Militär und Militärismus in der Weimarer Republik*, ed. Klaus-Jürgen Müller (Düsseldorf, 1978), 193–222, esp. 200–03, and Benjamin Ziemann, *Front und Heimat. Ländliche Kriegserfahrungen im südlichen Bayern 1914–1923* (Essen, 1997), 394–437.

[84] Peter Bucher, "Zur Geschichte der Einwohnerwehren in Preußen 1918–1921," *Militärgeschichtliche Mitteilungen* 10 (1971): 15–59.

[85] On the patriotic movement in Bavaria, see Harold J. Gordon, Jr., *Hitler and the Beer Hall Putsch* (Princeton, NJ, 1972), 88–119, and Hans Fenske, *Konservatismus und Rechtsradikalismus in Bayern nach 1918* (Bad Homburg, 1969), 76–112, as well as James M. Diehl, *Paramilitary Politics in Weimar Germany* (Bloomington, IN, 1977), 69–88, 100–07.

A self-styled adventurer and outspoken anti-Communist,[86] Escherich had begun by organizing the counterrevolutionary defense units in his hometown of Isen after the end of the war. Orgesch was formally established at Regensburg on 8–9 May 1920 and cemented Escherich's place as the undisputed leader of the volunteer defense movement in all of Germany.[87] Although the leadership of Orgesch rested almost exclusively in the hands of Escherich and his associates from the Bavarian volunteer defense leagues, the two remained juridically independent of each other and served fundamentally different purposes. In the case of the Orgesch, that purpose was less the actual preservation of peace and order in the face of Bolshevism than the establishment of closer organizational ties between the Bavarian civilian defense leagues and similar groups in other parts of the country. The true nature of the new organization, however, was partly obscured by the fact that the four-point program Escherich proclaimed at Regensburg committed Orgesch, among other things, to the "defense of the constitution" and the "rejection of putschism from right or left."[88] Much of this was no doubt a ploy to shield the Orgesch and its affiliated organizations against the threat of suppression by the Reich in the wake of the Kapp putsch. In point of fact, the true spirit that animated the new organization had less to do with the preservation of the existing constitutional system than with the defense of the bourgeois social order against Bolshevism and socialism in any of their myriad forms.

In the weeks that followed, representatives from the Orgesch travelled throughout Germany in an attempt to solidify the ties that had been cultivated at Regensburg. Among those with whom Orgesch officials met was the DNVP's Alfred Hugenberg, who assured them of his support but declined to commit himself with respect to financing until after the Reichstag elections scheduled for June 1920 had taken place.[89] While Orgesch leaders felt sufficiently encouraged by their contacts with like-minded groups in the other parts of the country to continue their efforts on behalf of a national volunteer defense league modeled after the Bavarian prototype,[90] they also began to encounter strong resistance in Prussia, where neither the "ultra-reactionary" Right nor the socialist Left showed much interest in their plans. Orgesch, which Escherich and his associates continued to portray as a nonpartisan

---

[86] For example, see Georg Escherich, *Von Eisner bis Eglhofer. Die Münchener Revolution vom November 1918 bis zum Zusammenbruch der Räteherrschaft*, 6 vols. (Munich, 1922).

[87] Escherich's handwritten notes on the "Regensburger Tagung," 8–9 May 1920, records of the Einwohnerwehren Bayerns, Bayerische Hauptstaatsarchiv Munich, (hereafter cited as BHStA Munich), Abt. IV, EWB, 5/3a.

[88] Günther Axhausen, *Organisation Escherich. Die Bewegung zur nationalen Einheitsfront* (Leipzig, 1921), 16–19.

[89] Report by Kannengiesser on his trip to northern Germany, 25 May–5 June 1920, BHStA Munich, Abt. IV, EWB, 5/3a.

[90] Ibid.

"union of the middle" whose main goal was the defeat of Bolshevism,[91] was either too radical for the self-defense organizations that had surfaced under aristocratic leadership in Prussia's eastern provinces or too reactionary for those within the socialist labor movement who were loyal to the existing political system.[92] The most serious obstacle to the expansion of the Orgesch north of the Main, however, was Allied pressure for the disarmament of Germany's civilian population and the dissolution of all paramilitary combat leagues.[93] While Kahr continued to protect the Bavarian volunteer defense leagues against demands for their dissolution, officials serving the Reich and Prussia had little choice but to comply with Allied demands and ordered the dissolution of Orgesch and its affiliates in the spring and summer of 1920.[94] Kahr was able to resist pressure from Berlin until late May 1922, when he found it necessary to cut his political losses and asked Escherich to initiate a partial disarmament of the Bavarian volunteer defense units.[95] After a period of initial defiance and procrastination,[96] Escherich eventually realized that he had no alternative but to submit to Allied pressure and reluctantly began to comply with Kahr's orders. On 1 June 1921 Escherich ordered the disarmament of the Bavarian volunteer defense units, thus setting the stage for the official dissolution of the Orgesch four weeks later.[97]

At the time of their dissolution, the Bavarian volunteer defense leagues numbered over 360,000 members,[98] while the membership of the Orgesch and its Austrian counterpart, the Organization Kanzler (Organisation Kanzler), has been placed at nearly two million.[99] For those who went through this experience, the Orgesch and its affiliated defense leagues in Bavaria and other parts of the country constituted an important way-station on their path to more radical paramilitary organizations. Of the countless such organizations that flourished in the middle and late years of the Weimar Republic, none were

---

[91] Escherich, "Aufklärung über die Organisation Escherich," 5 Aug. 1920, BHStA Munich, Abt. IV, EWB, 5/3b.

[92] Kustermann to Orgesch business leaders, 6 Oct. 1920, BHStA Munich, Abt. IV, EWB, 5/3b.

[93] For further details, see Michael Salewski, *Entwaffnung und Militärkontrolle in Deutschland 1919–1927* (Munich, 1966), 137–46.

[94] Bucher, "Einwohnerwehren in Preußen," 53–58.

[95] Kahr to Escherich, 21 May 1921, BHStA Munich, Abt. IV, EWB, 3/11.

[96] For example, see Escherich to Kahr, 27 and 28 May 1921, BHStA Munich, Abt. IV, EWB, 3/11.

[97] Statement by Escherich, 29 June 1921, BHStA Munich, Abt. IV, EWB, 5/3d. For further details, See also Kanzler, *Bayerns Kampf,* 81–82, 108–18. On developments in Baden, see Helmut Neumaier, "Die Organisation Escherich in Baden. Zum Rechtsextremismus in der Frühphase der Weimarer Republik," *Zeitschrift für die Geschichte des Oberrheins* 137 (1989): 341–82.

[98] Kanzler, *Bayerns Kampf,* 162–63.

[99] Large, *Politics of Law and Order,* 77.

more important than the Stahlhelm and Young German Order (Jungdeutscher Orden). Like the Orgesch, these organizations emerged in the general chaos that accompanied the end of Word War I and were strongly committed to the reestablishment of "law and order" throughout the country. Each had received its baptism of fire in the defense of Germany's eastern borders against the threats of Bolshevism and Polish aggresion and worked closely with volunteer defense leagues in Bavaria and other parts of the country in the suppression of Bolshevism. Not surprisingly, both the Stahlhelm and the Young German Order recruited the bulk of their rank-and-file membership from those who had served at the front and were often experiencing difficulty adjusting to the demands of civilian life and the collapse of domestic political authority. Unlike the Orgesch, however, both the Stahlhelm and Young German Order were more than military combat leagues and espoused political goals that went far beyond the representation of veterans' interests or the reestablishment of law and order and the defeat of Bolshevism.

The Stahlhelm

The Stahlhelm – League of Front Soldiers (Stahlhelm – Bund der Frontsolda-ten) was founded in Magdeburg on 25 December 1918 on the initiative of Franz Seldte, a decorated reserve officer in the German infantry who had lost his left arm at the battle of the Somme.[100] Like most of those who had served at the front, Franz and his brother Georg had been swept up in the wave of national enthusiasm that had accompanied the outbreak of hostilities in August 1914. But by the end of 1915 – and particularly after the bloody battle of the Somme – the sense of euphoria they had experienced at the outbreak of the war began to crack under the hard realities of trench warfare and gave way to a new mood informed above all else by a sense of duty to nation and comrade. Like so many of their comrades, the Seldte brothers too began to believe that the heroism of the front was only a small part of a much larger struggle that was slowly, but surely, transforming the face of all mankind.[101]

---

[100] Facsimile of the handwritten protocol of the Stahlehlm's founding on 25 Dec. 1918 in *Der Stahlhelm. Erinnerungen und Bilder aus den Jahren 1918–1933*, ed. Franz Seldte, 2 vols., (Berlin, 1933), 1:169. See also Alois Klotzbücher, "Der politische Weg des Stahl-helms, Bund der Frontsoldaten, in der Weimarer Republik. Ein Beitrag zur Geschichte der 'Nationalen Opposition' 1918–1933" (Ph.D. diss., Universität Erlangen-Nürnberg, 1964), 1–30; and Volker R. Berghahn, *Der Stahlhelm – Bund der Frontsoldaten 1918–1935* (Düsseldorf, 1966), 13–53.

[101] On the mythos of the "front experience," see Richard Bessel, "The 'Front Generation' and the Politics of Weimar Germany," in *Generations in Conflict: Youth Revolt and Generation Formation in Germany, 1770–1968*, ed. Mark Roseman (Cambridge, 1995), 121–36.

Not even the news of the general strike, the Kaiser's abdication, or the proclamation of the republic could shake the strength of this conviction. It was to sustain their faith in the transformative power of the front experience and to fulfill their commitment to those of their comrades who had fallen at the front that the Seldte brothers and associates launched the Stahlhelm in the first days of the November Revolution.

In its initial attempt at self-definition, the Stahlhelm proclaimed three goals: to represent the interests of the front soldier so that he might find the place he rightfully deserved in public and professional life, to provide for law and order so that the task of national reconstruction could begin, and to provide mutual support for those who had served at the front without regard for class or party affiliation.[102] In the immediate context, the second of these three goals took clear precedence over the other two. The phrase "restoration of law and order" was little more than a euphemism for the suppression of Marxism and provided the Stahlhelm with all the justification it needed to intervene against the revolutionary Left in the turmoil of the postwar period. By its own account, the Stahlhelm played a major role in the "liberation" of Magdeburg, Halle, and much of central Germany from the threat of Marxist insurrection.[103] At the same time, Seldte had begun to cultivate close ties with Escherich and represented the north German civilian defense leagues at the Orgesch's founding ceremonies in Regensburg.[104] The fact that the Stahlhelm defined itself as an organization for the promotion of veterans' interests, however, helped shield it from the fate that befell the Free Corps and Germany's other paramilitary combat leagues when the government ordered their dissolution in late 1919 and early 1920. As its ranks swelled through the influx of new members who had formerly belonged to organizations now banned by the state, the Stahlhelm spread from its original stronghold in and around Magdeburg across the rest of central Germany and into eastern Prussia. Between March 1920 and January 1922 the Stahlhelm grew from an organization with thirty local chapters to one with approximately six hundred.[105] The Stahlhelm's greatest success occurred in the fall of 1924 when the Westphalian League (Westfalenbund), which had been founded in the summer of 1921 out of the

---

[102] Franz Seldte, "Der Stahlhelm," n.d., [ca. 1926–27], records of the Stahlhelm, BA Berlin, Bestand R 72 22/229–31.

[103] *Sechs Jahre Stahlhelm in Mitteldeutschland*, ed. Stahlhelm, Landesverband Mittel-deutschland (Halle, 1926), 11–16.

[104] Press release issued by Orgesch on the Regensburg conference, n.d. [9 May 1920], BHStA Munich, Abt. IV, EWB, 5/3a. See also Seldte to Escherich, 21 Jan. 1920, ibid., 3/1c, and Seldte to Escherich, 8 Apr. 1920, ibid., 5/3a.

[105] Sigmund Graff, "Gründung und Entwicklung des Bundes," in *Der Stahlhelm. Erinne-rungen und Bilder aus den Jahren 1918–1933*, ed. Franz Seldte, 2 vols., (Berlin, 1933), 1:19–107, here 38–40.

remnants of the Westphalian chapter of Organization Escherich and stood under the leadership of Baron Ferdinand von Lüninck, formally dissolved itself to become the Stahlhelm's regional affiliate.[106]

Initially the Stahlhelm had typically recruited the bulk of its membership from the ranks of veterans who had managed the transition to postwar civilian life with relative ease and never experienced the deep-seated alienation from postwar bourgeois society that most of those who gravitated to the more militant combat leagues had felt. Ridiculed by its rivals on the political Left as an organization of "milksops" and "bemedalled old men," the Stahlhelm's rank-and-file displayed little of the militancy in the first years of the Weimar Republic that would become the hallmark of Germany's paramilitary Right.[107] Over time, however, the Stahlhelm began to attract the support of aristocrats whose dreams of a career in the German officer corps or the state civil service had been cut short by the revolutionary upheaval of 1918-19 and who remained implacably opposed to the changes that had taken place in Germany's political system.[108] This, however, did not take place without a certain price. For whereas beforehand the Stahlhelm had opened its ranks to all of those – including Jews and Social Democrats – who had served a minimum of six months in the armed services, the sudden influx of new members from more radical organizations such as the League of Nationalist Soldiers (Verband nationalgesinnter Soldaten) had a dramatic effect on the Stahlhelm's political profile and quickly transformed it into a vanguard of counterrevolutionary and revanchist sentiment.[109] The storm of national protest that greeted ratification of the Versailles Peace Treaty in the summer of 1919 greatly accelerated the radicalization and growth of the Stahlhelm. Still, the Stahlhelm continued to profess an official policy of neutrality, or Überparteilichkeit, with respect to the existing political parties. Its nonpartisan character was further underscored by the fact that Seldte, the driving force behind its founding and early expansion, was a member of the German People's Party, while Theodor Duesterberg, rapidly emerging as the leader of the Stahlhelm's more radical elements, was chairman of the DNVP district organization in

---

[106] Seldte, "Der Stahlhelm," (see n. 102). See also Gerd Krüger, "Von den Einwohnerwehren zum Stahlhelm. Der nationale Kampfverband 'Westfalenbund e.V.' (1921-1924)," Westfälische Zeitschrift 147 (1997): 405-32. On the paramilitary Right in Westphalia, see Gerd Krüger, 'Treudeutsch allewege!' Gruppen, Vereine und Verbände der Rechten in Münster (1887-1929/30) (Münster, 1992), esp. 71-134.

[107] Mennen, "'Milksops' and 'Bemedalled Old Men'," 31.

[108] Marcus Funck, "Schock und Chance. Der preußische Militäradel in der Weimarer Republik zwischen Stand und Profession," in Adel und Bürgertum in Deutschland II. Entwicklungslinien und Wendepunkte im 20. Jahrhundert, ed. Heinz Reif (Berlin, 2001), 127-71.

[109] See Berghahn, Stahlhelm, 26-39, and Diehl, Paramilitary Politics, 96-97.

Halle-Merseburg.[110] But nonpartisanship had a peculiar meaning for the leaders of the Stahlhelm and was not synonymous with neutrality. For while the Stahlhelm claimed to stand above the sordid world of party politics, its policy of nonpartisanship was a discriminatory strategy that consistently favored those parties whose national pedigree was above reproach at the expense of those that had allowed themselves to become too closely identified with the defense of Germany's new republican order.[111]

As the Stahlhelm gravitated more and more into the orbit of the radical Right, it came under increasingly close scrutiny from officials of the central and state governments and was one of the first organizations to be officially banned as an enemy of the republic in the wake of Rathenau's assassination.[112] The ban on the Stahlhelm remained in effect for the next six months and did much to enhance its popularity as a member of the national movement. It was not until after Seldte took it upon himself to publicly reaffirm the Stahlhelm's loyalty to the existing system of government that the Stahlhelm was allowed to resume its role in the public sphere.[113] In the meantime, Seldte was finding it increasingly difficult to control the more radical elements that had begun to attach themselves to Duesterberg's political star. In April 1923 Duesterberg was appointed leader of the Stahlhelm organization in Halle-Merseburg as part of an arrangement whereby he agreed to resign his post as chairman of the DNVP district party organization.[114] This provided Duesterberg's followers with a foothold within the Stahlhelm organization from which they could undercut Seldte and his proclamations of loyalty for the Weimar Republic. As a result, the Stahlhelm pursued an uncertain and sometimes confused policy that only mirrored the differences that existed at the upper echelons of its national leadership. While Duesterberg and the leaders of the Stahlhelm's radical wing flirted with Bavarian putschists hoping to emulate Mussolini's "March on Rome" with a march on Berlin and even advocated the cultivation of closer ties with the National Socialists,[115] Seldte and his supporters pressed first Stresemann and then General Hans von Seeckt for the creation of a

---

[110] On Duesterberg, see his letter to Westarp, 21 Dec. 1922, NL Westarp, Gärtringen, VN 87. Resolution by the Stahlhelm executive committee, 6 Oct. 1925, reprinted in Graff, "Gründung und Entwicklung des Bundes," 58–59.

[111] For example, see the resolution adopted by the Stahlhelm leadership on the "Stahlhelm und nationale Parteien," 3 Oct. 1926, and the programmatic statement by Heinz Brauweiler, "Stahlhelm und Politik," in *Stahlhelm-Handbuch 1927*, ed. Walter Kellner and Heinrich Hildebrandt (Berlin, 1927), 45–46, 51–57.

[112] Graff, "Gründung und Entwicklung," 40–44.

[113] Berghahn, *Stahlhelm*, 37.

[114] *Sechs Jahre Stahlhelm in Mitteldeutschland*, 52.

[115] Hans Langermann, "Kampf und Sieg des Stahlhelm in Mitteldeutschland," in *Deutschlands Erwachen. Das Buch vom Niedergang und Aufstieg des deutschen Volkes 1918–1933*, ed. Hans Henning Grote (Essen, n.d. [ca. 1933]), 296.

national dictatorship capable of leading Germany out of the morass in which it currently found itself.[116] These differences became increasingly apparent as the situation in the Reich continued to deteriorate throughout the course of 1923.

The Young German Order

The Stahlhelm's principal rival for the leadership of the paramilitary Right in the early years of the Weimar Republic was the Young German Order.[117] Like the Stahlhelm, the Young German Order had surfaced in the chaos that immediately followed the end of the World War I. But whereas the Stahlhelm tended to be strongest in the Prussian provinces to the east of the Elbe River, the Young Germans experienced their greatest success in the western and central parts of Germany. The Young German Order owed its founding to the initiative of Artur Mahraun, a young lieutenant colonel who had served in the Prussian army since 1908 and a former activist in the prewar German youth movement. On 10 January 1919 Mahraun formed a volunteer unit consisting of about 200 officers, non-commissioned officers, and soldiers from his home-town of Kassel to combat the threat of social revolution and to assist in the restoration of law and order.[118] This unit, which officially rechristened itself the Young German Order on 17 March 1920, went on to play a significant role in suppressing left-wing unrest in Hesse and Thuringia following the collapse of the Kapp putsch. In the summer of 1920 the Order affiliated itself with the Organization Escherich and joined forces with the more militant combat leagues in the suppression of Marxism until it, like the Orgesch, was officially banned in parts of Prussia later that August.[119] From all appearances, the Young German Order was scarcely distinguishable from other organizations on Germany's paramilitary Right and had to be regarded, along with the Stahlhelm, as one of Weimar's most resolute enemies.

For all of their similarities, the Young German Order and Stahlhelm differed in several important respects. In the first place, the Young German

---

[116] See the text of Seldte's telegram to Stresemann, 4 Nov. 1923, reprinted in Heinz Brauweiler, "Der Anteil des Stahlhelm," in Curt Hotzel, ed., *Deutscher Aufstand. Die Revolution des Nachkriegs* (Stuttgart, 1934), 221.

[117] On the history of the Young German Order, see Klaus Hornung's *Der Jungdeutsche Orden* (Düsseldorf, 1958), as well as the more reliable accounts by Diehl, *Paramilitary Politics*, 95–100, 118–19, and Brian E. Crim, *Antisemitism in the German Military Community and the Jewish Response, 1916–1938* (Lanham, MD, 2014), 65–96.

[118] Artur Mahraun, *Gegen getarnte Gewalten. Weg und Kampf einer Volksbewegung* (Berlin, 1928), 13–19.

[119] On ties between the Young German Order and Escherich, see Krayse, "Bericht über meinen Empfang in München am 30.8.21," 5 Sept. 1921, records of the Young German Order, BA Koblenz, Bestand R 161, 1.

Order saw itself as a bridge to the prewar German youth movement and, like the *Wandervögel* before it, evinced a general disdain for the social and political values of the all but moribund bourgeois order.[120] Mahraun and the Young Germans characteristically dissociated themselves from efforts to restore things to the way they had been before 1914 and called for a more fundamental rebirth of state and society on the basis of the *Volksgemeinschaft*.[121] Secondly, high-ranking officers and members of Germany's industrial and agricultural elites were never as prominently represented in the Young German Order as they were in the Stahlhelm, a fact that helped explain the more superficial differences in style between the two organizations. By the same token, the Young German Order was more sincerely committed to winning the support of the German worker, although it, like the Stahlhelm, remained a predominantly middle-class organization that sought to accomplish this objective not so much by raising the banner of class warfare as by appealing to the worker's sense of national solidarity.[122] Thirdly, the Young German Order's commitment to the preservation of German Christian culture and its statutory ban against membership for Jews made it something of a haven for racists and political antisemites, many of whom had been affiliated with the German-Racist Protection and Defense League. Even though Mahraun and his closest associates did not sympathize with the more virulent expressions of antisemitic feeling that had surfaced in Germany since the end of the war, the Young German leadership routinely recommended antisemitic tracts such as Theodor Fritsch's *Handbuch zur Judenfrage* and Adolf Bartel's *Rasse und Volkstum* for the edification of its rank-and-file membership.[123] Its identification with the revolutionary élan of the prewar German youth movement, its appeal across class lines for the support of the German worker and its defense of Germany's Christian culture against those "un-German" elements that threatened to subvert it all tended to highlight the differences that separated the Young German Order from the more traditional fusion of

---

[120] Kurt Pastenaci, "Der Jungdeutsche Orden und die Jugendbewegung," *Süddeutsche Monatshefte* 23, no. 9 (June 1926): 177–80.

[121] [Artur Mahraun], "Ein Wendepunkt," in Jungdeutscher Orden, *Rundbriefe des Hochmeisters Nr. 1* (Berlin, n.d. [ca. 1925–26]), 1–6.

[122] For example, see [Jungdeutscher Orden], *Denkschrift zur westdeutschen Kundgebung des Jungdeutschen Ordens am 17. und 18. Juni 1922 in Barmen-Elberfeld* (N.p., 1922), 16.

[123] For a statement of Young German racial policy, see Mahraun, "Jungdeutsch-völkische Politik," in Artur Mahraun, *Reden und Aufsätze*, 3 vols. (Kassel, n.d. [1923–24]), 2:16–21. See also Crim, *Antisemitism*, 81–91, and Wieland Vogel, *Katholische Kirche und nationale Kampfverbände in der Weimarer Republik* (Mainz, 1989), 13–20, as well as the regional study by Werner Neuhaus, "Der Jungdeutsche Orden als Kern der völkischen Bewegung im Raum Arnsberg in den Anfangsjahren der Weimarer Republik," *Sauerland. Zeitschrift des Sauerländer Heimatbundes* 43, no. 1 (Mar. 2010): 15–20.

nationalism and bourgeois conservatism that lay at the heart of the Stahlhelm's ideological orientation.

United Patriotic Leagues

The period from 1919 to 1923 marked the heyday of Germany's patriotic movement. The Pan-German League, Stahlhelm, and Young German Order represented only a small fraction of the vast array of patriotic associations that dotted Germany's political landscape in the early 1920s. By the end of 1922 there were more than a hundred such organizations scattered throughout the Reich, some small with little more than a local or regional profile, others with a mass membership and a broad base of popular support. Their existence constituted an increasingly serious threat to established political authority to which the government and the parties supporting it did their best to respond. Following Rathenau's assassination inJ une 1922 the Wirth government moved quickly and forcefully against the threat that extremist organizations on the right posed to the stability of the republic. The chancellor proceeded to use presidential emergency powers to enact two decrees aimed at curtailing the activities of right-wing and anti-republican groups throughout the country by establishing a new federal court responsible for political crimes and threats against the republic. The government parties also began work on a "Law for the Protection of the Republic" that was approved by the Reichstag on 21 July 1922 and that provided legal justification for perpetuating the measures contained in Wirth's initial emergency decree. Armed with these powers, the government went after the German-Racist Protection and Defense League with such vehemence that the DSTB was eventually forced to dissolve itself in early 1923, while the Pan-Germans were obliged to curtail much of their activities in order to escape a similar fate. At the same time, both the Stahlhelm and the Young German Order were banned throughout much of the Reich, along with a number of other paramilitary organizations.[124]

It quickly became increasingly apparent that the various organizations on Germany's patriotic and paramilitary Right would benefit from tighter and more effective organization among themselves. During the war more than fifty such organizations had come together to form the Central Office of Patriotic Leagues (Zentralstelle vaterländischer Verbände) under the leadership of Count Friedrich von Baudissin. After Baudissin's death in February 1921, the Central Office of Patriotic Leagues merged in December 1922 with the Alliance for Patriotic Enlightenment (Arbeitsgemeinschaft für vaterländische Aufklärung) and the National Unity Front (Nationale Einheitsfront) to form

---

[124] Gotthard Jasper, *Der Schutz der Republik. Studien zur staatlichen Sicherung der Demokratie in der Weimarer Republik* (Tübingen, 1963), 56-69.

the United Patriotic Leagues of Germany (Vereinigte vaterländische Verbände Deutschlands or VVVD).[125] The VVVD's immediate objective was "the creation of a national unity front inside and outside of parliament with the ultimate goal of restoring Germany's freedom, unity, power, and greatness." In pursuit of this goal, the VVVD professed a policy of complete neutrality with respect to Germany's political parties and the various branches of the Christian faith.[126] What the VVVD actually meant by this, however, was highly selective and extended only to those parties whose national credentials were beyond reproach. The VVVD was, if nothing else, militantly anti-Marxist and sought to free Germany from the Bolshevik curse that had descended upon it with the defeat and collapse of 1918.[127] This, however, entailed a series of far-reaching domestic changes that included the elimination of the existing parliamentary system, the creation of a strong hereditary monarchy, and a return to a modified form of the constitutional arrangements that Bismarck had devised more than a half-century earlier. In the area of international affairs, the VVVD called for the repudiation of Versailles, the restoration of Germany's colonial empire, and the creation of a greater German Reich through the absorption of the German-speaking areas adjacent to Germany's postwar borders. Only the relatively moderate tone of the VVVD's appeal for a struggle against the Jewish spirit in scholarship, art, and the press distinguished its program from that of the Pan-Germans.[128]

The leadership of the VVVD rested in the hands of Fritz Geisler, a one-time member of the DVP Reichstag delegation and a prominent figure in the "yellow" trade-union movement.[129] The yellow unions were company unions that had been established in the last decade before the outbreak of World War I in an attempt to check the spread of the Christian and socialist labor movements.[130] In the late summer of 1920 Geisler succeeded in consolidating what remained of the prewar yellow unions into a new organization calling itself the National Federation of German Unions (Nationalverband deutscher

[125] Schultz-Oldendorf (Zentralstelle Vaterländischer Verbände), circular of 11 Dec. 1922, NL Westarp, Gärtringen, VN 86. See also James M. Diehl, "Von der 'Vaterlandspartei' zur 'Nationalen Revolution.' Die Vereinigten Vaterländischen Verbände Deutschlands (VVVD) 1922–1932," *Vierteljahrshefte für Zeitgeschichte* 33 (1985): 617–39.

[126] "Richtlinien der Vereinigten vaterländischen Verbände Deutschlands," May 1924, BHStA Munich, Abt. IV, EWB, 10/2.

[127] See Geisler's remarks in "Ein Jahr Vereinigte vaterländische Verbände," 26 Jan. 1924, BHStA Munich, Abt. IV, EWB, 10/2, as well as *Jahresbericht der Vereinigten Vaterländischen Verbände Deutschlands für das Berichtsjahr 1923* (Berlin, n.d. [1924]), 3–4.

[128] "Richtlinien der Vereinigten vaterländischen Verbände Deutschlands," n.d. [May 1924], BHStA Munich, Abt. IV, EWB, 10/2.

[129] See Rüdiger von der Goltz, "Die vaterländische Verbände," in *Volk und Reich der Deutschen*, ed. Bernhard Harms, 3 vols. (Berlin, 1929): 2:155–77, esp. 173–77.

[130] For further details, see Klaus J. Mattheier, *Die Gelben. Nationale Arbeiter zwischen Wirtschaftsfrieden und Streik* (Düsseldorf, 1973).

Gewerkschaften). The purpose of this organization, as Geisler explained in a speech in Hamburg in late August, was to promote Germany's national renewal by liberating the German worker from the spirit of self-interest that had come to dominate both the socialist and Christian labor movements.[131] But by the end of 1922 Geisler's advocacy of the yellow labor unions had so severely strained his ties to DVP national chairman Gustav Stresemann that he left the party to join the more militantly anti-republican DNVP.[132] Under Geisler's leadership, the VVVD struck a militantly anti-Marxist and antiso-cialist tone that appealed to a broad cross-section of Germany's conservative and nationalist associational life. Among the more than the hundred or so organizations affiliated with the VVVD were the Pan-German League, the National Rural League, the German National Youth League, the National Association of German Officers (Nationalverband Deutscher Offiziere), the National League of German White-Collar Professional Associations (Reichs-bund Deutscher Angestellten-Berufsverbände), the National Farm Workers' League (Reichlandarbeiterbund), and the National Alliance of Patriotic Workers' Clubs (Reichsbund vaterländischer Arbeitervereine). More than any other organization of its day, the VVVD served as a magnet to which right-wing organizations of all kinds were immediately attracted.[133]

The VVVD's rapid growth in the first year of its existence stemmed in no small measure from its ability to capitalize upon the upsurge in national feeling that had greeted the Franco-Belgian occupation of the Ruhr in January 1923. In appealing to this sentiment, the leaders of the VVVD made conveni-ent use of the "stab-in-the-back legend" and exhorted the various elements on the German Right to join forces in the struggle to free the Fatherland from the liberal and Marxist forces they held responsible for Germany's political and military collapse. Racism and antisemitism, on the other hand, played a relatively subordinate role in the VVVD's political calculations and were never as important in terms of its self-definition as they were for the Pan-German League, the Young German Order, and other right-wing organizations. Though by no means free of antisemitic prejudice, Geisler and the leaders of

[131] Fritz Geisler, *Die nationale, wirtschaftsfriedliche Gewerkschaftsbewegung beim Wieder-aufbau Deutschlands. Rede gehalten im National-Klub von 1919 in Hamburg am 31. August 1920* (Hamburg, n.d. [1920]), 39–40. See also Geisler's letter to the VVVD, Feb. 1, 1923, PA AA Berlin, NL Stresemann, 256/145106–08, as well as Geisler to Stresemann, 25 Aug. 1922, BA Koblenz, R 45 II, 37/133–35, and Geisler to Jarres, 1 Sept. 1924, BA Koblenz, NL Jarres, 54.

[132] See Geisler, "Eine Warnung an die Deutsche Volkspartei," *Das freie Wort*, 10 Sept. 1922, no. 37, as well as Geisler's letter to Heyl von Herrensheim, 6 Dec. 1922, BA Koblenz, NL Dingeldey, 72/103. On the final break between Geisler and the DVP in February 1923, see Stresemann to Uebel, 15 Mar. 1923, PA AA Berlin, NL Stresemann, 257/145240–42, as well as the report in the *Nationalliberale Correspondenz*, 15 Mar. 1923, no. 22.

[133] Goltz, "Die vaterländische Verbände," 155–73.

the VVVD argued that the "Jewish problem" was secondary to the larger task of uniting all national forces into a comprehensive political front capable of freeing the German people from the domination of Social Democracy at home and the shackles of Versailles abroad.[134]

Born of the sense of national desperation that accompanied Germany's military defeat, the patriotic societies took their place alongside political parties and economic interest organizations as the third pillar of organized conservatism in the Weimar Republic. To be sure, relations between these three pillars were fraught with all sorts of tensions, and it was never easy to reconcile the brand of radical nationalism articulated by the patriotic societies to the more mundane concerns that political parties and economic interest organizations faced as part of their everyday agenda. Indeed, the fate of political conservatism in the Weimar Republic would depend upon the extent to which it succeeded in harnessing the activism of the patriotic societies to its own political agenda. At no point would this challenge be more daunting than during the crisis year of 1923. The descent into hyperinflation, the Franco-Belgian occupation of the Ruhr, the omnipresent specter of Communism, the challenge of Bavarian separatism, and the rise of National Socialism culminating in the abortive "Beer Hall putsch" of November 1923 would all create new opportunities for the leaders of both the German National People's Party and the other organizations that stood on Germany's radical Right. At the same time, these developments would only exacerbate the rift between those on the German Right who were now prepared to cooperate with Germany's fledgling republican order for fear of what might happen if they failed to do so and those who remained implacably opposed to any accommodation with the hated Weimar system and indeed hoped to use the ever deepening crisis of 1923 to overthrow that system.

---

[134] Reichsgeschäftsstelle der vereinigten vaterländischen Verbände Deutschlands, *Deutschvölkische Freiheitspartei und vaterländische Bewegung. Ein Wort der Abwehr und Mahnung zur Einigkeit der vaterländischen Bewegung* (Berlin, 1923).

6

1923 – A Missed Opportunity?

The years from 1919 to 1923 were heady years for the German Right. The general crisis that surrounded the founding of the Weimar Republic provided the various organizations on the German Right with an opportunity to adjust to the dramatic changes that had taken place in Germany's political structure as a result of the November Revolution and to lay the foundations for a sustained offensive against Germany's fledgling republican institutions. Not only had the founders of the Weimar Republic left the social and economic bases of conservative power essentially intact, but the fact that the various factions in the German National People's Party were united in opposition to the new political order temporarily shielded it from the threat that acceptance of political responsibility would have posed to its unity. The DNVP's remarkable success in the early years of the Weimar Republic stemmed in no small measure from its ability to establish itself as the party of "national opposition" to the dramatic changes that had taken place in Germany's domestic and international situation following its defeat in World War I.[1] Its unconditional opposition to the Weimar Republic and the policy of fulfillment had allowed the DNVP to reclaim much of the nationalist terrain that political conservatism had surrendered in the last years of the Wilhelmine Empire and to forge a new alliance between governmental conservatives and radical nationalists. At the same time, the DNVP was able to reach across the ecological limits of prewar German conservatism to embrace soal groups that had previously remained outside its orbit. Much of the DNVP's success in this regard was fueled by the runaway inflation of the early 1920s. What remained uncertain as the German inflation drew to its frenetic climax in the summer and fall of 1923 was not the DNVP's growing popularity as an alternative to the more moderate bourgeois parties but whether or not the DNVP would be able to translate its political mandate into an effective and coherent program of political action.

---

[1] See the official party history by Axel von Freytagh-Loringhoven, *Deutschnationale Volkspartei* (Berlin, 1931), 10–16, as well as Max Maurenbrecher, *Die Taktik der Parteien 1920–1924. Betrachtungen über die parlamentarische Politik der nationalen Opposition* (Berlin, 1924), esp. 45–49, 93–95.

Coping with Inflation

The social and political consequences of the German inflation were enormous. The inflation originated not just in wartime shortages of food, raw materials, and other commodities but, more importantly, in the government's decision to finance the war by selling war bonds instead of increasing direct or indirect taxation beyond the limits of the tax model established in the 1913 budget. By the end of the war Germany's national indebtedness – mostly to its own citizens and domestic financiers – had reached unmanageable proportions, with the result that monetary depreciation had become an inescapable fact of German life. Given the fact that the military victory with which the German government had planned to repay this debt failed to materialize, the governments of the early Weimar Republic were left with no alternative but to repay the debt with currency that was no longer worth as much as it had been when the debt was originally contracted.[2] An inflationary fiscal policy also had political benefits in that it enabled the German economy to remain more or less at full employment and thus avoided the mass unemployment with all of its attendant consequences that had accompanied economic demobilization in Great Britain and France.[3] The acceptance of the London Ultimatum in May 1921 and the establishment of Germany's reparations burden at 132 billion gold marks dramatically intensified the inflationary pressures already at work in the German economy and set the stage for a new round of attacks on the stability of the German mark in the summer and fall of 1921.[4] Efforts to stabilize the mark – most notably in the spring of 1922 when the Wirth government fashioned a tax compromise designed to bring the inflationary spiral of the postwar era to a sudden halt – failed in part for the lack of a domestic consensus that was willing to accept the higher taxes it would have taken to balance the budget but also because the Allies were unwilling to negotiate a reduction in Germany's reparations burden that would have afforded the German government the time it needed to put its financial house back in order.[5] The assassination of German Foreign Minister Walther

---

[2] On the German inflation, see the authoritative synthesis by Gerald D. Feldman, *The Great Disorder: Politics, Economics, and Society in the German Inflation, 1914–1924* (Oxford, 1993), 25–96. On its international context, see Charles S. Maier, *Recasting Bourgeois Europe: Stabilization in France, Germany, and Italy in the Decade after World War I* (Princeton, NJ, 1975), 358–63, 385–86.

[3] Gerald D. Feldman, "The Political Economy of Germany's Relative Stabilization during the 1920/21 World Depression," in *Die deutsche Inflation. Eine Zwischenbilanz/The German Inflation Reconsidered*, ed. by Gerald D. Feldman, Carl-Ludwig Holtfrerich, Gerhard A. Ritter, and Peter-Christian Witt (Berlin and New York, 1982), 180–206.

[4] Feldman, *Great Disorder*, 309–417.

[5] For further details, see Peter-Christian Witt, "Staatliche Wirtschaftspolitik in Deutschland 1918 bis 1923. Entwicklung und Zerstörung einer modernen wirtschaftspolitischen

Rathenau by right-wing extremists in the summer of 1922 destroyed the last vestige of international confidence in Germany's ability to restore fiscal and economic solvency and accelerated the flight of foreign capital from the mark into more stable currencies. As a result, the inflation rapidly degenerated into a hyperinflation that over the course of the next sixteen months was to reduce the German mark to an infinitesimal fraction of its original worth.[6]

The net effect of the inflation was to accelerate the disintegration of those social strata that constituted the backbone of the German middle class and to intensify the degree of social and economic antagonism at all levels of German society. The social fabric of German political life dissolved into a Hobbesian state of *bellum omnium contra omnes* with organized economic interests serving as the principal solvent. In the meantime, the inflation greatly radicalized those social strata upon which the more moderate bourgeois parties depended for the bulk of their popular and electoral support. This was particularly true of the two liberal parties, both of which saw the social constituencies upon which they had traditionally relied decimated by the inflation.[7] The leaders of the DNVP, on the other hand, moved quickly to mobilize middle-class frustration over the deteriorating economic situation into a mandate for political change. The fact that the second wave of inflation in the summer and fall of 1921 coincided with the publication of Allied reparations demands made it easy for the Nationalists to explain the inflation as a consequence of Allied intransigence on reparations and the compliance of Germany's republican government in fulfilling the terms of the Versailles Peace Treaty and London Ultimatum. With Helfferich setting the tone, the leaders of the DNVP made reparations the ultimate cause of the inflationary spiral that was pressing so heavily upon the German middle classes. At the same time, Helfferich and the DNVP vehemently opposed any new taxes on Germany's propertied classes that might have alleviated the government's budgetary crisis.[8] From Helfferich's perspective, not only was the inflation part of a conspiracy by the Social Democrats and Allied powers to confiscate the wealth of Germany's propertied classes for the payment of reparations, but those who supported the policy of fulfillment were witting accomplices in the expropriation of the German middle classes. Only by ending the policy of fulfillment and the system of government that had made it possible, argued

---

Strategie," in *Die deutsche Inflation/The German Inflation Reconsidered*, ed. Feldman et al., (Berlin and New York, 1982), 151–79.

[6] Feldman, *Great Disorder*, 513–697.

[7] Larry Eugene Jones, "Democracy and Liberalism in the German Inflation: The Crisis of a Political Movement, 1918–1924," in *Konsequenzen der Inflation/Consequences of Inflation*, ed. Gerald D. Feldman, Carl-Ludwig Holtfrerich, Gerhard A. Ritter, and Peter-Christian Witt (Berlin, 1989), 3–43.

[8] Karl Helfferich, *Steuerkompromiß und nationale Opposition. Reichstagsreden vom 16. und 20. März 1922* (Berlin, 1922).

Helfferich, could one put an end to the suffering of the German middle classes.[9]

By blaming the inflation and the economic misery it had left in its wake on the Allies and those domestic politicians who were committed to fulfilling Allied reparations demands, the Nationalists were able to shift the focus of middle-class anxiety over the collapse of the German currency from the economic to the political arena. The implicit assumption that lay at the heart of the Nationalist position was that only by bringing the DNVP into the government would it be possible to marshal the national resources necessary to put an end to the policy of fulfillment and to resist future reparations demands. In a larger sense, however, this presupposed a fundamental realignment of the existing party system. For at the heart of Germany's political weakness, argued the Nationalists, lay a party system in which the balance of power rested with the parties of the middle or parliamentary center. Not only did these parties lack the resolve to join the DNVP in the creation of a united national front capable of bringing the revolutionary state of affairs that had existed in Germany since November 1918 to a close,[10] but the parties that supported the Weimar Republic were all in such a state of internal dissolution that neither the unification of the Independent and Majority Socialists nor the creation of the Coalition of the Constitutional Middle (Arbeitsgemeinschaft der verfassungstreuen Mitte) by the DDP, DVP, Center, and Bavarian People's Party in the summer of 1922 could provide Germany with the political stability it so sorely needed. Only through the creation of a united German Right on the broadest possible basis, the Nationalists insisted, could one reconcile the class antagonisms that had become so deeply embedded in the fabric of German society in the spirit of a genuine *Volksgemeinschaft*.[11]

Cuno, the DNVP, and the Patriotic Right

On 14 November 1922 the Wirth government submitted its resignation after efforts to bring the German People's Party into the cabinet had foundered on the opposition of the Majority Socialists. Two days later Reich President

---

[9] See Karl Helfferich, *Deutschlands Not und Rettung. Reichstagsrede gehalten am 26. Januar 1923* (Berlin, 1923), and Karl Helfferich, *Steuern, Geldentwertung und Sozialdemokratie. Reichstagsrede gehalten am 15. März 1923* (Berlin, 1923), as well as Helfferich's most sustained polemic against the policy of fulfillment in Karl Helfferich, *Die Politik der Erfüllung* (Berlin, 1922), esp. 81–90.

[10] Georg von Below, *Politik der Mitte – Politik der Schwäche*, Deutschnationale Flugschrift, no. 129 (Berlin, 1922), 7–8.

[11] For example, see Walther Lambach, *Die breitere Front im politischen Kampf*, Deutschnationale Flugschrift, no. 132 (Berlin, 1922), 22–23, and Max Wallraf, *Die deutschen Parteien am Scheidewege! Rede auf dem vierten Deutschnationalen Reichsparteitage in Görlitz am 28. Oktober 1922*, Deutschnationale Flugschrift, no. 139 (Görlitz, 1922), 4–11.

Friedrich Ebert entrusted the task of forming a new government to Wilhelm Cuno, the politically unaffiliated general director of the Hamburg-America Line (Hamburg-Amerikanische Packetfahrt-Actien-Gesellschaft or HAPAG). Chosen primarily because of his business and economic acumen, Cuno announced the formation of a new government consisting of representatives from the three parties of the Coalition of the Constitutional Middle and the Bavarian People's Party on 22 November. The DNVP party leadership greeted the fall of the Wirth government with a collective sigh of relief and welcomed Cuno's appointment as chancellor. Cuno was the first chancellor in Weimar's short history who enjoyed close personal ties to the leaders of the DNVP. Both Westarp and Helfferich could look back upon a long and warm relationship with both Cuno and his foreign minister, Frederic von Rosenberg, and they moved quickly to bring DNVP party chairman Oskar Hergt into their circle of confidence. At the same time, the Nationalists remained deeply suspicious of the chancellor's ties to Reich President Ebert and the four middle parties that had come together in the Coalition of the Constitutional Middle, and they vigorously resisted efforts by the presidential palace to draw the Social Democrats into the governmental coalition.[12] As a result, the declaration of support with which Hergt greeted the new cabinet upon its presentation to the Reichstag on 24 November 1922 was tempered by private misgivings on the part of Westarp and other party leaders about its ability to pursue an independent course of action.[13]

All of this dramatically changed when Germany was declared in default on the payment of reparations and French and Belgian troops occupied the Ruhr on 11 January 1923. The leaders of the DNVP fully anticipated the Allied action and had already begun to prepare the public for the struggle that lay ahead with appeals for national unity in face of the threat that occupation of the Ruhr posed to the existence of the Reich.[14] The DNVP rallied quickly to the support of the Cuno government and worked behind the scenes to stiffen its resolve to carry the policy of passive resistance in the Ruhr to a successful conclusion.[15] This was particularly true of Helfferich, who had served as Cuno's superior in the Office of the Treasury during the war and whose views

[12] Manuscript of Westarp's unpublished memoir from 1944–45, "Der Ruhrkampf. Kapitel 1: Regierung Cuno," NL Westarp, Gärtringen, VN 93, 1–5.

[13] Ibid., 7–9. See also the DNVP's statement on the formation of the Cuno government, [24] Nov. 1922, BA Berlin, R 8005, 9/114–19, as well as Brauer to Heydebrand, 1 Dec. 1922, NL Westarp, Gärtringen, II/83.

[14] For example, see Helffferich, "Um Leben und Tod," *Der deutsche Führer. Nationale Blätter für Politik und Kultur* 2, no. 3 (Feb. 1923): 63–65. See also Westarp, "Der Ruhrkampf. Kapitel 1: Regierung Cuno," NL Westarp, Gärtringen, VN 93, 32–38.

[15] See Hergt's memorandum of 3 Feb. 1923 of a meeting with Cuno on the previous day, BA Berlin, R 8005, 2/36, as well as Brauer to Heydebrand, 21 Mar. 1923, NL Westarp, Gärtringen, II/83.

on foreign policy and reparations coincided closely with those of the new chancellor. Helfferich not only exhorted the government in public to respond to the Allied occupation of the Ruhr with vigorous and decisive action,[16] but he consulted with Cuno and other cabinet officials on a regular basis through the spring and early summer of 1923 in an effort to shore up their support for efforts in the Ruhr at a time when the struggle was not going as well as they had hoped.[17] At the same time, Helfferich and the DNVP party leadership pressed the other parties from the Social Democrats to the racists on the DNVP's right to unite behind the chancellor in his struggle to save the Ruhr from Allied aggression. National unity, in the eyes of Westarp and his associates, constituted an indispensable prerequisite for success in the Ruhr, and they were unsparing in their attacks against the German Left for having placed partisan political interests before the struggle to preserve Germany's territorial integrity from Allied designs on the Ruhr.[18]

Throughout all of this, the leaders of the DNVP pursued a policy of "tempered opposition" with respect to the Cuno cabinet. What this meant was trying to keep the chancellor in power as long as possible and working through him to strengthen the backbone of resistance in the Ruhr.[19] At the same time, Westarp and the DNVP party leadership worked behind the scenes to restrain the more militantly anti-republican elements on their party's right wing from attacking the Cuno government too aggressively for its failure to check the fall of the mark or break the deadlock in the Ruhr. But if Helfferich and Westarp were able to soften criticism of Cuno within the ranks of the DNVP, neither they nor anyone else in the party were able to do much to dampen the aspirations of Germany's patriotic Right. With Fritz Geisler setting the tone, the newly founded United Patriotic Leagues of Germany immediately tried to position itself at the forefront of the national opposition to the Franco-Belgian occupation of the Ruhr. But the VVVD's propaganda was directed less against the occupying powers than against the Social Democrats for having allegedly undermined the German worker's will to resist. To address this situation, the VVVD sponsored the creation of local action committees in the Ruhr for the three-fold purpose of countering the effects of socialist subversion, destroying the French front in the Ruhr, and

---

[16] Helfferich, "Entschlossenheit im Ruhrkampf und Aktivität in der Außenpolitik," 18 Apr. 1923, in Karl Helfferich, *Reichstagsreden 1922–1924*, ed. J. W. Reichert (Berlin, 1925), 133–53.

[17] Hergt to Westarp, 28 May 1923, NL Westarp, Gärtringen, II/9. See also Williamson, *Helfferich*, 373–78.

[18] For further details, see Westarp's unpublished manuscript "Der Ruhrkampf. Kapitel 2: Auftakt Januar 1923," NL Westarp, Gärtringen, VN 93, 13–28.

[19] Brauer to Heydebrand, 7 May 1923, NL Westarp, Gärtringen, II/84.

forwarding reports on the situation in the Ruhr to the VVVD leadership in Berlin.[20] At the same time, the VVVD attacked the leaders of Germany's more moderate bourgeois parties for having failed to recognize the true motives of Social Democracy and for having deluded themselves into thinking that the socialists could overcome the crass egoism of the free trade-unions to take their place in the fight for German freedom.[21] As it became increasingly clear by the summer of 1923 that the policy of passive resistance had failed to free the Ruhr from foreign occupation, the VVVD called upon its allies on the patriotic Right to intensify their propaganda in order to prevent a complete breakdown of resistance in the Ruhr.[22]

Nowhere was the role of the patriotic Right more controversial than in Bavaria. The experience of the Munich soviet and its violent suppression in the spring of 1919 had done much to radicalize Bavarian political culture and to implant the fear of Bolshevism far more firmly in the psyche of Bavaria's propertied classes than in other parts of the country. After the Kapp putsch in the spring of 1920 the BVP's Gustav von Kahr, a political neophyte with close ties to Bavaria's paramilitary Right, assumed the post of Bavarian minister president. Kahr had been in office less than a month when he created a sensation by publicly raising the possibility that Bavaria might secede from the Reich if Berlin caved into Allied pressure for the dissolution of the civilian defense units, or *Einwohnerwehren*, and other paramilitary organizations that had taken refuge in Bavaria.[23] Although Kahr could not, in the final analysis, shield the *Einwohnerwehren* from Allied demands for their dissolution and eventually had to step down as Bavarian minister president in September 1921 in favor of the more compliant Count Hugo von Lerchenfeld,[24] Bavaria nevertheless became a haven for those on the radical Right who were prepared to use force to overthrow the Weimar Republic and replace it with a more

---

[20] VVVD Geschäftsstelle, "Bericht über die Zersetzungsversuche der Sozialdemokratie im Ruhrrevier," 1 Feb. 1923, NL Westarp, Gärtringen, VN 42. On the VVVD's struggle in the Ruhr, see *Jahresbericht der Vereinigten Vaterländischen Verbände Deutschlands für das Berichtsjahr 1923* (Berlin, n.d. [1924]), 6–14.

[21] VVVD Geschäftsstelle, "Was wollen wir?," Mar. 1923, NL Westarp, VN Gärtringen, VN 42.

[22] VVVD Geschäftsstelle, "Bericht über den Stand der Ruhrkampf," 28 June 1923, NL Westarp, VN Gärtringen, VN 42.

[23] See Kahr's remarks at a reception for the leaders of the civilian defense leagues, 9 Apr. 1920, *Frankfurter Zeitung*, 13 Apr. 1920, no. 267. See also Gustav von Kahr, *Reden zur bayerischen Politik. Ausgewählte Reden*, Politische Zeitfragen, nos. 22–24 (Munich, 1920), esp. 384–91.

[24] Wolfgang Zorn, *Bayerns Geschichte im 20. Jahrhundert. Von der Monarchie zum Bundesland* (Munich, 1986), 240–45.

authoritarian system of government.[25] At the same time, Bavarian authorities were vehemently opposed to the "Law for the Protection of the Republic" that the Reichstag had adopted in the wake of Rathenau's assassination and steadfastly refused to execute its provisions against the right-wing organizations that had sought refuge in Bavaria.[26] In the summer of 1922 twenty-one of the patriotic and veteran associations that maintained a presence in Bavaria came together to found the United Patriotic Leagues of Bavaria (Vereinigte Vaterländische Verbände Bayerns or VVVB) with none other than the venerable Kahr as its honorary chairman. With "Through White-Blue against Red-Gold-Black to Black-White-Red" as its motto, the founders of the VVVB sought nothing less than to revoke the social and political legacy of the November Revolution and restore the German imperial order beginning with the restoration of the Wittelsbach dynasty in Bavaria.[27]

All of this had enormous implications for the future of the Bavarian Middle Party, as the state chapter of the DNVP was generally known. Founded in the immediate aftermath of the November Revolution, the BMP had officially reconstituted itself as the DNVP's Bavarian chapter shortly before the June 1920 Reichstag elections. The DNVP national leadership would invest a great deal of energy and resources in establishing a foothold in Bavaria, a region in which conservatives had not done particularly well before 1914. As it was, the BMP's organization was largely confined to predominantly Protestant Franconia, and party leaders were eager to extend their party's influence into Upper Bavaria and those parts of the state with a predominantly Catholic population. The choice of Munich as the site of the DNVP's 1921 party congress was part of a calculated attempt to achieve a breakthrough into the ranks of Bavarian Catholics. Energized by Cardinal Michael von Faulhaber's caustic denunciation of the Weimar Constitution at the 1922 German Catholic Congress (Deutscher Katholikentag) in Munich as a product of "perjury and high treason" that bore the "mark of Cain,"[28] the leaders of the DNVP's Reich

---

[25] For further details, see Bruno Thoß, *Der Ludendorff-Kreis 1919–1923. München als Zentrum der mitteleuropäischen Gegenrevolution zwischen Revolution und Hitler-Putsch* (Munich, 1978), and Gordon, *Hitler and the Beer Hall Putsch,* 3–21.

[26] Gotthard Jasper, *Der Schutz der Republik. Studien zur staatlichen Sicherung der Demokratie in der Weimarer Republik* (Tübingen, 1963), 92–100.

[27] Untitled report on the paramilitary Right in Bavaria, 28 Apr. 1923, BA Berlin, R 8005, 27/69–71. See also the circular from the VVVB, 26 Oct. 1923, NL Westarp, Gärtringen, VN 42. For further details, see Gordon, *Hitler and the Beer Hall Putsch,* 88–119, and Hans Fenske, *Konservatismus und Rechtsradikalismus,* 164–69.

[28] Faulhaber's remarks in *Die Reden gehalten in den öffentlichen und geschlossenen Versammlungen der 62. General-Versammlung der Katholiken Deutschlands zu München 27. bis 30. August 1922* (Würzburg, 1923), 4.

Catholic Committee hoped that this would provide them with a decisive breakthrough into the ranks of Bavaria's Catholic population.[29]

All of this came to naught as the racist crisis that erupted within the DNVP in the summer and early fall of 1922 set the stage for a full-fledged fight for control of the BMP between the party's racist faction around Rudolf von Xylander and Rudolf Buttmann and the state party chairman Hans Hilpert. Although Hilpert, a secondary school teacher who had headed the party since its founding in 1918, managed to hang on to his position as BMP's chairman,[30] the secession of Graefe-Goldebee and his associates at the DNVP's Görlitz party congress and the subsequent expulsion of the group around Xylander and Buttmann from the BMP left the party vulnerable to the agitation of a new player on the Bavarian scene, the National Socialist German Workers' Party under the leadership of Adolf Hitler. The NSDAP had made significant gains ever since Hitler assumed control of the party in the summer of 1921 and appealed in large part to precisely the same voters whom the BMP hoped to attract. Hitler's appeal was not lost upon the DNVP's Bavarian supporters, many of whom began to express a private admiration for his tactical and oratorical skills at the same time that the BMP leadership were becoming increasingly concerned about the inroads of Hitler's party into the ranks of the BMP.[31] As the BMP's situation continued to deteriorate through the spring and early summer of 1923 with continued losses to the NSDAP in places like Kulmbach, Bayreuth, and Hof, its future effectiveness as a force in Bavarian political life became increasingly uncertain.[32]

From Cuno to Stresemann

As it became clear by the summer of 1923 that passive resistance had failed to dislodge the French and Belgians in the Ruhr and that the costs of passive resistance had made it impossible to stabilize the German mark, Cuno's hold on power became increasingly tenuous. Not only had the Allied rejection of

---

[29] Lejeune-Jung to Westarp, 28 Aug. 1922, "Dokumentation Lejeune-Jung," StA Paderborn, S2/125/32.

[30] Report on the extraordinary BMP party congress, 18 Nov. 1922, BA Berlin, R 8005, 26/56–60.

[31] Minutes of the BMP executive committee, 20 Dec. 1922, BA Berlin, R 8005, 26/46–49. On the appeal of Hitler to the DNVP's Bavarian supporters, see Traub, "Die Hitlersche Bewegung," *Eiserner Blätter* 4, no. 33 (11 Feb. 1923): 501–05, as well as Traub to Tirpitz, 21 Oct. 1922, BA-MA Freiburg, Nachlass Alfred von Tirpitz, 265/110–12.

[32] Hopp to Weilnböck, 13 Apr. 1923, BA Koblenz, NL Weilnböck, 4c. For two exemplary local studies, see Robert F. Hopwood, "Mobilization of a Nationalist Community, 1919–23," *German History* 10 (1992): 149–76, and Alex Burkhardt, "Postear 'Existential Conflict' and Right-Wing Politics in Hof an der Saale, 1918–1924," *German History* 36 (2018): 522–43.

the government's reparations note from 2 May 1923 made Germany's diplomatic isolation more apparent than ever, but by late summer the mark had fallen to a mere twentieth of what it had been worth only months before. At the same time, there were ominous signs that support for passive resistance was beginning to unravel. In late July a wave of wildcat strikes and rioting spread throughout the Ruhr and parts of unoccupied Germany, with the result that the Social Democrats began to waver in their support of passive resistance. No less ominous were the growing strength of the radical Left in Saxony and Thuringia and the increasing popularity of separatist movements in Bavaria and the Rhineland.[33] As rumors of Cuno's impending resignation became more and more persistent in the first week of August 1923, Helfferich met with the chancellor on 10 August in an ultimately futile attempt to persuade him to remain in office and take the lead in introducing a new currency based upon the value of Germany's rye production, a move that would have greatly enhanced the status and influence of the landowning aristocracy.[34] At the same time, Germany's paramilitary Right and their patrons in Berlin and Munich were busy at work hatching plans for a military coup and the establishment of a national dictatorship more or less along the lines of what Benito Mussolini had accomplished the previous fall in Italy.[35] The leaders of the DNVP did little to discourage these schemes, no doubt expecting that the collapse of the Cuno government would remove the last obstacle on their road to power. But when Reich President Ebert chose not one of their own but the DVP's Gustav Stresemann to assume responsibility for the formation of a new cabinet following Cuno's resignation on 11 August 1923, the leaders of the German Right suddenly found themselves confronted with a new situation that required an entirely new set of strategic calculations.[36]

Stresemann and the leaders of the DVP had begun to lay the foundation for a transfer of power in early July 1923 by suggesting that under certain circumstances they were prepared to discuss sharing governmental responsibility with the Social Democrats.[37] Realizing that Germany could ill afford the

---

[33] On the plight of the Cuno government, see Maier, *Recasting Bourgeois Europe*, 364–73, and Rupieper, *Cuno and Reparations*, 174–99.

[34] On Helfferich's meeting with Cuno, see Westarp's unpublished manuscript entitled "Inflation" from 1944–45, NL Westarp, Gärtringen, VN 93, 30–31. See also Cuno to Gildemeister, 26 Feb. 1924, StA Hamburg, records of the Hapag-Lloyd Rederei, Handakten Cuno, 1489.

[35] For further details, see Raffael Scheck, "Politics of Illusion: Tirpitz and Right-Wing Putschism, 1922–1924," *German Studies Review* 18 (1995): 29–49. See also Bruno Thoß, "Nationale Rechte, militärische Führung und Diktaturfrage in Deutschland 1913–1923," *Militärgeschichtliche Mitteilungen* 42 (1987): 27–76.

[36] On Cuno's resignation, see Rupieper, *Cuno and Reparations*, 211–17.

[37] Stresemann's speech before the DVP central executive committee, 7 July 1923, in *Nationalliberalismus in der Weimarer Republik*, ed. Kolb and Richter, 1:467–74. For

strain of a prolonged cabinet crisis, the Social Democrats indicated that they too were prepared to enter a government of the Great Coalition with a nonsocialist as chancellor.[38] Although the idea of coalition with the Social Democrats met with strong opposition from the leaders of the DVP's right wing, Stresemann persuaded a majority of his colleagues at a meeting of the DVP Reichstag delegation on 10 August 1923 to seek a government of the Great Coalition with a nonsocialist as chancellor should efforts to keep the Cuno government in office fail.[39] Ignoring pressure from within his own party, Ebert accepted the recommendation of the Coalition of the Constitutional Middle and entrusted Stresemann with the task of forming a new government. With remarkable dispatch, Stresemann was able to organize his cabinet in time for its installation in office on the evening of 13 August 1923. To be sure, Stresemann would have preferred the formation of a national unity front reaching from the Social Democrats to the Nationalists, but the latter, in Stresemann's eyes, had taken themselves out of the running as a prospective coalition partner by virtue of their relentless and unscrupulous agitation against the Social Democrats.[40] Under the circumstances, Stresemann felt that the Nationalists had left him with no alternative but to reach an accommodation with the Social Democrats that saw them receive four cabinet posts, including the all-important ministries of finance and interior.[41]

The Nationalists were infuriated by the way in which they had been passed over in favor of the Social Democrats in the reorganization of the national cabinet. They were particularly concerned that Stresemann's appointment as chancellor foreshadowed the end of passive resistance in the Ruhr,[42] and in his official interpellation in the Reichstag on 14 August Hergt not only criticized the new government's dependence upon the Social Democrats in the Reich and Prussia but exhorted it to intensify the struggle against the French in the Ruhr.[43] But the party was far from united in its position on the Stresemann cabinet. At a meeting on 14 August the DNVP Reichstag delegation had split

further details, see Wright, *Stresemann*, 195–212, and Richter, *Deutsche Volkspartei*, 267–72.

[38] On Stresemann's contacts with the Social Democrats, see his letters to Kempkes, 29 July 1923, PA AA Berlin, NL Stresemann, 260/145780–84, and Leidig, 29 July 1923, ibid., 145788–90.

[39] Minutes of the DVP Reichstag delegation, 10 Aug. 1923, PA AA Berlin, NL Stresemann, 87/171264–65.

[40] Henry Bernhard, *Das Kabinett Stresemann* (Berlin, 1924), 5.

[41] For the composition of the first Stresemann cabinet, see Gustav Stresemann, *Vermächtnis. Der Nachlaß in drei Bänden*, ed. Henry Bernhard and with the collaboration of Walter Goetz, 3 vols. (Berlin, 1932–33), I:88–89.

[42] Unpublished memoir by Westarp from 1945, "Ruhrkampf und Regierung Stresemann," NL Westarp, Gärtringen, VN 93, 1–3.

[43] Ibid., 82–83.

down the middle in a vote on the wording of its official response to the formation of the Stresemann cabinet and ultimately opted for the more measured tone that Hergt had taken in his interpellation before the Reichstag.[44] For the moment, the DNVP party leadership was content to temper its criticism of the Stresemann cabinet in the hope that some sort of accommodation with the new government might still be possible. As a conciliatory gesture, Stresemann invited Helfferich to meet with members of his cabinet on 18 August to present the outlines of his proposal for stabilization of the mark.[45] But a formal proposal that Helfferich submitted to the cabinet three days later was referred to a committee of experts, where it languished until the confusion surrounding the formation of the new government could resolve itself. In the meantime, the Social Democrats launched a major press attack against the Helfferich proposal under the slogan "Los von Helfferich und seinem Projekt." From the DNVP's perspective, these attacks were politically motivated and designed, in Westarp's words, "to keep this exceptionally energetic and dangerous leader of the national opposition [i.e. Helfferich] from showing the governing majority the way to salvation" and thus prevent his party from receiving the "credit and fame to which it was entitled."[46] Whatever its motives might have been, the Social Democratic campaign against Helfferich's currency proposal was not without effect upon the coalition parties, with the result that it never made it out of the committee to which it had been referred.[47]

The Nationalists responded to their exclusion from the Stresemann cabinet and its dismissal of Helfferich's proposal for a reform of the German currency with a fourteen-point action program on 28 August 1923. The "Aktionsprogramm der Deutschnationalen Volkspartei" denounced the Stresemann government for its dependence upon the Social Democrats and called for a vigorous foreign policy aimed at intensifying national resistance in the Ruhr and Rhineland. At the same time, the Nationalists warned against a second German revolution and demanded measures to restore of the authority of the state not only by making it independent of the mood of the masses but, more radically, by placing extraordinary powers in the hands of a special office that could "save the honor and future of the German people" free from the pressure

---

[44] Entry in Gallwitz's diary, 14 Aug. 1923, BA-MA Freiburg, NL Gallwitz, 39.

[45] Reichert's protocol of a meeting between representatives of the Stresemann cabinet and a three-man delegation from the DNVP, 18 Aug. 1923, in *Akten der Reichskanzlei: Die Kabinette Stresemann I u. II. 13. August bis 6. Oktober 1923. 6. Oktober bis. 30. November 1923*, ed. Karl Dietrich Erdmann and Martin Vogt, 2 vols. (Boppard am Rhein, 1978), 1:23–29.

[46] Westarp, "Inflation," NL Westarp, Gärtringen, VN 93, 33–34.

[47] For further details, see Claus-Dieter Krohn, "Helfferich contra Hilferding. Konservative Geldpolitik und die sozialen Folgen der deutschen Inflation 1918–1923," *Vierteljahrsschrift für Sozial- und Wirtschaftsgeschichte* 62 (1975): 62–92.

of the streets, parties, and party coalitions. At the same time, the program also advocated a number of specific measures aimed at providing tax relief for agriculture, creating an "honest currency," improving domestic productivity, and halting, if not reversing, the flood of alien – in particular east European Jewish – elements into Germany.[48] The publication of this program represented nothing less than a declaration of war against the Stresemann cabinet and committed the DNVP to a course of unconditional opposition to both its domestic and foreign policies.[49]

Within the DNVP, Stresemann's most determined opponent was Alfred Hugenberg, whose enmity towards the new chancellor dated back to the last years of the Second Empire. Writing to the DVP's Hugo Stinnes two days before Stresemann's appointment as chancellor, Hugenberg explained:

> I have nothing against the person of Stresemann. But he has neither nerve nor inner strength nor political instinct; in decisive moments (see his vacillation at the time of the [London] Ultimatum) he never does the right thing. In himself he embodies all that is weak and politically immature in the German bourgeoisie. I think it is therefore highly likely – if not certain – that if he becomes Reich Chancellor at this point in time, this would be the fateful end [*Verhängnis*] of the German bourgeoisie. I therefore implore you, before I travel away for the next forty-eight hours, to do your best to see that not he but [Albert] Vögler – after all I have to name another name – becomes Reich Chancellor.[50]

Hugenberg's hostility towards Stresemann had less to do with the latter's alleged lack of nerve or political instinct than with the fact that the two men represented fundamentally different strategies for resolving the crisis in which Germany found itself. Stresemann was convinced that the painful measures necessary to stabilize the currency and restore economic productivity could be implemented only on the basis of a broad parliamentary mandate that included the Social Democrats as the representative of that group most likely to bear the brunt of Germany's fiscal and economic stabilization.[51] Hugenberg, on the other hand, was adamantly opposed to any sort of collaboration with the Social Democrats and believed that the entire parliamentary system had to be dismantled before Germany could begin its recovery from the deepening

[48] Albrecht Philipp, *Von Stresemann zu Marx. Sechs Monate deutschnationaler Politik (August 1923–Januar 1924)*, Deutschnationale Flugschrift, no. 146 (Berlin, 1924), 4–8. See also Westarp, "Ruhrkampf und Regierung Stresemann," NL Westarp, Gärtringen, VN 93, 100.

[49] For the mood in the DNVP, see Westarp to Helfferich, 1 Sept. 1923, NL Westarp, Gärtringen, II/9, as well as the memorandum appended to Lindeiner-Wildau to Hergt, 4 Sept. 1923, BA Berlin, R 8005, 2/32–35.

[50] Hugenberg to Stinnes, 11 Aug. 1923, ACDP Sankt-Augustin, NL Stinnes I-220/022/2.

[51] Stresemann to Schultz, 9 Oct. 1923, PA AA Berlin, NL Stresemann, 87/171367–69.

economic crisis.[52] Hugenberg also disagreed with the fundamental premise of Stresemann's foreign policy by insisting that Germany should not negotiate with the Allies over the revision of Versailles and the reduction of her reparations burden but should repudiate them outright.[53] Underlying these differences lay an even more fundamental difference in that Hugenberg was fully prepared to use the crisis that had descended upon Germany to destroy the republican system of government while Stresemann remained deeply committed to the principles of parliamentary government and eventually hoped to stabilize the Weimar Republic by winning the cooperation of the German Right.

The conflict between Stresemann and Hugenberg was to become the defining feature of German bourgeois politics for the next half decade. In his efforts to undercut Stresemann's position as head of the German government, Hugenberg found ready allies in the chancellor's own party, where no fewer than twenty-two members of the DVP Reichstag delegation had registered their disapproval of Stresemann's coalition with the Social Democrats by abstaining in the formal vote of confidence that took place in the Reichstag on 14 August 1923.[54] The driving force behind the anti-Stresemann fronde in the DVP was Stinnes, who had been on a collision course with the party leader ever since he entered the Reichstag in the summer of 1920.[55] As one of Germany's most powerful industrialists, Stinnes was convinced that the stabilization of the German currency should not take place until certain conditions designed to improve the nation's industrial productivity had been satisfied. First and foremost among those measures was a repeal of the eight-hour day, a reform that organized labor had rightfully come to regard as the most important social achievement of the November Revolution.[56] Stinnes opposed Stresemann's "Great Coalition" with the Social Democrats for the simple reason that the composition of the new government would prevent it from enacting the reforms he thought essential for Germany's economic recovery. Neither the appointment of Rudolf Hilferding, a prominent Social Democratic fiscal specialist, to the all-important ministry of finance nor the fact that Hans von

---

[52] Hugenberg, "Parteien und Parlamentarismus," in Alfred Hugenberg, *Streiflichter aus Vergangenheit und Gegenwart* (Berlin, 1927), 79–83.

[53] Hugenberg, "Locarno," ibid., 88–91.

[54] For further details, see Jones, *German Liberalism*, 197, and Richter, *Deutsche Volkspartei*, 273–75.

[55] Gerald D. Feldman, "Hugo Stinnes, Gustav Stresemann, and the Politics of the DVP in the Early Weimar Republic," in *Gestaltung des Politischen. Festschrift für Eberhard Kolb*, ed. Wolfram Pyta and Ludwig Richter (Berlin, 1998), 421–42.

[56] See Hugo Stinnes, *Mark-Stabilisierung und Arbeitsleistung. Rede gehalten am 9. November 1922 im Reichswirtschaftsrat* (Berlin, 1922), as well as the memorandum of his conversation with Stresemann, 19 Mar. 1923, PA AA Berlin, NL Stresemann, 257/145243–45.

Raumer, the DVP's most eloquent spokesman for cooperation with the Social
Democrats, had been entrusted with the ministry of economics helped assuage
the fears of Stinnes and his associates that, if Stresemann was to have his way,
the stabilization of the mark would take place on terms they could ill afford to
accept.[57]

At a meeting of the DVP Reichstag delegation on 12 September 1923,
Stinnes fired the first salvo in what would quickly develop into a virtual
rebellion on the party's right wing when he attacked the national government
for its passivity during the past five weeks and warned that if it did not take
immediate action to create more work, stabilize the currency, and remove the
left-wing governments in Saxony and Thuringia, then civil war would erupt in
the next fourteen days.[58] With the termination of passive resistance in the
Ruhr, the campaign against Stresemann would become even more heated.
Stresemann's announcement on 26 September 1923 that the government
would no longer support passive resistance in the Ruhr provoked a storm of
protest throughout right-wing circles across the country. The anti-Stresemann
forces in the DVP responded by intensifying their campaign against his
chancellorship and leadership of the party. At a meeting of the DVP Reichstag
delegation on 25 September – the day before the termination of passive
resistance was officially announced – Reinhold Quaatz, a Stinnes protégé with
close ties to Hugenberg, denounced the government's decision as an act of
"capitulation ultima forma" that could only end in the formation of a separate
Rhenish state. Quaatz demanded nothing less than the repudiation of the
Versailles Peace Treaty and preparations for a struggle that Germany could
not yet afford to fight. "Whoever does not want to cooperate in these preparations in the nation at large," continued Quaatz, "must be beaten to the
ground with a mailed fist [bewaffneter Hand]."[59]

Within the DNVP Stresemann's decision to terminate passive resistance in
the Ruhr met with almost universal condemnation.[60] As late as two days
before the official announcement terminating passive resistance in the Ruhr,
Westarp and his associates in the DNVP leadership had reason to believe that
Ernst Scholz, chairman of the DVP Reichstag delegation, and Karl Jarres,
Reich commissar for the occupied territories, would succeed in persuading
Stresemann to abandon plans for the termination of passive resistance and

[57] For further details, see Peter Wulf, *Hugo Stinnes. Wirtschaft und Politik 1918–1924*
(Stuttgart, 1979), 425–65, and Gerald D. Feldman, *Hugo Stinnes. Biographie eines Industriellen 1870–1924* (Munich, 1998), 884–905.

[58] Minutes of the DVP Reichstag delegation, 12 Sept. 1923, PA AA Berlin, NL Stresemann,
87/171307.

[59] Minutes of the DVP Reichstag delegation, 25 Sept. 1923, ibid., 87/171326–31. See also
Günter Arns, "Die Krise des Weimarer Parlamentarismus im Frühherbst 1923," *Der Staat*
8 (1969): 181–216.

[60] Entry in Gallwitz's diary, 10 Sept. 1923, BA-MA Freiburg, NL Gallwitz, 39.

that he would break with the Social Democrats in favor of a coalition with the DNVP.[61] The Nationalists denounced the end of passive resistance as an act of capitulation to the French and blasted the Stresemann cabinet for having abandoned the struggle against the Allied occupation of the Ruhr without significant concessions from the enemy. All of this the Nationalists attributed to Stresemann's dependence upon the Social Democrats, who had consistently refused to join the DNVP and other groups on the German Right in a united national front against Allied aggression in the Ruhr. By allying himself with the Social Democrats, the Nationalists claimed, Stresemann had become their willing accomplice in orchestrating Germany's defeat in the Ruhr. Now, Westarp argued in a lead article for the Neue Preußische (Kreuz-) Zeitung, only a complete break of diplomatic relations with France could compensate for the humiliation of defeat in the Ruhr, as he exhorted Stresemann to sever all ties with the Social Democrats so that the next phase in the struggle for Germany's national rehabilitation could begin.[62]

Putschism on the Right

Stresemann's decision to terminate passive resistance in the Ruhr galvanized the German Right both within and outside of parliament. This was particularly true in Bavaria, where the state government reacted to the termination of passive resistance by declaring a state of emergency and investing Gustav von Kahr with special executive powers as general state commissar. Kahr, who had served as Bavarian minister president for fifteen months from the spring of 1920 to the summer of 1921, was an outspoken monarchist with little love for the Weimar Republic who had played a leading role in organizing the various patriotic organizations that had taken refuge in Bavaria into the United Patriotic Leagues of Bavaria.[63] While Kahr's appointment had the effect of placing an official stamp of approval on the patriotic leagues' struggle against the so-called Weimar system, it was also an attempt to contain the more radical elements on the patriotic Right that had coalesced behind the NSDAP's Adolf Hitler and war hero Erich Ludendorff in the German Combat League (Deutscher Kampfbund) at the beginning of September 1923.[64] Kahr's appointment greatly exacerbated the tensions

---

[61] Westarp, "Ruhrkampf und Regierung Stresemann," NL Westarp, Gärtringen, VN 93, 87. See also Brauer to Heydebrand, 24 Sept. 1923, NL Westarp, Gärtringen, II/84.

[62] Westarp, "Ruhrkampf und Regierung Stresemann," NL Westarp, Gärtringen, VN 93, 31–36. In a similar vein, see Wir Deutschnationalen und die Regierung Stresemann. Sonderabdruck aus der "Hessischen Landeszeitung," Darmstadt, Nr. 217 und 222 vom 17. und 22. September 1923 (n.p. [Darmstadt], n.d. [1923]).

[63] Fenske, Konservatismus und Rechtsradikalismus, 188–223.

[64] Kahr to Stegmann, 14 Oct. 1923, BA Koblenz, Nachlass Hermann Stegmann, 1.

between Munich and Berlin and revived the specter of a new constitutional crisis when on 27 September Kahr refused to execute a federal order from Reich Defense Minister Otto Gessler to ban the *Völkischer Beobachter*, the official Nazi party organ, because of its seditious attacks against officials of the central government.[65]

Figure 5. Photograph of Adolf Hitler at a rally of right-wing forces at the Deutscher Tag in Nuremburg, 1 September 1923. This is the earliest photograph of Hitler as leader of the Nazi party. Reproduced with permission from the Bundesarchiv Berlin, Bild 102-16148

[65] Gordon, *Hitler and the Beer Hall Putsch*, 212–37.

It was against the background of these developments that the Reichswehr's
Hans von Seeckt, one of the most enigmatic figures in Weimar politics,
became more actively involved in efforts to seek a solution to the crisis that
had paralyzed Germany's parliamentary institutions. Ever since his appointment as chief of army command in the aftermath of the Kapp putsch, Seeckt
had pursued one overriding goal, namely, to keep the Reichswehr from being
drawn into the domestic political conflict so that at the proper moment it
could serve as an instrument of German foreign policy. As much as Seeckt
sought to immunize the Reichswehr against the factionalism of Weimar
political life, he also remained a profoundly conservative individual who
believed that monarchy was the form of government best suited to the
traditions and psychology of the German people.[66] With the virtual collapse
of state authority during the course of 1923, Seeckt found himself under
growing pressure from various factions on the German Right to assume a
more active role in the search for a solution to the political crisis that
threatened the complete paralysis of Germany's national life. On 23 September
Seeckt received Hergt and Westarp from the DNVP party leadership and
might have responded more favorably to their suggestion that he become
chancellor had it not been for the counsel of his closest advisors.[67] But when
the Pan-German League's Heinrich Claß implored him to take matters into his
own hands and seize power by force, Seeckt countered in such a way as to
suggest that he regarded the radical Right a threat to the unity of the Reich that
was every bit as serious as the radical Left.[68] From beginning to end, Seeckt
remained unalterably opposed to the putschist ambitions of the radical Right.

As much as Seeckt was committed to preserving the political neutrality of the
Reichswehr, he deeply despised Stresemann and anxiously awaited the failure of
his misguided experiment with the Social Democrats. Whatever initial reticence
Seeckt may have had about becoming more actively involved in the domestic
political arena, however, quickly evaporated in the wake of Stresemann's decision to terminate passive resistance in the Ruhr and the crisis this triggered in
the Reich's relations with Bavaria. When the Bavarian government responded
to the termination of passive resistance by proclaiming a state of emergency,
Seeckt saw this as a clear and unequivocal threat to the unity of the Reich and
the authority of its central government. Despite his deep-seated aversion to
politics and his desire to preserve the political neutrality of the Reichswehr,
Seeckt began to entertain the possibility of assuming the chancellorship himself
and turned to Friedrich Minoux, one of Stinnes's closest political associates, for

[66] F. L. Carsten, *The Reichwehr and Politics 1918 to 1923* (Oxford, 1966), 103–24. See also
William Mulligan, "The *Reichswehr*, the Republic, and the Primacy of Foreign Policy,
1918–1923," *German History* 21 (2003): 347–68.
[67] Hans Meier-Welcker, *Seeckt* (Frankfurt, 1967), 374.
[68] Ibid., 374–75. On Claß's contacts with Seeckt, see Leicht, *Claß*, 315–23.

advice on fiscal and economic matters. Minoux's influence on Seeckt's thinking was reflected in two lengthy memoranda – one entitled "Ein Regierungspro-gramm" and the other "Entwürfe zur etwaigen Regierungsübernahme" – that Seeckt composed on or around 27 September. Here Seeckt outlined a series of far-reaching constitutional and economic changes that included a reform of Germany's federal structure aimed at ending the dualism between the Reich and Prussia, an increase in the voting age to twenty-five, the creation of a national chamber of estates (*Reichs-Ständekammer*), the prohibition of cartels and trusts, the cancellation of collective labor agreements, and the replacement of trade unions by occupational chambers (*Berufskammer*).[69] The implemen-tation of these reforms would be entrusted to a transitional cabinet, or direc-torium, appointed by Reich President Ebert and vested with special emergency powers authorized by Article 48 of the Weimar Constitution. The three men whom Seeckt had in mind for the directorium were himself, Minoux, and the former director of the Krupp Steel Works and current ambassador to the United States, Otto Wiedfelt.[70]

In the meantime, events in Berlin were assuming a momentum of their own. The newspapers under the control of Hugenberg and Stinnes had been quick to seize upon the termination of passive resistance to launch a series of attacks against the Social Democrats just as Hilferding and Raumer were putting the finishing touches on a special enabling act designed to stabilize the mark. Frustrated by the Social Democrats' refusal to include a provision extending the length of the work day in the proposed enabling act, Stinnes and his supporters were so abusive in their attacks against the government's economic policy that on 2 October Hilferding and Raumer resigned from the cabinet.[71] Two days later – thus at a point in the negotiations when it was still unclear whether Stresemann would succeed in retaining the support of the Social Democrats – the leaders of the DVP Reichstag delegation approached the DNVP to determine if it would support a Stresemann cabinet without formal ties to individual political parties and if it would vote to authorize the special emergency powers the cabinet needed to deal with the rapidly deteriorating

---

[69] These two documents, the originals of which are in BA-MA Freiburg, Nachlass Hans von Seeckt, 139/6–15, have been reprinted in *Kabinette Stresemann*, ed. Erdmann and Vogt, 2:1203–10.

[70] Eberhard Kessel, "Seeckts politisches Programm von 1923," in *Spiegel der Geschichte. Festgabe für Max Braubach zum 10. April 1964*, ed. Konrad Repgen and Stephan Skalweit (Münster, 1964), 887–914. On Seeckt's plans for the creation of a directorium, see Meier-Welcker, *Seeckt*, 390–94, 400–04, 412–15, and Cartsen, *Reichswehr and Politics*, 153–95. On the relationship between Stinnes and Seeckt, see Wulf, *Stinnes*, 452–65, and Feldman, *Stinnes*, 889–93, 902–05.

[71] Raumer to Stresemann, 2 Oct. 1923, in *Kabinette Stresemann*, ed. Erdmann and Vogt, 1:446.

situation in central Germany and Bavaria.[72] Just two days earlier all but one member of the DNVP Reichstag delegation – Gustav Roesicke – had rejected their party's participation in a cabinet that was not formally tied to individual political parties.[73] Now, on the question of the DNVP's participation in a bourgeois coalition government under Stresemann's leadership the delegation split down the middle with twenty-seven deputies in support and twenty-eight opposed.[74] But all of this fell apart when on 6 October Stresemann, contrary to all expectations, reached a compromise with the Social Democrats on the contentious issue of work hours that secured their participation in a second Stresemann cabinet with a profile decidedly more conservative than that of the first.[75]

The Nationalists responded to this turn of events with a bitter invective that was directed not just against the concept of the "Great Coalition" but against the parliamentary system of government itself.[76] None of this did much to mollify Stresemann's enemies on the right wing of his own party. Neither the appointment of Count Gerhard von Kanitz and Karl Jarres – both politicians with impeccable conservative credentials – to the ministries of agriculture and interior respectively nor the transfer of Hans Luther, an influential municipal politician with close ties to the Ruhr industrial establishment, from the ministry of agriculture to the all-important ministry of finance could assuage the frustration that Stinnes and the leaders of the DVP's right wing felt over the fact that, despite their best efforts, the Social Democrats were still members of a national government in which the DVP was represented by no less than the chairman of their own party.[77]

The Crisis Peaks

While the Stresemann cabinet used the emergency powers it had received on 13 October to order federal troops into Saxony and Thuringia to depose the

---

[72] Westarp, "Ruhrkampf und Regierung Stresemann," NL Westarp, Gärtringen, VN 93, 88–89. See also the letter from Ada Gräfin von Westarp to Gertraude Freifrau Hiller von Gaertingen, 4 Oct. 1923, NL Westarp, Gärtringen, as well as Philipp, *Von Stresemann zu Marx*, 12–16.

[73] Entry in Gallwitz's diary, 2 Oct. 1923, BA-MA Freiburg, NL Gallwitz, 39.

[74] Entry in Gallwitz's diary, 4 Oct. 1923, ibid.

[75] For further details, see Jones, *German Liberalism*, 200–02; Wright, *Stresemann*, 223–26; and Richter, *Deutsche Volkspartei*, 284–86.

[76] Westarp, "Ruhrkampf und Regierung Stresemann," NL Westarp, Gärtringen, VN 93, 92–97.

[77] See the sharp exchange of letters between Stinnes and Stresemann, 7–11 Oct. 1923, PA AA Berlin, NL Stresemann, 2/154192–94, 154226–28, as well as Feldman, *Stinnes*, 883–905.

left-wing governments that had assumed power there,[78] the Bavarian government refused to recognize the legitimacy of the cabinet's emergency powers.
For his own part, Kahr hoped that the defiance of the Bavarian government
would pave the way for Stresemann's dismissal or resignation.[79] To Kahr's
supporters in the patriotic movement, it seemed as if the moment for which
they had been waiting had at long last arrived. Not only did it seem as if Kahr
and his shadow government were about to emulate Mussolini's celebrated
"March on Rome" with their own "March on Berlin," but it would be an event
in which the patriotic associations would fulfill their historic destiny by freeing
Berlin from the grip of the November criminals and by demolishing the
system of government they held responsible for Germany's national weakness.[80] Emboldened by his success in Bavaria, Kahr began to cultivate contacts
with Seeckt and other prominent conservatives outside his home state. One of
those with whom Kahr made contact was the retired admiral and former
secretary of the navy Alfred von Tirpitz, whom he had met at a conference on
"National Propaganda for the Countryside" that a trio of right-wing intellectuals – Paul Nikolaus Coßmann of the prestigious *Münchner Neueste
Nachrichten*, Martin Spahn from the newly founded Political College for
National Political Training and Pedagogy (Politisches Kolleg für nationalpo-
litische Schulungs- und Bildungsarbeit) in Berlin, and the celebrated neoconservative historian Oswald Spengler – had organized for approximately sixty
supporters of the German Right in Munich for three days in early November
1922.[81] Over the course of the next several months Tirpitz intensified his
contacts with Kahr[82] and other representatives of the Bavarian Right and lent
his support to the establishment of a new right-wing press office known as the
Joint Committee (Gemeinsamer Ausschuß or GA, later as Gäa) that was
founded in Munich on 14 December 1922.[83] Like Kahr and Stinnes, Tirpitz
was to remain a key player in the conspiratorial calculations of the German
Right through the fall of 1923 and into the spring of the following year.[84]

---

[78] Wright, *Stresemann*, 238–44. See also Donald B. Pryce, "The Reich Government versus
Saxony, 1923: The Decision to Intervene," *Central European History* 10 (1977): 112–47,
and Benjamin Lapp, *Revolution from the Right: Politics, Class and the Rise of Nazism in
Saxony, 1919–1933* (Atlantic Highlands, NJ, 1997), 76–110.

[79] Kahr to Stegmann, 14 Oct. 1923, BA Koblenz, NL Stegmann, 1.

[80] Remarks by Geisler and Bauer at the VVVD delegate conference in Berlin, 13 Oct. 1923,
NL Westarp, Gärtringen, VN 42.

[81] "Tagung über nationale Aufklärung auf dem flachen Land," Nov. 1922, BA-MA Freiburg,
NL Tirpitz, 293/156–57. On Tirpitz's involvement, see Scheck, *Tirpitz*, 82–94.

[82] For example, see Tirpitz to Kahr, 12 Nov. 1922, BA-MA Freiburg, NL Tirpitz, 254.

[83] On the founding and goals of the Gäa, see Oettingen-Wallenstein to Tirpitz, 16 Feb. 1923,
BA-MA Freiburg, NL Tirpitz, 296/13–14, as well as Karl Alexander von Müller, *Im
Wandel einer Welt. Erinnerungen 1919–1932* (Munich, 1966), 120–24.

[84] Scheck, *Tirpitz*, 95–113.

Throughout all of this, Hergt and the leaders of the DNVP had maintained a conspicuously low profile. The Nationalists had steadfastly resisted Stresemann's entreaties to accept a share of governmental responsibility in a broadly based cabinet of national concentration and strongly opposed the emergency authorization the chancellor received from the Reichstag on 13 October.[85] Westarp in particular remained adamantly opposed to the DNVP's participation in a Stresemann cabinet despite the fact that a number of his colleagues in the DNVP Reichstag delegation were prepared to enter into the national government if Stresemann were replaced as chancellor by someone like the decidedly more conservative Jarres.[86] Having met with Seeckt on several occasions in late September and early October, Hergt and Westarp became convinced that only the replacement of the Stresemann cabinet with a national dictatorship of one sort or another would put an end to the existing political crisis.[87] Hugenberg, on the other hand, remained ambivalent about the dictatorial schemes of Tirpitz and his entourage and discreetly dissociated himself from their plans for a national dictatorship.[88] But, as the crisis persisted into the first and second weeks of October, the Nationalists threw their full support behind the Bavarian government in its defiance of Berlin in the hope that Kahr would succeed in harnessing the energies of Hitler and his followers without having to suppress them by force.[89] Still, many Nationalists feared that Kahr's antics would lead to Bavaria's secession from the Reich and sought to steer his efforts into what they regarded as a more positive direction, namely, the overthrow of Germany's republican system and its replacement by a more authoritarian form of government. The leaders of the DNVP were convinced that Stresemann's days as chancellor were indeed numbered and that it was only a matter of time before they were entrusted with the reins of power.

In the meantime, the crisis in Berlin was quickly drawing to a climax. The federal government's intervention against the left-wing governments in Saxony and Thuringia in late October and early November was bitterly denounced by the Social Democrats and led to their resignation from the second Stresemann cabinet on 2 November. Contrary to all expectations, Ebert reappointed Stresemann as head of a rump cabinet supported by the two liberal parties, the Center, and the Bavarian People's Party that would oversee

---

[85] Philipp, *Von Stresemann zu* Marx, 16–21. See also Helfferich, "Diktatorische Ermächtigung des Kabinetts," 9 Oct. 1923, in *Helfferichs Reichstagsreden*, ed. Reichert, 177–96.

[86] Brauer to Heydebrand, 10 Oct. 1923, NL Westarp, Gärtringen, II/84, 344.

[87] For further details, see Meier-Welcker, *Seeckt*, 374–75.

[88] Correspondence between Tirpitz and Hugenberg, 14–22 Sept. 1923, BA-MA Freiburg, NL Tirpitz, 192.

[89] For indications of Nationalist sympathy for Kahr, see Traub to Kahr, 29 Sept. 1923, BA Koblenz, NL Traub, 64/47, as well as Westarp, "Ruhrkampf und Regierung Stresemann," NL Westarp, Gärtringen, VN 93, 121–22.

the affairs of state until the political situation had sorted itself out.[90] Stresemann, however, found himself under increasingly heavy pressure from the
leaders of his party's right wing to extend the governmental coalition to the
right even if this meant that their own party leader would had to be sacrificed
in order to placate his enemies in the DNVP.[91] The DNVP party leadership,
on the other hand, remained adamantly opposed to the DNVP's participation
in a Stresemann cabinet and would only consider his retention as chancellor if
he broke with the Social Democrats in both the Reich and Prussia. Many
Nationalists were in fact so confident that they would be asked to assume the
reins of power that in the DNVP Reichstag delegation they had already begun
to allocate the cabinet posts among themselves.[92] Throughout all of this, the
Nationalist party leadership was in constant contact with Seeckt, who had
resuscitated his plans for the establishment of a directorium – this time, with
Ebert's express approval – and had reestablished contact with those to whom
he had originally broached the idea.[93]

In reviving his plans for a national dictatorship, Seeckt was motivated by his
concern over the continuing deterioration of relations between the Reich and
Bavaria and his fear that this might result in the establishment of an independent Bavarian state.[94] On 3 November Colonel Hans von Seißer from the
Bavarian state police went to Berlin on behalf of Kahr and the third member
of their triumvirate, commander-in-chief of the Bavarian Reichswehr Otto von
Lossow, to meet with Seeckt and Minoux as well as with representatives of the
patriotic leagues and the National Rural League. What these meetings revealed
was a total lack of consensus as to what sort of government should take the
place of the Stresemann cabinet once it had been forced from office. While all
of those with whom Seißer met agreed that Stresemann should be forced out of
office at the earliest possible opportunity, Minoux rejected the idea of a
military coup and expressed little confidence in men like Hitler and Erich
Ludendorff, whereas Seeckt stressed the importance of resolving the crisis
without violating the constitutional chain of command. In the final analysis,
all seemed to hinge upon the attitude of the Reichswehr, for none of those
whom Seißer contacted, including the leaders of the patriotic leagues and
National Rural League, were prepared to act without the support and cooperation of the military. On this point Seeckt's adherence to the form, if not the

[90] Wright, *Stresemann*, 238–44.
[91] Remarks by Scholz and Albrecht at a meeting of the DVP Reichstag delegation, 5
Nov. 1923, PA AA Berlin, NL Stresemann, 87/171432–37. See also Quaatz, "Illusionen,"
Der Tag, 4 Nov. 1923, no. 251.
[92] Brauer to Heydebrand, 30 Oct. 1923, NL Westarp, Gärtringen, II/84.
[93] Handwritten draft of Seeckt to Wiedfeldt, 4 Nov. 1923, BA-MA Freiburg, NL Seeckt, 179/
88. On the DNVP's contacts with Seeckt, see Brauer to Heydebrand, 30 Oct. 1923, NL
Westarp, Gärtringen, II/84.
[94] Handwritten draft of Seeckt to Kahr, 2 Nov. 1923, BA-MA Freiburg, NL Seeckt, 108/3–5.

substance, of legality proved the major stumbling block in the calculations of the antirepublican Right.[95]

Seißer returned to Munich convinced that the northern leaders of the anti-Stresemann fronde lacked the resolve and resources to take the decisive action that was necessary to bring about the fundamental changes in Germany's political system that Kahr and the leaders of the Bavarian government were planning to implement. This left Kahr and his entourage with no alternative but to act on their own despite strong words of caution from Seeckt and without appreciable support from their counterparts in the north.[96] In the meantime, a veritable mutiny had erupted within the DVP Reichstag delegation where Quaatz, Alfred Gildemeister, Oskar Maretzky, and other members of the party's right wing had launched a vicious attack against Stresemann's performance as chancellor and DVP party leader.[97] With his own party on the verge of repudiating his chancellorship, Stresemann's position could not possibly have been weaker than it was in the first week of November 1923. It was against the background of these developments that Kahr and his associates finalized plans for a major rally in Munich's fashionable Bürger-bräukeller for the evening of 8 November. The purpose of this rally would be to provide Kahr and his allies in the Bavarian general state commissariat with an overwhelming demonstration of support by Bavaria's political and economic elites. But all of this began to unravel when Hitler, as leader of the more militant German Combat League, refused to heed the warnings of Kahr, Seißer, and Lossow and went ahead with his plans to use Bavaria as the staging base for a "March on Berlin" in the spirit of what Mussolini had accomplished in Rome scarcely a year earlier. In hopes that Kahr and his allies might still be persuaded to join him in his plans for a strike on Berlin, Hitler wrangled an invitation to the rally in the Bürgerbräukeller, interrupted Kahr approximately thirty minutes into his speech, and took the general state commissar, Seißer, and Lossow into an anteroom where he extracted under great duress a promise of cooperation and support.[98] When the Bavarian triumvirate failed to honor

[95] Memorandum on Seißer's conversations in Berlin, 3 Nov. 1923, in *Der Hitler-Putsch. Bayerische Dokumente zum 8./9. November 1923*, ed. Ernst Deuerlein (Stuttgart, 1962), 301–04. See also Gordon, *Hitler and the Beer Hall Putsch*, 247–49. On Seißer's meeting with Minoux, see the report by Kroeger, 4 Nov. 1923, ACDP Sankt-Augustin, NL Stinnes, I-220/029/1.

[96] Gordon, *Hitler and the Beer Hall Putsch*, 250–51, 255–58.

[97] Minutes of the DVP Reichstag delegation, 6 Nov. 1923, PA AA Berlin, NL Stresemann, 87/171457–58, 1171442. For further details, see Jones, *German Liberalism*, 204–05, and Richter, *Deutsche Volkspartei*, 289–98.

[98] For Kahr's account of these events, see "Zum Vorgang in der Nacht vom 8. auf 9. Nov. 1923 im Bürgerbräu[keller] in München," n.d. [Dec. 1923], as well as the report of the Bavarian government, "Der Putsch am 8. November 1923. Vorgeschichte und Verlauf," n.d., appended to Kahr to Stegmann, 1 Jan. 1924, both in BA Koblenz, NL

this promise on the following day, a desperate Hitler and the venerable, if not unstable, Ludendorff tried to salvage what remained of their political fantasies by staging a "March on Munich" that ended in disaster on the steps of the Feldherrnhalle.[99] All hopes of uniting the patriotic movement, both in Bavaria and in the Reich as a whole, had collapsed.

The implications of Hitler's beer hall fiasco on the future development of the German Right were enormous. In the short term, the abortive putsch had the effect of temporarily stabilizing Stresemann's position as chancellor and DVP party chairman. As the VVVD's Fritz Geisler laconically remarked at a delegate conference of the United Patriotic Leagues of Germany in Berlin on 17 November 1923: "Stresemann had every reason to be thankful to Hitler for his attempted coup because, if nothing else, it momentarily strengthened Stresemann's position."[100] Chastened by news of the events in Munich, all but the most irascible of Stresemann's opponents within the DVP Reichstag delegation closed ranks behind the beleaguered chancellor.[101] At the same time, Stresemann responded to criticism of his "rump cabinet" from his party's right wing by reopening negotiations with the DNVP in the hope that the recent events in Munich had made its leaders more amenable to a coalition with the other nonsocialist parties. Ernst Scholz and Rudolf Heinze from the DVP Reichstag delegation met with Hergt and Westarp on the evening of 9 November, but the Nationalists, who continued to advocate the creation of a directorium that was independent of the Reichstag and vested with special emergency powers, refused to enter a cabinet in which Stresemann remained on as either chancellor or foreign minister.[102] Stresemann, on the other hand, continued to insist that considerations of foreign policy made the creation of a directorium along the lines suggested by Seeckt or Minoux impossible and

Stegmann, 1. For eye-witness accounts of these events, see Müller, *Im Wandel einer Welt*, 160–66; Traub, *Erinnerungen*, 323–32; and Lehmann to his daughter, 10 Nov. 1923, in *Verleger J. F Lehmann. Ein Leben im Kampf für Deutschland. Lebenslauf und Briefe*, ed. Melanie Lehmann (Munich, 1935), 188–96. For further details, see Gordon, *Hitler and the Beer Hall Putsch*, 270–312, and Zorn, *Bayerische Geschichte*, 270–88.

[99] Gordon, *Hitler and the Beer Hall Putsch*, 313–65.
[100] Report on the VVVD delegate conference, 17 Nov. 1923, NL Westarp, Gärtringen, VN 42.
[101] Minutes of the DVP Reichstag delegation, 9–10 Nov. 1923, PA AA Berlin, NL Stresemann, 87/171465–79. See also the entries in Gallwitz's diary, 13–14 Nov. 1923, BA-MA Freiburg, NL Gallwitz, 39.
[102] Philipp, *Von Stresemann zu Marx*, 21–23. See also Stresemann's remarks at a cabinet meeting, 19 Nov. 1923, in *Die Kabinette Stresemann*, ed. Erdmann and Vogt, 2:1130–33. See also the remarks by Scholz, Gildemeister, and Lersner before the DVP Reichstag delegation, 6 Nov. 1923, PA AA Berlin, NL Stresemann, 87/171457–58, 1171442, as well as the resolution adopted by the delegation, 9 Nov. 1923, BA Koblenz, R 45 II, 338/77–78.

resolved to remain in office, if only as the head of a "rump cabinet" that no longer commanded a parliamentary majority, as long as his party continued to support him.[103]

Stresemann was to remain in office for the next two weeks until his failure to secure a positive vote of confidence in the Reichstag on the evening of 23 November finally forced him from office. Not even his own party would close ranks behind him as six members of the DVP Reichstag delegation, including Stinnes and Quaatz, were conspicuously absent from the plenary session when the decisive vote was taken.[104] These were nevertheless extremely productive days for the Stresemann cabinet and included some of its most notable accomplishments, not the least of which was the establishment of the *Rentenbank* on 15 November 1923 and the issuance of a new currency with an exchange rate of one *Rentenmark* to a trillion paper marks. The creation of the *Rentenmark* represented one of the decisive events in ending the inflation and helped restore at least a modicum of public confidence in the value of German money. Combined with earlier measures to reduce the size of Germany's civil administration and to introduce consumption taxes of such items as sugar, salt, playing cards, and tobacco, Germany had taken the first tentative steps toward the stabilization of its currency and a return to economic normalcy.[105] At the same time, the restoration of federal authority in the renegade states of Saxony, Thuringia, and Bavaria and the defeat of the anti-republican challenge on both the Left and the Right augured well for the future of German democracy and suggested that Germany had indeed begun to emerge from the dark crisis that had gripped it from the early 1920s. This – and not the turmoil and tumult that had descended upon Germany in the fall of 1923 – was the true legacy of Stresemann's hundred days as chancellor.

At the Crossroads

The abortive Hitler-Ludendorff putsch gave the Stresemann cabinet the respite it needed to establish the *Rentenbank* and take the first critical steps toward Germany's economic and political stabilization. At the same time, the Munich fiasco had a sobering effect on the German Right and forced its leaders to reevaluate their political options and strategies. For although the VVVD persisted in its putschist fantasies and denounced Hitler for having sabotaged

---

[103] Stresemann's speech before the DVP central executive committee, 18 Nov. 1923, in *Nationalliberalismus in der Weimarer Republik*, ed. Kolb and Richter, 1:476–85.

[104] Wright, *Stresemann*, 253–58.

[105] For further details, see Holtfrerich, *Inflation*, 298–314, and Feldman, *Great Disorder*, 780–802.

a process that in time would have led to the overthrow of the Weimar Republic,[106] other right-wing organizations began to reconcile themselves to the stabilization of Germany's beleaguered republican system and to make the necessary strategic adjustments in their quest for political power. This was particularly true in the case of the DNVP, whose leaders had peered into the abyss into which Germany had nearly fallen and now began to negotiate in earnest about assuming a share of governmental responsibility despite their deep-seated hostility toward Stresemann.[107] Following Stresemann's defeat in the Reichstag on 23 November, Ebert met privately with the leaders of the various parties from the SPD to DNVP to determine if and under what conditions they might be willing to serve in a caretaker government that would remain in office at least until new national elections were held the following spring. In his meeting with Ebert, the DNVP party chairman Oskar Hergt expressed his party's willingness not only to take on the responsibility of forming a new government but also to allow its members to participate in a government led by someone from another party if certain conditions regarding its future political course could be met. Over the course of the next several days, however, the DNVP rejected first the DVP's Siegfried von Kardorff and then Heinrich Albert, a politically unaffiliated former cabinet officer who hoped to organize a nonpartisan government of experts, after Ebert had asked them each to try their hand at forming a new government.[108]

Following the collapse of Albert's efforts on 27 November the Nationalists urged the president to call for new elections so that the nation as a whole might have an opportunity to determine the composition of the Reichstag and, with it, the shape of the new government that was to follow the Stresemann cabinet.[109] Ebert, however, turned to the Center's Adam Stegerwald in hopes that he might be able to reach an accommodation with the DNVP. Not only had Stegerwald taken a public stand in favor of a coalition with the DNVP, but he also enjoyed close ties to influential elements in the Nationalist party leadership. On the evening of 27 November the Nationalists indicated that they were prepared to enter into negotiations with Stegerwald but made their entry into a cabinet under his leadership conditional upon the simultaneous reorganization of the state government in Prussia. Although the Nationalists no longer insisted upon Stresemann's resignation as German foreign minister

---

[106] Report by Geisler, "Die bayerischen Vorgänge und die vaterländischen Verbände," at the VVVD delegate conference in Berlin, 17 Nov. 1923, NL Westarp, Gärtringen, VN 42.

[107] See Helfferich to Westarp, 19 Nov. 1923, NL Westarp, Gärtringen, II/9, as well as the entry in Gallwitz's diary, 20 Nov. 1923, BA-MA Freiburg, NL Gallwitz, 39.

[108] DNVP Parteivorstand, "Darstellung der Mitwirkung der Deutschnationalen Volkspartei bei den Verhandlungen zur Neubildung der Reichsregierung in der Woche von 23.–30. November 1923," BA Berlin, R 8005, 9/59–79, esp. 59–63.

[109] Hergt to Ebert, n.d., BA Berlin, R 8005, 9/88.

as a precondition for their cooperation in forming a new government, they nevertheless demanded specific guarantees regarding the character and political course of a Stegerwald cabinet in return for their party's participation and showed little inclination to commit themselves either to the Weimar Constitution or to the binding character of the international obligations Germany had assumed since the end of the war.[110] When the Nationalists' demand for a reorganization of the Prussian government was summarily rejected by the three parties represented in the Coalition of the Constitutional Middle, the Nationalists refused to reconsider their negotiating posture. At this point Stegerwald announced that his efforts to reach an understanding with the DNVP had failed and withdrew as a candidate for the chancellorship.[111]

At this point Ebert had become so frustrated with the DNVP's negotiating tactics that he turned to the only remaining option, a bourgeois minority government supported by the parties of Coalition of the Constitutional Middle and promptly entrusted Wilhelm Marx, the Center Party national chairman and a strong supporter of Stresemann's domestic and foreign policies, with the task of forming such a government. After assuring himself of Stresemann's willingness to serve in his cabinet, Marx proceeded to organize a government that was virtually identical to the cabinet that the Nationalists, Social Democrats, and right-wing racists groups had so unceremoniously voted out of office a week earlier.[112] At the same time, Marx had not abandoned hope that the Nationalists might be persuaded to support his government and approached Martin Schiele, a prominent DNVP Reichstag deputy and an influential figure in the leadership of the National Rural League, with an invitation to join his cabinet as minister of agriculture. Following Schiele's initial rebuff, Marx tried to sweeten his offer by agreeing to appoint another Nationalist to the ministry of transportation if Schiele would join his cabinet. After consulting with his party's Reichstag delegation on 30 November, Schiele withdrew his name from further consideration, thus putting an end to Marx's efforts to secure the DNVP's support.[113] In explaining his party's decision before the Reichstag several days later, Hergt cited the refusal of the middle parties to undertake a reorganization of the Prussian government as the principal reason for the failure of Marx's efforts to bring the DNVP into the national government. As a result, Hergt continued, the DNVP would not be

[110] DNVP Parteivorstand, "Darstellung der Mitwirkung der DNVP ...," BA Berlin, R 8005, 9/64–79. See also Philipp, *Von Stresemann zu Marx*, 23–32.

[111] Forster, *Stegerwald*, 344–49.

[112] Ulrich von Hehl, *Wilhelm Marx 1963–1946. Eine politische Biographie* (Mainz, 1987), 249–55. See also the introduction by Günter Abramowski in *Die Akten der Reichskanzlei: Die Kabinette Marx I und II. 30. November 1923 bis 3. Juni 1924. 3. Juni 1924 bis 15. Januar 1925*, ed. Günter Abramowski, 2 vols. (Boppard am Rhein, 1973), 1:vii–xi.

[113] Schiele to Marx, 29 and 30 Nov. 1923, in *Der Nachlaß des Reichskanzlers Wilhelm Marx*, ed. Hugo Stehkämper, 4 vols. (Cologne, 1968), 1:324.

able to support the government in the use of presidential emergency authority to solve the myriad problems that currently confronted the German people.[114]

Throughout the negotiations Hergt, Schiele, and the leaders of the DNVP Reichstag delegation were hamstrung by the vociferous opposition of local party leaders, particularly in the east, to any accommodation with the government that did not grant the DNVP everything that it had hoped to accomplish. This was clearly the intent of the resolution the DNVP district organization in Potsdam II adopted on 27 November.[115] By the same token, Hans Schlange-Schöningen, a landowner from Pomerania, conceded that the DNVP had become the hostage of its own rhetoric but expressed more than just a silent sigh of relief when the negotiations at the end of November 1923 failed to produce a break in the deadlock that had developed in relations between the government and the DNVP.[116] For most party members, their visceral dislike of Stresemann and their reluctance to be part of a government in which he held a prominent post were so great that an accommodation with Marx without Stresemann's removal would be seen as a betrayal of the DNVP's most fundamental principles and sense of mission. The Nationalists were also determined to use their leverage at the national level to force a change of government in Prussia and to replace the "Great Coalition" with a right-wing coalition. This, of course, encountered strong opposition from Marx and the leaders of the Prussian Center Party and ultimately became the issue that led to the collapse of cabinet negotiations in late November 1923.[117] At the same time, however, it was imperative for the Nationalists to join the national government at the earliest possible opportunity in order to influence the shape of Germany's fiscal and economic stabilization and to make certain that the various constituencies that composed their party's electoral base did not have to accept an inordinate share of the social cost of stabilization. The DNVP party leadership did not expect the existing state of affairs in Berlin to last for long and fully anticipated another cabinet crisis at the end of January 1924 with new elections later that spring.[118] By that time the DNVP would presumably be in a stronger position to press its bid for power.

In the meantime, the various organizations on Germany's patriotic Right had also begun to ponder the implications of the failed putsch in Munich. To the leaders of the patriotic movement, as well as to most of those at the helm of the DNVP, it seemed that the events of the fall of 1923 added up to a lost opportunity. At no point in the early history of the Weimar Republic had the conditions for a right-wing seizure of power been more propitious than in the

---

[114] Philipp, *Von Stresemann zu Marx*, 35–36.
[115] Steinhoff to Westarp, 28 Nov. 1923, NL Westarp, Gärtringen, VN 37.
[116] Schlange-Schöningen to Hergt, 3 Dec. 1923, BA Berlin, R 8005, 9/85.
[117] Hehl, *Marx*, 251–52.
[118] Brauer to Heydebrand, 11 Dec. 1923, NL Westarp, Gärtringen, II/84.

early fall of 1923. The Weimar regime had thoroughly compromised itself, if not by its inability to stem the fall of the mark, then certainly by its weakness vis-by the French in the Ruhr and its passivity in the face of the Marxist Left in Saxony and Thuringia and the secessionists in Bavaria. The Reich seemed threatened with nothing less than total dissolution, and only firm, decisive action by the forces of the German Right – or so they claimed – could rescue the nation from the increasingly desperate situation in which it found itself. But when the dust had settled, the Right had little to show for itself. By the end of 1923 the Weimar regime seemed well on its way to restoring order. The first, tentative steps toward stabilization of the mark had been taken, the threat of Marxism in central Germany had been met, and the collapse of the Hitler-Ludendorff putsch had made it all that much easier for the federal government in Berlin to dispel the specter of Bavarian separatism and normalize relations with Munich.

What, from the perspective of the German Right, had gone wrong? Why had the German Right failed to take advantage of the rare confluence of events in the summer and early fall of 1923 to overthrow the Weimar regime and replace it with a more authoritarian system of government, military or civilian? In answering these questions, pundits on the Right had more than enough blame to spread around. A favorite target was the Reichswehr's Hans von Seeckt, who was criticized not just for having failed to take a decisive stand against Stresemann, Ebert, and the policies of the "Great Coalition" in the critical period leading up to abortive Hitler-Ludendorff putsch but also for his reluctance to use the special emergency powers he had received after the putsch to execute a coup against the government and to undertake a fundamental change in Germany's political system.[119] Even then, however, criticism of Seeckt was generally tempered by a recognition of his role in suppressing the Marxist regimes in Saxony and Thuringia and his success in preserving the integrity of the Reichswehr as an instrument of national power during a troubled and turbulent time.[120] In the case of Kahr, however, sentiment was not so generous. Gottfried Traub, a prominent Nationalist who had been unceremoniously dispatched to Bavaria after his involvement in the 1920 Kapp putsch to assume editorship of the *Münchner-Augsburger Abendzeitung*, denounced Kahr for having betrayed the patriotic leagues "with the handshake of Judas" by failing to act in the decisive days of November 1923 and demanded that he step aside so that the patriotic movement could rise to prominence once again.[121] But the harshest words by far were reserved for Adolf Hitler. Speaking at a delegate assembly of the United Patriotic Leagues

---

[119] For example, see Scheibe to Ludendorff, 12 Apr. 1924, BA-MA Freiburg, NL Tirpitz, 171/77–81.
[120] Geisler, "Die bayerischen Vorgänge . . .," 17 Nov. 1923, NL Westarp, Gärtringen, VN 42.
[121] Traub to Kahr, 6 Dec. 1923, BA Koblenz, NL Traub, 64/37.

of Germany on 17 November 1923, VVVD chairman Fritz Geisler bitterly denounced the Nazi party leader for having carelessly destroyed months of hard work and preparation with his ill-advised and hastily organized coup on the night of 8 November. Not only had Hitler's impetuosity prolonged Stresemann's tenure in office, but the Nazi party leader was oblivious to the deep rift his action would leave within the ranks of those upon whom the rebirth of Germany ultimately depended. From Geisler's perspective, Hitler's abortive putsch was a national tragedy whose implications had yet to be fully comprehended.[122]

Most of those on the German Right recognized that the defeat of the Munich putsch in November 1923 represented a decisive turning point in the history of the Weimar Republic. But the lessons they drew from the failure of 1923 varied greatly. For all but the most intractable opponents of the hated Weimar system, the events of 1923 had a sobering effect that led them to realize just how close Germany had come to the abyss. Had Hitler succeeded with his coup in Munich and then proceeded with his "March on Berlin," this could very easily have brought Germany to the brink of civil war with disastrous consequences for survival of the Reich itself. Now that Germany had survived the crisis and seemed on its way to political and economic recovery, Germany's conservative leaders now faced the question of how they would respond to the challenges of working within a system of government to which many of them remained irreconcilably opposed but that had received a new breath of life from having survived the ordeal of 1923.

---

[122] Geisler, "Die bayerischen Vorgänge . . .," 17 Nov. 1923, NL Westarp, Gärtringen, VN 42.

7

From Triumph to Schism

As the year 1923 drew to a close, an uneasy calm settled over Germany's political landscape. The inflation was over – or so it seemed for the moment – although precisely how the social cost of the inflation was to be distributed throughout German society as a whole was yet to be determined. At the same time, the abortive Hitler-Ludendorff putsch had thoroughly discredited the idea of a military coup among all but the most obtuse of Weimar's right-wing enemies. All of this would require a strategic adjustment on the part of the German Right. Now that the inflation was over and the social cost of the inflation was to be allocated among the different sectors of German society, it was imperative for the Nationalists to gain access to the corridors of power in order to influence the shape of Germany's stabilization program and make certain that the various constituencies that constituted their party's material base were not forced to accept an inordinate share of the social cost of stabilization. The failure of the Munich putsch and the resultant stabilization of Germany's parliamentary system left the Nationalists with no choice but to strike an accommodation with the non-socialist parties that supported the Weimar Republic. Yet it was clear from the DNVP's posture in the negotiations that led to the formation of the Marx cabinet at the end of 1923 that the party was not yet quite prepared to take such a step or share the burden of governmental responsibility on terms other than those it itself dictated. The winds of change were nevertheless slowly, but surely, at work on the German Right.

The Politics of Stabilization

When the Marx cabinet assumed office in early December 1923, its most pressing task was to bring the process of stabilizing the mark to a successful conclusion and to prevent another wave of inflation from wreaking havoc upon Germany's fragile economy.[1] The initial step toward stabilizing the mark

---

[1] Gerald D. Feldman, "The Politics of Stabilization in Weimar Germany," *Tel-Aviver Jahrbuch für Deutsche Geschichte* 17 (1988): 19–42.

had been taken by the Stresemann cabinet with the termination of passive resistance in the Ruhr. Further measures to strengthen the mark had been stymied by a bitter conflict within the Stresemann cabinet between Finance Minister Rudolf Hilferding, a Social Democrat who believed that the solution to Germany's fiscal and economic crisis lay in reducing the amount of money in circulation through tight controls over domestic and foreign currencies, and Agricultural Minister Hans Luther, who subscribed to Helfferich's thesis that fiscal stability could be accomplished only through the creation of a new currency tied to the value of "real assets" such as rye.[2] After the reorganization of the Stresemann cabinet in early October 1923 responsibility for drafting the legislation to stabilize the currency shifted to Luther, now serving as the new finance minister. An unaffiliated politician who stood to the right of center on most of the major political issues, Luther was certainly far more acceptable to Germany's industrial and agricultural elites than his Social Democratic predecessor. Moreover, the fundamental premise of Luther's strategy for fiscal and economic recovery was that the industrial and agricultural sectors had already been taxed to the full extent of their capacity to pay and that the national budget could be balanced only through a sharp reduction in the general level of government spending and a modest increase in taxation for those sectors of society that had escaped the inflation more or less unharmed.[3] The net effect of Luther's tax policy would be to shift the social cost of stabilizing the mark from industry and agriculture to the German middle classes.

Luther proceeded to incorporate elements of Helfferich's plan for stabilizing the mark into the government's currency reforms, with the result that the government's stabilization program took on an increasingly conservative character. On 13 October 1923 the Reichstag passed an enabling act that gave the Stresemann cabinet emergency authorization to implement the measures it deemed necessary to stabilize the mark. The cabinet used this authorization on 27 October to issue a "Decree for the Reduction of Public Personnel" that initiated a dramatic reduction in the size of Germany's civil administration and implemented far-reaching cuts in civil service pensions.[4] This was accompanied by the introduction of new taxes on the consumption of such items as sugar, salt, and *Zündwaren* such as playing cards and tobacco. By far the most important step Stresemann and his cabinet took to stabilize the mark, however, was the creation of a new currency known as the *Rentenmark*, a currency

---

[2] Reichert's notes on a meeting between representatives of the government and DNVP, 18 Aug. 1923, in the records of the Association of German Iron and Steel Industrialists (Verein Deutscher Eisen- und Stahlindustrieller), BA Berlin, Bestand R 13, 278/204–07. For further details, see Feldman, *Great Disorder*, 708–36.

[3] Hans Luther, *Feste Mark – Solide Wirtschaft. Rückblick auf die Arbeit der Regierung während der Wintermonate 1923/24* (Berlin, 1924), 5–13.

[4] Feldman, *Great Disorder*, 750–60.

that was not based, as Helfferich had wished, on the value of rye but created from the proceeds of a compulsory mortgage, or *Zwangshypothek*, on all landed property, agricultural as well as industrial. The establishment of the *Rentenbank* on 15 November 1923 and the issuance of a new currency with an exchange rate of one *Rentenmark* for one trillion paper marks represented the decisive event in ending the inflation and restoring at least a modicum of public confidence in the value of German money.[5]

As finance minister in the Marx cabinet, Luther's primary responsibility was to ensure that the measures the Stresemann government had taken to stabilize the mark would not be jeopardized by a return to the deficit spending that had plagued government finances in the first years of the Weimar Republic. Luther's stabilization program from the winter of 1923–24 imposed new and, in many cases, unexpected economic hardships upon the German middle strata. Not only was the size of the German civil service significantly reduced in order to curtail the general level of government spending, but new and onerous taxes had been imposed upon the more traditional elements of Germany's middle-class economy. Even farmers, who had used the inflation to liquidate approximately 80 percent of Germany's agricultural indebtedness, were hurt by a stipulation requiring them to pay their taxes, as well as the compulsory mortgages that had been levied against their property to finance the creation of the *Rentenmark*, in the new currency despite the fact that virtually all of their harvest from the summer and fall of 1923 had been sold for paper marks that were now all but worthless.[6] Nor was the worker spared the burden of stabilization, for he was obliged to accept the terms of an agreement the government had reached with representatives from management and labor on 13–14 December 1923 to reintroduce the ten-hour work-day and the two-shift system in all areas where they had been in effect before the war.[7] Yet for all of the consternation this aroused among those who regarded the eight-hour day as the greatest accomplishment of the November Revolution, the most controversial feature of the government's stabilization program pertained to the revalorization of those paper mark assets that had been destroyed by the inflation. In response to a ruling by the German Supreme Court on 28 November 1923 that opened up the possibility that every single revaluation dispute could be taken to court where it would be

---

[5] Ibid., 780–802. For Helfferich's influence on the government's stabilization program, see Williamson, *Helfferich*, 383–94.

[6] Robert G. Moeller, "Winners as Losers in the German Inflation: Peasant Protest over the Controlled Economy, 1920–1923," in *Die deutsche Inflation: Eine Zwischenbilanz/The German Inflation Reconsidered*, ed. Gerald D. Feldman, Carl-Ludwig Holtfrerich, Gerhard A. Ritter, and Peter-Christian Witt (Berlin, 1982), 255–88.

[7] Gerald D. Feldman and Irmgard Steinisch, "Die Weimarer Republik zwischen Sozial- und Wirtschaftsstaat. Die Entscheidung gegen den Achtstundentag," *Archiv für Sozialgeschichte* 18 (1978): 353–439.

adjudicated according to its individual merits and the debtor's ability to make financial restitution,[8] Luther drafted a special provision for the Third Emergency Tax Decree that limited the revalorization of mortgages and other private debts to 15 percent of their gold mark value while exempting all government debts, including war bonds, from revaluation until after a final settlement of the reparations question.[9] To middle-class investors who had traditionally set aside as much as a sixth of their income in one form of investment or another, this amounted to nothing less than an act of betrayal by the very government in which they had been asked to place their trust.[10]

Whatever damage the antisocial character of the government's stabilization program had done to public confidence in Germany's republican institutions was only compounded by the manner in which the program was enacted into law. From the outset, the architects of Germany's fiscal stabilization were convinced that the government's inability to command the support of a majority in the Reichstag left them with no alternative but to circumvent parliament in implementing the measures they deemed necessary to stabilize the mark. This was presumably necessary not only because of the hardships that stabilization entailed for politically influential sectors of German society but also because the kind of quick and decisive action necessary to restore governmental authority precluded the slow and measured procedures of conventional parliamentary rule. In return for their support of the enabling act that the Reichstag passed on 8 December 1923, the Social Democrats had insisted that measures protecting the prerogatives of parliament be incorporated into the language of the bill. This led to the creation of a special fifteen-member committee consisting of representatives from all of Germany's major political parties that was supposed to advise the government in formulating its stabilization program and to review the specific executive decrees by which this program was enacted into law. In practice, however, this committee exercised little influence over the actual course of governmental deliberations and never fulfilled any of the expectations that had accompanied its creation. As a result, both the Reichstag and the various political parties that belonged to it were effectively excluded from any sort of meaningful role in determining just how the mark was to be stabilized or how its effect upon the different

---

[8] For further details, see David Southern, "The Impact of the Inflation: Inflation, the Courts, and Revaluation," in *Social Change and Political Development in Weimar Germany*, ed. Richard Bessel and E. J. Feuchtwanger (London, 1981), 55–76.

[9] Luther, *Feste Mark – Solide Wirtschaft*, 37–48. See also Hans Luther, *Politiker ohne Partei. Erinnerungen* (Stuttgart, 1960), 229–33.

[10] For example, see Reinhard Wüst, *Das Aufwertungsproblem und die 3. Steuernotverordnung. Eine gemeinverständliche Betrachtung* (Halle, 1924). See also Larry Eugene Jones, "Inflation, Revaluation, and the Crisis of Middle-Class Politics: A Study in the Dissolution of the Weimar Party System, 1923–28," *Central European History* 12 (1979): 143–68, esp. 149–53.

sectors of German society might be ameliorated. The legitimacy of Germany's parliamentary institutions, therefore, was severely compromised not only by the antisocial character of the government's stabilization program but also by the authoritarian manner in which this program had become law.[11]

Stabilization under Fire

All of this helped create a situation ripe for exploitation by Germany's anti-republican Right. For the right-wing DNVP, the situation was doubly fortuitous. On the one hand, Helfferich's participation in the deliberations of both the Cuno and Stresemann cabinets over how the mark was to be stabilized made it possible for the Nationalists to claim a major share of the credit for the introduction of the *Rentenmark* and the subsequent stabilization of the German currency. On the other hand, the fact that the Stresemann cabinet had replaced a currency based on rye with one capitalized through a compulsory mortgage on industrial and agricultural assets provided the Nationalists with a convenient pretext for rejecting the currency reforms of November 1923 as a retreat from what Helfferich had originally counseled. By the same token, the Nationalists were able to claim that stabilization would have taken place much earlier and with much less economic hardship had Stresemann not been fettered by his ties to the Social Democrats.[12] This ploy made it possible for the Nationalists to dissociate themselves from the antisocial consequences of the government's stabilization program at the same time they portrayed their party as the last hope of the German middle classes. To underscore this claim, the DNVP Reichstag delegation boycotted parliamentary chambers on 8 December in an attempt to deprive the newly installed Marx government of the two-thirds quorum it needed to secure passage of the enabling act that would enact the tax reforms necessary to complete the stabilization process. This, the Nationalists hoped, would then force the chancellor into dissolving the Reichstag and calling for new elections.[13] When this failed, the Nationalists were still in a position to dissociate themselves from all the Draconian measures that were to follow, including the severe and extremely unpopular provisions of the Third Emergency Tax Decree.

---

[11] Larry Eugene Jones, "In the Shadow of Stabilization: German Liberalism and the Legitimacy Crisis of the Weimar Party System, 1924–30," in *Die Nachwirkungen der Inflation auf die deutsche Geschichte 1924–1933*, ed. Gerald D. Feldman (Munich, 1985), 21–41.

[12] *Die Wahrheit über die Rentenmark*, Deutschnationale Flugschrift, no. 164 (Berlin, 1924). See also Helfferich's Reichstag speech, 9 Oct. 1923, in Karl Helfferich, *Reichstagsreden 1922–1924*, ed. J. W. Reichert (Berlin, 1925), 177–96.

[13] Albrecht Philipp, *Von Stresemann zu Marx. Sechs Monate deutschnationaler Politik (August 1923–Januar 1924)*, Deutschnationale Flugschrift, no. 146 (Berlin, 1924), 35–41.

In the six months since the formation of the Stresemann cabinet, the Nationalists had consistently walked a thin line between the politics of responsibility and the politics of demagogy. If, on the one hand, Helfferich and other DNVP party leaders had supported the government in its efforts to stabilize the mark, they went to great pains to dissociate themselves from the more unpopular aspects of the stabilization process and frequently resorted to demagogic flourishes to put distance between themselves and those who were responsible for Germany's fiscal stabilization. This position was all the more remarkable in light of the fact that the terms upon which the mark had been stabilized were effectively dictated by conservative economic interests that had generally supported the DNVP.[14] Athough Helfferich failed to have the value of the new currency tied to Germany's rye production in a move that would have greatly enhanced the status and political influence of the landowning aristocracy, neither agriculture nor industry could complain about the way in which the economic burden of stabilizing the mark had been shifted from them to the German middle class. The irony of the DNVP's role in Germany's fiscal stabilization in the winter of 1923–24, therefore, was that it continued to portray itself as the champion of those who had been hurt by the government's stabilization program at the same time that those interests that were most closely tied to the DNVP party leadership – namely, large landed agriculture and heavy industry – had emerged from the stabilization process with their social and economic position significantly strengthened.

When the government's emergency powers expired on 15 February 1924, the Nationalists joined the Social Democrats, Communists, and racists on the radical Right in refusing to renew or extend the enabling act. Marx promptly ordered the dissolution of the Reichstag and scheduled new elections for the first week of May. The campaign opened amidst a mood of increasing uneasiness on the part of Germany's middle-class electorate. Although many middle-class voters could derive a measure of consolation from the fact that the inflation had indeed ended, there was lingering uncertainty as to whether or not the measures the government had taken to end the inflation would succeed in permanently stabilizing the value of the mark. These fears were compounded by a general feeling within middle-class circles that the mark had been stabilized at their expense and that their chief antagonists in the struggle over how the social cost of the lost war was to be allocated – namely, big business and organized labor – were among the principal beneficiaries of the great inflation. Moreover, the highly authoritarian manner in which the mark had been stabilized undermined the legitimacy of Germany's parliamentary institutions and severely compromised the integrity of those political parties

[14] Claus-Dieter Krohn, "Helfferich contra Hilferding. Konservative Geldpolitik und die sozialen Folgen der deutschen Inflation 1918–1923," *Vierteljahresschrift für Sozial- und Wirtschaftsgeschichte* 66 (1975): 62–92

most closely identified with the republican system of government. Germany's more moderate bourgeois parties were hurt both by the fact that they had abdicated responsibility for the formulation and implementation of the government's stabilization program and by their failure to protect middle-class economic interests during the inflation and the stabilization process.[15]

From the outset, the Nationalists conducted the campaign as a referendum on the government's stabilization program in an attempt to transform middle-class resentment over the way in which the mark had been stabilized into a mandate for radical political change. Quick to dissociate themselves from the antisocial consequences of the government's stabilization program, the Nationalists not only denounced the steps the government had taken to reduce the size of the German civil service,[16] but criticized the revaluation provisions of the Third Emergency Tax Decree as a betrayal of the German middle class and made vague promises of a "full and equitable" restoration of those paper mark assets that had been destroyed by the inflation.[17] At the same time, the Nationalists appealed for the support of the German farmer by denouncing the failure to dismantle the system of price controls and mandatory delivery quotas that had been imposed during the war as evidence of governmental discrimination against Germany's agricultural producers.[18] All of this, they argued, only underscored the need for a radical change in the existing political system if the German farmer was ever to escape the grip of those who, behind the facade of popular sovereignty, celebrated the disenfranchisement of the German people with the use of presidential emergency powers.[19]

The National Liberal Revolt

The leaders of Germany's more moderate bourgeois parties came under heavy attack for their failure to protect Germany's rural and urban middle classes

[15] Jones, "In the Shadow of Stabilization," 27–30. On the general climate in which the elections took place, see Maier, *Recasting Bourgeois Europe*, 440–50, and Thomas Childers, *The Nazi Voter: The Social Foundations of Fascism in Germany, 1919–1933* (Chapel Hill, NC, and London, 1983), 50–64.

[16] Kurt Deglert, *Wider den Beamtenabbau. Rede, gehalten im Reichstage am 10. März 1924*, Deutschnationale Flugschrift, no. 154 (Berlin, 1924).

[17] "Aufwertungsfrage und Deutschnationale Volkspartei," DNVP-Werbeblatt, no. 287, BA Koblenz, NL Weilnböck, 34.

[18] Josef Kaufhold, *Die politischen Parteien und die Landwirtschaft*, Deutschnationale Flugschrift, no. 158 (Berlin, 1924), 11–27.

[19] Reinhold Dieckmann, *Wen soll der Landwirt wählen? Entwurf eines Vortrags vor ländlichen Wählern*, Deutschnationale Flugschrift, no. 155 (Berlin, 1924), 21–22. In a similar vein, see Martin Schiele, *Deutschnationale Volkspartei und Landwirtschaft*, Deutschnationales Rüstzeug, no. 9 (Berlin, 1924).

against the ravages of inflation and stabilization.[20] No one, however, came in for more abuse than Gustav Stresemann, Germany's foreign minister and DVP party chairman. Stresemann was attacked not only for sharing governmental responsibility with the Social Democrats but, more importantly, for the collapse of the struggle in the Ruhr and on the occupied west bank of the Rhine. These attacks coincided with a determined attempt on the part of Hugenberg and his associates to drive a wedge between Stresemann and the right wing of his own party. Relations between Stresemann and the leaders of his party's right wing had become increasingly strained ever since his appointment as chancellor at the end of the previous summer.[21] In hopes that this might develop into a full-fledged secession on the DVP's right wing, Hugenberg and Helfferich met with Hugo Stinnes and Reinhold Quaatz from the DVP Reichstag delegation in the third week of February to enlist their help in the campaign to undercut Stresemann's political position.[22] The founding of the National Liberal State Party of Bavaria (Nationalliberale Landespartei Bayern) on 17 February 1924 by a group of dissidents from the DVP's Bavarian organization only underscored the depth of anti-Stresemann sentiment within the party at large and evoked the specter of a general secession on the DVP's right wing.[23]

On 12 March 1924 the leaders of the DVP's right wing tried to force the issue by announcing the founding of the National Liberal Association of the German People's Party (Nationalliberale Vereinigung der Deutschen Volkspartei or NLV) at a small gathering in Berlin's Hotel Esplanade.[24] Although poor health and a desire not to antagonize Stresemann kept Stinnes from taking part in the NLV's founding ceremonies, the fact that both Quaatz and Albert Vögler, another Stinnes protégé who sat in the DVP Reichstag delegation, played prominent roles in launching the new organization bore ample testimony to his influence behind the scenes.[25] Moreover, the vast majority of

---

[20] For further details, see Larry Eugene Jones, "Democracy and Liberalism in the German Inflation: The Crisis of a Political Movement, 1918–1924," in *Konsequenzen der Inflation/ Consequences of Inflation*, ed. Gerald D. Feldman, Carl-Ludwig Holtfrerich, Gerhard A. Ritter, and Peter-Christian Witt (Berlin, 1989), 3–43, esp. 36–42.

[21] For further details, see Jones, *German Liberalism*, 195–207, 213–16, as well as Richter, *Deutsche Volkspartei*, 273–302, and Wright, *Stresemann*, 217–59.

[22] Entry in Quaatz's diary, 21 Feb. 1924, BA Koblenz, Nachlass Reinhold Quaatz, 16.

[23] "Wahlprogramm der Nationalliberalen Partei Bayern (Beschlossen vom Ersten 'Landesvertretertag' in Nürnberg am 17. Februar 1924)," BHStA Munich, Abt. V, Flugblätter-Sammlung, F84.

[24] Report on the NLV's founding, 2 Mar. 1924, PA AA Berlin, NL Stresemann, 89/ 171762-63. See also the entries in Quaatz's diary, 12–13 Mar. 1924, BA Koblenz, NL Quaatz, 16.

[25] On Vögler and the NLV, see Manfred Rasch, "Über Albert Vögler und sein Verhältnis zur Politik," *Mitteilungsblatt des Instituts für soziale Bewegungen. Forschungen und Forschungsberichte* 28 (2003): 127–56, esp. 133–35.

whose who affiliated themselves with the NLV, including no less than twenty of the twenty-five participants in the NLV's official founding, were either directly or indirectly tied to the Ruhr industrial establishment.[26] Only the presence of two prominent DVP agrarians, Karl Hepp from Hesse-Nassau and Friedrich Döbrich from Thuringia, disturbed the NLV's predominantly industrial profile. Yet with the exception of a small clique around Quaatz and Oskar Maretzky, few of those involved in the founding of the NLP sought or desired a break with the DVP.[27] In outlining the NLV's goals at its first public demonstration on 26 March, DVP Reichstag deputy Alfred Gildemeister stressed that the NLV did not seek to hurt or split the DVP but only to return it to the principles upon which it had been founded. Its ultimate objective, Gildemeister continued, was to lay the foundation for the creation of a broad bourgeois front in the upcoming Reichstag elections and to prepare the way for the formation of a new national government that would no longer require the support or cooperation of the socialist Left. And this, he concluded, could only be achieved by working within the DVP to bring about its political reorientation to the right.[28]

Despite Gildemeister's assurances that the NLV had no intention of reconstituting itself as a new political party, Stresemann moved quickly to counter what he perceived as a direct threat to his control of the party. On 13 March the DVP party executive committee condemned the existence of a separate organization within the party as incompatible with its solidarity and political effectiveness and instructed all party members who belonged to the NLV to resign or face the threat of disciplinary action.[29] This action left the dissidents around Gildemeister and Quaatz with no choice but to leave the NLV or face expulsion from the party. While Gildemeister and his associates promptly resigned from the NLV as part of a reconciliation agreement with the DVP Reichstag delegation,[30] Quaatz and the more irascible of Stresemann's critics opposed any accommodation with the DVP party leadership and called for a general secession on the DVP's right wing behind the slogan "Heraus aus der

---

[26] Report on the NLV's founding, 12 Mar. 1924, PA AA Berlin, NL Stresemann, 89/171762–63. For further details, see Richter, *Deutsche Volkspartei*, 303–22, as well as Roland Thimme, *Stresemann und die Deutsche Volkspartei 1923–25* (Lübeck and Hamburg, 1961), 50–55, and Horst Romeyk, "Die Deutsche Volkspartei in Rheinland und Westfalen," *Rheinische Vierteljahrsblätter* 39 (1975): 189–236, here 229. On Stinnes's role, see Feldman, *Stinnes*, 912–22.

[27] Gildemeister to Stresemann, 14 Mar. 1924, PA AA Berlin, NL Stresemann, 88/171714–15.

[28] Alfred Gildemeister, *Was wir wollen! Rede auf der Tagung der Nationalliberalen Vereinigung der Deutschen Volkspartei am Mittwoch, den 26. März 1924* (Berlin, n.d. [1924]), 3–9. See also the report in the *Berliner Börsen-Zeitung*, 26 Mar. 1924, no. 146. See also Quaatz, "Die nationalliberale Vereinigung der D.V.P.," *Der Tag*, 15 Mar. 1924, no. 65.

[29] *Nationalliberale Correspondenz*, 17 Mar. 1924, no. 30.

[30] Undated memorandum from the spring of 1924, BA Koblenz, R 45 II, 339/41–42.

Stresemann-Partei."[31] Quaatz was in close contact with both Stinnes and Hugenberg throughout this period,[32] and there can be little doubt that his call for a secession on the DVP's right wing carried their stamp of approval.[33] But Stinnes's death on 10 April 1924 dealt the NLV a blow from which it never recovered. Although the NLV proceeded to field its own slate of candidates in Berlin and several other parts of the country in the upcoming Reichstag elections,[34] its fate as an independent political force was effectively sealed when Quaatz and Moritz Klönne, an influential Ruhr industrialist who had also belonged to the DVP, accepted Hugenberg's offer of secure candidacies on the DNVP's national ticket.[35] Those who remained with the NLV proceeded to conclude an electoral alliance with regional farm organizations in Thuringia, Hesse, Baden, and Württemburg that assigned any *Reststimmen* – votes these organizations could not count toward the election of their own candidates at the district level – to a national slate of candidates headed by the NLV's Oskar Maretzky and Baron Kurt von Lersner.[36]

Playing the Racist Card

In the meantime, the Nationalists moved to shore up their defenses with regard to what many party leaders saw as the most serious single obstacle to a Nationalist victory at the polls, namely, the radical racists who had broken away from the DNVP in the fall of 1922 and who were now attacking it from the extreme right. Following the collapse of the Munich "Beer Hall Putsch" and Hitler's subsequent incarceration, Albrecht von Graefe-Goldebee and the leaders of the German-Racist Freedom Party moved quickly to unite their followers with the remnants of the NSDAP in northern and central Germany under the umbrella of an organization calling itself the Racist-Social Bloc

---

[31] Entry in Quaatz's diary, 2 Apr. 1924, BA Koblenz, NL Quaatz, 16. See also "Betreff: Geheimrat Dr. Quaatz," n.d. [Feb.–Mar. 1924], PA AA Berlin, NL Stresemann, 267/147061–68.

[32] Entries in Quaatz's diary, 27 Mar.–2 Apr. 1924, BA Koblenz, NL Quaatz, 16.

[33] See Wulf, *Stinnes*, 524–26, and Holzbach, *Das "System Hugenberg,"* 172–74.

[34] Circular from Maretzky on behalf of the National Liberal Campaign Committee (Nationalliberaler Wahlausschuß), 16 Apr. 1924, PA AA Berlin, NL Stresemann, 89/171873–74. See also "Ade, Deutsche Volkspartei!" n.d. [Apr. 1924]; NLV, "Entschließung!" 9 Apr. 1924; "Wir klagen die Deutsche Volkspartei an," n.d. [Apr. 1924], Geheimes Staatsarchiv Preußischer Kulturbesitz, Berlin-Dahlem (hereafter cited as GStA Berlin-Dahlem), ZSg. XIII/IV, no. 153.

[35] Entry in Quaatz's diary, 15 Apr. 1924, BA Koblenz, NL Quaatz, 16.

[36] RLB, Parlamentsabteilung, to Helmot (Hessischer Bauernbund), Mackeldey (Thüringer Landbund), and Füller (Badischer Landbund), 12 Apr. 1924, BA Berlin, R 8034 I, 116/15–16.

(Völkisch-Sozialer Block or VSB).[37] Although Graefe ultimately failed to unite Nazi and non-Nazi racists into a single political party, the leaders of the two factions signed an agreement on 24 February 1924 providing for closer cooperation between their respective organizations at the district and provincial levels.[38] This, in turn, served as the basis of a cooperative effort between the DVFP and what remained of the NSDAP in the upcoming Reichstag elections under the auspices of an electoral alliance known as the National Socialist Freedom Party (Nationalsozialistische Freiheitspartei or NSFP).[39] Like the DNVP and the various splinter parties that had surfaced since the last national election, the racists assailed the government's stabilization program as a betrayal of the German middle class and denounced the policy of fulfillment as a conspiracy to perpetuate the enslavement of the German people. These charges were invariably combined with general broadsides against the twin shibboleths of Marxism and finance capital and supplemented by specific recommendations aimed at breaking the power of international Jewry over German economic life.[40] At the same time, the racists denounced the DNVP as an elitist party that lacked the ideological commitment and grass-root support necessary to transform the struggle for racial purity into a revolutionary movement of the people. Only a revolutionary racism rooted in the heart and soul of the *Volk* could ever free Germany from the grip of the Jew at home and abroad.[41]

The leaders of the DNVP recognized the racist challenge as a clear threat to their own party's hopes for victory in the May 1924 Reichstag elections, particularly after the racists' strong performance in the Mecklenburg and Thuringian state elections earlier in the year.[42] From the outset the leaders

---

[37] For further details, see Jeremy Noakes, *The Nazi Party in Lower Saxony, 1921–1933* (Oxford, 1971), 41–44.

[38] Text of the agreement between the DVFP and NSDAP, 22 Feb. 1924, NSDAP Hauptarchiv, BA Berlin, Bestand NS 26, 843. See also David Jablonsky, *The Nazi Party in Dissolution: Hitler and the Verbotzeit, 1923–1925* (London, 1989), 54–63.

[39] For further details, see Reimer Wulff, "Die Deutschvölkische Freiheitspartei 1922–1928" (Ph.D. diss., Universität Marburg, 1968), 38–40, and Stephanie Schrader, "Vom Partner zum Widerpart. Die Deutschvölkische Freiheitspartei und ihr Wahlbündnis mit der NSDAP," in *Wegbereiter des Nationalsozialismus. Personen, Organisationen und Netzwerke der extremen Rechten zwischen 1918 und 1933*, ed. Daniel Schmidt, Michael Sturm, and Massimiliano Livi (Essen, 2015), 55–69, esp. 56–60.

[40] See "Wahlaufruf der DFVP (Völkisch-Sozialer Block)," n.d. [Apr. 1924], GStA Berlin-Dahlem, ZSg XII/IV, no. 212, and "Was will der völkisch-sozialer Block?" n.d. [Apr. 1924], BA Koblenz, ZSg. 1-45/13. See also Childers, *Nazi Voter*, 53–55, 66–69, and Wulff, "Die deutschvölkische Freiheitspartei," pp. 40–42.

[41] For example, see Joachim Haupt, *Völkisch oder national? Eine grundlegende Auseinandersetzung mit der deutschen-"nationalen" Oberschicht*, Völkisches Rüstzeug, no. 4 (Munich, n.d. [1924]), 20–32.

[42] Brauer to Heydebrand, 23 Feb. 1924, NL Westarp, Gärtringen, II/84.

of the DNVP's National Racist Committee were determined to move the issues of race and anti-Semitism to the forefront of the Nationalist campaign not just to counter the challenge of the racist Right but for the sake of the issue itself.[43] In this respect, the DNVP racists benefited from an apparent change of heart by DNVP party chairman Oskar Hergt. Having previously opposed efforts to tie the party too closely to a racist agenda, Hergt announced his full and unequivocal support for the aspirations of the party's racist wing at a meeting of the DNVP's National Racist Committee in Berlin on 17 February 1924.[44] With the encouragement of Hergt and the DNVP party leadership, the leaders of the DNVP's National Racist Committee proceeded to to draft a set of guidelines, or *Leitsätze*, on the *völkisch* principle and its place in the party's public profile.[45] Although the original draft was too radical for Hergt and underwent further revision at the hands of the party's national leaders,[46] it nevertheless served as the basis for the position the DNVP took on racism and antisemitism for the duration of the campaign. This position was rooted in a biological racism that stressed not just the unique properties of the German national character but also the need to preserve the purity of the nordic-German blood that flowed through the veins of the German nation as the foremost responsibility of the state. This was to be accomplished by purifying the German national community of all alien elements from the bottom up, that is, from the family to the clan, from the clan to the tribe, from the tribe to the state, and from the state to the empire. Through a program of racial hygiene, those of alien racial stock were to be segregated from the nation as a whole and rendered morally harmless. This, would be accompanied by the introduction of a new educational curriculum with the five-fold objective of strengthening the Christian foundations of Germany's national culture, developing a greater understanding of the history of the German race and its place in the history of the world, fostering a greater appreciation of the German language and its impact upon the cultures of other races, promoting a German sense of beauty in the fine arts, and instructing the German nation

---

[43] Westarp to Wedell, 19 Mar. 1924, NL Westarp, Gärtringen, VN 49. For the broader context, see Jones, "Conservative Antisemitism," 85–88, as well as Jackisch, *Pan-German Leauge*, 96–100, and Hofmeister, "Between Monarchy and Dictatorship, 273–79.

[44] Hergt's opening statement in the minutes of the DNVP's National Racist Committee, 17 Feb. 1924, BA Berlin, R 8048, 223/41. See also Brauer to Heydebrand, 19 Feb. 1924, NL Westarp, Gärtringen, II/84.

[45] For the original draft of this statement, see "Leitsätze der völkischen Welt- und Staatsauffassung," n.d., appended to the meeting announcement from Graef, 2 Feb. 1924, BA Berlin, R 8048, 223/32–37. See also the minutes of the DNVP's National Racist Committee, 17 Feb. 1924, ibid., 41–45.

[46] Brauer to Heydebrand, 16 Mar. 1924, NL Westarp, Gärtringen, II/84. See also the critique of the "Leitsätze" in Pfannkuche to the DNVP National Racist Committee, 12 Feb. 1924, BA Berlin, R 8048, 223/36–40.

in the sciences of biology and racial hygiene. But to accomplish this it would first be necessary to liberate the state from the grip of those currently in power and to create a genuine German people's state, or *Volksstaat*, free from the insidious influence of alien elements.[47]

On 21 February 1924 the DNVP tried to steal the racists' political thunder by introducing a resolution in the Prussian Landtag that would have required all Jews who had entered Prussia since 1 August 1914 to register with the police by 15 April in preparation for their removal from the state by 1 July. Those Jews who did not comply with this ordinance would be subject to confinement in detention camps prior to their expulsion from Prussian territory.[48] While this was an obvious ploy to capitalize upon the resentment many Germans felt over the large-scale influx of East European Jews into Germany after the end of World War I, Nationalist propagandists were anxious to meet the racist Right on the latter's own terms and stressed their party's commitment to the *völkisch* principle at every conceivable opportunity.[49] Speaking at a party rally in Stettin, estate owner Hans Schlange-Schöningen lapsed into demagogy that was scarcely discernible from that of the racist Right. "Jewry," Schlange-Schöningen exclaimed, "not only brought us the war and delivered us into slavery but it keeps us in this deplorable situation because it serves its oldest purposes ... In the final analysis it was not France, not England, not even America but the international Jewish stock market that was the true victor in the war."[50] Even relative moderates like Lindeiner-Wildau, a member of the DNVP delegation to the Prussian Landtag campaigning for a seat in the Reichstag, cloaked his critique of the modern democratic state and his defense of the conservative conception of the state in the language of the racist antisemite.[51] Yet for all of the passion with which they embraced the racist cause and exposed the clandestine machinations of international and German Jewry, the Nationalists drew a crucial distinction between their brand of antisemitism and that of the racists to their right. The Nationalists were

[47] "Die völkischen Ziele der Deutschnationalen Volkspartei," n.d. [Apr. 1924], DNVP-Werbeblatt, no. 217, BA Koblenz, NL Weilnböck, 5b. See also Bayerische Mittelpartei,"-Positive völkische Arbeit," n.d. [Apr. 1924], DNVP-Werbeblatt, no. 212, NL Westarp, Gärtringen, VN 49.

[48] Georg Negenborn, *Die jüdische Gefahr*, Deutschnationale Flugschrift, no. 153 (Berlin, 1924), 2–3.

[49] For example, see [Deutschnationale Volkspartei], *Der völkisch-nationale Gedanke im Kampfe mit der Republik (Vier Jahre deutschnatl. Reichstagsarbeit)*, Deutschnationale Flugschrift, no. 147 (Berlin, 1924).

[50] Hans Schlange-Schöningen, *Wir Völkischen! Rede in Stettin 1924*, Deutschnationale Flugschrift, no. 142 (Berlin, n.d. [1924]), 9–10.

[51] Hans Erdmann von Lindeiner-Wildau, *Aufgaben völkischer Politik. Vortrag vor dem Amt für staatspolitische Bildung der Studentenschaft der Universität Berlin am 27. Februar 1924*, Deutschnationale Flugschrift, no. 148 (Berlin, 1924), 10–14.

particularly critical, for example, of the hostility the leaders of the racist parties manifested towards religion, the monarchy, and the capitalist economic system. At the same time, there was a plebeian quality to racist agitation against the Jews and their place in German economic life that the leaders of the Nationalist party found difficult to accept.[52]

Nowhere did the racist Right pose a more serious threat to the DNVP's electoral prospects than in Bavaria, where the situation was complicated by the fact that state elections were scheduled to take place a month or so earlier than the national elections. The Bavarian Middle Party, as the DNVP's Bavarian chapter was generally known, was still recoiling from the racist crisis at the end of 1922 and the desertion of Rudolf von Xylander, Rudolf Buttmann, and other outspoken racists to the rival German-Racist Freedom Party.[53] At the same time, a serious strain had developed in relations between the BMP and the Bavarian Rural League, which had affiliated itself with the BMP in the aftermath of the November Revolution and had worked closely with the party in the 1919 and 1920 parliamentary elections.[54] But the abortive Hitler-Ludendorff putsch at the end of 1923 had sent shock waves through the ranks of Bavaria's conservative establishment and afforded the BMP an opportunity to repair its relationship with the BLB before new state and national elections took place the following spring. Here the initial impulse came not from the BMP but from the leaders of the Bavarian Rural League, who in January 1924 proposed an alliance of all right-wing forces for the upcoming state elections.[55] Ideally this alliance would include the racists, but should they refuse to cooperate, the fall-back position would be an alliance of all other right-wing groups including the BMP, the DVP, the National Liberal secession, and several lesser-known monarchist and conservative organizations.[56] But the unexpectedly heavy losses the BMP suffered in the Bavarian Landtag elections on 6 April 1924 caused a virtual panic within the DNVP party organization.[57] To shore up their party's position in Bavaria, the DNVP's

---

[52] See Schwarzer, "Das Ziel der Wahl," *Der Tag*, 9 Mar. 1924, no. 60, as well as Walther von Graef-Anklam, *Völkische Mittel- oder deutschnationale Rechtspartei?*, Deutschnationale Flugschrift, no. 150 (Berlin, 1924), and [Deutschnationale Volkspartei], *Die Deutschvölkische Freiheitspartei*, Deutschnationales Rüstzeug, no. 1 (Berlin, 1924).

[53] Minutes of the expanded BMP executive committee, 20 Dec. 1922, BA R 8005, 26/46–49.

[54] For example, see Hopp to Weinlböck, 3 Jan. and 12 Sept. 1923, BA Koblenz, NL Weinlböck, 4a. See also Kittel, "Zwischen völkischem Fundamentalismus und gouvrenmentaler Taktik, 849–901.

[55] Hilpert to Weinlböck, 12 Jan. 1924, as well as the minutes of the BLB executive committee, 29 Nov. 1923, BA Koblenz, NL Weinlböck, 5b.

[56] Bayerische Mittelpartei, "Positive deutschvölkische Arbeit," n.d., appended to Otto to Westarp, 26 April 1924, NL Westarp, Gärtringen, VN 49.

[57] On the BMP's losses in the 1924 Bavarian state elections, see Elina Kiiskinen, *DNVP in Bayern*, 244–48.

national leadership intervened in the nomination of candidates for the upcoming Reichstag elections on behalf of retired admiral Alfred von Tirpitz in the hope that a man of his stature could unite the splintered forces of the Bavarian Right and help the DNVP win back the votes it had lost to the radical racists.[58]

A "Second Versailles"

At issue in all of this was not so much the question of racism itself as whether the struggle against the domination of German and international Jewry could be waged more effectively by single-issue parties like the DVFP or by larger, more inclusive parties like the BMP and its national affiliate, the DNVP. But this and the other domestic issues that dominated the early stages of the campaign for the May 1924 Reichstag elections quickly receded into the background when on 9 April 1924 an international commission headed by the American banker Charles G. Dawes presented its recommendations for a solution to Germany's reparations problem. The central feature of the Dawes report was a schedule for the payment of reparations structured in such a fashion that it would not overwhelm Germany's admittedly limited capacity to pay. Annual payments would rise from one billion marks in 1925–26 to a maximum of 2.5 billion marks by 1928–29, although the Germany could, given suitable economic conditions, make supplemental payments over and above what the plan stipulated. In return for accepting the plan, the German government would receive an international loan of 800 million marks that would be used by the Reichsbank to reimburse German producers for the payment of reparations in kind and to inject badly needed capital into the German economy. A further inducement to accepting the plan was the belief that this would clear the way for the reestablishment of German economic sovereignty in the Ruhr and Rhine basins and that implementation of the plan would be followed by the evacuation of Allied troops from the occupied territories east of the Rhine River within a year of acceptance.[59]

The national government headed by Centrist Wilhelm Marx was anxious to take advantage of the new plan's economic benefits and indicated its willingness to accept the Dawes committee recommendations as the basis for a provisional solution of the reparations problem on 14 April 1924. From this point on, the controversy over acceptance or rejection of the Dawes committee recommendations almost totally eclipsed the domestic issues that had figured so prominently in the early stages of the campaign. At an extraordinary party

[58] Hergt to the members of the DNVP executive committee, 8 Apr. 1924, NL Westarp, Gärtringen, VN 44. On the Tirpitz candidacy, see Scheck, *Tirpitz*, 144–50.
[59] For further details, see Jon Jacobson, "The Reparations Settlement of 1924," in *Konsequenzen der Inflation/Consequences of Inflation*, ed. Gerald D. Feldman, Carl-Ludwig Holtfrerich, Gerhard A. Ritter, and Peter-Christian Witt (Berlin, 1989), 79–108.

congress in Hamburg at the end of March and beginning of April, Hergt and the DNVP party leadership had taken a strong and unequivocal stand against acceptance of the committee's recommendations.[60] The government's announcement two weeks later that it was prepared to accept the Dawes recommendations as the basis of renewed negotiations with the Allies triggered a storm of protest throughout the Nationalist party organization. The tone was set by Helfferich, who on 12 April publicly denounced the new plan as a "Second Versailles" and dismissed the benefits the government hoped to reap from its implementation as illusory.

Not only did Helfferich argue that the material burden of meeting the payment schedule outlined in the new plan exceeded Germany's capacity to pay even under the most favorable economic conditions, but he insisted that whatever benefits Germany was to receive from its adoption were more than offset by the controls it imposed upon the German economy. Helfferich was particularly critical of the proposal to reorganize the German railway system as a private corporation under the control of an international holding company whose dividends were to be counted towards the payment of reparations. By the same token, Helfferich attacked the plan because it failed to specify a timetable for the evacuation of foreign troops from the Ruhr and the other parts of Germany that were still under Allied occupation. In conclusion, Helfferich argued:

> Responsibility for the rejection of the experts report is every bit as great as it was for the rejection of the Versailles dictate. By the same token, responsibility for the acceptance of the experts report is as great as it was for the acceptance of Versailles. The curse of accepting unfulfillable conditions and the curse of the sins against the spirit of national self-affirmation have oppressed Germany for five long years and have led the German people to the brink of collapse. The German people is lost without salvation if it saddles itself with this curse once again.[61]

When Helfferich was killed in a railway accident in northern Italy twelve days later, this became the legacy his party carried into the campaign for the May 1924 Reichstag elections.[62]

---

[60] Oskar Hergt, *Wege zur Rettung. Rede auf dem außerordentlichen Reichsparteitage in Hamburg am Bismarcktage 1924*, Deutschnationale Flugschrift, no. 160 (Berlin, 1924), 9–16. For the official proceedings of the Hamburg party congress, 30 Mar.–1 Apr. 1924, see *Korrespondenz der Deutschnationalen Volkspartei*, 2 Apr. 1924, no. 40.

[61] Karl Helfferich, "Das zweite Versailles," in Karl Helfferich and Jakob Wilhelm Reichert, *Das zweite Versailles. Das Reparationsgutachten der alliierten Experten*, Deutschnationale Flugschrift, no. 175 (Berlin, 1924), 3–11.

[62] For example, see Westarp, "Helfferich und sein letztes Vermächtnis," *Korrespondenz der Deutschnationalen Volkspartei*, 26 Apr. 1924, no. 57.

Figure 6. "Frei von Versailles!" DNVP campaign placard designed by an unidentified graphic artist for the May 1924 Reichstag elections. Reproduced with permission from the Bundesarchiv Berlin, Plakat, 002-029-039

By stigmatizing the recommendations of the Dawes committee as a "Second Versailles," the Nationalists sought to mobilize popular sentiment against those parties that continued to support Stresemann's efforts to reach a diplomatic understanding with the Allies. This tactic, however, backfired against the DNVP in two important respects. In the first place, it shifted the focus of the campaign away from the domestic arena where the DNVP could play upon the anxiety and anger of those who had been hurt by the government's stabilization program to that of foreign policy where the material consequences of accepting or rejecting the Dawes Plan were far less clearly defined. As a result, the government parties were able to regain the offensive by attacking the DNVP for its unprincipled demagogy and unreliability in matters of Germany's national interest.[63] Secondly, the DNVP's highly emotional and unconditional condemnation of the Dawes Plan produced a severe strain in its relations with those sectors of the German industrial establishment that stood to benefit from the implementation of the Dawes committee recommendations. On 24 April 1924 the presidium and executive committee of the National Federation of German Industry adopted a resolution recognizing the recommendations of the Dawes committee as "a suitable basis for the solution of the reparations problem" and approving the use of these recommendations as the point of departure for the government's negotiations with the Allies.[64] This action constituted a direct rebuff to the DNVP party leadership and prompted a sharp rebuke from Hugenberg, who in his capacity as chairman of the Committee of German National Industrialists issued a tersely worded statement dissociating himself from the RDI's resolution and rejecting the notion that it reflected the sentiments of German industry as a whole.[65]

All of this was symptomatic of a much deeper split within the German industrial establishment between those who were prepared to work within the existing system of government in order to achieve specific social, economic, and political objectives and those who remained categorically opposed to any form of collaboration with Germany's republican institutions. In the immediate context, however, this split had virtually no effect upon the extent of industrial support for the DNVP in the May 1924 Reichstag elections. In fact, industry's willingness to support the DNVP was much greater in light of the strain that had developed in relations between Ruhr heavy industry and the DVP party leadership. Not only had Stresemann's decision to terminate passive resistance in the fall of 1923 prompted at least one prominent Ruhr

---

[63] See Stresemann, "Politische Ostern," in *Die Zeit*, [ca. 20 April 1924], in Stresemann, *Vermächtnis*. ed. Bernhard, 1:391–95.

[64] *Geschäftliche Mitteilungen für die Mitglieder des Reichsverbandes der Deutschen Industrie* 6, no. 10 (1 May 1924): 72, BA Koblenz, ZSg 1–14/2. For further details, see Weisbrod, *Schwerindustrie in der Weimarer Republik*, 273–76.

[65] Holzbach, *Das "System Hugenberg,"* 171–72.

industrialist – Paul Reusch from the Gutehoffnungshütte – to resign from the DVP in protest,[66] but the Stinnes concern moved to terminate its support of the party in the spring of 1924.[67] Moreover, the special fund that Vögler had created for Ruhr heavy industry in March 1924 for the purpose of supporting candidates who could be expected to represent industrial interests in the new Reichstag[68] was much more sympathetically disposed to the DNVP than to the DVP and routinely diverted funds earmarked for the DVP to candidates running on the National Liberal ticket in Berlin and other parts of the country.[69] Relations between Germany's industrial leadership and the DVP were further strained by that fact that the party no longer accorded prominent industrialists such as RDI president Kurt Sorge preferential treatment in the placement of candidates for the upcoming Reichstag elections and thereby weakened their chances of being returned to parliament.[70] The net effect of these developments was to solidify the DNVP's position as the party of preference for an increasingly large sector of the Ruhr industrial establishment.

A similar shift in support could be detected in the behavior of the patriotic and paramilitary Right. The most ambitious of the patriotic associations that stood on the German Right in the spring of 1924 was the United Patriotic Leagues of Germany under the leadership of former DVP Reichstag deputy Fritz Geisler. Following the collapse of the Munich "Beer Hall Putsch" in the fall of 1923, the United Patriotic Leagues of Germany had intensified its efforts to consolidate the patriotic and conservative forces that were currently scattered among a number of different parties and organizations into a united German Right.[71] Its ultimate objectives, however, were still the overthrow of the Weimar Constitution, the establishment of some form of right-wing dictatorship, and the eradication of Marxism from Germany's national life.[72] Though ostensibly neutral with respect to Germany's non-Marxist parties, the VVVD understood neutrality in a very selective way and was interested only in cultivating closer ties with the parties of the bourgeois Right. In the campaign

---

[66] Reusch to Blumberg, 26 Sept. 1923, RWWA Cologne, Abt. 130, NL Reusch, 30019393/0.
[67] Edmund Stinnes to Büxenstein, Thomas, Lehmann, Schliewen, Hoffmann, Osius, and Hilpert, 7 Apr. 1924, ACDP Sankt-Augustin, NL Stinnes, I-220/002/7.
[68] Circular from Wiskott (Bergbau-Verein), 18 Mar. 1924, RWWA Cologne, Abt. 130, Allgemeine Verwaltung der GHH, 400106/83.
[69] Raumer to Vögler, 29 Apr. 1924, BA Koblenz, NL Kardorff, 14/19–22.
[70] Bücher to Stresemann, 7 Apr. 1924, PA AA Berlin, NL Stresemann, 89/171829. On the fate of Sorge's candidacy, see Richter, *Deutsche Volkspartei*, 326.
[71] Report by Geisler at the VVVD delegate conference, 16 Feb. 1924, BHStA Munich, Abt. IV, EWB, 10/2. See also Diehl, "Von der 'Vaterlandspartei' zur 'Nationalen Revolution'," 623–25.
[72] "Richtlinien der Vereinigten vaterländischen Verbände Deutschlands," Feb. 1924, BHStA Munich, Abt. IV, EWB, 10/2.

for the May 1924 Reichstag elections, the leaders of the VVVD called for the unification of all those parties that were unequivocally committed to cleaning up the "Marxist system" that had presumably ruled Germany since November 1918 but were stymied by the refusal of the DVFP and other radical racist groups to participate in any such alliance.[73] Whereas the DVP had severely compromised its political pedigree by sharing governmental responsibility with the Social Democrats, the Nationalists made a concerted effort to win the support of Germany's paramilitary associations and praised them for their role in the resurgence of German national awareness within the younger generation.[74] Like the DNVP, the VVVD was adamantly opposed to the Dawes committee recommendations and joined the Nationalists in denouncing the new plan as a "Second Versailles."[75] Of all of major Germany's political parties, only the German National People's Party received the VVVD's unqualified support. Carefully crafted in the vocabulary of *Überparteilichkeit*, this and similar endorsements from other paramilitary associations clearly helped legitimate the DNVP as the party of "national opposition" to Weimar, Versailles, and the Dawes committee recommendations.

From Victory to Frustration

All of these factors – the increasingly desperate plight of Germany's urban and rural middle classes, the emotionally charged crusade against acceptance of the Dawes Plan, industrial disaffection from the DVP, and the tacit support of Germany's patriotic and paramilitary Right – combined to provide the German National People's Party with a stunning victory in the May 1924 Reichstag elections. In the four years since the last national elections, the DNVP had increased its electorate by nearly two million votes and could now claim the support of 19.5 percent of the total popular vote as opposed to 15.1 percent in 1920. The DNVP was now entitled to ninety-six seats in the Reichstag in contrast to the sixty-six seats it had received in 1920. Multivariate regression analysis of the June 1920 and May 1924 election results reveals that Nationalist gains seem to have been strongest in the agrarian sector, where the

---

[73] Report by Goltz at the VVVD delegate conference, 5 Apr. 1924, BHStA Munich, Abt. IV, EWB, 10/2.

[74] Otto Schmidt-Hannover, *Die vaterländische Bewegung und die Deutschnationale Volkspartei. Vortrag, gehalten in Berlin am 28. März 1924*, Deutschnationale Flugschrift, no. 167 (Berlin, 1924). See also Schlange-Schöningen's speech at the DNVP party congress in Hamburg, 30 Mar.–1 Apr. 1924, in *Korrespondenz der Deutschnationale Volkspartei*, 2 Apr. 1924, no. 40.

[75] For example, see Fritz Geisler, *Die falsche Front. Klassenkampf und Landesverrat. "Reichsbanner Nollet." Rede in der Reichs-Vertreterversammlung der Vereinigten vaterländischen Verbände Deutschlands am 30. Juni 1924 zu Berlin*, ed. Reichsgeschäftsstelle der Vereinigten Vaterländischen Verbände Deutschlands (Berlin, n.d. [1924]), 7–8.

retention of wartime controls over agricultural prices and production and a discriminatory tax policy had done much to turn small and middle-sized family farmers against the republic and those parties most closely identified with it.[76] These gains came almost exclusively at the expense of the two liberal parties, which in 1919–20 had experienced considerable success in attracting the support of rural voters in the central and western parts of the country.[77] Another group that rallied behind the Nationalist banner in the May 1924 Reichstag elections was the professional civil service, which had become increasingly disaffected from the republic first as a result of the material losses it had suffered during the runaway inflation of the early 1920s and then more recently by virtue of the layoffs that the Stresemann and Marx governments had ordered as part of their efforts to stabilize the mark.[78] By the same token, the DNVP was also able to capitalize upon the sense of betrayal that Germany's small investors felt towards the government as a result of its refusal to consider a full and equitable restoration of those paper marks assets that had been destroyed by the inflation.[79] Germany's white-collar employees, on the other hand, tended to support the DNVP with about the same degree of enthusiasm they had demonstrated in 1920, while the so-called old middle class of artisans, shopkeepers, and small-scale entrepreneurs had already begun to abandon the party in favor of the more radical groups that stood to the right of the Nationalists.[80]

Only the fact that the coalition of Nazi and non-Nazi racists known as the National Socialist Freedom Party scored significant gains of its own kept the Nationalist victory in the May 1924 Reichstag elections from being even more impressive than it actually was. In fact, many of those from the urban "old middle class" who had supported the DNVP in 1920 voted for the racist coalition four years later. Despite a conspicuous lack of success in the countryside, the racists received 1.9 million votes – or 6.5 percent of the popular vote – and elected thirty-two deputies to the new Reichstag.[81] The National Liberal Association, on the other hand, failed to elect so much as a single deputy, although the alliance it had concluded with conservative farm

---

[76] Childers, *Nazi Voter*, 72–76. For the raw data, see Falter, Lindenberg, and Schumann, *Wahlen und Abstimmungen*, 68–69.

[77] See the lament by the DVP's Otto Hugo before the DVP central executive committee, 6 July 1924, BA Koblenz, R 45 II, 339/345–51.

[78] Childers, *Nazi Voter*, 98–102. See also Andreas Kunz, *Civil Servants and the Politics of Inflation in Germany 1914–1924* (Berlin and New York, 1986), 366–82, and Rainer Fattmann, *Bildungsbürger in der Defensive. Die akademische Beamtenschaft und der "Reichsbund höherer Beamten" in der Weimarer Republik* (Göttingen, 2001), 113–29.

[79] Jones, "Inflation, Revaluation, and the Crisis of Middle-Class Politics," 152–56.

[80] Childers, *Nazi Voter*, 69–71, 87–92.

[81] See Wulff, "Die deutschvölkische Freiheitspartei," 42–43, and Jablonsky, *Nazi Party in Dissolution*, 85.

organizations in Hesse, Thuringia, Baden, and Württemberg polled nearly 600,000 votes and captured ten seats in the newly elected Reichstag. In the meantime, Germany's two liberal parties registered heavy losses of their own. The Democrats, for example, lost 29.1 percent of their popular vote from the 1920 Reichstag elections and saw their parliamentary representation slip from thirty-nine to twenty-five deputies. The People's Party, by comparison, lost 31.3 percent of its 1920 vote along with twenty of its sixty-five parliamentary mandates. Between them, the two liberal parties lost nearly two million votes in the May 1924 Reichstag elections and saw their share of the national electorate decline from 22.9 percent in 1919 and 22.2 percent in 1920 to a disappointing 14.9 percent in 1924.[82] By no means, however, did all of those who abandoned the liberal parties in the May 1924 Reichstag elections switch their allegiance to the DNVP. Many chose instead to vote instead for the Business Party of the German Middle Class (Wirtschaftspartei des deutschen Mittelstandes or WP) or one of the other special-interest or regional splinter parties that had surfaced in Germany since the last national elections. All told, special-interest and regional parties accounted for nearly 10 percent of the national vote in the May 1924 elections in what was essentially another symptom of the structural instability that plagued the German party system in the early and middle years of the Weimar Republic.[83]

The outcome of the May 1924 Reichstag elections left the German National People's Party in a commanding political position. With the addition of ten deputies who had won election as candidates of regional farm organizations, the DNVP was now the strongest party in the Reichstag and could claim the support of 106 deputies in parliament. Only the Social Democrats with their 100 parliamentary mandates were in a position to challenge the DNVP for political supremacy. But the SPD was still nursing its wounds from its participation in Stresemann's Great Coalition and showed little inclination to trade the advantages of opposition for the burden of governmental responsibility. In the meantime, the DNVP found itself caught on the horns of its own campaign rhetoric. After all, how could the DNVP, as the party that had branded the Dawes Plan a second Versailles, participate in a government whose first item of business would be the implementation of its recommendations for a

---

[82] Jones, *German Liberalism*, 220–22.

[83] In this respect, see Thomas Childers, "Inflation, Stabilization, and Political Realignment in Germany, 1924–1928," in *Die deutsche Inflation – eine Zwischenbilanz/The German Inflation Reconsidered – A Preliminary Balance*, ed. Gerald D. Feldman, Carl-Ludwig Holtfrerich, Gerhard A. Ritter, and Peter-Christian Witt (Berlin and New York, 1982), 409–31, and Thomas Childers, "Interest and Ideology: Anti-System Politics in the Era of Stabilization, 1924–1928," in *Die Nachwirkungen der Inflation auf die deutsche Geschichte 1924–1933*, ed. Gerald D. Feldman (Munich, 1985), 1–20. On the WP, see Martin Schumacher, *Mittelstandsfront und Republik. Die Wirtschaftspartei – Reichspartei des deutschen Mittelstandes 1919–1933* (Düsseldorf, 1972), 80–86, 89–107.

solution to the reparations problem? Or, in more fundamental terms, how could the DNVP enter a government that derived its legitimation from the Weimar Constitution without compromising its integrity as a party of "national opposition"?[84] As long as these questions remained unanswered, Nationalist hopes of translating their success at the polls into a lasting political advantage would remain unfulfilled. For Germany's republican leadership, the critical question was one of bringing the Nationalists into the government, particularly in light of its newly discovered political muscle, without compromising the integrity of Germany's republican institutions. This was a situation fraught with risk for Nationalists and republicans alike.

The Nationalist response to this situation was anything but encouraging. Given the fact that the four parties supporting the Marx government commanded less than a third of the seats in the Reichstag, there were compelling reasons for an extension of the existing governmental coalition to the right. For his own part, Stresemann was optimistic that the DNVP's recent electoral success would bring with it a greater sense of responsibility on the part of the Nationalist party leadership and a more positive attitude towards the Dawes committee recommendations.[85] But the government's efforts to secure a positive commitment from the DNVP regarding the future course of German foreign policy were frustrated by the lack of any sort of coherent position on the part of the Nationalist leadership.[86] The resolution released by the DNVP Reichstag delegation on 7 May 1924 indicated the party's willingness to share the burden of governmental responsibility but failed to clarify its position on acceptance or rejection of the Dawes committee recommendations.[87] Nor did the Nationalists help their cause when in their first meeting with representatives from the four government parties on 21 May they insisted that the task of forming a new government should be placed in the hands of the former head of the German navy, Great Admiral Alfred von Tirpitz.[88] Given Tirpitz's political past and outspoken hostility toward the republican system of

---

[84] In this respect, see the confidential memorandum prepared by Schlange-Schöningen for Hugenberg, 19 May 1924, BA Koblenz, NL Hugenberg, 28/134–37, as well as Axel von Freytagh-Loringhoven, *Nationale Opposition* (Munich, 1924).

[85] Stresemann to Jarres, 9 May 1924, PA AA Berlin, NL Stresemann, 90/171964–69. See also Larry Eugene Jones, "Stabilisierung von Rechts: Gustav Stresemann und das Streben nach politischer Stabilität 1923–1929," in *Politiker und Bürger. Gustav Stresemann und seine Zeit*, ed. Karl Heinrich Pohl (Göttingen, 1992), 162–93.

[86] Stresemann to Hembeck, 13 May 1924, PA AA Berlin, NL Stresemann, 90/171986–88.

[87] Resolution of the DNVP Reichstag delegation, 7 May 1924, NL Westarp, Gärtringen, VN 50.

[88] Protocol of a conversation between representatives from the DNVP and the German middle parties, 21 May 1924, BA Koblenz, Nachlass Anton Erkelenz, 136. For the Nationalist position, see Hans Erdmann von Lindeiner-Wildau, "Die Deutschnationalen und die Regierungskrise," n.d. [June 1924], DNVP-Werbeblatt, no. 255, NL Westarp, Gärtringen, VN 45.

government, the Nationalist proposal was hardly credible and did little to reassure the leaders of the more moderate bourgeois parties of the sincerity of Nationalist intentions.[89] When Hergt and the Nationalist leaders failed at a second meeting two days later to commitment themselves to a foreign policy based upon acceptance of the Dawes committee recommendations,[90] Marx concluded that the DNVP was not seriously interested in joining his government and tendered his cabinet's resignation on 26 May 1924.[91]

It is unlikely the Nationalists ever thought that Tirpitz would be given an opportunity to form a new government.[92] In all likelihood, his nomination was little more than a ploy that sought to reassure the more militantly antirepublican elements on the DNVP's right wing that if the party did enter the government, it would be on terms they could easily accept. Since there was little reason to believe the more moderate bourgeois parties would ever accept Tirpitz as chancellor, his candidacy had the further advantage of delaying serious discussion of a Nationalist entry into the cabinet until after the Dawes committee recommendations had been formally accepted. The Nationalists would thus be able to join the government and influence the distribution of the benefits accruing from the implementation of the Dawes Plan without ever being tainted by the odium of acceptance. Whatever hopes the Nationalists might have had that DNVP party chairman Hergt would be chosen to form a new cabinet following the collapse of the Marx government were quickly dispelled when on 28 May Reich President Ebert reappointed Marx to the task of organizing a new government. This led to a new round of negotiations in which the Nationalists dropped their demands for a Tirpitz chancellorship but still made their willingness to join the cabinet contingent upon Stresemann's resignation as foreign minister, a fundamental change in the direction of German foreign policy, and an end to the "Great Coalition" in Prussia.[93] When Marx rejected these conditions as unacceptable, the Nationalists announced the collapse of efforts to form a new government on the evening

---

[89] Remarks by Marx at a ministerial conference, 24 May 1924, in *Akten der Reichskanzlei: Die Kabinette Marx I und II. 30. November 1924 bis 3. Juni 1924. 3. Juni 1924 bis 15. Januar 1925*, edited by Günter Abramowski, 2 vols. (Boppard am Rhein, 1973), 1: 659–60.

[90] Protocol of a conversation between representatives from the DNVP and the German middle parties, 23 May 1924, BA Koblenz, NL Erkelenz, 136. See also Hergt to Schulz, 24 May 1924, BA Berlin, R 8005, 9/17–18.

[91] Marx's report at a ministerial conference, 31 May 1924, in *Die Kabinette Marx I und II*, ed. Abramowski, 1:671–73. For further details, see Michael Stürmer, *Koalition und Opposition in der Weimarer Republik 1924–1928* (Düsseldorf, 1967), 41–49, and Robert P. Gratwohl, *Stresemann and the DNVP: Reconciliation or Revenge in German Foreign Policy, 1924–1928* (Lawrence, KS, 1980), 21–30.

[92] Freytagh-Loringhoven to Goldacker, 12 Sept. 1924, BA Koblenz, Nachlass Otto Schmidt-Hannover, 34.

[93] Hergt to Scholz, 2 June 1924, BA Berlin, R 8005, 9/4–5.

of 30 May. Following one last effort to reach an understanding with the Nationalists, Marx informed Ebert that further negotiations had no purpose, whereupon the Reich President promptly accepted Marx's suggestion that the previous cabinet be reinstated in office.[94]

The Dawes Crisis

Although the Nationalists had temporarily avoided the odium of having to serve in a government whose first item of business would have been the ratification and implementation of the Dawes committee recommendations, the dilemma in which the Nationalist party leadership found itself refused to go away. Over the next several months, Stresemann and his associates in the national government finalized the details of the Dawes Plan in a series of extended negotiations with Allied representatives in London. In the course of these negotiations, Stresemann and the German delegation were able to secure a number of essential improvements in the terms of the proposed treaty, not the least of which was the provision that the military evacuation of the Ruhr was to begin within a year of ratification. Moreover, the German delegation was able to nail down the financial commitments from British and American bankers that were essential for Germany's economic recovery.[95] Whether or not all of this would be sufficient to win Nationalist acceptance – or, at least, Nationalist acquiescence – in the Reichstag remained to be seen.[96] Such support was essential in light of the fact that a constitutional amendment requiring a two-thirds majority in the Reichstag was necessary to transfer ownership of the German railway system from the public to the private sector. Without Nationalist support or large-scale Nationalist defections, the London Treaty stood no chance of securing the two-thirds majority necessary for ratification.

On 16 July the Allies reconvened in London to put the finishing touches on a treaty implementing the recommendations of the Dawes committee. In the meantime, the situation within the DNVP became increasingly confused as three distinct positions on the acceptance or rejection of the London Treaty had begun to emerge. In the first place, there were the Pan-German and militantly anti-republican elements on the DNVP's extreme right wing that demanded a policy of absolute and unconditional opposition. This faction was irreconcilably opposed to the new plan and insisted that the German Right

---

[94] For further details, see Stürmer, *Koalition und Opposition*, 45–49, and Hehl, *Marx*, 286–87.

[95] Krüger, *Außenpolitik*, 243–47.

[96] See Westarp's reservations in a meeting with Stresemann and other party leaders, 4 July 1924, NL Westarp, Gärtringen, VN 50.

should not compromise itself by taking part in the voluntary enslavement of the German people and that the DNVP could not afford to betray those voters who had rallied behind its call for the rejection of the Dawes Plan in the recent Reichstag elections.[97] The second faction consisted of those who enjoyed close ties to outside economic interests and who described themselves as political pragmatists anxious to protect the German economy against the convulsions they feared might result from rejection of the plan.[98] Between these two factions stood the DNVP party leadership, which was prepared to provide the government with the votes necessay to secure ratification of the controversial treaty if this would pave the way for the DNVP's entry into the national government on terms that would assure it of a lasting influence upon Germany's political future.[99]

At the urging of Tirpitz and other party leaders, Hergt decided to take advantage of the temporary lull in the domestic political scene to convene a special session of the DNVP Reichstag delegation from 17 to 22 July. With Reinhold Quaatz and Martin Spahn leading the way, the delegation began to harden its position against acceptance of the so-called Dawes Plan.[100] Even Hergt, who was still hoping that it might be possible to leverage Nationalist support for acceptance of the Dawes committee recommendations into an invitation for the DNVP to join the government on terms commensurate with its recent success at the polls, capitulated to the passions of the moment. At a joint meeting of the Reichstag delegation and representatives of the party's state and regional organizations on 22 July, the Nationalist party chairman outlined seven demands with respect to the Dawes committee recommendations that would have to be met before the DNVP could support the plan in parliament. Among other things, these demands stipulated that the Allies must begin the immediate withdrawal from the military and economic control of the so-called sanction areas, that German sovereignty must be fully and immediately restored in the Rhineland, that the Allies give assurances that no

[97] Schmidt-Hannover to Ritgen, 23 Aug. 1924, BA Koblenz, NL Schmidt-Hannover, 32.
[98] Baerwolff to Tirpitz, 7 June 1924, BA-MA Freiburg, NL Tirpitz, 60/61–63. In this respect, see also Stresemann's appeal for the support of German industry in a speech before the Iron and Steel Goods Industrial Association (Eisen- und Stahlwaren-Industriebund) in Elberfeld, 10 July 1924, NL Westarp, Gärtringen, VN 47.
[99] Hergt to the DNVP district organization in West Prussia, 9 Sept. 1924, BA-MA Freiburg, NL Tirpitz, 60/386–92. On the mood at the upper echelons of the DNVP party leadership, see Westarp to Hergt, 17 July 1924, NL Westarp, II/13.
[100] For further details, see the entry in Quaatz's diary, 27 July 1924, BA Koblenz, NL Quaatz, 16, as well as Freytagh-Loringhoven to Goldacker, 12 Sept. 1924, BA Koblenz, NL Schmidt-Hannover, 34, and Keudell to Tirpitz, 27 July 1924, BA-MA Freiburg, NL Tirpitz, 278/6–7. See also Reinhold Quaatz and Martin Spahn, *Deutschland unter Militär-, Finanz- und Wirtschaftskontrolle* (Berlin, 1925), esp. 74–121.

further sanctions will be imposed in the future, and that the Allies disavow the war-guilt clause of the Versailles Peace Treaty.[101]

In the meantime, outside pressure on the DNVP Reichstag delegation for acceptance of the Dawes Plan continued to mount from three different directions. On 2 July 1924 the executive committee of the National Federation of German Industry voted overwhelmingly to reaffirm the position it had taken on 24 April in support of the Dawes committee recommendations.[102] This action, which ran into strong opposition from Hugenberg and a small contingent of his supporters from the Ruhr industrial establishment,[103] placed those DNVP Reichstag deputies with close ties to German industry under increasingly heavy pressure to vote for acceptance of the plan when it came before parliament for ratification in the fourth week of August. Agents for the Krupp Steel Works, for example, were particularly active in pressuring Nationalist deputies like Jakob Wilhelm Reichert from the Association of German Iron and Steel Industrialists into voting for the plan.[104] Similarly, organized agriculture seemed no less intent upon using the conflict over acceptance or rejection of the Dawes Plan as a lever to extract important concessions from the government on the future direction of German trade policy. Anticipating the moment when Germany would regain full tariff autonomy on 1 January 1925, the leaders of the National Rural League and other agricultural interest organizations had already begun to press the government for a return to the agricultural protectionism of the prewar period.[105] At the same time, Krupp's

[101] "Die sieben Forderungen der Deutschnationalen," *Korrespondenz der Deutschnationalen Volkspartei,* 23 July 1924, no. 104. For a defense of the DNVP's position, see Otto Hoetzsch, *Die Deutschnationalen und das Dawes-Gutachten. Reichstagsrede am 26. Juli 1924,* Deutschnationale Flugschrift, no. 178 (Berlin, 1924). On the situation within the DNVP Reichstag delegation, see the entry in Quaatz's diary, 27 July 1924, BA Koblenz, NL Quaatz, 16.

[102] *Geschäftliche Mitteilungen für die Mitglieder des Reichsverbandes der Deutschen Industrie* 6, no. 16 (15 July 1924): 113–15, BA Berlin, ZSg 1-14/2. For further details, see Weisbrod, *Schwerindustrie in der Weimarer Republik,* 273–80, and Stephanie Wolff-Rohé, *Der Reichsverband der Deutschen Industrie 1919–1924/25* (Frankfurt am Main, 2001), 355–87.

[103] Hugenberg's remarks at the meeting of the RDI main committee (Hauptausschuß), 2 July 1924, BA Koblenz, NL Silverberg, 355/84–93. See also the entry in Quaatz's diary for 3 July 1924, BA Koblenz, NL Quaatz, 16.

[104] See the exchange of telegrams between Krupp and Haniel, 24–25 Aug. 1924, Historisches Archiv Krupp, Essen (hereafter cited as HA Krupp Essen), Bestand FAH, IV E 789. On Reichert, see his letter to Cuno, 13 Aug. 1924, StA Hamburg, Hapag-Rederei, Handakten Cuno, 1489. For Reichert's defense of the pact, see J. W. Reichert, *Zur deutschnationalen Wirtschaftspolitik,* Deutschnationale Flugschrift, no. 193 (Berlin, 1924), 14–23.

[105] Karl Hepp and Eberhard von Kalckreuth, *Wege zur Aktivierung der deutschen Wirtschaftsbilanz. Die Vorschläge des Reichs-Landbundes* (Berlin, 1925). See also the memorandum from Hepp and Kalckreuth of the RLB to the national government, 21 June 1924, in *Kabinette Marx I und II,* ed. Abramowski, 2:729–30.

allies in the German agricultural community – most notably his brother-in-law and RLB official Baron Tilo von Wilmowsky – sought to break down the RLB's opposition to the Dawes Plan by pointing out the benefits that acceptance of the plan held for German agriculture.[106] Under these circumstances, the RLB leadership became convinced that a return to agrarian protectionism would be possible only if the Nationalists were represented in the government. As RLB president Eberhard von Kalckreuth expressed it to Westarp in a conversation less than a week before the decisive vote in the Reichstag, "if this required accepting the plan, then so be it."[107] The third source of outside pressure on the DNVP Reichstag delegation for acceptance of the Dawes recommendations came from the German Trade-Union Federation and its associates in the Christian labor movement. The leaders of the DGB looked upon the Dawes Plan as a means of attracting the foreign capital necessary to recover from the massive unemployment that had accompanied Germany's return to economic and fiscal stability in the winter of 1923–24. Consequently, the leaders of the DNVP's Christian-social labor wing found themselves under increasingly heavy pressure from the DGB and its affiliated unions to support the controversial report when it came before the Reichstag for a final vote.[108]

Under these circumstances, the unity of the Nationalist delegation to the Reichstag began to crack.[109] As it became increasingly clear by the second or third week of August that the government had no intention of meeting the seven demands the DNVP Reichstag delegation had announced on 22 July, the Nationalist party leadership became more and more uncertain in its handling of the crisis. On 21 August the DNVP Reichstag delegation reaffirmed the position it had taken against ratification of the London accords a month earlier and insisted upon complete fulfillment of its seven demands before any change in its current stance could be considered.[110] But Nationalist hopes of maintaining a united front against ratification of the London Treaty received a

---

[106] Wilmowsky to Krupp, 13 May 1924, HA Krupp, FAH 23/500/235–36. See also Wolfgang Zollitsch, "Das Scheitern der 'gouvernementalen' Rechten. Tilo von Wilmowsky und die organisierten Interessen in der Staatskrise von Weimar," in *Demokratie in Deutschland. Chancen und Gefährdungen im 19. und 20. Jahrhundert. Historische Essays*, ed. Wolther von Kieseritzky and Klaus-Peter Sick (Munich, 1999), 254–74.

[107] Westarp's report of his conversation with Klackreuth in a letter to his wife, 23 Aug. 1924, NL Westarp, NL Gärtringen.

[108] Roder, *Gewerkschaftsbund*, 405–06.

[109] For an insightful analysis of the dilemma in which Hergt and the DNVP party leadership found themselves, see Philipp Nielsen, "Verantwortung und Kompromiss. Die Deutschnationalen auf der Suche nach einer konservativen Demokratie," in *Normalität und Fragilität. Demokratie nach dem Ersten Weltkrieg*, ed. Tim B. Müller and Adam Tooze (Hamburg, 2015), 294–314, here 303–13.

[110] *Neue Preußische (Kreuz-)Zeitung*, 22 Aug. 1924, no. 393.

severe blow when the National Rural League issued a deliberately ambiguous statement that reaffirmed its opposition to acceptance of the Dawes committee recommendations and its call for a reorganization of the national government but fell short of instructing its representatives in the DNVP and other political parties to vote against the recommendations in the upcoming Reichstag vote.[111] The language of the RLB statement might very well have been even more forthright in its support of the plan had it not been for the tireless efforts of Quaatz, who met with Kalckreuth and members of the DNVP Reichstag delegation with close ties to the RLB – Hans von Goldacker, Prätorius von Richthofen-Boguslawitz, and Walther von Keudell – in an attempt to stiffen thier opposition to the plan's acceptance and to minimize the damage caused by the ambiguity of the RLB's statement.[112] Given the fact that as many as 52 of the DNVP's 106 deputies belonged to the RLB, the RLB's announcement greatly increased the threat of an open split within DNVP party ranks.

At this point, the Nationalist party leadership tried to salvage whatever they could out of what was quickly becoming an impossible situation by approaching Stresemann and the leaders of the DVP on the evening of 23 August with an offer to provide the government with the votes it needed for ratification of the London accords if the DVP would reciprocate by issuing a statement committing it to a reorganization of the national government when the Reichstag reconvened in October.[113] By making such an offer, Hergt and the leaders of the DNVP Reichstag delegation were trying not only to extract maximum political advantage from the likelihood that Nationalist deputies might vote for the Dawes recommendations despite instructions to the contrary but also to minimize the extent of such defections by insisting that party unity was an essential precondition for the success of its negotiations with the government.[114] It was a risky ploy that met with little enthusiasm from the leaders of the DNVP's right wing,[115] but under the circumstances it was about the only strategic option open to Hergt and the DNVP party leadership. Although Stresemann agreed to present the Nationalist offer to the chancellor, his initial inclination was to reject it and let the Nationalists suffer the

---

[111] "Stellungnahme des Präsidiums des Reichs-Landbundes zur gegenwärtigen politischen Lage," n.d. [Aug. 1924], appended to Kalckreuth to Westarp, 23 Aug. 1924, NL Westarp, Gärtringen, VN 46.

[112] Entry in Quaatz's diary, 22 Aug. 1924, BA Koblenz, NL Quaatz, 16. See also to Krupp, 31 Aug. 1924, HA Krupp Essen, FAH 23/500/283–86.

[113] Stresemann's memorandum of a conversation with Curtius and Zapf from the DVP Reichstag delegation, 24 Aug. 1924, PA AA Berlin, NL Stresemann, 15/156931–32. See also Wright, Stresemann, 290–92, and Richter, Deutsche Volkspartei, 343–45.

[114] For Hergt's strategy, see his letter to the DNVP district organization in East Prussia, 9 Sept. 1924, NL Westarp, Gärtringen, II/13.

[115] Entry in Quaatz's diary, 23 Aug. 1924, BA Koblenz, NL Quaatz, 16.

consequences of their own demagogy.[116] For even if Stresemann may not have felt that he had the votes necessary for ratification of the London accords, he clearly looked forward to the prospect of new national elections at a time when the Nationalists were badly divided and very much on the defensive.

In the meantime, confusion continued to reign within the ranks of the DNVP. Hergt's Reichstag speech of 25 August did little to clarify the situation and consisted of little more than a restatement of the DNVP's previous position, though with sufficient ambivalence to suggest his party's willingness to support the controversial legislation if it received the necessary concessions from the government.[117] Over the course of the next several days pressure on the DNVP Reichstag delegation continued to mount as even the German chief of command, General Hans von Seeckt, began to counsel moderation on the part of the DNVP.[118] But entreaties of this sort had little effect upon the determination of the DNVP's extreme right wing. On 26 August Hugenberg interrupted his convalescence from a mild heart attack he had suffered the night before to fire off an impassioned letter imploring the DNVP party chairman to remain firm in his resolve to block ratification of the London accords.[119] Hergt and the leaders of the DNVP Reichstag delegation, on the other hand, continued to vacillate between declarations of unconditional opposition to the London accords and suggestions that they might vote for acceptance if certain demands, such as the revocation of the war guilt clause and a postponement in the treaty's implementation until the evacuation of the Ruhr, were met. This did little to inspire confidence in Hergt's ability to lead the party.[120]

Throughout all of this, the situation in the DNVP continued to deteriorate. At a meeting of the DNVP Reichstag delegation on the afternoon of 27 August, twenty-two Nationalist deputies indicated that they were prepared to vote for acceptance of the Dawes recommendation despite the almost unanimous opposition to such a step fact that the leaders of the party's district organizations had voiced at a caucus with the delegation earlier that morning. Those deputies inclined to vote for acceptance had begun to coalesce behind the leadership of Max Wallraf and included such party stalwarts as Otto Hoetzsch, Gottfried von Dryander, and Count Prätorius von Richthofen-Boguslawitz

---

[116] Stresemann's memorandum of a conversation with Curtius and Zapf, 24 Aug. 1924, PA AA Berlin, NL Stresemann, 15/156931–32.

[117] Freytagh-Loringhoven to Goldacker, 12 Sept. 1924, BA Koblenz, NL Schmidt-Hannover, 34. For the text of Hergt's speech, see Oskar Hergt, *Der Weg zur einer richtigen Regierungspolitik. Reichstagsrede am 25. August 1924*, Deutschnationale Flugschrift, no. 181 (Berlin, 1924).

[118] Hans Meier-Welcker, *Seeckt* (Frankfurt am Main, 1967), 446–47.

[119] Alfred Hugenberg, *Streiflichter aus Vergangenheit und Gegenwart* (Berlin, 1927), 96–97.

[120] Freytagh-Loringhoven to Goldacker, 12 Sept. 1924, BA Koblenz, NL Schmidt-Hannover, 34.

from the Silesian Rural League (Schlesischer Landbund).[121] Their position was influenced in no small measure by the fact that the DVP Reichstag delegation had tried to break the impasse by sending the DNVP a letter in which it promised to join the Nationalists in forming a new government if they provided the votes necessary for ratification of the London accords.[122] Hergt, who was still hopeful of preventing a schism within the DNVP Reichstag delegation,[123] met with representatives from the Center and DVP on 28 August but was unable to secure terms for the DNVP's entry into the government that would have been acceptable to all the factions in the DNVP Reichstag delegation. Most importantly, the government parties were no longer willing to consider Nationalist demands for the chancellorship or for a change in the leadership of the German foreign office.[124]

Within hours of the final and decisive vote in the Reichstag, Hergt met with the chancellor in the early hours of 29 August to determine to the extent to which the DVP's action actually signaled a change in the government's position. But this meeting produced still another deadlock when Hergt made his party's support in the upcoming Reichstag vote conditional not only upon the formation of a new government with Westarp at its head but also upon the transfer of the Prussian minister presidency and the Prussian ministry of interior into Nationalist hands. Citing the opposition of his own party and the negative reaction that such a step would almost certainly encounter abroad, Marx rejected the Nationalist demands and broke off further negotiations.[125] At this point Hergt returned to the DNVP Reichstag delegation and, with the full support of Westarp, called upon his colleagues to reject the London accords along with all the legislation necessary for their implementation.[126] By now, however, it was too late to salvage the unity of the delegation. The two factions had met separately that morning, and there was no longer any reason to believe, as Hergt apparently did, that the delegation would unanimously reject acceptance of the London accords if its demands for the revocation of the war guilt clause and other modifications in the terms of the treaty were not met. Hergt's assumption that the delegation would remain united against the accords if its demands were not met received a rude shock when Wilhelm Bazille, a Nationalist deputy from Württemberg, announced on

---

[121] Ibid. See also Bachmann to Weilnböck, 27 Aug. 1924, BA Koblenz, NL Weilnböck, 5a.

[122] *Nationalliberale Correspondenz*, 1 Sept. 1924, no. 145.

[123] Hergt to the DNVP district organization in East Prussia, 9 Sept. 1924, NL Westarp, Gärtringen, II/13.

[124] Freytagh-Loringhoven to Goldacker, 12 Sept. 1924, BA Koblenz, NL Schmidt-Hannover, 34.

[125] Undated memorandum by Hergt on the negotiations of 28–29 Aug. 1924, NL Westarp, Gärtringen, II/12. See also Hergt to Zapf, 29 Aug. 1924, BA Berlin, R 8005, 10/117–18.

[126] Hergt to the DNVP district organization in East Prussia, 9 Sept. 1924, NL Westarp, Gärtringen, II/13.

behalf of those who favored acceptance of the Dawes recommendations that they would vote for the treaty's ratification when it came before the Reichstag later that afternoon.[127]

Much to the dismay of those who stood on the party's right wing, Hergt seemed resigned to a split in the delegation and made little attempt to use his authority as DNVP party chairman to force those who had coalesced behind Hoetzsch, Wallraf, and Bazille into going along with the rest of the delegation.[128] The indecisiveness of the DNVP party leadership combined with pressure from the National Federation of German Industry, the National Rural League, and other outside economic interests to produce widespread confusion and uncertainty within the ranks of the party's Reichstag delegation. The fate of the Ruhr and Rhineland in the event that the London accords were not accepted, the specter of a new round of credit restrictions by the finance ministry and German National Bank, and warnings from the ministry of agriculture about the dire consequences of the treaty's rejection for Germany's small and middle-sized farmers all played a major role in undermining Nationalist resolve to fight ratification of the treaty.[129] As a result, the unity of the delegation completely collapsed in the voting on the Dawes Plan on the afternoon of 29 August. Nowhere was this more apparent than in the fateful vote on the Federal Railway Law (Reichsbahngesetz). For, as in the case of all other votes on the various pieces of legislation related to the implementation of the Dawes Plan, the Nationalist delegation split right down the middle, thereby providing the government with the two-thirds majority necessary for the controversial railway bill to take effect. Of the hundred Nationalist deputies who voted on the bill, forty-eight voted for acceptance and fifty-two for rejection. Nationalist unity was now in shambles.[130]

Party leaders moved quickly to contain the damage caused by the split in the Nationalist vote on the railway bill by sending a circular to district and precinct party leaders that stressed the gravity of the situation in which the fateful vote had taken place and urged the party faithful not to attack the integrity of those who had voted one way or the other.[131] To the leaders of the DNVP's right wing, however, the collapse in party unity in the fateful vote on 29 August 1924 was a source of deep embarrassment. In their eyes, the split in the Nationalist vote constituted nothing less than a betrayal of the "national

[127] Freytagh-Loringhoven to Goldacker, 12 Sept. 1924, BA Koblenz, NL Schmidt-Hannover, 34.
[128] Ibid.
[129] Schmidt-Hannover to Ritgen, 17 Oct. 1924, BA Koblenz, NL Schmidt-Hannover, 32.
[130] Hans Erdmann von Lindeiner-Wildau, *Nach der Entscheidung*, Deutschnationale Flugschrift, no. 182 (Berlin, 1924).
[131] Circular from Lindeiner-Wildau to the DNVP district and precinct organizations, 29 Aug. 1924, NL Westarp, Gärtringen, II/12.

opposition" and served as a classic example of the way in which special economic interests were able to subvert the will of the party and subordinate it to their own specific agenda.[132] At the same time, how one had voted on 29 August 1924 became a litmus test of one's commitment to Germany's struggle for national liberation. The individual deputies who had voted for acceptance of the London accords were stigmatized as *Ja-Sager* who had placed the welfare of special economic interests before that of the nation as a whole. But the most vicious attacks were reserved for Hergt. Not even the fact that Hergt himself had voted against acceptance could shield him from the wrath of his party's right wing. Hergt now became a symbol of the vacillation and indecisiveness that had led to the split in the first place, and he was under mounting pressure from the Pan-German League and the more militantly antirepublican elements on the DNVP's right wing to resign from the party chairmanship as an act of public penance for his failure to preserve party unity. Such sentiment was particularly strong at the local and regional levels of the Nationalist party organization, where the Pan-Germans and old-line conservatives not only demanded Hergt's resignation but insisted that those deputies who had voted for the Dawes recommendations be summarily purged from the Reichstag delegation.[133] The split in the vote on the Dawes Plan threatened to erupt into a major crisis within the party as a whole.

The events of 29 August 1924 and the recriminations that reverberated throughout the Nationalist party organization were indicative of a much deeper schism within the ranks of the German Right. From 1919 to 1924 the German Right had been united in its opposition to the symbols and institutions of Germany's new republican order. Governmental conservatives and radical nationalists stood together in their rejection of the sweeping changes that had taken place in Germany's constitutional system as a result of the November Revolution. But as Germany reemerged from the abyss of 1923 and began to take the first tentative steps towards political and economic stability, the "unity of the no" began to lose much of its integrative potential. For many of those on the German Right, opposition became a luxury they could no longer afford. This was particularly true of large and influential economic interest organizations like the National Federation of German Industry, the National Rural League, and the German National Union of Commercial Employees. For as much as the leaders of these organizations may have distrusted the republican form of government, they had no choice but to work

---

[132] Freytagh-Loringhoven, *Deutschnationale Volkspartei*, 24–26.
[133] For example, see Arnim-Boitzenburg to Westarp, 30 Aug. 1924, NL Westarp, Gärtringen, VN 43, as well as the letter from the DNVP Harburg to Schmidt-Hannover, 28 Sept. 1924, BA Koblenz, NL Schmidt-Hannover, 34.

within the framework of the constitutional arrangements that had been established at Weimar to defend and represent the vested interests of their respective constituencies. This, in turn, placed them on a collision course with those elements on the German Right that remained irreconcilably opposed to any form of collaboration with the Weimar Republic.

8

Stabilization from the Right?

The ratification of the London accords and the implementation of the Dawes committee recommendations represented an important step towards the political and economic stabilization of the Weimar Republic. It also represented a vindication of the strategy that Stresemann and other government officials had adopted with respect to the German Right following its impressive gains in the May 1924 Reichstag elections. From the height of the Dawes crisis in the summer of 1924 through the end of 1925, Stresemann and his associates pursued a deliberate policy of trying to stabilize the republic from the right by coopting the support of influential economic interest organizations like the National Federation of German Industry and the National Rural League in the hope that this would force the DNVP party leadership into adopting a more constructive attitude towards Germany's republican system of government. If successful, this strategy would oblige the Nationalists to foreswear the demagogy that had served them so well in the most recent Reichstag elections and to square their rhetoric with the hard realities of Germany's political and economic situation.[1] The extent to which this strategy would work depended not merely upon the effectiveness with which the various interest groups in the DNVP were able to press their case at the upper echelons of the Nationalist party leadership but, more importantly, upon the specific benefits that the DNVP's participation in the national government would bring to its various constituencies. Whether or not this would be possible under the restrictive conditions of Germany's economic stabilization remained to be seen.

---

[1] For the general outlines of Stresemann's strategy with respect to the DNVP, see Gustav Stresemann, *Nationale Realpolitik. Rede auf dem 6. Parteitag der Deutschen Volkspartei in Dortmund am 14. November 1924*, Flugschriften der Deutschen Volkspartei, no. 56 (Berlin, 1924), 32–34, as well as the manuscript of his article, "Zur Regierungskrise," *Hamburger Fremdenblatt*, 25 Dec. 1924, PA AA Berlin, NL Stresemann, 18/157792–806. See also Larry Eugene Jones, "Stabilisierung von Rechts: Gustav Stresemann und das Streben nach politischer Stabilität 1923-1929," in *Politiker und Bürger. Gustav Stresemann und seine Zeit*, ed. Karl Heinrich Pohl (Göttingen, 2002), 162–93. For a somewhat different reading of Stresemann's political strategy, see Wright, *Stresemann*, 296–301.

Stalemate in Berlin

Efforts to bring the DNVP into the government received new life after the Nationalists had helped it to secure ratification of the London accords and begin implementation of the Dawes committee recommendations.[2] But the position of DNVP party chairman Oskar Hergt had been severely weakened by his failure to maintain party unity in the decisive vote on the Dawes Plan. Hergt accepted responsibility for the split in the vote on the Dawes Plan and was fully prepared to step down as party chairman. Only the fact that the DNVP was about to enter into exploratory negotiations with the DVP and Center that could conceivably lead to its entry into the national government kept Hergt from going ahead with this decision.[3] Nevertheless, the DNVP remained bitterly divided as opponents of the Dawes Plan tried to mobilize the party's rank-and-file membership against those deputies who had supported the controversial bill in the Reichstag.[4] All of this made Stresemann increasingly skeptical as to whether or not the Nationalists would be able to assume a responsible and constructive role in a new governmental coalition.[5] The leaders of the DVP Reichstag delegation, on the other hand, remained firmly committed to an extension of the existing governmental coalition to the right and entered into exploratory negotiations with the Nationalist party leadership in the second week of September.[6] But the leaders of the DNVP responded to DVP's overtures with little enthusiasm, if for no other reason than the simple fact that their ability to influence the composition and policies of the national cabinet had been severely compromised by the DNVP's ambiguous role in the passage of the Dawes Plan.[7] Still, when the DVP Reichstag delegation publicly reaffirmed its pledge to support the DNVP's entry into the national government in return for the role it had played in the ratification of the London accords,[8] the DNVP party leadership responded positively to the DVP's overture and agreed to take part in negotiations aimed at an extension of the government to the right as long as their party's representation in a reorganized

[2] For further details, see Stürmer, *Koalition und Opposition*, 73–78; Richter, *Deutsche Volkspartei*, 334–49, and Ohnezeit, *Zwischen "schärfster Opposition,"* 272–77.

[3] Report by Brauer (Central Association of German Conservatives), 2 Oct. 1924, Brandenburgisches Landeshauptstaatsarchiv, Potsdam (hereafter cited as BLHA Potsdam) Nachlass Count Dietlof von Arnim-Boitzenburg, Rep. 37, 4426/89–90.

[4] Brauer to Westarp, 9 and 19 Sept. 1924, NL Westarp, Gärtringen, VN 46. See also the entry in Gallwitz's diary, 10 Sept. 1924, BA-MA Freiburg, NL Gallwitz, 39.

[5] Stresemann to Campe, 8 Sept. 1924, PA AA Berlin, NL Stresemann, 157093–96.

[6] Scholz's report at a meeting of the executive committee of the DVP Reichstag delegation, 24 Sept. 1924, BA Koblenz, R 45 II, 366/22–23.

[7] See the correspondence between Hergt and Westarp, 15–18, 1924, BA Berlin, R 8005, 10/96–103, and Westarp to Lindeiner-Wildau, 25 Sept. 1924, ibid., 10/88–89.

[8] Deutsche Volkspartei, Reichsgeschäftsstelle, ed., *Nachtrag zum Wahlhandbuch 1924* (Berlin, 1924).

Marx cabinet be commensurate with the strength it had demonstrated by its recent victory at the polls.[9]

For his own part, Marx had little interest in a one-sided extension of his cabinet to the right and immediately tried to dampen the effect of the DVP's overtures to the DNVP by inviting the Social Democrats to participate in a reorganization of his cabinet. Hergt promptly denounced Marx's overtures to the Social Democrats at a meeting of the DNVP Reichstag delegation on 8 October as a breach of the promise the chancellor had made to the DNVP at the time of the Dawes vote.[10] By then, a small but vociferous minority that strongly opposed the DNVP's entry into a reorganized Marx cabinet had begun to crystallize within the DNVP Reichstag delegation around the person of Count Westarp.[11] The Nationalists then proceeded to torpedo Marx's overtures to the SPD by attaching three conditions to their participation in a reorganization of his cabinet. Specifically, the Nationalists demanded that the government parties accept Christianity as the basis of German political life, reject the notion of class conflict in favor of a commitment to the principle of the *Volksgemeinschaft*, and disavow Germany's alleged responsibility for the outbreak of World War I.[12] The first and second of these demands were clearly directed at the Social Democrats and sought to exclude them from future cabinet negotiations. Even after the Social Democrats expressed disinterest in a reorganization of the Marx cabinet, efforts to extend the existing governmental coalition to the right became bogged down in disagreements over the future conduct of German foreign policy.[13] When the Center made the participation of the German Democratic Party a precondition of its willingness to go along

[9] *Korrespondenz der Deutschnationalen Volkspartei*, 7, no. 164 (1 Oct. 1924). See also Westarp's report to the executive committee of the Central Association of German Conservatives, 11 Oct. 1924, reported by Brauer, 14 Oct. 1924, BLHA Potsdam, NL Arnim-Boitzenburg, 4426/87–88, as well as the entries in Quaatz's diary, 29–30 Sept. 1924, BA Koblenz, NL Quaatz, 16, and Keudell to Tirpitz, 2 Oct. 1924, BA-MA Freiburg, NL Tirpitz, 60/178–82. For the official party account of these negotiations, see *Regierungskrise und Reichstagsauflösung (August bis Oktober 1924)*, Deutschnationale Flugschrift, no. 185 (Berlin, 1924), 3–4.

[10] Hergt at a meeting of the DNVP Reichstag delegation, 8 Oct. 1924, BA Koblenz, NL Quaatz, 16.

[11] Westarp's report to the executive committee of the Central Association of German Conservatives, 11 Oct. 1924, cited above, no. 9.

[12] Resolution of the DNVP Reichstag delegation, 8 Oct. 1924, in *Korrespondenz der Deutschnationalen Volkspartei*, 9 Oct. 1924, no. 171. See also *Regierungskrise und Reichstagsauflösung*, 5.

[13] Protocol of a meeting between representatives of the government and a four-man delegation from the DNVP, 10 Oct. 1924, in *Kabinette Marx I und II*, ed. Abramowski, 2:1105–06. See also the memorandum on this meeting by an unidentified DNVP partici-pant, 10 Oct. 1924, NL Westarp, Gärtringen, II/12. For the Nationalist version of these negotiations, see *Regierungskrise und Reichstagsauflösung*, 6–8.

with an extension of the existing cabinet to the right, the DVP Reichstag delegation signalled its frustration with the deadlock that had developed in the government's negotiations with the Nationalists by issuing a declaration later in the afternoon that effectively terminated its support of the existing cabinet.[14] When the DDP reiterated its refusal to serve in a government in which the Nationalists were also represented at a meeting of its executive committee on 20 October,[15] Marx declared his efforts to form a new government at an end and petitioned the Reich President to dissolve the Reichstag and call for new elections.[16]

The outcome of the cabinet negotiations in October 1924 represented a stinging rebuff to the DNVP party leadership and its efforts to translate its victory in the May elections into a decisive political advantage. Anxious to avoid a leadership crisis in the midst of a national election campaign, Hergt tendered his resignation as DNVP party chairman on 23 October, thus fulfilling a promise he had made at the start of the cabinet negotiations.[17] His successor, chosen on a provisional basis until an official election could be conducted, was Friedrich Winckler, chairman of the DNVP delegation to the Prussian Landtag and president of the Lutheran General Synod. In a parallel move, Tirpitz was chosen to serve at Winckler's side with responsibility for restoring and maintaining the unity of the DNVP party organization.[18] None of this, however, signaled an abrupt turn to either the left or the right on the part of the DNVP national leadership. In fact, Winckler's principal qualification for the party chairmanship was that he had had no part in the conflicts that had torn the DNVP apart since the summer of 1924 and that he could not be identified with either of the two factions that were vying for control of the party. Moreover, Winckler's election tended to reaffirm the conservative social and religious values that lay at the heart of the DNVP's political *Weltanschauung* and upon which all elements of the party could comfortably agree. In the matter of coalition politics, Winckler's position was scarcely distinguishable from that of his predecessor. Speaking before the party executive committee and representatives of the DNVP party organization in Berlin on 4 November, Winckler reiterated his party's willingness to accept responsibility for the formulation and conduct of national policy but warned that this could not

[14] DVP, Reichsgeschäftsstelle, ed., *Nachtrag zum Wahlhandbuch 1924*, 99–100. See also Julius Curtius, "Politische Umschau: Der Kampf um eine Mehrheitsregierung," *Deutsche Stimmen* 36, no. 21 (5 Nov. 1924): 339–46.

[15] Report by Koch-Weser at a meeting of the DDP executive committee, 21 Oct. 1924, in *Linksliberalismus in der Weimarer Republik. Die Führungsgremien der Deutschen Demokratischen Partei und der Deutschen Staatspartei 1918–1933*, ed. Lothar Albertin and Konstanze Wegner (Düsseldorf, 1980), 330–31.

[16] Hehl, *Marx*, 314–16.

[17] Entry in Gallwitz's diary, 24 Oct. 1924, BA-MA Freiburg, NL Gallwitz, 39.

[18] Entry in Quaatz's diary, 22 Oct. 1924, BA Koblenz, NL Quaatz, 16.

take place at the expense of its principles or on terms inconsistent with its recently demonstrated strength at the polls. At the same time, Winckler criticized the more moderate bourgeois parties for trying to exclude the DNVP from the government and for refusing to accord it the role and influence to which it was rightfully entitled.[19] While Winckler's speech may have reassured the party's moderates, it revealed a lack of direction to those who stood on the DNVP's right wing and promised little relief from the confusion that had plagued party affairs since the May elections.[20]

Back to the Polls

The campaign for the December 1924 Reichstag elections was conducted along essentially the same lines as that of the previous spring. From beginning to end, the campaign was dominated by the issue of the Dawes Plan, as the more moderate bourgeois parties tried to capitalize upon the DNVP's split in the Reichstag vote of 29 August 1924 as a sign of its unreliability on matters of foreign policy. The Center ridiculed the DNVP as the "party of the faltering banner" and attributed its inability to pursue a consistent course of action to a fatal disparity between its "hunger for cabinet posts" and a legacy of antirepublican demagogy.[21] In a similar vein, Stresemann structured the DVP's campaign around a vigorous defense of the foreign policy he had pursued since assuming office and chided the Nationalists for not knowing whether they were a party of opposition or one of responsible and constructive cooperation.[22] The collapse of the cabinet negotiations in the fall of 1924, however, had done much to repair the damage that the Dawes crisis had done to relations between the DNVP party leadership and the party's right wing and to defuse the possibility of a new right-wing party that the more recalcitrant elements in the Central Association of German Conservatives were threatening to launch as a protest against the DNVP's move to the middle.[23] At the same time, the Nationalists benefitted from an electoral truce the

[19] Friedrich Winckler, *Rede des Parteivorsitzenden vor dem Parteivorstande und Vertretern der Parteiorganisation am 4. November 1924 in Berlin*, Deutschnationale Flugschrift, no. 188 (Berlin, 1924).
[20] Entry in Quaatz's diary, 27 Oct. 1924, BA Koblenz, NL Quaatz, 16.
[21] See *Die Anderen und wir*, ed. Deutsche Zentrumspartei, Reichsgeneralsekretariat (Berlin, n.d. [1924]), 3–22.
[22] Gustav Stresemann, *Nationale Realpolitik. Rede auf dem 6. Parteitag der Deutschen Volkspartei in Dortmund am 14. November 1924*, Flugschriften der Deutschen Volkspartei, no. 56 (Berlin, 1924), 32–34.
[23] On the threat of a new party, see Arnim-Boitzenburg to Westarp, 30 Aug. 1924, NL Westarp, Gärtringen, VN 43, as well as Westarp's report before the executive committee of the Central Association of German Conservatives, 16. Nov. 1924, BLHA Potsdam, NL Arnim-Boitzenburg, 4426/72–80.

United Patriotic Leagues of Germany had brokered between the DNVP, DVP, and other "national parties" in hopes that this would lead to the creation of a united German Right once the elections were over.[24] This arrangement did much to temper the tone of the DVP's campaign against the DNVP at the same time that it allowed the Nationalists to concentrate the bulk of their efforts on the racist elements that stood to the DNVP's immediate right.

Throughout the campaign, the Nationalists tried desperately to shift voter attention away from those foreign policy issues that had proven so divisive in the struggle over the Dawes Plan to questions of domestic social and economic policy on which there was more in the way of fundamental agreement within the ranks of the party. No issue served the Nationalists better in this regard than that of revaluation.[25] The leaders of the DNVP were anxious to exploit the fact that efforts to redress the inequities of the revaluation provisions of the Third Emergency Tax Decree had broken down as a result of the parliamentary stalemate created by the outcome of the May 1924 Reichstag elections. In the meantime, Germany's small investors had begun to organize themselves into their own political parties. In an effort to prevent a further splintering of the revaluation movement, the Protective Association of Mortgagees and Savers for the German Reich (Hypotheken-Gläubiger- und Sparer-Schutzverband für das Deutsche Reich) approached the leaders of the various nonsocialist parties to determine which, if any, warranted its endorsement in the upcoming national elections. Of the parties contacted, only the Center, the DNVP, and the newly constituted National Socialist German Freedom Party (Nationalsozialistische Deutsche Freiheitspartei or NSDFP) were deemed worthy of endorsement.[26] The Nationalists went one step further in their efforts to win the support of Germany's small investors by offering a secure candidacy to Georg Best, a prominent Darmstadt jurist who had played a major role in the early stages of the revaluation struggle and an honorary chairman of the Mortgagees and Savers' Protective Association.[27] Best's candidacy did much to enhance the DNVP's visibility in the revaluation issue and

---

[24] Flyer circulated by the VVVD's Geisler under the title "Überparteilicher Vaterländischer Wahldienst der Vereinigten vaterländischen Verbände Deutschlands," 15 Nov. 1924, BHStA Munich, Abt. IV, EWB, 10/1. See also Weiss to Westarp, 6, Dec. 1924, NL Westarp, Gärtringen, VN 44.

[25] For example, see "Aufwertungsfrage und Deutschnationale Volkspartei," n.d. [Oct.–Nov. 1924], BA Koblenz, NL Weilnböck, 34. For further details, see Larry Eugene Jones, "Inflation, Revaluation, and the Crisis of Middle-Class Politics," 155–57.

[26] "Richtlinien zur Wahl," in Die Aufwertung. Offizielles Organ des Hypotheken-Gläubiger- und Sparer-Schutzverbandes 1, no. 24 (7 Nov. 1924): 185–86. See also the report of the meeting of the central executive committee of the Mortgagees and Savers' Protective Association, 26 Oct. 1924, ibid., 187–88.

[27] On the details of this arrangement, see Meyer to Best, 20 May 1925, in Der Kampf um die Aufwertung, Deutschnationale Flugschrift, no. 215 (Berlin, 1925), 30–31.

greatly helped the Nationalists attract the support of those who felt they had been victimized by the revaluation provisions of the Third Emergency Tax Decree.

The DNVP was no less committed to winning the support of the German farmer. The German farmer had been one of the principal beneficiaries of the runaway inflation of the early 1920s. Credit was easy, and farmers were able to liquidate the debt that had accumulated against their property with a currency that was worth far less than the currency in which those debts had originally been contracted. But all of that had come to a crashing halt with the stabilization of the mark in late 1923 and the insolvency of the agricultural credit institutions through which the farmer had traditionally secured the credit he needed to purchase grain seed and farm equipment. As a result, the farmer now had to compete for credit in the much more expensive credit market that had been organized for big business and industry.[28] All of this placed an increasingly heavy strain on relations between organized agriculture, the government, and the political parties that had traditionally mediated between the two. Count Gerhard von Kanitz, minister of agriculture in the first Marx cabinet, had come under heavy fire from organized agricultural interests despite impeccable conservative credentials.[29] As the largest of Germany's agricultural interest organizations, the National Rural League was statutorily prevented from identifying itself with any particular political party, while its regional affiliates were free to support any candidates or parties they deemed acceptable. In the May 1924 Reichstag elections RLB affiliates in Baden, Hesse, Württemburg, and Thuringia had endorsed candidates from both the DNVP and the renegade National Liberal Association that had broken away from the German People's Party in protest against Stresemann's alliance with the Social Democrats.[30] By the fall of 1924, however, the National Liberal Association was no longer a factor as its principal spokesmen had either gone over to the DNVP, made their peace with the DVP, or withdrawn from partisan politics altogether. In the campaign for the December elections, RLB affiliates in Thuringia, Württemberg, Baden, and Hesse concluded a series of alliances with state DNVP leaders that guaranteed first that the deputies elected on their own state tickets would affiliate themselves with the DNVP Reichstag delegation and second that all votes not needed for the election of farm candidates at the state level

---

[28] Lothar Meyer, *Die deutsche Landwirtschaft während der Inflation und zu Beginn der Deflation* (Tübingen, 1924), 23–32.

[29] See Kanitz to Winckler, 8 Nov. 1924, appended to Kanitz to Schleicher, 17 Nov. 1924, BA-MA Freiburg, Nachlass Kurt von Schleicher, 29/43–48.

[30] RLB, Parlamentsabteilung, to Helmot, Mackeldey, and Füller, 12 Apr. 1924, BA Berlin, R 8034 I, 115/15–16.

would be transferred to the DNVP national ticket.[31] In Bavaria and Saxony, on the other hand, the RLB affiliates decided not to run a spearate slate of candidates and allied themselves directly with the DNVP.[32] At the same time, the RLB presented the DNVP with a short list of prospective candidates whom they would like to have seen nominated to secure candidacies on the DNVP ticket.[33] The alliance between the DNVP and the RLB could not have been firmer.

On a different front, the DNVP greatly intensified its efforts to secure a breakthrough into the ranks of Germany's Catholic electorate in Bavaria and elsewhere. The leaders of the DNVP's Reich Catholic Committee had become increasingly frustrated by the fact that Germany's Catholic episcopacy had apparently reconciled itself to the changes that had taken place in Germany's political system since the summer of 1917 and continued to support the Center as the political representative of German Catholicism. In the spring of 1924 the Fulda Bishops' Conference (Fuldaer Bischofskonferenz), the assembly of German bishops from outside Bavaria that convened twice a year under the presidency of Cardinal Adolf von Bertram from Breslau to clarify and formulate positions on issues of importance to the church, had declared that Catholics who wished to remain in good standing with the church should not join or become otherwise involved in the activities of right-wing paramilitary organizations like the Stahlhelm and Young German Order.[34] In the eyes of the DNVP Catholics, this betrayed a bias against the German Right they hoped to correct by petitioning the Catholic bishops to reconsider their support of the Center and their indifference, if not outright opposition, to the aspirations of the nationalist Right. Dispatched in July 1924, this petition carried the signatures of twenty-one members of the DNVP Reich Catholic Committee and began by reminding the episcopacy that for every four Catholics who belonged to the Center there was another who belonged to the DNVP. The petition complained about the partisanship of the Catholic clergy and protested against the way in which their own credentials as Catholics had been maligned because of their refusal to support the Center. To correct this situation, the petition demanded the withdrawal of the clergy from political life, the "depoliticization" of Catholic institutions throughout the country, and

[31] Kalckreuth to the DNVP party leadership, 7 Nov. 1924, BA Berlin, R 8034 I, 116/91–92. See also the letter from the RLB, Parlamentsabteilung, to the Mittelrheinischer Landbund, 5 Dec. 1924, ibid., 116/127–28,

[32] On arrangements in Bavaria, see Weilnböck, "Zu den Reichstagswahlen Dezember 1924," n.d. [Oct. 1924]. BA Koblenz, NL Weilnböck, 5a. For Saxony, see Alvin Domsch and Albrecht Philipp, *Sächsische Landwirtschaft und Reichstagswahl 1924. Ein Rückblick und Ausblick*, Schriften der Deutschnationalen Volkspartei in Sachsen (Arbeitsgemeinschaft), no. 6 (Dresden, 1924).

[33] Kalckreuth to the DNVP party leadership, 1 Nov. 1924, BA Berlin, R 8034 I, 116/85–86.

[34] Vogel, *Kirche und Kampfverbände*, 34–55.

the creation of a non-partisan parliamentary coalition, or *Arbeitsgemeinschaft*, of Catholics for the more effective representation of their religious and cultural interests. This and only this, the petition concluded, would end discrimination against Catholics who had broken with the Center and church efforts to salvage "Catholic peace through the rape of a party [*aus der Vergewaltigung einer Partei*]."[35]

The fact that the Fulda Bishops' Conference dismissed the petition of the DNVP Reich Catholic Committee without so much as a formal debate and never issued an official response came as no surprise to most of its sponsors and only confirmed their assertion of bias on the part of Germany's Catholic episcopacy.[36] In the meantime, DNVP Catholics continued to make significant gains within their own party. The leaders of the DNVP Reich Catholic Committee were gratified by the special consideration that Catholics had received in the selection of candidates for the Nationalist ticket in the May 1924 Reichstag elections[37] and expressed great satisfaction that no fewer than ten of the 107 Nationalist deputies who entered the new Reichstag were practicing Catholics.[38] DNVP Catholics were similarly pleased with the placement of Catholic candidates on the Nationalist ticket for the December 1924 Reichstag elections and looked forward to consolidating their position within the DNVP Reichstag delegation.[39] In return, the leaders of DNVP National Catholic Committee waged an energetic and hard-hitting campaign against the Center in which they not only disputed the exclusive claims the Center made with respect to the representation of Germany's Catholic interests but also documented the party's dramatic swing to the left since the summer of 1917 and the deep gulf this had created between the party and an increasingly large sector of Germany's Catholic population. At the same time, they took issue with efforts by the Center to discredit the DNVP's credentials as a Christian party by lumping it together with the racist Right.[40]

---

[35] "Eingabe an die in Fulda sich versammelnden Hochwürdigsten Erzbischöfe und Bischöfe Deutschlands," July 1924, BA Koblenz, NL Spahn, 177. See also the entry in Gallwitz's diary, 2 Apr. 1924, BA-MA Freiburg, NL Gallwitz, 41.

[36] For further details, see Vogel, *Kirche und Kampfverbände*, 109–10, n. 22. See also Landsberg's report at a meeting of the DNVP's Reich Catholic Committee, 13 Mar. 1925, VWA Münster, NL Landsberg, E1.

[37] Lejeune-Jung to Buchner, 13 Mar. 1924, BA Koblenz, Nachlass Max Buchner, 18.

[38] Lejeune-Jung to Buchner, 26 May 1924, ibid.

[39] Lejeune-Jung to Fischer, 5 Nov. 1924, StA Paderborn, "Dokumentation Lejeune-Jung," S2/125/258–61.

[40] See Johannes Pritze, *Das Zentrum*, Deutschnationales Rüstzeug, no. 3 (Berlin, 1924), esp. 11–20. The target of Pritze's pamphlet was a brochure by Friedrich Grebe, *Zentrum und die deutschnationalen Katholiken*, Flugschriften der Deutschen Zentrumspartei 1924 (Berlin, 1924).

Perhaps the most suprising aspect of the DNVP's campaign for the December 1924 Reichstag elections was the greatly diminished role of the racist and antisemitic rhetoric that had played such a prominent role the previous spring. Even though antisemitism was never totally absent from the Nationalist campaign,[41] it no longer figured as prominently in the architecture of the DNVP's campaign for the December elections as it had in previous campaigns. Two factors accounted for the DNVP's strategic turn-about. First, the state of almost total disarray in which the racist elements on the extreme right of Germany's political spectrum found themselves in the summer and fall of 1924 greatly reduced the threat they posed to the DNVP's electoral pro-spects,[42] with the result that party leaders may no longer have felt obliged to compete with the racists on their own terrain. To be sure, the leaders of the racist Right assailed the DNVP for its role in the acceptance of the Dawes Plan as an act of high treason that sacrificed Germany's national honor on the altar of international finance,[43] but the Nationalists were quick to counter by portraying their party as a party of "constructive opposition" that alone possessed the potential to bring about a genuine change in the existing political system. Second, the exigencies of coalition politics and the fact that the leaders of the DNVP were actively seeking a place for their party in a new national government required that it make itself more palatable to potential coalition partners by disentangling it as discreetly as possible from the racist Right. Although this may not have sat well with the more militantly racist elements on the DNVP's right wing,[44] the party's national leaders proceeded to mute the antisemitism that had served the party so well in the campaign for the May elections in favor of a more general appeal that called upon Germany's propertied classes to unite in the DNVP as their only reliable bulwark against the parties of the Marxist Left.

The results of the December 1924 Reichstag elections were particularly difficult for the leaders of the DNVP to interpret. For whereas the parties that had supported ratification of the Dawes Plan – from the Social Democrats to the DDP, DVP, and Center – all emerged from the campaign significantly strengthened, it was the DNVP that produced the greatest surprise of the election by posting a remarkable 9.0 percent gain over the number of votes it had received in May. This, in turn, increased the size of its parliamentary

---

[41] For example, see *Hieb- und Stichwaffen für den Wahlkampf*, 28 Nov. 1924, no. 8, in BA Koblenz, NL Weilnböck, 34.

[42] For further details, see Jablonsky, *Nazi Party in Dissolution*, 129–47.

[43] Christian Mergenthaler, *Das Dawes-Gutachten und der Deutschnationale Volksverrat. Nach einem Vortrag gehalten in Stuttgart in September 1924* (Leipzig, Berlin, and Stuttgart, n.d. [1924]), esp. 21–25.

[44] Correspondence between Kriping and the Pan-German leadership, 19–29 Oct. 1924, BA Berlin, R 8048, 210/94–95, 107. See also Vietinghoff-Scheel to Gebsattel, 20 Oct. 1924, ibid., 210/97, and Claß to Mündler, 1 Nov. 1924, ibid., 210/110.

delegation from 95 to 103 seats – or 111 seats, if one includes the eight deputies who were elected on regional agrarian tickets and subsequently affiliated themselves with the DNVP Reichstag delegation. Only the fact that the Social Democrats improved upon its performance in the May elections by a dramatic 31.2 percent and now held 131 parliamentary mandates prevented the DNVP from reclaiming its place as the largest party in the Reichstag. The DDP and DVP, in the meantime, increased their share of the popular vote by 16.1 and 13.2 percent respectively and now claimed a total of 83 seats in the Reichstag, while the Center received 5.0 percent more votes in December than it had received the previous May. For the most part, the gains of the Social Democrats and more moderate bourgeois parties could be attributed not only to a record voter turnout in the December 1924 elections but also to cross-over votes from the radical parties at both ends of the political spectrum. The Communists lost 26.6 percent of their May vote, while the Nazi-racist coalition campaigning as the National Socialist Freedom Movement of Greater Germany (Nationalsozialistische Freiheitsbewegung Großdeutschlands) lost 52.7 percent of what its predecessor had received in May.[45] What this revealed was a clear trend away from the more extremist parties in favor of those that articulated a more measured respone to the myriad problems that confronted Germany in the second half of the 1920s.

The DNVP's success in the December 1924 Reichstag elections stemmed from three factors. By far the most important was the disarray of the racist elements on the extreme right and their inability to mount a coherent and effective campaign, with the result that many of those who had supported the National Socialist Freedom Party in May 1924 either stayed at home or switched their support to the DNVP.[46] A second factor was the DNVP's success in mobilizing the support of Catholic conservatives who had become disillusioned with the Center's move to the left since the last years of World War I. One contemporary analysis concluded that approximately 11.9 percent of the popular vote the DNVP received in the December 1924 elections had been cast by Catholics. Although this represented just 8.7 percent of all Catholic voters taking part in the election and 19.5 percent of those Catholic voters who supported neither of the two Catholic parties, Catholics nevertheless constituted a significant component of the Nationalist electorate and accounted for as many as a dozen of its seats in the Reichstag.[47] Third, the DNVP continued to receive a disproportionate share of the support of women

---

[45] These calculations are based upon statistics from Falter, Lindenberger, and Schumann, *Wahlen und Abstimmungen*, 41. See also Thomas Childers, *The Nazi Voter*, 50–118.

[46] Jablonsky, *Nazi Party in Dissolution*, 150–51.

[47] Johannes Schauff, *Das Wahlverhalten der deutschen Katholiken im Kaiserreich und in der Weimarer Republik. Untersuchungen aus dem Jahre 1928*, ed. Rudolf Morsey (Mainz, 1975), 129–33.

voters despite the disappointment of the DNVP's National Women's Committee over what its leaders perceived as "the obvious exclusion of female
candidates from the party's electoral slates" and a lack of appreciation at the
local levels of the DNVP's national organization for the contribution that
women had made to the party's organizational life.[48] By August 1922 the
DNVP's National Women's Committee had established thirty-eight provincial
affiliates, or *Landesfrauenausschüsse*, throughout the country with nearly two
thousand local chapters and another 2,700 confidants, or *Vertrauensfrauen*,
performing the tasks of a local chapter in areas where none existed.[49] In the
two 1924 elections the DNVP's National Women's Committee launched a full-
scale campaign to mobilize its supporters with an appeal that affirmed, as it
had in 1919 and 1920, a traditional image of women that stood in sharp
contrast to the more emancipatory impulses generally associated with Weimar
culture.[50] The way this resonated among women voters was reflected in the
fact that the DNVP continued to receive more of its votes from women than
from men. In December 1924 approximately 54 percent of all the DNVP's
votes came from women voters. Only the Center and Bavarian People's Party
received a higher percentage of its votes from women in the two 1924 elections
than the DNVP.[51]

Compromise at Last

The disarray of the racists no doubt helped to insulate the DNVP against
losses that might otherwise have turned its performance in the December
1924 Reichstag elections from a positive to a negative balance. The leaders of
the DNVP, however, failed to recognize the true nature of their party's good
fortune and immediately interpreted its strong performance at the polls as a
mandate to continue the course they had pursued since the May Reichstag
elections.[52] Moreover, the DNVP's success at the polls had greatly thinned the
ranks of those within the DNVP Reichstag delegation who were still prepared
to fight the party's entry into the national government. According to one
informed party source, no more than six Nationalist deputies continued to
oppose such an eventuality.[53] While all of this augured well for a more
constructive Nationalist response to a resumption of efforts aimed at bringing

---

[48] Lehmann to Westarp, 28 June 1924, NL Westarp, Gärtringen, VN 48.
[49] "Deutschnationale Frauenarbeit im Lande," *Frauenkorrespondenz der Deutschnationalen Volkspartei* 3, no. 23 (23 Aug. 1922).
[50] Sneeringer, *Winning Women's Votes*, 110–15.
[51] Joachim Hofmann-Götig, *Emanzipation mit dem Stimmzettel. 70 Jahre Frauenwahlrecht in Deutschland* (Bonn, 1986), 32.
[52] Confidential circular on the cabinet negotiations, 16 Jan. 1925, BA Berlin, NL Mumm, 279/467–74.
[53] Axel von Freytagh-Loringhoven, *Deutschnationale Volkspartei* (Berlin, 1931), 27.

the DNVP into the government, it was Stresemann who brought matters to a head by announcing at a ministerial conference on 10 December 1924 that his party could no longer support the present cabinet and that it would therefore work for the creation of a bourgeois government with the DNVP, Center, and other nonsocialist parties.[54] On the following day Marx tendered his resignation so that efforts to form a new government with the support of a parliamentary majority could begin in earnest. Negotiations with the Nationalists extended over the course of the next week but failed to dispel the reservations of the Center and DDP about serving in a coalition with the DNVP. Frustrated by the lack of progress towards a coalition with the DNVP, the leaders of the DVP Reichstag delegation announced on 17 December that their party was leaving the governmental coalition, thereby depriving the Marx cabinet of its mandate to govern.[55]

This marked the second of four successive "Christmas crises" that Germany's parliamentary institutions would experience from 1923 to 1926. The stalemate in efforts to form a new government persisted through the remainder of December and was only broken when Stresemann suggested on 9 January 1925 that the task be handed over to Hans Luther, a politically unaffiliated municipal politician who had served as minister of finance under both Stresemann and Marx. Luther, who enjoyed close ties to Ruhr heavy industry and enjoyed the confidence of influential conservative circles, was committed to the formation of a cabinet that was free of formal ties to the individual political parties that were prepared to support it. In this sense, Luther embodied the highest principles of conservative nonpartisanship, or *Überparteilichkeit*.[56] Moreover, Luther's notion of a cabinet of experts free of formal commitments to the parties that supported it corresponded in large measure to what the Nationalists themselves had advocated for the better part of a year, a fact that made it that much easier for him to reach an understanding with the DNVP party leadership.[57]

The Nationalist representative in the cabinet negotiations was Martin Schiele, a highly respected farm leader who had assumed the chairmanship of the DNVP Reichstag delegation on 17 December 1924.[58] Schiele had

[54] Minutes of a ministerial conference, 10 Dec. 1924, in *Kabinette Marx I und II*, ed. Abramowski, 2:1219–20. See also the manuscript of Stresemann's article, "Zur Regierungskrise," *Hamburger Fremdenblatt*, 25 Dec. 1924, PA AA Berlin, NL Stresemann, 18/157792–806.
[55] Protocol of two conversations between Marx and a DVP delegation, 18 Dec. 1924, in *Kabinette Marx I und II*, ed. Abramowski, 2:1227–31. For further details, see Stürmer, *Koalition und Opposition*, 78–83, and Richter, *Deutsche Volkspartei*, 359–65.
[56] Hans Luther, *Politiker ohne Partei* (Stuttgart, 1960), 316–17.
[57] Freytagh-Loringhoven, *Deutschnationale Volkspartei*, 32–36.
[58] On Schiele's election as chairman of the DNVP Reichstag delegation, see the letter from Westarp's wife to their daughter, 18 Dec. 1924, NL Westarp, Gärtringen.

originally belonged to that group of Nationalist deputies who opposed ratification of the Dawes Plan, but he had since come to the conclusion that the
DNVP would have to join the government in order to protect the vital
interests of the social constituencies upon which it was politically dependent.
In an attempt to expedite a resolution of the current cabinet crisis, Schiele and
Luther agreed that formal commitments between the government and the
parties that supported it should be replaced with an arrangement whereby
each of the government parties would be represented in the cabinet by a
special liaison, or *Vertrauensmann*. The remaining cabinet posts would then
be occupied by ostensibly nonpolitical specialists, or *Fachmänner*, who were to
be chosen not for their party affiliation but for the professional qualifications
they brought to the post they held.[59] The irony of this arrangement was that it
weakened the role of the political parties in the governmental process – thus
fulfilling one of the DNVP's professed campaign objectives – at the precise
moment the DNVP chose to enter the government.

When the new government assumed office on 15 January 1925, the Nationalists were represented by Schiele as the party's liaison with the cabinet and
three nonpolitical experts in finance minister Otto von Schlieben, economics
minister Albert Neuhaus, and agricultural minister Count Gerhard von
Kanitz.[60] While Nationalist participation in the Luther cabinet provided
conservative moderates who had been impressed by the republic's recovery
from the collapse of 1923 with an opportunity to work for a reform of the
existing governmental system from within the system itself,[61] many Nationalists remained profoundly ambivalent about their party's entry into the
national government and openly criticized Schiele and other party leaders
for having failed to secure more in return for the DNVP's surrender of
principle. The Nationalists were particularly concerned about becoming too
closely identified with Stresemann's foreign policy and sought to avoid a
public airing of Germany's military and security situation for fear that this
might expose the weakness of their current position.[62] Even then, the DNVP's
defense of its decision to work within the framework of a governmental
system to which it remained fundamentally and ideologically opposed was

---

[59] Luther, *Politiker ohne Partei*, 316.

[60] On the composition of the first Luther cabinet, see *Akten der Reichskanzlei: Die Kabinette
Luther I und II. 15. Januar 1925 bis 20. Januar 1926. 20. Januar 1926 bis 17. Mai 1926*, ed.
Karl-Heinz Minuth, 2 vols. (Boppard am Rhein, 1977), 1:xxiii–xxiv. On the DNVP's role
in the formation of the Luther cabinet, see Albrecht Philipp, "Mein Weg: Rückschau eines
Siebzigjährigen auf allerlei Geschenisse und Menschen," Dritte Teil: "Abgeordnetenjahre
in der Weimarer Republik (1919–1930)," SHStA Dresden, NL Philipp, 4/157–59.

[61] See Franz Behrens, *Die Deutschnationalen zur Sozialpolitik. Reichstagsrede am 22. Januar
1925*, Deutschnationale Flugschrift, no. 203 (Berlin, 1925).

[62] For example, see Keudell to Tirpitz, 5 Feb. 1925, BA-MA Freiburg, NL Tirpitz, 278/
18–21.

particularly tortured and did little to insulate it against charges of opportunism and unreliability.[63] But for Stresemann and the DVP, the DNVP's decision to join the Luther cabinet represented an unequivocal triumph for their strategy of "stabilization from the right" and was, they hoped, the harbinger of a new era in Germany's postwar political development.

The Struggle for the Presidency

The DNVP's entry into the Luther government was soon followed by a development that was to have even more profound implications for the success of Stresemann's strategy, namely, the sudden and unexpected death of Reich President Friedrich Ebert and the opportunity to elect a successor more amenable to the various factions on the German Right. Even before Ebert's death, elements on the German Right had already been hard at work laying the groundwork for the election of a new Reich President more sympathetic to their own political agenda. Here the initial impetus came from two principal directions. Following the split in the DNVP Reichstag delegation in the August 1924 vote on the Dawes Plan, Germany's paramilitary Right had begun to coalesce behind Baron Wilhelm von Gayl, a Nationalist deputy in the Prussian State Council (Preußischer Staatsrat), in hopes of restoring the unity of the German Right. As their first practical goal, Gayl and his associates hoped to unify Germany's paramilitary combat leagues and conservative economic interest organizations behind a single candidate in the presidential elections that were scheduled to take place sometime in the summer of 1925.[64] This effort paralleled a no less ambitious undertaking by the National Citizens' Council (Reichsbürgerrat), an ostensibly nonpartisan but aggressively middle-class and antisocialist forum for constitutional and political reform that had been founded in the immediate aftermath of the November Revolution.[65] The leaders of the National Citizens' Council were critical of the way in which the German party system had developed since the founding of the Weimar Republic and sought a remedy for the "tyranny of political parties" in a constitutional reform that would create a second legislative chamber consisting of corporate, state, and legislative appointees and expand the powers of the

---

[63] See Kuno von Westarp, *Die Deutschnationalen zur Regierungspolitik. Reichstagsrede vom 20. Januar 1925* Deutschnationale Flugschrift, no. 202 (Berlin, 1925), esp. 3–5, 14–16.

[64] Eight-page handwritten note by Gayl, n.d., BA Koblenz, Nachlass Baron Wilhelm von Gayl, 23. For a more detailed account of Gayl's relationship with the paramilitary Right, see ibid., 4/17–29.

[65] On the Reich Citizens' Council, see *Verhandlungsbericht über die Ersttagung des Reichsbürgerrats im Preußischen Abgeordnetenhause zu Berlin am 5. Januar 1919* (n.p. [Berlin], n.d. [1919]), 26–41, 110–14.

Reich presidency at the expense of the Reichstag and national cabinet.[66] To implement such a reform, however, it was first necessary to elect a new Reich president who, free from the petty party politics of his day, would use the powers of his office to effect a fundamental transformation in the fabric of German public life.[67]

The recommendations of the National Citizens' Council for a reform of the Weimar Constitution implied tacit recognition of the fact that the conservative cause could no longer be effectively served either by remaining in opposition until the Right had finally achieved a majority in the Reichstag or by conspiring to overthrow the republic in the fashion of Kapp and Hitler. The upcoming presidential campaign, on the other hand, afforded the German Right a rare opportunity to correct Germany's political course by electing a conservative activist who would expand the powers of the Reich presidency and use them to undertake a fundamental revision of the Weimar Constitution. It was with this in mind that Friedrich Wilhelm Loebell, a former Prussian minister of interior who had recently assumed leadership of the National Citizens' Council, scheduled a series of meetings in December 1924 with the leaders of the various nonsocialists parties as well as with representatives of Germany's most influential economic interest organizations and patriotic associations.[68] Of the various organizations that Loebell consulted, only the DDP rejected his proposal out of hand. Encouraged by an otherwise positive response, Loebell scheduled a meeting of those who had expressed interest in his project for 12 February 1925,[69] at which time the idea of a bourgeois *Sammelkandidatur* received strong support from all of the attending organizations with the exception of the Center.[70]

When Ebert's unexpected death at the end of February accelerated the timetable for new presidential elections, the Loebell Committee held three

---

[66] See the series of articles by Loebell, "Der Kampf um den Staat," *Der Deutschen-Spiegel. Politische Wochenschrift* 1, no. 1 (1 Sept. 1924): 12–15; no. 3 (19 Sept. 1924): 10–13; no. 12 (21 Nov. 1924): 30–32; and no. 13 (28 Nov. 1924): 26–29, as well as Kriegk, "Der Weg zur Staatspolitik," ibid., 1, no. 12 (21 Nov. 1924): 8–23.

[67] Loebell, "Die Reichspräsidentenwahl," *Der Deutschen-Spiegel* 1, no. 15 (12 Dec. 1924): 13–19. For further details, see Noel D. Cary, "The Making of the Reich President, 1925: German Conservatism and the Nomination of Paul von Hindenburg," *Central European History* 23 (1990): 179–204.

[68] See Loebell to Hepp, 29 Dec. 1924, BA Berlin, Nachlass Karl Hepp, BA Berlin, 2/128, and Loebell to Bredt, 29 Dec. 1924, Stadtarchiv Wuppertal, Nachlass Johann Victor Bredt, Bestand NDS 263, 59. On Loebell, see the recent biography by Peter Winzen, *Friedrich Wilhelm von Leobell (1885–1931). Ein Leben gegen den Strom der Zeit* (Vienna, Cologne, and Weimar, 2019), esp. 340–46.

[69] Loebell to Hepp, 2 Feb. 1925, BA Berlin, NL Hepp, 2/129–30.

[70] Minutes of the first meeting of the ad-hoc committee for the presidential election in the offices of the Reich Citizens' Council, 12 Feb. 1925, StA Hamburg, Hapag-Lloyd Reederei, Handakten Cuno, 1503. See also Zapf's memorandum for Stresemann, 12 Feb. 1925, appended to Zapf to Stresemann, 13 Feb. 1925, PA AA Berlin, NL Stresemann, 20/158154–56.

meetings in the first week of March to determine whom it would support for the presidency.[71] With the first meeting on 3 March devoted exclusively to organizational matters, it was not until the second meeting two days later that the committee turned its attention to the selection of a candidate. Of the politicians whose names surfaced in the course of the deliberations, only the DVP's Karl Jarres, the former Reich minister of interior and the lord mayor of Duisburg, met with the approval of all the participating organizations with the exception of the Democrats.[72] Loebell informed Jarres on 9 March that he had been selected as his committee's candidate,[73] but postponed announcing Jarres's nomination when the leaders of the Bavarian People's Party asked for additional time to respond to the idea of a Jarres candidacy. In the meantime, the leaders of the German Democratic Party indicated that they too might be interested in cooperating with the Loebell Committee in its search for a candidate who could command the support of all sectors of the German people. This, along with persistent doubts as to whether or not Jarres could be elected on the first ballot, prompted Loebell and his associates to turn their attention to Otto Gessler, a member of the DDP's right wing who had served as minister of defense since 1920. Not only was Gessler an experienced and capable politician who, like Loebell and the leaders of the National Citizens' Council, recognized the need for a reform of the Weimar Constitution,[74] but as a Bavarian, a Catholic, and a Democrat he appealed to sectors of the German population whose support was essential for the ultimate success of Loebell's strategy.[75] Gessler's candidacy, however, ran into stiff opposition from both the Nationalists and Stresemann – the former because of his party affiliation and the latter out of concern for what his election might mean for his foreign policy[76] – with the result that on 12 March he was dropped in favor

---

[71] For further details, see Friedrich von Loebell, "Die Verhandlungen des Loebell-Ausschusses. Eine objective Darstellung," *Der Deutschen-Spiegel* 2, no. 13 (27 Mar. 1925): 581–87.
[72] Hepp's handwritten notes on the meeting of the Loebell committee, 6 Mar. 1925, BA Berlin, NL Hepp, 2/140. For the Nationalist perspective, see Westarp to Tirpitz, 7 Mar. 1925, NL Westarp, Gärtringen, VN 98.
[73] Loebell to Jarres, 9 Mar. 1925, BA Koblenz, Nachlass Karl Jarres, 23. See also Loebell, "Warum Jarres," n.d., BA Koblenz, NL Gayl, 23. On the Jarres candidacy with excerpts and facsimiles of much of the relevant documentation, see Jürgen D. Kruse-Jarres, *Karl Jarres. Ein bewegtes Politikerleben – vom Kaiserreich zur Bundesrepublik* (Munich, 2006), 162–90.
[74] Gessler's remarks at a ministerial conference, 19 Dec. 1924, BA Koblenz, Nachlass Otto Gessler, 50/60–63.
[75] Heiner Möllers, *Reichswehrminister Otto Geßler. Eine Studie zu "unpolitischer" Militärmacht in der Weimarer Republik* (Frankfurt a.M. and New York, 1998), 289–306.
[76] Stresemann to Gessler, 11 Mar. 1925, BA Koblenz, NL Gessler, 9/62–64. See also Henry A. Turner, *Stresemann and the Politics of the Weimar Republic* (Princeton, NJ, 1963), 193–95, and Wright, *Stresemann*, 307–10.

of Jarres, a politician whose conservative credentials were impeccable but who lacked Gessler's impressive profile.[77]

Although both the DVP and DNVP were quick to declare their support for the Jarres candidacy,[78] Jarres stood little chance of securing the absolute majority that was necessary for election on the first ballot. Jarres, in turn, seemed almost apologetic about having been chosen to run for the presidency and would have willingly stepped aside if the Loebell committee could have settled on a more suitable candidate.[79] The Center and DDP both refused to endorse his candidacy and proceeded to field candidates of their own, as did the Bavarian People's Party in an ostensible protest against the allegedly sectarian character of Jarres's candidacy.[80] Even the Nationalists, who tried to portray Jarres as a conservative activist who was every bit as committed to a fundamental change in the existing political system as they themselves,[81] were lukewarm in their support of his candidacy, in large part because they feared it would help consolidate Stresemann's political influence. At the same time, Jarres's nomination encountered strong opposition from the Young German Order, which withheld its endorsement until the last week of March in hopes that the Loebell Committee might reconsider its decision and nominate the commander-in-chief of the Reichswehr, General Hans von Seeckt.[82] All in all, the Jarres candidacy failed to generate the popular enthusiasm for which the leaders of the Reich Bloc (Reichsblock) – as the Loebell Committee had reconstituted itself on 12 March – had been hoping. For although Jarres received 38.8 percent of the popular vote in the first trip to the polls on 29 March 1925 and thus outdrew his rivals by a substantial margin, he still fell considerably short of an absolute majority. Moreover, the fact that the three candidates representing the parties of the Weimar coalition – Otto Braun from the SPD, Marx from the Center, and Willy Hugo Hellpach from the DDP – received 49.2 percent of the popular vote meant that Jarres stood virtually no chance of being elected if the three parties were to unite behind a single candidate in the runoff elections scheduled for 26 April.[83]

---

[77] Loebell, "Verhandlungen des Loebell-Ausschusses," 581–87.

[78] *Mitteilungsblatt des Reichsblocks zur Durchführung des Reichspräsidentenwahl*, 17 Mar. 1925, no. 2, and 19 Mar. 1925, no. 3.

[79] See Jarres to Gayl, 17 Mar. 1925, BA Koblenz, NL Gayl, 23, and Cuno, 18 Mar. 1925, StA Hamburg, Hapag-Reederei, Handakten Cuno, 1503.

[80] Hauss, *Volkswahl*, 65–72.

[81] For example, see Westarp, "Jarres," *Mitteilungsblatt des Reichsblocks zur Durchführung der Reichspräsidentenwahl*, 17 Mar. 1925, no. 2.

[82] See the correspondence between Mahraun and Gayl, 13–28 Mar. 1925, as well excerpts from the protocol of a meeting of the paramilitary combat leagues held under Gayl's chairmanship, 13 Mar. 1925, both in BA Koblenz, NL Gayl, 23.

[83] Hauss, *Volkswahl*, 72–77.

The Second Round

Five days after the first round of voting, the parties of the Weimar coalition coalesced to form the People's Bloc (Volksblock) and announced that they would support the Center's Wilhelm Marx in the run-off election for the presidency.[84] Since the candidates of these three parties had received nearly fifty percent of the popular vote in the first ballot, it was clear to Jarres's supporters and detractors alike that he stood little chance of defeating Marx, with the result that the Nationalists began to press their case for another candidate who in their eyes stood a better chance of winning.[85] The person to whom the Nationalists immediately turned was retired war hero Paul von Hindenburg. Hindenburg's name had surfaced in the initial round of deliberations but had been dropped for several reasons. In the first place, Hindenburg was an unreconstructed monarchist whose disdain for the world of practical politics and uncompromising hostility to the Weimar Republic hardly recommended him to Loebell and his associates as a man capable of carrying out the vigorous reform program they expected of the new Reich president. Secondly, Hindenburg's deep-seated opposition to the policy of fulfillment and his close identification with the Prussian military establishment posed precisely the same sort of problems that had led Stresemann to oppose Gessler's nomination in the initial stages of the search for a bourgeois unity candidate. Thirdly, there was the question of Hindenburg's age and his willingness to take on the burdens of political office. By 1925 Hindenburg was already seventy-seven years old, and it was by no means certain that he would accept the nomination even if it were offered him. At the same time, however, Hindenburg personified the traditions that were associated with Germany's rise to greatness in the previous century and that, in Nationalist eyes, now held the key to redresssing the horrible shame that Germany had suffered with the defeat and collapse of November 1918.[86]

In their pursuit of Hindenburg, the Nationalists faced two major problems. First, they had to convince the other members of the Reich Bloc that Hindenburg stood a better chance of winning against Marx than Jarres and that his election would be consistent with the general goals for which the Loebell Committee had been constituted. Here the Nationalists would have to outmaneuver the DVP and coopt its leaders into supporting a candidate for

---

[84] Ibid., 77–84. See also Hehl, *Marx*, 335–41.

[85] Rheinbaben to Bredt, 25 Mar. 1925, in Johann Victor Bredt, *Erinnerungen und Dokumente von Joh. Victor Bredt 1914 bis 1933*, ed. Martin Schumacher (Düsseldorf, 1970), 347–49. See also Sorge to Jarres, 3 Apr. 1925, BA Koblenz, NL Jarres, 23.

[86] Weiß to Westarp, 4 Mar. 1925, NL Westarp, Gärtringen, VN 55. On Hindenburg's career before 1932, see Larry Eugene Jones, *Hitler versus Hindenburg: The 1932 Presidential Elections and the End of the Weimar Republic* (Cambridge, 2016), 16–42, as well as the authoritative biography by Pyta, *Hindenburg*, esp. 381–458.

whom they felt little genuine enthusiasm. Second, the Nationalists would have to persuade Hindenburg that it was in Germany's national interest for him to run for the presidency. Hindenburg's position, as expressed in a series of meetings with different DNVP delegations at the end of March, was that he was "not disinclined" to run for the presidency but would do so only if the Reich Bloc was united behind his candidacy and if Jarres agreed to go along with his nomination.[87] This stipulation, however, made it awkward for the Nationalists to press their case for his candidacy with the other members of the Reich Bloc. Neither the DVP nor the patriotic associations that had coalesced behind Gayl's leadership were particularly supportive when the DNVP Reichstag delegation voted on 2 April to intensify its efforts on behalf of a Hindenburg candidacy and dispatched DNVP Reichstag deputy Otto Schmidt-Hannover to meet with the retired war hero in hopes of persuading him to run for the presidency.[88] In fact, efforts to draft Hindenburg as a candidate for the Reich Presidency would very likely have collapsed had it not been for a group of deputies from the Bavarian People's Party who declared that they were prepared to support Hindenburg against Marx and that they would use their influence within the BVP to secure its endorsement for the retired war hero should he agree to stand for election.[89] Given the fact that the BVP had balked at supporting Jarres in the preliminary elections on 29 March, this announcement was of enormous significance and immediately prompted a new round of negotiations between the DNVP, the Reich Bloc, and Hindenburg's entourage.

Throughout all of this, the Nationalists were driven by their desire to secure the nomination of a candidate whose election would not help Stresemann in consolidating his domestic political position.[90] Hindenburg, on the other hand, continued to pledge his support of Jarres and disclaimed any interest

---

[87] On Nationalist negotiations with Hindenburg, see Dieter von der Schulenburg, *Welt um Hindenburg. Hundert Gespräche mit Berufenen* (Berlin, 1935), 57–70, and Hans Schlange-Schöningen, *Am Tage danach* (Hamburg, 1946), 30. On Hindenburg's reluctance to run for the presidency, see his letter to Cramon, 27 Mar. 1925, BA-MA Freiburg, Nachlass August von Cramon, 24/14.

[88] Otto Schmidt-Hannover, *Umdenken oder Anarchie. Männer – Schicksäle – Lehren* (Göttingen, 1959), 185–91.

[89] Hauss, *Volkswahl*, 92–95. See also Klaus Schönhoven, *Die Bayerische Volkspartei 1924-1932* (Düsseldorf, 1972), 122–31.

[90] On the Nationalist strategy, see Westarp to Tirpitz, n.d. [Apr. 1925], BA-MA Freiburg, NL Tirpitz, 176. See also the entries for 7–8 Apr. 1925, in a handwritten memorandum by Westarp for the period from 20 Mar. to 9 Apr. 1925, NL Westarp, Gärtringen, VN 121. For further information, see Ohnezeit, *Zwischen "schärfster Opposition,"* 310–19, as well as Raffael Scheck, "Höfische Intriqe als Machtstrategie in der Weimarer Republik. Paul v. Hindenburgs Kandidatur zur Reichspräsidentschaft 1925, "in *Adel und Moderne. Deutschland im europäischen Vergleich im 19. und 20. Jahrhundert*, ed. Eckart Conze and Monika Weinfort (Cologne, Weimar, and Vienna, 2004), 107–18.

in the nomination as long as Stresemann and the DVP remained opposed to his candidacy. Hindenburg thus informed Loebell on 7 April that in light of his advanced age he wished to have his name withdrawn from further consideration and reiterated his support for Jarres.[91] When a statement to this effect appeared against Hindenburg's explicit instructions in the German press later that afternoon, the Nationalists dispatched another delegation, this time headed by the venerable Tirpitz, to his home in Hanover in hopes of persuading him to rescind his decision. Whereas other Nationalist delegations had failed to overcome Hindenburg's reservations, Tirpitz's intervention seems to have been decisive. Not only did Tirpitz appeal to Hindenburg's patriotism and underscore the importance of his candidacy to the strategic objectives of the German Right, but he pointed to the strong support the retired war hero enjoyed among conservative Catholics who were almost certain to choose him over Marx if he stood for election. Impressed by the force of Tirpitz's logic, Hindenburg agreed to retract his decision but only if the Reich Bloc was no longer prepared to support Jarres.[92]

For his own part, Jarres was fully prepared to step down as a candidate for the Reich presidency if it appeared that the German Right could be united behind another candidate whose chances of defeating Marx were better than his.[93] Increasingly annoyed by Nationalist intrigues on Hindenburg's behalf, Jarres informed Loebell on the evening of 7 April that he would withdraw as a candidate if his nomination encountered difficulties at the meeting of the Reich Bloc that was scheduled for the following day. Although spokesmen for the DVP, the patriotic associations, and Germany's industrial leadership reaffirmed their support for Jarres at the outset of the meeting of the Reich Bloc on 8 April, the Nationalists pressed their case for Hindenburg's nomination and announced that they had succeeded in persuading Hindenburg to retract the decision he had communicated to Loebell the day before. At this point, Loebell read the communication from Jarres announcing his withdrawal as a candidate. Fearful that his committee might be left without a candidate to oppose Marx, Loebell then placed a telephone call to Hindenburg, in which he prevailed upon the retired war hero to accept the Reich Bloc's nomination and stand for election. After a further exchange of telephone calls in which Jarres and Hindenburg agreed upon the precise wording of a statement confirming the former's withdrawal from the race, the Reich

---

[91] Schulenburg, *Welt um Hindenburg*, 64–65.
[92] Ibid., 66. See also Keudell, "Mit Tirpitz in Hannover bei Hindenburg," from 1968, BA Koblenz, Nachlass Walther von Keudell, 102, as well as Schmidt-Hannover to Spahn, 11 Apr. 1925, BA Koblenz, NL Schmidt-Hannover, 73. See also Scheck, *Tirpitz*, 194–202.
[93] Jarres to Sorge, 6 Apr. 1925, BA Koblenz, NL Jarres, 23.

Bloc concluded its deliberations by formally endorsing Hindenburg for the presidency.[94]

The Reich Bloc's nomination of Hindenburg as its candidate for the Reich presidency represented a clear and unequivocal triumph for the German National People's Party and its new chairman, Friedrich Winckler. The indefatigable Winckler had worked long and hard behind the scenes first to persuade Hindenburg to stand for election and then to prevent the Reich Bloc from renominating Jarres.[95] To Loebell, Gayl, and the leaders of the National Citizens' Council, on the other hand, Hindenburg's nomination came as something of a disappointment. For although they could console themselves with the argument that Hindenburg's nomination represented a triumph of *Staatspolitik* over *Parteipolitik*,[96] both Loebell and Gayl harbored lingering resentment over the way in which the DNVP had monopolized their overtures on behalf of a truly nonpartisan candidacy.[97] Their reservations over the wisdom of a Hindenburg candidacy only mounted when the grizzled war hero let it be known that he had no intention of taking an active part in the Reich Bloc's campaign on his behalf and left the management of his campaign in the hands of a special committee in Hanover under the direction of his adjutant, retired Lieutenant Colonel Otto von Feldmann.[98] Aside from his annual Easter Address on 11 April, Hindenburg confined his activity during the campaign to a speech and press conference in Hanover and a radio address to the nation. The tone of these statements was remarkably moderate, particularly in light of the more extreme expectations that had attached themselves to Hindenburg's candidacy. Speaking in Hanover, Hindenburg took special pains to underscore the nonpartisan character of his candidacy and surprised his critics by expressing a commitment to excercise the powers of the presidency "on the basis of the existing constitutional foundation and Germany's present situation in the world." What ultimately mattered, Hindenburg contended, was "not the form of government but the spirit that animated the form of government."[99]

---

[94] Meeting of the Reich Bloc, 8 Apr. 1925, BA Koblenz, R 45 II, 311/217–25. See also the account by Baltrusch, "Geschichtliches zur Wahl Hindenburgs," BA Koblenz, Nachlass Fritz Baltrusch, 11, as well as "Bericht über Sitzungen des Loebell-Ausschusses," 31 Mar.–7 May 1925, in Bredt, *Erinnerungen und Dokumente*, ed. Schumacher, 349–51.

[95] Schulenburg, *Welt um Hindenburg*, 70.

[96] Kriegk, "Hindenburg," *Der Deutschen-Spiegel* 2, no. 16 (17 Apr. 1925): 726–30.

[97] Handwritten note by Gayl, n.d., BA Koblenz, NL Gayl, 23.

[98] Memorandum of a conversation with Hindenburg, 9 Apr. 1925, BA Koblenz, NL Gayl, 23. See also Otto von Feldmann, *Turkei, Weimar, Hitler. Lebenserinnerungen eines preußischen Offiziers und deutschnationalen Politikers*, ed. Peter von Feldmann (Bosdorf, 2013), 259–74.

[99] [Paul von Hindenburg], *Hindenburg: Briefe, Reden, Berichte*, ed. Fritz Endres (Munich, 1934), 144–45.

Over the course of the next several days, virtually all of the organizations that belonged to the Reich Bloc rallied to Hindenburg's support. Even the Stahlhelm, which continued to express a preference for Jarres right up until the eve of Hindenburg's nomination, overcame the severe strain that had developed in its relations with the Young German Order as a result of the latter's behavior during the nominating process and joined the rest of the patriotic movement in supporting Hindenburg's bid for the presidency.[100] By the same token, the Bavarian People's Party officially joined the Reich Bloc and called upon its followers to vote for Hindenburg after having refused to support Jarres in the initial ballot.[101] Of the various organizations that had supported Jarres's presidential campaign, only the DVP remained aloof from the excitement that greeted the news of Hindenburg's candidacy. While Stresemann was no doubt concerned about foreign reaction to Hindenburg's election, he was also embarrassed by the way in which the DNVP tried to transform the campaign into a referendum on Germany's form of government and withheld his personal endorsement until the last week of the campaign.[102] The Nationalists, in the meantime, hailed Hindenburg as the "savior of the German people" whose election would mark the beginning of Germany's national recovery at home and abroad. Those who voted for Marx, on the other hand, were stigmatized as "reactionaries" responsible for perpeutating a "rotten and corrupt system" of government.[103]

At the same time that Nationalist hyperbole reflected the tremendous importance the DNVP attached to Hindenburg's election, it also had the effect of greatly increasing the political stakes involved in the outcome of the election. If, for example, Hindenburg were to be defeated, this would be a great victory for Germany's republican forces and an unmitigated defeat for those who continued to oppose the principles enshrined in the Weimar Constitution, in all likelihood a defeat from which the German Right might never have recovered. Consequently, the leaders of the DNVP – and particularly Winckler, Westarp, and those governmental conservatives who were in control of the party – committed themselves and the resources at their disposal without any reservation whatsoever to the task of securing Hindenburg's election. At the same time, the leaders of the Stahlhelm, the Young German Order, and other elements on the paramilitary Right were able to set aside

---

[100] Circular from Seldte to the leaders of the Stahlhelm local organizations, 10 Apr. 1925, BA Koblenz, NL Gayl, 23.

[101] Hauss, *Volkswahl*, 103–24. On the BVP, see Cuno to Jarres, 15 Apr. 1925, BA Koblenz, NL Jarres, 23, as well as Schönhoven, *Bayerische Volkspartei*, 123–28.

[102] Stresemann, "Deutsche Volkspartei und Reichspräsidentenwahl," *Die Zeit*, 19 Apr. 1925, no. 160. See also Turner, *Stresemann*, 191–200.

[103] Manfred Dörr, "Die Deutschnationale Volkspartei 1925 bis 1928" (Ph.D. diss., Universität Marburg, 1964), 126–28.

their deep-seated antipathy towards the world of Weimar party politics to provide massive logistic support for the Hindenburg campaign. These efforts were rewarded when on 26 April 1925 Hindenburg captured more than 14.6 million votes – or 48.3 percent of the total popular vote – and defeated Marx by slightly more than 900,000 votes. The secret to Hindenburg's victory lay not only in his ability to attract the support of many of those who had stayed at home on 29 March – approximately three million more voters went to the polls in April than the month before – but also in his popularity with Bavarian Catholics who may have shared Marx's religion but not his ties to the Social Democrats.[104]

Organized Interests and Stabilization

Although Hindenburg's election was doubtlessly a major triumph for the German Right, its immediate impact on German political life was ambiguous and difficult for contemporaries to assess. The confusion here stemmed in no small measure from the fact that Hindenburg took special pains to defuse fears of a new assault against the social and political legacy of the November Revolution by reaffirming his commitment to exercise the powers of his office within the framework of the existing constitutional order.[105] But if Hindenburg's remarks helped reassure the defenders of the Weimar Republic that his election did not signal an immediate swing to the right in domestic and foreign policy, they found little favor with the more irascible elements on the DNVP's extreme right wing. Even before the conclusion of the campaign, many Nationalists had expressed private fears that the election of a man of Hindenburg's mythic stature as president of the German republic would only expedite its political legitimation and thus make its replacement by a more authoritarian political system all the more difficult.[106] Not only did Hindenburg's oath of loyalty to the Weimar Constitution tend to confirm such fears, but Hindenburg's election demonstrated to influential elements within Germany's conservative establishment just how much one could accomplish by working within rather than outside the existing political system. In the words of the DNVP's Martin Schiele, Hindenburg's election "greatly strengthened the structure of German state power" at the same time that it demonstrated

[104] On this point, see John K. Zeender, "The German Catholics and the Presidential Election of 1925," *Journal of Modern History* 35 (1963): 366–81, and Karl Holl, "Konfessionalität, Konfessionalismus und demokratische Republik – zu einigen Aspekten der Reichspräsidentenwahl von 1925," *Vierteljahrshefte für Zeitgeschichte* 17 (1969): 254–75.
[105] [Hindenburg], *Briefe, Reden, Berichte*, ed. Endres, 150–51.
[106] For example, see Martin Spahn, "Die Wahl zum Reichspräsidenten: Das Amt und der Mann," in Friedrich Wilhelm Loebell, ed., *Hindenburg. Was er uns Deutschen ist. Eine Festgabe zum 80. Geburtstag* (Berlin, 1927), 113.

"support for the state [*Staatsbejahung*]" and "a sense of national feeling" that "offers the strongest guarantee for the strength and permanence of our state system."[107]

The immediate effect of Hindenburg's election was thus to encourage the reconciliation of the more moderate elements within the DNVP to Germany's new republican order and to isolate those on the party's right wing who remained irreconcilably opposed to any form of collaboration with the existing political system. Coming on the heels of the split in the Nationalist vote on the ratification of the Dawes Plan and the DNVP's entry into the Luther cabinet, Hindenburg's election represented another step in the gradual accommodation of Germany's conservative establishment to the possibility of pursuing its social and political objectives within the existing system of government and bore dramatic testimony – though not without a touch of irony in light of his opposition to Hindenburg's candidacy – to the success of Stresemann's strategy of stabilizing the republic from the Right. The success of Stresemann's strategy could also be seen in the changes in the leadership of Germany's two most influential nonsocialist special-interest organizations, the National Federation of German Industry and the National Rural League. In the early years of the Weimar Republic, both organizations had been under the control of elements that were strongly opposed, if not openly hostile, to the changes that had taken place in Germany's political system since the collapse of November 1918. In the summer of 1924, however, both the RDI and the RLB had played an important role in securing the ratification of the Dawes Plan, in the first case to gain access to international capital markets and in the latter case to gain a measure of influence over the formulation of German trade policy. Now, in deference to Weimar's apparent stabilization, both the RDI and RLB began to make tactical adjustments to what they perceived as the changed realities of Germany's domestic political situation.

By and large, the German industrial community was one of the principal beneficiaries of Germany's political and economic stabilization. If nothing else, the adoption of the Dawes Plan provided German industry with access to international capital markets and enabled it to compensate for the acute capital shortage that had resulted from the runaway inflation of the early 1920s. Still, Germany's industrial leadership was far from united in its support of Stresemann's domestic and foreign policies. Not only had Ruhr heavy industry backed the short-lived National Liberal Association in its efforts to undermine Stresemann's position as DVP party chairman,[108] but influential Ruhr industrialists such as Paul Reusch, Fritz Thyssen, and Albert Vögler had strongly opposed ratification of the Dawes Plan for fear that this would place

---

[107] Martin Schiele, "Innere Politik," in *Politische Praxis 1926*, ed. Walther Lambach (Hamburg, n.d. [1926]), 48–57.
[108] Rasch, "Über Albert Vögler," 134.

German heavy industry at a permanent competitive disadvantage in future international trade.[109] All of this, in turn, tended to threaten the unity of the National Federation of German Industry, which in April 1924 had given its tentative approval to the Dawes committee recommendations as "a suitable basis for the solution of the reparations problem."[110] The most direct threat to the RDI's unity came in the form of the German Industrialists' Association (Deutsche Industriellen-Vereinigung or DIV), which Hugenberg's associates in the German industrial community founded in Berlin's Hotel Esplanade on 14 May 1924 under the leadership of Paul Bang and Eduard Stadtler. The DIV was militantly opposed to the tone and substance of the Dawes committee recommendations and sought to block their implementation not only by mobilizing industrial opposition to Stresemann's stabilization strategy but also by fomenting a rebellion within the RDI against Hermann Bücher and those officials it held responsible for the RDI's disastrous political course.[111]

Although the German Industrialists' Association remained a splinter organization that never established itself as a serious rival to the RDI, its founding bore dramatic testimony to the sharp cleavage that had developed between Ruhr heavy industry and the more moderate elements of the German industrial establishment. Much of the RDI's internal discord was attributed to the ineffective leadership of Kurt Sorge, president of the RDI since its founding in 1919. Sorge, who had served as a member of the DVP Reichstag delegation until earning Stresemann's ire for his involvement in the NLV, was in the process of divesting himself of his positions within the German industrial establishment and asked to be relieved of his responsibilities as RDI president in the early fall of 1924.[112] The search for a successor who could command the respect of both Ruhr heavy industry and the other branches of German industry continued throughout the remainder of the year before the RDI finally settled upon Carl Duisberg, chairman of the board of directors of one of Germany's largest chemical firms.[113] Duisberg's subsequent election as RDI

---

[109] For further details, see Weisbrod, *Schwerindustrie in der Weimarer Republik*, 273–82.

[110] *Geschäftliche Mitteilungen für die Mitglieder des Reichsverbandes der Deutschen Industrie* 6, no. 10 (1 May 1924): 72, BA Koblenz, ZSg 1-142.

[111] On the DIV, see Eduard Stadtler, *"Reichsverband der Deutschen Industrie" und "Deutsche Industriellen-Vereinigung"* (Berlin, n.d. [1924]), esp. 15–29. See also Bang to Claß, 25 May 1924, BA Potsdam, ADV, 287/233–34.

[112] Sorge to the members of the RDI presidium, 20 Sept. 1924, Bayer-Archiv Leverkusen, RDI-Akten, 62/10.2.

[113] *Geschäftliche Mitteilungen für die Mitglieder des Reichsverbandes der Deutschen Industrie* 7, no. 1 (21 Jan. 1925): 1, BA Koblenz, ZSg 1-14/2. On Duisberg's election, see Weisbrod, *Schwerindustrie in der Weimarer Republik*, 217–45, as well as Stephanie Wolff-Rohé, *Der Reichsverband der Deutschen Industrie 1919-1924/25* (Frankfurt am Main, 2001), 387–95, and Werner Plumpe, *Carl Duisberg 1861-1935. Anatomie eines Industriellen* (Munich, 2016), 721–27.

president in January 1925 represented a clear triumph for the more moderate elements within the organization. For although Duisberg may have taken pride in being temperamentally unsuited for politics and took great pains to reaffirm the RDI's essentially nonpartisan character,[114] he was at the same time one of Stresemann's strongest supporters within the German industrial community and a severe critic of the policies Ruhr heavy industry had pursued during the 1923 crisis.[115] Moreover, Duisberg was strongly committed to improving industry's effectiveness in its relations with the Reichstag and took immediate steps upon his election as RDI president to establish a parliamentary advisory council (*Beirat*) that would facilitate the flow of information between industry and parliament.[116] Notwithstanding the fact that German heavy industry continued to exercise an unofficial veto over the policies of the RDI and could still block any initiative by the RDI leadership that might jeopardize its own interests,[117] Duisberg's election to the RDI presidency and his willingness to promote industry's welfare within the framework of the existing political system validated the significance of Stresemann's efforts at stabilizing the German republic from the Right.[118]

Developments within the RDI's principal agrarian counterpart, the National Rural League, were more difficult to interpret. Despite an arrangement that granted small and middle-sized family farmers in southern and western Germany the semblance of parity, the RLB's policies ever since its founding in 1921 had been effectively dictated by the large landowning interests from east of the Elbe River.[119] Under the leadership of Gustav Roesicke, the RLB had allied itself with the DNVP, where it took its place among those elements most resolutely opposed to any sort of accommodation with Germany's new republican system.[120] In the fall of 1923 the RLB had sympathized with the efforts to replace Germany's republican order with a more authoritarian system of government and had even established contact with Seeckt in the

[114] Remarks by Duisberg at a press conference, 17 June 1925, in Carl Duisberg, *Abhandlungen, Vorträge und Reden aus den Jahren 1922–1933* (Berlin, 1933), 13.
[115] Duisberg to Weinberg, 24 Sept. 1923, Bayer-Archiv Leverkusen, I.G. Farben-Vorakten, 4B/20.
[116] Duisberg to Kalle, 17 Jan. 1925, Bayer-Archiv Leverkusen, RDI-Akten, 62/10.2. See also Duisberg to Siemens, 13 Mar. 1925, SHI Berlin, NL Siemens, 4/Lf 665, and Duisberg to Silverberg, 13 Mar. 1925, BA Koblenz, NL Silverberg, 259/13–18, as well as Plumpe, *Duisberg*, 728–29.
[117] Bernd Weisbrod, "Economic Power and Political Stability Reconsidered: Heavy Industry in Weimar Germany," *Social History* 4 (1979): 241–63.
[118] Wolfram Pyta, "Vernunftrepublikanismus in den Spitzenverbänden der deutschen Industrie," in *Vernunftrepublikanismus in der Weimarer Republik. Politik, Literatur, Wissenschaft*, ed. Andreas Wirsching and Jürgen Eder (Stuttgart, 2008), 87–108.
[119] Flemming, *Landwirtschaftliche Interessen und Demokratie*, 252–322.
[120] For example, see Kriegsheim to Ziemke, 21 Jan. 1924, BA Berlin, R 72, 263/54.

hope that he might take the initiative in bringing this about.[121] All of this, however, began to change during the Dawes crisis in the summer of 1924. The threat of a new credit restrictions by the German National Bank placed the leaders of the German agricultural community under heavy pressure to support acceptance of the Dawes commitee recommendations. Moreover, the leaders of the RLB were anxious to influence the general contours of German trade policy after Germany regained full tariff autonomy at the beginning of 1925 and were determined to make certain that agricultural interests would be shielded as much as possible from the new taxes that would result from implementation of the Dawes Plan.[122] None of this would be possible if the DNVP continued to disqualify itself as a potential coalition partner by blocking acceptance of the Dawes committee recommendations. Under these circumstances, the more moderate elements around the DVP's Karl Hepp managed to gain the upper hand over Roesicke and his supporters from the RLB's East Elbian affiliates to force a critical change in the RLB's position on the Dawes Plan. In late August the RLB executive committee formally released its representatives in the Reichstag to vote according to their conscience, thereby helping to clear the way for acceptance of the controversial plan.[123]

The moderate tendency within the RLB was greatly strengthened not only by the appointment of one of their own, the DNVP's Martin Schiele, as the new minister of agriculture in January 1925 but also by Hindenburg's election as Reich president three months later. Not only did these developments demonstrate the possibility, if not the wisdom, of working within the existing political system, but they were accompanied by an important change in the RLB's national leadership.[124] With Roesicke's death in February 1925 and that of his long-time friend and associate Conrad von Wangenheim fifteen months later, the RLB lost the two men whose politics and reputation most closely identified it with the prewar Agrarian League. Their departure from the scene cleared the way for the ascendancy of a new generation of agrarian politicians, the most important of whom were Schiele, Hepp, Count Eberhard von Kalckreuth, and Arno Kriegsheim. Hepp, who had languished in Roesicke's shadow as part of an arrangement that had the two men share presidential authority, became increasingly assertive in setting the course for the RLB after 1925, while Kalckreuth, an East Elbian aristocrat chosen as Roesicke's successor in the two-man RLB presidium, tended to defer to Hepp in most political matters

---

[121] Wangenheim to Roesicke, 15 Dec. 1923, BA Berlin, NL Wangenheim, 17/34.

[122] *Wege zur Aktivierung der deutschen Wirtschaftsbilanz. Die Vorschläge des Reichs-Landbundes* (Berlin, 1925).

[123] "Stellungnahme des Präsidiums des Reichs-Landbundes zur gegenwärtigen politischen Lage," n.d. [ca. 22–23 Aug. 1924], appended to Kalckreuth to Westarp, 23 Aug. 1924, NL Westarp, Gärtringen, VN 46.

[124] Flemming, *Landwirtschaftliche Interessen und Demokratie*, 241–45.

so that he could concentrate his efforts on rescuing the organization's numerous economic institutions from fiscal collapse.[125] The person who did more than anybody else to set the tone at the helm of the RLB was Kriegsheim. Having come to the RLB by way of the German Rural League, Kriegsheim was the consummate *Verbandstaktiker* who placed the corporate welfare of the German agricultural community ahead of all other political considerations.[126] Although he himself belonged to the DNVP, Kriegsheim had flirted with the idea of a new agrarian party in the summer of 1924 and sought to relax the RLB's close ties to the DNVP so that it might pursue a more independent course of action in the defense of agricultural economic interests.[127]

The change of leadership both here and at the National Federation of German Industry represented part of a more general accommodation on the part of Germany's conservative economic elites to the realities of Weimar's political and economic stabilization after 1924. This becomes even more apparent when these developments are placed in the context of the August 1924 split in the Nationalist vote on the Dawes Plan, the DNVP's entry into the Luther cabinet in January 1925, and Hindenburg's election as president of the German republic the following April. Taken together, these developments foreshadowed a new era in the history of the Weimar Republic, one in which the more moderate elements on the German Right could be persuaded through an appeal to their economic self-interest to work within the framework of a political system they continued to reject on ideological grounds. To be sure, this was anything but an ideal solution to the problem of Weimar's political stability. In the first place, it rested upon the assumption that the special-economic interests willing to collaborate with the existing system of government would be rewarded for their sacrifice of political principle with tangible benefits in the field of social and economic policy. Whether or not this condition would hold, particularly in light of the harsh realities of Germany's economic stabilization in the second half of the 1920s, remained to be seen. Secondly, any move in the direction of an accommodation with the Weimar Republic was almost certain to provoke a fierce reaction from those on the extreme Right who refused to countenance any sort of collaboration with the existing political system. All of this suggests that the efforts to stabilize the republic from the right rested upon extremely fragile premises and that the success of this gambit was far from certain.

---

[125] In this respect, see Hugenberg to Kalckreuth, 22 Dec. 1925, BA Koblenz, NL Schmidt-Hannover, 73.

[126] In this respect, see Arno Kriegsheim, "Die politische Bedeutung des Reichs-Landbundes," in *Politische Praxis 1926*, ed. Walther Lambach (Hamburg, 1926), 295–303, and Arno Kriegsheim, "Die politische Sendung der Berufsstände," *Politische Wochenschrift* 3, no. 12 (24 Mar. 1927): 246–48.

[127] Entry in Quaatz's diary, 5 July 1924, BA Koblenz, NL Quaatz, 16.

9

Paladins of the Right

With the political and economic stabilization of the Weimar Republic in the middle of the 1920s and the split that this produced within the ranks of Germany's conservative elites, the mobilization of culture in the war against democracy became more important than ever before. From beginning to end, the Weimar Republic was the scene of a pitched battle for cultural hegemony, though one waged not so much between different social classes as one waged within Germany's bourgeois intelligentsia between those who believed in cooperation across class lines on the basis of parliamentary democracy and those who categorically rejected the social and political compromises upon which the Weimar Republic had been founded.[1] No group in the Weimar Republic attached greater significance to winning the struggle for cultural and intellectual hegemony than Germany's conservative intelligentsia. To the paladins of the Right, the immediate task was to challenge whatever legitimacy the newly founded Weimar Republic enjoyed in the eyes of the German bourgeoisie and to lay the foundation for what they embraced as the "conservative revolution." The term conservative revolution was first introduced into Weimar's political vocabulary by the Austrian poet and dramatist Hugo von Hofmannstahl in a speech at the University of Munich in January 1927. Against the fragmentation of German social and political life Hofmannstahl sought to invoke the healing power of German culture. Here he called for a conservative revolution that could overcome the estrangement of spirit (*Geist*) from life and create "a new German reality in which the entire nation could take part."[2] In its

---

[1] For overviews of Weimar culture, see Peter Gay, *Weimar Culture: The Insider as Outsider* (New York, 1968), and Walter Laqueur, *Weimar: A Cultural History* (New York, 1974), as well as the relevant chapters in Eric D. Weitz, *Weimar Germany: Promise and Tragedy* (Princeton, NJ, and Oxford, 2007), 169–330. For more nuanced readings of the paradoxes of Weimar culture, see the essays in Moritz Föllmer and Rüdiger Graf, eds., *Die 'Krise' der Weimarer Republik. Zur Kritik eines Deutungsmusters* (Frankfurt a.M. and New York, 2005), as well as Benjamin Ziemann, "Weimar was Weimar: Politics, Culture, and the Emplotment of the German Republic," *German History* 28 (2010): 542–71.

[2] Hugo von Hofmannstahl, *Das Schrifttum als geistiger Raum der Nation* (n.p. [Munich], n.d. [1927]), 31.

more blatant manifestations, the doctrine of the conservative revolution was directed not merely against the individualistic and materialistic trappings of modern mass democracy but also against the reactionary social vision of old-line conservatives such as those who were in control of the DNVP. In a broader sense, the conservative revolution defined itself in essentially moral and spiritual terms and sought nothing less than the rebirth of the human spirit.[3]

At the forefront of this crusade stood a small group of conservative intellectuals who alternately called themselves "young" or "revolutionary" conservatives as a way of distinguishing themselves from that the prewar conservative establishment. This particular mode of conservative thought had surfaced in the late nineteenth-century as a rival to both the governmental and radical nationalist strains of Wilhelmine conservatism. It drew much of its inspiration from Nietzsche's ruthless dissection of European cultural decadence and was characterized by a degree of cultural pessimism that was conspicuously absent from the more influential and established forms of German conservatism.[4] Similarly, the young conservatives felt a certain affinity for the apocalyptic impulse that had manifested itself so vividly in the German expressionist movement at the beginning of the twentieth century. Like the expressionists, the young conservatives longed for some sort of apocalyptic breakthrough, or *Durchbruch*, out of a decadent and moribund society into a new world of the spirit. For the young conservatives, however, this breakthrough into the new world of the spirit was to be accompanied by the creation of a new political order in which the historic separation of *Staat* and *Volk* would dissolve in a celebration of national unity. The young conservatives thus appropriated the millenarian and apocalyptic imagery of German expressionism and harnessed it to their own political aspirations. For many of those in the vanguard of modernist culture, World War I would be the catalyst that would set in motion the series of events that would presumably culminate

---

[3] The classic study of the "conservative revolution" is Armin Mohler, *Die konservative Revolution in Deutschland. Grundriß ihrer Weltanschauungen* (Stuttgart, 1950). See also Keith Bullivant, "The Conservative Revolution," in *The Weimar Dilemma: Intellectuals in the Weimar Republic*, ed., Anthony Phelan (Manchester, 1985), 47–70, as well as Stefan Breuer, *Anatomie der konservativen Revolution* (Darmstadt, 1993), and Roger Woods, *The Conservative Revolution in the Weimar Republic* (London and New York, 1996).

[4] In this respect, see Fritz Stern, *The Politics of Cultural Despair: A Study in the Rise of the Germanic Ideology* (Berkeley, CA, and Los Angeles, 1961). Nietzsche's relationship to the conservative revolution is the focus of a collection of essays that recently appeared under the title *Nietzsche und die Konservative Revolution*, ed. Sebastian Kaufmann and Andreas Urs Sommer (Berlin, 2018). In particular, see the editors' introduction, "Nietzsche und die Konservative Revolution: Zur Einführung," 1–12.

in the realization of their highest hopes for the spiritual, cultural, and political rebirth of the German nation.[5]

The June Club

By far the most important center of young conservative activity in the early Weimar Republic was the June Club (Juniklub). The June Club was founded on 28 June 1919 through the merger of two other young conservative organizations, the Association for National and Social Solidarity (Vereinigung für nationale und soziale Solidarität) under the leadership of Heinrich von Gleichen-Russwurm and the League for the Defense of German Culture (Liga zum Schutz der deutschen Kultur), more commonly known as the Anti-Bolshevist League (Antibolschewistische Liga), under the leadership of Eduard Stadtler. Founded as a symbolic protest against Germany's acceptance of the Versailles Peace Treaty, the June Club was a relatively small organization that never numbered more than 150 active members.[6] Its membership was recruited exclusively from the ranks of Germany's conservative elite and included not only prominent politicians such as Hans Erdmann von Lindeiner-Wildau and Otto Hoetzsch from the DNVP, Reinhold Quaatz from the DVP, and Martin Spahn, Heinrich Brüning, and occasionally Adam Stegerwald from the Center but also influential conservative publicists such as Walther Schotte from the *Preußische Jahrbücher*, Rudolf Pechel from the *Deutsche Rundschau*, Paul Fechter from the *Deutsche Allgemeine Zeitung*, and Franz Röhr from the *Deutsche Arbeit*, the leading journal of the Christian-national labor movement. Meeting weekly at the club's Berlin fashionable headquarters at Motzstraße 22, club members would discuss topics of both political and literary interest in what was part of a conscious effort to bring the leading conservative intellectuals of the day into closer contact with the men whose policies would ultimately shape the direction of political conservatism in the Weimar Republic.[7] As a forum that provided young conservative intellectuals with informal, yet direct, access to Germany's economic and political elites, the June Club quickly assumed a significance that greatly exceeded the size of its membership.[8]

---

[5] For example, see Frederick S. Levine, *The Apocalyptic Vision: The Art of Franz Marc as German Expressionism* (New York, 1979): 138–69.

[6] An undated membership list in BA Koblenz, Nachlass Rudolf Pechel, 144, indicates that the June Club had ninety members with full voting rights and another forty-five extraordinary members without voting rights.

[7] For the club's goals, see Juni-Klub, "Die dreiunddreissig Sätze," n.d., BA Koblenz, NL Pechel, 144.

[8] For further details, see Manfred Schoeps, "Der Deutsche Herrenklub. Ein Beitrag zur Geschichte des Jungkonservativismus in der Weimarer Republik" (Ph.D. diss., Universität Erlangen-Nürnberg, 1974), 11–34; and Joachim Petzold, *Wegbereiter des deutschen Faschismus*.

From the outset, the driving intellectual force in the June Club was Arthur Moeller van den Bruck, a young conservative intellectual who went on to earn more than his share of posthumous notoriety for his book *Das dritte Reich*. Born in 1876, Moeller belonged to that generation of Germans who had been born in the first decade after the founding of the Second Empire and who reached political maturity around the turn of the century. Unlike the vast majority of those in his cohort group, however, Moeller felt little attachment to the symbols and institutions of imperial Germany and remained profoundly alienated from what he perceived as the decadence of Wilhelmine culture. A literary and cultural critic who had earned a measure of distinction for his comprehensive survey of German literature after Nietzsche and for his authoritative German edition of Dosteoevsky's collected writings, Moeller viewed the world through a prism that refracted the underlying disenchantment of an entire generation of German intellectuals with the materialism, philistinism, and facile nationalism of Wilhelmine Germany. In his self-imposed exile from 1902 until the outbreak of World War I, Moeller developed increasingly close ties to leading representatives of the expressionist movement – Edvard Munch and Ernst Barlach in particular – and came to share their longing for some sort of apocalyptic resolution to the crisis of modern culture.[9] In the meantime, Moeller reserved his most scathing remarks for liberalism, which, with its promise of equality and freedom for all, was both source and symptom of the decay and dissolution of European cultural life. At the core of Moeller's rejection of liberalism lay a deeply pessimistic view of human nature and a profound lack of faith in the powers of human reason. Nor did conservatism, the movement to which Moeller felt the greatest emotional attachment, escape his scorn. For not only was conservatism guilty of failing to address the problems of the modern age but it had degenerated into the preserve of a privileged caste. Of the political movements of his day, only Social Democracy evoked a positive response from Moeller,

---

Die Jungkonservativen in der Weimarer Republik (Cologne, 1978), 99–106, as well as two more recent studies by Berthold Petzinna, *Erziehung zum deutschen Lebensstil. Ursprung und Entwicklung des jungkonservativen "Ring"-Kreises 1918-1933* (Berlin, 2000), 118–42, and André Postert, *Von der Kritik der Parteien zur außerparlamentarischen Opposition. Die Jungkonservative Klub-Bewegung in der Weimarer Republik und ihre Auflösung im National-sozialismus* (Baden-Baden, 2014), 107–43.

[9] On Moeller's early development, see Stern, *Politics of Cultural Despair*, 231–55, and Hans-Joachim Schwierskott, *Arthur Moeller van den Bruck und der revolutionäre Natio-nalismus in der Weimarer Republik* (Göttingen, 1962), 13–36, as well as the more recent studies by André Schlüter, *Moeller van den Bruck. Leben und Werk* (Cologne, Weimar, and Vienna, 2010), 29–86; Volker Weiß, *Moderne Antimoderne. Arthur Moeller van den Bruck und der Wandel des Konservatismus* (Paderborn, 2012), 102–211; and Claudia Kemper, *Das "Gewissen" 1919-1925. Kommunikation und Vernetzung der Jungkonserva-tiven* (Munich, 2011), 61–106.

though not so much for its commitment to the social and political equality of the worker as for its Prussian discipline and sense of duty.[10]

Throughout all of this, Moeller retained the esthete's disdain for the world of practical politics. Politics, Moeller suggested, was nothing more than the constant wrangling of different political parties for the material benefit of the special economic interests they represented. Politics in the modern state had thus surrendered the welfare of the nation as a whole to a parliamentary marketplace in which interests, not ideas, drove the course of events. With the outbreak of World War I and Germany's military collapse four years later, Moeller overcame his aversion to politics and began to stake out a position for himself and those who were prepared to follow him. Moeller and his associates remained deeply indebted to what they called "the ideas of 1914." By this they meant first and foremost the deep and abiding sense of national unity that had surfaced almost inexplicably in the first days of the war, a sense of unity, as Moeller was quick to point out, that did not stop with the propertied classes but embraced the worker as well. This sense of national unity, with its concomitant emphasis upon the essential equality of all of those who belonged to the German nation, stood in naked contrast to the partisan bickering of Wilhelmine political life and provided the young conservatives who had rallied behind Moeller's banner with their distinctive vision of Germany's political future.[11] By the same token, Moeller and his associates were profoundly touched by the events of November 1918. If old-line conservatives were deeply shaken by the collapse of the monarchy and the triumph of Social Democracy, the young conservatives rejoiced at the death of a corrupt and moribund political order and welcomed the November Revolution as an opportunity to translate "the ideas of 1914" into practice.[12]

The heady euphoria that the young conservatives felt at the collapse of the old order lasted for precisely eight months, that is, until Germany yielded to the threat of dismemberment and signed the Versailles Peace Treaty. To the young conservatives, Versailles became a symbol of Germany's national humiliation without whose total and unconditional repudiation the task of national regeneration could never begin. From this point on, Moeller and his followers became unrelenting opponents not only of Versailles but also of the political system they held responsible for its acceptance, the Weimar Republic.

---

[10] On Moeller's political ideas, see Schwierskott, *Moeller van den Bruck*, 88–141; Schlüter, *Moeller van den Bruck*, 115–73; and Weiß, *Moderne Antimoderne*, 73–77, 80–86, 94–101.

[11] On the "ideas of 1914," see Jeffrey Verhey, *The Spirit of 1914: Militarism, Myth, and Mobilization in Germany* (Cambridge, 2000).

[12] Peter Fritzsche, "Breakdown or Breakthrough? Conservatives and the November Revolution of 1918," in *Between Reform, Reaction, and Resistance: Studies on the History of German Conservatism from 1789 to 1945*, ed. Larry Eugene Jones and James N. Retallack (Oxford and New York, 1993), 299–328.

All that Moeller had had to say about liberalism in the prewar period took on new intensity in the wake of Versailles. Nowhere was this more apparent than in a famous essay entitled "An Liberalismus gehen die Völker zugrunde" that Moeller wrote for *Die neue Front*, the collective manifesto that thirty-eight members of the June Club issued in 1922. Here Moeller not only reiterated his more theoretical arguments against the liberal concepts of man, state, and society, but applied them to the specific conditions that existed in Germany after the end of the war. While Moeller continued to equate liberalism with the decadence and leveling of contemporary German culture, he also decried the way in which the ideas of 1914 and the revolution of 1918 had been betrayed by the forces of liberalism at home and abroad. To rectify this situation, Moeller called upon his followers to complete the revolution that the liberal architects of Germany's new constitutional order had done their best to subvert and to lay the foundation for a new German Reich through the consolidation of all who were prepared to sacrifice their own self-interest for the sake of Germany's national destiny.[13]

By no means did Moeller's disciples confine their work to Berlin. In 1919 and 1920 representatives of the June Club held colloquia and workshops throughout Germany in an effort to educate a broader public about the club's goals and to recruit new followers to its crusade for a rebirth of German cultural and political life. At the same time, club members established contact not just with like-minded intellectuals from other parts of the country but also with representatives of Germany's industrial and agricultural elites. But its primary focus remained the younger generation, the generation that had served so valiantly at the front during the recent war and that was now trying to make its way back into civilian life. As Max Hildebert Boehm, one of the June Club's most committed activists, wrote in 1920, the task of rescuing the German nation from the nihilistic despair, crass materialism, and relentless mechanization of the postwar period had fallen to that generation that had proven its mettle in the trenches of the great war and that was now being called upon to forge a new *Volksgemeinschaft* out of the universal misery that had befallen the German people.[14] It was in this spirit that Boehm sent Westarp, Stresemann, and other leaders of the bourgeois Right a memorandum extolling the virtues of the soldiers' and worker's councils that had sprung up first in the Russian revolution of 1917 and then more recently in the much pilloried November Revolution, praising them as an alternative to the moribund system of bourgeois parliamentarism that Germany had

---

[13] Moeller van den Bruck, "An Liberalismus gehen die Völker zugrunde," in *Die neue Front*, ed. Arthur Moeller van den Bruck, Heinrich von Gleichen-Rußwurm, and Max Hildebert Boehm (Berlin, 1922), 5–34. On Moeller's involvement in the June Club, see Schlüter, *Moeller van den Bruck*, 289–318, and Weiß, *Moderne Antimoderne*, 225–31.

[14] Boehm, "Die Front der Jungen," *Süddeutsche Monatshefte* 8, no. 1 (1920–21): 8–12.

inherited from the nineteenth century. Denouncing parliamentarism as "the legitimate off-spring of the mechanist-atomist western theory of the state," Boehm called upon the parties of the German Right to embrace the younger generation and its search for new forms of social and political organization that would enable the German people to translate the "ideas of 1914" into concrete reality.[15]

Of the conservative intellectuals who suddenly rose to prominence after the collapse of 1918, only Oswald Spengler rivaled Moeller van den Bruck in influence and popularity. Spengler's fame stemmed from his authorship of *Der Untergang des Abendlandes*, an ambitious and highly speculative exercise in universal history that captured the sense of despair that gripped Germany in the aftermath of World War I as powerfully as any book of its time.[16] Spengler, however, was anything but a clear thinker, and there was always an unresolved tension between the implicit pessimism of his universal history and his passionate espousal of right-wing political causes.[17] As a political thinker, Spengler was best known for a book he published in 1919 under the title of *Preußentum und Sozialismus*. Here Spengler argued that conservatism and socialism were not irreconcilable opposites but elements of a new political synthesis that would enable Germany to overcome the fragmentation of western parliamentary democracy and the individualistic ethos of nineteenth-century liberalism. Rejecting the Marxist doctrine of class conflict along with Social Democratic demands for the expropriation of the rich and economically powerful, Spengler called upon conservatives and workers to recognize their common commitment to the creation of a new political order in which service to the state as a whole replaced economic self-aggrandizement as the basis upon which Germany's national regeneration would take place.[18] Superficial differences aside, these ideas had much in common with Moeller's

---

[15] Boehm, "Die Rechtsparteien und das Rätesystem," n.d., appended to his letter to Westarp, 17 Feb. 1919, BA Berlin, NL Westarp, 33/64-73, reprinted in Max Hildebert Boehm, *Ruf der Jungen. Eine Stimme aus dem Kreise um Moeller van den Bruck* (Freiburg im Breisgau, 1933), 66-73. See also Ulrich Prehn, *Max Hildebert Boehm. Radikales Ordnungsdenken vom Ersten Weltkrieg bis in die Bundesrepublik* (Göttingen, 2013), 134-81.

[16] On Spengler, see Clemens Vollnhals, "Praeceptor Germaniae. Spenglers politische Publizistik," in *Völkische Bewegung – Konservative Revolution – Nationalsozialismus. Aspekte einer politisierten Kultur*, ed. Walter Schmitz and Clemens Vollnhals (Dresden, 2005), 117-37.

[17] For Spengler's attempt to rescue his faith in the efficacy of human agency from the fatalism of his philosophy of world history, see Oswald Spengler, *Pessimismus?* (Berlin, 1922). In this respect, see Felix Schönherr, "Zum Menschenbild des 'Pessimismus der Stärke': Nietzsche, Spengler und die Konservative Revolution," in *Nietzsche und die Konservative Revolution*, ed. Kaufmann and Sommer, 218-30.

[18] Oswald Spengler, *Preußentum und Sozialismus* (Munich, 1922), esp. 97-99. On Spengler's political ideas, see Klemens von Klemperer, *Germany's New Conservatism: Its History and Dilemma in the Twentieth Century* (Princeton, NJ, 1957), 170-79, and

appeal for the creation of a distinctly German socialism. But Moeller rejected the underlying pessimism of Spengler's *magnum opus* and criticized its author for the almost casual way in which he had linked Germany's fate to that of the West as a whole.[19] At the heart of this dispute lay not only the personal rivalry of two extremely self-centered and ambitious men but also the fact that Moeller retained a much greater faith in the redemptive power of the "ideas of 1914" and a much greater attachment to the millenarian ethos of modernist culture than the more prosaic Spengler. Although a week-long meeting between the two men in the summer of 1920 failed to overcome the differences that separated Spengler from the June Club and its peculiar brand of revolutionary conservatism, the two parted on good terms with Spengler returning to southern Germany to function as the club's Munich liaison.[20]

For all intents and purposes, Spengler remained outside the immediate orbit of the June Club and would over the course of the next several years drift further and further away from the circle of Berlin-based intellectuals around Moeller van den Bruck. In Munich Spengler cultivated close ties to a wide range of right-wing intellectuals and politicians and became actively involved in the affairs of Bavaria's counter-revolutionary Right. Not only did he play an active role in the affairs of the Joint Committee (Gaä-Gesellschaft or Gaä) that Paul Nikolaus Coßmann and his associates had founded in late 1922 with massive support from Paul Reusch, Karl Haniel, and the Ruhr industrial establishment,[21] but he championed the cause of Georg Escherich, the onetime leader of the Bavarian civilian defense leagues, in his struggle with rivals on Bavaria's paramilitary Right.[22] In all of these endeavors Spengler was able to count upon strong financial and moral support from benefactors in the Ruhr, the most influential of whom was the Gutehoffnungshütte's Paul Reusch. Reusch was arguably the most politically active of the Ruhr industrial magnates, and in 1922 he formed a close relationship with Spengler that was to last until the latter's death in 1936.[23] As the relationship with Reusch and the Ruhr

Walter Struve, *Elites against Democracy: Leadership Ideals in Bourgeois Political Thought in Germany, 1890–1933* (Princeton, NJ, 1973), 232–73.

[19] Stern, *Politics of Cultural Despair*, 293–95.

[20] On the meeting between Moeller and Spengler, see Ringleb to Schwierskott, n.d., in Schwierskott, *Moeller van den Bruck*, 163–65, and Detlev Felken, *Oswald Spengler. Konservativer Denker zwischen Kaiserreich und Diktatur* (Munich, 1988), 135–36.

[21] Vollnhals, "Praeceptor Germaniae," 124. Karl Alexander von Müller recalls in his memoirs that Spengler delivered the main address at the Gaä's second congress in early September 1923. See Karl Alexander von Müller, *Im Wandel einer Welt. Erinnerungen 1919–1932*, ed. Otto Alexander von Müller (Munich, 1966), 120–23.

[22] On Spengler's Munich activities in the early 1920s, see Felken, *Spengler*, 134–56.

[23] For further information, see Bodo Herzog, "Die Freundschaft zwischen Oswald Spengler und Paul Reusch," in *Spengler-Studien. Festgabe für Manfred Schröter zum 65. Geburtstag*, ed. Anton Koktanek (Munich, 1965), 77–97.

industrial elite became more and more intimate, the gulf that separated him from Moeller van den Bruck and the revolutionary conservatism of the June Club became ever more pronounced.

The Ring Movement

If Moeller van den Bruck was the driving intellectual force behind the June Club, its most effective organizer was Heinrich von Gleichen. For all of his intellectual prowess, Moeller was temperamentally unsuited to take on the responsibility of organizing the young conservatives and was perfectly content to leave this to the younger Gleichen. During the last years of the war, Gleichen had served at Rathenau's recommendation as secretary of the Association of German Academics and Artists (Bund deutscher Gelehrter und Künstler), an agency created for the purpose of mobilizing Germany's intellectual elite in support of the war effort.[24] The contacts that Gleichen developed in this capacity were to prove invaluable once he turned his attention after the end of the war to the task of organizing Germany's young conservative intelligentsia. Gleichen's principal contribution in this regard was the creation of what came to be known as the Ring Movement (Ring-Bewegung). Whereas the purpose of the June Club was to forge strong and lasting ties between men of conservative political persuasion, the Ring Movement sought to extend young conservative ideas into all parts of the country and to consolidate national-minded Germans on the broadest possible basis. With the ring as a symbol of the unity it sought to forge throughout the nation as a whole, the Ring Movement aimed for a much wider audience than the June Club was ever able to reach and placed particular emphasis upon winning the support of the younger generation.[25] To enhance its public effectiveness, the Ring-Movement founded its own journal, *Das Gewissen*, in April 1919. As its name suggested, this journal functioned as the self-proclaimed "conscience of the German Right," a function it fulfilled by repeatedly remonstrating the leaders of Germany's conservative parties whenever they deviated from the young conservatives' political agenda.[26]

---

[24] Schoeps, "Herrenklub," 14–22.

[25] On the Ring Movement and its relationship to the June Club, see Moeller van den Bruck to Grimm, 10 Oct. 1919, Deutsches Literaturarchiv Marbach (hereafter cited as DLA Marbach), Nachlass Hans Grimm, A17b. See also Petzinna, *Erziehung zum deutschen Lebensstil*, 77–107, and Volker Mauersberger, *Rudolf Pechel und die "Deutsche Rundschau." Eine Studie zur konservativ-revolutionären Publizistik in der Weimarer Republik (1919–1933)* (Bremen, 1971), 46–54.

[26] For further details, see Hans-Joachim Schwierskott, "'Das Gewissen'. Ereignisse und Probleme aus den ersten Jahren der Weimarer Republik im Spiegel einer politischen Zeitschrift," in *Lebendiger Geist. Hans-Joachim Schoeps zum 50. Geburtstag von Schülern dargebracht*, ed. Hellmut Diwald (Leiden and Cologne, 1959), 161–76. On its relationship

From the outset, the Ring Movement proved remarkably successful in attracting the support of Catholic conservatives who, for the most part, had stood well outside the orbit of prewar German conservatism. None of these was more important than Eduard Stadtler, a Catholic conservative who spent his entire life in the service of one right-wing cause after another.[27] First as a Russian prisoner of war and then as an official at the German embassy in St. Petersburg, Stadtler had witnessed the collapse of the Russian Empire and the Bolshevik seizure of power at first hand. Profoundly shaken by the magnitude of these events, Stadtler was convinced that the triumph of Bolshevism in Russia marked the beginning of a world revolution that threatened to sweep the western world and its distinctly Christian culture into what Marx and Engels had disparagingly called the dustbin of history. The revolutionary wave that had begun in Russia was now at the doorsteps of the German people, whom it threatened with the same fate that had befallen Imperial Russia. All of this – and this was the underlying premise of Stadtler's subsequent political career – underscored the obsolescence of the German party system as it had evolved since the last years of the Second Empire just as it dramatized the need "to unite the productive, hard-working and intellectually vibrant elements of the entire German nation behind a leadership that has boldly broken with the old party schema in search of new political paths consistent with the spirit of the times."[28] As editor of *Das Gewissen* from 1920 until its demise in 1925 and as one of the Ring Movement's most effective public speakers, Stadtler took his appeal for the creation of a national leadership free from ties to an obsolete and ossified party system to all corners of the country and, in doing so, articulated a theme that by the end of the Weimar Republic would occupy a prominent place in the intellectual arsenal of the radical Right.[29] At the same time, Stadtler was instrumental in recruiting the support of Hugo Stinnes, Albert Vögler, and other influential industrialists for the ideals of Ring Movement and in mobilizing their economic resources for its various projects.[30]

to the June Club, see Karlheinz Weißmann, "Das 'Gewissen' und der 'Ring' – Entstehung und Entwicklung des jungkonservativen 'Zentralorgans' der Weimarer Republik," in *Konservative Zeitschriften zwischen Kaiserreich und Diktatur. Fünf Fallstudien*, ed. Hans-Christof Kraus (Berlin, 2003), 115–54, as well as Kemper, *Das "Gewissen,"* 61–169.

[27] Rüdiger Stutz, "Stetigkeit und Wandlungen in der politischen Karriere eines Rechtsextremisten. Zur Entwicklung Eduard Stadtlers von der Novemberrevolution bis 1933," *Zeitschrift für Geschichtswissenschaft* 34 (1986): 796–806. For further details, see Kemper, *Das "Gewissen,"* 121–30, 245–84.

[28] Eduard Stadtler, *Die Revolution und das alte Parteiwesen*, Revolutions-Streitfragen, no. 6 (Berlin, n.d. [1919]), 15. On Stadtler's hostility to the German party system, see Stadler to Spahn, 27 June 1919, BA Koblenz, NL Spahn, 3, as well as Eduard Stadtler, *Volkswille und Parteiwesen* (Leipzig, 1920).

[29] On Stadtler's activities on behalf of the June Club, see his letters to Spahn, 6 and 21 Oct. 1920, BA Koblenz, NL Spahn, 3.

[30] See Stadtler to Spahn, 2 and 12 Aug. 1920, BA Koblenz, NL Spahn, 3.

No less passionate in his commitment to the ideals of the Ring Movement was another Catholic intellectual, Heinz Brauweiler. A member of the Center Party before and during World War I, Brauweiler had become increasingly disenchanted with the party's sharp swing to the left following the passage of the Peace Resolution in the summer of 1917. Here he worked closely with Martin Spahn and members of the Rhenish-Westphalian aristocracy in a futile effort to return the Center to the tried and true principles that had served it so well since its founding in the 1870s.[31] By the end of 1919 Brauweiler had become convinced that the situation within the Center was indeed hopeless and that there was no realistic prospect of reversing the party's drift to the left. Over the course of the next several years Brauweiler would take part in a number of different attempts to create a new political home for Catholic conservatives like himself who found it difficult to countenance the direction in which the Center was headed.[32] In the spring of 1920 Brauweiler joined forces with Baron Hermann von Lüninck and Baron Clemens von Loë-Bergerhausen, two prominent Catholic aristocrats with extensive ties to organized agriculture in the Rhineland and Westphalia, in founding the Christian People's Party as an alternative for right-wing Catholics who had become disenchanted with the Center.[33] After a promising debut in the 1920 Reichstag elections, the CVP failed to sustain its momentum in the 1921 Prussian Landtag elections and subsequently disappeared from the political stage. Brauweiler then cooperated with Hermann von Lüninck's older brother Ferdinand in establishing the Ketteler League (Ketteler-Bund) in early May 1921 as a non-partisan association of Catholic men committed to promoting the social and political teachings of the Catholic faith through the concerted action of all those who, regardless of party affiliation, embraced these teachings as the heart and soul of their political credo.[34] Then, in the spring of 1922, Brauweiler founded the Society for Corporatist Reform (Gesellschaft für berufsständischen Aufbau) in hopes of creating a public forum for the discussion and dissemination of ideas related to Germany's search for a third way

---

[31] Brauweiler, "Vor dem Reichsparteitag," 28 Sept.–5 Oct. 1919, StA Mönchen-Gladbach, NL Brauweiler, 120. For further information on Brauweiler's activities in the early and mid-1920s, see Simon, "Brauweiler," 78–157.

[32] Brauweiler's memorandum to the members of the coordinating committee of the West German Publishers' Trust Company (Westdeutsche Verlags- und Treuhandgesellschaft), 31 Dec. 1920, VWA Münster, NL Lüninck, 709.

[33] In this respect, see Hermann von Lüninck to Count Hermann zu Stolberg-Stolberg, 26 Feb. 1920, VWA Münster, NL Hermann zu Stolberg-Stolberg, 167, and to Josef Stolberg zu Stolberg, 12 Apr. 1920, VWA Münster, NL Josef Stolberg zu Stolberg, 330.

[34] Minutes of the founding ceremonies of the Ketteler League, 3 May 1921, StA Mönchen-Gladbach, NL Brauweiler, 133. See also "Aufruf des Ketteler-Bundes," *Görres-Korrespondenz für Zentrumswähler und Zentrumspresse*, June 1921, nos. 29–30. For its objectives, see Ferdinand von Lüninck, "Zur Einführung," *Görres-Korrespondenz*, July 1921, no. 1.

between the equally idolatrous doctrines of laissez-faire capitalism and Marxist socialism.[35]

All of these projects were driven by Brauweiler's deep-seated antipathy toward the capitalist economic system and the parliamentary democracy that Germany had inherited from the November Revolution.[36] Brauweiler's projects received strong support from the more conservative elements of Germany's Catholic aristocracy, particularly in the Rhineland and Westphalia. Not only had the two Lüninck brothers played an important role in helping to found the Christian People's Party and the Ketteler League, but even those Catholic nobles like Baron Engelbert Kerckerinck zur Borg who had remained loyal to the Center sympathized with Brauweiler's efforts to define a new sense of mission for Catholic conservatives who no longer felt comfortable in the postwar Center.[37] Brauweiler's efforts paralleled those of another prominent Catholic conservative, Martin Spahn, whose defection from the Center to the DNVP in October 1921 created something of a political sensation. Spahn was a highly respected Catholic intellectual whose appointment to a chair of history at the newly founded University of Cologne in 1920 provided him with credentials that few in the young conservative movement could match.[38] From his new post in Cologne Spahn assiduously cultivated the support of the Rhenish-Westphalian aristocracy for his efforts first to reverse the direction in which the Center was headed and then, once that no longer seemed feasible, to provide those German Catholics who were no longer willing to follow the course of Erzberger and Wirth with a new sense of political mission.[39] In April 1923 Spahn was invited to speak on the problems of German foreign policy at the first of four conferences the Rhenish-Westphalian aristocracy held over the

---

[35] Minutes of the constitutive meeting of the Society for Corporatist Reform, 19 Apr. 1922, StA Mönchen-Gladbach, NL Brauweiler, 134. On agricultural and industrial support for this undertaking, see Brauweiler to Schorlemer, 26 Oct. 1921, as well as the minutes of the meeting of the Coordinating Committee of Rhenish-Westphalian Vocational Estates (Arbeitsausschuß der rheinisch-westfälischen Berufsstände), 30 Dec. 1921, StA Mönchen-Gladbach, NL Brauweiler, 120.

[36] For example, see Heinz Brauweiler, Die ständische Bewegung und die Landwirtschaft. Vortrag gehalten in der Versammlung des Bezirkverbandes Düsseldorf 2 des Rheinischen Bauernvereins (Cleve, n.d. [1921]), and Heinz Brauweiler, Berufsstand und Staat. Betrachtungen über eine neuständische Verfassung des deutschen Staates (Berlin, 1925).

[37] Kerckerinck zur Borg to Brauweiler, 25 Dec. 1921, StA Mönchen-Gladbach, NL Brauweiler, 125. For further details, see Jones, "Catholic Conservatives in the Weimar Republic," 64–68.

[38] Rudolf Morsey, "Martin Spahn (1875–1945)," in Zeitgeschichte in Lebensbildern. Aus dem deutschen Katholizismus des 19. und 20. Jahrhunderts, ed. Jürgen Aretz, Rudolf Morsey, and Anton Rauscher, vol. 4 (Mainz, 1980), 143–58.

[39] In this respect, see Spahn's correspondence with Kerckerinck zur Borg, 28 Feb. 1920–17 Mar. 1921, BA Koblenz, NL Spahn, 88.

course of the next two years in an effort to clarify its position on a wide range of issues confronting German Catholics.[40] At the same time, Spahn functioned as a liaison linking the Catholic conservatives in the Rhineland and Westphalia to the June Club and the young conservatives in Berlin who had come together in the Ring Movement. No doubt this played a major role in the selection of Spahn as director of the Ring Movement's most important project, the Political College (Politisches Kolleg).

The Political College

The Political College for National Political Training and Pedagogy was launched in November 1920 as a conservative response to the German Academy for Politics (Deutsche Hochschule für Politik) that had been founded the preceding August under ostensibly liberal auspices by Ernst Jäckh.[41] From the outset the Political College received massive support from a consortium of conservative industrialists who had originally hoped to take over the German Academy for Politics but were thwarted by the refusal of Jäckh and his associates to accept the conditions upon which they had made financing contingent. Most of the funding for the Political College came through contacts that Stadtler had cultivated with Germany's industrial elite in the early years of the June Club's existence.[42] Led by an informal triumvirate consisting of Stinnes, Vögler, and Hugenberg, the consortium raised enough money to fund at first five and then later seven full-time positions at the Political College.[43] In the meantime, Hugenberg and his associates prevailed

[40] For a summary of Spahn's speech, see the official protocol of the National Political Course for the Rhenish-Westphalian Aristocracy in Willebadessen, 23–25 Apr. 1923, VWA Münster, Nachlass Max Heereman von Zuydtwyck, Haus Surenburg, 494/37–38. An abridged version of this protocol, including Spahn's speech on foreign policy, can be found in BA Koblenz, NL Spahn, 177. Speeches from the four conferences were published in *Katholische Politik. Eine Sammlung von Vorträgen, gehalten bei Zusammenkünften des rheinisch-westfälischen Adels*, 3 vols. (Cologne, 1924–25).
[41] On the founding of the Political College, see Moeller van den Bruck to Grimm, 6 Oct. 1920, DLA Marbach, NL Grimm, A17b. On its history, see Klaus-Peter Hoepke, "Das 'Politische Kolleg'," *Mitteilungen der Technischen Universität Carlo-Wilhelmina zu Braunschweig* 11 (1976), no. 2, 20–25, and Berthold Petzinna, "Das Politische Kolleg. Konzept, Politik und Praxis einer konservativen Bildungsstätte in der Weimarer Republik," in *"Die Erziehung zum deutschen Menschen." Völkische und nationalkonservative Erwachsenenbildung in der Weimarer Republik*, ed. Paul Ciupke et al. (Essen, 2007), 101–18.
[42] On Stadtler's contacts with Stinnes and other Ruhr industrialists, see Stadtler to Spahn, 2 and 12 Aug. 1920, BA Koblenz, NL Spahn, 3.
[43] On Hugenberg's interest in the project, see Gleichen to Spahn, 21 Oct. 1919, BA Koblenz, NL Spahn, 80. For further information, see Holzbach, *Das "System Hugenberg,"* 154–66. On Vögler's support, see Freundt to Spahn, 7 Oct. 1920, BA Koblenz, NL Spahn, 194.

upon the Prussian Ministry of Culture to appoint Spahn its academic director.[44] The choice of Spahn was particularly fortuitous for a number of reasons. In the first place, the fact that Spahn was a Catholic and – for the moment at least – a member of the German Center Party lent at least a modicum of credibility to the college's claims of political nonpartisanship. Secondly, Moeller van den Bruck and the leaders of the young conservative movement readily accepted Spahn as an intellectual whose political convictions were not all that different from their own and as a man with whom they could easily cooperate.[45] Spahn's appointment as the Political College's academic director was therefore certain to enhance its legitimacy in the eyes of those in the younger generation in whom the leaders of the Ring Movement had placed their hopes. And lastly, Spahn enjoyed Hugenberg's personal confidence and was a person upon whose loyalty he felt he could count in moments of political difficulty.[46] All of this no doubt reassured Hugenberg and his associates that the Political College would remain a reliable vehicle for the intellectual legitimation of the conservative and nationalist point of view.

The goal of the Political College, as Gleichen explained in an article written for the *Deutsche Rundschau* in the spring of 1921, was to forge a new political will within that generation into whose hands history had placed the fate of the German nation. Molded by the cardinal lessons of war, collapse, and deprivation, this will stood in sharp contrast to the "impotent intellectualism" that had found such pathetic expression in the fragmentation of the German party system and the resultant dissipation of the nation's political energies. The Political College sought to overcome the spirit of partisanship that had already wrought so much havoc upon the German people by creating a new political elite emboldened by a reawakened sense of community and a heightened awareness of its responsibilities to the welfare of the nation as a whole.[47] The college's claims of nonpartisanship, however, were disingenuous and conveniently ignored the role that Hugenberg and other politicians with close ties to the right-wing DNVP had played in its establishment. To foster this sense of nonpartisanship, Spahn and his associates organized a series of courses, lectures, and seminars on a variety of topics ranging from foreign policy and the problem of German nationalities abroad to corporatism, labor unions, and the German party system.[48] The college's salaried faculty represented an impressive cross-section of

---

[44] On the circumstances of Spahn's appointment, see Grimm to Hugenberg, 16 Juli 1921, BA Koblenz, NL Hugenberg, 14/176–77.

[45] Moeller van den Bruck to Grimm, 10 Oct. 1919, DLA Marbach, NL Grimm, A17b.

[46] Clemens, *Spahn*, 151–55.

[47] Gleichen, "Das Politische Kolleg," *Deutsche Rundschau* 187, no. 7 (Apr. 1921): 104–09.

[48] Spahn, "Bericht über das Politische Kolleg, sein Amt und Tätigkeit," *Mitteilungen des Politischen Kollegs* 1, no. 2 (Dec. 1925): 14–20. See also Petzold, *Wegbereiter*, 123–24.

Germany's young conservative intelligentsia that included the likes of Glei-
chen and Moeller van den Bruck as well as lesser known figures such as
Brauweiler, Boehm, and Heinrich Herrfahrdt. The college also afforded
political activists like Stadtler or parliamentarians like the DVP's Reinhold
Quaatz and the DNVP's Otto Hoetzsch an opportunity to offer their own
courses on topics of current political interest.[49] Even the future chancellor
Heinrich Brüning, at that time Stegerwald's right-hand man in the German
Trade-Union Federation and co-author of the "Essen Program" for a reform
and reorganization of the German party system, was an occasional partici-
pant in the Political College's activities before discreetly dissociating himself
from the organization in the fall of 1923.

   That Christian labor leaders like Stegerwald and Brüning might take part in
the institute's activities was not surprising given the importance that Spahn
himself attached to winning the support of the German working class. For
Spahn the German working class represented the "keystone for the reconstruction of the German fatherland" if only it could be rescued from the
spiritual poverty of Marxist socialism and capitalist materialism.[50] In the
1920 Reichstag elections Stegerwald had vigorously supported Spahn's bid
for a place on the Center's Westphalian ticket only to meet with a cold
response from the party's district leaders.[51] Brüning too cultivated close ties
to Spahn in the early years of the Weimar Republic and had warned Spahn
against becoming too closely allied with political reactionaries like the two
Lüninck brothers for fear that he might become a pariah in the eyes of the
Christian labor movement.[52] Spahn's failure to heed Brüning's warning, however, did not prevent the latter from frequenting the June Club's familiar
haunts on the Motzstraße[53] or from incorporating its ideas on the German
party system into the "Essen Program" that Stegerwald proclaimed with such
great fanfare at the Essen congress of the Christian labor unions in the fall of
1920.[54] With the founding of the Political College that November, the leaders

[49] For example, see the *Vorlesungsverzeichnis für das Politische Kolleg e.V./Hochschule für nationale Politik* from 13 Nov. 1922–18 May 1923, records of the Politisches Kolleg, BA Koblenz, Bestand R 118, 42/27–32, and from 5 Nov. 1923–31 May 1924, ibid., 42/20–25.
[50] Martin Spahn, *Die deutsche Arbeiterschaft und der Aufbau*, Ring-Flugschriften, no. 3 (Berlin, n.d., [1920–21]), 23–24.
[51] Correspondence between Stegerwald and Brand from the Westphalian Center Party, 29 Apr.–11 May 1920, ACDP Sankt-Augustin, NL Stegerwald, I-206, 014/1–2. See also Brüning to Spahn, 30 Apr. 1920, BA Koblenz, NL Spahn, 22.
[52] Brüning to Spahn, 16 July 1920, BA Koblenz, NL Spahn, 22.
[53] For example, see Gleichen to Spahn, 11 Dec. 1920 and 10 Feb. 1921, BA Koblenz, NL Spahn, 80.
[54] Brüning's contacts with the Ring Movement and the role that its ideas played in the concept of the "Essen Program" have not received the attention they deserve. For example, see Willam L. Patch, Jr., *Heinrich Brüning and the Dissolution of the Weimar*

of the Ring Movement made a concerted effort to reach out to the leaders of the German Trade-Union Federation – and in particular to Brüning – in an attempt to determine just how far to the left they might be able to extend their movement.[55] In the summer of 1921 Gleichen worked closely with Brüning and Franz Behrens from the Central Association of Farm Laborers to put the final touches on plans for special colloquium on corporatism that the DGB was scheduled to hold the following September.[56] But relations between the Ring Movement and the DGB soured when Spahn's defection from the Center to the DNVP in early September 1921 severely compromised the movement's pretense of nonpartisanship.[57] A contributing factor may also have been Hugenberg's decision to pass over Behrens in favor of DNVP ideologue Friedrich Brunstäd as head of the Evangelical-Social Academy (Evangelisch-soziale Hochschule) that provided the Political College with the use of its physical facilities in Spandau.[58] Relations between the Ring Movement and the DGB were never again as good as they had been in the spring and summer of 1921 and continued to deteriorate over the next two years as Brüning began to distance himself from the movement's activities.[59]

In November 1922 the Political College reconstituted itself as the Academy for National Politics (Hochschule für nationale Politik) and was accorded legal status as an institute of higher learning by the German and Prussian governments. As in the case of the Political College, the Academy for National Politics continued to receive virtually all of its funding through a consortium that stood under Hugenberg's personal control. In addition to Hugenberg and Spahn, the consortium included Vögler, Quaatz, and industrialist Ernst von Borsig as well as two representatives of the Prussian DNVP – Friedrich von Winterfeld and Baron Wilhelm von Gayl – and two East Elbian landowners with close ties to the National Rural League.[60] The college's dependence upon

---

Republic (Cambridge, 1998), 24–38, and Herbert Hömig, *Brüning. Kanzler in der Krise der Republik. Eine Weimarer Biographie* (Paderborn, 2000), 72–76.

[55] Gleichen to Spahn, 2 Oct. 1920, BA Koblenz, NL Spahn, 80.

[56] Gleichen to Spahn, 27 June 1921, ibid., 80.

[57] Evers to Pechel, 10 Sept. 1921, BA Koblenz, NL Pechel, 57.

[58] On the plans for the academy, see Gleichen to Spahn, 16 July 1921, BA Koblenz, NL Spahn, 80, and Gleichen to Hugenberg, 16 July 1921, BA Koblenz, NL Hugenberg, 14/176–77, as well as Hugenberg to Vögler, 11 Oct. 1921, ibid., 49/3. On the negotiations with Behrens, see Gleichen to Hugenberg, 16 July 1921, ibid., 14/176–77, and Gleichen to Spahn, 25 Aug. 1921, BA Koblenz, NL Spahn, 80.

[59] See the correspondence between Gleichen and Brüning, 19–28 Oct. 1922, BA Koblenz, R 118, 10/32–33, as well as Brüning to Gleichen, 20 Oct. 1923, ibid., 10/31.

[60] Details on the finances of the Political College are vague. On sources of its support, see Brocker to Spahn, 22 June 1922, BA Koblenz, R 118, 35/152, and Hugenberg to Spahn, 25 Sept.–4 Oct. 1922, ibid., 36/53–56. On the involvement of Stinnes, see Moeller van den Bruck to Grimm, 6 Oct. 1920, DLA Marbach, NL Grimm, A17b. For further information, see Petzold, *Wegbereiter*, 119–23.

the financial largesse of Hugenberg and his associates, however, posed a serious threat to its integrity. Many young conservatives saw a fundamental contradiction between the revolutionary vision of those who had launched the June Club back in 1919 and the fact that not only Hugenberg but the vast majority of those who served on the consortium overseeing the Political College's financing were so-called old conservatives with close ties to vested economic interests. Many of those within the young conservative movement became increasingly concerned over the way in which representatives of established economic elites were using their control over the movement's finances to subvert the revolutionary elan of the June Club and the organizations it had spawned under the auspices of the Ring Movement. As much as Moeller van den Bruck liked to praise the newly discovered national feeling of Germany's industrial elite,[61] his movement's dependence upon Hugenberg and his associates produced a severe strain not only in relations between the June Club and the Political College but within the June Club itself.

The Fichte Society

By no means was the June Club the only center of young conservative activity in the early years of the Weimar Republic. Another organization with similar objectives but a different base of operations was the Fichte Society of 1914 (Fichte-Gesellschaft von 1914). Founded in Hamburg on 10 May 1916 by young conservative activists with close ties to the German National Union of Commercial Employees,[62] the society was conceived in the spirit of Johann Gottlieb Fichte, whose impassioned call for Germany's national rebirth during the darkest days of the Napoleonic occupation served as a model for national liberation that all Germans, regardless of social class or political affiliation, should emulate in their nation's struggle against the Allies a hundred years later.[63] Although the founders of the Fichte Society rivaled Moeller van den Bruck and the ideologues of the June Club both in the vehemence of their attacks against the bourgeois liberal order and in the intensity of their

---

[61] Moeller van den Bruck to Ziegler, 21 Jan. 1924, BA Koblenz, R 118, 34/32–33.

[62] *Aufruf zur Bildung der Fichte-Gesellschaft von 1914*, Flugblätter der Fichte Gesellschaft von 1914, no. 1 (Hamburg, 1916). On the history of the Fichte Society, see Nelson Edmondson, "The Fichte Society: A Chapter in Germany's Conservative Revolution" (Ph.D. diss., Harvard University, 1963), as well as the summary of his dissertation under the same title in the *Journal of Modern History* 38 (1966): 161–80. References to Edmondson's work are to the dissertation. Edmundson's work has since been superceded by Postert, *Von der Kritik der Parteien*, 283–332.

[63] Bruno Bauch, *Fichte und der deutsche Gedanke*, Flugschriften der Fichte-Gesellschaft von 1914, no. 4 (Hamburg, 1917). See also Edmondson, "Fichte Society," 37–53.

commitment to the cultural renewal of the German nation,[64] there were a number of subtle differences between the two movements, not the least of which was the way in which they each related to Germany's conservative economic elites. For whereas the June Club and the various organizations that had been established under the aegis of the Ring Movement were heavily dependent upon the financial largesse of Hugenberg and German heavy industry, the Fichte Society received the bulk of its financial and organizational support from the German National Union of Commercial Employees and frequently evinced an antipathy toward capitalism that in the case of the Ring Movement had been muted by its dependence upon capitalistic economic interests.[65] Secondly, the Fichte Society was much more firmly rooted in the tradition of Christian and racial, or *völkisch*, nationalism than the June Club and espoused a species of antisemitism that had been conspicuously absent from the theoretical pronouncements of Moeller van den Bruck and his associates. Although the Fichte Society did not explicitly bar Jews from membership, its appeal for the creation of a distinctly *völkisch* German culture held implications for the status of German Jewry that required little elaboration.[66]

By far and away the most important intellectual associated with the Fichte Society was Wilhelm Stapel. A prolific neo-conservative publicist perhaps best known for his book *Der christliche Staatsmann* from 1932,[67] Stapel assumed editorship of *Deutsches Volkstum* in December 1918 and worked closely with the DHV's Max Habermann in putting together a comprehensive program of political pedagogy for the Fichte Society and its affiliated organizations.[68] Born in 1882 and raised in a conservative Lutheran tradition, Stapel belonged to that generation of young conservatives who believed that revolution was necessary to cleanse Germany of the stigma of military defeat but rejected the November revolution of 1918 as a pseudo-revolution alien to the spirit of the German

---

[64] Hans Gerber, "Das Wesen und die Ziele der Fichte-Gesellschaft," in *Deutsche Volkserziehung. Zwei Vorträge über das Wollen und Wirken der Fichte-Gesellschaft* (Hamburg, n.d. [1920]), 4–23.

[65] On the DHV's social and economic philosophy, see Max Habermann, *Die neue Ordnung von Kapital und Arbeit. Vortrag gehalten auf der Tagung des Ausschusses des Deutschen Handlungsgehilfentages am 22. Mai 1921* (Hamburg, 1921), esp. 52–54. On the DHV and the founding of the Fichte Society, see Edmondson, "Fichte Society," 59–63, 92–95, and Hamel, *Völkischer Verband*, 125–35.

[66] Edmondson, "Fichte Society," 58. See also Louis Dupeux, "Der Kulturantisemitismus von Wilhelm Stapel," in *Protestantismus und Antisemitismus in der Weimarer Republik*, ed. Kurt Nowak and Gérard Raulet (Frankfurt a.M., and New York, 1998), 167–76.

[67] Wilhelm Stapel, *Der christliche Staatsmann. Eine Theologie des Nationalismus* (Hamburg, 1932).

[68] See Heinrich Kessler, *Wilhelm Stapel als politischer Publizist. Ein Beitrag zur Geschichte des konservativen Nationalismus zwischen den beiden Weltkriegen* (Nuremburg, 1967), 37–83.

people. Stapel categorically rejected any revolution that was based upon political concepts imported from abroad and insisted that any genuine revolution in Germany required a reaffirmation of those conservative values that were inseparable from the essence of the German *Volk*.[69] Such a revolution, Stapel reminded Germany's conservative elites, was not synonymous with the simple restoration of the social, economic, and political relationships that had existed in Germany before the war but involved nothing less than the spiritual rebirth of the German nation through the offices of an entirely new leadership cadre that had emancipated itself from the narrow perspective of political parties and organized economic interests.[70] It was the task of the Fichte Society to provide this new generation of political leaders with a program of political education that emphasized both the intellectual and moral components of genuine political leadership. And this, Stapel argued in a book entitled *Volksbürgerliche Erziehung* that was published with the society's imprimatur in 1920, meant restoring that vital link between the state and *Volk* that the liberalism, secularism and materialism of the nineteenth century had done so much to destroy.[71]

The Fichte Society regarded the regeneration of Germany's national culture as an essential prerequisite for the nation's recovery from the twin calamities of military defeat and social revolution. The society hoped to serve as the catalyst for Germany's cultural and national rejuvenation by endowing a new generation of conservative politicians with the moral and intellectual resources it needed to lead Germany out of the morass in which it found itself following the dual collapse of 1918. The task of educating this cadre of future conservative leaders fell to the Fichte Academy (Fichte-Hochschule), an evening school the Fichte Society had founded with the DHV's assistance in the fall of 1917 for the purpose of providing Hamburg's politically minded adults with a "scientific" approach to the study of Germany's national culture.[72] Similarly, the Fichte Society also promoted the appreciation of German classics by Goethe, Schiller, and others through the establishment of the Association for a German Stage (Verein Deutsche Bühne) in 1920.[73] In the same year the DHV also founded the Hanseatic Publishing Institute (Hanseatische Verlags-Anstalt) as a vehicle for the dissemination of the neo-conservative ideology. Not only did a close working relationship develop between the Hanseatic

[69] St. [Stapel], "Wohin geht die Fahrt?" *Deutsches Volkstum* 21, no. 1 (Jan. 1919): 1–3.

[70] Stapel, "Volk und Volkstum," in *Die neue Front*, ed. Moeller van den Bruck et al., 80–89.

[71] Wilhelm Stapel, *Volksbürgerliche Erziehung*, 2nd ed. (Hamburg, n.d. [1920]), esp. 37–109.

[72] For further details, see Emil Engelhardt, *Die Fichte-Hochschule in Hamburg. Aufbau, Verwaltung und Arbeit 1917 bis 1919*, Beiträge zur Gestaltung der Deutschen Volkshochschule, no. 2 (Hamburg, n.d. [1919]), esp. 7–35.

[73] Gerber, "Die praktische Arbeit der Fichte-Gesellschaft," in *Deutsche Volkserziehung*, 34–53.

Publishing Institute and Stapel's *Deutsches Volkstum*, but the institute also provided established neo-conservative publicists such as Hans Blüher, Ernst Jünger, and August Winnig as well as Hans Grimm, author of the enormously popular *Volk ohne Raum*, with the resources they needed to reach the largest possible audience.[74]

The leaders of the Fichte Society – and behind them those of the DHV as well – were also involved in helping Otto de le Chevallerie launch a new political academy for university students and young academics with the official name of Hochschulring deutscher Art but more commonly referred to as the German University Ring (Deutscher Hochschulring or DHR). The DHR had been founded in the summer of 1920 when student government leaders from eighteen German universities came together in Göttingen to stress the need for a reform of the German university system and to voice their opposition to the deplorable conditions in which the German fatherland found itself after World War I.[75] The DHR's purpose, as de la Chevallerie explained in his introductory remarks at a special training week for an estimated eighty DHR activists at Schloß Elgersburg in Thuringia in April 1921, was to counter the fragmentation and lack of direction of Germany's national life by forging new ties between the most promising of Germany's young academics in the hope that this would spark Germany's national rebirth and the creation of a genuine *Volksgemeinschaft* that transcended the social, economic, and political divisions within the German nation.[76] De la Chevallerie was joined on the podium by two activists from the Fichte Society, Hans Gerber and Karl Bernhard Ritter. German youth, Gerber argued, must not be drawn into the partisan political conflicts of the day and could fulfill its mission as the agent of Germany's national rebirth only by maintaining its complete independence from the existing party system.[77] Ritter, on the other hand, exhorted the new generation of German students to look past the historic divide between bourgeois and proletarian and devote itself to the creation of a *Volksgemeinschaft* that brought all segments of German society together in a

---

[74] Gary D. Stark, *Entrepreneurs of Ideology: Neoconservative Publishers in Germany, 1890–1933* (Chapel Hill, NC, 1981), 22–32.

[75] For a brief history of the DHR, see Harald Lönnecker, "Deutsche Akademikerschaft," in *Handbuch der völkischen Wissenschaften. Akteure, Netzwerke, Forschungsprogramme*, ed. Michael Fahlbusch, Ingo Haar, and Alexander Pinwinkler, 2nd ed., 2 vols. (Berlin, 2017), 2:1775–83.

[76] Otto de la Chevallerie, "Ziele und Gedanken des Deutschen Hochschulrings," in *Um deutsche Volksgemeinschaft. Die Schulungswoche des deutschen Hochschulrings auf Schloß Elgersburg in Thüringen vom 3.–9. April 1921*, ed. Kanzlei des Deutschen Hochschulrings and Deutscher Hochschulring Nachrichtenblatt, no. 4 (Erlangen, 1921), 6–9. See also Hans Ellenbeck, *Student, Volk und Staat*, Schriftenreihe des Deutschen Hochschulringes, no. 1 (n.p. [Berlin], 1926).

[77] Gerber, "Hochschulringbewegung und Jugend," in *Um deutsche Volksgemeinschaft*, 9–11.

celebration of national unity inspired by the idealism and sacrifice of German youth.[78] While the DHR professed complete neutrality toward the various parties that dotted the political landscape of the Weimar Republic, its attitude toward the German party system was actually more one of disdain than neutrality. To the leaders of the DHR, political parties were simply manifestations of the increasingly powerful role that the masses had come to play in the life of the modern state and stood in sharp contrast to the elitism that was part and parcel of its political identity.[79]

Like the DHR, the Fichte Society remained committed to the political education of a new German elite and to preparing it for the political and intellectual leadership of the German nation. It was with this in mind that Gerber and a fellow Fichte Society activist Frank Glatzel drafted an elaborate proposal for the creation of a new institute tentatively entitled the Leadership Academy for German Politics (Führer-Schule für deutsche Politik) for the education of Germany's political elite. Like Gerber, Glatzel had been active in the German youth movement before the war, and they joined forces with Stapel to launch the Young German League (Jungdeutscher Bund) under the auspices of the Fichte Society at Burg Lauenstein in August 1919.[80] But while Glatzel belonged to the DNVP and in fact addressed the party's Hanover national party congress in October 1920 on the task of winning the support of the younger generation,[81] Gerber warned against becoming too closely associated with any political party and advocated instead the creation of a national community that embraced the best elements of all the parties from the Democrats to the Nationalists.[82] Whatever differences that might have separated them on this particular issue, however, were completely overshadowed by their shared antipathy toward the capitalistic economic system and their concern about the effects that the unrestrained pursuit of profit had upon the social and moral fabric of Germany's national character. In their proposal for the establishment of a Leadership Academy for German Politics, Gerber and Glatzel stressed the need for a new cadre of political leaders uncorrupted

---

[78] Ritter, "Die Not unserer Zeit und unsere Aufgaben," ibid., 11–15.

[79] Lölhöffel, "Politisches Parteiwesen," ibid., 22–26.

[80] See Frank Glatzel, "Der Jungdeutsche Bund," and Hans Gerber, "Nationale Pflichten," in *Jungdeutsches Wollen. Vorträge gehalten auf der Gründungstagung des Jungdeutschen Bundes auf Burg Lauenstein vom 9.–12. August 1919*, ed. Bundesamt des Jungdeutschen Bundes (Hamburg, 1920), 11–55. See also Glatzel, "Die deutsche Jugendbewegung," in *Deutsche Volkserziehung*, 23–34. For further details, see Edmondson, "Fichte Society," 130–43, and Postert, *Von der Kritik der Parteien*, 324–27.

[81] Speech by Glatzel at the DNVP Hanover party congress, 25 Oct. 1920, BA Berlin, R 8005, 53/332–34.

[82] Hans Gerber, "Nationale Sozialpolitik" (June 1920), in idem, *Auf dem Wege zum neuen Reiche. Eine Sammlung politischer Vorträge und Aufsätze aus deutscher Notzeit 1919-1931* (Stuttgart and Berlin, 1934), 26–36.

by the partisanship, factionalism, and materialistic pursuit of self-interest that had come to define modern political life. To accomplish this, it was necessary not only to educate this elite in the techniques of modern politics but, more importantly, to instill in it the selflessness, love of nation, and devotion to the *Volksgemeinschaft* embodied in the social and political teachings of the Fichte Society.[83]

Given the similarity in their goals and ideological orientation, the leaders of the June Club moved quickly to establish a cooperative relationship with the Fichte Society so as to avoid competing with each other for funding and resources. Gerber and Glatzel met with representatives from the June Club on at least two occasions in the winter of 1920–21, but were fearful that the latter might be falling too heavily under the influence of social reactionaries in the DNVP and chose to keep their distance.[84] Eventually Gleichen succeeded in forging a loose tie between the two groups through the appointment of the Ring Movement's Johann Wilhelm Mannhardt as a liaison to the inner councils of both the June Club and the Fichte Society.[85] Even then, the Fichte Society's plans for a special leadership academy cut across those that the leaders of the Ring Movement had for the future of the Political College, with the result that the two organizations were frequently competing with each other for the limited resources that Germany's industrial establishment had available for projects of this nature.[86] As Rudolf Blohm, the director of the Blohm and Voß ship construction firm who had agreed to take on the responsibility of raising funds for the proposed political academy, soon discovered, it was not uncommon for prospective benefactors to decline to take part in funding the Fichte Society's Leadership Academy for German Politics on the grounds that their resources were already committed elsewhere.[87] As it became increasingly clear toward the end of 1921 that Blohm and Gerber had not been able to develop the resources necessary to secure the financial independence of the proposed leadership academy in Hamburg,[88] the Fichte Society severed all legal ties to the project and entered into an arrangement with the German Bourse in Marburg (Deutsche Burse zu Marburg) whereby

---

[83] Gerber and Glatzel, "Denkschrift über die Errichtung einer Führer-Schule für deutsche Politik durch die Fichte-Stiftung in Hamburg," n.d. [1921], StA Hamburg, Blohm und Voß GmbH, 1206.

[84] Gleichen to Spahn, 11 Dec. 1920, BA Koblenz, NL Spahn, 80, and Stadtler to Spahn, 26 Feb. 1921, ibid., 3.

[85] Petzinna, *Erziehung zum deutschen Lebensstil*, 156.

[86] Sorge to Blohm, 6 Oct. 1921, StA Hamburg, Blohm und Voß GmbH, 1206.

[87] For example, see Hugenberg to Blohm, 25 Aug. 1921, and Duisberg to Blohm, 29 Aug. 1921, both in StA Hamburg, Blohm und Voß GmbH, 1206. On the sources of this support, see Blohm to Gerber, 8 Oct. and 10 Dec. 1921, ibid.

[88] Blohm's report of a conversation with Hugenberg in his letter to Gerber, 22 Nov. 1921, StA Hamburg, Blohm and Voß GmbH, 1206.

the latter would house the academy in its Marburg facilities with Gerber serving as its director.[89]

The move to Marburg removed the Leadership Academy for German Politics from the immediate proximity and influence of the Fichte Society and thus provided it with easier access to the resources of conservative industrialists like the Gutehoffnungshütte's Paul Resuch.[90] Although this represented something of a setback to the leaders of the Fichte Society, they continued to support the academy and covered approximately 20 percent of the academy's operating budget for 1922.[91] In the meantime, Habermann and the leaders of the DHV continued to stress their commitment to the principle of political pedagogy as emphatically as possible.[92] From their perspective, the major problem plaguing the German Right in the postwar era was the lack of ideological clarity within the ranks of Germany's conservative elite. To help rectify this situation, the Fichte Society convened the first Conference for German National Education (Tagung für Deutsche Nationalerziehung) in Hamburg in the first week of October 1924.[93] Devoted to the topic of "*Volkstum* and state," the conference sought, as Stapel himself stressed, not just to give form and substance to a specifically German concept of the state derived from the teachings of Luther, Fichte, Kant, and Hegel, but also to explore the ways in which this concept might be translated into practical reality as a corrective to "a monstrous German formlessness" that left him deeply pessimistic about Germany's political future.[94] Two years later the society convened its second Conference on German National Education, this time on the theme of Christianity and national education with keynote addresses and commentary by prominent representatives of both the Catholic and Lutheran faiths as a first step toward healing the confessional cleavages that had become so deeply embedded in the fabric of Germany's national life.[95]

---

[89] Gerber to Blohm, 11 Jan. 1922, StA Hamburg, Blohm und Voß GmbH, 1206.

[90] See the correspondence between Reusch and Hugenberg, 24–26 July 1922, RWWA Cologne, Abt. 130, NL Reusch, 30019390/17.

[91] Fichte Schule (Marburg), "Bericht über das 1. Geschäftsjahr 1922," 2 Jan. 1923, StA Hamburg, Blohm und Voß GmbH, 1206.

[92] For example, see Max Habermann, *Die Erziehung zum deutschen Menschen. Einführung in die Bildungsarbeit des Deutschnationalen Handlungsgehilfen-Verbandes. Vortrag gehalten auf dessen 19. Verbandstag am 28. Juni 1924 in Königsberg* (Hamburg, 1924).

[93] Georg Kleibömer, "Erste Tagung für deutsche Nationalerziehung," *Mitteilungsblatt der Fichte-Gesellschaft e.V., Nov. 1924* (Hamburg, n.d. [1924]), 1–3.

[94] Wilhelm Stapel, "Deutsche Nationalerziehung," in *Volkstum und Staat. Die Verhandlungen der Ersten Tagung für deutsche Nationalerziehung, veranstaltet von der Fichte-Gesellschaft in Hamburg vom 3. bis 5. Oktober 1924* (Hamburg, n.d. [1924]), 27–31, 37. For further details, see Edmondson, "Fichte Society," 118–30.

[95] See in particular the lectures by Ritter, Getzeny, and Althaus, in *Christentum und Nationalerziehung. Vorträge und Aussprache der 2. Tagung für deutsche Nationalerziehung, von der*

The Great Caesura: 1923

As the Fichte Society braced itself for a sustained assault against the Weimar state in the second half of the 1920s, the situation within the June Club continued to deteriorate throughout the course of 1923.[96] At no point was the internal dissolution of the June Club more apparent than in the events surrounding the infamous Munich beer hall putsch at the beginning of November. As the authority of the Reich began to crumble with the occupation of the Ruhr and the collapse of the German currency, Gleichen traveled to Munich in the spring of 1923, where he met with Escherich and the leaders of the Bavarian patriotic movement in an attempt to lay the foundation for a right-wing putsch that, if successful in Munich, would be followed by a similar strike in Berlin.[97] When these plans failed to materialize, Stadtler traveled to Munich in the fall of 1923 to meet with Spengler, the nominal leader of the local June Club whose fame in right-wing circles was exceeded only by that of Moeller van den Bruck. Stadtler had come to plead his case for the creation of a three-man dictatorship consisting of Escherich in Munich, Seeckt in Berlin, and Stinnes in the Ruhr, but his initiative evoked little enthusiasm on the part of those whom he had hoped to impress.[98] As self-appointed emissaries from the Berlin June Club, Gleichen and Stadtler did their best to encourage the counterrevolutionary fantasies of some of the most reactionary elements in Bavarian political life.

At the heart of the counterrevolutionary cabal in Munich stood Oswald Spengler. Not only had Spengler developed close ties with Escherich and Bavaria's paramilitary Right,[99] but he actively supported the efforts of the Gutehoffnungshütte's Paul Reusch and other conservative industrialists to gain a controlling interest over Bavaria's right-wing press through the creation of the Joint Committee in late 1922.[100] As the crisis in Reich-Bavarian relations drew to a climax in the fall of 1923, Spengler admonished Reusch to mobilize the opposition of German industry to Stresemann and his policy of

---

Fichte-Gesellschaft veranstaltet in Halle am 5. und 6. März 1926 (Hamburg, n.d. [1926]), 7–51.

[96] See Pechel to Stolberg, 27 Oct. 1923, BA Koblenz, NL Pechel, 144. For further details, see Petzinna, *Erziehung zum deutschen Menschen*, 138–42.

[97] Spengler to Pechel, 7. Oct 1923, BA Koblenz, NL Pechel, 144. For further details, see Petzold, *Wegbereiter*, 140–49; Postert, *Von der Kritik der Parteien*, 134–40; and Maurensberger, *Pechel und die "Deutsche Rundschau,"* 40–41.

[98] See Pechel's account of these developments in an undated memorandum attached to his letter to Spengler, 12 Sept. 1923, BA Koblenz, NL Pechel, 144.

[99] Correspondence between Spengler and Escherich, 21 Sept.–30 Oct. 1922, in Oswald Spengler, *Briefe 1913–1936*, ed. Anton Koktanek (Munich, 1963), 214–23.

[100] Fur further details, see Paul Hoser, "Ein Philosoph im Irrgarten der Politik. Oswald Spenglers Pläne für eine geheime Lenkung der nationalen Presse," *Vierteljahrshefte für Zeitgeschichte* 38 (1990): 435–58.

weakness and compromise.[101] At the same time, he implored the DVP's Quaatz to do everything in his power to bring about the fall of the Stresemann cabinet for fear that otherwise Kahr and his supporters would not be able to stave off the radicals around Hitler and Ludendorff.[102] But Spengler quickly found himself swept up in the events of the day without a viable response to the crisis unfolding before his very eyes. Originally he had supported the creation of a national dictatorship under Seeckt but had become increasingly critical of the general's lack of resolve and had lost faith in his ability to lead Germany out of the crisis in which it found itself trapped.[103]

Spengler and the leaders of the Munich June Club were caught off-guard by the events of 8-9 November 1923. For even though the June Club's most resolute opponents of Germany's republican system were quick to dissociate themselves from Hitler's Munich folly,[104] it was also clear that whatever hopes they may have had for the overthrow of the existing political system had been irrevocably shattered. The effect of these developments on the June Club was disastrous. Not only did Gleichen and Stadtler come under heavy fire for their involvement in the series of events that had led up to Hitler's abortive coup,[105] but Rudolf Pechel, editor of the influential *Deutsche Rundschau* and former chairman of the Berlin June Club, was so embarrassed by the disrepute into which Gleichen and Stadtler had brought the young conservative movement that he and a number of his associates resigned from the club.[106] But the greatest casualty was Spengler himself. For although Spengler tried to salvage his reputation with a speech before student sympathizers in Würzburg in which he rejected a politics of intoxication and called upon his audience to substitute the hard study of politics for the "colors and insignia, the music and parades, the theatrical vows and amateurish appeals and theories" of the so-called national movement,[107] he had so thoroughly discredited himself by his antics in the summer and fall of 1923 that he could no longer be taken seriously as an agent of the political Right.[108] By the same token, Moeller van den Bruck tried to rehabilitate the June Club's political reputation by dissociating himself from Hitler's dilettantism, though without disclaiming

---

[101] Spengler to Reusch, 17 Aug. 1923, in Spengler, *Briefe*, ed. Koktanek, 260.

[102] Spengler to Quaatz, 30 Oct. 1923, ibid., 282-83.

[103] For further details, see Felken, *Spengler*, 141-52. For a defense of his role in these developments, see Spengler to Cossmann, 1 Dec. 1923, BHStA Munich, Abt. V, Nachlass Paul Nicholas Cossmann, 6.

[104] Moeller van den Bruck to Grimm, 10 Mar. 1924, DLA Marbach, NL Grimm, A17b.

[105] Pechel to Stolberg-Wernigerode, 27 Oct. 1923, BA Koblenz, NL Pechel, 144.

[106] Pechel to Spengler, 19 Nov. 1923, BA Koblenz, NL Pechel, 144. For further details, see Mauersberger, *Pechel und die "Deutsche Rundschau,"* 39-41.

[107] Oswald Spengler, *Politische Pflichten der deutschen Jugend. Rede gehalten am 26. Februar vor dem Hochschulring deutscher Art in Würzburg* (Munich, 1924), 21-25.

[108] Felken, *Spengler*, 152-56.

authorship of much of what the Nazis supposedly stood for.[109] But Moeller, whose own animus toward Hitler stemmed in no small measure from his fear that the Nazi party leader might appropriate the title of the book he had published on the eve of the Munich putsch – *Das Dritte Reich* – for his own political purposes, was a sick and exhausted man whose energy and emotional reserves were quickly running dry.[110] In the fall of 1924 Moeller suffered a nervous breakdown, and the following May he committed suicide at a sanatarium in the outskirts of Berlin where, it was hoped, he might recover from the deep depression that had descended upon him. For a man who had supposedly once said that he would rather commit suicide than see Hitler abuse his concept of the Third Reich,[111] Moeller's death had a peculiarly prophetic quality to it.

By the time that Moeller van den Bruck died in the spring of 1925, the June Club had ceased to exist. Not only had the collapse of the Munich putsch done much to exacerbate divisions at the upper echelons of the club's leadership, but the despair and emotional turmoil that afflicted Moeller in the aftermath of the Munich fiasco robbed the club of its most dynamic and highly regarded intellectual spokesman. The club's isolation was compounded by the resentment that many of its members – and particularly those who stressed the nonpartisan character of their movement – felt about the way in which Spahn and Hugenberg had supposedly transformed the Political College into an instrument of the Germany's economic elites.[112] In the meantime, the movement's financial backers had begun to cut back on their subsidies to the Political College and the Ring Publishing House (Ring-Verlag) as a result of the economic difficulties they had experienced in the wake of Germany's fiscal and economic stabilization.[113] All of this placed the future of the June Club in such serious doubt that an emergency meeting of the club's national membership to determine whether or not the club should be dissolved was set for

---

[109] For Moeller's response to these developments, see his letter to Grimm, 27 Nov. 1923, DLA Marbach, NL Grimm, 17b.

[110] For conflicting interpretations of Moeller's assessment of Hitler in the aftermath of the Munich putsch, see Schwierskott, *Moeller van den Bruck*, 145–46, and Petzold, *Wegbereiter*, 160–61.

[111] Klemperer, *Germany's New Conservatism*, 193–94. At Gleichen's invitation, Moeller and several other members of the June Club apparently met with Hitler in June 1921. See Gleichen to Stadtler, Boehm, Moeller van den Bruck, and Evers, 30 May 1921, BA Koblenz, NL Pechel, 144. According to Pechel, Moeller was impressed neither by Hitler's tirades against the existing political system nor by his praise for the June Club's political and intellectual format. The meeting has been generally dismissed as a failure by all of those who have left any record of it. See also Rudolf Pechel, *Deutscher Widerstand* (Erlenbach-Zurich), 277–80.

[112] For example, see Spahn's reaction to this line of criticism in his letter to Schürholz, 21 Jan. 1924, BA Koblenz, R 118, 34/32.

[113] For example, see Spahn to Gleichen, 25 June 1924, BA Koblenz, R 118, 35/92.

23 April 1924.[114] The meeting generated a heated and indeed embittered debate over the future of the young conservative movement but produced no consensus as to what the club should do.[115] Much of the uncertainty surrounding the club's fate was related to plans on the part of Gleichen and Walther Schotte to transform it into a sort of gentlemen's salon that would serve as a meeting place for Germany's social and economic elites.[116] These plans encountered strong resistance not only from Moeller, who argued that this would deliver the young conservative movement into the hands of Germany's prewar conservative elites,[117] but also from Spahn, who complained that he and his colleagues at the Political College would have a difficult time defending their involvement with such a costly and socially ostentatious club at a time of general economic distress.[118] The June Club languished on the periphery of Germany's conservative establishment without any clear idea of where it was headed until it quietly disappeared from the political scene in the summer of 1924.

The German Gentlemen's Club

Neither the demise of the June Club nor the criticism of Moeller van den Bruck and Spahn could deter Gleichen and Schotte from their plans for the creation of a salon that would serve as a place where representatives of Germany's highest social strata could meet on a regular and informal basis. After extensive negotiations with potential financial backers in the late spring and summer of 1924,[119] Gleichen and his associates capped their efforts with the official founding of the German Gentlemen's Club (Deutscher Herrenklub or DHK) in Berlin's fashionable Hotel Bristol on 12 December 1924.[120] Although the Gentlemen's Club regarded itself as the heir to the young conservative legacy of the June Club, it differed from its predecessor in both its ideological profile and social composition. For whereas the June Club had been founded by avowed conservative revolutionaries who sought to translate the egalitarian spirit of August 1914 into political reality, the Gentlemen's

---

[114] Invitation of 15 Apr. 1924 to an extraordinary meeting of the June Club membership on 23 Apr. 1924, BA Koblenz, R 118, 12/29.

[115] Memorandum to the members of the June Club, 2 May 1924, BA Koblenz, NL Pechel, 144.

[116] Gleichen to Spahn, 16 and 30 Apr. 1924, BA Koblenz, R 118, 35/102, 98–99.

[117] Schwierskott, *Moeller van den Bruck*, 72.

[118] Spahn to Gleichen, 14 Apr. 1924, BA Koblenz, R 118, 35/103.

[119] See Gleichen's memorandum for Spahn, 30 Apr. 1924, BA Koblenz, R 118, 35/98–99.

[120] On the DHK, see Schoeps, "Herrenklub," as well as Petzold, *Wegbereiter*, 175–82; Petzinna, *Erziehung zum deutschen Lebensstil*, 220–30; Yuji Ishida, *Jungkonservative in der Weimarer Republik. Der Ring-Kreis 1928–1933* (Frankfurt am Main, 1988), 55–77; and Postert, *Von der Kritik der Parteien*, 144–88.

Club became the preserve of political reactionaries who sought to reestablish the social and political hegemony of Germany's prewar conservative elites. The demise of the June Club and the founding of the Gentlemen's Club thus revealed a fundamental shift from the revolutionary to the restorative strain of German conservatism.[121] This shift in emphasis was further reflected in the differences between the social composition of the two organizations. For if the June Club had recruited the bulk of its members from the ranks of Germany's young conservative intelligentsia without regard for their social pedigree, the Gentlemen's Club restricted its membership to socially and politically influential representatives of Germany's conservative elites and served in particular as a magnet for disaffected aristocrats determined to rid Germany of the hated Weimar regime and, in so far as it was still possible, to restore the hegemonic relations of the old imperial order.[122]

In a larger sense, the dissolution of the June Club and the eclipse of its peculiar brand of revolutionary conservatism corresponded to a fundamental change in Germany's political environment that obliged Germany's conservative elites to develop new strategies in their bid for political power. If nothing else, the collapse of the Munich putsch meant that attempts to gain power by revolutionary means stood little, if any, chance of success. Moreover, the defeat of the insurrection in Munich was part of a process of political and economic stabilization that was to continue in Germany until the outbreak of the world economic crisis at the very end of the 1920s. While all of this may have recommended a more accommodationist strategy on the part of Germany's conservative elites, Gleichen and the leaders of the Gentlemen's Club remained implacably opposed to the democratic ethos of the Weimar Republic and worked in close concert with those in the DNVP who sought to return the party to the path of unconditional opposition. The Gentlemen's Club saw itself as a forum where representatives of Germany's conservative elites in government, industry, agriculture, and academe could meet on a purely social basis and thus forge a sense of social solidarity that overrode the material concerns that frequently divided them. Its professed goal remained the rebirth of the German nation through a return to tried and true conservative principles and

[121] See the bitter criticism of this development in Grimm to Gleichen, 12 Jan. 1925, as well as Gleichen's response to Grimm, 3 Mar. 1925, both in DLA Marbach, NL Grimm, A17b.
[122] For examples of the DHK's unabashed elitism, see Heinrich von Gleichen, "Adel eine politische Forderung," *Preußische Jahrbücher* 197, no. 2 (July–Sept. 1924): 131–45, and Heinrich von Gleichen, "Oberschicht und Nation," in *Die Einheit der Nationalen Politik*, ed. Alfred Bozi and Alfred Niemann (Stuttgart, 1925), 233–49. See also Stephan Malinowski, "'Führertum' und 'neuer Adel'. Die Deutsche Adelsgenossenschaft und der Deutsche Herrenklub in der Weimarer Republik," in *Adel und Bürgertum in Deutschland II. Entwicklungslinien und Wendepunkte im 20. Jahrhundert* (Berlin, 2001), 173–211, esp. 197–211.

to promote this objective not by holding demonstrations or taking public stands on the issues of the day but by facilitating closer social contacts between those who, regardless of social background or party affiliation, subscribed to a conservative philosophy of the state.[123] At the same time, the DHK and its affiliated organizations waged an unrelenting struggle against the terms upon which Germany's economic and political stabilization in the second half of the 1920s had taken place. The young conservatives were united in their contempt for the political system that Germany had inherited from the November Revolution and in their determination to free the state from the grip of those party bosses who had handed it over to special economic interests, most notably organized labor.

The young conservatives from Moeller van den Bruck, Brauweiler, and Stapel to Gleichen, Stadtler, and Spahn played a decisive role in depriving the Weimar system of the moral and intellectual legitimacy it needed to transform the political and economic stabilization of the mid-1920s into a permanent state of affairs. In the war of position that characterized German political life in the second half of the 1920s, the "treason of the clerks" – to use the famous phrase of Julian Benda – not only dealt a critical blow to Weimar's chances of survival but sowed the seeds of something ultimately far more ominous. Yet for all of the success they may have enjoyed in delegitimizing Germany's experiment in democracy at that point in time when it seemed that the Weimar Republic had recovered from the trauma of its birth and was on its way to achieving some measure of stability, the young conservatives proved incapable of translating their vision of the German future into political reality. At the heart of their problem lay not just their unabashed elitism but also their refusal to recognize the political concomitants of the social, economic, and cultural modernization that Germany had experienced since the middle of the previous century. In this respect, the young conservatives remained something of a curious anachronism that mirrored the longings of all too many Germans but whose grasp of practical politics was too limited for them to give form and content to those longings.

---

[123] "Richtlinien für den Deutschherrenklub," 11 Nov. 1924, BA Koblenz, R 118, 35/62.

10

A Resurgent Nationalism

The eighteen months between the collapse of the Munich beer hall putsch and Hindenburg's election as Reich president had a profound impact upon the organizations that formed the backbone of Germany's patriotic and paramilitary movement. Most of these organizations had been severely compromised if not by their actual involvement in the preparations for the putsch, then certainly by their sympathy for the aspirations of the putschists. The leaders of Germany's three largest patriotic organizations – the Stahlhelm, the Young German Order, and the United Patriotic Leagues – all seemed disoriented by this turn of events and were slow to formulate a strategy for dealing with the new political realities created by Weimar's economic and political stabilization. To the more prescient of Germany's paramilitary leaders, it seemed not only that they had squandered a rare opportunity to overthrow the hated Weimar system but also that the revolutionary tide that had descended upon Germany after the end of the great war had crested and entered a second and less violent phase in which the forces of bourgeois capitalism had supplanted the revolutionary Left as the dominant force in German political life.[1]

Germany's patriotic and paramilitary Right would demonstrate remarkable resilience in rebounding from the malaise that gripped it in the immediate aftermath of the Munich fiasco. The revival of the so-called national movement in the second half of the 1920s was directed in large part against the role that conservative economic interests had played in the economic and political stabilization of the Weimar Republic. The architects of this revival sought not only to free the German state from the tyranny of special economic interests but also to reassert the primacy of the political and national moment in German public life over the purely economic. In this respect, they drew much of their inspiration from the revolutionary conservatism of the early 1920s and articulated their political strategy in the idiom of what Ernst Jünger and other right-wing intellectuals hailed as the "new nationalism." This strain of nationalist thought stood in sharp contrast to the crass materialism of the liberal

---

[1] See the particularly revealing analysis from the Stahlhelm's Franke to Tirpitz, 4 June 1924, appended to Franke to Stresemann, 25 June 1924, PA AA Berlin, NL Stresemann, 10/ 156049–64.

epoch and sought to supplant the alliance that had developed between liberalism and nationalism in the nineteenth century with a new alliance between
nationalism and revolutionary conservatism. In doing so, the champions of
the new nationalism sought to invoke a sense of national feeling so powerful in
terms of its emotional appeal that it would override the social, political, and
economic cleavages that had become so deeply entrenched within the German
nation.[2]

The Quest for Right-Wing Unity

Of all the problems that faced the leaders of the patriotic Right in the second
half of the 1920s, none was more pressing than that of restoring the unity of
the patriotic movement. Not only had the Munich fiasco produced widespread
confusion within the ranks of the patriotic movement, but the struggle over
the Dawes Plan had driven a wedge between those who belonged to the DVP
and tacitly supported the basic principles of Stresemann's foreign policy and
those who belonged to the DNVP and remained irreconcilably opposed to any
form of collaboration with the existing system of government. In an attempt to
heal these divisions and repair the damage the Nationalist split on the Dawes
Plan had done to the unity of the German Right, Baron Wilhelm von Gayl
from the DNVP invited representatives from the Stahlhelm, Young German
Order, and United Patriotic Leagues to a series of meetings in the fall and
winter of 1924.[3] These negotiations drew to a preliminary climax on 28 January
1925, when the leaders of the Stahlhelm, the Young German Order, the
National Federation of German Professional Unions (Nationalverband
Deutscher Berufsverbände or NDB), and a handful of delegates supposedly
representing the Christian labor movement formed an alliance known simply
as the National Committee (Nationalausschuß) with a central office in Berlin
under the direction of the NBD's Fritz Geisler. By uniting Germany's two
largest paramilitary organizations and the "yellow" labor unions under the
aegis of the National Committee, Geisler hoped to provide the United Patriotic
Leagues, an organization he had headed since its establishment in 1922, with
the mass following it needed if it was ever to have a measurable effect upon the
course of developments in Berlin.[4]

---

[2] For a brief overview, see Stefan Breuer, "Neuer Nationalismus in Deutschland," in
Rechtsextreme Ideologien in Geschichte und Gegenwart, ed. Uwe Backes (Cologne,
Weimar, and Vienna, 2003), 53–72.

[3] Gayl's handwritten memoir on his relations with the paramilitary combat leagues from the
spring of 1923 to the 1925 presidential elections, n.d., BA Koblenz, NL Gayl, 4/17–29.

[4] Geisler to the patriotic leagues and their supporters, 4 Feb. 1925, BA Koblenz, NL Pechel,
144, also in BHStA Munich, EWB, 10/2.

Geisler's experiment in right-wing unity proved short-lived for several reasons. First of all, the leaders of the United Patriotic Leagues were suspicious of Geisler's intentions and criticized the way in which he had identified the VVVD with the agenda of the "yellow" labor movement. As a result, Geisler was obliged to resign from the VVVD presidium – he had already stepped down as the organization's national chairman – after a particularly heated meeting of VVVD representatives from throughout the country on 12 February.[5] With the subsequent election of former army officer Count Rüdiger von der Goltz as Geisler's successor, the VVVD fell under the influence of unreconstructed reactionaries with close ties to the Prussian military, East Elbian aristocracy, and the Hohenzollern court. In so far as they had a program of their own, those now in control of the VVVD were committed to little more than restoring things to the way they had been before the war. This, along with the VVVD's close ties to the Pan-German League and "yellow" trade-union movement, did much discredit the VVVD in the eyes of both the Stahlhelm and Young German Order and blocked any further movement in the direction of closer cooperation between the three organizations.[6] In point of fact, the VVVD remained little more than a loose federation of organizations representing a very narrow stratum of German society and commanding little in the way of direct popular support. Although the occupation of the Ruhr and the crisis of Germany's republican institutions throughout the course of 1923 had done much to enhance the VVVD's political profile, the niche that it had hoped to carve out for itself on the German Right was ultimately usurped by an entirely new type of political organization, the paramilitary combat league or *Kampfbund*. Unable to match the dynamism of numerically stronger and more tightly organized paramilitary combat leagues like the Stahlhelm and Young German Order, the VVVD found itself relegated more and more to the periphery of the German Right and entered a period of relative eclipse that was to continue for the remainder of the decade.[7]

In a parallel effort, the leaders of the Ring Movement also tried to foster a greater sense of unity among the various organizations on the German Right. Less than a month after the fateful split in the Nationalist vote on the Dawes Plan, more than forty representatives of various right-wing organizations,

---

[5] For Geisler's account of these developments, see his letter to the VVVD presidium, 19 Feb. 1925, BA Koblenz, NL Jarres, 36/51–55. See also the circular from the VVVD to the patriotic leagues and sympathizers, 14 Feb. 1925, BHStA Munich, Abt. IV, EWB, 10/2, as well as the police report on the VVVD, n.d., appended to Geisler to Westarp, 19 Jan. 1925, NL Westarp, Gärtringen, VN 97.

[6] Frank Glatzel, "Wehrverbände und Politik," in *Politische Praxis 1926*, ed. Walther Lambach (Hamburg, n.d. [1926]), 322. See also Laudahn, "V.V.V.D.," *Der Meister. Jungdeutsche Monatsschrift für Führer und denkende Brüder* 1, no. 9 (July 1926): 19–22.

[7] For further details, see Weiß to Westarp, 6 Dec. 1924, NL Westarp, Gärtringen, VN 44. See also Diehl, "Von der 'Vaterlandspartei' zur 'nationalen Revolution'," 617–39.

including the VVVD and the German Industrial Association, met in Berlin's Hotel Continental at the invitation of the Stahlhelm's Theodor Duesterberg, the Ring Movement's Bodo von Alvensleben, and the DNVP's Friedrich von Zitzewitz-Kottow. The purpose of the meeting was to map out a strategy that would enable the right wing of the DNVP to regain control of the party and return it to the path of unconditional opposition to the Weimar Republic that had served it so well in the period before 1924. The meeting concluded with the formation of a political action committee that sought to reverse the direction in which the DNVP was currently headed by bringing members of the DNVP Reichstag delegation and other influential party leaders together with representatives of the patriotic leagues, the Ring Movement, the German Industrial Association, and the prewar German Conservative Party.[8] This committee met for the first time on 7 October 1924 and was immediately expanded to twenty-five members, including a seven-man contingent from the DNVP Reichstag delegation headed by Westarp. While the ostensible purpose of this committee was to help the DNVP's right wing regain control of the party,[9] the task of developing a broader base of support for conservative principles outside the DNVP was assigned to Heinrich von Gleichen and the leaders of the Ring Movement.[10] It was in this spirit that Gleichen and the leaders of the German Gentlemen's Club staged a rally in Berlin on 21–22 February 1925 for members and associates of the various organizations that were affiliated with the Ring Movement.[11] The principal speakers – Heinz Brauweiler, Gustav Roethe, Walther Schotte, Martin Spahn, and Eduard Stadtler – all came from the ranks of Germany's young conservative intelligentsia and made a concerted effort to articulate the ideological foundations upon which the unification of the German Right should take place with lectures on such topics as the national movement, constitutional reform, and the struggle for the state.[12]

Neither the creation of the National Committee nor the Ring Movement's rally in Berlin succeeded in generating the emotional elan it would have taken

---

[8] Circular from the Mittelstelle des Ringes, 17 Sept. 1924, appended to the letter from Gleichen to Schmidt-Hannover, 17 Sept. 1924, BA Koblenz, NL Schmidt-Hannover, 33. See also Brauer to Westarp, 19 Sept. 1924, NL Westarp, Gärtringen, VN 46.

[9] This was implicit in the circular from the Mittelstelle des Ringes, 28 Jan. 1925, NL Westarp, Gärtringen, VN 97.

[10] Circular from the Mittelstelle des Ringes, 14 Oct. 1924, BA Koblenz, NL Schmidt-Hannover, 33. See also Gleichen to Spahn, 10 Oct. 1924, BA Koblenz, R 118, 35/76.

[11] Rosenberger, invitation to the Ring-Tagung, Feb. 1925, BA Berlin, NL Hepp, 4/80.

[12] On the rally in Berlin, see "Bericht über die Ring-Tagung 21. und 22. Februar 1925 im Herrenhaus in Berlin," in the circular from the Mittelstelle des Ringes, 3 Mar. 1925, NL Westarp, Gärtringen, VN 97. See also the report in the *Deutsche Arbeitgeberzeitung*, 1 Mar. 1925, no. 9, in BA Koblenz, R 118/40, as well as Gleichen to Grimm, 3 Mar. 1925, DLA Marbach, NL Grimm, A17b. For further details, see Simon, "Brauweiler," 203–08.

to overcome the deep-seated divisions that had developed within the ranks of the patriotic movement. At no point was this more apparent than during the course of the 1925 presidential campaign. Initially the Young German Order, the Stahlhelm, and other right-wing organizations that had coalesced behind Gayl in the fall and winter of 1924 supported the nomination of Reichswehr commander-in-chief Hans von Seeckt as a unity candidate whose election would keep the parties of the Weimar coalition from retaining control of the Reich presidency.[13] Seeckt's candidacy, however, ran into strong opposition from members of the Loebell Committee who doubted that he was sufficiently popular to win the election, with the result that he was passed over in favor of the DVP's Karl Jarres for the first round of voting on 29 March 1925. While the Stahlhelm and the other paramilitary organizations represented by Gayl quickly rallied to the support of Jarres's candidacy, Artur Mahraun and the Young Germans continued to press the case for Seeckt's nomination, even going so far as to attack Gayl for his failure to adequately represent the paramilitary Right in his dealings with the Loebell committee.[14]

In an attempt to minimize the damage the Young Germans had done to the Jarres candidacy, Seeckt dissociated himself from efforts to enlist him as a presidential candidate and declared his support for Jarres.[15] Although the Young Germans ultimately joined the Stahlhelm and other paramilitary organizations in supporting Jarres's bid for the presidency,[16] a new conflict erupted in the preparations for the runoff election on 26 April when the Young Germans chastised both Gayl and the Stahlhelm for their lack of enthusiasm for a Hindenburg candidacy and denounced Gayl as an agent of capitalistic economic interests intent upon perpetuating their control of the existing political system by supporting Jarres.[17] At the heart of the conflict between the Stahlhelm and the Young German Order lay not merely the fact that both were jockeying for position in the struggle for leadership of the patriotic movement but a far more fundamental dispute over the strategy the patriotic Right should pursue in the quest for a change in the existing political system. Whereas the Young Germans regarded Hindenburg's election as an opportunity to heal the wounds that so badly divided the German body politic

[13] Statement by Sodenstern from the National Association of German Officers (Nationalverband deutscher Offiziere) in an excerpt from the protocol of the meeting of the patriotic organizations on 13 Mar. 1925, BA Koblenz, NL Gayl, 23.
[14] Mahraun to Gayl, 13 Mar. 1925, BA Koblenz, NL Gayl, 23. See also Loebell, "Die Verhandlungen des Loebell-Ausschusses: Eine objektive Darstellung," *Der Deutschen-Spiegel* 2, no. 13 (Mar. 27, 1925): 583.
[15] Hans Meier-Welcker, *Seeckt* (Frankfurt am Main, 1967), 463–66.
[16] Jarres to Gayl, 17 Mar. 1925, BA Koblenz, NL Gayl, 23. See also Gayl to Mahraun, 28 Mar. 1925, ibid.
[17] Handwritten notes by Gayl on the 1925 presidential campaign, n.d., BA Koblenz, NL Gayl, 23.

and to put an end to the conflict over the form of government,[18] the leaders of
the Stahlhelm were fearful that the election of someone of Hindenburg's
stature would have precisely that effect and thereby facilitate the republic's
legitimation in the eyes of those who were already seeking some sort of
accommodation with the existing system of government.[19] But these differences would become moot once Hindenburg had been elected. The Stahlhem
immediately hailed Hindenburg's election as the beginning of a new era in
German history in which it and the thousands of front soliders allied with it
would serve as one of the "firmest cornerstones in the reconstruction of the
state and Reich" in the struggle for the "liberation of the fatherland from
infamy and bondage."[20]

Aristocratic Offensive

Nowhere was the role the DNVP had played in the economic and political
stabilization of the Weimar Republic more deeply resented than within the
ranks of Germany's landowning and military aristocracy. For the most part,
the aristocracy had been relegated to the margins of German political life
during the first years of the Weimar Republic. To be sure, Westarp had
succeeded in carving out a niche for the Prussian aristocracy in the DNVP,
but the Central Association of German Conservatives had maintained little
more than a shadow existence in the early years of the Weimar Republic and
exercised little direct influence over the affairs of the party. But with the eclipse
of putschism and the stabilization of the republic in 1923–24 the German
aristocracy began to show signs of renewed vigor as it positioned itself for a
new and more sustained assault against the social and political legacy of the
November Revolution. The founding of the German Gentlemen's Club as a
forum where representatives of Germany's bourgeois and feudal elites could
meet on a purely social basis and Goltz's election as the new chairman of the
United Patriotic Leagues of Germany were simply two aspects of a resurgence
of aristocratic politics in the wake of Germany's economic and political
stabilization in the middle years of the Weimar Republic.

  The German aristocracy was anything but a cohesive and monolithic force
in Germany's national life. The German aristocracy was deeply fragmented
along regional, confessional, and socio-economic lines and never enjoyed the
degree of social and political homogeneity that has been popularly associated

---

[18] Artur Mahraun, *Gegen getarnte Gewalten. Wege und Kampf einer Volksbewegung* (Berlin,
   1928), 199–200.
[19] Circular from Ausfeld and Seldte to the leaders of the Stahlhelm's local chapters, 10
   Apr. 1925, BA Koblenz, NL Gayl, 23.
[20] H. Ludwig, "Die Gegenwartsaufgaben des 'Stahlhelm'," Apr. 1925, BA Berlin, R 72, 32/
   297.

with it. The founding of the German Nobles' Association (Deutsche Adels-genossenschaft or DAG) by East Elbian landowners in February 1874 repre-sented the first significant attempt to unite the German aristocracy into a single organization. But the DAG, which had a membership of approximately 2,400 by the end of World War I, appealed primarily to those elements of the aristocracy that had been marginalized by the course of German economic development and manifested a strong antipathy toward the wealthier and more politically influential magnates from east of the Elbe.[21] At the same time, the DAG never succeeded in bridging the confessional divide that separated it from the Catholic nobles in west Prussia or southern and south-west Germany who in 1869 had founded the Association of Catholic Nobles of Germany (Verein katholischer Edelleute Deutschlands or VKE) in an effort to forge a sense of common purpose at the height of Prussia's *Kulturkampf* against the Catholic Church.[22] These divisions persisted well into the Weimar Republic, where the elitism, religious piety, and strong sense confessional solidarity that defined the self-image of Germany's Catholic aristocracy hampered the establishment of closer organizational ties with the DAG despite their shared hostility toward the social and political legacy of the November Revolution.[23] In the meantime, the membership of the predominantly Prot-estant DAG had swelled to nearly 17,000 as a result of the increasingly desperate situation in which more and more nobles found themselves after the political collapse of 1918.[24]

The loss of political privilege combined with economic marginalization to radicalize increasingly large sectors of the German aristocracy in the early and

---

[21] On the DAG, see Georg H. Kleine, "Adelsgenossenschaft und Nationalsozialismus," *Vierteljahrshefte für Zeitgeschichte* 26 (1978): 100–43, and Stefan Malinowski, "'Führer-tum' und 'Neuer Adel.' Die Deutsche Adelsgenossenschaft und der Deutsche Herrenklub in der Weimarer Republik," in *Adel und Bürgertum in Deutschland II. Entwicklungslinien und Wendepunkte im 20. Jahrhundert*, ed. Heinz Reif (Berlin, 2001), 173–211. On the impoverishment of the lesser nobility, see Stefan Malinowski, "'Wer schenkt uns wieder Kartoffeln?' Deutscher Adel nach 1918 – eine Elite?" in *Deutscher Adel im 19. und 20. Jahrhundert. Büdinger Forschungen zur Sozialgeschichte 2002 und 2003*, ed. Günther Schulz and Markus A. Denzel (St. Katharinen, 2004), 503–37.

[22] On the VKE, see Klemens von Oer, *Der Verein katholischer Edelleute Deutschlands. Eine ÜberFblick über seine Entstehungsgeschichte und Entwicklung 1869-1919*, als Handschrift gedruckt (Münster, 1919), as well as Horst Conrad, "Stand und Konfession. Der Verein der katholischen Edelleute. Teil 1: Die Jahre 1857-1918," *Westfälische Zeitschrift* 158 (2008): 125–86.

[23] Malinowski, *Vom König zum Führer*, 358–67. For the sense of mission of the Catholic aristocracy, see Franz von Galen, *Ritterlichkeit in alter und neuer Zeit. Vortrag gehalten in der Generalversammlung des Vereins katholischer Edelleute, Abt. Münster, am 1. Septem-ber 1921* (Warendorf i.W., n.d. [1921]).

[24] See Kleine, "Adelsgenossenschaft und Nationalsozialismus," 105, and Malinowski, *Vom König zum Führer*, 321–22.

middle 1920s.[25] This could be seen first and foremost in the development of the German Nobles' Association, which not only adopted a position of uncompromising hostility toward Germany's fledgling republican order but fell more and more under the influence of the racist Right. Although anti-semitism had been a distinctive feature of Germany's aristocratic culture long before the collapse of 1918, it would become even more prominent with the dramatic spread of anti-Semitic and racist thought in the first years of the Weimar Republic.[26] In December 1920 the DAG not only amended its statutes to make racial purity a prerequisite for membership, but it introduced the *Eisernes Buch deutschen Adels deutscher Art*, more commonly known by the shorter designation EDDA, to certify the racial pedigree of those who claimed noble heritage.[27] Antisemitic prejudice had perhaps an even longer history within Germany's Catholic aristocracy, but here it had less to do with race than with religion. Even if anti-Semitism retained much of its potency within the Catholic aristocracy in the immediate postwar period,[28] neither the Cen-tral Association of Catholic Nobles (Hauptverein katholischer Edelleute Deutschlands) – as the VKE had renamed itself in February 1918 – nor the Association of Catholic Nobles in Bavaria (Genossenschaft katholischer Edel-leute in Bayern or GKE) was willing to make racial purity a prerequisite for membership.[29]

Germany's Catholic aristocracy was far more divided than the predomin-antly Protestant DAG on a wide range of strategic and tactical issues. While the Rhenish-Westphalian aristocracy had become progressively disenchanted

[25] Malinowski, *Vom König zum Führer*, 260–82. See also Zollitsch, "Erosion des traditio-nellen Konservativismus," 162–82.

[26] Stefan Malinowski, "Vom blauen zum reinen Blut. Antisemitischer Adelskritik und adliger Antisemitismus 1871–1944," *Jahrbuch für Antisemitismusforschung* 12 (2003): 147–68.

[27] See section one paragraph three of *Satzung der Deutschen Adelsgenossenschaft* (2 Dec. 1920), 4, and *Überblick über die Entwicklung der Adelsschutzeinrichtung, Potsdam 1921*, both in VWA Münster, NL Lüninck, 815.

[28] For example, see Count Hermann zu Stolberg-Stolberg, *Judengeist und Judenziele. Als Aufsatz in einem im Verein katholischer Edelleute zu Münster i.W. am 22. August 1919 gehaltenen Vortrage ausgearbeitet* (Paderborn, 1919), as well as Count Josef zu Stolberg-Stolberg's remarks in *Protokoll der außerordentlichen General-Versammlung des Hauptvereins katholischer Edelleute Deutschlands Abteilung Münster am 1. September 1921 in Münster* (Münster, 1921), 5–9, records of the Genossenschaft katholischer Edelleute in Bayern, BHStA Munich, Abteilung V, GKE, 7/2, and idem, "Freimaurerei, Judentum und Presse" in "Bericht über den nationalpolitischen Kursus für den rheinisch-westfälischen Adel in Willibadessen 23.–25. April 1923," BA Koblenz, NL Spahn, 177.

[29] Malinowski, *Vom König zum Führer*, 340. On the contours of Catholic antisemitism, see Olaf Blaschke, "Wider die 'Herrschaft des modernen jüdischen Geistes.' Der Katholizis-mus zwischen traditionellen Antijudaismus und modernem Antisemitismus," in *Deutscher Katholizismus im Umbruch zur Moderne*, ed. Wilfried Loth (Stuttgart, Berlin, and Cologne, 1991), 236–61.

with the German Center Party since the summer of 1917 and publicly disputed its commitment to restoring the primacy of Christian values in Germany's national life on the eve of the 1920 Reichstag elections,[30] the GKE enjoyed much closer ties to the Center's more conservative Bavarian counterpart, the Bavarian People's Party, and was thus insulated against the full effect of the radicalization that had taken place within the Catholic aristocracy in the Rhineland and Westphalia.[31] The differences between the Rhenish-Westphalian and Bavarian branches of Germany's Catholic aristocracy proved in fact so great that in the spring of 1922 the Central Association of Catholic Nobles divided itself into five regional associations that remained only loosely affiliated with each other under the umbrella of the Central Committee of Catholic German Noble Associations (Hauptausschuß katholischer Deutscher Adelsgenossenschaften).[32] Of these, by far the most influential and the most radical was the Rhenish-Westphalian Association of Catholic Nobles (Rhenisch-Westfälischer Verein katholischer Edelleute) with its headquarters in Münster. Even here, however, there was discernible tension between those like Baron Engelbert Kerckerinck zur Borg and his protégé Franz von Papen who had remained loyal to the Center and those like the two Lüninck brothers Ferdinand and Hermann who were moving more and more into the orbit of the radical Right. At the heart of this tension, as Kerckerinck zur Borg explained at a meeting of the Rhenish-Westphalian Association of Catholic Nobles in August 1922, lay the question as to whether it would be more effective to pursue opposition from the outside through a party like the DNVP or from the inside by defending the aristocratic point of view in a party that supported the government.[33]

---

[30] "Eine Kundgebung des katholischen Adels," 24 Feb. 1920, in *Protokoll der ordentlichen Generalversammlung des Vereins katholischer Edelleute Deutschlands in 1920* (Münster, 1920), 6–7, in VWA Münster, NL Lüninck, 807. See also Ferdinand von Lüninck, "Gedanken zur Zentrumspolitik," 20 June 1920, BA Koblenz, NL Spahn, 93.

[31] See the attempt to soften the tone of the VKE's statement of 24 Feb. 1920, in Löwenstein, "Der katholische Adel Deutschlands und die Politik," *Allgemeine Rundschau* 17, no. 14 (3 Apr. 1920): 184–86.

[32] See the two letters from Stolberg to Löwenstein, 7 Mar. 1922, VWA Münster, NL Hermann zu Stolberg-Stolberg, 246. See also Löwenstein to the Central Association of Catholic Nobles of Germany, 9 May 1921, BHStA Munich, Abt. V, GKE, 7/2, as well as *Protokoll der außerordentlichen General-Versammlung des Hauptvereins katholischer Edelleute Deutschlands am 2. März 1922 in Münster in Westfalen i.W.* (Münster, 1922), 3–4, VWA Münster, NL Hermann zu Stolberg-Stolberg, 245.

[33] Remarks by Kerckerinck zur Borg in *Protokoll der außerordentlichen General-Versammlung des Rheinisch-Westfälischen Vereins kath. Edelleute am 12. August 1922 in Münster* (Münster, 1922), 6–7, archives of the Verein katholischer Edelleute Deutschlands, VWA Münster, 19. For further details, see Horst Conrad, "Stand und Konfession. Der Verein der katholischen Edelleute. Teil 2: Die Jahre 1918–1949," *Westfälische Zeitschrift* 159 (2009): 91–154.

In the early years of the Weimar Republic the German aristocracy, whether Catholic or Protestant, found itself relegated to the periphery of German political life. Only in Bavaria did the aristocracy enjoy access to the corridors of power, and then only as a consequence of an accommodation with the Bavarian People's Party that did not extend to all sectors of the Bavarian nobility.[34] But all of this began to change with the relative stabilization of the Weimar Republic in the middle of the 1920s. Stresemann's efforts to stabilize the republic from the Right effectively redefined Weimar's political landscape in the second half of the decade and created an entirely new set of strategic and tactical priorities for the German Right. For the German aristocracy, this did little to soften its hostility toward the existing political order and only added to the sense of urgency it felt about Germany's political future. Nowhere was this expressed more forcefully than in a letter that Ferdinand von Lüninck wrote to an unknown recipient in late January 1924:

> After – as everyone today readily concedes – the great moment at the end of last October was allowed to slip away, the disastrous [heillose] Munich affair has resulted in such far-reaching fragmentation and apathy that virtually the entire patriotic movement has been neutralized by its internal conflicts ... From where I stand, the most important thing is for leadership to recognize that since last fall the lines of combat have dramatically changed. For all intents and purposes socialism and Marxism are finished. Now a new and more ominous enemy threatens the national concept, i.e., the threat of enslavement to international capital as represented by the firm of Schacht and Stresemann, the collapse of our national economy, and with it our absolute dependence upon international Jewry. That this takes place under the mantle of democracy changes nothing whatsoever about the essence of the existing situation.[35]

The collapse of putschism and the subsequent stabilization of the Weimar Republic under conservative auspices marked the beginning of a new and more militant phase in the aristocracy's struggle against the hated Weimar system. Over the course of the next several years, conservative aristocrats who refused to accept the changes that had taken place in Germany's political order at the end of World War I would intensify their efforts to subvert the terms upon which Weimar's political stabilization had taken place and to rally Germany's conservative forces for a new assault against the symbols and institutions of Weimar democracy. For the large landowners from the east of the Elbe, the immediate and indeed most pressing task was to return the DNVP to the course of unconditional opposition to the existing system of government. The DNVP's split in the vote on the Dawes Plan and its

[34] Malinowski, *Vom König zum Führer*, 367–85.
[35] Letter from Lüninck, 26 Jan. 1924, VWA Münster, NL Lüninck, 822.

subsequent entry into the Luther cabinet only fueled the fears of the East
Elbian aristocracy that the party had betrayed the principles that had inspired
its founding.[36] To reverse the direction in which they saw the party headed,
the East Elbian nobles worked through the Central Association of German
Conservatives and its chairman Count Ernst Julius von Seidlitz-Sandreczki.[37]
Seidlitz had taken part in the strategy sessions that Gleichen and the leaders of
the Ring Movement had organized in the late fall of 1924 and vigorously
supported their efforts to return the DNVP to a path of unconditional
opposition to the Weimar Republic.[38] The DNVP's decision to enter the first
Luther cabinet had met with strong opposition from Seidlitz and his allies in
the Ring Movement and only strengthened their resolve to assert themselves
more forcefully within the party.[39]

Within the Catholic aristocracy a different set of strategic and tactical
objectives existed. The more conservative elements of Germany's Catholic
aristocracy were every bit as strongly opposed to the postwar political system
as their East Elbian counterparts. Speaking to the Association of Catholic
Nobles in Bavaria in the summer of 1925, Lüninck categorically rejected the
principle of popular sovereignty as enshrined in Article I, Paragraph 2, of the
Weimar Constitution and denounced the modern democratic state as a *Zah-
lendemokratie* that did little more than tally up the votes of atomized individuals. Lüninck maintained that all power, including temporal power, was
derived from the majesty of God and that no secular institution – and
particularly not a parliament that derived its legitimacy from the will of the
people – could lay claim to the sovereign powers of the Lord or usurp the
rights of those whom He had ordained to rule in His stead. At the same time,
Lüninck subscribed to an organic theory of the state and society in which the
rights and privileges of the individual were limited by the welfare of the whole
and in which the illusory equality of the democratic age would be replaced by
respect for the authority of God's moral law. It was the task of Germany's
Catholic nobility, Lüninck insisted, to take the lead in the struggle for Christian and conservative values in an age of increasing democratization and
secularization. And this, he concluded, had nothing to do with the party to
which one belonged but was a mission that presupposed a unity of purpose
and a commitment to action that transcended all party lines.[40]

---

[36] Flemming, "Konservativismus als 'nationalrevolutionäre Bewegung'," 295–331. See also
Rainer Pomp, "Brandenburgischer Landadel," 186–218.
[37] Memorandum of 14 Oct. 1924 on a meeting of the executive committee of the Central
Association of German Conservatives, 11 Oct. 1924, NL Westarp, Gärtringen, VN 50.
[38] Circular from the Mittelstelle des Ringes, 14 Oct. 1924, BA Koblenz, NL Schmidt-
Hannover, 33.
[39] Circular from the Mittelstelle des Ringes, 28 Jan. 1925, NL Westarp, Gärtringen, VN 97.
[40] Ferdinand von Lüninck, "Der moderne Staat und die Stellung des Adels zu ihm," in
Genossenschaft katholischer Edelleute in Bayern, ed., *Sozialpolitischer Kurse zu*

Lüninck's speech represented a virtual declaration of war against the Weimar state at a time when moderate conservatives in the DNVP, the National Federation of German Industry, the National Rural League, and even the Stahlhelm were all seeking an accommodation with the Weimar Republic as part of the general realignment of political forces that had begun in 1923–24. For Lüninck and his associates, the immediate objective was not so much to drive the DNVP out of the governmental coalition in Berlin as to replace the alliance that had developed between the Center and the parties of the political Left with a new alliance between the Center and the German Right. Catholic conservatives hoped to leverage the DNVP's impressive show-ing in the December 1924 Reichstag elections into a far-reaching realignment of political forces in the Reich and Prussia that would put a definitive end to the domination of Social Democracy and the Weimar Coalition.[41] The key player in all of this was Franz von Papen, a former diplomat and army officer who had been elected to the Prussian Landtag in 1921 as a liaison between the Westphalian Peasants' League and the German Center Party.[42] While Papen shared Lüninck's deep-seated antipathy toward the political system that Germany had inherited from the November Revolution, he also insisted that a Christian and conservative regeneration of the German state could take place only on the basis of the existing constitutional order and rejected the putschist proclivities of the radical Right.[43] At the same time, Papen exhorted his peers in the Catholic aristocracy to take a more active role in "the systematic concentration [*planmäßige Sammlung*]" of the "conservative elem-ents of the Catholic Volk" into a united front capable of freeing Germany from the liberal-democratic morass in which it was currently entrapped.[44]

Kleinheubach 15.–17. Juni 1925 (n.p, n.d. [1925]), 3–11, BHStA Munich, Abt. V, GKE, 13. For further details, see Jones, "Catholic Conservatives in the Weimar Republic," 68–70. On Lüninck, see Ekkehard Klausa, "Vom Bündnispartner zum 'Hochverräter.' Der Weg des konservativen Widerstandskämpfer Ferdinand von Lüninck," *Westfälische Forschun-gen* 43 (1993): 530–71, and Peter Möhring, "Ferdinand Freiherr von Lüninck," *Westfä-lische Lebensbilder* 17 (2005): 60–102.

[41] In this respect, see Ferdinand von Lüninck to his brother Hermann, 21 Jan. 1925, as well as his letters to Schley, 21 Jan. 1925, and Bornemann (Young German Order), 29 Jan. 1925, VWA Münster, NL Lüninck, 838.

[42] On Papen's career prior to his appointment as chancellor in the summer of 1932, see Joachim Petzold, *Franz von Papen. Ein deutsche Verhängnis* (Munich and Berlin, 1995), 15–62.

[43] Papen to Escherich, 2 June 1926, BHStA Munich, Abt. IV, EWB, 7/2.

[44] Papen, "Der Staat von heute und der Einsatz der konservativen Kräfte des katholischen Volkes," in *Wechselburger Tagung 1927*, ed. Hauptausschuß der katholischen Adelsge-nossenschaften Deutschlands (Munich, n.d. [1927]), 6–11, VWA Münster, NL Lüninck, 811. For further details, see Larry Eugene Jones, "Franz von Papen, the German Center Party, and the Failure of Catholic Conservatism in the Weimar Republic," *Central European History* 38 (2005): 191–217.

In January 1925 Papen used his influence as a member of the Center delegation to the Prussian Landtag to sabotage the appointment of Center party chairman Wilhelm Marx as Prussian minister president in hopes that this would clear the way for the creation of a cabinet of civil servants, or *Beamtenkabinett*, without formal ties to the parties that supported it.[45] Papen further infuriated the Center's national leadership when he circulated a petition in the Westphalian Center Party endorsing not Marx but Hindenburg in the presidential elections later that spring.[46] While this did not provide Hindenburg with the votes he needed to defeat Marx, Papen was nevertheless pleased with the outcome of the election and its implications for Germany's political future.[47] For the most part, however, Papen remained isolated within the Center and never succeeded in reconciling the differences that separated it from his peers in the Rhenish-Westphalian aristocracy. His appeals, most notably after a highly publicized meeting of the Center's executive committee and party council in Erfurt in 1926, for a Christian-conservative reorientation of the Center evoked little in the way of a positive response from the party leadership and only reinforced his sense of isolation within the party.[48] Still, Papen's exhortations to Germany's Catholic nobility to assume a more active role in the crusade for a Christian and conservative reconstruction of the German state served as important barometers of an aristocratic resurgence that would contribute in no small measure to reshaping Weimar's political landscape over the course of the next decade.

The Burden of Power

The increased assertiveness of the German nobility in the wake of Weimar's economic and political stabilization came at a time when the leaders of the DNVP were still wrestling with the implications of their party's entry into the national cabinet. One of the many ironies of the DNVP's victory in the May and December 1924 Reichstag elections was that at the very moment the party commanded the parliamentary strength to force its way into the national government, the position of those elements in the DNVP Reichstag delegation

---

[45] For further details, see Papen to Kerckerinck zur Borg, 8 Jan. 1925, as well as his reports on the meetings of the Center delegation to the Prussian Landtag, 7 and 10 Feb. 1925, VWA Münster, NL Kerckerinck zur Borg, 145. See also Ruppert, *Im Dienst von Weimar*, 101–08.

[46] This appeal appeared until the title "Zentrum und Sozialdemokratie. Ein Mahnruf rheinisch-westfälischer Katholiken," *Kölnische Zeitung*, 20 Apr. 1925. For the rationale behind this action, see Kerckerinck zur Borg to Marx, 19 Apr. 1925, VWA Münster, NL Kerckerinck zur Borg, 145.

[47] Papen to v. Löe, 17 June 1925, VWA Münster, NL Kerckerinck zur Borg, 145.

[48] Papen, "Erfurt und der konservative Gedanke," *Allgemeine Rundschau* 24, no. 1 (8 Jan. 1927): 3–4.

that opposed the party's experiment at governmental participation had been greatly strengthened by the influx of new deputies with an aristocratic pedigree. Of the 106 Nationalists who had been elected to the Reichstag in May 1924, no less than thirteen belonged to the titled nobility.[49] In the December elections the number of Nationalist deputies with a noble pedigree had risen to fifteen.[50] By the same token, the number of Nationalist deputies who were either landowners or otherwise had close ties to organized agriculture had increased significantly since 1920. One estimate placed no less than forty of those who had been elected to the DNVP Reichstag delegation in May 1924 in this category. Moreover, the new generation of agrarian spokesmen who had been elected to the Reichstag for the first time in 1924 – Johann-Georg von Dewitz from the Pomeranian Rural League (Pommerscher Landbund), Count Botho-Wendt zu Eulenburg from Gallingen in East Prussia, Hans von Goldacker from Weberstedt in Thuringia, and Baron Prätorius von Richthofen-Boguslawitz from Silesia – were far more aggressive and confrontational in their political style than the older generation of farm leaders represented by Roesicke and Schiele.[51] The enhanced status of large landed agriculture in the DNVP Reichstag delegation could also be seen in the election of Count Kuno von Westarp in early February 1925 to succeed Schiele as delegation chairman after his resignation to accept a position in the Luther cabinet.[52] Though not a landowner himself, Westarp had played a critical role in helping the East Elbian aristocracy secure a place for itself within the DNVP. The composition of the newly elected DNVP Reichstag delegation – and in particular the increased leverage that Germany's landed aristocracy enjoyed within the delegation – did not augur well for the success of the party's first experiment in sharing government responsibility.

The DNVP's decision to join the Luther cabinet in January 1925 was predicated upon the assumption that this would result in more effective representation for the special-economic interests that constituted the the party's material base.[53] In this respect, however, two issues proved particularly vexing: revaluation and trade policy. The revaluation issue was especially agonizing to the leaders of the DNVP. Not only had the anger of Germany's

---

[49] Germany, Bureau des Reichstags, ed., *Reichstags-Handbuch. II. Periode 1924* (Berlin, 1924), 351–52.

[50] Germany, Bureau des Reichstags, ed., *Reichstags-Handbuch. III. Periode 1924* (Berlin, 1925), 172–73.

[51] On the composition of the Nationalist delegation, see Albrecht Philipp, "Mein Weg: Rückschau eines Siebzigjährigen auf allerlei Geschenisse und Menschen," Dritte Teil: "Abgeordnetenjahre in der Weimarer Republik (1919-1930)," SHStA Dresden, NL Philipp, 4/134–42.

[52] Ibid., 4/159.

[53] Gottfried R. Treviranus, *Deutschnationale Innenpolitik im Reichstag*, Deutschnationale Flugschrift, no. 223 (Berlin, 1925).

middle-class investors over the revaluation provisions of the Third Emergency Tax Decree played a major role in the DNVP's success at the polls in the May and December 1924 Reichstag elections, but once in power the Nationalists quickly discovered that there was no way they could possibly satisfy investors' demands for a full and equitable revaluation of the paper mark assets that had been destroyed during the runaway inflation of the early 1920s.[54] If nothing else, the desperate state of German finances in 1925 precluded a revaluation of worthless paper mark assets on a scale and magnitude sufficient to satisfy the expectations of the savers' organizations that had rallied to the DNVP's support in the 1924 Reichstag elections.[55] Moreover, the leaders of the revaluation movement found themselves blocked within the DNVP by a powerful coalition of agricultural and industrial interests that was opposed to any settlement of the revaluation question that might prejudice the gains they had recorded as a result of the inflation.[56] Unable to follow through on their campaign promises from the previous year, the Nationalists came under increasingly heavy attack not just from the opposition parties but also from the various revaluation groups that had sprung up throughout the country since the end of 1922.[57]

In March 1925 the Nationalist party leadership tried to assuage the anger of Germany's small investors by agreeing to a revision of the revaluation provisions of the Third Emergency Tax Decree that increased the revalorization rate for mortgages and other forms of private indebtedness from fifteen to twenty-five percent of their original gold mark value. At the same time, the agreement established revalorization rates of fifteen percent for industrial obligations and five percent – a figure later reduced to two-and-a-half percent for assets that had changed hands since 1 July 1920 – for war bonds and other forms of

---

[54] Much of the following is taken from Jones, "Inflation, Revaluation, and the Crisis of Middle-Class Politics," 152–61. See also Michael Hughes, *Paying for the German Inflation* (Chapel Hill, NC, 1988), 102–58, as well as Ohnezeit, *Zwischen "schärfster Opposition,"* 290–96, and Dörr, "Deutschnationale Volkspartei," 325–33.

[55] Remarks by the German finance minister, Hans August von Schlieben, at a meeting of the Reichstag's budget committee, 28 Jan. 1925, BA Koblenz, Nachlass Hermann Dietrich, 295/365–71.

[56] See the report of the meeting of the DNVP Reichstag delegation, 10 Feb. 1925, in Reichert to Meyer, Reusch, and Blohm, 12 Feb. 1925, along with the enclosure, "Zur Aufwertungsfrage: Drei Ministerreden in der deutschnationalen Fraktion am 10.II.25," RWWA Cologne, Abt. 130, NL Reusch, 400101295/16.

[57] See Hirsch to Westarp, 18 Jan. 1925, and the letter from the Revaluation and Reconstruction Party (Aufwertungs- und Aufbau-Partei) to Westarp, 4 Mar. 1925, both in NL Westarp, Gärtringen, II/17, as well as the petition from the Osnabrück district organization of the Mortgagees and Savers' Protective Association (Hypothekengläubiger- und Sparerschutzverband, Bezirk Osnabrück) to the DNVP executive committee, 17 Mar. 1925, Niedersächsisches Staatsarchiv Osnabrück, records of the DNVP, Landesverband Osnabück (hereafter cited as NSSA Osnabrück), Bestand C1, 90/9.

public indebtedness. This represented a compromise between government parties anxious to escape the wrath of those who had been dispossessed by the inflation and a government determined to limit the scope of revaluation so as not to aggravate Germany's already desperate fiscal situation.[58] Even then, the leaders of the National Rural League criticized the revaluation compromise on the grounds that it, along with other proposed taxes, constituted an intolerable burden for German farmers and seriously jeopardized their chances of full recovery in Germany's post-inflation economy.[59] Large landowners like Reichstag deputy Hans von Goldacker criticized the striking discrepancy in the revaluation compromise between the revalorization rates for government and private debts and warned party leaders that agriculture's bitterness over the terms of the revaluation settlement would come back to haunt them if they did not pay more attention to the welfare of the German farmer.[60] By the same token, the Coordinating Committee of German National Industrialists expressed grave concern about the fiscal implications of the revaluation bill and warned against additional concessions to the revaluation movement that might adversely affect the private sector's ability to raise the capital necessary for economic expansion.[61]

Given the strong opposition of organized agricultural and industrial interests to the revaluation bill, there was little likelihood of further concessions that might have made it more palatable to the leaders of the revaluation movement. The compromise of March 1925 fell far short of the movement's demands for a full and equitable restoration of those paper mark assets that had been destroyed by the inflation and provoked a storm of protest from savers' organizations from throughout the country when its terms were made public in early May. Much of this anger was directed against the DNVP, where Georg Best, a prominent Darmstadt jurist elected to the Reichstag in December 1924 as the party's liaison to the revaluation movement, refused to go along with the compromise bill and vowed to oppose it when it came before the Reichstag's revaluation committee. The conflict drew to a dramatic head on 13–14 May 1925 when Best announced his resignation from the DNVP

---

[58] Minutes of a meeting between representatives of the government and the leadership of the government parties, 18 Mar. 1925, in *Akten der Reichskanzlei: Die Kabinette Luther I u. II. 15. Januar 1925 bis 20. Januar 1926. 20. Januar 1926 bis 17. Mai 1926*, edited by Karl-Heinz Minuth, 2 vols. (Boppard am Rhein, 1977), 1:185–97.

[59] Kalckreuth and Hepp (RLB) to the executive committee of the DNVP Reichstag delegation, 11 May 1925, BA Berlin, NL Hepp, 4/145–46. See also Reichs-Landbund e.V., *Landbund und Aufwertungsgesetz*, Vortrags-Material für Landbundführer- und Redner, no. 4 (Berlin, 1926).

[60] Goldacker to Westarp, 2 June 1925, NL Westarp, Gärtringen, VN 55.

[61] "Stellungnahme des Arbeitsausschusses Deutschnationaler Industrieller zur Aufwertungsfrage," 4 June 1925, NSSA Osnabrück, C1, 90/34–36.

Reichstag delegation after it had voted to accept the revaluation compromise that had been hammered out with the other government parties.[62] To Best, the DNVP's support of this compromise represented a breach of faith with the revaluation movement that he, as a man of his word, could no longer countenance.[63] To those in the DNVP organization with their fingers on the pulse of the party's grass-roots support, the disaffection of Best and his supporters was a cause for great concern.[64]

The revaluation issue was to haunt the leaders of the DNVP over the course of the next three years and left their party exposed to charges of duplicity and electoral opportunism. For their own part, the Nationalists continued to maintain that they had done everything in their power to meet the demands of the revaluation movement and that without the party's constant pressure no revision of the revaluation provisions of the Third Emergency Tax Decree would have taken place.[65] Though disingenuous at best, these claims held true for at least one prominent Nationalist, former party chairman Oskar Hergt who, as minister of justice in the Luther cabinet, had worked tirelessly on behalf of what he thought to be a fair and equitable settlement of the revaluation question.[66] And, as fate would have it, the unpleasant task of defending the DNVP's role in the adoption of the revaluation compromise fell to none other than Hergt. Speaking before the Reichstag on 10 July, Hergt insisted that the bill under consideration was the best that one could expect in view of Germany's economic situation and denounced Social Democratic charges that the DNVP had abandoned the small investor to the avarice of big business and large-scale agriculture as pure and simple demagogy. At the same time, Hergt argued that if anything stood in the way of an equitable settlement of the revaluation question, it was the financial burden Germany had incurred with the acceptance of the Dawes Plan. Accordingly, it was this, and not a lack of commitment on the part of the government or the DNVP, that had made it impossible to do more for the German saver than what the current bill had to offer.[67] Six days later the DNVP joined the other government parties in voting

---

[62] Best to the DNVP executive committee, 14 May 1925, reprinted along with the party's response and other correspondence in *Der Kampf um die Aufwertung*, Deutschnationale Flugschrift, no. 215 (Berlin, 1925), 29–30.

[63] Best, "Das Kompromiß in der Aufwertungsfrage und seine Väter," *Die Aufwertung* 2, no. 23 (12 July 1925): 197–99.

[64] For example, see Vogt to Westarp, 17 May 1925, NL Westarp, Gärtringen, II/13.

[65] For example, see *Ohne Deutschnationale keine Aufwertung! Was jeder von der Aufwertung wissen muß*, Deutschnationale Flugschrift, no. 219 (Berlin, 1925).

[66] Oskar Hergt, *Zur Aufwertungsfrage. Reichstagsrede am 7. März 1925*, Deutschnationale Flugschrift, no. 206 (Berlin, 1925).

[67] Oskar Hergt, *Der Endkampf um die Aufwertung. Reichstagsrede am 10. Juli 1925*, Deutschnationale Flugschrift, no. 217 (Berlin, 1925).

for the controversial revaluation bill ad it came to the Reichstag for a final vote on 16 July 1925.[68]

The DNVP's failure to live up to the promises it had made to the revaluation movement during the 1924 election campaigns highlighted the increasingly prominent role that organized economic interests had come to play not just in the DNVP's internal affairs but in German political life as a whole. This could also be seen in the way the DNVP responded to organized agriculture's demands for tariff protection against foreign agricultural imports. Landowners who had originally benefited from the runaway inflation of the early 1920s now found themselves confronted with a whole new set of problems that adversely affected their ability to operate at a profit. Not only had many farmers sold their 1923 harvests for paper marks that were subsequently rendered all but worthless by the introduction of the *Rentenmark* in November 1923, but the inflation had also destroyed the capital reserves of the private credit cooperatives through which the German farmer had traditionally obtained the inexpensive, short-term loans he needed for the purchase of seed, fertilizer, and farm machinery. This coincided with the virtual collapse of agricultural prices on the world market and the specter of massive agricultural imports from the United States, Canada, and eastern Europe.[69] If German agriculture was to survive the deepening crisis left in the wake of Weimar's fiscal and economic stabilization, argued conservative farm leaders like RLB president Count Eberhard von Kalckreuth and DNVP Reichstag deputy Prätorius von Richthofen-Boguslawitz, it was absolutely imperative to provide the German farmer with effective tariff protection against the sheer volume of foreign agricultural products that would soon flood the domestic market.[70]

The DNVP's decision to join the Luther cabinet at the beginning of the year was driven in large part by the desire of its agrarian wing to have a hand in formulating German trade policy after Germany regained full tariff autonomy in January 1925.[71] Luther's minister of agriculture, Count Gerhard von Kanitz, recognized the danger that the threat of foreign agricultural imports posed to the stability of Germany's agricultural economy and readily conceded the need

[68] Paul Moldenhauer, *Die Regelung der Aufwertungsfrage* (Cologne, 1925).
[69] On the plight of German agriculture, see Franz Schenk von Stauffenberg, *Bauernnot! Ein Mahnruf*, Wirtschaftsfragen der Zeit, nos. 4–5 (Berlin, n.d. [1925]).
[70] See Eberhard von Kalckreuth, *Ernährung und Schutzzoll*, Wirtschaftsfragen der Zeit, no. 3 (Berlin, 1925), and Prätorius von Richthofen-Boguslawitz, *Zur Zollfrage* (Schweibnitz, 1925), esp. 10–11.
[71] Martin Schiele, "Die Agrarpolitik der Deutschnationalen Volkspartei in den Jahren 1925/1928," in Max Weiß, ed., *Der Nationale Wille. Werden und Wirken der Deutschnationalen Volkspartei 1918–1928* (Essen, 1928), 291–306.

for tariff protection for large landowner and small farmer alike.[72] Under Kanitz's guidance, the Luther government began to work with representatives from the DVP and DNVP on formulating the general guidelines of a new tariff policy aimed at reconciling the interests of industry and agriculture. This was to be achieved by establishing minimum tariffs for a wide range of agricultural products at the same time that the domestic market for industrial goods was to be protected against "unnecessary" foreign competition. The situation within the DNVP was far from unanimous, and it was only after Westarp went through the motions of resigning the delegation chairmanship in late May that the delegation finally agreed on the terms of the bill that he had negotiated with the leaders of the other government parties.[73] As expected, the proposed bill encountered strong opposition from the two working-class parties on the Left as well as from a solid majority within the DDP Reichstag delegation. In the final analysis, however, it was the leaders of the DNVP's Christian-national labor wing who tipped the balance in favor of passage by mobilizing the support of Christian labor leaders in the Center, with the result that the controversial tariff bill was adopted by a narrow margin in the Reichstag on 12 August 1925.[74]

Although the Nationalists were quick to claim credit for the passage of the 1925 tariff bill,[75] they were well aware of its limitations and regarded it as a little more than a provisional measure that would have to be supplemented by further action in the future.[76] Germany's large grain producers were particularly displeased with the new tariff bill because it failed to provide them with the same protection against foreign grain imports that small family farmers had received for meat and dairy products.[77] All of this tended to reinforce the suspicion in influential agrarian circles that the true beneficiary of the new tariff bill was not agriculture but those sectors of the German industrial establishment that were most interested in gaining access to international markets. As a result, serious doubts over the wisdom of the DNVP's decision

---

[72] Gerhard von Kanitz, *Die Lage der deutschen Landwirtschaft und ihr Verhältnis zur Industrie. Vortrag im Industrie-Club Düsseldorf gehalten am 7. März 1925* (Düsseldorf, n.d. [1925], 6–11.

[73] Letter from Ada Gräfin von Westarp to Gertraude Freifrau Hiller von Gaertringen, 27 May 1925, NL Westarp, Gärtringen.

[74] For further details, see Stürmer, *Koalition und Opposition*, 98–107, as well as Ohnezeit, *Zwischen "schärfster Opposition,"* 299–306, and Gessner, *Agrarverbände*, 46–81.

[75] G. R. Treviranus, "Landwirtschaft," in *Politische Praxis 1926*, ed. Walther Lambach (Hamburg, n.d. [1926]), 211–38, esp. 223–24.

[76] See Otto Rippel, "Die Deutschnationalen als Regierungspartei," in *Politische Praxis 1926*, ed. Walther Lambach (Hamburg, n.d. [1926]), 66–71, here 68, and Hans Schlange-Schöningen, "Die Deutschnationale Volkspartei und die Landwirtschaft," in *Der nationale Wille. Werden und Wirken der Deutschnationalen Volkspartei 1918–1928*, ed. Max Weiß (Essen, 1928), 307–18, esp. 311–13.

[77] Comments by Arnim-Rittgarten at a meeting of the executive committee of the Brandenburg Rural League, 19 Aug. 1925, BA Berlin, R 8034 I, 268/462–77.

to enter the national government began to surface within the ranks of organized agriculture. Whereas Karl Hepp and the more moderate elements of the RLB leadership defended the government's trade initiative as a positive step towards restoring agriculture's economic viability, many farm leaders – and particularly those who had opposed the DNVP's entry into the Luther government in the first place – argued that agriculture had given away too much to industry in arriving at the compromise upon which the new tariff law was based.[78] This criticism seemed particularly warranted in light of the way in which the interests of the German wine industry had been shortchanged in the bilateral trade treaty that Germany had negotiated with Spain in August 1924 and that the DNVP and Bavarian People's Party had categorically rejected in committee earlier that spring.[79]

Foreign Policy Challenges

To many Nationalists, it seemed that the DNVP's record of accomplishment entry as a member of the Luther government had not justified the sacrifice of political principle this had entailed. Agriculture's uneasiness over the future course of German trade policy and the frustration the Nationalists felt over their inability to satisfy the expectations of the revaluation movement left party leaders increasingly vulnerable on what was to become the litmus test of the DNVP's reliability as a coalition partner, the proposed Rhineland security pact with France and Belgium. In early 1925 the German Foreign Office had sent the British and French the general outlines of a proposal whereby Germany would join Great Britain, France, and Belgium in signing a Rhineland security pact that would not only end military occupation of the Rhine but, more importantly from the Allied standpoint, would guarantee existing boundaries between Germany and her former enemies in the west.[80] When the details of this proposal were made public at the beginning of March, the leaders of the DNVP voiced reservations about the proposed security pact but scrupulously avoided a public debate on the matter for fear of jeopardizing their position in the Luther cabinet.[81] In meeting with the leaders of the

---

[78] See the exchange between Hepp and Wangenheim at a meeting of the RLB tariff and trade committee, 15 Apr. 1925, BA Koblenz, NL Weilnböck, 37.

[79] For example, see Hepp to Stresemann, 24 May 1925, PA AA Berlin, NL Stresemann, 93/172762–63.

[80] For further details, see Peter Krüger, *Die Aussenpolitik der Weimarer Republik* (Darmstadt, 1985), 269–84, as well as Jonathan Wright, "Stresemann and Locarno," *Contemporary European History* 4 (1995): 109–31.

[81] For example, see Schiele to Stresemann, 21 Mar. 1925, NL Westarp, Gärtringen, VN 121, and to Westarp, 21 Mar. 1925, ibid., II/19, as well as Schultz-Bromberg to Westarp, 21 Mar. 1925, ibid. For further details, see Dörr, "Deutschnationale Volkspartei," 100–10, and Ohnezeit, *Zwischen "schärfster Opposition,"* 319–28.

DNVP Reichstag delegation on 2 April, Stresemann was thus able to secure their tentative support for his foreign policy initiative by stressing how the proposed security pact would tie the French to a specific schedule for the evacuation of the Rhine, eliminate the threat of future unilateral French action like the occupation of the Ruhr, and preempt the conclusion of an Anglo-Franco-Belgian pact directed against the threat of German revanchism.[82]

Although the leaders of the DNVP Reichstag delegation remained faithful to the terms of their compromise with the Luther cabinet through the spring of 1925, they came under increasingly heavy attack from both within and outside the party for their tacit support of Stresemann's foreign policy initiative. For Germany's patriotic and paramilitary Right, the controversy over the proposed security pact would test the DNVP's willingness to defend Germany's national honor even if this meant forsaking the material benefits of remaining in the government. Of all the organizations on the radical Right, none was more aggressive in its attacks on Stresemann's foreign policy than the Pan-German League.[83] Here the objective was not merely to block the proposed security pact but, more importantly, to use the fight over the conduct of German foreign policy to force the DNVP out of the cabinet and to bring its first experiment in government participation to an ignominious end. After the 1922 racist crisis the Pan-Germans had staked their entire political strategy on building up a strong position within the DNVP and transforming it into an instrument of the racist cause. After having played a major role in designing the party's successful strategy for the May 1924 Reichstag elections, the party's racist wing resented the way in which its message had been muted in the Nationalist campaign for the December 1924 elections and how they had been relegated to the sidelines in the negotiations that accompanied the DNVP's entry into the national government in January 1925.[84] For the Pan-Germans, the conflict over the proposed security pact with France and Belgium thus afforded them an opportunity to reclaim their place in the party and to reverse the course in which the DNVP was apparently headed.

---

[82] Protocol of a discussion between Luther, Stresemann, and the leaders of the DNVP Reichstag delegation, 2 Apr. 1925, PA AA Berlin, NL Stresemann, 23/158577–85. For further details, see Gratwohl, *Stresemann and the DNVP*, 58–75, and Wright, *Stresemann*, 301–48.

[83] For further details, see Barry A. Jackisch, "Kuno Graf von Westarp und die Auseinandersetzungen über Locarno. Konservative Aussenpolitik und die deutschnationale Parteikrise 1925," in *"Ich bin der letzte Preuße": Der politische Lebensweg des konservativen Politikers Kuno Graf von Westarp*, ed. Larry Eugene Jones and Wolfram Pyta (Cologne, Weimar, and Vienna, 2006), 147–62, here 150–57.

[84] See Claß's remarks at a meeting of the ADV managing committee, 30 Jan.–1 Feb. 1925, BA Berlin, R 8048, 141/36–39, 41–44. See also Jackisch, *Pan-German League*, 111–31, and Hofmeister, "Between Monarchy and Dictatorship," 275–82.

Meeting in Dresden on 21–22 March 1925, ADV managing committee decided to bring as much pressure as possible to bear upon the DNVP Reichstag delegation and the Nationalist ministers in the Luther cabinet in an attempt to block approval of Stresemann's proposed security pact for the Rhineland.[85] This was accompanied by a so-called German Evening in Dresden's Wettiner Hall that attracted over a thousand participants and that was highlighted by speeches by ADV chairman Heinrich Claß and DNVP Reichstag deputy Carl Gottfried Gok in which they subjected Stresemann's foreign policy to a scathing attack.[86] This marked the beginning of a public crusade against Stresemann that grew in intensity through the spring and early summer of 1925. In June the ADV leadership intensified its efforts at the local and regional levels of the DNVP's national organization to make it all the more difficult for the party's parliamentary leadership to ignore the Pan-German agenda.[87] By then, other right-wing organizations had also begun to take up the struggle against Stresemann and the proposed security pact. On 23 May 1925 the leaders of the United Patriotic Leagues denounced the proposed security pact as well as efforts to join the League of Nations as steps that would lead to Germany's servitude and military enslavement to its mortal enemies.[88] Privately the VVVD's national chairman Count Rüdiger von der Goltz exhorted the DNVP party leadership to do everything in its power to strengthen the party's political resolve in seeing the struggle against the security pact to a successful conclusion. A repeat of the fateful split of 29 August 1924, he warned, would have disastrous consequences not just for the DNVP but for the entire nationalist Right.[89]

In the meantime, the most visible of Germany's paramilitary organizations, the Stahlhelm, felt that it could no longer remain on the sidelines and reluctantly added its voice to the rising cacophony of right-wing demands for a repudiation of Stresemann's foreign policy. Following Hitler's abortive Beer Hall putsch in November 1923, the Stahlhelm had moved quickly to establish itself as a formidable force in the struggle for control of public space in towns and middle-sized cities and came to represent a voice in German national

---

[85] Minutes of the ADV managing committee, 21–22 Mar. 1925, BA Berlin, R 8048, 142/73–102. See also Vietinghoff-Scheel to Leopold, 3 Aug. 1925, NL Westarp, Gärtringen, VN 54.

[86] Jackisch, *Pan-German League*, 118.

[87] Claß's remarks in the minutes of the ADV managing committee, 4–5 July 1925, BA Berlin, R 8048, 143/52–56.

[88] Resolution adopted at the conclusion of the meeting of VVVD delegate conference, 23 May 1925, NL Westarp, Gärtringen, VN 97.

[89] Goltz to Westarp, 15 July 1925, NL Westarp, Gärtringen, VN 95.

politics that could not be easily ignored.[90] The Stahlhelm's decision to align itself with the forces opposed to the proposed pact represented a fundamental reversal of the political course that Franz Seldte and the leaders of the Stahlhelm had set for themselves following the collapse of efforts in the fall of 1923 to establish a national dictatorship under the tutelage of Seeckt or some other right-wing leader. Throughout 1924 and the first half of 1925, Seldte had remained on cordial terms with Stresemann and seemed perfectly content to allow the foreign minister to use the Stahlhelm and its demands for a more aggressive foreign policy as a way of reminding the Allies of the domestic constraints under which he as foreign minister had to operate.[91] All of this, however, began to change when the executive committee of the Stahlhelm met on 4–5 July 1925 to discuss the proposed security pact. Here Seldte found himself under heavy pressure from Duesterberg and those members of the Stahlhelm leadership cadre with close ties to the DNVP's right wing to take a more aggressive stance against Stresemann and his foreign policy.[92] The meeting concluded with the adoption of a resolution that condemned "the voluntary recognition of the provisions of the Versailles Treaty, as well as the abandonment of German nationals or any of the stolen territories, as an offense against German honor and dignity, which [the Stahlhelm] must combat with all the means at its disposal."[93] Although the leaders of the Stahlhelm tried to avert an open break with Stresemann and the DVP,[94] it was clear from the tone and language of the resolution that it stood firmly opposed to any foreign policy initiative that purchased a diplomatic understanding with the Allies by guaranteeing the boundaries of 1919.[95]

Developments on Germany's patriotic Right received close attention not only from Stresemann but also from the leaders of the DNVP. The Nationalists had assiduously cultivated the support of the various organizations that belonged to the patriotic movement ever since the early 1920's and enjoyed particularly close ties to the Stahlhelm and the United Patriotic Leagues

---

[90] Peter Fritzsche, "Between Fragmentation and Fraternity: Civic Patriotism and the Stahlhelm in Bourgeois Neighborhoods during the Weimar Republic." *Tel Aviver Jahrbuch für deutsche Geschichte* 17 (1988): 123–44.

[91] Franke (Stahlhelm) to Bernhard, 8 Jan. 1924, PA AA Berlin, NL Stresemann, 265/156674–75. See also Berghahn, *Stahlhelm – Bund der Frontsoldaten 1918–1935* (Düsseldorf, 1966), 75–91.

[92] Remarks by Duesterberg and Eulenburg-Wicken in the minutes of the Stahlhelm executive committee, 4–5 July 1925, BA Potsdam, R 72, 4/33–35, 53–55, 58–62.

[93] Resolution of the Stahlhelm executive committee, 4 July 1925, reprinted in *Stahlhelm-Handbuch*, ed. Walter Kettner and Heinrich Hildebrandt, 3rd ed. (Berlin, 1927), 45.

[94] Ausfeld to Stresemann, 13 July 1925, PA AA Berlin, NL Stresemann, 27/159377–78.

[95] For example, see the letter from Hampe to the Stahlhelm's national leadership, 1 Apr. 1925, BA Berlin, R 72, 279/65–66.

despite their ostensibly nonpartisan character.[96] The leaders of the DNVP were particularly sensitive to the positions these organization adopted on issues like the proposed Rhineland security pact and Germany's entry into the League of Nations. Their agitation against the security pact struck a particularly responsive chord among those Nationalists who had opposed their party's participation in the national cabinet and were looking for a suitable pretext that would allow them to return to the relative comfort of an opposition party.[97] The leaders of the DNVP Reichstag delegation, who were in the final stages of guiding the revaluation and tariff bills through parliament, were wary of launching a full-scale attack against Stresemann's foreign policy that, in all likelihood, would lead to the collapse of the government. Though adamantly opposed to a security pact that entailed formal recognition of Germany's western boundaries, Westarp was reluctant to force a cabinet crisis in the summer of 1925 that might lead to the collapse of the national government and preferred instead to wait and see what course future developments would take.[98] The Nationalists thus found themselves obliged to give their tacit approval – though subject to explicit reservations that Westarp spelled out in a speech before the Reichstag on 22 July 1925 – to Stresemann's efforts to reach a diplomatic accommodation with the French on the security of Germany's western borders.[99] Even then, the DNVP Reichstag delegation remained unanimously opposed to the proposed security pact and was determined to prevent it from being signed without significant modifications on a wide range of issues. In the meantime, the Nationalists would use the public debate that the proposed security pact had spawned to revisit the issue of Germany's alleged guilt for the outbreak of World War I and the legitimacy of the Versailles Treaty until a more propitious moment for attacking Stresemann's conduct of German foreign policy presented itself.[100]

---

[96] For example, see Otto Schmidt-Hannover, *Die vaterländische Bewegung und die Deutschnationale Volkspartei. Vortrag, gehalten in Berlin am 28. März 1924*, Deutschnationale Flugschrift, no. 167 (Berlin, 1924), and Max Weiß, "Wir und die vaterländische Bewegung," in *Der nationale Wille. Werden und Wirken der Deutschnationalen Volkspartei 1918–1928*, ed. Max Weiß (Essen, 1928), 351–61.

[97] For example, see the report on the meeting of the DNVP's National Racist Committee, 5 July 1925, appended to a circular from the DNVP's Racist Committee to its members and affiliated regional chapters, 10 July 1925, BA Berlin, R 8005, 361/192–94.

[98] Westarp's speech at a meeting of the executive committee of the Central Association of German Conservatives, 6 June 1925, BLHA Potsdam, Rep. 37, NL Arnim-Boitzenburg, 4429/42–49.

[99] Kuno von Westarp, *Keine neue Ketten! Rede zum Sicherheitspakt am 22. Juli 1925 im Reichstag*, Deutschnationale Flugschrift, no. 218 (Berlin, 1925). On Westarp's dilemma, see Gasteiger, *Westarp*, 270–88.

[100] Westarp to the *Nationale Rundschau* in Bremen, 22 July 1925, NL Westarp, Gärtringen, VN 97. See also the entries in Stresemann's diary for 3, 7 and 17 July 1925, in Stresemann, *Vermächtnis*, ed. Bernhard, 2:143–45, 151–55.

The Locarno Predicament

Pressure on the Nationalist party leadership to dissociate itself from the proposed Rhineland security pact continued to mount through the late summer and early fall of 1925.[101] On 22 September Martin Schiele, the Nationalist minister of the interior and the DNVP's official liaison to the Luther cabinet, presented the government with four demands that had to be met before his party would consent to any treaties that Germany might conclude with the Allies at the upcoming conference at Locarno. The most contentious of these was a demand for the formal repudiation of the war guilt clause by the signatories of the proposed Rhineland security pact.[102] The fact that these demands were, by Stresemann's own admission, remarkably mild in tone and substance suggests that they were formulated not so much to create difficulties for the government as to assuage the leaders of the DNVP's district and provincial organizations who, by no strange coincidence, were scheduled to meet in Berlin later that afternoon. Schiele's conciliatory attitude was no doubt informed by the fact that, as a high-ranking official in the National Rural League, he believed that the DNVP should remain in the government so that organized agriculture could exercise a decisive influence on the formulation of Germany's future trade policy. This position stood in sharp contrast to the militancy of those party leaders who had been subjected to a steady barrage of anti-Stresemann propaganda from the Pan-German League and the patriotic Right. Although Schiele tried to appease the anti-Stresemann elements on the DNVP's right wing by adopting a tougher posture in subsequent negotiations with the foreign minister and other members of the Luther cabinet, he was reluctant to press the matter to its logical conclusion and ultimately relented in his efforts to have the DNVP's demands adopted as the basis of the guidelines that were to define the position of the German delegation at Locarno.[103] Only Schiele's insistence upon the inclusion of the DNVP's demands for the repudiation of the war guilt clause in the government's acceptance of the invitation to Locarno succeeded in reconciling an

[101] Claß's report to the ADV managing committee, Sept. 4, 1925, BA Berlin, R 8048, 144/ 9–19. See also the account in Albrecht Philipp, "Mein Weg: Rückschau eines Siebzig-jährigen auf allerlei Geschenisse und Menschen," Dritte Teil: "Abgeordnetenjahre in der Weimarer Republik (1919–1930)," SHStA Dresden, NL Philipp, 4/178–85. For further details, see Dörr, "Deutschnationale Volkspartei," 158–201.

[102] Westarp, "Ein Jahr Außenpolitik," in Politische Praxis 1926, ed. Walther Lambach (Hamburg, n.d. [1926]), 26–47, here 40–41. On contacts with the government, see Lindeiner-Wildau to Schiele, 11 Sept. 1925, NL Westarp, Gärtringen, VN 120. For further details, see Ohnezeit, Zwischen "schärfster Opposition," 328–39.

[103] Minutes of the ministerial conference, 1 Oct. 1925, and cabinet meeting, 2 Oct. 1925, Kabinette Luther, ed. Minuth, 1:600–05, 657–66.

increasingly contentious DNVP Reichstag delegation to Germany's participation in the conference.[104]

By the time the Locarno conference opened on 5 October 1925, the Nationalists felt isolated within the Luther cabinet and were frustrated by their inability to reconcile the imperative for governmental participation with the commitment to defend Germany's national honor. More than anything else, the leaders of the DNVP were determined to prevent a repeat of what had happened the preceding August when the DNVP Reichstag delegation had split down the middle in the vote on ratification of the Dawes Plan. The specter of another split was never far from their minds and remained very much part of the political baggage that Westarp and other party leaders brought with them as they approached the problems confronting their party's options in the fall of 1925.[105] In the early stages of the negotiations at Locarno, Schiele was able to keep the DNVP Reichstag delegation lined up behind the German delegation at Locarno despite strong opposition from Hugenberg and the leaders of the party's right wing.[106] But as reports from Locarno began to make their way back to Berlin, concerns that Stresemann and the German delegation were not giving sufficient credence to the Nationalist position on matters like the war guilt clause or Germany's entry into the League of Nations began to take hold within the DNVP Reichstag delegation. This, in turn, left Schiele with little choice but to accommodate Westarp and other party leaders who were fundamentally opposed to what Stresemann was trying to accomplish at Locarno. Even then, Westarp was reluctant to precipitate a break with the Luther cabinet for fear that this would clear the way for Social Democratic participation in a new government in which there would have been little, if any, resistance to Stresemann's foreign policy. If a break with the government was to take place, then it would have to be after and not before the conclusion of negotiations at Locarno.[107]

In the meantime, the leaders of Germany's patriotic Right had begun to mobilize their supporters for a crusade against the proposed Rhineland security pact. At the heart of this activity stood the Pan-German League and its

---

[104] On the situation in the DNVP Reichstag delegation, see Westarp to his wife, 24 Sept. 1925, NL Westarp, Gärtringen, as well as also his notes on a meeting of the DNVP Reichstag delegation, 25 Sept. 1925, ibid., VN 121.

[105] Westarp to the DNVP district organization in Bremen, 12 Oct. 1925, NL Westarp, Gärtringen, VN 94.

[106] Schiele to Luther, 5 Oct. 1925, in *Kabinette Luther*, ed. Minuth, 2:668–69, n. 5. For Hugenberg's position, see his letter to Hergt, 5 Oct. 1925, NL Westarp, Gärtringen, VN 53.

[107] Westarp to Traub, 12 Oct. 1925, NL Westarp, Gärtringen, II/17. See also the exchange of letters between Westarp and Schiele in the *Deutsche Allgemeine Zeitung*, 28 Mar. 1931, no. 142.

allies in the DNVP's National Racist Committee and the patriotic leagues.[108] On 22 September the United Patriotic Leagues sent the DNVP Reichstag delegation a resolution urging the Nationalists to resign from the cabinet if their point of view on the upcoming Locarno conference did not prevail. The Stahlhelm and the German Kyffhäuser League of Imperial Warriors (Deutscher Reichskriegerbund Kyffhäuser), an organization for retired army officers that dated back to the early 1890s, immediately endorsed this position with an addendum calling upon the DNVP not to betray the memory of their fallen comrades by submitting to a pact that so grievously violated Germany's national honor.[109] On 6 October the executive committee of the Stahlhelm amplified its position on the Locarno negotiations by adopting a resolution that specifically enjoined the German delegation from acceding to anything that might compromise the restoration of Germany's national honor and singled out the war guilt clause as a matter upon which no compromise was possible.[110] This was directed first and foremost against those Nationalists who, like Schiele, sought a compromise formula that would have made it possible for the DNVP to remain in the government and reinforced the strong stand that the leaders of the party's right wing had taken against Germany's participation in the Locarno conference. The agitation of the patriotic Right produced widespread uneasiness at the local and regional levels of the DNVP's national organization and made it all the more difficult for the DNVP party leadership to devise a formula that would allow it to remain in the government while swallowing what now loomed as an unmitigated foreign policy disaster.[111]

The German delegation returned home from Locarno on 17 October after having initialed an agreement that fell far short of satisfying Nationalist demands regarding the proposed security pact. At a cabinet meeting two days later, Schiele gave a indication of what was soon to follow when he refused to give his stamp of approval or that of his party to the results of the Locarno

[108] Correspondence between Freytagh-Loringhoven and Prince Wilhelm Friedrich, 19–21 Sept. 1925, BA Berlin, R 8048, 223/84–87. On the role of the Pan-Germans in the crusade against Locarno, see Jackisch, "Westarp und die Auseinandersetzungen über Locarno," 155–60.
[109] VVVD to the DNVP Reichstag delegation, 22 Sept. 1925, NL Westarp, Gärtringen, VN 97.
[110] Resolution by the Stahlhelm executive committee, 6 Oct. 1925, reprinted in Sigmund Graff, "Gründung und Entwicklung des Bundes," in Der Stahlhelm. Erinnerungen und Bilder aus den Jahren 1918–1933, ed. Franz Seldte, 2 vols. (Berlin, 1932–33), 1:58–59.
[111] Treviranus to Jarres, 26 Oct. 1925, BA Koblenz, NL Jarres, 54. On unrest at the grass-roots of the DNVP party organization, see Hergt to Westarp, 16 Sept. 1925, NL Westarp, Gärtringen, VN 53, and the resolution "Die Deutschnationalen Sachsens zum Sicher-heitspakt," n.d. [15 Sept. 1925], appended to Kürbs to Westarp, 17 Sept. 1925, ibid., VN 94.

conference.[112] Schiele's position – and that of Westarp as well – was that the DNVP should remain in the cabinet as long as it could use its influence as a member of the governmental coalition to reshape the Locarno agreements in accordance with its own sense of Germany's national honor. But their efforts to prevent a break with the Luther cabinet were undercut by the determination of those on DNVP's right wing to use the Locarno accords to force their party out of the government. Schiele and Westarp won the first skirmish when on 21 October they succeeded in persuading the DNVP Reichstag delegation to go along with their strategy until it had become clear that no improvement in the terms of the Locarno treaty world be forthcoming.[113] But they could not escape the wrath of the party's extreme right wing. On 22 October the executive committee of the DNVP's National Racist Committee and a bastion of Pan-German influence within the party met in Berlin to formulate a resolution denouncing the proposed security pact that would then be presented at a joint meeting of the party executive committee and the leaders of the DNVP's state and regional organizations that was scheduled for the following day. The resolution rejected the results of the Locarno negotiations as irreconcilable with the conditions that the DNVP had attached to its willingness to take part in the negotiations in the first place and demanded that the Reichstag delegation reverse the position it had taken the day before by withdrawing from the governmental coalition.[114] The battle lines between the party leadership and the extremists on the DNVP's right wing could not have been more clearly drawn.

The meeting of the DNVP party executive committee with the leaders of the party's state and regional organizations on the morning of 23 October was tumultuous from beginning to end, so tumultuous that Schiele, in a move that reflected his growing desperation over the situation in the party, turned to Luther in hopes that the chancellor might provide him with a statement on the future status of Alsace-Lorraine that might appease his critics on the DNVP's right wing.[115] But there was little that Luther could do to accommodate his beleaguered cabinet officer, with the result that the representatives of the DNVP's district and local organizations proceeded to adopt a resolution that bluntly rejected the outcome of the Locarno negotiations as "unacceptable for the party."[116] This placed the party's organizational base on a collision course with the party's national leadership and those within the DNVP Reichstag

[112] Minutes of the cabinet meeting, 19 Oct. 1925, in *Kabinette Luther*, ed. Minuth, 2:780–89.
[113] *Korrespondenz der Deutschnationalen Volkspartei*, 22 Oct. 1925, no. 229.
[114] Resolution adopted by the DNVP's National Racist Committee, 22 Oct. 1925, NL Westarp, Gärtringen, VN 55.
[115] Memorandum by Kempner, 23 Oct. 1925, in *Kabinette Luther*, ed., Minuth, 2:795–96.
[116] *Korrespondenz der Deutschnationalen Volkspartei*, 24 Oct. 1925, no. 231.

delegation who were prepared to accept the Locarno agreement as part of the price they had to pay for remaining in the national government. But the real question was whether the party could afford to risk another split reminiscent of the one that had occurred a scant year earlier in the vote on the Dawes Plan. At a stormy meeting of the DNVP Reichstag delegation on the afternoon of 25 October, Westarp demanded that for the sake of party unity his colleagues should set aside their personal feelings and authorize the DNVP's resignation from the existing governmental coalition. Although several deputies proceeded to voice their anger over the way in which the DNVP's district and local leaders had meddled in the delegation's affairs, the delegation nevertheless followed Westarp's directive and instructed Schiele and the other cabinet officers who belonged to the DNVP – Hergt at the ministry of justice along with finance minister Otto von Schlieben and economics minister Albert Neuhaus – to resign from the Luther cabinet.[117] In justifying this step, the official party press insisted that the Locarno accords did not follow the guidelines the cabinet itself had given to the German delegation at Locarno and that the DNVP was therefore not bound by the results of the conference. Responsibility for the collapse of the government coalition, the Nationalists insisted, rested with the government and not with the DNVP.[118]

At the same time that the Nationalists tried to avoid responsibility for the crisis of the Luther cabinet, they appealed to Reich President von Hindenburg in hopes that he could be persuaded not only to block ratification of the Locarno Treaty but also to initiate a full-scale reversal of Germany's political course. Ever since his election to the Reich presidency, Hindenburg had been besieged by congratulatory telegrams and letters from prominent Nationalist leaders hopeful that he would use the powers of his office to support their political agenda.[119] But Hindenburg's activity in the first months of his Reich presidency had done little to justify such hopes. Not only had he ignored Nationalist objections to the retention of Otto Meißner as state secretary in the bureau of the Reich presidency, but he proved extremely reluctant to use the powers of his office to bring about the political changes for which the Nationalists had been hoping. For those Nationalists who had grown disenchanted with Hindenburg's performance at the presidential palace, the Locarno crisis afforded the Reich president an excellent opportunity to erase

---

[117] Ibid., 26 Oct. 1925, no. 232. See also Treviranus to Jarres, 26 Oct. 1925, BA Koblenz, NL Jarres, 54.

[118] *Korrespondenz der Deutschnationalen Volkspartei*, 31 Oct. 1925, no. 237. See also *Erfüllte und unerfüllte Forderungen der deutschen Außenpolitik*, Heft 2, *Locarno*, Deutschnationales Rüstzeug, no. 27 (Berlin, 1925), esp. 9–12, 15–17, as well as the articles by Westarp from late October 1925 in Kuno von Westarp, *Locarno. Authentische und kritische Darstellung*, Deutschnationale Flugschrift, no. 243 (Berlin, 1925), 3–16.

[119] For example, see Westarp to Hindenburg, 29 Apr. 1925, NL Westarp, Gärtringen, II/66, and Spahn to Hindenburg, n.d. [ca. 30 Apr. 1925], BA Koblenz, NL Spahn, 173.

those doubts and reassure the leaders of the German Right of his commitment to their political aspirations. No less a figure than the DNVP Reichstag deputy and former head of the German navy Alfred von Tirpitz urged Hindenburg to use his constitutional authority as Reich president to end the current political crisis by appointing an interim government that was consistent with his own political views and that would refuse to implement the Locarno accords.[120]

By resigning from the government, the Nationalists hoped to precipitate a crisis of sufficient gravity that Hindenburg would have no alternative but to intervene on their behalf. That such hopes were indeed poorly founded became increasingly clear when Hindenburg not only refused to disavow the accomplishments of the German delegation at Locarno but severely chastised the Nationalists for their own political foolishness. Writing to Tirpitz on 5 November 1925, Hindenburg did not hesitate to voice his frustration over developments within the DNVP and to question the political foresight of those who claimed to be his most loyal supporters:

> Through their unexpectedly premature and brash action, the Nationalists have excluded themselves from their hard-fought role in the national government and have postponed any change in the composition of the Prussian government. I fear that such an attitude in today's difficult times will not find universal sympathy, but rather encourage internal discord to the great joy of our enemies. Whether the old "conservatives" would have acted in such a manner is something I leave for you to decide. One already hears patriots speaking of "bulls in a china closet [Elefanten im Porzellanladen]." How unfortunate![121]

Hindenburg's admonition had less to do with the Nationalists' opposition to the Locarno accords than with his dissatisfaction over their choice of tactics.[122] Though angered by the DNVP's decision to leave the Luther cabinet, the Reich president remained sympathetic to the Nationalist position on Locarno and freely acquiesced in their efforts to mobilize his influence in preventing Germany's entry into the League of Nations.[123] Still, his reluctance to act publicly in the matter of Locarno left him vulnerable to attacks from the Pan-German League and the more militantly antirepublican organizations in the so-called patriotic front. In the meantime, the public debate over the Locarno pact seemed to be reaching a crescendo. The Nationalists felt obliged to justify

[120] Tirpitz to Hindenburg, 26 Oct. 1925, BA-MA Freiburg, NL Tirpitz, 176/33–36. See also Scheck, *Tirpitz*, 200–04. For further details, see Harald Zaun, *Paul von Hindenburg und die deutsche Außenpolitik 1925–1934* (Cologne and Vienna, 1999), 387–410, as well as Pyta, *Hindenburg*, 490–94.

[121] Hindenburg to Tirpitz, 5 Nov. 1925, BA-MA Freiburg, NL Tirpitz, 176/37.

[122] Keudell to Tirpitz, 10 Nov. 1925, BA-MA Freiburg, NL Tirpitz, 278/23–24.

[123] Memorandum of a conversation between Hindenburg and Tirpitz, 27 Nov. 1925, BA-MA Freiburg, NL Tirpitz, 176/42–44.

their resignation from the Luther cabinet and dispel rumors of a split within the party by escalating their attacks against the Locarno accords.[124] Moreover, the Allied refusal to implement the corollaries, or so-called *Rückwirkungen*, of the Locarno Treaty until after the treaty had been signed only provided Stresemann's enemies in the DNVP with added incentive for fighting the treaty's acceptance in parliament. Speaking at the DNVP's national party congress in Berlin on 16 November 1925, Westarp cited the failure to implement the corollaries before the treaty was signed as an indication of continued Allied bad faith toward Germany and criticized the treaty as an ill-conceived expedient that severely curtailed Germany's freedom of movement in securing a more thorough revision of the Versailles Treaty at some point in the future. Whatever benefits the DNVP may have reaped from its participation in the Luther cabinet – and here Westarp was clearly defending the decision to enter the government in the first place – were overshadowed by the ominous implications the Locarno Treaty held for the future conduct of German foreign policy.[125]

With the formal ratification of Locarno 27 November 1925, a particularly irksome chapter in the history of the German Right had been closed. In the final analysis, neither the DNVP's increasingly histrionic attacks against the Locarno Treaty nor Hindenburg's involvement in the efforts to block its acceptance were to much avail. Nevertheless, the episode's implications for Germany's future political development and in particular for the success of Stresemann's efforts to stabilize the republic from the Right were enormous. Not only did the DNVP's refusal to support Locarno and its subsequent resignation from the national government constitute a severe setback for Stresemann's efforts to stabilize the Weimar Republic from the right,[126] but this represented a decisive triumph for the Stahlhelm and its sister organizations on the patriotic Right. By mobilizing popular sentiment against the treaty at the district and local levels of the Nationalist party organization, the Stahlhelm and its affiliates in the patriotic movement played a decisive role in forcing the DNVP's resignation from the Luther cabinet.[127] At the same time, the fight over Locarno had done much to energize the patriotic movement and to mobilize it against those special economic interests whose

---

[124] For example, see Westarp's articles from Nov. 1925, reprinted in Westarp, *Locarno*, 16–28.

[125] Kuno von Westarp, *Unser Ziel: Deutschlands Befreiung! Rede auf dem Reichsparteitage in Berlin am 16. November 1925*, Deutschnationale Flugschrift, no. 246 (Berlin, 1925), 13–20.

[126] For Stresemann's reaction, see his letter to Keudell, 27 Nov. 1925, PA AA Berlin, NL Stresemann, 32/160613–15.

[127] Treviranus to Jarres, 26 Oct. 1925, BA Koblenz, NL Jarres, 54.

influence had been instrumental in the ratification of the Dawes Plan and the DNVP's entry into the Luther cabinet. The net effect of all of this was to undermine the unity of the German Right and to exacerbate the differences between those governmental conservatives who were prepared, albeit with personal and ideological reservations of the greatest magnitude, to pursue their objectives within the framework of the existing system of government and those radical nationalists who remained irreconcilably opposed to any form of collaboration with the hated Weimar system.

11

The Road Back to Power

The struggle over Locarno constituted a defining moment in the history of the German Right. Not only had the DNVP's resignation from the Luther cabinet in October 1925 dealt a severe blow to Stresemann's hopes of stabilizing the Weimar Republic from the Right, but the struggle over Locarno had done much to energize the various patriotic and paramilitary organizations that constituted the nucleus of Germany's radical Right. At the same time, the collapse of the first Luther cabinet came as a bitter disappointment to those special economic interests in agriculture, industry, and the Christian labor movement that had underwritten the DNVP's first experiment at government participation and that were anxious to return to the corridors of power at the first suitable opportunity. Caught between the demands of agriculture, industry, and Christian labor for a return to government and the agitation of the patriotic Right against Stresemann's foreign policy, the leaders of the DNVP found it increasingly difficult to chart a steady course for the German Right in the post-Locarno era and floundered in a sea of uncertainty and indecision. At the heart of this indecisiveness lay the paradox that in order to promote and protect the welfare of those interests that constituted its material base the DNVP was obliged to work within the framework of a governmental system to which it was fundamentally and ideologically opposed. Whether or not the DNVP would ever succeed in resolving this paradox would ultimately determine the fate of the Weimar Republic.

All of this coincided with a subtle, yet perceptible, intensification of the legitimacy crisis that had plagued the Weimar Republic ever since its founding in the wake of the November Revolution. Not only had the antisocial character of the government's stabilization program done much to embitter the very constituencies upon which Germany's nonsocialist parties relied for their electoral support, but the authoritarian manner in which it had been implemented undermined public confidence in the viability of Germany's republican institutions. At the same time, the increasingly prominent role that organized economic interests like the National Federation of German Industry and the National Rural League began to play in the political process as well as the increasing fragmentation of the Weimar party system along lines of economic self-interest lent renewed credence to charges from the radical Right that the existing system of government offered an inadequate framework for the conduct of national policy. The net effect of all this was both to make it all the more difficult for Weimar's political leadership to forge a viable domestic consensus for the conduct of national policy and to erode whatever legitimacy the Weimar party system still possessed in the eyes of Germany's nonsocialist electorate.[1]

In the Wake of Locarno

By no means was the general course of Germany's social and economic development in the second half of the 1920s all that conducive to the success of Stresemann's stabilization strategy. The years from 1924 to 1928/29 were years of economic contraction that contained the seeds of future collapse. The measures that had been taken to stabilize the mark in 1923–24 triggered an economic recession that drew to a climax towards the end of 1925 and the beginning of 1926. The most dramatic symptom of the crisis was a sharp increase in unemployment from 636,000 in October 1925 to 2,270,000 in February 1926. This was accompanied by an unprecedented number of business failures in 1925 and 1926. No sector of the economy managed to escape the recession unscathed, although agriculture and heavy industry were more severely affected than banking, manufacturing, and commerce.[2] At the heart of these difficulties lay an acute capital shortage that stemmed not just from the weakness of the German stock market as a source of investment capital but also from the restrictive credit policies of the German National Bank. Further compounding the situation was the erosion of corporate profits through the high tax rates that had been introduced as part of the government's stabilization program in 1923–24.[3] Similarly, agriculture was still reeling from the collapse of its credit cooperatives during the runaway inflation of the early 1920s and found itself forced to compete with industry on essentially unfavorable terms for the little capital that was still available. With the collapse of agricultural prices on the international market and rising domestic prices for fertilizer, fuel, and farm machinery, the German farmer was caught in a price and credit squeeze that left him with no alternative but to go into debt. Whatever gains the German farmer had

---

[1] Larry Eugene Jones, "In the Shadow of Stabilization: German Liberalism and the Legitimacy Crisis of the Weimar Party System, 1924–1930," in *Die Nachwirkungen der Inflation auf die deutsche Geschichte 1924–1933*, ed. Gerald D. Feldman (Munich, 1985), 21–41.

[2] For further details, see Blaich, *Die Wirtschaftskrise 1925–26 und die Reichsregierung. Von der Erwerbslosenfürsorge zur Konjunkturpolitik* (Kallmünz, 1977).

[3] Harold James, *The German Slump: Politics and Economics, 1924–1936* (Oxford, 1986), 130–31.

experienced as a result of the inflation were now threatened by the specter of rising rural indebtedness.[4]

The recession that struck Germany in 1925–26 was anomalous in the sense that it did not conform to the general pattern of international economic development. The realization that the German slump was not part of an international economic downturn but a specifically German phenomenon that could be understood only in terms of the specific structural weaknesses of the German economy gave rise to increased pressure from various sectors of the German economy for more active state intervention in the economic process. In December 1925 the leaders of the National Federation of German Industry intensified their campaign on behalf of tax relief for business and industry by publishing a set of comprehensive recommendations for economic and fiscal reform. For the RDI the key to economic recovery lay in facilitating the process of capital formation through a dramatic reduction in taxation and government spending.[5] In a similar vein, the leaders of the National Rural League pinned their hopes of recovery on increased tariff protection for the German farmer and called for a reversal of German trade policy that would make the defense of the home market and not the conquest of new markets for industrial and manufactured goods its chief aim.[6] Neither these demands stood any chance of making it through the Reichstag as long as the DNVP, the largest of Germany's nonsocialist parties, remained outside the government.

After the DNVP's resignation from the national government in the fall of 1925, the Luther cabinet reconstituted itself as a bourgeois minority cabinet that was to remain in office until the Locarno accords had been ratified and implemented.[7] This was little more than a political expedient that underscored the inherent weaknesses of Germany's republican institutions and confirmed right-wing claims that parliamentary democracy was incapable of producing a stable domestic consensus for the conduct of national policy. No one was more

---

[4] Ibid., 253–59.

[5] *Deutsche Wirtschafts- und Finanzpolitik*, Veröffentlichungen des Reichsverbandes der Deutschen Industrie, no. 29 (Berlin, 1925), esp. 13–16. See also Weisbrod, *Schwerindustrie in der Weimarer Republik*, 226–45.

[6] Eberhard von Kalckreuth, *Ernährung und Schutzzoll*, Wirtschaftsfragen der Zeit, no. 3 (Berlin, n.d. [1925–26]). See also Dirk Stegmann, "Deutsche Zoll- und Handelspolitik 1924/5–29 unter besonderer Berücksichtigung agrarischer und industrieller Interessen," in *Industrielles System und politische Entwicklung. Verhandlungen des Internationalen Symposiums in Bochum vom 12–17. Juni 1973*, ed. Hans Mommsen, Dietmar Petzinna, and Bernd Weisbrod (Düsseldorf, 1974), 499–513.

[7] Stürmer, *Koalition und Opposition*, 127–40. See also the memorandum drafted for Hindenburg, "Bemerkungen zur Regierungs-Umbildung," 2 Dec. 1925, records of the Office of the Reich Presidency, BA Berlin, Bestand R 601, 401/18–23.

disturbed by the implications of the DNVP's decision to leave the government than the leaders of the National Rural League. At a demonstration in Berlin just three days after the DNVP's resignation from the Luther cabinet, Reich Agricultural Minister Gerhard von Kanitz listened to a steady stream of speakers from the various parts of the country who deplored the increasingly desperate situation in which German farmers found themselves since the end of the inflation and called for immediate state intervention to prevent the total collapse of German agriculture. Friedrich von Zitzewitz-Kottow from the Pomeranian nobility, Johannes Wolf from the National Farm Workers' League, Heimcke from Ravenstedt in Hanover, and DNVP Reichstag deputy Georg Bachmann from Westheim in Bavaria spoke in telling detail of how the deepening agricultural crisis had affected large landowners, farm laborers, and small and middle-sized farmers alike. To conclude the conference, RLB president Eberhard von Kalckreuth introduced a three-point resolution that called for governmental action to reestablish the system of agricultural credit that had been ruined by the inflation, an energetic price policy aimed at restoring prewar parity between the production costs of agricultural and industrial commodities, and strict controls over unproductive and superfluous administrative costs at the national, state, and municipal levels. All of this was necessary, Kalckreuth insisted, to restore the health of German agriculture and with it the health of the German nation.[8]

By the end of 1925 the moderates within the RLB were apparently prepared to support Stresemann's foreign policy in return for increased tariff protection for domestic farm products.[9] At the same time, they had become so distressed by the implications the DNVP's withdrawal from the government held for the future of German trade policy that they began to promote the candidacy of Karl Hepp, one of the RLB's two presidents and a member of the DVP Reichstag delegation, for the ministry of agriculture in the Luther cabinet.[10] But this initiative ran into strong opposition at the upper echelons of the RLB leadership from conservative farm leaders with close ties to the DNVP who feared that any positive overture toward the national government might be

---

[8] *Bauer in Not. Herrenhaus-Tagung des Reichs-Landbundes, Mittwoch, den 28. Oktober 1925* (Berlin, 1925). For Kalckreuth's resolution, see 41–42. In a similar vein, see Karl Böhme, *Der Bauern Not – des Reiches Tod!* (Nowawes, n.d. [1925]), and Franz Schenk von Stauffenberg, *Bauernnot! Ein Mahnruf*, Wirtschaftsfragen der Zeit, nos. 4/5 (Berlin, n.d. [1925–26]).

[9] Stresemann's memorandum of a conversation with Richard von Flemming-Paatzig from the Pomeranian Chamber of Agriculture (Landwirtschaftskammer für die Provinz Pommern), 6 Dec. 1925, PA AA Berlin, NL Stresemann, 272, cited in Stürmer, *Koalition und Opposition*, 133.

[10] Handwritten notes on the meeting of the RLB executive commitee, 13 Jan. 1926, NL Westarp, Gärtringen, II/24.

interpreted as a sign of support for Stresemann's foreign policy.[11] At the same time, the Brandenburg Rural League (Brandenburgischer Landbund), one of the RLB's most conservative regional affiliates, sent the RLB's national leadership a petition criticizing the DNVP for its failure to pay sufficient attention to the vital interests of German agriculture and urging the RLB to continue its cooperation with the government and the parties that supported it despite the DNVP's resignation from the cabinet.[12] This only fueled rumors that the leaders of the RLB were about to found a new party of their own as a way of extricating themselves from the difficult situation in which the DNVP's resignation from the Luther cabinet had left them.[13]

Throughout all of this, the Nationalists remained resolutely opposed to any accommodation with the Luther cabinet as long as this entailed explicit support for Stresemann's foreign policy and refused to go along with Germany's entry into the League of Nations unless specific conditions accelerating the timetable for the evacuation of the Rhineland were met.[14] When efforts to reorganize the Luther cabinet following the ratification of the Locarno accords in December 1925 ended in deadlock,[15] the DNVP went into "active opposition" to the new Luther cabinet and demanded that it withdraw its petition for acceptance into the League of Nations as a condition of its toleration or support.[16] But Nationalist polemics against the second Luther cabinet did little to repair the damage the DNVP's resignation from the national government in the fall of 1925 had done to its relations with the German agriculture. In the late winter and spring of 1926 the specter of an agrarian secession loomed increasingly large as Baron Prätorius von Richthofen-Boguslawitz, chairman of the Silesian Rural League (Schlesischer Landbund) and a member of the RLB presidium, resigned his seat in the DNVP Reichstag delegation and called upon his followers to align themselves behind the policies of Luther and Hindenburg.[17]

[11] Memorandum by Goldacker, 12 Dec. 1925, NL Westarp, Gärtringen, VN 52. See also Goldacker to Kalckreuth, 12 Dec. 1925, ibid., II/24.
[12] "Entschließung des Gesamtvorstandes des Brandenburgischen Landbundes zur Politik der Deutschnationalen Volkspartei," n.d. [late 1925]," NL Westarp, Gärtringen, VN 54. For further details, see Pomp, *Bauern und Grossgrundbesitzer*, 244–50.
[13] On rumors to this effect, see Alvensleben to Stresemann, 1 Dec. 1925, PA AA Berlin, NL Stresemann, 32, cited in Stürmer, *Koalition und Opposition*, 133.
[14] See Westarp to Stegmann, 30 Jan. 1926, NL Westarp, Gärtringen, VN 76, and Westarp to Knebusch, 8 Feb. 1926, ibid., VN 78.
[15] Stürmer, *Koalition und Opposition*, 127–40.
[16] Protocol of a conversation between Luther, Schiele, and Westarp, 28 Jan. 1926, BA Koblenz, Nachlass Hans Luther, 362. See also Westarp, "Außenpolitik," in *Politische Praxis 1927*, ed. Walther Lambach (Hamburg, n.d. [1927]), 12–13.
[17] Richthofen first announced his intent to resign his Reichstag mandate in early December 1925. See Goßler to Westarp, 9 Dec. 1925, NL Westarp, Gärtringen, VN 52. For his reasons, see Richthofen to Nicholas (Brandenburg Rural League), 7 Apr. 1926, BA Berlin,

As chairman of the DNVP Reichstag delegation, Westarp tried to reassure the party's farm leaders that the government's weakness in parliament made it even more as responsive to Nationalist pressure on economic issues than it would have been had the DNVP remained in the government.[18] Even as the National Rural League commended the DNVP party leadership for helping to rectify inequities in German tax policy that disciminated against the German farmer,[19] disgruntlement on the party's agrarian wing continued to grow.[20]

These developments only underscored the lack of direction at the upper echelons of the DNVP's national organization and set the stage for a change in the Nationalist party leadership. In late February 1926 Friedrich Winckler, the DNVP's national party chairman since the fall of 1924, asked to be relieved of his responsibilities as party leader so that he could return to his work in the Lutheran Church.[21] Over the course of the next several weeks, most of those who had been mentioned as Winckler's possible successor – Schiele, Hugenberg, and estate owner Hans Schlange-Schöningen from the party's Pomeranian organization – withdrew from consideration for one reason or another, so that in the final analysis only Westarp, chairman of the DNVP Reichstag delegation since the formation of the first Luther cabinet in January 1925, remained in contention. The party chairmanship, however, was not a position that Westarp actively sought or particularly wanted. Westarp had always conceived of himself as a liaison between the DNVP and the Prussian conservatives who had regrouped after World War I in the Central Association of German Conservatives, and he had worked with great determination to carve out a niche in the postwar DNVP for those who had formerly belonged to the German Conservative Party. Moreover, his conservative pedigree represented a distinct liability in the eyes of the DNVP's Christian-social labor wing, which, along with the young conservatives, remained decidedly cool to the prospect of his election as party chairman. It was only after Schiele, who had prevailed over Westarp by a narrow margin in a preliminary vote on 5 March,[22] formally withdrew his name from

---

R 8034 I, 268/327–31. For further details, see Dörr, "Deutschnationale Volkspartei," 216–17.

[18] Westarp to Weilnböck, 13 Feb. 1926, BA Koblenz, NL Weilnböck, 2a. See also Westarp's memorandum, 13 Mar. 1926, NL Westarp, Gärtringen, II/24.

[19] Kalckreuth to Westarp, 10 Mar. 1926, NL Westarp, Gärtringen, II/24.

[20] Weilnböck to Westarp, 12 Mar. 1926, NL Westarp, Gärtringen, VN 76. See also Hilpert to Weilnböck, 14 Mar. 1926, BA Koblenz, NL Weilnböck, 2a.

[21] Winckler to the members of the DNVP party representation, 26 Feb. 1926, BA Koblenz, NL Spahn, 174.

[22] Letter from Westarp's wife to his daughter, 6 Mar. 1926, NL Westarp, Gärtringen.

Figure 7. Photograph of Count Kuno von Westarp, DNVP Reichstag deputy from 1920 to 1930, chairman of the DNVP Reichstag delegation from 1925 to 1929, and DNVP national party chairman from 1926 to 1928. Reproduced with permission from the Bundesarchiv Berlin, Bild 146-1976-067-19A

consideration that party leaders closed ranks behind Westarp as the new party chairman.[23]

Westarp's formal installation as DNVP party chairman took place by acclamation at a meeting of the DNVP party representation on 24 March.[24] Westarp inherited a party that was deeply divided, in no small measure as a result of his own tactics during the Locarno crisis in the fall of 1925.[25] A district-by-district survey of the DNVP's national organization by the party's Berlin headquarters shortly after Westarp assumed office revealed widespread exhaustion and frustration among the party's rank-and-file membership. Local party leaders complained not only of a lack of resources but also of a general malaise at all levels the party organization.[26] It was unclear

---

[23] Letter from 19 Mar. 1926, ibid. See also the report from Linau to Buff on the meeting of the DNVP party leadership, 17 Mar. 1926, NSSA Osnabrück, C1, 27-II.

[24] Letter from Westarp's wife to his daughter, 24 Mar. 1926, NL Westarp, Gärtringen.

[25] For example, see Keudell to Westarp, 1 Mar. 1926, BA-MA Freiburg, NL Tirpitz, 278/34–37.

[26] Five-page report appended to Weiß to Westarp, Jacobi, and Treviranus, 29 Apr. 1926, NL Westarp, Gärtringen, VN 73. See also Neubergt to Jacobi, 29 Apr. 1926, ibid., VN 98.

whether Westarp possessed the personal mandate necessary to restore party unity. To moderates on the party's left wing, Westarp's ties to old-line Prussian conservatism and his opposition to the aspirations of the Christian-national labor movement in the first years of the Weimar Republic made him particularly suspect. To the militantly antirepublican elements on the party's right wing, Westarp was too closely identified with the compromise of political principle that had accompanied the DNVP's entry into the Luther government. Still, the party's local leaders were relieved by his election and hoped that he could reinvigorate the party and infuse it with the sense of purpose necessary to lead the crusade against the twin evils of Versailles and Weimar to a successful conclusion.[27]

What Westarp brought to the party chairmanship was an unwavering commitment to the restoration and preservation of party unity, a commitment demonstrated both during the 1922 racist crisis and in the aftermath of the 1924 split on the Dawes Plan.[28] Moreover, Westarp was an accomplished negotiator with a conciliatory style of leadership that made it easy for him to work with the different factions in the party. But his election as DNVP party chairman did not bring an end to the strife that was tearing the party apart. For while those on the party's right wing hoped that Westarp would return the DNVP to the path of unconditional opposition to the Weimar Republic,[29] the continued deterioration of Germany's agricultural economy led the leaders of the party's agrarian wing to think that only rejoining the government at the earliest possible opportunity could possibly help.[30] East Elbian conservatives like Count Friedrich von der Schulenburg-Tressow were particularly concerned that farmers and independent peasants, radicalized by the deteriorating economic situation in the countryside, were falling under the influence of the racist Right.[31] The crisis came to a head when on 30 March 1926 more than 250 conservatives from Brandenburg, most of whom belonged to the land-owning aristocracy, met in Berlin to protest the state of affairs that existed in the DNVP. The meeting had been called by Count Dietlof von Arnim-Boitzenburg, one of Brandenburg's largest landowners and an outspoken critic of the DNVP's apparent accommodation with Germany's republican system of government. Arnim-Boitzenburg's objectives were two-fold, first to energize the efforts of those who, like him, sought to return the DNVP to the path of unconditional opposition to the Weimar Republic and second to encourage

---

[27] For example, see Würtz to Spahn, 13 Apr. 1926, BA Koblenz, NL Spahn, 176.
[28] Gasteiger, *Westarp*, 229–358. See also Jones, "Kuno Graf von Westarp und die Krise des deutschen Konservativismus," 118–29.
[29] Exchange of letters between Westarp and the ADV's Vietinghoff-Scheel, 26–27 Mar. 1926, NL Westarp, Gärtringen, VN 96.
[30] Wilmowsky to Krupp, 11 Apr. 1926, HA Krupp Essen, FAH 23/501/83–89.
[31] Schulenburg to Westarp, 15 Aug. 1926, NL Westarp, Gärtringen, VN 75.

the land-owning aristocracy to assert itself more vigorously within both the DNVP and the National Rural League.[32] The results of the meeting, however, were ambiguous. For whereas between twenty-five and thirty of those present supported Arnim-Boitzenburg in his campaign to reverse the direction in which the DNVP and RLB appeared to be headed, his efforts ran into strong opposition from his namesake, Count Dietloff von Arnim-Rittgarten-Ragow, and other Brandenburg conservatives who embraced the political strategy espoused by those in control of the RLB.[33] Among those who rejected the obstructionist tactics of Arnim-Boitzenburg and his associates was none other than Jean Nicolas, chairman of the Brandenburg Rural League, who reaffirmed his commitment to the basic principles of governmental conservatism in a pamphlet distributed to estate owners in Brandenburg.[34]

While the meeting in Berlin exposed the divisions that existed within the ranks of the Prussian aristocracy and thus failed to fulfill the expectations of its instigators,[35] it nevertheless sent a signal to Westarp that he could ill afford to ignore. Although Westarp continued to rely upon his relationship with Arnim-Boitzenburg to keep the disgruntlement of the East Elbian aristocracy from developing into a full-scale mutiny against the DNVP,[36] he also realized that in the long run these developments only underscored the need for the DNVP to return to the government at the first suitable opportunity so that it could do what was necessary to prevent the complete collapse of Germany's rural economy.[37] But as the DNVP intensified its attacks against the Luther cabinet in preparation for its return to power, it found itself drawn more closely to the national government on a number of practical issues. Not only did the DNVP join the government in denouncing socialist and communist efforts to conduct a referendum authorizing the uncompensated expropriation of Germany's dynastic houses,[38] but they both opposed the campaign of former DNVP Reichstag deputy Count Arthur von Posadowsky-Wehner and the leaders of the Savers' Association for the German Reich (Sparerbund

---

[32] Arnim-Boitzenburg to Nicolas, Mar. 1926, BA Berlin, R 8034 I, 268/332. For Arnim-Boitzenburg's criticism of the DNVP, see his letters to Wischnöwski, 4 May 1925, and Westarp 10 May 1926, BLHA Potsdam, Rep. 37, NL Arnim-Boitzenburg, 4428/88–90. For further details, see Flemming, "Konservatismus als 'nationalrevolutionäre Bewegung'," 295–331.

[33] No protocol of the meeting has survived. On the strategic split that developed at the meeting, see Pomp, "Brandenburgischer Landadel," 188–95.

[34] Nicolas, "Landbundarbeit und Politik," n.d. [Apr. 1926], NL Westarp, Gärtringen, VN 79.

[35] Arnim-Boitzenburg to Westarp, 27 Apr. 1926, NL Westarp, Gärtringen, VN 96.

[36] Correspondence between Westarp and Arnim-Boitzenburg, Apr.–June 1926, NL Westarp, Gärtringen, VN 96.

[37] See Westarp to Schulenburg, 22 Apr. 1926, and Treviranus to Schulenburg, 23 Apr. 1926, NL Westarp, Gärtringen, VN 75.

[38] Undated nine-page report appended to Weiß to Westarp, 26 June 1926, NL Westarp, Gärtringen, VN 73.

für das Deutsche Reich) to revise the 1925 revaluation settlement by means of a popular referendum.[39] Perhaps most telling, however, was the DNVP's failure to come to the government's rescue by abstaining on a vote of no-confidence that the leaders of the DDP introduced on 12 May in response to the government's decision to permit Germany's diplomatic missions to display not just the new republican flag with its historic black, red, and gold colors but also a modified version of the old imperial banner that served as Germany's commercial flag. As a result, Luther cabinet was forced to resign on 18 May 1926.[40]

The Economic Imperative

Its disclaimers to the contrary notwithstanding, the DNVP had played a decisive role in staging the collapse of the second Luther cabinet. Yet while this turn of events cleared the way for a reorganization of the national government, it found the Nationalists as indecisive as ever. The DNVP remained strongly opposed to Germany's entry into the League of Nations and balked at participating in the formation of a new government as long as this entailed explicit acceptance of Stresemann's foreign policy.[41] The Social Democrats, on the other hand, were no more eager than the Nationalists to surrender the benefits of opposition for the dubious honor of entering the government. This left Germany's republican leadership with the unhappy prospect of organizing still another minority cabinet based upon the parties of bourgeois middle. Although the Nationalists opposed the formation of another minority cabinet that, in the worst of scenarios, might be totally dependent upon the toleration of the Social Democrats and found themselves under heavy pressure from their supporters in industry and agriculture to rejoin the government,[42] the DNVP Reichstag delegation remained divided pretty much down the middle as to whether it should seek a role in the government. As a result, the DNVP proved incapable of staking out a coherent position in the negotiations that followed the collapse of the Luther cabinet

---

[39] For example, see Westarp to the Savers' Association (Sparerbund), 11 June 1926, NSSA Osnabrück, C1/90/71–73, and 17 June 1926, NL Westarp, Gärtringen, VN 72.

[40] Stürmer, *Koalition und Opposition*, 146–51. On Luther's relations with the DNVP during the flag crisis, see his letter to Richthofen, 3 July 1926, BA Koblenz, NL Jarres, 37/2–12. For further details, see Dörr, "Deutschnationale Volkspartei," 225–30.

[41] In this respect, see Axel von Freytagh-Loringhoven, *Von Locarno nach Genf und Thoiry* (Berlin, 1926), esp. 16–20, and Paul Bang, *Die Deutschen als Landsknechte. Eine Bilanz des neuesten Kurses* (Dresden, n.d. [1926]), esp. 45–63.

[42] Letter from Ada Gräfin von Westarp to Gertraude Freifrau Hiller von Gaertringen, 14 May 1926, NL Westarp, Gärtringen. See also Wilmowsky to Krupp, 15 May 1926, HA Krupp Essen, FAH 23/501/91–94.

and languished on the sidelines as the former chancellor Wilhelm Marx proceeded to organize another bourgeois minority government that was officially presented to the Reichstag on 17 May 1926.[43]

From the outset, the third Marx cabinet was nothing more than a temporary expedient that would eventually be replaced by a majority cabinet if and when either the Nationalists or the Social Democrats managed to overcome their aversion to political responsibility. In the meantime, conservative economic interests worked vigorously both behind the scenes and in public to lay the foundation for the DNVP's return to power. No effort was more important in this respect than that undertaken by the National Federation of German Industry to resolve the differences that separated it from the National Rural League in the matter of trade and tariff policy. Organized agriculture continued to complain about the preferential treatment that Germany's export-oriented industries had supposedly received in a series of bilateral trade treaties that Germany had concluded with Russia, Spain, and the three Scandinavian countries since the passage of the new tariff bill in August 1925.[44] The more prescient of Germany's industrial leaders were well aware of the danger that such sentiment posed to the unity of the German Right and were anxious to avert a conflict over trade policy that might complicate Nationalist efforts to rejoin the government. The key figure in this endeavor was Paul Reusch, director of the Gutehoffnungshütte in Oberhausen who organized a series of informal meetings in December 1926 between Germany's industrial and agricultural leaders in an attempt to improve relations between the two factions of Germany's conservative infrastructure.[45] Reusch's chief liaison to organized agriculture was Baron Tilo von Wilmowsky, a moderate conservative who, as the brother-in-law of Ruhr industrialist Gustav Krupp von Bohlen und Halbach and chairman of the RLB's regional affiliate in Prussian Saxony, was uniquely positioned to mediate between Germany's largest and most influential industrial and agricultural interest organizations.[46] With industry apparently willing to concede the necessity of a limited agricultural tariff as long as this did not increase overall production costs, preliminary efforts to reach an understanding between industry and agriculture on the contentious issue of trade policy bode well for the stabilization of conservative power in the late Weimar Republic.

---

[43] For further details, see Stürmer, *Koalition und Opposition*, 151–55, and Hehl, *Marx*, 376–79.

[44] Minutes of the RLB committee for tariff and trade questions, 15 Apr. 1926, BA Koblenz, NL Weilnböck, 37.

[45] Reusch's remarks at a meeting of representatives of industry and agriculture, 9 Dec. 1926, RWWA Cologne, Abt. 130, NL Reusch, 40010124/0. For further details, see Gessner, *Agrarverbände*, 72–74.

[46] See Zollitsch, "Das Scheitern der 'gouvernmentalen' Rechten," 255–59.

A further sign of movement on the Right was an initiative taken by the DNVP's Baron Wilhelm von Gayl and the DVP's Karl Jarres in the summer of 1926. The two men, both highly regarded in conservative circles, shared the leadership of a five year-old coalition, or *Arbeitsgemeinschaft*, between the DNVP and DVP in the Prussian State Council (Preußischer Staatsrat), a body whose principal functions were consultative rather than legislative. On 30 June 1926 Gayl and Jarres approached the leaders of the two parties with the proposal for the creation of an *Arbeitsgemeinschaft* in the Reichstag and Prussian Landtag similar to the one that existed in the Prussian State Council. Such a step, they contended, would ultimately lead to the consolidation of the German bourgeoisie on a platform that was national, Christian, and conservative.[47] Not only did their proposal meet with a positive response from the leaders of the Nationalist delegations in both the Reichstag and Prussian Landtag,[48] but it also received strong public support from influential spokesmen on the DVP's right wing.[49] Stresemann, however, was particularly wary of the implications that closer political and organizational ties with the DNVP held for his own party's freedom of action. Writing to Jarres on 30 July, Stresemann explained that the proposed *Arbeitsgemeinschaft* would deprive the DVP of the influence it currently enjoyed as an independent party of the German middle and would eventually force it, as the smaller of the two parties in question, to resign from the national government. Rather than join the DVP and DNVP in a new coalition of the bourgeois Right, Stresemann argued, the Center would opt instead for a return to the Weimar Coalition. The net effect of the proposed *Arbeitsgemeinschaft* would not be to strengthen the conservative element in German political life but to precipitate a swing to the left within the Center and the reestablishment of the Weimar Coalition as the arbiter of Germany's political future.[50]

Stresemann's rebuke did little to dampen the enthusiasm of Gayl and his friends for a parliamentary *Arbeitsgemeinschaft* with the DVP. With strong encouragement from Kalckreuth, Wilmowsky, and the leaders of the National Rural League, Gayl scheduled a meeting for August 28, to which Albert Vögler, one of Germany's most politically engaged industrialists, was also invited. The

---

[47] Gayl and Jarres to Stresemann, 30 June 1926, BA Koblenz, R 45 II, 303/7–11. See also Jarres to Stresemann, 5 July 1926, BA Koblenz, NL Jarres, 37. For further details, see Jones, *German Liberalism*, 275–78; Richter, *Deutsche Volkspartei*, 429–31; and Wright, *Stresemann*, 369–72.

[48] For example, see Westarp to Gayl, 5 July 1926, NL Westarp, Gärtringen, VN 125, and Winkler to Gayl and Jarres, 5 July 1926, BA Koblenz, NL Jarres, 37, as well as Gayl to Jarres, 2 July 1926, ibid.

[49] For example, see Gildemeister, "Arbeitsgemeinschaft der Rechten," *Kölnische Zeitung*, 13 July 1926, no. 512, and Eduard Dingeldey, "Die Arbeitsgemeinschaft der Bürgerlichen," *Rheinisch-Westfälische Zeitung*, 29 July 1926, no. 521.

[50] Stresemann to Jarres, 30 July 1926, PA AA Berlin, NL Stresemann, 95/173105–14.

purpose of the meeting was to form a five-man committee to oversee the creation of a special body that would mediate between the various right-wing parties in hopes of establishing a united front.[51] Gayl's initiative received active support from Westarp and the leaders of the DNVP but failed to overcome Stresemann's resistance to the idea of closer political ties with the DNVP. Gayl and his associates tried to reassure Stresemann and the DVP party leadership that they had no intention of unifying the two parties and insisted that their immediate objective was simply the creation of a loose parliamentary coalition that would facilitate closer cooperation between the two parties on a number of practical political issues.[52] Similarly, G. R. Treviranus, a rising moderate in the DNVP Reichstag delegation, tried to soften the DVP's resistance to the proposed *Arbeitsgemeinschaft* by suggesting that it be expanded to include to the Center as well.[53] These efforts notwithstanding, the project was already in serious trouble when it suffered what proved to be a fatal blow from an entirely unexpected direction, the National Federation of German Industry.

The RDI held its annual membership convention in Dresden on 4–5 September 1926. Upon his election to the federation's presidency in early 1925, Carl Duisberg had initiated a change in the RDI's political orientation that would draw to a climax at Dresden with a formal declaration of loyalty to the Weimar Constitution and the republican system of government. In light of the bitter opposition of certain sectors of Ruhr heavy industry to Germany's new republican order, Duisberg felt that he had to secure the cooperation of at least one major representative of the Ruhr industrial establishment when the RDI affirmed its acceptance of the Weimar Republic at Dresden. When ill health caused Vögler to back out of the speech he was scheduled to give, Duisberg turned to Paul Silverberg, a former Stinnes associate who had established himself as a dominant figure in the German soft coal industry.[54] Speaking at Dresden on 4 September, Silverberg caused a sensation when toward the end of his remarks he went beyond a simple affirmation of the RDI's willingness to work within the framework of the existing constitutional system to call for the revival of the *Zentralarbeitsgemeinschaft* and the reentry of the Social Democrats into the national government. To be sure, Silverberg prefaced his remarks with an attack on the social welfare system as it had evolved during the Weimar Republic and criticized the Social Democrats for their reluctance to accept their fare share of the governmental burden. At the same time, Silverberg argued that in a parliamentary democracy it was

[51] Gayl to Jarres, 14 Aug. 1926, BA Koblenz, NL Jarres, 37.
[52] Gayl to Jarres, 26 Aug. 1926, ibid.
[53] Treviranus to Jarres, 18 Aug. 1926, ibid. See also Treviranus, "Weg mit den Scheuklappen," *Berliner Börsen-Zeitung*, 23 July 1926, no. 337.
[54] Correspondence between Kastl and Silverberg, 22–23 July 1926, BA Koblenz, NL Silverberg, 235/20–22.

intolerable for a party in which the overwhelming majority of the German working class found its political representation to escape the burden of political responsibility. The Social Democrats must therefore turn their backs upon the politics of the street and join hands with Germany's industrial leadership in revitalizing the German economy and restoring to it the full flower of its productive potential.[55]

Silverberg's speech – and particularly his declaration of loyalty to the republican system of government – represented the culmination of a concerted effort by Duisberg and the more moderate elements in the German industrial establishment to bring the policies of the largest and most influential of Germany's industrial interest organizations in line with the realities of Weimar's economic and political stabilization. Industry moderates like Clemens Lammers from the German Center Party derived great satisfaction from the outcome of the Dresden convention and hoped that it signaled the beginning of an harmonious new relationship between industry, labor, and the state.[56] The leaders of Ruhr heavy industry, on the other hand, felt betrayed by the entire thrust of Silverberg's speech and countered with a major campaign aimed at undercutting its impact.[57] The attack was spearheaded by Reusch and Max Schlenker, chairman and executive secretary respectively of the Langnamverein, who mobilized their resources for a decisive showdown with Silverberg at a meeting of the Langnamverein in Düsseldorf on 1 October 1926.[58] Here Silverberg came under a sharp attack from Reusch and steel magnate Fritz Thyssen that left him with little choice but to qualify some of the positions he had staked out at Dresden. In the meantime, Reusch continued to argue that industry should not, as Silverberg had suggested, enter into an alliance with the German working class but should seek instead an accommodation with organized agriculture on tariff policy that would expedite the DNVP's reentry into the national government. All of this only underscored the extent of Silverberg's isolation within Ruhr

---

[55] Paul Silverberg, "Das deutsche industrielle Unternehmertum in der Nachkriegszeit," in *Mitglieder-Versammlung des Reichsverbandes der Deutschen Industrie am 3. und 4. September 1926 in Dresden*, Veröffentlichungen des Reichsverbandes der Deutschen Industrie, no. 32 (Berlin, 1926), 55–65. For further details, see Reinhard Neebe, *Großindustrie, Staat und NSDAP 1930–1933. Paul Silverberg und der Reichsverband der Deutschen Industrie in der Weimarer Republik* (Göttingen, 1981), 35–49, and Boris Gehlen, *Paul Silverberg (1876–1959). Ein Unternehmer* (Stuttgart, 2007), 362–66.

[56] Lammers to Fonk, 18 Oct. 1926, BA Koblenz, NL ten Hompel, 21.

[57] For example, see Blank to Reusch, 6 Sept. 1926, RWWA Cologne, Abt. 130, NL Reusch, 4001012024/3a.

[58] For further details, see Schlenker to Reusch, 25 and 27 Sept. 1926, RWWA Cologne, Abt. 130, NL Reusch, 400101221/4, as well as Schlenker to Silverberg, 21 Sept. 1926, BA Koblenz, NL Silverberg, 414/110–11.

heavy industry and set the stage for a strategic retreat from the goals he had enunciated at Dresden when the RDI leadership met to discuss the matter on 14 October 1926.[59]

Although Ruhr heavy industry succeeded in blunting the thrust of Silverberg's Dresden initiative, his appeal for the creation of a coalition with the Social Democrats spread confusion throughout the ranks of the German Right and undercut efforts on behalf of closer political and organizational ties between the DVP and DNVP.[60] In his keynote address at the Nationalist Party congress in Cologne in the second week of September, DNVP party chairman Westarp tried to salvage what he could from the notion of a parliamentary *Arbeitsgemeinschaft* with the DVP by reiterating his party's willingness to participate in the creation of a greater German Right.[61] By now, however, many of those within the DVP who had originally embraced the Gayl-Jarres proposal had begun to cool on the idea of closer ties with the DNVP.[62] Consequently, when the DVP held its annual party congress in Cologne at the beginning of October, the delegates effectively killed the proposed *Arbeitsgemeinschaft* by adopting a unanimous resolution that reaffirmed Stresemann's concept of an independent and liberal German People's Party.[63] In the meantime, Silverberg's speech – and particularly his appeal for the creation of a new coalition government that included not only the "state-supporting" bourgeois parties but also the Social Democrats – had had a sobering effect upon the situation within the DNVP. For although Hugenberg and the leaders of the DNVP's industrial wing were quick to criticize Silverberg for misusing the RDI as a forum for propagating political views with which a substantial portion of its membership did not agree,[64] his speech nevertheless served notice on the DNVP that if it could not overcome its ambivalence toward government participation, then industry might have no alternative but to reach an accommodation of its own with the Social Democrats.

---

[59] Weisbrod, *Schwerindustrie in der Weimarer Republik*, 256–66. See also Dirk Stegmann, "Die Silverberg-Kontroverse 1926. Unternehmerpolitik zwischen Reform und Restauration," in *Sozialgeschichte heute. Festschrift für Hans Rosenberg zum 70. Geburtstag*, ed. Hans-Ulrich Wehler (Göttingen, 1974), 594–610.

[60] Jarres to Loebell, 9 Sept. 1926, BA Koblenz, NL Jarres, 37.

[61] Kuno von Westarp, *Klar das Ziel, fest das Wollen! Rede auf dem Reichsparteitage in Köln am 9. September 1926*, Deutschnationale Flugschrift, no. 260 (Berlin, 1926), 18–19.

[62] For example, see Scholz, "Innere Entwicklung und Deutsche Volkspartei," *Kölnische Zeitung*, 1 Oct. 1926, no. 732.

[63] Minutes of the DVP central executive committee, 1 Oct. 1926, in *Nationalliberalismus in der Weimarer Republik*, ed. Kolb and Richter, 2:652–710.

[64] *Kölnische Zeitung*, 10 Sept. 1926, no. 673. See also the report of the meeting of the Coordinating Committee of German National Industrialists (ADI) at the DNVP party congress in Cologne, 9 Sept. 1926, StA Hamburg, Blohm und Voß GmbH, 1215.

Rumblings on the Radical Right

Throughout the fall of 1926 pressure for a reorganization of the national government continued to mount. Not only would Germany's formal acceptance into the League of Nations on 10 September 1926 remove the single most serious obstacle to the DNVP's participation in a new national government, but the Nationalists found themselves under heavy pressure from Germany's most influential industrial and agricultural interest organizations to set aside their differences with Stresemann over the conduct of German foreign policy and rejoin the cabinet. If anything, the Silverberg controversy only intensified heavy industry's interest in an accommodation with organized agriculture that would expedite the Nationalists' return to power.[65] But as the DNVP moved almost inexorably toward a second experiment at government participation, the forces on the patriotic Right regrouped for another offensive against Stresemann's foreign policy and his efforts to stabilize the republic from the Right. The struggle against Locarno and the DNVP's resignation from the first Luther cabinet had done much to energize the Pan-German League, the Stahlhelm, and other organizations on the patriotic Right.[66] That this did not bode well for the DNVP's participation in a future government could not have been more apparent than in the case of the Stahlhelm.

In the wake of Hitler's abortive "Beer Hall putsch" in the fall of 1923, the Stahlhelm had quickly established itself as the largest and most influential organization on Germany's paramilitary Right. Regional paramilitary organizations that had stood on the fringes of the putsch subsequently affiliated themselves with the Stahlhelm and were integrated into its national organizational structure. The Stahlhelm's original strength had been concentrated in central Germany with its most important strongholds in Saxony and Magdeburg, but now it began to develop a truly national profile with chapters in virtually every part of the country. After having absorbed the Westphalian League in the fall of 1924, the Stahlhelm continued to expand its organization into northern Germany with the creation of new chapters in Schleswig-Holstein, Oldenburg, and Lower Saxony. In 1926 the Stahlhelm absorbed the remnants of Hermann Ehrhardt's newly rejuvenated Viking League (Bund Wiking) after a number of its leaders had become implicated in a crudely conceived putsch to overthrow established political authority in the Reich and Prussia, and the following year it merged with the Nuremberg-based Reich Flag (Reichsflagge). And in 1930 the largest of Bavaria's paramilitary organizations, the League Bavaria and Reich (Bund Bayern und Reich), finally suc-

---

[65] Reichert's remarks before the executive committee of the Association of German Steel and Iron Industrialists, 16 Sept. 1926, BA Koblenz, R 13 I, 101/110–11.
[66] Treviranus to Jarres, 26 Oct. 1925, BA Koblenz, NL Jarres, 54.

cumbed to its overtures and agreed to its incorporation into the Stahlhelm.[67] With an estimated half million members, the Stahlhelm was far and away the largest of the various organizations on Germany's paramilitary Right with only the Young German Order as a serious rival.[68]

The large-scale influx of new members from the Viking League and other paramilitary organizations with a profile more radical than that of the Stahlhelm itself posed a serious challenge to Franz Seldte's control of the organization. The situation was compounded by the fact that by 1926 more than two-thirds of the Stahlhelm's district leaders were former officers from aristocratic backgrounds who felt that they and not a one-time bourgeois reserve officer like Seldte should head the organization.[69] The ensuing conflict for control of the Stahlhelm continued right up until the end of the Weimar Republic and placed an increasingly heavy strain on the Stahlhelm's relations with more moderate bourgeois organizations and parties. With the election of DNVP activist Theodor Duesterberg in April 1923 as leader of the Stahlhelm district organization in Halle-Merseburg, Seldte and his supporters found it increasingly difficult to contain the forces of political radicalization that had begun to make their presence felt throughout the organization. The radicals around Duesterberg and retired general Georg Maercker dealt Seldte and his supporters a major political defeat when, at a meeting of Stahlhelm district leaders in March 1924, they pushed through a resolution that explicitly barred Jews from membership in the organization.[70] This represented a radical break with the Stahlhelm's earlier position that any German who had spent at least six months in military service during World War I could belong to the organization and led to a heated exchange between Seldte and Duesterberg at a meeting of the Stahlhelm executive committee in late May.[71] In July 1925 the forces around Duesterberg succeeded in pressuring Seldte to dissociate himself from Stresemann's foreign policy and to issue a public statement repudiating charges that the Stahlhelm had become politically dependent upon the

---

[67] On developments in Westphalia, Schlewig-Holstein, Lower Saxony, and Bavaria, see Gerd Krüger, "Von den Einwohnerwehren zum Stahlhelm. Der nationale Kampfverband 'Westfalenbund e.V' (1921–1924)," *Westfälische Zeitschrift* 147 (1997): 406–32, esp. 425–30; Lawrence D. Stokes, "'Wegbereiter des neuen nationalen Werdens'. Der 'Stahlhelm, Bund der Frontsoldaten' in Eutin 1923–1934," *Informationen zur Schleswig-Holsteinischen Zeitgeschichte* 31 (1997): 3–28; Fritzsche, *Rehearsals for Fascism*, 166–89; and Hans Fenske, *Konservatismus und Rechtsradikalismus*, 255–60.

[68] Diehl, *Paramilitary Politics*, 232–33.

[69] Heinz Brauweiler, "Meine Tätigkeit im 'Stahlhelm'," 22 Dec. 1965, StA Mönchen-Gladbach, NL Brauweiler, 110. See also Berghahn, *Stahlhelm*, 64–115, and Klotzbücher, "Der politische Weg des Stahlhelm," 103–11.

[70] Minutes of the meeting of Stahlhelm district leaders, 9 Mar. 1924, BA Berlin, R 72, 4/111–14. See also Crim *Antisemitism*, 45–47.

[71] Minutes of the meeting of Stahlhelm executive committee, 29 May 1924, BA Berlin, R 72, 4/89–109.

German foreign minister.[72] Both of these developments underscored the increasingly influence of the more radical elements around Duesterberg in the Stahlhelm's internal affairs.

The Stahlhelm's shift to the right in 1924–25 was accompanied by a concerted effort by its leaders and allies on the paramilitary Right to break the Center Party's hold over Germany's Catholic electorate. In their disillusionment with the Center's sharp swing to the left in the summer of 1917, many conservative Catholics – but most notably those from the nobility and intelligentsia – had gravitated toward the paramilitary Right. The significance of this development was not lost upon the hierarchy of the Catholic Church, and in March 1924 the Fulda Bishops' Conference (Fuldaer Bischofskonferenz), the assembly of German bishops from outside of Bavaria that met twice a year under the presidency of Cardinal Adolf von Bertram from Breslau to formulate positions on issues of concern to the episcopacy, issued a decree urging the Catholic clergy to exercise restraint with respect to the patriotic movement. Then, in August 1924, the conference hardened its position against Catholic involvement in any of the numerous organizations on Germany's patriotic Right.[73] This, along with the fact that the annual meeting of the German Catholic Congress in Hanover a month later was dominated by representatives of the Center to the exclusion of anyone who represented a different political position, provoked charges of partisanship within both the Stahlhelm and the Young German Order.[74] In an attempt to provide Catholics who no longer felt at home in the Center with a new organization of their own, the Young German Order's Otto Bornemann, himself a Catholic and Mahraun's right-hand man in the order's chain of command, founded the Ring of National German Catholics (Ring nationaler deutscher Katholiken) in early January 1925.[75] This organization, whose very name suggested a certain affinity with the goals of the Ring Movement, received active support not only from prominent Westphalian nobles such as Ferdinand von Lüninck and Alexander von Elverfeldt but also from the DNVP's Reich Catholic

---

[72] See the remarks by Duesterberg and Eulenburg before the Stahlhelm executive committee, 4–5 July 1925, BA Berlin, R 72, 4/33–35, 49–55, as well as the resolution of the Stahlhelm executive committee, 4 July 1925, reprinted in *Stahlhelm-Handbuch*, 3rd ed., ed. Walter Kellner and Heinrich Hildebrandt (Berlin, 1927), 45.

[73] Heinrich Czeloth, *Klarheit und Wahrheit. Warum wir Katholiken die vaterländischen Verbände ablehnen müssen!* (Cöthen and Berlin, n.d. [1924]), 255–66. For further details, see Vogel, *Kirche und Kampfverbände*, 34–55, 106–10.

[74] Exchange of letters between Lüninck and the Young German Order's Otto Bornemann, 26–30 Sept. 1924, VWA Münster, NL Lüninck, 713.

[75] For the goals of this organization, see "Richtlinien für den 'Ring nationaler deutscher Katholiken'," n.d., BA Koblenz, NL Spahn, 185. On its founding, see Karp to Lüninck, 28 Oct.–3 Nov. 1924, VWA Münster, NL Lüninck, 713. See also Vogel, *Kirche und Kampfverbände*, 121–45.

Committee.[76] But the venture met with a cool response from the Catholic episcopacy and never succeeded in generating the public enthusiasm for which its founders had hoped.[77]

In the meantime, the struggle against Locarno had done much to push the Stahlhlem more and more into the orbit of the radical Right. In November 1925 the leaders of the Stahlhelm entered into a coalition, or *Arbeitsgemeinschaft*, with the United Patriotic Leagues whereby the two would cooperate with each other in matters of Germany's national interest.[78] At the same time, spokesmen for the right wing of the DNVP praised the Stahlhelm for its stand against Locarno and expressed the hope that this foreshadowed an era of even closer cooperation between the two organizations.[79] Anxious to avoid becoming too closely identified with the DNVP, the Stahlhelm continued to reaffirm its nonpartisan character by inviting those Reichstag deputies from the DNVP, DVP, and Business Party who belonged to their organization to a meeting that, by pure coincidence, took place on the morning of the final vote on the Locarno Treaty.[80] Ratification of the Locarno accords played directly into the hands of the activists around Duesterberg and strengthened their position in what was quickly developing into a major struggle for control of the Stahlhelm. Whatever solidarity the Stahlhelm had shown in the struggle against Locarno quickly evaporated as Duesterberg and his supporters continued to undercut Seldte's position at the regional and local levels of the Stahlhelm organization.[81] Frustrated by the lack of political élan the Stahlhelm had demonstrated under Seldte's leadership, Duesterberg sought to transform it from a staid, predominantly "bourgeois" – and here the term was used pejoratively – veterans' organization into a vanguard of revolutionary nationalism. For Duesterberg the ultimate objective was to infuse the state with the activism of the front generation and to free it from the control of outside

---

[76] Minutes of a meeting of the Catholic Ring (Katholischer Ring), 8 Jan. 1925, BA Koblenz, NL Spahn, 185. On ties to the DNVP's Reich Catholic Committee, see Karp to Lüninck, 6 Oct. 1924, VWA Münster, NL Lüninck, 713.

[77] For the episcopacy's response, see Bertram to Lüninck, 7 Oct. 1925, VWA Münster, NL Lüninck, 710/711.

[78] Exchange of letters between Goltz and Seldte, 14–19 Nov. 1925, BA Berlin, R 72, 280/5–6.

[79] For example, see Schmidt-Hannover to Seldte, 15 Dec. 1925, NL Westarp, Gärtringen, VN 123, and Scheibe to Duesterberg, 25 Jan. 1926, BA-MA Freiburg, NL Tirpitz, 171/191–95.

[80] Minutes of a meeting of the Stahlhehm executive committee with Reichstag deputies who belonged to the Stahlhelm, 27 Nov. 1925, BA Berlin, R 72, 14/2–17. See also Seldte to the executive committees of the Reichstag delegations of the DNVP, DVP, and Business Party, 30 Nov. 1925, VWA Münster, BA Berlin, R 72, 280/7–8, as well as the correspondence between Treviranus and Ludwig, 23–30 Dec. 1925, ibid., 32/342–43.

[81] Duesterberg to Hammerstein, 16 Apr. 1926, BA Koblenz, R 72, 2302. See also the manuscript of Duesterberg's unpublished memoirs, BA Koblenz, Nachlass Theodor Duesterberg, 46/91–93.

economic interests so that it might be rebaptized in the spirit of those who had served so heroically and selflessly at the front.[82]

The task of defining the Stahlhelm's new mission fell to a group of revolutionary nationalists under the intellectual tutelage of Ernst Jünger. Jünger was one of the most prolific and popular writers of the postwar period,[83] and in late 1925 he became a major contributor to *Die Standarte*, a new journal that the Stahlhelm had launched in an attempt to lend its enterprise an aura of intellectual and literary legitimacy. Jünger quickly gathered around himself a number of like-minded intellectuals including Helmut Franke, Wilhelm Kleinau, Franz Schauwecker, and his brother Friedrich Georg Jünger. Under their leadership, *Die Standarte* emerged as a major forum for the dissemination of what Jünger and his associates proudly hailed as the "new nationalism."[84] Born in the trenches of World War I, Jünger's new nationalism differed from the patriotism of the Wilhelmine era in that it placed a total claim on the energies and loyalties of the individual and demanded that he subordinate everything – and particularly his material self-interest – to the sacred task of Germany's national salvation. Seen from this perspective, the war had been a spiritual event that produced an entirely new species of man in the person of the front soldier. Not only had the war exposed the spiritual poverty of the so-called bourgeois epoch, but it had liberated those who received their baptism of fire at the front from the sterile conventions and obsolete ideologies of a dying social order so that they might take part in their nation's spiritual rebirth. The front generation thus represented a new elite that had been hardened by the horrors of trench warfare to the point where it and it alone possessed the ruthlessness necessary to save Germany from national ruin. At the same time, the war had exposed the front generation to a new and indeed revolutionary sense of solidarity that was to serve as a model and inspiration for the organization of social life in the future German Reich, a solidarity in which all social distinctions were dissolved in the mystical unity of the German nation, a solidarity forged by the fire of combat and watered by the blood of national self-renewal. But to give this concrete form, it was first necessary for the front soldier to become a revolutionary. For it was only

---

[82] See Wilhelm Kleinau, *Stahlhelm und Staat. Eine Erläuterung der Stahlhelm-Botschaften* (Berlin, 1929), 27–37, and Alexander Pache, *Der Stahlhelm – Bund der Frontsoldaten. Sein Werden/Sein Wesen/Seine Ziele* (Zwickau, n.d. [1929]), 8–12.

[83] On Jünger's political thought in the Weimar era, see Hans-Peter Schwarz, *Der konservative Anarchist. Politik und Zeitkritik Ernst Jüngers* (Freiburg in Breisgau, 1962), 17–94; Roger Woods, *Ernst Jünger and the Nature of Political Commitment* (Stuttgart, 1982), 99–231; and Thomas Nevin, *Ernst Junger and Germany: Into the Abyss, 1914–1945* (Durham, NC, 1996), 75–114.

[84] Marjatta Hietala, *Der neue Nationalismus. In der Publizistik Ernst Jüngers und des Kreises um ihn 1920–1933* (Helsinki, 1975), esp. 42–57, 97–127.

through the systematic and ruthless annihilation of the existing political order that the rebirth of the German nation could ever be achieved.[85]

For all of its rhetorical force, the "front experience" as depicted in the writings of Jünger and his associates bore little resemblance to the actual experience of those who had served at the front in World War I. For all intents and purposes, the concepts of the "front experience" and "front generation" were political and literary constructs of the late 1920s designed to mobilize the support of those who were too young to have served in the war and to harness their frustration to a conservative political agenda.[86] At the same time, Jünger's idealization of the "front experience" and his call for greater activism on the part of the front generation represented an attempt to redefine the polity on essentially masculine terms to the exclusion of anything associated with the feminine weakness he held responsible for the collapse of the German home front in 1917–18.[87] Jünger's brazen contempt for the existing political order struck at the basic assumptions of Seldte's political strategy and clearly reflected the direction in which Duesterberg and his associates wished to take the Stahlhelm. None of this, however, did much to clarify the situation in the Stahlhelm. At no point was the confusion at the upper echelons of the Stahlhelm leadership more apparent than in the fall of 1926, when, much to the dismay of friends and enemies alike, the Stahlhelm executive committee announced a new strategic gambit with the motto "Hinein in den Staat!"[88] The immediate assumption was that this signaled the Stahlhelm's implicit recognition of the Weimar Constitution and that it too, like other organizations on the German Right, was about to make its peace with the republican form of government. Such an interpretation could not have been further from the truth. For, as the leaders of the Stahlhelm reassured their followers throughout the country, the true meaning of the motto lay in its exhortation to infiltrate the state and to reshape it in the spirit of the Stahlhelm's ideals. "We must," explained the Stahlhelm's Hans Ludwig at a meeting of the organization's state and district leaders in early October 1926, "conquer

[85] For Jünger's political views, see Ernst Jünger, "Grundlagen des Nationalismus," in *Stahlhelm-Jahrbuch 1927*, ed. Franz Schauwecker (Magdeburg, 1927), 68–88. On Jünger and the Stahlhelm, see Klotzbücher, "Der politische Weg des Stahlhelm," 72–79, and Berghahn, *Stahlhelm*, 91–101, as well as Susanne Meinl, *Nationalsozialisten gegen Hitler. Die nationalrevolutionäre Opposition um Friedrich Wilhelm Heinz* (Berlin, 2000), 94–106.

[86] Richard Bessel, "The 'Front Generation' and the Politics of Weimar Germany," in *Generations in Conflict. Youth Revolt and Generational Formation in Germany, 1770–1968*, ed. Mark Roseman (Cambridge, 1995), 121–36.

[87] Bernd Weisbrod, "Kriegerische Gewalt und männlicher Fundamentalismus. Ernst Jüngers Beitrag zur konservativen Revolution," *Geschichte in Wissenschaft und Unterricht* 49 (1998): 542–58.

[88] *Der Stahlhelm*, 10 Oct. 1926, no. 41.

the state from within."[89] As these remarks and subsequent clarifications in the official Stahlhelm press clearly indicated, the ultimate objective that lay behind the new motto was the subversion of the existing system of government for the purpose of transmuting it into an authoritarian state in which the Reichstag and the political parties that belonged to it would be stripped of effective political power.

The Saxon Interlude

The motto "Hinein in den Staat" was fully consistent with Jünger's call for greater activism on the part of the front generation, and its promulgation revealed the extent to which the balance of power within the Stahlhelm had begun to shift from the moderates around Seldte to Duesterberg and the organization's more radical wing.[90] Precisely what all of this was supposed to mean and how the newly proclaimed strategy of "Hinein in den Staat" was to be implemented remained unclear. The first opportunity to test the new strategy quickly presented itself in the Saxon Landtag elections scheduled for 31 October 1926. Saxony provided a perfect laboratory for the testing the Stahlhelm's new strategy. The absence of a substantial Catholic population meant that the German Center Party was not available to perform its customary role as a mediator between different social classes in the interest of political stability. As a result, the processes of fragmentation and polarization that ultimately led to the collapse of the bourgeois party system throughout Germany as a whole were more advanced in Saxony than in states like Prussia, Württemberg, or Bavaria, where the Catholic parties mediated between middle-class and working-class elements in a way that inhibited the process of political polarization that would lead to the collapse of effective parliamentary government throughout much of the country.[91] By the same token, the victory of the Saxon Left in the November 1922 Landtag elections and the subsequent inclusion of the Communists in the state government in the fall of 1923 put a face on the specter of social revolution that continued to haunt Saxony's propertied classes.[92]

---

[89] Minutes of the meeting of the Stahlhelm's state and district leaders, 2–3 Oct. 1926, BA Berlin, R 72, 5/51–53. See also Graff, "Gründung und Entwicklung des Bundes," 62–64.

[90] Remarks by Ausfeld (Stahlhelm) in a conversation with Stresemann's secretary Bernhard, 27 Oct. 1926, PA AA Berlin, NL Stresemann, 45/162823–26.

[91] Much of the following is based on Larry Eugene Jones, "Saxony, 1924–1930: A Study in the Dissolution of the Bourgeois Party System in Weimar Germany," in *Saxony in German History: Culture Society, and Politics, 1830–1933*, ed. James Retallack (Ann Arbor, MI, 2000), 336–55. See also Benjamin Lapp, *Revolution from the Right: Politics, Class, and the Rise of Nazism in Saxony, 1919–1933* (Atlantic Highlands, NJ, 1997).

[92] Benjamin Lapp, "Remembering the Year 1923 in Saxon History," in *Saxony in German History: Culture, Society, and Politics, 1830–1933*, ed. James Retallack (Ann Arbor, MI, 2000), 322–35.

After federal officials intervened in late October 1923 to remove the socialist Erich Zeigner and his government from power, Saxony was governed by a bourgeois minority cabinet with the DNVP as the only non-socialist party in opposition.[93] Efforts to stabilize the Weimar Republic from the Right by co-opting influential economic interest organizations such as the National Federation of German Industry and the National Rural League found little resonance in Saxony, which remained something of an economic backwater during the Weimar Republic and never shared in the benefits of Germany's short-lived "return to normalcy" in the second half of the 1920s. As a result, special-interest parties like the Business Party of the German Middle Class and the Reich Party for People's Justice and Revaluation (Reichspartei für Volksrecht und Aufwertung or VRP) succeeded in establishing themselves much more quickly in Saxony than in the Reich as a whole. Founded in September 1920 on the initiative of Berlin master baker Hermann Drewitz, the Business Party quickly attracted the interest of organized housing interests headed by the former DNVP politician Johann Victor Bredt. Bredt's benefactors in the Prussian chapter of the Central Association of Home and Property Owners' Organization (Zentralverband der deutschen Haus- und Grundbesitzervereine) threw their full support behind the Business Party in the 1921 Prussian Landtag elections and were rewarded when the WP received over 192,000 votes and elected four deputies to the state parliament.[94] But it was in Saxony that the WP experienced its greatest success. After a disappointing showing in the 1922 Landtag elections, the WP polled 2.8 and 4.7 percent of the popular vote in the three Saxon electoral districts in the May and December 1924 Reichstag elections, figures that compared favorably to the 1.8 and 2.3 percent of the national electorate the party received in the same two elections.[95] The Business Party was not the only party competing for the votes of Saxony's disaffected middle class. In the fall of 1924 Reinhard Wüst, a lawyer from Halle, helped launch the German Revaluation and Recovery Party (Deutsche

---

[93] J. Siegert, *16 Monate sächsischer Landtag. Ein politischer Überblick*, Schriften der Deutschnationalen Volkspartei in Sachsen (Arbeitsgemeinschaft), no. 2 (Dresden, 1924).

[94] For the official history of the WP, see Hermann Drewitz, "Die politische Standesbewegung des deutschen Mittelstandes vor und nach dem Kriege," in *Jahrbuch der Reichspartei des deutschen Mittelstandes*, ed. Reichspartei des deutschen Mittelstandes (Berlin, 1929), 13–32, here 19–22. See also Jürgen Weber, "Ziele, Handlungsbedingungen und Ergebnisse mittelständischer Interessenpolitik am Beispiel der 'Wirtschaftspartei' (Reichspartei des deutschen Mittelstandes) 1924–1933" (Wissenschaftliche Hausarbeit, Berlin, 1979) 75–85. On Bredt, see Martin Grosch, *Johann Victor Bredt. Konservative Politik zwischen Kaiserreich und Nationalsozialismus. Eine politische Biographie* (Berlin, 2014), 186–93. On the plight of Germany's middle-class homeowners, see Daniel P. Silverman, "A Pledge Unredeemed: The Housing Crisis in Weimar Germany," *Central European History* 3 (1970): 112–39.

[95] See the tables in Schumacher, *Mittelstandsfront und Republik*, 228, 230–31.

Aufwertungs- und Aufbaupartei) as a protest against the revaluation provisions of the Third Emergency Tax Decree that had taken effect the preceding February.[96] Although the new party's impact in the December 1924 Reichstag elections was negligible, its emergence underscored the frustration that an increasingly large segment of Germany's middle-class electorate had begun to feel over the terms of Germany's political and economic stabilization.

The Saxon Landtag elections on 31 October 1926 provided Germany's middle-class splinter parties with an excellent forum for validating themselves as legitimate voices of middle-class discontent. In the summer of 1925 the Business Party had rebaptized itself the Reich Party of the German Middle Class (Reichspartei des deutschen Mittelstandes or WP) in attempt to escape the odium of special interest and to broaden its appeal among Germany's middle-class voters. The following July the WP held its first national party congress in Görlitz – no doubt with an eye to the upcoming Landtag elections – and used the occasion to launch a new party program called the "Görlitzer Richtlinien." The work of Saxon party leader Walther Wilhelm, the "Görlitzer Richtlinien" sought to embellish the party's ideological profile by reformulating the traditional demands of homeowners, artisans, and small businessmen in the language of German corporatism. With the adoption of the new party program, the Business Party's transformation from a party easily stigmatized as an agent for organized housing interests into one that claimed to represent the German middle class in all of its social and economic heterogeneity was essentially complete.[97] All of this, including the choice of Görlitz as the site where this transformation supposedly culminated in the promulgation of a new party program, was part of a calculated effort to position the WP as advantageously as possible in the campaign for the upcoming Saxon state elections. In the meantime, the various revaluation groups that had surfaced throughout the country since the enactment of the Third Emergency Tax Decree in February 1924 had begun to coalesce into a national revaluation party. These efforts, which capitalized upon the sense of betrayal that Germany's middle-class investors felt toward the DNVP as a result of its role in

---

[96] See the two pamphlets by Reinhard Wüst, *Das Aufwertungsproblem und die 3. Steuernotverordnung. Eine gemeinverständliche Betrachtung* (Halle, 1924), and Reinhard Wüst, *Im Aufwertungskampf für Wahrheit und Recht gegen "Luthertum" und "Marxismus." Eine gemeinverständliche Auseinandersetzung mit den Trugschlüssen und Schlagworten der Aufwertungsgegner* (Halle, 1924).

[97] Reichspartei des deutschen Mittelstandes, *Die Satzungen und Görlitzer Richtlinien der Reichspartei des deutschen Mittelstandes e.V. (Wirtschaftspartei)* (Berlin, [1929]), 18–31. For the WP's "middle-class ideology," see Walther Waldemar Wilhelm and Willy Schlüter, *Die Mission des Mittelstandes. 99 Thesen für das schaffende Volk*, ed. Eugen Fabricus (Dresden, 1925), as well as Johann Victor Bredt, "Das politische Parlament und die berufsständischen Vertretungen," in *Volk und Reich der Deutschen*, ed. Bernhard Harms, 2 vols. (Berlin, 1929), 2: 282–300.

the passage of the 1925 revaluation law, drew to a climax in late August 1926 with the founding of the Reich Party for People's Justice and Revaluation under the leadership of Stuttgart school inspector Adolf Bauser at a delegate conference of the Savers' Association in Erfurt.[98] Speaking in Erfurt, the one-time DNVP patriarch Count Arthur von Posadowsky-Wehner assailed the more established bourgeois parties for having betrayed the trust of Germany's small investor and exhorted those who had been victimized by this betrayal to seek their revenge at the polls.[99]

By using the Saxon campaign to thrust themselves into the national political spotlight, the WP and VRP transformed the campaign for the 1926 Saxon Landtag elections into a referendum on the future of the more established and ideologically oriented "people's" parties like the DDP, DVP, and DNVP. Still reeling from the heavy losses it had suffered in the Mecklenburg Landtag elections in August 1926,[100] the Nationalists moved quickly to counter the appeal of the special-interest parties by arguing that they not only isolated the German middle class from those parties that were committed to the defense of its legitimate social and economic interests but, more importantly, that their emergence only frustrated the need for greater bourgeois cohesiveness in the struggle against Marxism. The WP's efforts to unite the German middle class into a single political party were dismissed as a frivolous distraction that undermined the effectiveness with which the DNVP could defend the interests of its middle-class constituents.[101] By the same token, the Nationalists argued that single-issue parties like the VRP could not possibly defend the interests of their supporters as effectively as a larger party like the DNVP.[102]

The phenomenon of special-interest parties also aroused widespread concern outside the parties that were directly affected by this process. Both the Stahlhelm and the Young German Order lamented the fragmentation of Germany's political culture and were fearful that the Saxon elections would produce an even greater fragmentation of Germany's bourgeois forces. As the

[98] Adolf Bauser, "Notwendigkeit, Aufgaben und Ziele der Volksrechtspartei," in *Für Wahrheit und Recht. Der Endkampf um eine gerechte Aufwertung. Reden und Aufsätze*, ed. Adolf Bauser (Stuttgart, 1927), 90–91. See also Hans Peter Müller, "Adolf Bauser (1880–1948), der Sparerbund und die Volksrechtspartei," *Zeitschrift für Württembergische Landesgeschichte* 75 (2016): 247–76, here 248–53, 256–59.
[99] Speech by Posadowsky-Wehner, "Ansprache, gehalten auf der Reichsdelegiertentagung des Sparerbundes zu Erfurt am 28. August 1926," in Arthur von Posadowsky-Wehner, *Die Enteignung des Gläubiger-Vermögens. Eine Sammlung von Aufsätzen* (Berlin, n.d. [1928]), 42–46.
[100] Report on the Mecklenburg Landtag elections of 6 Aug. 1926, NL Westarp, Gärtringen, VN 75.
[101] "Entwurf zu einer Diskussionsrede in Versammlungen der Wirtschaftspartei," n.d., SHStA Dresden, NL Philipp, 20.
[102] Philipp, "Aufwertung und Landtagswahl," *Leipziger Abendpost*, 16 Oct. 1926, no. 242.

elections drew near, the leaders of Saxony's paramilitary Right called upon the
so-called patriotic parties to set aside their differences and unite in a crusade to
free Saxony – and, by extension, the rest of Germany – from the insidious yoke
of Marxism.[103] When this effort at "bourgeois consolidation from below"
foundered on Stresemann's refusal to countenance any electoral alliance that
might jeopardize the prospects of the "Great Coalition" in the Reich,[104] the
Saxon Citizens' Council (Sächsischer Bürgerrat), with strong support from the
League of Saxon Industrialists (Verband sächsischer Industrieller) and other
bourgeois interest organizations, tried to salvage what it could of the campaign
for bourgeois unity by proposing the creation of an electoral truce for the
duration of the campaign.[105] Much less threatening to Stresemann and the
DVP's national leadership than what the paramilitary leagues had in mind,
this attempt at "bourgeois consolidation from above" eventually produced an
agreement to which the DVP, DNVP, and Business Party all adhered.[106]

   In the final analysis, the experiment in "bourgeois consolidation from
above" failed to insulate the more established bourgeois parties against the
centrifugal forces that more than a decade of economic hardship had
unleashed within the Saxon middle classes. When the votes were counted,
the DDP, DVP, and DNVP had suffered losses amounting to 42.0, 28.7, and
37.6 percent of what they had each received in Saxony in the December
1924 Reichstag elections. The Business Party, on the other hand, more than
doubled the number of votes it had received in 1924, from 124,193 to 237,462
(10.1 percent), and entered the newly elected Landtag with a complement of
ten deputies, while the fledgling People's Justice Party polled 98,258 votes (4.2
percent) and received four Landtag mandates.[107] The dramatic gains the two
middle-class splinter parties recorded in the Saxon elections represented a
stinging indictment of the ideological foundations upon which the Weimar
party system rested and constituted a direct threat not just to the two liberal
parties but to the DNVP as well. Plagued by lingering resentment over its role

---

[103] Brückner (Stahlhelm, Landesverband Sachsen) to the DVP, Wahlkreisverband Leipzig,
     29 July 1926, PA AA Berlin, NL Stresemann, 96/173150-51. See also Frank to Strese-
     mann, 9 Aug. 1926, ibid., 173144-46, as well as the memorandum of a conversation
     between the Young German leadership and Stresemann's secretary Henry Bernhard, 16
     Aug. 1926, ibid., 173179-82.
[104] Stresemann to Dieckmann, 25 Aug. 1926, PA AA Berlin, NL Stresemann, 96/173225-28.
[105] For further details, see Frank to Stresemann, 24 Aug. 1926, PA AA Berlin, NL Strese-
     mann, 96/173213-14, and Dieckmann to Stresemann, 24 and 28 Aug. 1926, ibid.,
     173221-24, 173236-43, as well as the memorandum on the meeting organized by the
     Saxon Citizens' Council, 22 Aug. 1926, ibid., 96/173215-17. The phrases "consolidation
     from below" and "above" have been taken from Lapp, Revolution from the Right, 143-50.
[106] Arthur Graefe, 3 Jahre Aufbaupolitik. Zu den Sachsenwahlen 1926, ed. Sächsische
     Wahlkreisverbände der Deutschen Volkspartei (Dresden, 1926), 59-62.
[107] Wirtschaft und Statistik 6, no. 21 (18 Nov. 1926): 783-84.

in the passage of the 1925 revaluation legislation, the DNVP was unable to shake charges that it was nothing more than the party of big agriculture and industry and sustained massive losses among those petty bourgeois elements that had rallied to its support in 1924. The VRP, on the other hand, proved remarkably adept in establishing itself, in the words of the DNVP's Walther Rademacher, as a "rallying point for all of those disgruntled elements . . . that because of their background were either unwilling or unable to support the Socialists or Communists."[108] What this would have on the balance of power on the Reich as a whole to be seen.

The Return to Power

Throughout the fall of 1926 pressure for a reorganization of the national government continued to mount. Not only had Germany's acceptance into the League of Nations on 10 September 1926 removed the single most serious obstacle to the DNVP's participation in a new national government, but Nationalist party leaders found themselves under heavy pressure from Germany's most influential industrial and agricultural interest organizations to rejoin the cabinet. Westarp's keynote address at the DNVP's Cologne party congress in September 1926 laid the foundation for his party's reentry into the national government by reaffirming the Nationalists' unconditional willingness to enter into negotiations with the other government parties. While reiterating the DNVP's opposition to Germany's entry into the League of Nations, Westarp stressed that it was also important for Germany to conduct its foreign policy as forcefully as possible in order to take advantage of the opportunities that league membership now afforded it. But an essential prerequisite for the conduct of such a foreign policy, Westarp continued, was a healthy and growing economy. Alluding to the economic difficulties that had plagued Germany since the DNVP had left the government in October 1925, Westarp argued that the strong and effective political leadership that was necessary to put Germany's economic house in order was inconceivable without the active participation of the DNVP.[109]

Westarp's speech affirmed in no uncertain terms the DNVP's willingness to accept its share of the governmental responsibility and invited the cabinet and government parties to enter into serious negotiations aimed at bringing the DNVP into the government. In a closed caucus, the DNVP leadership endorsed their party's reentry into the national government and authorized the leaders of the Reichstag delegation to initiate negotiations directed toward

---

[108] Rademacher, "Zur Frage der Aufwertung," 19 Nov. 1926, NL Westarp, Gärtringen, II/24.

[109] Kuno von Westarp, *Klar das Ziel, fest das Wollen! Rede auf dem Reichsparteitage in Köln am 9. September 1926*, Deutschnationale Flugschrift, no. 260 (Berlin, 1926), 2–12.

that end at the earliest appropriate opportunity.[110] At the same time, DNVP moderates like Hans Erdmann von Lindeiner-Wildau tried to reassure the party's prospective coalition partners by publicly stating that there was no point in trying to change the existing form of government until the more urgent social and economic problems that confronted the German people had been addressed.[111] Similarly, the party's criticism of Stresemann's foreign policy was notably more moderate in tone in comparison to its previous diatribes against the policy of fulfillment and and its campaign against Germany's entry into the League of Nations.[112] Nevertheless, neither the chancellor Marx nor Stresemann were all that eager to bring the DNVP into the government. Stresemann was still smarting from the DNVP's behavior over Locarno and would almost certainly have preferred the maintenance of the existing governmental coalition.[113] Marx and the leaders of the Center, on the other hand, were far more favorably disposed to an expansion of the coalition to the Left than to the Right and showed little interest in reorganizing the government once it became clear that the Social Democrats would not be part of the solution.[114] But efforts to reach an understanding with the SPD that would have allowed Marx to remain in office with or without its official blessing were sabotaged first by revelations in the British press about German violations of the armament provisions of the Versailles Treaty and then by public attacks against the Social Democrats for their views on social and military policy by Ernst Scholz, chairman of the DVP Reichstag delegation.[115] The government's last hopes of a reconciliation with the Social Democrats evaporated when on 16 December Philipp Scheidemann, the SPD's expert on military affairs, disclosed German violations of the Versailles Treaty, including secret military collaboration with the Red Army, in a sensational speech before the Reichstag. On the following day the Social Democrats and Communists introduced a motion of no-confidence in the Marx government that passed by a 249 to 171 margin.[116]

[110] Lindeiner-Wildau to Westarp, 3 Feb. 1927, BA Koblenz, Nachlass Hans Erdmann von Lindeiner-Wildau, 3/34, also in NL Westarp, Gärtringen, II/25.
[111] Hans Erdmann von Lindeiner-Wildau, *Die Ziele der Deutschnationalen. Vortrag in der Lessing-Hochschule zu Berlin am 19. Oktober 1926*, Deutschnationale Flugschrift, no. 270 (Berlin, 1926), 17.
[112] For example, see Otto Hoetzsch and Axel Freytagh von Loringhoven, *Deutsche Außenpolitik und nationale Opposition. Reichstagsreden*, Deutschnationale Flugschrift, no. 276 (Berlin, 1926).
[113] Stresemann to Marx, 14 Jan. 1927, PA AA Berlin, NL Stresemann, 49/163560–66.
[114] Karsten Ruppert, *Im Dienst am Staat von Weimar. Das Zentrum als regierende Partei in der Weimarer Demokratie 1923–1930* (Düsseldorf, 1992), 230–35. See also Hehl, *Marx*, 389–91.
[115] Richter, *Deutsche Volkspartei*, 444–46.
[116] Stürmer, *Koalition und Opposition*, 162–81.

At the suggestion of Reich President Hindenburg, negotiations on the formation of a new government were postponed until after the Christmas recess.[117] In the meantime, the various parties began to stake out the positions they would take once the Reichstag had reconvened. Although Scheidemann's revelations had eliminated the SPD as a coalition partner for the more moderate bourgeois parties, neither the Center nor Stresemann was particularly interested in sharing power with the Nationalists and would have preferred the maintenance of a bourgeois minority government that would ally itself alternately with the Left or the Right.[118] But the Nationalists found such an arrangement unacceptable and refused to tolerate a minority cabinet based upon the parties of the so-called bourgeois middle even if this meant risking new elections in order to secure their party's return to power.[119] When negotiations were finally resumed in the second week of January 1927, the Center remained steadfast in its commitment to a cabinet of the middle and refused to go along with the DVP's Julius Curtius in his efforts to organize a right-wing majority government that would have included the DNVP.[120] At this point, Hindenburg tried to break the deadlock by calling upon Marx to undertake the formation of a government that rested upon a majority of the bourgeois parties in the Reichstag and appealed to the parties that would belong to such a government to resolve their differences as quickly as possible.[121] The fact that Marx and not Curtius was now in line for the chancellorship helped soften the Center's opposition to a coalition with the DNVP.[122]

Sensitive to charges from their party's left wing that a coalition with the Nationalists was tantamount to a betrayal of the Center's republican principles and an abandonment of its commitment to the welfare of the German working class, the leaders of the Center Reichstag delegation formulated two

---

[117] Meissner, "Bemerkungen zur Regierungsbildung," 18 Dec. 1926, BA Berlin, R 601, 402/7–9.

[118] On the government's options, 28 Dec. 1926, BA Koblenz, Nachlass Hermann Pünder, 27/160–67.

[119] For the Nationalist position, see Treviranus to Tirpitz, 30 Dec. 1926, BA-MA Freiburg, 265/152, and Hugenberg, 30 Dec. 1926, NL Westarp, VN 76, as well as Westarp to Seidlitz, 31 Dec. 1926, ibid., VN 40.

[120] On Hindenburg's initiative, see "Aktennotiz über die Besprechungen des Herrn Reichspräsidenten, betreffend die Neubildung der Reichsregierung am 10. Januar 1927," BA Berlin, R 601, 402/26–36, and Meissner, "Aktennotiz," 15 Jan. 1927, ibid., 402/42–46. For the position of the Center, see the mintues of the Center Reichstag delegation and its executive committee, 11–14 Jan. 1927, in *Protokolle der Reichstagsfraktion und des Fraktionsvorstandes der Deutschen Zentrumspartei 1926–1933*, ed. Rudolf Morsey (Mainz, 1969), 80–84, as well as Gehrig to Weber, 7 Jan. 1927, ACDP Sankt-Augustin, NL Gehrig, I-087, 001/2.

[121] Hindenburg to Marx, n.d. [20 Jan. 1927], BA Berlin, R 601, 402/74–75.

[122] Minutes of the Center Reichstag delegation, 20 Jan. 1927, in *Protokolle der Reichstagsfraktion*, ed. Morsey, 89–90.

documents – a national political manifesto and a social political manifesto – that the Nationalists would have to accept before the Center would join them in a new coalition government.[123] The Center further sought to limit the DNVP's potential for mischief by securing its commitment to set of guidelines, or *Leitsätze*, whose acceptance entailed implicit recognition of the existing system of government and a pledge of support for the basic principles of Stresemann's foreign policy.[124] When Westarp met with Marx on the afternoon of 18 January to reassure the chancellor of his party's willingness to work within the framework of the existing constitutional system and subsequently agreed to accept the Center's guidelines as part of an arrangement that would provide the Nationalists with four cabinet posts,[125] the internal unity of the DNVP began to unravel. But as Hugenberg and the leaders of the DNVP's right wing began to mobilize their supporters within the DNVP Reichstag delegation for a showdown,[126] they found themselves virtually isolated within the party. At the decisive meeting of the DNVP Reichstag delegation on 28 January, the leaders of the party's right wing were able to muster only thirteen votes in a futile effort to block acceptance of the guidelines that had been formulated by the Center as the political and ideological cornerstone of the new cabinet.[127] Not only did this remove the last obstacle to the DNVP's participation in the formation of a bourgeois majority government under Marx and Stresemann, but the outcome of the meeting represented a moment

[123] Minutes of the executive committee of the Center Reichstag delegation, 21 Jan. 1927, in *Protokolle der Reichstagsfraktion*, ed. Morsey, 91. See also Josef Joos, *Die politische Ideenwelt des Zentrums* (Karlsruhe, 1928), 67–72. For further details, see Ruppert, *Im Dienst am Staat von Weimar*, 243–45.

[124] For the text of these guidelines, see BA Koblenz, NL Pünder, 33/65–68. See also Pünder's memorandum, 23–31 Jan. 1927, ibid., 41–51. For further details, see Stürmer, *Koalition und Opposition*, 188, and Ruppert, *Im Dienst am Staat von Weimar*, 245–46.

[125] On the DNVP's negotiations with Marx and other government officials, see Pünder's memorandum of a meeting between Westarp and Marx, 18 Jan. 1927, BA Koblenz, NL Pünder, 95/91, as well as Pünder's memorandum on the cabinet negotiations from 23–30 Jan. 1927, BA Koblenz, ibid., 33/41–51, and the memorandum of a conversation between Stresemann and a delegation from the DNVP, 25 Jan. 1927, PA AA Berlin, NL Stresemann, 49/163627–35.

[126] See the postscript to Hugenberg's letter to Westarp, 15 Jan. 1927, NL Westarp, VN 62, and Hugenberg to Wegener, 15 Jan. 1927, BA Koblenz, Nachlass Leo Wegener, 65/48, as well as Hugenberg's notes for a speech before the DNVP executive committee, Jan. 1927, BA Koblenz, NL Hugenberg, 113. For further details, see the entry in Quaatz's diary, 17–18 Jan. 1927, BA Koblenz, NL Quaatz, 16, and the letter from Ada Gräfin von Westarp to Gertraude Freifrau Hiller von Gaertringen, 17 Jan. 1927, NL Westarp, Gärtringen.

[127] Entry in Quaatz's diary, 28 Jan. 1927, BA Koblenz, NL Quaatz, 16. See Lindeiner-Wildau to Westarp, 3 Feb. 1927, BA Koblenz, NL Lindeiner-Wildau, 3/14–36, as well as Westarp's memorandum, "Meine persönliche Einstellung zu dem Vorschlag v. Lindeiner's als Reichsminister," n.d. [Feb. 1927], NL Westarp, Gärtringen, II/25.

of supreme humiliation to Hugenberg and the militantly antirepublican elements on the party's extreme right wing.[128]

Frustrated by their failure to block the party's decision to rejoin the government, the leaders of the DNVP's right wing set out to influence the selection of the four men who were to represent the party in the new cabinet. Although it was generally conceded that Schiele would receive the ministry of agriculture and Christian labor leader Wilhelm Koch the ministry of transportation, a bitter fight developed over the appointees to the ministries of justice and the interior.[129] The party's right wing hoped to block the appointment of Lindeiner-Wildau as minister of the interior but agreed to go along with this if the ultra-conservative Walther Graef-Anklam was tapped as the minister of justice. But this compromise fell apart when Marx and the Center vetoed the appointment of Graef-Anklam, whereupon the Nationalists nominated former party chairman Oskar Hergt as his replacement. Though amenable to the Center, Hergt's nomination infuriated the leaders of the DNVP's right wing, who provoked a crisis so severe that at one point the Reich President threatened the Nationalists with new national elections if they could not settle their petty internal differences. The stalemate was eventually broken when the DNVP Reichstag delegation settled on Walther von Keudell, an East Prussian landowner and close associate of retired admiral Alfred von Tirpitz who was acceptable to both Hindenburg and the other coalition parties, to replace Lindeiner-Wildau as its nominee for the ministry of interior.[130]

The new government with Marx as chancellor and Stresemann as foreign minister was formally installed in office on 3 February 1927. The fact that the DNVP was represented in the cabinet by four ministers – Hergt, Keudell, Schiele, and Koch – reflected the party's parliamentary strength and was consistent with what Westarp and the DNVP party leadership had hoped to accomplish. Many Nationalists, however, still found the conditions that had been attached to their party's entry into the government humiliating and difficult to accept. Never was the awkwardness of the DNVP's position more apparent than in the tortured defense of his party's decision to enter the government that Westarp offered in the parliamentary debate that accompanied the cabinet's installation. For while

---

[128] Axel von Freytagh-Loringhoven, *Deutschnationale Volkspartei* (Berlin, 1931), 41–42.

[129] On the haggling over the DNVP's cabinet appointments, see the memoirs of Albrecht Philipp, "Mein Weg: Rückschau eines Siebzigjährigen auf allerlei Geschenisse und Menschen," Dritte Teil: "Abgeordnetenjahre in der Weimarer Republik (1919–1930)," SHStA Dresden, NL Philipp, 4/191–94, as well as see the letters from Ada Gräfin von Westarp to Gertraude Freifrau Hiller von Gaertringen, 20 Jan.–1 Feb. 1927, NL Westarp, Gärtringen.

[130] See the entries in Quaatz's diary, 26–28 Jan. 1927, BA Koblenz, NL Quaatz, 16, as well as the correspondence between Lindeiner-Wildau and Westarp, 3 Feb.–9 Mar. 1927, BA Koblenz, NL Lindeiner-Wildau, 3/2–36, 58–66. See also Dörr, "Deutschnationale Volkspartei," 270–87.

Westarp had no choice but to concede that the DNVP's entry into the government was predicated upon de facto acceptance of the existing political system as the framework within which it would pursue its short-term political objectives, he went to great pains to reassure the leaders of his party's right wing that this did not mean that the DNVP had abandoned its struggle for a restoration of the monarchy. The DNVP's ultimate commitment, Westarp argued, was to serve the state regardless of the particular form in which that state might exist. But agreeing to serve the state on the basis of the republican form of government, he continued, was by no means the same thing as making an emotional commitment to that form of government and all its emblems, symbols, and organs. The DNVP, therefore, would continue to fight for the principles upon which it had been founded and for the defense of German dignity, German freedom, and German interests.[131] Bromides like this, however, did little to conceal or heal the deep divisions that had developed within the party and that had only been exacerbated by the its entry into the fourth Marx cabinet.[132]

Ever since the DNVP's resignation from the first Luther cabinet as a result of its opposition to the Locarno accord, party leaders – and particularly the organized interests allied with the party – worked long and hard at plotting a course that would end with the DNVP's return to power. This enterprise was driven by the conviction of Westarp and his supporters that only a return to power would make it possible for the DNVP to provide the various interests that constituted their party's material base with the effective protection they needed during a period of increasing economic hardship. But the calculus of interest politics that lay at the heart of the DNVP's second experiment in governmental participation encountered strong resistance from the various nationalist pressure groups that stood on the extreme right of Germany's political spectrum. From their perspective, the very idea of using the state as a mechanism for promoting the material interests of specific sectors of German society constituted a heresy they could not reconcile with their concept of the nation as a sacred entity in which the distinctions of class, confession, and region were somehow mystically dissolved. The dividing line between these two distinctly different approaches to politics ran right through the heart of the the DNVP. Once again, the ability of the party and its leaders to strike a balance between these two political concepts would be severely tested.

---

[131] *Verhandlungen des Reichstags*, vol. 391, 8804–06. See also Lambach, "Um die Führung im Reiche," in *Politische Praxis 1927*, ed. Walther Lambach (Hamburg, n.d. [1927]), 60–61, as well as Walther Graef-Anklam, "Der Werdegang der Deutschnationalen Volkspartei 1918–1928," in *Der nationale Wille. Werden und Wirken der Deutschnationalen Volkspartei 1918–1928*, ed. Max Weiß (Essen, 1928), 50.

[132] For the reaction to Westarp's speech, see the letter from Ada Gräfin von Westarp to Gertraude Freifrau Hiller von Gaertringen, 3 Feb. 1927, NL Westarp, Gärtringen.

12

The Burden of Responsibility

The installation of the fourth Marx cabinet in January 1927 marked the beginning of the DNVP's second experiment with governmental responsibility. For the next thirteen months the DNVP would serve as an integral member of the governmental coalition and as the party that provided the Marx cabinet with the parliamentary majority it needed to secure passage of its legislative agenda. This experiment in governmental participation, however, differed from the DNVP's earlier attempt in 1925 in several important respects. In the first place, the DNVP was now a full-fledged member of a governmental coalition with formal ties to the cabinet, whereas in 1925 the first Luther cabinet had presented itself as a cabinet of experts in which each of the four parties supporting it was represented by one cabinet officer apiece. Second, the fourth Marx cabinet was based on formal political commitments that had been negotiated by the parties that supported it, the most important being the agreements that had been reached by the DNVP and Center. In the case of the Luther cabinet two years earlier, no such commitments had existed. Third, the general economic climate at the beginning of 1927 was generally better than it had been in 1925, although the deterioration of Germany's rural economy would only intensify during the tenure of the Marx cabinet. Fourth, the diplomatic controversies that had figured so prominently during the DNVP's first experiment at government participation had faded into the background. For all intents and purposes, 1927 was a year of relative inactivity on the diplomatic front, with the result that the disruptive potential of disputes over foreign policy had been greatly reduced, if not eliminated altogether. All of this augured well for the success of the DNVP's second experiment at government participation.

Still, things were not as easy for the Nationalist party leadership as they might have seemed. First of all, the DNVP was far less united in 1927 than it had been at the time of its entry into the first Luther cabinet in January 1925, when even Hugenberg, arguably the most influential figure on the DNVP's right wing, had gone along with the decision to join the government.[1] The

---

[1] Hugenberg's remarks at a meeting of the DNVP Reichstag delegation, 12 June 1928, BA Koblenz, NL Schmidt-Hannover, 35.

DNVP's right wing was far better organized in 1927 than it had been two years earlier and enjoyed a broad base of support at the local and regional base of the DNVP's national organization that could be mobilized against the party's parliamentary leadership with telling effect.[2] The pressure the leaders of the DNVP's right wing could bring to bear upon the party leadership was further enhanced by their ties to the Pan-German League, the Stahlhelm, and other organizations on the patriotic Right. The struggle against Locarno had moved the Pan-German League back into the political limelight, and its leaders were determined to reverse the direction in which the DNVP was headed and bring its second experiment at government participation to a quick and decisive end. Similarly, the radicalization of the Stahlhelm was to continue unabated through 1927–28 as the radical nationalists behind former DNVP activist Theodor Duesterberg intensified their campaign against Franz Seldte and the more traditional species of bourgeois nationalism he represented.

Initial Successes, Initial Challenges

The key figure in the DNVP's second experiment at governmental participation was Count Kuno von Westarp. Ever since his election as DNVP party chairman in March 1926 Westarp had steadfastly steered the DNVP toward a return to power, and the DNVP's entry into the fourth Marx cabinet represented a great personal triumph for Westarp for which he received the plaudits of most of his colleagues in the DNVP Reichstag delegation.[3] Despite his deep-seated aversion to the republican system of government, Westarp was not only fully initiated into what Thomas Mergel has called the parliamentary culture of the Weimar Republic but became one of its most effective practitioners.[4] As chairman of the parliamentary coordinating committee, or *Interfraktioneller Ausschuß*, that oversaw the flow of legislation to and from the floor of the Reichstag, Westarp excercised more direct influence upon the legislative process than the chancellor himself. His office in the Reichstag became a virtual clearing house for all the legislation that reached the floor of the Reichstag or the chambers of its various and sundry committees. His disdain

---

[2] For example, see the report on the Mecklenburg party organization, n.d. [after 6 Aug. 1926], NL Westarp, Gärtringen, VN 75, as well as Fleischauer to Westarp, 9 Dec. 1926, ibid., II/24.

[3] On Westarp's role in the formation of the Marx cabinet, see the letters from Ada Gräfin von Westarp to Gertraude Freifrau Hiller von Gaertringen, 21 Jan.–1 Feb. 1927, NL Westarp, Gärtringen.

[4] On the concept of parliamentary culture and its place in the history of the Weimar Republic, see Thomas Mergel, *Parlamentarische Kultur in der Weimarer Republik. Politische Kommunikationen, symbolische Politik und Öffentlichkeit im Reichstag* (Düsseldorf, 2002), 13–31.

for the republican system of government notwithstanding, Westarp used the position he had carved out for himself as power broker for the fourth Marx cabinet to advance the agenda of the German Right at every conceivable opportunity – and nowhere more so than in the areas of social, economic, and agricultural policy.[5]

Of the various factions within the DNVP, none embraced the Nationalists' entry into the Marx cabinet more enthusiastically than the leaders of the Christian-national labor movement. Walther Lambach, a member of the DNVP Reichstag delegation who doubled as its chief liaison to the German National Union of Commercial Employees, hailed the new government as a "people's conservative coalition" in which the consolidation of workers and peasants on a Christian-national basis had finally been achieved. Lambach and his associates took credit for having used their ties to the working-class elements in the Center to wear down its resistance to a coalition with the DNVP.[6] Having served as midwife to the birth of the new government, the DNVP's working-class and white-collar wings now expected to see their efforts rewarded with new laws expanding and improving the existing body of social welfare legislation. But the new-found militancy of the Christian labor movement and its embrace of the government as the vehicle for initiating a new round of social welfare legislation posed a direct threat to the position of industry and agriculture in the governmental coalition and threatened to undermine their ties to the coalition parties. From the outset, the fourth Marx cabinet rested upon a fragile and inherently unstable coalition of disparate social and economic interests that, if subjected to sufficient stress, could fall apart with little or no warning.

The DNVP's decision to enter the Marx cabinet had been driven by the party's desire to assume a more active role in the formulation and implementation of state social and economic policy. Yet all of this assumed that the various interests that constituted the DNVP's material base could be reconciled to each other without threatening the unity of the party. As the DNVP's Paul Lejeune-Jung, an industrialist and outspoken Catholic conservative, stressed in a programmatic speech before the Reichstag on 4 February 1927, the fundamental premise of the DNVP's social and economic program was that there was no contradiction between the social and economic needs of the German nation and that the former could be satisfied only on the basis of a

---

[5] On Westarp's role in shaping the legislative agenda of the fourth Marx cabinet, see Albrecht Philipp, "Mein Weg: Rückschau eines Siebzigjährigen auf allerlei Geschenisse und Menschen, Dritte Teil: Abgeordnetenjahre in der Weimarer Republik (1919–1930)," SHStA Dresden, NL Philipp, 4/198–200.

[6] Walther Lambach, "Um die Führung im Reiche," in Politische Praxis 1927, ed. Walther Lambach (Hamburg, n.d. [1927]), 60–61.

vigorous and healthy economic policy.[7] This premise would be severely tested in late February 1927 when the cabinet revived a bill that sought to restore the eight-hour workday as the norm for industrial labor and to establish a new and less generous formula for the compensation of overtime work. This bill, the essential outlines of which had been agreed upon in the last days of the previous government, aroused such intense opposition from Ruhr heavy industry that the DNVP's industrial supporters threatened to curtail their subsidies to the party if it capitulated to the trade-union elements on its left wing and helped secure passage of the bill in the Reichstag.[8] In an attempt to offset the influence of the Christian labor unions, the DNVP joined forces with the DVP in allowing deputies with close ties to German industry to take the lead in working out the final details of the bill in the parliamentary committee to which it had been assigned. Representatives of the two parties were thus able to pressure the Center into accepting a weakened version of the bill that eliminated many of the provisions on overtime that organized industrial interests had found so offensive.[9] Despite the fact that Hugenberg and sixteen other members of the DNVP Reichstag delegation signaled their disapproval of the proposed bill by staying away from the Reichstag at the time during the decisive vote, the compromise saved the governmental coalition and paved the way for the bill's eventual acceptance by a narrow 196–184 margin on 8 April 1927.[10]

The struggle over the Provisional Work Hours Law in the spring of 1927 only foreshadowed the difficulties the DNVP would continue to have as a member of the governmental coalition. Even as this law was making its way through parliament, Heinrich Brauns and the ministry of labor were preparing another bill aimed at softening the social and economic hardships the German worker had experienced as a result of the currency stabilization of 1923–24. Designed to protect the German worker against the vicissitudes of an uncertain labor market, the Unemployment Insurance Act enjoyed a broad base of support that extended from the Social Democrats to the left wing of the DNVP and was approved by an overwhelming margin in the Reichstag on

---

[7] Paul Lejeune-Jung, *Gegenwartsaufgaben deutscher Wirtschafts- und Sozialpolitik. Reichstagsrede am 4. Februar 1927*, Deutschnationale Flugschrift, no. 283 (Berlin, 1927), esp. 6–12.

[8] For example, see Kirdorf to Westarp, 26 Feb. 1927, and Hugenberg to Westarp, 2 Mar. 1927, both in NL Westarp, Gärtringen, II/25, as well as circular no. 5 from the ADI, 10 Mar. 1927, HA Krupp Essen, FAH IV C 178.

[9] For further details, see Rademacher to Westarp, 1 Mar. 1927, and Westarp to Kirdorff, 10 Mar. 1927, both in NL Westarp, Gärtringen, II/25. See also Michael Stürmer, *Koalition und Opposition*, 203–10, and Ohnezeit, *Zwischen "schärfster Opposition,"* 368–70.

[10] See Hugenberg's speech before the DNVP economic conference in Bielefeld, 24 Apr. 1927, BA Koblenz, NL Hugenberg, 113/96–112.

7 July 1927.[11] The passage of this act marked the high-point of the legislative influence of Christian labor and provided dramatic proof that the DNVP was not the party of social reaction its rivals had always made it out to be. But if the leaders of the DNVP's Christian-national labor wing hailed the bill's passage as a major triumph for workers and white-collar employees throughout the country,[12] spokesmen for the DNVP's industrial and agrarian wings resented the way in which the party's national leadership had been outmaneuvered by the forces of organized labor.

Sentiment to this effect was particularly strong among the leaders of the party's industrial wing. In the spring of 1927 – indeed, at the precise moment that the work hours bill was making its way through the Reichstag – Ruhr heavy industry had tried to shore up its position within the DNVP by agreeing to provide the DNVP and DVP with two 50,000 mark subsidies each to help them sustain their national organizations in the period of relative inactivity between national elections.[13] Given the severe financial difficulties the DNVP had experienced through 1925 and 1926,[14] this support was critical to the party's long-term financial stability.[15] But Fritz Thyssen, the industrialist responsible for steering this money to the DNVP, was so enraged by the passage of the Unemployment Insurance Act that he warned Westarp in July 1927 that the financial arrangements of the previous spring were in jeopardy.[16] The Coordinating Committee of German National Industrialists (ADI), which had been founded at the DNVP's 1921 Munich party congress, tried to placate the party's industrial supporters by defending the DNVP's role in blunting the thrust of Brauns's legislative agenda. Had not the DNVP been in the government, the ADI's Anton Scheibe argued in a circular that was widely distributed throughout the German industrial establishment, the legislation in question would have been far more damaging to industry than it actually was. The ultimate problem, continued Scheibe, lay not with a lack of commitment on the part of the DNVP but rather with the parliamentary system of government

---

[11] Stürmer, *Koalition und Opposition*, 210–12. See also Dörr, "Deutschnationale Volkspartei," 335–39, and Ohnezeit, *Zwischen "schärfster Opposition,"* 371–73.

[12] Karl Dudey, *Deutschnationale Sozialpolitik. Vortrag gehalten auf dem Deutschnationalen Parteitag in Königsberg am 22. Sept. 1927*, Deutschnationale Flugschrift, no. 302 (Berlin, 1927), 10–12.

[13] For further details, see Kirdorf to Krupp, 14 Mar. 1927, HA Krupp Essen, FAH IV C 178, as well as Thyssen's correspondence with Westarp, 11–14 Apr. 1927, NL Westarp, Gärtringen, II/23. On the rationale behind this arrangement, see Wilmowsky to Krupp, 12 Nov. and 15 Dec. 1927, HA Krupp Essen, FAH 23/501.

[14] Report by Widenmann at the DNVP party congress in Cologne, 9 Sept. 1926, BA-MA Freiburg, NL Tirpitz, 60/330–37.

[15] Remarks by Westarp at a meeting with a group of Ruhr industrialists, Düsseldorf, 18 Mar. 1927, NL Westarp, Gärtringen, VN 59.

[16] Correspondence between Thyssen and Westarp, 18–23 July 1927, NL Westarp, Gärtringen, VN II/23.

in which the DNVP was obliged to operate. Only a radical overhaul of the existing political system and the establishment of a more authoritarian form of government, Scheibe concluded, would free German industry from the fetters under which it was forced to operate so that it might realize the full flower of its productive potential.[17]

The Price of Compromise

As the struggle over the Work Hours Law of April 1927 and the Unemployment Insurance Act three months later clearly indicated, the task of reconciling the respective demands of social and economic policy was by no means as easy as Lejeune-Jung had intimated in his Reichstag speech earlier that February. This was no less true of the DNVP's relations to German agriculture. One of the compelling reasons behind the DNVP's decision to rejoin the government had been the need to provide the party's agricultural interests with more effective representation than the party could do in opposition. The need to do so was all the more urgent in light of the continued deterioration of Germany's rural economy since the stabilization of the currency in 1923–24.[18] With more than 1.7 million members, the National Rural League was far and away the largest of Germany's agricultural interest organizations, and it stood fully behind the DNVP's reentry into the national government, though with the important caveat that this not be construed as acceptance of the existing constitutional system.[19] In his maiden speech as Reich agricultural minister, the Schiele outlined a comprehensive program of agrarian relief that envisaged not only more vigorous tariff protection against agricultural imports from the rest of Europe, Canada, and the United States but also fundamental structural changes that would reverse a decade of governmental neglect and restore agricultural productivity to its prewar levels. To accomplish this, Schiele proposed a series of measures designed to reduce the high level of rural indebtedness that had resulted from the inflationary turmoil of the early 1920s and restore the profitability of small and middle-sized agricultural enterprises. The net effect of these reforms, Schiele argued, would be to revitalize German agriculture so that it could serve as a catalyst of Germany's national economic recovery.[20]

---

[17] ADI, circular no. 6, Aug. 1927, StA Hamburg, Blohm und Voß GmbH, 1215. See also Anton Scheibe, *Wirtschaft und Parlamentarismus. Ein Beitrag zur Kritik an der Partei*, Deutschnationale Flugschrift, no. 300 (Berlin, 1927).

[18] For further details, see Harold James, *German Slump*, 246–59.

[19] *Reichs-Landbund* 6, no. 48 (27 Nov. 1926): 545–46, and no. 50 (11 Dec. 1926): 573–74.

[20] Martin Schiele, *Die Agrarpolitik der Deutschnationalen Volkspartei in den Jahren 1925/ 1928*, Deutschnationale Flugschrift, no. 320 (Berlin, 1928), 5–9, 15. See also Schiele, "Deutsche Agrarpolitik nach dem Kriege," *Nationalwirtschaft. Blätter für organischen Wirtschaftsaufbau* 1, no. 4 (Apr. 1928): 493–507.

Despite Schiele's deep and abiding commitment to the social and economic welfare of the German farmer, organized agriculture became increasingly impatient with the pace of the government's farm program. On 18 March 1927 Ernst Brandes, president of the German Chamber of Agriculture (Deutscher Landwirtschaftsrat), wrote a long letter to Westarp in which he warned the DNVP party chairman of the depressed mood that existed throughout the German countryside and implored him to do what he could to expedite the implementation of the government's farm program. While praising Schiele for the scope and vision of his farm program, Brandes questioned the DNVP's resolve and unity of purpose "to create the necessary economic prerequisites for its successful implementation."[21] Brandes's letter constituted a direct challenge to Schiele and the DNVP party leadership and exhorted them to fulfill the promises that had accompanied their return to the national government. On 4 April Westarp met with representatives from the other coalition parties to draft the outlines of a new tariff policy aimed at securing the livelihood of German agriculture, increase its productive capabilities, strengthen the domestic market, and create the prerequisites for new settlement in the east.[22] Over the course of the next several months Schiele succeeded in securing improvements benficial to agriculture in commercial treaties that Germany was in the process of negotiating with Spain, France, Poland, and Canada. At the same time, he was able to persuade the cabinet to reduce taxes on the consumption of sugar and rye in an attempt to expand the market for domestically produced agricultural products.[23] Responding to Brandes in April 1927, Westarp cited this as proof of the DNVP's commitment to the welfare of German agriculture and reassured him that the DNVP would continue to do everything in its power to rescue the German farmer from the increasingly desperate situation in which he currently found itself.[24]

The exchange between Brandes and Westarp revealed just how fragile the relationship between the DNVP and organized agriculture had become. Brandes's dissatisfaction over the speed with which Schiele was implementing his farm program underlined a deeper frustration that conservative economic interest organizations in both industry and agriculture had come to feel about the exigencies of coalition politics. For, as Westarp reminded Brandes, the DNVP was a member of a coalition government and had to respect the interests and concerns of its coalition partners.[25] At no point was the poignancy of Westarp's statement more apparent than in the party's agonizing

---

[21] Brandes to Westarp, 18 Mar. 1927, NL Westarp, Gärtringen, VN 59.
[22] Memorandum by Westarp, 4 Apr. 1927, NL Westarp, Gärtringen, VN 66.
[23] Schiele, *Agrarpolitik der DNVP*, 7–9. For further details, see Dörr, "Deutschnationale Volkspartei," 339–46.
[24] Westarp to Brandes, 11 Apr. 1927, NL Westarp, Gärtringen, VN 59.
[25] Ibid.

struggle to come to terms with the renewal of the 1922 Law for the Protection of the Republic. This law, which had been enacted in the aftermath of Rathenau's assassination and gave the state extensive powers to monitor the activities of anti-republican organizations, was scheduled to expire in the summer of 1927. The struggle over its renewal dramatized the dilemma in which the DNVP found itself as a member of the governmental coalition. For Marx and his supporters, Nationalist acceptance of the controversial bill was a sign of the DNVP's good faith as a coalition partner and a *conditio sine qua non* for the Center's continued collaboration with the DNVP.[26] For the Nationalists, on the other hand, the Law for the Protection of the Republic had always been a thorn in their side and an affront to their monarchist principles. As Westarp reminded the party faithful at a rally in Berlin in the second week of May, the DNVP was a monarchist party whose fundamental opposition to the republican form of government had been compromised in no way whatsoever by its participation in the national government. If the DNVP was to fulfill its mission as the bearer of Germany's conservative tradition, Westarp insisted, then it had no choice but to remain true to the principles that had inspired its founding, not the least of which was its commitment to the monarchical form of government as the form of government best suited to the character of the German nation.[27]

The Nationalists came under heavy pressure to support renewal of the Law for the Protection of the Republic from the Center, where Joseph Wirth and the party's left wing were on the verge of an open revolt as a consequence of their party's coalition with the DNVP.[28] Marx was fully prepared to resign as chancellor if renewal of the law failed to receive the necessary two-thirds majority in the Reichstag and demanded that the Nationalists demonstrate their reliability as a member of the national government by making a declaration of loyalty to the Weimar Constitution that went beyond Westarp's pallid reassurances before the Reichstag on 3 February.[29] Although Westarp and the leaders of the DNVP Reichstag delegation were anxious to prevent the collapse of the governmental coalition, they regarded the controversial law as a measure directed against their own party and registered strong opposition to its renewal at a meeting with their coalition partners 11 May 1927.[30] The DVP

[26] Hehl, *Marx* , 416–22.

[27] Kuno von Westarp, *Die Sendung der Deutschnationalen Volkspartei. Ansprache in der Werbewoche des Landesverbandes Berlin am 9. Mai 1927*, Deutschnationale Volkspartei, no. 294 (Berlin, 1927), 9–12. See also Kuno von Westarp, *Deutschnationale Innenpolitik in der Regierungskoalition*, Deutschnationale Flugschrift, no. 292 (Berlin, 1927), 27–31.

[28] Josef Becker, "Joseph Wirth und die Krise des Zentrums während des IV. Kabinetts Marx (1927–28)," *Zeitschrift für die Geschichte des Oberrheins* 109 (1961): 371–92.

[29] Hehl, *Marx*, 416–22.

[30] Westarp's remarks at a meeting of government party leaders, 11 May 1927, in *Akten der Reichskanzlei: Die Kabinette Marx III und IV. 17. Mai 1926 bis 29. Januar 1927. 29 Januar*

and BVP tried to break the deadlock with an amendment that permitted extension of the law for another two years but abolished the special courts that had been set up for the purpose of investigating and suppressing anti-republican organizations. The so-called Kaiser paragraph prohibiting the return of the emperor or members of the other ruling dynasties to Germany, on the other hand, would be retained over strenuous objections from the Nationalists.[31] Anxious to avoid the onus of bringing about the fall of the government, the Nationalist party leadership reluctantly agreed to this compromise, and in the decisive vote on 17 May all but six members of the DNVP Reichstag delegation voted for it, thereby assuring its passage by the necessary two-thirds majority.[32]

For the Nationalists all of this was a particularly bitter pill to swallow. The retention of the Kaiser paragraph ignited a storm of protest throughout the DNVP party organization and prompted threats of resignation from several prominent party members.[33] The imperial household was particularly distraught over the DNVP's alleged betrayal of the monarchist cause and protested vigorously from its exile in Doorn.[34] In an attempt calm the waters, Westarp undertook an energetic defense of the compromise he had negotiated with the other government parties at a particularly stormy meeting of the DNVP executive committee on 2 June 1927. Not only did Westarp dismiss the Kaiser paragraph as a measure of little practical import, but he reiterated his fear that the DNVP's failure to support an extension of the controversial law would lead to the collapse of the existing governmental coalition and the formation of a new left-wing government under Social Democratic influence. For the DNVP it was essential to prevent the Center from falling once again under the control of Wirth and the elements on its extreme left wing, and this, Westarp insisted, was almost certain if the DNVP persisted in its opposition to an extension of the Law for the Protection of the Republic.[35] Although the leaders of the DNVP district organizations in central and western Germany tended to accept the arguments with which Westarp defended the DNVP's role in the renewal of the Law for the

---

1927 bis 29. Juni 1928, ed. Günther Abramowski, 2 vols. (Boppard am Rhein, 1988), 1:730–33.

[31] Minutes of a meeting of government party leaders, 12 May 1927, ibid., 1:745–47.

[32] Undated memorandum by Westarp, May 1927, NL Westarp, Gärtringen, 61. For further details, see Dörr, "Deutschnationale Volkspartei," 303–13.

[33] Ada Gräfin von Westarp to Gertraude Freifrau Hiller von Gaertringen, 12 May 1927, NL Westarp, Gärtringen.

[34] Dommes to Westarp, 26 May 1927, NL Westarp, Gärtringen, VN 60.

[35] Westarp's speech at the meeting of the DNVP executive committee, 2 June 1927, BA-MA Freiburg, NL Tirpitz, 60/155–56. See also Westarp to Dommes, 4 June 1927, NL Westarp, Gärtringen, VN 60, as well as Westarp, Deutschnationale Innenpolitik, 24–27.

Protection of the Republic,[36] his words did little to assuage the bitterness that those who stood on the party's right wing felt over what they regarded as an unconscionable sacrifice of political principle for the sake of preserving a governmental coalition that had yet to fulfill its promise.[37]

Revolt on the Patriotic Right

Westarp had come to recognize that the exigencies of coalition politics sometimes took precedence over the DNVP's ideological opposition to the republican form of government and believed that compromises were unavoidable in order to protect the welfare of those interests that were essential for the future of the conservative movement. This sort of thinking, however, found little favor on the patriotic Right, where opposition to any form of collaboration with the existing political system was deeply suspect. Of the various organizations on Germany's patriotic Right, none was more incensed over the DNVP's participation in the Marx cabinet that the Pan-German League. The Pan-Germans were particularly frustrated by their exclusion from any sort of meaningful role in the deliberations that had preceded the DNVP's entry into the fourth Marx cabinet. Westarp had met with ADV chairman Heinrich Claß on several occasions in the second half of December 1926, leaving him with the distinct impression that the DNVP was not interested in becoming part of a government based upon a parliamentary majority and sought instead the formation of a right-wing minority government in which the DNVP would replace the Center as the dominant force.[38] But when the DNVP, contrary to all expectations, joined the Center and other parties of the middle and moderate Right in a new government that rested on a Reichstag majority, this struck the Pan-Germans an act of capitulation to the very system the DNVP had pledged to overthrow. Meeting in Berlin on 12–13 February 1927, the leaders of the ADV denounced the DNVP's decision to join the Marx cabinet as a betrayal of the struggle against the existing system of government and called upon the their supporters throughout the country to rededicate themselves to the task of building a strong "national opposition" at the local and regional levels of the DNVP organization.[39] Claß was particularly critical of

---

[36] Ada Gräfin von Westarp to Gertraude Freifrau Hiller von Gaertringen, 2 June 1927, NL Westarp, Gärtringen.

[37] Remarks of Lineau (Hamburg), Averdunk (Potsdam I), Schiele-Naumburg, and Steinhoff (Potsdam II), in the minutes of the DNVP executive committee, 2 June 1927, BA-MA Freiburg, NL Tirpitz, 60/156–58.

[38] Remarks by Claß at a meeting of the ADV managing committee, 12–13 Feb. 1927, BA Berlin, R 8048, 149/42–56.

[39] "Alldeutsche Kundgebung zur Lage," Deutsche Zeitung, 14 Feb. 1927, no. 37. For further details, see Jackisch, Pan-German League, 150–51.

Westarp's role in the creation of the new cabinet and accused the DNVP of having betrayed the very principles upon which the it had been founded.[40] The proper response, according to ADV secretary general Baron Leopold von Vietinghoff-Scheel, would not be to leave the DNVP for the sake of a new political party as some had suggested but to mobilize the party's rank-and-file membership against the policies of the party's national leadership and to refashion the DNVP as a radical opposition party capable of winning back the support of those who had abandoned it in disapppointment over its current political course.[41]

The situation within the Pan-German League was not substantially different from that within the United Patriotic Leagues of Germany under the leadership of retired major Count Rüdiger von der Goltz. Ever since he assumed leadership of the organization in early 1925, Goltz had led the VVVD more and more decisively into the orbit of the radical Right.[42] In the dispute over Locarno the VVVD had done its part in forcing the DNVP out of the Luther government, and it continued to press the party to take a strong stand on matters of national interest even after the DNVP had left the government.[43] Lke the Pan-Germans, the VVVD had been caught off-guard by the DNVP's decision to join the Center in forming a new government that derived its mandate from a majority in the Reichstag. For Goltz and his associates, the net effect of this had been to "paralyze the national opposition in parliament," a situation that could be corrected only by mobilizing and unifying the forces of the national opposition.[44] Stunned by the Nationalist entry into the Marx cabinet, the VVVD immediately tried to embellish its credentials as a member of the national opposition by enlisting retired general and field marshall August von Mackensen as its honorary protector or *Schirmherr*.[45] Mackensen was one of Germany's most venerated heroes of World War I, and the leaders of the VVVD hoped that his patronage would enable their organization to reestablish itself as the unquestioned leader of the patriotic movement.[46]

---

[40] Claß at the meeting of the ADV managing committee, 12–13 Feb. 1927, BA Berlin, R 8048, 149/42–56.

[41] Remarks by Vietinghoff-Scheel, ibid., 56–59.

[42] Report by Goltz at the VVVD national delegate conference, 25 Aug. 1926, BA Berlin, R 8005, 86/24–26.

[43] For example, see Goltz to Westarp, 13 Mar. 1926, NL Westarp, Gärtringen, VN 76.

[44] Resolution adopted by the VVVD national delegate conference, 16 Mar. 1927, Nachlass August von Mackensen, BA-MA Freiburg, 337/28–29.

[45] Goltz to Mackensen, 25 Mar. 1927, BA-MA Freiburg, NL Mackensen, 337/32. See also Theo Schwarzmüller, *Zwischen Kaiser und "Führer." Generalfeldmarschall August von Mackensen. Eine politische Biographie* (Paderborn, 1998), 202–31.

[46] Goltz, "Beurteilung der Lage der vaterländischen Bewegung im Spätsommer 1927," 2 Sept. 1927, records of the Dresden chapter of the Pan-German League, Stadtarchiv Dresden (hereafter cited as StA Dresden), 10. For Mackensen's political stance, see Cramon to Seldte, 19 Dec. 1926, BA Berlin, R 72, 55/114–16.

In the meantime, the struggle for the control of the largest of Germany's paramilitary organizations, the Stahlhelm, drew to its inexorable climax. The struggle against Locarno had done much to energize the Stahlhelm's more radical elements and to fuel their challenge to Seldte's leadership of the organization. Critical of Seldte's inability to articulate a clear political line for the Stahlhelm to follow, Duesterberg and his supporters and were intent upon transforming the Stahlhelm from a staid, predominantly bourgeois veterans' organization into a vanguard of revolutionary nationalism.[47] At the same time, Duesterberg sought to tie the Stahlhelm more closely to Goltz and the more militantly antirepublican elements in charge of the VVVD.[48] Emboldened by their earlier successes, the forces around Duesterberg launched a direct challenge to Seldte's leadership of the Stahlhelm in the spring of 1927 in a determined effort to drive him from control of the organization and to bring about a fundamental change in its political orientation.[49] These efforts would almost certainly have succeeded had not Seldte taken legal precautions to tie the designation "Stahlhelm" to his own person, thereby making it impossible for his opponents to remove him as its leader without changing the organization's name. As a result, Duesterberg was forced to accept a compromise whereby he and Seldte would share responsibility for leadership of the Stahlhelm with Duesterberg as its second leader, but with powers and responsibilities equal to those of its first leader Seldte.[50]

This arrangement represented a clear triumph for the activists around Duesterberg and completed the Stahlhelm's transformation from an ostensibly non-partisan veteran's organization into a political combat league. In the course of this, the Stahlhelm had abandoned the pretense of political neutrality to become, as Seldte wrote defiantly to Stresemann in April 1927, "a political national freedom movement."[51] This transformation reached its climax in May 1927 at the eighth Reich Front Soldiers' Congress (Reichsfrontsoldatentag) in Berlin.[52] Here, in the presence of four Hohenzollern princes, the leaders of the Stahlhelm issued a special proclamation, or *Botschaft*, outlining the Stahlhelm's program for Germany's national renewal at home and abroad. Not only did the proclamation underscore the Stahlhelm's refusal to accept the conditions that had been created by Versailles and subsequent diplomatic agreements, but it demanded the unconditional repudiation of the war guilt clause as a necessary precondition

---

[47] Duesterberg to Hammerstein, 16 Apr. 1926, BA Koblenz, R 72/2305.
[48] Exchange of letters between Duesterberg and Ausfeld, 10–15 Jan. 1927, BA Berlin, R 72, 53/141–42.
[49] Brauweiler to Lüninck, 16 Mar. 1927, VWA Münster, NL Lüninck, 768.
[50] Brauweiler, "Meine Tätigkeit im 'Stahlhelm'," 22 Dec. 1965, StA Mönchen-Gladbach, NL Brauweiler, 110. For further details, see Berghahn, *Stahlhelm*, 103–14; Klotzbücher, "Der politische Weg des Stahlhelm," 72–111; and Simon, "Brauweiler," 210–16.
[51] Seldte to Stresemann, 29 Apr. 1927, PA AA Berlin, NL Stresemann, 53/164031.
[52] Seldte, "Der 8. Reichsfrontsoldatentag," *Der Stahlhelm*, 8 May 1927, no. 19.

for German membership in the League of Nations. At the same time, the proclamation reaffirmed the Stahlhelm's commitment to the black, red, and gold colors of the imperial flag and called for a constitutional reform to strengthen the powers of the Reich President so that he could protect the national welfare against the arbitrariness of parliamentary government. In the area of social and economic policy, the Stahlhelm denounced the Marxist concept of class conflict at the same time that it advocated a policy of internal colonization and the settlement of Germany's eastern mark with peasants from other parts of the country to correct the problem of "over-industrialization" and "the progressive detachment of healthy national energy [*Volkskraft*] from its native soil [*Heimatboden*]."[53]

As the Stahlhelm fell more and more under the influence of Duesterberg and the elements on its extreme right wing, its relations with Artur Mahraun and the Young German Order became increasingly strained. The Young Germans had already begun to extricate themselves from the so-called national opposition on the grounds that it had fallen so thoroughly under the influence of reactionaries like Hugenberg and Claß that it was no longer capable of satisfying the German people's longing for political rejuvenation.[54] This was to become a recurrent refrain in Mahraun's attacks against the Pan-Germans, the Stahlhelm, and the other groups on the patriotic Right, and in the fall of 1926 it provided the Young Germans with all the justification they needed to dissociate themselves from the Stahlhelm's initiative on behalf of a bourgeois unity ticket in the Saxon state elections.[55] The Young Germans also refused to join the Stahlhelm, the VVVD, and other right-wing organizations in public demonstrations against the Locarno accords once the treaty had been ratified and dissociated themselves as forcefully as possible from the vilification to which the patriotic Right subjected Reich President von Hindenburg for his failure to block Germany's acceptance of the controversial treaty.[56] At the same time, the Young German Order remained deeply contemptuous of the existing party system and carefully avoided becoming entangled in partisan political controversy. What ultimately separated the Young German Order from its former allies in the patriotic movement was not so much their

---

[53] Brauweiler, "Die Stahlhelm-Botschaft," *Die Standarte. Zeitschrift des neuen Nationalismus* 2, no. 9 (26 June 1927): 271–75.

[54] Mahraun, "Jungdeutscher Orden und nationale Opposition," *Der Meister* 1, no. 2 (Dec. 1925): 46–50. See also Laudahn, "Jungdeutscher Orden und vaterländische Verbände," ibid., 1, no. 6 (Apr. 1926): 24–27, and "V.V.V.D.," ibid., 1, no. 9 (July 1926): 19–22.

[55] Memorandum of a conversation between Bernhard, Mahraun, and Bornemann, 16 Aug. 1926, PA AA Berlin, NL Stresemann, 96/173179–82.

[56] Laudahn, "Die Haltung des jungdeutschen Ordens gegenüber dem Vertrage von Locarno," *Der Meister* 1, no. 2 (Dec. 1925): 26–31.

respective attitudes toward parliamentarism and the German party system as its call for the peaceful evolution of the Weimar Republic into a higher and more perfect form of democracy that derived its spiritual legitimacy from the experience of those who had served at the front in World War I and that envisaged the dissolution of all social, confessional, and political differences in a deep and abiding love of the nation.[57]

The defection of the Young Germans from the patriotic front was of no immediate consequence and did little to temper the militancy of the other organizations on the patriotic Right. Both the Stahlhelm and the VVVD escalated their attacks against the so-called Weimar system through the latter half of 1927 at the same time that the Pan-Germans were steppimg up their efforts to reassert themselves within the DNVP and reverse the direction in which the party appeared to be moving. All of this placed an increasingly heavy burden on the DNVP's relations with the patriotic Right and posed a threat to its effectiveness as a member of the Marx cabinet. Although Westarp and the DNVP party leadership sought to cultivate close relations with all of Germany's patriotic associations with the notable exception of the Young German Order, this began to wear increasingly thin in light of the anti-system histrionics of the patriotic Right and its hostility to the DNVP's collaboration with the existing system of government. With new national elections scheduled for the spring of 1928, the need to clarify this situation and normalize relations between the DNVP and the patriotic Right would become ever more urgent.

A Restless Party

By the time the Reichstag broke for its summer recess in late July 1927, the DNVP party leadership had become increasingly concerned about the lethargy of the party organization and the apparent indifference of large sectors of the Nationalist electorate. For the most part, the DNVP's rank-and-file member-ship seemed more interested in issues of immediate import than in the more fundamental questions of ideology and national policy that lay at the heart of the party's identity. The task confronting party leaders, therefore, was to reinvigorate the DNVP's popular base without driving those who were motiv-ated primarily by their own economic self-interest into the arms of special-interest parties like the Business Party or People's Justice Party. This task was not made any easier by the fact that there were no longer foreign policy issues like the Dawes Plan or Locarno that could be used to infuse new energy into the local and regional levels of their party's national organization. By the same

---

[57] Artur Mahraun, *Das jungdeutsche Manifest. Volk gegen Kaste und Geld. Sicherung des Friedens durch Neubau der Staaten* (Berlin, 1927), esp. 7–10, 95–107, 139–42, 197–203.

token, the fact that the DNVP was a member of the national government meant that it could no longer avail itself of the often inflammatory anti-government rhetoric that had served it so well in the past. Whether the DNVP could somehow square the circle and recapture its emotional élan remained to be seen.[58]

In his capacity as DNVP national chairman, Westarp continued to offer a vigorous defense of the Nationalists' accomplishments as a member of the governmental coalition, though always with the cavaet that the exigencies of coalition politics made it difficult, if not impossible, for the party to achieve everything it had set out to achieve.[59] At the same time, Westarp categorically rejected the argument that this had compromised the party's ideological integrity and insisted that the DNVP remained as committed as ever to the restoration of the monarchy. But as the party concluded preparations for its annual party congress in Königsberg – a site carefully selected to reaffirm the DNVP's identification with the symbols and traditions of Prussian power – in the third week of September 1927, hopes of restoring unity within the DNVP were again jeopardized by the antics of the party's right wing.[60] Through the summer and fall of 1927 ADV chairman Heinrich Claß had met with Alfred Hugenberg, the putative leader of the party's right wing, on several occasions to persuade him to become more actively involved in the struggle for control of the party.[61] Hugenberg had always preferred to stay out of the political limelight and rely upon his influence over Germany's right-wing press, his extensive contacts in the German business community, and his control of party finances to achieve his objectives. An embittered opponent of the Dawes Plan, Hugenberg had nevertheless supported the DNVP's entry into the Luther cabinet in 1925 only to break with Westarp and the leaders of the DNVP Reichstag delegation at the height of the Locarno crisis by lending the full weight of his authority to the efforts of those who sought to force the DNVP out of the government.[62] But more than anything else, it was the

---

[58] See Scheibe, "Für Reichsparteitag und Werbewoche," n.d., appended to Scheibe to Tirpitz, 12 Aug. 1927, BA-MA Freiburg, NL Tirpitz, 171/208, 211–29.

[59] Kuno von Westarp, *Die deutschnationale Arbeit in der Regierungskoalition. Sommerta-gung 1927*, Deutschnationale Flugschrift, no. 296 (Berlin, 1927). In a similar vein, see Treviranus, "Bilanz der deutschnationalen Regierungsarbeit," *Politische Wochenschrift* 3, no. 37 (15 Sept. 1927): 199–203.

[60] Correspondence between Westarp and Dommes, 11 Aug.–3. Sept. 1927, NL Westarp, Gärtringen, VN 32. See also Westarp to Schlange-Schöningen, 13 Sept. 1927, ibid., VN 63.

[61] See the unpublished second volume of Claß's memoirs "Wider den Strom," BA Berlin, Nachlass Heinrich Claß, 3/879–81.

[62] Hugenberg to Hergt, 5 Oct. 1925, NL Westarp, Gärtringen, VN 53. See also Hugenberg, "Locarno," 15 Nov. 1925, in Alfred Hugenberg, *Streiflichter aus Vergangenheit und Gegenwart* (Berlin, 1927), 88–90.

DNVP's decision to join the fourth Marx cabinet that prompted Hugenberg to set aside whatever reservations he might have had and to challenge Westarp for control of the party.

On 17 September 1927 Hugenberg threw down the gauntlet with a highly charged letter to Westarp in which he insisted that the party must end the contradiction that lay at the heart of its present strategy and return to a policy of uncompromising opposition to the existing system of government. Hugenberg categorically rejected the premise that the party had to work within the framework of a governmental system to which it was fundamentally opposed in order to defend and promote the welfare of those interests that were vital to the DNVP's growth and development. "Whoever," wrote Hugenberg in a passage that reflected his scorn for the professional politicians he held responsible for the crisis that had taken hold of the DNVP, "affirms the need for a thorough reorganization and reconstruction of our existing state life … and accordingly scorns today's state only to base his personal career and future on collaboration with parliamentarism is an inner cripple whose ambition will soon triumph over all theories and convictions …" The deep schism that had developed within the ranks of the DNVP, he continued, could only be ended by committing the party without any reservation whatsoever to "the establishment of a new state compatible with the German character." To do this, however, one only had to listen to those who made up the party's popular base throughout the country. "Give the party that exists in the nation at large," Hugenberg exhorted Westarp, "a genuine life of its own alongside that of its parliamentary delegations, and let the unparliamentary party in the country as a whole serve as the conscience of those delegations that sit in parliament today! Then at least a formal line," he concluded, "will have been drawn from which we can free and consolidate the forces for a solution to the real tasks of our party."[63]

Hugenberg's letter represented a frontal attack upon the political course the DNVP had charted ever since the summer of 1924 and marked the beginning of a pitched battle for control of the party that would continue for the better part of the next three years. But the immediate effect of Hugenberg's letter, copies of which were sent to a number of his associates on the DNVP's right wing,[64] was only to underscore his isolation within the party as a whole.[65] In the meantime, the Königsberg party congress passed without further incident. In his keynote address on the afternoon of 20 September, Westarp delivered a speech that was carefully crafted to heal the divisions that had developed

---

[63] Hugenberg to Westarp, 17 Sept. 1927, BA Koblenz, NL Hugenberg, 113/78–83, reprinted in Leo Wegener, *Hugenberg. Eine Plauderei* (Solln-Munich, 1930), 53–54.

[64] For a list of recipients, see Hugenberg to Westarp, 15 Nov. 1927, NL Westarp, Gärtringen, II/25.

[65] Wegener to Bang, 8 Oct. 1927, BA Koblenz, NL Wegener, 23/70.

within the party in the wake of its two experiments at government participation. Westarp not only reminded the party faithful of the DNVP's achievements as a member of the government but stressed that the party's work was not yet finished and outlined an ambitious agenda for the months ahead. Concentrating on those issues that were most likely to reinforce the party's inner unity, Westarp struck a notably strident tone by criticizing the Allies for their failure to fulfill the commitments they had made at Locarno, Geneva, and Thoiry and called for an end to all talk about future "compensations" until England and France had begun to live up to their own promises. At the same time, Westarp identified a number of domestic issues, the most prominent of which were the passage of a Reich School Law and a reform of the criminal justice system, that the DNVP hoped to accomplish in what still remained of the current legislative period. None of this, he reassured his audience, compromised the DNVP's political and ideological integrity in the slightest, for the DNVP remained unshakably committed to the restoration of the monarchy and to the defense of Germany's imperial legacy against all who sought to drag it down into the muck of partisan politics. Yet to do all of this and at the same time prepare for the upcoming national elections, it was essential for the party to strengthen its organization and internal solidarity. Therein, concluded Westarp, lay the keys to the DNVP's success and future.[66]

Cultural Politics and the End of the Coalition

Of all the issues that Westarp touched upon in his Königsberg address, none was more critical than the Reich School Law. The DNVP's participation in the fourth Marx cabinet was premised upon a series of compromises with the Center that, among other things, envisaged the introduction of a new school law that would authorize the establishment of denominational schools throughout the entire Reich.[67] This was an issue upon which virtually every sector of the DNVP could agree, though some, like the party's two confessional committees, obviously ascribed much greater significance to it than others. For the leaders of the party's Catholic wing, the introduction of a new national school law was obviously a more effective way of advancing their political agenda than pursuing a concordat with the Holy See, a move that was certain to encounter strong opposition from the DNVP's Lutheran

---

[66] Kuno von Westarp, *Unser Weg zur Macht in Reich und Ländern! Rede auf dem Reichsparteitag in Königsberg Pr. am 20. September 1927*, Deutschnationale Flugschrift, no. 304 (Berlin, 1927). See also Westarp to Hugenberg, 8 Oct. 1927, NL Westarp, Gärtringen, VN 62.

[67] For further details, see Günther Grünthal, *Reichsschulgesetz und Zentrumspartei in der Weimarer Republik* (Düsseldorf, 1968), 196–207.

leadership.[68] For Reinhard Mumm and the leaders of the DNVP's Evangelical Reich Committee, on the other hand, the struggle for the national school law afforded them an opportunity to reassert the primacy of cultural policy over the social and economic issues that had thus far dominated the DNVP's agenda in the Marx cabinet.[69] But these considerations were secondary to the broader strategic goals of the party's national leadership. For by placing themselves at the head of the crusade for a national school law, Westarp and his supporters in the DNVP Reichstag delegation hoped that they would be able to restore the unity of their own party and inject new energy into the flagging fortunes of the national movement.[70]

Responsibility for drafting the new law lay within the purview of the DNVP's Walther von Keudell and the Reich ministry of the interior. After some initial delay, Keudell presented his draft of the school bill to the cabinet on 22 June 1927.[71] Inspired by the Christian and conservative values that lay at the heart of the DNVP's sense of identity, Keudell's bill had been crafted in obvious deference to demands of the Catholic and Lutheran churches for legal recognition of their claims to a more direct role in the German educational system. Keudell's bill sought to rewrite the compromise on public education that had been incorporated into the language of the Weimar Constitution. For not only did Keudell's bill privilege denominational schools at the expense of the non-denominational Christian common schools, or *Simultanschulen*, that had been established by the Weimar Constitution as one of the three alternate modes of public education, but it also made provisions for the direct involvement of Catholic and Lutheran clergy in shaping the curricula for religious instruction in the schools. Moreover, the Keudell bill established denominational schools as the norm throughout the country, thereby forcing Christian common schools in areas like Baden, Hesse-Darmstadt, and the former duchy of Hesse-Nassau to conform to the national standard.[72] But this came as a

---

[68] Minutes of the DNVP's Reich Catholic Committee, 12 July 1927, VWA Münster, NL Landsberg, E1.

[69] Reinhard Mumm, *Der christlich-soziale Gedanke. Bericht über eine Lebensarbeit in schwerer Zeit* (Berlin, 1933), 127-30.

[70] Correspondence between Tiling and Westarp, 21 Feb.-1 Mar. 1927, NL Westarp, Gärtringen, II/23. See also Ellenbeck, "Das Reichsschulgesetz und der Vormarsch der nationalen Bewegung," *Politische Wochenschrift* 3, no. 28 (14 July 1927), 598-601, as well as Wilhelm Kähler, "Die Kulturpolitik der Deutschnationalen Volkspartei," *Jahrbuch der Erziehungswissenschaft und Jugendkunde*, ed. Erich Stern, 3 (1927), 5-30, esp. 19-29. For further details, see Ohnezeit, *Zwischen "schärfster Opposition,"* 399-410.

[71] Minutes of the minsterial conference, 22 June 1927, in *Die Kabinette Marx III und IV*, ed. Abramowski, 2:808-10.

[72] Walther von Keudell, "Unser Kampf um das Reichsschulgesetz," in *Der nationale Wille. Werden und Wirken der Deutschnationalen Volkspartei 1918-1928*, ed. Max Weiß (Essen, 1928), 204-07.

sharp slap in the face to the leaders of the DVP and their representatives in the Marx cabinet, Stresemann and economics minister Julius Curtius. In celebrating the sixtieth anniversary of the founding of its predecessor, the National Liberal Party, earlier that spring, the DVP had made a concerted effort to reaffirm the national and liberal values that lay at the heart of its political heritage.[73] The proposed school law threatened to compromise the very principles upon which the DVP had been founded, and at a ministerial conference on 13 July Stresemann indicated that, while he and his party supported the bill, they would not be able to go along with the conversion of the Christian common schools in southwest Germany into denominational schools.[74]

For Stresemann, who was generally satisfied with the DNVP's performance as a member of the governmental coalition,[75] the conflict over the national school bill constituted a genuine threat to the success of his efforts to stabilize the republic from the Right. The situation was complicated even further by the fact that the Center was anxious to reverse the series of electoral defeats it had suffered since the beginning of the decade by using the school issue to mobilize Catholic parents who might not otherwise support the party.[76] Stresemann was understandably irritated with Keudell and the leaders of the Center Party they proceeded to rescue the national school bill from the hands of the Federal Council, or *Reichsrat*, where delegates of the Prussian government had taken the lead in first rejecting it and then rewriting it in such a way that it that no longer reflected the original intentions of the DNVP and Center. After the revised draft of Keudell's bill was rejected in the Federal Council on 14 October by a 37 to 31 vote, the Marx cabinet voted over the vigorous objections of the DVP to take the original version of the bill to the Reichstag in hopes that the threat of a collapse of the governmental coalition would leave the DVP with no choice but to allow passage of the controversial bill.[77] To Stresemann, this turn of events not only represented an affront to his party's most deeply held

[73] "Das Manifest der Deutschen Volkspartei," in *60 Jahr-Feier der Nationalliberalen Partei am 19. und 20. März 1927 in Hannover*, ed. Reichsgeschäftsstelle der Deutschen Volkspartei (Berlin, n.d. [1927]), 8–9. See also Richter, *Deutsche Volkspartei*, 464–69.
[74] Statement by Stresemann at the ministerial conference, 13 July 1927, in *Die Kabinette Marx III und IV*, ed. Abramowski, 2:856–58. See also Stephen G. Fritz, "'The Center Cannot Hold.' Educational Politics and the Collapse of the Democratic Middle in Germany: The School Bill Crisis in Baden," *History of Education Quarterly* 25 (1985): 413–37.
[75] Stresemann to Jänecke, 15 Aug. 1927, PA AA Berlin, NL Stresemann, 285/150326–31.
[76] Ellen L. Evans, "The Center Wages *Kulturpolitik*: Conflict in the Marx-Keudell Cabinet of 1927," *Central European History* 2 (1969): 139–58. See also Hehl, *Marx*, 428–37, and Ruppert, *Im Dienst am Staat von Weimar*, 287–99.
[77] Minutes of the ministerial conference, 14 Oct. 1927, in *Die Kabinette Marx III und IV*, ed. Abramowski, 2:999–1001.

ideological convictions but, more importantly, seriously jeopardized the success of his own stabilization strategy.[78]

The resuscitation of the national school bill in its original and unrevised form constituted a direct threat to the survival of the fourth Marx cabinet. Given the DVP's unremitting opposition to the provisions of the proposed school law affecting the status of the Christian common schools in southwest Germany, it was only a matter of time until the governmental coalition fell apart. A number of other issues unrelated to the controversial school bill also threatened the survival of the Marx cabinet. A sweeping reform of Germany's civil servant salary structure in October 1927 had met with strong opposition from Adam Stegerwald and the leaders of the Christian trade unions and inflamed tensions between Christian labor and civil servant representatives in both the Center and DNVP.[79] At the same time, organized agriculture had become increasingly dissatisfied with the benefits of the government's trade policy and intensified its pressure upon the cabinet for the more vigorous representation of agrarian interests in bilateral trade treaty negotiations with Poland and other east European states.[80] None of this augured well for the future of the Marx cabinet, and in January 1928 Keudell effectively sealed its fate when he brought the controversial school bill before the Reichstag for final action.[81] A new round of high-level conferences between representatives of the government parties in the middle of February failed to break the deadlock,[82] and on 15 February the Center's Theodor von Guérard, a vigorous defender of his party's alliance with the DNVP and a champion of the proposed school law, announced that for him and his party the governmental coalition had been dissolved.[83] Although the cabinet would remain in office until new elections the following spring, the DNVP's second experiment at government participation had ended in failure.

---

[78] Stresemann's speech before the DVP central executive committee, 21 Nov. 1927, in *Nationalliberalismus in der Weimarer Republik*, ed. Kolb and Richter, 2:732–36.

[79] Adam Stegerwald, *Zur Reform der Beamtenbesoldung*, 2nd printing (Berlin-Wilmersdorf, 1928). See also Ruppert, *Im Dienst am Staat von Weimar*, 274–87.

[80] For further details, see Stresemann to Marx, 24 Nov. 1927, PA AA Berlin, NL Stresemann, 284/150286–97.

[81] For Keudell's position, see his letter to Traub, 7 Jan. 1928, BA Koblenz, NL Traub, 64/52. For his defense of the bill, see Walther von Keudell, *Eltenrecht und christliche Schule. Rede in Dresden am 4. März 1928* (Berlin, 1928).

[82] "Bericht über die interfraktionellen Verhandlungen vom 13.–19. Februar 1928," Nachlass Alfred Zapf, BA Koblenz, 32.

[83] Statement by Guérard at a meeting of representatives of the government parties and cabinet members, 15 Feb. 1928, in *Die Kabinette Marx III und IV*, ed. Abramowski, 2:1310–12.

Crisis in the Countryside

The collapse of the governmental coalition and the preparations for new elections in the spring of 1928 could not have come at a more difficult time for the leaders of the DNVP. The party was still deeply divided over its participation in the Marx cabinet, and its record of accomplishment since the embarrassment of having to support the Law for the Protection of the Republic in May 1927 seemed hardly adequate to justify either the high hopes that had accompanied its entry into the national government or the compromises that governmental participation had necessarily entailed. No problem was more vexing to the leaders of the DNVP than the deepening crisis in the German countryside. The DNVP had entered the Marx cabinet in large part because of pressure from the National Rural League for the more vigorous representation of agricultural economic interests at the upper echelons of Germany's national government. While the RLB concentrated its efforts primarily upon German trade policy in hopes of providing Germany's agricultural producers with more effective tariff protection against farm imports from the rest of Europe, the United States, and Canada, German agriculture was besieged by a host of other problems, not the least of which were the collapse of agricultural prices on the world market, rising production costs at home, an oppressive tax burden, and the lack of access to inexpensive credit. The result was an extraordinarily high level of indebtedness that was particularly acute among the large estate owners from east of the Elbe.[84] While Marx and his cabinet were not insensitive to the difficulties in which the German farmer found himself, none of the measures the government had undertaken on his behalf in the second half of 1927 afforded the relief he so desperately needed. This, in turn, had a radicalizing effect upon the mood of the German farmer and severely strained the DNVP's ties to the German agricultural community.[85]

With the approach of new national elections, the leaders of the DNVP and their allies in the National Rural League faced a difficult challenge in containing the rising tide of rural unrest to which the deepening agrarian crisis had given birth. Peasant unrest reached a dramatic climax on 28 January 1928 when more than 140,000 farmers, artisans, and small shopkeepers from Schleswig-Holstein demonstrated throughout the province to protest high taxes, high interest rates, and inadequate protection against foreign agricultural imports.[86] The rally in Schleswig-Holstein was quickly followed by

---

[84] James, *German Slump*, 246–82.
[85] For example, see Winkler to Westarp, 21 Jan. 1928, NL Westarp, Gärtringen, VN 64. For further details, see Gessner, *Agrarverbände*, 83–181, and Müller, "*Fällt der Bauer, stürzt der Staat*," 58–77.
[86] Jacobi to Westarp, 2 Feb. 1928, NL Westarp, Gärtringen, VN 64.

similar demonstrations in Thuringia, Württemberg, and other parts of the country as the leaders of the RLB's regional affiliates tried to keep the rising wave of agrarian discontent under their own control.[87] Similarly, the RLB's national leadership moved quickly to finalize preparations for its annual congress in Berlin at the very end of January.[88] The RLB's two presidents, Count Eberhard von Kalckreuth and Karl Hepp, would use the congress as a forum to outline a series of additional measures they deemed necessary to restore the profitability of German agriculture, while Schiele, acting in his capacity as the RLB's minister in the Marx cabinet, reaffirmed the government's commitment to the welfare of the German farmer and called upon the German agricultural community to stay the course in the struggle for social and economic rehabilitation.[89]

Efforts on the part of Germany's rural conservatives to keep the rising tide of agrarian protest under their protective wing received a rude shock when Anton Fehr and the leaders of the Bavarian Peasants' League outlined plans of their own for the founding of a new peasants' party. Speaking at a demonstration of the Silesian Peasants' League (Schlesischer Bauernbund) in Breslau on 12 February 1928, Fehr announced that the Bavarian Peasants' League would present a full slate of candidates under the name of the German Peasants' Party (Deutsche Bauernpartei or DBP) in the Reichstag elections that were scheduled to take place later that spring.[90] This represented the culmination of

[87] On the demonstrations in Rudolstadt (Thuringia) and Stuttgart (Württemberg), see *Thüringer Landbund. Thüringer Bauernzeitung für die im Thüringer Landbund zusammengeschlossenen Bauernvereinigungen* 9, no. 12 (11 Feb. 1928): 1, and *Der württembergische Bauernfreund. Ein Wegweiser und Jahrbuch für unsere bäuerlichen und gewerblichen Mittelstand für das Jahr 1929*, ed. Württembergischer Bauern- und Weingärtnerbund (Stuttgart, n.d. [1929]), 90–91. For the broader context, see Jürgen Bergmann and Klaus Mergerle, "Protest and Aufruhr der Landwirtschaft in der Weimarer Republik (1924–1933). Formen und Typen der politischen Agrarbewegung im regionalen Vergleich." In Regionen im historischen Vergleich. Studien zu Deutschland im 19. und 20. Jahrhundert, ed. Jürgen Bergmann et al., Opladen, 1989, 221–28.

[88] Report on the meeting of the RLB executive commitee, 14 Dec. 1927, BA Koblenz, NL Weilnböck, 29b.

[89] For the speeches of Kalckreuth, Hepp, and Schiele, see *Der 8. Reichs-Landbund-Tag. Die Reden der Präsidenten und des Ernährungsministers Schiele* (Berlin, n.d. [1928]), esp. 1–36.

[90] See the text of Fehr's speech in the *Bayerischer Bauern- und Mittelstandsbund. Beilage der "Neuen freien Volkszeitung" in München*, 22 Feb. 1928, no. 5, as well as the correspondence between Lübke and Hiltmann, 28 Feb.–1 Mar. 1928, BHStA Munich, Abt. V, Nachlass Anton Fehr, 29. See also Larry Eugene Jones, "Crisis and Realignment: Agrarian Splinter Parties in the Weimar Republic, 1928–33," in *Peasants and Lords in Modern Germany: Recent Studies in Agricultural History*, ed. Robert G. Moeller (London, 1986), 198–232, and Arno Panzer, "Parteipolitische Ansätze der deutschen Bauernbewegung bis 1933," in *Europäische Bauernparteien im 20. Jahrhundert*, ed. Heinz Gollwitzer (Stuttgart and New York, 1977), 524–42.

a development that had begun the previous summer when the leaders of the Silesian Peasants' League first explored the possibility of a new peasants' party in negotiations with Fehr and the leadership of the BBB.[91] Fehr, who had served as Bavarian minister of agriculture since the summer of 1924, stood considerably to the left of the rural conservatives in control of the RLB, and the founding of the new German Peasants' Party under his auspices aroused widespread concern within the ranks of Germany's conservative agrarian elite. Not only did the Bavarian Peasants' League, the driving force behind the founding of the DBP, represent a nascent agrarian populism for which Germany's more conservative leaders felt little sympathy, but they feared it foreshadowed a further radicalization of the German countryside.

The decentralized structure of the RLB made it difficult for Germany's conservative farm leaders to formulate a concerted response to the radicalizing effect the deepening agricultural crisis was having upon Germany's rural population. Moreover, several of the RLB's regional affiliates – most notably in Thuringia and Württemberg – had run their own slate of candidates in virtually every state and national election since the founding of the Weimar Republic and thus exercised considerably more influence over their local constituencies than the RLB itself. In November 1927 the leaders of the Thuringian Rural League had petitioned the RLB's national leadership on behalf of a national agrarian ticket for the Reichstag elections that were set for the following spring.[92] This proposal encountered fierce opposition from the RLB leaders with close ties to the DNVP, and it was shelved at a meeting of the RLB executive committee on 14 December 1927 in favor of a resolution that left the question of electoral strategy in the hands of the RLB's affiliates themselves.[93] As a result, confusion reigned at the RLB headquarters in Berlin and in the offices of its regional affiliates throughout the country.[94] It was only after a demonstration by 36,000 Thuringian peasants in Rudolstadt on 7 February 1928 and Fehr's announcement five days later that the Bavarian

---

[91] For further details, see Paul Hiltmann, "Tatsachen und Probleme der Bauernbewegung," *Die grüne Zukunft. Zeitschrift für deutsche Bauernpolitik* 1, no. 1 (Oct. 1928): 3–5, and no. 2 (Nov. 1928): 18–24.

[92] Resolution from the TLB executive committee, 24 Nov. 1927, appended to Mackeldey to the RLB, 28 Nov. 1927, BA Koblenz, NL Weilnböck, 42. On the TLB, see the official history "Der Thüringer Landbund in den ersten zehn Jahren," in *Zehn Jahre Thüringer Landbund. Festschrift zum 10jährigen Gedenktag der Gründung des Thüringer Landbundes*, ed. Thüringer Landbund, Hauptgeschäftsstelle (Weimar, n.d. [1929]), 26–36, as well as Guido Dressel, *Der Thüringer Landbund – Agrarischer Berufsverband als politische Partei in Thüringen 1919–1933* (Weimar, 1998), esp. 46–56.

[93] Report on the meeting of the RLB executive committee, 14 Dec. 1927, BA Koblenz, NL Weilnböck, 29b.

[94] Report by Nicolas at the delegate assembly of the Brandenburg Rural League, 25 Jan. 1928, BA Berlin, R 8034 I, 50/40–49. On the situation in Brandenburg, see Pomp, *Bauern und Grossgrundbesitzer*, 265–71.

Peasants' League would join the DBP in presenting a national slate of candidates in the forthcoming Reichstag elections that the leaders of the TLB decided that they could no longer afford to wait for the official sanction of the RLB leadership in Berlin. On 17 February Franz Hänse and Friedrich Döbrich from the Thuringian Rural League along with Wilhelm Dorsch from the Hessian Rural League (Hessischer Landbund) took matters into their own hands by announcing their resignation from the DNVP Reichstag delegation to join a new agrarian party that called itself the Christian-National Peasants' Party (Christlich-nationale Bauernpartei).[95]

The fact that the three principals involved in the founding of the Christian-National Peasants' Party – Franz Hänse, Döbrich, and Dorsch – were all former members of the DNVP Reichstag delegation gave rise to immediate suspicions that the new party was nothing but a Nationalist front organization created for the purpose of duping unwitting peasants into voting for candidates who, once they had been elected, would immediately rejoin the DNVP. The new party's credibility, however, was greatly enhanced when the three former Nationalists were joined by Karl Hepp, a member of the DVP Reichstag delegation from Hesse-Nassau and a farm leader of truly national stature.[96] Having served as one of the RLB's two national presidents ever since its founding in 1921, Hepp had long sought to organize the small and middle-sized farmers from central and southwestern Germany into a force sufficiently powerful to prevent the RLB from falling under the domination of the large landowners from east of the Elbe.[97] Buoyed by Hepp's defection, the official founding of the new agrarian party – now known as the Christian-National Peasants and Farmers' Party (Christlich-nationale Bauern- und Landvolkpartei or CNBLP) – took place in the Thuringian capital of Weimar on 8 March 1928.[98] Contrary to Nationalist fears that this foreshadowed a further radicalization of the German peasantry,[99] the founders of the CNBLP showed little interest in overtures from Fehr and left his queries about the possibility of a merger of the two new agrarian parties into a united peasant party unanswered.[100] In point of fact, the impulse that lay behind the founding of the CNBLP was profoundly conservative and had little in common with the

---

[95] *Thüringer Landbund* 9, no. 15 (22 Feb. 1928): 1. For further details, see Markus Müller, *Die Christlich-Nationale Bauern- und Landvolkpartei 1928–1933* (Düsseldorf, 2001), 23–48.

[96] On Hepp's defection, see Kempkes to Stresemann, 24 Feb. 1928, PA AA Berlin, NL Stresemann, 99/173883–89.

[97] Hepp to Stresemann, 4 Sept. 1921, PA AA Berlin, NL Stresemann, 231/141458–60.

[98] *Thüringer Landbund* 9, no. 20 (10 Mar. 1928): 1.

[99] Stauffenberg to Westarp, 24 Feb. 1928, NL Westarp, Gärtringen, VN 100.

[100] Fehr's report in the minutes of the DBP delegate conference in the Reichstag, 23 Mar. 1928, BHStA Munich, Abt. V, NL Fehr, 29. See also Hiltmann to Fehr, 12 Apr. 1928, ibid.

agrarian populism of the Bavarian Peasants' League. As Ernst Höfer, chairman of the Thuringian Rural League, explained in an article written shortly after the CNBLP's founding, the party to which he and his associates had given birth was essentially an attempt to contain the wave of agrarian unrest that was spreading across the countryside by providing the farmer with the effective political representation he needed in order to survive the deepening agricultural crisis. Given the way in which all of Germany's nonsocialist parties had consistently sacrificed the welfare of the German farmer to that of other social groups, Höfer concluded, it was only through the consolidation of the entire agricultural community into a united agrarian party that the radicalization of the German countryside could be held in check.[101]

Heavy Industry to the Rescue

The founding of the Christian-National Peasants and Farmers' Party sent shock waves through the ranks of the DNVP and posed a clear threat to its prospects in the upcoming national elections. In the meantime, a similar strain had developed in its relations to German industry with severe implications for the party's financial situation.[102] In his report on the state of party finances at the DNVP's Cologne party congress in September 1926, party treasurer Wilhelm Widenmann had identified a revenue shortfall of approximately 780,000 marks that resulted in large part from the failure of the DNVP's district organizations to keep up with their payments to the party's national headquarters in Berlin.[103] Westarp addressed this situation by meeting with the party's backers from Ruhr heavy industry in the spring of 1927 and proceeded to negotiate an agreement whereby the DNVP would receive two 50,000 mark subsidies to help sustain its national organization in the period of relative inactivity before the next national election.[104] But this arrangement began to unravel as a result of the DNVP's role in the passage of the Unemployment Insurance Act in the summer of 1927, and in October 1927 Fritz Thyssen, the Ruhr magnate responsible for steering this money to the DNVP, decided to punish the party for its failure to block the passage of social legislation detrimental to the vital interests of German industry by

---

[101] Höfer, "Zur Gründung der Christlich-Nationalen Bauernpartei," *Thüringer Landbund* 9, no. 23 (21 Mar. 1928): 1. See also Karl Dorsch, "Zur Gründung der Christlich-Nationalen Bauern- und Landvolkpartei," ibid., no. 32 (21 Apr. 1928): 1.

[102] For example, see Winnacker to Westarp, 25 June 1926; Dryander to Winnacker, 10 July 1926; and Kellermann to Westarp, 13 July 1926, all in NL Westarp, Gärtringen, VN 78.

[103] Report by Widenmann at the DNVP party congress in Cologne, 9 Sept. 1926, BA-MA Freiburg, NL Tirpitz, 60/330–37.

[104] For further details, see Kirdorf to Krupp, 14 Mar. 1927, HA Krupp Essen, FAH IV C 178, as well as the correspondence between Thyssen and Westarp, 11–14 Apr. 1927, NL Westarp, Gärtringen, II/23.

refusing to pay the second of the two 50,000 mark installments to which the party was entitled.[105] In November 1927 Widenmann tried to negotiate an agreement with Hugenberg whereby the latter would restrict his solicitation of party funds to the iron, steel, and coal mining industries, while responsibility for raising funds from the other branches of German industry would rest with the DNVP party leadership for the intervals between elections and the Coordinating Committee of German National Industrialists during the campaigns themselves. But this arrangement was rejected by Hugenberg, who was determined to use his control over party finances to bring about a change in the direction in which the DNVP was headed and thus refused to countenance any change in the collection of industrial contributions that might undermine his leverage within the party.[106]

Panicked by the prospect of facing new national elections with empty campaign coffers, Westarp and the leaders of the DNVP turned once again to Ruhr heavy industry for its help in the upcoming campaign. Not only was Westarp able to persuade the Ruhr industrial elite to restore the 50,000 marks the DNVP was supposed to have received in October 1927,[107] but he inadvertently prompted Ruhr heavy industry to become more actively involved in efforts to curtail Hugenberg's growing influence over party affairs. The key figure in this regard was Paul Reusch, director of the Gutehoffnungshütte in Oberhausen and a bitter and inveterate opponent of Hugenberg.[108] Reusch, who had belonged to the German People's Party until his resignation from the party in protest over the termination of passive resistance in the Ruhr in the fall of 1923,[109] is best described as a conservative nationalist whose differences with Hugenberg had less to do with their ultimate objectives than with the means by which they proposed to achieve those objectives. Although both remained fundamentally opposed to the changes that had taken place in the

---

[105] Reichert to Reusch, 31 Oct. 1927, RWWA Cologne, Abt. 130, NL Reusch, 400101293/8b. On the DNVP's financial difficulties, see Thyssen to Wilmowsky, 8 Nov. 1927, and Wilmowsky to Reusch, 11 Nov. 1927, ibid., and Wilmowsky to Krupp, 12 Nov. 1927, HA Krupp Essen, FAH 23/501, as well as Thyssen to Scheibe, 28 Nov. 1927, NL Westarp, Gärtringen, II/23.

[106] For further details, see Widenmann to Westarp, 14 Nov. 1927, and the three appendices attached to his letter, NL Westarp, Gärtringen, VN 61.

[107] Wilmowsky to Krupp, 15 Dec. 1927, HA Krupp Essen, FAH 23/501. See also Springorum to Westarp, 19 Feb. 1928, NL Westarp, Gärtringen, II/28.

[108] On Reusch, see Gerald D. Feldman, "Paul Reusch and the Politics of German Heavy Industry 1908-1933," in *People and Communities in the Western World*, ed. Gene Brucker, 2 vols. (Homewood, IL, and Georgetown, ON, 1979), 2:293–331. On Reusch's political activities, see Langer, *Macht und Verantwortung. Der Ruhrbaron Paul Reusch* (Essen, 2012), esp. 361–64, 389–98, and Christian Marx, *Paul Reusch und die Gutehoffnungshütte. Leitung eines deutschen Großunternehmens* (Göttingen, 2013), 308–47.

[109] Reusch to Blumberg, 26 Sept. 1923, RWWA Cologne, Abt. 130, NL Reusch, 400101293/4.

structure of German political life after the end of World War I, Reusch rejected the "all-or-nothing" strategy that characterized Hugenberg's political agenda in favor of a more differentiated approach that included working within the existing party system to promote a conservative and nationalist political agenda. Though very much out of the public eye, the conflict between Reusch and Hugenberg would become one of the defining features of conservative politics in the late Weimar Republic.

In the fall and early winter of 1927 Reusch would undertake three separate projects, all of which had as either their explicit or implicit objective the isolation of Hugenberg and the neutralization of his influence on the politics of the German Right. The most ambitious of these was the founding of the League for the Regeneration of the Reich (Bund zur Erneuerung des Reiches or BER) under the chairmanship of former chancellor Hans Luther. In July 1927 Reusch outlined a grandiose plan to Hamburg banker Max Warburg for "a full-scale [*regelrecht*] crusade against the Dawes Plan," which he and his fellow industrialists regarded as economically impracticable. In the course of his remarks, Reusch identified tax and administrative reform as an essential prerequisite for the success of his plan, if for no other reason than the fact that defenders of the Dawes Plan could argue that the economic problems associated with its implementation resulted not from the provisions of the plan itself but from the fiscal irresponsibility of state and municipal governments throughout the country.[110] As discussion unfolded in the summer and early fall of 1927, Reusch revised his original plan to incorporate Warburg's suggestion that they enlist Luther to head a movement dedicated to a sweeping reform of Germany's federal structure with the goal of reducing administrative costs and taxation at all levels of government. Plans for the creation of a new organization that would both educate the public about the necessity of structural reform and win the political support necessary for its implementation were finalized at a meeting between Reusch, Warburg, Luther, the RDI's Ludwig Kastl, and Count Siegfried von Roedern at Reusch's Württemberg estate on 19–20 September 1927.[111] The official founding of the League for the Regeneration of the Reich took place on 6 January 1928 at a convention in Berlin to which eighty guests from all walks of German economic and political life had been invited. Luther, who no doubt hoped to use the League to launch his return to active political life, was tapped as chairman of the BER with Baron Tilo von Wilmowsky, the brother-in-law of industrial magnate Gustav

---

[110] Reusch to Warburg, "Undurchführbarkeit des Dawesplans," 8 July 1927, RWWA Cologne, Abt. 130, NL Reusch, 400101293/15.

[111] Hak-Ie Kim, *Industrie, Staat und Wirtschaftspolitik. Die konjunkturpolitische Diskussion in der Endphase der Weimarer Republik 1930–1932/33* (Berlin, 1999), 20–24. See also Warburg to Reusch, 21 and 23 Oct. 1927, and Reusch to Cossmann, 21 Dec. 1927, RWWA Cologne, Abt. 130, NL Reusch, 400101293/15.

Krupp von Bohlen und Halbach and a conservative moderate with close ties to the German agricultural community, as its vice chairman.[112]

Although the inspiration for the founding of the League for the Regeneration of the Reich came from Reusch and his associates in the German business community, it afforded reform-minded elements from all of Germany's non-socialist parties a bipartisan forum from which they could address the need for federal, administrative, and constitutional reform.[113] With an estimated three hundred members, the League for the Regeneration of the Reich represented a genuine cross-section of Germany's bourgeois leadership that stretched from the National Federation of German Industry and National Rural League to the Christian labor movement and the German National Union of Commercial Employees. At the same time, the organization's membership was drawn from the DDP and Center as well as from the DVP and DNVP.[114] The political and ideological diversity of the BER membership stood in sharp contrast to Hugenberg's own political agenda and generated little enthusiasm among his supporters, one of whom – Rudolf Blohm from the Hamburg ship-building industry – discreetly dissociated himself from the BER in private correspondence with Reusch.[115] Hugenberg and representatives of Germany's radical Right were conspicuously absent from BER membership lists, a fact that only underscored the extent to which the new organization represented an implicit repudiation of the "all-or-nothing" politics of the extreme Right in favor of a reformist strategy that presumed tacit, though by no means unqualified, acceptance of the existing constitutional order.

Despite the fact that the founders of the League for the Regeneration of the Reich included representatives of the industrial and agricultural elites that stood behind the DNVP, the BER's proposal for a reform of the Weimar Constitution met with a cool response from the Nationalist party leadership. At its Königsberg party congress in September 1927 the DNVP had empaneled

[112] Most to Reusch, 7 Jan. 1928, RWWA Cologne, Abt. 130, NL Reusch, 400101293/15. On Luther's involvement, see his letters to his supporters, 12 and 25 Nov. 1927, TKA Dortmund, NL Springorum, B 1a 60, as well as Hans Luther, *Vor dem Abgrund. Reichsbankpräsident in Krisenzeiten 1930–1933* (Berlin, 1964), 37–48. On Wilmowsky's involvement, see Zollitsch, "Das Scheitern der 'gouvernementalen' Rechten," 254–73, here 259–60.

[113] For the BER's goals, see Hans Luther, "Die Reichsreformvorschläge des Bundes zur Erneuerung des Reiches," *Der deutsche Volkswirt. Zeitschrift für Politik und Wirtschaft* 3, no. 2 (12 Oct. 1928): 44–47.

[114] Kim, *Industrie, Staat und Wirtschaftspolitik*, 25–30. For a list of conservative farm leaders affiliated with the BER, see Nagel to Weilnböck, 23 Dec. 1927, BA Koblenz, NL Weilnböck, 42.

[115] Blohm to Reusch, 6 Nov. 1928, StA Hamburg, Blohm und Voß GmbH, 1218. For Hugenberg's rejection of the BER's proposals for constitutional reform, see his letter to Frowein, 24 June 1928, BA Koblenz, NL Hugenberg, 114/137–40.

a special committee under the chairmanship of DNVP Reichstag deputy Walther Rademacher to prepare recommendations for a comprehensive reform of the existing constitutional system. This was perfectly in line with the strategic objectives of the governmental conservatives, who rejected calls for the forcible overthrow of the Weimar Republic in favor of working to for its revision within the existing constitutional system. The leaders of the DNVP, however, felt pressured by the pace of events to move up their schedule for the publication of their party's program for a revision of the Weimar Constitution so as to position the DNVP at the head of the movement for constitutional reform.[116] Despite Hugenberg's criticism that the committee's recommendations did not go far enough in curtailing the tyranny of parliament or in calling for an end to the "war of all against all" that dominated Germany's political life,[117] the preliminary draft of the DNVP's proposal was essentially complete by the end of November 1927 and was formally adopted by party leaders at a special meeting of the DNVP party representation on 9 December. The DNVP's proposal proceeded from the assumption that a restoration of the monarchy was not in Germany's immediate future and that the party had to resign itself to pursuing its objectives within the framework of the existing constitutional order. In this respect, however, the DNVP explicitly rejected the idea of a unitary state and strongly opposed measures aimed at undermining the sovereignty of the individual German states. At the same time, the Nationalists proposed consolidating the office of the chancellor with that of the Prussian minister president and increasing the executive powers of the Reich president and his counterparts at the state level as a corrective to the monopoly of power currently invested in the Reichstag and various state parliaments. Similarly, the Nationalist proposal called for strengthening the legislative prerogatives of the Federal Council, or Reichsrat, to counter the influence of constantly fluctuating parliamentary majorities in the Reichstag.[118]

The grand design that lay behind the founding of the League for the Regeneration of the Reich was to unite Germany's middle and moderate Right behind an ambitious program of federal, administrative, and constitutional reform. If successful – and this was clearly Reusch's unspoken hope – this would neutralize Hugenberg's growing influence over the politics of the German Right. At the same time, Reusch was directly involved in two other

---

[116] Rademacher to Westarp, 20 Nov. 1927, NL Westarp, Gärtringen, II/26.

[117] Memorandum from 30 Nov. 1927, appended to Hugenberg to Westarp, 1 Dec. 1927, NL Westarp, Gärtringen, II/26.

[118] "Wege zur Verfassungsreform. Ein deutschnationales Programm," *Unsere Partei* 5, no. 24 (15 Dec. 1927): 201–02. See also "Verhandlungsprogramm des Verfassungs-ausschusses der D.N.V.P. Nach dem Ergebnis der Generaldebatte am 25. November 1927," NL Westarp, Gärtringen, II/26.

projects aimed at curtailing Hugenberg's influence. After meeting with Westarp, Thyssen, Wilmowsky, and Fritz Springorum from the Hoesch Steel Works in Dortmund on 15 December 1927, Reusch proposed the creation of a special committee consisting of five industrialists – Springorum, Ernst Brandi from the United Steel Works in Dortmund, Ernst von Simson from the Berlin chemical industry, Heinrich Retzmann from the League of Saxon Industrialists, and Carl Jordan from the textile industry in Upper Bavaria – and four parliamentarians, two each from the DVP and DNVP to be nominated by Westarp.[119] From the DNVP Westarp chose himself and Walther Rademacher from mining interests in Saxony, from the DVP Ernst Scholz, chairman of the party's delegation to the Reichstag, and Hans von Raumer from the Berlin electrical industry.[120] The ostensible purpose of this committee, known as the Joint Committee of the German National People's Party and German People's Party (Gemeinsamer Ausschuß der Deutschnationalen Volkspartei und der Deutschen Volkspartei), was to coordinate the representation of industrial interests by the two right-wing parties in the hope that this would strengthen industry's position in parliament. Whatever hopes Reusch and his associates might have had that the creation of the new committee might also undercut the influence that Hugenberg enjoyed as chair of the Coordinating Committee of German National Industrialists, however, were thwarted when Westarp, in response to a nudge from Brandi, belatedly invited Hugenberg to join the committee.[121]

Reusch's efforts to bring together industrialists and parliamentarians outside the orbit of Hugenberg's influence never achieved their intended goal. To be sure, the joint committee established for this purpose continued to meet through most of 1928, but it had faded into insignificance by the end of the year.[122] In the meantime, Reusch moved on still another front to counter Hugenberg's growing influence on the politics of the German Right. In November 1927 Reusch, along with Krupp and Thyssen, announced the creation of an exclusive club of Ruhr industrialists known as the "Ruhrlade" and invited nine of their fellow industrialists to join.[123] The purpose of this organization, which met for the first time in early January 1928 and which continued to meet on a monthly basis for the balance of the Weimar Republic,

[119] Reusch to Westarp, 15 Dec. 1927, NL Westarp, Gärtringen, VN 39. Jordan declined to join the committee and was replaced by Hans Dietrich from the German banking community. See Reusch to Westarp, 26 Dec. 1927, ibid., and Reusch to Dietrich, 31 Dec. 1927, RWWA Cologne, Abt. 130, NL Reusch, 400101293/8b.

[120] Westarp to Reusch, 17 Dec. 1927, NL Westarp, Gärtringen, VN 39.

[121] Westarp to Hugenberg, 14 Jan. 1928, NL Westarp, Gärtringen, VN 39. See also Brandi to Reusch, 24 Dec. 1927, RWWA Cologne, Abt. 130, NL Reusch, 400101293/8b.

[122] For a record of the committee's meetings and activities, see RWWA Cologne, NL Reusch, 400101293/8b.

[123] Reusch to Springorum, 22 Nov. 1927, TKA Dortmund, NL Springorum, F1 i 3.

was to bridge the differences that existed within the ranks of the Ruhr industrial elite and to forge, in so far as possible, a united front for the more effective
representation of industry's vital interests at all levels of government. The
"Ruhrlade" was truly bipartisan in character and included those who were
aligned with the DVP, the DNVP, and the Center as well as several who
preferred to remain politically unaffiliated. Of the twelve industrialists who
belonged to the "Ruhrlade," only Thyssen openly sympathized with Hugenberg's political agenda, although none, with the possible exception of Peter
Klöckner who belonged to the Center Party, felt much in the way of loyalty to
Germany's republican institutions. By bringing the twelve together for regular
meetings that were primarily social but invariably political as well, Reusch
hoped to foster a greater sense of social and political solidarity within the
ranks of the Ruhr industrial elite.[124]

As 1927 drew to a close, the situation in the DNVP was far from clear. The
extent to which Reusch and his associates would be able to hold Hugenberg
and his supporters in check would depend in large part upon the outcome of
the Reichstag elections that were scheduled to take place later that spring. The
elections would test whether the economic benefits of reentering the government outweighed the cost of having to work within a system of government to
which the DNVP remained fundamentally opposed. As the gains that middle-
class splinter parties had recorded since 1924 and the unrest in the German
agricultural community clearly suggested, the situation in which the DNVP
found itself was indeed precarious, all the more so because of the deep and
unresolved divisions within the party itself.

---

[124] Henry Ashby Turner, Jr., "The *Ruhrlade*, Secret Cabinet of Heavy Industry in the
Weimar Republic," *Central European History* 3 (1970): 195–228. On the anti-Hugenberg
animus of Reusch and Ruhr heavy industry, see Wilmowsky to Krupp, 15 Dec. 1927, HA
Krupp Essen, FAH 23/501.

13

From Defeat to Crisis

The call for new elections in the spring of 1928 found the German Right more deeply divided than ever before. With the economic and political stabilization of the Weimar Republic in the second half of the 1920s a deep and increasingly bitter gulf had developed within the German Right between those who were prepared to work within the framework of Germany's republican system to promote interests vital to the conservative cause and those who denounced any such accommodation as an betrayal of Germany's sacred national trust. This split ran right through the middle of the German National People's Party, where the party's national leaders struggled valiantly to bridge the gap between the two strands of right-wing political commitment until they themselves became a target of right-wing invective. In the meantime, the disintegration of the DNVP's social base continued unabated as first the economic and commercial middle class, then the small investor, and finally the farmer began to desert the DNVP in favor of parties that claimed to represent their special interests more effectively than the DNVP.[1] Moreover, the general climate in which the campaign opened was not as favorable to the forces of the German Right as they had been in 1924. The relative stability that Germany had enjoyed since the end of 1923 tended to favor the parties that identified themselves with the Republic and robbed the Nationalist campaign of much of its emotional force. To be sure, the Nationalists would wage a furious attack against reparations and Stresemann's policy of understanding, but this no longer resonated as powerfully as it had four years earlier when the debate the Dawes Plan occupied center stage. Without the benefit of a foreign policy issue they could use to arouse the passions of the Nationalist electorate, the leaders of the DNVP were forced back on to the terrain of domestic politics where they were vulnerable to attack from the various special-interest parties that had surfaced during the course of the 1920s.

[1] For further details, see Attila Chanady, "The Disintegration of the German National People's Party, 1924–1930," *Journal of Modern History* 39 (1967): 65–80.

The Challenge of Special Interests

The campaign for the May 1928 Reichstag elections was dominated above all else by the assault of the special-interest parties. The Business Party, which had whittled away at the margins of the Nationalist electorate ever since its emergence in the early 1920s, continued to press its bid for the support of those middle-class elements that had been excluded from the benefits of Germany's economic stabilization in the second half of the decade.[2] On 18 March 1928 WP party chairman Hermann Drewitz and the leaders of an ostensibly nonpartisan organization known as the Reich Cartel of the German Middle Class (Reichskartell des deutschen Mittelstandes) opened the WP's campaign with a series of demonstrations throughout the country under the slogan "Mittelstand in Not." This initiative reached its high point in Berlin, where several thousand demonstrators closed their shops and took to the streets in protest against high taxes, rent controls, and excessive government spending.[3] Though presumably nonpartisan in character, these demonstrations afforded Drewitz and the leaders of the WP an excellent forum for carrying their attack to the other nonsocialist parties. The DNVP was singled out in particular for having capitulated to organized labor in supporting the Work Hours Law in the spring of 1927, for having blocked the creation of a state secretary for the artisanry in the ministry of economics, and for having failed to live up to all the promises it had made over the years to German homeowners. All of this, WP campaign strategists argued, was part of a consistent pattern of middle-class neglect by the DNVP and other nonsocialist parties that could be remedied only through the unification of the German middle class behind the banner of a new political party that was unequivocally committed to the defense of its vital interests.[4]

In a similar vein, the various revaluation groups that had come together in late August 1926 to form the People's Justice Party were determined to take their measure of revenge upon the Nationalists for their in the passage of the 1925 revaluation law. The VRP enjoyed closed ties to the Savers' Association

---

[2] Hermann Drewitz, "Die politische Standesbewegung des deutschen Mittelstands vor und nach dem Kriege," in *Jahbruch der Reichspartei des deutschen Mittelstandes 1929* (N.p., n.d. [1929]), 13–32. See also Schumacher, *Mittelstandsfront und Republik. Die Wirtschaftspartei – Reichspartei des deutschen Mittelstandes 1919–1933* (Düsseldorf, 1972), 31–112.

[3] Ibid., 30. See also the *Kölner Nachrichten. Wochenschrift der Reichspartei des deutschen Mittelstandes (Wirtschaftspartei)*, 24 Mar. 1928, no. 12.

[4] *Wahrheiten 1928. Wahlhandbuch der Reichspartei des deutschen Mittelstandes (Wirtschaftspartei)*, ed. Reichspartei des deutschen Mittelstandes (Berlin, 1928), 3–8, 90–92, 164–65. See also the broadsides in the *Kölner Nachrichten*, 14 and 21 Apr. 1928, nos. 15 and 16, as well as the WP's last-minute election appeal, ibid., 19 May 1928, no. 20, as well as Benjamin Lieberman, "Turning against the Weimar Right: Landlords, the Economic Party, and the DNVP," *German History* 15 (1997): 56–79.

Figure 8. WP campaign placard with a quote from Bismarck designed by Paul Jürgens for the May 1928 Reichstag elections. Reproduced with permission from the Bundesarchiv Berlin, Plakat 002-031-013

for the German Reich and sought to mobilize the outrage of those small investors who had been hurt by the runaway inflation of the early 1920s and felt betrayed by the DNVP's failure to honor its commitment to a "full and equitable" revaluation of those paper mark assets that had been destroyed by the inflation. From the perspective of the revaluation movement, the DNVP's role in securing passage of the 1925 revaluation settlement only underscored the extent to which the party was willing to sacrifice the welfare of the small investor to the interests of big business and large landed agriculture. Like the WP, the VRP had also recorded dramatic gains at the DNVP's expense in the October 1926 Saxon Landtag elections, and now it hoped to build upon its success in Saxony to compete for the votes of Germany's disaffected middle class as a party with a national profile.[5] At the same time, the VRP tried to escape the odium of a splinter party by insisting that in a larger sense its objective was to restore the sense of right and justice that had been violated with the passage of the 1925 revaluation legislation. The VRP was therefore not just for the rights of the dispossessed investor but also for the ethical principles that lay at the heart of Germany's national culture.[6]

Westarp and the leaders of the DNVP responded to the attack of the middle-class splinter parties with a vigorous defense of their own party's record of accomplishment on behalf of the German middle class.[7] At the same time, they warned that the continued splintering of Germany's middle-class electorate only weakened the strongest of Germany's nonsocialist parties and thus played directly into the hands of the German Left.[8] This particular admonition, however, was not directed just at the urban middle classes but was also pregnant with meaning for Germany's rural voters whose economic situation had continued to deteriorate throughout the second half of the 1920s. The outburst of widespread rural protest in the first months of 1928 and the subsequent founding of the Christian-National Peasants and Farmers' Party sent shock waves through the ranks of the DNVP party organization and threatened the party with the loss of its largest and most significant voting

---

[5] Adolf Bauser, "Auf zur Wahl!," *Deutsches Volksrecht. Zentralorgan des Sparerbundes/ Offizielles Nachrichtenblatt der Volksrechts-Partei*, 19 May 1928, no. 40. See also Adolf Bauser, "Notwendigkeit, Aufgaben und Ziele der Volksrechtspartei," in *Für Wahrheit und Recht. Der Endkampf um eine gerechte Aufwertung. Reden und Aufsätze*, ed. Adolf Bauser (Stuttgart, 1927), 90–96, as well as Müller, "Adolf Bauser," 259–62.

[6] "Wahlaufruf der Volksrechts-Partei," *Deutsches Volksrecht*, 16 May 1928, no. 39.

[7] In this respect, see Johann Howe, *Zur Abwehr wirtschaftsparteilicher Angriffe!* (Kiel, n.d. [1928]), 1–4, as well as Deutschnationale Volkspartei, Landesverband Schleswig-Holstein. *Die Sozialisierung der deutschen Wirtschaft! Rechenschaftsbericht über die Wohnungspolitik des Verbandes Schleswig-Holsteinischer Haus- und Grundbesitzer-Vereine*, ed. Howe (Kiel, n.d. [1928]). For further details, see Dörr, "Deutschnationale Volkspartei," 363–70.

[8] Kuno von Westarp, *Die Deutschnationale Volkspartei und der gewerbliche Mittelstand*, Deutschnationale Flugschrift, no. 306 (Berlin, 1927).

Figure 9.   VRP campaign placard designed by an unidentified graphic artist for the May 1928 Reichstag elections. Reproduced with permission from the Bundesarchiv Berlin, Plakat 002-031-017

bloc, the German farmer. The leaders of the CNBLP attacked the DNVP's performance as a member of the national government and lamented about how little it had done to provide the farmer with the help he so desperately needed.[9] The DNVP responded with an emergency farm program that Westarp introduced from the floor of the Reichstag on 22 February and that, among other things, called for the consolidation of agricultural debt, the conversion of short-term personal indebtedness into mortgages and other forms of long-term credit, a reduction of the income tax and estate taxes on agricultural property, government subsidies to rationalize the market for agricultural products, and tariffs to protect the domestic market for agricultural products against unfair competition from foreign imports.[10] Similarly, Martin Schiele and other party leaders highlighted what the DNVP had

---

[9] Erwin Baum, "Was will die Christlich-Nationale Bauern- und Landvolkpartei?," *Nassauische Bauern-Zeitung. Organ und Verlag des Bezirksbauernschaft für Nassau und den Kreis Wetzlar e.V.*, 5 May 1928, no. 105.

[10] Kuno von Westarp, *Bauernnot – Volksnot. Das Arbeitsprogramm des Reichstages und das landwirtschaftliche Programm der Deutschnationalen Volkspartei. Reichstagsrede vom 22. Februar 1928*, Deutschnationale Flugschrift, no. 317 (Berlin, 1928), 7–16.

accomplished for the farmer by virtue of its participation in the national government and reaffirmed their party's deep and abiding commitment to the material and spiritual welfare of the German agricultural community.[11] At the same time that they dismissed the CNBLP as a splinter party whose existence only undermined the effectiveness with which the DNVP could represent the interests of the German agricultural community,[12] party leaders like Saxony's Albrecht Philipp warned against a splintering of Germany's conservative forces that would only make it that much easier for the German Left to regain the reins of power.[13]

To Westarp and his associates, the most troubling aspect of the CNBLP's sudden emergence as a rival for the votes of the German farmer was that its founding enjoyed the support of influential regional affiliates of the National Rural League, most notably in Thuringia and Hesse-Nassau. Fearing that this was the beginning of a trend that might spill over into other parts of the country,[14] the leaders of the DNVP urged the RLB's national leadership to dissociate itself from the CNBLP and to reaffirm in no uncertain terms its alliance with the DNVP.[15] But in its initial response to the founding of the CNBLP, the National Rural League chose instead to reaffirm its long-standing policy of bipartisan neutrality toward all political parties and stated that its position on any particular party would depend upon that party's "engagement for the welfare of German agriculture and the Fatherland."[16] This statement, no doubt adopted in deference to the deep-seated distrust that certain sectors of the German agricultural community felt toward toward the DNVP and other Weimar parties,[17] met widespread resentment from the leaders of the DNVP, who criticized the RLB for its vacillation and insisted that it disavow the efforts of the new party to establish itself in areas where the RLB's regional

[11] Martin Schiele, *Die Agrarpolitik der Deutschnationalen Volkspartei 1925/1928*, Deutsch-nationale Flugschrift, no. 320 (Berlin, 1928).
[12] Lothar Steuer, *Die deutsche Landwirtschaft und die politische Parteien. Eine Wahlkampf-betrachtung* (Kassel, 1928), 12–15.
[13] Albrecht Philipp, *Die Zukunft der deutschen Landwirtschaft. Nach einer Rede gehalten am 30. April 1928 zu Gethain auf der Generalversammlung des Landbundes Borna*, Schriften der Deutschnationalen Volkspartei in Sachsen (Arbeitsgemeinschaft), no. 26 (Borna, 1928), 13–14.
[14] Schmidt-Hannover to Treviranus, 14 Feb. 1928, NL Westarp, Gärtringen, VN 67.
[15] Westarp to Wilmowsky, 23 Feb. 1928, NL Westarp, Gärtringen, II/29.
[16] Statement by the RLB executive committee, 18 Feb. 1928, in *Reichs-Landbund. Agrarpolitische Wochenschrift* 8, no. 8 (25 Feb. 1928): 101. See also the minutes of the RLB executive committee, 18 Feb. 1928, Landeshauptarchiv Sachsen-Anhalt, Abteilung Magdeburg/Wernigerode (hereafter cited as LHA Magdeburg-Wernigerode), Marienthal Gutsarchiv, 319/219ff.
[17] Wendhausen to the RLB presidium and the chairmen of the RLB's regional affiliates, 20 Feb. 1928, BA Berlin, R 8034 I, 132/35.

affiliates had remained loyal to the DNVP.[18] When the RLB revisited the issue at a meeting of its executive committee on 21 March, sentiment was so deeply divided that all it could do was to reiterate the RLB's neutrality toward all of those parties, the CNBLP included, that were prepared to fight for the vital interests of German agriculture. As a concession to the DNVP, the RLB executive committee also stipulated that the expansion of the CNBLP into areas other than those where it was already established required the express approval of the RLB's regional affiliate.[19]

It was no longer possible to deny that the founding of the CNBLP had produced a deep rift within the ranks of the RLB leadership.[20] The defection of RLB president Karl Hepp to the CNBLP in mid-February 1928 evoked the specter of an open conflict between those like Schiele and Kalckreuth who continued to support the DNVP and those like Hepp and the leaders of the Thuringian Rural League had come out in support of the new party.[21] The state and provincial leaders of the DNVP party organization entered into direct negotiations with the RLB's regional affiliates in an attempt to prevent other RLB affiliates from supporting the CNBLP and to discourage them from sponsoring the creation of special agarian tickets.[22] But this proved more difficult than the leaders of the DNVP had anticipated. For while the Württemberg Peasants and Wine Growers' League under the leadership of Theodor Körner alt moved quickly to reaffirm an alliance with the DNVP that had been in effect since the first years of the Weimar Republic,[23] things were not so easy with the RLB's affiliates in states like Bavaria or Saxony. In Bavaria, for example, Hans Hilpert and the leaders of the Bavarian Middle Party, as the DNVP's state organization was commonly known, were fearful even before the founding of the CNBLP that the Bavarian Rural League might run its own slate

---

[18] Wilmowsky to the RLB presidium, 15 Mar. 1928, BA Koblenz, NL Weilnböck, 29b. See also Schmitt-Stettin to Hepp, 26 Mar. 1928, ibid., 29a, and Richthofen to Hepp, 25 Apr. 1928, ibid., 29b.

[19] Report on the meeting of the RLB executive committee, 21 Mar. 1928, LHA Magdeburg-Wernigerode, Marienthal Gutsarchiv, 319/186ff. See also Feldman to Hepp, 27 Mar. 1928, NL Westarp, Gärtringen.

[20] Wangenheim's notes on a meeting of the RLB leadership, 17 Mar. 1928, BA Koblenz, NL Weilnböck, 29b. For further details, see Merkenich, Grüne Front gegen Weimar, 287–300.

[21] For example, see Hepp to Weilnböck, 11 Feb. 1928, BA Koblenz, NL Weilnböck, 29b. For the Thuringian context, see Jochen Grass, Studien zur Politik der bürgerlichen Parteien Thuringens in der Weimarer Zeit 1920–1932. Ein Beitrag zur Landesgeschichte (Hamburg, 1997), 168–83, and Guido Dressel, Der Thüringer Landbund – Agrarischer Berufsverband als politische Partei in Thüringen (Weimar, 1998), 54–56.

[22] Westarp to Wilmowsky, 23 Feb. 1928, NL Westarp, Gärtringen, II/29.

[23] Wahlhandbuch für das Wahljahr 1928. Zum Gebrauch und zur Aufklärung für die württembergischen Wähler, ed. Württembergischer Bauern- und Weingärtnerbund/Bund der Landwirte in Württemberg (Stuttgart, 1928), 24.

of candidates in the state and national elections scheduled for later that spring.[24] Hilpert and his associates in the BMP redoubled their efforts in the last two weeks of February to keep the Bavarian Rural League from fielding its own slate of candidates, eventually signing an agreement on 3 March 1928 that contained far-reaching concessions to the BLB in the placement of rural candidates on a joint BMP-BLB ticket in both the state and national elections.[25] An open break was thus avoided, all but eliminating the threat of large-scale defections to the CNBLP in the DNVP's Franconian strongholds.

Nor was the situation much different in Saxony, where local party leaders were concerned that the enthusiastic support the founding of the CNBLP had received in the neighboring state of Thuringia might spill over into the Saxon peasantry and inflict a defeat upon the DNVP even more severe than the one it had suffered in the 1926 state elections.[26] The leaders of the Saxon Rural League, most of whom remained loyal to the SLB's alliance with the local DNVP,[27] worked hand in hand with the local DNVP leadership to check the spread of the new party by running their own slate of candidates on a list entitled the Saxon Landvolk (Sächsisches Landvolk) with the understanding that those elected on this ticket would join the DNVP Reichstag delegation in the new national parliament.[28] When the leaders of the Thuringian Rural League carried their campaign on behalf of the CNBLP across state borders and began to set up a Saxon chapter of the new agrarian party, Otto Feldmann and the leaders of the SLB complained bitterly that this violated the terms of the position the RLB's national leadership had taken in its resolution of 21 March and exhorted RLB headquarters in Berlin to disavow the renegades

[24] Hilpert to the BLB executive committee (Vorstandschaft), 2 Feb. 1928, BA Koblenz, NL Weilnböck, 29a. For further information, see Brosius to Weilnböck, 21 Feb. 1928, and Hopp (BLB) to Brügel, 23 Feb. 1928, ibid., 29a, as well as Hopp to Weilnböck, 1 Mar. 1928, ibid., 50.

[25] Agreement between the BLB and the Bavarian DNVP, 3 Mar. 1928, BA Koblenz, NL Weilnböck, 29b. See also the minutes of the meeting of the BLB executive committee, 3 Mar. 1928, BA Berlin, R 8034 I, 170/42, as well as Hans Hilpert, "Meinungen und Kämpfe. Meine politische Erinnerungen," BHStA Munich, Abt. V, Nachlass Hans Hilpert, 18/3222–24.

[26] For example, see Rademacher to Beutler, 7 Mar. 1928, appended to Rademacher to Westarp, 10 Mar. 1928, and Rademacher to Westarp, 23 Mar. 1928, NL Westarp, Gärtringen, VN 101. For the position of the Saxon DNVP, see Lüttichau to Westarp, ibid., VN 67, as well as "Grundsätzliches zur Reichstagswahl 1928 für die Rechtsgruppen in Sachsen," n.d., SHStA Dresden, NL Philipp, 20.

[27] Feldmann to Höfer, 27 Mar. 1928, NL Westarp, Gärtringen, VN 99. See also Feldmann to Kriegsheim, 23 Feb. 1928, BA Berlin, R 8034 I, 132a/7–10.

[28] Feldmann to Westarp, 24 Mar. 1928, NL Westarp, Gärtringen, VN 99. For the details of this arrangement, see Lüttichau to Westarp, 24 Mar. 1928, ibid., and 17 Apr. 1928, ibid., VN 67. See also "Warum: Sächsisches Landvolk?" Sächsische Bauern-Zeitung. Amtliches Organ des Sächsischen Landbundes e.V. 35, no. 17 (22 Apr. 1928): 166–67.

in Thuringia.[29] Although the leaders of the RLB, in the words of Bodo von Alvensleben from the RLB's affiliate in Magdeburg, regarded the founding of the CNBLP as an act of "political stupidity [*eine politische Dummheit*],"[30] they clearly feared that the rivalry between the DNVP and CNBLP might destroy their own organization and quickly reaffirmed the declaration of neutrality they had issued at the beginning of the campaign.[31]

Campaign Dilemmas

The belligerence of the CNBLP's campaign forced the DNVP on to the defensive throughout much of the countryside and severely undermined the effectiveness of its efforts to retain the support of the German farmer. The common thread that united the CNBLP with the other middle-class splinter parties in the 1928 elections was their implicit rejection of the existing political system as the source of the social and economic hardships that had been visited upon their respective constituencies. Anti-system sentiment had become an increasingly widespread feature of German political culture in the second half of the 1920s and formed the essential subtext of much of what was said and done during the 1928 campaign.[32] For the DNVP this represented a paradox from which it had to extricate itself if its campaign was ever going to be successful. By joining the national government, the DNVP had effectively abdicated its place in German political life as the anti-system party of choice, with the result that it now found itself the target of precisely the same rhetoric that had served it so well in the early years of the republic. This paradox affected not just those constituencies that had broken away from the DNVP in search of a more effective way of securing their social and economic interests but also those that had remained loyal to the party. The DNVP's civil service wing, for example, was indignant over the way in which the party leadership had acquiesced to the Center in the passage of the civil service salary reform in the fall of 1927 but, unlike the civil servants within the Center itself, abstained from any sort of overt public demonstration that might have embarrassed the party leadership. Though critical of the political course the DNVP had pursued over the last several years, the Association of German Nationalist Higher Civil Servants of the Reich (Vereinigung der

---

[29] Feldman to the presidents of the RLB, 28 Mar. 1928, NL Westarp, Gärtringen, VN 99.

[30] Memorandum dated 4 Apr. 1928 on a meeting of the Magdeburg Rural League with representatives of the CNBLP, 2 Apr. 1928, ibid., VN 99.

[31] Comments by Alvensleben and Schiele, 2. Apr. 1928, ibid. See also Schmidt-Stettin to Hepp, 26 Mar. 1928, BA Koblenz, NL Weilnböck, 29a, and Nicolas (Brandenburg Rural League) to Stützner-Karbe, 23 Apr. 1928, NL Westarp, Gärtringen, VN 68.

[32] Thomas Childers, "Interest and Ideology: Anti-System Politics in the Era of Stabilization, 1924–1928," in *Die Nachwirkungen der Inflation auf die deutsche Geschichte 1924–1933*, ed. Gerald D. Feldman (Munich, 1985), 1–20.

deutschnationalen höheren Beamten des Reichs) that had been founded in November 1926 denounced those who had left the party in search of a more effective way of representing their material interests and remained committed to working within the party for the welfare of the civil service and the German nation in all of its manifold complexity.[33]

The position of the DNVP's civil servant contingent did not differ materially from that of the working-class and white-collar elements that formed the nucleus of the party's left wing. No faction within the party had benefited more from the DNVP's two experiments at government participation than the workers and white-collar employees who had joined the DNVP under the banner of Christian-Socialism.[34] But the leaders of the DNVP's Christian-Social faction were uneasy over the increased assertiveness of the Hugenberg wing, in part because Hugenberg's entourage included outspoken critics of the postwar labor movement like Paul Bang from the League for National Economics and Industrial Peace (Bund für Nationalwirtschaft und Werkgemeinschaft) and Wilhelm Schmidt from the National Alliance of Patriotic Workers' Clubs (Reichsbund vaterländischer Arbeitervereine or RvA). These elements were fundamentally opposed to the special recognition that German industry had accorded the socialist, Christian, and liberal labor unions in the compact that had established the *Zenralarbeitsgemeinschaft* at the end of 1918.[35] In their struggle with the Christian labor for parity within the DNVP, Schmidt and the leaders of the so-called yellow workers' unions had Hugenberg in the hope that this would provide them with the leverage they need to challenge the preferential treatment Christian labor had received from the DNVP party leadership.[36] The DNVP's Christian-Social faction saw this as nothing less than a concerted effort by the social reactionaries around Hugenberg to undermine the independence and vitality of the German trade-union

---

[33] Memorandum appended to Lammers to Westarp, 13 Apr. 1928, NL Westarp, Gärtringen, VN 99. For a defense of the DNVP's record on behalf of the civil service, see Otto Schmidt-Stettin, "Beamtenfragen im Reichstage," in *Politische Praxis 1927*, ed. Walther Lambach (Hamburg, n.d. [1927]), 188–90.

[34] Lambach, "Von Köln bis Königsberg. Deutschnationaler Kampf um die Führung im Reich," *Politische Wochenschrift* 3, no. 37 (15 Sept. 1927): 196–98. See also Stupperich, *Volksgemeinschaft oder Arbeitersolidarität*, 98–121.

[35] For example, see Wilhelm Schmidt, *Die deutsche Arbeiterbewegung der Vorkriegs- und der Revolutionsjahre in besonderer Berücksichtigung des Werkgemeinschafts-Gedankens* (Berlin, n.d. [1925]), 24–40, and Wilhelm Schmidt, *Der Werkgemeinschafts-Gedanke in Staat und Wirtschaft. Vortrag gehalten auf der 1. Reichstagung des Reichsbundes vaterländischer Arbeiter- und Werkvereine, e.V., in Halle a. Saale, 18. bis 21. September 1925* (Berlin, n.d. [1925]).

[36] For example, see the letters from the Coalition of Nationalist Workers (Arbeitsgemeinschaft nationaler Arbeitnehmer) to Westarp, 19 Mar. 1928, NL Westarp, Gärtringen, II/19, and Wolf from the Workers' Group of the Pomeranian Rural League (Arbeitnehmergruppe des Pommerschen Landbundes) to Westarp, 22 Mar. 1928., ibid., VN 67.

movement. In response, Walther Lambach and the leaders of the DNVP's working-class and white-collar wing published a "Bekenntnis zur Christlich-nationalen Selbsthilfe" in January 1928 to reaffirm the Christian and social principles that lay at the heart of the DNVP's political program in the hope that this would help them stake out their position in time for the upcoming national elections.[37]

The German National Workers' League and its allies in the Christian-national labor movement had been one of the DNVP's most important sources of electoral support since the first years of the Weimar Republic. Even a staunch conservative like Westarp readily conceded that without the support of right-wing workers the DNVP would never have increased its popular vote from three to over six million between January 1919 and December 1924.[38] But the position that Christian labor had managed to carve out for itself within the DNVP was deeply resented by other sectors of the party that felt that this had come at their expense. This sentiment was particularly strong among those who served as representatives of the independent middle class. Robert Hampe, a Nationalist deputy who functioned as the DNVP's liaison to the hotel and restaurant industry, relayed the frustration that his supporters had experienced as a result of new government regulations that in some cases had been supported by representatives of his own party's labor wing.[39] Even more revealing was the case of Gustav Budjühn, one of the DNVP's most persistent and dedicated spokesmen for middle-class economic interests and chairman of the DNVP's Reich Middle-Class Committee. In the nomination of candidates for the 1928 Reichstag elections in his home district of Potsdam I, Budjühn had been passed over in favor of the Stahlhelm's Eduard Stadtler, a Catholic conservative who stood on the DNVP's extreme right wing without any ties whatsoever to Germany's beleagured middle class.[40] "How am I to behave during the campaign," Budjühn wrote to Westarp on 18 April 1928, "when I run into the argument that the party's empathy for the middle class expresses itself best not just by denying a secure candidacy to one of its middle-class leaders but even worse by dropping him down in the placement of candidates [on its national ticket]?"[41] The irony that lay at the heart of Budjühn's

---

[37] "Bekenntnis zur christlich-nationalen Selbsthilfe," n.d., BA Berlin, NL Mumm, 286/195–98, reprinted in *Politische Wochenschrift* 4, no. 4 (26 Jan. 1928): 70–76. See also the letter from Lambach, 12 Feb. 1928, FZH Hamburg, Nachlass Alfred Diller, 7, as well as the report on the DNVP white-collar conference in Berlin, 29 Jan. 1928, appended to Lambach to Westarp, 1 Feb. 1928, NL Westarp, Gärtringen, VN 71. For further details, see Stupperich, *Volksgemeinschaft oder Arbeitersolidarität*, 134–40, and Roder, *Gewerkschaftsbund*, 447–52.

[38] Westarp, *Konservative Politik*, ed. Hiller von Gaertringen, 119.

[39] See the two letters from Hampe to Westarp, 4 Feb. 1928, NL Westarp, Gärtringen, II/29.

[40] Budjühn to Westarp, 4 and 12 Apr. 1928, ibid., II/29.

[41] Budjühn to Westarp, 18 Apr. 1928, ibid., II/29.

rhetorical question did not augur well for the DNVP's ability to meet the challenge of the Business Party and other middle-class interest parties.

Although Westarp, Schiele, and other Nationalist leaders offered a vigorous defense of their party's record of achievement in the fourth Marx cabinet and took great pride in what it had been able to accomplish for the various constituencies that constituted their party's social base,[42] party strategists also hoped to recapture the political high ground that the DNVP's had enjoyed as an opposition party from 1918 to 1924.[43] In an effort to reclaim their party's legacy as an opposition party, the Nationalists focused the full force of their fury on the situation in Prussia, where the parties of the Weimar Coalition had governed almost without interruption since the founding of the Weimar Republic.[44] At the same time, the Nationalists called for a fundamental reform of the Weimar Constitution that, if successfully implemented, would have stripped the Reichstag of much of its power and decoupled the exercise of executive authority from the will of the people as manifest in the constantly fluctuating party configurations of the Reichstag. Here the Nationalists went to great pains to identify themselves as closely as possible with Hindenburg's mystic aura and the call for "More power to the Reich president" in the hope that this would somehow insulate the DNVP against the appeal of the special-interest parties.[45] On a parallel front, Annagrete Lehmann and the leaders of the DNVP's women's movement complained bitterly about the "Bolshevization" of German public life and projected an inherently conservative vision of the German woman and her role in the family, nation, and state as an antidote to the moral decay of modern society.[46] All of this was

---

[42] Westarp to Finckenstein, 23 Feb. 1928, NL Westarp, Gärtringen, VN 65. See also the manuscript of an undated speech by Westarp from the spring of 1928, ibid., VN 66, as well as Kuno von Westarp, *14 Monate Deutschnationale Regierungsarbeit. Rückblick und Ausblick. Reichstagsrede vom 29. März 1928*, Deutschnationale Flugschrift, no. 322 (Berlin, 1928), and Alfred Hanemann, *Materialien für deutschnationale Wahlredner* (Freiburg im Breisgau, 1928), 10–16.

[43] See the speeches by Westarp and Treviranus at the DNVP Training Week (Schülungswoche), 28 Mar. 1928, BA Berlin, R 8005, 58/73–96, and 59/33–73.

[44] Hans Schlange-Schöningen, *Die große Abrechnung mit den Zuständen in Preußen. Rede am 27. März 1928 im Preußischen Landtag*, Deutschnationale Flugschrift, no. 321 (Berlin, 1928).

[45] Axel von Freytagh-Loringhoven, *Verfassungsreform*, Deutschnationale Flugschrift, no. 314 (Berlin, 1928). See also Rademacher to Westarp, 27 Dec. 1927 and 13 Jan. 1928, NL Westarp, Gärtringen, II/26.

[46] Annagrete Lehmann, *Der Kampf gegen die Bolschewisierung von Sitte und Sittlichkeit*, Aus Deutschlands Not und Ringen, no. 2 (Berlin, 1928). See also Käthe Schirmacher, *Was verdankt die deutsche Frau der deutschen Frauenbewegung? Die deutschen Frau in Familie, Volk, und Staat*. No. 7 (Querfurt, 1927), and Magdalene von Tiling, *Wir Frauen und die christliche Schule* (Berlin, 1928). See also Heinsohn, *Konservative Parteien in Deutschland 1912 bis 1933. Demokratisierung ind Partizipation in geschlecthistorischer Perspektive* (Düsseldorf, 2010), 147–52, and Sneeringer, *Winning Women's Votes:*

Figure 10. DNVP campaign placard designed by Herbert Rothgaengel for the May 1928 Reichstag elections. Reproduced with permission from the Bundesarchiv Berlin, Plakat 002-029-053

carefully crafted to reestablish the DNVP's credentials as the party of national opposition to the changes that had taken place in Germany's political, social, and cultural life since the end of World War I. That this ran counter to what party leaders were saying about the DNVP's accomplishments as a member of two national governments only helped create a mixed message that amplified the deeper divisions that existed at all levels of the DNVP party organization.

Campaign Financing

The difficulties the DNVP experienced in reconciling its self-image as a party of national opposition with its two stints in the national government were further reflected in its relationship to the German industrial community. In November 1927 the DNVP party leadership had tried to free the party from its financial dependence upon Hugenberg and his supporters by negotiating an arrangement whereby Hugenberg would restrict his solicitation of funds to the coal and steel industries while the Coordinating Committee of German National Industrialists, or ADI, would be responsible for the collection of all other funds. But Hugenberg was reluctant to relinquish control over the collection of party funds and balked at going along with the proposed changes in the way the DNVP solicited contributions from its industrial backers.[47] Just how Hugenberg proposed to exercise this control became abundantly clear when he threatened to withhold campaign funds from the party if one of his closest associates, Paul Bang from the ADV, was not nominated to a secure candidacy in Saxony.[48] In February 1928 Westarp turned once again to the Ruhr industrial elite with the complaint that Hugenberg had failed to honor his financial commitments and pleaded for its help in financing the party's campaign for the upcoming Reichstag elections.[49] The situation in the DNVP and the problem of party financing were discussed at length at a meeting of the "Ruhrlade" on 5 March, at which time it was decided to create a special fund that could be used, among other things, to help finance the

Proaganda and Politics in Weimar Germany (Chapel Hill, NC, London, 2002), 134–35, 140–41, 160–62.

[47] Widenmann to Westarp, 14 Nov. 1927, NL Westarp, Gärtringen, VN 61. On Hugenberg's role in soliciting funds for the 1928 campaign, see the circular from Hugenberg, Reichert, and Scheibe to the DNVP's industrial backers, Mar. 1928, StA Hamburg, Blohm und Voß GmbH, 1215.

[48] For further details, see Philipp to Westarp, 9 and 14 Mar. 1928, NL Westarp, Gärtringen, VN 71, and Lüttichau to Westarp, 27 Mar. 1928, ibid., VN 67.

[49] On the difficulties with Hugenberg, see Widenmann to Westarp, 4 Mar. 1928, NL Westarp, Gärtringen, II/28.

campaigns of candidates sympathetically disposed to the concerns of Ruhr heavy industry.[50]

In doing this, the "Ruhrlade" was establishing a campaign fund that was beyond Hugenberg's control and free from his machinations. An account bearing the name "Wirtschaftshilfe" was established under Springorum's signature at the Berlin office of the German Bank and Discount Society (Deutsche Bank und Diskonto-Gesellschaft), and a levy of 1.11 marks for each ton of raw steel produced in February 1928 was imposed upon all members of the "Ruhrlade."[51] The "Ruhrlade" proceeded to raise several hundred thousand marks for use in the 1928 elections and made campaign contributions to the DVP, DNVP, and Center according to the number of candidates from industry that each party nominated to secure candidacies in the upcoming Reichstag elections. According to this arrangement, the DNVP received 200,000 of the 487,000 marks it spent in the 1928 campaign from the account administered by Springorum.[52] Another 50,000 marks came from Hugenberg, who begrudgingly honored his commitment to the DNVP from the funds that had been placed at his disposal by Ruhr heavy industry.[53] At the same time, individual candidates for the DNVP received another 184,000 marks from Ruhr heavy industry, 47,000 marks from a consortium of Berlin banks, and 67,000 marks from the Curatorium for the Reconstruction of German Economic Life, as well as several smaller contributions from industrialists who stood outside the orbit of either the "Ruhrlade" or the Siemens Curatorium.[54] Hugenberg, in turn, was so aggravated by his lack of influence over the nomination of candidates for the Reichstag that he not only refused to provide another 50,000 marks from his own reserves but a scant two weeks before the election demanded repayment of the 50,000 marks that he had donated to the party leadership earlier in the campaign.[55]

The success with which Westarp and his associates in Ruhr heavy industry were able to circumvent Hugenberg's control over the DNVP's campaign finances afforded the party leadership a measure of independence in its

---

[50] See Haniel to Reusch, 5 Mar. 1928, RWWA Cologne, Abt. 130, NL Reusch, 40010124/11, and Silverberg to Reusch, 6 Mar., 1928, ibid., 400101290/35a, as well as Springorum to Westarp, 29 Feb. 1928, NL Westarp, Gärtringen, II/28.

[51] Springorum to Reusch, 3 Apr. 1928, RWWA Cologne, Abt. 130, NL Reusch, 400101290/36a.

[52] "Einzahlungen auf den Wahlfonds 1928," 25 June 1928, NL Westarp, Gärtringen, II/28.

[53] Hugenberg to Westarp, 29 Feb. 1928, ibid., II/28.

[54] "Einzahlungen auf den Wahlfonds 1928," 25 June 1928, ibid., II/28. On the DNVP's support from the Siemens Curatorium, see "Unterlagen zur Sitzung des Kuratoriums zum Wiederaufbau des deutschen Wirtschaftslebens am 2. November 1928," SHI Berlin, NL Siemens, 4/Lf 646.

[55] Hugenberg to Westarp, 6 May 1928, NL Westarp, Gärtringen, VN 67. In a similar vein, see Hugenberg to Westarp, 19 May 1928, ibid.

conduct of the campaign for the 1928 elections. Still, the fight over control of industrial campaign contributions to the DNVP was only the opening skirmish in a conflict that would continue for at least the next two years. In the short run, however, Hugenberg's machinations only exacerbated the chronic financial difficulties the DNVP had experienced since the stabilization of the mark in 1923–24 and severely limited its ability to counter the appeal of the special-interest parties with a dynamic and effective counter-offensive of its own. This did not augur well for its prospects in the May 1928 Reichstag elections.

The Anatomy of Defeat

Throughout the campaign for the 1928 Reichstag elections the leaders of the DNVP walked a fine line between the Scylla of highlighting their party's accomplishments as a member of the governmental coalition and the Charibidis of reclaiming the DNVP's role as the leader of the so-called national opposition.[56] That was a problematic strategy at best could be seen in the outcome of the elections. For when all the votes had been tallied, the DNVP had lost more than 1.8 million votes – or approximately 30 percent of what it had received four years earlier – and saw its share of the popular vote fall from 20.5 percent in December 1924 to 14.2 percent in May 1928. In terms of its parliamentary strength, this translated into the loss of 30 of the 103 mandates the DNVP had won in December 1924. The party's losses extended to all but one of Germany's thirty-five electoral districts – the lone exception was Cologne-Aachen – and as a general rule were substantially heavier in those areas in central and western Germany where independent farmers constituted the most important voting bloc than in urban areas or the predominantly agricultural areas east of the Elbe where the social and political hegemony of the local aristocracy was still relatively intact. The DNVP suffered its heaviest losses in a broad swath of territory stretching from the three Saxon districts of Dresden-Bautzen (–49.6 percent), Leipzig (–62.8 percent), and Chemnitz-Zwickau (–51.6 percent) through East and South Hanover (–48.6 percent and –47.5 percent respectively) and Weser-Ems (–45.0 percent) to Hesse-Darmstadt (–57.2 percent), Hesse-Nassau (–47.7 percent), and Württemberg (–44.6 percent). The DNVP fared much better in areas east of the Elbe with substantially lighter losses in East Prussia (–20.3 percent), Potsdam I and II (–20.9 percent and –16.5 percent respectively), Frankfurt an der Oder (–24.4 percent), and the three Silesian districts of Breslau (–18.7 percent), Liegnitz (–16.5 percent), and Oppeln (–18.4 percent). In Berlin the DNVP managed to keep its losses to 25.2 percent of its December 1924 vote, whereas in East and

---

[56] For example, see Albrecht Philipp, *Bilanz und Aufgaben deutschnationaler Arbeit 1928. Eine politische Übersicht.* Schriften der Deutschnationalen Volkspartei in Sachsen (Arbeitsgemeinschaft), no. 27 (Dresden, 1928), 6–13.

West Düsseldorf Nationalist losses amounted to 18.1 and 20.2 percent of what the party had received in 1924.[57] Even if the reasons for the DNVP's defeat differed significantly from district to district, it all added up to an electoral disaster that was unprecedented in the annals of German conservatism.

By no means was the DNVP the only party to experience the bitter pill of defeat in the May 1928 Reichstag elections. In point of fact, all of the more established, ideologically oriented non-socialist parties like the Center, German Democratic Party, and German People's Party incurred heavy losses in the face of what on the surface appeared to be a massive swing to the left highlighted by a particularly strong performance by the Social Democrats. The DDP and DVP lost 21.7 and 12.1 percent respectively of the popular vote they had tallied in December 1924, whereas the Center lost 9.9 percent of its 1924 vote.[58] The principal beneficiaries of this were the Business Party, the Christian-National Peasants and Farmers' Party, and the other middle-class splinter parties that had risen to prominence since the last national elections. The WP more than doubled the popular vote it had polled in the December 1924 Reichstag elections and increased its representation in the Reichstag from eleven to twenty-three deputies, whereas the CNBLP and the German Peasants' Party received a combined total of more than a million votes and elected seventeen deputies to the Reichstag. The People's Justice Party, on the other hand, polled nearly half a million votes in the 1928 Reichstag elections, while another 830,000 votes were cast for parties that were too small to receive so much as a single mandate. All told, middle-class splinter parties received nearly 12 percent of the popular vote, or more than twice what they had received in December 1924. Combined with a particularly high rate of voter abstention of over 25 percent, this inflicted unexpectedly heavy losses on all of Germany's more established nonsocialist parties.[59] A major factor in all of this was the lethargy of the so-called younger generation. Not only the Nationalists but Stresemann and the leaders of all other parties with the exception of the Communists lamented the fact that their parties had failed to excite the imagination of Germany's younger voters. For some, this reflected the estrangement of the younger generation from the increasing materialism of German political life.[60] For the Nationalists, on the other hand, this was was a

---

[57] The raw data for this has been taken from *Statistisches Jahrbuch des Deutschen Reiches* 46 (1927): 498–99, and 47 (1928): 580–81. See also Dörr, "Deutschnationale Volkspartei," 387–90. On the party's losses in Saxony, see Rademacher to Westarp, 21 May 1928, NL Westarp, Gärtringen, VN 101. On the situation in Hanover, see Jaeger to Westarp, 29 May 1928, ibid., VN 99.

[58] Falter, Lindenberger, and Schumann, *Wahlen und Abstimmungen*, 41, 70–71.

[59] Ibid., 40, 70–71.

[60] Larry Eugene Jones, "Generational Conflict and the Problem of Political Mobilization in the Weimar Republic," in *Elections, Mass Politics, and Social Change in Germany: New Perspectives*, ed. Larry Eugene Jones and James Retallack (New York, 1992), 347–69.

signal that maybe their party's crusade for a restoration of the monarchy no longer resonated as powerfully with those who had risen to political consciousness since the end of World War I as it had with their fathers.[61]

Westarp and the leaders of the DNVP could find little solace in the losses of the other bourgeois parties. The sheer magnitude of their own party's defeat was totally unexpected and left them in a state of deep shock.[62] The DNVP's defeat at the polls stemmed from a variety of factors, the common denomiator of which was its inability to satisfy the expectations of those socio-economic groups whose support had catapulted it to victory in May and December of 1924. In his post-mortem before the DNVP Reichstag delegation on 12 June 1928 Westarp attributed the Nationalists' defeat to the increasingly materialistic attitude of significant sectors of the German electorate – particularly the farmers and independent middle class – and their lack of interest in the larger ideological and foreign policy issues around which the DNVP had structured its campaign. Westarp offered a vigorous defense of the policies the DNVP had pursued as a member of the national government and argued that the party's losses at the polls were part of the cost it had to bear for accepting its share of governmental responsibility. Had it not been for the relentless agitation of special-interest parties like the CNBLP and WP, he concluded, these losses would have been held within acceptable limits and would not have prejudiced the party's return to power.[63] But Westarp's analysis of his party's debacle at the polls was immediately challenged by Hugenberg and his supporters on the DNVP's right wing. Claiming that Westarp had misrepresented the reasons for the DNVP's defeat, Hugenberg argued that the party's entry into the government in 1927 had diverted it from its long-range goal of bringing about a fundamental change in the existing system of government

[61] Undated memorandum appended to Hoetzsch to Westarp, 30 May 1928, NL Westarp, Gärtringen, II/34.

[62] This is clearly reflected in the letter from Ada Gräfin von Westarp to Gertraude Freifrau Hiller von Gaertringen, 21 May 1928, NL Westarp, Gärtringen.

[63] Westarp's remarks at a meeting of the DNVP Reichstag delegation, 12 June 1928, BA Koblenz, NL Schmidt-Hannover, 35. This analysis of the DNVP's losses at the polls is confirmed in large part by a memorandum from the Berlin headquarters of the German National Workers' League, appended to Lindner to Westarp, 12 June 1928, NL Westarp, Gärtringen, VN 69. According to his analysis, the party had lost approximately 450,000 votes to the VRP, another 240,000 to middle-class interest parties, and 120,000 to the CNBLP and DBP. For further information, see Lothar Steuer, *Die Deutschnationale Wahlniederlage am 20. Mai 1928. Ihre Ursachen, Zusammenhänge, Folgerungen* (Anklam, 1928), as well as Lambach, "Wie ist eine Verjüngung der Parteien zu erzielen?," Lejeune-Jung, "Gehen die deutschnationalen Verlüste auf Abwanderung oder Enthaltung zurück?," and Treviranus, "Was wurde an den Deutschnationalen am meisten kritisiert?," all in the *Deutsche Allgemeine Zeitung*, 27 May 1928, nos. 243–44. For the best analysis of the DNVP's defeat at the polls, see Ohnezeit, *Zwischen "schärfster Opposition,"* 414–24.

and that henceforth the DNVP should forswear all attempts to reenter the government in that this would fatally compromise not just the ideals and fundamental principles upon which the party was based but, more importantly, the integrity and effectiveness of its struggle against the hated Weimar system.[64]

Hugenberg and the Pan-Germans

The reverberations from the shock of the Nationalist defeat in the 1928 Reichstag elections targeted the one person who was most closely identified with the party's move to the center between 1924 and 1928, Count Kuno von Westarp. The first slap against Westarp's leadership of the party had come during the campaign itself and in fact from some of his oldest associates in the Central Association of German Conservatives. A bastion of reactionary conservativism that refused to accept the new republican system that Germany had adopted after the end of World War I, the Central Association had been a thorn in the side of the DNVP ever since the party's founding in November 1918 despite the fact that Westarp himself had served as its chairman until his election as chairman of the DNVP Reichstag delegation in early 1925. Even then, Westarp continued to function as the Central Association's honorary chairman and principal liaison to the party, often finding himself in the uncomfortable position of having to defend the DNVP's more unpopular policies before some of the party's most outspoken critics.[65] The anger that hard-line conservatives like Count Dietlof von Arnim-Boitzenburg and Count Ernst Julius von Seidlitz-Sandrecski felt over the DNVP's acquisence in the extension of Law for the Protection of the Republic in the summer of 1927 continued to simmer within the Central Association until the spring of 1928, when on 31 March it refused to endorse the DNVP and encouraged its members to support those parties and candidates who in their opinion best represented conservative values and thought. For Westarp this was the final straw, and on 13 April he resigned from the organization in a letter to Seidlitz-Sandrecski that gave full vent to the anquish and pain he felt over the break with his erstwhile comrades-in-arms.[66]

---

[64] Hugenberg's remarks, ibid. See also the remarks of Schmidt-Hannover and Freytagh-Loringhoven, ibid., as well as [Wegener], "Betrachtungen über die und Folgerungen aus der Reichstagswahl vom 20.5.1928," n.d., BA Koblenz, NL Wegener, 42/1–20. In a similar vein, see Ernst Oberfohren, *Auf zur Opposition. Reichstagrede am 5. Juli 1928*, Deutschnationale Flugschrift, no. 328 (Berlin, 1928).

[65] For further details, see Flemming, "Konservatismus als 'nationalrevolutionäre Bewegung'," 295–331.

[66] Exchange between Westarp and Seidlitz-Sandrecski, 12–13 Apr. 1928, NL Westarp, Gärtringen, VN 40. See also Daniela Gasteiger, "From Friends to Foes: Count Kuno von Westarp and the Transformation of the German Right," in *The German Right in the*

While the break between the Central Association and DNVP was symptomatic of the problems that bedeviled the DNVP in the wake of its two experiments at governmental participation, the driving force in the anti-Westarp campaign in the DNVP came from the Pan-German League. Having been pushed pretty much to the periphery of German political life since the founding of the Weimar Republic, Heinrich Claß and the leaders of the ADV were bitterly opposed to the republican institutions that Germany had inherited from the November Revolution and sought nothing less than the repeal of universal suffrage, an end to parliamentarianism and the party system, and a restoration of the monarchy as the keys to Germany's national salvation.[67] Following the DNVP's return to the national government in January 1927, the Pan-Germans redoubled their efforts to gain control of the DNVP and transform it into an instrument of Pan-German policy.[68] There was, however, a curious anomaly in all of this since the Pan-Germans decided to launch their campaign to gain control of the DNVP at a time when its fortunes could not have been lower. The ADV's membership had declined steadily from a peak of 38,000 in 1922 to approximately 16,000 by the end of 1928 as a result of its inability to compete with the more militant forms of mass mobilization on the extreme Right.[69] Confronted by what appeared to be an irreversible decline in its membership and with limited resources to rectify this problem, the Pan-Germans decided to concentrate what remained of their political capital on a last-ditch effort to build up a strong base of support within the DNVP in hopes of eventually capturing control of the party. It was a peculiar feature of Weimar political culture that an organization so obviously in the grip of decline as the Pan-German League should seek and achieve such a decisive role in the affairs of the German Right.

The key figure in the Pan-German calculations was press and film magnate Alfred Hugenberg. Hugenberg's ties to the ADV dated back to the period before World War I, when he had played a major role first in the founding of

Weimar Republic: Studies in the History of German Conservatism, Nationalism, and Antisemitism, ed. Larry Eugene Jones, (New York and Oxford, 2014), 48–78, esp. 59–71.

[67] Heinrich Claß, "Alldeutsche Ziele für Deutschlands Rettung," *Deutschlands Erneuerung* 12, no. 10 (Oct. 1928): 575–80.

[68] Remarks by Claß before the ADV managing committee, 12–13 Feb. 1927, BA Berlin, R 8048, 146/55.

[69] Jackisch, *Pan German League*, 88. See also the detailed discussion of the ADV's membership trends in the minutes of the ADV managing committee, 1–2 Dec. 1928, BA Berlin, R 8048l, 156/55–56. For further details, see Björn Hofmeister, "Realms of Leadership and Residues of Social Mobilization: The Pan-German League, 1918–33," in *The German Right in the Weimar Republic. Studies in History of German Conservatism, Nationalism, and Antisemitism*, ed. Larry Eugene Jones (New York and Oxford, 2014), 134–65, esp. 142–47.

its predecessor, the General German League, in 1891 and then in its recon-
stitutation as the Pan-German League three years later. Unlike Westarp, who
possessed a noble pedigree and identified himself with the world-view and
values of the East Prussian land-owning aristocracy, Hugenberg came from
an unabashedly bourgeois background and belonged to that cadre of erstwhile liberals who in the 1890s embraced radical nationalism as an antedote
to the ossification and sterility of Wilhelmine politics.[70] Hugenberg used his
unquestioned managerial skills to build up a massive press empire that was
without parallel in Germany and that included such high-circulation newspapers as the *Berliner Lokal-Anzeiger* and *Der Tag* as well as a large portion
of Germany's provincial press.[71] Hugenberg had also developed substantial
interests in the German coal industry, took part in the founding of the
National Federation of German Industry, and was soon to be elected to
high-ranking executive positions in Germany's two largest interests organizations for mining, the Association for Mining Interests (Verein für bergbau-
liche Interessen) and the organization of Ruhr employers known as the
Zechenverband.[72] By the end of the war and well into the first years of the
Weimar Republic Hugenberg was recognized as one of Germany's most
influential industrial leaders. But for many he epitomized all that was wrong
with German capitalism.

After the collapse of 1918 Hugenberg cast his lot with the DNVP, where he
joined Oskar Hergt, Karl Helfferich, and Otto Hoetzsch in the so-called 4-H
consortium that effectively ran party affairs from 1919 to 1924. Although he
stood on the party's right wing, he rejected the Kapp putsch in the spring of
1920 and supported the expulsion of the racists from the DNVP in the fall of
1922. At the same time, Hugenberg supported a wide array of right-wing
organizations, including young conservative projects like the June Club,
Martin Spahn's Political College, and the Evangelical-Social Academy of
Friedrich Brunstäd. Hugenberg's largesse even extended to elements on the
right wing of the Christian labor movement around Franz Behrens and the
Central Association of Farm Laborers. In all of this Hugenberg was driven by
the determination to unite all of those who shared his love for Germany and
longed for its political rebirth into a broadly based and cohesive political
movement that would sweep those responsible for Germany's misery from

---

[70] On Hugeberg's early career, see John A. Leopold, *Alfred Hugenberg: The Radical Nationalist Campign against the Weimar Republic* (New Haven and London, 1977), 1–20.
[71] For further details, see Dankwart Guratsch, *Macht durch Organisation. Die Grundlegung
   des Hugenbergschen Presseimperiums* (Düsseldorf, 1974), 344–93. See also Holzbach, *Das
   "System Hugenberg."* 259–89.
[72] Stefan Przigoda, *Unternehmerverbände im Ruhrbergbau. Zur Geschichte von Bergbau-
   Verein und Zechenverband 1858–1933* (Bochum, 2002), 163–66, 234–55.

Figure 11.   Photograph of Alfred Hugenberg, DNVP Reichstag deputy from 1920 to 1933 and DNVP national party chairman from 1928 to 1933. Reproduced with permission from the Bundesarchiv, Bild 183-2005-0621-500

power.[73] But this would all change with the fateful split in the DNVP Reichstag delegation on the vote on the Dawes Plan. Hugenberg was bitterly opposed to the Dawes Plan and had done his best to prevent its ratification with an impassioned plea from his sickbed at home.[74] Furious with those in the delegation who had placed their own special interests ahead of the national welfare, Hugenberg began to withdraw support from those whom he held responsible for the betrayal of Germany's national trust. Still, he was reluctant to be drawn into the Pan-German intrigues against Westarp and steadfastly resisted efforts to draw him into the feud that was consuming his party. It was probably not until a series of high-level discussions in the summer of 1927 that Claß was finally able to overcome Hugenberg's reticence and persuade him to accept the charge the Pan-Germans had given him.[75] With the letter that Hugenberg wrote to Westarp on the eve of the DNVP's Königsberg party congress and in which he demanded that "the unparliamentary party throughout the country as a whole serve as the conscience of those delegations that sit

---

[73] Hozlbach, *Das "System Hugenberg,"* 136–66.
[74] Hugenberg to Hergt, 26 Aug. 1924, in Alfred Hugenberg, *Streiflichter aus Vergangenheit und Gegenwart* (Berlin, 1927), 96–97.
[75] Claß, "Wider den Strom," BA Berlin, NL Claß, 3/880. See also Leicht, *Claß*, 362–63.

in parliament today," Hugenberg threw down the gauntlet and began his fight for control of the party.[76]

Westarp's Retreat

The conflict that had been building within the party for the better part of a year and a half would come to a dramatic head at a meeting of the DNVP Reichstag delegation on 12 June 1928. Having worked diligently to organize support for Hugenberg at the local and district levels of the DNVP's national organization and to secure the election of candidates who would reinforce his position in the DNVP Reichstag delegation, the Pan-Germans were confident that the moment to reverse the direction in which the party was headed had arrived.[77] The prospect of a Hugenberg bid for control of the party sent chills through the ranks of the DNVP's white-collar and working-class supporters. This animus stemmed in large part from the fact that Hugenberg's entourage included men like Paul Bang, a long-time Pan-German activist who was renown for his involvement in the yellow trade-union movement as chairman of the League for National Economics and Industrial Peace and as a propogandist for a new concept in labor relations called the "work community" or *Werkgemeinschaft*. Modelled after the *carto del lavoro* that Mussolini had instituted in Fascist Italy, Bang's concept of the "work community" sought to reestablish a paternalistic relationship between employer and employee through the creation of factory unions under the direct control of the factory owner himself.[78] To Christian labor leaders both within and outside the DNVP, the notion of the "work community" was little more than a fraud

---

[76] Hugenberg to Westarp, 17 Sept. 1927, NL Westarp, Gärtringen, II/25, also in BA Koblenz, NL Hugenberg, 113/78-83, reprinted in Leo Wegener, *Hugenberg. Eine Plauderei* (Solln-Munich, 1930), 53-54. For further details, see John A. Leopold, "The Election of Alfred Hugenberg as Chairman of the German National People's Party," *Canadian Journal of History* 7 (1972): 149-71, and Larry Eugene Jones, "German Conservatism at the Crossroads: Count Kuno von Westarp and the Struggle for Control of the DNVP, 1928-30." *Contemporary European History* 18 (2009): 147-77, as well as Dörr, "Deutschnationale Volkspartei 1925 bis 1928," 410-65; Holzbach, *Das "System Hugenberg."* 192-253; Ohnezeit, *Zwischen "schärfster Opposition,"* 386-94, 425-48, and Mergel, "Das Scheitern des deutschen Tory-Konservatismus, Die Umformung der DNVP zu einer rechtsradikalen Partei 1928-1932." *Historische Zeitschrift* 276 (2003): 341-45.

[77] On the Pan-German strategy in the 1928 elections, see the resolution that Claß introduced at the meeting of the ADV managing committee, 26-27 Nov. 1927, BA Berlin, R 8048, 152/23-24, as well as Claß's remarks before the ADV managing committee in Eisenach, 21 Apr. 1928, BA Berlin, R 8048, 154/70-71, and his reflections in Claß, "Wider den Strom," BA Berlin, NL Claß, 3/881-83. See also Jackisch, *Pan-German League,* 151-53, and Hofmeister, "Between Monarchy and Dictatorship," 269-98.

[78] Bang, "Werkgemeinschaft," *Nationalwirtschaft. Blätter für organischen Wirtschaftsaufbau* 1 (1927): 149-73.

perpertrated upon Germany's working and white-collar classes by social reactionaries intent upon destroying their ability to negotiate for themselves when it came to wages and work conditions.[79]

In September 1926 the DNVP party leadership had negotiated a truce between the two factions at the DNVP's Cologne party congress. But this truce broke down in the spring of 1928 amid complaints from the German National Workers' League (DNAB), the organizational home of the Christian labor movement in the DNVP, about the aggressiveness of the "yellow" unions in the selection of candidates for the upcoming Reichstag elections.[80] The belligerence of the "yellow" unions was a matter of particular concern to the leaders of the German National Union of Commercial Employees, the largest of Germany's white-collar unions with more than 375,000 members and the architect of an elaborate network of *Querverbindungen* that it had built up since the early 1920s and that extended to all of the established bourgeois parties with the exception of the DDP.[81] The DHV's chief liaison to the DNVP was Walther Lambach, a Reichstag deputy since 1920 who also served as chairman of the DNVP's National White-Collar Committee. As a self-proclaimed young conservative, Lambach was particularly distressed by the fact that in the 1928 Reichstag elections the established bourgeois parties, including the DNVP, appeared to have lost the confidence of the younger generation, something that in his mind only confirmed the need for a sweeping reform and rejuvenation of the German party system.[82]

Lambach would return to this theme in an article he wrote for the *Politische Wochenschrift* in which he had the temerity to challenge the DNVP's commitment to the principle of monarchism. The central thrust of Lambach's argument was that monarchism as a political issue had lost all appeal for the German voter and especially for the German youth. For those who had reached political maturity after 1918, the monarchy was little more than a symbol they had come to know only through stage and screen. The election of Hindenburg to the Reich Presidency in 1925, argued Lambach, had given the

[79] For example, see Max Habermann, "Zur Werkgemeinschaftsfrage," *Deutsche Handels-Wacht* 34, no. 23 (7 Dec. 1927): 539–42.
[80] Memorandum from the DNAB to the DNVP party leadership, 12 Mar. 1928, appended to Lindner to Westarp, 13 Mar. 1928, NL Westarp, Gärtringen, VN 71. On the animus between the two trade-union factions, see Richter to Behrens, 25 Feb. 1924, appended to Richter to Westarp, 26 Feb. 1924, ibid., VN 48, and Schmidt to Hergt, Helfferich, Wallraf, and Westarp, 4 Apr. 1928, ibid., VN 44. See also Stupperich, *Volksgemeinschaft oder Arbeitersolidarität*, 131–34.
[81] For further details, see Larry Eugene Jones, "Between the Fronts: The German National Union of Commerical Employees from 1928 to 1933," *Journal of Modern History* 48 (1976): 462–82, and Iris Hamel, *Völkischer Verband*, 167–238.
[82] Lambach, "Wie ist eine Verjüngung der Parteien zu erzielen?" *Deutsche Allgemeine Zeitung*, 27 May 1928, nos. 243–44.

German people a substitute Kaiser, who as a living symbol of Germany's past greatness completely overshadowed all memory of the royal family. The DNVP's recent defeat at the polls only confirmed the demise of the monarchist cause. If the party were ever to regain the support of the younger generation, then it must realize that the restoration of the monarchy is little more than a dream which can never be realized in the foreseeable future. The DNVP, concluded Lambach, had no choice but to adapt to the new situation by opening its ranks to monarchists and conservative republicans alike.

> In the future we of the German National People's Party ... must direct our appeal to the entire German electorate. Monarchists and republicans, join our ranks! And at the same time that we revise our attitude concerning the form of government, we must also change our program and our party leadership. The DNVP must approach the future not as a one-sided party of the past, but as a new conservative party that represents the entire nation.[83]

Published without the foreknowledge of the DHV's chief political strategist Max Habermann,[84] Lambach's article struck a sensitive nerve with the champions of the monarchist cause and brought the conflict that had been building within the DNVP for the past several years to a dramatic head. The anti-Westarp forces on the DNVP's right wing seized upon Lambach's indiscretion to intensify their attacks against Westarp's leadership of the party in the hope of blocking his reelection as chairman of the DNVP Reichstag delegation. Speaking before the DNVP organization in his home district of North Westphalia on 16 June, Hugenberg complained bitterly about Westarp's leadership of the party and warned that if he were reinstalled as its parliamentary leader, the party could no longer count on his financial support.[85] Meeting privately with Westarp on 23 June, Hugenberg demanded Lambach's expulsion as a precondition for an end to the turmoil in the party.[86] As a dedicated monarchist, Westarp was deeply offended by the thrust of Lambach's argument and publicly reaffirmed the DNVP's unequivocal commitment to the

---

[83] Lambach, "Monarchismus," *Politische Wochenschrift* 4, no. 24 (14 June 1928): 485–87. See also Lambach, "Die Stellung des Verbandes im öffentlichen Leben," *Deutsche Handels-Wacht* 35, no. 12 (25 June 1928): 230–31.

[84] Habermann, "Der Deutschnationale Handlungsgehilfen-Verband im Kampf um das Reich," DHV-Archiv Hamburg, 68.

[85] Ada Gräfin von Westarp to Gertraude Freifrau Hiller von Gaertringen, 17 June 1928, NL Westarp, Gärtringen. See also Westarps's undated memorandum to the DNVP's district chairmen, appended to Westarp to Tirpitz, 25 June 1928, BA-MA Freiburg, NL Tirpitz, 60/1–3.

[86] Ada Gräfin von Westarp to Gertraude Freifrau Hiller von Gaertringen, 24 June 1928, NL Westarp, Gärtringen.

restoration of the monarchy.[87] At the same time, however, Westarp was reluctant to take disciplinary action against the dissident trade-union secretary for fear of precipitating a general secession on the DNVP's left wing and counseled prudence on the part of those who were trying to drive Lambach from the party.[88] Westarp's restraint only played into the hands of his opponents on the DNVP's right wing, who cited his refusal to take action against Lambach as only one more example of the weak and indecisive leadership responsible for the DNVP's precipitous decline between 1924 and 1928.[89]

Efforts by Hugenberg and his supporters to block Westarp's reelection as chairman of the DNVP Reichstag delegation and thus put an end to the personal union of delegation chairman and party chairman suffered an embarrassing setback when all but nine members of the delegation – among them Hugenberg, Bang, Quaatz, and Freytagh-Loringhoven – voted on 2 July to reinstall Westarp as chairman of the delegation.[90] At the same time, Lambach moved to appease his more moderate critics within the delegation by reading a statement in which he reaffirmed his personal loyalty to the monarchist principle and was let off with a mere reprimand for his article in the *Politische Wochenschrift*.[91] This only infuriated the forces around Hugenberg, who intensified their efforts in preparation for a meeting of the DNVP party representation that was scheduled to take place in Berlin on 8–9 July. As a result of the vigorous campaign the Pan-Germans had waged on his behalf at the local levels of the DNVP organization, Hugenberg could now count on the support of at least ten of the party's thirty-five state and provincial organizations with another five leaning in his direction.[92] Westarp's tepid response to Lambach's indiscretion had had the effect of tipping several district organizations that had initially supported Westarp in Hugenberg's direction. A case in point was the DNVP district organization in Potsdam II, whose chairman Werner Steinhoff had originally supported Westarp's reelection to both the

---

[87] Westarp, "Der monarchische Gedanke und die Deutschnationale Volkspartei," *Neue Preußische (Kreuz-)Zeitung*, 26 June 1928, no. 196. See also Westarp's correspondence with G. W. Schiele, 26–30 June 1928, NL Westarp, Gärtringen, VN 100.

[88] Ada Gräfin von Westarp to Gertraude Freifrau Hiller von Gaertringen, 17 June 1928, NL Westarp, Gärtringen.

[89] For further details, see Blank to Springorum, 22 June 1928, RWWA Cologne, Abt. 130, NL Reusch, 400101293/8b.

[90] Ada Gräfin von Westarp to Gertraude Freifrau Hiller von Gaertringen, 2 July 1928, NL Westarp, Gärtringen. For Westarp's credo, see Kuno von Westarp, *Um die christlichen, sozialen und nationalen Güter der Nation. Oppositionsrede im Reichstag am 4. Juli 1928*, Deutschnationale Flugschrift, no. 327 (Berlin, 1928).

[91] *Neue Preußische (Kreuz-)Zeitung*, 3 July 1928, no. 309.

[92] Wegener to Rojahn-Wabnitz, 25 July 1928, BA Koblenz, NL Wegener, 11.

chairmanship of the DNVP Reichstag delegation and the DNVP party chairmanship,[93] but which now not only aligned itself with Hugenberg in his efforts to unseat Westarp but initiated expulsion proceedings against Lambach on 10 July for having damaged the image of the party.[94]

By this time, the principal objective of the forces behind Hugenberg was no longer just to force Lambach's expulsion from the party, but to use the Lambach affair to prevent Westarp's reelection as DNVP national chairman.[95] A spokesman for the fifteen district organizations that supported Hugenberg opened the meeting by reading a statement demanding Lambach's immediate expulsion from the party with vague threats of a general secession on the DNVP's right wing if Westarp and the party leadership failed to take decisive action in the Lambach affair. When Hugenberg refused to retract this statement, Westarp announced that he no longer possessed the support necessary to lead the party and announced his resignation as its chairman. After Westarp left the room in obvious disgust with the tactics of the Hugenberg faction, Max Wallraf assumed the chairmanship and succeeded in restoring a modicum of unity as Hugenberg and his supporters relented in their attacks against Westarp. The assembly then proceeded to adopt a unanimous resolution beseeching Westarp to resume his functions as DNVP party chairman. On the following day, however, the newly found sense of unity fell apart when the fifteen district organizations aligned with Hugenberg and under the leadership of retired general Wilhelm von Dommes presented Westarp with a new resolution on the Lambach affair that was promptly rejected because it deviated from established procedures for dealing with matters of party discipline. When Hugenberg and Dommes refused to withdraw their resolution or amend it in a manner acceptable to the DNVP party leadership, Westarp tendered his resignation once again, this time making his decision irrevocable. Westarp, however, would remain at the post until a new party chairman could be elected later that fall.[96]

---

[93] Blank to Springorum, 22 June 1928, RWWA Cologne, Abt. 130, NL Reusch, 400101293/8b.

[94] "Beschluß des Landesverbandes Potsdam II der Deutschnationalen Volkspartei, nach §19 der Parteisatzung vom Amts wegen ein Ausschlußverfahren gegen das im Bezirk des Landesverbandes wohnhafte Parteimitglied, Herrn Walther Lambach, MdR, mit Bezugnahme auf §17 der Parteisatzung zu eröffnen," signed by Steinhoff, 10 July 1928, BA Koblenz, Nachlass Walther Lambach, 10/72–74.

[95] Reusch to Springorum, 5 July 1928, RWWA Cologne, Abt. 130, NL Reusch, 400101293/9. See also Reichert to Reusch, 17 July 1928, BA Koblenz, NL Lambach, 24.

[96] Westarp's memorandum on the developments on 8–9 July 1928 to the chairmen of the DNVP state and provincial organizations, 12 July 1928, NL Westarp, II/30. See also Reichert to Wesenfeld, 9 July 1928, BA Koblenz, NL Lambach, 24, as well as the account in Hilpert, "Meinungen und Kämpfe," BHStA Munich, Abt. V, NL Hilpert, 18/3666–78. For the perspective of the Hugenberg faction, see the entries in Quaatz's diary, 8–9 July 1928, BA Koblenz, NL Quaatz, 16. The Quaatz diary has been published as *Die*

The Battle Lines Form

The meeting of the DNVP party representation in July 1928 represented a decisive triumph for Hugenberg and those who sought to return their party to a policy of uncompromising opposition to the Weimar Republic. A final resolution of the crisis, however, was still not in sight. Hugenberg's ultimate objective, perhaps best summed up by his slogan "Block, nicht Brei," was to transform the DNVP from a socially heterogeneous reservoir of Christian, conservative, and national sentiment into a strong, compact bloc "fused together by the iron hammer of *Weltanschauung*."[97] This aim ran sharply counter to Westarp's conception of the DNVP as a conservative *Sammelpartei* that stood above the clash of antagonistic social and economic interests and that sought sought to fuse these interests into a stable and harmonious whole.[98] The key to Hugenberg's campaign to transform the DNVP from a socially heterogeneous conservative *Sammelpartei* into a strong and united bloc lay in the support he received at the local and district levels of the DNVP's national organization. Relying in large part upon the resources of his Pan-German allies, Hugenberg's confederates had been hard at work organizing grass-roots support for his political agenda ever since the DNVP reentered the national government in January 1927. Invariably this had been accompanied by bitter fights at the local and district levels of the DNVP's national organization between those who supported and those who opposed Hugenberg's program for a reform of the party. In March 1927, for example, the leaders of the party's right wing in Württemberg were able to unseat long-time state party chairman Gustav Beißwänger in what was a rebuff to the role the DNVP had played in the stabilization of Weimar parliamentarism both in the Reich under Westarp and in Württemberg under Wilhelm Bazille, the Nationalist minister president of Württemberg since 1924.[99] In East Saxony pro-Hugenberg forces were able to force the Bang's candidacy down the throats of the local party leaders in the spring of 1928, with the result that the district party chairman and Westarp supporter Kurt Philipp resigned in protest.[100] And in Pomerania Hugenberg's forces waged a full-scale offensive against Reichstag deputy Hans Schlange-Schöningen and his right-hand man Karl Passarge in

---

Deutschnationalen und die Zerstörung der Weimarer Republik. Aus dem Tagebuch von Reinhold Quaatz 1928–1933, ed. Hermann Weiß and Paul Hoser (Stuttgart, 1989), but for reasons of economy only the unpublished diary in the Bundesarchiv has been cited.

[97] Hugenberg, "Block oder Brei?" *Berliner Lokal-Anzeiger*, 26 and 28 Aug. 1928, nos. 404 and 406.

[98] Kuno von Westarp, *Die Aufgaben der Deutschnationalen Volkspartei*, Deutschnationale Flugschrift, no. 330 (Berlin, 1928), 4–11.

[99] On the coup in Württemberg, see Müller, "Bürgerpartei," 405–17.

[100] Philipp to Westarp, 20 Mar. 1928, NL Westarp, Gärtringen, VN 67.

what was ultimately an unsuccessful attempt to drive Schlange-Schöningen from the chairmanship of the DNVP's district organization.[101] All of this was part of a pattern that had repeated itself in one district after another before the fateful meeting of the DNVP representation on 8–9 July 1928.

When the DNVP party representation concluded its deliberations in July, Hugenberg could count on the support of fifteen of the DNVP's thirty-five district organizations.[102] Of the remaining district organizations, ten were in the hands of party moderates who supported Westarp and ten remained uncommitted.[103] In the time before the DNVP party representation reconvened later that fall to elect a new party chairman, Hugenberg's supporters hoped that they would be able to win over two, if not more, of the undecided district organizations, thereby giving Hugenberg a virtual mandate when it came to shaping the DNVP's future political course.[104] But while Hugenberg hoped to rally sufficient support at the local levels of the DNVP party organization to reverse the direction in which the party was headed, it was unclear just how Hugenberg was going to exercise his control of the party in light of his own ambivalence about serving as party chairman. To address this quandry, Reinhold Quaatz, a strong Hugenberg ally from the outset, proposed in late July 1928 that leadership of the party be entrusted to a three-man presidium consisting of Hugenberg, Westarp, and Friedrich von Winterfeld, chairman of the DNVP delegation to the Prussian Landtag. Not only would this effectively subordinate Westarp to Hugenberg and the policies of the DNVP's right wing, but the presence of Westarp in the proposed triumvirate would minimize the dangers of a secession on the party's left wing. For Hugenberg Quaatz's proposal had the added advantage of allowing him to dictate party affairs without having to leave the relative obscurity in which he was accustomed to operating.[105]

The support he enjoyed at the grass-roots level of the DNVP's national organization notwithstanding, Hugenberg still encountered formidable resistance from the representatives of the three most important special-interest groups in the DNVP party organization: agriculture, industry, and Christian-social labor. The leaders of the National Rural League, the vast majority of whom still regarded themselves as loyal adherents of the DNVP, were fearful that Hugenberg's uncompromising opposition to any sort of accommodation with Germany's republican system of government would

[101] Report on the annual meeting of the DNVP Pomeranian district organization in Stettin, 23 June 1928, BA Koblenz, NL Schlange-Schöningen, 19/10–25.
[102] For the districts aligned with Hugenberg, see Hilpert, "Meinungen und Kämpfe," BHStA Munich, Abt. V, NL Hilpert, 18/3667.
[103] Reichert to Reusch, 17 July 1928, BA Koblenz, NL Lambach, 10a.
[104] Wegener to Rojahn-Wabnitz, 25 July 1928, BA Koblenz, NL Wegener, 11.
[105] Entries in Quaatz's diary, 27 July and 7 Aug. 1928, BA Koblenz, NL Quaatz, 16.

make it difficult for them to advance their legislative agenda in the Reichstag. No issue in this regard was more pressing than the upcoming negotiations on the German-Polish trade treaty.[106] At the same time, the RLB's ties to the DNVP were also strained by virtue of the fact that there was no longer one, but two conservative parties with a strong commitment to the welfare of the German farmer, the DNVP and CNBLP.[107] In cognizance of this fact, the RLB approved a sweeping reorganization of its leadership structure 1 August 1928, the central feature of which was the creation of a three-person presidium in which each of the three major sectors of the German agricultural community – estate agriculture from east of the Elbe, the middle-sized peasanty of central Germany, and small peasant proprietors from the northern and western parts of the country – would be represented by its own president. Accordingly, Schiele was chosen to serve in the presidium as the representative of estate agriculture, Hepp for the small and middle-sized peasants in the west, and Albrecht Bethge from Mark Brandenburg for the small, independent peasantry.[108] The genial and accommodating Schiele, who had served as minister of agriculture in the fourth Marx cabinet, would soon emerge as one of Hugenberg's sharpest critics within the DNVP.

By the same token, the leadership struggle within the DNVP was also having a profound impact on the party's relationship to German industry. For the most part, Germany's industrial magnates did not look with favor upon Hugenberg's bid for control of the DNVP. Among the twelve coal and steel industrialists who comprised the "Ruhrlade," only Fritz Thyssen sympathized with Hugenberg's political agenda, while the Gutehoffnungshütte's Paul Reusch and Fritz Springorum from Hoesch Steel Works in Dortmund supported Westarp in his efforts to retain control of the party. Meeting with Westarp on 5 July 1928, Reusch indicated that the Ruhr steel industry was willing to help the DNVP cover the deficit in its operating budget with a substantial contribution in the second half of the year but stipulated that this

---

[106] For example, see the letter from the members of the RLB presidium to Reich Chancellor Müller, 9 Nov. 1928, NL Westarp, Gärtringen, VN 99. See also Andreas Müller, *"Fällt der Bauer, stürzt der Staat." Deutschnationale Agrarpolitik 1928–1933* (Hamburg, 2003), 113–22.

[107] Kriegsheim, "Schlußfolgerungen des Reichs-Landbundes auf Grund der Wahlergebnisse vom 20. Mai 1928," 28 June 1928, BA Koblenz, NL Weilnböck, 17. See also the memorandum from Kriegsheim to the members of the RLB executive committee, 6 June 1928, ibid., 15.

[108] Nicolas, "Die Neuorganisation der Führungsorgane des Reichs-Landbundes," 16 Aug. 1928, BA Koblenz, NL Weilnböck, 15. See also the minutes of the meeting of the RLB regional chairmen, 31 July 1928, BA Berlin, R 8034 I, 50/105a–105d, as well as the report in *Reichs-Landbund* 8, no. 31 (4 Aug. 1928): 351–52. For further information, see Wilmowsky to Krupp, 2 Aug. 1928, HA Krupp Essen, FAH 23/502, and Reusch, 2 Aug. 1928, RWWA Cologne, Abt. 130, NL Reusch, 400101290/39.

commitment was to him personally and would not be honored if there was a change in the party leadership.[109] When Westarp formally resigned from the DNVP party chairmanship four days later, Reusch exploded with a bitter invective against the architect of Westarp's demise, Hugenberg. "I have," Reusch wrote to Springorum, "been following the activity of this man for more than twenty years, activity which has been neither fruitful nor useful for either his party or industry. On the contrary, it is now and has always been my conviction that Hugenberg's activities have inflicted enormous damage upon industry in the west."[110] Yet for all of his fury, Reusch had little leverage within the DNVP and was unable to use the resources at his disposal to influence the outcome of the leadership crisis.

No one in the DNVP felt more threatened by the prospect of Hugenberg's elevation to the party chairmanship than the party's Christian-Social faction. The Christian-Socials were deeply suspicious of Hugenberg's ties to Bang and the leaders of the "yellow" trade union movement and feared that his ascendancy to the party leadership would legitimate the struggle to undo all that organized labor had managed to accomplish since the fall of the Second Empire.[111] Moreover, the fact that one of their own – the DHV's Walther Lambach – had become a special target of the party's extreme right wing and was threatened with expulsion from the party for having questioned the DNVP's embrace of monarchism only exacerbated the uneasiness that the Christian-Socials felt about their prospects in a party under Hugenberg's control.[112] Lastly, the leaders of the DNVP's Christian-Social faction had already taken what many saw as the first step toward the creation of a new political party when they met on 14 June 1928 under the leadership of theologian Karl Veidt to found the Christian-Social Union (Christlich-soziale Vereinigung) as the crystallization point around which all of those within the DNVP who shared a commitment to the social gospel of Lutheran pastor Adolf Stoecker could unite.[113] On 18–19 August the Christian-Socials met in Bielefeld to finalize arrangements for the founding of the new organization, now known as the Christian-Social Reich Union (Christlich-soziale Reichsvereinigung or CSRV), and appointed a three-man committee consisting of DNVP Reichstag deputies Reinhard Mumm and Gustav Hülser along with

<hr/>

[109] Reusch to Springorum, 5 July 1928, RWWA Cologne, Abt. 130, NL Reusch, 400101293/9.
[110] Reusch to Springorum, 11 July 1928, RWWA Cologne, Abt. 130, NL Reusch, 400101290/36a.
[111] On Bang's hostility toward Lambach and his supporters, see his letter to Lambach, 16 June 1928, BA Koblenz, NL Lambach, 10/69–70.
[112] See Hartwig to Jacobi, 7 Aug. 1928; Rippel to Treviranus, 9 Aug. 1928; and Treviranus to Westarp, 8 Aug. 1928, NL Westarp, Gärtringen, VN 91.
[113] Circular from Veidt and Drebes, June 1928, BA Berlin, NL Mumm, 282/114.

Count Leopold von Baudissin from the Bodelschwingh Institute in Bethel to share its leadership responsibilities.[114] All of this raised the spectre of a Christian-Social secession from the DNVP should Hugenberg and the social reactionaries supporting his candidacy succeed in taking over control of the party.

Hugenberg's Road to Victory

In the meantime, the Lambach affair worked its way through the various levels of the DNVP party organization. On 24 July 1928 – two weeks after the DNVP district organization in Potsdam II had initiated expulsion proceedings against Lambach for having supposedly damaged the image of the party with his attack on monarchism – Lambach was officially expelled from both the party and the Reichstag delegation and given four weeks in which to appeal this decision.[115] The matter was now referred to a special party court that could either annul the decision or let it stand. The reaction to this development was predictable. Baron Axel von Freytagh-Loringhoven, chairman of the DNVP's National Racist Committee and a close Hugenberg ally, applauded Lambach's expulsion as an important step toward the creation of a German Right that made up in unity for what it might have lacked in size,[116] while the DHV's Max Habermann warned that the triumph of Hugenberg's monolithic conception of the party could only lead to a rapid deterioration of his own organization's relations with the DNVP and the collapse of the *Querverbindungen* that the DHV and its allies in the Christian labor movement had built up since the end of the war.[117] The gravity of the crisis became apparent as most of the DNVP's white-collar organizations throughout the country came out in support of Lambach's reinstatement and in some cases even evoked the specter of a general secession on the DNVP's left wing should his explusion be upheld.[118] No doubt pressure of this sort played a role when on 29 August the

---

[114] On developments in Bielefeld, see the report on the meeting of the Christian-Social leadership, 18 Aug. 1928, and the national conference of the Christian-Socials, 19 Aug. 1928, BA Berlin, NL Mumm, 282/167–71, 185–92, as well as the official report of the Bielefeld congress in *Angestelltenstimme und Arbeiterstimme*, ed. Deutschnationaler Angestelleten- und Arbeiter-Bünde 8, no. 9 (Sept. 1928): 2–4. On the aims of the Christian-Socials, see Hülser, "Die Arbeiterschaft und die neue Rechte," *Der Tag*, 7 Aug. 1928, no. 188.

[115] *Deutsche Allgemeine Zeitung*, 26 July 1928, nos. 345–46.

[116] Freytagh-Loringhoven, "Nicht große, sondern starke Rechte," *Der Tag*, 25 July 1928, no. 177.

[117] Habermann, "Querverbindungen. Eine politische Betrachtung zum 'Fall Lambach'," *Deutsche Handels-Wacht* 35, no. 14 (25 July 1928): 281–82.

[118] *Einige Stimmen aus der durch den Aufsatz Monarchismus von Walther Lambach, M.d.R., im Gang gebrachten Aussprache* (Hamburg, 1928), 38–48.

party court to which Lambach had appealed his expulsion announced that it had reversed the decision of the DNVP district organization in Potsdam II and had reinstated the deputy to full membership in the party and Reichstag delegation with little more than a reprimand for impropriety.[119]

Westarp had hoped that Lambach's reinstatement would give the DNVP an opportunity to restore discipline in the party, clarify its basic values with a reaffirmation of its commitment to monarchism, and announce an aggressive social policy that would solidy its position within the Christian-national working class.[120] But the immediate effect of Lambach's reinstatement was to energize the oppositionist elements on the DNVP's right wing in their assault against Westarp's leadership of the party. On 5 September representatives from the fifteen DNVP state and provincial organizations that had supported Hugenberg earlier that summer met in Berlin under Dommes's chairmanship to pass a resolution condemning Lambach's reinstatement as a betrayal of the principles for which the DNVP had always stood. At the same time, they petitioned Westarp to convene another meeting of the DNVP party representation so that the leadership crisis that currently paralyzed the party could be resolved for once and for all.[121] In the meantime, Hugenberg's confederates stepped up their efforts at the local level of the DNVP organization so that by the end of the summer the number of state and provincial organizations firmly committed to Hugenberg had risen to seventeen with another four leaning heavily in his direction.[122] At a minimum, Hugenberg's supporters hoped to implement a plan drafted by Steinhoff and Quaatz for a full-scale reorganization of the party's leadership structure that would undercut the influence that Westarp had amassed through the personal union of the party chairmanship with that of the Reichstag delegation. Not only would this presumably result in significant budgetary savings, but more importantly it would have the effect of weakening the DNVP's character as a parliamentary party and make its parliamentary delegations more responsive to the demands of its state and provincial organizations.[123]

As Hugenberg and his supporters forged ahead with their sundry schemes to gain control of the DNVP, they too became increasingly concerned about

---

[119] Decision of the DNVP party court, 29 Aug. 1928, NL Westarp, Gärtringen, VN 91.

[120] Kuno von Westarp, *Aufgaben der Deutschnationalen Volkspartei*, Deutschnationale Flugschrift, no. 330 (Berlin, 1928), 6–12.

[121] Kreisverein Potsdam der DNVP, "Bericht über die heutige Besprechung in Berlin, Dessauerstraße 14," 5 Sept. 1928, records of the DNVP county organization in Aurich, Niedersächsisches Staatsarchiv Aurich, Depositum 51, 1/523–26. See also Hilpert, "Meinungen und Kämpfe," BHStA Munich, Abt. V, NL Hilpert, 18/3694–95.

[122] Wegener to Rojahn-Wabnitz, 25 July 1928, and Hassel, 31 July 1928, both in BA Koblenz, NL Wegener, 11.

[123] Steinhoff and Quaatz, "Denkschrift zur Reform der Parteiorganisation," 1 Oct. 1928, BA Koblenz, NL Wegener, 31, also in NL Westarp, Gärtringen, II/30.

the possibility of a secession that might extend far beyond the Christian trade-union elements on the party's left wing. In marked contrast to the situation on the party's right wing, Hugenberg's opponents on the DNVP's left wing found themselves in a state of complete disarray. On 4 September Martin Schiele and Wilhelm Koch, both former ministers in the fourth Marx cabinet and spokes-men for the DNVP's agrarian and Christian-Social labor wings respectively, met with Westarp in an attempt to persuade him to stand for reelection to the DNVP party chairmanship.[124] Two days later Westarp received a delegation of Christian-Social labor leaders including Koch and DNAB chairman Emil Hartwig, who pleaded with him to challenge Hugenberg and his supporters and stand for reelection in so far as that was the only possible solution to the DNVP's leadership crisis.[125] But Westarp, who still harbored a great deal of anger over the way in which he had been treated by Hugenberg, remained non-committal and did nothing to encourage further efforts on his behalf. In the meantime, another candidacy surfaced in the person of former Reich minister of the interior Walther von Keudell, who had the gall to present himself as the candidate of the "younger generation."[126] Gradually Hugen-berg's opponents began to crystallize into a small group under the leadership of Koch and Pomeranian landowner Hans Schlange-Schöningen. A one-time antisemite and an outspoken opponent of Germany's republican system, Schlange-Schöningen had emerged as one of the DNVP's most committed and eloquent moderates.[127] On 8 October he and Bernhard Leopold, an industrialist and member of the DNVP Reichstag delegation, met with repre-sentatives from the district organizations that were not yet under Hugenberg's control and other party moderates to formulate a strategy for retaining control of the party. Not only did those around Schlange-Schöningen reject the idea of a triumvirate as incompatible with the goal of effective political leadership, but they sent a delegation to Hugenberg and his supporters recommending that the two factions unite behind Westarp's reelection as DNVP party chair-man.[128] Three days later, however, Westarp instructed Schlange-Schöningen and his associates to suspend their efforts on his behalf and categorically

[124] Ada Gräfin von Westarp to Gertraude Freifrau Hiller von Gaertringen, 4 Sept. 1928, NL Westarp, Gärtringen.

[125] Ibid., 6 Sept. 1928, NL Westarp, Gärtringen.

[126] On the Keudell candidacy, see the letters from Otto von Keudell to Tirpitz, 21 Aug. and 25 Sept. 1928, BA-MA Freiburg, NL Tirpitz, 278/68–69, 74–75.

[127] Entry in diary of Karl Passarge, 14 Oct. 1928, BA Koblenz, Nachlass Passarge, 1/49–53. On Schlange-Schöningen, see Günter J. Trittel, "Hans Schlange-Schöningen. Ein ver-gessener Politiker der 'Ersten Stunde'," *Vierteljahrshefte für Zeitgeschichte* 35 (1987): 25–63, esp. 26–32.

[128] Memorandum on the meeting of DNVP moderates, 8 Oct. 1928, appended to Leopold to Westarp, 16 Oct. 1928, NL Westarp, Gärtringen, II/30.

dissociated himself from the idea of a triumvirate as propagated by Quaatz and other Hugenberg supporters.[129]

Westarp's refusal to seek reelection to the DNVP party chairmanship or to participate in the proposed triumvirate dealt a severe blow to the efforts of party moderates to keep Hugenberg from gaining control of the party. In the meantime, the forces around Hugenberg moved quickly to exploit the disorganization of their opponents. As late as the first week of October Hugenberg had been contemplating the possibility of organizing a secession from the DNVP should his efforts to bring about a change in the party leadership fail.[130] The following day, however, Hugenberg informed Quaatz that Dommes would present his name as a candidate for the party chairmanship, presumably as a way of frightening his opponents into accepting the creation of a triumvirate as an alternative to his own election.[131] When the seventeen DNVP district organizations supporting his candidacy met on 8 October to give unanimous approval to a resolution endorsing Hugenberg's election as DNVP party chairman, Hugenberg reserved judgement and declined to commit himself to accepting the chairmanship.[132] The following day Hugenberg wrote to Maximilian von Dziembowski, the Saxon envoy in Munich with close ties to both the DNVP and Stahlhelm, and encouraged the leaders of the Bavarian Middle Party – as the DNVP's Bavarian chapter was generally known – to endorse the creation of a triumvirate as the best possible solution to the leadership crisis.[133] The BMP had generally supported Westarp's political line from 1924 to 1928 only to suffer abnormally heavy losses in the state and national elections in the spring of 1928.[134] Hans Hilpert, chairman of the state party organization, saw a direct connection between his party's decline and its participation in state and national governments and had begun, much against his initial inclination, to slide into the Hugenberg camp.[135] Consequently, when the leaders of the DNVP's Bavarian state organization met on 13 October to determine the position their delegates would take when

---

[129] Ada Gräfin von Westarp to Gertraude Freifrau Hiller von Gaertringen, 11 Oct. 1928, NL Westarp, Gärtringen. See also Westarp's memorandum, "Parteiführung oder Parteivorsitzender," appended to Weiß, "Erwiderung auf die 'Denkschrift zur Reform der Parteiorganisation'," 15 Oct. 1928, ibid., II/30.

[130] Notes by Wegener, 4 Oct. 1928, BA Koblenz, NL Wegener, 65/285.

[131] Entry in Quaatz's diary, 5 Oct. 1928, BA Koblenz, NL Quaatz, 16.

[132] Report on the meeting of seventeen DNVP district organizations in Berlin, 8 Oct. 1928, appended to a circular from Dommes, 8 Oct. 1928, NL Westarp, Gärtringen, II/30. See also Hilpert, "Meinungen und Kämpfe," BHStA Munich, Abt. V, NL Hilpert, 18/3696–3700.

[133] Hugenberg to Dziembowski, 9 Oct. 1928, BHStA Munich, Abt. V, Nachlass Maximilian Dziembowski, 16.

[134] Kiiskinen, DNVP in Bayern, 244–313.

[135] On Hilpert's dilemma, see Manfred Kittel, "Zwischen völkischem Fundamentalismus und gouvernementaler Taktik," 882–85.

the DNVP convened to elect a new party leader, they forced Hilpert's hand by adopting a resolution that expressed "full confidence in the person of Hugenberg" and announced its support "for a new leadership of the party with Hugenberg."[136] Although the phrase "with Hugenberg" left open the question whether this would take the form of a triumvirate or Hugenberg's outright election as DNVP party chairman, the action of the Bavarian DNVP nevertheless tipped the balance in Hugenberg's favor.

Hugenberg's election was far from certain when the DNVP representation convened in Berlin on 20–21 October 1928 to resolve the party's leadership crisis. By now it was possible to distinguish between at least three different factions in the party. First, there were the seventeen DNVP district organizations that had consistently supported Hugenberg in his efforts to gain control of the party and reverse the direction in which it had been headed since 1924–25. Second, there was a smaller contingent of ten more moderate district organizations that had coalesced behind Schlange-Schöningen and Leopold and rejected the Hugenberg faction's not so subtle threats of a secession as a crude attempt to unilaterally impose Hugenberg upon the DNVP as its new party chairman.[137] Between these two factions stood a third and even smaller group of technically uncommitted district organizations led by Bavaria and Württemberg that sought to preserve party unity through a compromise that was amenable to the other two groups.[138] But, as the resolution adopted by the leaders of the Bavarian DNVP clearly demonstrated, local party leaders there were sympathetic to Hugenberg's candidacy even though they had not gone so far as to formally endorse his bid for the party chairmanship. Three days after the Bavarian DNVP had met, Hugenberg's supporters scored a similar success with Walther Hirzel and the leaders of the DNVP's Württemberg affiliate, the Württemberg Burgher Party.[139] Just as everything seemed to be falling in place for Hugenberg and his associates, his opponents were still without a viable candidate and pinned what remained of their hopes of stopping Hugenberg on convincing a reluctant Oskar Hergt, the former DNVP party chairman from 1918 to 1924, to challenge Hugenberg for the leadership of the party.[140]

[136] Minutes of the meeting of the state executive committee of the Bavarian DNVP, 13 Oct. 1928, BHStA Munich, Abt. V, NL Hilpert, 1/10–14, as well as Hilpert's memoirs, "Meinungen und Kämpfe," ibid., 18/3706–08. See also Dziembowski to Lüttichau, 14 Oct. 1928, BHStA Munich, Abt. V, NL Dziembowski, 14. For further details, see Kiiskinen, DNVP in Bayern, 314–28.
[137] Resolution circulated by Lüttichau from the DNVP district organization in East Saxony, 13 Oct. 1928, NL Westarp, Gärtringen, VN 15.
[138] Hilpert, "Meinungen und Kämpfe," BHStA Munich, Abt. V, NL Hilpert, 18/3693–94.
[139] Entry in Quaatz's diary, 16 Oct. 1928, BA Koblenz, NL Quaatz, 16.
[140] Ada Gräfin von Westarp to Gertraude Freifrau Hiller von Gaertringen, 17 Oct. 1928, NL Westarp, Gärtringen.

"What happens today in this room may very well be a turning point in the history of the entire German nation." With these words Westarp opened the meeting of the DNVP party representation in Berlin on 20 October 1928.[141] But even as Westarp began his remarks, Hugenberg's followers began to distribute copies of Hugenberg's letter to Westarp from September 1927 and of his article "Bloc oder Brei?" among the more than 300 delegates in attendance along with a cover letter in which Hugenberg claimed that the moment had arrived for the DNVP to decide "whether it was to be reborn as the great ideological movement it had once been or would continue to degenerate into a tool of Germany's parliamentary system."[142] At the outset, however, it seemed as if the moderates had gained the upper hand as the result of a skillful counterattack orchestrated by Siegfried Lüttichau from the party's East Saxon organization against the proposal of four pro-Hugenberg, yet technically uncommitted provincial organizations – Bavaria, Württemberg, East Prussia, and Frankfurt an der Oder – to entrust the party leadership to a triumvirate consisting of Hugenberg, Westarp, and a representative from the party in Prussia.[143] The goal of this action, as Lüttichau explained to a colleague in Bavaria, was to protect the party against the convulsions that Hugenberg's election to the party chairmanship would almost certainly bring and to work out a compromise that would enable Westarp to maintain his firm hand at the helm of the party.[144] But whatever headway the moderates had made in derailing the idea of a triumvirate quickly evaporated when Keudell took the podium to launch a bitter personal attack against Hugenberg. Keudell alleged that Hugenberg was nothing but the pawn of special economic interests whose easy access to the campaign coffers of Ruhr heavy industry had severely irreparably tarnished the party in the eyes of the younger generation.[145]

[141] Westarp's speech before the DNVP party representation, 20 Oct. 1928, NL Westarp, NL Gärtringen, II/30. On the meeting, see the entry in Quaatz's diary, 21 Oct. 1928, BA Koblenz, NL Quaatz, 16, as well as the account in Hilpert, "Meinungen und Kämpfe," BHStA Munich, Abt. V, NL Hilpert, 18/3717–28, and Reichert to Reusch, 22 Oct. 1928, RWWA Cologne, Abt. 130, NL Reusch, 400101293/9.

[142] These documents, in addition to Hugenberg's cover letter of 18 Oct. 1928, are in BA Koblenz, NL Wegener, 31, also in NL Westarp, Gärtringen, II/30.

[143] See the text of Lüttichau's resolution as an attachment to his note to Westarp, 13 Oct. 1928, NL Westarp, Gärtringen, VN 15. On the fate of this proposal, see Schlange-Schöningen to Passarge, 21 Oct. 1928, BA Koblenz, NL Passarge, 11/21, and Mumm's statement on Hugenberg's election to the DNVP party chairmanship, n.d., NL Westarp, Gärtringen, II/30.

[144] Lüttichau to Dziembowski, 11 Oct. 1928, BHStA Munich, Abt. V, NL Dziembowski, 14.

[145] For the text of Keudell's remarks, see "Betrifft: Die Differenz zwischen Herrn Reichsminister a.D. von Keudell und Herrn Geheimen Finanzrat Dr. Hugenberg, beide Mitglieder der Deutschnationalen Reichstagsfraktion," n.d. [fall 1929], NL Westarp, Gärtringen, II/30. For Keudell's possible motives, see the letter from Otto von Keudell to Tirpitz, 11 Nov. 1928, BA-MA Freiburg, NL Tirpitz, 278/76–80.

Hugenberg responded to Keudell's attacks not in kind but with a magnanimity that dismarmed his opponents and reassured his supporters that he was indeed the man of the hour.[146] Even a shocked and exasperated Westarp rose to Hugenberg's defense against Keudell's allegations.[147] The tide had indeed turned in Hugenberg's favor, and after a brief recess the four provincial organizations that had originally proposed the formation of a triumvirate withdrew their motion and recommended that Hugenberg be elected as the sole leader of the DNVP. At this point Hergt, the man upon whom the moderates had pinned their last hopes of keeping Hugenberg from the party chairmanship, withdrew his name from consideration, leaving the moderates without a candidate. Sensing that their moment had at long last arrived, Hugenberg's backers immediately moved that the assembly simply vote yes or no on Hugenberg's candidacy. In the subsequent vote Hugenberg prevailed, but by a margin so narrow that it was never made public and that may have been no more than a single vote.[148]

Hugenberg's election to the DNVP party chairmanship on 20 October 1928 represented a critical turning in the history of the German Right. Not only did it spell the definitive collapse of Stresemann's efforts to stabilize the republic from the right, but it left a party that was deeply divided between governmental conservatives and radical nationalists, between those like Schiele, Treviranus, and Lindeiner-Wildau who sought to pursue conservative objectives within the framework of the German republic and who who behind the banner of Hugenberg and the Pan-Germans rejected any sort of compromise with the existing political order and were determined to transform the DNVP into an instrument of the radical Right. The latent antipathy that had existed between these two factions on the German Right ever since the founding of the Weimar Republic had now been transformed into an open split that threatened not just the unity of the DNVP but the future of Weimar democracy itself.

[146] Entry in Quaatz's diary, 21 Oct. 1928, BA Koblenz, NL Quaatz, 16.
[147] "Erklärung, abgegeben von Graf Westarp nach der Rede des Ministers v. Keudell am 20.10.1928," BA NL Westarp, Gärtringen, II/30.
[148] Gottfried Reinhold Treviranus, *Das Ende von Weimar. Heinrich Brüning und seine Zeit* (Düsseldorf, 1968), 99.

14

Reverberations and Realignment

On 9 November 1928 the Weimar Republic celebrated the tenth anniversary of the fall of the Second Empire and the proclamation of the German Republic. Whereas in republican circles the events of a decade earlier were celebrated in a subdued and respectful manner that reflected the strength of republican conviction, on the radical Right this signaled the beginning of a renewed offensive against the social and political legacy of the November Revolution as conservatives and nationalists alike joined in a rising crescendo of condemnation of Germany's republican order.[1] Hugenberg's election to the chairmanship of the German National People's Party in the fall of 1928, therefore, was not an isolated incident but must be seen in the context of a renewed militancy on the part of the radical Right that extended well beyond the boundaries of the DNVP. The effects of Hugenberg's election to the DNVP party chairmanship were by no means confined to his own party but would be felt throughout the bourgeois spectrum of German party life. The deteriorating economic situation, particularly in the countryside and the independent middle class, only intensified the forces of social and political disintegration that were at work within the bourgeois party system, with the result that the integrative potential of those parties that conceived of themselves as sociologically heterogeneous "people's parties" would be severely challenged. The magnitude of the socialist victory in the 1928 elections and the transfer of power to a new government headed by the Social Democrats had set in motion a pronounced shift to the right that could be seen in differing degrees in all of the parties from the DDP to the DNVP. Seen from this perspective, the Lambach affair in the DNVP was not an isolated event

---

[1] For example, see memorial speeches by Kuno von Westarp, *Zehn Jahre republikanische Unfreiheit. Das Verbrechen vom 9. November und seine Folgen* (Berlin, n.d. [1928]); Martin Hauffe, *Rede gehalten am 9. November 1928 in der großen nationalen Kundgebung des Stahlhelms Dresden in Zirkus Sarrasani* (N.p., n.d. [1928]); and Rüdiger von der Goltz, *Ernste Gedanken zum 10. Geburtstag der deutschen Republik 9.11.1928* (Berlin, n.d. [1928]).

but part of a more general process that mirrored events in the DVP and Center.[2] And throughout all of this, Hugenberg and his supporters on the patriotic Right were doing what they could to polarize the German party system into two mutually antagonistic camps and to push the crystallization point around which an increasingly fractured German bourgeoisie might reconstitute itself more and more to the right.

Turmoil in the People's Party

Hugenberg's election as DNVP party chairman had immediate repercussion on the situation in the ranks of its one-time coalition partner, the German People's Party. The DVP had been in the grip of a crisis ever since the 1928 Reichstag elections and its participation in the cabinet that Social Democrat Hermann Müller formed with Stresemann's strong support in the last week of June. Stresemann's willingness to collaborate with the Social Democrats had met with strong opposition from the DVP's right wing and the influential chairman of the DVP Reichstag delegation Ernst Scholz.[3] Although Stresemann moved quickly to reassert his authority as the party's chairman as forcefully as possible, the conflict with his party's right wing gave him pause to look beyond the current party crisis into the future development of the German party system. Not only did Stresemann cultivate closer ties with DDP party chairman Erich Koch-Weser in the hopes that this might help hold his party's right wing in check,[4] but he also reached out to August Weber and the leadership of the Liberal Association (Liberale Vereinigung), an organization founded in 1924 that sought to bring unite the DDP and DVP into a single liberal party.[5] But Stresemann was interested in far more than the simple merger of the DDP and DVP and hoped ultimately for the creation of a comprehensive bourgeois party that extended from the right wing of the DDP to the more moderate elements on the DNVP's left wing. Only through

---

[2] See Patch, *Christian Trade Unions*, 125–56, and Hartmut Roder, *Der christlich-nationale Deutsche Gewerkschaftsbund (DGB) im politisch-ökonomischen Kräftefeld der Weimarer Republik* (Frankfurt a.M., Bern, and New York, 1986), 441–53.

[3] For further details, see Jones, *German Liberalism*, 314–16, and Wright, *Stresemann*, 421–28, as well as Ludwig Richter, "Führungskrise in der DVP. Gustav Stresemann im Kampf um die 'Große Koalition' 1928/29," in *Demokratie in Deutschland. Chancen und Gefährdungen im 19. und 20. Jahrhundert. Historische Essays*, ed. Wolther von Kieseritzky and Klaus-Peter Sick (Munich, 1999), 202–27.

[4] Correspondence between Koch-Weser and Stresemann, 16–25 June 1928, PA AA Berlin, NL Stresemann, 68/167019–22, 167937.

[5] Stresemann to Weber, 5 July 1928, PA AA Berlin, NL Stresemann, 105/175126–27. See also Stresemann's remarks at a banquet organized by the Liberal Association on 1 February 1926, in *Die Liberale Vereinigung* (Berlin, n.d. [1926]), 13–14. For further details, see Jones, *German Liberalism*, esp. 271–78, 309–14.

the creation of such a party, Stresemann wrote to the Saxon industrialist Rudolf Schneider, would it be possible to check the growing influence of organized economic interests and reverse the decline of Germany's liberal parties.[6]

Before Stresemann had an opportunity to follow up on his overtures to the DDP and Liberal Association, his party was rocked by another crisis involving the German Right, in this case the Stahlhelm. Stresemann had always tried to cultivate good relations with the Stahlhelm and other organizations on the paramilitary Right in the hope that they might eventually be won over to the support of the Republic and his foreign policy.[7] But the ourcome of the 1928 Reichstag elections and particularly the strong showing by the Social Democrats had come as a rude shock to the leaders of the Stahlhelm and had only intensified their sense of urgency about the plight of the national cause.[8] At the same time, Hugenberg's bid for the DNVP party chairmanship had done much to excite the antirepublican fervor of the Stahlhelm leadership and to frustrate Stresemann's hopes of stabilizing the republic from the Right. At no point was this more apparent than when Elhard von Morosowicz, the leader of the Stahlhelm's Brandenburg section, issued his infamous "Fürsten-wald Hate Declaration" at a demonstration in early September 1928. "We hate the present form of government," Morosowicz exclaimed, "with all our hearts – its form and content, its appearance and essence... For us there is only the uncompromising struggle against the system that dominates today's state."[9] The "Fürstenwald Hate Declaration" came as the last and most blatant in a long series of developments that threatened to end in a complete rupture of his party's relations with the veterans' association .[10]

Stresemann reacted to Morosowicz's declaration of hatred against Ger-many's republican system by insisting that those members of the DVP Reichstag and Prussian Landtag delegations who still belonged to the Stahl-helm must announce their resignation with a public statement that, he hoped, would ignite a general secession from the organization on the part of DVP members throughout the country.[11] At the time, no less than seven

---

[6] Stresemann to Schneider, 11 July 1928, PA AA Berlin, NL Stresemann, 101/174305–06.

[7] Bernhard's protocol of a meeting between Stresemann, Seldte, and Duesterberg, 1 Oct. 1927, PA AA Berlin, NL Stresemann, 354/488. See also Stresemann to Carl, 7 Nov. 1927, ibid., 98/173687–88.

[8] Jüttner to the Stahlhelm leadership, 11 July 1928, StA Mönchen-Gladbach, NL Brauweiler, 117.

[9] Morosowicz, "Fürstenwalder Botschaft," n.d. [Sept. 1928], BA-MA Freiburg, Nachlasssplitter Elhard von Morosowicz, MSg 2/11675. For the text of Morosowicz's speech, see Elhard von Morosowicz, Die "Haß"-Botschaft von Fürstenwalde (Oranienberg and Beinau, n.d. [1928]).

[10] Stresemann to Kempkes, 23 Sept. 1928, PA AA Berlin, NL Stresemann, 102/174412–13.

[11] Stresemann to Scholz, 26 Sept. 1928, PA AA Berlin, NL Stresemann, 102/174418–20.

of the DVP's forty-five Reichstag deputies, including its chairman Ernst Scholz, were members of the Stahlhelm and had seen no contradiction between belonging to the DVP and belonging to the Stahlhelm. But Scholz, who had had his differences with Stresemann over the course of the preceding months, agreed with his party chairman that a break with the Stahlhelm could no longer be avoided. With Scholz taking the lead, the DVP Reichstag delegation proceeded to adopt a resolution that recommended that all office-holders in the DVP party organization – this referred first and foremost to those who sat in the Reichstag or a state legislature – should resign from the Stahlhelm. The fact that the resolution did not also call upon party members to follow their lead reflected a desire on the part of the DVP party leadership not to make the situation any worse than it already was and to minimize the damage that Morosowicz's declaration had already done to relations between the two organizations.[12]

Furstrated by what was happening on the German Right, Stresemann began to show renewed interest in the theme of bourgeois concentration. To Stresemann and his circle of associates, the recent developments in the DNVP and Stahlhelm only underscored the imperative of strengthening the political middle through the establishment of closer ties between the various non-confessional parties and organizations that stood to the left of the DNVP. Writing to his colleague Alfred Zapf in the wake of Hugenberg's victory, Stresemann characterized the party's failure to release the margin of Hugenberg's victory as "an monstrosity [*eine Groteske*] that was unprecedented in [German] party life," adding that "the beginning is dark and the end could be civil war."[13] To address this situation, Stresemann proposed a reform of the DVP's national organization that would not only prevent a recurrence of the crisis that had erupted earlier that summer but free the party from the control of the business interests that had entrenched themsvles on its right wing in the hope that this would attract the support of the disaffected white-collar and working-class elements from the DNVP. Stresemann immediately enlitsted the cooperation of Otto Thiel, a member of the DVP Reichstag delegation who, like Lambach, functioned as a liaison between his party and the German National Union of Commercial Employees. Thiel shared Stresemann's concerns about the future of the DVP, and at a meeting of its central executive committee in November

[12] Minutes of the executive committee of the DVP Reichstag delegation, 2 Oct. 1928, BA Koblenz, R 45 II, 366/125–38. See also Scholz to Stresemann, 1 Oct. 1928, PA AA Berlin, NL Stresemann, 102/174429, and Karl von Schoch, "Stahlhelm, Deutsche Volkspartei und Volksbegehren," *Deutsche Allgemeine Zeitung*, 19 Oct. 1928, nos. 489–90. For further details, see Richter, *Deutsche Volkspartei*, 509–16, and Berghahn, *Stahlhelm*, 103–14.
[13] Stresemann to Zapf, 23 Oct. 1928, PA AA Berlin, NL Stresemann, 102/174478–80.

1928 he presented plans for a organizational reform of the party that would strengthen the position of its younger, middle-class, and working-class elements within the DVP party organization and check the influence of the industrial interests that stood on its right wing.[14]

Before Stresemann had an opportunity to act on Thiel's plans for an organizational reform of the DVP, the party was convulsed by yet another internal crisis that struck at Stresemann's authority as party chairman. In November 1928 Reich chancellor Hermann Müller reopened negotiations with the Center to fulfull a promise he had made the previous summer to reorganize his government and broaden its base basis at the earliest possible opportunity. Still embittered over its failure to secure a seat in the Prussian government in return for its support of the Müller cabinet, the DVP Reichstag delegation saw in this an excellent opportunity not only to revisit the Prussian question once again but also to voice its concerns in the areas of budgetary and tax policy.[15] Although Stresemann was eventually able to rescue the "Great Coalition" from the antics of his party's right wing,[16] the episode left him deeply discouraged about the future of his party and revived his interest in a comprehensive bourgeois party reaching from the right wing of the DDP to the left wing of the DNVP.[17] Pinning his hopes on the idealism of the younger generation, Stresemann threw his full support behind a new political club known as the "Front 1929" that his biographer and protégé Baron Rochus von Rheinbaben had founded in the early spring of 1929.[18] Meeting with Rheinbaben and the founders of the "Front 1929" in late April, Stresemann encouraged them not to limit their efforts to the development of closer ties between the two liberal parties but to seek the support and cooperation of the anti-Hugenberg dissidents on the DNVP's left wing. The future of the German party system and with it the fate of the German republic, Stresemann argued, lay in the hands of the younger generation and its ability to fuse like-minded elements across the political spectrum into a dynamic force capable of transforming German political life.[19]

---

[14] Otto Thiel, "Die Deutsche Volkspartei," in *Internationales Handwörterbuch des Gewerkschaftswesens*, ed. Ludwig Heyde, 2 vols. (Berlin, 1931–32) 1:347–49. For the details of Thiel's plans, see "Denkschrift über die Reorganisation der Deutschen Volkspartei," 31 Dec. 1928, appended to Thiel, to the members of the DVP executive committee, 5 Jan. 1929, BA Koblenz, NL Jarres, 41.

[15] Scholz, "Sachlichkeit," *Nationalliberale Correspondenz*, 6 Mar. 1929, no. 49.

[16] For further details, see Jones, *German Liberalism*, 319–22; Wright, *Stresemann*, 445–61; and Richter, *Deutsche Volkspartei*, 530–40, as well as the article by Richter cited in n. 2.

[17] Stresemann to Kahl, 13 Mar. 1929, PA AA Berlin, NL Stresemann, 104/174722–33.

[18] In this respect, see Rheinbaben to Stresemann, 23 Mar. 1929, ibid., 78/169430–35.

[19] Memorandum of a conversation between Stresemann, Bernhard, Rheinbaben, and Stein, 26 Apr. 1929, ibid., 105/174987–88. In a similar vein, see Stresemann to Zöphel, 15 Apr. 1929, ibid., 105/174941–44.

The Center's Confessional Gambit

By no means was the ferment that existed within the ranks of the DVP and DNVP in the late 1920s confined to these two parties. To the contrary, the German Center Party, outwardly the healthiest and most stable of Germany's nonsocialist parties, found itself in the grips of a crisis that was every bit as ominous as those that were tearing apart the predominantly Protestant parties to its immediate right.[20] To be sure, the Center's close identification with the values and institutions of the Catholic faith gave it a measure of internal coherence that its Protestant counterparts sorely lacked.[21] But not even this had adequately insulated the Center against the processes of social and political disintegration that were at work throughout Germany's bourgeois party system. The Center too had sustained heavy losses in the 1928 Reichstag elections, seeing its share of the popular vote fall from 13.6 in December 1924 to 12.0 percent in 1928 and losing seven of its sixty-nine deputies in the Reichstag. Center loyalists were quick to interpret this as "the breakthrough of class conflict" into the ranks of the party, a development that placed its long-term prospects in serious doubt. Whether the Center's losses had stemmed from defections to the Social Democrats by Catholic workers in the Rhineland and Westphalia or from defections to the Business Party on the part of its middle-class supporters or from the estrangement of the Catholic peasantry, the common denominator underlying each of these trends was the increasingly high priority that important segments of Germany's Catholic electorate had come to place upon economic as opposed to confessional issues. The most alarming statistic of all was the fact that the percentage of eligible Catholic voters who supported the Center or the Bavarian People's Party had fallen from 85 percent in 1870 and 55 percent in 1912 to 48 percent in 1928. But even this concealed the true extent of the Center's deteriorating position within the Catholic electorate, for it included women voters who had been enfranchised only in 1919 and who generally supported the Center more enthusiastically than their male counterparts. Of male Catholic voters, only 39 percent still supported the Center in 1928.[22]

In October 1928 Wilhelm Marx tendered his resignation as party chairman in order to expedite a resolution of the crisis in which the Center found itself.[23] The hier apparent to the position Marx had held for the previous seven years

---

[20] Becker, "Wirth und die Krise des Zentrums," 361–482.

[21] Karsten Ruppert, "Die weltanschaulich bedingte Politik der Deutschen Zentrumspartei in ihrer Weimarer Epoche," *Historische Zeitschrift* 285 (2007): 49–97.

[22] Johannes Schauff, *Das Wahlverhalten der deutschen Katholiken im Kaiserreich und in der Weimarer Republik. Untersuchungen aus dem Jahre 1928*, ed. and with an introduction by Rudolf Morsey (Mainz, 1975), 191–204. See also Ruppert, *Im Dienst am Staat von Weimar*, 315–29.

[23] Hehl, *Marx*, 455–62.

was Adam Stegerwald, the acting chairman of the Center Reichstag delegation. Stegerwald had remained faithful to the spirit of his "Essen Program" from 1920 and still envisaged the creation of a large, socially heterogeneous, inter-confessional "people's bloc" as the only viable solution to the problem of Germany's social and political fragmentation.[24] Stegerwald, who continued to serve as chairman of both the United Federation of Christian Trade Unions and the German Trade-Union Federation, launched his candidacy with a programmatic speech at a party conference in Alternberg on 23–24 September 1928. Here Stegerwald deplored the fragmentation of Germany's Catholic electorate into factions both within and outside the Center that placed primary emphasis on the representation of special economic interests and not on the welfare of the state and nation as a whole. What this reflected, Stegerwald lamented, was an inadequate sense on the part of the vast majority of the German people – Catholics included – of what it meant to be a citizen whose primary loyalties lay not with the class, estate, or special-interest group to which one belonged but to the state and the national community, or *Lebens-gemeinschaft*, it served. To remedy this deficiency in Germany's political culture, Stegerwald argued, the Center must rebaptize itself as a party that no longer conceived of itself as the representative of specifically Catholic interests but as one whose primary responsibilities lay in reconciling the interests and welfare of all those who made up the German nation as a party that represented the entire German family in all of its social, regional, and confessional diversity.[25]

When the executive committee of the Center met in Berlin first on 17 November and then again on 1 December, a clear majority of the party's leaders supported Stegerwald's candidacy. At this point, only the question of separating the party chairmanship from the chairmanship of the Reichstag delegation seemed to stand in the way of Stegerwald's election.[26] But Steger-wald's candidacy had begun to encounter strong opposition from many in the party who were reluctant to entrust the party chairmanship to someone so closely identified with the Christian labor unions. Opposition was particularly strong among the Center's civil servants, whose wrath Stegerwald had incurred toward the end of the previous year with his vociferous opposition to any increase in civil servant salaries that ignored Germany's fiscal realities and

[24] Adam Stegerwald, *Arbeiterschaft, Volk und Staat. Vortrag, gehalten auf dem elfster Kongreß der christlichen Gewerkschaften in Dortmund* (Berlin-Wilmersdorf, 1926), 15–27.
[25] Stegerwald, "Geistige und politische Grundlagen der Zentrumspartei," n.d. [23–24 Sept. 1928], ACDP Sankt-Augustin, NL Stegerwald, I-206, 004/2. See also Forster, *Stegerwald*, 453–54.
[26] Kaiser, "Aufzeichnungen zur Wahl des ersten Vorsitzenden der Deutschen Zentrumspartei auf dem 5. Reichsparteitag in Köln, im Dezember 1928," 12 Jan. 1929, ACDP Sankt Augustin, NL Stegerwald, I-206, 5/606.

exceeded increases in the private sector for workers and white-collar employees.[27] Stegerwald's tirade against the proposed civil service salary reform was all the more regrettable because the bill had originated in the ministry of finance headed by another member of the Center, Heinrich Köhler.[28] At a meeting of Center party leaders from the Rhineland on 16 November, spokesmen for the party's civil servant wing took a strong stand against Stegerwald's candidacy but were not able to come up with a credible alternative except to urge Marx to reconsider his resignation.[29] Then, at a meeting of the Center executive committee on 6 December a delegation from the party's National Civil-Servant Advisory Council (Reichsbeamtenbeirat der Deutschen Zentrumspartei) read a declaration in which they stated that Stegerwald's election to the party chairmanship could only be interpreted as a repudiation of the civil service by the party as a whole. In the ensuing vote only fifteen of the committee's twenty-eight members endorsed Stegerwald's candidacy. Stegerwald suffered another defeat on the following day when the party's national committee passed a resolution to separate the office of the party chairman from the chairmanship of the party's delegation to the Reichstag by an overwhelming 120 to 40 margin. Infuriated by the party's rejection of Stegerwald, union spokesman Johannes Giesberts read a declaration at a meeting the Center executive committee on 7 December in which he denounced the treatment that Stegerwald had received at the hands of the national committee as a repudiation of the Catholic working class and announced that he and his colleagues would not take part in further deliberations and left the meeting with five of his associates.[30]

All of this took place as the Center was making final preparations for its national party congress that was set to open in Cologne on 8 December. In a desperate attempt to salvage party unity and to prevent a major secession on the part of either its civil servant or working-class constituencies, the leaders of the Center decided to entrust leadership of the party to a special three-man collegium. This effort, however, collapsed when a petition calling for the immediate election of the new party chairman was circulated at the opening session of the Cologne party congress and received the requisite number of signatures. By then, two other candidates for the party chairmanship had surfaced in Joseph Joos, a Catholic labor leader who was too closely identified

---

[27] Adam Stegerwald, *Zur Reform der Beamtenbesoldung* (Berlin-Wilmersdorf, 1928), 3–12, 19–27.

[28] Ruppert, *Im Dienst am Staat von Weimar*, 274–87.

[29] Bachem to Müller, 17 Nov. 1928, in Rudolf Morsey, "Die Deutsche Zentrumspartei," *Das Ende der Parteien 1933*, ed. Erich Matthias and Rudolf Morsey (Düsseldorf, 1960), 281–453, here 418.

[30] Kaiser, "Aufzeichnungen zur Wahl," 12 Jan. 1929, ACDP Sankt Augustin, NL Stegerwald, I-206, 5/606.

with the People's Association for Catholic Germany to satisfy the Center's middle-class constituencies, and Monseigneur Ludwig Kaas, an experienced church diplomat and constitutional expert who offered himself as a compromise candidate. In the election that took place without any further debate, Kaas received 184 votes – twenty-four more than the absolute majority required for election – while Joos and Stegerwald received 92 and 42 votes respectively.[31] While Stegerwald's election would have most likely exacerbated the social and economic divisions that were already eating away at the party's internal cohesiveness, Kaas's election had the effect of reaffirming those confessional principles that lay at the heart of the Center's unique *Weltanschauung*. The obvious hope here was that this might hold in check the forces of social and political disintegration that were at work within the party. "The solidarity of all those who believe in Christ," stressed Kaas in his acceptance speech at Cologne, "must be greater than that which separates us from one another."[32]

The symbolism of Kaas's election was immediately apparent. In choosing Kaas over Joos and Stegerwald, the Center had opted for a leader who stood above the conflict that was eating away at the unity of the party and whose election afforded it the best chance of reversing its electoral decline and attracting new support from disaffected Catholic voters.[33] His election was immediately hailed by Catholic nobles who had remained loyal to the Center and who hoped that his election signaled a turn to the right that might make the party more attractive to those of their peers who had abandoned it after the end of World War I.[34] But as difficult as it was to situate Kaas in a left-right sprectrum, the signature feature of his political world-view was a deep and abiding loyalty to the principles of constitutional government. Kaas was acutely sensitive to the legacy of the *Kulturkampf* of the 1870s and believed as early as 1919 that the best way to secure the interests of Germany's Catholic minority was through legally binding agreements or concordats with duly constituted political authority. But unlike the Catholic Right, Kaas was not wedded to the monarchical form of government and never questioned the legitimacy of the republican institutions that Germany had inherited from the November Revolution.[35] Beyond that, Kaas embraced the concept of concentration, or *Sammlung*, as a way not only of uniting German Catholics on the

---

[31] *Offizieller Bericht des fünften Parteitages der Deutschen Zentrumspartei. Tagung zu Köln am 8. und 9. Dezember 1928*, ed. Reichsgeneralsekretariat der Deutschen Zentrumspartei (Trier, n.d. [1929]), 43. See also Ruppert, *Im Dienst am Staat von Weimar*, 335–47, and Forster, *Stegerwald*, 455–64.

[32] Deutsche Zentrumspartei, *Offizieller Bericht 1928*, 76.

[33] Bachem to Müller, 10 Dec. 1928, reprinted in Morsey, "Deutsche Zentrumspartei," 419.

[34] For example, see the letter from the future Bishop of Münster, Clemens August von Galen, to his brother Franz, 9 Dec. 1928, WVA Münster, NL Galen, 227.

[35] Ludwig Kaas, *Staat und Kirche im neuen Deutschland. Rede gehalten auf dem Trierer Katholikentag am 12. Okt. 1919* (Trier, n.d. [1919]).

basis of the Center but also of uniting the German nation across class and confessional lines into a political unity that could withstand the centrifugal forces that were slowly, but surely eroding the fabric of Germany's national life. Precisely what Kaas's concept of *Sammlung* meant in practical terms was imprecise, but in the immediate context it meant reorganizing the Müller government so that the Center received the full complement of cabinet posts to which it was entitled as the second largest party in the governmental coalition.[36] In a broader sense, however, *Sammlung* implied the consolidation of all those who, regardless of their party affiliation, shared similar a commitment to the defense of Germany's Christian culture and envisaged the cultivation of closer ties to parties and organizations outside the Center. Whether or not Kaas's strategy with its implications for the Center's relations with the DNVP represented a viable response to the fragmentation and polarization of German party life, particularly in the light of Hugenberg's election as DNVP party chairman, remained unclear.[37]

For Stegerwald Kaas's election was a slap in the face,[38] and the reaction of his supporters in the Christian trade unions was as quick as it was ominous. On the second day of the Cologne party congress, the Center's working-class delegates met separately under Giesberts's chairmanship to vent their anger over what had happened the day before with a sharply worded statement in which they equated the rejection of Stegerwald's candidacy with a rejection of the Catholic worker. A conference of Centrist labor leaders in Essen was set for 16 December to subject the question of the party's ties to the Christian trade-union movement to a thorough reexamination.[39] Throughout all of this Jakob Kaiser, a prominent Catholic labor leader from the Rhineland and one of Stegerwald's most trusted associates, worked diligently to repair the damage that Stegerwald's defeat had done to the Centers relations with the Catholic working class.[40] But the driving force behind this effort at reconciliation was Stegerwald himself, who at the conference in Essen unequivocally reaffirmed

---

[36] Kaas to Stresemann, 20 Feb. 1929, PA AA Berlin, NL Stresemann, 77/169252–54. See also the exchange of letters between Kaas and Wirth, 29–30 Oct. 1929, BA Koblenz, Nachlass Joseph Wirth, 73.

[37] For one of the more cogent statements of this concept, see Ludwig Kaas, *Nicht rückwärts – vorwärts* (Berlin, n.d. [1931]), 8–10. For further insight, see Martin Menke, "Ludwig Kaas and the End of the German Center Party," in *From Weimar to Hitler: Studies in the Dissolution of the Weimar Republic and the Establishment of the Third Reich, 1932–1934*, ed Hermann Beck and Larry Eugene Jones (New York and Oxford, 2018), 79–109, esp. 81–83.

[38] Forster, *Stegerwald*, 463.

[39] Kaiser, "Aufzeichnungen zur Wahl," 12 Jan. 1929, ACDP Sankt Augustin, NL Stegerwald, I-206, 5/606.

[40] Circular from Kaiser, 10 Dec. 1928, ACDP Sankt Augustin, NL Stegerwald, I-206, 5/607. For further details, see Patch, *Christian Trade Unions*, 133–41.

his loyalty to the Center and its new party chairman. Explaining that Kaas had always been committed to the principle of class reconciliation, Stegerwald dismissed the notion that his defeat represented a rejection of the Catholic worker or of the ideals of the Christian labor movement. At the same time, Stegerwald criticized the Center for its failure to respond to the changes that were taking place in the structure of German society and evoked, as he had done at Essen eight years earlier, the vision of a Christian-social people's party that would unite Catholics and Protestants to defend the basic values of Germany's Christian heritage and to lay the foundation for the creation of a genuine people's state. Only Stegerwald's contention that the Center was the prototype of such a party and the seed out of such a party could develop robbed his comments of the sting they might otherwise have held for Kaas and the Center party leadership.[41]

Stegerwald's allusion to the "Essen Program" of 1920 notwithstanding, his speech at the Essen conference of Centrist labor leaders was a clear attempt to put the bitterness of defeat behind him and to reassure his audience that the struggle for the future of the party was still very much ahead of them. In a similar vein, industrialist Rudolf ten Hompel proposed at a meeting of the party's Advisory Council for Trade and Industry (Handels- und Industrie-Beiräte der Deutschen Zentrumspartei) on 6 December 1928 that representatives from the Christian trade-unions, the Catholic Worker's Associations (Katholische Arbeitervereine), and the party's industrial supporters should meet on a regular basis in an attempt to promote social harmony and party unity.[42] The first such meeting took place on 21 January 1929 with Stegerwald, Kaiser, and Bernhard Otte from the Christian labor movement and Joos for the Catholic Workers' Associations in attendance.[43] Kaas too helped reduce tensions within the party by offering Stegerwald the chairmanship of the Center delegation to the Reichstag with the understanding that he would support Stegerwald for the party chairmanship should the opportunity present itself in the future.[44] With Kaas's endorsement, Stegerwald election as chairman of the Center Reichstag delegation took place by acclamation on 25

---

[41] Adam Stegerwald, *Zentrumspartei, Arbeiterschaft, Volk und Staat* (Berlin-Wilmersdorf, n.d. [1928]), esp. 7–11. See also Kaiser to Giesberts, Imbusch, and Stegerwald, 17 Dec. 1928, BA Koblenz, NL Kaiser, 247. For further details, see Forster, *Stegerwald*, 464–69.

[42] Minutes of the meeting of the Center's Advisory Council for Trade and Industry, 6 Dec. 1928, in *Mitteilungen der Handels- und Industrie Beiräte der Deutschen Zentrumspartei*, 22 Dec. 1928, BA Koblenz, NL ten Hompel, 38.

[43] Minutes of the meeting of Center Party industrialists and labor leaders, 21 Jan. 1929, BA Koblenz, NL ten Hompel, 33.

[44] Kaas to Stegerwald, 9 Jan. 1929, ACDP Sankt Augustin, NL Stegerwald, I-206, 014/13. See also Heinrich Teipel, "Kaas und Stegerwald," *Deutsche Republik*, 3, no. 18 (1 Feb. 1929): 549–54.

January, whereupon he resigned his chairmanships of both the United Feder-ation of Christian Trade Unions and the German Trade-Union Federation.[45] What these three developments – Stegerwald's conciliatory speech at Essen, ten Hompel's proposal for regular meetings between representatives of the party's working-class and industrial interests, and Stegerwald's election to the chairmanship of the Reichstag delegation – all underscored was a willingness on the part of the Center leadership and the various interest groups that comprised the party's material base to strive for a genuine resolution of the social antagonisms that nearly fifteen years of unrelieved economic pressure had produced within the ranks of their party. It was precisely this willingness, sustained no doubt by a shared commitment to confessional and religious values that transcended private economic interests, that helped insulate the Center so effectively against the forces of social and political disintegration that were ravaging the other bourgeois parties.

Still, Kaas's election as Center party chairman presented a host of problems whose ultimate resolution would have a profound impact on the future of political Catholicism in Germany. In the first place, Kaas's election signaled a shift to the right that may not have been as dramatic as what had happened in the DNVP but nevertheless raised questions about the stability of Germany's republican institutions. Second, Kaas had not previously held a leadership position in the Center, and his genial and non-confrontational manner of dealing with his colleagues left him ill-suited to assume the responsibilities of leading a party beset by the myriad problems facing the Center. Third, Kaas was a cleric whose election to the Center party chairmanship represented part of a more general trend that Stegerwald would later decry as the "clericaliza-tion" of the Germany's Catholic parties.[46] Fourth, Kaas was no ordinary cleric but one whose close friendship with the Papal Nuncio in Germany, Eugenio Pacelli, raised concerns about the independence of the Center vis-à-vis the Vatican. Like Kaas, Pacelli was a canon lawyer and diplomat who operated on the premise that it was only through diplomatic arrangements with secular states that the interests of the church could be secured. Pacelli had played a major role in negotiating the concordat with the state of Bavaria in 1924 and was hopeful that a similar arrangement could be worked out with Prussia.[47]

---

[45] Minutes of the Center Reichstag delegation, 25 Jan. 1929, in *Protokolle der Reichstags-fraktion und des Fraktionsvorstandes der Deutschen Zentrumspartei 1926–1933*, ed. Rudolf Morsey (Mainz, 1969), 256–57.

[46] Stegerwald, "Aus meinen Erlebnissen im Kampf gegen den Integralismus und die poli-tische Reaktion in katholisch kirchlichen Kreisen," 1945, ACDP Sankt Augustin, NL Stegerwald, I-206, 016/4.

[47] See Karsten Ruppert, "Interaktionen von politischem Katholizismus, Kirche und Vatikan während der Weimarer Republik," in *Eugenio Pacelli als Nuntius in Deutschland. For-schungsspektiven und Ansätzen zu einem internationellen Vergleich*, ed. Hubert Wolf (Paderborn, 2012), 215–46, here 17–21.

But Pacelli was no friend of parliamentary democracy and enjoyed close ties to the anti-democratic elements on the Catholic Right, having, for example, officiated at the marriage of one of Franz von Papen's daughters in 1926.[48] Given Kaas's close relationship with Pacelli, it was unclear just how much the latter's aversion to parliamentary democracy would undercut Kaas's commitment to working within the framework of duly constituted political authority.

Towards a "Hugenberg Party"

The turmoil within the DVP and Center mirrored the situation within the German National People's Party. Developments within the three parties were all part of a more general crisis within the German party system that could seen in part as a reaction to the socialist victory in the 1928 Reichstag elections but was also a sign of growing frustration of Germany's nonsocialist electorate with the government's ineffectiveness in dealing with the country's economic stagnation. Hugenberg's confederates were quick to take note of these developments and easily convinced themselves that this could only work to the advantage of their own party.[49] Two days after his election as DNVP party chairman Hugenberg outlined his goals and methods at a special meeting of nearly three hundred party strategists in Berlin. Here Hugenberg set three objectives for himself and his party: first, a sweeping reform of party finances that would require more in the way of contributions from individual party members to make the party less dependent upon outside economic interests; second, a reexamination of the factors responsible for the DNVP's defeat in the May 1928 Reichstag elections as part of a plan to regain the confidence of the general populace; and third, "the ordering of ideas and the creation of a battle plan with clear lines of conflict for the solution of the great problems facing the party." Hugenberg then proceeded to review the strengths and weakness of the party press, the party's progaganda apparatus, and the party organization as a whole.[50] Hugenberg was followed by Lothar Steuer, a member of the DNVP delegation to the Prussian Landtag from Hesse-Kassel who provided a more detailed analysis of the 1928 election results with particular emphasis upon the appeal of special-interest parties, the high rate of voter non-participation, and the alienation of the younger generation.[51] Subsequent speakers then turned their attention to matters of special concern such as the party's relationship to the middle class and workers, its efforts to

---

[48] Pacelli to Papen, 12 June 1926, BA Koblenz, Nachlass Max von Stockhausen, 2.

[49] For example, see Wegener to Claß, 1 Nov. 1928, BA Koblenz, NL Wegener, 23/99–100.

[50] Hugenberg, "Rückblick und Ausblick," in Deutschnationale Volkspartei, Hauptgeschäftsstelle, *Wahlkampftagung der Deutschnationalen Volkspartei im Reichstag am Montag, den 22. Oktober 1928* (Berlin, 1928), 1–5, in BA Koblenz, ZSg 1-44/6 (16).

[51] Steuer, "Gründe für den Wahlausfall," ibid., 5–8.

solicit the support of women and youth, and its involvement in the patriotic movement.[52]

Hugenberg and his associates in the DNVP party leadership focused much of their attention on the German middle class. The leaders of the DNVP were particularly concerned about the inroads that the Business Party had made into the ranks of their party's middle-class constituency and linked their party's recovery at the polls "to leading middle-class circles back into the bosom of the party."[53] The DNVP's middle-class representatives complained bitterly about the "irresponsible demagoguery of the WP" and struggled to find a formula that would allow it to stress what it had done on behalf of the independent middle class without compromising its character as an opposition party. Only by squaring the fight for middle-class economic interests with the struggle for Germany's highest national goals, argued Wilhelm Jaeger as the party's specialist on middle-class issues, would the DNVP ever be able to win back the support of the German middle class and fulfill its responsibilities to the German fatherland.[54] Another group that was every bit as important to the fate of the DNVP as the independent middle-class was the German farmer. Here the leaders of the DNVP were facing an animated challenge from the newly founded Christian-National Peasants and Farmers Party. Nationalist efforts to persuade the leaders of the CNBLP to resolve their differences with the DNVP and and join forces in the struggle for the welfare of the German farmer met with little reaction from the CNBLP,[55] whose leaders were convinced that the wave of the future was a fundamental reorganization of the German party system along vocational and corporatist lines.[56] Speaking at a conference of the DNVP's Agricultural National Committee in Berlin on 10 November 1928, Hugenberg reassured his party's farm leaders that he was every bit as committed to the welfare of the German farmer as they. At the same time, however, he insisted that agricultural recovery could not be secured by piece-meal measures but only through a thorough overhaul of German trade and reparations policy.[57]

---

[52] Speeches by Jaeger, Lindner, Hertwig, Müller-Loebnitz, and Krause, ibid., 10–17.

[53] Remarks by Jaeger, 19 Oct. 1928, in Deutschnationale Volkspartei, Reichsausschuß für den Mittelstand, *Deutschnationale Mittelstandstagung in Berlin* (Berlin, 1928), 1.

[54] Jaeger, "Unsere Werbung in Mittelstandskreisen," in *Wahlkampftagung der Deutschnationalen Volkspartei*, 10–11.

[55] Correspondence between Richthofen and Westarp, 6–16 July 1928, and in particular Richthofen to Hepp, 6 July 1928, NL Westarp, Gärtringen, VN 100.

[56] See Hepp's programmatic speech, "Die Ziele der Christlich-Nationale Bauern- und Landvolkpartei," Hanover, 9 Sept. 1928, in the *Nassauische Bauern-*Zeitung, 4 and 5 Oct. 1928, nos. 230–31.

[57] Hugenberg's remarks to the DNVP's Agricultural National Committee, 10 Nov. 1928, BA Koblenz, NL Hugenberg, 114/78–88.

If the DNVP was going to fend off the challenges of special-interest parties like the WP and CNBLP, an essential prerequisite in the eyes of Hugenberg and his supporters was a comprehensive reform of the DNVP party organization. Even party leaders from the Westarp era had begun to realize that the decentralized party structure the DNVP had developed in the aftermath of the November Revolution was badly outmoded and in need of a complete overhaul.[58] In the wake of the DNVP's defeat in the May 1928 Reichstag elections two of Hugenberg's lieutenants, Reinhold Quaatz and Werner von Steinhoff, had been entrusted with the task of developing a comprehensive plan for a reorganization of the party. Action on their proposals, which were presented to the DNVP party representation in October 1928,[59] was shelved until the turmoil that surrounded the election of the new party chairman had subsided. It was not until this body had an opportunity to meet again on 8 December that the party revisited the proposals for a reform of the DNVP party organization. The reforms proposed by Quaatz and Steinhoff had as much to do with the party's internal politics as they did with the efficiency of the party organization. The most important feature of the proposal was a recommendation to eliminate the thirty-two man party leadership council (Parteileitung) with its veto power over the policies of the party chairman in favor of an expanded executive committee (Parteivorstand) in which the chairmen of the DNVP's state and provincial organizations enjoyed *ipso jure* membership.[60] As a move that greatly strengthened the influence of Hugenberg's supporters at the upper levels of the party organization, it encountered strong opposition from a group of Reichstag deputies that had coalesced behind the leadership of Lindeiner-Wildau. But this group was powerless to block the efforts of Hugenberg and his confederates to bring the party more firmly under the new chairman's personal control and went down to an lop-sided defeat in the final and decisive vote.[61]

The outcome of the meeting of the DNVP party representation on 8 December 1928 represented a clear victory for Hugenberg and his efforts to transform the party into an instrument of his political will.[62] Westarp, who had stayed on

---

[58] Dewitz (Pomeranian Rural League) to Westarp, 4 Jan. 1928, NL Westarp, Gärtringen, II/31.

[59] Steinhoff and Quaatz, "Denkschrift zur Reform der Parteiorganisation," 1 Oct. 1928, NL Westarp, Gärtringen, II/30. On the origins of this memorandum, see Westarp's circular to the members of the DNVP party representation, 12 Oct. 1928, ibid.

[60] Documents on the reorganization of the party for the meeting of the DNVP party representation, 8 Dec. 1928, FZG Hamburg, NL Diller, 9.

[61] *Unsere Partei*, 6, no. 27 (15 Dec. 1928): 397–99. See also Blank to Reusch, 7 Dec. 1928, RWWA Cologne, Abt. 130, NL Reusch, 4001012024/4b.

[62] Entry in Quaatz's diary, 8 Dec. 1928, BA Berlin, NL Quaatz, 16.

as chairman of the DNVP Reichstag delegation with Hugenberg's apparent blessing,[63] avoided becoming involved in the dispute over the reorganization of the party but was concerned that the centralization of power in the hands of Hugenberg and the newly reconstituted party executive committee threatened the autonomy of the delegation.[64] These fears proved fully justified when in the spring of 1929 Hugenberg moved to curtail the freedom of the DNVP Reichstag delegation. On 18 March 1929 Westarp met with Reich President von Hindenburg to discuss, among other things, the possibility of a new right-wing government under the leadership of Lindeiner-Wildau or one of his colleagues on the DNVP's left wing.[65] Hugenberg regarded Westarp's action as a circumvention of his own authority, and at a meeting of the DNVP executive committee in early April one of his lieutenants introduced a resolution that made the decisions of the party chairman in all important political questions, including that of participating in the government, binding upon the DNVP Reichstag delegation and the DNVP's other parliamentary delegations throughout the country.[66] Westarp, who was determined to preserve the autonomy of the Reichstag delegation, succeeded in blocking acceptance of Hugenberg's motion by a narrow margin at a special caucus of the DNVP Reichstag delegation in early May 1929.[67] Hugenberg then proceeded to mobilize his supporters in the DNVP executive committee in June 1929 to override the delegation's vote in a move that formally subordinated Westarp and the DNVP Reichstag delegation to the control of the DNVP party chairman.[68] To Westarp this represented an unwarranted infringement of the delegation's freedom of action, but he lacked the leverage within the party's

[63] Letter from Ada Gräfin von Westarp to Gertraude Freifrau Hiller von Gaertringen, 23 Oct. 1928, NL Westarp, Gärtringen.
[64] Westarp to his son-in-law Berthold Freiherr Hiller von Gaertringen, 5 Dec. 1928, NL Hiller, Gärtringen. For further details, see Larry Eugene Jones, "Conservatism at the Crossroads: Count Kuno von Westarp and the Struggle for Control of the German National People's Party," *Contemporary European History* 18 (2009): 147–77.
[65] Memorandum of Westarp's conversation with von Hindenburg, 18 Mar. 1929, NL Westarp, Gärtringen, II/61.
[66] Diller's handwritten notes on the meeting of the DNVP executive committee, 8–9 Apr. 1929, FZG Hamburg, NL Diller, 7.
[67] Entry in Quaatz's diary, 2 May 1929, BA Koblenz, NL Quaatz, 16. See also Westarp's correspondence with Hugenberg, 19–22 Apr. 1929, NL Westarp, Gärtringen, VN 122, as well as his letters to Traub, 4 May 1929, ibid., II/37, and Natzmer, 14 May 1929, ibid., VN 102. For a breakdown of the anti-Hugenberg forces in the DNVP Reichstag delegation, see Traub to Hilpert, 22 May 1929, BA Koblenz, NL Traub, 50/8–15.
[68] Report of the meeting of the DNVP executive committee, 15 June 1929, in *Unsere Partei* 7, no. 13 (1 July 1929): 207–09. See also the entry in Quaatz's diary, 18 June 1929, BA Koblenz, NL Quaatz, 16, as well as Quaatz to Westarp, 19 June 1929, NL Westarp, VN 102.

governing bodies to reverse what he saw an intolerable situation.[69] Hugenberg had taken another step toward transforming the DNVP into an instrument of his political will.

Christian-Social Unrest

Hugenberg's efforts to bring the DNVP more and more under his personal control aroused deep-seated misgivings in various sectors of the party. Not only was Westarp concerned about the autonomy of the DNVP Reichstag delegation, but the reforms that the new party chairman had pushed through the DNVP executive committee at the beginning of December 1928 only reinforced the fears that the leaders of the party's working-class wing had already voiced about their party's future development. The first group to break the uneasy truce that had existed between Hugenberg and his opponents on the DNVP's left wing was the Christian-Social faction led by Emil Hartwig, Gustav Hülser, and Reinhard Mumm.[70] Ever since the Lambach affair in the summer of 1928, the Christian-Socials had been moving toward a break with the DNVP. In August 1928 the leaders of the DNVP's Christian-Social faction met in Bielefeld to found the Christian-Social Reich Association as the first step toward uniting all of those in the DNVP who embraced the social and political gospel of the late Adolf Stoecker in a move that designed to strengthen Christian-Social influence at all levels of the DNVP party organiza- tion.[71] Although the founders of the new organization remained committed to pursuing their objectives within the framework of the DNVP, they were hoped to establish closer ties to like-minded groups from Württemberg and other parts of the country that stood outside the immediate orbit of the DNVP.[72]

The fact that Hugenberg's immediate entourage included outspoken social reactionaries like Paul Bang from the League for National Economics and Industrial Peace and a champion of Germany's management-controlled "yellow unions" and Gustav Hartz, author of a controversial proposal to dismantle the existing system of social legislation in favor of a compulsory

---

[69] Westarp to Quaatz, 24 June 1929, NL Westarp, Gärtringen, VN 102.

[70] On the goals of the DNVP's Christian-Social faction, see Hülser, "Die volks- und staatspolitische Bedeutung der Gewerkschaften," *Politische Wochenschrift* 5, no. 5 (31 Jan. 1929): 100–04, as well as Reinhard Mumm, *Die entscheidende Frontstellung* (Berlin, n.d. [ca. 1928]). See also Stupperich, *Volksgemeinschaft oder Arbeitersolidarität*, 98–194.

[71] Protocol of the national congress (*Reichstreffen*) of the Christian-Socials in Bielefeld, 19 Aug. 1928, NL Mumm, 282/181–95. See also Friedrich, "*Die christlich-soziale Fahne empor!*," 230–56.

[72] Büchenschütz's remarks at the national congress of the Christian-Socials, 19 Aug. 1928, BA Berlin, NL Mumm, 282/185. For further details, see Günter Opitz, *Der Christlich- soziale Volksdienst. Versuch einer protestantischen Partei in der Weimarer Republik* (Düsseldorf, 1969), 33–133.

savings program out of which Germany's social-welfare needs would be met,[73] only fueled Christian-Social fears that the social and economic progress of the previous decade was under siege. Two days after Hugenberg's election approximately thirty members of the DNVP's Christian-Social Reich Union held a special conference in Berlin to put their final stamp of approval on the organizational statutes and guidelines they had adopted two months earlier at Bielefeld.[74] By the following spring Hülser had already begun to characterize himself and his followers as "unwilling rebels" and did not hesitate to criticize Hugenberg in public for his lack of a commitment to the material and moral welfare of the German worker.[75] At the same time, the leaders of the DNVP's Christian-Social Reich Union continued to reaffirm their loyalty to the DNVP and disclaimed any interest in the founding of a new party.[76] All of this drew to a climax in April 1929 when Hartwig and the leaders of the German National Workers' League brought their complaints about the Hartz program to the DNVP executive committee only to be rebuffed when the committee referred the matter to a special commission created for the purpose of reviewing Hartz's proposals and the feasibility of their implementation.[77] Hugenberg's refusal to dissociate himself from Hartz's recommendations came as a slap in the face to the leaders of the DNVP's Evangelical labor wing, who now began to fear that it might be necessary for them to leave the party if they were to remain faithful to their Christian-Social ideals.[78] All of this, as Mumm wrote to Hugenberg in February 1929, was part of a larger question as to whether the German party system would organize itself on a spiritual or a material basis, whether the values of the Christian faith would still have

[73] Gustav Hartz, *Irrwege der deutschen Sozialpolitik und der Weg zur sozialen Freiheit* (Berlin, 1928), esp. 95–133, 149–210.
[74] Minutes of the first meeting of the CSRV, 21 October 1928, BA Berlin, NL Mumm, 282/301–02. See also the report in *Christlich-soziale Stimmen. Mitteilungsblatt der Christlich-sozialen Reichsvereinigung*, 15 Feb. 1929, no. 1, as well as Hartwig, "Vorwärts! Trotz allem!" *Angestelltenstimme und Arbeiterstimme*, ed. Deutschnationale Angestellten- und Arbeiterbünde, 8, no. 11 (Nov. 1928): 1–2.
[75] Hülser, "Rebellen wider Willen," *Politische Wochenschrift*, 5, no. 14 (6 Apr. 1929): 324–25. See also Hülser, "Positive Kritik und Mitarbeit an der Sozialpolitik!" *Der Reichsbote*, 14 Dec. 1928, and Hülser, "Ein Herold des christlich-sozialen Gedankens. Zu Adolf Stoeckers 20. Todestag," *Der Deutsche*, 8 Feb. 1929, no. 33.
[76] Heinz-Dietrich Wendland, *Christlich-soziale Grundsätze. Gedanken zu einem neuen christlich-sozialen Programm* (Berlin, 1929).
[77] *Unsere Partei* 7, no. 9 (1 May 1929): 132. For the Christian-Social position, see "Sozial-versicherung oder Sparzwang?" *Angestelltenstimme und Arbeiterstimme*, 9, no. 5 (May 1929): 1–4, as well as Lambach's letter of 26 Mar. 1929, FZG Hamburg, NL Diller, 7.
[78] For example, see Baudissin's remarks at the CSRV's first annual congress in Bielefeld, 2 Aug. 1929, in DNVP, Mitteilungen no. 36, 30 Aug. 1929, FZG Hamburg, NL Diller, 10.

meaning in a political system dominated by the one-sided representation of special economic interests.[79]

Agrarian Activism and the "Green Front"

Of the various social and economic interests that supported the DNVP, none was more important than organized agriculture. With the stabilization of the mark in 1923–24 the German farmer began to encounter economic difficulties that were to become even more severe than those he had experienced during the runaway inflation of the early 1920s. As a result, ties between organized agriculture and the parties through which it had traditionally sought to represent its vital interests became increasingly strained. The demonstrations in Schleswig-Holstein and other parts of the country in the early winter and spring of 1928 came as a rude shock to Germany's conservative establishment and constituted a direct threat to conservative hegemony in the countryside. A particularly disturbing aspect of this development was the emergence of the Rural People's Movement, or *Landvolkbewegung*, as a radical and sometimes violent alternative to the more traditional forms of rural protest. This phenomenon – which surfaced in the wake of the first mass demonstrations in Schleswig-Holstein and then spread to Pomerania, Thuringia, and East Prussia – featured the threat of boycott, silent marches, attacks on government finance offices, and the occasional use of bombs. All of this raised the specter of a peasant insurrection, the likes of which had not been seen since the great revolt of 1524–25.[80]

The peasant uprising in the late 1920s caught Germany's conservative agrarian elites off-guard and forced them to take immediate action to contain it before it wreaked havor with their own organizations. The founding of the CNBLP with support from the leaders of the regional affiliates of the National Rural League in Thuringia and Hesse posed a direct threat to the RLB's internal cohesion and obliged its leaders to look for a formula that would both preserve the unity of their organization and make it possible for them to contain the wave of social and political radicalization that was sweeping the countryside.[81] Efforts to reorganize the RLB's leadership structure had been under way for some time before drawing to a concluions at a meeting of the RLB full executive committee (Gesamtvorstand) on 5 July 1928. Here RLB

[79] Mumm to Hugenberg, 27 Feb. 1929, BA Berlin, NL Mumm, 300/50–53.
[80] Hans Beyer, "Die Landvolkbewegung Schleswig-Holsteins und Niedersachsens 1928-1932," *Jahrbuch der Heimatgemeinschaft des Kreises Ecken-förde e.V.* 15 (1957): 173–202. For the broader context, see Bergmann and Megerle, "Protest und Aufruhr der Landwirtschaft in der Weimarer Republik," 200–87.
[81] Memorandum by Kriegsheim for the members of the RLB executive committee, 6 June 1928, BA Koblenz, NL Weilnböck, 15.

president Count Eberhard von Kalckreuth proposed that the dual presidency that had been in effect since 1925 be replaced by a new three-person presidium consisting of the former Reich agricultural minister Martin Schiele and two subordinate presidents, the identity of whom was yet to determined.[82] Despite protests from the representatives of the small peasant proprietors from western Germany that this arrangement bestowed preferential treatment upon large landowning interests from east of the Elbe, the RLB overwhelmingly approved a slightly modified version of Kalckreuth's proposal in a series of meetings on 31 July 1928 and 1 August.[83] According to the compromise embodied in this arrangement, Schiele would serve as the RLB's executive president (geschäftsführender Präsident) with CNBLP Reichstag deputy Karl Hepp from Hesse-Nassau and estate owner Albrecht Bethge from Pomerania as his deputy presidents. The fact that Hepp came from the west and Bethge from the east represented a compromise that would satisfy the concerns of large landowners and independent peasants alike and thus salvage the unity of the RLB.[84]

Schiele's election as RLB executive president was immediately hailed as a victory for the more moderate elements within the German agricultural community over those who sympathized with the more radical elements of the *Landvolkbewegung*.[85] Schiele's election was particularly well received by German industrialists who saw in him "a calm, well-balanced, and thoroughly objective individual ... who would strive to reach a compromise with industry" on matters of common concern.[86] At the same time, the election of Hepp and Bethge as Schiele's deputies was an attempt to depoliticize the RLB and to insulate it against the increasingly bitter rivaly between the CNBLP and DNVP. But Schiele's reputation as a moderate and as a man of compromise would set him on a collision course with Hugenberg and his "all-or-nothing" policy as the DNVP's newly elected national chairman. Such a collision seemed all the more likely in view of Schiele's interest in establishing closer ties with agricultural interest organizations of different political persuasions as a way of enhancing the effectiveness of the agrarian lobby at all levels of government. Negotiations toward this end were already under way at the

[82] Minutes of the full executive committee of the RLB, 5 July 1928, LHA Magdeburg-Wernigerode, Marienthal Gutsarchiv, 319/119–26. See also memorandum from Nicolas, "Die Neuorganisation der Führungsorgane des Reichs-Landbundes. Denkschrift für den Gesamtvorstand des Brandenburg. Landbundes zur Vorstandssitzung vom 22.8.1928," 16 Aug. 1928, BA Koblenz, NL Weilnböck, 15.

[83] Nicholas, "Die Neuorganisation der Führungsorgane des Reichs-Landbundes," 16 Aug. 1928, BA Koblenz, NL Weilnböck, 15.

[84] *Reichs-Landbund* 8, no. 31 (4 Aug. 1928): 351.

[85] Wilmowsky to Krupp, 2 Aug. 1928, Krupp-Archiv Essen, FAH 23/502. See also Wilmowsky to Reusch, 2 Aug. 1928, RWWA Cologne, Abt. 130, NL Reusch, 400101290/39.

[86] Reusch to Wilmosky, 4 Aug. 1928, RWWA Cologne, Abt. 130, NL Reusch, 400101290/39.

regional level in the Rhineland, where in 1927–28 the predominantly Catholic Rhenish Peasants' Union (Rheinischer Bauern-Verein) under the leadership of Baron Clemens von Loë-Bergerhausen, a Catholic conservative with close ties to the DNVP, seceded from its parent organization in Berlin, the Association of German Peasant Unions (Vereinigung der Deutschen Bauernvereine or VDBV), to pursue closer organizational ties with the RLB's regional affiliate, the Rhenish Rural League (Rheinischer Landbund).[87] Similar developments were under foot in the neighboring province of Westphalia, where efforts to merge the predominantly Catholic Westphalian Peasants' Union (Westfälischer Bauernbund or WBB) with the politically more conservative and Protestant-led Westphalian Rural League (Westfälischer Landbund) enjoyed strong support from elements of Westphalia's Catholic aristocracy.[88]

All of this was part of an attempt by the more conservative elements of Germany's Catholic aristocracy to shore up their social and political hegemony in the face of mounting peasant unrest. These developments, however, caused great concern not just among the leaders of both the National Rural League, who feared that the numerically stronger Catholic peasant unions in the Rhineland and Westphalia would overwhelm their Protestant counterparts in the RLB's regional affiliates,[89] but also within the Association of German Peasant Unions, whose leaders were apprehensive that the two largest Catholic peasant unions outside of Bavaria might fall under conservative domination.[90] In response to grass-roots pressure for the creation of a single organization for all of German agriculture, Schiele met with Andreas Hermes, the recently elected chairman of the VDBV and a member of the Center Party, to explore the possibility of closer cooperation between their respective organizations. Hermes, who had replaced Baron Engelbert Kerckerinck zur Borg as VBDV chairman earlier in the year, was more open than his predecessor to the

---

[87] See the detailed memorandum by the Rheinischer Bauernverein, Hauptforstand, *Bericht über die Vorgänge, die zum Austritt des Rheinischen Bauernvereins aus der Vereinigung der deutschen Bauernvereine geführt haben* (n.p. [Cologne], 1927), ACDP Sankt Augustin, Bestand VI-051, 768. See also [Clemens von Loë-Bergerhausen], *Der Rheinische Bauern-Verein und seine Gesamtorganisation* (n.p. [Cologne], n.d. [1929]), 61. For further information, see Klaus Müller, "Agrarische Interessenverbände in der Weimarer Republik," *Rheinische Vierteljahrsblätter* 38 (1974): 386–405, and Jens Flemming, "Landwirtschaftskammer und ländliche Organisationspolitik in der Rheinprovinz, 1918–1927. Ein Beitrag zur Geschichte der 'Grünen Front'," in *Von der Reichsgründung bis zur Weimarer Republik*, ed. Kurt Düwell and Wolfgang Köllmann, 2 vols. (Wuppertal, 1984), 2:314–32.
[88] See Papen to Lüninck, 16 Feb. 1928, VWA Münster, NL Lüninck, 732, and Lüninck to Schorlemer, 20 Feb. 1928, ibid., 834.
[89] Merkenich, *Grüne Front gegen Weimar*, 259.
[90] Heide Barmeyer, *Andreas Hermes und die Organisation der deutschen Landwirtschaft. Christliche Bauernvereine, Reichslandbund, Grüne Front, Reichsnährstand 1928–1933* (Suttgart, 1971), 59–73.

possibility of an arrangement with the RLB and had already taken an important step toward toward that end when in October 1928 he succeeded in negotiating an arrangement whereby Loë and the Rhenish Peasants' Union would rejoin the parent organization in Berlin.[91]

In late January 1929 Schiele set events in motion by calling for the creation of a united agrarian front in his keynote address at the RLB's annual convention.[92] The negotiations that followed dragged on until 20 February when Schiele, Hermes, Anton Fehr for the German Peasantry (Deutsche Bauernschaft), and Ernst Brandes for the German Chamber of Agriculture (Deutscher Landwirtschaftsrat) agreed to issue a joint appeal on behalf of a united solution to the deepening agricultural crisis.[93] At a mass rally in Cologne later that month Schiele announced that the four organizations would henceforth work "shoulder to shoulder" to promote the welfare of all of German agriculture under the aegis of a new umbrella organization known as the "Green Front." Although Hermes and Schiele were careful to discourage speculation that this foreshadowed a merger of their respective organizations, their dementi did little to deter Loë and the organizers of the rally from releasing a resolution of their own that called for "the creation of a united economic-political organization for all German farmers without regard for size, confession, or party."[94] The creation of the "Green Front," however, fell far short of this goal and represented instead a compromise by which Schiele and Hermes sought to insulate their respective organizations against the growing pressure from below for the creation of a single interest organization for the entire agricultural community.[95] On 20 March the four leaders of the "Green Front" finalized the details of a comprehensive farm program that covered everything from indexing of agricultural prices and increased tariff protection for the domestic market to tax relief, easier access to credit, and resettlement policy.[96] At the same time, both Schiele and Hermes were quick

---

[91] See Loë to Lüninck, 11 June 1928, WVA Münster, NL Lüninck, 732, as well as Loë's correspondence with Hermes, 23 June 1928–8 Oct. 1928, ibid., 733.

[92] Schiele's speech at the RLB's annual conference in Berlin, 28 Jan. 1929, reported in *Reichs-Landbund* 9, no. 5 (2 Feb. 1929): 45–48.

[93] Wilmowsky to Krupp, 20 Feb. 1929, HA Krupp, FAH 23/502. See also Hopp to Weilnböck, 22 Feb. 1929, BA Koblenz, NL Weilnböck, 16b.

[94] On the Cologne rally, see the report in the *Rheinischer Bauer* 47, no. 9 (2 Mar. 1929): 70–74, as well as Schiele, Hepp, and Bethge, "Zur Entwicklung des Einigungsgedankens in Westfalen," n.d. [April 1929], BA Kobelnz, NL Weilnböck, 16b. See also Barmeyer, *Hermes*, 75–79.

[95] Ibid., 83–89. See also Dieter Gessner, "Industrie und Landwirtschaft 1928–30," in *Industrielles System und politische Entwicklung in der Weimarer Rebublik. Verhandlungen des Internationalen Symposiums in Bochum von 12.–17. June 1973*, ed. Mommsen, Petzinna, and Weisbrod (Düsseldorf, 1974), 762–78.

[96] Wilmowsky to Krupp, 20 Mar. 1929, HA Krupp, FAH 23/502. See also Barmeyer, *Hermes*, 89–94.

to reassure their supporters that the formation of the "Green Front" infringed in no way whatsoever upon the integrity or independence of the participating organizations.[97] Not even this could satisfy the leaders of the Catholic peasant unions and RLB affiliates in the Rhineland and Westphalia, who met in Hagen on 11 March to issue an ultimatum to their counterparts in Berlin that if they had not succeeded in creating a united national agricultural interest organization by the beginning of October, they would invite all of the agricultural associations throughout the country to join them in negotiations aimed at the creation of such an organization.[98]

The Hagen ultimatum was the handiwork of Catholic nobles like Loë and the two Lüninck brothers who sought to pressure Hermes and the Berlin leadership of the Christian peasant unions into carrying the unification of the German agricultural community, presumably under conservative auspices, further than either Hermes or Schiele had originally intended.[99] Infuriated by the impudence of the Hagen ultimatum, Hermes summoned the leaders of the Rhenish and Westphalian Peasants' Unions to a meeting of the executive committee of the Association of German Peasant Unions in Berlin on 20 March, where the very future of VDBV was at stake.[100] Here Hermes mobilized the support of the twenty-five other peasant unions that belonged to the VDBV to isolate the delegations from the Rhineland and Westphalia and to hand them a sharp and unequivocal rebuff.[101] Under no circumstances, stressed the resolution the VDBV released at the close of the meeting, should cooperation with the RLB and other agrarian interest organizations in the common struggle to provide the German farmer with the relief he so desparately needed be jeopardized by the agitation for the creation of a single agricultural interest organization. Nor would the Christian peasant unions, the resolution continued, ever be part of a merger that in any way whatsoever compromised their distinctly Christian character and sense of Christian mission.[102]

---

[97] See Schiele's remarks before the RLB executive committee, 13 Mar. 1929, and Hermes's statement at a committee meeting of the Westphalian Peasants' Union, 26 Mar. 1929, both reprinted in Schiele, Hepp, and Bethge, "Zur Entwicklung des Einigungsgedankens in Westfalen," n.d. [Apr. 1929], BA Koblenz, NL Weilnböck, 16b.

[98] For the text of the Hagen ultimatum, see [Loë-Bergerhausen], Der Rheinische Bauern-Verein (see n. 91), 62, as well as Schiele, Hepp, and Bethge, "Zur Entwicklung des Einigungsgedankens in Westfalen," n.d. [Apr. 1929], BA Koblenz, NL Weilnböck, 16b.

[99] Report by Golte at a meeting of the central committee of the Westphalian Peasants' Union, 1 Mar. 1929, VWA Münster, NL Kerckerinck, 252.

[100] Hermes to Kerckerinck, 13 Mar. 1929, VWA Münster, NL Kerckerinck, 289.

[101] See Hermes to Kerckerinck zur Borg, 28 Mar. 1929, VWA Münster, NL Kerckerinck, 280, and the reports by Dieckmann and Golte at the meeting of the executive committee of the Westphalian Peasants' Union, 25 Mar. 1929, VWA Münster, NL Lüninck, 744.

[102] Resolution of the VDBV executive committee, 20 Mar. 1929, appended to the circular from Hermes to the Peasants' Union, 21 Mar. 1929, BA Koblenz, Nachlass Karl Herold,

Despite the sharp rebuff the leaders of the Rhenish and Westaphalian peasant unions received at the hands of the VDBV executive committee, the agitation for the creation of a single interest organization for all of German agriculture continued and would not relent until after Loë's death in early 1930. The Rhenish Peasants' Union would in fact conclude an alliance with the Rhenish Rural League on 1 July 1929,[103] while in Westphalia the leaders of Westphalian Peasants' Union would beat a tactical retreat in the face of heavy pressure not just from Hermes but also from the organization's former chairman Kerckerinck zur Borg.[104] All of this underscored the highly volatile situation that existed in much of the German countryside as a result of the deepening agricultural crisis and heightened the likelihood of a collision between the pragmatic leadership of the "Green Front" and the "all-or-nothing" strategy of Hugenberg. In fact, the leaders of the DNVP's agrarian wing were already growing wary of the direction in which Hugenberg seemed to be taking the party and feared that relations between organized agriculture and the DNVP would continue to deteriorate.[105]

Ordeal of the Catholic Right

The reverberations of Hugenberg's election to the DNVP party chairmanship also extended to the leadership of the party's Catholic wing. Although the DNVP was and remained a predominantly Protestant party, it had experienced remarkable success in attracting the support of Catholic conservatives who had become disenchanted with the Center's turn to the left during and after World War I. Much of this could be attributed directly to the work of the DNVP's National Catholic Committee, which had been founded in 1920–21 under the leadership of Count Engelbert von Landsberg-Velen. Although Landsberg and his supporters had contributed in no small measure to the DNVP's victories in the May and December 1924 Reichstag elections,[106] they were obliged to temper their attacks on the Center for the sake of coalition etiquette and assumed a less conspicuous role in the party's internal affairs after the DNVP's entry into the national government first in January 1925 and

---

24. See also the official protocol of this meeting, ACDP Sankt Augustin, Nachlass Andreas Hermes, I-090-2

[103] Müller, "Agrarische Interessenverbände," 399.

[104] Kerckerinck zur Borg to Dieckmann, 14 Mar. 1929, VWA Münster, NL Kerckerinck, 252. See also the exchange of letters between Hermes and Kerckerinck, 28 Mar.–20. Apr. 1929, ibid., 280, as well as Lüninck's remarks at a meeting of the WBB executive committee, 6 Nov. 1929, VWA Münster, NL Lüninck, 744.

[105] Lind to Hugenberg, 6 May 1929, NL Westarp, Gärtringen, VN 102.

[106] For further information, see Jones, "Catholics on the Right: The Reich Catholic Committee of the German National People's Party, 1920–33," *Historisches Jahrbuch* 126 (2006): 221–67, and Hübner, *Rechtskatholiken*, 235–64, 352–73.

then two years later in January 1927.[107] Westarp's resignation as DNVP party chairman in July 1928 plunged the party's Catholic leaders into the middle of the bitter fight for control of the party that ensued. Martin Spahn, arguably the most prominent DNVP Catholic after his defection to the party at the Munich party congress in September 1921, had actively supported Hugenberg's candidacy for the party chairmanship.[108] Landsberg, on the other hand, was among those who did not vote for the new party chairman in the decisive meeting of the DNVP party representation in October 1928, although he quickly reconciled himself to Hugenberg's election in the hope that under the new party chairman the DNVP's Reich Catholic Committee might reclaim for itself the role it had played in the early 1920s.[109] This, however, never materialized. Although the leaders of the DNVP's Catholic committee received exemption from the organizational reforms that Hugenberg introduced as DNVP party chairman at the end of 1928,[110] they soon found themselves embroiled in a bitter conflict with the party leadership over its position on the ratification of the Concordat that the Prussian state government negotiated with the Holy See in June 1929.

After the end of World War I the Vatican launched a determined effort to secure the legal status of the Catholic Church wherever possible through the conclusion of special treaties or concordats with secular political authorities. Following the defeat of the national school bill in early 1928, the Prussian government under the leadership of Social Democrat Otto Braun – no doubt in an attempt to bind the Center more firmly to the existing governmental coalitions in both Prussia and the Reich – negotiated a concordat with the Holy See in June 1929 that contained a number of far-reaching concessions on the legal status and prerogatives of the Catholic Church in Prussia.[111] Although the treaty discreetly avoided any mention of the role of the churches in the Prussian educational system, it encountered widespread opposition from Protestant groups affiliated with the DNVP that greatly exacerbated confessional tensions throughout the party organization. All of this placed the leaders of the DNVP's Reich Catholic Committee in a difficult situation. For while the Catholic members of the DNVP delegation to the Prussian

---

[107] Spahn to Hugenberg, 23 Apr. 1930, BA Koblenz, NL Spahn, 86.

[108] On Spahn's relationship to Hugenberg, see his letter to Hugenberg, 3 Jan. 1928, BA Koblenz, NL Spahn, 86.

[109] Landsberg to Hugenberg, 15 Nov. 1928, VWA Münster, NL Landsberg, II. This designation refers to the second of two volumes of correspondence with the DNVP in the Landsberg Nachlass that do not carry any special identification.

[110] Landsberg's remarks in the minutes of the DNVP Reich Catholic Committee, 10 Mar. 1929, VWA Münster, NL Landsberg, E1.

[111] For further details, see Stewart Stehlin, *Weimar and the Vatican, 1919–1933: German-Vatican Diplomatic Relations in the Interwar Years* (Princeton, NJ, 1983), 412–29.

Landtag would most likely vote for the proposed concordat if it met their expectations,[112] the party's Protestant leaders remained strongly opposed to any arrangement with the Vatican that was not accompanied by a parallel arrangement with the Lutheran Church.[113] In December 1928 Hugenberg brought the leaders of the two factions together in an attempt to resolve their differences and formulate a common position on the question of the Prussian concordat.[114] The net result of this was a resolution adopted by the DNVP party representation on 8 December 1928 whereby the party endorsed the principle of a concordat with the Catholic Church but only if it were accompanied by a similar agreement with the Lutheran Church and did not infringe upon either the sovereign rights of the Prussian state or Germany's national interest.[115]

The Prussian government had little interest in an arrangement with the Prussian Lutheran Church and saw no point in including the DNVP in the concordat negotiations. The concordat that Prussia concluded with the Vatican on 14 June 1929 fell far short of the DNVP's demands for parity with the Lutheran Church and provoked immediate condemnation from the DNVP party leadership. Since ratification of the concordat in the Prussian Landtag was by no means certain, the ten Catholics who belonged to the DNVP's Prussian delegation found themselves caught between the insistence of the party leadership that they must maintain solidarity with the delegation majority by voting against ratification and pressure from the local and district leaders of the party's Catholic committees to join the Center in voting for ratification.[116] For the leaders of the DNVP Reich Catholic Committee, their "trial by fire," as Landsberg put it at a hastily convened meeting of the

[112] Minutes of the DNVP Reich Catholic Committee, 5 Dec. 1928, VWA Münster, NL Landsberg, E1.

[113] For example, see Albrecht Philipp, *Betrachtungen zur Konkordatsfrage*, Schriften der Deutschnationalen Volkspartei Sachsen, no. 21 (Dresden, 1927). See also Norbert Friedrich, "'National, Sozial, Christlich'. Der Evangelische Reichsausschuß der Deutschnationalen Volkspartei in der Weimarer Republik," *Kirchliche Zeitgeschichte* 6 (1993): 290–311, esp. 297–301, and Jonathan Wright, *"Above Parties": The Political Attitudes of the German Protestant Church Leadership, 1918–1933* (Oxford, 1974), 38–42.

[114] Minutes of Hugenberg's meeting with representatives from the DNVP's Reich Catholic and Evangelical Reich Committees, 6 Dec. 1928, VWA Münster, NL Landsberg, E1.

[115] "Entschließung zur Konkordatsfrage," 8 Dec. 1928, BA Berlin, R 8005, 15/18. See also "Gutachten in der Sache des preußischen Konkordats," n.d., appended to a letter from Mumm to Westarp, 28 Mai 1929, NL Westarp, Gärtringen, VN 102. For further information, see *Die Konkordatsfrage*, Deutschnationales Rüstzeug, no. 14 (Berlin, 1928), 18–21, 26–30.

[116] Glasebock and Klövekorn from the DNVP State Catholic Committee for the Lower Rhein (Landes-Katholikenausschuß Niederrhein der Deutschnationalen Volkspartei) to the DNVP Prussian Landtag delegation, 27 June 1929, BA Berlin, NL Mumm, 655/252–54.

committee on 19 June 1929, had arrived.[117] Virtually the entire committee supported Landsberg's argument that the Catholic members of the Prussian delegation should be allowed to vote according to the dictates of their conscience and denounced the efforts of the party's Prussian leadership to impose party discipline upon the Catholics in the DNVP delegation. Only Spahn, one of Hugenberg's closest confidants in the party, struck a dissenting note when he claimed that the concordat was essentially a ploy by the Social Democrats to play one confession off against the other and sew disunity in the ranks of the nationalist Right. For Spahn the highest priority was to preserve the unity of the Prussian delegation regardless of whether it voted to support or reject ratification of the concordat.[118]

At a joint meeting of the DNVP's two confessional committees under Keudell's chairmanship later that afternoon, Wilhelm Koch and the leaders of the party's Lutheran faction reaffirmed their party's commitment to the principle of confessional parity and insisted that the delegation abide by the resolution of the DNVP party representation from 8 December 1928. In the face of strong opposition from the DNVP's Lutheran leadership, Landsberg and his supporters insisted that the Catholic members of the Prussian delegation should be allowed to vote their conscience and that the party would be ill-advised to force them to do otherwise.[119] On the following day Landsberg wrote to Hugenberg to register the severity with which the DNVP Reich Catholic Committee and the Catholic members of the Prussian delegation viewed the situation. Not only did Landsberg stress that his committee had neither the desire nor the power to impose any sort of discipline on the Catholic members of the Prussian delegation, but he warned that those Catholic deputies who failed to support the concordat would find themselves alienated from the rest of the committee by such a profound gulf that future cooperation within the framework of the committee would be impossible.[120] Hugenberg, who felt that party unity and tactical considerations took priority

---

[117] Landsberg's remarks at the meeting of the DNVP Reich Catholic Committee, 19 June 1929, VWA Münster, NL Landsberg, E1. See the entry in Gallwitz's diary, 19 June 1929, BA-MA Freiburg, NL Gallwitz, 49. On the dilemma of DNVP Catholics, see Landsberg to Mumm, 9 June 1929, BA Berlin, NL Mumm, 655/232. For further details, see Hübner, *Rechtskatholiken*, 541–70.

[118] Minutes of the DNVP Reich Catholic Committee, 19 June 1929, VWA Münster, NL Landsberg, E1. For Landsberg's account of this meeting, see [Engelbert von Landsberg-Steinfurth], *Der Reichskatholikenausschuß und das Konkordat. Eine Rechenschaftsbericht* (N.p., n.d. [1929]), 4–5, in VWA Münster, NL Landsberg, E4.

[119] Minutes of a meeting between representatives from the DNVP Reich Catholic Committee and the DNVP Evangelical Reich Committee, 19 June 1929, VWA Münster, NL Landsberg, E1.

[120] Landsberg to Hugenberg, 20 June 1929, VWA Münster, NL Landsberg, E1. The text of this letter has been published as appendix IIa in [Landsberg-Velen], *Reichskatholikenausschuß und das Konkordat*, 11–12.

over the sectarian concerns of the DNVP's Catholics, responded coolly to Landsberg's entreaties and simply repeated the well rehearsed arguments of those within the DNVP's Prussian delegation who opposed ratification of the concordat.[121]

On 1 July Landsberg and Max Wallraf from the DNVP's Reich Catholic Committee met with Hugenberg and other party leaders in a last-ditch effort to break the impasse over the concordat. Hugenberg and the party leadership remained firm in making the DNVP's support of the concordat with the Catholic Church in Prussia contingent upon the simultaneous conclusion of a similar arrangement with the Prussian Lutheran Church.[122] Whatever hopes Landsberg may have had of averting an open break with the DNVP party leadership were definitively dashed when at the close of a tumultuous meeting of the DNVP Prussian Landtag delegation on 5 July Hugenberg announced that "in the final vote no deputy, as long as he is a member of the delegation, may vote for acceptance of the concordat." The delegation then incorporated Hugenberg's statement into a resolution it adopted over the strenuous objections of its Catholic members.[123] To Landsberg, Hugenberg's action infringed upon the individual deputy's freedom of conscience, and he protested vigorously that this constituted a breach of the party's faith with its Catholic supporters.[124] One member of the delegation, Franz Goldau, was so aggrieved by Hugenberg's handling of the matter that on the day before the decisive vote in the Prussian Landtag he announced that he would vote for the concordat regardless of the consequences this might have for his membership in the DNVP's Prussian delegation.[125] The remaining Catholics in the DNVP's Prussian delegation, however, submitted to party discipline and voted against the proposed concordat when it came up for ratification on 9 July 1929.[126]

Although Hugenberg's opposition was not sufficient to keep the concordat from finding the votes it needed for ratification, his refusal to allow the Catholic members of the Prussian delegation to vote according to their conscience represented the final indignity for Landsberg and his supporters. Frustrated by the lack of support his efforts at a compromise had received at

---

[121] Brackel to Landsberg, 21 June 1929, VWA Münster, NL Landsberg, II.

[122] For Landsberg's account of his meeting, see [Landsberg-Velen], *Reichskatholikenausschuß und Konkordat*, 5–6. See also Landsberg to Buchner, 4 July 1929, VWA Münster, NL Landsberg, II, also in BA Koblenz, Nachlass Max Buchner, 66.

[123] For a defense of the resolution, see "Die Wahrheit über die Konkordats-Verhandlungen!," n.d. [July 1929], BA Berlin, NL Mumm, 655/289. See also Hugenberg to Landsberg, 10 July 1929, 10 July 1929, VWA Münster, NL Landsberg, II.

[124] Landsberg to Hugenberg, 6 July 1929, VWA Münster, NL Landsberg, II.

[125] Statement by Goldau, 8 July 1929, BA Berlin, R 8005, 474/12. See also the memorandum by Brackel, n.d. [July 1929], VWA Münster, NL Landsberg, II.

[126] Entry in Gallwitz's diary, 10 July 1929, BA-MA Freiburg, NL Gallwitz, 41. See also *Unsere Partei* 7, no. 14 (15 July 1929): 238–39.

the upper echelons of the party leadership, Landsberg informed Hugenberg that it was no longer possible for him to function as a representative of the party's Catholic interests and that he was resigning both as chairman of the DNVP Reich Catholic Committee and from the committee itself.[127] Landsberg was immediately joined in his decision to leave the committee by its deputy chairman Paul Lejeune-Jung, Reichstag deputy Max Wallraf, Max Buchner from Bavaria, Willy Glasebock from the Rhineland, Viktor Lukassowitz and Kurt Ziesché from Silesia, and retired general Max von Gallwitz from southwest Germany.[128] Aside from Goldau, none of the party's Catholic leaders went so far as to leave the party, although their disenchantment with Hugenberg's political leadership was indeed great. The leaders of the DNVP's Catholic wing were demoralized by these events, and their loyalty to the party, particularly under Hugenberg's leadership, could no longer be taken for granted.

The DNVP Catholics were the first casualties of Hugenberg's efforts to transform the DNVP from a sociologically and confessionally heterogeneous conservative *Sammelpartei* into a block forged by "the iron hammer of *Weltanschauung*." As his first major test of strength with those who did not fully share his political agenda, the dispute over the Prussian concordat exposed Hugenberg's shortcomings as a political leader and in particular his inability to compromise when that was clearly the reasonable course of action. But as developments within the German People's Party and Center clearly indicated, the unrest that existed within the DNVP was by no means confined to that party alone. In fact, the entire spectrum of bourgeois politics seemed to be in a state of ferment that suggested that far-reaching changes in the structure of the German party system were at hand. For Hugenberg and the leaders of the radical Right, the question was whether they could turn this to their own advantage and transform the uneasiness that had made itself manifest in various sectors of Germany's party system into a mandate for political change.

[127] Landsberg to Hugenberg, 9 July 1929, VWA Münster, NL Landsberg, II, reprinted in [Landsberg-Steinfurt], *Reichskatholikenausschuß und Konkordat. Ein Rechenschaftsbericht*, 13. See also the entries in Gallwitz's diary, 8–10 July 1929, BA-MA Freiburg, NL Gallwitz, 41.
[128] Ibid. See also Lejeune-Jung to Hugenberg, 6 July 1929, in [Landsberg-Steinfurt], *Reichskatholikenausschuß und Konkordat*, 13, as well as Lukassowitz to Landsberg, 11 July 1929, and Gallwitz to Landsberg, 7 and 16 July 1929, both in VWA Münster, NL Landsberg, II. On Gallwitz, see Jakob Jung, *Max von Gallwitz (1952-1937). General und Politiker* (Osnabrück, 1995), 175–84.

15

The Chimera of Right-Wing Unity

Speaking before the DVP central executive committee in February 1929, Gustav Stresemann exclaimed: "Let us not delude ourselves: We stand in a crisis of parliamentarism that is far more than a mere crisis of confidence or no confidence in a particular government."[1] DDP party chairman Erich Koch-Weser echoed these sentiments several months later when in his keynote address at the DDP's Mannheim party congress in early October 1929 he stated: "The [Weimar] Constitution is good. But what the parties have made of it is a mockery."[2] Coming from two of Germany's most highly respected liberal statesmen, these comments reflected the growing uneasiness that even those who were most deeply committed to the existing constitutional order were beginning to feel about the way in which it had developed over the course of the previous decade. At the heart of the problem lay the fact that Germany's political parties had been transformed more and more into instruments of the special economic interests that constituted their material base. This was very much a legacy of the role that organized economic interests had played in the stabilization of the mark in 1923–24 and in the return to a measure of economic normalcy in the second half of the 1920s. But with the onset of the great depression, the level of social and economic conflict was intensified to the point where Germany's parliamentary system was no longer capable of generating a viable domestic consensus for the conduct of national policy, a fact that had become all too apparent in the torturous negotiations that accompanied the reorganization of the Müller cabinet in the spring of 1929. The crisis to which Stresemann and Koch-Weser were alluding had suddenly become a fact of German political life.[3]

---

[1] Stresemann's speech before the DVP central executive committee, 26 Feb. 1929, PA AA Berlin, NL Stresemann, 103/174673–90, reprinted in an abridged version as "Die Krise des Parlamentarismus," *Deutsche Stimmen* 41, no. 5 (5 Mar. 1929): 134–41.

[2] Koch-Weser's speech at the DDP's Mannheim party congress, 4 Oct. 1929, in *Der Demokrat. Mitteilungen aus der Deutschen Demokratischen Partei* 10, no. 20 (20 Oct. 1929): 486–96.

[3] For various iterations of this argument, see Werner Conze, "Die Krise des Parteienstaates in Deutschland 1928/30," *Historische Zeitschrift* 178 (1954): 47–83; Lothar Albertin, "Die Auflösung der bürgerlichen Mitte und die Krise des parlamentarischen Systems von

Overtures to Right-Wing Unity

The increasing paralysis of Germany's parliamentary system clearly worked to the advantage of the German Right. No organization on the German Right was more eager to move into the vacuum created by the paralysis of Weimar democracy than the Stahlhelm. The outcome of the 1928 Reichstag elections and the formation of a new national government under Social Democratic leadership had produced a backlash against those within the Stahlhelm who had staked their organization's future on the cultivation of close ties with the various right-wing parties. Seldte, the more moderate of the Stahlhelm's two national leaders, signaled that he had lost all hope in Stresemann's leadership of the DVP and that he no longer saw any point in trying to work with the German Foreign Minister.[4] At the same time, the activists around Duesterberg had grown increasingly frustrated with their organization's political ineffectiveness and were pressing for a more aggressive stance in the struggle against democracy and the legacy of the November Revolution.[5] The growing radicalization of the Stahlhelm in the wake of the 1928 Reichstag elections could be seen not only in Morosowicz's infamous "Fürstenwald Hate Declaration" but also in the widespread sympathy that Hugenberg's bid for the DNVP party chairmanship enjoyed among the more militant elements in the Stahlhelm organization.

In an attempt to channel the frustration of those within the Stahlhelm who advocated a more aggressive course of action, the Stahlhelm executive committee decided at a meeting in late September 1928 to initiate a popular referendum for a revision of the Weimar Constitution.[6] The author of this proposal was Heinz Brauweiler, a Catholic conservative who had joined the Stahlhelm in 1926 to become the editor of its national newspaper before being appointed head of the Stahlhelm's political division a year or so later.[7] A neo-conservative activist with close ties to the Ring Movement, Brauweiler had championed a reform of the Weimar Constitution along corporatist lines in

Weimar," in *Demokratie in der Krise. Parteien im Verfassungssystem der Weimarer Republik*, ed. Eberhard Kolb and Walter Mühlhausen (Munich, 1997), 59–111; and Andreas Wirsching, "Koalition, Opposition, Interessenpolitik. Probleme des Weimarer Parteienparlamentarismus," in *Parlamentarismus in Europa. Deutschland, England und Frankreich*, ed. Marie-Luise Recker (Munich, 2004), 41–64.

[4] Wegener to Hugenberg, 31 Aug. 1928, BA Koblenz, NL Wegener, 65/295–96.

[5] For example, see Loewe to the Berlin headquarters of the Stahlhelm, 11 July 1928, and Borck to Seldte and Duesterberg, 11 July 1928, StA Mönchen-Gladbach, NL Brauweiler, 117, as well as Lüninck to Brauweiler, 11 Aug. 1928, VWA Münster, NL Lüninck, 769.

[6] Minutes of the Stahlhelm executive committee, 22–23 Sept. 1928, BA Berlin, R 72, 9/90–95. For further details, see Klotzbücher, "Der politische Weg des Stahlhelm," 169–86, and Berghahn, *Stahlhelm*, 103–22.

[7] Brauweiler, "Meine Tätigkeit im 'Stahlhelm'," 22 Dec. 1965, StA Mönchen-Gladbach, NL Brauweiler, 110.

the early years of the Weimar Republic and in 1925 had outlined a comprehensive proposal for the reorganization of state, society, and economy in his book *Berufsstand und Staat.*[8] Brauweiler's proposed reform of the Weimar Constitution had two central features: first, a call to strengthen the powers of the Reich President by vesting him with the authority to appoint the chancellor without the consent of the Reichstag and, second, a proposal to lift the immunity of deputies charged with high treason.[9] To be sure, all of this fell far short of the sweeping constitutional reforms that Brauweiler had originally envisaged in his publications from the early 1920s, but it nevertheless represented the common denominator upon which not just the various factions within the Stahlhelm but all of the right-wing parties and organizations that the Stahlhelm hoped to bring together could agree.

The strategic objective that lay at the heart of Brauweiler's proposal was to place the Stahlhelm at the head of the national movement and to establish it as the focal point around which the various organizations that belonged to the national movement would revolve. Even the more activist elements around Duesterberg and Morosowicz lined up in support of Brauweiler's proposal, and on 22–23 September 1928 the Stahlhelm executive committee issued a resolution announcing its plans to initiate a referendum for a reform of the Weimar Constitution.[10] The leaders of the Stahlhelm immediately entered into negotiations with other organizations on the German Right to determine to what extent they were willing to join the Stahlhelm in launching a referendum for a revision of the constitution.[11] On 18 October Seldte, Duesterberg, and Brauweiler met with Schiele, Hepp, and Arno Kriegsheim from the National Rural League and received tentative commitments of support for the proposed referendum.[12] In a parallel move, the leaders of the Stahlhelm took steps to

---

[8] Heinz Brauweiler, *Berufsstand und Staat. Betrachtungen über eine neuständische Verfassung des deutschen Staates* (Berlin, 1925). See also Brauweiler, "Parlamentarismus und berufsständische Verfassungsreform," *Preußischer Jahrbücher* 202, no. 1 (Oct. 1925): 58–72.

[9] Brauweiler before the Stahlhelm executive committee, 22–23 Sept. 1928, BA Berlin, R 72, 9/90–95. For further details, see Simon, "Brauweiler," 221–30, as well as Volker R. Berghahn, "Das Volksbegehren gegen den Young-Plan und die Ursprünge des Präsidialregimes, 1928–1930," in *Industrielle Gesellschaft und politisches System. Beiträge zur politischen Sozialgeschichte. Festschrift für Fritz Fischer zum siebzigsten Geburtstag,* ed. Dirk Stegmann, Bernd-Jürgen Wendt, and Peter-Christian Witt (Bonn, 1978), 431–46.

[10] In this respect, see Friedrich Everling, *Warum bekämpfen wir den Parlamentarismus?,* Stahlhelm-Flugschrift, no. 1 (n.p. [Berlin], n.d. [1929]), and Alexander Pache, *Die Krisis der Verfassung. Ein aufklärendes Wort zum Volksbegehren* (Zwickau, n.d. [1929]).

[11] Duesterberg to Seldte, 27 Sept. 1928, BA Berlin, R 72, 300/4. See also Duesterberg to Wagner, 26 Sept. 1928, ibid., 300/30–31.

[12] Protocol of a meeting between leaders of the Stahlhelm and RLB, 18 Oct. 1928, BA Berlin, R 72, 49/25–33. See also Kriegsheim to the RLB district and local offices, 13 Oct. 1928, BA Berlin, R 8034 I, 74/2.

repair its relations with the DVP through the offices of Erich von Gilsa, a member of the DVP Reichstag delegation who also belonged to the Stahlhelm and enjoyed good relations with its leaders.[13] Of the organizations with which Brauweiler and the leaders of the Stahlhelm established contact in the fall of 1928, only the Young German Order refused to make so much as a tentative commitment to the Stahlhelm's proposed referendum, with the result that relations between the two organizations were on the brink of an open break.[14]

In the meantime, Seldte traveled extensively throughout the country lining up commitments from prominent businessmen and industrialists, not the least of whom was Wilhelm Cuno, the former chancellor and currently chief executive of the Hamburg-American Shipping Lines (Hamburg-Amerikanische Packetenfahrt-AG or HAPAG) in Hamburg.[15] Cuno had maintained a low profile ever since his resignation as chancellor in the late summer of 1923. But after the dismal showing of Germany's right-wing parties in the 1928 national elections, Cuno launched a political comeback that his supporters hoped would end in his election to the Reich presidency.[16] In October 1928 Cuno invited representatives of various right-wing organizations from northern Germany for a steamer trip on the Elbe. The outing was organized under the auspices the Hamburg National Club of 1919 (Hamburger Nationaler Klub von 1919), and its purpose was to discuss what could be done to restore the unity and striking force of the German Right. The participants represented a cross-section of Germany's conservative elite and included spokesmen for the National Club's sister organizations in Augsburg, Berlin, and Saxony, the German Gentlemen's Club in Berlin and its affiliated societies, or *Herrengesellschaften*, from throughout the Reich, as well as a delegation from the United Patriotic Associations of Germany under the leadership of Count Rüdiger von der Goltz. Most of those in attendance were committed to a restoration of the monarchy, although for some this was more a goal for the distant rather than the immediate future. Setting aside whatever differences there may have been on the appropriate form of government, the participants not only agreed to support Cuno's candidacy for the Reich Presidency but also encouraged the immediate creation of a nonpartisan "Reich Committee of German Men from the Parties of the Right and Middle" to counter the splintering of Germany's bourgeois forces.[17]

---

[13] Wagner to Czettritz, 27 Oct. 1928, BA Berlin, R 72, 35/28–29.

[14] Ibid.

[15] Seldte to Wegener, 19 Nov. 1928, BA Koblenz, NL Wegener, 28/49.

[16] On Cuno's activities in the late Weimar Republic, see Gerhard Granier, *Magnus von Levetzow. Seeoffizier, Monarchist und Wegbereiter Hitlers. Lebensweg und ausgewählte Dokumente* (Boppard, 1982), 129–70.

[17] On the outing on the Elbe, see the report by Holten (?), n.d. [May–June 1930], BA-MA Freiburg, Nachlass Magnus von Levetzow, 54/28–34, and Levetzow to Wildgrube, 8 Oct. 1928, ibid., 51/187. See also Manfred Asendorf, "Hamburger Nationalklub,

A particularly important player in the efforts to unify the German Right in the late 1920s was the retired admiral Magnus von Levetzow. Levetzow enjoyed close ties to the imperial household in Doorn, and in October 1928 he began to receive regular subsidies from the exiled Kaiser for the support of patriotic projects as part of a plan to lay the groundwork for a return of the monarchy.[18] Though unequivocally committed to the restoration of the monarchy, Levetzow did not believe that this lay in the Germany's immediate future and believed that in the interim he should concentrate his energies on the unification of the German Right.[19] By the fall of 1928 Cuno, Levetzow, and the VVVD's Goltz had developed a close working relationship in establishing a broadly based alliance of all right-wing organizations in Germany. Among other things, Levetzow helped Cuno gain access to Bavarian monarchist circles, although a meeting in Munich of Cuno and his entourage with representatives of the south Germany's landed aristocracy in early December 1928 to solicit their support for the creation of a national umbrella organization for the German Right foundered on the latter's particularist sympathies. Still, the two groups affirmed a far-reaching consensus on most other political issues, including the possibility of a Cuno candidacy for the Reich Presidency.[20]

The efforts of Cuno, Levetzow, and Goltz paralleled those of the Stahlhelm. In late September 1928 Levetzow established contact with Seldte and apprised him of the plans for the creation of an umbrella organization for the entire German Right.[21] Levetzow had taken notice of the "Fürstenwald Hate Declaration" and the Stahlhelm's plans to initiate a popular referendum for a revision of the Weimar Constitution and looked upon the Stahlhelm as a potential ally in his efforts to unify the German Right.[22] Seldte, Duesterberg, and Brauweiler took part in the second meeting of the Cuno circle in Hamburg in late November 1928. Seldte and Duesterberg were appointed to the steering committee that took shape in January 1929 under the chairmanship of the VVVD's Goltz to lay the foundation for the creation of a large national committee embracing all of the political parties, economic interest

Keppler-Kreis, Arbeitsstelle Schacht und der Aufstieg Hitlers," *1999. Zeitschrift für Sozialgeschichte des 20. und 21. Jahrhunderts* 2 (1987): 106–50, esp. 106–16.

[18] On the terms of Levetzow's support, see Sell to Levetzow, 24 Aug. 1928, BA-MA Freiburg, NL Levetzow, 51/159–60. See also Holger H. Herwig, "From Kaiser to Führer: The Political Road of a German Admiral, 1923–33," *Journal of Contemporary History* 9 (1974): 107–20.

[19] See Levetzow to Hugenberg, 23 Oct. 1928, BA-MA Freiburg, NL Levetzow, 51/207, and Sell, 27 Oct. 1928, ibid., 51/214–15.

[20] Holten's report, May–June 1930, ibid., 54/28–34.

[21] Ibid.

[22] Levetzow to Donnersmark, 27 Oct. 1928, BA-MA Freiburg, NL Levetzow, 82/103–05.

organizations, patriotic associations, and political clubs that sought a change in the existing political system.[23] At its first meeting on 11 January the committee discussed the Stahlhelm's proposed referendum for a revision of the Weimar Constitution but made its participation contingent upon that of the National Rural League and DNVP.[24] Although Seldte had sought good relations with Hugenberg following the latter's election to the DNVP party chairmanship in late October 1928,[25] the leaders of the Stahlhelm were apprehensive that the DNVP might try to preempt their referendum for a revision of the Weimar Constitution by coming out with their own proposals for constitutional reform.[26]

A Modest Proposal

The Stahlhelm's negotiations with the DNVP both before and after Hugenberg's election to the party chairmanship proved far more difficult than its leaders had ever anticipated. In the lead-up to the election of the new party chairman, Westarp had sought an alliance that was closer than the leaders of the Stahlhelm were willing to accept and remained cool to their idea of a referendum for constitutional revision.[27] After his election as DNVP party chairman, Hugenberg expressed initial support for the Stahlhelm's referendum[28] but began to waver about making a formal commitment as the date for publication of the appeal drew near. The Stahlhelm chose 13 November 1928, the tenth anniversary of the Stahlhelm's founding in Magdeburg, to present the formal text of the proposed referendum and announced that it would form a National Committee for the Referendum (Reichsausschuß für das Volksbegehren) in which all of those organizations that supported the campaign for a revision of the Weimar Constitution would be represented.[29] The Stahlhelm officially launched the campaign at a national leadership conference (Reichsführertagung) in Magdeburg on 19 January 1929, the tenth anniversary of the elections to the Weimar National Assembly and the symbolic birth date of the

---

[23] For Goltz's objectives, see Goltz, "Was wollen die Vereinigten vaterländischen Verbände Deutschlands," 24 July 1929, BA Berlin, Zsg 1, E87.

[24] Holten's report, May–June 1930, BA-MA Freiburg, NL Levetzow, 54/28–34.

[25] Correspondence between Seldte and Wegener, 19 Oct.–16 Nov. 1928, BA Koblenz, NL Wegener, 28/44–49.

[26] Brauweiler to Seldte, 4 Oct. 1928, StA Mönchen-Gladbach, NL Brauweiler, 117.

[27] Ibid. See also Seldte to Brauweiler, 26 Sept. 1928, ibid. For Westarp's assessment of the proposed referendum, see his letter to Hiller von Gaertringen, 6 Feb. 1929, NL Westarp, Gärtringen, VN 82.

[28] Seldte to Wegener, 16 Nov. 1928, BA Koblenz, NL Wegener, 28/44–45.

[29] Brauweiler's remarks at a meeting of the Stahlhelm executive committee, 24–25 Nov. 1928, BA Berlin, R 72, 9/17–20.

Weimar Republic.[30] But the flurry of activity that accompanied the official promulgation of the referendum at the turn of the new year provoked a sharp rebuke from a totally unexpected quarter, the DNVP. In late February 1929 Baron Axel von Freytagh-Loringhoven, a Hugenberg loyalist and the party's expert on constitutional affairs, caught everyone off guard when he categorically rejected the proposed referendum before a large crowd of VVVD supporters in Berlin.[31] Although Hugenberg moved quickly to censor the dissident DNVP deputy and thus prevent a further strain in his party's relations with the Stahlhelm,[32] the prevailing sentiment within the DNVP was that both the Stahlhelm and the National Rural League would have to subordinate themselves to its leadership if the creation of a united German Right and the struggle for a change in the existing political system were to be successful.[33]

For the leaders of the Stahlhelm, what mattered the most was not so much the actual language of the referendum itself as the sense of right-wing unity to which they hoped the referendum campaign would give rise.[34] In a memorandum prepared for the leaders of the Stahlhelm in mid-March 1929, Brauweiler reviewed the progress the Stahlhelm had made in securing commitments from the parties and organizations on the German Right. According to Brauweiler, firm commitments of support had been received from twelve nationalist associations, including the VVVD, the Pan-German League, the German Noble's Society, the German Gentlemen's Club, the Reich Citizens' Council, and the National Association of German Officers. Only Mahraun's Young German Order and the Tannenburg League (Tannenburg-Bund) under the leadership of Erich Ludendorff of World War I fame declined to take part. Of the various political parties, both the DNVP and CNBLP promised their full support, while negotiations with spokesmen for the DVP, the Business Party, the German-Hanoverian Party (Deutsch-Hannoversche Partei), and the Bavarian People's Party were still under way. Brauweiler also noted that the National Socialists had expressed reservations about the proposed referendum and were apparently fearful that its defeat might have a negative impact upon their movement's prospects. Of the various economic interest organizations, both the National Rural League and the Rhenish and Westphalian peasant

---

[30] W[ilhelm] K[leinau], "Reichsführertagung des Stahlhelms," *Die Standarte* 4, no. 4 (26 Jan. 1929): 75–76. See also the two flyers "Warum Stahlhelm-Volksbegehren? Ein Wort an Alle!," n.d., and "Warum Stahlhelm-Volksbegehren? Ein Wort an die Führer!," n.d., both in the Hoover Institution Archives, Special Collections, Box 8, Folder 183.

[31] Ausfeld to Marklowski, 20 Feb. 1929, BA Berlin, R 72, 55/82–83.

[32] Ausfeld to Marklowski, 8 Mar. 1929, ibid., 55/75–77.

[33] Leopold Reisner, *Stahlhelm, Landbund und Deutschnationale Volkspartei*, ed. Deutschnationale Volkspartei, Landesverband Frankfurt (Oder) (Landsberg a.W., n.d. [1929]).

[34] Ausfeld to Marklowski, 8 Mar. 1929, BA Berlin, R 72, 55/75–77.

unions had committed their full support, but negotiations with the German National Union of Commercial Employees had reached an impasse, in large part because the DHV feared that support of the referendum might jeopardize its ties to the Christian labor movement. The support of industry, Brauweiler continued, was contingent upon the position of the DVP, although Cuno had promised to use his contacts with Germany's industrial leadership on behalf of the referendum.[35]

Brauweiler and the leaders of the Stahlhelm planned to announce the composition of the National Committee for the Referendum by the middle of March. But differences with the National Rural League over the wording of the statement that was to be released in conjunction with the appointment of the committee made it impossible for the leaders of the Stahlhelm to meet this deadline.[36] To maintain a sense of momentum, the leaders of the Stahlhelm decided to go ahead with the publication of an appeal that would carry the signatures of prominent individuals who supported the referendum but without listing the various organizations that would constitute the National Referendum Committee.[37] In the meantime, negotiations with the German People's Party drew to a standstill despite Gilsa's efforts to repair the damage that the "Fürsterwald Hate Declaration" had done to its relations with the Stahlhelm.[38] A far more serious obstacle, however, was the attitude of the National Socialists and their leader Adolf Hitler. In late April 1929 Hitler sent the Stahlhelm a twenty-six page position paper in which he outlined in great detail the NSDAP's reasons for not supporting the proposed referendum. With characteristic scorn, Hitler argued that the proposal to strengthen the powers of the Reich Presidency could easily benefit the Social Democrats if they were ever to regain control of the presidency. Hitler also expressed doubts that the campaign for a revision of the Weimar Constitution could ever generate the emotional momentum necessary for success. Even should it succeed, he continued, its effect would only be to distract the national opposition from the struggle for a fundamental and indeed revolutionary change in the system of government to which the German people were now subject.[39]

[35] Brauweiler, "Betrifft: Stahlhelm-Volksbegehren," 12 Mar. 1929, BA-MA Freiburg, NL Levetzow, 52/92-96.
[36] Wagener to Levetzow, 21 Mar. 1929, BA-MA Freiburg, NL Levetzow, 52/103. See also Brauweiler's remarks before of the Stahlhelm executive committee, 16-17 Feb. 1929, BA Berlin, R 72/11/240-41, as well as Seldte and Duesterberg to an unidentified recipient, 21 Mar. 1929, appended to Friedrichs (VVVD) to Levetzow, 22 Mar. 1929, BA-MA Freiburg, NL Levetzow, 53/112-13.
[37] Brauweiler to Lüninck, 21 Mar. 1929, VWA Münster, NL Lüninck, 769.
[38] Gilsa to Seldte, 16 Mar. 1929, BA Berlin, R 72, 35/55.
[39] Hitler to the Stahlhelm leadership, n.d. [Apr. 1929], BA Berlin, NS 26, 863. See also Hess to the Stahlhelm leadership, 27 Apr. 1929, StA Mönchen-Gladbach, NL Brauweiler, 114.

Stunned by the substance and tone of Hitler's statement,[40] the leaders of the Stahlhelm refused to let this deter them from their plans to initiate a popular referendum for a revision of the Weimar Constitution. On 17 May Hugenberg reached agreement with the RLB's Martin Schiele and the leaders of the Stahlhelm on the creation of the National Referendum Committee.[41] Six days later Seldte announced that their organizations, along with the Christian-National Peasants and Farmers' Party and the United Patriotic Leagues, had come together to form the National Referendum Committee and invited prominent politicians from a wide array of right-wing parties, interest groups, and patriotic associations to join the committee and sign a public appeal in support of its to referendum for constitutional reform.[42] But Hitler's arguments against the Stahlhelm's referendum had struck a responsive chord not just among the Stahlhelm rank and file[43] but also with Hugenberg and the leaders of the DNVP. Insisting that a referendum for a revision of the Weimar Constitution lacked the emotional charge necessary to galvanize the German Right into a cohesive political force, Hugenberg used a meeting of the DNVP executive committee on 15 June 1929 to propose that the forces of the German Right use the referendum provisions of the Weimar Constitution not to seek a revision of the constitution but to force a change in the conduct of German foreign policy. Specifically Hugenberg recommended the introduction of a popular referendum to block ratification of an international treaty that Stresemann was negotiating with the Allies for a revision of the Dawes Plan be followed by a referendum aimed at the revocation of the War Guilt Clause of the Versailles Treaty.[44] Hugenberg and his supporters hoped to reignite their campaign against Weimar parliamentarism by using those emotionally charged foreign policy issues upon which the various factions on the German Right could all agree and with which the fate of Germany's republican system of government had become inextricably intertwined.

The leaders of the Stahlhelm were incensed by the way in which they had been blindsided by Hugenberg and the DNVP party leadership. But what

---

[40] Wagner to Levetzow, 28 Apr. 1929, BA-MA Levetzow, 52/239. See also Allesandro Salvador, "The Political Strategies of the Stahlhelm Veterans' League and the National Socialist German Workers' Party, 1918–1933," in *Movements and Ideas of the Extreme Right in Europe: Positions and Continuities*, ed. Nicola Kristina Karcher and Anders G. Kjøstvedt (Frankfurt a.M., 2012), 57–78.

[41] Draft of an agreement between Hugenberg, Schiele, Duesterberg, and Seldte, 17 May 1929, NL Westarp, Gärtringen, II/37. See also excerpts from the minutes of the RLB executive committee, 1 May 1929, BA Berlin, R 8034 I, 120/213–17.

[42] Invitation from Seldte, 23 May 1929, StA Mönchen-Gladbach, NL Brauweiler, 114. For the strategic objectives behind the appeal, see Sell to Levetzow, 9 May 1929, BA-MA Freiburg, NL Levetzow, 52/274–76,

[43] Lenz to the Stahlhelm, 24 June 1929, StA Mönchen-Gladbach, NL Brauweiler, 114.

[44] *Unsere Partei* 7, no. 13 (1 July 1929): 207–09.

made their situation even more awkward was the fact that Hugenberg then proceeded to constitute a new committee of his own, the National Committee for the German Referendum (Reichsausschuß für das deutsche Volksbegehren), to oversee the crusade he planned to launch against Stresemann and the policy of fulfillment.[45] The Stahlhelm tried to save face by agreeing to postpone its referendum for a revision of the Weimar Constitution in order to clear the way for Hugenberg's initiative on the conduct of German foreign policy.[46] Even then, this was a bitter pill for Seldte, Brauweiler, and the more moderate forces in the Stahlhelm to swallow.[47] For while the leaders of the Stahlhelm clearly recognized the importance of the campaign against Stresemann's foreign policy, they were embittered by how first Hitler had dismissed their plans for a revision of the Weimar Constitution and then Hugenberg had bypassed their referendum committee to create one of his own.[48] What this reflected was a dramatic radicalization in the politics of the Germany's anti-parliamentary Right. The Stahlhelm's referendum for a revision of the Weimar Constitution was originally conceived as an attempt to contain the more radical elements in the Stahlhelm, but the initiative in using the referendum provisions of the Weimar Constitution had now passed into the hands of those looked upon the popular referenda as a way of radicalizing and polarizing the German public. A referendum against Stresemann's conduct of German foreign policy would not only preclude cooperation with the German People's Party and the more moderate groups that might have supported the Stahlhelm's campaign for a revision of the Weimar Constitution, but also shift the balance of power among the organizers of the referendum from the Stahlhelm to Hugenberg and the National Socialists.

Against the Young Plan

On 16 September 1928 Germany and the Allies agreed at Geneva to open negotiations for a revision of the Dawes Plan and a final settlement of Germany's reparations obligations. These negotiations would take place simultaneously with negotiations for an end to the Allied occupation of the Rhineland, although the German government stipulated that the two issues were to be handled separately and that there was to be no *quid pro quo*

---

[45] Brauweiler to the members of the Stahlhelm executive committee, 2 Aug. 1929, BA Berlin, R 72, 43/37–41.

[46] For example, see Morocowicz to Blank, 27 July 1929, RWWA Cologne, Abt. 130, NL Reusch, 4001012024/6.

[47] Goltz to Cuno, 22 June 1929, BA-MA Freiburg, NL Levetzow, 52/348–51.

[48] Brauweiler to the members of the Stahlhelm executive committee, 2 Aug. 1929, BA Berlin, R 72, 43/37–41. For further details, see Simon, "Brauweiler," 233–35.

between a settlement of the reparations question and the evacuation of the Rhineland.[49] Stresemann was optimistic that a new agreement on reparations would bring Germany substantial benefits, including an end to the Allied occupation of the Rhineland before the deadlines stipulated in the Versailles Peace Treaty and Locarno accords of 1925. At the same time, German industry and its supporters on the DVP's right wing were hopeful that such an agreement would provide a measure of relief from the increasingly heavy burden of its unemployment insurance program.[50] Accordingly, the Müller cabinet appointed Albert Vögler from the United Steel Works and the RDI's Ludwig Kastl to the committee of experts responsible for drafting the new reparations plan that would replace the Dawes Plan. Vögler enjoyed close relations with Hugenberg, and Stresemann obviously hoped that his appointment, along with that of Kastl, would create "a wall of personalities capable of withstanding the storm of the Hugenberg press."[51] But Vögler resigned from the committee of experts on 23 May once it became clear that the new round of negotiations would not provide the government the fiscal latitude it needed to trim management's contributions to the government's unemployment insurance program. This was an embarrassing public relations setback for Stresemann and the Müller cabinet, but neither Vögler's resignation nor the bizarre negotiating tactics of Reichsbank president Hjalmar Schacht, the most prominent member of the German delegation, kept the German authorities from accepting the terms of the new plan – now known as the Young Plan – on 31 May or initialing the final text of the agreement on 7 June 1929.[52]

The German Right would fire its first salvo in what would quickly develop into a general broadside against Stresemann's foreign policy long before the official start of negotiations in Paris in the early spring of 1929. In September 1928 the DNVP, Stahlhelm, and other patriotic associations organized a demonstration in Berlin to protest the Geneva agreement. Speaking before an estimated 12,000 participants, Westarp denounced the bankruptcy of Stresemann's foreign policy and the Geneva accord as a painful reminder of

---

[49] Peter Krüger, *Die Aussenpolitik der Republik von Weimar* (Darmstadt, 1985), 428–43.

[50] Jorg-Otto Spiller, "Reformismus nach rechts. Zur Politik des Reichsverbandes der Deutschen Industrie in den Jahren 1927–1930 am Beispiel der Reparationspolitik," in *Industrielles System und politische Entwicklung in der Weimarer Republik. Verhandlungen des Internationalen Symposiums in Bochum vom 12.–17. Juni 1973*, ed. Mommsen, Petzinna, and Weisbrod (Düsseldorf, 1974), 593–602.

[51] Stresemann to Silverberg, 4 Jan. 1929, PA AA Berlin, NL Stresemann, 76/168925–26. See also the correspondence between Vögler and Stresemann, 23–28 December 1928, ibid., 75/168814–15, 168829–31, as well as Silverberg to Stresemann, 31 Dec. 1928, ibid., 75/168864–68. For further details, see Wright, *Stresemann*, 444.

[52] Krüger, *Aussenpolitik*, 476–83. On Schacht's antics, see Christopher Kopper, *Hjalmar Schacht. Aufstieg und Fall von Hitlers mächtigsten Bankier* (Munich and Vienna, 2006), 141–57.

the humiliation that Germany had suffered at Allied hands.[53] In a speech to the Reichstag two months later Westarp hailed the end of the Locarno era and, after listing the dangers that lurked in the new round of reparations negotiations, called for an "strong, steadfast no" to Allied demands that Germany commit itself to a firm and binding schedule for the payment of reparations. Westarp ended his speech with a call for a new German offensive on reparations, the revision of Germany's eastern boundaries, and the revocation of the War Guilt Clause.[54] In a similar vein, DNVP Reichstag deputy Reinhold Quaatz denounced the new reparations plan as a "second Dawes Plan" that only perpetuated the war guilt lie, while Paul Bang, like Quaatz one of Hugenberg's strongest supporters in the DNVP Reichstag delegation, focused on the enormous economic devastation that would almost certainly result from implementation of the new reparations plan.[55] The attacks intensified as the recommendations of the Young committee of experts were published in early 1929. By now, however, the Nationalists had begun to focus more and more attention on the economic and fiscal implications of the new plan with specific emphasis on whether or not the German economy was sufficiently strong to meet the fiscal burden imposed by the new reparations plan. As Bang argued in an article from April 1929, the committee of experts had greatly overestimated Germany's capacity to pay. Compliance with the reparations provisions of the Young Plan, he concluded, would result in the complete collapse of the German economy.[56]

Against the background of these developments, Hugenberg decided to go ahead with the referendum against the Young Plan and to give it priority over the Stahlhelm's proposed referendum for a revision of the Weimar Constitution. On 15 June 1929 the DNVP executive committee decided by a near unanimous vote – only DNVP labor leader Emil Hartwig dissented – to take up the struggle against the Paris tribute plan, as the Nationalists frequently referred to the Young Plan, in accordance with the procedure outlined in Articles 72 and 73 of the Weimar Constitution.[57] The goal of this initiative would be to block implementation of the reparations plan that Germany and the Allies had approved in Paris, though not as a single party acting on its own

---

[53] Kuno von Westarp, *Die deutschnationale Reichstagsfraktion und die Pariser Tributver-handlungen* (Berlin, n.d. [1929]), 8–11.

[54] Westarp, "Kriegsschuldlüge, Kriegsächtungspankt und Tributverhandlungen," 12 Feb. 1929, ibid., 27–29. See also *Die Deutschnationalen und die Kriegstribute* (Berlin, 1928), 15–33.

[55] Ibid., 34–73.

[56] Bang, "Angebliche Leistungsfähigkeit Deutschlands," *Unsere Partei* 7, no. 7 (1 Apr. 1929): 109–10.

[57] Entry in Quaatz's diary, 18 June 1929, BA Koblenz, NL Quaatz, 16. On Hartwig's dissent, see his correspondence with Mumm, 6–16 July 1929, BA Berlin, NL Mumm, 283/143, 156.

but as a member and strongest parliamentary representative of the national movement.[58] After three weeks of furious negotiations, Hugenberg and the leaders of the "national opposition" met on 9 July 1929 in the former upper house, or Herrenhaus, of the Prussian state legislature in Berlin to announce the creation of the National Committee for the German Referendum and the beginning of their crusade against the Young Plan. In addition to Hugenberg and the Stahlhelm's Franz Seldte, the list of speakers included RLB president Martin Schiele, the VVVD's Count Rüdiger von der Goltz, the NSDAP's Adolf Hitler, the CNBLP's Albrecht Wendhausen, Paul Rüffer as a representative of the nationalist workers' movement, Annagrete Lehmann from the DNVP's National Women's Committee, and Ruhr industrialist Fritz Thyssen.[59] Conspicuous by his absence was Wilhelm Cuno, who had hoped to use the referendum to launch his campaign for the Reich Presidency but whom the organizers of the Herrenhaus demonstration had not invited for fear that this might lend his bid for the presidency a semi-official stamp of approval they were not prepared to give.[60]

The demonstration in the Herrenhaus concluded with the publication of a two paragraph resolution that announced first that the National Committee for the German Referendum had assumed responsibility for the Stahlhelm's referendum for a revision of the Weimar Constitution and second that its first priority would be to use all legal at its disposal, but particularly the referendum provisions of the Weimar Constitution, to prevent implementation of the Paris tribute plan.[61] The presidium that was to provide strategic oversight of the referendum campaign included representatives from all of the participating organizations from the DNVP and NSDAP to the Stahlhelm, the Unitied Patriotic Leagues, and Pan-German League as well as the National Rural League and the Christian-National Peasants and Farmers' Party. They were complemented by Thyssen as a spokesman for Ruhr heavy industry, Baron Ludwig von Gebsattel and Baron Hermann von Lüninck as representatives of the Bavarian and Rhenish aristocracy respectively, and a yet to be named representative for university students.[62] A task force, or *Arbeitsausschuß*, with considerable overlap in personnel with the presidium was also created to deal

---

[58] *Unsere Partei*, 7, no. 13 (1 July 1929): 208–09.
[59] *Unsere Partei* 7, no. 14 (15 July 1929): 230–33. See also the circular from Hugenberg, 11 July 1929, BA Berlin, R 8048, 262/11–12, as well as the memorandum from Brauweiler to members of the Stahlhelm executive committee, 2 Aug. 1929, BA Berlin, R 72/37–41. On Hitler's role, see Claß's unpublished memoirs, "Wider den Strom," BA Berlin, NL Claß, 3/Anhang, 37–41.
[60] Entry in Quaatz's diary, 9 July 1929, BA Koblenz, NL Quaatz, 16.
[61] *Unsere Partei* 7, no. 14 (15 July 1929): 233.
[62] Undated memorandum on the composition of the committee's presidium, BA Berlin, R 8048, 262/59.

with the tactical and organizational aspects of the anti-Young Plan crusade.[63] In addition, there were three subcommittees: a finance committee under the chairmanship of the Stahlhelm's Erich Lubbert, a judicial committee chaired by the Stahlhelm's Heinz Brauweiler, and a propaganda committee under the direction Max Weiß and Hans Brosius from the DNVP.[64] Overseeing the day-to-day operations of the National Referendum Committee was retired army officer Jenó von Egan-Krieger, a Hugenberg loyalist who enjoyed close ties to the Stahlhelm. Egan-Krieger's role in the referendum campaign was to prove critical. For although leadership of the referendum campaign clearly lay in the hands of the Stahlhelm and DNVP, Seldte and the leaders of the Stahlhelm were still angry over the way in which they had been shunted aside by Hugenberg and remained wary of the DNVP's chairman increasing dependence upon Hitler and the National Socialists.[65]

From the outset, Hugenberg attached great value to the participation of the National Socialists in the crusade against the Paris tribute plan. Accordingly, the NSDAP's Reich organizational leader Gregor Strasser was co-opted into the subcommittees for finance and propaganda and Wilhelm Frick into the judicial committee.[66] All of this ran counter to the reserve with which the DNVP had historically treated the NSDAP. In the 1928 Reichstag elections the Nationalists had portrayed Hitler as a petty demagogue whose agitation only contributed to the fragmentation of Germany's national bourgeoisie and denounced the NSDAP as a party of self-styled revolutionaries that must "be opposed with all sharpness."[67] But Hugenberg and his supporters in the Pan-German League looked beyond the NSDAP's social radicalism to the national values they believed to be at the core of Hitler's political *Weltanschauung* and were prepared to make far-reaching concessions to keep the National Socialists in the "national front."[68] Hugenberg not only cleared early drafts of the

[63] *Unsere Partei* 7, no. 14 (15 July 1929): 233.

[64] Brauweiler's circular to the Stahlhelm executive committee, 2 Aug. 1929, BA Berlin, R 72, 43/37–41. See also Blank to Springorum, 22 July 1929, RWWA Cologne, Abt. 130, NL Reusch, 4001012924/6.

[65] Brauweiler, memorandum entitled "Bemerkungen zur Lage" for Duesterberg, Czettritz, and Wagner, 23 Aug. 1929, StA Mönchen-Gladbach, NL Brauweiler, 114, also in BA Berlin, R 72, 43/121–25. On the tension between Hugenberg and the Stahlhelm, see Hugenberg to Claß, 13 July 1929, BA Berlin, R 8048, 262/24–25, and Seldte, ibid., 26–27, as well as Brauweiler's circular to the Stahlhelm executive committee, 2 Aug. 1929, BA Berlin, R 72, 43/37–41.

[66] Hitler, declaration of 26 July 1929, in Adolf Hitler, *Reden, Schriften, Anordnungen. Februar 1925 bis Januar 1933*, ed. Institute für Zeitgeschichte, 5 vols. in 12 parts (Munich, London, New York, and Paris, 1992–98) vol. 3, pt. 2, 303.

[67] [Deutschnationale Volkspartei], *Nationalsozialistische Arbeiterpartei*, Deutschnationales Rüstzeug, no. 11a (Berlin, 1928), esp. 14–1PP5.

[68] For example, see the letters from the Pan-German publicist F. J. Lehmann to Claß, 13 Aug. 1929, BA Berlin, R 8048, 262/165–66, and the VVVD, 17 Aug. 1929, BA-MA

referendum with the Nazi party leader before presenting them to the National Referendum Committee,[69] but he hoped to launch the crusade against the Young Plan by staging a major rally with Hitler as his co-speaker at the Hermann Monument near Detmold, the historic site of the battle where the Germans defeated the Roman legions of Varus at the battle of the Teutoburg forest in AD 9.[70] Hitler, on the other hand, had problems in his own party as a result of his alliance with "social reactionaries" like Hugenberg and Claß, and it only with great difficulty that he and Strasser were able to justify their participation in the National Referendum Committee to those on the NSDAP's left wing.[71] At the same time, Hugenberg's deference to the Nazi party leader rankled the leaders of the Stahlhelm and met with widespread skepticism within the ranks of his own DNVP, not the least among those with close ties to organized agriculture and the Christian-national labor movement.[72]

In the meantime, Hugenberg had begun to experience difficulties of his own with his financial backers in German industry. The leaders of Ruhr heavy industry were concerned about the fiscal and economic implications of the new reparations plan and sought a way to highlight its "economic impossibility [*Untragbarkeit*]" without compromising the position of the German government in its negotiations with the Allies.[73] The annual meeting of the Langnam-verein scheduled for 8 July 1929 was carefully orchestrated by its chairman Paul Reusch and executive secretary Max Schlenker to give both supporters and opponents of the new plan – in the latter case Vögler – an opportunity to present their respective positions for fear that their silence might otherwise be

Freiburg, NL Levetzow, 53/96–97. See also Claß's recollections of the struggle against the Young Plan in "Wider den Strom," BA Berlin, NL Claß, 3/900–07. For the attitude of the Stahlhelm, see Brauweiler, "Stahlhelm und Nationalsozialisten," *Norddeutsche Blätter. Nationale Monatsschrift* 9, no. 2 (Sept. 1929): 237–42. For further details, see Jackisch, *Pan-German League*, 160–69, and Hofmeister, "Between Monarchy and Dictatorship," 341–61.

[69] Hugenberg to Hitler, 14 Aug. 1929, in BA Berlin, Sammlung personenbezogener Unterlagen bis 1945, Bestand R 9354, 647.

[70] Ibid. For Hitler's refusal, see Hess to Hugenberg, 13 Aug. 1929, ibid.

[71] For example, see Strasser to Reinhardt, 12 Aug. 1929, BA Berlin, Sammlung Schumacher, Bestand R 187, 206.

[72] Patch, *Christian Trade Unions*, 149–50. For the most important secondary literature on the DNVP party crisis, see the unpublished dissertation by Elisabeth Friedenthal, "Volksbegehren und Volksentscheid über den Young-Plan und die deutschnationale Sezession" (Ph.D. diss., Universität Tübingen, 1957), as well as Attila A. Chanady, "The Disintegration of the German National People's Party, 1924–1930," *Journal of Modern History* 39 (1967): 65–91, and Denis Walker, "The German Nationalist People's Party: The Conservative Dilemma in the Weimar Republic," *Journal of Contemporary History* 14 (1979): 627–47.

[73] Schlenker to Reusch, 26 June 1929, RWWA Cologne, Abt. 130, NL Reusch, 400101221/9.

interpreted as acceptance.[74] Despite their strong reservations about the fiscal and economic consequences of the new reparations plan,[75] Reusch and most of his associates in Ruhr heavy industry remained decidedly cool to Hugenberg's National Committee for the German Referendum and its plans for a referendum against the Young Plan.[76] Writing to his Berlin associate Martin Blank on 24 July 1929, Reusch denounced the proposed referendum as a "great stupidity" and stated with characteristic bluntness that he had no intention of giving so much as "a single farthing [*einen roten Heller*]" to the referendum campaign.[77] Acting on Reusch's explicit instructions, Blank resigned from the finance subcommittee of the National Committee for the German Referendum with immediate repercussions on industry's willingness to underwrite the costs of Hugenberg's crusade against the Young Plan.[78] Of Germany's more prominent industrial leaders, only Thyssen and Emil Kirdorf were prepared to put their names and fortune behind Hugenberg's referendum.[79] And Albert Vögler, an outspoken and uncompromising opponent of the Young Plan in the form that it had taken by the summer of 1929,[80] was furious with the way in which Hugenberg had orchestrated the campaign against the Young Plan, although he refrained from going so far as to follow the example of his fellow industrialist Ernst Poengsen by resigning from the National Referendum Committee.[81] The disaffection of the more conservative elements in the German industrial establishment from Hugenberg's crusade against the Young Plan did not augur well for the crusade's ultimate success.

[74] Ibid. See also Schlenker to Silverberg, 25 June 1929; Vögler to Schlenker, 27 June 1929; and Vögler to Reusch, 1 July 1929, all in BA Koblenz, NL Silverberg, 415/205–09. See also Weisbrod, *Schwerindustrie in der Weimarer Republik*, 457–77.

[75] For example, see August Heinrichsbauer, "Die Konzequenzen aus dem Young-Plan," *Ruhr und Rhein* 10, no. 27 (5 July 1929): 868–73.

[76] For example, see Springorum to Hugenberg, 22 June 1929, RWWA Cologne, Abt. 130, NL Reusch, 4001012024/5b.

[77] Reusch to Blank, 24 July 1929, RWWA Cologne, Abt. 130, NL Reusch, 4001012024/6. For an elaboration of Reusch's reasons, see his letter to Miguel, 27 July 1929, ibid., 400101293/9a.

[78] Reusch to Blank, 24 July 1929, RWWA Cologne, Abt. 130, NL Reusch, 4001012024/6. See also Wilmowsky to Reusch, 15 Aug. 1929, HA Krupp Essen, FAH, 23/503.

[79] See the text of Thyssen's speech at the Herrenhaus demonstration on 9 July 1929 in *Fort mit dem Pariser Tributplan*, Kampfschrift no. 1, Berlin, 1 Aug. 1929, 6–8, a copy of which is to be found in NL Hiller, Gärtringen. See also Thyssen to the RDI, 28 May 1929, RWWA Cologne, Abt. 130, NL Reusch, 400102220/6b. On Thyssen, see Carl-Friedrich Baumann, "Fritz Thyssen und der Nationalsozialismus," *Zeitschrift des Geschichtsvereins Mühlheim a.d. Ruhr* 70 (1998): 139–54. On Kirdorf, see Henry Ashby Turner, Jr., "Emil Kirdorf and the Nazi Party," *Central European History* 1 (1968): 324–44.

[80] Vögler to Schlenker, 27 June 1929, BA Koblenz, NL Silverberg, 415/207–08.

[81] Krupp to Wilmowsky, 28 Sept. 1929, HA Krupp Essen, FAH 23/503.

A Fragile Consensus

Flanked by the ADV's Rudolf von Xylander and the Stahlhelm's Siegfried Wagner, Hugenberg launched the campaign against the Young Plan on 1 September 1929 with a speech at the monument in the Teutoburg forest that had been constructed in the 1840s to commemorate the German hero Arminius and his defeat of the Roman legions. Pointing to Arminius's sword, Hugenberg claimed that Germany's sword had been taken but would be returned when German hearts were once strong again. It was now the task of the German people, he continued, to assume the mantle of Arminius and take up the struggle against foreign domination by rejecting the Young Plan. Not only would the new tribute plan destroy Germany economically, but even more importantly, Hugenberg argued, it would sap the spiritual strength and vitality of the German people. Then, in a purely rhetorical gesture, Hugenberg asked if the German people were willing to accept the consequences of the Paris tribute plan – the terrible spiritual affliction, the new bondage, the economic ruin, the unemployment, and new currency convulsions.[82] Yet for all of the fanfare with which Hugenberg opened his crusade against the new reparations plan, the campaign revealed incipient fault lines within the anti-Young Plan coalition from the very outset. For not only did Hitler decline to join Hugenberg at the rally in the Teutoburg forest,[83] but the Stahlhelm held a separate demonstration in Brunswick, where Duesterberg, Morosowicz, and Wagner spoke before an estimated 15,000 loyalists in support of the referendum against the Young Plan.[84] Annoyed by Duesterberg's decision to hold a separate demonstration for the Stahlhelm, Hugenberg blamed Brauweiler for sabotaging the unity of the German Right.[85] Even the Pan-Germans held a demonstration of their own at Würzburg, where the ADV chairman Heinrich Claß and DNVP Reichstag deputy Paul Bang denounced the Paris tribute plan as an Allied ploy to perpetuate the enslavement of the German people.[86]

In the meantime, Hugenberg and his associates were hard at work on the text of the law that would take effect if the referendum proved successful. Hugenberg's *modus operandi* was to involve as few people as possible in preparing the text of the law – provocatively entitled the "Law against the Enslavement of the German People (Gesetz gegen die Versklavung des deutschen Volkes)" but more commonly known as the "Freedom Law

---

[82] On the demonstration at the Hermann Monument, see the report in the *Berliner Lokal-Anzeiger*, 2 Sept. 1929, no. 413.

[83] Hess to Hugenberg, 13 Aug. 1929, BA Berlin, R 9354, 647.

[84] *Volksbegehren. Pressedienst des Reichsausschusses*, ed. J. von Egan-Krieger, 8 Sept. 1929, no. 8. See also Duesterberg to Hugenberg, 15 Aug. 1929, BA Berlin, R 8048, 262/187, as well as his unpublished memoirs, BA Koblenz, NL Duesterberg, 46/144.

[85] Hugenberg to Claß, 16 Aug. 1929, BA Berlin, R 8048, 262/186.

[86] *Berliner Lokal-Anzeiger*, 2 Sept. 1929, no. 413.

(Freiheitsgesetz)" – and to circulate it to a small circle of associates before sending it to the presidium of the National Committee for the German Referendum for review at its first meeting in Nuremberg on 28 August 1929.[87] In this way, Hugenberg sought not only to bypass the National Referendum Committee's judicial subcommittee under Brauweiler but also to present a united front in the referendum committee against those in the RLB and CNBLP who might have counseled a less confrontational course of action. Brauweiler protested against his committee's exclusion from the preparation of the bill but was unable to overcome Hugenberg's refusal to submit the text of his proposed "Freedom Law" to the scrutiny of his committee.[88] Hugenberg, however, did send a copy of his draft to Westarp,[89] who as chairman of the DNVP Reichstag delegation had been left off the presidium of the National Referendum Committee on the pretext that its composition was already too heavily weighted in favor of the DNVP to justify the addition of still another Nationalist.[90] Westarp responded with a long letter that contained a number of specific recommendations for changes in the text of the proposed law, not the least of which was that Hugenberg drop a paragraph demanding that Reich authorities responsible for signing the Paris tribute plan should be tried for high treason (Landesverrat) and imprisoned according to the provisions of the federal penal code. In Westarp's words, such a provision was simply "impossible."[91]

In response to Westarp's carefully argued criticism, Hugenberg replied that he might be willing to drop the imprisonment paragraph from the text of the proposed "Freedom Law."[92] In the meantime, a group of Stahlhelm leaders including Duesterberg, Brauweiler, and Wagner met in Halle on 27 August and agreed not only that the imprisonment paragraph should be dropped but also that the wording of the proposed referendum required the unanimous consent of all the groups in the National Referendum Committee.[93] But at its meeting in Nuremberg on 28 August the presidium of the referendum committee formally approved the text of Hugenberg's "Law Against the

---

[87] In this respect, see Hugenberg to Hitler, 14 Aug. 1929, BA Berlin, R 9354, 647, as well as Hugenberg to Claß, 16 Aug. 1929, BA Berlin, R 8048, 262/189.

[88] On Brauweiler's overtures to Hugenberg, see his "Bericht über Kissingen," 19 Aug. 1929, BA Berlin, R 72, 43/131–35. See also Brauweiler to Hugenberg, 15 Aug. 1929, BA Berlin, R 8048, 262/190, and 23 Aug. 1929, StA Mönchen-Gladbach, NL Brauweiler, 114.

[89] "Gesetz gegen die Versklavung des Deutschen Volkes. Entwurf 21.8.29," appended to Hugenberg to Westarp, 21 Aug. 1929, NL Westarp, Gärtringen, VN 122.

[90] Hugenberg to Westarp, 1 Aug. 1929, NL Westarp, Gärtringen, VN 122. See also Westarp to Hugenberg, 11 July and 19 Aug. 1929, ibid.

[91] Westarp to Hugenberg, 22 Aug. 1929, ibid.

[92] Hugenberg to Westarp, 23 Aug, 1929, ibid.

[93] Brauweiler, "Historischer Bericht über die Verhandlungen betr. das Volksbegehren," 15 Sept. 1929, StA Mönchen-Gladbach, NL Brauweiler, 112.

Enslavement of the German People," including the imprisonment paragraph to which Westarp had raised such strong objection. Illness prevented Hitler from attending the meeting, and Hugenberg was unwilling to drop the offending paragraph without first securing the consent of the Nazi party leader. The other provisions of the proposed "Freedom Law" renounced Germany's acceptance of sole responsibility for the war, stipulated that Allied evacuation of Germany's occupied territories should not be contingent upon the liquidation of its reparations burden, and rejected the Young Plan on the grounds that German authorities should sign no new treaties or undertake no new obligations based upon the "War Guilt Clause." At the same time, the presidium voted that the text of the proposed referendum should not be referred to the judicial committee of the National Referendum Committee for review and possible revision.[94]

Brauweiler was furious when he learned not only that the imprisonment paragraph had not been dropped against the express wishes of the Stahlhelm leadership but also that his committee would not be given an opportunity to review the text of the proposed referendum. Brauweiler immediately convened a meeting of the National Referendum Committee's judicial subcommittee to register its opposition to the wording of the so-called Freedom Law and its frustration over Hugenberg's handling of the matter.[95] On 6 September Hugenberg traveled to Halle, where he met with the leaders of the Stahlhelm to inform them that the publication of the "Freedom Law" would take place on the following Thursday and that the National Socialists had made their participation in the referendum campaign conditional upon retention of the imprisonment paragraph. Brauweiler's judicial subcommittee, he continued, would be permitted to review the text of the proposed referendum but could do no more than make technical recommendations for changes in the text of the bill.[96] In doing so, Hugenberg effectively swept aside the Stahlhelm's reservations against the inclusion of the imprisonment paragraph in the so-called Freedom Law and coopted the leaders of Germany's largest para-military organization into a campaign that was considerably more radical than anything they had envisaged when they first proposed a referendum for a revision of the Weimar Constitution in the fall of 1928.

---

[94] No record of the Nuremberg meeting of the presidium of the National Referendum Committee on 28 August 1929 exists. For what transpired here, see Brauweiler to Duesterberg, 5 Sept. 1929, StA Mönchen-Gladbach, NL Brauweiler, 114, and Brauweiler, "Historischer Bericht...," 15 Sept. 1929, ibid., 112., as well as Hugenberg to Westarp, 29 Aug. 1929, NL Westarp, Gärtringen, VN 122. For the appeal issued at the close of the meeting, see "Aufruf des Reichsassuchusses für das Deutsche Volksbegehren," n.d. [28 Aug. 1929], BA Berlin, R 8034 I, 120/133.

[95] Brauweiler to Duesterberg, 5 Sept. 1929, StA Mönchen-Gladbach, NL Brauweiler, 114.

[96] Brauweiler, "Historischer Bericht ...," 15 Sept. 1929, StA Mönchen-Gladbach, NL Brauweiler, 112.

The damage the Stahlhelm would have suffered by withdrawing from the campaign against the Young Plan far outweighed the embarrassment of being associated with the imprisonment paragraph, and its leaders acquiesced, albeit begrudgingly, in Hugenberg's *fait accompli*.[97] Nor were Goltz, Levetzow, and the leaders of the United Patriotic Leagues pleased with the way in which Hugenberg's action had effectively preempted their efforts to mobilize the German Right in support of Cuno's future candidacy for the Reich presidency.[98] Gebsattel and Cuno's circle of supporters in Bavaria were particularly incensed by Hugenberg's action and regarded it as a "catstrophe."[99] Even more serious difficulties had surfaced in Hugenberg's relations with the leaders of the National Rural League and the Christian-National Peasants and Farmers' Party. Neither the RLB's Schiele nor Karl Hepp or Friedrich Döbrich from the CNBLP had attended the meeting of the presidium of the National Referendum Committee on 28 August and therefore had no opportunity to prevent the inclusion of the controversial imprisonment paragraph in the final text of Hugenberg's "Freedom Law."[100] On 4 September Hepp and the CNBLP's Günther Gereke met with Brauweiler to voice their opposition not only to the imprisonment paragraph but also to the way in which Hugenberg had deliberately bypassed the judicial subcommittee of the National Referendum Committee in drafting the "Freedom Law."[101] Anxious to capitalize upon what they expected to be another German diplomatic setback at The Hague, Hugenberg and his allies pressed forward with their plans to release the text of the referendum on 12 September.[102] In the late afternoon of 11 September, Schiele and the CNBLP's Albrecht Wendhausen met with Hugenberg and two of his closest associates, Schmidt-Hannover and Quaatz, in a desperate, last-minute effort to block inclusion of the imprisonment paragraph in the so-called Freedom Law, only to be rebuffed by Hugenberg with the explanation that not only was it too late to make any alterations in the wording of the referendum but also that the inclusion of the imprisonment paragraph was the basis upon which the accord with Hitler had been reached.[103]

---

[97] Wagner to Duesterberg, 23 Aug. 1929, StA Mönchen-Gladbach, NL Brauweiler, 114.
[98] Correspondence between Friedrichs and Levetzow, 2–20 Sept. 1929, BA-MA Freiburg, NL Levetzow, 53/106, 120–21.
[99] Gebsattel to Levetzow, 23 Sept. 1929, BA-MA Freiburg, NL Levetzow, 53/125.
[100] Hugenberg to Westarp, 29 Aug. 1929, NL Westarp, Gärtringen, VN 122.
[101] Brauweiler's notes on his meeting with Hepp and Gereke, 4 Sept. 1929, StA Mönchen-Gladbach, NL Brauweiler, 110. See also Brauweiler to Duesterberg, 5 Sept. 1929, ibid., 114.
[102] Hugenberg to the members of the presidium of the National Committee for the German Referendum, 10 Sept. 1929, BA Berlin, R 8048, 263/37–38.
[103] Entry in Quaatz's diary, 11 Sept. 1929, BA Koblenz, NL Quaatz, 16. See also Hugenberg to the presidium of the National Committee for the German Referendum, 15 Sept. 1929, BA Berlin, R 8048, 263/74–76. For conflicting accounts of this meeting, see Schiele to the

Undeterred by Schiele's opposition to the inclusion of the imprisonment paragraph in his "Law against the Enslavement of the German People," Hugenberg published the full text of the proposed law on the morning on 12 September 1929. On the following day, Schiele wrote to headquarters of the National Committee for the German Referendum to reiterate the RLB's strong opposition to the imprisonment paragraph and called for an immediate meeting of the referendum committee's presidium to deal with the problems that had been created by its inclusion in the published text of the "Freedom Law."[104] Schiele and the leaders of the RLB were particularly concerned that their support for a referendum that included the inflammatory language of the imprisonment paragraph would seriously endanger their ties to the more moderate groups in the newly created "Green Front" and undermine the effectiveness with which it could represent the interests of the German agricultural community.[105] A serious strain could also be seen in relations between the National Referendum Committee and the leaders of the CNBLP. Speaking at a CNBLP rally in Dortmund on 15 September, Gereke sharply criticized the imprisonment paragraph and warned that its wording was such that not even Reich President von Hindenburg was exempt from the threat of imprisonment.[106] Relations between the CNBLP and DNVP became increasingly frayed as the latter insinuated that the CNBLP leadership had put economic self-interest ahead of the national welfare.[107] In response, CNBLP activists attacked the DNVP for having failed to recognize the extent to which the German farmer was part of the national movement or to appreciate the increasingly desperate situation in which Germany's rural population currently found itself.[108] Nor was the DNVP immune from the increasingly heated conflict

---

presidium of the National Committee for the German Referendum, 20 Sept. 1929, BA Berlin, R 8034 I, 284/320–23, and Hugenberg to Schiele, 30 Sept. 1929, BA Koblenz, NL Weilnböck, 16b.

[104] Schiele to the presidium of the National Committee for the German Referendum, 13 Sept. 1929, NL Westarp, Gärtringen, VN 122. See also the statement of the RLB presidium, "Stellungnahme gegen §4 des Gesetzvorschlages gegen die Versklavung des deutschen Volkes," 17 Sept. 1929, BA Berlin, R 8034 I, 284/324–28. For further details, see Wilmowsky to Krupp, 14 Sept. 1929, HA Krupp Essen, FAH 23/503.

[105] See the letter from Nicolas (Brandenburg Rural League) to Schiele, 8 Nov. 1929, BA Berlin R 8034 I, 18/274–78, as well as Schiele to the DVP's Alfred Zapf, 12 Oct. 1929, BA Koblenz, NL Zapf, 37. For further details, see Andreas Müller, *"Fällt der Bauer, stürzt der Staat." Deutschnationale Agrarpolitik 1928–1933* (Hamburg, 2003), 123–56, and Gessner, *Agrarverbände*, 222–27, as well as Markus Müller, *Landvolkpartei*, 118–38.

[106] *Schulthess' Europäischer Geschichtskalender*, ed. Ulrich Thürauf (Munich, 1860ff.), 70 (1929): 166–67.

[107] For example, see Georg Wilhelm Schiele-Naumburg to his cousin Martin Schiele, 20 Sept. 1929, BA Berlin, R 8034 I, 266/576–77.

[108] "Weshalb Christlich-nationale Bauern- und Landvolkpartei?," *Politische Wochenschrift* 5, no. 39 (28 Sept. 1929): 921–24.

that had erupted within the ranks of the so-called national opposition.[109] On 17 September Westarp wrote to Hugenberg to reiterate his opposition to the inclusion of the imprisonment paragraph in the text of the "Freedom Law," adding pessimistically that the controversy over the paragraph had greatly weakened the publicity value of the referendum. Westarp was particularly sensitive to the danger the imprisonment paragraph posed to the party's standing in the German agricultural community and urged Hugenberg to soften the offending language for the sake of a compromise that would satisfy both parties.[110]

Hugenberg remained impervious to the storm of criticism that greeted publication of the "Freedom Law" and refused to consider any changes in its wording that might make it more palatable to Schiele, Westarp, and their supporters.[111] Infuriated by what he perceived as a deliberate attempt on the part of Schiele and the RLB leadership to sabotage the unity of the "national front,"[112] Hugenberg traveled to Munich on 18 September to reassure himself of Hitler's support in the struggle over the form and substance of the "Freedom Law."[113] In the meantime, Westarp tried to defuse the deepening crisis that threatened to tear his party apart by calling an emergency meeting of party leaders on 20 September.[114] But Hugenberg, who had just returned from Munich where he had met with Nazi party leader Adolf Hitler, insisted on the retention of the imprisonment paragraph with all of its objectionable language and remained adamantly opposed to any change in the text of the proposed Freedom Law that might endanger the unity of the "national front."[115] Later that evening and then again on the following morning Hugenberg met with CNBLP national chairman Erwin Baum and Reichstag deputy Friedrich Döbrich in an attempt to repair relations between their respective organizations and to negotiate the terms of a compromise that would exempt Hindenburg from the threat of imprisonment. This would then make it possible for the CNBLP and RLB to support the referendum against the Young Plan

[109] See Schultz-Bromberg to Westarp, 15 Sept. 1929, and Lindeiner-Wildau to Westarp, 17 Sept. 1929, both in NL Westarp, Gärtringen, VN 122.
[110] Westarp to Hugenberg, 17 Sept. 1929, NL Westarp, Gärtringen, VN 122.
[111] Hugenberg to the presidium of the National Committee for the German Referendum, 15 Sept. 1929, BA Koblenz, NL Weilnböck, 50.
[112] See Hugenberg to Duesterberg, 14 and 16, 1929, BA Berlin, R 8048, 263/56-59, 67-69.
[113] Hugenberg's remarks at a meeting of DNVP party leaders, 20 Sept. 1929, NL Westarp, Gärtringen, II/35.
[114] Invitation from Westarp, 18 Sept. 1929, NL Westarp, Gärtringen, II/35.
[115] Westarp's notes on a meeting of DNVP party leaders, 20 Sept. 1929, NL Westarp, Gärtringen, II/35. In a similar vein, see Hugenberg to Nagel, 15 Sept. 1929, BA Berlin, R 8048, 263/62-66, as well as the draft of Hugenberg's unpublished article, "Zerfall der nationalen Front," n.d., BA Koblenz, NL Hugenberg, 115/65.

despite the retention of the imprisonment paragraph in the text of the "Freedom Law."[116] While Schiele's last-ditch effort to have the obnoxious paragraph deleted from the text of the "Freedom Law" was voted down at a meeting of the executive committee of the National Referendum Committee despite the strong support he received from the leaders of the Stahlhelm,[117] Hugenberg did at least agree to an amendment in the language of the imprisonment paragraph so that it no longer pertained to the person of the Reich President.[118]

The meeting of the presidium of the National Referendum Committee on 21 September 1929 did little more than restore a façade of right-wing unity in the struggle against the Young Plan. Unable to shake Hugenberg's control of the presidium yet unwilling to incur the odium of abandoning the anti-Young Plan campaign altogether, the leaders of the CNBLP accepted Hugenberg's olive branch and issued a statement that despite their reservations about the imprisonment paragraph they would "fight shoulder to shoulder" with the other organizations of the National Referendum Committee in the struggle against the Young Plan and the war guilt lie.[119] Four days later the RLB executive committee met in Berlin to reiterate not just the RLB's opposition to the imprisonment paragraph but, more importantly, its determination to carry the crusade against the Young Plan to a successful conclusion.[120] Still, relations between Hugenberg and the RLB remained profoundly strained. Hugenberg's refusal to drop the controversial paragraph had come as a sharp rebuff to Schiele and the leaders of the RLB, who complained bitterly about the way in which the matter had been misrepresented in the Hugenberg press and how their legitimate concerns about the political implications of the imprisonment paragraph had been brushed aside by Hugenberg and his allies.[121] Schiele nevertheless remained hopeful that an accommodation with Hugenberg might still be possible and urged his followers to stay the course in the

---

[116] Copy of a letter from Pf[eil] to the CNBLP executive committee and to Hepp, Wendhausen, and Oheimb, 22 Sept. 1929, records of the CNBLP, BA Berlin, Bestand R 8001, 1/32–33. See also Müller, *Landvolkpartei*, 118–30.

[117] Entry in Quaatz's diary, 21 and 23 Sept. 1929, BA Koblenz, NL Quaatz, 16. See also DNVP, Mitteilungen no. 40, 24 Sept. 1929, NL Westarp, Gärtringen, VN 82, as well as the minutes of the judicial subcommittee of the National Referendum Committee, 19 Sept. 1929, BA Berlin, R 8048, 263/109–14.

[118] Resolution of the presidium of the National Committee for the German Referendum, n. d. [21 Sept. 1929], appended to the letter cited in n. 117, BA Berlin, R 8001, 1/35.

[119] Ibid.

[120] Resolution of the RLB executive committee, 25 Sept. 1929, BA Koblenz, NL Weilnböck, 16b. See also the report in the *Neue Preußische (Kreuz-)Zeitung*, 26 Sept. 1929, no. 310.

[121] In this respect, see the correspondence between Schiele and Hugenberg, 25 Sept.–4 Oct. 1929, NL Westarp, Gärtringen, VN 122.

campaign against the Young Plan.[122] In the meantime, Hugenberg had begun to mobilize his own supporters within the RLB in an attempt to undercut Schiele's position as the organization's national chairman, with the result that the unity of the RLB itself was threatened by the conflict between those who supported Schiele and his brand of conservative pragmatism and those who remained loyal to Hugenberg's wholesale assault against the Weimar system and the policy of fulfillment.[123]

A Pyrrhic Victory?

The controversy over the imprisonment paragraph of the "Law against the Enslavement of the German People" severely handicapped the effectiveness of Hugenberg's crusade against the Young Plan from the very outset. In order for the "Freedom Law" to go forward, it required the signatures of ten percent of the eligible German electorate, in this case approximately 4,127,800 voters. Those who supported the proposed law had two weeks from 16 to 29 October 1929 in which they could attach their signatures to a referendum that, if successful, would require the Reichstag to debate and vote on the "Freedom Law." Then, if the Reichstag rejected the proposed law, it would go back to the electorate in the form of a plebiscite, or *Volksentscheid*, that would become law with the support of fifty percent of the German electorate. By the first week of October, the campaign was in full swing, as all of the organizations represented in the National Committee for the German Referendum mobilized their followers to register for the referendum in what was a massive propaganda campaign against the Young Plan, the war guilt lie, and Stresemann's foreign policy.[124] To be sure, Hugenberg set the tone by speaking on every second day and traveling from one end of the country to the other during the two-week registration period.[125] But he was joined in this effort by the leaders of the Stahlhelm, who hoped that the campaign for the referendum against the Young Plan would solidify ties between the organizations of the German Right

---

[122] Wilmowsky to Krupp, 25 Sept. 1929, HA Krupp Essen, FAH 23/503. See also Schiele, "Vorwärts mit aller Kraft für das Volksbegehren," *Sächsische Bauern-Zeitung* 36, no. 42 (20 Oct. 1929): 424–25.

[123] See minutes of the RLB executive committee, 1 Nov. 1929, BA Berlin, R 8034 I, 120/ 123–37, also in Dieter Gessner, "'Grüne Front' oder ,'Harzburger Front.' Der Reichs-Landbund in der letzten Phase der Weimarer Republik zwischen wirtschaftlicher Interessenpolitik und nationalistischem Revisionsanspruch," *Vierteljahrshefte für Zeitgeschichte* 29 (1981): 110–23, here 116–23.

[124] For an optimistic assessment of the campaign's initial successes, see the report by the Stahlhelm district leaders to the Stahlhelm executive committee, 1–2 Oct. 1929, BA Berlin, R 72, 11/51–57.

[125] See the manuscripts of Hugenberg's speeches in the last half of October 1929, BA Koblenz, NL Hugenberg, 116/89–154.

and shared the podium whenever they could with representatives from the other organizations in the National Referendum Committee.[126]

The National Socialists, on the other hand, were under specific instructions from the party leadership not to participate in demonstrations where other representatives of the National Referendum Committee were involved and to wage their campaign against the Young Plan at a discreet distance from the rest of the national front.[127] Hitler himself maintained a conspicuously low profile throughout the campaign, speaking only once when he and Hugenberg took part in a rally in Munich toward the very end of the registration period.[128] The official explanation for Hitler's absence from the early stages of the campaign was that the Nazi party leader was nursing a sore throat that had made it difficult for him to speak.[129] Hitler's reticence, however, did not prevent other high-ranking Nazi officials such as Gregor Strasser or Joseph Goebbels from doing their part,[130] although here the intention was less to prevent the Young Plan from becoming law than to secure a breakthrough into the ranks of the other parties on the moderate and radical Right.[131] No doubt this was also what the party leadership had in mind when it invited Duesterberg and Goltz to appear as honored guests at the Nazi party congress in Nuremberg at the beginning of August 1929.[132]

All of this was accompanied by a veritable flood of anti-Young Plan propaganda in the form of handouts, placards, brochures, and even a film that crested in the last two weeks of October 1929.[133] The central theme around which Hugenberg and the leaders of the National Referendum

---

[126] See Seldte's speech in the Herrenhaus demonstration, 9 July 1929, reported in *Fort mit dem Pariser Tributplan*, Kampfschrift no. 1, 1 Aug. 1929, 2–3, as well as the report of a demonstration in the Berlin Sports Palace in late September 1929 where the featured speakers were Duesterberg and Hugenberg, *Der Stahlhelm* 11, no. 39 (29 Sept. 1929): 1–2.

[127] Entries for 5 and 12 July 1929 in *Die Tagebücher von Joseph Goebbels*, ed. Elke Fröhlich, Part I: *Aufzeichnungen 1924–1941*, 5 vols. (Munich and New York, 1987–2004), vol. 1/III, 280–81, 284–85. See also Otmar Jung, "Plebizitärer Durchbruch 1929? Zur Bedeutung von Volksbegehren und Volksentscheid gegen den Youngplan für die NSDAP," *Geschichte und Gesellschaft* 15 (1989): 489–510, here 492.

[128] Hitler, "Rede auf Kundgebung des bayerischen Landesausschusses für das deutsche Volksbegehren in München," 25 Oct. 1929, in Hitler, *Reden, Schriften, Anordnungen*, vol. 3, pt. 2, 411–20.

[129] Hess to Hugenberg, 13 Aug. 1929, BA Berlin, R 9354, 647.

[130] For example, see Gregor Strasser, *58 Jahre Young-Plan! Eine quellenmäßige Betrachtung über Inhalt, Wesen und Folgen des Young-Plans* (Berlin, n.d. [1929]), and Joseph Goebbels, *Der Kampf gegen Young – eine Sache des deutschen Arbeiters. Rede gehalten am 26. September 1929 im Kriegervereinshaus Berlin* (Berlin, 1929).

[131] Jung, "Plebizitärer Durchbruch 1929?," 502–09.

[132] *Völkischer Beobachter*, 5 Aug. 1929, no. 180.

[133] In this respect, see "Überblick über die Agitation der Rechtsparteien gegen den Young-Plan zusammengestellt auf Grund der Berichte der Landesabteilungen durch die Reichszentrale für Heimatdienst," 14 Oct. 1929, records of the Reich Ministry of

Committee crafted their campaign was the theme of enslavement. Not only was the Young Plan based upon the war-guilt lie of the Versailles Treaty, but it contained a schedule for the payment of reparations that perpetuated the enslavement of the German people for another sixty years.[134] The burden the Young Plan imposed upon the German economy, so argued Hugenberg and his supporters, was even more onerous than that of the Dawes Plan, whose adoption in 1924 had sacrificed the economic welfare of the German people to the vindictiveness of the Allies at the same time it had left a deep rift within the ranks of the nationalist Right.[135] By rejecting the Young Plan, the German people would be taking the first step toward regaining its freedom from Allied domination and restoring its sense of national honor.[136] Acceptance of the Young Plan, on the other hand, meant economic disaster not just for German industry but for broad sectors of the German populace, but most of all for the already beleaguered German farmer and the independent middle class.[137] This, insisted the architects of the anti-Young Plan campaign, was tantamount to nothing less than a new act of treason by those politicians who had betrayed the German people in 1918 and whose treachery now manifested itself in their determination to perpetuate Germany's economic enslavement through the imposition of a new tribute plan that promised relief and security but delivered only suffering and hardship.[138]

The National Referendum Committee's campaign against the Young Plan combined highly charged appeals to German national feeling with a picture of Germany's economic future that was intentionally designed to instill fear and a sense of desperation in the hearts of the average German if the new plan were to take effect. Yet for all of its emotional power, the crusade against the Young Plan failed to strike a responsive chord with the German electorate. At least four factors accounted for this failure. In the first place, the lingering resentment that Schiele and the RLB leadership felt over the

---

Interior, Bundesarchiv Berlin, Bestand R 1501, 125717a/114–23, reprinted in *Das Kabinett Müller II*, ed. Vogt, 2: 1035–40.

[134] Reichsausschuß für das deutsche Volksbegehren, "Soll das wahr werden?," Flugblatt no. 8, NL Hiller, Gärtringen.

[135] *Die Wahrheit über den Young-Plan. Nach Aufsätzen von Dr. Graf Brockdorff und Dr. Quaatz, M.d.R.*, ed. Landesverband Baden der Deutschnationalen Volkspartei (Freiburg im Breisgau, n.d. [1929]), esp. 18–20. See also Westarp, "Dawes-Plan oder Young-Plan," *Neue Preußische (Kreuz-)Zeitung*, 20 Sept. 1929, no. 304.

[136] Reichsausschuß für das deutsche Volksbegehren, "Durch Volksbegehren und Volksentscheid zur deutschen Freiheit!," n.d., Flugblatt no. 21, NL Hiller, Gärtringen.

[137] Reichsausschuß für das deutsche Volksbegehren, "Landleute," Flugblatt no. 5, and "Pariser Tributplan und deutscher Mittelstand," Flugblatt no. 10, both in NL Hiller, Gärtringen.

[138] Rudolf von Xylander, *Deutschland und der Youngplan* (Munich, n.d. [1929]), 11–12.

Figure 12.   Placard designed by an unidentified graphic artist in support of the
referendum against the Young Plan, 1 October 1929. Reproduced with permission from
the Bundesarchiv Berlin, Plakat 002-015-019

way in which they had been manipulated into supporting a referendum with
whose language they did not agree undermined its willingness to support
Hugenberg's campaign against the Young Plan. Nothing revealed the disillusionment of the RLB's more moderate elements with the campaign than the

Figure 13. Placard designed by Herbert Rothgaengel, in support of the referendum against the Young Plan, October 1929. Reproduced with permission from the Bundesarchiv Berlin, Plakat 002-015-020

resignation of Baron Tilo von Wilmowsky, chairman of the RLB's regional affiliate in provincial Saxony and the RLB's principal liaison to Ruhr heavy industry, from the National Referendum Committee on 11 October.[139] Secondly, Germany's industrial leadership remained cool to the referendum and refused to commit the financial resources upon which Hugenberg had been counting. The National Referendum Committee was always short of money, and Hugenberg had to dip into his own pockets on at least one occasion to help cover the committee's operational expenses.[140] The campaign also lost much of its emotional impetus when on 3 October 1929 German Foreign Minister Gustav Stresemann died of a stroke after a Herculean effort to rally his badly divided German People's Party behind a compromise on unemployment insurance that temporarily ensured the survival of the Müller cabinet.[141] The predicament in which the architects of the anti-Young Plan crusade found themselves after Stresemann's death was further complicated by the Hindenburg's refusal to support the "Freedom Law" even after the objectionable language threatening him with trial and imprisonment had been removed from its text. Hindenburg was convinced that despite all of its shortcomings the Young Plan represented an improvement on the Dawes Plan and steadfastly resisted pressure from the leaders of the Stahlhelm and other elements on the German Right to assume a more public role in the struggle against its ratification. On 16 October Hindenburg issued a public statement dissociating himself from the agitation of the National Referendum Committee and asserting his neutrality in the conflict over the Young Plan.[142]

Fully cognizant of the threat that the campaign against the Young Plan posed to the stability of Germany's republican order, the governments in the Reich and Prussia responded with a vigorous counter-offensive of their own.[143] Responsibility for coordinating the various aspects of the government's counter-offensive was placed in the hands of Carl Severing, the Social

[139] Wilmowsky to Hugenberg, 11 Oct. 1929, BA Berlin, R 8034 I, 120/148–49. See also Zollitsch, "Das Scheitern der 'gouvernementalen' Rechten," 259–61.
[140] On the campaign's financial difficulties, see Lord to Wagner, 10 Aug. 1929, BA Berlin, R 72, 40/247–49, as well as the minutes of the budget committee of the National Referendum Committee, 10 Oct. 1929, BA Berlin, R 8048, 263/139.
[141] Minutes of the DVP national committee, 30 Sept. 1929, in *Nationalliberalimus in der Weimarer Republik*, ed. Kolb and Richter, 2:837–63.
[142] Hindeburg to Müller, 16 Oct. 1929, in *Das Kabinett Müller II*, ed. Vogt, 2:1043–44. See also Hindenburg to Schröder, 4 Nov. 1929, BHStA Munich, Abt. V, NL Dziembowksi, 19. On the Stahlhelm's overtures to Hindenburg, see Duesterberg's unpublished memoirs, BA Koblenz, NL Duesterberg, 46/147–49.
[143] For further details, see "Plan für die Aufklärungsarbeit anläßlich des Volksbehrens," n.d., appended to a memorandum from Abegg to the Prussian provincial presidents and Berlin police chiefs, 12 Oct. 1929, BA Berlin, R 1501, 125717a/80–83.

Democratic minister of interior in the Müller cabinet. The Müller cabinet placed nearly 495,000 marks at Severing's disposal to combat the propaganda of the National Referendum Committee and authorized a vigorous campaign that included, among other things, the extensive use of the radio by cabinet officers and other high-ranking government officials.[144] The government also organized an appeal in support of the Young Plan that carried the signatures of all the cabinet officers and other well-known public figures, including industrialist Robert Bosch, Albert Einstein and Max Planck from the German scientific community, historians Hermann Oncken and Friedrich Meinecke, dramatist Gerhard Hauptmann, and Nobel laureate Thomas Mann.[145] The fact, however, that a number of prominent industrialists, including Carl Duisberg and Carl Friedrich von Siemens, as well as former chancellor Hans Luther declined to sign the appeal despite their opposition to the tone and substance of Hugenberg's referendum revealed a reluctance to become publicly identified with a campaign that, in their eyes at least, had been monopolized by the Social Democrats at the expense of the government's nonsocialist supporters.[146] Lacking the resources at the government's disposal, the various nonsocialist parties that supported the Müller cabinet confined their role to issuing public statements denouncing the so-called Freedom Law as a "laughable miscarriage [lächerlicher Mißgeburt)" that sought only to divide rather than unite the German people.[147]

As the registration deadline for the referendum against the Young Plan drew near, not even its most vigorous supporters were confident of success. As late as 31 October the NSDAP's Joseph Goebbels noted in his diary: "Defeat. Most likely instead of the prescribed 10 percent only 8 percent."[148] Even as the final tally was being taken on 3 November Goebbels was still in doubt as to the outcome of the referendum.[149] When the final tally was announced, the referendum had, to the surprise of all but a handful of Hugenberg diehards, succeeded with the signatures of 10.02 percent of Germany's eligible voters.

[144] Minutes of the ministerial conference, 3 Oct. 1929, in Das Kabinett Müller II, ed. Vogt, 2:998–1001. See also the summary of the government's campaign finances dated 15 Jan. 1930, BA Berlin, R 1501, 125717d/87.

[145] See the text of the appeal dated 10 Oct. 1929, in Das Kabinett Müller II, ed. Vogt, 2:1032–34.

[146] For example, see Siemens to Severing, 15 Oct. 1929, BA Berlin, R 1501, 125717b/91–93; Duisberg to Severing, 12 Oct. 1929, ibid., 105; and Luther to Severing, 15 Oct. 1929, ibid., 106. See also Koch-Weser to Müller, 17 Oct. 1929, in Das Kabinett Müller II, ed. Vogt, 2:1044–45.

[147] Koch-Weser's speech at the DDP's Mannheim party congress, 4 Oct. 1929, in Der Demokrat. Organ der Deutschen Demokratischen Partei 10, no. 20 (20 Oct. 1929): 486–96, here 491.

[148] Entry for 31 Oct. 1929, in Goebbels Tagebücher, ed. Fröhlich, 1/3, 361.

[149] Entry for 3 Nov. 1929, ibid., 363.

But this was hardly a cause for celebration. Not only had the referendum carried by the narrowest of margins with only 9,925 more votes than the 10 percent required to send the "Freedom Law" to the Reichstag, but the number of registrants fell more than a million short of the combined total of 5,191,690 votes the DNVP and NSDAP had received in the 1928 Reichstag elections. The referendum's success was confined almost entirely to traditional conservative strongholds east of the Elbe. In Pomerania, East Prussia and Mecklenburg, for example, 32.9, 23.9, and 20.9 percent of the voters respectively had registered for the referendum. In twelve other districts the referendum received less than five percent of the signatures of the eligible electorate, with its poorest showing in predominantly Catholic districts such as Cologne-Aachen and Koblenz-Trier.[150] If Hugenberg and the leaders of the National Committee for the German Referendum had hoped to use the referendum provisions of the Weimar Constitution to ignite a popular insurrection against the Young Plan, the policy of fulfillment, and the hated Weimar system, this had clearly failed to materialize.

The success of the referendum, in so far as it could be termed a success, meant that the "Freedom Law" would now go to the Reichstag, where it faced certain defeat. For Hugenberg, Hitler, and their associates, this would nevertheless afford them a welcome opportunity to continue and intensify their agitation against the Young Plan and the system of government with which it had become inextricably identified. As Goebbels noted in his diary with his characteristic cynicism: "Now the dance goes on."[151]

Hugenberg's referendum against the Young Plan left a legacy that was both irrevocable and of enormous consequence. Ever since the last years of the Second Empire the German Right had embraced two fundamentally different camps, one a governmental conservatism associated with the names of men like Karl Helfferich, Oskar Hergt, and Martin Schiele and a radical Pan-German nationalism represented by the likes of Alfred Hugenberg and the ADV's Heinrich Claß. In the early years of the Weimar Republic both were housed within the German National People's Party, where they had been fused together by what DNVP moderate Hans Erdmann von Lindeiner-Wildau called the "unity of the no."[152] But with the stabilization of the Weimar Republic in the second half of the 1920's and the DNVP's two experiments at government participation, Lindeiner's "unity of the no" began to lose its

---

[150] The statistics upon which this analysis is based have been taken from Falter, Lindenberger, and Schumann, *Wahlen und Abstimmungen*, 41, 71, 80.

[151] Entry for 3 Nov. 1929, in *Goebbels Tagebücher*, ed. Fröhlich, 1/3, 363.

[152] Hans Erdmann von Lindeiner-Wildau, "Konservatismus," in *Volk und Reich der Deutschen*, ed. Bernhard Harms, 3 vols. (Berlin, 1929), 2:35–61, here 58–61.

integrative force. The referendum against the Young Plan, with all its attendant feuding over strategy and tactics, only exacerbated the tensions within the
DNVP and drove a wedge deep into the ranks of the German Right. Whether
or it might still be possible to repair this rift not just within the DNVP but
within the German Right as a whole remained to be seen.

16

Schism and Fragmentation

For all of its heat and passion, the campaign against the Young Plan was little more than a side-show in the second half of 1929. By far the most important problem challenging Germany's political leadership was the deteriorating economic situation and the strain it placed upon public finances. Increases in unemployment, though modest for the period from January to December 1929, greatly exceeded the projections that had been incorporated into the 1927 Unemployment Insurance Law, with the result that whatever financial benefits Germany's political leaders had hoped to reap from the Young Plan fell far short of what was needed to restore fiscal stability. At the same time, Stresemann's death in early October 1929 had created an irreparable void in the ranks of Germany's political leadership and robbed the Weimar Republic of one of its most ardent defenders at the precise moment that his talents as a champion of liberal democracy were most urgently needed. But the crisis that descended upon Germany in the fall and early winter of 1929 found the forces of the anti-parliamentary Right more divided than ever. Hugenberg's crusade to unite the various parties, interest organizations, and patriotic associations that made up the German Right into a powerful phalanx that would sweep away the institutions of Weimar democracy in favor of a more authoritarian system of government only exacerbated the divisions that already existed in the ranks of the German Right. As the campaign against the Young Plan so clearly revealed, Hugenberg's political agenda set him on a collision course with the special economic interests that constituted the DNVP's material base and that were prepared to work within the framework of the existing system of government in order to defend the vital interests of their constituencies. Now that the first stage of the referendum process was over and Hugenberg's "Freedom Law" made its way to the Reichstag, the unity of the DNVP was once again at risk.

The Hardening of Dissent

Disclaimers to the contrary notwithstanding, the founding of the Christian-Social Reich Union in August 1928 was the first step toward the creation of a new party by the leaders of the DNVP's Christian-Social faction and

493

sympathizers who stood outside the immediate orbit of the DNVP.[1] The presence of outspoken social reactionaries like Paul Bang and Gustav Hartz in Hugenberg's immediate entourage only fueled Christian-Social fears that the social and economic achievements of the previous decade were under siege. Nowhere was this more apparent than in the sharp attack that Gustav Hülser, a member of the DNVP Reichstag delegation and a leading spokesman for the party's Christian-Social faction, levelled against Hartz – and against Hugenberg by association – at the Frankfurt congress of the Christian Labor Unions in mid-September 1929.[2] Hülser would become one of the driving forces in the struggle against Hugenberg and in efforts to organize Christian-Socials throughout the country into a new party of their own. Having once belonged to the Young German Order, Hülser was on close personal terms with its high master Artur Mahraun and made no secret of his sympathy for the "People's National Action" that the Young Germans had launched with such fanfare earlier that spring.[3] Still, Hülser and his associates were reluctant to break away from the DNVP despite increasing pressure from local Evangelical parties in Baden and Württemberg to join them in the creation of a new Christian-Social party.[4]

All of this would come to a head at the CSRV's second national congress in Bielefeld in early August 1929. Although Treviranus had succeeded in dissuading Hülser from threatening Hugenberg and the DNVP with the founding of a Christian-Social party,[5] this did not keep Hülser and the Young National Ring's Heinz Dähnhardt, the two principal speakers at Bielefeld, from openly criticizing the DNVP leadership's indifference to the aspirations of the Christian-Social movement. In deference to Treviranus, they drew the line at founding a new Christian-Social Party for fear that this would compress the movement into an organizational mold that would cripple its overall

---

[1] On the founding of the CSRV, see the protocol of the Bielefeld national congress (*Reichstreffen*) of the Christian-Socials, 19 Aug. 1928, BA Berlin, NL Mumm, 282/181–85. On the CSRV's goals, see Heinz-Dietrich Wendland, *Christlich-soziale Grundsätze. Gedanken zu einem neuen christlich-sozialen Programm* (Berlin, 1929).

[2] Hülser, "Die Sozialpolitik und ihre Gegner," in *Niederschrift der Verhandlungen des 12. Kongresses der christlichen Gewerkschaften Deutschlands. Frankfurt a. Main 15. bis 18. September 1929* (Berlin-Wilmersdorf, n.d. [1929]), 249–67.

[3] See Hülser, "Christlich-soziale Realpolitik," *Der Deutsche*, 24 July 1929, no. 171, and Hülser, "Christlich-sozialer Aufbruch," *Der Jungdeutsche*, 30 July 1929, no. 175. I am further indebted to Hülser for his letter of 24 August 1967 and information on his ties to Mahraun and the Young Germans.

[4] See Mumm, "Wir Christlich-sozialen und die Parteikrise in der Gegenwart," n.d. [July 1929], BA Berlin, NL Mumm, 283/157–62, as well as Mumm to Dähnhardt, 21 Oct. 1929, ibid., 283/325–26. See also Kandzia, "Die Christlich-soziale Reichsvereinigung," *Kölnische Zeitung*, 2 Aug. 1929, no. 419a, and Hülser, "Politische Umgruppierung," *Politische Wochenschrift*, 5, no. 31 (3 Aug. 1929): 733–34.

[5] Treviranus to Westarp, 10 Aug. 1929, NL Westarp, Gärtringen, II/37.

effectiveness. In the ensuing discussion, Count Leopold von Baudissin from the Bodelschwingh Institutes in Bethel triggered a lively and often heated discussion when he called for a complete break with the existing political parties and the consolidation of all Christian-Social forces in a separate organization of their own. Baudissin's remarks, which found strong support among the more than 200 delegates attending the convention, prompted DNVP parliamentarians like Mumm, Lambach, and Hartwig to intervene in order to prevent an open break with the DNVP.[6] Over the course of the next several months, the leaders of the CSRV would struggle to define their relationship to Christian-Social groups throughout the rest of the country.[7] The unexpectedly strong showing of the Evangelical People's Service (Evangelischer Volksdienst) in the Baden state elections on 27 October 1929 would only aggravate the dilemma in which the leaders of the DNVP's Christian-Social faction found themselves.[8] The was no less true of the agitation of the Christian People's Service (Christlicher Volksdienst or CVD) in the Rhineland and Westphalia in preparation for municipal elections that were scheduled to take place throughout Prussia on 17 November.[9]

This conflict inevitably spilled over into the DNVP Evangelical Reich Committee, where Hugenberg and his supporters began to press for a full-scale attack against the Christian People's Service and its sister organizations throughout the country.[10] The conflict reached a climax at the end of October, when Reinhard Mumm, the committee chairman and a Lutheran pastor who had been at the forefront of the Christian-Social movement since before the war, and Magdalene von Tiling, a prominent Lutheran theologian who had served in the DNVP delegation to the Prussian Landtag since 1921, squared off at a closed meeting of over a hundred committee members in Berlin on 30 October. Whereas Tiling accused Mumm of pursuing Evangelical interest politics and called for a strict separation of Christianity and politics, Mumm vigorously reaffirmed his commitment to infusing all aspects of German life – and in particular the political – with the spirit of the Evangelium.[11] Like most

---

[6] DNVP, Mitteilungen, no. 36, 30 Aug. 1929, BA Berlin, NL Mumm, 291/138–47. See also the reports in the *Christlicher Volksdienst*, 10 and 17 Aug. 1929, nos. 32–33.

[7] Minutes of the meeting of the CSRV executive committee, 15 Sept. 1929, BA Berlin, NL Mumm, 283/293–98.

[8] On the results in Baden, see Kraus's remarks to the DNVP's Evangelical Reich Committee, 30 Oct. 1929, BA Berlin, R 8005, 458/26–33.

[9] See Karl Dudey of the Christian Metal Workers' Union (Christlicher Metalarbeiter-Verband) to Mumm, 25 Sept. 1929, BA Berlin, NL Mumm, 283/299–301.

[10] See Bartelheim's remarks before the executive committee of the DNVP's Evangelical Reich Committee, 11 Sept. 1929, BA Berlin, R 8005, 465/82–88, as well as Thadden to Mumm, 7 Aug. 1929, ibid., 465/25.

[11] Report of the meeting of the Evangelical Reich Committee, 30 Oct. 1929, in *Der Reichsbote*, 31 Oct. 1929, no. 261. See also the minutes of the CSRV executive committee, 29

of the women in the DNVP leadership, Tiling had lined up behind Hugenberg in his struggle with the party moderates and strongly supported his efforts to return the DNVP to a course of uncompromising opposition to the Weimar Republic. Her altercation with Mumm was only one more sign of the deepening rift within the ranks of the DNVP's Evangelical supporters and that a parting of the ways was imminent.[12]

Whatever reluctance the DNVP's Christian-Social faction might have felt about a break with the DNVP quickly evaporated during the referendum against the Young Plan in the fall of 1929. In September an organization identifying itself as the Young National Ring (Jungnationaler Ring) published a pamphlet entitled *Der Niedergang der nationalen Opposition* in which it attacked Hugenberg as an aspirant dictator whose extremism only guaranteed the continuation of Stresemann's disastrous foreign policies. The only solution to the catastrophic situation in which the German political system found itself, argued the pamphlet's author, lay in the consolidation of the German Right behind the banner of Reich President von Hindenburg in a new conservative party that, like the fabled phoenix of classical mythology, would rise from the ashes of the old DNVP to lead the way to a rebirth of the German nation and the historic values it embodied.[13] Such sentiments resonated with the moderates on the DNVP's left wing, who by the end of October had begun to coalesce under the leadership of Lindeiner-Wildau and Treviranus with an eye toward using Hugenberg's anticipated defeat in the referendum against the Young Plan to force his removal as DNVP party chairman.[14] By now, the dissidents were in close contact with elements in the Reichswehr, the Christian labor movement, and the German industrial establishment that strongly

---

Oct. 1929, BA Berlin, NL Mumm, 283/339–43. For further details, see Norbert Friedrich, "'National, Sozial, Christlich'. Evangelischer Reichsausschuß der Deutschnationalen Volkspartei in der Weimarer Republik," *Kirchliche Zeitgeschichte* 6 (1993): 290–311, here 306–08.

[12] Gury Schneider-Ludorff, *Magdalene von Tiling. Ordnungstheologie und Geschlechterbeziehungen. Ein Beitrag zum Gesellschaftsverständnis des Protestantismus in der Weimarer Republik* (Göttingen, 2001), 213–15. On Hugenberg's support from the party's women leaders, see Heinsohn, *Konservative Parteien*, 206–13.

[13] *Der Niedergang der nationalen Opposition. Ein Warnruf aus den Reihen der Jugend*, ed. Jungnationaler Ring (Berlin, n. d. [1929]), esp. 34–39.

[14] See Westarp's recollection of a conversation with Lindeiner-Wildau in late October 1929 in an untitled twenty-four page memorandum on the DNVP party crisis in November–December 1929 (hereafter cited as Westarp, "Niederschrift über die DNVP-Parteikrise"), NL Westarp, Gärtringen, II/61. See also the detailed report from Blank to Reusch, 30 Oct. 1929, RWWA Cologne, Abt. 130, NL Reusch, 4001012024/6, as well as Mumm to Rippel, 19 Nov. 1929, BA Berlin, NL Mumm, 139/211. The most detailed treatment of the DNVP party crisis in 1929–30 remains the unpublished dissertation by Elizabeth Friedenthal, "Volksbegehren und Volksentscheid über den Young Plan und die deutschnationale Sezession (Ph.D. diss., Universität Tübingen, 1957).

supported efforts to force a change in the DNVP party leadership and initiate a fundamental realignment of forces on the German Right.[15] Not even the fact that the referendum had defied all expectations in receiving the more than four million signatures that were required to bring the "Freedom Law" to the floor of the Reichstag would deter them.

Throughout all of this, the leaders of the DNVP's agrarian wing continued to bide their time. Although the leaders of the party's agrarian wing had become increasingly critical of Hugenberg and the DNVP party leadership,[16] Schiele did not think that the time or pretext for a break with the DNVP had arrived and recused himself from an active role in the preparations for a secession on the party's left wing.[17] In the meantime, Hugenberg and his associates were busy at work rallying their supporters for a showdown with the dissidents at the upcoming party congress that was to take place in Kassel in the last week of November. From their perspective, what the DNVP most needed was an ideological cement that could bind the party together at the precise moment it seemed to be falling apart. If the Center had succeeded in insulating itself against the centrifugal forces that were at work within the other bourgeois parties by reaffirming its commitment to the social and moral values of the Catholic faith, what might the DNVP use as its ideological cement? Moreover, what sort of appeal might enable the DNVP to reach across existing party lines and close ranks with parties and groups outside its immediate orbit in a common effort to change once and for all the direction in which the ship of state seemed to be heading?

The Kassel Debacle

In his quest for a magic formula that would enable him to reassert his control over a badly fractured DNVP, Hugenberg fell back on a bromide that had worked well in the past: anti-Marxism. Here the initiative seems to have come from retired naval officer Wilhelm Widenmann, who in his capacity as DNVP party treasurer had begun to solicit the support of Vögler, Poengsen, and other Hugenberg backers in the German industrial community for the creation of anti-Marxist front that would also include the Center, the DVP, and the

---

[15] On Schleicher, see Gottfried R. Treviranus, "Zur Rolle und zur Person Kurt von Schleichers," in *Staat, Wirtschaft und Politik in der Weimarer Republik. Festschrift für Heinrich Brüning*, ed. Ferdinand A. Hermens and Theodor Schieder (Berlin, 1967), 363–82, here 371. See also Brüning to Gehrig, 1 Nov. 1929, ACDP Sankt-Augustin, NL Gehrig, I-087/001/2; and the correspondence between the RDI's Duisberg and Baron Werner von Alvensleben, 28 Nov.–3 Dec. 1929, Bayer-Archiv Leverkusen, Autographen-Sammlung Duisberg.

[16] For example, see Lind to Hugenberg, 6 May 1929, NL Westarp, Gärtringen, VN 83, and Richthofen-Boguslawitz to Westarp, 6 May 1929, ibid., VN 102.

[17] Westarp, "Niederschrift über die DNVP-Parteikrise," NL Westarp, Gärtringen, II/61.

various middle-class splinter parties that stood to the left of the DNVP. The purpose of such a front, as Widenmann explained to the Bavarian Minister of Justice Franz Gürtner, would be to lay the foundation for a change of government in both the Reich and Prussia that would effectively exclude the Marxists – namely, the Social Democrats – from any role whatsoever in Germany's political future.[18] Vögler warmed quickly to Widenmann's proposal, as did Hugenberg after meeting with Gürtner and a Vögler confidant during his summer retreat in Bad Kreuth.[19] It was also in this context that Hugenberg wrote to the Center party chairman Ludwig Kaas on 20 November 1929. After a brief allusion to a speech in which Kaas had voiced reservations about the wisdom of a long-term alliance with the Social Democrats, Hugenberg wrote "that from the core of my own being I regard a strong anti-Marxist bloc with the capacity to assume the reins of government as the accepted course of future development and as the foundation for order and a healing of German affairs as long as this extends to Prussia as well and carries within it a guarantee of permanence." Such a front, Hugenberg continued, was all the more necessary in light of the enormous burden that acceptance of the Young Plan would impose upon all sectors of German society and how this would impact the process of forming a new government. All of this, concluded the DNVP party chairman, would only intensify the deep gulf that already existed between management and labor and push the realization of a true German *Volksgemeinschaft* decades into the future.[20]

The DNVP's Kassel party congress convened on 21 November 1929 amidst widespread speculation that Hugenberg's opponents would use the congress as a forum for staging their exodus from the party.[21] Hugenberg did little to help the situation when at a meeting of the DNVP executive committee on the first day of the congress he introduced a resolution stipulating that all organs of the party, including the Reichstag delegation, must support the proposed Freedom Law in its entirety and that any member of the delegation who either voted against the controversial imprisonment paragraph or abstained from voting on it would be subject to disciplinary action.[22] This came as a sharp rebuff to Westarp, who had struggled valiantly as chairman of the DNVP Reichstag delegation to

---

[18] Widenmann to Gürtner, 7 Nov. 1929, BA-MA Freiburg, Nachlass Wilhelm Widenmann, 17/82–84. In a similar vein, see Gerhard Raab, *Konservativismus. Bemerkungen über Idee und Weg der deutschen Rechten* (Wetzlar an der Lahn, 1929), esp. 13–19.

[19] Widenmann to Poengsen, 8 Nov. 1929, BA-MA Freiburg, NL Widenmann, 17/75–77. See also Widenmann to Vögler, 10 Nov. 1929, ibid., 17/71.

[20] Hugenberg to Kaas, 20 Nov. 1929, BA Koblenz, NL Hugenberg, 192/389–91.

[21] Blank to Reusch, 30 Oct. 1929, RWWA Cologne, Abt. 130, NL Reusch, 4001012024/6.

[22] Hugenberg's speech before the DNVP executive committee, 21 Nov. 1929, BA Berlin, R 8005, 54/3–5.

salvage what remained of party unity and sharply criticized Hugenberg's resolution.[23] But Hugenberg's supporters on the DNVP party executive committee, many of whom were intent upon driving Hugenberg's opponents from the party,[24] rallied behind the beleaguered party chairman and rejected Westarp's efforts at mediation by a decisive, if not overwhelming, margin.[25] The committee then turned its attention to an incident involving Treviranus, a one-time Hugenberg protégé who had emerged as a leader of the anti-Hugenberg faction on the party's left wing. In a letter written earlier that November to a long-time family friend in Bremen, Treviranus had sharply criticized Hugenberg's leadership of the party and alluded to the growing interest of civil servants, industrialists, and white-collar employees in a secession from the DNVP. Treviranus suggested that if a change in the DNVP party leadership was no longer possible, it would be necessary to find "a new form from which a progressive conservative politics that is not afraid to call itself conservative could be pursued."[26] Through an indiscretion Treviranus's letter had fallen into the hands of a Hugenberg confederates and led to the introduction of expulsion proceedings against the disgruntled deputy. Westarp objected vehemently to the use of a private letter in a situation like this and urged all parties to accept a compromise on the imprisonment paragraph that would preserve party unity in the upcoming vote on the referendum against the Young Plan.[27] Once again Hugenberg and his supporters ignored Westarp's admonitions and went ahead with proceedings to expel Treviranus from the party.[28]

The meeting of the DNVP executive committee on the eve of the Kassel party congress did little to ease the tensions that had been building within the party. If anything, the meeting revealed how deep the gulf separating Hugenberg from his critics on the party's left wing actually was. In his keynote address on the following evening Hugenberg stressed first and foremost the

---

[23] Westarp's first statement before the DNVP executive committee, 21 Nov. 1929, NL Westarp, Gärtringen, II/61. See also Jones, "German Conservatism at the Crossroads," 157–60.

[24] Resolution adopted by the DNVP district executive committee (Landesvorstand) in Potsdam II, 6 Nov. 1929, NL Westarp, Gärtringen, 1929, II/35.

[25] Westarp to Wallraf, 26 Nov. 1929, NL Westarp, Gärtringen, II/37.

[26] Treviranus to Ahlefeld, 1 Nov. 1929, BA Koblenz, NL Schmidt-Hannover, 73, also in G. R. Treviranus, *Rückblick* (n.p., n.d. [1930]), 4, NL Westarp, Gärtringen, as well as in VWA Münster, NL Lüninck, 823. See also Horst Möller, "Gottfried Reinhold Treviranus. Ein Konservativer zwischen den Zeiten," in *Um der Freiheit Willen. Eine Festgabe für und von Johannes und Karin Schauff zum 80. Geburtstag*, ed. Paulus Gordan (Pfullingen, 1983), 118–46.

[27] Westarp's second statement before the DNVP executive committee, 21 Nov. 1929, NL Westarp, Gärtringen, II/61.

[28] Treviranus, "Rückblick," 7. For Hugenberg's position, see Traub to Tirpitz, 2 Jan. 1930, BA-MA Freiburg, NL Tirpitz, 221/8–9.

need for unity not only if the campaign against the Young Plan was to succeed but even more ominously if it should fail. Here Hugenberg highlighted the theme of anti-Marxism as the ideological axis around which the unification of the national opposition should take place. It was only through the creation of a strong and effective anti-Marxist front, Hugenberg insisted, that Germany could free itself from the yoke of foreign domination and deal with the enormous economic consequences of the Young Plan should it be accepted.[29] Over the course of the next several days Hugenberg's supporters would return to the theme of anti-Marxism time and time again: Magdalene von Tiling in her speech on what Christianity had to say to Marxism,[30] Christian-Social pastor and CSRV chairman Karl Veidt in his speech on the new *Kulturkampf* between Christianity and Marxism,[31] and World War I veteran Otto Schmidt-Hannover in his speech on the role of the front generation and youth in the struggle against Marxism.[32] Even Emil Hartwig, chairman of the German National Workers' League and a leading spokesman for the Christian-Social movement, delivered an impassioned speech in which he too identified the crusade against Marxism as the highest priority of the German Right, though tempered with a warning that fratricidal conflicts like that over the imprisonment paragraph only sewed disunity within the ranks of the national opposition and robbed it of the cohesiveness it needed to carry the struggle against Marxism to victory.[33]

None of this did much to assuage the depression of Westarp, who, according to one observer, sat through Hugenberg's speech with a face full of the greatest concern and deep solemnity. Only once did Westarp do so much as to applaud silently during the standing ovations that were being orchestrated by Hugenberg's confederates.[34] In reflecting back upon the Kassel

[29] Alfred Hugenberg, *Klare Front zum Freiheitskampf! Rede gehalten auf dem 9. Reichsparteitag der Deutschnationalen Volkspartei in Kassel am 22. November 1929*, Deutschnationale Flugschrift, no. 339 (Berlin, 1929), esp. 7–8. For the official record of the Kassel party congress, see *Unsere Partei* 7:23 (1 Dec. 1929): 389–413.

[30] Magdalene von Tiling, *Was hat das Christentum zum Marxismus zu sagen? Rede, gehalten auf dem 9. Reichsparteitag der Deutschnationalen Volkspartei in Kassel am 22. November 1929*, Deutschnationale Flugschrift, no. 341 (Berlin, 1929).

[31] Karl Veidt, *Der Kulturkampf unserer Zeit: Christentum und Marxismus. Rede, gehalten auf dem 9. Reichsparteitag der Deutschnationalen Volkspartei in Kassel am 22. November 1929*, Deutschnationale Flugschrift, no. 338 (Berlin, 1929).

[32] Otto Schmidt-Hannover, *Frontgeneration und Jugend im Freiheitskampf gegen den Marxismus. Rede, gehalten auf dem 9. Reichs-Partei-Tage der D.N.V.P. in Kassel am 23. November 1929* (Berlin, 1929).

[33] Hartwig's speech before the DNVP party congress, Kassel, 22 Nov. 1929, BA Berlin, R 8005, 55/44–53.

[34] Breuer, "Bericht über den deutschnationalen Parteitag in Kassel vom 21.–23.11.1929," BA Berlin, R 43 I, 2654/288–96.

congress, Westarp lamented the lack of support that his efforts on behalf of party unity had received from the DNVP party leadership and criticized Hugenberg in particular for his refusal to drop expulsion proceedings against Treviranus.[35] In point of fact, the Kassel party congress did little to heal the divisions that had developed within the DNVP during the campaign against the Young Plan. Even though the Christian-Socials, including Hülser and Hartwig, had gone to great lengths to reaffirm their loyalty to the DNVP and its struggle against Marxism in the report the German National Workers' League presented to the congress on 22 November,[36] they remained bitterly opposed to Hugenberg's leadership of the party and seemed resolved to use the conflict over the imprisonment paragraph as the pretext for leaving the party once it was clear that a change in the party leadership could no longer be expected. By the same token, Hugenberg's refusal to drop expulsions proceedings against Treviranus meant that any secession on the DNVP's left wing would not be confined to the Christian-Socials but would most likely involve the party's young conservative faction as well. Throughout all of this, the leaders of the DNVP's agrarian wing continued to bide their time, no doubt the outcome of the crisis with an eye on the Christian-National Peasants and Farmers' Party as a likely refuge if the situation in the DNVP did not resolve itself in their favor.

The December Secession

As the parliamentary debate on the "Freedom Law" drew near, a group of approximately twenty dissidents from the DNVP's left wing met under Lindeiner-Wildau's leadership in Berlin's Hotel Continental on the evening of 27 November to formulate a strategy for the upcoming vote in the Reichstag. The participants also included Westarp, who as chairman of the DNVP Reichstag delegation hoped that the deputies who refused to support the controversial imprisonment paragraph – here the estimates ranged from a dozen or so to more than thirty – could be prevented from leaving the party by allowing them to read a statement to the Reichstag in which they explained the reasons for their action. Westarp, however, rejected a draft statement that had been prepared for this purpose by Lindeiner-Wildau on the grounds that it was too incendiary and highlighted the reasons for opposing the imprisonment paragraph without underscoring the extent to which the dissidents too were opposed to the Young Plan and the policy of fulfillment. At the same

---

[35] Westarp to Wallraf, 26 Nov. 1929, NL Westarp, Gärtringen, II/37.

[36] *Von Bielefeld bis Kassel. Bericht der Bundesleitung des Deutschnationalen Arbeiterbundes, erstattet auf der 9. Reichstagung in Kassel am 21. November 1929*, ed. Bundesvorstand des Deutschnationalen Arbeiterbundes, Arbeiterbundschriften, no. 15 (Berlin, 1929), 11.

time, Westarp announced his intention to vote for the "Freedom Law" in its entirety and urged those who opposed the imprisonment paragraph to remain in the party despite their differences with the party chairman. Westarp then fashioned a statement for the dissidents that stressed their unequivocal opposition to the Young Plan despite differences over the language of the imprisonment paragraph in the hope that this might be acceptable to all factions in the party.[37]

Westarp's efforts at a compromise received strong support from Schiele, who had decided that he would not take part in the vote on the imprisonment paragraph but would explain his action in a statement to the Reichstag. In a private conversation with Schiele on 29 November Hugenberg indicated that he was amenable to this solution as long as the dissidents supported all other provisions of the "Freedom Law" and did not vote against the imprisonment paragraph but simply absented themselves from the Reichstag when the decisive vote took place.[38] When this proposal had been floated at a meeting of the DNVP Reichstag delegation on the previous evening, it had provoked a storm of criticism from Hugenberg's confederates, most of whom seemed more intent upon purging the party of its unreliable elements than salvaging party unity. This was particularly true of Hugenberg's close associate Reinhold Quaatz, who attacked Westarp not just for having taken part in meetings with the dissidents but also for having consistently failed to preserve the unity of the delegation at critical points in the party's history. What began as criticism of Westarp's efforts to placate the anti-Hugenberg elements on the DNVP's left wing quickly escalated into a full-scale attack upon Westarp's performance first as the party's national chairman and then as its leader in the Reichstag.[39] Westarp's efforts to prevent a secession on the DNVP's left wing were further undercut by the unresolved status of the Treviranus affair. At the meeting of the DNVP Reichstag delegation on 28 November Treviranus had taken the floor to defend his indiscretion as a purely private remark to a personal associate and denied any involvement in preparations for the founding of a new party.[40] But Treviranus's disclaimer only infuriated the pro-Hugenberg elements on the party's right wing and did nothing to ease tensions within the party.

When the DNVP Reichstag delegation resumed its deliberations on the morning of 29 November, Hugenberg's supporters intensified their attacks

---

[37] Westarp, "Niederschrift über die DNVP-Parteikrise," NL Westarp, Gärtringen, II/61.

[38] Ibid. See also Mumm to Rippel, 28 Nov. 1929, BA Berlin, NL Mumm, 139/218. On Westarp's efforts to avoid a split, see Gasteiger, *Westarp*, 352–55. See also Mergel, "Das Scheitern des deutsche Tory-Konservatismus," 351–55.

[39] Westarp, "Niederschrift über die DNVP-Parteikrise," NL Westarp, Gärtringen, II/61. See also the entry in Quaatz's diary, n.d. [29 Nov. 1929], BA Koblenz, NL Quaatz, 16.

[40] Ibid. See also Treviranus, "Rückblick" (see n. 26), 7–9.

against the dissidents and their plans to release a statement explaining their reasons for not supporting the controversial imprisonment paragraph. At the urging of Westarp and Schiele, all of the dissidents with the exception of Hülser relented and agreed simply to absent themselves during the critical vote without issuing an explanation of their behavior. This represented a modest victory for Westarp and Schiele, who earned expressions of gratitude from Hugenberg and several of his supporters for their efforts on behalf of party unity.[41] This arrangement, however, fell apart when after the decisive vote on the so-called Freedom Law on the morning of 30 November – a vote in which thirteen Nationalist deputies including Treviranus and Lindeiner-Wildau abstained from voting, while another ten, some for reasons of poor health, missed the session altogether – Hartwig, Hülser, and Lambach released a statement in which they identified themselves with the position taken by Schiele, declared their solidarity with Treviranus, and criticized the DNVP party leadership for its inability to tolerate differences of political opinion.[42] The release of this statement was a clear breach of the arrangement to which Hugenberg had reluctantly assented, whereupon the DNVP party chairman called an emergency session of the DNVP executive committee on 3 December for the purpose of initiating explusion proceedings against the three renegade deputies.[43]

Over the weekend Westarp negotiated furiously with all concerned parties in an attempt to prevent the crisis from developing into a major secession on the DNVP's left wing. But he was repeatedly frustrated not just by the intransigence of both Hugenberg and the Christian-Socials but also by the lingering uncertainty regarding the disposition of the Treviranus affair.[44] Consequently, when the DNVP executive committee convened on the morning of 3 December to deal with the consequences of the split in the vote on the "Freedom Law," the lines had hardened to the point where compromise was no longer possible.[45] Hugenberg opened the meeting with a motion calling for the expulsion of three Christian-Socials for having damaged the image of the party.[46] At this point Hartwig took the floor to announce that he already considered himself expelled from the party, offered an impassioned defense of

[41] Westarp, "Niederschrift über die DNVP-Parteikrise," NL Westarp, Gärtringen, II/61.
[42] For the text of this statement, see *Klärung und Sammlung. Der Wortlaut der wichtigeren Veröffentlichungen gelegentlich der Klärung im deutschnationalen Lager. Als Handschrift gedruckt* (N.p., n.d. [1929–30]), 8.
[43] Ibid., 8.
[44] Westarp, "Niederschrift über die DNVP-Parteikrise," NL Westarp, Gärtringen, II/61.
[45] See the article by Lambach, "Gegen Erstarrungserscheinungen im politischen Leben," *Berliner Börsen-Zeitung*, 2 Dec. 1929, no. 562, reprinted in *Klärung und Sammlung*, 3–6, as well as the entry in Quaatz's diary, 2 Dec. 1929, BA Koblenz, NL Quaatz, 16.
[46] *Klärung und Sammlung*, 9. For the perspective of the DNVP party leadership, see DNVP, Mitteilungen, no. 51, 5 Dec. 1929, FZH Hamburg, NL Diller, 10.

the statement he and his colleagues had issued in the Reichstag, and complained bitterly about the way in which the so-called Freedom Law had come into existence without the cooperation or involvement of the DNVP Reichstag delegation. All of this, concluded Hartwig, underscored the lack of genuine leadership skills on the part of the DNVP party chairman who had failed to build the necessary consensus for an action as ambitious as the referendum against the Young Plan.[47] In response, Westarp expressed disappointment with the dissidents' decision to issue a public statement in defense of their vote, for in his mind this left the party leadership with no alternative but to introduce expulsion proceedings against them. Drawing a parallel to the situation before and during World War I when the splintering of the German Right had resulted in its total impotence, Westarp implored the party leadership and the dissidents to resolve their differences for the sake of party unity.[48] Such entreaties were to little avail, as Hugenberg and his supporters prevailed by a 65 to 9 margin with three abstentions, including that of Westarp, to initiate expulsion proceedings against the three Christian-Socials and Treviranus for the damage they had allegedly done to the image of the party and the unity of the national front.[49]

All of this represented a clear repudiation of the strategy that Westarp had pursued since the beginning of the crisis. At a meeting of the DNVP Reichstag delegation later that afternoon Westarp appealed once again for the various factions within the party to set aside their differences for the sake of party unity in the struggle against the Young Plan.[50] As in the past, Westarp's words went unheeded, this time by the Christian-Socials, who were determined to bolt the party and were no longer interested in any compromise that might save party unity. Immediately after the end of the meeting, Hülser and Lambach announced their resignation from the party and the DNVP Reichstag delegation, to be followed shortly thereafter by Mumm and Behrens in a demonstration of solidarity with their Christian-Social colleagues.[51] Over the next twenty-four hours they were joined by eight other DNVP Reichstag deputies, among them several of Westarp's most trusted associates in the party. In addition to Treviranus, Lindeiner-Wildau, and Hartwig, the secessionists also included industrialist Moritz Klönne, foreign policy expert Otto Hoetzsch, former interior minister

---

[47] Hartwig's speech before the DNVP executive committee, 3 Dec. 1929, BA Berlin, R 8005, 55/19–27, reprinted in *Klärung und Sammlung*, 9–18.

[48] Westarp's speech before the DNVP executive committee, 3 Dec. 1929, NL Westarp, Gärtringen, II/61.

[49] DNVP, Mitteilungen, no. 51, 5 Dec. 1929, FZH Hamburg, NL Diller, 10.

[50] Westarp to Wallraf, 5 Dec. 1929, NL Westarp, Gärtringen, II/37.

[51] Mumm, "Zum 30. November 1929," BA Berlin, NL Mumm, 283/359–61.

Walther von Keudell, farm leader Hans Schlange-Schöningen, and the Catholic young conservative Paul Lejeune-Jung.[52]

The number of deputies leaving the party might very well have been much greater had not Schiele decided to remain with the DNVP in the hope that it still might be possible to force a change in the party's national leadership.[53] As it was, Westarp felt that his efforts to salvage party unity had received so little support from Hugenberg and his supporters that he had no choice but to resign as chairman of the DNVP Reichstag delegation.[54] Westarp was succeeded in this capacity by Ernst Oberfohren, a Hugenberg confederate who strongly supported the so-called Freedom Law as the first step toward freeing Germany from Allied bondage.[55] In the meantime, however, the secessionists' hopes of triggering a full-scale rebellion against Hugenberg at the grassroots of the DNVP party organization failed to materialize as the leaders of one district organization after another rallied to Hugenberg's support.[56] This was due in large part to the aggressive campaign that Hugenberg's Pan-German allies had waged for control of the party's local organizations, with the result that the party's moderates no longer enjoyed the support they once had at the local and district levels of the DNVP party organization.[57] For Hugenberg and his confederates, the secession was less a leadership crisis than a purge by which the DNVP had cleansed itself of unreliable elements that were superfluous in the struggle for a fundamental change in the existing political order.[58]

[52] Blank to Reusch, 5 Dec. 1929, RWWA Cologne, Abt. 130, NL Reusch, 4001012024/6. For the text of their statements and resignation letters, see *Klärung und Sammlung*, 18–30, and the official DNVP publication, *Die Abtrünnigen. Die Geschichte einer Absplitterung, die die Festigung einer Partei brachte*, Deutschnationales Rüstzeug, no. 16 (Berlin, 1930), 13–20, as well as Lambach, "Gegen Erstarrungserscheinungen im politischen Leben," *Berliner Börsen-Zeitung*, 2 Dec. 1929, no. 562, and Klönne, "Die deutschnationale Parteikrise," *Deutsche Allgemeine Zeitung*, 4 Dec. 1929, no. 562.

[53] Wilmowsky to Krupp, 7 Dec. 1929, HA Krupp Essen, FAH 23/503.

[54] Memorandum by Westarp, 14 Dec. 1929, NL Westarp, Gärtringen, VN 104. See also Westarp to Pückler, 5 Feb. 1930, ibid., VN 20.

[55] Ernst Oberfohren, *Zum Freiheitsgesetz. Rede in der Sitzung des Reichstags vom 6. Dezember 1929*, Deutschnationale Flugschrift, no. 342 (Berlin, 1929).

[56] "Kundgebung der deutschnationalen Führer," *Mitteilungen der Deutschnationalen Volkspartei*, 6 Dec. 1929, in *Unsere Partei* 7, no. 24 (15 Dec. 1929): 417–28.

[57] Claß to Wegener, 24 May 1929, BA Koblenz, NL Wegener, 23. See also Hilpert, "Meinungen und Kämpfe," BHStA Munich, NL Hilpert, 20/4025–31.

[58] See Seidlitz-Sandreczki, chairman of the Central Association of German Conservatives, to Westarp, 6 Dec. 1929, NL Westarp, Gärtringen, II/37, as Bang, "Nicht Führerkrise, sondern Fraktionskrise," *Deutsche Zeitung*, 7 Dec. 1929, no. 287. See also the accounts of the secession by Hugenberg loyalists Lothar Steuer, *Absplitterung von der D.N.V.P.*, Volk und Vaterland, nos. 160–62 (Kassel, 1930), 1–8, and Axel von Freytagh-Loringhoven, *Deutschnationale Volkspartei* (Berlin, 1931), 63–70.

The Quest for Conservative Unity

The crisis within the DNVP and the secession of twelve Reichstag deputies in December 1929 was but one more symptom of the advanced state of dissolution in which the bourgeois party system found itself at the end of the 1920s. All of this posed a severe challenge to the political influence of Germany's conservative economic elites. Not only was Hugenberg's style of leadership directed against the role that organized economic interests had played in the economic and political stabilization of the Weimar Republic, but both agriculture and industry required a strong and cohesive political Right to defend and assert their interests against those of organized labor. But the situation for organized agriculture, which had already developed a fallback position in the Christian-National Peasants and Farmers' Party, was not as ominous as it was for German industry. The Ruhr iron conflict in the fall of 1928 marked the beginning of an intensified assault by Ruhr heavy industry against the social and economic achievements of organized labor since the end of World War I. Although the outcome of this conflict was ambiguous at best, it was only the prelude to a renewed industrial offensive against unemployment insurance in the fall and early winter of 1929. Germany's industrial leadership had hoped that adoption of the Young Plan would bring a measure of relief from Germany's reparations obligations under the Dawes Plan and a reduction in industry's tax burden. When this failed to materialize, Germany's industrial leadership took the position that only through a thorough reorganization of public finances and a reduction in public spending would it be possible for the German economy to fulfill the terms of the Young Plan.[59] At the same time, German industry remained adamantly opposed to any increase in its mandatory contributions to the state unemployment insurance program. But all of this, as industrialists of varying political stripes clearly recognized, meant an end to the "Great Coalition" in the Reich, if not also in Prussia, and a reorganization of the national government on the basis of a broad coalition of parties from the middle and moderate Right.[60]

The only real leverage that German industry enjoyed in the last months of 1929 was on the right wing of the German People's Party, where Reusch and

---

[59] Jakob Wilhelm Reichert, *Young-Plan, Finanzen und Wirtschaft* (Berlin, 1930), esp. 66–68. For further details, see Weisbrod, *Schwerindustrie in der Weimarer Republik*, 415–77.

[60] For further details, see Helga Timm, *Deutsche Sozialpolitik und der Bruch der großen Koalition im März 1930* (Düsseldorf, 1952) and Ilse Maurer, *Reichsfinanzen und große Koalition. Zur Geschichte des Kabinetts Müller (1928–1930)* (Bonn and Frankfurt a.m. Main, 1973), as well as James, *German Slump*, 39–109.

his factotum Erich von Gilsa were hard at work trying to bring about an end to the DVP's participation in the "Great Coalition."[61] Their chances of success, however, depended to a large extent upon what happened in the DNVP. The leaders of Germany's industrial establishment followed developments in the DNVP in the fall and early winter of 1929 closely but were divided in their assessment of what should be done. Some like Albert Vögler and Ernst Poengsen from the United Steel Works, as well as a sizable contingent within the Ruhr coal industry, enthusiastically endorsed Hugenberg's call for the creation of an anti-Marxist front and had little sympathy for the aspirations of the secessionists on the DNVP's left wing.[62] Others such as the Gutehoffnungshütte's Paul Reusch, steel magnate Gustav Krupp von Bohlen und Halbach, and RDI president Carl Duisberg were critical of Hugenberg's leadership style and sympathized with the secessionists in their efforts to found a new conservative party.[63] Both groups, however, lamented the fragmentation of the DNVP at a time when the battle over unemployment insurance seemed to be drawing to a head. It was no accident when the National Federation of German Industry prefaced the publication of its proposal for economic and fiscal reform under the title "Aufstieg oder Niedergang" in mid-December 1929 with an appeal for the "consolidation of all the constructive forces of our nation [*Sammlung aller aufbauenden Kräfte unseres Volkes*]."[64]

Although the more moderate elements within the German industrial establishment may have felt that the December secession had been premature and regretted that it had not been more extensive,[65] they were anxious that the secessionists reconstitute themselves as a viable political force at the earliest possible opportunity. To assist in this process, Duisberg provided the secessionists with 20,000 marks from the RDI's own resources through an

[61] Peter Langer, "'v. Gilsa an Reusch (Oberhausen)': Wirtschaftsinteressen und Politik am Vorabend der Großen Krise," in *Abenteuer Industriestadt. Oberhausen 1874–1999. Beiträge zur Stadtgeschichte* (Oberhausen, 2001), 103–24. See also Richter, *Deutsche Volkspartei*, 595–604.

[62] See the letters from Widenmann to Gürtner, 7 Nov. 1929; to Poengsen, 8 Nov. 1929; and to Vögler, BA-MA Freiburg, NL Widenmann, 17/82–84, 75–77, 71.

[63] For example, see Wilmowsky to Krupp, 22 Nov. 1929, HA Krupp Essen, FAH 23/503.

[64] Duisberg's introductory remarks at an extraordinary meeting of the RDI membership, 12 Dec. 1929, Bayer-Archiv Leverkusen, 62/10.9c. For the text of the RDI's program, see *Aufstieg oder Niedergang? Deutsche Wirtschafts- und Finanzreform 1929. Eine Denkschrift des Reichsver-bandes der Deutschen Industrie*, Veröffentlichungen des Reichsverbandes der Deutschen Industrie, no. 49 (Berlin, 1929). See also Jorg-Otto Spiller, "Reformismus nach rechts. Zur Politik des Reichsverbandes der Deutschen Industrie in den Jahren 1927–1930 am Beispiel der Reparationspolitik," in *Industrielles System und politische Entwicklung*, ed. Mommsen, Petzina, and Weisbrod, 593–602.

[65] Wilmowsky to Krupp, 7 Dec. 1929, HA Krupp, FAH 23/503.

intermediary, Baron Werner von Alvensleben.[66] Even more lucrative offers of financial support came from the military, where General Kurt von Schleicher, the Reichswehr's political adjutant, offered Treviranus 300,000 marks to assist in the founding of a new conservative party, an offer that was declined for fear that it would compromise the new party's freedom of movement.[67] In order for the secessionists to continue their parliamentary activity, it was imperative that they find new allies in the Reichstag so that they would be recognized as a delegation, or *Fraktion*, with its full complement of committee assignments and related privileges. This problem was quickly solved when the twelve secessionists joined the nine deputies from the CNBLP to form a parliamentary delegation known as the Christian-National Coalition (Christlich-nationale Arbeitsgemeinschaft) under the chairmanship of Treviranus.[68] But this was little more than a temporary expedient that did not solve the far more serious problem of building a strong national organization that would make it possible for them to continue their parliamentary activity beyond the current legislative period. To be sure, the group around Treviranus and Lindeiner-Wildau were anxious to hold the secessionists together in some form of loose coalition until the organizational foundation for a comprehensive moderate conservative party could be developed. But strong centrifugal forces were already at work among the secessionists inasmuch as both the Christian-Socials and leaders of the DNVP's agrarian wing had begun to gravitate toward different centers of political activity. This development constituted a particularly ominous threat to the young conservatives, for without the support of organized agriculture or the Evangelical bloc their movement lacked a solid sociological and organizational foundation.

Originally the young conservatives around Treviranus and Lindeiner-Wildau had hoped to unite the Christian-Socials, the CNBLP, and the other groups that had broken away from the DNVP into a loose federation of conservative forces called the "German Right" as a short-term step leading to the creation of a new moderate conservative party.[69] The roots of such an idea went back to the "Essen Program" that Stegerwald had outlined at the tenth congress of the Christian trade unions in November 1920 and was popular with young-conservative intellectuals such as Friedrich Glum, Hans

---

[66] Duisberg to Alvensleben, 29 Nov. 1929, Bayer-Archiv Leverkusen, Autographensammlung Duisberg.

[67] Treviranus, "Schleicher" (see n. 15), 371.

[68] *Aufruf und Gründung*, Volkskonservative Flugschriften, no. 1 (Berlin, 1930), 4–5. See also Mumm to Rippel, 12 Dec. 1929, and 2 Jan. 1930, BA Berlin, NL Mumm, 284/79, 201–02.

[69] Entry in Passarge's diary, 5 Jan. 1930, BA Koblenz, NL Passarge, 2/9. See also Treviranus, "Unsere Aufgabe," *Politische Wochenschrift* 5, no. 50 (14 Dec. 1929): 981–82, and Treviranus, "Das Fähnlein der Zwölf," *Das Staatsschiff*, 1, no. 5 (16 Jan. 1930): 176–78. See also Jonas, *Volkskonservativen 1928–1933. Entwicklung, Struktur, Standort and staatspolitische Zielsetzung* (Düsseldorf, 1965), 57–63.

Zehrer, and Hermann Ullmann.[70] Unlike their rivals on the radical Right, as Lindeiner-Wildau reminded the Reichstag in a programmatic speech on 12 December, the young conservatives were committed to pursue a regeneration of German political life within the framework of the existing form of government, its obvious imperfections notwithstanding.[71] It was precisely this strong sense of loyalty to the state regardless of the form in which it existed that separated the young conservatives from the obstructionist tactics of Hugenberg and his Pan-German allies. In their eyes, Hugenberg was a 'hopeless reactionary and the "grave-digger of German conservatism." Out of the ruins of the struggle against the Young Plan, so argued Hermann Ullmann in a pamphlet aptly entitled *Die Rechte stirbt – es lebe die Rechte!*, would emerge a new conservatism that reached across the boundaries of confession and class to embrace conservative elements within Germany's Catholic population and the Christian-national labor movement. Only such a conservatism, and not the sham conservatism offered by Hugenberg and his confederates, would lead the German nation out of the depths of despair into which it had fallen.[72]

Initially the young conservatives had hoped to solicit at least five hundred signatures for a public appeal calling for the founding of a comprehensive conservative party committed to the preservation of the state against the forces of social and political radicalism that were at work in the German nation. But by the beginning of January 1930 efforts to consolidate the various conservative groups that had broken away from the DNVP into a new, united German Right had drawn to a complete standstill as a result of strong resistance from both the CNBLP and the Christian-Socials. Uncertain as to whether or not the plans to this effect should be abandoned, Treviranus called a meeting of the twelve secessionists and their closest political supporters on the afternoon of 9 January with the clear intention of placing them before an "either–or" decision.[73] In addition to the twelve secessionists, the meeting was attended

---

[70] In this respect, see Friedrich Glum, *Das geheime Deutschland. Die Aristokratie der demokratischen Gesinnung* (Berlin, 1930), 101–14; Hans Zehrer, "Grundriß einer neuen Partei," *Die Tat* 21, no. 9 (Dec. 1929): 641–61; Hermann Ullmann, *Das werdende Volk. Gegen Liberalismus und Reaktion* (Hamburg, 1929), 97–103, 130–37. On Glum, see Bernd Weisbrod, "Das 'Geheime Deutschland' und das 'Geistige Bad Harzburg.' Friedrich Glum und das Dilemma des demokratischen Konservatismus am Ende der Weimarer Republik," in *Von der Aufgabe der Freiheit. Politische Verantwortung und bürgerliche Gesellschaft im 19. und 20. Jahrhundert. Festschrift für Hans Mommsen zum 5. November 1995*, ed. Christian Jansen, Lutz Niethammer, and Bernd Weisbrod (Berlin, 1995), 285–308.

[71] Hans Erdmann von Lindeiner-Wildau, *Erneuerung des politischen Lebens. Reichstagsrede gehalten am 13. Dezember 1929*, Schriften der Deutschnationalen Arbeitsgemeinschaft, no. 1 (Berlin-Charlottenburg, 1929), 7–8.

[72] Hermann Ullmann, *Die Rechte stirbt – es lebe die Rechte!* (Berlin, 1929), esp. 20–44.

[73] Entry in Passarge's diary, 5 Jan. 1930, BA Koblenz, NL Passarge, 2/10.

by a delegation from the DHV headed by its ch[74]ief political stratagist Max Habermann. The largest of Germany's white-collar unions with an estimated 380,000 members by the end of 1929,[75] the DHV had long pursued its social, economic, and political objectives through an elaborate network of interrelationships, or *Querverbindungen*, with the various political parties that stood to the right of Social Democracy only to see this network fall completely apart in the wake of Hugenberg's election to the DNVP's party chairmanship. Habermann and the DHV, however, rejected the proposal for a loose confederation of conservative forces along the lines of Treviranus's united German Right and supported instead the creation of a "people's conservative state party."[76] This proposal ignited a heated debate that required all of Treviranus's talents as a mediator to keep the meeting from degenerating into a complete debacle. The Christian-Socials not only rejected the DHV's proposal outright but refused to take part even in the more modest united German Right advocated by Treviranus and his supporters. With no more than four of the original twelve secessionists in support of the creation of a "people's conservative state party," the meeting closed on a note of bitterness that was particularly strong among the leaders of the DHV.[77]

The outcome of the meeting on 9 January signaled the collapse of young-conservative efforts to create either a new conservative party or a united conservative front along the more modest lines of the "German Right." Still hopeful that some sort of an accommodation might be possible in the event of new national elections, the young conservatives suspended plans for the founding of a new political party and concentrated their efforts instead upon launching a new organization entitled the People's Conservative Association (Volkskonservative Vereinigung or VKV). The official founding of the VKV took place in Berlin on 28 January and was attended by more than 200 supporters and interested guests. According to its founding charter, the primary purpose of the new organization was "to bring the Christian and conservative elements in the German nation to greater effectiveness in politics, legislation, and administration at all levels of government in order to

---

[74] On Habermann, see Peter Rütters, "Max Habermann und der gewerkschaftliche Widerstand gegen den Nationalsozialismus. Probleme einer biographischen Rekonstruktion," *Historisch-politische Mitteilungen* 20 (2013): 37–70, esp. 42–47.

[75] Walther Lambach, "Deutschnationaler Handlungsgehilfenverband (DHV)," in *Internationales Handwörterbuch des Gewerkschaftswesens*, ed. Ludwig Heyde, 2 vols. (Berlin, 1931–32), 1:393–399, here 394.

[76] In this respect, see Habermann "Der Deutschnationale Handlungsgehilfen-Verband im Kampf um das Reich," DHV-Archiv, Hamburg, as well as the unpublished biography by Albert Krebs, "Max Habermann. Eine biographische Studie," FZH Hamburg, 12/H.

[77] Entry in Passarge's diary, 12 Jan. 1930, ibid., 2/16–18.

promote the cause of national independence abroad and inner renewal at home."[78] As the convention's keynote speaker and the newly elected chairman of the VKV, Treviranus elaborated upon the movement's political objectives as well as on its relationship to other conservative groups. Treviranus stressed that the VKV was not a political party but a bipartisan association of like-minded men and women dedicated to a consolidation of all conservative forces in a greater German Right without regard to their current party affiliation.[79] The Christian-National Coalition that had just been created in the Reichstag, Treviranus continued, represented in microcosm what the People's Conservative Association hoped to achieve on a broader basis, namely the unification of all conservative forces – peasant, worker, artisan, and intelligentsia – on the basis of positive action within the existing system of government.[80] The goal of positive action, as opposed to Hugenberg's nihilistic obstructionism, was stressed even more emphatically by Otto Hoetzsch in the final speech of the day. Comparing the goals of the young-conservative movement with those of the British Conservative Party, Hoetzsch proclaimed: "We want to be the German 'Tory Democracy' – with all of the national, civic, and social connotations that are associated with this concept."[81]

Although its founders insisted that the VKV was not a political party but a movement that transcended existing party lines, they hoped that the new organization, presumably in close cooperation with the CNBLP and CSVD, would be able to run its own slate of candidates in any future elections.[82] At the VKV's official founding in Berlin, both the CNBLP's Günther Gereke and the CSVD's Franz Behrens pledged their full support and willingness to

---

[78] *Aufruf und Gründung*, Volkskonservative Flugschriften, no. 1 (Berlin, 1930), 3–5. For comprehensive reports on the founding of the VKV, see *Volkskonservative Stimmen*, 1 Feb. 1930, no. 1, and *Neue Preußische (Kreuz-)Zeitung*, 30 Jan. 1930, no. 31.

[79] Lambach to Classen, 23 Jan. 1930, BA Koblenz, NL Lambach, 2. See also Hans-Peter Müller, "Sammlungsversuche *charaktervoller* Konservativer. Die Volkskonservativen in Württemberg 1930–1932," *Zeitschrift für Württembergische Landesgeschichte* 64 (2005): 339–54.

[80] Treviranus, *Auf neuen Wegen*, Volkskonservative Flugschriften, no. 2 (Berlin, 1930), 3–8. On the VKV's attitude toward the republican form of government, see Treviranus, "Konservatismus in der Demokratie," *Volkskonservative Stimmen. Zeitschrift der Volkskonservativen Vereinigung*, 26 Apr. 1930, nos. 12–13. See also Walther Lambach, "Volkskonservative Vereinigung (Konservative Volkspartei)." in *Internationales Handwörterbuch des Gewerkschaftswesens*, ed. Ludwig Heyde, 2 vols. (Berlin, 1931–32), 2:1930–32.

[81] Hoetzsch, "Deutsche Tory-Demokratie," *Politische Wochenschrift* 5, no. 6 (8 Feb. 1930): 56–58. For a fuller statement of Hoetzsch's views on the solutions to the problems confronting Germany, see Otto Hoetzsch, *Germany's Domestic and Foreign Policies* (New Haven, CT, 1929).

[82] Lambach to Classen, 23 Jan. 1930, BA Koblenz, NL Lambach, 2.

cooperate in the struggle for the realization of conservative values.[83] The young conservatives were particularly interested in on the establishment of close ties with the CNBLP and relied heavily upon the services of Hans Schlange-Schöningen, one of the twelve secessionists who officially joined the CNBLP on the day after the founding of the VKV.[84] Deeply committed to the idea of a progressive conservative party supported by all sectors of the population, Schlange realized that the prospects of the VKV and the greater German Right for which it stood were virtually non-existent without the support of German agriculture.[85] But the young conservatives' dependence upon the financial and organizational support of the DHV severely handicapped their efforts to attract a diversified popular base. Nowhere was the extent of this support more apparent than when the VKV executive committee was elected in the middle of February, no less than twelve of its fifteen members were affiliated either directly or indirectly with the white-collar union.[86] That the DHV was so heavily involved in the founding of the VKV did not augur well for its efforts to develop a united conservative front that transcended the social and economic cleavages that were so deeply embedded in the fabric of Germany's national life.

Realignment in the Countryside

Nowhere were the centrifugal forces at work in the German party system more apparent than in the German agricultural community, where in early 1928 two new agrarian splinter parties, the German Peasants' Party and the decidedly more conservative Christian-National Peasant and Farmers' Party, made their appearance on the political stage.[87] The founding of the CNBLP constituted a direct threat to the DNVP's position in the countryside, and in the May 1928 Reichstag elections the party received over 580,000 votes and elected nine deputies to the Reichstag. The CNBLP's hopes of establishing a parliamentary alliance, or *Frationsgemeinschaft*, with the more democratically oriented German Peasant's Party, however, collapsed when Anton Fehr, the chairman of the Peasants' Party, opted in favor of a coalition with the Business Party.[88] The CNBLP's resultant isolation in the Reichstag, however, did not

---

[83] *Volkskonservative Stimmen*, 1 Feb. 1930, no. 1.

[84] Entry in Passarge's diary, 30 Jan. 1930, BA Koblenz, NL Passarge, 2/25–26.

[85] *Volkskonservative Stimmen*, 1 Feb. 1930, no. 1.

[86] Entry in Passarge's diary, 22 Feb. 1930, BA Koblenz, NL Passarge, 3/51–52, 55–57.

[87] For an overview, see Larry Eugene Jones, "Crisis and Realignment: Agrarian Splinter Parties in the Late Weimar Republic, 1928–33," in *Peasants and Lords in Modern Germany: Recent Essays in Agricultural History*, ed. Robert G. Moeller (Boston, 1986), 198–232. On the CNBLP, see Markus Müller, *Landvolkpartei*, 23–70.

[88] *Die grüne Zukunft. Zeitschrift für Deutsche Bauernpolitik*, 1, no. 2 (Nov. 1928): 28.

lead to an improvement in its relations with the DNVP despite repeated overtures from the Nationalists.[89] In the meantime, the rivalry between the DNVP and CNBLP had become so intense by the end of the summer that the National Rural League found it necessary to undertake a major overall of its internal leadership structure that placed responsibility for charting the RLB's political course in the hands of a three-man presidium consisting of the DNVP's Martin Schiele, the CNBLP's Karl Hepp, and the ostensibly neutral Albrecht Bethge.[90] The appearance of RLB director Heinrich von Sybel at the CNBLP's national delegate congress (Reichsvertretertag) in Hanover on 8–9 September 1928 and Hepp's vigorous defense of the CNBLP's independence vis-à-vis Germany's other political parties in his keynote address on the first day of the congress could only have reinforced Nationalist fears that the new party was headed in a direction that did not bode well for the future of their own party.[91]

Efforts to "depoliticize" the National Rural League and thus insulate it from the conflict between the DNVP and CNBLP all but collapsed in the wake of Hugenberg's election to the chairmanship of the DNVP, with the result that the balance in the RLB now began to swing toward the CNBLP. The creation of the "Green Front" in the spring of 1929 reflected a further deterioration of the DNVP's traditional ties with the German agricultural community and gave new impetus to the CNBLP's campaign on behalf of a united agrarian party.[92] Efforts to create a new agrarian party organized along corporatist and vocational lines received another boost in the summer of 1929 when Günther Gereke, founder and president of the German Association of Rural Municipalities (Deutscher Landgemeindetag), resigned from the DNVP to join the CNBLP.[93] Gereke, whose bid for reelection to the Reichstag in May 1928 had ended in disappointment both for him and his backers in the

---

[89] For example, see Richthofen to Hepp, 7 July 1928, and to Westarp, 7 and 19 July 1928, NL Westarp, Gärtringen, VN 100, as well as Joseph Kaufhold, "Die Christlich-nationale Bauernpartei," *Unsere Partei*, 4, no. 27 (15 Dec. 1928): 386–88.

[90] *Reichs-Landbund*, 8, no. 31 (4 Aug. 1928): 351–52.

[91] Report on the CNBLP's Hanover delegate conference, 8–9 Sept. 1928, BA Berlin, R 8034 I, 50/78–84. See also the press reports in the *Thüringer Landbund* 9, no. 73 (12 Sept. 1928), and the *Nassauische Bauern-Zeitung*, 15 Sept. 1928, no. 214.

[92] See Sybel to Kurzrock, 26 Mar. 1929, BA Berlin, R 8034 I, 152/42–44. For further details, see Andreas Müller, "*Fällt der Bauer,*" 110–12, 123–39.

[93] Gereke to Westarp, 28 June 1929, NL Westarp, Gärtringen, II/35. On Gereke's motives, see Westarp to Oppenfeld, 25 Oct. 1929., ibid., VN 102. For Gereke's account of his activities, see the "Lebenslauf" he prepared in connection with his 1933 trial in the records of the Generalstaatsanwaltschaft, Prozeßakten Gereke, Landesarchiv Berlin (hereafter cited as LA Berlin), Repertorium A, 358-01, 76, 14, as well as the less reliable account in Günther Gereke, *Ich war königlich-preußischer Landrat* (Berlin, 1970), 91–105, 122–28, 148–53.

German agricultural community,[94] was a capable organizer who used his extensive contacts in central and eastern Germany to help establish and finance a CNBLP organization in East Prussia, Saxony, Thuringia, and other areas previously dominated by the DNVP.[95] Not only did Gereke's efforts to broaden the CNBLP's organizational base at the expense of the DNVP receive financial support from steel magnate Gustav Krupp von Bohlen und Halbach and the directorate of I. G. Farben, but he also received considerable encouragement from General Kurt von Schleicher, the Reichswehr's chief political strategist and a determined opponent of Hugenberg.[96]

By the end of the summer DNVP party leaders were becoming increasingly annoyed by the agitation of the CNBLP and its affect upon their party's rural electorate.[97] It was almost inevitable that Gereke's activities should lead to a clash with the DNVP, and in August 1929 he came under a sharp attack from Georg Wilhelm Schiele, chairman of the DNVP provincial organization in Halle-Merseburg and one of Hugenberg's strongest supporters in his conflict with the DNVP's left wing.[98] An even more serious source of friction was the reluctance with which Gereke and other CNBLP leaders supported the infamous imprisonment paragraph of the so-called Freedom Law.[99] Last-minute efforts by Schiele and the CNBLP's Albrecht Wendhausen to prevent the inclusion of the imprisonment paragraph in the final text of the "Freedom Law" were to no avail, so that the full text of the proposed law was published on the morning of 12 September without RLB and CNBLP consent.[100] At a CNBLP rally in Dortmund on 15 September, Gereke sharply criticized the imprisonment paragraph and warned that the language of the "Freedom Law" was so indiscriminate that not even Reich President von Hindenburg was exempt from the threat of imprisonment.[101] CNBLP national chairman Erwin

---

[94] On the Gereke candidacy, see the detailed letter from Schellen to Westarp, 17 July 1928, NL Westarp, Gärtringen, VN 67.

[95] For example, see the reports in *Der Landbürger. Kommunalpolitisches Organ der Christlich-nationalen Bauern- and Landvolkpartei*, 4, no. 15 (2 Aug. 1929): 225; no. 17 (2 Sept. 1929): 258; and no. 29 (2 Oct. 1929): 290. On the financial support that Gereke steered to the CNBLP's district organizations, see the correspondence in LA Berlin, Prozeßakten Gereke, Rep. A, 358–01, 76/16, Anlage 2.

[96] Gereke, *Ich war königlich-preußischer Landrat*, 153–55.

[97] For example, see Boedicker to Westarp, 9 Aug. 1929, NL Westarp, Gärtringen, II/35.

[98] DNVP, Mitteilungen no. 36, 30 Aug. 1929, FZH Hamburg, NL Diller, 10. See also *Der Landbürger*, 4, no. 17 (2 Sept. 1929): 257.

[99] See Brauweiler's notes on his meeting with Hepp and Gereke, 4 Sept. 1929, StA Mönchen-Gladbach, NL Brauweiler, 110, as well as a speech by Gereke in Hamm, n.d., reported in *Der Landbürger*, 4, no. 19 (2 Oct. 1929): 289–90. See also Müller, *Landvolkpartei*, 118–30

[100] Entry in Quaatz's diary, 11 Sept. 1929, BA Koblenz, NL Quaatz, 16.

[101] *Schulthess' Europäischer Geschichtskalender*, ed. Ulrich Thü_rauf (Munich, 1859ff.), 70 (1929): 166–67.

Baum and Reichstag deputy Friedrich Döbrich met with Hugenberg on the evening of 21 September and then again the following morning in an effort to negotiate a compromise that would have exempted Hindenburg from the threat of imprisonment.[102] In a rare and indeed uncharacteristic retreat from his hand-line position, Hugenberg took it upon himself to approve an amendment in the language of the "Freedom Law" that removed the Reich President from the threat of imprisonment and, in so doing, secured the CNBLP's agreement to support the referendum.[103]

Throughout all of this, the CNBLP continued to attack the DNVP for an "all-or-nothing" strategy that failed to appreciate the increasingly desperate situation in which the German farmer found himself.[104] The conflict between the two parties reached a climax in the weeks before the elections to the provincial, county, and municipal parliaments throughout Prussia on November 17. In a particularly sharp attack against the DNVP a week before the elections, Gereke asserted that the real issue was not so much the struggle against the Weimar Republic as the fact that German agriculture stood little to gain from a policy of uncompromising opposition, jingoistic fantasies, and political machinations that only polarized the nation at a time when solidarity was the order of the day.[105] What the CNBLP had to offer, on the other hand, was a sober, objective *Realpolitik* aimed at improving the material welfare of the German farmer in the hope that parity between town and country might eventually be achieved. The leaders of the CNBLP maintained that the course of German economic development since the middle of the previous century had consistently favored the large urban areas at the expense of Germany's rural population. Not only the existing system of taxation, but also the current method of financing public education discriminated against the German farmer, a situation the leaders of the CNBLP hoped to correct through greater austerity on the part of local governments and the introduction of a tax reform aimed at distributing the burden of government financing more equitably among the different sectors of the population.[106] Skeptical as to whether this

---

[102] Copy of a letter from Pf[eil] to the CNBLP executive committee and to Hepp, Wendhausen, and Oheimb, 22 Sept. 1929, records of the CNBLP, BA Berlin, Bestand R 8001, 1/32–33.

[103] Resolution of the presidium of the National Committee for the German Referendum, n. d. [21 Sept. 1929], appended to the letter cited in n. 102, BA Berlin, R 8001, 1/35.

[104] "Weshalb Christlich-nationale Bauern- und Landvolkpartei?," *Politische Wochenschrift* 5, no. 39 (28 Sept. 1929): 921–24.

[105] *Der Landbürger*, 4, no. 2 (16 Nov. 1929): 342.

[106] *Weshalb Landvolkpartei? Richtlinien und Arbeitsmethoden*, ed. Landbürger-Verlag (Berlin, n.d. [1929]), esp. 7–16, 18–19. See also "Einfachheit und Sparsamkeit. Die kommunalpolitische Richtlinien der Christlich-nationalen Bauern- und Landvolkpartei," *Der Landbürger*, 4, no. 19 (16 Oct. 1929): 306–10, as well as Gereke's speech in Querfurth, 10 Nov. 1929, in *Der Landbürger*, 4, no. 22 (16 Nov. 1929): 341–42.

could be accomplished on the basis of the existing party system, the leaders of the CNBLP saw their own party's growth as part of a far more fundamental transformation in the very structure of the German party system.[107]

The Prussian municipal elections on 17 November 1929 and the Thuringian Landtag elections three weeks later resulted in substantial CNBLP gains at the expense of the DNVP. The election results also revealed that in areas like Schleswig-Holstein and Thuringia where rural discontent was particularly strong the CNBLP's chief rival was no longer the DNVP, but the more radical National Socialist German Worker's Party. The leaders of the CNBLP were quick to take notice of the threat that the NSDAP's growing appeal presented to their own party's political prospects, and in the late summer of 1929 the Thuringian Rural League – an organizational bulwark of the CNBLP ever since the party's founding in 1928 – published a sharply worded pamphlet entitled *Nationalsozialismus und Bauerntum* in which the NSDAP was denounced as a "socialist workers' party" whose social and economic program was inimical to the interests of the German farmer.[108] But for the most part the CNBLP leadership concentrated their attention instead on building up their own party organization in former Nationalist strongholds such as Saxony and East Prussia.[109] Even then, most of the DNVP's farm leaders did not take part in the secession of December 1929 and chose to follow the lead of RLB president Martin Schiele, who thought the secession was premature and believed that it still might be possible to force a change in the leadership of the party.[110] The lone exception to this trend was Hans Schlange-Schöningen, a Pomeranian landowner and one-time Hugenberg protégé who left the DNVP to affiliate himself with the CNBLP. Unlike most of those in the new party's leadership, Schlange favored the cultivation of close ties with the other groups that had broken away from the DNVP and took part in the founding of the People's Conservative Association in late January 1930.[111]

Immediately after the conclusion of the third stage in the referendum process – a national plebiscite on 22 December 1929 in which the "Freedom

---

[107] Speech by Döbrich, 11 Nov. 1929, in *Der Landbürger*, 4, no. 23 (2 Dec. 1929): 357–58.

[108] *Nationalsozialismus und Bauerntum. Ein Handbuch zur Klärung der nationalsozialistischen Frage*, ed. Otto Weber (Weimar, 1929).

[109] Report by Gereke before the Saxon provincial organization of the CNBLP, 21 Dec. 1929, in *Der Landbürger*, 5, no. 1 (2 Jan. 1930): 2.

[110] Wilmowsky to Krupp, 7 Dec. 1929, HA Krupp, FAH 23/503. See also Schiele to Traub, 4 Feb. 1930, BA Koblenz, NL Traub, 67/106–07.

[111] See Schlange's speech at the founding of the VKV in *Volkskonservative Stimmen*, 1 Feb. 1930, no. 1. On his negotiations with the CNBLP, see the entry in Passarge's diary, 30 Jan. 1930, BA Koblenz, NL Passarge, 2/25–26. See Günter J. Trittel, "Hans Schlange-Schöningen. Ein vergessener Politiker der 'Ersten Stunde'," *Vierteljahrshefte für Zeitgeschichte* 35 (1987): 25–63, esp. 28–30.

Law" received the support of over 5,800,000 voters but still fell far short of what was needed to be enacted into law[112] – the National Rural League announced its resignation from the National Referendum Committee and claimed that the committee's work was done.[113] In January 1930 the CNBLP followed suit, thus severing its organizational ties to Hugenberg and the forces of the radical Right.[114] But aside from Schlange-Schöningen and Gereke there was little interest in the CNBLP leadership for close organizational ties with the other groups that had broken away from the DNVP. The most outspoken critic of such ties was Karl Hepp, who at a party rally in Münster in late February 1930 stressed that in light of the profound structural transformation that was taking place throughout the German party system the CNBLP should not risk diluting its unique vocational orientation by affiliating itself with groups of a different ideological persuasion.[115] The CNBLP continued to insist that the Christian-National Coalition it had formed with the twelve National-ist secessionists in December 1929 was nothing more than a short-term expedient necessitated by the parliamentary weakness of the two groups. In no way, CNBLP strategists insisted, did this arrangement compromise the CNBLP's distinctive ideological orientation or infringe upon its organizational integrity.[116] Throughout all of this, the CNBLP continued to win new recruits from the ranks of the DNVP's agrarian wing as disgruntlement over Hugen-berg's leadership of the party continued to fester through the spring of 1930.[117]

Christian-Socials in Revolt

At the same time that the DNVP's agrarian leaders began to regroup along vocational and corporatist lines, the party's Christian-Social wing moved in the direction of closer ties with the various Evangelical circles that had broken away from the DNVP over the course of the previous decade. Disillusionment with the DNVP had been strong in Evangelical circles ever since the early 1920s, but it was not until the spring of 1924 that an open break materialized in the form of a public appeal from Samuel Jaeger, pastor of the Evangelical

---

[112] Falter, Lindenburger, and Schumann, *Wahlen und Abstimmungen*, 47.

[113] Bethge, Schiele, and Hepp to the presidium of the National Committee for the German Referendum, 23 Dec. 1929, BA Berlin, R 8034 I, 120/104–05. This decision was reaffirmed at a meeting of the RLB executive committee on 15 Jan. 1930, ibid., 120/60–67. See also the report in *Reichs-Landbund* 10, no. 3 (18 Jan. 1930): 28–29.

[114] Höfer to the National Referendum Committee, 14 Jan. 1930, cited in Otto Schmidt-Hannover "DNVP und nationale Organisationen," June 1932, BA Koblenz, NL Schmidt-Hannover, 72/38.

[115] *Der Landbürger*, 5, no. 6 (16 Mar. 1930): 83.

[116] Remarks by Gereke, 21 Dec. 1929, in *Der Landbürger*, 5, no. 1 (2 Jan. 1930): 2.

[117] In this respect, see *Der Landbürger*, 5, no. 7 (16 Mar. 1930): 83, and no. 7 (2 Apr. 1930): 98.

theological seminary in Bethel, for the founding of Christian-Social Faith Communities, or *Gesinnungsgemeinschaften*, as the first step towards infusing German public life with the spirit of the Evangelium.[118] Although the leaders of the DNVP's Christian-Social faction remained cool to Jaeger's appeal, it evoked considerable interest outside official party circles. Interest was particularly strong in Württemberg, where a small Evangelical group under the leadership of Paul Bausch and Wilhelm Simpfendörfer were quick to establish contact with Jaeger and founded a Christian-Social Faith Community for Stuttgart and its environs in April 1924.[119] A similar group calling itself the Christian People's Service (Christlicher Volksdienst) was founded in Nuremburg shortly thereafter under the chairmanship of Hans Oberdörfer, who in 1925 had been elected to the city council on a separate Evangelical ticket.[120] Still, efforts to consolidate these and other Evangelical groups into a national organization foundered until the fall of 1927 when the Evangelical movement, under Bausch and Simpfendörfer, formally reconstituted itself as the Christian People's Service at a national congress of the Christian-Social Faith Communities in Nuremburg.[121]

Although the outcome of the Nuremburg congress represented an important step towards the creation of a national organization with the potential of

---

[118] Samuel Jaeger, *Gott allein die Ehre! Gesammelte Aufsätze*, ed. Theodor Schlatter (Bethel bei Bielefeld, 1930), 108–09. In particular, see Jaeger's appeal, "Christlich-soziale Gesinnungsgemeinschaften," 13 Mar. 1924, and his essay, "Gottesherrschaft im öffentlichen Leben," n.d. [Apr. 1924], BA Koblenz, Nachlass Paul Bausch, BA Koblenz, 7. See also Bausch's memoirs, *Lebenserinnerungen und Erkenntnisse eines schwäbischen Abgeordneten* (Korntal, n.d. [1970]), 299–300. The following account has been supplemented by materials in the possession of the late Wilhelm Simpfendörfer. The originals of some of these documents have been lost, but copies in the author's possession have been deposited in Landesarchiv Baden-Württemberg, Hauptstaatsarchiv Stuttgart (hereafter cited as HStA Stuttgart) Nachlass Wilhelm Simpfendörfer, Bestand Q 1/14. See also Günther Opitz, *Der Christlich-soziale Volksdienst. Versuch einer protestantischen Partei in der Weimarer Republik* (Düsseldorf, 1969).

[119] On developments in Württemberg, see Bausch and Simpfendörfer to Jaeger, 15 Mar. and 28 Apr. 1924, as well as Bausch to Schlatter, 20 Mar. 1924, and Jaeger, 13 Apr. 1924, all in BA Koblenz, NL Bausch, 7. See also Bausch, *Lebenserinnerungen*, 70–73.

[120] Simpfendörfer, "Über Entstehung, Entwicklung und Arbeit des Volksdienstes," HStA Stuttgart, NL Simpfendörfer, 374. On similar developments in Frankfurt and Hesse-Nassau, see Oberschmidt, "Der Evangelische Volksdienst," in *Evangelischer Volkstag Frankfurt a.M. 6. Sept. 1925*, ed. Evangelischer Volksdienst (Frankfurt a.M., n.d. [1925]), 88–92.

[121] Opitz, *Volksdienst*, 45–62, 80–85. See also Bausch, *Lebenserinnerungen*, 75–78, and Simpfendörfer, "Über Entstehung, Entwicklung und Arbeit des Volksdienstes," HStA Stuttgart, NL Simpfendörfer, 374. On the CVD's political orientation, see "Voraussetzungen und Ziele der Arbeit des Christlichen Volksdienstes. Beschlossen auf der Nürnberger Tagung des Christlichen Volksdienstes vom 12. und 13. November 1927," BA Koblenz, NL Bausch, 8.

developing into a new political party, the founders of the Christian People's Service were adamant that their organization was not another political party but represented the beginnings of a popular movement inspired by the social teachings of Jesus Christ and dedicated to a spiritual reformation of Germany's political life.[122] On the question of Germany's form of government, the leaders of the CVD criticized the anti-republican fulminations of both the DNVP and the established Lutheran Church and called for a policy of constructive cooperation within the new republican order as the best means of serving the German nation and God's divine plan.[123] Their endorsement of the Weimar Republic notwithstanding, the leaders of the CVD were highly critical of the existing party system and categorically rejected the practice of interest representation as an activity wholly incompatible with the political responsibilities of a devout Christian. By the same token, the People's Service steadfastly refused to associate itself with the schemes of big business and other propertied interests for the creation of an anti-Marxist front that was little more than an ill-disguised attempt to exclude the German worker from his rightful role in Germany's political life. Although the CVD was no less anti-Marxist than the other groups on the German Right, it maintained that the spread of Marxism could be checked only through the full integration of the German worker into the social and political fabric of the nation. "Neither socialist nor bourgeois, but Christian" was the slogan that inspired the CVD in its efforts to emancipate the German worker from the influence of Marxism and to secure not only for the worker, but for all of those who comprised the German nation their rightful place in its political and economic life.[124]

The founding of the Christian People's Service came under sharp criticism from Mumm, Veidt, and the leaders of the DNVP's National Evangelical Committee on the grounds that it presaged a further splintering of Germany's Evangelical forces.[125] The CVD did not take part in the 1928 Reichstag

---

[122] *Was will der Christliche Volksdienst?*, Schriften des Christlichen Volksdienstes, no. 1 (Korntal-Stuttgart, n.d. [1927]), 5–21. In a similar vein, see Heinrich Mosel, *Christen an die Front! Vortrag auf der Hauptversammlung des Landesverbandes Berlin-Brandenburg des Christlichen Volksdienstes am 27. Januar 1928 in Berlin* (Berlin, 1928), and Adolf Schlatter, *Was fordert die Lage unseres Volkes von unserer evangelischer Christenheit?* (Korntal-Stuttgart, 1929).

[123] Simpfendörfer, "Von Politik, von politischen Programmen und vom politischen Weg des Christlichen Volksdienstes," *Christlicher Volksdienst. Evangelisch-soziales Wochenblatt Süddeutschlands*, 17 Mar. 1928, no. 11.

[124] Paul Bausch, *Der Kampf um die Freiheit des evangelischen Christen im politischen Leben. Sozialistisch? Bürgerlich? Oder Christlich?*, Schriften des Christlichen Volksdienstes, no. 4 (Korntal-Stuttgart, n.d. [1929]), 20–29.

[125] For example, see Reinhard Mumm, *Christlich-soziale und deutschnational! Ein Wort gegen die Zersplitterungssucht*, and Karl Veidt, *Eine evangelische Partei? Ein offenes Wort an den "Christlichen Volksdienst" und andere Leute*, Deutschnationale Flugschrift, no. 315 (Berlin, 1928).

elections due to strong opposition from Simpfendörfer and the Württemberg CVD to any national campaign until an adequate organizational structure had been developed.[126] After the elections the leaders of the Württemberg CVD traveled extensively throughout Germany in an attempt to establish closer ties with other Evangelical groups and to build up the CVD's national organization. In Baden this led to the founding of the Evangelical People's Service (Evangelischer Volksdienst), which in the state elections on 27 October 1929 surprised even its most ardent supporters by polling more than 35,000 votes and electing three deputies to the state parliament.[127] By the same token, the CVD and affiliated Evangelical groups managed to score impressive gains in the Prusssian municipal elections on 17 November even though their efforts were handicapped by strong opposition from the local Evangelical clergy, inadequate financial support, and the lack of experienced leadership.[128]

The leaders of the Christian People's Service were also at work cultivating closer ties to the Christian-Social faction within the DNVP. But, as the outcome of the Bielefeld congress of the Christian-Social Reich Union in early August 1928 revealed, none of the prominent Nationalists affiliated with the Christian-Social movement were prepared to leave the DNVP despite the outspoken sympathy of many with the CVD's goals and aspirations.[129] This would all change with the crisis over the imprisonment paragraph of Hugenberg's so-called "Freedom Law," as the leaders of the DNVP's Christian-Social faction began to show less restraint in their criticism of Hugenberg and moved closer to leaving the DNVP should efforts to depose him as party chairman fail.[130] When Hartwig, Hülser, and Lambach ignited the secession of some of the party's leading moderates in early December 1929, their action enjoyed the full support of the Christian-Social Reich Union, which met in Berlin on the evening of 30 November to discuss the situation within the DNVP.[131] After the first wave of Christian-Social resignations on 3–4 December that included the venerable Mumm,[132] Hülser and Veidt traveled to Stuttgart to meet with the leaders of the Evangelical movement from Württemberg and Baden on 6 December.[133]

---

[126] Simpfendörfer, "Der Christliche Volksdienst und die Reichstagswahlen," *Christlicher Volksdienst. Evangelisch-soziales Wochenblatt Süddeutschlands*, 5 May 1928, no. 18.

[127] *Christlicher Volksdienst*, 2 Nov. 1929, no. 44.

[128] *Christlicher Volksdienst*, 23 Nov. 1929, no. 47.

[129] DNVP, Mitteilung No. 36, 30 Aug. 1929, FZH Hamburg, NL Diller, 10.

[130] Mumm, "Wir Christlich-sozialen und die Parteikrisis in der Gegenwart," n.d. [July 1929], BA Berlin, NL Mumm, 283/157–62. See also Hartwig to Mumm, 16 July 1929, ibid., 283/156.

[131] *Christlicher Volksdienst*, 7 Dec. 1929, no. 49.

[132] Mumm to Westarp, 4 Dec. 1929, BA Berlin, NL Mumm, 284/61. See also Reinhard Mumm, *Die christich-soziale Fahne empor! Ein Wort zur gegenwärtigen Lage* (Siegen, 1930).

[133] Kling to Keudell, 6 Dec. 1929, BA Berlin, NL Mumm, 284/15.

Nine days later a second meeting with more than twenty representatives from the two groups in attendance took place in Frankfurt, where they reached agreement on virtually every major issue with the exception of monarchism.[134] The fact that illness prevented Mumm, Adolf Stoecker's son-in-law and the most outspoken monarchist in the Christian-Social faction,[135] from taking part in the Frankfurt deliberations meant that Simpfendörfer and the leaders of the Christian People's Service were able to secure the adoption of a program that was fully compatible with their republican sympathies and that avoided any direct mention of monarchism.[136] Confronted with what amounted to a fait accompli, Mumm and his supporters decided that discretion was the better part of valor and acquiesced at a joint demonstration of the two organizations in Berlin on 27–28 December 1929 to found of a new political party calling itself the Christian-Social People's Service (Christlilch-sozialer Volksdienst or CSVD).[137]

Over the course of the next several weeks, the founders of the CSVD concentrated on building up a broad base of popular support among the Evangelical working-class and white-collar elements still nominally affiliated with the DNVP. But by the middle of January 1930 it had become clear that Hartwig's efforts to split the German National Workers' League off from the parent DNVP had run into serious legal complications,[138] while Lambach's campaign to reorganize the DNVP's working-class and white-collar constituencies into a new organization entitled the Christian-National Self-Help

---

[134] *Christlicher Volksdienst*, 21 Dec. 1929, no. 51. For the text of the preliminary agreement, 22 Dec. 1929, see BA Berlin, NL Mumm, 284/31. See also Mumm's letters to Simpfendörfer, 13 Dec. 1929, ibid., 284/18–20, and Rippel, 18 and 20 Dec. 1929, ibid., 284/28, 42, as well as Hülser, "Sammlung und Führung," *Aufwärts*, 17 Dec. 1929, no. 295, and Hülser, "Die neue christlichsoziale Bewegung," *Das Staatsschiff* 1, no. 3 (17 Dec. 1929): 176–78.

[135] For example, see Reinhard Mumm, *Unser Programm. Christentum – Vaterland – Volksgemeinschaft – Kaisertum* (Berlin, n.d. [1928]), 2–6. See also Bausch, *Lebenserinnerungen*, 87–89.

[136] Reinhard Mumm, *Der christlich-soziale Gedanke. Bericht über eine Lebensarbeit in schwerer Zeit* (Berlin, 1933), 142. For Mumm's position, see his letter to Dähnhardt, 20 Dec. 1929, BA Berlin, NL Mumm, 284/42. For further details, see Frei, *"Die christlich-soziale Fahne empor!"* 247–56.

[137] For the stenographic record of this demonstration, see *Um die neue Front. Die Vereinigung der Stöckerschen Christlich-sozialen (Christlich-soziale Reichsvereinigung) mit dem Christlichen Volksdienst. Ein Rückblick auf die Berliner Verhandlungen vom 27./28. Dezember 1929*, Schriften des Christlichen Volksdienstes, no. 5 (Korntal-Stuttgart, n.d. [1930]), 11–52. See also Gustav Hülser, "Christlich-sozialer Volksdienst," *Internationales Handwörterbuch des Gewerkschaftswesens*, ed. Ludwig Heyde, 2 vols. (Berlin, 1931–32), 2:1922–23.

[138] DNVP, Mitteilungen, no. 3, 25 Jan. 1930, FZH Hamburg, NL Diller, 10. For further information, see DNVP, Mitteilungen, no. 53, 10 Dec. 1929, ibid., as well as the one-sided account in *Die Abtrünnigen*, 114–29.

(Christlich-nationale Selbsthilfe) had not progressed much beyond the initial planning stage.[139] Still, this did not prevent prominent Nationalist labor leaders such as Wilhelm Lindner and Else Ulrich from defecting to the CSVD in early 1930.[140] In the meantime, Mumm hoped that the former Reich minister of the interior Walther von Keudell could be persuaded to accept the chairmanship of the new party in the hope that a man of his stature could bring the various factions within the Christian-Social movement together.[141] But the founders of the new party soon discovered that residual friction between the CVD and CSRV made a merger of their respective organizations a great deal more difficult than they had anticipated. As a result, it was not until March 1930 that the Christian-Social Club (Christlich-sozialer Verein) in Berlin and Brandenburg, a bastion of Stoeckerite sentiment in the Christian-Social movement, finally agreed to join the CSVD.[142]

The leaders of the new party now turned their attention to the challenge of ideological solidarity. The Christian-Social People's Service did not conceive of itself as a political party in the traditional sense of the word, but rather as a spiritual movement that drew its inspiration from the social and political teachings of Jesus Christ. Consequently, as CSVD's new chairman Wilhelm Simpfendörfer stressed in his keynote address at the CSVD's first national congress in Kassel over the 1930 Easter weekend, the leaders of the CSVD were determined not to compromise the spiritual integrity of their movement through close political and organizational ties with other German parties.[143] This was particularly true of the CSVD's attitude towards the efforts on behalf of a united liberal party. Not only was the CSVD outspokenly anti-liberal in matters of educational and cultural policy, but it explicitly rejected the individualistic premises upon which the liberal conception of government was based. At the same time, the leaders of the CSVD regarded the various appeals from Hugenberg and other right-wing politicians for a united bourgeois front

---

[139] Lambach to the members of the DNVP National Employee Committee, 6 Dec. 1929, FZH Hamburg, NL Diller, 7. See also Gonschorek and Franke to the members of the DNVP Employee Committee in Leipzig, n.d., and the letter from Gonschorek to the DNVP's white-collar members in Saxony, 19 Dec. 1929, ibid.

[140] Die Abtrünnigen, 24–30.

[141] Mumm to Keudell, 18 Dec. 1929, BA Berlin, NL Mumm, 284/28, and to Rippel, 28 Mar. 1930, ibid., 139/178.

[142] Minutes of the merger meetings between representatives of the Christian-Social Club and the CVD, 25 Jan. and 13 Mar. 1930, BA Berlin, NL Mumm, 332/80, 29–32.

[143] Simpfendörfer, Politik aus Glauben und Gehorsam. Vortrag Über die grundsätzliche Einstellung des Christlich-sozialen Volksdienstes auf der Reichsvertretertagung in Kassel zu Ostern 1930, Schriften des Christlich-sozialen Volksdienstes, no. 6 (Korntal-Stuttgart, n.d. [1930]), 11–16. On the Kassel congress, see the Kölnische Zeitung, 22–25 Apr. 1930, nos. 221–24.

against Marxism as little more than a conspiracy to harden existing class lines at the expense of the German worker.[144] The CSVD reserved its sharpest criticism, however, for those who sought to effect a realignment of the German party system along class and vocational lines and advocated the creation of a separate occupational chamber in which the clash of antagonistic social interests was to be resolved in the interests of national solidarity. The leaders of the CSVD looked upon special-interest parties like the Business Party, the CNBLP, the People's Justice Party, and the Württemberg Peasant's League as manifestations of a materialistic egoism that was corrupting the fabric of German political life and that was inimical to the spirit of the Christian faith. What all of these efforts lacked, argued the CSVD's Bausch in a lengthy speech at Kassel, was the necessary spiritual cement. It was not on the basis of economic self-interest or any of the pre-war ideologies such as liberalism or conservatism, but only through a return to the Gospel and the social teachings of Jesus Christ that a genuine consolidation of the German people could ever take place.[145]

With the progressive dissolution of German society into a Hobbesian state of *bellum omnium contra omnes*, the question confronting Germany's political leadership was not just whether the various elements to the right of Social Democracy could be reunited into a cohesive political force but, more importantly, on which foundation and around which axis this would take place. That the secession had not shaken Hugenberg's control of the party dealt a severe blow to those who still staked their hopes on the creation of a progressive conservative party that could serve as a platform from which the more moderate elements on the German Right could pursue a conservative agenda within the framework of the existing system of government. By the same token, the disunity of those who had broken away from the DNVP made the task of bringing them back under the fold of a single political party all the more difficult. This did not augur well for Germany's political future as the demise of the Müller cabinet and the transfer of power to the middle and moderate Right appeared imminent.

---

[144] Bausch, "Was fordert die politische Lage von uns?," *Christlicher Volksdienst*, 25 Jan. 1930, no. 4. See also Simpfendörfer, "Um die neue Front," ibid., 14 Dec. 1929, no. 50.

[145] Paul Bausch, *Die politischen Gegenwartsaufgaben des Christlich-sozialen Volksdienstes. Vortrag gehalten auf der Reichsvertretertagung des Christlich-sozialen Volksdienstes in Kassel zu Ostern 1930*, Schriften des Christlich-sozialen Volksdienstes, no. 8 (Korntal-Stuttgart, n.d. [1930]), 7–9, 22–26.

17

The Brüning Gambit

The most pressing question confronting Germany's political leadership at the end of 1929 and beginning of 1930 was whether a viable domestic consensus for the formulation and conduct of national policy on the basis of the existing system of government could still be found. Even though Hugenberg's campaign against the Young Plan had ended in a failure, the parties that belonged to the Müller cabinet were still far from agreement over how the social and economic cost of fulfilling the terms of the Young Plan was to be distributed among the different sectors of German society. The fact that more than two million German workers were without employment placed an enormous strain on state finances and made the SPD's left wing all the more intractable in its opposition to any changes in the existing system of state unemployment insurance that might further weaken the economic situation of the German worker. At the same time, the German industrial establishment and its allies on the DVP's right wing had become increasingly insistent that implementation of the Young Plan was possible only if it was accompanied by a far-reaching reform of German finances and by a drastic reduction in the general level of public spending at all levels of government. The situation was further complicated by a restrictive credit policy on the part of the national bank that together with the collapse of agricultural prices on the international market produced widespread insolvency and an increasingly large number of foreclosures on properties belonging to farmers who could no longer meet their financial obligations.[1] The net effect of these developments was the paralysis of German democracy and its inability to produce a stable domestic consensus upon which the formulation and conduct of national policy could take place. It was precisely this convergence of economic and political crisis that gave the situation in Germany its fascist potential.

From Müller to Brüning

Against the background of these developments, both the Reichswehr and the presidential palace would become more actively involved in the search for an

[1] James, *German Slump*, 246–82.

alternative to the "Great Coalition." For the most part, the Reichswehr had been a source of stability for the republic ever since its role in the suppression of the Spartacist uprising in January 1919. The new cadre of military leaders that rose to prominence in the wake of Germany's defeat did not settle for the "stab-in-the-back legend" as an explanation for the German defeat but also placed blame on the antiquated command structure of the imperial army. They had little desire to return to the way things had been done before 1914 but sought instead to provide Germany with the most modern and professional armed force on the European continent. Nor were they wedded to the monarchal form government or sympathetic to those who hoped for the return of the Hohenzollerns. Still, they were frustrated by the restrictions that Versailles had placed on the size and capacities of Germany's military forces and were committed to restoring to restore Germany's sovereignty over its military affairs through the peaceful revision of the Versailles Peace Treaty. In the domestic political arena, the Reichswehr leadership refused to identify itself with any single political party and was prepared to work with any party or constellation of parties that might be used to promote its own interests, and generally prided itself on its ability to remain above the fray of partisan political conflict.[2] Even then, the German military establishment was not immune from the feelings of "fear and loathing" that had come to grip Germany's conservative intellectual elites at the turn of the 1930s.[3]

No one better epitomized the military's willingness to adapt to the realities of Weimar democracy than Wilhelm Groener, the former chief of the German general staff during the last days of World War I who in January 1928 had been called out of retirement to become minister of defense. Groener was a convinced democrat from southwest Germany whose Achilles heel was his faith in Hindenburg and his embrace of the Hindenburg myth to help stabilize Germany's fledgling republic. As he stated to the young British historian John Wheeler-Bennett after his dismissal from office in 1932: "It was necessary that one great German figure should emerge from the war free from all blame that was attached to the General Staff. That figure had to be Hindenburg."[4] Behind Groener the most influential person in the German military establishment was Major General Kurt von Schleicher, who as chief of the newly created office for ministerial affairs (Ministeramt) in the ministry of defense was responsible for coordinating and implementing the Reichswehr's strategy for dealing with the

---

[2] William Mulligan, "The Reichswehr and the Weimar Republic," in *Weimar Germany*, ed. Anthony McElligott (Oxford, 2009), 78–101.

[3] Emre Sencer, "Fear and Loathing in Berlin: German Military Culture at the Turn of the 1930s," *German Studies Review* 37 (2014): 19–39.

[4] John Wheeler-Bennett, *Knaves, Fools, and Heroes: Europe Between the Wars* (London, 1974), 57. On Groener, see Johannes Hürten, *Wilhelm Groener. Reichswehrminister am Ende der Weimarer Republik (1928–1932)* (Munich, 1993), esp. 199–306.

cabinet, the Reichstag, the various political parties, and, perhaps most importantly, the office of the Reich President.[5] Schleicher's ultimate goal was to rebuild and modernize Germany's military capacities and to restore Germany's sovereignty over its military affairs in so far as this was possible within the limits imposed by the Versailles Peace Treaty. In late 1926 Schleicher and his associates in the ministry of defense had toyed with the idea of using the special emergency powers that Article 48 of the Weimar Constitution vested in the office of the Reich presidency to install a cabinet whose mandate to govern would depend not upon the authority of the Reichstag but upon that of the Reich President.[6] Although the formation of the fourth Marx government in January 1927 made such an expedient unnecessary, Schleicher did not hesitate to dust off plans for a presidential cabinet in preparation for the demise of the Müller cabinet. Only this time, as Schleicher lamented in a private conversation with the Stahlhelm's Siegfried Wagner in October 1928, the German Right was far more fragmented than it had been at the end of 1926.[7]

As the paralysis of Germany's parliamentary institutions became more and more apparent in early 1930, Schleicher·worked through Groener to mobilize the resources of the presidential palace in support of his efforts to lay the foundation for a new government based upon the parties of the middle and moderate Right. For his own part, Hindenburg had become increasingly disenchanted with the performance of the Müller cabinet and was already involved in the search for an alternative to the "Great Coalition."[8] On 15 January 1930 Hindenburg met with Westarp to assess the situation in the DNVP and to determine whether under Hugenberg's leadership the Nationalists might be willing to participate in a new coalition government that would derive its legitimacy not from a majority in the Reichstag but from the authority of the Reich President. Westarp responded that while the DNVP would certainly welcome an end to the socialist presence in the national government, he doubted that the DNVP would participate in a new government as long as Hugenberg remained at the helm of the party – and, if so, then only under conditions that the president would find difficult to accept. Westarp added that he did not foresee a change in the DNVP leadership at any time in the near future inasmuch as the recent secession from the DNVP Reichstag delegation had only strengthened Hugenberg's position as leader of

[5] On Schleicher, see Peter Hayes, "'A Question Mark with Epaulettes'? Kurt von Schleicher and Weimar Politics," *Journal of Modern History* 52 (1980): 35–65. On Schleicher and the fall of the Müller cabinet, see Thilo Vogelsang, *Reichswehr, Staat und NSDAP. Beiträge zur Deutschen Geschichte 1930–1932* (Stuttgart, 1962), 65–75.
[6] Josef Becker, "Zur Politik der Wehrmachtabteilung in der Regierungskrise 1926/27. Zwei Dokumente aus dem Nachlass Schleicher," *Vierteljahrshefte für Zeitgeschichte* 14 (1966): 69–78.
[7] Wagner to Duesterberg, 4 Oct. 1928, BA Berlin, R 72, 264/30–33.
[8] For further details, see Pyta, *Hindenburg*, 555–76.

the party. In light of Hugenberg's intractable opposition to any accommodation with the existing political system, Westarp saw little chance that the DNVP would play any sort positive role in the political changes the Reich President and Schleicher were contemplating.[9]

That Hugenberg could not be counted upon to take part in the realignment of political forces that Hindenburg and Schleicher had in mind would become a cardinal principle of Schleicher's strategic thinking in the spring of 1930. In fact, Hugenberg and his Pan-German acolytes had thoroughly disqualified themselves for a role in the government by virtue of their relentless attacks against the Young Plan and their adamant refusal to support any of the measures required for its implementation.[10] Speculation about Müller's possible successor focus instead on three men: former chancellor Hans Luther, Centrist Heinrich Brüning, and Ernst Scholz, Stresemann's successor as DVP party chairman. Luther had been staging a political comeback ever since his election as chairman of the League for the Regeneration of the Reich at the beginning of 1928 had given him a forum from which he could expound upon his ideas for a reform and regeneration of German political life. After Stresemann's death Luther emerged as a candidate for the DVP party chairmanship and enjoyed strong support not just from the party's industrial backers[11] but also from the reform-minded elements on the party's left wing.[12] But once it became clear that Scholz had recovered from the ill health that had incapacitated him in the fall of 1929, Luther withdrew as a candidate for the party chairmanship and endorsed Scholz as Stresemann's successor.[13] It was only when Luther agreed in early March to succeed Hjalmar Schacht as president of the German Reich Bank that his candidacy for the chancellorship came to a definitive end.[14]

Although Luther was the clear favorite of the German business community to succeed Müller as chancellor, it is doubtful that he ever figured all that prominently in the calculations of Schleicher and his entourage. By the time that Luther removed himself from consideration, Schleicher had already begun

[9] Memorandum by Westarp, 15 Jan. 1930, NL Westarp, Gärtringen, II/61. See also the correspondence between Westarp and his son-in-law Berthold Freiherr Hiller von Gaertringen, Jan. 1930, ibid., II/51.
[10] For example, see Heinrich Claß, Die außenpolitischen Wirkungen des neuen Tributsystems (Munich, 1930).
[11] Reusch to Gilsa, 9 Nov. 1929, RWWA Cologne, Abt. 130, NL Reusch, 400101293/4. See also Jones, German Liberalism, 348–49, and Richter, Deutsche Volkspartei, 590–92.
[12] See Dieckmann to Luther, 28 Nov. 1929, as well as the memorandum of a conversation between Luther, Hardt, and Schroeder, 30 Nov. 1929, BA Koblenz, NL Luther, 363.
[13] Report on the meeting of the DVP national committee, 3 Dec. 1929, appended to Luther to Kempkes, 4 Dec. 1929, RWWA Cologne, Abt. 130, NL Reusch, 400101290/29.
[14] On Luther's calculations, see Jänecke's memorandum, 9 Mar. 1930, BA Koblenz, NL Luther, 365.

to focus his attention on Brüning with Scholz as the fallback in the event that Brüning's candidacy ran into difficulty.[15] Brüning's assets as a candidate for the chancellorship were obvious. As a veteran of the Great War, the forty-nine year-old Brüning would be the first of the so-called front generation to serve as chancellor, a fact that was not lost upon the Reich President.[16] Moreover, Brüning had received his political apprenticeship in the Christian trade-union movement and enjoyed close ties to Adam Stegerwald and other prominent Christian labor leaders from both the Center and other political parties. Brüning had nurtured close ties with the young conservative movement in the early years of the Weimar Republic and for several months in 1920–21 was intensely involved in an ultimately unsuccessful effort to build bridges between the Ring Movement and the Christian labor movement.[17] In May 1924 Brüning was elected to the Reichstag, where he quickly earned for himself a reputation as one of the party's most highly respected specialists in the fields of taxation and finance. Within the Center Brüning distinguished himself as a fiscal conservative whose views on the need to balance the budget through the systematic reduction of government spending at the federal, state, and municipal levels made his candidacy for the chancellorship particularly attractive to the leaders of Germany's industrial establishment.[18] After Stegerwald joined the Müller cabinet in April 1929, Brüning succeeded him as head of the Center Reichstag delegation, first in an interim capacity and then by a unanimous vote of the entire delegation on 5 December 1929.[19] The following month Brüning resigned his post as secretary general of the German Trade-Union Federation so that he could devote his full attention to his responsibilities as chairman of the Center's delegation to the Reichstag.[20]

It is unclear just when Brüning first caught Schleicher's eye as Müller's possible successor. In his memoirs Brüning recalls a conversation with Schleicher at Easter in 1929 where the latter outlined his views on the impending

---

[15] On Schleicher's strategy in the early spring of 1930, see the undated notes composed by his aide Ferdinand Noeldechen, BA-MA Freiburg, Nachlass Kurt von Schleicher, 29/1–3.

[16] On Brüning's youth, academic preparation, and early political career, see Patch, *Brüning*, 14–48, and Herbert Hömig, *Brüning: Kanzler in der Krise der Republik. Eine Weimarer Biographie* (Paderborn, 2001), 27–114.

[17] Brüning's ties to the young conservative movement in the early Weimar Republic have been discussed above in chapter 9. See also Peer Oliver Volkmann, *Heinrich Brüning (1995–1970). Nationalist ohne Heimat* (Düsseldorf, 2007), 48–58.

[18] See Heinrich Brüning, "Die Arbeit der Zentrumspartei auf finanzpolitischem Gebiet," in *Nationale Arbeit. Das Zentrum und sein Wirken in der deutschen Republik*, ed. Karl Anton Schulte (Berlin and Leipzig, n.d. [1929]), 354–88. See also Rudolf Morsey, "Brünings Kritik an der Reichsfinanzpolitik 1919-1929," in *Geschichte – Wirtschaft – Gesellschaft. Festschrift für Clemens Bauer zum 75. Geburtstag*, ed. Erich Hassinger, J. Heinz Müller, and Hugo Ott (Berlin, 1974), 359–73.

[19] Minutes of 5 Dec. 1929, in *Protokolle der Reichstagsfraktion*, ed. Morsey, 348–49.

[20] Hömig, *Brüning*, 131.

political crisis and tried to enlist Brüning's support for the formation of a cabinet that would use the special emergency powers authorized by Article 48 of the Weimar Constitution. Schleicher also envisaged a far-reaching revision of the Weimar Constitution that would strengthen the powers of the executive at the expense of the legislature. By his own account, Brüning expressed skepticism not so much about the thrust and intent of Schleicher's plans – the two supposedly even agreed on the ultimate desirability of restoring the monarchy – as about the general's sense of timing and warned that any move in the direction of a constitutional reform would have to await ratification of the Young Plan and evacuation of the last Allied troops from the Rhine. In the meantime, Brüning continued, it would be best to proceed with the necessary reforms in the areas of fiscal and economic policy on the basis of the existing governmental coalition for as long as it could be held together.[21]

Although Schleicher remained in contact with Brüning through the summer of 1929,[22] it was not until after the secession on the left wing of the DNVP that he resumed his efforts to enlist Brüning's support for the plans he had outlined the previous spring. Brüning had paid close attention to developments within the DNVP, sympathized with the aspirations of the anti-Hugenberg elements around Treviranus, and hoped that "clarification on the Right" would make it possible to govern without the SPD.[23] On 26 December Brüning met with Schleicher, Treviranus, and Hindenburg's state secretary Otto Meißner – Groener had been invited but was unable to attend – in the Berlin home of Schleicher's close associate Baron Friedrich Wilhelm von Willisen. According to Treviranus's account of the meeting, Schleicher pressed his case for the immediate formation of a presidential cabinet armed with Article 48 emergency powers but was unable to overcome either Brüning's deep sense of loyalty to Müller or his visceral aversion to a departure from established parliamentary procedures. Brüning insisted that the Müller cabinet should remain in office at least until after the evacuation of the Rhineland later that fall and predicted that a new right-wing government saddled with responsibility for the unpopular fiscal and social reforms that were necessary for the implementation of the Young Plan would almost certainly fail, as it had in 1925 and 1927–28.[24]

Brüning's coolness toward Schleicher's overtures at the end of 1929 meant at the very least that no reorganization of the national government could be expected until after ratification of the Young Plan. Brüning remained

---

[21] Heinrich Brüning, *Memoiren 1918–1934* (Stuttgart, 1970), 145–47.
[22] For example, see Schleicher to Brüning, 14 Dec. 1929, BA-MA Freiburg, NL Schleicher, 76/158.
[23] Brüning to Gehrig, 1 Nov. 1929, ACDP Sankt-Augustin, NL Gehrig, I-087/001/2.
[24] Gottfried Reinhold Treviranus, *Das Ende von Weimar. Heinrich Brüning und seine Zeit* (Düsseldorf and Vienna, 1968), 114–15. See also Brüning, *Memoiren*, 150–52.

committed to the maintenance of the Müller cabinet and used all the resources
at his disposal both within the Center and with the Social Democrats to build a
consensus for the passage of the fiscal reforms, including unpopular tax
increases, that would be necessary to stabilize Germany's financial situation.[25]
In the meantime, Hugenberg and the National Committee for the German
Referendum were pressuring Hindenburg to use the influence of his office to
block ratification of the Young Plan.[26] Hindenburg, however, remained resolute in his determination to see the Young Plan enacted into law but expected
a reorganization of the national government as compensation for the odium
he had brought upon himself by virtue of his unpopular stand in support of
the new reparations plan. On 1 March 1930 Hindenburg met with Brüning for
the first time in an official capacity to overcome his resistance to ending the
"Great Coalition" and forming a new cabinet that rested upon the parties of
the middle and moderate Right. Brüning reiterated his party's commitment to
the preservation of the existing governmental coalition and his reluctance to
undertake the task of fiscal, social, and economic reform without Social
Democratic participation. At the same time, Brüning indicated that the Center
would not turn its back on a patriotic appeal from the Reich President to take
part in the formation of a new government should the Müller cabinet prove
incapable of implementing the reforms that were essential for Germany's
financial and economic recovery.[27] By the time the two met for a second time
on 11 March, Brüning had emerged as the clear favorite to succeed Müller.
Hindenburg stipulated that ratification of the Young Plan would require more
than a narrow majority and that the support of the Center was therefore
necessary if he was going to sign it. Hindenburg also acknowledged the
legitimacy of the Center's concerns regarding the fiscal reforms that were
necessary to implement the new plan and assured Brüning of his full support
in securing their passage.[28]

---

[25] Breitscheid's protocol of a conversation with Brüning, 1 Feb. 1930, reprinted in Rudolf
Morsey, "Neue Quellen zur Vorgeschichte der Reichskanzlerschaft Brünings," in *Staat,
Wirtschaft und Politik in der Weimarer Republik. Festschrift für Heinrich Brüning*, ed.
Ferdinand A. Hermens and Theodor Schieder (Berlin, 1967), 207–31, here 210–12.

[26] On Hindenburg's meeting with Hugenberg and Oberfohren on 17 Feb. 1930, see his letter
to Müller, 18 Feb. 1930, in *Das Kabinett Müller II*, ed. Vogt, 2:1471–72. See also
Hugenberg's report of this meeting in Claß, "Wider den Strom," BA Berlin, NL Claß,
3/906, as well as the speeches by Hugenberg and Quaatz, *Gegen die marxistisch-liberale
Unterwerfungspolitik! Die Reden von Dr. Hugenberg und Dr. Quaatz, am 11. und 12.
Februar 1930 im Reichstag*, DNVP-Flugblatt, no. 538, BA Koblenz, NL Wegener, 31/
145–48.

[27] Brüning's protocol of 4 Mar. 1930 on his conversation with Hindenburg, 1 Mar. 1930, in
Morsey, "Neue Quellen," in *Staat, Wirtschaft und Politik*, ed. Hermens and Schieder,
213–15.

[28] "Wie es zur Regierung Brüning kam," in *Das Zentrum. Mitteilungsblatt der Deutschen
Zentrumspartei* 1, no. 4 (Apr. 1930): 75–81, here 79–80.

On the morning of 13 March 1930 Hindenburg signed the documents that formally ratified the Young Plan and enacted its provisions into German law. Later than afternoon the Reich President sent Müller a polite, yet forcefully worded, letter in which he outlined his political agenda and insisted, among other things, upon a reform of German finances with the goal of eliminating the mounting deficit in the national budget.[29] Over the course of the next several weeks, the Müller cabinet wrestled with the implications of Hindenburg's demarche before finally settling on a compromise that Brüning had hammered out with an eye toward the incipient mutiny that was taking shape among the pro-business elements on the DVP's right wing. According to the terms of this compromise, the government would loan 150 million marks to the unemployment compensation fund while the premiums that German business firms were required to pay into the fund would remain the same. Not only did the cabinet, with the exception of the Social Democratic Labor Minister Rudolf Wissel, approve the compromise at a meeting on 27 March,[30] but Scholz surprised all pundits when in his keynote address at the DVP's Mannheim party congress in the third week of March he emphatically reaffirmed the DVP's commitment to the preservation of the existing governmental coalition.[31] But hopes that this might salvage the Müller cabinet were definitively dashed when representatives of the socialist labor unions sided with the leaders of the party's left wing at a stormy session of the SPD Reichstag delegation on 27 March to reject the Brüning compromise, thereby sealing the fate of the Müller cabinet. On the following morning, the chancellor submitted his resignation in a private audience with Hindenburg.[32]

Throughout the crisis Brüning had used all of the influence at his disposal to salvage the "Great Coalition." At no point during the course of the deliberations that accompanied the collapse of the Müller cabinet did Brüning advance a personal agenda or his candidacy for the chancellorship. Yet when the dust had settled, Brüning had clearly emerged as the candidate most likely to succeed Müller, and Hindenburg summoned him to his office on the morning of 28 March to commission him with the task of forming a new government. In doing this, the Reich president assured him of his willingness to use the special emergency powers vested in his office by Article 48 of the

---

[29] Hindenburg to Müller, 13 Mar. 1930, in *Das Kabinett Müller II*, ed. Vogt, 2:1580–82.
[30] Minutes of a ministerial conference, 27 Mar. 1930, ibid., 2:1605–07. On Brüning's efforts to salvage the Müller cabinet, see Patch, *Brüning*, 67–71.
[31] Scholz, "Deutsche Politik," in *8. Reichsparteitag der Deutschen Volkspartei in Mannheim vom 21. bis 23. März 1930*, ed. Reichsgeschäftsstelle der Deutschen Volkspartei (Berlin, n.d. [1930]), 3–5.
[32] For further details, see Ilse Maurer, *Reichsfinanzen und grosse Koalition. Zur Geschichte des Reichskabinetts Müller (1928–1930)* (Bern and Frankfurt a.M., 1973), 129–39, as well as Donna Harsch, *German Social Democracy and the Rise of Nazism* (Chapel Hill, NC, and London, 1993), 51–59.

Weimar Constitution to solve the enormous problems that confronted the German state.[33] The Brüning era had begun.

Brüning and the Hindenburg Mythos

The new chancellor was a profoundly conservative politician whose core values were rooted in the twin wellsprings of his Catholic faith and the Prusso-German tradition. He was clearly a man of the Right, though one schooled in the principles of discipline and self-sacrifice associated with Prussia's national greatness and not in the nationalist fantasies of Hugenberg and the Pan-Germans. Though a member of the Center Party, Brüning was in every sense of the phrase a constitutional conservative who was committed to a return of Germany to great power status through a systematic revision of the Weimar Constitution, a sharp reduction of spending at all levels of government, and, if possible, a negotiated end to Germany's reparations obligations. Brüning remained deeply suspicious of parliamentary democracy and its ability to deal with the myriad problems that had descended upon Germany with the outbreak of the great depression. At the same time, Brüning saw the deepening economic crisis as an opportunity to bring about a fundamental reorientation of German fiscal and economic policy and to convince the Allies that Germany lacked the resources to fulfill the reparations burden it had inherited from the lost war. But it was first necessary to decouple the exercise of executive authority from the vicissitudes of the popular will as manifest in the party configurations of the Reichstag by anchoring the ship of state to the one person who stood above the troubled waters of German party politics, Reich President Paul von Hindenburg.[34]

The fate of the Brüning experiment rested upon the strength of the new chancellor's relationship with the Reich President. Hindenburg's place in the politics of the German Right has long been one of the more vexing problems in

---

[33] Brüning's report to the executive committee of the Center Reichstag delegation, 27 Mar. 1930, in *Protokolle der Zentrumsfraktion 1926–1933*, ed. Morsey, 425–26. See also Brüning's account of this meeting in his *Memoiren*, 161–62.

[34] This reading of Brüning is deeply indebted to Hans Mommsen, "Staat und Bürokratie in der Ära Brüning," in *Tradition und Reform in der deutschen Politik. Gedenkschrift für Waldemar Besson*, ed. Gotthard Jasper (Frankfurt a.M., 1976), 81–137, and Hans Mommsen, "Heinrich Brünings Politik als Reichskanzler: Das Scheitern eines politischen Alleingangs," in *Wirtschaftskrise und liberale Demokratie. Das Ende der Weimarer Republik und die gegenwärtige Situation*, ed. Karl Holl (Göttingen, 1978), 16–45. See also Werner Conze, "Die Reichsverfassungsreform als Ziel der Politik Brünings," *Der Staat* 11 (1972): 209–17, and Josef Becker, "Heinrich Brüning und das Scheitern der konservativen Alternative," *Aus Politik und Geschichte. Beilage zum Parlament*, no. 22 (May 1980): 3–17. For more recent scholarship, see Patch, *Brüning*, 1–13; Hömig, *Brüning*, 224–29; and Volkmann, *Brüning*, 110–74.

the historical literature on the Weimar Republic. If the more traditional literature tended to characterize Hindenburg as a prototypical representative of the Prusso-German tradition with its emphasis upon the martial values of Prussian military greatness,[35] more recent work has focused on the cultivation of a mythos that enabled Hindenburg to exercise a charismatic claim upon the loyalties of the German people. According to this narrative, Hindenburg had assiduously cultivated a public persona ever since the last years of World War I that at one and the same time insulated him from responsibility for Germany's military defeat in 1918 and legitimated his return to German public life with his election to the Reich presidency in 1925. Hindenburg presumably personified the virtues that lay at the heart of Germany's national greatness in the decades before the outbreak of World War I and that constituted the basis upon which the reconstruction of German public life and Germany's return to great power status would take place. Hindenburg thus contrived to project an image of himself that transcended the partisan cleavages of Weimar political life and that would serve as a beacon lighting the way to Germany's national rehabilitation.

Hindenburg's careful and deliberate cultivation of a charismatic bond between himself and the German nation stood in sharp contrast to the more time-honored traditions of German conservatism associated with men like Julius Friedrich Stahl and the two Gerlach brothers Ernst and Leopold. Conservatives in this tradition such as Westarp, Hergt, and Schiele were legitimists who remained committed to hereditary monarchy as the form of government best suited to the traditions and character of the German people. Hindenburg, on the other hand, had turned his back on the Kaiser in the last days of World War I and was at best ambivalent about restoring the Hohenzollerns to the throne. Instead Hindenburg saw himself as a charismatic leader whose bond with the German people superseded established political prerogatives and endowed him with the right, if not the duty, to assert the full weight of his personality in times of acute crisis such as the one in which Germany currently found itself.[36]

In his meeting with the Reich President on the morning of 28 March, Brüning had received Hindenburg's support for the formation of a new cabinet that was not bound by formal commitments to the parties in the Reichstag and received the president's assurance that, if necessary, he would

---

[35] For example, see Andreas Dorpalen, *Hindenburg and the Weimar Republic* (Princeton, NJ, 1964), esp. 6–15.

[36] Wolfram Pyta, "Paul von Hindenburg als charismatischer Führer der deutschen Nation," in *Charismatische Führer der deutschen Nation*, ed. Frank Möller (Munich, 2004), 109–47. See also Jesko von Hoegen, *Der Held von Tannenberg. Genese und Funktion des Hindenburg-Mythos* (Cologne, Weimar, and Vienna, 2007), esp. 77–156.

use the special emergency powers vested in his office to implement the new chancellor's fiscal and economic program. At the same time, the president gave Brüning considerable latitude in the choice of his ministers with the stipulation that he wished to see Schiele appointed as minister of agriculture, Treviranus assigned to another cabinet post, and Groener and the BVP's Georg Schätzel retained at the defense and postal ministries respectively.[37] The key figure was Schiele, who as president of the National Rural League was unequivocally committed to restoring the profitability of German agriculture.[38] On 20 March Schiele had met with Hindenburg to outline an ambitious program of agrarian relief that envisaged tariff protection for cereal grains and meat products along with financial relief for East Elbian agriculture through a reduction of interest on outstanding indebtedness and a cut in taxes and other costs.[39] In his subsequent negotiations with Brüning, Schiele made his appointment as minister of agriculture contingent upon an iron-clad agreement to implement his program even if this required the use of presidential emergency powers.[40] The conditions that Schiele attached to his entry into the cabinet and the strong support he enjoyed from the Reich President severely limited the new chancellor's freedom of maneuver in dealing with the deepening economic crisis. The implementation of Schiele's program would almost certainly require the diversion of funds that were needed to cover deficits in other areas of the national budget. Not only did this severely restrict Brüning freedom of movement in restoring fiscal sanity through a sharp reduction in the overall level of government spending, but it also revealed the extent to which the new government's fiscal priorities were hostage to the interests of Hindenburg's peers in the East Elbian aristocracy.

Brüning's goal was to form a cabinet that would command a majority in the Reichstag yet remain free of formal political commitments to the parties that supported it. A tried and proven parliamentarian who recognized the strengths and weaknesses of parliamentary government, Brüning did not share Schleicher's appetite for decoupling the exercise of executive authority from control of the Reichstag. Instead, Brüning hoped that his program for fiscal and economic recovery would find sufficient support in the Reichstag that it

---

[37] Brüning, *Memoiren*, 161–62. See also Breitscheid's memorandum of his conversation with Brüning, 29 Mar. 1930, in Morsey, "Neue Quellen," 227–28.

[38] Martin Schiele, *Wie kann die Landwirtschaft wieder rentabel werden? Eine Rede* (Berlin, n.d. [1928–29]).

[39] Schiele to Meissner, 20 Mar. 1930, BA Berlin, R 601, 777/68–74.

[40] Schiele to Brüning, 29 Mar. 1930, BA Koblenz, NL Pünder, 131/231–34. A copy of this letter was also sent to Hindenburg. See Schiele to Hindenburg, 29 Mar. 1930, BA Berlin, R 601, 404/9–14. For further details, see Gessner, *Agrarverbände*, 183–218.

would not be necessary to take the extraordinary step of invoking presidential emergency powers.[41] Over the two days following his meeting with Hindenburg, Brüning negotiated feverishly with various politicians before presenting his cabinet to the Reich President on 30 March 1930. In many respects, the new cabinet was not all that different from its predecessor. Not only did Brüning keep Groener as his minister of defense, but he also retained the services of the DDP's Hermann Dietrich and Julius Curtius and Paul Moldenhauer from the DVP at the economics ministry, foreign office, and finance ministry respectively. The new cabinet was even more remarkable for its additions. The appointments of Schiele to the ministry of agriculture, Treviranus to the ministry of occupied territories, the Business Party's Johann Victor Bredt to the ministry of justice represented a concerted overture to those elements on the German Right that rejected the all-or-nothing politics of the DNVP's Hugenberg. At the same time, Brüning went out of his way to preserve good relations with the Social Democrats by appointing Stegerwald and Joseph Wirth, the nominal leader of the Center's left wing, as his ministers of labor and the interior respectively. That these appointments were designed to reassure the Social Democrats did little to alter the fact that in terms of its composition and political orientation the Brüning cabinet stood further to the right than any other cabinet in the history of the Weimar Republic with the exception of the fourth Marx cabinet of 1927–28.[42]

In his maiden speech as chancellor, Brüning identified the task of balancing the budget as his government's highest priority and threatened that if no parliamentary majority for fiscal reform could be found, he would have no alternative but to invoke presidential emergency powers under Article 48 of the Weimar Constitution. A reform of German finances, Brüning insisted, was necessary not just to facilitate implementation of the Young Plan but also to provide industry and the commercial middle class with the relief they so desperately needed and to alleviate unemployment in all sectors of the German economy. At the same time Brüning honored his commitment to Hindenburg and Schiele by promising a comprehensive program of agrarian relief that included, among other things, special measures to alleviate the distress in which agriculture east of the Elbe currently found itself. Though short on details, Brüning's speech underscored the urgency with which the problems

[41] In this respect, see Brüning's speech in the protocol of the information conference of the executive committee of the German Center Party, 27 July 1930, ACDP Sankt Augustin, VI-051, 280/58–67.

[42] See Brüning's account of these developments in his *Memoiren*, 163–68. See also Hömig, *Brüning*, 149–56, as well as the introduction by Tilman Koops in *Akten der Reichskanzlei: Die Kabinette Brüning I u. II. 30. März 1930 bis 10. Oktober 1931. 10. Oktober 1931 bis 1. Juni 1932*, ed. Tilman Koops, 3 vols. (Boppard am Rhein, 1985 and 1989), 1:1–4.

that confronted the government would have to be solved before Germany's position both at home and abroad could be expected to improve.[43]

Tightening the Grip on the DNVP

The DNVP had just begun to recover from the effects of the December secession when the installation of the Brüning government and Schiele's appointment as Reich minister of agriculture were announced. Hugenberg and his associates had moved quickly to reassert their control over the DNVP party organization but continued to meet with heavy resistance in certain sectors of the party. In Saxony, for example, the leaders of the state DNVP organization had stubbornly refused to give Hugenberg the vote of confidence his supporters were seeking from the DNVP's state and local organizations throughout the country.[44] In Bavaria, on the other hand, it was only with great difficulty that Hans Hilpert, chairman of the state DNVP organization, was able to win the support of three Reichstag deputies – Christian-Social Hermann Strathmann and two delegates from the Bavarian Rural League, Georg Bachmann and Kurt Fromm – for a resolution endorsing Hugenberg's position in his struggle with the dissidents on the party's left wing.[45] Even then, Hilpert had to withstand a furious attack from Hugenberg's opponents in the National Liberal State Organization of Bavaria (Nationalliberale Landesverband Bayern) that sought Hilpert's removal from the state party leadership and a repudiation of Hugenberg's policies as DNVP national chairman.[46] For the most part, however, Hugenberg and his associates were able to isolate the secessionists and prevent them from securing a significant breakthrough into the ranks of the party faithful.

Over the course of the next several months Hugenberg's supporters redoubled their efforts to purge the DNVP's state and local organizations of those who sympathized with the secessionists and to complete the task of transforming the DNVP into a compliant instrument of Hugenberg's political will.[47] At the same time, they focused much of their attention on reviving three of the DNVP's special committees, or *Fachausschuße*, that had been

---

[43] Brüning's statement to the Reichstag, 1 Apr. 1930, in Heinrich Brüning, *Zwei Jahre am Steuer des Reichs. Reden aus Brünings Kanzlerzeit* (Cologne, 1932), 9–12.

[44] For further details, see Kurt Philipp to Albrecht Philipp, 13 Dec. 1929, SHStA Dresden, NL Philipp, 20.

[45] Minutes of the state executive committee of the Bavarian DNVP, 7 Dec. 1929, BHStA Munich, NL Hilpert, 1/57–68. See also Hilpert, "Meinungen und Kämpfe," ibid., 20/4025–31.

[46] Report in the *Münchener Post*, 18 Feb. 1930, no. 40. See also Kittel, "Zwischen völkischem Fundamentalismus und gouvernementaler Taktik, 887–88, and Kiiskinen, *DNVP in Bayern*, 339–41.

[47] Steinhoff to Westarp, 24 Feb. 1930, NL Westarp, Gärtringen, VN 13.

particularly hard hit by the December secession: the German National Workers' League, the DNVP's Evangelical Reich Committee, and the DNVP's Reich Catholic Committee. In the case of the Workers' League, the secession had triggered a bitter legal battle for control of the organization between DNAB chairman Emil Hartwig and Hugenberg loyalists Paul Rüffer, Gustav Wischnövski, and Wilhelm Koch. Following the December secession, the DNAB executive committee had come out in strong support of Hartwig and his associates at a hastily convened meeting on 7 December 1929.[48] Through the remainder of December and into the first two weeks of January 1930, more and more of the DNVP's Evangelical labor leaders – most prominently Wilhelm Lindner and Else Ulrich – chose to leave the party, reducing the DNAB to a rump of what it had been before Hugenberg had assumed chairmanship of the party.[49] At a series of meetings in Berlin on 19 January 1930, Hugenberg's supporters quickly reestablished control over what remained of the DNAB. The resolution from the previous December was officially rescinded, and the DNAB leadership was reconstituted with Wischnövski and Rüffer as chairman and secretary respectively.[50] Although Hugenberg and his supporters were thus able to keep the DNAB falling into the hands of the secessionists, the organization was but a shadow of its former self.

The situation was only slightly better in the DNVP's two confessional organizations. Like the DNAB, the Evangelical Reich Committee had been hit hard by the December secession with the defection of one its most prominent members, Reinhard Mumm, to the newly founded Christian-Social People's Service. Hugenberg's supporters were anxious to isolate Mumm from the rest of the organization and refused to let him use it as a forum for explaining his reasons for leaving the party.[51] At the same time, they closed ranks behind their beleaguered party chairman by electing Karl Koch, president of the Westphalian synod of the Evangelical Church, as its new chairman with Magdalene von Tiling and Reinhold von Thadden as his two co-deputies.[52] Tiling, who had emerged as Mumm's principal antagonist in the

---

[48] See the report of the special meeting of the DNAB executive committee, 8 Dec. 1929, in *Unsere Partei* 8, no. 1 (1 Jan. 1930): 3–4, as well as the account in *Die Abtrünnigen. Die Geschichte einer Absplitterung, die die Festigung der Partei brachte*, Deutschnationales Rüstzeug, no. 16 (Berlin, 1930), 115–17.

[49] See Lindner to Winterfeld, 15 Jan. 1930, and Ulrich to Laverrenz, 10 Jan. 1930, in DNVP, *Die Abtrünnigen*, 24–28.

[50] See appendix 4 to Mitteilungen der DNVP-Parteizentrale, no. 3, 25 Jan. 1930, FGZ Hamburg, NL Diller, 10, as well as DNVP, *Die Abtrünnigen*, 127–29.

[51] Nagel to Hugenberg, 7 Jan. 1930, BA Koblenz, NL Hugenberg, 38/121–24.

[52] Minutes of the meeting of the DNVP's Evangelical Reich Committee, 24 Jan. 1930, BA Berlin, R 8005, 465/27–28. See also the circular from Koch to the DNVP's state Evangelical Reich Committee, 19 Feb. 1930, ibid., 465/19, as well as Thadden, "Denkschrift über die gegenwärtige politische Lage der Partei in bezug auf die evangelischen Kreise," 27

months leading up to the December secession, proceeded to launch a full-scale offensive against the concept of an Evangelical party. Tiling operated from the perspective of a Lutheran theologian who rejected a self-conscious Evangelical politics in the style of the CSVD in favor of professional competence by men and women for whom faith was an important but by no means the sole factor. The CSVD, Tiling asserted, was little more than a special-interest party intent upon pursuing a sectarian agenda of its own without regard for the welfare of the German nation as a whole.[53] With arguments like these Hugenberg's supporters in the Evangelical Reich Committee hoped to neutralize the effects of Mumm's resignation and hold defections to the CSVD to a minimum. But the committee no longer played an important role in the DNVP's internal affairs and served as little more than a vehicle for attacking the CSVD.[54]

A similar fate lay in store for the DNVP's Reich Catholic Committee under Baron Engelbert von Landsberg-Velen. The leaders of the DNVP's Catholic faction were still recoiling from the fall-out over Hugenberg's refusal to support the concordat between the Vatican and the Prussian government and were just beginning to rebuild their organization when the fight over the "Freedom Law" and the December secession struck.[55] On 22–23 October 1929 Landsberg and his supporters traveled to Berlin, where they met under Hugenberg's chairmanship with Martin Spahn, Ludwig Schwecht, and the leaders of the state Catholic committees from throughout the country. Much to their surprise, Hugenberg demonstrated a remarkably conciliatory attitude and agreed, despite constant sniping from Spahn and Schwecht, to an arrangement that would return Landsberg to the leadership of the DNVP Reich Catholic Committee and entrust him with its rejuvenation.[56] Although the general outlines of this arrangement were subsequently ratified at the DNVP's Kassel party congress in late November 1929,[57] it quickly unraveled in the wake of the December secession and the loss of one of the committee's most dedicated activists in Reichstag deputy Paul Lejeune-Jung.[58]

Jan. 1930, ibid., 465/34–38. For further details, see Norbert Friedrich, "'National, Sozial, Christlich.' Der Evangelische Reichsausschuß der Deutschnationalen Volkspartei in der Weimarer Republik," *Kirchliche Zeitgeschichte* 6 (1993): 290–311, here 308–09.

[53] Tiling, "Evangelische Partei oder nicht," *Unsere Partei* 8, no. 4 (15 Feb. 1930): 34; no. 5 (1 Mar. 1930): 43–44; no. 6 (15 Mar. 1930): 55–57; and no. 8 (16 Apr. 1930): 80–81.

[54] For example, see *Die religiösen Grundanschauungen des Christlich-Sozialen Volksdienstes. Herrschaft Gottes oder Herrschaft des "Christlichen Gewissens"?*, ed. Vorstand des Evangelischen Reichsausschusses der Deutschnationalen Volkspartei (Berlin, n.d. [1930]).

[55] Brackel to Stotzingen, 24 Sept. 1929, BA Berlin, R 8005, 478a/1, and Brackel to Jaeckel, 14 Nov. 1929, ibid., 472/4–5. For further details, see Jones, "Catholics on the Right," 252–55.

[56] Minutes of the DNVP Reich Catholic Committee, 22–23 Oct. 1929, VWA Münster, NL Landsberg, E1.

[57] *München-Augsburger Abendzeitung*, 2 Dec. 1929, no. 328.

[58] On Lejeune-Jung, see Franz-Josef Weber, "Paul Lejeune-Jung (1882–1944)," in *Deutsche Patrioten im Widerstand und Verfolgung 1933–1945. Paul Lejeune-Jung – Theodor*

On 6 January 1930 approximately thirty prominent Catholic politicians of differing political persuasions met in the Kettelerhaus in Cologne to see if there might not be some sort of common denominator upon which they could all agree. The meeting had been called by Joseph Joos from the Center Party at the suggestion of the most recent meeting of the German Catholic Congress (Deutscher Katholikentag) in Freiburg.[59] Those in attendance included Lejeune-Jung, Prince Alois von und zu Löwenstein from the Center party, and a sizable delegation from the DNVP led by Landsberg, Baron Hermann von Lüninck, Max von Gallwitz, and Julius Doms. Emil Ritter, editor of *Der deutsche Weg* and a prominent figure on the Catholic Right, opened the meeting with remarks in which he lamented the political fragmentation of German Catholics and intimated that the goal of those present should be the creation of a united Catholic Center Party based upon the cultural heritage that all Catholics held in common. This prompted an immediate response from Gallwitz, who questioned the extent to which the Center would be able to accomplish anything by itself in the areas of legislation, administration, and wages and spoke in favor of cooperation with the Right and against fraternization with the Left. Gallwitz's comments triggered a heated discussion that only confirmed how deeply divided the participants were on secular political issues. At the heart of the dispute was the automatic equation of Catholic with Center, an equation that clerics took for granted and that the Nationalists vigorously disputed. It was only through the skillful intervention of Joos, a leader from the Catholic workers' movement who enjoyed the reputation of being a young conservative, that a measure of harmony was finally restored.[60] This, however, did little to assuage the disappointment that Joos and Ritter felt over the way in which the larger goal of Catholic unity had been subverted by the spirit of partisanship and the deep-seated animosity that Catholics in the DNVP felt toward their co-religionists in the Center.[61]

None of this augured well for the success of the DNVP's efforts to infuse new life into the party's Reich Catholic Committee. In February Landsberg drafted a program for the rejuvenation of the DNVP's Reich Catholic Committee that would have restored the committee to the quasi-independent status it had enjoyed before the conflict over the Prussian concordat. Landsberg's proposal, however, placed greater emphasis upon the defense

---

Roeningh – Josef Wirmer – Georg Frhr. von Boeselager. Ein Gedenkschrift der Stadt Paderborn, ed. Friedrich Gerhard Hohmann (Paderborn, 1986), 7–19.

[59] Invitation from Joos, 28 Dec. 1929, Kommission für Zeitgeschichte, Bonn (hereafter cited as KfZ Bonn), Nachlass Emil Ritter, C2/040.

[60] Entry in Gallwitz's diary, 6 Jan. 1930, BA-MA Freiburg, NL Gallwitz, 42.

[61] For Ritter's disappointment, see the letter he wrote but never sent to those who had attended the meeting, 7 Jan. 1930, KfZ Bonn, NL Ritter, C2/043–46. See also his correspondence with Loewenstein, 11–20 Jan. 1930, ibid., C2/047–48, 51, and Doms, 4 Feb. 1930, ibid., C2/049–50.

and representation of Catholic interests within the framework of the DNVP than it did upon the recruitment of right-wing Catholics to the DNVP party banner.[62] This did not sit well with Hugenberg's Catholic supporters, who were primarily interested in using a revitalized committee to enhance the effectiveness of the party's recruitment of Catholic voters at the expense of the Center. Hugenberg and his supporters continued to view the Center as the greatest single obstacle to the success of their political strategy and regarded neutralization as a viable political force an indispensable prerequisite for the triumph of the radical Right.[63] At no point did this reading of Germany's political situation seem more fraught with meaning than in the wake of Brüning's appointment as chancellor.

Hugenberg's Dilemma

Schiele's decision to enter the Brüning cabinet and the strong support his efforts to rehabilitate East Elbian agriculture had received from the Reich President confronted Hugenberg and the leaders of the DNVP with a difficult dilemma. A political pragmatist who sought to accomplish what could be accomplished on the basis of the existing governmental system, Schiele remained deeply skeptical of both the style and substance of Hugenberg's all-or-nothing strategy.[64] Schiele had protested vehemently against the language of the imprisonment paragraph in the so-called Freedom Law but stayed with the party through the December secession in the hope that it still might be possible to force a change in the DNVP party leadership.[65] As executive president of the National Rural League, Schiele commanded enormous respect on the DNVP's agrarian wing, which looked to him for leadership in the struggle to restore Germany's badly battered agricultural sector to economic and fiscal viability. Anxious to avoid a conflict of interests, Schiele moved to extricate himself from any commitments that might compromise his freedom of action as Reich minister of agriculture by resigning his seat in the DNVP Reichstag delegation along with all other party offices. As Schiele explained in a private letter to Hugenberg on 31 March, the increasingly desperate situation of German agriculture and the president's appeal to do whatever was necessary to prevent its collapse had left him with no alternative but to accept this heavy responsibility and to free himself from any commitments that might interfere with his ability to fulfill this mandate.[66]

---

[62] "Arbeitsprogramm für den Reichsausschuß der Katholiken in der Deutschnationalen Volkspartei," 1 Feb. 1930, WVA Münster, NL Landsberg, II.

[63] For example, see Spahn to Hugenberg, 23 Apr. 1930, BA Koblenz, NL Spahn, 86.

[64] Schiele to Traub, 4 Feb. 1930, BA Koblenz, NL Traub, 67/106–07.

[65] Westarp, "Niederschrift über die DNVP-Parteikrise," NL Westarp, Gärtringen, II/61.

[66] Schiele to Hugenberg, 31 Mar. 1930, BA Berlin, R 8005, 36/120–21.

Schiele's appointment to the Brüning cabinet played an important role in Schleicher's political calculations. Like the Reich President, Schleicher harbored a deep-seated antipathy toward Hugenberg and was determined to do what he could to break or weaken his control over the DNVP. Schiele's appointment was part of calculated strategy to pressure Hugenberg into supporting the Brüning cabinet – in which case his credentials as the self-anointed leader of the national opposition would have been severely compromised – or, failing that, to drive a wedge between him and the leaders of his party's agrarian wing, who for the most part had remained loyal to the DNVP.[67] The dilemma in which Hugenberg and the DNVP party leadership found themselves became even more critical when the Social Democrats greeted the installation of the Brüning cabinet with a motion of no-confidence when the Reichstag reconvened on 1 April. In two heated sessions of the DNVP Reichstag delegation on the following day, Hugenberg could muster the support of only twenty-eight deputies for a resolution expressing support for the Social Democratic motion, while another eighteen members, including the leaders of the party's agrarian faction, rejected the harsh wording of Hugenberg's resolution and called for a more conciliatory attitude toward the Brüning cabinet.[68] To complicate the situation even further, the executive committee of the National Rural Union fanned the fire within the DNVP Reichstag delegation by publishing a resolution of its own that expressed full and unequivocal support of Schiele and his decision to join the Brüning cabinet.[69]

On the morning of 3 April Ernst Oberfohren, Westarp's successor as chairman of the DNVP Reichstag delegation, met with Brüning, Schiele, and Hermann Pünder from the Reich Chancery to present the chancellor with a series of conditions that would have to be met before the DNVP would support him against the Social Democrats. Not only did Brüning reject the Nationalist demands, but he proceeded to inform Oberfohren that he and his cabinet had every intention of enacting its program for agricultural relief by the Easter recess with or without approval of the Reichstag.[70] Oberfohren returned to his delegation to report that the cabinet had accepted the Nationalist conditions in what was a clear misrepresentation of what had transpired

---

[67] This is implicit in Noeldechen's undated notes "Gedanken zur Politik," [ca. Mar. 1930], BA-MA Freiburg, NL Schleicher, 29/1–3.

[68] Entry in Quaatz's diary, 2 Apr. 1930, BA Koblenz, NL Quaatz, 16. See also the minutes of the DNVP Reichstag delegation, 2 Apr. 1930, BA Koblenz, NL Schmidt-Hannover, 72a. See also Blank to Reusch, 2 Apr. 1930, RWWA Cologne, Abt. 130, NL Reusch, 4001012024/6, For further details, see Müller, "Fällt der Bauer," 158–76.

[69] Reichs-Landbund 10, no. 14 (1 May 1930): 162.

[70] Memorandum prepared by Pünder, 1 May 1930, BA Berlin, R 43 I, 2654/217–20, as well as the entry for 4 Apr. 1930, in Herman Pünder, Politik in der Reichskanzlei. Aufzeichnungen aus den Jahren 1929–1932, ed. Thilo Vogelsang (Stuttgart, 1962), 47–48.

in the meeting with Brüning and Schiele.[71] This, however, was sufficient to prompt a tactical reverse by Hugenberg that made it possible for the DNVP to support the new cabinet in the vote of confidence that took place in the Reichstag later that afternoon on the pretext that this would provide Brüning and Schiele the time they needed to prepare a comprehensive program of agrarian relief.[72]

The DNVP's support enabled the Brüning cabinet to survive the Social Democratic motion of no-confidence by a comfortable margin of sixty-six votes. Hugenberg and his supporters immediately claimed credit for having saved the Brüning cabinet from certain defeat at the hand of the Social Democrats and for having salvaged its emergency farm program.[73] But all of this blew up in Hugenberg's face when Hitler reacted to the news of the DNVP's support for the Brüning cabinet with what Nazi propaganda chief Joseph Goebbels called "a *Scheißwut*" and declared the NSDAP's resignation from the National Referendum Committee. After meeting with Hugenberg on the morning of 4 April, Hitler softened his position and agreed to postpone announcing his decision for fourteen days in order to give the DNVP party chairman an opportunity to bring down the Brüning cabinet.[74] Stunned by these developments, Hugenberg and the DNVP party leadership resolved to return their party to the policy of uncompromising opposition to any form of collaboration with the existing system of government.[75] But efforts at a rapprochement between the DNVP and NSDAP fell apart when Gregor Strasser, the putative leader of the NSDAP's left wing and an outspoken critic of the party's collaboration with conservative right-wing elements like the DNVP, broke party discipline and announced, much to Hitler's irritation, the NSDAP's resignation from the National Referendum Committee in his own organ.[76]

What Hugenberg failed to mention in his pledge to Hitler was that his decision to support Brüning on 3 April had averted a major secession on the

[71] Minutes of the DNVP Reichstag delegation, 3 Apr. 1930, BA Koblenz, NL Schmidt-Hannover, 72a. See also Westarp's memorandum on the formation of the Brüning cabinet, n.d. [Apr. 1930], NL Westarp, Gärtringen, II/61, as well as the entry in Quaatz's diary, 3 Apr. 1930, BA Koblenz, NL Quaatz, 16.

[72] Hugenberg's interpellation in the Reichstag, 3 Apr. 1930, in *Unsere Partei* 8, no. 7 (4 Apr. 1930): 61. See also Westarp, "Das Kabinett Brüning und die Deutschnationale Volkspartei," *Neue Preußische (Kreuz-)Zeitung*, 6 Apr. 1930, no. 98.

[73] Commentary on Hugenberg's speech of 3 April 1930 in *Unsere Partei* 8, no. 7 (4 Apr. 1930): 61–62.

[74] Entry for 4 Apr. 1930, in *Die Tagebücher von Joseph Goebbels*, ed. Elke Fröhlich, Part I: *Aufzeichnungen 1924–1941*, 5 vols. (Munich and New York, 1987–2004), vol. 2/I, 124.

[75] See Hitler's letter to the presidium of the National Committee for the German Referendum, 3 Apr. 1930, as well as Hugenberg to Hitler, 4 and 11 Apr. 1930, all in BA Koblenz, NL Schmidt-Hannover, 30.

[76] Entry for 5 Apr. 1930, in *Goebbels Tagebücher*, ed, Fröhlich, 2/I, 125.

DNVP's left wing, one that would have been far more damaging than the secession of the twelve dissident deputies at the end of the previous year. On 8–9 April the DNVP executive committee and the DNVP party representation met in Berlin to reassure Hugenberg of their support in his conflict with the dissidents in the Reichstag delegation.[77] But Brüning, who was fully cognizant of the situation within the DNVP and was by no means adverse to putting so much pressure on the party that it would break in two,[78] felt even more strongly about the need to address the budgetary crisis than agrarian relief and was fully prepared to dissolve the Reichstag if the Reichstag failed to approve his fiscal reforms. At a meeting with the leaders of the parties that supported his cabinet on 11 April, Brüning announced plans to introduce a bill linking agrarian relief to the passage of a sweeping reform of German finances that included, among other things, unpopular increases in consumption taxes.[79] Hugenberg's supporters, for whom this came as no surprise and who suspected Brüning of conspiring to split the party in two,[80] immediately attacked the chancellor's linkage of the two bills as a ploy to secure the imposition of new taxes that otherwise would have been rejected in the Reichstag.[81] Hugenberg subsequently instructed his party's parliamentary deputies to vote against the proposed tax bill when it came to the floor of the Reichstag on 12 April even though this almost certainly meant the defeat of the government's farm bill.[82] Hugenberg's action provoked a storm of protest from the DNVP's agrarian deputies and threated a general secession on the party's agrarian wing. The storm was fueled in no small measure by the intervention of the National Rural League, whose leaders implored those deputies with close ties to German agriculture to ignore whatever instructions they had received from the DNVP party leadership and vote for the Brüning–Schiele program.[83]

---

[77] Minutes of the DNVP party representation, 9 Apr. 1930, BHStA Munich, NL Dziembowski, 18. See also Hilpert, "Meinungen und Kämpfe," BHStA Munich, NL Hilpert, 22/4263–68, and the entries in Quaatz's diary, 8–9 Apr. 1930, BA Koblenz, NL Quaatz, 16, as well as the report in *Unsere Partei* 8, no. 8 (16 Apr. 1930): 78–79.

[78] See Pünder's memorandum of a conversation with Schleicher, 30 Apr. 1930, BA Koblenz, NL Pünder, 131, reprinted in *Politik und Wirtschaft*, ed. Maurer and Wengst, 1:150.

[79] Minutes of a meeting with the parliamentary leaders of the government parties, 11 Apr. 1930, BA Berlin, in *Die Kabinette Brüning*, ed. Koops, 1:50–51. See also the entry for 13 Apr. 1930 in Pünder, *Politik in der Reichskanzlei*, 49–50.

[80] Entries in Quaatz's diary, 31 Mar. and 5 Apr. 1930, BA Koblenz, NL Quaatz, 16.

[81] Quaatz, "Kabinett Brüning und deutsche Bauernnot," *Der Tag*, 12 Apr. 1930, no. 88.

[82] Hugenberg's statement before the DNVP executive committee, 25 Apr. 1930, BA Koblenz, NL Schmidt-Hannover, 72a.

[83] See Hepp, Bethge, and Kriegsheim to the RLB's regional and local offices, 16 Apr. 1930, NL Westarp, Gärtringen, VN 10, as well as the handwritten notes by Schmidt-Hannover, "Landbund und Regierung," n.d. [after 19 Apr. 1930], BA Koblenz, NL Schmidt-Hannover, 75. See also Bethge to Nagel, 17 Apr. 1930, appended to Kriegsheim to the

While Hugenberg and his associates did not seem overly concerned about the prospects of a second secession and may have actually been eager to have it over and done with, the loss of the party's agrarian wing was something that Westarp desperately sought to prevent. Ever since the December secession, Westarp had chosen to stay in the background where he could use whatever influence he still had to soothe tensions within the DNVP and to work for conciliation between the different factions in the party.[84] Determined to prevent Hugenberg's intransigence from further weakening the DNVP, Westarp led a contingent of thirty-one deputies who ignored the instructions of the party leader and voted for the controversial tax bill when it came to the floor of the Reichstag on 12 April, thus securing its passage by a slim eight-vote margin. Only twenty-three DNVP deputies supported the party chairman while another nine were absent at the time of the vote and six others simply failed to vote. This scenario repeated itself throughout the rest of the day and then again on 14 April as the moderates led by Westarp continued to support the various measures that Brüning brought to the floor of the Reichstag, all of which passed by margins ranging from four to forty-six votes.[85] Although Westarp succeeded in averting what would certainly have been another secession from the DNVP Reichstag delegation, he earned not Hugenberg's gratitude for having salvaged the unity of the party but the enmity of the Hugenberg camp for having helped the Brüning cabinet survive its first parliamentary test of strength.[86] Nor had Westarp's action done much to temper the lingering resentment of the party's agrarian leaders toward Hugenberg and the

RLB's main offices, 22 Apr. 1930, NL Westarp, Gärtringen, II/40, and the circular from the RLB headquarters in Berlin, 16 Apr. 1930, ibid., VN 10. For the ensuing polemic, see Stubbendorf-Zapel, "Der Streit zwischen Landbund und Partei," *Der Tag*, 1 May 1930, no. 104.

[84] Westarp to Berg, 19 Jan. 1930, NL Westarp, Gärtringen, VN 1. See also Jones, "German Conservatism at the Crossroads," 166–69, and Mergel, "Scheitern des deutsche Tory-Konservatismus," 357–59.

[85] *Verhandlungen des Reichstags*, vol. 427, 4950–59, 5000–11. For Westarp's position, see his article "Agrarprogramm und Steuervorlage," *Neue Preußische (Kreuz-)Zeitung*, 17. Apr. 1930, no. 108, as well as his letter to Hugenberg, 16 Apr. 1930, BA Berlin, R 8005, 11/46–51. See also the entries in Quaatz's diary, 12 and 14 Apr. 1930, BA Koblenz, NL Quaatz, 16. For differing perspectives on these developments, see Reichert, "Die parlamentarischen Vorgänge in den Tagen vom 1. bis 14. April 1930," appended to Reichert to the ADI membership, 16 Apr. 1930, RWWA Cologne, Abt. 130, NL Reusch, 400101293/10a, and Bang's circular to the ADI membership, 18 Apr. 1930, NL Westarp, Gärtringen, VN 14, as well as Steiniger, "Betrifft die Reichstagsverhandlungen der letzten Tage," 17 Apr. 1930, BA Koblenz, NL Spahn, 174.

[86] Comments of Steinhoff, Laverrenz, Spuler, Hilpert, and Stubbendorf before the DNVP executive committee, 25 Apr. 1930, BA Koblenz, NL Schmidt-Hannover, 72a.

Nationalist party leadership for an obstructionist policy that threatened the German agricultural community with economic disaster.[87]

The People's Conservatives

Of the various groups, parties, and organizations that dotted Germany's political landscape at the beginning of the 1930s, none stood to benefit more from this turn of events than the People's Conservatives. The split within the DNVP Reichstag delegation over Brüning's tax and farm policies greatly increased the likelihood of a second secession that would afford the People's Conservatives new opportunities to expand their political base at the expense of the DNVP. The key figure in this regard was Treviranus, who served both as chairman of the newly founded People's Conservative Association and as parliamentary leader of the Christian-National Coalition that the twelve deputies who had seceded from the DNVP in December 1929 formed with the parliamentary representatives of the Christian-National Peasants and Farmers' Party. Treviranus's appointment to the Brüning cabinet met with enthusiasm from the deputies who had seceded from the DNVP in December 1929 and helped validate the People's Conservatives as a legitimate option to the *Katastrophenpolitik* of Hugenberg and the DNVP party leadership.[88] Hopeful that the Christian-National Coalition might serve as the prototype of a new united German Right,[89] Treviranus was disappointed that both the CNBLP and the Christian-Socials had chosen to assert their own political pedigree and avoid ties with other political groups that might compromise their distinctive ideological orientations.[90]

The collapse of efforts in January 1930 to unite the various factions that had broken away from the DNVP into a united political party left the VKV increasingly dependent upon the German National Union of Commercial Employees for the financial and organizational support. The driving force behind this alliance was the DHV's Max Habermann, who, like Treviranus,

---

[87] See Richthofen-Boguslawitz to Hindenburg, 13 Apr. 1930, BA Koblenz, NL Schmidt-Hannover, 74, and Lind to Kriegsheim with supporting documentation, 2 May 1930, BA Berlin, R 8034 I, 99/4–24, as well as the memorandum from Nicolas to the Brandenburg Rural League's county offices and other league officials, 9 May 1930, ibid., 36/43–51. See also Richthofen, *Speckzölle über Nationalpolitik. Aufklärung und Klärung*, printed as a manuscript (Boguslawitz, 1930).

[88] For example, see Walther Lambach, *Katastrophe – oder Rettung?*, Volkskonservative Flugschriften, no. 3 (Berlin, 1930). See also Ulrich Roeske, "Brüning und die Volkskonservativen (1930)," *Zeitschrift für Geschichtswissenschaft* 19 (1971): 904–15, and Erasmus Jonas, *Die Volkskonservativen 1928–1933. Entwicklung, Struktur, Standort und staatspolitische Zielsetzung* (Düsseldorf, 1965), 63–65.

[89] Treviranus, "Unsere Aufgabe," *Politische Wochenschrift* 5, no. 50 (14 Dec. 1929): 981–82.

[90] Entry in Passarge's diary, 12 Jan. 1930, BA Koblenz, NL Passarge, 2/16–18.

belonged to the circle of new chancellor's intimate advisors and had played a major role in persuading a reluctant Brüning to accept the chancellorship.[91] Appointed the DHV's chief political strategist in the fall of 1927, Habermann had sought to build up an elaborate network of interrelationships, or *Querverbindungen*, between the DHV, the Christian labor movement, and the various non-socialist parties as a vehicle for representing the material and spiritual welfare of Germany's white-collar employees.[92] But the Lambach affair and Hugenberg's election as DNVP party chairman, Stresemann's death and the ascendancy of heavy industry within the DVP, and the defeat of Stegerwald's bid for the Center party chairmanship had dealt Habermann's strategy a severe blow, with the result that he and the DHV leadership now concentrated their energies on the creation of a new political party that embodied the basic principles of the People's Conservative world-view.[93] The DHV's relations with the DNVP had in the meantime deteriorated to such a point that in late March 1930 Habermann ordered all union members who had been elected to municipal assemblies on the DNVP ticket to sever their ties with the party.[94]

The DHV's close identification with the VKV alienated many industrial leaders who might otherwise have been attracted to the new organization.[95] Treviranus had hoped to offset the DHV's influence in the new organization by reaching out to Catholic conservatives like Baron Ferdinand von Lüninck, but his entreaties were rebuffed with the argument that a truly conservative reconstruction of the German state could never take place on the basis of the existing system of government.[96] Lüninck's response was symptomatic of the obstacles the People's Conservatives began to encounter as they tried to develop a broad and socially heterogeneous popular base upon which a genuine consolidation of the German Right could take place. By the middle of March the VKV, whose total membership still languished around two thousand, had become so moribund that many of those who had greeted its founding two months earlier with enthusiasm were on the verge of

---

[91] Habermann, "Der DHV im Kampf um das Reich," DHV-Archiv Hamburg, 70–71. See also Habermann, "Reichskanzler Heinrich Brüning," *Deutsche Handels-Wacht* 37, no. 17 (10 Apr. 1930): 129–30.

[92] Habermann, "Querverbindungen. Eine politische Betrachtung zum 'Fall Lambach'," *Deutsche Handels-Wacht* 35, no. 14 (25 July 1928): 281–82. See also Krebs, "Habermann," FZG Hamburg, 12/H, 38–41.

[93] Krebs, "Habermann," 41–44. See also Jones, "Between the Fronts," 465–71.

[94] Habermann to the DHV district leaders, 24 Mar. 1930, FGZ Hamburg, NL Diller, D9.

[95] Entry in Passarge's diary, 22 Feb. 1930, BA Koblenz, NL Passarge, 3/58–62. For the concerns of German heavy industry, see Blank to Reusch, 17 Apr. 1930, RWWA Cologne, Abt. 130, NL Reusch, 4001012024/6.

[96] Correspondence between Lüninck and Treviranus, 4–7 Feb. 1930, VWA Münster, NL Lüninck, 823.

abandoning the project altogether.[97] Much of resulting blame fell on Treviranus, who in the eyes of one sympathizer may have been an effective public
speaker, a competent negotiator, and a politician with influence and connections but most certainly not a skilled organizer with the command of detail
required to launch a new organization like the VKV. Perhaps what was most
disturbing in this regard was the almost total absence of a grass-roots
organization outside of Berlin, Hamburg, and one or two other urban
centers.[98]

The formation of the Brüning government breathed new life into a movement that was on the brink of total obscurity. The Christian-National
Coalition embraced the formation of the Brüning cabinet with a promise to
help secure passage of the new chancellor's tax and farm programs, though
with the caveat that this be done in the spirit of a renewed commitment to "the
imperishable and life-giving values of the Christian faith."[99] The mutiny
within the DNVP Reichstag delegation in the votes on Brüning's tax and farm
initiatives raised the distinct possibility of a second and more extensive secession by DNVP moderates who could no longer tolerate Hugenberg's flirtation
with disaster. By this time a group of about twenty-five deputies, including
such party stalwarts as Max Wallraf, Jakob Wilhelm Reichert, and Bernhard
Leopold along with Heinrich Lind and Baron Prätorius von Richthofen-
Boguslawitz from the party's agrarian wing, began to meet regularly to lay
the foundation for a second secession from the DNVP.[100] Hugenberg, on the
other hand, had already begun to mobilize his supporters at the local and
district levels of the DNVP party organization in an attempt to impose even
tighter discipline upon the party's Reichstag delegation.[101] After offering his
resignation as DNVP national chairman in a blatantly transparent ploy to
solidify support behind his chairmanship,[102] Hugenberg convened an emergency session of the DNVP executive committee on 25 April to secure the
adoption of a resolution that would make the decisions of the party executive
committee and party leader binding upon all members of the party's delegations to the Reichstag and sundry state parliaments. Failure to observe these

---

[97] Entry in Passarge's diary, 16 Mar. 1930, BA Koblenz, NL Passarge, 3/60. On the
composition of the VKV leadership, see "Zusammensetzung des Reichsausschusses,"
appended to Langhoff to Gerland, 7 May 1930, BA Koblenz, Nachlass Heinrich
Gerland, 8.

[98] Entries in Passarge's diary, 22 Feb.–19 Mar. 1930, BA Koblenz, NL Passarge, 3/51–62.

[99] Reichstag declaration by Hülser, 2 Apr. 1930, BA Berlin, NL Mumm, 333/54–57.

[100] Westarp, "Betr. Trennungsabsichten," [undated notes from before July 1930], NL
Westarp, Gärtringen, II/61.

[101] Resolution adopted by the DNVP district organization in Potsdam II, reprinted in *Der
Tag*, 22 Apr. 1930, no. 96.

[102] Blank to Reusch, 17 Apr. 1930, RWWA Cologne, Abt. 130, NL Reusch, 4001012024/6.

decisions would result in expulsion from the party.[103] Westarp and his supporters protested vigorously against the resolution, denouncing it as "a tyrannical suppression of the deputy's responsibility to his conscience, to his electorate, to the interests standing behind him, and to the other political parties."[104] Such entreaties were to no avail as an overwhelming four-fifths majority of the committee members proceeded to vote for the resolution.[105]

Three days later Reichert, Leopold, and Walther Rademacher from the dissident faction in the DNVP Reichstag delegation met with Schiele, who insisted that the group's first priority should be Hugenberg's removal as DNVP party chairman. In the event that this was no longer possible, Schiele proposed the creation of a "conservative people's party" more or less along the lines of what the DNVP had been before Hugenberg's takeover of the party. But Schiele also stressed that the recent action of the DNVP executive committee did not constitute a suitable pretext for leaving the party and that the dissidents should wait for a more auspicious moment when the weight of public opinion was on their side. Then and only then, Schiele argued, would the dissidents be able to bring a significant portion of the DNVP party organization along with them.[106] In a more defiant mood, Westarp and his supporters sent Hugenberg an open letter in which they expressed disappointment with the resolution that had been adopted by the DNVP executive committee and reserved for themselves the right to vote according to their conscience and personal sense of political responsibility.[107] Convinced that less than a half-dozen of the DNVP's district organizations were sympathetic to the plight of the dissidents,[108] Westarp tried to dissuade his colleagues from leaving the party until they could reasonably expect to take a significant part of the DNVP's local and regional organization with them. Like Wallraf, Reichert, and most of the DNVP's farm leaders, Westarp had become convinced that a break with the party could no longer be avoided; it was only a matter of finding the appropriate pretext.[109] The People's Conservatives, on the other hand, had become increasingly frustrated by Westarp's indecisiveness and Schiele's naïve hope that the DNVP would

---

[103] Hugenberg's remarks before the DNVP executive committee, 25 Apr. 1930, BA Koblenz, NL Schmidt-Hannover, 72a.

[104] Westarp's speech before the DNVP executive committee, 25 Apr. 1930, NL Westarp, Gärtringen, II/61.

[105] *Unsere Partei* 8, no. 9 (1 May 1930): 86–87.

[106] Westarp, "Betr. Trennungsabsichten," NL Westarp, Gärtringen, II/61.

[107] Westarp to Hugenberg, 2 May 1930, FZG Hamburg, NL Diller, 9. See also Westarp's letter to thirty-five members of the DNVP Reichstag delegation, 26 Apr. 1930, SHStA Dresden, NL Philipp, 24.

[108] Westarp, "Betr. Trennungsabsichten," NL Westarp, Gärtringen, II/61.

[109] Westarp's unpublished memorandum composed between 25 Apr. and 18 July 1930, NL Westarp, Gärtringen, II/61.

"drop into his lap like a ripe fruit" once Hugenberg had thoroughly discredited himself as DNVP party leader.[110]

The predicament in which the People Conservatives found themselves was further complicated by the fact that the first secession from the DNVP in December 1929 and the formation of the Brüning cabinet has also energized efforts at bourgeois concentration. At the end of February 1930 party leaders from Treviranus to the DDP's Erich Koch-Weser met to explore the creation of a new "state party" under the leadership of former chancellor Hans Luther.[111] In his report to the DVP national committee at the beginning of March Scholz proposed that the "state-supporting" bourgeois parties – namely, the Democrats, the Christian-National Coalition, the Business Party, and his own DVP – should test their ability to work together in the form of a parliamentary coalition, or *Arbeitsgemeinschaft*, to secure passage of the various measures in the areas of finance and tax policy that would be required for implementation of the Young Plan.[112] By all accounts, Scholz's sudden embrace of bourgeois concentration reflected the influence of Luther and the leaders of the DVP's young liberal wing, so much so that he returned to the theme at the DVP's Mannheim party congress from 21 to 23 March to issue an appeal "to all of those parties that share our goal for positive and constructive cooperation . . . for a closer union [*Zusammenschluß*] – a union that under certain circumstances does not have to stop at existing party lines."[113]

Scholz's initiative at Mannheim received warm support from Brüning and his circle of supporters.[114] But his efforts to position himself and the DVP at the head of the movement for bourgeois concentration presented problems for both the Democrats and the People's Conservatives. Though among the first to champion the cause of bourgeois concentration, the leaders of the DDP remained adamantly opposed to any form of bourgeois concentration that was directed against the German working class and, more specifically, against the Social Democrats.[115] The People's Conservatives, on the other hand, were now being asked to take a position on the question of bourgeois concentration before their own organization had had an opportunity to get off the ground and

[110] Blank to Reusch, 24 May 1930, RWWA Cologne, Abt. 130, NL Reusch, 4001012024/6.
[111] Memorandum by Pünder of a telephone conversation with Brüning, 1 Mar. 1930, in Morsey, "Neue Quellen," 216–17.
[112] Scholz's speech before the DVP national committee, 2 Mar. 1930, BA Koblenz, R 45 II, 332/25–27.
[113] Scholz, "Deutsche Politik" (n. 31), 3–5. On Scholz's embrace of bourgeois concentration, see Mansfeld's report to the editorial board of the *Kölnische Zeitung*, 25 Mar. 1930, in the "Büchner-Protokolle. Redaktionssitzungen der Kölnischen Zeitung 22. März 1929 bis 2. Dezember 1935," archives of the *Kölner Stadt-Anzeiger*, Cologne, made accessible through the generosity of Kurt Weinhold.
[114] See Brüning to Pünder, 22 Apr. 1930, BA Koblenz, NL Pünder, 30/53–57.
[115] Koch-Weser, "Material zu einem Programm für eine neu zu gründende Partei," n.d. [Apr. 1930], BA Koblenz, NL Koch-Weser, 101/149–59.

were justifiably concerned about the loss of their political identity should they become too closely tied to the other political parties.[116] The first round of formal talks did not take place until the third week of April, at which time Scholz met with Koch-Weser, Lindeiner-Wildau, and the Business Party's Hermann Drewitz met to discuss an electoral truce in the event of new national elections.[117] The four party leaders would meet on several more occasions over the course of the next six weeks, although by then the focus of the discussion had shifted from the question of electoral strategy to that of a parliamentary alliance in support of the Brüning cabinet.[118] The Democrats, their ranks already badly divided by their party's participation in the Brüning cabinet, became increasingly uneasy about an alliance with the more conservative bourgeois parties and announced their withdrawal from the proposed Arbeitsgemeinschaft at a meeting of the four party leaders on 28 May.[119] When the project also encountered strong opposition from the leaders of the CNBLP, Lindeiner-Wildau reluctantly announced his organization's withdrawal from the proposed parliamentary alliance as well. Even though Scholz and the WP's Drewitz were prepared to proceed with the project even if the Democrats opted out, Lindeiner-Wildau's announcement effectively sealed the fate of the proposed Arbeitsgemeinschaft and left the two party leaders with no alternative but to suspend efforts on behalf of a parliamentary alliance with the other state-supporting bourgeois parties.[120]

Many of those in the People's Conservative movement were privately relieved that Scholz's efforts to create a parliamentary alliance of the so-called "state-supporting" elements in the spring of 1930 had ended in failure. Although the People's Conservatives were among Brüning's most reliable political allies, they were nevertheless fearful that their distinctive ideological profile might be lost through the establishment of closer ties with other political parties.[121] For the People's Conservatives, the one positive note to all of this was their success in enlisting at least the moral support of dissident Democrats like the former Reichstag deputy Heinrich Gerland and, more importantly for the immediate context, Willy Hugo Hellpach. The Democratic

---

[116] Treviranus at a meeting of bourgeois party leaders and representatives of the young liberal movement, 17 Mar. 1930, StA Braunschweig, GX6, 612.

[117] DVP Reichsgeschäftsstelle, circular no. 2, 25 Apr. 1930, BA Berlin, R 45 II, 225/168.

[118] On the course of these negotiation, see Gilsa to Reusch, 1 May 1930, RWWA Cologne, Abt. 130, NL Reusch, 400101293/4.

[119] "Arbeitsgemeinschaft der Mittelparteien?," Der Demokrat 11, no. 11 (5 June 1930): 258. See also Koch-Weser to Scholz, 9 July 1930, BA Koblenz, NL Koch-Weser, 105/116–18.

[120] Scholz's report to the DVP Reichstag delegation, 28 May 1930, BA Koblenz, R 45 II, 367/ 240–41, and to the DVP central executive committee, 4 July 1930, ibid., 346/75–77.

[121] Lindeiner-Wildau, "Wandlungen im Parteileben," Volkskonservative Stimmen, 7 June 1930, no. 9. See also Blank to Reusch, 17 July 1930, RWWA Cologne, Abt. 130, NL Reusch, 4001012024/7, as well as the report of Treviranus's speech at a VKV rally in Frankfurt, 12 May 1930, Kölnische Zeitung, 13 May 1930, no. 261a.

candidate for the Reich presidency in 1925 and a highly visible member of the DDP Reichstag delegation, Hellpach had celebrated the founding of the People's Conservative Association in January 1930 with an oft cited article in the *Neue Zürcher Zeitung* in which he espoused the virtues of a "conservative democracy."[122] In early March 1930 Hellpach established ties with Artur Mahraun and the leaders of the People's National Reich Association (Volksnationale Reichsvereinigung or VNR) that Mahraun and the Young Germans had launched earlier in the year as the first step toward the concentration of the German *Staatsbürgertum*.[123] Frustrated by his party's inactivity in the matter of bourgeois concentration, Hellpach caused a sensation when he resigned from the DDP Reichstag delegation on 3 March.[124] Lindeiner-Wildau subsequently approached the renegade Democrat later that spring in the hope that the recruitment of a politician of Hellpach's stature might provide the VKV with the political boost it needed to revive its flagging fortunes. While these overtures revealed a sense of common purpose, Hellpach's response fell far short of the firm commitment Lindeiner was seeking.[125] If the People's Conservatives were going to expand their political base, then it would not be in the middle but at the expense of the DNVP.

The July Secession

The passage of his government's tax and farm bills in April 1930 had given Brüning a brief respite from the pressures of Weimar party politics but certainly not a lasting and fundamental solution to the fiscal and economic problems that confronted the German people. It would only be a matter of time before the conflict over the rising costs of Germany's unemployment insurance program would resurface, this time resulting in a mutiny in the DVP Reichstag delegation and Moldenhauer's resignation as the Reich finance minister on 18 June.[126] The crisis then drew to a climax in the second and

---

[122] Hellpach, "Konservative Demokratie," *Neue Zürcher Zeitung*, 4 Feb. 1930, no. 218. On Hellpach and the People's Conservatives, see [Willy Hellpach], *Hellpach-Memoiren 1925–1945*, ed. Christoph Führ and Hans Georg Zieher (Cologne and Vienna, 1987), 99–108. See also Claudia-Anja Kaune, *Willy Hellpach (1877–1955). Biographie eines liberalen Politikers der Weimarer Republik* (Frankfurt a.m. Main, 2005), 292–99.

[123] [Hellpach], *Hellpach-Memoiren*, ed. Führ and Zieher, 106.

[124] Hellpach to Meyer, 3 Mar. 1930, Landesarchiv Baden-Württemberg, Generallandesarchiv Karlsruhe (hereafter cited as GLA Karlsruhe), Nachlass Willy Hellpach, 257. For further details, see Jones, *German Liberalism*, 359–63.

[125] Correspondence between Lindeiner-Wildau and Hellpach, 20 May–12 June 1930, GLA Karlsruhe, NL Hellpach, 257.

[126] On Moldenhauer's resignation, see his remarks before the cabinet, 18 June 1930, in *Die Kabinette Brüning*, ed. Koops, 1:209–12, and excerpts from his unpublished memoirs, BA Koblenz, NL Moldenhauer, 3.

third weeks of July as the Social Democrats intensified their efforts to prevent the Brüning cabinet from using presidential emergency powers to implement a tax program to which they were irreconcilably opposed. The fate of Brüning's tax program would depend upon the number of deputies in the DNVP who were prepared to defy Hugenberg by voting against the SPD's efforts to block the cabinet's use of Article 48. Against the background of these developments Brüning met first with Oberfohren, chairman of the DNVP Reichstag delegation, on 12 July and then again with Oberfohren and Hugenberg four days later but to no avail as the Nationalists remained unconditionally opposed to the government's tax bill.[127] Four days later a majority of the deputies in the DNVP Reichstag delegation joined forces with the Social Democrats, the Communists, and the National Socialists in defeating Brüning's proposed tax increase in the Reichstag. At this point, the chancellor proceeded to enact the bill that had just been rejected by the Reichstag by invoking the special emergency powers that had been invested in the office of the Reich Presidency by Article 48 of the Weimar Constitution. Brüning's use of presidential emergency powers to enact a bill that had been rejected by the Reichstag represented a dramatic break with historical precedent and was, in the eyes of the Social Democrats and other contemporary observers, of dubious constitutional legitimacy. Brüning's efforts to assuage these concerns by making minor modifications in the text of his proposed tax bill did little to mollify his critics in the SPD, who immediately introduced a motion to rescind the government's emergency powers. Should this motion pass, Brüning was fully prepared to dissolve the Reichstag, call for new elections, and govern by means of presidential emergency powers until a new parliament had been elected.[128]

The historic vote on the Social Democratic motion to revoke the government's emergency powers was set for the afternoon of 18 July. In forcing a confrontation with the Reichstag, Brüning was hoping to ignite a rebellion against Hugenberg's leadership of the DNVP that, if it did not produce a change in the party leadership, would leave Hugenberg's control of the party severely weakened. Under these circumstances, tensions within the DNVP Reichstag delegation quickly reached the boiling point. At a meeting of the delegation on the morning of 17 July Hugenberg tried to disarm his opponents by proposing a letter to the chancellor in which he urged the start of negotiations aimed at breaking the deadlock. But such a move, Hugenberg insisted, made sense only if he could count on the unconditional support of the entire delegation for the Social Democratic motion rescinding the government's

[127] On contacts between the Brüning government and DNVP party leadership, see Pünder's memoranda from 12 and 19 July 1930, in *Die Kabinette Brüning*, ed. Koops, 1:301–03, 326–29.
[128] For further details, see Patch, *Brüning*, 90–95; Hömig, *Brüning*, 177–82; and Harsh, *Social Democracy*, 59–62.

emergency powers. Although most of the delegation strongly endorsed the idea of negotiations with the chancellor, Westarp and his followers refused to commit themselves to supporting the Social Democratic motion without knowing in advance what Hugenberg hoped to accomplish or precisely what circumstances might require them to vote against the government. In short, the group around Westarp lacked sufficient confidence in Hugenberg's intentions to provide him with the authority he sought and suspected that all of this was little more than a ploy to force the dissidents to toe the line in any vote against the Brüning cabinet.[129]

The discussion continued into the early hours of the following morning but did not produce a break in the deadlock between Hugenberg and his opponents on the DNVP's left wing. When the Reichstag delegation resumed its deliberations early on the morning of 18 July, Westarp read a statement on behalf of himself and twenty-one members of the delegation announcing that they would not support the Social Democratic motion to lift the government's emergency powers and that, pursuant to the resolutions adopted by the DNVP executive committee on 25 April, they were prepared to leave the party. Westarp implored Hugenberg to reconsider his position or at the very least accept a postponement in the crucial vote until the fall, a strategem that would have averted a second secession on the DNVP's left wing.[130] When Hugenberg remained adamant in his determination to force the dissolution of the Reichstag, Westarp and approximately thirty Reichstag deputies refused to capitulate to what they denounced as the tyranny of the party chairman and announced their resignation from the DNVP.[131] Not even this, however, was sufficient to rescue the cabinet from defeat in the Reichstag, leaving the chancellor with no alternative but to dissolve parliament and call for new elections.

The secession of Westarp and his supporters from the DNVP Reichstag delegation in the summer of 1930 had been long expected and set the stage for a further realignment of forces on the German Right. The shape of the German Right that would ultimately emerge from the turmoil of 1930 would be determined by the way in which three separate endeavors intersected cut across each other. The first of these was the struggle of the People's Conservatives to establish themselves into a viable political force by uniting the other

---

[129] Minutes of the DNVP Reichstag delegation, 17 July 1930, BA Koblenz, NL Schmidt-Hannover, 72a.

[130] Westarp's statement before the DNVP Reichstag delegation, 18 July 1930, NL Westarp, Gärtringen, II/61. See also Westarp's letters to Oldenburg-Janaschau, 26 July 1930, ibid., II/46, and Schulenberg, 1 Aug. 1930, ibid., VN 15, as well as Gasteiger, *Westarp*, 366.

[131] For Westarp's reasons for leaving the DNVP, see his two-part article, "Die Gründe der Trennung von der Deutschnationalen Volkspartei," *Neue Preußische (Kreuz-)Zeitung*, 24 Aug. 1930, nos. 238–39.

groups that had broken away from the DNVP into a comprehensive and socially heterogeneous conservative *Sammelpartei* modeled after what the DNVP had been before Hugenberg's election to the party chairmanship. The second was the tenacity with which Hugenberg and the leaders of the DNVP struggled to retain control of the DNVP party organization and to isolate the secessionists from any support they may have enjoyed at the state, provincial, and local levels of the party apparatus. And the last was the determination of Germany's industrial elite to use its control over campaign finances to force closer ties between the various groups that now existed between the Social Democrats on the Left and the DNVP on the Right. Just how all of this would shake out in time for the upcoming Reichstag elections remained to be seen.

18

The September Earthquake

The campaign for the 1930 Reichstag election opened under a cloud of deepening economic crisis and increasing radicalization of the German electorate. Capital flight, mass unemployment, and agricultural insolvency placed an enormous strain upon Germany's parliamentary institutions and threatened the complete breakdown of the governmental system. Brüning's decision to invoke presidential emergency powers to enact his fiscal and economic program after it had been rejected by the Reichstag represented a radical departure from the fundamental tenets of Weimar democracy and signaled the end of effective parliamentary government in Germany. Brüning's use of Article 48 greatly expanded the prerogatives of executive power at the expense of the Reichstag and created an opening that not just Hugenberg and the DNVP party leadership but also the Reichswehr and Germany's industrial leadership were eager to exploit. At the same time, the evacuation of the last contingents of French and Belgian troops from the Rhineland in August 1930 – the crowning achievement of Brüning's foreign policy – meant that Germany's conservative elites were free from external restraints that might have kept them from replacing Germany's democratic institutions with an authoritarian system of government more in line with their values and inter-ests. But the increasing fragmentation of Germany's conservative milieu and the general disarray that existed on the German Right after two secessions on the DNVP's left wing had left those elites without a reliable political base from which they could pursue their agenda. The dilemma in which Germany's conservative elites found themselves was further compounded by the emer-gence of an even more radical alternative to the existing political system in the form of Adolf Hitler and the NSDAP. Just how the leaders of the various parties and organizations that made up Germany's non-Nazi Right would deal with the phenomenon of Nazism would ultimately decide just how the crisis of Weimar parliamentarism would resolve itself.

An Inauspicious Debut

Much depended upon the outcome of the September 1930 Reichstag elections. For Brüning and his supporters, the critical question was whether the more moderate elements on the German Right would garner enough support at the polls to implement the government's program for fiscal and economic recovery within the framework of established parliamentary praxis. Otherwise the cabinet would have no recourse but to enact its programs through the use of presidential emergency powers in defiance of the Reichstag and whatever party political configurations the new elections might produce. Most likely Brüning would have preferred to resolve the political stalemate that had led to the dissolution of the Reichstag by parliamentary means, but Schleicher and many of his closest advisors were already pressing for a more authoritarian solution to the existing political crisis.[1] In their pre-election assessment of what would be needed to avoid the use of Article 48, Brüning and his associates estimated that the Center and the Bavarian People's Party have would to gain approximately ten seats in the Reichstag, that the remaining middle parties with the exception of the DVP would need to hold their own, and that the various groups that had broken away from the DNVP would need to win at least fifty seats. All of this was predicated upon the expectation that between them the DNVP and NSDAP would win approximately a hundred seats and that the two Marxist parties would return to the Reichstag with a combined strength of about two hundred deputies. If this prognosis held true, the government would still be approximately eighty deputies short of a parliamentary majority and would require the support of either the SPD or DNVP to avoid the use of Article 48.[2]

From the chancellor's perspective, it was imperative that the various groups that had splintered off from the DNVP make as strong a showing as possible. The key figure in Brüning's calculations was his minister of agriculture, Martin Schiele. On the afternoon of 19 July Schiele received Westarp, Treviranus, and a number of their closest supporters in his Berlin office, where he announced that the National Rural League would be founding a new agrarian party uniting the Christian-National Peasants and Farmers' Party with those members of the Westarp faction with ties to German agriculture. For urban areas Schiele proposed the creation of a sister party that would draw its support from the People's Conservative movement and those elements of the Westarp group without ties to agriculture. According to Schiele's proposal, the two parties would then cooperate with each other both within and outside of parliament.[3] Up until this point, Treviranus and the People's Conservatives had been careful to avoid contact with the dissidents in the DNVP Reichstag

---

[1] Blank's summary of a conversation between Schleicher and Gerhard Erdmann from the Federation of German Employer Associations in his report to Reusch, 24 July 1930, RWWA Cologne, Abt. 130, NL Reusch, 4001012024/7.

[2] Entry for 14 Sept. 1930, in Hermann Pünder, *Politik in der Reichskanzlei. Aufzeichnumgen aus den Jahren 1929–1932,* ed. Thilo Vogelsang (Stuttgart, 1961), 58–59.

[3] Blank to Reusch, 21 July 1930, RWWA Cologne, Abt. 130, NL Reusch, 4001012024/7.

delegation for fear of compromising their standing in the party.[4] Now that there was no longer any reason for such scruple, the leaders of the People's Conservative delegation responded favorably to Schiele's proposal and granted Treviranus authority to enter into exploratory negotiations with the various groups that had broken away from the DNVP on 21 July.[5] These negotiations culminated two days later in the founding of the Conservative People's Party (Konservative Volkspartei or KVP) at a demonstration in Berlin's Hotel Kaiserhof. The demonstration was a modest affair, attended by less than a hundred supporters plus a sizeable delegation from the German press. The principal speakers were Westarp and Schiele, both of whom stressed the imperative of close ties with the German agricultural community, and Treviranus, who commented briefly on the conservative goals that lay at the heart of the new party's ideological orientation. While Treviranus went to great lengths to stress the KVP's loyalty to the state regardless of the form in which it happened to exist, he carefully avoided any mention of the one issue over which the KVP's founders had not been able to agree, the issue of monarchism.[6]

The founders of the KVP – and none more so than Westarp – were committed to restoring the historic ties that had always existed between organized agriculture.e and German conservatism.[7] Westarp and his associates had a willing partner in the person of Schiele, who as minister of agriculture in the Brüning cabinet and president of the National Rural League was the single most influential individual in the German agricultural community. Like Westarp, Schiele deeply regretted the rupture of ties between organized agriculture and the DNVP, and he regarded the restoration of those ties between agriculture and German conservatism as one of his highest priorities.[8] But at a heated meeting of the RLB executive committee on 22 July Schiele's plan for the creation of a new agrarian party that would cooperate with the People's Conservatives both during and after the election encountered strong

---

[4] Treviranus to Westarp, 14 July 1930, NL Westarp, Gärtringen, II/57.

[5] Blank to Reusch, 21 July 1930, RWWA Cologne, Abt. 130, NL Reusch, 4001012024/7. See also the report of this meeting in the *Volkskonservative Stimmen. Zeitschrift der Volkskonservativen Vereinigung*, 26 July 1930, no. 26.

[6] On the founding of the KVP, see the *Neue Preußische (Kreuz-) Zeitung*, 25 July 1930, no. 208, as well as the report from Blank to Reusch, 24 July 1930, RWWA Cologne, Abt. 130, NL Reusch, 4001012024/7, and the entry in Passarge's diary, 28 July 1930, BA Koblenz, NL Passarge, 4/101–03. On the new party's goals, see Konservative Volkspartei, *Das Wollen und Wirken der Konservativen Volkspartei* (Hamburg, 1930).

[7] Westarp, "Das Ziel konservativen Zusammenschlusses," *Neue Preußische (Kreuz-)Zeitung*, 25 July 1930, no. 208.

[8] In this respect, see Schiele, "Schließt die Reihen! Ein Appell an das Landvolk," *Reichs-Landbund* 10, no. 33 (16 Aug. 1930): 385, as well as his letter to Seeckt, 20 Aug. 1930, BA-MA Freiburg, NL Seeckt, 131.

Figure 14. KVP campaign placard designed by Henry Boothby for the September 1930 Reichstag elections. Reproduced with permission from the Bundesarchiv Berlin, Plakat 002-031-002

opposition from Hepp and those members of the RLB leadership who had cast their lot with the CNBLP. Hepp and the CNBLP leadership advocated a fundamental realignment of the German party system along corporatist lines and were adamantly opposed to any and all proposals for the reestablishment of close ties between organized agriculture and the more ideologically oriented political parties.[9] Their intransigence left Schiele with no alternative but to abandon plans for the creation of a new agrarian party that would align itself with the party that Treviranus and Westarp were in the process of founding. The resolution that the RLB executive committee released at the conclusion of the meeting called upon the RLB membership, in a clear and deliberate departure from the practices of the past, to follow the "appeal for vocational solidarity [*Sammelparole des Berufsstandes*]" and to support, in so far as local circumstances permitted, the election of candidates on regional agrarian tickets throughout the country.[10] Efforts to restore the historic ties between agriculture and German conservatism that Hugenberg's policies as DNVP party chairman had done so much to destroy had been effectively stymied.

Consolidation or Splintering?

Developments within the RLB came as a bitter disappointment not just to Westarp and those of his allies who were trying to launch a new conservative party but also to the leaders of the German industrial establishment who were prepared to use the resources at their disposal to pressure the various parties between the Center and DNVP into some sort of alliance for the upcoming elections.[11] In this regard, Reusch and the anti-Hugenberg elements in the Ruhr industrial establishment pursued a two-pronged strategy that sought both to bolster the electoral prospects of the People's Conservatives and to encourage the other groups that stood between the Center and DNVP to present a united front in the upcoming campaign. To make their point, Reusch and his associates threatened to withhold campaign contributions from those parties that refused to resolve their differences for the sake of a joint effort in the campaign for the September elections.[12] Against the background of these developments, Westarp met with DVP chairman Ernst Scholz on the afternoon of July 21 to lay the groundwork for a more concerted campaign effort. Much to Westarp's surprise, Scholz took the initiative by proposing the

[9] Report of CNBLP party chairman Ernst Höfer's speech "Neue Sorgen, neue Wege" in St. Goarshausen, 27 July 1930, *Nassauische Bauern-Zeitung*, 29 July 1930, no. 173.
[10] *Reichs-Landbund* 10, no. 30 (26 July 1930): 360.
[11] For example, see Krupp to Wilmowsky, 19 July 1930, HA Krupp Essen, FAH 23/503.
[12] Blank to Reusch, 23 July 1930, RWWA Cologne, Abt. 130, NL Reusch, 4001012024/7. See also Turner, "The *Ruhrlade*," 208–09; Langer, *Macht und Verantwortung*, 463–66; and Neebe, *Grossindustrie, Staat und NSDAP*, 73–76.

creation of a single slate of candidates stretching from the Democrats to the People's Conservatives. Though skeptical that this could be done in the short time that remained before the election, Westarp nevertheless agreed to bring Scholz's proposal for an electoral truce, a joint election appeal, and a parliamentary alliance after the elections to the attention of his associates the following morning.[13] All of this met with strong, if not skeptical, support from Reusch and his associates in the Ruhr industrial establishment. But with encouragement from the leaders of his own party's right wing,[14] Scholz decided to take his cause one step further, and on 22 July he sent the leaders of the DDP, the Christian-National Coalition, the Westarp faction, and the Business Party an open letter inviting them to join his party in conversations aimed at satisfying the "strong yearning for the concentration of all state-supporting forces" that existed in broad sectors of the German populace.[15]

In the meantime, Westarp was heavily involved in preparations for the founding of the KVP and regarded the unification of the various groups that had broken away from the DNVP as his first and most pressing political priority.[16] Still, the People's Conservatives were desperately short of funds and could ill afford to ignore the offer of support from Reusch and his associates in return for their participation in an electoral alliance with the other moderate bourgeois parties. Meeting with a select group of business and banking leaders that included Hjalmar Schacht, Georg Solmssen, and Ernst von Borsig shortly before the KVP's official founding on the afternoon of 23 July, Westarp and Treviranus went to great lengths to stress that although they had little interest in a merger with the DVP and other political parties, they were not opposed to an agreement aimed at minimizing inter-party animosity during the campaign. By the same token, Westarp and his associates did not rule out the possibility of a parliamentary coalition, or *Fraktionsgemeinschaft*, between the non-Catholic parties that supported the Brüning government once the elections were over.[17] But this interest in the possibility of closer ties with the other political parties that stood between the Center and

---

[13] Blank to Reusch, 21 July 1930, RWWA Cologne, Abt. 130, NL Reusch, 4001012024/7.

[14] For example, see Jarres to Scholz, 21 July 1930, and Treviranus, 25 July 1930, both in BA Koblenz, NL Jarres, 45. In a similar vein, see Schmidt to Westarp, 20 July 1930, NL Westarp, Gärtringen, II/40, and Brandes to Scholz, 21 July 1930, BrStA Brunswick, GX6/606.

[15] The text of Scholz's letter is appended to Scholz to Brüning, 22 July 1930, BA Berlin, R 43 I, 1006/8–9, and reprinted in *Mit Hindenburg für Deutschlands Rettung!*, ed. Reichsgeschäftsstelle der Deutschen Volkspartei (Berlin, n.d. [1930]), 24–26. For further details, see Richter, *Deutsche Volkspartei*, 651–52.

[16] Westarp, "Meine Verhandlungen zwischen dem 18. Juni und 18. Oktober 1930," n.d. [Oct. 1930], NL Westarp, Gärtringen, II/61.

[17] *Berliner Börsen-Courier*, 24 July 1930, no. 340. See also Treviranus to Jarres, 26 July 1930, BA Koblenz, NL Jarres, 45.

DNVP did not extend to the other groups that had emerged from the ruins of the DNVP's left wing. The Christian-Social People's Service had consistently dissociated itself from the movement for bourgeois unity and remained adamantly opposed to any ties to other political parties that might compromise its confessional orientation. When pressed on the matter of bourgeois concentration, the leaders of the CSVD stressed their commitment to a Christian social policy that transcended existing class lines and specifically rejected efforts to create a united bourgeois front that would have been directed against the German worker. Meeting in Eisenach in the last week of July, the CSVD national executive committee (*Reichsvorstand*) reiterated its commitment to preserving the CSVD's independence vis-à-vis other political parties and announced that the CSVD would enter the upcoming Reichstag campaign free of arrangements or obligations that might infringe upon its political and organizational integrity.[18]

Even more disturbing in this regard was the position of the CNBLP. At the meeting of the RLB executive committee on 22 July Schiele and his supporters had failed to overcome the opposition of those like Hepp, Heinrich von Sybel, and Albrecht Wendhausen who insisted that the political realignment of the German agricultural community should take place on a vocational rather than an ideological basis.[19] As a result, Schiele's efforts to launch an new agrarian party that would unite the CNBLP with those farm leaders who, like himself, intended to work with the Conservative People's Party both before and after the elections were placed on hold until the CNBLP leadership could meet to discuss its options the following week.[20] On the following day Westarp and Schiele met with the CNBLP's newly elected chairman Ernst Höfer and Günther Gereke, a driving force in the CNBLP, in one last attempt to salvage something of the efforts to negotiate an alliance between the KVP and CNBLP. With Gereke's vigorous support, Schiele and Westarp were able to persuade Höfer to go along with an arrangement whereby the CNBLP would reserve places on the new agrarian ticket's national slate, or *Reichswahlvorschlag*, for candidates from the KVP so that it would receive the full complement of mandates to which it was entitled under Weimar electoral law without having to elect so much as a single deputy at the district level.[21]

---

[18] See the report on the meeting of the CSVD national executive committee in Eisenach, 26–27 July 1930, as well as Simpfendörfer, "Neubildung der Fronten," both in the *Christlicher Volksdienst*, 2 Aug. 1930, no. 31.

[19] Westarp, "Meine Verhandlungen zwischen dem 18. Juni und 18. Oktober 1930," n.d. [Oct. 1930], NL Westarp, Gärtringen, II/61.

[20] Blank to Reusch, 21–24 July 1930, RWWA Cologne, Abt. 130, NL Reusch, 4001012024/7. See also Westarp to Hiller von Gaertringen, 28 July 1930, NL Hiller, Gärtringen.

[21] Westarp, "Meine Verhandlungen zwischen dem 18. Juni und 18. Oktober 1930," n.d. [Oct. 1930], NL Westarp, Gärtringen, II/61.

Figure 15. CSVD campaign placard designed by H. P. Schnorr for the September 1930 Reichstag elections. Reproduced with permission from the Bundesarchiv Berlin, Plakat 002-031-033

In the meantime, Reusch and his associates in the "Ruhrlade" intensified their efforts to keep the movement for conservative unity on track. Industrial leaders from moderates like Carl Duisberg and Carl Friedrich von Siemens to Reusch and the leaders of Ruhr heavy industry had long supported the consolidation of those parties that stood to the right of the Center, though it was no longer clear just how Hugenberg's DNVP would factor into their plans.[22] The fragmentation of the DNVP's left wing and the proliferation of parties on the moderate Right had lent a new sense of urgency to their efforts on behalf of a united bourgeois front in the upcoming Reichstag elections. Reusch and his associates were critical of the political course Hugenberg had steered since his election as DNVP party chairman, and they strongly supported Westarp's efforts to organize the various elements that had broken away from the DNVP into a new conservative party that would be sympathetic to the interests of German industry. This, they hoped, would serve as the prelude to a much broader bourgeois constellation that would include not just Westarp's new conservative party but also the DVP, WP, and other political parties between the Center and DNVP. To underscore their commitment to the success of these efforts, the "Ruhrlade" resolved at a meeting on 28 July to provide support to all non-socialist parties from the Democrats on the Left to the DNVP on the Right if they agreed to suspend polemics against each other for the duration of the campaign.[23]

On 28 July Martin Blank from the Gutehoffnungshütte's Berlin office and Martin Sogemeier from the Alliance of Northwest German Business Representatives (Zweckverband nordwestdeutscher Wirtschaftsvertreter) met with Gereke to honor his role in the struggle against Hepp with a campaign contribution of 30,000 marks with reassurances that more would be forthcoming if the CNBLP executive committee gave its approval to an electoral alliance with the KVP.[24] As the chief conduit of funds from German industry to the CNBLP, Gereke would then redirect this money to the party's state and district organizations to help underwrite their campaign expenses.[25] The leaders of the CNBLP could ill afford to turn their back on offers of this magnitude and agreed after a series of heated meetings of the its party leadership on 29 July to an arrangement whereby the CNBLP would join forces with regional conservative agrarian organizations under the banner of a united agrarian ticket known as the German Rural People (Deutsches Landvolk). The CNBLP party

---

[22] For example, see the speeches by Duisberg and Wieland at a meeting of the RDI central committee, 23 May 1930, WA Bayer, 62/10.5.
[23] Blank to Springorum, 29 July 1930, RWWA Cologne, Abt. 130, NL Reusch, 4001012024/7.
[24] Blank to Reusch, 28 July 1930, RWWA Cologne, Abt. 130, NL Reusch, 4001012024/7.
[25] See Gereke to Tiemann, 15 July 1930, LA Berlin, Prozeßakten Gereke, Rep. A, 358-01, 76/16, Anlage 12, and Ohm to Gereke, 30 Aug. 1930, ibid., Anlage 26.

leadership also agreed to accept the terms of the electoral alliance that Höfer had negotiated with Schiele and Westarp six days earlier.[26] All of this represented a modest, but nonetheless important victory for Schiele, who officially endorsed the CNBLP and agreed to head its ticket in a number of districts across the country.[27]

As the negotiations with the CNBLP were running their course, Scholz's efforts on behalf of a more broadly based bourgeois unity front received a rude shock when on the morning of 28 July Erich Koch-Weser, chairman of the left-liberal DDP, and the Young German Order's Artur Mahraun announced that they had joined forces to launch a new party of their own bearing the name German State Party (Deutsche Staatspartei or DStP).[28] The founders of the DStP hoped to infuse German party life with the selfless idealism and activism of the "front generation" to galvanize the forces of the German middle into a cohesive political front capable of rescuing the German nation from the twin threats of international Marxism and world plutocracy.[29] Although the negotiations between Koch-Weser and the Young Germans had been going on since the dissolution of the Reichstag, the founding of the German State Party hit Scholz and those who championed the creation of a bourgeois unity front for the upcoming Reichstag elections like a bombshell. Scholz was furious with Koch-Weser for what he regarded as a clear act of betrayal and an attempt to split the elements on his party's left wing off from the rest of the DVP.[30] Reusch and the leaders of the Ruhr industrial establishment were no less shocked by the founding of the new party, criticized the secretive and disloyal way in which it had been founded, and excluded it from financial support from the funds at their disposal as well as from the efforts to forge a bourgeois unity ticket for the September elections.[31]

For Scholz, it was now a question of whether the movement for bourgeois concentration would regain the momentum it seemed to be building before the founding of the DStP had taken place. At a series of meetings with various

---

[26] Resolution published by the CNBLP executive committee, 29 July 1930, in the *Thüringer Landbund* 11, no. 62 (2 Aug. 1930): 1. See also Wilmowsky to Krupp, 1 Aug. 1930, HA Krupp, Essen, 23/504. See also Höfer, "Offener Brief an die deutschen Bauern," 1 Sept. 1930, BA Koblenz, ZSg 1–647/4 (8).

[27] Interview with Schiele in the *Deutsche Allgemeine Zeitung*, 2 Aug. 1930, nos. 355–56.

[28] On the founding of the DStP, see Jones, *German Liberalism*, 366–77. On Koch-Weser's role, see Gerhard Papke, *Der liberale Politiker Erich Koch-Weser in der Weimarer Republik* (Baden-Baden, 1989), 175–81.

[29] Artur Mahraun, *Die Deutsche Staatspartei. Eine Selbsthilfeorganisation des deutschen Staatsbürgertums* (Berlin, 1930), esp. 25–29.

[30] Scholz's remarks before the DVP central executive committee, 31 July 1930, BA Koblenz, R 45 II, 332/245–55, reprinted in *Nationalliberalismus in der Weimarer Republik*, ed. Kolb and Richter, 2:1056–58.

[31] Reusch to Weinlig, 5 Sept. 1930, RWWA Cologne, Abt. 130, NL Reusch, 400101293/10b. See also Reusch to Hamm, 2 Aug. 1930, ibid., 40010123/25b.

party leaders on 31 July and 1 August Scholz succeeded in securing the agreement of Treviranus, Gereke, and the WP's Hermann Drewitz to the publication of a joint election appeal in support of the reforms that had come to be known as the "Hindenburg Program." The DVP's Adolf Kempkes was given the task of drafting the text of the proposed appeal for presentation to the four party leaders at their next meeting on 7 August.[32] But Gereke, who supported the proposed action, encountered such strong opposition from the forces around Hepp and Höfer in the CNBLP party leadership that he had no choice but to announce at the meeting on 7 August that his party would not be participating in a joint election appeal with the other three parties.[33] Upon hearing this, Gotthard Sachsenberg from the Business Party responded that Gereke's announcement made it impossible for the WP, as the only remaining vocational party, to proceed with the project, whereupon Scholz and the KVP's Lindeiner-Wildau declared efforts to forge an electoral alliance among the moderate bourgeois parties for the upcoming Reichstag elections at an end.[34]

Bitterly disappointed by the outcome of the meeting on 7 August, Reusch and his associates in the Ruhr industrial establishment immediately mobilized their resources in an attempt to rectify the situation.[35] This led to a second round of negotiations in the third week of August that culminated in the publication of an appeal on 21 August that carried the signatures of the DVP, KVP, and WP in support of the so-called Hindenburg Program. In signing the appeal, the three parties committed themselves to cooperating with each other in the implementation of the reform package that Brüning had launched in the name of the Reich president with the prospect of formal political ties in the new Reichstag.[36] In no way whatsoever, as Westarp explained in a letter to a KVP sympathizer, did this agreement compromise the organizational or political independence of the participating parties.[37] In terms of its immediate impact, the publication of the "Hindenburg Appeal" meant that the three parties would not squander their limited resources – and more importantly those of their industrial backers – on fruitless polemics against each other. The People's Conservatives – and above all Treviranus – had fully invested

---

[32] Westarp, "Bericht über Verhandlungen mit der DVP wegen Zusammenwirkens für das Hindenburg-Programm," n.d. [Aug. 1930], NL Westarp, Gärtringen, II/40.

[33] Ibid. See also the report of Hepp's speech in Usingen, 28 Aug. 1930, *Nassauische Bauern-Zeitung*, 30 Aug. 1930, no. 200.

[34] DVP, Reichsgeschäftsstelle, circular no. 11, 9 Aug. 1930, BA Berlin, R 45 II, 225/143–46. See also Blank to Reusch, 9 Aug. 1930, RWWA Cologne, Abt. 130, NL Reusch, 4001012024/7.

[35] Blank to Springorum, 13 Aug. 1930, RWWA Cologne, Abt. 130, NL Reusch, 4001012024/7.

[36] Report by Scholz to the DVP central executive committee, 24 Aug. 1930, BA Koblenz, R 45 II, 347/49–57.

[37] Westarp to Kropatscheck, 2 Sept. 1930, NL Westarp, Gärtringen, VN 15.

themselves in the efforts to reach an understanding with the moderate bourgeois parties and were doubtlessly satisfied with the successful conclusion of
the negotiations.[38] In point of fact, however, the tedious and often contentious
negotiations that accompanied the publication of the "Hindenburg Appeal"
only underscored the confusion and disorder that existed on Germany's
moderate Right. In as much as neither the State Party nor the Christian-
Social People's Service signed the appeal,[39] it remained an empty gesture that
offered the appearance but not the substance of bourgeois unity.

DNVP on the Counterattack

With characteristic intransigence, Hugenberg greeted the call for new elections
with a public appeal in which he claimed credit for the dissolution of the
Reichstag, denounced the second wave of secessionists as renegades who had
traded the banner of the DNVP for that of the Center, and protested against
the misuse of Hindenburg's name to advance a partisan political agenda. At
the same time, Hugenberg reaffirmed the DNVP's commitment to the struggle
against Marxism and called for a reversal in the conduct of German foreign
policy and a radical change of the existing political system if a "catastrophe of
unimaginable magnitude" was to be avoided.[40] But the secession from the
DNVP that followed the dissolution of the Reichstag in July 1930 was far more
extensive than the one that had taken place the previous December. Of the
seventy-eight Nationalist deputies who had been elected to the Reichstag in
1928, only thirty-five remained after the dust had settled from the altercation
over Hugenberg's decision to support the suspension of the government's
emergency powers. The list of those who had left the party included such
party stalwarts as Wilhelm Bazille, Gottfried von Dryander, Jakob Haßlacher,
Bernhard Leopold, Jakob Wilhelm Reichert, Georg Schultz-Bromberg, and
Max Wallraf in addition to Westarp and Schiele.[41] Of the five DNVP deputies
from Saxony only Paul Bang remained with the DNVP while the four others –
Alvin Domsch, Georg Hartmann, Albrecht Philipp, and Walther Rademacher – had left the party.[42] The same was true in Bavaria, where Georg

---

[38] See the statement by Treviranus, 11 Aug. 1930, in the *Neue Preußische (Kreuz-)Zeitung*,
12 Aug. 1930, no. 437, as well as his article, "Gemeinsame Verantwortung," *Deutsche
Allgemeine Zeitung*, 12 Aug. 1930, nos. 371–72.

[39] Blank to Reusch, 28 Aug. 1930, RWWA Cologne, Abt. 130, NL Reusch, 4001012024/7.

[40] Hugenberg, "Es, geht um Freiheit und Schicksal der Nation! Der Wahlaufruf des Führers
der Deutschnationalen Volkspartei!," n.d., Flugblatt no. 554, NL Hiller, Gärtringen, also
in *Unsere Partei* 8, Wahlkampf-Sondernummer 1 (23 July 1930): 157.

[41] "Hugenbergs Verlustliste," *Volkskonservative Stimmen*, 2 Aug. 1930, no. 27. See also
Mergel, "Das Scheitern des deutsche Tory-Konservatismus," 359–62.

[42] Domsch, Hartmann, Philipp, and Rademacher to the DNVP Saxon state committee, n.d.,
in the *Dresdener Nachrichten*, 23 July 1930, no. 341. On the situation in Saxony, see

Bachmann, Kurt Fromm, Paul von Lettow-Vorbeck, and Hermann Strathmann along with the long-time DNVP loyalist Walter Otto all cast their lot
with the secession,[43] while in Württemberg Bazille, Wilhelm Dingler, Heinrich
Haag, and Wilhelm Vogt announced that they too were leaving the party.[44] By
no means, however, was the secession confined to deputies from central and
western Germany. Of the DNVP's once powerful agrarian wing, only a
handful of deputies stayed with the DNVP, most notably Hans von Goldacker
from Thuringia and Walther Stubbendorf from Potsdam. But the rest of the
DNVP's agrarian support had evaporated in what amounted to a mass exodus
of the party's farm leaders, including seven members of the DNVP's delegation
to the Prussian Landtag.[45] One curious exception to this trend was the fact that
the party's most prominent women's leaders – Annagrete Lehmann, Paula
Müller-Otfried, Käthe Schirmacher, and Magdalene von Tiling – continued to
support Hugenberg, as they had in his bid for the DNVP party chairmanship
and in his crusade against the Young Plan.[46] This, however, did little to change
the fact that in terms of its parliamentary representation the secession had
been an unmitigated disaster for the DNVP.

Hugenberg and his loyalists scrambled to immunize the party's national
organization against the effects of the secession. Hugenberg summoned district leaders from throughout the country to Berlin for a series of high-level
strategy conferences on 24–25 July. He opened the meeting of the DNVP
executive committee on 24 July with a vigorous defense of the policies he had
pursued since the formation of the Brüning cabinet and characterized the
departure of Westarp and his associates as part of a purification process
through which the DNVP had to pass if it was to assume the lead in the
struggle against Marxism. The immediate task, he continued, was to take the
struggle to those middle parties like the Center whose very existence had
contributed to the persistence of Social Democratic power in Prussia and the
Reich.[47] Hugenberg continued his tirade against Brüning, the Social
Democrats, and the parties he held responsible for the stranglehold of Marxism over German economic and political life the following day at a meeting of

Maltzahn to Westarp, 26 July 1930, NL Westarp, Gärtringen, II/57, and Kurt Philipp to
Lüttichau, 28 July 1930, SHStA Dresden, NL Philipp, 24.

[43] For further details, see Kiiskinen, *DNVP in Bayern*, 346–53. See also Otto to Westarp,
27 July 1930, NL Westarp, Gärtringen, VN 106.

[44] Müller, "Bürgerpartei," 416–17.

[45] *Volkskonservative Stimmen*, 9 Aug. 1930, no. 28.

[46] Schirmacher, Tiling, and Müller-Otfried at the meeting of the DNVP executive committee, 24 July 1930, BA Berlin, R 8005, 56/5–6, 32, 35. For further details, see Süchting-
Hänger, *"Gewissen der Nation,"* 317–33.

[47] Hugenberg's comments before the DNVP executive committee, 24 July 1930, BA
Koblenz, NL Schmidt-Hannover, 72a. For the discussion that followed, see the minutes
of the DNVP executive committee, 24 July 1930, BA Berlin, R 8005, 56/1–38.

the DNVP party representation.[48] With nearly three hundred members from all corners of the Reich, the party representation was the largest and most representative body in the DNVP organization and voted by an overwhelming 283 to 4 margin to approve a resolution expressing full confidence in Hugenberg's performance as party chairman.[49] The resounding votes of confidence Hugenberg received from the leaders of his party's national organization reassured him of his party's rank and file and only strengthened him in his determination to stay the course in his attacks against Brüning.

The next task facing Hugenberg and his supporters was to minimize the damage the most recent secession from the Reichstag delegation had done to the party's district, regional, and local organizations. In Württemberg, for example, the secession had claimed the state's most prominent conservative politician, Wilhelm Bazille. In many respects Bazille's career mirrored that of Westarp. Not unlike Westarp, Bazille had evolved from one of Weimar democracy's most outspoken critics into a governmental conservative who served first as Württemberg state president from 1924 to 1928 and then as Württemberg minister of culture until 1933.[50] Throughout his early career, Bazille had enjoyed the strong support of the Württemberg Burgher Party, but by the late 1920s increasing resistance to Bazille and his brand of governmental conservatism had begun to crystallize within the WBP around the person of Fritz Wider, a Hugenberg loyalist who had faithfully supported the DNVP party chairman in the inner-party conflicts of 1928–30.[51] Increasingly disenchanted with Hugenberg's leadership during the crusade against the Young Plan and in the struggle with the Reichstag delegation in the first half of 1930, Bazille emerged as one of the most vocal and readily identifiable members of the so-called Westarp group.[52] Like Westarp, Bazille refused to go along with the party chairman in supporting Social Democratic efforts to suspend Brüning's use of presidential emergency powers and left the party following the fateful Reichstag vote and call for new elections on 18 July 1930.[53] Given his stature in Württemberg politics, Bazille had every reason to expect that a

[48] Hugenberg's speech "Freiheitspolitik statt Tributpolitik" before the DNVP party representation, 25 July 1930, in *Unsere Partei* 8, Wahlkampf-Sondernummer 2 (6 Aug. 1930): 182–83.

[49] *Unsere Partei* 8, no. 15 (1 Aug. 1930): 163.

[50] Müller, "Bazille," 501–09.

[51] See Wider to Westarp, 26 Nov. and 19 Dec. 1929, both in NL Westarp, Gärtringen, II/37. For further details, see Müller, "Bürgerpartei," 412–21.

[52] Bazille's remarks at the meetings of the DNVP Reichstag delegation, 11–12 Apr. and 10 July 1930, BA Koblenz, NL Schmidt-Hannover, 72a.

[53] Bazille to Hirzel, open letter, 26 July 1930, in the *Frankfurter Zeitung*, 27 July 1930, no. 553. See also Wilhelm Bazille, "Die Tragödie der Deutschnationalen Volkspartei," *Nationale Volksgemeinschaft* 1, no. 2 (Sept. 1930), Stadtarchiv Stuttgart, Nachlass Wilhelm Kohlhaas, Bestand 2134, 77.

significant portion of the Burgher Party would follow him in his decision to leave the DNVP. But at a meeting of the WBP state committee on 27 July an overwhelming majority of the committee members threw their support behind Hugenberg and Wider in an embarrassing rebuff to the most prominent and well-known Württemberg conservative. Only a small number of highly placed state civil servants joined Bazille in leaving the party, while the rest of the WBP organization rallied almost without exception behind the party leaders in Berlin and Stuttgart.[54]

A similar situation existed in Bavaria, where the Bavarian Middle Party had functioned as the DNVP's state affiliate ever since its merger with the national party in early 1920. Like its Württemberg counterpart, the BMP had been a member of the state government almost without interruption from 1920 to 1928. But unlike the WBP where Hugenberg's election as DNVP national chairman had been accompanied by increased tensions within the state party organization, the Bavarian Middle Party and its chairman Hans Hilpert supported Hugenberg's candidacy and were quick to close ranks behind him once he had been elected.[55] Moreover, the leaders of the BMP state organization had staunchly supported Hugenberg in his conflicts with the party moderates both during and after the campaign against the Young Plan despite the increasing strain this produced between the state party and its supporters in the Bavarian Rural League.[56] But by the spring of 1930 all of this had begun to take its toll on the state party organization, which found itself without money and facing the defection of its younger members to either the NSDAP or People's Conservatives.[57] Following the secession of the Westarp faction and all five Bavarian members of the DNVP Reichstag delegation in July 1930,[58] the KVP established a state organization under the mentorship of neo-conservative publicist Edgar Julius Jung to support the Reichstag

---

[54] Ernst Marquardt, "Kaempfe fuer Deutschlands Zukunft und Ehre. Umrisszeichnungen aus der Geschichte der deutschnationalen Volkspartei Württembergs," unpublished manuscript in the Württembergische Landesbibliothek, Stuttgart, 77. See also the report of this meeting in the WBP campaign leaflet "Der deutschnationale Wahlaufruf," n.d. [Aug.–Sept. 1930], NL Hiller, Gärtringen, as well as the circular letter from Wider and Sontheimer, Aug. 1930, ibid.

[55] Minutes of the BMP state committee, 13 Oct. and 8 Dec. 1928, BHStA Munich, Abt. V, NL Hilpert, 1/10–23. See also Kiiskinen, DNVP in Bayern, 332–34, and Kittel, "Zwischen völkischem Fundamentalismus und gouvernementaler Taktik," 885–87.

[56] See the exchange between Hilpert and Bachmann in the minutes of the BMP state committee, 9 Dec. 1929, and 10 May 1930, BHStA Munich, Abt. V, NL Hilpert, 1/57–79, as well as the more detailed analysis by Kiiskinen, DNVP in Bayern, 341–46.

[57] Dziembowski to Brosius, n.d. [8 May 1930], BHStA Munich, Abt. V, NL Dziembowski, 18.

[58] Kiiskinen, DNVP in Bayern, 347–48. See also Schmidt-Hannover to Dziembowski, 11 July 1930, BHStA Munich, Abt. V, NL Dziembowski, 18.

candidacy of retired general Paul von Lettow-Vorbeck.[59] A highly decorated hero of the African campaign in World War I, Lettow-Vorbeck had belonged to the DNVP Reichstag delegation since 1920 and was among those who had left the party in July 1930.[60] The founders of the Bavarian KVP no doubt hoped that Lettow-Vorbeck's popularity would not just serve as a rallying point for the anti-Hugenberg elements within the BMP but would also attract the support of voters who stood outside the immediate orbit of Bavarian conservatism. But Hilpert and the leaders of the BMP moved quickly to shore up their organization against the threat of further defections. Meeting in Munich on 2 August, the BMP state committee reaffirmed its unequivocal loyalty to Hugenberg and the party's national leadership, criticized those who had recently left the party for having undermined the unity of the national front, and rededicated the Bavarian Middle Party as a "*Kampfgemeinschaft* against Marxism and cultural Bolshevism, against unitarism and alien [*volksfremder*] republicanism and parliamentarism, against tribute slavery, and against the debilitating economic and tax policies of the post-revolutionary period."[61]

Disarray on the Moderate Right

The most serious problem the leaders of the DNVP faced in their efforts to contain the damage that the July secession had done to their party's grassroots organization was the estrangement of the party's agrarian wing. Following the dissolution of the Reichstag in July 1930 the executive committee of the National Rural League had called upon its regional affiliates throughout the country to run candidates on separate agrarian tickets in the spirit of vocational solidarity.[62] In Württemberg the RLB affiliate, the

---

[59] Jung to Pechel, 25 July 1930, BA Koblenz, NL Pechel, 79. On Jung and the People's Conservative movement, see Roshan Magub, *Edgar Julius Jung: Right-Wing Enemy of the Nazis. A Political Biography* (Rochester, NY, 2017), 133–50.

[60] See the drafts of Lettow-Vorbeck's letters of resignation to Hugenberg and Hilpert, both dated 19 July 1930, BA-MA, Freiburg, Nachlass Paul von Lettow-Vorbeck, 58, and Lettow-Vorbeck to Einem, 9 Sept. 1930, BA-MA Freiburg, Nachlass Karl von Einem, 28/60–67, as well as Paul Lettow-Vorbeck, *Warum ich aus der DNVP. austrat* (Berlin, n.d. [1930]), BA Koblenz, ZSg 1–275/2 (4). See also Uwe Schulte-Varendorff, *Kolonialheld für Kaiser und Führer. General Lettow-Vorbeck – Mythos und Wirklichkeit* (Berlin, 2006), 100–01.

[61] "'Unter Schwarz-weiß-rot gegen Marxismus und Versailles.' Landesausschuß der Deutschnationalen Volkspartei i.B.," n.d. [Aug. 1930], BHStA Munich, Abt. V, Flugblätter-Sammlung 60/1930. See also the minutes of the BMP state committee, 2 Aug. 1930, BHStA Munich, Abt. V, NL Hilpert, 1/80–96, as well as Hilpert's recollection of this meeting in Hilpert, "Meinungen und Kämpfe," ibid., 22/4371–73.

[62] *Reichs-Landbund* 10, no. 30 (26 July 1930): 360.

Württemberg Peasants and Wine Growers' League, severed its decade-long ties with the Württemberg Burgher Party and announced that in accordance with the RLB's appeal for vocational solidarity it would run its own slate of candidates in the upcoming national elections under the rubric "German Rural People" with the understanding that the deputies elected on this ticket would subsequently affiliate themselves with the CNBLP Reichstag delegation.[63] In a parallel move Karl Prieger, president of the Bavarian Rural League, announced at a meeting of the BLB's general membership on 10 August that the increasing fragmentation of the German Right had left his organization with no choice but to "go it alone" in the upcoming campaign and that it too would field its own slate of candidates.[64] And in Saxony, where four of the DNVP's six Reichstag deputies had left the party and where the Pan-Germans were busy at work purging the party's state organization of those who still harbored sympathies for Westarp and his supporters,[65] the Saxon Rural League declared on 31 July that it would follow the RLB's appeal for vocational solidarity and run its own slate of candidates in the campaign for the September elections.[66] Even in Pomerania, where the regional RLB affiliate was among the most reactionary in the entire organization, local farm leaders including representatives of the land-owning nobility turned their backs on the DNVP after it refused to enter into an electoral alliance with the CNBLP at the provincial level.[67]

All of this dealt a severe blow not just to the DNVP's prospects in the upcoming Reichstag elections but also to the electoral hopes of urban conservatives like Saxony's Albrecht Philipp who had pinned their chances of

---

[63] WBVB, "Wahlaufruf zur Reichstagswahl am 14. Sept. 1930," n.d. [Aug. 1930], NL Hiller, Gärtringen. See also *Das grüne Buch der Bauernpolitik. Ein politisches Handbuch für Wähler in Stadt und Land*, ed. Theodor Körner alt (Stuttgart, 1931), 22–24. On relations between the WBWB and local KVP, see Körner to Hiller von Gärtringen, 7 Aug. 1930, NL Hiller, Gärtringen.

[64] *Bayerischer Landbund* 32, no. 33 (17. Aug. 1930).

[65] For further details, see the letter to Hugenberg, 23 July 1930, BA Berlin, R 8048, 216/158–62, and Beutler to Claß, 9 Sept. 1930, ibid., 194–95. See also Larry Eugene Jones, "Saxony, 1924–1930: A Study in the Dissolution of the Bourgeois Party System in Weimar Germany," in *Saxony in German History: Culture, Society, and Politics, 1830–1933*, ed. James Retallack (Ann Arbor, MI, 2000), 336–55, here 343–54.

[66] *Sächsische Bauern-Zeitung* 37, no. 31 (3 Aug. 1930): 315. See also Domsch, "Reichstagsauflösung und Neuwahl," ibid., 316–17, as well as Domsch to Philipp, 27 July, 1930, SHStA Dresden, NL Philipp, 24.

[67] *Sächsischer Bauern-Zeitung* 37, no. 33 (17 Aug. 1930): 338. On developments in Pomerania, see Knebel-Döberitz to Schiele, 31 Aug. (sic July) 1930, NL Westarp, Gärtringen, VN 15, and Brosius to Hugenberg, 12 Aug. 1930, BA Koblenz, NL Hugenberg, 189/273–74, as well as the entries in Passarge's diary, 4 and 23 Aug. 1930, BA Koblenz, NL Passarge, 4/104–09.

reelection upon the support of organized agriculture.[68] Not surprisingly, a bitter polemic erupted between the DNVP and RLB over the latter's support of the CNBLP and affiliated agrarian tickets throughout the country. DNVP propagandists claimed that Schiele and the leaders of the National Rural League had abandoned the RLB's long-standing policy of bipartisan neutrality by its support of the CNBLP and that its sabotage of the national front had left German agriculture defenseless in the struggle against Marxism.[69] The RLB responded with a vigorous defense of Schiele's accomplishments as Reich minister of agriculture and implored the German agricultural community to rally behind Hindenburg and Schiele as "the best guarantee for the continuation of efforts to save German agriculture."[70] For its part, the CNBLP contrasted the positive steps that had been taken under Schiele's leadership to rescue German agriculture from the brink of disaster with the *Katastrophenpolitik* of Hugenberg and those in control of the DNVP. Whereas Hugenberg and his supporters, the CNBLP alleged, was intent upon plunging Germany into a full-scale economic crisis in order to bring down the existing political system, the leaders of the CNBLP argued that the struggle against Marxism could never be won without a healthy German peasantry and that the first order of business was the rehabilitation of German agriculture. And this, they insisted, could only take place through the consolidation of the German agricultural community into a single agrarian party.[71]

Yet for all of its passion, the CNBLP's appeal to the vocational identity of the German peasantry met with a mixed reception from the different constituencies within the German agricultural community. Not only did some DNVP farm leaders like the Westphalian Ludwig Schwecht decline to follow Schiele and remained loyal to Hugenberg and the DNVP,[72] but the Association of

---

[68] See Philipp, "Landvolk und Reichstagswahl," *Sächische Bauern-Zeitung* 37, no. 33 (17 Aug. 1930), 338–40, and his letters to Schiele, 24 July and 24 Aug. 1930, SHStA Dresden, NL Philipp, 24.

[69] *Der Landbund im Wahlkampf* (Berlin, n.d. [1930]), BA Koblenz, ZSg 1/E77. See also Müller, "*Fällt der Bauer,*" 185–95.

[70] Reichs-Landbund e.V., *Agrarpolitische Zwischenbilanz. Entwicklung der Lage der Landwirtschaft seit dem Amtsantritt Schieles*, Berlin, 30 July 1930, 1–7. In a similar vein, see *Für Ar und Halm!* (Berlin, n.d. [1930]), as well as "Wahlaufruf zur Reichstagswahl am 14. Sept. 1930," ed. Vorstand und Landesauschuss des Württ. Bauern- und Weingärnterpartei, n.d. [Aug. 1930], NL Hiller, Gärtringen.

[71] *Die Sendung des Landvolkes* (Berlin, n.d. [1930]), 12–18. See also Döbrich, "Christlich-Nationale Bauern- und Landvolkpartei und Neuwahlen," *Thüringer Landbund* 11, nos. 69 (27 Aug. 1930), and 70 (20 Aug. 1929), and Ohm, "Landvolk und Reichstagswahl," *Reichs-Landbund* 10, no. 16 (3 Aug. 1930): 244–45, as well as the campaign speeches by Gereke, "Die Ziele der Landvolkpartei," *Der Landbürger* 5, no. 16 (16 Aug. 1930): 241–42, and Hepp, "Was wird die Landvolkpartei im neuen Reichstag tun?," *Nassauische Bauern-Zeitung*, 30 Aug. 1930, no. 200.

[72] Schwecht to Schiele, 2 Aug. 1930, BA Koblenz, ZSg 1–44/13 (1).

German Peasant Unions, Germany's second largest agricultural interest organization, went to great pains to reaffirm its neutrality with respect to the existing political parties and urged its members to work within those parties to ensure that the interests of German agriculture were well represented in the selection of candidates for the upcoming Reichstag elections.[73] Nor did the CNBLP's appeal for vocational solidarity sit well with the leaders of the German Peasants' Party, who argued that the preponderance of nobility and large landowners in the CNBLP leadership and on its slate of candidates for the upcoming election had left the DBP, as the party of the small and middle-sized peasant, with no alternative but to enter the campaign under its own banner.[74] The logic of vocational solidarity was apparently not as clear to all sectors of the German agricultural community as it was for the leaders of the RLB and CNBLP.

If the agitation of the CNBLP posed a serious threat to the DNVP's prospects in the September 1930 Reichstag elections, the same was no less true in the case of the Christian-Social People's Service.[75] The leaders of the CSVD portrayed their party as "a calming pole of stability" in the midst of the confusion and turmoil that bedeviled Germany's other non-socialist, non-Catholic parties.[76] While recognizing that the German party system was in the midst of a profound structural and spiritual transformation and that all of the parties to the right of the Social Democrats and Center were in an advanced state of internal dissolution, the leaders of the CSVD reserved their sharpest attacks for the DNVP. Not only had Hugenberg and his associates employed methods in their struggle against the CSVD that were unworthy of a supposedly Christian party, but the DNVP had betrayed its crusade against Marxism by voting for the Social Democratic and Communist motion to revoke the Brüning cabinet's presidential emergency powers. The political cynicism and moral bankruptcy that existed at the upper echelons of the DNVP party leadership had left Evangelical Christians, claimed the CSVD, with no alternative but to seek a new political home in the Christian-Social

---

[73] See the two circulars from Hermes, president of the Association of German Peasant Unions, 21 and 29 July, 1930, in Landesarchiv Nordrhein-Westfalen Münster, Archiv des Landschaftsverbandes Westfalen-Lippe (Bestand C113), Bestand B: Restakten der Vereinigung der deutschen Bauernvereine, 103.

[74] Hiltmann to Fehr, 24 July 1930, BHStA Munich, Abt. V, NL Fehr, 30. See also Hillebrand, "Vom alten zum neuen Reichstag," *Die grüne Zukunft. Zeitschrift für deutsche Bauernpolitik* 3, nos. 7–8 (July–Aug. 1930): 81–86.

[75] In this respect, see Hülser, "Die derzeitige Lage des Volksdienstes. Interne Betrachtung für die Reichsleitung," 1 July 1930, BA Berlin, NL Mumm, 333/121–28, as well as Mumm to Hül the leaders of the CSVD ser, 5 July 1930, ibid., 121/19–21. See also Simpfendörfer to party supporters, 19 July 1930, HStA Stuttgart, NL Simpfendörfer. 374.

[76] Hülser, "Umgruppierungen," *Christlicher Volksdienst*, 9 Aug. 1930, no. 32.

People's Service.[77] At the same time, the CSVD dissociated itself as unequivocally as possible from efforts at liberal or bourgeois concentration into an anti-Marxist front as well as from special-interest parties like the Business Party and CNBLP. All of this, the CSVD charged in a campaign leaflet from the pen of Paul Bausch, was but another manifestation of the increasingly pervasive role that material rather than spiritual values had come to play at all levels of German public life.[78] And this, Bausch continued, only underscored the need for a Christian renewal of German political life and for a reaffirmation of Evangelical Christian values as the key to Germany's redemption from the morass into which it had descended.[79]

The success with which the CNBLP and CSVD were able to mobilize the agrarian and Evangelical sectors of the DNVP's national electorate significantly narrowed the field in which the People's Conservatives could operate. Relations between the KVP, CSVD, and CNBLP had been on a positive footing before the campaign and displayed little of the bitterness that generally characterized relations between the different parties on the German Right.[80] But as it became increasingly clear by late July 1930 that the KVP's hopes of reuniting all of those who had broken away from the DNVP into a new conservative party would go unfulfilled, the party became more and more dependent upon Habermann and the German National Union of Commercial Employees for financial and organizational support.[81] The alliance between the KVP and DHV, however, was problematic in two critical respects. In the first place, the DHV was a white-collar union established on the principle of bipartisan neutrality with respect to the individual political parties, a principle that it had taken special pains to reaffirm at its most recent national congress in Cologne on 27–28 June 1930.[82] Second, the prominent role the DHV had played in the founding of the KVP was seen as a blemish, or *Schönheitsfehler*, in the eyes of more traditional conservatives like Westarp who were offended by the new party's ambivalence on the issue of monarchism.[83] Many

---

[77] CSVD, "Der Christlich-soziale Volksdienst und die Hugenberg-Partei," n.d. [Aug.–Sept. 1930], HStA Stuttgart, NL Simpfendörfer. 374.

[78] CSVD, "Die Neugliederung der politischen Fronten in Deutschland," n.d. [Aug.–Sept. 1930], ibid.

[79] CSVD, "Was will der Christlich-soziale Volksdienst?," n.d. [Aug.–Sept. 1930], ibid.

[80] For example, see Lambach to Hülser, Hartwig, Mumm, and seven other CSVD leaders, 17 June 1930, BA Berlin, NL Mumm, 333/89.

[81] Westarp to Wallraf, 28 July 1930, NL Westarp, Gärtringen, VN 5. See also Albert Krebs, "Max Habermann. Eine biographische Studie," FGZ Hamburg, 49.

[82] "22. Verbandstag des Deutschnationalen Handlungsgehilfen-Verbandes am 27. Juni 1930 in Köln," BA Koblenz, NL Lambach, 12, also in *Deutsche Handels-Wacht* 37, no. 13 (15 July 1930): 251–52.

[83] Westarp to Oldenburg-Janaschau, 26 July 1930, NL Westarp, Gärtringen, II/46. See also Alvensleben to Schleicher, 25 July 1930, BA-MA Freiburg, NL Schleicher, 76/20–23.

prominent Catholic conservatives, including the long-time chairman of the DNVP's Reich Catholic Committee Baron Engelbert von Landsberg-Velen and the Würzburg historian Max Buchner who had left the DNVP during the most recent secession, also found it difficult to embrace the new party because of its unclear position on the question of monarchism.[84] Treviranus tried to clarify the KVP's stand on monarchism with an article in the *Berliner Börsen-Courier* in which he argued not only that monarchism was an important, if not indispensable, component of German conservatism but also that a conservative reconstruction of the German state entailed much more than the restoration of the monarchy.[85] Statements like this did little to assuage the concerns of German monarchists and only complicated the KVP's efforts to enlist the support from the ranks of the monarchist movement.[86]

Its various shortcomings notwithstanding, the Conservative People's Party still received massive support from German industry and banking in the campaign for the 1930 Reichstag elections. As Eduard Hamm, a former Democrat who served as executive secretary of the German Chamber of Industry and Commerce, wrote to Reusch on 28 July 1930, the KVP appeared to be a party in which his organization's views on economic policy would find "a not unfriendly reception."[87] Ruhr heavy industry, the Curatorium for the Reconstruction of German Economic Life, and the Berlin banks would funnel substantial sums into the KVP's campaign coffers over the course of the next month and a half in an attempt to provide the conservative moderates who had been driven from the DNVP with a new and reliable political base from which they could continue their work on behalf of the Brüning cabinet. The bulk of these funds ran through Reichert, a former member of the DNVP Reichstag delegation who had served as a liaison between the party and the

---

[84] For Landsberg's resignation, see his letter to Hugenberg, 25 July 1930, VWA Münster, NL Landsberg, II. See also Bucher to Hilpert, 7 Aug. 1930, BA Koblenz, NL Buchner, 13. For indications of Catholic conservative ambivalence toward the KVP, see Landsberg to Westarp, 10 and 15 Aug. 1930, NL Westarp, Gärtringen, VN 10, as well as the correspondence between Landsberg and Buchner, 22–27 Aug. 1930, BA Koblenz, NL Buchner, 66. On Buchner, see Jens Flemming, "'Vollprozentige Katholiken und Deutsche': Max Bucher, die *Gelben Hefte* und der Rechtskatholizismus zwischen Demokratie und Diktatur," in *Le milieu intellectuel catholique en Allemagne, sa presse et ses réseaux (1871–1963)/Das katholische Intellektuellen-Milieu in Deutschland, seine Presse und seine Netzwerke (1871–1963)*, ed. Michael Grunewald and Uwe Puschner (Bern, 2006), 363–94, here 382–87.

[85] Treviranus, "Konservative Volkspartei und Monarchismus," *Berliner Börsen-Courier*, 12 Aug. 1930, no. 372. See also the statement on monarchism in *Konservative Stichworte*, ed. Konservative Volkspartei (Berlin, n.d. [1930]), BA Koblenz, ZSg 1-275/1 (3a).

[86] For example, see Buchner to Guttenberg, 22 Aug. 1930, BA Koblenz, NL Buchner, 51.

[87] Hamm to Reusch, 28 July 1930, RWWA Cologne, Abt. 130, NL Reusch, 40010123/25b. See also Wolfgang Hardtwig, *Freiheitliches Bürgertum in Deutschland. Der Weimarer Demokrat Eduard Hamm zwischen Kaiserreich und Widerstand* (Stuttgart, 2018), 322–33.

Ruhr industrial establishment before leaving it in the summer of 1930.[88] As executive secretary of the Association of German Iron and Steel Industrialists with close ties to Reusch and the Ruhr industrial elite, Reichert joined the KVP, where he campaigned for a Reichstag seat in the district of Magdeburg-Anhalt and served as party treasurer to play an instrumental role in funneling funds to the KVP from his associates in the German business community.[89] Ties between the KVP and the Ruhr industrial establishment were further cemented by the candidacy of Ludwig Grauert, executive secretary of the Employers Association for the Northwestern Branch of German Iron and Steel Industrialists (Arbeitgeberverband für den Bezirk der nordwestlichen Gruppe des Vereins Deutscher Eisen- und Stahlindustrieller or VDESI), in Cologne-Aachen and Koblenz-Trier.[90]

In the meantime, the DNVP was experiencing financial difficulties of its own as funding from erstwhile supporters in Ruhr heavy industry and other sectors of the German industrial establishment began to dry up.[91] Not even the Blohm und Voß Ship Building Firm in Hamburg, a long-time source of funding for Hugenberg and his Pan-German allies, was able to keep up its contributions to the campaign chest of the DNVP's national headquarters in Berlin.[92] By no means, however, were the financial difficulties the DNVP experienced in the 1930 election campaign a unique or isolated incident. All of Germany's non-socialist parties were severely affected by the fact that their former backers in industry, commerce, and finance were reluctant to see their increasingly precious resources squandered in fruitless polemics among the parties they supported. What the German business community expected more than anything else from the parties it supported was an end to their fratricidal polemics and greater solidarity in support of a sweeping reform of Germany's financial and economic policy.[93] From the outset, the "Ruhrlade" had made its support contingent upon a positive commitment to the principle of bourgeois concentration and was willing to support only those parties that demonstrated both in word and deed their willingness to cooperate with each other in

---

[88] For Reichert's reasons, see "Warum fort von Hugenberg? Die Gründe für die Spaltung der Deutschnationalen," n.d., appended to Reichert to Krupp, 8 Sept. 1930, HA Krupp Essen, FAH IV E 962, also in SHI Berlin, NL Siemens, 4 Lf/670.

[89] Reichert to Witzleben, 19 Aug. 1930, SHI Berlin, NL Siemens, 4 Lf/646.

[90] See Ludwig Grauert, *Worum geht es am 14. September?* (N.p., n.d. [1930]).

[91] See Scheibe to Blohm, 14 Aug. 1930, StA Hamburg, Blohm und Voß GmbH, 1223, and Scheibe to Gok, 26 Aug. and 4 Sept. 1930, ibid., 1219.

[92] Blohm to Scheibe, 16 Aug. 1930, StA Hamburg, Blohm und Voß GmbH, 1223. See also Gok to Scheibe, 5 Sept. 1930, ibid., 1219.

[93] See the appeal issued by the RDI presidium, 16 Aug. 1930, BA Koblenz, NL Silverberg, 268/208, as well as the circular from the Bavarian Industrialists' Federation (Bayerischer Industriellen-Verband) to its members, 19 Aug. 1930, RWWA Cologne, Abt. 130, NL Reusch, 400106/104. See also Neebe, *Silverberg*, 67–76.

support of Brüning's reform program.[94] But by the end of August Carl
Friedrich von Siemens and his associates in the Curatorium for the Reconstruction of German Economic Life had become so frustrated with the lack of
movement toward the goal of bourgeois consolidation that they decided not to
collect any new funds and to cease operations after distributing the monies on
hand. According to the formula it used for allocating the funds at its disposal,
the Curatorium allotted 24,000 marks each to the DNVP, KVP, DVP, and
DDP/DStP and 6,000 marks to the Business Party.[95] The Center, which had
been overlooked in the original dispersal of funds, subsequently received two
donations totaling 25,000 marks.[96] But for the Borsig Locomotive Works, a
long-time member of the Curatorium, the situation in which the machine
construction industry found itself was so desperate that it suspended contributions to individual political parties for the duration of the campaign.[97]

All told, the amount of money the Curatorium for the Reconstruction of
German Economic Life allocated in the 1930 campaign was less than half of
what it had given in 1928, and in September 1930 it formally dissolved itself
and suspended solicitations for financial support.[98] The demise of the Curatorium and the general decline in the level of industrial support for the parties
of the middle and moderate Right in the campaign for the 1930 elections were
symptomatic of a more fundamental breakdown in the relationship between
economic interest organizations and the political parties that had traditionally
served as vehicles for the representation of their social and economic interests.
The same was true of the National Rural League and the German National
Union of Commercial Employees, both of which found it increasingly difficult
to work through the existing political parties and now sought a more effective
representation of their vital interests in new political parties like the CNBLP
and KVP respectively. The consequences of this were two-fold. Not only did it
obviously undermine the electoral effectiveness of the large, sociologically
diverse people's parties like the DNVP and DVP, but it left the interest
organizations themselves susceptible to penetration and subversion by the
most radical of the parties on the German Right, the NSDAP.

---

[94] Blank to Reusch, 28 July 1930, RWWA Cologne, Abt. 130, NL Reusch, 4001012024/7. See
also Brandi to Schifferer, 9 Aug. 1930, Landesarchiv Schleswig-Holstein, Schleswig,
Nachlass Anton Schifferer, 27g.

[95] Memorandum on the meeting of the executive committee of the Curatorium for the
Reconstruction of German Economic Life, 28 Aug. 1930, SHI Berlin, NL Siemens, 4/Lf
646. See also Witzleben to Borsig, 1 Sept. 1930, LA Berlin, Zentralverwaltung Borsig
GmbH, 5/24–25.

[96] Correspondence between Siemens and the Center Party's Rudolf ten Hompel, 8–18
Sept. 1930, SHI Berlin, NL Siemens, 4/Lf 670.

[97] Heinrich to Bennigsen, 28 Aug. 1930, LA Berlin, Zentralverwaltung Borsig GmbH, 8/183.

[98] Memorandum by Witzleben, 10 Oct. 1930, SHI Berlin, NL Siemens, 4 Lf/670.

Misreading the Nazi Threat

As the parties of the middle and moderate Right jostled for position in the lead-up to the September 1930 Reichstag elections, those on the radical Right prepared their assault against the Marxist citadel that had been erected on the foundation of Weimar parliamentarism. For the DNVP, the immediate objective of the campaign was to break the political power of the Center in the Reich and Prussia without which the Marxist domination of German political life would not have been possible. As Hugenberg wrote to fellow Pan-German and Essen lord major Theodor Reismann-Grone four days before the election, "For me the reason behind the dissolution of the Reichstag and the election campaign is to crush the insidious policy of the Center [*dem Zentrum seine hinterlistige Politik zu erschlagen*] and to make certain that we no longer continue to fool around in the old ways [*in dem bisherigen Trane weiter dahin dusseln*]."[99] To accomplish this, however, it was first necessary to pulverize the various splinter parties in the middle and moderate Right upon which the influence of the Center ultimately depended. Speaking in the Berlin Sports Palace on 14 August, Hugenberg intoned what was to become the dominant motif of his party's campaign for the September elections when he declared anti-Marxism as the ideological axis around which the German bourgeoisie should unite in its crusade to rescue Germany from collapse. Dismissing those who had turned their backs on the DNVP as "marionettes of the Center," Hugenberg held the Center and its habit of alternating coalitions first with the Left and then with the Right responsible for the Marxist hold on German political life. By implication, it was only through the ruthless destruction of the smaller parties to the left of the DNVP that the Center's political leverage could be broken. Calling for the consolidation of the German bourgeoisie into "an anti-Marxist freedom front" under strong and resolute leadership, Hugenberg invoked the maxim of the famed military strategist Count Alfred von Schlieffen: "Make my right wing strong!"[100]

In its efforts to polarize the German party system into two mutually antagonistic camps, one Marxist and the other nationalist, the DNVP

---

[99] Hugenberg to Reismann-Grone, 10 Sept. 1930, Stadtarchiv Essen, Nachlass Theodor Reismann-Grone, 12.

[100] "Was will die Deutschnationale Volkspartei? Die Rede Dr. Hugenbergs im Berliner Sportpalast am 14. August 1930," StA Hamburg, Blohm und Voß GmbH, 1221, also in *Unsere Partei* 8, no. 16 (15 Aug. 1930): 197–201. In a similar vein, see Hilpert, "Klarheit und Entschlossenheit," n.d. [Aug.–Sept. 1930], BHStA Munich, Abt. V, Flugblätter-Sammlung, 60/1930. For further evidence of DNVP hostility toward the Center, see Reinhard G. Quaatz, *Die politische Entwicklung der letzten Jahre. Rede auf der Schulungstagung am 7. August 1930 in Berlin*, Deutschnationale Flugschrift, no. 346 (Berlin, n.d. [1930]).

targeted the various parties that stood between the DNVP and Social Democracy for annihilation. The DNVP was especially dismissive in its treatment of the Conservative People's Party, which, with support from the arch-reactionary Central Association of German Conservatives, it attacked as a mockery of the true and tried principles of German conservatism that had laid a false claim to the word "conservative" in a ploy to deceive the German electorate.[101] The DNVP employed a more subtle approach in its propaganda against the Christian-National Peasant and Farmers' Party. Not only did the Nationalists claim credit for the enactment of Brüning's farm program, but they insisted that the effectiveness of the government's farm program had been undercut by the chancellor's refusal to break with the Social Democrats.[102] In supporting the Brüning cabinet, therefore, the CNBLP was only perpetuating the stranglehold the Marxist Left held over the conduct of national policy. It was not until those who had left the DNVP had returned to the fold, argued Hugenberg and his associates, that it would be possible to break this stranglehold and provide the German farmer the help he so desperately needed.[103] But Hugenberg and the DNVP reserved their strongest venom for the Christian-Social People's Service. Not only did the DNVP take issue with the CSVD's claim that it was not a political but a religious movement, but it directly challenged the theological assumptions about the state and political authority that lay at the heart of the CSVD's Christian *Weltanschauung*. In particular, the DNVP disputed the emphasis the Christian-Socials placed upon the Christian's responsibility to act according to the dictates of conscience in all matters political as an affront to the majesty of God as the source of all political authority.[104] On a more mundane level, the DNVP contested the CSVD's depiction of Hugenberg and his associates as plutocrats whose easy access to money had corrupted the moral fiber of German political life and accused the CSVD not only of fostering a fratricidal war among Evangelical Christians but also of complicity in implementing the tax policies of the Brüning cabinet. Its protestations

---

[101] "Wer ist konservativ?," n.d. [Aug. 1930], Flugblatt no. 558, reprinted in *Unsere Partei* 5, Wahlkampf-Sondernummer 2 (6 Aug. 1930): 184. See also Richthofen-Mertschütz, "Die Konservativen und die neue 'Konservative Volkspartei'," ibid., 5, Wahlkampf-Sondernummer 3 (22 Aug. 1930): 220–21.

[102] "Das Kabinett Brüning und die deutsche Bauernnot," n.d. [Aug. 1930], Flugblatt no. 545, NL Hiller, Gärtringen.

[103] *Landvolkpartei*, Deutschnationales Rüstzeug, no. 25 (Berlin, 1930), esp. 8–9. See also Hilpert, "Macht den rechten Flügel stark! Ein Appell an das Landvolk," n.d. [Aug.–Sept. 1930], BHStA Munich, Abt. V, Flugblätter-Sammlung, 60/1930.

[104] *Die religiösen Grundanschauungen des Christlich-Sozialen Volksdienstes. Herrschaft Gottes oder Herrschaft des "Christlichen Gewissens"?*, ed. Vorstand des Evangelischen Reichsausschusses der Deutschnationalen Volkspartei (Berlin, n.d. [1930]).

to the contrary, the CSVD was a political party no different from all the others that dotted Germany's political landscape.[105]

For all of the fury the DNVP directed against the parties of the middle and moderate Right, Hugenberg and his associates took relatively little notice of its erstwhile ally and incipient rival, the National Socialist German Workers' Party. Of all the pamphlets, leaflets, and handbills the DNVP's national party headquarters in Berlin circulated during the campaign, only one dealt directly with the NSDAP.[106] What this suggests is that Hugenberg and the DNVP party leadership still viewed the NSDAP as a prospective ally in the struggle against Weimar democracy and wished to avoid a further strain in their party's relationship with the NSDAP despite their growing distrust of Nazi motives and tactics.[107] The NSDAP, on the other hand, had shown much less restraint in its polemics against the DNVP ever since Hitler had resigned from the National Committee for the German Referendum in early April 1930.[108] In the campaign guidelines the Reich Propaganda Leadership (Reichspropagandaleitung or RPL) of the NSDAP issued to the party's district and local organizations on 23 July, it conceded that, of the four groups that had formerly made up the DNVP, the one around Hugenberg was by far the most reliable in the struggle against Weimar parliamentarism and the legacy of Versailles. At the same time, however, RPL guidelines drew attention to the thoroughly reactionary and capitalistic character of Hugenberg's rump party and dismissed it as a force with no future in the revolutionary transformation of the German state for which the National Socialists were striving. Although the guidelines discouraged personal attacks against Hugenberg and his entourage, it stressed that ideological differences between the NSDAP and the Hugenberg faction should be highlighted as much as possible. The other three factions that had emerged from the ruins of the DNVP were anathema to the aspirations of the Nazi movement and should receive no mercy in the NSDAP's assault upon the remnants of the hated Weimar system.[109]

---

[105] For example, see Agnes Riesner (WBP), "Deutschnationale und Christlicher Volksdienst," n.d. [Sept. 1930], and Johanna Beringer (DNVP Stuttgart), "Offener Brief an Herrn Rechnungsrat Bausch, Korntal," n.d. [Sept. 1930], HStA Stuttgart, NL Simpfendörfer. 374.

[106] For an overview of DNVP's campaign literature in the 1930 elections, see *Unsere Partei* 8, Wahlkampf-Sondernummer 3 (22 Aug. 1930): 231–32, and 8, no. 17 (1 Sept. 1930): 248. For the lone exception, see *Wir und die Nationalsozialisten*, Vortragsentwurf, no. 14 (Berlin, n.d. [1930]), BA Koblenz, ZSg 1–44/18 (8).

[107] For example, see Hugenberg to Hitler, 4 and 11 Apr. 1930, BA Koblenz, NL Schmidt-Hannover, 30.

[108] Hitler, "Prinzip und Taktik. Zur Krise der Deutschnationalen Volkspartei," *Völkischer Beobachter*, 9 Apr. 1930, no. 83.

[109] Reichspropagandaleiter, Ausserordentliches Rundschreiben der Reichspropagandaleitung zur Vorbereitung des Wahlkampfes zur Reichstagswahl am 14. Sept. 1930, 23 July 1930, BA Koblenz, Nachlass Julius Streicher, 24. See also Goebbels, "Das patriotische

The lack of attention the DNVP devoted to the NSDAP was a strategic oversight of enormous proportions. Among other things, the DNVP seemed oblivious to the fact that following its dismal showing in the 1928 Reichstag elections the NSDAP had developed the most elaborate and sophisticated party organization in all of Germany.[110] The architect of the Nazi party organization was Gregor Strasser, who in 1928 had been appointed Reich Organization Leader (Reichsorganisationsleiter) of the NSDAP to develop a comprehensive and effective party organization that would make it possible for Goebbels and his co-workers to carry their propaganda message to all corners of the Reich. Strasser's organizational reforms were in place well before the onset of the Great Depression and left the NSDAP well positioned to exploit the distress the deepening economic crisis had produced within Germany's urban and rural middle classes.[111] The result of all this was a dramatic breakthrough into the ranks of the German middle classes and a string of victories at the state and local level beginning with the Saxon Landtag elections in May 1929, when the NSDAP polled 4.9 percent of the popular vote and elected five deputies to the new state parliament. This scenario would repeat itself in Baden five months later when the NSDAP, possibly benefiting from its alliance with the DNVP and other right-wing organizations in the campaign against the Young Plan, received 7.0 percent of the popular vote and elected six deputies to the Baden state parliament. Then, in the Thuringian state elections of December 1929 the NSDAP increased its share of the popular vote to 11.3 percent and sent six deputies to the state parliament. The NSDAP's greatest success would come in Saxony, where new state elections in June 1930 provided Hitler and his followers with 14.4 percent of the popular vote and fourteen deputies in the Saxon Landtag. There can be little doubt that the NSDAP was well on its way to achieving a full-scale breakthrough into the ranks of Germany's middle-class electorate before the full effect of the Great Depression would make itself felt.[112] All of this underscored the DNVP's folly in not taking the challenge of Nazism and the danger that the NSDAP posed to its own electoral base more seriously than it did.

Bürgertum," *Nationalsozialistische Monatshefte* 1, no. 5 (Aug. 1930): 221–29. For further details, see David A. Hackett, "The Nazi Party in the Reichstag Election of 1930" (Ph.D. diss., University of Wisconsin, 1971), 195–331, and Childers, *Nazi Voter*, 137–42.

[110] For an overview of the Nazi party organization, see "Die Organisation der N.S.D.A.P.," *Nationalsozialistische Monatshefte* 1, no. 1 (Apr. 1930): 35–46.

[111] For further details, see Udo Kissenkoetter, *Gregor Straßer und die NSDAP* (Stuttgart, 1978), 48–54, and Peter Stachura, *Gregor Strasser and the Rise of Nazism* (London, 1983), 67–73, as well Dietrich J. Orlow, *The History of the Nazi Party, 1919-1933* (Pittsburgh, PA, n.d. [1969]), 128–84, and Wolfgang Horn, *Führerideologie und Parteiorganisation in der NSDAP (1919-1933)* (Düsseldorf, 1972), 278–327.

[112] Childers, *Nazi Voter*, 119–91.

Figure 16. NSDAP campaign placard designed by an unidentified graphic artist for the September 1930 Reichstag elections. Reproduced with permission from the Bundesarchiv Berlin, Plakat 002-039-025

The Nazi success in the various state and local elections in late 1929 and early 1930 stemmed in no small measure from its ability to penetrate and mobilize important sectors of Germany's conservative Protestant milieu.[113] The key to this success lay in the NSDAP's ability to co-opt the support of four key groups that played a critical role in influencing the voting patterns of Germany's rural population: the large peasant or *Großbauer*, the manor lord or *Gutsherr*, the country parson, and the village school teacher. Not only did the support the NSDAP received from these groups help validate it as a legitimate claimant to the political loyalties of Germany's rural voters, but it afforded the Nazis easy access to the influence that rural elites traditionally exercised over the political and electoral behavior of Germany's conservative milieu.[114] Whereas the DNVP was slow to recognize the threat that this posed to its standing in the German countryside and responded with a defense of its position that was lukewarm at best, the various parties that had drifted away from the DNVP during the second half of the 1920s took the threat of Nazi radicalism far more seriously and mounted fierce counterattacks of their own. This was particularly true in the case of the Christian-Social People's Service, which took direct aim at the enthusiasm with which increasingly large sectors of Germany's Protestant population had embraced National Socialism by challenging the NSDAP's Christian credentials in a widely circulated handbill entitled "Hakenkreuz oder Christenkreuz?" Specifically, the CSVD denounced the NSDAP for its "anti-Christian glorification and absolutization [Verabso-lutierung] of race," for equating the love of God with the love of nation, for propagating "an excessive, un-Christian hatred of Jews," and for presenting National Socialism as a surrogate religion divorced from the moral content of the Christian faith. For the leaders of the CSVD, any compromise between Christianity and National Socialism, between Cross and Swastika, was inconceivable.[115]

Few of Germany's non-socialist parties, particularly as early as 1930, were as outspoken in their rejection of Nazism as the Christian-Social People's Service. Only the Center, which like the CSVD defined itself as a Christian party, took the challenge of Nazism as seriously. For Kaas and Brüning, the real challenge facing the Center was not just to position itself as well as possible for the upcoming election, but to lay the foundation for the consolidation, or

[113] Wolfram Pyta, "Politische Kultur und Wahlen in der Weimarer Republik," in *Wahlen und Wahlkämpfe in Deutschland. Von den Anfängen im 19. Jahrhundert bis zur Bundesrepublic*, ed. Gerhard A. Ritter (Düsseldorf, 1997), 197–239, esp. 229–39.
[114] For further details, see Pyta, *Dorfgemeinschaft und Parteipolitik*, 324–471.
[115] Christlicher Volksdienst Korntal, "Hakenkreuz oder Christenkreuz? Eine ernste Frage an die evangelische Christenheit," [Aug.–Sept. 1930], HStA Stuttgart, NL Simpfendörfer, 374. See also Paul Bausch, *Lebenserinnerungen und Erkenntnisse eines schwäbischen Abgeordneten* (Korntal, n.d. [1969]), 313–14.

Sammlung, of all those elements that were prepared to cooperate with each other in support of Brüning's program for Germany's fiscal and economic recovery.[116] In its campaign propaganda, the Center portrayed Brüning in almost heroic terms as the last line of defense against radicalism and party dictatorship.[117] At the same time, the Center denounced the NSDAP as a revolutionary party whose commitment to the violent overthrow of the existing social, economic, and political order would only lead Germany deeper and deeper into chaos.[118] Special-interest parties like the CNBLP and WP, on the other hand, articulated their attacks against the NSDAP in the language of economic self-interest. For the CNBLP it was a question of whether the interests of the German farmer could be best served by a party that preached the gospel of social revolution and threatened to plunge all of Germany into political and economic chaos or by a party that had placed itself unconditionally behind the reform program of the Brüning-Schiele cabinet.[119] For the Business Party, it was a question of whether the NSDAP as party that relied more on demagogy than reason was genuinely committed to the welfare of Germany's middle-class electorate.[120] In both parties, however, the confrontation with National Socialism took second place to the struggle against Marxism, which from the perspective of all parties to the right of the Center represented the most palpable threat to Germany's propertied classes.[121] The preoccupation with the threat that Marxism presumably posed to the

---

[116] Speech by Kaas at the information conference of the executive committee of the German Center Party, 27 July 1930, ACDP Sankt Augustin, VI-051, 280/1–3.

[117] *Mit Brüning gegen Radikalismus und Parteiherrschaft für Wahrheit und Verantwortung* (Cologne, n.d. [1930]).

[118] For example, see *Die NSDAP als Umsturzpartei* (Berlin, n.d. [1930]), 14–24, and *Der Nationalsozialismus. Der Weg ins Chaos*, ed. Reichsgeneralsekretariat der Deutschen Zentrumspartei (Berlin, n.d. [1930]), esp. 6–7, as well as "Der Nationalsozialismus. Entwicklung, Grundlagen, Organisation und Arbeitsmethoden der N.S.D.A.P.," *Das Zentrum* 1, nos. 7–8 (July–Aug. 1930): 219–38.

[119] *Die Sendung des Landvolkes* (Berlin, n.d. [1930]), 12–18. In a similar vein, see Theodor Körner-Herrenburg, "Bauernbund und Nationalsozialisten," ed. Württembergischer Bauern- und Weingärtnerbund, Flugblatt no. 16, NL Hiller, Gärtringen, and "Warum Nationalsozialist?," *Thüringer Landbund* 11, no. 70 (30 Aug. 1930): 1, as well as Hepp's remarks in a debate with the NSDAP's Willy Seipel in Aumenau, 5 Sept. 1930, in *Nassauische Bauern-Zeitung*, 7 Sept. 1930, no. 207.

[120] H. A. Hömberg, *Hitlerpartei oder Wirtschaftspartei – Phrase oder Vernunft?* (Recklinghausen, n.d. [1930]). See also *Unsere Arbeit und unsere Gegner. 1930 Wahlhandbuch der Reichspartei des deutschen Mittelstandes (Wirtschaftspartei)* (Berlin, n.d. 1930), 123–29.

[121] For example, see Willy Ohm, *Der Schicksalsruf: Bauern, an die Front!* (Berlin, n.d. [1930]), 4–7. In this same context, see Theodor Körner alt, "Der 'Marxismus' und der 'Christliche Volksdienst.' Eine Entgegnung auf die Landtagsrede des Abgeordneten Bausch," ed. Württembergischer Bauern- und Weingärtnerbund, Flugblatt no. 15, NL Hiller, Gärtringen.

bourgeois social and political order only obscured the real danger of National Socialism and left the parties between the Center and NSDAP more vulnerable to Nazi penetration than might otherwise have been the case.

The Nazi Breakthrough

While Germany's non-socialist parties generally tended to minimize the threat that Nazism posed to their prospects in the 1930 Reichstag elections, the Nazi campaign was reaching a crescendo of its own. Between 18 August and 14 September the NSDAP held more than 30,000 separate demonstrations in every corner of the Reich.[122] In the last ten days before the elections Hitler addressed large and enthusiastic crowds in Königsberg, Hamburg, Nuremburg, Augsburg, Berlin, Breslau, and finally in Munich on the last day of the campaign.[123] A recurrent motif in all of Hitler's speeches from the last week of the campaign was the political fragmentation of the German electorate and the failure of the existing political parties to forge the unity that a badly divided German nation needed to survive the increasingly desperate situation in which it found itself. Speaking on 6 September before an estimated 10,000 supporters in Hamburg, Hitler deplored the deep cleavage that had developed within the German people between "bourgeois nationalism" and "Marxist socialism." Neither the nationalist nor the socialist camp, Hitler continued, had succeeded in forging the unity Germany so desperately needed. It was only by healing the cleavage between nationalism and socialism in the spirit of the two million German soldiers who had fallen in the battlefields of the Great War could the fragmentation of the German nation be ended and the unity of the German nation at long last restored.[124] Hitler returned to this theme on the following day in a speech before 15,000 followers in Nuremburg: "Nationalism and socialism must become one [*zu einer Einheit werden*]!"[125] This was invariably combined with a stinging indictment of the existing political parties for having placed their own salvation before that of the nation. Dismissing the old parliamentary parties as "rotten and fragile [*morsch und faul*]," Hitler demanded their elimination as an essential prerequisite for the rebirth of the German nation.[126] This was something that neither the Marxist Left nor the bourgeois Right could accomplish. Both, Hitler claimed before an enthusiastic crowd of 16,000 in the Berlin Sports Palace on 10 September, had become hostage to the rhetoric of economic self-interest and were incapable of

---

[122] Hackett, "Nazi Party in the Election of 1930," 224.
[123] For the content of these speeches, see Hitler, *Reden, Schriften, Anordnungen*, vol. 3, part 3, 382–83, 384–94, 408–18.
[124] Hitler, speech in Hamburg, 6 Sept. 1930, ibid., 384–86.
[125] Hitler, speech in Nuremburg, 7 Sept. 1930, ibid., 387–90, here 388.
[126] Hitler, speech in Augsburg, 8 Sept. 1930, ibid., 390–94, here 393.

articulating a sense of national unity that transcended the cleavages of class, confession, and region.[127] It was precisely therein, Hitler reiterated in one speech after another, that the historic mission of the NSDAP lay.

What Hitler and the leaders of the NSDAP articulated was a sense of national unity so powerful in terms of its emotional appeal that it overrode more traditional patterns of voting behavior based upon the pursuit of economic self-interest. The appeal of National Socialism lay not merely in the fact that it had identified itself with the material welfare of the German middle classes but, more importantly, that it had done this not as an interest party but as a *Sammelpartei* dedicated to the welfare of the German nation as a whole. All of this was reinforced by the personal charisma that Hitler had nurtured ever since his start in politics in the immediate postwar period. The effect of Hitler's charisma was to disrupt and eventually override patterns of behavior based on tradition or the rational subordination of means to ends. The force of Hitler's charisma was only enhanced by the confluence of economic crisis and political paralysis as his party mobilized the support of those who had abandoned hope in the existing political system with promises of salvation through the agency of a great leader who stood above all of the conflicts real or imagined that were ripping apart the fabric of the German nation.[128]

The net effect of this was a dramatic breakthrough into the ranks of the German middle classes and a victory of unexpected proportions. When the votes were finally tallied, the NSDAP had polled approximately 6.4 million votes – or 18.3 percent of the total popular vote – and elected 107 deputies to the Reichstag. Suddenly a party that had received scarcely 2 percent of the popular vote in 1928 and held no more than mere twelve seats in the national parliament had catapulted itself to the center of the political stage as the second largest party in the Reichstag. Of the more established non-socialist parties, only the Center and Bavarian People's Party managed to hold their own in the face of the Nazi onslaught. The two liberal parties, by comparison, saw their share of the national vote plummet from 13.5 percent in May 1928 to 8.4 percent in 1930. Not even the DDP's alliance with the Young German Order and its rebaptism as the German State Party could shield it from losses

---

[127] Hitler, speech in Berlin, 10 Sept. 1930, ibid., 408–12.

[128] On Hitler's charisma and the creation of the Hitler myth, see M. Rainer Lepsius, "The Model of Charismatic Leadership and Its Applicability to the Rise of Adolf Hitler," *Totalitarian Movements and Politics Religions* 7 (2006): 175–90, and Ludolf Herbst, *Hitlers Charisma und die Erfindung eines deutschen Messias* (Frankfurt a.m. Main, 2010). On the messianic impulse in the late Weimar Republic, see Klaus Schreiner, "'Wann kommt der Retter Deutschlands?' Formen und Funtionen von politischem Messianismus in der Weimarer Republik," *Saeculum* 49 (1998): 107–60, and Thomas Mergel, "Volksgemeinschaft und Maschine. Politische Erwartungsstrukturen in der Weimarer Republik und der Nationalsozialismus 1918–1936," in *Politische Kulturgeschichte der Zwischenkriegszeiten 1928–1939*, ed. Wolfgang Hardtwig (Göttingen, 2005), 91–127.

that amounted to approximately a fifth of the votes the DDP had received in 1928. But the heaviest losses of all were sustained by the DNVP, which lost nearly two million of the 4.4 million votes it had received in 1928 and saw its share of the popular vote plunge from 14.2 in 1928 to 7.0 percent two years later. Of the splinter parties that had broken away from the DNVP's left wing, the CNBLP improved upon its performance in the 1928 elections by over a half million votes with 3.2 percent of the total popular vote and twenty-two deputies in the Reichstag, whereas the CSVD received over 860,000 votes for 2.5 percent of the popular vote and elected fourteen deputies to the Reichstag in its national electoral debut. The Conservative People's Party, by contrast, went down to a devastating defeat, polling slightly less than 315,000 votes and electing only four deputies to the Reichstag.[129]

The NSDAP's gains in the 1930 Reichstag elections came almost exclusively at the expense of the DNVP and the parties of the middle and moderate Right. The party appealed across class and vocational lines to diverse sectors of the German electorate as what Thomas Childers has called "a catch-all party of protest whose constituents were united by a vehement rejection of an increasingly threatened present."[130] The NSDAP drew its greatest strength from the predominantly Protestant areas in the northern and eastern parts of Germany where it was able to capitalize upon the distress of the local peasantry and other groups that were dependent upon the vitality of the rural economy. In Schleswig-Holstein, where it had experienced its first successes in 1928, the NSDAP received 27.0 percent of all votes cast, while to the east of the Elbe in one-time DNVP strongholds such as East Prussia, Pomerania, Breslau, and Frankfurt an der Oder the NSDAP consistently polled more than 20 percent of all eligible votes. The party also did well in predominantly Protestant Franconia and Hesse-Nassau, where it received 20.5 and 20.8 percent of the popular vote respectively. In predominantly Catholic areas or in districts with large working-class populations, on the other hand, the NSDAP's performance at the polls lagged significantly behind its national average.[131] The Nazis also benefited from the fact that voter participation in the 1930 election was

---

[129] Alfred Milatz, "Das Ende der Parteien im Spiegel der Wahlen 1930 bis 1933," in *Das Ende der Parteien 1933*, ed. Erich Matthias and Rudolf Morsey (Düsseldorf, 1960), 743–93, here 744–58. See also Hackett, "Nazi Party in the Election of 1930," 332–58.

[130] Thomas Childers, "The Social Bases of the National Socialist Vote," *Journal of Contemporary History* 11 (1976): 17–42, here 31.

[131] For a regional, confessional, and class breakdown of the Nazi vote in the 1930 elections, see John O'Loughlin, Colin Flint, and Luc Anselin, "The Geography of the Nazi Vote: Context, Confession, and Class in the Reichstag Election of 1930," *Annals of the Association of American Geographers* 84 (1994): 351–80. See also Jürgen W. Falter and Reinhard Zintl, "The Economic Crisis of the 1930s and the Nazi Vote," *Journal of Interdisciplinary History* 19 (1988): 55–83. On the social and geographical composition of the Nazi electorate, see Falter, *Hitlers Wähler* (Munich, 1991), 30–34, 101–25.

significantly higher than at any time since the 1919 elections to the National Assembly. Over 4.2 million more voters went to the polls in 1930 than in 1928 as the percentage of the eligible electorate that voted increased from 74.6 to 81.4 percent between 1928 and 1930. The success with which the Nazis were able to mobilize the support of new voters as well as that of voters who had abstained from voting in previous national elections contributed in no small measure to the party's dramatic victory at the polls in the 1930 elections.[132]

The magnitude of the Nazi victory on 14 September 1930 sent shock waves through the ranks of the German Right. In this respect, three factors were particularly relevant. The first was the defeat of the DNVP, which no matter how Hugenberg might try to sugarcoat his party's performance at the polls returned to the Reichstag with only forty-four of the seventy Reichstag seats it had held in 1928. As much satisfaction as Hugenberg's opponents might take from his party's setback at the polls, the fact remained that the parties on the moderate Right had failed to establish themselves as a viable political force. This, in turn, severely limited the political options that were available to the Brüning cabinet. Brüning and his supporters had hoped that the parties of the middle and moderate Right would be able to coalesce into a solid phalanx of support that would make him less dependent upon the toleration of either the Social Democrats or the radical Right. This was clearly not the case. All of this left the leaders of the German Right with a situation radically different from the one that had existed before the election. Although the collapse of Germany's parliamentary democracy had created unprecedented opportunities for the German Right, it remained deeply divided as to how these opportunities were to be exploited.

---

[132] Jürgen W. Falter, "The National Socialist Mobilisation of New Voters: 1928–1933," in *The Formation of the Nazi Constituency, 1919–1933*, ed. Thomas Childers (Totowa, NJ, 1986), 202–31.

~

Epilogue

The Price of Disunity

The 1930 Reichstag elections represented a major and ultimately irreversible turning point in the history of the German Right. At no point in the history of the Weimar Republic had the splintering of the German Right and its disastrous consequences become more apparent than in the outcome of the September 1930 elections. Neither the DNVP nor any of the splinter parties that had emerged on the moderate Right since the middle of the 1920s had succeeded in establishing itself as the crystallization point around which all of those who were opposed to the Weimar state and sought to replace it with a more authoritarian order of one sort or another could coalesce. The situation in which the more traditional elements of the German Right found themselves was further complicated by the unexpectedly strong performance of the NSDAP. The NSDAP's exact relationship to the German Right was always ambiguous. From the perspective of many of those on the German Right, the NSDAP did not belong to the Right as such but was a revolutionary force that rejected the existing social and economic order in favor of socialist schemes that were scarcely discernible from those of the Marxist Left.[1] What the more traditional elements of the German Right shared with the NSDAP was deep-seated animosity toward the system of government that Germany had inherited from the November Revolution and a commitment to returning Germany to great power status by breaking the chains of Versailles in a powerful and vigorous assertion of the rights to which Germany had been denied by the victors of World War I. But whether or not this would be sufficient to overcome the deep-seated apprehension that influential elements on the German Right felt with respect to Nazi radicalism on social and economic question was far from clear.

The magnitude of Nazi gains in the 1930 Reichstag elections sent shock waves throughout Germany's conservative establishment. Just how the more

---

[1] For example, see Anton Scheibe, *DNVP und NSDAP. Was uns einigt und was uns trennt*, Deutschnationale Flugschrift, no. 307 (Berlin, 1932), and Irmgard Wrede, *Deutschnationale und Nationalsozialisten. Die Unterschiede auf wirtschafts- und sozialpolitischem Gebiete. Vortrag, gehalten am 12. Juni 1932 auf der Tagung des Erweiterten Reichsfrauenausschusses* (Berlin, Deutschnationale Flugschrift, no. 365 (Berlin, 1932).

traditional elements of the German dmost important single question that its leaders would have to face. It was to this question that Westarp, the parliamentary leader of the small People's Conservative faction in the newly elected Reichstag, turned his attention in a lead arti3cle entitled "Was nun?" for his party's official organ, the *Volkskonservative Stimmen*. Here Westarp urged Brüning to initiate negotiations with the National Socialists in an attempt to determine if they were prepared to abandon their obstructionist tactics and make a positive contribution to the solution of the myriad problems that confronted the German nation. Specifically, Westarp hoped that the National Socialists could be persuaded to join the Center and the other parties between the DNVP and Social Democrats in supporting Brüning's reform program. Not only would this provide a way out of the impasse in which Germany's parliamentary system found itself as a result of the most recent national elections, but it also offered the only possibility of separating the Center from the Social Democrats in Prussia and making possible the long-awaited realignment of the Center with the forces of the German Right. More importantly, it would determine whether Hitler and the NSDAP were indeed prepared to accept the mantle of responsibility that their recent victory at the polls had bestowed upon them and wrest leadership of a badly divided German Right from Hugenberg and his minions in control of the DNVP. As Westarp himself expressed it: "In all seriousness, it will now be incumbent upon [the National Socialists] to show proof whether they, with their new strength so surprisingly won at the polls, will find the will and ability to accept a responsible role in the conduct of foreign and domestic affairs."[2]

Westarp's article contained the germ of what would come to be known as "the taming strategy" for dealing with the challenge of National Socialism. The essential premise of this strategy was that bringing the National Socialists into the government would deprive them of the advantages they enjoyed as an opposition party and force them to accept a responsible role in the solution of the problems that faced the German nation. This, in turn, would transform the Nazi movement with all of its energy and dynamism from a revolutionary force that threatened the established social and economic order into a force of stability that could be mobilized in support of a conservative agenda for the reorganization of the German state.[3] This strategy was quickly embraced by the leaders of the German business community. While a handful of prominent German businessmen and industrialists openly sympathized with the program and aspirations of the Nazi movement, most were deeply suspicious of the NSDAP's social and economic programs and would have countenanced the

---

[2] Westarp, "Was nun?," *Volkskonservative Stimmen*, 20 Sept. 1930, no. 36. See also Westarp to Fumetti, 20 Sept. 1930, NL Westarp, Gärtingen, II/40.

[3] For further details, see Gotthard Jasper, *Die gescheiterte Zähmung. Wege zur Machtergreifung Hitlers 1930–1934* (Frankfurt a.M., 1986).

party's entry into the national government only if it was accompanied by guarantees that effectively limited its potential for social and economic mischief. More importantly, industry's plans for "taming the NSDAP" always assumed that the Nazis would not be the dominant force within the governmental coalition but subject to control by their more conservative coalition allies.[4] But the strongest and most persistent advocacy of the taming strategy came not from the ranks of Germany's economic elites but from the German military. Here the key figure was the Reichswehr's enigmatic political strategist and architect of the Brüning cabinet, Kurt von Schleicher. After the NSDAP's dramatic breakthrough in the 1930 Reichstag elections, Schleicher and his associates felt that they could no longer afford to dismiss Hitler as a political incompetent and began to formulate the general outlines of a strategy for containing the threat that he and his movement posed. Like Westarp and Germany's industrial leadership, Schleicher believed not only that the radicalism of the Nazi movement could be mitigated by saddling it with political responsibility but also that this would oblige Hitler and his party to moderate the tone and intensity of their rhetoric against the government. At the same time, bringing the Nazis into the government would provide Germany's conservative elites with the mantle of popular legitimacy they needed to carry out a fundamental revision of Germany's constitutional system, a revision that had already begun under Hindenburg's aegis with Brüning's appointment as chancellor in March 1930.[5]

An indispensable prerequisite for the success of the taming strategy that Schleicher and the leaders of the German business community devised for containing the threat of Nazism was a large, well-established conservative party sufficiently powerful to contain the Nazi movement and subordinate it to the agenda of Germany's conservative elites. The fact of the matter, however, was that by the fall of 1930 no such party in Germany existed. The chronic and unmitigated disintegration of the German National People's Party since 1924 had left it so weak that by 1930 it was no longer in a position to contain the incomparably more dynamic National Socialist German Workers' Party despite Hugenberg's assertion that he and not Hitler was the leader of the national movement. To be sure, there had been moments in the earlier history of the DNVP when it appeared on the verge of developing into the kind of party that would have been necessary to contain the NSDAP. As early

---

[4] For example, see August Heinrichsbauer, *Schwerindustrie und Politik* (Essen-Kettwig, 1948), 40–42. See also, Henry A. Turner, *German Big Business and the Rise of Hitler* (New York and Oxford, 1985), 313–39.

[5] For further details, see Larry Eugene Jones, "Taming the Nazi Beast: Kurt von Schleicher and the End of the Weimar Republic," in *From Weimar to Hitler: Studies in the Dissolution of the Weimar Republic and the Establishment of the Third Reich*, ed. Hermann Beck and Larry Eugene Jones (New York and Oxford, 2018), 23–51.

as the fall of 1918 there had been a concerted attempt by progressive-minded young conservatives under the leadership of Ulrich von Hassell to fashion an entirely new kind of conservative party that was unburdened by the follies of the past and tailored to the exigencies of the democratic age. But this effort encountered strong resistance from old-line conservatives like Westarp and been effectively muted by the time the DNVP formally adopted its new party program in April 1920. Though symbolically important, the secession of the Free Conservatives around Siegfried von Kardorff and Johann Victor Bredt had little impact on the DNVP's efforts to transform itself into a sociologically heterogeneous people's party that reflected the social, economic, and confessional diversity of the German people. Fueled by the runaway inflation of the early 1920's and the national uproar over the imposition of the London Ultimatum and the transfer of large sections of Upper Silesia to Poland, this process drew to a preliminary climax at the DNVP's Munich party congress in September 1921. Highlighted by the defection of the Center's Martin Spahn in what was a calculated effort to woo the support of right-wing Catholics disillusioned by the Center's embrace of the Weimar Republic, the Munich party congress testified to just how far German conservatism had come since the outbreak of World War I in transforming itself from an instrument of feudal self-interest into an expression of the popular will.

The first real blip on this trajectory occurred with the racist crisis and the subsequent secession of the leaders of the DNVP's racist wing in the summer and fall of 1922. But party leaders – most notably DNVP party chairman Oskar Hergt, Karl Helfferich and Westarp – were able to negotiate this crisis with great aplomb and minimize its damage on the party organization as a whole. The irony of the situation was that despite the racist secession in September–October 1922 racism and antisemitism were to become an even more prominent feature of the DNVP's public profile over the course of the next year and a half. With the continued collapse of the German mark, the Franco-Belgian occupation of the Ruhr, and the resurgence of the Communist threat in the summer and fall of 1923, the DNVP experienced little difficult in establishing itself as *the* party of national opposition to the Weimar system and all that supposedly represented. With a steady dose of antisemitism to underpin its appeal to the anxiety of all those who had been victimized by the great inflation, the DNVP scored a sensational victory in the 1924 Reichstag elections that fully vindicated all the time, energy, and money that had gone into the creation of a truly comprehensive party organization. But now the DNVP suddenly found itself confronted with a host of new problems. For with success comes responsibility. As the largest of Germany's non-socialist parties, the DNVP faced the challenge of transforming itself from a party that had flourished in opposition to one that would have to accept responsibility as a member of a coalition government that included other political parties. Among other things, this meant that the party would have to mute the antisemitism that had played such an essential role in its victory in the May elections so that it could present itself as a credible candidate for a role in the national government. The challenge here was to make the transition from an opposition to a government party without alienating those elements whose opposition to the Weimar Republic had made its success at the polls possible in the first place. Or in the words of DNVP moderate Hans Erdmann von Lindeiner-Wildau, could the DNVP transform the "unity of the no" that had served it so well in the first years of the Weimar Republic into a "unity of the yes" that would enable the party to find the same unity in governmental participation that it had found in opposition?"[6]

The first test of the party's ability to make this transition came with the August 1924 Reichstag vote on the Dawes Plan. And as the 48–52 split in the Nationalist vote revealed, the party had clearly failed. With the economic and political stabilization of the Weimar Republic from 1924 to 1928, the problems that had bedeviled the DNVP in the vote on the Dawes Plan were only exacerbated. Here party leaders would find themselves confronted with two closely intertwined challenges: first, that of preserving party unity while working within a governmental system to which the party was unconditionally opposed and, second, that of reconciling the different and often conflicting expectations that the various social and economic interests that constituted the DNVP's material base attached to the party's entry into the national government. The task of the DNVP party leadership was further complicated by the fact that they faced increasingly heavy pressure not just from special-interest organizations like the National Federation of German Industry, the National Rural League, and the German National Union of Commercial Employees but also from the Pan-German League, the Stahlhelm, and the various organizations on the patriotic Right. Nowhere was the party's inability to reconcile the exigencies of interest politics with the anti-system rhetoric of the patriotic Right more apparent than in its withdrawal from the first Luther cabinet in the fall of 1925 as a result of the controversy over Locarno. In the meantime, the party's middle-class constituencies became increasingly embittered over what they perceived as the preferential treatment accorded industry, agriculture, and organized labor and began to abandon the DNVP in favor of special-interest parties like the Business Party and the People's Justice Party. The fragmentation of the DNVP's material base continued even after the party entered the government for a second time in January 1927 when conservative farm leaders disgruntled with the party's failure to address the deepening agrarian crisis launched the Christian-National Peasants Farmers' Party in early 1928 with support from local and state branches of the National Rural League.

---

[6] Hans Erdmann von Lindeiner-Wildau, "Konservatismus," in *Volk und Reich der Deutschen*, ed. Bernhard Harms, 3 vols. (Berlin, 1929), 2:35–61, here 29.

All of this came together to inflict a massive defeat on the DNVP in the May 1928 Reichstag elections, the first in the party's history since its founding in 1918. As the outcome of the election clearly showed, the disintegration of the DNVP's social base was highly advanced, so much so that its prospects of developing into a political force sufficiently powerful to contain the rise of Nazism had been severely compromised. Moreover, the shock and scale of the party's defeat triggered a bitter internal conflict that would culminate in the triumph of those forces that were most adamantly opposed to any sort of collaboration with the existing political order. Hugenberg and those now in control of the DNVP eschewed all ties to those parties that sought to stabilize Germany's republican order for the sake of closer relations with elements on Germany's anti-republican Right, including the NSDAP. To be sure, Hugenberg envisaged himself as the unquestioned leader of the so-called national opposition and fully expected Hitler and the NSDAP to assume a role subordinate to the DNVP in the struggle against Weimar democracy. But this scheme, like so much of what Hugenberg hoped to accomplish in the last years of the Weimar Republic, rested upon a fundamental misreading of Hitler and the Nazi calculus for the seizure of power. More importantly, Hugenberg's ascendancy to the DNVP party chairmanship in October 1928 took place in the face of bitter opposition from the party's more moderate elements and resulted in two secessions on the DNVP's left wing, the first in December 1929 and the second in July 1930. In the fall of 1930 the party's strength in the Reichstag was reduced to less than half of what it had been after the December 1924 national elections, a fact that underscored just how miserably the DNVP had failed as a truly comprehensive conservative *Sammelpartei* that could have facilitated the transition from autocratic to democratic government or, at the very least, have contained the threat of Nazism. As it was, the DNVP was too divided to do the former and too weak to do the latter.

The reasons for this were many and complex. In the first place, the German Right was never all that united to begin with. The divisions that had marked the development of the German Right in the Second Empire carried over into the Weimar Republic and were papered over only by virtue of the fact that all of the various factions that made up the German Right categorically rejected the republican system of government that Germany had inherited from the November Revolution. But the glue that had held the party together while the party was in opposition began to lose its cohesive strength once the DNVP had to enter the government and assume the role of a responsible coalition partner. At the same time, the general course of German economic development during the Weimar Republic intensified the level of interest conflict at all levels of German society, with the result that it became increasingly difficult for Germany's non-socialist parties to mediate between the divergent and often antagonistic interests that constituted their material base. This was particularly true of the DNVP, which of all of Germany's non-socialist parties with the possible exception of the Center and BVP had the most diverse and highly differentiated social base. From this perspective, the fate of DNVP was hardly different from that suffered by the other non-Catholic bourgeois parties of the Weimar Republic. And like its non-Catholic counterparts, the DNVP suffered from chronic financial problems that only became more acute with the stabilization of the mark in second half of the 1920s and that made it increasingly difficult for it to sustain the elaborate organizational apparatus that it had built up in the first years of the Weimar Republic. In the case of the DNVP, the situation was further complicated by a decentralized organizational structure that afforded party leaders in Berlin little direct influence over what was happening at the local and regional levels of the party. This, in turn, created sanctuaries within the party organization for extremist elements that were then in a position to obstruct or block initiatives on the part of the DNVP's national leadership that might have contributed to the stability of the Weimar Republic. It was precisely the decentralized character of the DNVP party organization that explains the success of the insurgency candidacy that elements on the party's right wing unfurled in support of Hugenberg and his bid for the DNVP party chairmanship in the summer and fall of 1928. The organizational structure of the DNVP left the party vulnerable to a right-wing assault from within that would – and ultimately did – render it incapable of rallying conservative forces to the support of Germany's republican order.[7]

The fragmentation of the DNVP's left wing in 1929 and 1930 doomed efforts to stabilize the Weimar Republic from the Right to failure. To be sure, there would be repeated attempts over the course of the next several years to fuse the various splinter parties that had broken away from the DNVP and the other non-socialist parties into a united middle party or some kind of united political front. Much to the annoyance of the Brüning government and Germany's economic elites, these efforts invariably ended in failure as it proved impossible to bridge the gap between those who remained loyal to the principles of democratic government and still hoped to unite in support of Germany's beleaguered republican system and those who were more interested in an alliance with the anti-democratic forces on the radical Right.[8] The split between the two ran right through the middle of the movement for bourgeois unity at a time when the popular longing for unity was stronger than ever. In this respect, the disunity of the DNVP only mirrored that of the German Right as a whole. The campaign against the Young Plan was supposed to bring together the various elements on the German Right, including

---

[7] On this point, see Ohnezeit, *Zwischen "schärfster Opposition,"* 47–59, and Daniel Ziblatt, *Conservative Parties and the Birth of Democracy* (Cambridge, 2016), 280–85, 301–14.

[8] For further details, see Larry Eugene Jones, "Sammlung oder Zersplitterung? Die Bestrebungen zur Bildung einer neuen Mittelpartei in der Endphase der Weimarer Republik 1930–1933," *Vierteljahrshefte für Zeitgeschichte* 25 (1977): 265–304.

patriotic leagues like the Stahlhelm and Pan-German League, into a common crusade against Stresemann's foreign policy, but it too foundered on the conflict between organizations like the RLB and DHV that functioned as the representatives of special economic interests and those like the Stahlhelm and Pan-German League that were committed to a national agenda that had little, if anything, in common with the representation of special economic interests. This was a fundamental division that had run through the heart of the German Right since the founding of the Weimar Republic and that had been intensified by the political and economic stabilization of the republic in the second half of the 1920s. Whether or not it could ever be overcome remained to be seen.

All of this had profound consequences for the success or failure of the taming strategy that not just Schleicher, but influential elements of Germany's conservative elites had adopted for dealing with the rise of National Socialism. If nothing else, the disunity of the German Right meant that those conservatives who hoped to domesticate the Nazis by bringing them into the national government lacked the means to keep Hitler and his minions under control once they were in power. Only if the architects of this strategy had had at their disposal a large and well organized conservative party that could serve as a bulwark against Nazi radicalism would it have been possible to enforce the terms of the covenant under which the Nazis were allowed into the government. But by the end of 1930 it was clear that neither the DNVP nor any other constellation of forces on the German Right was capable of performing in this capacity. Consequently, when Papen and Schleicher first tried to negotiate with the Nazis in the summer of 1932 in an attempt to entice them into the government, the absence of a strong and united conservative party at their backs meant that they were negotiating from a position of weakness and that they lacked the leverage necessary to hold the Nazis in check. As it was, Hitler was able to extract concessions from Papen and Schleicher – namely, the dissolution of the Reichstag, the repeal of the ban on the SA and other Nazi paramilitary organizations, and the removal of the Prussian government from office – in return for promises that he had no intention of fulfilling once his own demands had been met. Nowhere were the tragic implications of this situation more apparent than in January 1933 when Papen – this time without Schleicher's backing – succeeded in reaching an agreement with Hitler whereby the Nazi party leader would assume the leadership of a government in which all but three positions would be held by conservatives. Hitler's appointment as chancellor was based on the premise that the conservatives in the Hitler cabinet would have sufficient leverage to contain the activism of the Nazi movement and harness it to their own political agenda. But without the support of a strong and united conservative party behind them, this proved to be a devastating illusion. This was particularly apparent in the spring of 1933 when the more militant elements with the Nazi movement unleashed an assault that not only destroyed the last vestiges of Germany's republican order but targeted Hitler's conservative allies as well. By the end of the summer all of Germany's conservative organizations had either been dissolved or coordinated into the institutional structure of the Nazi state on terms that amounted to their virtual subjugation to the Nazi will.[9] Had the conservatives enjoyed the support of a strong and well-organized party at their back, this might very well have been averted. But such was not the case.

---

[9] Hermann Beck, *The Fateful Alliance: German Conservatives and Nazis in 1933. The Machtergreifung in a New Light* (New York and Oxford, 2008), 146–73, 259–93.

SELECT BIBLIOGRAPHY

Archival Sources

Archiv der Freiherren Hiller von Gaertringen, Gärtringen
  Nachlass Berthold Freiherr Hiller von Gaertringen
  Nachlass Kuno Graf von Westarp
  Briefwechsel Ada Gräfin von Westarp-Gertraude Freifrau Hiller von Gaertringen
Archiv des Deutschen Handels- und Industrieangestellten Verband (DHV-Archiv), Hamburg
  Max Habermann, "Der Deutschnationale Handlungsgehilfen-Verband im Kampf um das Reich 1918–1933. Ein Zeugnis seines Wollens und Wirkens." N.p., 1934
Archiv für Christlich-Demokratische Politik an der Konrad-Adenauer-Stiftung, Sankt-Augustin
  Bestand Zentrum (VI-051)
  Nachlass Otto Gehrig (I-087)
  Nachlass Andreas Hermes (I-090)
  Nachlass Adam Stegerwald (I-206)
  Nachlass Hugo Stinnes (I-201)
Bayerisches Hauptstaatsarchiv, Munich
  Abteilung IV (Kriegsarchiv)
    Akten der Einwohnerwehren Bayerns
    Akten des Stahlhelm, Landesverband Bayern
  Abteilung V (Nachlässe und Sammlungen)
    Flugblätter-Sammlung
    Archiv der Genossenschaft katholischer Edelleute in Bayern
    Akten der Deutschnationalen Volkspartei in Bayern
    Nachlass Maximilian Dziembowski
    Nachlass Georg Escherich
    Nachlass Anton Fehr
    Nachlass Hans Hilpert
    Nachlass Edgar Julius Jung
Brandenburgisches Hauptlandesarchiv, Potsdam
  Rep. 37 (Boitzenburg)
    Nachlass Dietlof Graf von Arnim-Boitzenburg

Bundesarchiv, Berlin-Lichterfelde
 Akten der Reichskanzlei (R 43 I)
 Akten der Deutschen Volkspartei (R 45 II)
 Akten der Deutschen Demokratischen Partei/Deutschen Staatspartei
   (R 45 III)
 Akten des Stahlhelm, Bund der Frontsoldaten (R 72)
 Akten des Jungdeutscher Ordens (R 161)
 Sammlung Schumacher (R 187)
 Büro des Reichspräsidenten (R 601)
 Akten des Reichsministerium des Innen (R 1501)
 Akten der Christlich-Nationalen Bauern- und Landvolkpartei (R 8001)
 Akten der Deutschkonservativen Partei (R 8003)
 Akten der Deutschnationalen Volkspartei (R 8005)
 Akten des Reichs-Landbundes (R 8034 I)
 Akten des Alldeutschen Verbandes (R 8045)
 Akten des Volksvereins für das katholische Deutschland (R 8115 I)
 Sammlung personenbezogener Unterlagen bis 1945 (R 9354)
 Akten der NSDAP-Reichsorganisationsleitung (NS 22)
 Akten des NSDAP-Hauptarchivs (NS 26)
 Nachlass Heinrich Claß
 Nachlass Johannes Giesberts
 Nachlass Karl Hepp
 Nachlass Reinhard Mumm
 Nachlass Gustav Roesicke
 Nachlass Conrad von Wangenheim
 Nachlass Kuno Graf von Westarp
Bundesarchiv, Koblenz
 Nachlass Fritz Baltrusch
 Nachlass Paul Bausch
 Nachlass Max Buchner
 Nachlass Theodor Duesterberg
 Nachlass Wilhelm Freiherr von Gayl
 Nachlass Heinrich Gerland
 Nachlass Otto Gessler
 Nachlass Gottfried Gok
 Nachlass Rudolf ten Hompel
 Nachlass Karl Herold
 Nachlass Alfred Hugenberg
 Nachlass Karl Jarres
 Nachlass Jakob Kaiser
 Nachlass Wolfgang Kapp
 Nachlass Siegfried von Kardorff
 Nachlass Walther von Keudell
 Nachlass Erich Koch-Weser

Nachlass Walther Lambach
Nachlass Hans Erdmann von Lindeiner-Wildau
Nachlass Hans Luther
Nachlass Karl Passarge
Nachlass Rudolf Pechel
Nachlass Hermann Pünder
Nachlass Reinhold Quaatz
Nachlass Hans Schlange-Schöningen
Nachlass Otto Schmidt-Hannover
Nachlass Paul Silverberg
Nachlass Martin Spahn
Nachlass Hermann Stegmann
Nachlass Julius Streicher
Nachlass Gottfried Traub
Nachlass Leo Wegener
Nachlass Luitpold von Weilnböck
Nachlass Alfred Zapf
Zeitgeschichtliche Sammlungen (ZSg)
    1/2 ADV
    1/8 BVP
    1/14 RDI
    1/42 DVP
    1/44 DNVP
    1/88 Stahlhelm
    1/275 VKV/KVP
    1/E87 VVVD
    1/E92 RLB
Bundesarchiv-Militärarchiv, Freiburg im Breisgau
Nachlass August von Cramon
Nachlass Karl von Einem
Nachlass Max von Gallwitz
Nachlass Rüdiger Graf von der Goltz
Nachlass Paul von Lettow-Vorbeck
Nachlass Magnus von Levetzow
Nachlass August von Mackensen
Nachlass Hans von Seeckt
Nachlass Kurt von Schleicher
Nachlass Alfred von Tirpitz
MSG 2/11675: Nachlasssplitter Elhard von Morosowicz
Forschungsstelle für Zeitgeschichte in Hamburg, Hamburg
Albert Krebs, "Max Habermann. Eine biographische Studie" (Bestand 12/H)
Nachlass Alfred Diller (Bestand 11/D1)
Generallandesarchiv Karlsruhe
Nachlass Willy Hugo Hellpach

Historisches Archiv, Friedrich Krupp GmbH, Essen
  Briefwechsel Gustav Krupp von Bohlen und Halbach und Tilo Freiherr von
    Wilmowsky (FAH 23)
  Familienarchiv Hügel (FAH)
Institut für Zeitgeschichte, Munich
  Akten zum Bayerischen Landbund (BLB-Akten)
Kommission für Zeitgeschichte, Bonn
  Nachlass Emil Ritter
Landesarchiv Baden-Württemberg, Hauptstaatsarchiv Stuttgart
  Nachlass Wilhelm Simpfendörfer (Q1/14)
Landesarchiv Berlin, Berlin
  Akten der Generalstaatsanwaltschaft, Prozeß Gereke (Reportorium A,
    358-01)
  Akten der Zentralverwaltung August Borsig AG
Landesarchiv Nordrheinland-Westfalen, Münster
  Bestand B: Restakten der Vereinigung der deutschen Bauernvereine
    (Bestand 113)
  Nachlass Count Clemens von Schorlemer-Lieser
Landesarchiv Schleswig-Holstein, Schleswig
  Nachlass Anton Schifferer
Landeshauptarchiv Sachsen-Anhalt, Abteilung Magdeburg, Depositum Wernigerode
  Marienthal Gutsarchiv (Reportorium H)
Niedersächsisches Staatsarchiv. Aurich
  Akten der Deutschnationalen Volkspartei Aurich (Reportorium 227/8)
Niedersächsisches Staatsarchiv, Osnabrück
  Akten der Deutschnationalen Volkspartei, Landesverband Osnabrück
    (Bestand CI)
Politisches Archiv des Auswärtigen Amts, Berlin
  Nachlass Gustav Stresemann
Rheinisch-Westfälisches Wirtschaftsarchiv zu Köln, Cologne
  Historisches Archiv der Gutehoffnungshütte (Abteilung 130)
    Akten der Allgemeinen Verwaltung
    Nachlass Paul Reusch
Sächsisches Hauptstaatsarchiv Dresden, Dresden
  Nachlass Albrecht Philipp
Siemens Historical Institute, Berlin
  Nachlass Carl Friedrich von Siemens
Staatsarchiv Hamburg, Hamburg
  Archiv Firma Blohm und Voß GmbH
  HAPAG-Lloyd Reederei, Handakten Wilhelm Cunos
Stadtarchiv Braunschweig
  Akten der Deutschen Volkspartei, Landesverband Braunschweig (Bestand GX6)
Stadtarchiv Dresden, Dresden
  Archiv des Alldeutschen Verbandes, Ortsgruppe Dresden

Stadtarchiv Mönchen-Gladbach
    Nachlass Heinz Brauweiler (Bestand 15/13)
Stadtarchiv Nürnberg
    Bestand KV-Prozesse, Fall 6
Stadtarchiv Paderborn
    Dokumentation Paul Lejeune-Jung (Bestand S 2/125)
Stadtarchiv Stuttgart
    Nachlass Wilhelm Kohlhaas (Bestand 2134)
Stadtarchiv Wuppertal
    Nachlass Johann Victor Bredt (Bestand NDS 263)
ThyssenKrupp Konzernarchiv, Außenstelle Hoesch-Archiv, Dortmund
    Nachlass Fritz Springorum
Unternehmensarchiv Bayer A.G., Leverkusen
    Autographen-Sammlung Carl Duisberg
    Vorakten der I. G. Farben
    Akten des Reichsverbandes der Deutschen Industrie
Vereinigte Westälische Adelsarchive, Münster
    Archiv des Vereins katholischer Edelleute Deutschlands
    Nachlass Franz Graf von Galen
    Nachlass Max Heereman von Zuydtwyck
    Nachlass Engelbert Freiherr von Kerckerinck zur Borg
    Nachlass Engelbert Freiherr von Landsberg-Steinfurt
    Nachlass Ferdinand Freiherr von Lüninck
    Nachlass Hermann Graf zu Stolberg-Stolberg
    Nachlass Josef Graf zu Stolberg-Stolberg
Verlagsarchiv M. DuMont Schauberg, Cologne
    Protokolle der Redaktionskonferenzen der Kölnischen Zeitung, 19 Sept.
      1929–11 Oct. 1933
Württembergische Landesbibliothek, Stuttgart
    Ernst Marquardt, "Kaempfer fuer Deutschlands Zukunft und Ehre.
      Umrißzeichnungen aus der Geschichte der Deutsch-nationalen Volkspartei
      Württembergs."

The following contains published sources and scholarly works that are cited multiple times in multiple chapters. A complete bibliography of contemporary political literature, including periodicals and newspapers, and memoir literature as well the secondary scholarship consulted in preparation of the monograph may be accessed at www.cambridge.org/thegermanright.

Published Sources

Akten der Reichskanzlei
    Die Kabinette Stresemann I u. II. 13. August bis 6 Oktober 1923. 6. Oktober
      bis. 30. November 1923, ed. Karl Dietrich Erdmann and Martin Vogt. vols.
      Boppard am Rhein, 1978.

Die Kabinette Marx I und II. 30. November 1923–3. Juni 1924. 3. Juni 1924–15. Januar 1925, ed. Günter Abramowski. 2 vols. Boppard am Rhein, 1973.

Die Kabinette Luther I und II. 15. January 1925 bis 20. Januar 1926. 20 Januar 1926 bis 17. Mai 1926, ed. Karl-Heinz Minuth. 2 vols. Boppard am Rhein, 1977.

Die Kabinette Marx III und IV. 17. Mai 1926 bis 29. Januar 1927. 29 Januar 1927 bis 29. Juni 1928, ed. Günter Abramowski. 2 vols. Boppard am Rhein, 1988.

Das Kabinett Müller II. 28. Juni 1928 bis 27. März 1930, ed. Martin Vogt. 2 vols. Boppard am Rhein, 1970.

Die Kabinette Brüning I u. II. 30. März 1930 bis 10. Oktober 1931. 10. Oktober 1931 bis 1. Juni 1932, ed. Tilman Koops. 3 vols. Boppard am Rhein, 1985 and 1989.

Albertin, Lothar, and Wegner, Konstanze, eds. *Linksliberalismus in der Weimarer Republik. Die Führungsgremien der Deutschen Demokratischen Partei und der Deutschen Staatspartei 1918–1933.* Düsseldorf, 1980.

Falter, Jürgen, Lindenberger, Thomas, and Schulmann, Siegfried. *Wahlen und Abstimmungen in der Weimarer Republik. Materialien zur Wahlverhalten 1919–1933.* Munich, 1986.

Goebbels, Joseph. *Die Tagebücher von Joseph Goebbels*, ed. Elke Fröhlich. Part I: Aufzeichnungen 1923–1941. 5 vols. Munich and New York, 1997–2004.

Hitler, Adolf. *Reden, Schriften, Anordnungen. Februar 1925 bis Januar 1933*, ed. Institut für Zeitgeschichte. 5 vols. in 12 parts. Munich, London, New York, and Paris, 1992–98.

Kolb, Eberhard, and Richter, Ludwig, eds. *Nationalliberalismus in der Weimarer Republik. Die Führungsgremien der Deutschen Volkspartei 1918–1933.* 2 vols. Düsseldorf, 1999.

Morsey, Rudolf, ed. "Neue Quellen zur Vorgeschichte der Reichskanzlerschaft Brüning." In *Staat, Wirtschaft und Politik in der Weimarer Republik. Festschrift für Heinrich Brüning*, ed. Ferdinand A. Hermans and Theodor Schieder, 207–32. Berlin, 1967.

——— ed. *Protokolle der Reichstagsfraktion und des Fraktionsvorstandes der Deutschen Zentrumspartei 1926–1933.* Mainz, 1969.

Pünder, Hermann. *Politik in der Reichskanzlei. Aufzeichnungen aus den Jahren 1929–1932*, ed. Thilo Vogelsang. Stuttgart, 1961.

[Quaatz, Reinhold]. *Die Deutschnationalen und die Zestörung der Weimarer Republik. Aus dem Tagebuch von Reinhold Quaatz 1928–1933*, ed. Hermann Weiß and Paul Hoser. Stuttgart, 1989.

Stresemann, Gustav. *Vermächtnis. Der Nachlass in drei Bänden*, ed. Henry Bernhard with the collaboration of Walter Goetz. 3 vols. Berlin, 1932–33.

Westarp, Kuno von. *Konservative Politik im Übergang vom Kaiserreich zur Weimarer Republik*, ed. Friedrich Freiherr Hiller von Gaertringen with assistance from Karl J. Mayer and Reinhold Weber. Düsseldorf, 2001.

Frequently Cited Secondary Scholarship

Becker, Josef. "Joseph Wirth und die Krise des Zentrums während des IV. Kabinetts Marx (1927–28)," *Zeitschrift für die Geschichte des Oberrheins* 109 (1961): 361–482.

Berghahn, Volker R. *Der Stahlhelm – Bund der Frontsoldaten 1918–1935*. Düsseldorf, 1966.

Bergmann, Jürgen, and Megerle, Klaus. "Protest und Aufruhr der Landwirtschaft in der Weimarer Republik (1924–1933). Formen und Typen der politischen Agrarbewegung im regionalen Vergleich." In *Regionen im historischen Vergleich. Studien zu Deutschland im 19. und 20. Jahrhundert*, ed. Jürgen Bergmann et al., 200–87. Opladen, 1989.

Breuer, Stefan. *Die Völkischen in Deutschland. Kaiserreich und Weimarer Republik*. Darmstadt, 2008.

Childers, Thomas. *The Nazi Voter: The Social Foundations of Fascism in Germany*. Chapel Hill, NC, and London: 1983.

Clemens, Gabriele. *Martin Spahn und der Rechtskatholizismus in der Weimarer Republik*. Mainz, 1983.

Crim, Brian E. *Antisemitism in the German Military Community and the Jewish Response, 1916–1938*. Lanham, MD, 2014.

Diehl, James M. *Paramilitary Politics in the Weimar Republic*. Bloomington, IN, 1977.

"Von der 'Vaterlandspartei' zur 'Nationalen Revolution.' Die Vereinigten Vaterländischen Verbände Deutschlands (VVVD) 1922–1932," *Vierteljahrshefte für Zeitgeschichte* 33 (1985): 617–39.

Dörr, Manfred. "Die Deutschnationale Volkspartei 1925 bis 1928." Ph.D. diss., Universität Marburg, 1964.

Feldman, Gerald D. *Hugo Stinnes: Biographie eines Industriellen 1870–1924*. Munich, 1998.

The Great Disorder: Politics, Economics, and Society in the German Inflation, 1914–1924. New York and Oxford, 1993.

Fenske, Hans. *Konservatismus und Rechtsradikalismus in Bayern nach 1918*. Bad Homburg, 1969.

Flemming, Jens. "Konservatismus als 'nationalrevolutionäre Bewegung.' Konservative Kritik an der Deutschnationalen Volkspartei 1918–1933." *Deutscher Konservatismus im 19. und 20. Jahrhundert. Festschrift für Fritz Fischer*, ed. Dirk Stegmann, Bernd-Jürgen Wendt, and Peter-Christian Witt, 295–331. Bonn, 1983.

Landwirtschaftliche Interessen und Demokratie. Ländliche Gesellschaft, Agrarverbände und Staat 1890–1925. Bonn, 1978.

Forster, Bernhard. *Adam Stegerwald (1874–1945). Christlich-nationaler Gewerkschafter – Zentrumspolitiker – Mitbegründer der Unionsparteien*. Düsseldorf, 2003.

Friedrich, Nobert. *"Die christlich-soziale Fahne empor!" Reinhard Mumm und die christlich-soziale Bewegung*. Stuttgart, 1997.

Gasteiger, Daniela. *Kuno von Westarp (1864–1945). Parlamentarismus, Monarchismus und Herrschaftsutopien im deutschen Konservatismus*. Berlin, 2018.

Gessner, Dieter. *Agrarverbände in der Weimarer Republik. Wirtschaftliche und soziale Voraussetzungen agrarkonservativer Politik vor 1933*. Düsseldorf, 1976.

Gratwohl, Robert P. *Stresemann and the DNVP. Reconciliation or Revenge in German Foreign Policy, 1924–1928.* Lawrence, KS., 1980.

Hagenlücke, Heinz, *Deutsche Vaterlandspartei. Die nationale Rechte am Ende des Kaiserreiches.* Düsseldorf, 1997.

Hamel, Iris. *Völkischer Verband und nationale Gesellschaft. Der Deutschnationale Handlungsgehilfen-Verband 1893–1933.* Hamburg, 1967.

Hartenstein, Wolfgang. *Die Anfänge der Deutschen Volkspartei 1918–1920.* Düsseldorf, 1962.

Hehl, Ulrich von. *Wilhelm Marx 1863–1946. Eine politische Biographie.* Mainz, 1987.

Heinsohn, Kirsten. *Konservative Parteien in Deutschland 1912 bis 1933. Demokratisierung und Partizipatioin in geschlechthistorischer Perspektive.* Düsseldorf, 2010.

Hertzman, Lewis. *DNVP: Right-Wing Opposition in the Weimar Republic, 1918–1924.* Lincoln, 1963.

Hildebrand, Daniel. *Landbevölkerung und Wahlverhalten. Die DNVP im ländlichen Raum Pommerns und Ostpreußens 1918–1924.* Hamburg, 2004.

Hofmeister, Björn, "Between Monarchy and Dictatorship: Radical Nationalism and Social Mobilization of the Pan-German League, 1914–1939" Ph.D. diss., Georgetown University, 2012.

Holzbach, Heidrun. *Das "System Hugenberg." Die Organisation bürgerlicher Sammlungspolitik vor dem Aufstieg der NSDAP.* Stuttgart, 1981.

Hübner, Christoph. Die Rechtskatholiken, die Zentrumspartei und die katholische Kirche in Deutschland bis zum Reichskonkordat von 1933. Ein Beitrag zur Geschichte des Scheiterns der Weimarer Republik. 2014.

Jackisch, Barry A. *The Pan-German League and Radical Nationalist Politics in Interwar Germany, 1918–1939.* Farmham, 2012.

James, Harold. *The German Slump: Politics and Economics, 1924–1936.* Oxford, 1986.

Jochmann, Werner. "Die Ausbreitung des Antisemitismus." In *deutsches Judentum in Krieg und Revolution 1916–1923. Ein Sammelband,* ed. Werner E. Mosse, 409–510. Tübingen, 1971.

Jones, Larry Eugene. "Adam Stegerwald und die Krise des deutschen Parteiensystems. Ein Beitrag zur Deutung des 'Essener Programms' vom November 1920." *Vierteljahrshefte für Zeitgeschichte* 27 (1979): 1–29.

"Between the Fronts: The German National Union of Commercial Employees from 1928–1933." *Journal of Modern History* 48 (1976): 462–82.

"Catholic Conservatives in the Weimar Republic: The Politics of the Rhenish-Westphalian Aristocracy, 1919–1933." *German History* 18 (2000): 61–85.

"Catholics on the Right: The Reich Catholic Committee of the German National People's Party, 1920–33." *Historisches Jahrbuch* 126 (2006): 221–67.

"Conservative Antisemitism in the Weimar Republic: A Case Study of the German National People's Party," in *The German Right in the Weimar*

Republic: Studies in the History of German Conservatism, Nationalism, and Antisemitism, ed. Larry Eugene Jones, 79–107, New York and Oxford, 2014.

"German Conservatism at the Crossroads: Count Kuno von Westarp and the Struggle for Control of the DNVP, 1928–30." *Contemporary European History* 18 (2009): 147–77.

German Liberalism and the Dissolution of the Weimar Party System, 1918–1933. Chapel Hill, NC, 1988.

"In the Shadow of Stabilization: German Liberalism and the Legitimacy Crisis of the Weimar Party System, 1924–30." In *Die Nachwirkungen der Inflation auf die deutsche Geschichte 1924–1933*, ed. Gerald D. Feldman, 21–41. Munich, 1985.

"Inflation, Revaluation, and the Crisis of Middle-Class Politics: A Study in the Dissolution of the Weimar Party System, 1923–28." *Central European History* 12 (1979): 143–68.

"Stabilisierung von Rechts: Gustav Stresemann und das Streben nach politischer Stabilität 1923–1929." In *Politiker und Bürger. Gustav Stresemann und seine Zeit*, ed. Karl Heinrich Pohl, 162–93. Göttingen, 2002.

Jones, Larry Eugene. ed. *The German Right in the Weimar Republic: Studies in the History of German Conservatism, Nationalism, and Antisemitism.* New York and Oxford, 2014.

Kiiskinen, Elina. *Die Deutschnationale Volkspartei in Bayern (Bayerische Mittelpartei) in der Regierungspolitik des Freistaats während der Weimarer Zeit (1918–1933).* Munich, 2005.

Kittel, Manfred. "Zwischen völkischem Fundamentalismus und gouvernementaler Taktik. DNVP-Vorsitzende Hans Hilpert und die bayerischen Deutschnationalen." *Zeitschrift für bayerischen Landesgeschichte* 59 (1996): 849–901.

Klotzbücher, Alois. "Der politische Weg des Stahlhelm, Bund der Frontsoldaten, in der Weimarer Republik. Ein Beitrag zur Geschichte der 'Nationalen Opposition' 1918–1933." Ph.D. diss., Universität Erlangen, 1965.

Langer, Peter. *Macht und Verantwortung. Der Ruhrbaron Paul Reusch.* Essen, 2012.

Leicht, Johannes. *Heinrich Claß 1868–1953. Die politische Biographie eines Alldeutschen.* Paderborn, 2012.

Leopold, John A. *Alfred Hugenberg: The Radical Nationalist Campaign against the Weimar Republic.* New Haven, 1977.

Liebe, Werner. *Die Deutschnationale Volkspartei 1918–1924.* Düsseldorf, 1963.

Lohalm, Uwe. *Völkischer Radikalismus: Die Geschichte des Deutschvölkischen Schutz- und Trutz-Bundes 1919–1923.* Hamburg, 1970.

Maier, Charles S. *Recasting Bourgeois Europe: Stabilization in France, Germany, and Italy in the Decade after World War I.* Princeton, NJ, 1975.

Malinowski, Stephan. *Vom König zum Führer: Sozialer Niedergang und politische Radikalisierung im deutschen Adel zwischen Kaiserreich und NS-Staat.* Berlin, 2003.

Mergel, Thomas. "Das Scheitern des deutschen Tory-Konservatismus. Die Umformung der DNVP zu einer rechtsradikalen Partei 1928–1932." *Historische Zeitschrift* 276 (2003): 323–68.

Merkenich, Stephanie. *Grüne Front gegen Weimar. Reichs-Landbund und agra-rischer Lobbyismus 1918–1933*. Düsseldorf, 1998.

Moeller, Robert G. *German Peasants and Agrarian Politics, 1914–1924: The Rhine-land and Westphalia*. Chapel Hill, NC, and London, 1986.

"Winners as Losers in the German Inflation: Peasant Protest over the Con-trolled Economy. In *Die deutsche Inflation: Eine Zwischenbilanz/ The German Inflation Reconsidered*, ed. Gerald D. Feldman, Carl-Ludwig Holtfrerich, Gerhard A. Ritter, and Peter-Christian Witt, 255–88. Berlin, 1982.

Mommsen, Hans; Petzina, Dietmar; and Weisbrod, Bernd, eds. *Industrielles System und politische Entwicklung in der Weimarer Republik. Verhandlungen des Internationalen Symposiums in Bochum vom 12–17. Juni 1973*. Düsseldorf, 1974.

Morsey, Rudolf. *Die Deutsche Zentrumspartei 1917–1923*. Düsseldorf, 1966.

Müller, Andreas. *"Fällt der Bauer, stürzt der Staat." Deutschnationale Agrarpolitik 1928–1933*. Hamburg, 2003.

Müller, Hans Peter. "Adolf Bauser (1880–1948), der Sparerbund und die Volks-rechtspartei," *Zeitschrift für Württembergische Landesgeschichte* 75 (2016): 247–76.

"Die Bürgerpartei/Deutschnationale Volkspartei (DNVP) in Württemberg 1918–1933. Konservative Politik und die Zerstörung der Weimarer Republik." *Zeitschrift für Württembergische Landesgeschichte* 61 (2002): 374–433.

"Wilhelm Bazille. Deutschnationaler Politiker, württembergischer Staatspräsi-dent." *Lebensbilder aus Baden-Württemberg* 21 (2005): 480–517

Müller, Markus. *Die Christlich-Nationale Bauern- und Landvolkpartei 1928–1933*. Düsseldorf, 2001.

Neebe, Reinhold. *Großindustrie, Staat und NSDAP 1930–1933. Paul Silverberg und der Reichsverband der Deutschen Industrie in der Krise der Weimarer Republic*. Göttingen, 1981.

Ohnezeit, Maik. *Zwischen "schärfster Opposition" und dem "Willen zur Macht." Die Deutschnationale Volkspartei (DNVP) in der Weimarer Republik 1918–1928*. Düsseldorf, 2011.

Opitz, Günther. *Der Christlich-soziale Volksdienst. Versuch einer protestantischen Partei in der Weimarer Republik*. Düsseldorf, 1969.

Patch, William L., Jr. *Christian Trade Unions in the Weimar Republic, 1918–1933. The Failure of "Corporate Pluralism."* New Haven, 1985.

Heinrich Brüning and the Dissolution of the Weimar Republic. Cambridge, 1998.

Pomp, Rainer. *Bauern und Grossgrundbesitzer auf ihrem Weg ins Dritte Reich. Der Brandenburgische Landbund 1919–1933*. Berlin, 2013.

"Brandenburgischer Landadel und die Weimarer Republik. Konflikte um Oppositionsstrategien und Elitenkonzepte," in *Adel und Staatsverwaltung in Brandenburg im 19. und 20. Jahrhundert. Ein historischer Vergleich*, ed. Kurt Adamy and Kristina Hübener. Berlin, 1996, 185–218.

Pyta, Wolfram. *Dorfgemeinschaft und Parteipolitik 1918–1933. Die Verschränkung von Milieu und Parteien in den protestantischen Landgebieten Deutschlands in der Weimarer Republik.* Düsseldorf, 1996.

Hindenburg. Herrschaft zwischen Hohenzollern und Hitler. Berlin, 2007.

Rasch, Manfred. "Über Albert Vögler und sein Verhältnis zur Politik." *Mitteilungsblatt des Instituts für soziale Bewegungen. Forschungen und Forschungsberichte* 28 (2003): 127–56.

Richter, Ludwig. *Die Deutsche Volkspartei 1918–1933.* Düsseldorf, 2002.

Roder, Hartmut. *Der christlich-nationale Deutsche Gewerkschaftsbund (DGB) im politisch-ökonomischen Kräftefeld der Weimarer Republik.* Frankfurt am Main, Bern, and New York, 1986.

Ruppert, Karsten. *Im Dienst am Staat von Weimar. Das Zentrum als regierende Partei in der Weimarer Demokratie 1923–1930.* Düsseldorf, 1992.

Scheck, Raffael. *Alfred von Tirpitz and German Right-Wing Politics, 1914–1930.* Atlantic Highlands, NJ, 1998.

Mothers of the Nation: Right-Wing Women in Weimar Germany. Oxford and New York, 2004.

Schumacher, Martin. *Land und Politik. Eine Untersuchung über politische Parteien und agrarische Interessen 1914–1923.* Düsseldorf, 1978.

Mittelstandsfront und Republik. Die Wirtschaftspartei – Reichspartei des deutschen Mittelstandes 1919–1933. Düsseldorf, 1972.

Simon, Carina. "Heinz Brauweiler. Eine politische Biographie im Zeichen des antidemokratischen Denkens." Ph.D. diss., Universität Kassel, 2016.

Sneeringer, Julie. *Winning Women's Votes: Propaganda and Politics in Weimar Germany.* Chapel Hill, NC, and London, 2002.

Striesow, Jan. *Die Deutschnationale Volkspartei und die Völkisch-Radikalen 1918–1922.* 2 vols. Frankfurt am Main, 1981.

Stupperich, Amrei. *Volksgemeinschaft oder Arbeitersolidarität. Studien zur Arbeitnehmerpolitik in der Deutschnationalen Volkspartei.* Göttingen and Zurich, 1982.

Stürmer, Michael. *Koalition und Opposition in der Weimarer Republik 1924–1928.* Düsseldorf, 1967.

Süchting-Hänger, Andrea. *Das "Gewissen der Nation." Nationales Engagement und politisches Handeln konservativer Frauenorganisationen 1900 bis 1937.* Düsseldorf, 2002.

Thimme, Annelise. *Flucht in den Mythos. Die Deutschnationale Volkspartei und die Niederlage von 1918.* Göttingen, 1969.

Turner, Henry Ashby, Jr. *German Big Business and the Rise of Hitler.* Oxford, 1985.

"The Ruhrlade: Secret Cabinet of Heavy Industry in the Weimar Republic." *Central European History* 3 (1970): 195–228.

Vogel, Wieland. *Katholische Kirche und nationale Kampfverbände in der Weimarer Republik.* Mainz, 1989.

Weisbrod, Bernd. *Schwerindustrie in der Weimarer Republik. Interessenpolitik zwischen Stabilisierung und Krise.* Wuppertal, 1978.

Williamson, John G. *Karl Helfferich, 1872–1924: Economist, Financier, Politician.* Princeton, NJ, 1971.

Wright, Jonathan. *Gustav Stresemann: Weimar's Greatest Statesman.* Oxford, 2002.

Zollitsch, Wolfgang. "Die Erosion des traditionellen Konservatismus. Ländlicher Adel in Preußen zwischen Kaiserreich und Weimarer Republik." In *Parteien im Wandel. Vom Kaiserreich zur Weimarer Republik,* ed. Dieter Dowe, Jürgen Kocka, and Heinrich August Winkler, 161–82. Munich, 1999.

"Das Scheitern der 'gouvernementalen' Rechten. Tilo von Wilmowsky und die organisierten Interessen in der Staatskrise von Weimar." In *Demokratie in Deutschland. Chancen und Gefährdungen im 19. und 20. Jahrhundert. Historische Essays,* ed. Wolther von Kieseritzky and Klaus-Peter Sick, 254–74.

INDEX